Geographers'
LONDON ATLAS

CONTENTS

REFERENCE

Motorway	M1		Built-up Area	BANK STREET
A Road	A2		Local Authority Boundary	
Under Construction			Posttown & London Postal District Boundary	
Proposed			Postcode Boundary (within Posttowns)	
B Road	B408			
Dual Carriageway			Map Continuation	56
One-way Street			Church or Chapel	†
Traffic flow on A Roads is indicated by a heavy line on the drivers' left.	→		Fire Station	■
Junction Name	MARBLE ARCH		Hospital	H
Restricted Access			House Numbers A & B Roads only	51 19 22 48
Pedestrianized Road			Information Centre	i
Track & Footpath			National Grid Reference	530
Residential Walkway			Police Station	▲
Railway	Tunnel / Level Crossing		Post Office	★
			Toilet with Facilities for the Disabled	♿
Stations:			Educational Establishment	
National Rail Network			Hospital or Hospice	
Docklands Light Railway	DLR		Industrial Building	
Underground Station	⊖ is the registered trade mark of Transport for London		Leisure or Recreational Facility	
			Place of Interest	
Croydon Tramlink	Tunnel Stop		Public Building	
The boarding of Tramlink trams at stops may be limited to a single direction, indicated by the arrow.			Shopping Centre or Market	
			Other Selected Buildings	

SCALE

3.1 inches to 1 mile

0 ¼ ½ ¾ 1 Mile

0 250 500 750 Metres 1 Kilometre

1:20,438
7.87cm to 1 mile
4.89cm to 1 km

Geographers' A-Z Map Company Limited

Head Office : Fairfield Road, Borough Green, Sevenoaks, Kent TN15 8PP   Tel: 01732 781000   (General Enquires & Trade Sales)
Showrooms : 44 Gray's Inn Road, London WC1X 8HX   Tel: 020 7440 9500   (Retail Sales)
www.a-zmaps.co.uk

Ordnance Survey This product includes mapping data licensed from Ordnance Survey® with the permission of the Controller of Her Majesty's Stationery Office.

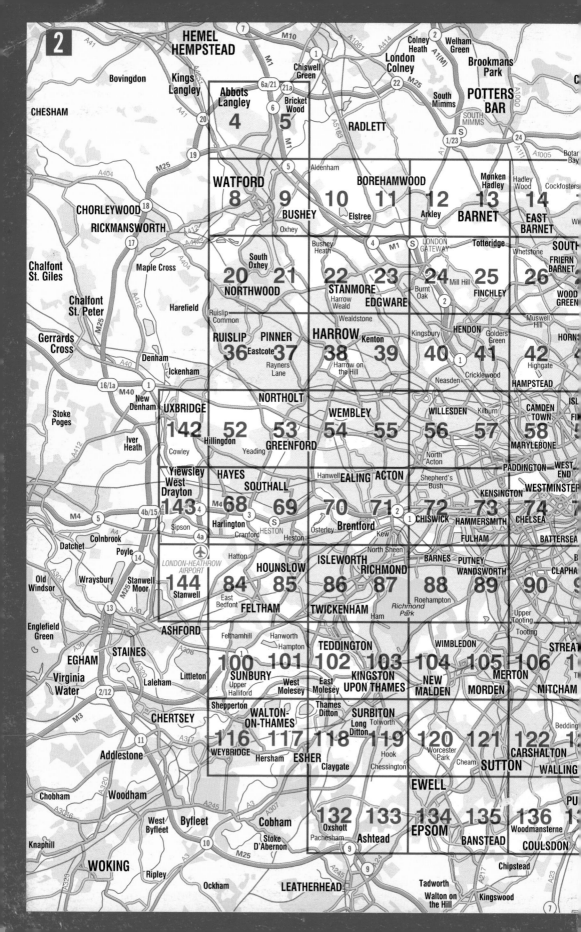

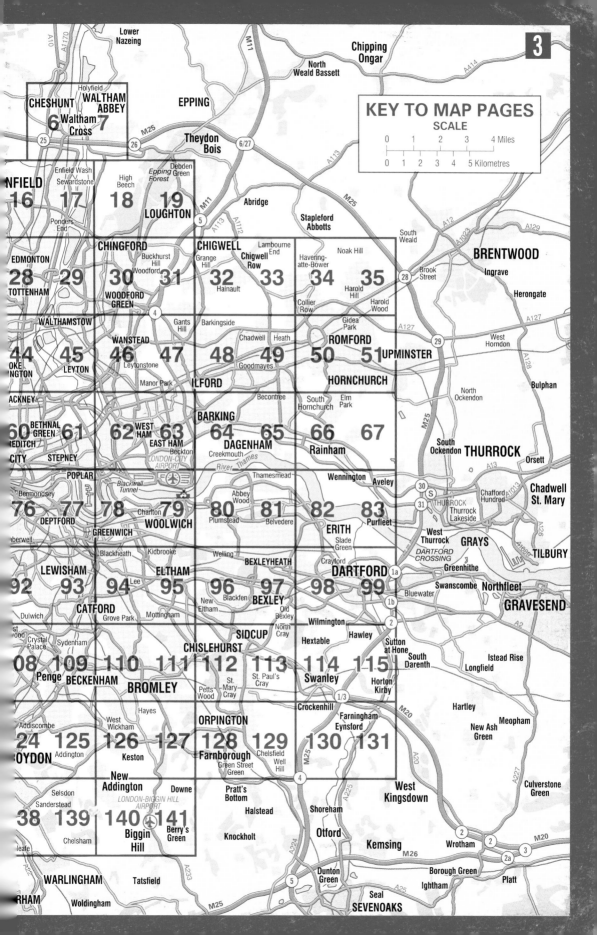

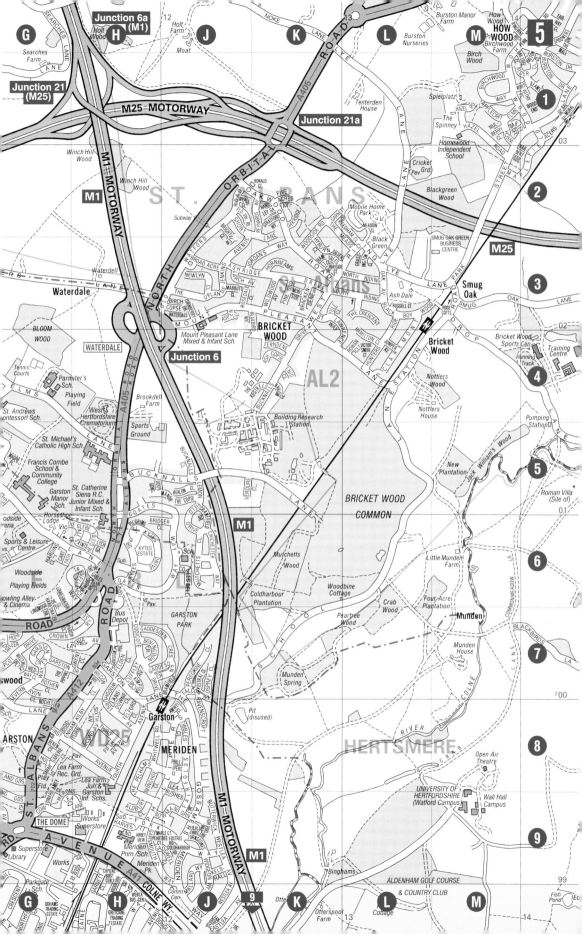

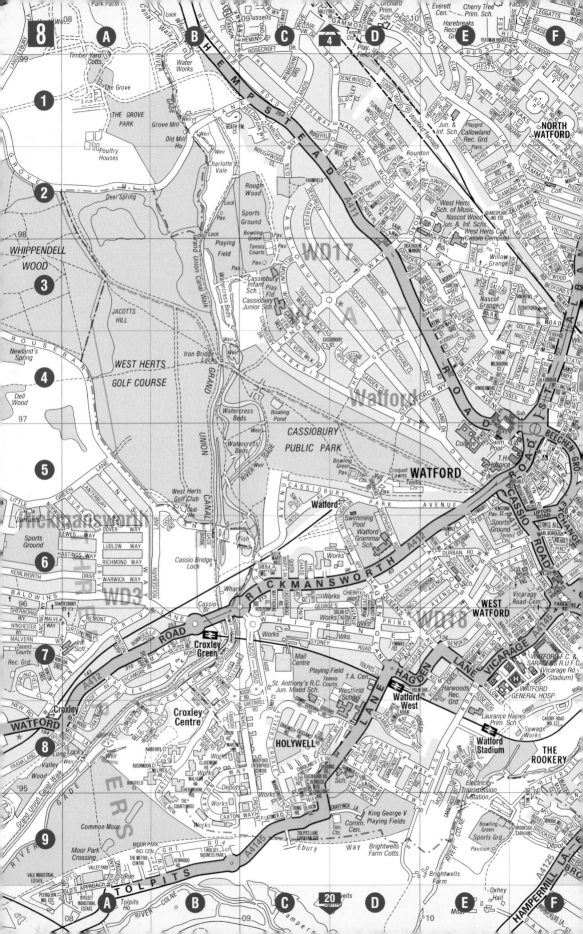

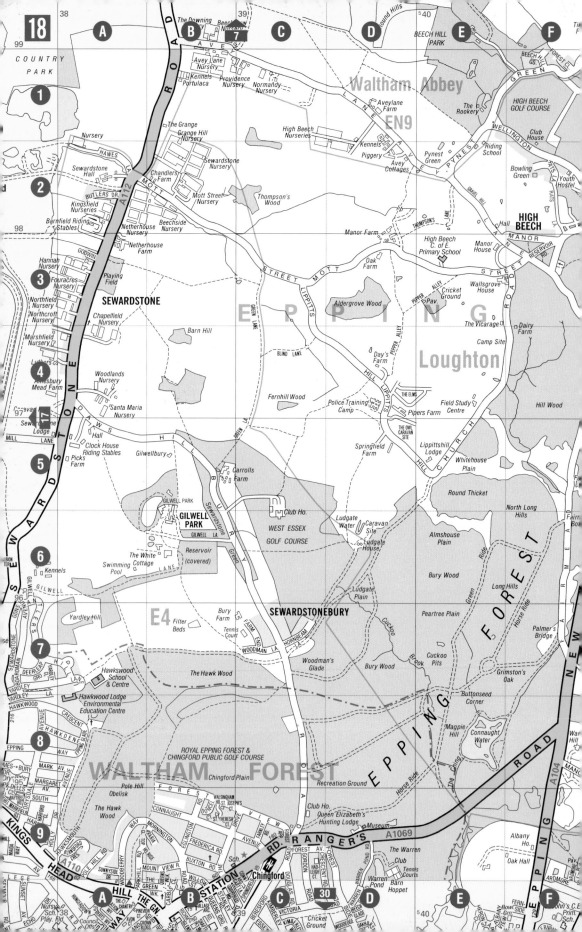

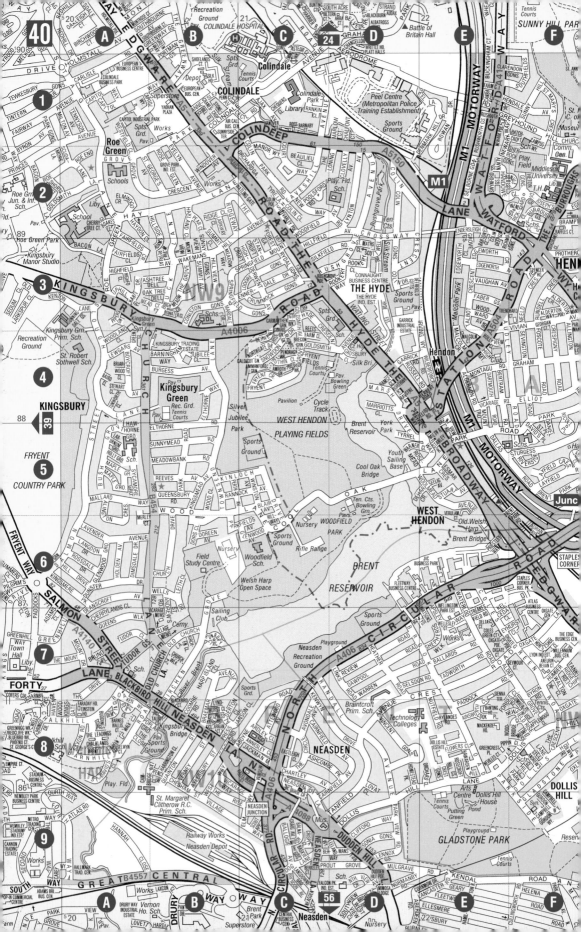

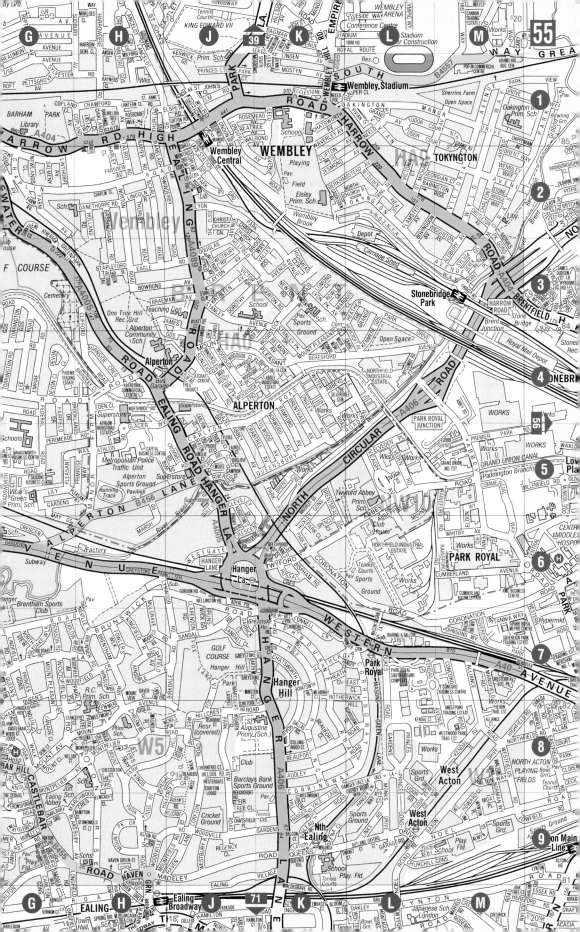

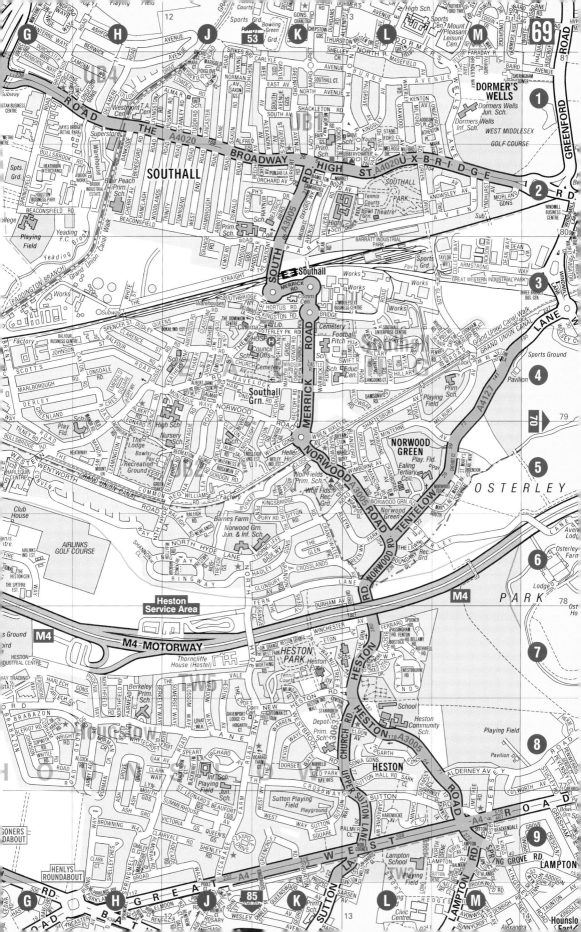

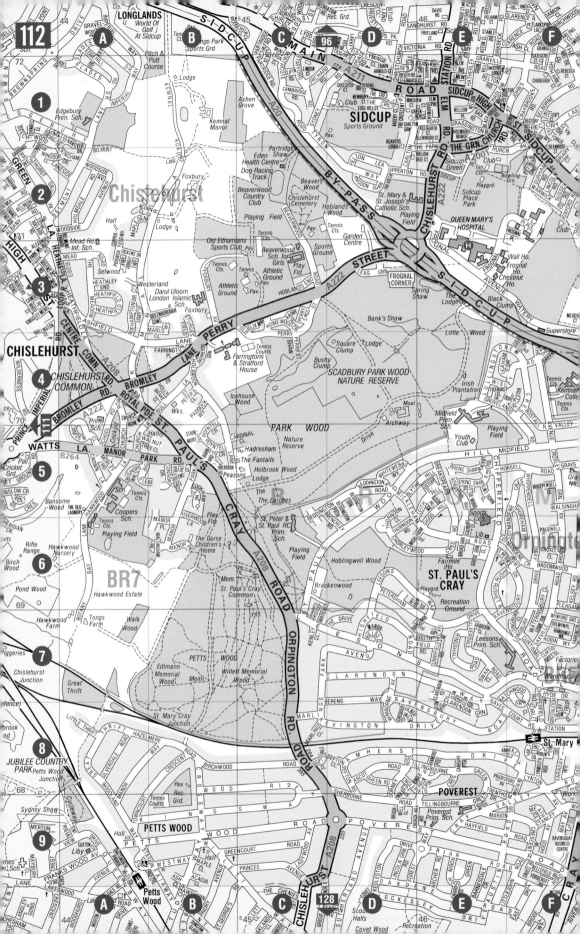

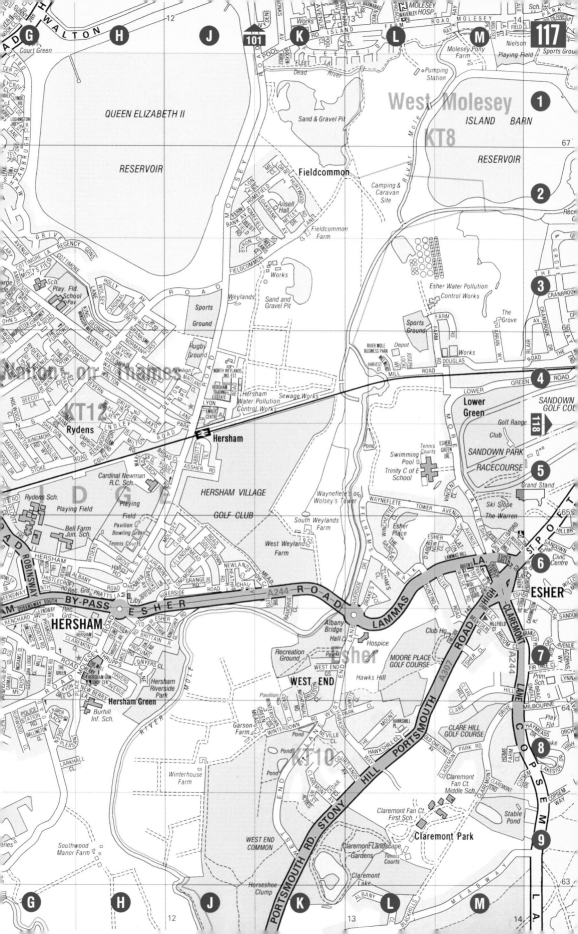

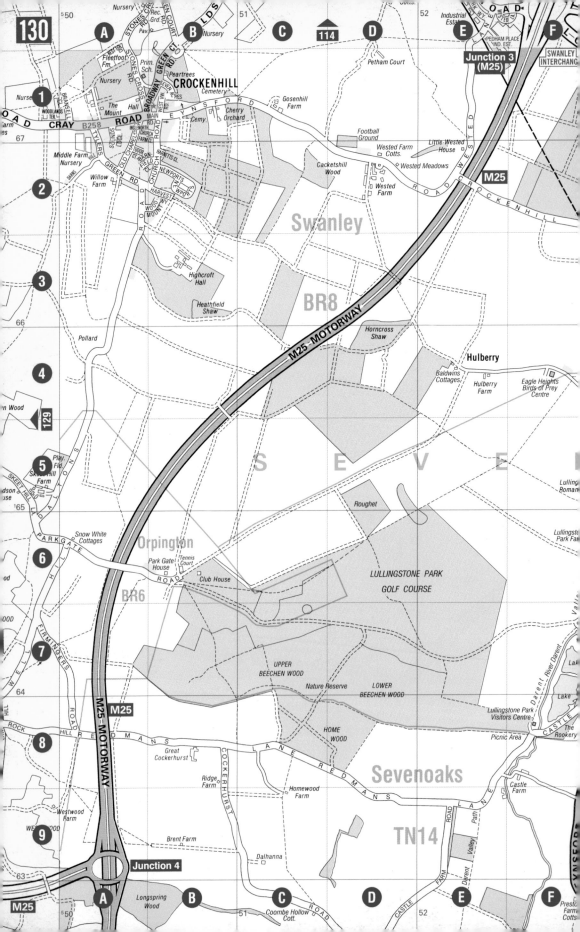

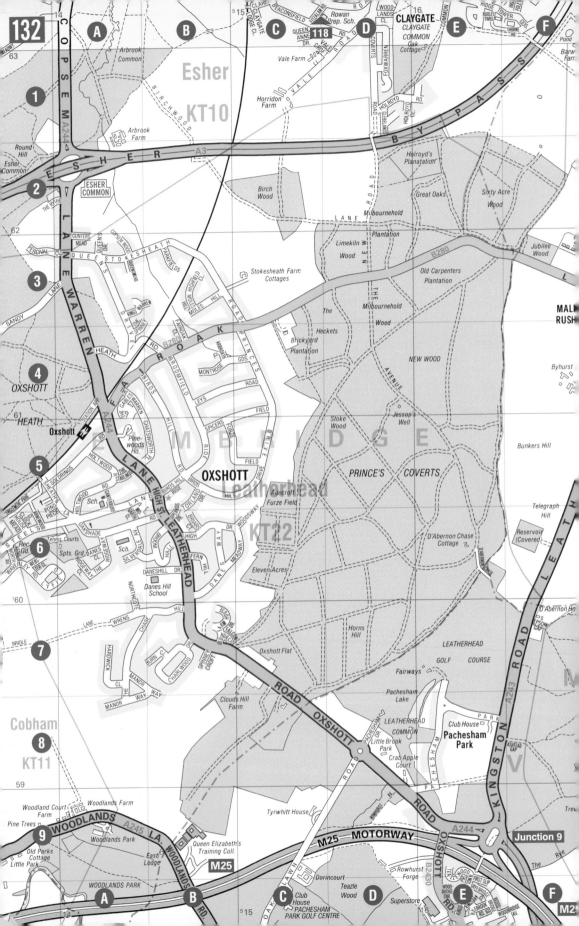

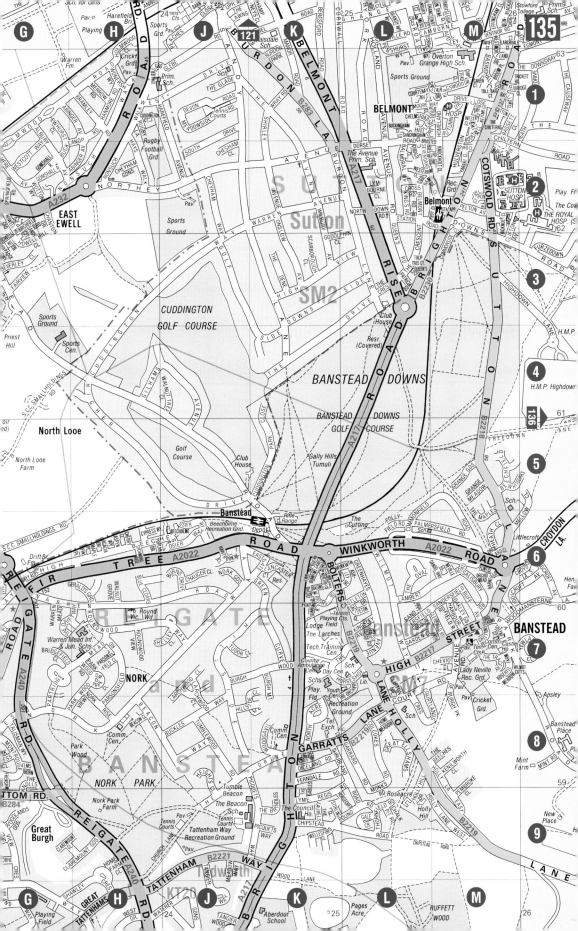

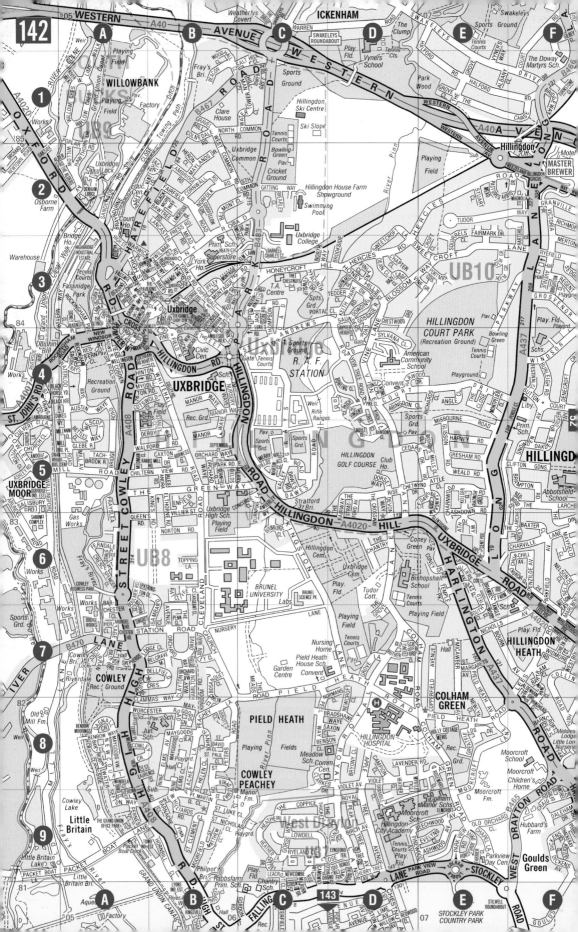

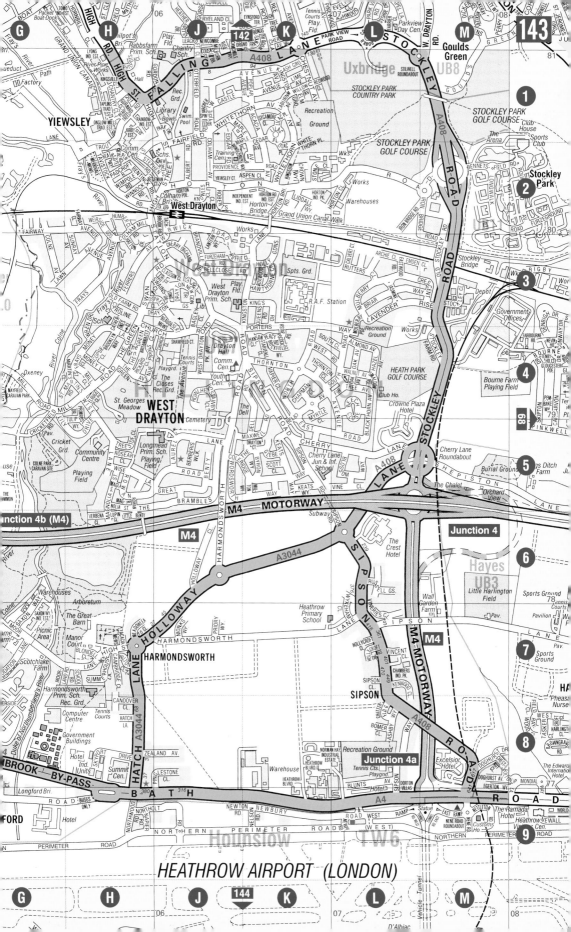

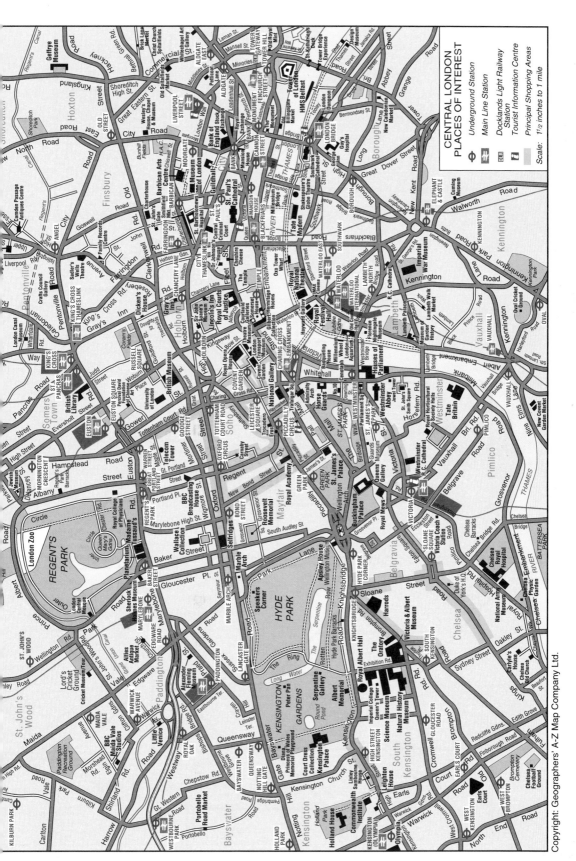

145

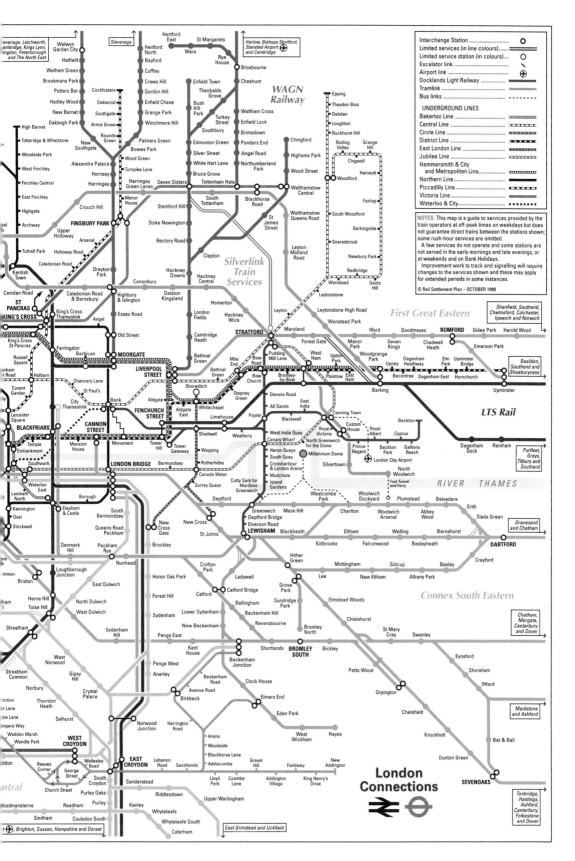

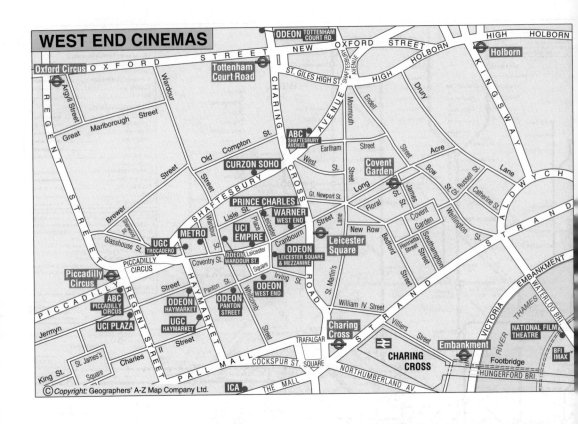

WEST END CINEMAS

Oxford Circus
Tottenham Court Road
Holborn
ABC SHAFTESBURY AVENUE
CURZON SOHO
Covent Garden
PRINCE CHARLES
WARNER WEST END
UCI EMPIRE
METRO
UGC TROCADERO
Leicester Square
ODEON Leicester Square & Mezzanine
ODEON WARDOUR ST.
ODEON WEST END
Piccadilly Circus
ABC PICCADILLY CIRCUS
ODEON HAYMARKET
ODEON PANTON STREET
UGC HAYMARKET
UCI PLAZA
Charing Cross
CHARING CROSS
Embankment
NATIONAL FILM THEATRE
BFI IMAX
ICA

© Copyright: Geographers' A-Z Map Company Ltd.

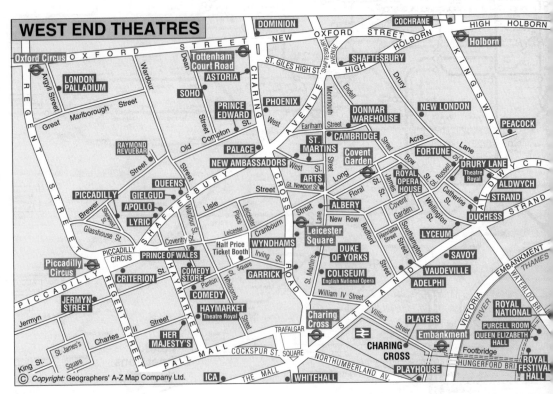

WEST END THEATRES

DOMINION
COCHRANE
Holborn
Oxford Circus
Tottenham Court Road
SHAFTESBURY
LONDON PALLADIUM
ASTORIA
SOHO
PHOENIX
NEW LONDON
PRINCE EDWARD
DONMAR WAREHOUSE
PEACOCK
RAYMOND REVUEBAR
PALACE
ST. MARTINS
CAMBRIDGE
Covent Garden
FORTUNE
NEW AMBASSADORS
DRURY LANE
Theatre Royal
QUEENS
ARTS
ROYAL OPERA HOUSE
ALDWYCH
PICCADILLY
GIELGUD
STRAND
APOLLO
ALBERY
DUCHESS
LYRIC
Leicester Square
LYCEUM
Piccadilly Circus
WYNDHAMS
Half Price Ticket Booth
DUKE OF YORKS
SAVOY
PRINCE OF WALES
GARRICK
VAUDEVILLE
CRITERION
Comedy Store
COLISEUM
English National Opera
ADELPHI
JERMYN STREET
COMEDY
PLAYERS
ROYAL NATIONAL
HAYMARKET
Theatre Royal
Charing Cross
PURCELL ROOM
QUEEN ELIZABETH HALL
HER MAJESTY'S
Embankment
CHARING CROSS
PLAYHOUSE
ROYAL FESTIVAL HALL
ICA
WHITEHALL

© Copyright: Geographers' A-Z Map Company Ltd.

INDEX

Including Streets, Places & Areas, Industrial Estates, Selected Subsidiary Addresses,
Junction Names and Selected Places of Interest.

HOW TO USE THIS INDEX

1. Each street name is followed by its Postal District (or, if outside the London Postal Districts, by its Posttown or Postal Locality), and then by its map reference;
   e.g. Aaron Hill Rd. *E6* —8L **63** is in the East 6 Postal District and is found in square 8L on page **63**. The page number being shown in bold type.
   A strict alphabetical order is followed in which Av., Rd., St. etc. (though abbreviated) are read in full and as part of the street name; e.g. Abbotsmede Clo. appears after
   Abbots Mead but before Abbots Pk.

2. Streets and a selection of Subsidiary names not shown on the Maps, appear in this index in *Italics* with the thoroughfare to which it is connected shown in brackets;
   e.g. *Abady Ho. SW1 —5H* **75** *(off Page St.)*

3. Places and areas are shown in the index in **bold type** the map reference referring to the actual map square in which the town or area is located and not to the place name;
   e.g. **Abbey Wood. —5G 81**

4. An example of a selected place of interest is Admiralty Arch. —2H 75

GENERAL ABBREVIATIONS

All : Alley	Cir : Circus	Gt : Great	M : Mews	Sq : Square
App : Approach	Clo : Close	Grn : Green	Mt : Mount	Sta : Station
Arc : Arcade	Comn : Common	Gro : Grove	Mus : Museum	St : Street
Av : Avenue	Cotts : Cottages	Ho : House	N : North	Ter : Terrace
Bk : Back	Ct : Court	Ind : Industrial	Pal : Palace	Trad : Trading
Boulevd : Boulevard	Cres : Crescent	Info : Information	Pde : Parade	Up : Upper
Bri : Bridge	Cft : Croft	Junct : Junction	Pk : Park	Va : Vale
B'way : Broadway	Dri : Drive	La : Lane	Pas : Passage	Vw : View
Bldgs : Buildings	E : East	Lit : Little	Pl : Place	Vs : Villas
Bus : Business	Embkmt : Embankment	Lwr : Lower	Quad : Quadrant	Vis : Visitors
Cvn : Caravan	Est : Estate	Mc : Mac	Res : Residential	Wlk : Walk
Cen : Centre	Fld : Field	Mnr : Manor	Ri : Rise	W : West
Chu : Church	Gdns : Gardens	Mans : Mansions	Rd : Road	Yd : Yard
Chyd : Churchyard	Gth : Garth	Mkt : Market	Shop : Shopping	
Circ : Circle	Ga : Gate	Mdw : Meadow	S : South	

POSTTOWN AND POSTAL LOCALITY ABBREVIATIONS

Ab L : Abbots Langley	*Chst* : Chislehurst	*Ham* : Ham	*Mit J* : Mitcham Junction	*Stai* : Staines
Abr : Abridge	*Clar P* : Claremont Park	*Hamp* : Hampton	*Mord* : Morden	*Stan* : Stanmore
A'ham : Aldenham	*Clay* : Claygate	*Hamp H* : Hampton Hill	*Nave* : Navestock	*Stanw* : Stanwell
Ark : Arkley	*Cob* : Cobham	*Hamp W* : Hampton Wick	*New Ad* : New Addington	*Stap A* : Stapleford Abbotts
Ashf : Ashford	*Cockf* : Cockfosters	*Hanw* : Hanworth	*New Bar* : New Barnet	*Stoke D* : Stoke D'Abernon
Asht : Ashtead	*Col R* : Collier Row	*Hare* : Harefield	*N Mald* : New Malden	*Stne* : Stone
Ave : Aveley	*Col S* : Colney Street	*Harm* : Harmondsworth	*Noak H* : Noak Hill	*S'leigh* : Stoneleigh
Badg M : Badgers Mount	*Coln* : Colnbrook	*H Hill* : Harold Hill	*N Har* : North Harrow	*Sun* : Sunbury-On-Thames
Bans : Banstead	*Coul* : Coulsdon	*H Wood* : Harold Wood	*N Mald* : New Malden	*Surb* : Surbiton
Bark : Barking	*Cow* : Cowley	*Harr* : Harrow	*N'holt* : Northolt	*Sutt* : Sutton
B'side : Barkingside	*Cran* : Cranford	*Har W* : Harrow Weald	*N Hth* : Northumberland Heath	*S at H* : Sutton At Hone
B'hurst : Barnehurst	*Cray* : Crayford	*H End* : Hatch End	*N'wood* : Northwood	*Swan* : Swanley
Barn : Barnet	*Crock* : Crockenhill	*Havw* : Havering-Atte-Bower	*Orp* : Orpington	*Tad* : Tadworth
B Hth : Batchworth Heath	*Crox G* : Croxley Green	*Hawl* : Hawley	*Oxs* : Oxshott	*Tats* : Tatsfield
Bean : Bean	*Croy* : Croydon	*Hayes* : Hayes (Kent)	*Park* : Park Street	*Tedd* : Teddington
Beck : Beckenham	*Cud* : Cudham	*Hay* : Hayes (Middlesex)	*Pet W* : Petts Wood	*Th Dit* : Thames Ditton
Bedd : Beddington	*Dag* : Dagenham	*H'row* : Heathrow	*Pil H* : Pilgrims Hatch	*T Hth* : Thornton Heath
Bedf : Bedfont	*Dart* : Dartford	*Hers* : Hersham	*Pinn* : Pinner	*Twic* : Twickenham
Bedm : Bedmond	*Den* : Denham	*Hex* : Hextable	*Pot B* : Potters Bar	*Upm* : Upminster
Belm : Belmont	*Dit H* : Ditton Hill	*High Bar* : High Barnet	*Prat B* : Pratts Bottom	*Uxb* : Uxbridge
Belv : Belvedere	*Dow* : Downe	*H Bee* : High Beech	*Purf* : Purfleet	*Wall* : Wallington
Berr G : Berrys Green	*E Barn* : East Barnet	*Hil* : Hillingdon	*Purl* : Purley	*Wal A* : Waltham Abbey
Bex : Bexley	*E Mol* : East Molesey	*Hin W* : Hinchley Wood	*Rad* : Radlett	*Wal X* : Waltham Cross
Bexh : Bexleyheath	*Eastc* : Eastcote	*Horn* : Hornchurch	*Rain* : Rainham	*W on T* : Walton-On-Thames
Big H : Biggin Hill	*Edgw* : Edgware	*Hort K* : Horton Kirby	*Rich* : Richmond	*War* : Warley
Borwd : Borehamwood	*Elm P* : Elm Park	*Houn* : Hounslow	*Rick* : Rickmansworth	*Warl* : Warlingham
Bren : Brentford	*Els* : Elstree	*Ick* : Ickenham	*Ridg* : Ridgeway, The	*Wat* : Watford
Brtwd : Brentwood	*Enf* : Enfield	*Ilf* : Ilford	*Romf* : Romford	*W'stone* : Wealdstone
Brick : Brickendon	*Epp* : Epping	*Iswth* : Isleworth	*Ruis* : Ruislip	*Well E* : Well End
Brick W : Bricket Wood	*Eps* : Epsom	*Iver* : Iver	*Rush G* : Rush Green	*Well* : Welling
Brim : Brimsdown	*Eri* : Erith	*Kenl* : Kenley	*St Alb* : St Albans	*Wemb* : Wembley
Brom : Bromley	*Esh* : Esher	*Kent* : Kenton	*St M* : St Mary Cray	*Wen* : Wennington
Buck H : Buckhurst Hill	*Ewe* : Ewell	*Kes* : Keston	*St P* : St Pauls Cray	*W Dray* : West Drayton
Bush : Bushey	*Eyns* : Eynsford	*Kew* : Kew	*Shenl* : Shenley	*W End* : West End
Bus H : Bushey Heath	*Farnb* : Farnborough	*K Lan* : Kings Langley	*Shep* : Shepperton	*W Ewe* : West Ewell
Cars : Carshalton	*F'ham* : Farningham	*King T* : Kingston Upon Thames	*Shor* : Shoreham	*W Mol* : West Molesey
Cat : Caterham	*Fawk* : Fawkham	*Kgswd* : Kingswood	*Short* : Shortlands	*W W'ck* : West Wickham
Chad H : Chadwell Heath	*Felt* : Feltham	*Knat* : Knatts Valley	*Sidc* : Sidcup	*W'ham* : Westerham
Chan X : Chandlers Cross	*Frog* : Frogmore	*Lea* : Leatherhead	*Slou* : Slough	*Wey* : Weybridge
Cheam : Cheam	*Gid P* : Gidea Park	*Leav* : Leavesden	*S Croy* : South Croydon	*W Vill* : Whiteley Village
Chels : Chelsfield	*G Oak* : Goffs Oak	*Let H* : Letchmore Heath	*S Dar* : South Darenth	*Whit* : Whitton
Chel : Chelsham	*Gnfd* : Greenford	*L Hth* : Little Heath	*S Harr* : South Harrow	*Whyt* : Whyteleafe
Chesh : Cheshunt	*Grnh* : Greenhithe	*H'row A* : London Heathrow Airport	*S Ock* : South Ockendon	*Wilm* : Wilmington
Chess : Chessington	*Grn St* : Green Street Green	*Lou* : Loughton	*S Ruis* : South Ruislip	*Wfd G* : Woodford Green
Chig : Chigwell	*Hack* : Hackbridge	*Mawn* : Mawneys	*S Wea* : South Weald	*Wor Pk* : Worcester Park
Chips : Chipstead	*Hals* : Halstead	*Mitc* : Mitcham	*S'hall* : Southall	*Yiew* : Yiewsley

INDEX

101 Bus. Units. *SW11* —2D **90**	Abbey Clo. *Hay* —2F **68**	Abbey Est. *NW8* —4M **57**	Abbey Ind. Est. *Wemb* —4K **55**	Abbey Pde. *W5* —6K **55**
198 Gallery. —5M **91**	Abbey Clo. *N'holt* —6K **53**	Abbeyfield Clo. *Mitc* —6C **106**	Abbey La. *E15* —5A **62**	Abbey Pde. *Beck* —4L **109**
(off Railton Rd.)	Abbey Clo. *Pinn* —1F **36**	Abbeyfield Est. *SE16* —5G **77**	Abbey La. *Beck* —4L **109**	Abbey Pl. *Dart* —4H **99**
	Abbey Clo. *Romf* —4E **50**	Abbeyfield Rd. *SE16* —5G **77**	Abbey La. Commercial Est. *E15*	Abbey Retail Pk. *Bark* —3M **63**
	Abbey Ct. *NW8* —5A **58**	*(in two parts)*	—5C **62**	Abbey Rd. *E15* —5B **62**
Aaron Hill Rd. *E6* —8L **63**	*(off Abbey Rd.)*	Abbeyfields Clo. *NW10* —6L **55**	Abbey Life Ct. *E16* —8F **62**	Abbey Rd. *NW6 & NW8* —3M **57**
Abady Ho. SW1 —5H **75**	Abbey Ct. *SE17* —6A **76**	Abbey Gdns. *NW8* —5A **58**	*Abbey Lodge. NW1* —6C **58**	Abbey Rd. *NW10* —4M **55**
(off Page St.)	*(off Macleod St.)*	Abbey Gdns. *SE16* —5E **76**	*(off Park Rd.)*	Abbey Rd. *SW19* —4A **106**
Abberley M. *SW4* —2F **90**	Abbey Ct. *Hamp* —4L **101**	Abbey Gdns. *W6* —7J **73**	Abbey Mead Ind. Est. *Wal A* —7J **7**	Abbey Rd. *Bark* —3M **63**
Abberton Wlk. *Rain* —4D **66**	Abbey Ct. *Wal A* —7H **7**	Abbey Gdns. *Chst* —5L **111**	Abbey M. *E17* —3L **45**	Abbey Rd. *Belv* —5H **81**
Abbess Clo. *E6* —8J **63**	Abbey Cres. *Belv* —5L **81**	Abbey Gro. *SE2* —5F **80**	Abbey Mills. *Wal A* —6H **7**	Abbey Rd. *Bexh* —3J **97**
Abbess Clo. *SW2* —7M **91**	Abbeydale Ct. *E17* —1B **46**	Abbey Hill Rd. *Sidc* —8G **97**	Abbey Orchard St. *SW1* —4H **75**	Abbey Rd. *Croy* —5M **123**
Abbeville M. *SW4* —3H **91**	*Abbeydale Ct. S'hall* —9M **53**	*Abbey Ho. E15* —5C **62**	Abbey Orchard St. Est. *SW1*	Abbey Rd. *Enf* —7C **16**
Abbeville Rd. *N8* —2H **43**	*(off Dormers Ri.)*	*(off Baker's Row)*	*(in two parts)* —4H **75**	Abbey Rd. *Ilf* —3B **48**
Abbeville Rd. *SW4* —5G **91**	Abbeydale Rd. *Wemb* —4K **55**	*Abbey Ho. NW8* —6A **58**	*Abbey Pde. SW19* —4A **106**	Abbey Rd. *S Croy* —2H **139**
Abbey Av. *Wemb* —5J **55**	Abbey Dri. *SW17* —2E **106**	*(off Garden Rd.)*	*(off Merton High St.)*	Abbey Rd. *Wal X* —7E **6**
Abbey Bus. Cen. *SW8* —9G **75**	Abbey Dri. *Ab L* —5E **4**	Abbey Ind. Est. *Mitc* —9D **106**		Abbey St. *E13* —7E **62**

149

Aldersey Gdns.—Altham Ct.

Aldersey Gdns. Bark —2B 64
Aldersford Clo. SE4 —4H 93
Aldersgate St. EC1 —8A 60
Alders Gro. E Mol —9B 102
Aldersgrove. Wal A —7L 7
Aldersgrove Av. SE9 —9H 95
Aldershot Rd. NW6 —4K 57
Aldershot Ter. SE18 —8L 79
Aldersmead Av. Croy —1H 125
Aldersmead Rd. Beck —4J 109
Alderson Pl. S'hall —2A 70
Alderson St. W10 —7J 57
Alders Rd. Edgw —5A 24
Alders, The. N21 —8L 15
Alders, The. SW16 —1G 107
Alders, The. Den —2A 142
Alders, The. Felt —1J 101
Alders, The. Houn —7K 69
Alders, The. W W'ck —3M 125
Alderton Clo. NW10 —8B 40
Alderton Clo. Lou —6L 19
Alderton Cres. NW4 —3F 40
Alderton Hall La. Lou —6L 19
Alderton Hill. Lou —7J 19
Alderton M. Lou —6L 19
Alderton Ri. Lou —6L 19
Alderton Rd. SE24 —2A 92
Alderton Rd. Croy —2D 124
Alderton Way. NW4 —3F 40
Alderton Way. Lou —7K 19
Alderville Rd. SW6 —1K 89
Alder Wlk. Ilf —1A 64
Alder Wlk. Wat —8F 4
Alder Way. Swan —6B 114
Alderwick Ct. N7 —2K 59
(off St Clement St.)
Alderwick Dri. Houn —2B 86
Alderwood Rd. SE9 —5B 96
Aldford Ho. W1 —2E 74
(off Park St.)
Aldford St. W1 —2E 74
Aldgate. (Junct.) —9D 60
Aldgate. E1 —9D 60
(off Whitechapel High St.)
Aldgate. EC3 —9C 60
Aldgate Av. E1 —9D 60
Aldgate Barrs. E1 —9D 60
(off Whitechapel High St.)
Aldgate High St. EC3 —9D 60
Aldgate Triangle. E1 —9E 60
(off Coke St.)
Aldham Ho. SE4 —1K 93
Aldine Ct. W12 —3G 73
(off Aldine St.)
Aldine Pl. W12 —3G 73
Aldine St. W12 —3G 73
Aldingham Ct. Horn —1F 66
(off Easedale Dri.)
Aldingham Gdns. Horn —1E 66
Aldington Clo. Dag —6G 49
Aldington Ct. E8 —3E 60
(off Lansdowne Dri.)
Aldington Rd. SE18 —4H 79
Aldis M. SW17 —2C 106
Aldis St. SW17 —2C 106
Aldred Rd. NW6 —1L 57
Aldren Rd. SW17 —9A 90
Aldrich Cres. New Ad —1A 140
Aldriche Way. E4 —6A 30
Aldrich Gdns. Sutt —5K 121
Aldrich Ter. SW18 —8A 90
Aldrick Ho. N1 —4K 59
(off Barnsbury Est.)
Aldridge Av. Edgw —3M 23
Aldridge Av. Enf —2L 17
Aldridge Av. Ruis —7G 37
Aldridge Av. Stan —8J 23
Aldridge Ri. N Mald —2C 120
Aldridge Rd. Vs. W11 —8K 57
Aldridge Wlk. N14 —9J 15
Aldrington Rd. SW16 —2G 107
Aldsworth Clo. W9 —7M 57
Aldwick Clo. SE9 —9B 96
Aldwick Rd. Croy —5K 123
Aldworth Gro. SE13 —5A 94
Aldworth Rd. E15 —3C 62
Aldwych. WC2 —9K 59
Aldwych Av. Ilf —2A 48
Aldwych Clo. Horn —6E 50
Aldwych Theatre. —9K 59
(off Aldwych)
Aldwyn Ho. SW8 —8J 75
(off Davidson Gdns.)
Alers Rd. Bexh —4H 97
Alesia Clo. N22 —7J 27
Alestan Beck Rd. E16 —9H 63
Alexa Ct. W8 —5L 73
Alexa Ct. Sutt —8L 121
Alexander Av. NW10 —3F 56
Alexander Clo. Barn —6B 14
Alexander Clo. Brom —3E 126
Alexander Clo. Sidc —5C 96
Alexander Clo. S'hall —2A 70
Alexander Clo. Twic —8C 86
Alexander Ct. Beck —5B 110
Alexander Ct. Stan —1K 39
Alexander Evans M. SE23 —8H 93
Alexander Fleming Mus. —9B 58
(off Praed St.)
Alexander Ho. E14 —4L 77
(off Tiller Rd.)
Alexander M. W2 —9M 57
Alexander Pl. SW7 —5C 74
Alexander Rd. N19 —8J 43
Alexander Rd. Bexh —1H 97
Alexander Rd. Chst —3M 111
Alexander Rd. Coul —7F 136
Alexander Sq. SW3 —5C 74
Alexander St. W2 —9L 57
Alexander Studios. SW11 —3B 90
(off Haydon Way)
Alexandra Av. N22 —8H 27
Alexandra Av. SW11 —9E 74
Alexandra Av. W4 —8B 72
Alexandra Av. Harr —6K 37
Alexandra Av. S'hall —1K 69
Alexandra Av. Sutt —5L 121
Alexandra Av. Warl —9K 139
Alexandra Clo. SE8 —7K 77
Alexandra Clo. Ashf —4B 100
Alexandra Clo. Harr —8L 37
Alexandra Clo. Swan —6C 114
Alexandra Clo. W on T —4E 116
Alexandra Cotts. SE14 —9K 77
Alexandra Ct. N14 —7G 15
Alexandra Ct. SW7 —4A 74
(off Queen's Ga.)
Alexandra Ct. W2 —1M 73
(off Moscow Rd.)
Alexandra Ct. W9 —7A 58
(off Maida Va.)
Alexandra Ct. Ashf —3B 100
Alexandra Ct. Chesh —3D 6
Alexandra Ct. Gnfd —5M 53
Alexandra Ct. Houn —1M 85
Alexandra Ct. Wat —4G 9
Alexandra Cres. Brom —3D 110
Alexandra Dri. SE19 —2C 108
Alexandra Dri. Surb —2L 119
Alexandra Gdns. N10 —2F 42
Alexandra Gdns. W4 —8C 72
Alexandra Gdns. Cars —9E 122
Alexandra Gdns. Houn —1M 85
Alexandra Gro. N4 —6M 43
Alexandra Gro. N12 —5M 25
Alexandra Ho. W6 —6G 73
(off Queen Caroline St.)
Alexandra Mans. SW3 —7B 74
(off Moravian Clo.)
Alexandra M. N2 —1D 42
Alexandra M. SW19 —3K 105
Alexandra Palace. —9H 27
Alexandra Pal. Way. N22 —2G 43
Alexandra Pde. Harr —9M 37
Alexandra Pk. Rd. N10 —9F 26
Alexandra Pk. Rd. N22 —8G 27
Alexandra Pl. NW8 —4A 58
Alexandra Pl. SE25 —9B 108
Alexandra Pl. Croy —3C 124
Alexandra Rd. E6 —6L 63
Alexandra Rd. E10 —8A 46
Alexandra Rd. E17 —4K 45
Alexandra Rd. E18 —1F 46
Alexandra Rd. N8 —1L 43
Alexandra Rd. N9 —9F 16
Alexandra Rd. N10 —8F 26
Alexandra Rd. N15 —3B 44
Alexandra Rd. NW4 —2H 41
Alexandra Rd. NW8 —4A 58
Alexandra Rd. SE26 —3H 109
Alexandra Rd. SW14 —2B 88
Alexandra Rd. SW19 —3K 105
Alexandra Rd. W4 —3B 72
Alexandra Rd. Ashf —4B 100
Alexandra Rd. Borwd —2B 12
Alexandra Rd. Bren —7H 71
Alexandra Rd. Chad H —4J 49
Alexandra Rd. Croy —3C 124
Alexandra Rd. Enf —6H 17
Alexandra Rd. Eps —5D 134
Alexandra Rd. Eri —7D 82
Alexandra Rd. Houn —1M 85
Alexandra Rd. King T —4L 103
Alexandra Rd. Mitc —4C 106
Alexandra Rd. Rain —4D 66
Alexandra Rd. Rich —1K 87
Alexandra Rd. Romf —4D 50
Alexandra Rd. Th Dit —9D 102
Alexandra Rd. Twic —5G 87
Alexandra Rd. Uxb —5B 142
Alexandra Rd. Warl —9K 139
Alexandra Rd. Wat —4E 8
Alexandra Rd. Ind. Est. Enf —6H 17
Alexandra Sq. Mord —9L 105
Alexandra St. E16 —8E 62
Alexandra St. SE14 —8J 77
Alexandra Ter. E14 —6M 77
(off Westferry Rd.)
Alexandra Wlk. SE19 —2C 108
Alexandra Way. Eps —3L 133
Alexandra Way. Wal X —7F 6
Alexandra Yd. E9 —4H 61
Alexandria Rd. W13 —1E 70
Alexis St. SE16 —5E 76
Alfan La. Dart —2B 114
Alfearn Rd. E5 —9G 45
Alford Ct. N1 —5A 60
(off Shepherdess Wlk.)
Alford Grn. New Ad —8B 126
Alford Ho. N6 —4G 43
Alford Pl. N1 —5A 60
Alford Rd. Eri —6A 82
Alfoxton Av. N8 —2M 43
Alfreda St. SW11 —9F 74
Alfred Clo. W4 —5B 72
Alfred Finlay Ho. N22 —9M 27
Alfred Gdns. S'hall —1J 69
Alfred Ho. E9 —1J 61
(off Homerton Rd.)
Alfred Ho. E12 —3J 63
(off Tennyson Av.)
Alfred M. W1 —8H 59
Alfred Nunn Ho. NW10 —4D 56
Alfred Pl. WC1 —8H 59
Alfred Prior Ho. E12 —9L 47
Alfred Rd. E15 —1D 62
Alfred Rd. SE25 —9E 108
Alfred Rd. W2 —8L 57
Alfred Rd. W3 —2A 72
Alfred Rd. Belv —6K 81
Alfred Rd. Buck H —2H 31
Alfred Rd. Dart —1J 115
(in two parts)
Alfred Rd. Felt —8G 85
Alfred Rd. King T —7J 103
Alfred Rd. Sutt —7A 122
Alfred's Gdns. Bark —5C 64
Alfred St. E3 —6K 61
Alfreds Way. Bark —6M 63
Alfred's Way Ind. Est. Bark —5E 64
Alfreton Clo. SW19 —9H 89
Alfriston. Surb —1K 119
Alfriston Av. Croy —2J 123
Alfriston Av. Harr —4L 37
Alfriston Clo. Surb —9K 103
Alfriston Rd. SW11 —4D 90
Algar Clo. Iswth —2E 86
Algar Clo. Stan —5D 22
Algar Ho. SE1 —3M 75
(off Webber Row)
Algar Rd. Iswth —2E 86
Algarve Rd. SW18 —7M 89
Algernon Rd. NW4 —4E 40
Algernon Rd. NW6 —4L 57
Algernon Rd. SE13 —3M 93
Algers Clo. Lou —7H 19
Algers Rd. Lou —7H 19
Alghers Mead. Lou —7H 19
Algiers Rd. SE13 —3L 93
Alibon Gdns. Dag —1L 65
Alibon Rd. Dag —1K 65
Alice Ct. SW15 —3K 89
Alice Gilliatt Ct. W14 —7K 73
(off Star Rd.)
Alice La. E3 —4K 61
Alice M. Tedd —2D 102
Alice Owen Technology Cen. EC1
(off Goswell Rd.) —6M 59
Alice Shepherd Ho. E14 —3A 78
(off Manchester Rd.)
Alice St. SE1 —4C 76
(in two parts)
Alice Thompson Clo. SE12
—8G 95
Alice Walker Clo. SE24 —3M 91
Alice Way. Houn —3M 85
Alicia Av. Harr —2F 38
Alicia Clo. Harr —3G 39
Alicia Gdns. Harr —2F 38
Alicia Ho. Well —9F 80
Alie St. E1 —9D 60
Alington Cres. NW9 —5A 40
Alington Gro. Wall —1G 137
Alison Clo. E6 —9L 63
Alison Clo. Croy —3H 125
Alison Ct. SE1 —6E 76
Aliwal Rd. SW11 —3C 90
Alkerden Rd. W4 —6C 72
Alkham Rd. N16 —7D 44
Allan Barclay Clo. N15 —4D 44
Allan Clo. N Mald —9B 104
Allandale Av. N3 —1J 41
Allandale Pl. Orp —5H 129
Allandale Rd. Enf —9D 6
Allandale Rd. Horn —5D 50
Allanson Ct. E10 —7L 45
(off Leyton Grange Est.)
Allan Way. W3 —8A 56
Allard Clo. Orp —2G 129
Allard Cres. Bus H —1A 22
Allard Gdns. SW4 —4H 91
Allardyce St. SW4 —3K 91
Allbrook Clo. Tedd —2C 102
Allcroft Rd. NW5 —1E 58
Allenby Av. S Croy —1A 138
Allenby Clo. Gnfd —6L 53
Allenby Dri. Horn —6J 51
Allenby Rd. SE23 —9J 93
Allenby Rd. Big H —9J 141
Allenby Rd. S'hall —9L 53
Allen Clo. Mitc —5F 106
Allen Clo. Sun —5F 100
Allen Ct. E17 —4L 45
(off Yunus Khan Clo.)
Allen Ct. Gnfd —1D 54
Allendale Av. S'hall —9L 53
Allendale Clo. SE5 —1B 92
Allendale Clo. SE26 —2H 109
Allendale Rd. Gnfd —2F 54
Allen Edwards Dri. SW8 —9J 75
Allenford Ho. SW15 —5D 88
(off Tunworth Cres.)
Allen Rd. E3 —5K 61
Allen Rd. N16 —9C 44
Allen Rd. Beck —6H 109
Allen Rd. Croy —3L 123
Allen Rd. Rain —5G 67
Allen Rd. Sun —5F 100
Allensbury Pl. NW1 —3H 59
Allens Rd. Enf —7G 17
Allen St. W8 —4L 73
Allenswood Rd. SE9 —2J 95
Allerford Ct. Harr —3A 38
Allerford Rd. SE6 —9M 93
Allerton Clo. Borwd —2K 11
Allerton Ho. N1 —6B 60
(off Provost Est.)
Allerton Rd. N16 —7A 44
Allerton Rd. Borwd —2J 11
Allerton St. N1 —6B 60
Allerton Wlk. N7 —7K 43
Allestree Rd. SW6 —8J 73
Alleyn Cres. SE21 —8B 92
Alleyndale Rd. Dag —7G 49
Alleyn Ho. SE1 —4B 76
(off Burbage Clo.)
Alleyn Pk. SE21 —8B 92
Alleyn Pk. S'hall —6L 69
Alleyn Rd. SE21 —9B 92
Allfarthing La. SW18 —5M 89
Allgood Clo. Mord —1H 121
Allgood St. E2 —5D 60
Allhallows La. EC4 —1B 76
Allhallows Rd. E6 —8J 63
All Hallows Rd. N17 —8C 28
Alliance Clo. Wemb —9H 39
Alliance Ct. W3 —8M 55
Alliance Rd. E13 —8G 63
Alliance Rd. SE18 —7E 80
Alliance Rd. W3 —7M 55
Allied Ind. Est. W3 —3C 72
Allied Way. W3 —3C 72
Allingham Clo. W7 —1D 70
Allingham St. N1 —5A 60
Allington Av. N17 —6C 28
Allington Av. Shep —7C 100
Allington Clo. SW19 —2H 105
Allington Clo. Gnfd —3A 54
Allington Ct. SW1 —4F 74
(off Allington St.)
Allington Ct. SW8 —1G 91
Allington Ct. Enf —7H 17
(in two parts)
Allington Rd. NW4 —3F 40
Allington Rd. W10 —6J 57
Allington Rd. Harr —3A 38
Allington Rd. Orp —4B 128
Allington St. SW1 —4F 74
Allison Clo. SE10 —9A 78
Allison Clo. Wal A —5M 7
Allison Gro. SE21 —7C 92
Allison Rd. N8 —3L 43
Allison Rd. W3 —9A 56
Alliston Ho. E2 —6D 60
(off Gibraltar Wlk.)
Allitsen Rd. NW8 —5C 58
(in two parts)
Allnutt Way. SW4 —4H 91
Alloa Rd. SE8 —6H 77
Alloa Rd. Ilf —7E 48
Allom Ho. W11 —1J 73
(off Clarendon Rd.)
Allonby Dri. Ruis —5A 36
Allonby Gdns. Wemb —6G 39
Allonby Ho. E14 —8J 61
(off Aston St.)
Alloway Rd. E3 —6J 61
Allport Ho. SE5 —2B 92
(off Denmark Hill)
All Saints Clo. N9 —2E 28
All Saints Clo. Chig —3E 32
All Saints Ct. E1 —1G 77
(off Johnson St.)
All Saints Ct. SW11 —8F 74
(off Prince of Wales Dri.)
All Saints Ct. Houn —9H 69
(off Springwell Rd.)
All Saints Cres. Wat —6H 5
All Saints Dri. SE3 —1C 94
All Saints Dri. S Croy —4D 138
All Saints Ho. W11 —8K 57
All Saints M. Harr —6C 22
All Saints Pas. SW18 —4L 89
All Saints Rd. SW19 —4A 106
(in two parts)
All Saints Rd. W3 —4A 72
All Saints Rd. W11 —8K 57
All Saints Rd. Sutt —5M 121
All Saints St. N1 —5K 59
All Saints Tower. E10 —5M 45
All Seasons Ct. E1 —2E 76
(off Aragon M.)
Allsop Pl. NW1 —7D 58
All Souls Av. NW10 —5F 56
All Souls' Pl. W1 —8F 58
Allum La. Els —7J 11
Allum Way. N20 —1A 26
Allwood Clo. SE26 —1H 109
Alma Av. E4 —7A 30
Alma Av. Horn —9J 51
Almack Rd. E5 —9G 45
Alma Clo. N10 —8F 26
Alma Ct. Borwd —2K 11
Alma Ct. Harr —7B 38
Alma Cres. Sutt —7J 121
Alma Gro. SE1 —5D 76
Alma Ho. Bren —7J 71
Alma Pl. NW10 —6F 56
Alma Pl. SE19 —4D 108
Alma Pl. T Hth —9L 107
Alma Rd. N10 —7F 26
Alma Rd. SW18 —3A 90
Alma Rd. Cars —7C 122
Alma Rd. Enf —7J 17
Alma Rd. Esh —3C 118
Alma Rd. Orp —4H 129
Alma Rd. Sidc —9E 96
Alma Rd. S'hall —1J 69
Alma Rd. Ind. Est. Enf —6H 17
Alma Row. Harr —8B 22
Alma Sq. NW8 —5A 58
Alma St. E15 —2B 62
Alma St. NW5 —2F 58
Alma Ter. SW18 —6B 90
Alma Ter. W8 —4L 73
Almeida St. N1 —4M 59
Almeida Theatre. —4M 59
(off Almeida St.)
Almeric Rd. SW11 —3D 90
Almer Rd. SW20 —4E 104
Almington St. N4 —6K 43
Almond Av. W5 —4H 71
Almond Av. Cars —4D 122
Almond Av. Uxb —8A 36
Almond Av. W Dray —4L 143
Almond Clo. SE15 —1E 92
Almond Clo. Brom —2L 127
Almond Clo. Felt —7E 84
Almond Clo. Hay —1C 68
Almond Clo. Ruis —8D 36
Almond Clo. Shep —6A 100
Almond Dri. Swan —6B 114
Almond Gro. Bren —8F 70
Almond Rd. N17 —7E 28
Almond Rd. SE16 —5F 76
Almond Rd. Eps —3B 134
Almonds Av. Buck H —2E 30
Almondsbury Ct. SE15 —8C 76
(off Newent Clo.)
Almond Way. Borwd —6M 11
Almond Way. Brom —2L 127
Almond Way. Harr —9M 21
Almond Way. Mitc —9H 107
Almorah Rd. N1 —3B 60
Almorah Rd. Houn —9H 69
Almshouse La. Chess —1G 133
Almshouses La. Enf —1F 16
Almshouses. Lou —3K 19
Almshouses, The. Chesh —3D 6
(off Turner's Hill)
Alnmouth Ct. S'hall —9A 54
(off Fleming Rd.)
Alnwick. N17 —7F 28
Alnwick Ct. Dart —5M 99
(off Osbourne Rd.)
Alnwick Gro. Mord —8M 105
Alnwick Rd. E16 —9G 63
Alnwick Rd. SE12 —5F 94
Alperton. —5J 55
Alperton La. Gnfd & Wemb —6G 55
Alperton St. W10 —7K 57
Alphabet Gdns. Cars —1B 122
Alphabet Sq. E3 —8L 61
Alpha Bus. Cen. E17 —3K 45
Alpha Clo. NW1 —7C 58
Alpha Est. Hay —3C 68
Alpha Gro. E14 —3L 77
Alpha Ho. NW1 —7C 58
(off Ashbridge St.)
Alpha Ho. NW6 —5L 57
Alpha Ho. SW9 —3K 91
Alpha Pl. NW6 —5L 57
Alpha Pl. SW3 —7C 74
Alpha Pl. Mord —3H 121
Alpha Rd. E4 —3L 29
Alpha Rd. N18 —6E 28
Alpha Rd. SE14 —9K 77
Alpha Rd. Croy —3C 124
Alpha Rd. Enf —6J 17
Alpha Rd. Surb —1K 119
Alpha Rd. Tedd —2B 102
Alpha Rd. Uxb —7F 142
Alpha St. SE15 —1E 92
Alphea Clo. SW19 —4C 106
Alpine Av. Surb —4A 120
Alpine Bus. Cen. E6 —8L 63
Alpine Clo. Croy —5C 124
Alpine Copse. Brom —6L 111
Alpine Rd. SE16 —5G 77
(in two parts)
Alpine Rd. W on T —2E 116
Alpine Vw. Cars —7C 122
Alpine Wlk. Stan —2C 22
Alpine Way. E6 —8L 63
Alric Av. NW10 —3B 56
Alric Av. N Mald —7C 104
Alroy Rd. N4 —5L 43
Alsace Rd. SE17 —6C 76
Alscot Rd. SE1 —5D 76
(in two parts)
Alscot Rd. Ind. Est. SE1 —4D 76
Alscot Way. SE1 —5D 76
Alsike Rd. SE2 & Eri —4H 81
Alsom Av. Wor Pk —6E 120
Alston Clo. Surb —2F 118
Alston Rd. N18 —5F 28
Alston Rd. SW17 —1B 106
Alston Rd. Barn —5J 13
Altair Clo. N17 —6D 28
Altair Way. N'wd —4D 20
Altash Way. SE9 —8K 95
Altenburg Av. W13 —4F 70
Altenburg Gdns. SW11 —3D 90
Alt Gro. SW19 —4K 105
Altham Ct. Harr —8M 21

Altham Rd.—Antigua Wlk.

Altham Rd. Pinn —7J 21
Althea St. SW6 —1M 89
Althorne Gdns. E18 —2D 46
Althorne Way. Dag —7L 49
Althorp Clo. Barn —9E 12
Althorpe M. SW11 —9B 74
Althorpe Rd. Harr —3A 38
Althorp Rd. SW17 —7D 90
Altior Ct. N6 —4G 43
Altmore Av. E6 —3K 63
Alton Av. Stan —7D 22
Alton Clo. Bex —7J 97
Alton Clo. Iswth —1D 86
Alton Cotts. F'ham —3J 131
Alton Gdns. Beck —4L 109
Alton Gdns. Twic —6B 86
Alton Rd. N17 —1B 44
Alton Rd. SW15 —7E 88
Alton Rd. Croy —5L 123
Alton Rd. Rich —3J 87
Alton St. E14 —8M 61
Altyre Clo. Beck —9K 109
Altyre Rd. Croy —4B 124
Altyre Way. Beck —9K 109
Aluna Ct. SE15 —2G 93
Alvanley Gdns. NW6 —1M 57
Alva Way. Wat —2H 21
Alverstoke Rd. Romf —7J 35
Alverstone Av. SW19 —8L 89
Alverstone Av. Barn & E Barn —9C 14
Alverstone Gdns. SE9 —7A 96
Alverstone Ho. SE11 —7L 75
Alverstone Rd. E12 —9L 47
Alverstone Rd. NW2 —3G 57
Alverstone Rd. N Mald —8D 104
Alverstone Rd. Wemb —6K 39
Alverston Gdns. SE25 —9C 108
Alverton St. SE8 —6K 77
(in two parts)
Alveston Av. Harr —1F 38
Alvey St. SE17 —6C 76
Alvia Gdns. Sutt —6A 122
Alvington Cres. E8 —1D 60
Alway Av. Eps —7B 120
Alwin Pl. Wat —6C 8
Alwold Cres. SE12 —5F 94
Alwyn Av. W4 —6B 72
Alwyn Clo. Els —8K 11
Alwyn Clo. New Ad —9M 125
Alwyne La. N1 —3M 59
Alwyne Pl. N1 —2A 60
Alwyne Rd. N1 —3A 60
Alwyne Rd. SW19 —3K 105
Alwyne Rd. W7 —1C 70
Alwyne Sq. N1 —2A 60
Alwyne Vs. N1 —3M 59
Alwyn Gdns. NW4 —2E 40
Alwyn Gdns. W3 —9M 55
Alyth Gdns. NW11 —4L 41
Alzette Ho. E2 —5H 61
(off Mace St.)
Amadeus Ho. Brom —7F 110
(off Elmfield Rd.)
Amalgamated Dri. Bren —7E 70
Amanda Clo. Chig —6B 32
Amanda M. Romf —3A 50
Amar Ct. SE18 —5D 80
Amar Deep Ct. SE18 —6D 80
Amazon St. E1 —9E 60
Ambassador Clo. Houn —1J 85
Ambassador Gdns. E6 —8K 63
Ambassadors' Ct. SW1 —2G 75
(off St James' Pal.)
Ambassador Sq. E14 —5M 77
Ambassadors Theatre. —1H 75
(off West St.)
Amber Av. E17 —8J 29
Amberden Av. N3 —1L 41
Ambergate St. SE17 —6M 75
Amber Gro. NW2 —6H 41
Amberley Clo. Orp —7D 128
Amberley Clo. Pinn —1K 37
Amberley Ct. Beck —4K 109
Amberley Ct. Sidc —2G 113
Amberley Gdns. Enf —9C 16
Amberley Gdns. Eps —6D 120
Amberley Gro. SE26 —2F 108
Amberley Gro. Croy —2D 124
Amberley Rd. E10 —5L 45
Amberley Rd. N13 —2K 27
Amberley Rd. SE2 —7H 81
Amberley Rd. W9 —8L 57
Amberley Rd. Buck H —1G 31
Amberley Rd. Enf —9D 16
Amberley Ter. Wat —8J 9
(off Villiers Rd.)
Amberley Way. Houn —4G 85
Amberley Way. Mord —2K 121
Amberley Way. Romf —2M 49
Amberley Way. Uxb —5C 142
Amberside Clo. Iswth —5B 86
Amberwood Clo. Wall —7J 123
Amberwood Ri. N Mald —1C 120
Amblecote Clo. SE12 —9F 94
Amblecote Meadows. SE12 —9F 94
Amblecote Rd. SE12 —9F 94
Ambler Rd. N4 —8M 43
Ambleside. NW1 —5F 58
(off Augustus St.)
Ambleside. Brom —3B 110
Ambleside Av. SW16 —1H 107
Ambleside Av. Beck —9J 109
Ambleside Av. Horn —1F 66
Ambleside Av. W on T —3G 117
Ambleside Clo. E9 —1G 61
Ambleside Clo. E10 —5M 45
Ambleside Cres. Enf —5H 17
Ambleside Dri. Felt —7D 84
Ambleside Gdns. SW16 —2H 107
Ambleside Gdns. Ilf —2J 47
Ambleside Gdns. S Croy —1H 139
Ambleside Gdns. Sutt —8A 122
Ambleside Gdns. Wemb —6H 39
Ambleside Point. SE15 —8G 77
(off Tustin Est.)
Ambleside Rd. NW10 —3D 56
Ambleside Rd. Bexh —1L 97
Ambleside Wlk. Uxb —4B 142
(off Cumbrian Way)
Ambrey Way. Wall —1H 137
Ambrooke Rd. Belv —4L 81
Ambrosden Av. SW1 —4G 75
Ambrose Av. NW11 —5J 41
Ambrose Clo. E6 —8K 63
Ambrose Clo. Cray —3D 98
Ambrose Clo. Orp —5D 128
Ambrose Ho. E14 —8L 61
(off Selsey St.)
Ambrose M. SW11 —1D 90
Ambrose St. SE16 —5F 76
Ambrose Wlk. E3 —5L 61
AMC Bus. Cen. NW10 —6M 55
Amelia Ho. W6 —6G 73
(off Queen Caroline St.)
Amelia St. SE17 —6A 76
Amen Corner. EC4 —9M 59
Amen Corner. SW17 —3D 106
Amen Ct. EC4 —9M 59
Amenity Way. Mord —2G 121
America Sq. EC3 —1D 76
America St. SE1 —2A 76
Amerland Rd. SW18 —4K 89
Amersham Av. N18 —6B 28
Amersham Clo. Romf —6K 35
Amersham Dri. Romf —6J 35
Amersham Gro. SE14 —8K 77
Amersham Ho. Wat —9C 8
(off Chenies Way)
Amersham Rd. SE14 —9K 77
Amersham Rd. Croy —1A 124
Amersham Rd. Romf —6J 35
Amersham Va. SE14 —8K 77
Amersham Wlk. Romf —6K 35
Amery Gdns. NW10 —4G 57
Amery Gdns. Romf —1H 51
Amery Ho. SE17 —6C 76
(off Kinglake St.)
Amery Rd. Harr —7E 38
Amesbury. Wal A —5M 7
Amesbury Av. SW2 —8J 91
Amesbury Clo. Wor Pk —3G 121
Amesbury Ct. Enf —4L 15
Amesbury Dri. E4 —8M 17
Amesbury Rd. Brom —7H 111
Amesbury Rd. Dag —3H 65
Amesbury Rd. Felt —8H 85
Amesbury Tower. SW8 —1G 91
Ames Cotts. E14 —8J 61
Ames Ho. E2 —5H 61
(off Mace St.)
Amethyst Rd. E15 —9B 46
Amherst Av. W13 —9G 55
Amherst Clo. Orp —8E 112
Amherst Dri. Orp —8D 112
Amherst Gdns. W13 —9G 55
(off Amherst Rd.)
Amherst Rd. W13 —9G 55
Amhurst Gdns. Iswth —1E 86
Amhurst Pk. N16 —5B 44
Amhurst Pas. E8 —1E 60
Amhurst Rd. E8 —1F 60
Amhurst Rd. N16 & E8 —9D 44
Amhurst Ter. E8 —9E 44
Amhurst Wlk. SE28 —2E 80
Amias Ho. EC1 —7A 60
(off Central St.)
Amidas Gdns. Dag —9F 48
Amiel St. E1 —7G 61
Amies St. SW11 —2D 90
Amigo Ho. SE1 —4L 75
(off Morley St.)
Amina Way. SE16 —4E 76
Amis Av. Eps —8M 119
Amity Gro. SW20 —5F 104
Amity Rd. E15 —3D 62
Ammanford Grn. NW9 —4C 40
Amner Rd. SW11 —5E 90
Amor Rd. W6 —4G 73
Amory Ho. N1 —4K 59
(off Barnsbury Est.)
Amott Rd. SE15 —2E 92
Amoy Pl. E14 —9K 61
(in two parts)
Ampere Way. Croy —2J 123
(in two parts)
Ampleforth Clo. Orp —6G 129
Ampleforth Rd. SE2 —3F 80
Ampthill Est. NW1 —5G 59
Ampthill Ho. H Hill —5H 35
(off Montgomery Cres.)
Ampton Pl. WC1 —6K 59
Ampton St. WC1 —6K 59
Amroth Clo. SE23 —7F 92
Amroth Grn. NW9 —4C 40
Amstel Ct. SE15 —8D 76
(off Garnies Clo.)
Amsterdam Rd. E14 —4A 78
Amundsen Ct. E14 —6L 77
(off Napier Av.)
Amunsden Ho. NW10 —3B 56
(off Stonebridge Pk.)
Amwell Clo. Enf —7B 16
Amwell Clo. Wat —8J 5
Amwell Ct. Wal A —6M 7
Amwell Ct. Est. N16 —7A 44
Amwell St. N1 —6L 59
Amwell Vw. Ilf —5F 32
Amyand Cotts. Twic —5F 86
Amyand La. Twic —6F 86
Amyand Pk. Gdns. Twic —6F 86
Amyand Pk. Rd. Twic —6E 86
Amy Clo. Wall —9J 123
Amy Johnson Ct. Edgw —9M 23
Amyruth Rd. SE4 —4L 93
Amy Warne Clo. E6 —7J 63
Anatola Rd. N19 —7F 42
Ancaster Cres. N Mald —1E 120
Ancaster M. Beck —7H 109
Ancaster Rd. Beck —7H 109
Ancaster St. SE18 —8C 80
Anchor. SW18 —3M 89
Anchorage Clo. SW19 —2L 105
Anchorage Ho. E14 —1B 78
(off Clove Cres.)
Anchorage Ho. E14 —3K 77
(off Cuba St.)
Anchorage Point Ind. Est. SE7 —4G 79
Anchor & Hope La. SE7 —4F 78
Anchor Bay Ind. Est. Eri —7E 82
Anchor Boulevd. Dart —3M 99
Anchor Brewhouse. SE1 —2D 76
Anchor Bus. Cen. Croy —5J 123
Anchor Clo. Chesh —1D 6
Anchor Ct. SW1 —5H 75
(off Vauxhall Bri. Rd.)
Anchor Ct. Enf —7C 16
Anchor Ct. Eri —8D 82
Anchor Dri. Rain —7F 66
Anchor Ho. E16 —8D 62
(off Barking Rd.)
Anchor Ho. E16 —9G 63
(off Prince Regent La.)
Anchor Ho. EC1 —7A 60
(off Old St.)
Anchor M. SW12 —5F 90
Anchor St. SE16 —5F 76
Anchor Wharf. E3 —8M 61
(off Yeo St.)
Anchor Yd. EC1 —7A 60
Ancient Almshouses. Wal X —3D 6
(off Turner's Hill)
Ancill Clo. W6 —7J 73
Ancona Rd. NW10 —5E 56
Ancona Rd. SE18 —6B 80
Andace Pk. Gdns. Brom —6G 111
Andalus Rd. SW9 —2J 91
Andaman Ho. E1 —8J 61
(off Duckett St.)
Ander Clo. Wemb —9H 39
Anderson Clo. N21 —7K 15
Anderson Clo. W3 —9B 56
Anderson Clo. Eps —4M 133
Anderson Clo. Sutt —3L 121
Anderson Ct. NW2 —6G 41
Anderson Dri. Ashf —1A 100
Anderson Ho. E14 —1A 78
(off Woolmore St.)
Anderson Ho. Bark —5B 64
Anderson Pl. Houn —3M 85
Anderson Rd. E9 —2H 61
Anderson Rd. Wey —5B 116
Anderson Rd. Wfd G —1H 47
Anderson Sq. N1 —4M 59
(off Gaskin St.)
Anderson St. SW3 —6D 74
Anderson Way. Belv —3A 82
Anderton Clo. SE5 —2B 92
Anderton Ct. N22 —9H 27
Andorra Ct. Brom —5G 111
Andover Av. E16 —9H 63
Andover Clo. Eps —3B 134
Andover Clo. Felt —7D 84
Andover Clo. Gnfd —7M 53
Andover Clo. Uxb —5A 142
Andover Pl. NW6 —5M 57
Andover Rd. N7 —7K 43
Andover Rd. Orp —3B 128
Andover Rd. Twic —7B 86
Andoversford Ct. SE15 —7C 76
(off Bibury Clo.)
Andreck Ct. Beck —6M 109
Andre St. E8 —1E 60
Andrew Borde St. WC2 —9H 59
Andrew Clo. Dart —4B 98
Andrew Clo. Ilf —6B 32
Andrew Ct. SE23 —8H 93
Andrewes Gdns. E6 —9J 63
Andrewes Highwalk. EC2 —8A 60
(off Fore St.)
Andrewes Ho. EC2 —8A 60
(off Fore St.)
Andrewes Ho. Sutt —6L 121
Andrew Pl. SW8 —8H 75
Andrew Reed Ct. Wat —4G 9
(off Keele Clo.)
Andrews Clo. Buck H —2G 31
Andrew's Clo. Eps —6D 134
Andrews Clo. Harr —5B 38
Andrew's Clo. Orp —6H 113
Andrews Clo. Wor Pk —4H 121
Andrews Crosse. WC2 —9L 59
(off Chancery La.)
Andrew's Ho. S Croy —8A 124
Andrew's La. G Oak & Chesh —1A 6
(in two parts)
Andrews Pl. SE9 —5M 95
Andrew's Rd. E8 —4F 60
Andrew St. E14 —9A 62
Andrews Wlk. SE17 —7M 75
Andringham Lodge. Brom —5F 110
(off Palace Gro.)
Andromeda Ct. H Hill —7G 35
Andwell Clo. SE2 —3F 80
Anerley. —6F 108
Anerley Gro. SE19 —4D 108
Anerley Hill. SE19 —3D 108
Anerley Pk. SE20 —4E 108
Anerley Pk. Rd. SE20 —4F 108
Anerley Rd. SE19 & SE20 —4E 108
Anerley Sta. Rd. SE20 —5F 108
Anerley St. SW11 —1D 90
Anerley Va. SE19 —4D 108
Aneurin Bevan Ct. NW2 —7F 40
Aneurin Bevan Ho. N11 —7H 27
Anfield Clo. SW12 —6G 91
Angas Ct. Wey —7A 116
Angel. (Junct.) —5L 59
Angela Davies Ind. Est. SE24 —3M 91
Angel All. E1 —9D 60
(off Whitechapel High St.)
Angel Cen., The. N1 —5L 59
(off St John St.)
Angel Clo. N18 —5D 28
Angel Corner Pde. N18 —4E 28
Angel Ct. EC2 —9B 60
Angel Ct. SW1 —2G 75
Angel Edmonton. (Junct.) —5E 28
Angelfield. Houn —3M 85
Angel Ga. EC1 —6M 59
(in three parts)
Angel Hill. Sutt —5M 121
(in two parts)
Angel Hill Dri. Sutt —5M 121
Angelica Clo. W Dray —9D 142
Angelica Dri. E6 —8L 63
Angelica Gdns. Croy —3H 125
Angelina Ho. SE15 —9E 76
(off Goldsmith Rd.)
Angel La. E15 —2B 62
Angel La. Hay —8B 52
Angell Pk. Gdns. SW9 —2L 91
Angell Rd. SW9 —2L 91
Angell Town. —9L 75
Angell Town Est. SW9 —1L 91
Angel M. E1 —1F 76
Angel M. N1 —5L 59
Angel M. SW15 —6E 88
Angel Pas. EC4 —1B 76
Angel Pl. N18 —4E 28
Angel Pl. SE1 —3B 76
Angel Rd. N18 —5E 28
Angel Rd. Harr —4C 38
Angel Rd. Th Dit —2E 118
Angel Rd. Works. N18 —5G 29
Angel Sq. N1 —5L 59
Angel St. EC1 —9A 60
Angel Wlk. W6 —5G 73
Angel Way. Romf —3C 50
Angel Yd. N6 —6E 42
Angerstein Bus. Pk. SE10 —5E 78
Angerstein La. SE3 —9D 78
Anglebury. W2 —9L 57
(off Talbot Rd.)
Angle Clo. Uxb —4E 142
Angle Grn. Dag —6G 49
Anglers Clo. Rich —1G 103
Angler's La. NW5 —2F 58
Anglers Reach. Surb —9H 103
Anglers, The. King T —7H 103
(off High St.)
Anglesea Av. SE18 —5M 79
Anglesea Ho. King T —8H 103
(off Anglesea Rd.)
Anglesea Rd. SE18 —5M 79
Anglesea Rd. King T —8H 103
Anglesea Rd. Orp —1G 129
Anglesey Clo. Ashf —9E 144
Anglesey Ct. W7 —7D 54
Anglesey Ct. Rd. Cars —8E 122
Anglesey Dri. Rain —7E 66
Anglesey Gdns. Cars —8E 122
Anglesey Ho. E14 —9L 61
(off Lindfield St.)
Anglesey Rd. Enf —6F 16
Anglesey Rd. Wat —5G 21
Anglesmede Cres. Pinn —1L 37
Anglesmede Way. Pinn —1L 37
Angles Rd. SW16 —1J 107
Anglia Clo. N17 —7F 28
Anglia Ct. Dag —6H 49
(off Spring Clo.)
Anglia Ho. E14 —9J 61
Anglian Clo. Wat —4G 9
Anglian Ind. Est. Bark —7D 64
Anglian Rd. E11 —8B 46
Anglia Wlk. E6 —4L 63
(off Napier Rd.)
Anglo Rd. E3 —5K 61
Angrave Ct. E8 —4D 60
(off Scriven St.)
Angrave Pas. E8 —4D 60
Angus Clo. Chess —7L 119
Angus Dri. Ruis —9G 37
Angus Gdns. NW9 —8B 24
Angus Ho. SW2 —6H 91
Angus Rd. E13 —6G 63
Angus St. SE14 —8J 77
Anhalt Rd. SW11 —8C 74
Ankerdine Cres. SE18 —8M 79
Anlaby Rd. Tedd —2C 102
Anley Rd. W6 —3H 73
Anmersh Gro. Stan —8H 23
Annabel Clo. E14 —9M 61
Anna Clo. E8 —4D 60
Annandale Gro. Uxb —8A 36
Annandale Rd. SE10 —7D 78
Annandale Rd. W4 —6C 72
Annandale Rd. Croy —4E 124
Annandale Rd. Sidc —6C 96
Annan Dri. Cars —1E 136
Anna Neagle Clo. E7 —9E 46
Annan Way. Romf —8C 34
Anne Boleyn Ct. SE9 —5B 96
Anne Boleyn's Wlk. King T —2J 103
Anne Boleyn's Wlk. Sutt —9H 121
Anne Case M. N Mald —7B 104
Anne Goodman Ho. E1 —9G 61
(off Jubilee St.)
Anne Nastri Ct. Romf —3F 50
(off Heath Pk. Rd.)
Anne of Cleeves Ct. SE9 —6B 96
Anne of Cleves Rd. Dart —4H 99
Annesley Av. NW9 —1B 40
Annesley Clo. NW10 —8C 40
Annesley Dri. Croy —5K 125
Annesley Ho. SW9 —9L 75
Annesley Rd. SE3 —9F 78
Annesley Wlk. N19 —7G 43
Anne St. E13 —7E 62
Anne Sutherland Ho. Beck —4J 109
Annett Clo. Shep —8C 100
Annette Clo. Harr —9C 22
Annette Rd. N7 —8K 43
(in two parts)
Annett Rd. W on T —2E 116
Annetts Cres. N1 —3A 60
Anne Way. Ilf —6A 32
Anne Way. W Mol —8M 101
Annie Besant Clo. E3 —4K 61
Annie Taylor Ho. E12 —9L 47
(off Walton Rd.)
Anning St. EC2 —7C 60
Annington Rd. N2 —1D 42
Annis Rd. E9 —2J 61
Ann La. SW10 —7B 74
Ann Moss Way. SE16 —4G 77
Ann's Clo. SW1 —3D 74
(off Kinnerton St.)
Ann's Pl. E1 —8D 60
(off Wentworth St.)
Ann St. SE18 —6A 80
(in two parts)
Annsworthy Av. T Hth —7B 108
Annsworthy Cres. SE25 —6B 108
Ansar Gdns. E17 —3K 45
Ansdell Rd. SE15 —1G 93
Ansdell St. W8 —4M 73
Ansdell Ter. W8 —4M 73
Ansell Gro. Cars —3E 122
Ansell Ho. E1 —8G 61
(off Mile End Rd.)
Ansell Rd. SW17 —9C 90
Anselm Clo. Croy —5D 124
Anselm Rd. SW6 —7L 73
Anselm Rd. Pinn —7K 21
Ansford Rd. Brom —2A 110
Ansleigh Pl. W11 —1H 73
Ansley Clo. S Croy —6F 138
Anson Clo. Kenl —9M 33
Anson Ho. E1 —7J 61
(off Shandy St.)
Anson Ho. SW1 —7G 75
(off Churchill Gdns.)
Anson Rd. N19 —9G 43
Anson Rd. NW2 —9F 40
Anson Ter. N'holt —2M 53
Anson Wlk. N'wd —4A 20
Anstead Dri. Rain —5E 66
Anstey Ct. W3 —3M 71
Anstey Rd. SE15 —2E 92
Anstey Wlk. N15 —2M 43
Anstice Clo. W4 —8C 72
Anstridge Path. SE9 —5B 96
Anstridge Rd. SE9 —5B 96
Antelope Rd. SE18 —4K 79
Antenor Ho. E2 —5F 60
(off Old Bethnal Grn. Rd.)
Anthony Clo. NW7 —4C 24
Anthony Clo. Wat —1G 21
Anthony Cope Ct. N1 —6B 60
(off Chart St.)
Anthony Ho. NW1 —7C 58
(off Ashbridge St.)
Anthony La. Swan —5E 114
Anthony Rd. SE25 —1E 124
Anthony Rd. Borwd —4K 11
Anthony Rd. Gnfd —6C 54
Anthony Rd. Well —9E 80
Anthony St. E1 —9F 60
Anthus M. N'wd —7C 20
Antigua Wlk. SE19 —2B 108

Antilles Bay—Arnold's La.

Antilles Bay. E14 —3A 78
Antill Rd. E3 —6J 61
Antill Rd. N15 —2E 44
Antill Ter. E1 —9H 61
Antlers Hill. E4 —7M 17
Antoinette Ct. Ab L —2D 4
Anton Cres. Sutt —5L 121
Antoneys Clo. Pinn —9H 21
Anton St. E8 —1E 60
Antony Ho. SE14 —8H 77
(off Barlborough St.)
Antony Ho. SE16 —5G 77
(off Raymouth Rd.)
Antrim Gro. NW3 —2D 58
Antrim Rd. NW3 —2D 58
Antrobus Clo. Sutt —7K 121
Antrobus Rd. W4 —5A 72
Anvil Clo. SW16 —4G 107
Anvil Rd. Sun —7E 100
Anworth Clo. Wfd G —6F 30
Apeldoorn Dri. Wall —1J 137
Aperfield. —9J 141
Aperfield Rd. Big H —9J 141
Aperfield Rd. Eri —7D 82
Aperfields. W'ham —9J 141
Apex Clo. Beck —5M 109
Apex Clo. Wey —5B 116
Apex Corner. (Junct.) —4B 24
(Edgware)
Apex Corner. (Junct.) —9K 85
(Hanworth)
Apex Ct. W13 —1E 70
Apex Ind. Est. NW10 —7D 56
Apex Pde. NW7 —4B 24
(off Selvage La.)
Apex Retail Pk. Felt —9K 85
Aphrodite Ct. E14 —5L 77
(off Homer Dri.)
Aplin Way. Iswth —9C 70
Apollo Av. Brom —5F 110
Apollo Av. N'wd —5E 20
Apollo Bus. Cen. SE8 —6H 77
Apollo Clo. Horn —7F 50
Apollo Ct. E1 —1E 76
(off Thomas More St.)
Apollo Ct. SW9 —9L 75
(off Southey Rd.)
Apollo Ho. E2 —5F 60
(off St Jude's Rd.)
Apollo Ho. N6 —5E 42
Apollo Ho. SW10 —8B 74
(off Riley St.)
Apollo Pl. E11 —8C 46
Apollo Pl. SW10 —8B 74
Apollo Theatre. —1H 75
(off Shaftesbury Av.)
Apollo Victoria Theatre. —4G 75
(off Wilton Rd.)
Apollo Way. SE28 —4B 80
Apostle Way. T Hth —6M 107
Apothecary St. EC4 —9M 59
Appach Rd. SW2 —4L 91
Apple Blossom Ct. SW8 —8H 75
(off Pascal St.)
Appleby Clo. E4 —6A 30
Appleby Clo. N15 —3B 44
Appleby Clo. Twic —8B 86
Appleby Dri. Romf —5G 35
Appleby Gdns. Felt —7D 84
Appleby Grn. Romf —5G 35
Appleby Ho. Eps —3B 134
Appleby Rd. E8 —3E 60
Appleby Rd. E16 —9D 62
Appleby St. E2 —5D 60
Applecroft. Park —1M 5
Appledore Av. Bexh —9A 82
Appledore Av. Ruis —8F 36
Appledore Clo. SW17 —8D 90
Appledore Clo. Brom —9D 110
Appledore Clo. Edgw —8L 23
Appledore Clo. Romf —8G 35
Appledore Cres. Sidc —9C 96
Appledown Ri. Coul —7G 137
Appleford Ho. W10 —7J 57
(off Bosworth Rd.)
Appleford Rd. W10 —7J 57
Apple Gth. Bren —5H 71
Applegarth. Clay —7D 118
Applegarth. New Ad —9M 125
(in two parts)
Applegarth Dri. Dart —8J 99
Applegarth Dri. Ilf —2D 48
Applegarth Ho. SE1 —3M 75
(off Nelson Sq.)
Applegarth Ho. SE15 —8E 76
(off Bird in Bush Rd.)
Applegarth Ho. Eri —1D 98
Applegarth Rd. SE28 —2F 80
Applegarth Rd. W14 —4H 73
Apple Gro. Chess —6J 119
Apple Gro. Enf —5C 16
Apple Mkt. King T —6H 103
Apple Orchard. Swan —8B 114
Apple Rd. E11 —8C 46
Appleshaw Ho. SE5 —2C 92
Appleton Dri. Dart —9F 98
Appleton Gdns. N Mald —1E 120
Appleton Rd. SE3 —2J 95
Appleton Rd. Lou —5M 19
Appleton Sq. Mitc —5C 106
Appleton Way. Horn —6H 51
Apple Tree Av. Uxb & W Dray —8D 142
Appletree Clo. SE20 —5F 108
Appletree Gdns. Barn —6C 14
Appletree Wlk. Wat —7F 4
Apple Tree Yd. SW1 —2G 75
Applewood Clo. N20 —1C 26
(in two parts)
Applewood Clo. NW2 —8F 40
Appleyard Ter. Enf —1G 17
Appold St. EC2 —8C 60
Appold St. Eri —7D 82
Apprentice Way. E5 —9F 44
Approach Clo. N16 —9C 44
Approach Rd. E2 —5G 61
Approach Rd. SW20 —6G 105
Approach Rd. Ashf —3A 100
Approach Rd. Barn —6B 14
Approach Rd. Edgw —6L 23
Approach Rd. Purl —4L 137
Approach Rd. W Mol —9L 101
Approach, The. NW4 —3H 41
Approach, The. W3 —9B 56
Approach, The. Enf —4F 16
Approach, The. Orp —4D 128
Approach, The. Upm —8M 51
Aprey Gdns. NW4 —2G 41
April Clo. W7 —1C 70
April Clo. Asht —9K 133
April Clo. Felt —9E 84
April Clo. Orp —7D 128
April Ct. E2 —5E 60
(off Teale St.)
April Glen. SE23 —9H 93
April St. E8 —9D 44
Apsley Clo. Harr —3A 38
Apsley Ho. E1 —8G 61
(off Stepney Way)
Apsley Ho. NW8 —5B 58
(off Finchley Rd.)
Apsley Ho. Houn —3K 85
Apsley Rd. SE25 —8F 108
Apsley Rd. N Mald —7A 104
Apsley Way. NW2 —7E 40
Apsley Way. W1 —3E 74
(in two parts)
Aquarius. Twic —7F 86
Aquarius Way. N'wd —5E 20
Aquila Clo. N'wd —4E 20
Aquila St. NW8 —5B 58
Aquinas St. SE1 —2L 75
Arabella Dri. SW15 —3C 88
Arabia Clo. E4 —9B 18
Arabian Ho. E1 —7J 61
(off Ernest St.)
Arabin Rd. SE4 —3J 93
Aragon Av. Eps —2F 134
Aragon Av. Th Dit —9D 102
Aragon Clo. Brom —3K 127
Aragon Clo. Enf —2K 15
Aragon Clo. Lou —8J 19
Aragon Clo. New Ad —2C 140
Aragon Clo. Romf —6M 33
Aragon Clo. Sun —3D 100
Aragon Ct. E Mol —8A 102
Aragon Ct. Ilf —7A 32
Aragon Dri. Ilf —7A 32
Aragon Dri. Ruis —6H 37
Aragon M. E1 —2E 76
Aragon Rd. King T —2J 103
Aragon Rd. Mord —1H 121
Aragon Tower. SE8 —5K 77
Aral Ho. E1 —7H 61
(off Ernest St.)
Aran Ct. Wey —4B 116
Arandora Cres. Romf —5F 48
Aran Dri. Stan —4G 23
Arapiles Ho. E14 —9B 62
(off Blair St.)
Arbery Rd. E3 —6J 61
Arbon Ct. N1 —4A 60
(off Linton St.)
Arbor Clo. Beck —6M 109
Arbor Ct. N16 —7B 44
Arborfield Clo. SW2 —7K 91
Arborfield Ho. E14 —1L 77
(off E. India Dock Rd.)
Arbor Rd. E4 —3B 30
Arbour Ho. E1 —9H 61
(off Arbour Sq.)
Arbour Rd. Enf —5H 17
Arbour Sq. E1 —9H 61
Arbour Way. Horn —1F 66
Arbroath Grn. Wat —3E 20
Arbroath Rd. SE9 —2J 95
Arbrook Chase. Esh —8A 118
Arbrook Clo. Orp —7E 112
Arbrook La. Esh —8A 118
Arbury Ct. SE20 —5F 108
Arbury Ter. SE26 —9E 92
Arbuthnot La. Bex —5J 97
Arbuthnot Rd. SE14 —1H 93
Arbutus St. E8 —4D 60
Arcade. Croy —4A 124
Arcade Pde. Chess —7H 119
Arcade Pl. Romf —3C 50
Arcade, The. E14 —9M 61
Arcade, The. E17 —2L 45
Arcade, The. EC2 —8C 60
(off Liverpool St.)
Arcade, The. Bark —3A 64
Arcade, The. Croy —5A 124
(off High St.)
Arcade, The. Romf —5H 35
(off Farnham Rd.)
Arcadia Av. N3 —9L 25
Arcadia Cen., The. W5 —1H 71
Arcadia Clo. Cars —6E 122
Arcadia Ct. E1 —8D 60
(off Old Castle St.)
Arcadian Av. Bex —5J 97
Arcadian Clo. Bex —5J 97
Arcadian Gdns. N22 —7K 27
Arcadian Rd. Bex —5J 97
Arcadia St. E14 —9L 61
Archangel St. SE16 —3H 77
Archbishop's Pl. SW2 —6K 91
Archdale Bus. Cen. Harr —7A 38
Archdale Ct. W12 —2F 72
Archdale Ho. SE1 —4C 76
(off Long La.)
Archdale Pl. N Mald —7M 103
Archdale Rd. SE22 —4D 92
Archel Rd. W14 —7K 73
Archer Clo. King T —4J 103
Archer Ho. SE14 —9J 77
Archer Ho. SW11 —9B 74
Archer Ho. W11 —1K 73
(off Westbourne Gro.)
Archer Ho. W13 —2F 70
(off Sherwood Clo.)
Archer M. Hamp H —3A 102
Archer Rd. SE25 —8F 108
Archer Rd. Orp —9E 112
Archers Ct. Brom —8F 110
Archers Ct. S Croy —7A 124
(off Nottingham Rd.)
Archers Dri. Enf —4G 17
Archers Lodge. SE16 —6E 76
(off Culloden Clo.)
Archer Sq. SE14 —7J 77
Archer St. W1 —1H 75
Archer Ter. W Dray —1J 143
Archer Way. Swan —6D 114
Archery Clo. W2 —9C 58
Archery Clo. Harr —1D 38
Archery Rd. SE9 —4K 95
Archery Steps. W2 —1C 74
(off St George's Fields)
Arches Bus. Cen., The. S'hall
(off Merrick Rd.) —3K 69
Arches, The. NW1 —3F 58
Arches, The. SW8 —8H 75
Arches, The. WC2 —2J 75
(off Villiers St.)
Arches, The. Harr —7M 37
Archgate Bus. Cen. N12 —5A 26
Archibald M. W1 —1E 74
Archibald Rd. N7 —9H 43
Archibald Rd. Romf —8L 35
Archibald St. E3 —6L 61
Archie Clo. W Dray —3L 143
Arch Rd. W on T —5H 117
Arch St. SE1 —4A 76
Archway. (Junct.) —7G 43
Archway. Romf —6F 34
Archway Bus. Cen. N19 —8H 43
Archway Clo. N19 —7G 43
Archway Clo. SW19 —9M 89
Archway Clo. W10 —8H 57
Archway Clo. Wall —5H 123
Archway Mall. N19 —7G 43
Archway Rd. N6 & N19 —4E 42
Archway St. SW13 —2C 88
Arcola St. E8 —1D 60
Arcon Ter. N9 —9E 16
Arctic St. NW5 —1F 58
Arcus Rd. Brom —3C 110
Ardbeg Rd. SE24 —4B 92
Arden Clo. Bus H —9D 10
Arden Clo. Harr —8B 38
Arden Ct. Gdns. N2 —4B 42
Arden Cres. E14 —5L 77
Arden Cres. Dag —3G 65
Arden Est. N1 —5C 60
Arden Grange. N12 —4A 26
Arden Gro. Orp —6M 127
Arden Ho. N1 —5C 60
(off Arden Est.)
Arden Ho. SE11 —5K 75
(off Black Prince Rd.)
Arden Ho. SW9 —1J 91
(off Grantham Rd.)
Arden M. E17 —3M 45
Arden Mhor. Pinn —2F 36
Arden Rd. N3 —1K 41
Arden Rd. W13 —1G 71
Ardent Clo. SE25 —7C 108
Ardent Ho. E3 —5J 61
(off Roman Rd.)
Ardesley Wood. Wey —6C 116
Ardfern Av. SW16 —7L 107
Ardfillan Rd. SE6 —7B 94
Ardgowan Rd. SE6 —6C 94
(in two parts)
Ardilaun Rd. N5 —9A 44
Ardingly Clo. Croy —5H 125
Ardleigh Clo. Horn —1H 51
Ardleigh Gdns. Sutt —2L 121
Ardleigh Green. —2G 51
Ardleigh Grn. Rd. Horn —4H 51
Ardleigh Ho. Bark —4A 64
Ardleigh M. Ilf —8M 47
Ardleigh Rd. E17 —8K 29
Ardleigh Rd. N1 —2C 60
Ardleigh Ter. E17 —8K 29
Ardley Clo. NW10 —8C 40
Ardley Clo. SE6 —9J 93
Ardley Clo. Ruis —5A 36
Ardlui Rd. SE27 —8A 92
Ardmay Gdns. Surb —9J 103
Ardmere Rd. SE13 —5B 94
Ardmore La. Buck H —9F 18
Ardmore Pl. Buck H —9F 18
Ardoch Rd. SE6 —8B 94
Ardra Rd. N9 —3H 29
Ardrossan Gdns. Wor Pk —5E 120
Ardross Av. N'wd —5C 20
Ardshiel Clo. SW15 —2H 89
Ardwell Av. Ilf —3A 48
Ardwell Rd. SW2 —8J 91
Ardwick Rd. NW2 —9L 41
Arena Bus. Cen. N4 —4A 44
Arena Est. N4 —4M 43
Arena, The. Enf —2K 17
Ares Ct. E14 —5L 77
(off Homer Dri.)
Arethusa Ho. E14 —5L 77
(off Cahir St.)
Arewater Green. —4L 19
Argali Ho. Eri —4J 81
(off Kale Rd.)
Argall Av. E10 —5H 45
Argall Way. E10 —6H 45
Argenta Way. NW10 —3M 55
Argenta Way. Wemb & NW10 —2L 55
Argent Cen., The. Hay —3E 68
Argent Ct. Chess —5L 119
Argon M. SW6 —8L 73
Argon Rd. N18 —5H 29
Argos Ct. SW9 —9L 75
(off Caldwell St.)
Argos Ho. E2 —5F 60
(off Old Bethnal Grn. Rd.)
Argosy Ho. SE8 —5J 77
Argosy La. Stanw —6B 144
Argus Clo. Romf —8M 33
Argus Way. N'holt —6J 53
Argyle Av. Houn —5L 85
(in two parts)
Argyle Clo. W13 —7E 54
Argyle Ct. Wat —6D 8
Argyle Ho. E14 —4A 78
Argyle Pas. N17 —8D 28
Argyle Pl. W6 —5F 72
Argyle Rd. E1 —7H 61
Argyle Rd. E15 —9C 46
Argyle Rd. E16 —9F 62
Argyle Rd. N12 —5M 25
Argyle Rd. N17 —8E 28
Argyle Rd. N18 —4E 28
Argyle Rd. Barn —6G 13
Argyle Rd. Gnfd & W13 —6D 54
Argyle Rd. Harr —4M 37
Argyle Rd. Houn —4M 85
Argyle Rd. Ilf —7L 47
Argyle Sq. WC1 —6J 59
Argyle St. NW1 —6J 59
Argyle Wlk. WC1 —6J 59
Argyle Way. SE16 —6E 76
(off St James Rd.)
Argyll Av. S'hall —2M 69
Argyll Clo. SW9 —2K 91
Argyll Gdns. Edgw —9M 23
Argyll Mans. SW3 —7B 74
Argyll Mans. W14 —5J 73
(off Hammersmith Rd.)
Argyll Rd. W8 —3L 73
Argyll St. W1 —9G 59
Arica Ho. SE16 —4F 76
(off Slippers Pl.)
Arica Rd. SE4 —3J 93
Ariel Ct. SE11 —5M 75
Ariel Rd. NW6 —2L 57
Ariel Way. W12 —2G 73
Ariel Way. Houn —2F 84
Aristotle Rd. SW4 —2H 91
Arkell Gro. SE19 —4M 107
Arkindale Rd. SE6 —9A 94
Arkley. —7E 12
Arkley Cres. E17 —3K 45
Arkley Dri. Barn —6E 12
Arkley La. Barn —2D 12
(in two parts)
Arkley Rd. E17 —3K 45
Arkley Vw. Barn —6F 12
Arklow Ho. SE5 —7B 76
(off Albany Rd.)
Arklow M. Surb —4J 119
Arklow Rd. SE14 —7K 77
Arklow Rd. Trad. Est. SE14 —7J 77
Arkwright Ho. SW2 —6J 91
(off Streatham Pl.)
Arkwright Rd. NW3 —1A 58
Arkwright Rd. S Croy —2D 138
Arlesey Clo. SW15 —4J 89
Arlesford Rd. SW9 —2J 91
Arlingford Rd. SW2 —4L 91
Arlington. N12 —3L 25
Arlington Av. N1 —4A 60
(in two parts)
Arlington Clo. SE13 —4B 94
Arlington Clo. Sidc —6C 96
Arlington Clo. Sutt —4L 121
Arlington Clo. Twic —5G 87
Arlington Ct. W3 —3M 71
(off Mill Hill Rd.)
Arlington Ct. Hay —6C 68
Arlington Cres. Wal X —7E 6
Arlington Dri. Cars —4D 122
Arlington Dri. Ruis —4B 36
Arlington Gdns. W4 —6A 72
Arlington Gdns. Ilf —6L 47
Arlington Gdns. Romf —8J 35
Arlington Ho. EC1 —6L 59
(off Arlington Way)
Arlington Ho. SE8 —7K 77
(off Evelyn St.)
Arlington Ho. SW1 —2G 75
Arlington Ho. W12 —2F 72
(off Tunis Rd.)
Arlington Lodge. SW2 —3K 91
Arlington Lodge. Wey —6A 116
Arlington M. Twic —5F 86
Arlington M. Wal A —6J 7
(off Sun St.)
Arlington Pk. Mans. W4 —6A 72
(off Sutton La. N.)
Arlington Pas. Tedd —1D 102
Arlington Pl. SE10 —8A 78
Arlington Rd. N14 —2F 26
Arlington Rd. NW1 —4F 58
Arlington Rd. W13 —9F 54
Arlington Rd. Rich —8H 87
Arlington Rd. Surb —1H 119
Arlington Rd. Tedd —1D 102
Arlington Rd. Twic —5G 87
Arlington Rd. Wfd G —8E 30
Arlington Sq. N1 —4A 60
Arlington St. W1 —2G 75
Arlington Way. EC1 —6L 59
Arliss Way. N'holt —4G 53
Arlow Rd. N21 —1L 27
Armada Ct. SE8 —7L 77
Armadale Clo. N17 —2F 44
Armadale Rd. SW6 —8L 73
Armadale Rd. Felt —4E 84
Armada St. SE8 —7L 77
(off McMillan St.)
Armada Way. E6 —1M 79
Armagh Rd. E3 —4K 61
Armand Clo. Wat —2D 8
Armfield Clo. W Mol —9K 101
Armfield Cres. Mitc —6D 106
Armfield Rd. Enf —3B 16
Arminger Rd. W12 —2F 72
Armistice Gdns. SE25 —7E 108
Armitage Rd. NW11 —6J 41
Armitage Rd. SE10 —6D 78
Armour Clo. N7 —2K 59
Armoury Rd. SE8 —1M 93
Armoury Way. SW18 —4L 89
Armsby Ho. E1 —8G 61
(off Stepney Way)
Armstead Wlk. Dag —3L 65
Armstrong Av. Wfd G —6C 30
Armstrong Clo. E6 —9K 63
Armstrong Clo. Brom —7J 111
Armstrong Clo. Dag —5H 49
Armstrong Clo. Pinn —4E 36
Armstrong Clo. W on T —1E 116
Armstrong Cres. Cockf —5B 14
Armstrong Rd. SW7 —4B 74
Armstrong Rd. W3 —2D 72
Armstrong Rd. Felt —2J 101
Armstrong Way. S'hall —3M 69
Armytage Rd. Houn —8H 69
Arnal Cres. SW18 —6J 89
Arncliffe. NW6 —5M 57
Arncliffe Clo. N11 —6E 26
Arncroft Ct. Bark —6F 64
Arndale Wlk. SW18 —4M 89
Arne Gro. Orp —5D 128
Arne Ho. SE11 —6K 75
(off Worgan St.)
Arne St. WC2 —9J 59
Arnett Sq. E4 —6K 29
Arne Wlk. SE3 —3D 94
Arneways Av. Romf —1H 49
Arneway St. SW1 —4H 75
Arnewood Clo. SW15 —7E 88
Arnewood Clo. Oxs —6A 132
Arneys La. Mitc —1E 122
Arngask Rd. SE6 —6B 94
Arnhem Av. Ave —2M 83
Arnhem Dri. New Ad —3B 140
Arnhem Pl. E14 —4L 77
Arnhem Way. SE22 —4C 92
Arnhem Wharf. E14 —4K 77
Arnison Rd. E Mol —8B 102
Arnold Av. E. Enf —2L 17
Arnold Av. W. Enf —2K 17
Arnold Cir. E2 —6D 60
Arnold Clo. Harr —5K 39
Arnold Ct. N22 —7J 27
Arnold Cres. Iswth —4B 86
Arnold Dri. Chess —8H 119
Arnold Est. SE1 —3D 76
(in two parts)
Arnold Gdns. N13 —5M 27
Arnold Ho. SE3 —8G 79
(off Shooters Hill Rd.)
Arnold Ho. SE17 —6M 75
(off Doddington Gro.)
Arnold Mans. W14 —7K 73
(off Queen's Club Gdns.)
Arnold Rd. E3 —6L 61
Arnold Rd. N15 —1D 44
Arnold Rd. SW17 —4D 106
Arnold Rd. Dag —3K 65
Arnold Rd. N'holt —2J 53
Arnold Rd. Wal A —8J 7
Arnold's La. S at H —3K 115

Arnold Ter.—Ashridge Gdns.

Arnold Ter. Stan —5D 22
Arnos Gro. N14 —4H 27
Arnos Gro. Ct. N11 —5G 27
(off Palmer's Rd.)
Arnos Rd. N11 —4G 27
Arnot Ho. SE5 —8A 76
(off Comber Gro.)
Arnott Clo. SE28 —2G 81
Arnott Clo. W4 —5B 72
Arnould Av. SE5 —3B 92
Arnsberga Way. Bexh —3L 97
Arnside Gdns. Wemb —6H 39
Arnside Rd. Bexh —9L 81
Arnside St. SE17 —7B 76
Arnulf St. SE6 —1M 109
Arnulls Rd. SW16 —3M 107
Arodene Rd. SW2 —5K 91
Arosa Rd. Twic —5H 87
(in two parts)
Arpley Sq. SE20 —4G 109
(off High St.)
Arragon Gdns. SW16 —4J 107
Arragon Gdns. W W'ck —5M 125
Arragon Rd. E6 —4H 63
Arragon Rd. SW18 —7L 89
Arragon Rd. Twic —6E 86
Arran Clo. Eri —7B 82
Arran Clo. Wall —6F 122
Arran Ct. NW9 —9D 24
Arran Ct. NW10 —8B 40
Arran Dri. E12 —6H 47
Arran Grn. Wat —4H 21
Arran Ho. E14 —2A 78
(off Raleana Rd.)
Arran M. W5 —2K 71
Arranmore Ct. Bush —6J 9
Arran Rd. SE6 —8M 93
Arran Wlk. N1 —3A 60
Arran Way. Esh —4M 117
Arras Av. Mord —9A 106
Arrol Ho. SE1 —4A 76
Arrol Rd. Beck —7G 109
Arrow Ct. SW5 —5L 73
(off W. Cromwell Rd.)
Arrowhead Ct. E11 —4B 46
Arrow Rd. E3 —6M 61
Arrowscout Wlk. N'holt —6J 53
Arrowsmith Clo. Chig —5D 32
Arrowsmith Ho. SE11 —6K 75
(off Wickham St.)
Arrowsmith Path. Chig —5D 32
Arrowsmith Rd. Chig —5C 32
Arsenal F.C. —8M 43
Arsenal Rd. SE9 —1K 95
Artemis Ct. E14 —5L 77
(off Homer Dri.)
Arterberry Rd. SW20 —4G 105
Arterial Av. Rain —7F 66
Arterial Rd. Purf —4L 83
Artesian Clo. NW10 —3B 56
Artesian Gro. Barn —6A 14
Artesian Rd. W2 —9L 57
Artesian Wlk. E11 —8C 46
Artespian Clo. Horn —4D 50
Arthingworth St. E15 —4C 62
Arthur Ct. SW11 —9E 74
Arthur Ct. W2 —9M 57
(off Queensway)
Arthur Ct. W10 —9H 57
(off Silchester Rd.)
Arthur Ct. Croy —5C 124
(off Fairfield Path)
Arthur Deakin Ho. E1 —8E 60
(off Hunton St.)
Arthurdon Rd. SE4 —4L 93
Arthur Gro. SE18 —5A 80
Arthur Henderson Ho. SW6 —1K 89
(off Fulham Rd.)
Arthur Horsley Wlk. E7 —1D 62
(off Tower Hamlets Rd.)
Arthur Rd. E6 —5K 63
Arthur Rd. N7 —9K 43
Arthur Rd. N9 —2D 28
Arthur Rd. SW19 —2K 105
Arthur Rd. Big H —7G 141
Arthur Rd. King T —4L 103
Arthur Rd. N Mald —9F 104
Arthur Rd. Romf —4G 49
Arthur St. EC4 —1B 76
Arthur St. Bush —5H 9
Arthur St. Eri —8D 82
Artichoke Hill. E1 —1F 76
Artichoke M. SE5 —9B 76
(off Artichoke Pl.)
Artichoke Pl. SE5 —9B 76
Artillery Clo. Ilf —4A 48
Artillery Ho. E15 —2C 62
Artillery Ho. SE18 —6L 79
(off Connaught M.)
Artillery La. E1 —8C 60
Artillery La. W12 —9E 56
Artillery Pas. E1 —8D 60
(off Artillery La.)
Artillery Pl. SE18 —6K 79
Artillery Pl. SW1 —4H 75
Artillery Pl. Harr —7A 22
Artillery Row. SW1 —4G 75
Artington Clo. Orp —6A 128
Artisan Clo. E6 —9M 63
Artizan St. E1 —9D 60
(off Harrow Pl.)
Arts & Unicorn Theatre. —1J 75
(off St Martin's St.)
Arun Ct. SE25 —9E 108
Arundale. King T —8H 103
(off Anglesea Rd.)
Arundel Av. Eps —2F 134
Arundel Av. Mord —8K 105
Arundel Av. S Croy —2E 138
Arundel Bldgs. SE1 —4C 76
(off Swan Mead)
Arundel Clo. E15 —9C 46
Arundel Clo. SW11 —4C 90
Arundel Clo. Bex —5K 97
Arundel Clo. Chesh —1C 6
Arundel Clo. Croy —5M 123
Arundel Clo. Hamp H —2M 101
Arundel Ct. N12 —6C 26
Arundel Ct. N17 —8E 28
Arundel Ct. SW3 —6C 74
(off Jubilee Pl.)
Arundel Ct. Short —6C 110
Arundel Ct. S Harr —9L 37
Arundel Dri. Borwd —6A 12
Arundel Dri. Harr —9K 37
Arundel Dri. Orp —7F 128
Arundel Dri. Wfd G —7E 30
Arundel Gdns. N21 —1L 27
Arundel Gdns. W11 —1K 73
Arundel Gdns. Edgw —7B 24
Arundel Gdns. Ilf —7E 48
Arundel Gt. Ct. WC2 —1K 75
Arundel Gro. N16 —1C 60
Arundel Ho. W3 —3M 71
(off Park Rd. N.)
Arundel Ho. Borwd —6A 12
(off Arundel Dri.)
Arundel Ho. Croy —7B 124
(off Heathfield Rd.)
Arundel Ho. Uxb —7A 142
Arundel Mans. SW6 —9K 73
(off Kelvedon Rd.)
Arundel Pl. N1 —2L 59
Arundel Rd. Ab L —5E 4
Arundel Rd. Cockf —5C 14
Arundel Rd. Croy —1B 124
Arundel Rd. Dart —3G 99
Arundel Rd. Houn —2G 85
Arundel Rd. King T —6M 103
Arundel Rd. Romf —7K 35
Arundel Rd. Sutt —9K 121
Arundel Rd. Uxb —5A 142
Arundel Sq. N7 —2L 59
Arundel St. WC2 —1K 75
Arundel Ter. SW13 —7F 72
Arun Ho. King T —5H 103
Arvon Rd. N5 —1L 59
(in two parts)
Asa Ct. Hay —4D 68
Ascalon Ho. SW8 —8G 75
(off Thessaly Rd.)
Ascalon St. SW8 —8G 75
Ascension Rd. Romf —6A 34
Ascham Dri. E4 —7M 29
Ascham End. E17 —8J 29
Ascham St. NW5 —1G 59
Aschurch Rd. Croy —2D 124
Ascot Clo. Els —7L 11
Ascot Clo. Ilf —6C 32
Ascot Clo. N'holt —1L 53
Ascot Ct. NW8 —6B 58
(off Grove End Rd.)
Ascot Ct. Bex —6K 97
Ascot Gdns. Enf —1G 17
Ascot Gdns. Horn —9J 51
Ascot Gdns. S'hall —8K 53
Ascot Ho. NW1 —6F 58
(off Redhill St.)
Ascot Ho. W9 —7L 57
(off Harrow Rd.)
Ascot Lodge. NW6 —4M 57
Ascot M. Wall —1G 137
Ascot Pl. Stan —5G 23
Ascot Rd. E6 —6K 63
Ascot Rd. N15 —3B 44
Ascot Rd. N18 —4E 28
Ascot Rd. SW17 —3E 106
Ascot Rd. Felt —7E 144
Ascot Rd. Orp —8D 112
Ascot Rd. Wat —7C 8
(in two parts)
Ascott Av. W5 —3J 71
Ascott Clo. Pinn —2E 36
Ashbee Ho. E2 —6G 61
(off Portman Pl.)
Ashbourne Av. E18 —2F 46
Ashbourne Av. N20 —2D 26
Ashbourne Av. NW11 —3K 41
Ashbourne Av. Bexh —8J 81
Ashbourne Av. Harr —7B 38
Ashbourne Clo. N12 —4M 25
Ashbourne Clo. W5 —8L 55
Ashbourne Ct. E5 —9J 45
Ashbourne Ct. N12 —4M 25
(off Ashbourne Clo.)
Ashbourne Gro. NW7 —5B 24
Ashbourne Gro. SE22 —3D 92
Ashbourne Gro. W4 —6C 72
Ashbourne Pde. NW11 —2K 41
Ashbourne Pde. W5 —7K 55
Ashbourne Ri. Orp —6B 128
Ashbourne Rd. W5 —7K 55
Ashbourne Rd. Mitc —4E 106
Ashbourne Rd. Romf —4G 35
Ashbourne Sq. N'wd —6C 20
Ashbourne Ter. SW19 —4K 105
Ashbourne Way. NW11 —2K 41
Ashbridge Rd. E11 —5C 46
Ashbridge St. NW8 —7C 58
Ashbrook. Edgw —6K 23
Ashbrook Rd. N19 —6H 43
Ashbrook Rd. Dag —8M 49
Ashburn Gdns. SW7 —5A 74
Ashburnham Av. Harr —4D 38
Ashburnham Clo. N2 —1B 42
Ashburnham Clo. Wat —3E 20
Ashburnham Ct. Beck —6A 110
Ashburnham Ct. Pinn —1H 37
Ashburnham Dri. Wat —3E 20
Ashburnham Gdns. Harr —4D 38
Ashburnham Gdns. Upm —6M 51
Ashburnham Gro. SE10 —8M 77
Ashburnham Mans. SW10 —8A 74
(off Ashburnham Rd.)
Ashburnham Pk. Esh —6A 118
Ashburnham Pl. SE10 —8M 77
Ashburnham Retreat. SE10 —8M 77
Ashburnham Rd. NW10 —6G 57
Ashburnham Rd. SW10 —8A 74
Ashburnham Rd. Belv —5A 82
Ashburnham Rd. Rich —9F 86
Ashburnham Tower. SW10
(off Worlds End Est.) —8B 74
Ashburn Pl. SW7 —5A 74
Ashburton Av. Croy —3F 124
Ashburton Av. Ilf —1C 64
Ashburton Clo. Croy —3E 124
Ashburton Enterprise Cen. SW15
—5G 89
Ashburton Gdns. Croy —4E 124
Ashburton Gro. N7 —9L 43
Ashburton Ho. W9 —7K 57
(off Fernhead Rd.)
Ashburton Memorial Homes.
Croy —2F 124
Ashburton Rd. E16 —9E 62
Ashburton Rd. Croy —4E 124
Ashburton Rd. Ruis —7E 36
Ashburton Ter. E13 —5E 62
Ashbury Dri. Uxb —8A 36
Ashbury Gdns. Romf —3H 49
Ashbury Pl. SW19 —3A 106
Ashbury Rd. SW11 —2D 90
Ashby Av. Chess —8L 119
Ashby Clo. Horn —6L 51
Ashby Ct. NW8 —7B 58
(off Pollitt Dri.)
Ashby Gro. N1 —3A 60
Ashby Ho. N1 —3A 60
(off Essex Rd.)
Ashby Ho. SW9 —1M 91
Ashby M. SE4 —1K 93
Ashby Rd. N15 —3E 44
Ashby Rd. SE4 —1K 93
Ashby Rd. Wat —2E 8
Ashby St. EC1 —6M 59
Ashby Wlk. Croy —1A 124
Ashby Way. W Dray —8L 143
Ashchurch Gro. W12 —4E 72
Ashchurch Pk. Vs. W12 —4E 72
Ashchurch Ter. W12 —4E 72
Ash Clo. SE20 —6G 109
Ash Clo. Ab L —5B 4
Ash Clo. Cars —4D 122
Ash Clo. Edgw —4A 24
Ash Clo. N Mald —6B 104
Ash Clo. Orp —9B 112
Ash Clo. Romf —7M 33
Ash Clo. Sidc —9F 96
Ash Clo. Stan —6E 22
Ash Clo. Swan —6A 114
Ash Clo. Wat —8F 4
Ashcombe Av. Surb —2H 119
Ashcombe Gdns. Edgw —4L 23
Ashcombe Pk. NW2 —8C 40
Ashcombe Rd. SW19 —2L 105
Ashcombe Rd. Cars —8E 122
Ashcombe Sq. N Mald —7A 104
Ashcombe St. SW6 —1M 89
Ash Copse. Brick W —4K 5
Ash Ct. NW5 —1G 59
Ash Ct. SW19 —4J 105
Ash Ct. W1 —9D 58
(off Harrowby St.)
Ash Ct. Eps —6A 120
Ashcroft. N14 —2H 27
Ash Cft. Pinn —6L 21
Ashcroft Av. Sidc —5E 96
Ashcroft Ct. N20 —2B 26
Ashcroft Ct. Dart —6L 99
Ashcroft Cres. Sidc —5E 96
Ashcroft Ho. SW8 —9G 75
(off Wadhurst Rd.)
Ashcroft Ri. Coul —8J 137
Ashcroft Rd. E3 —6J 61
Ashcroft Rd. Chess —5K 119
Ashcroft Sq. W6 —5G 73
Ashdale Clo. Stai —8C 144
Ashdale Clo. Twic —6A 86
Ashdale Gro. Stan —6D 22
Ashdale Ho. N4 —5B 44
Ashdale Rd. SE12 —7F 94
Ashdale Way. Twic —6M 85
Ashdene. SE15 —8F 76
Ashdene. Pinn —1G 37
Ashdene Clo. Ashf —4A 100
Ashdon Clo. Wfd G —6F 30
Ashdon Rd. NW10 —4D 56
Ashdon Rd. Bush —5H 9
Ashdown. W13 —8F 54
(off Clivedon Ct.)
Ashdown Clo. Beck —6M 109
Ashdown Clo. Bex —6A 98
Ashdown Ct. Sutt —8A 122
Ashdown Cres. NW5 —1E 58
Ashdown Cres. Chesh —1E 6
Ashdown Dri. Borwd —4K 11
Ashdowne Ct. N17 —8E 28
Ashdown Est. E11 —9B 46
Ashdown Gdns. S Croy —7F 138
Ashdown Ho. SW1 —4G 75
(off Victoria St.)
Ashdown Pl. Th Dit —2E 118
Ashdown Rd. Enf —4G 17
Ashdown Rd. Eps —5D 134
Ashdown Rd. King T —6J 103
Ashdown Rd. Uxb —5E 142
Ashdown Wlk. E14 —5L 77
(off Copeland Dri.)
Ashdown Wlk. Romf —8M 33
Ashdown Way. SW17 —8E 90
Ashe Ho. Twic —5H 87
Ashenden. SE1 —5A 76
(off Deacon Way)
Ashenden Rd. E5 —1J 61
Ashen Dri. Dart —6E 98
Ashen Gro. SW19 —9L 89
Ashen Gro. Rd. Knat —9M 131
Ashentree Ct. EC4 —9L 59
(off Whitefriars St.)
Ashen Va. S Croy —1H 139
Asher Loftus Way. N11 —6D 26
Asher Way. E1 —1E 76
Ashfield Av. Bush —8M 9
Ashfield Av. Felt —7F 84
Ashfield Clo. Beck —4L 109
Ashfield Clo. Rich —7J 87
Ashfield Ho. W14 —6K 73
Ashfield La. Chst —3M 111
(in three parts)
Ashfield Pde. N14 —1H 27
Ashfield Rd. N4 —4A 44
Ashfield Rd. N14 —3G 27
Ashfield Rd. W3 —2D 72
Ashfields. Lou —4K 19
Ashfields. Wat —8D 4
Ashfield St. E1 —8F 60
Ashfield Yd. E1 —8G 61
Ashford. —9D 144
Ashford Av. N8 —2J 43
Ashford Av. Hay —9H 53
Ashford Bus. Complex. Ashf
(Sandell's Av.) —2A 100
Ashford Bus. Complex. Ashf
(Shield Rd.) —1A 100
Ashford Clo. E17 —4K 45
Ashford Common. —4B 100
Ashford Ct. Edgw —3M 23
Ashford Cres. Ashf —9C 144
Ashford Cres. Enf —4G 17
Ashford Grn. Wat —5H 21
Ashford Ho. SE8 —7K 77
Ashford Ho. SW9 —3M 91
Ashford Park. —9A 144
Ashford Pas. NW2 —9H 41
Ashford Rd. E6 —3L 63
Ashford Rd. E18 —9F 30
Ashford Rd. NW2 —9H 41
Ashford Rd. Ashf —4A 100
Ashford Rd. Felt —1B 100
Ashford St. N1 —6C 60
Ash Gro. E8 —4F 60
(in two parts)
Ash Gro. N13 —3A 28
Ash Gro. NW2 —9H 41
Ash Gro. SE12 —7E 94
Ash Gro. SE20 —6G 109
Ash Gro. W5 —3J 71
Ash Gro. Enf —9C 16
Ash Gro. Felt —7C 84
Ash Gro. Hay —1B 68
Ash Gro. Houn —9H 69
Ash Gro. S'hall —8L 53
Ash Gro. Wemb —9E 38
Ash Gro. W Dray —1K 143
Ash Gro. W W'ck —4A 126
Ashgrove Ct. W9 —8L 57
(off Elmfield Way)
Ashgrove Ho. SW1 —6H 75
(off Lindsay Sq.)
Ashgrove Rd. Ashf —2A 100
Ashgrove Rd. Brom —3B 110
Ashgrove Rd. Ilf —6D 48
Ash Hill Clo. Bush —1M 21
Ash Hill Dri. Pinn —1G 37
Ash Ho. E14 —3A 78
(off E. Ferry Rd.)
Ash Ho. SE1 —5D 76
(off Longfield Est.)
Ash Ho. W10 —7J 57
(off Heather Wlk.)
Ashingdon Clo. E4 —3A 30
Ashington Ho. E1 —7F 60
(off Barnsley St.)
Ashington Rd. SW6 —1K 89
Ashlake Rd. SW16 —1J 107
Ashland Pl. W1 —8E 58
Ash La. Horn —2K 51
Ash La. Romf —6E 34
Ashlar Pl. SE18 —5M 79
Ashleigh Commercial Est. SE7
—4G 79
Ashleigh Ct. N14 —9G 15
Ashleigh Ct. W5 —5H 71
(off Murray Rd.)
Ashleigh Gdns. Sutt —4M 121
Ashleigh Point. SE23 —9H 93
Ashleigh Rd. SE20 —7F 108
Ashleigh Rd. SW14 —2C 88
Ashley Av. Eps —5B 134
Ashley Av. Ilf —9M 31
Ashley Av. Mord —9L 105
Ashley Cen. Eps —5B 134
Ashley Clo. NW4 —9G 25
Ashley Clo. Pinn —9F 20
Ashley Clo. W on T —3D 116
Ashley Ct. NW4 —9G 25
Ashley Ct. NW9 —9D 24
(off Guilfoyle)
Ashley Ct. SW1 —4G 75
(off Morpeth Ter.)
Ashley Ct. Barn —7A 14
Ashley Ct. Eps —5B 134
Ashley Ct. N'holt —4J 53
Ashley Cres. N22 —9L 27
Ashley Cres. SW11 —2E 90
Ashley Dri. Bans —6L 135
Ashley Dri. Borwd —7A 12
Ashley Dri. Iswth —7C 70
Ashley Dri. Twic —7M 85
Ashley Dri. W on T —5E 116
Ashley Gdns. N13 —4A 28
Ashley Gdns. SW1 —4G 75
(in three parts)
Ashley Gdns. Orp —7C 128
Ashley Gdns. Rich —8H 87
Ashley Gdns. Wemb —7J 39
Ashley Gro. Lou —5J 19
Ashley La. NW4 —7G 25
(in two parts)
Ashley La. Croy —6M 123
Ashley Park. —5E 116
Ashley Pk. Av. W on T —4D 116
Ashley Pk. Cres. W on T —3E 116
Ashley Pk. Rd. W on T —4E 116
Ashley Pl. SW1 —4G 75
(in two parts)
Ashley Ri. W on T —6D 116
Ashley Rd. E4 —6L 29
Ashley Rd. E7 —3G 63
Ashley Rd. N17 —1E 44
Ashley Rd. N19 —6J 43
Ashley Rd. SW19 —3M 105
Ashley Rd. Enf —4G 17
Ashley Rd. Eps —5B 134
Ashley Rd. Hamp —5L 101
Ashley Rd. Rich —2J 87
Ashley Rd. Th Dit —1D 118
Ashley Rd. T Hth —8K 107
Ashley Rd. Uxb —5A 142
Ashley Rd. W on T —6D 116
Ashley Sq. Eps —5B 134
(off Ashley Cen.)
Ashley Wlk. NW7 —7H 25
Ashling Rd. Croy —3E 124
Ashlin Rd. E15 —9B 46
Ashlone Rd. SW15 —2G 89
Ashlyn Clo. Bush —6J 9
Ashlyn Ct. Wat —6J 9
Ashlyn Gro. Horn —1H 51
Ashlyns Way. Chess —8H 119
Ashmead. N14 —7G 15
Ashmead Bus. Cen. E3 —7B 62
Ashmead Ga. Brom —5G 111
Ashmead Ho. E9 —1J 61
(off Homerton Rd.)
Ashmead Rd. SE8 —1L 93
Ashmead Rd. Felt —7E 84
Ashmeads. Lou —5K 19
Ashmere Av. Beck —6B 110
Ashmere Clo. Sutt —7H 121
Ashmere Gro. SW2 —3J 91
Ash M. Eps —5C 134
Ashmill St. NW1 —8C 58
Ashmole Pl. SW8 —7K 75
(in two parts)
Ashmole St. SW8 —7K 75
Ashmore. NW1 —3H 59
(off Agar Gro.)
Ashmore Ct. N11 —6D 26
Ashmore Ct. Houn —7L 69
Ashmore Gro. Well —2B 96
Ashmore Ho. W14 —4J 73
(off Russell Rd.)
Ashmore La. Kes —3G 141
Ashmore Rd. W9 —5K 57
Ashmount Est. N19 —5H 43
Ashmount Rd. N6 —5G 43
Ashmount Rd. N15 —3D 44
Ashmount Ter. W5 —5H 71
Ashmour Gdns. Romf —9B 34
Ashneal Gdns. Harr —8B 38
Ashness Gdns. Gnfd —2F 54
Ashness Rd. SW11 —4D 90
Ashpark Ho. E14 —9K 61
(off Norbiton Rd.)
Ashridge Clo. Harr —4G 39
Ashridge Ct. N14 —7G 15
Ashridge Ct. S'hall —9A 54
(off Redcroft Rd.)
Ashridge Cres. SE18 —8A 80
Ashridge Dri. Brick W —3J 5
Ashridge Dri. Wat —5G 21
Ashridge Gdns. N13 —5H 27
Ashridge Gdns. Pinn —2J 37

Avenue, The—Balmoral Rd.

Avenue, The. Eps & Sutt —9F 120
Avenue, The. Hamp —3K 101
Avenue, The. Harr —8D 22
Avenue, The. H End —6K 21
Avenue, The. Horn —7G 51
Avenue, The. Houn —4M 85
Avenue, The. Kes —6H 127
Avenue, The. Lou —8H 19
Avenue, The. N'wd —6A 20
Avenue, The. Orp —4D 128
Avenue, The. Oxs —3D 132
Avenue, The. Pinn —5K 37
Avenue, The. Rich —1K 87
Avenue, The. Romf —2B 50
Avenue, The. St P —4F 112
Avenue, The. Sun —5F 100
Avenue, The. Surb —1K 119
Avenue, The. Sutt —2K 135
Avenue, The. Twic —4F 86
Avenue, The. Wat —4E 8
Avenue, The. Wemb —6J 39
Avenue, The. W W'ck —2C 126
Avenue, The. Wor Pk —4D 120
Averil Gro. SW16 —3M 107
Averill St. W6 —7H 73
Avern Gdns. W Mol —8M 101
Avern Rd. W Mol —8M 101
Avery Farm Row. SW1 —5E 74
Avery Gdns. Ilf —3K 47
Avery Hill. —5B 96
Avery Hill Rd. SE9 —5B 96
Avery Row. W1 —1F 74
Avey La. Wal A & Lou —9K 7
Avia Pk. Felt —7F 144
Aviary Clo. E16 —8D 62
Aviemore Clo. Beck —9K 109
Aviemore Way. Beck —9J 109
Avignon Rd. SE4 —2H 93
Avington Ct. SE1 —5C 76
(off Old Kent Rd.)
Avington Gro. SE20 —4G 109
Avington Way. SE15 —8D 76
Avion Cres. NW9 —8E 24
Avior Dri. N'wd —4D 20
Avis Sq. E1 —9H 61
Avoca Rd. SW17 —1E 106
Avocet Clo. SE1 —6E 76
Avocet M. SE28 —4B 80
Avon Clo. Hay —7G 53
Avon Clo. Sutt —6A 122
Avon Clo. Wat —7G 5
Avon Clo. Wor Pk —4E 120
Avon Ct. E4 —1A 30
Avon Ct. N12 —5M 25
Avon Ct. Buck H —1F 30
Avon Ct. Gnfd —7M 53
Avon Ct. Pinn —7L 21
(off Avenue, The)
Avondale Av. N12 —5M 25
Avondale Av. NW2 —8C 40
Avondale Av. Barn —1D 26
Avondale Av. Esh —5E 118
Avondale Av. Wor Pk —3D 120
Avondale Clo. Lou —9K 19
Avondale Clo. W on T —7G 117
Avondale Ct. E11 —6C 46
Avondale Ct. E16 —8C 62
Avondale Ct. E18 —8F 30
Avondale Cres. Enf —5J 17
Avondale Cres. Ilf —3H 47
Avondale Dri. Hay —2E 68
Avondale Dri. Lou —9K 19
Avondale Gdns. Houn —4K 85
Avondale Ho. SE1 —6E 76
(off Avondale Sq.)
Avondale Pk. Gdns. W11 —1J 73
Avondale Pk. Rd. W11 —1J 73
Avondale Ri. SE15 —2D 92
Avondale Rd. E16 —8C 62
Avondale Rd. E17 —5L 45
Avondale Rd. N3 —8A 26
Avondale Rd. N13 —2L 27
Avondale Rd. N15 —3M 43
Avondale Rd. SE9 —8J 95
Avondale Rd. SW14 —2C 88
Avondale Rd. SW19 —2M 105
Avondale Rd. Ashf —9B 144
Avondale Rd. Brom —3C 110
Avondale Rd. Harr —1D 38
Avondale Rd. S Croy —8A 124
Avondale Rd. Well —1G 97
Avondale Sq. SE1 —6E 76
Avonfield Ct. E17 —1B 46
Avon Ho. W8 —4L 73
(off Allen St.)
Avon Ho. W14 —5K 73
(off Avonmore Rd.)
Avon Ho. King T —5H 103
Avonhurst Ho. NW2 —3J 57
Avonley Rd. SE14 —8G 77
Avon M. Pinn —7K 21
Avonmore Gdns. W14 —5K 73
Avonmore Pl. W14 —5J 73
(off Avonmore Rd.)
Avonmore Rd. W14 —5J 73
Avonmouth Rd. Dart —4H 99
Avonmouth St. SE1 —4A 76
Avon Path. S Croy —8A 124
Avon Pl. SE1 —3A 76
Avon Rd. E17 —1B 46
Avon Rd. SE4 —2L 93
Avon Rd. Gnfd —7L 53
Avon Rd. Sun —4D 100
Avonstowe Clo. Orp —5A 128
Avon Way. E18 —1E 46
Avonwick Rd. Houn —1M 85
Avril Way. E4 —5A 30
Avro Ho. SW8 —8F 74
(off Havelock Ter.)
Avro Way. Wall —9J 123
Awberry Ct. Wat —8B 8
Awlfield Av. N17 —8B 28
Awliscombe Rd. Well —1D 96
Axe St. Bark —4A 64
(in two parts)
Axholme Av. Edgw —8L 23
Axminster Cres. Well —9G 81
Axminster Rd. N7 —8J 43
Axtaine Rd. Orp —2H 129
Axtane Clo. S at H —5M 115
Axwood. Eps —7A 134
Aybrook St. W1 —8E 58
Aycliffe Clo. Brom —8K 111
Aycliffe Rd. W12 —2E 72
Aycliffe Rd. Borwd —3J 11
Ayerst Ct. E10 —5A 46
Aylands Clo. Wemb —7J 39
Aylands Rd. Enf —9C 6
Aylesbury Clo. E7 —2D 62
Aylesbury Ct. Sutt —5A 122
Aylesbury Ho. SE15 —7E 76
(off Friary Est.)
Aylesbury Rd. SE17 —6B 76
Aylesbury Rd. Brom —7E 110
Aylesbury St. EC1 —7M 59
Aylesbury St. NW10 —8B 40
Aylesford Av. Beck —9J 109
Aylesford Ho. SE1 —3B 76
(off Long La.)
Aylesford St. SW1 —6H 75
Aylesham Cen., The. SE15 —9E 76
Aylesham Clo. NW7 —7E 24
Aylesham Rd. Orp —2D 128
Ayles Rd. Hay & N'holt —6F 52
Aylestone Av. NW6 —3H 57
Aylett Rd. SE25 —8F 108
Aylett Rd. Iswth —1C 86
Ayley Cft. Enf —7E 16
Ayliffe Clo. King T —6L 103
Aylmer Clo. Stan —4E 22
Aylmer Ct. N2 —3D 42
Aylmer Dri. Stan —4E 22
Aylmer Ho. SE10 —6B 78
Aylmer Pde. N2 —3D 42
Aylmer Rd. E11 —6D 46
Aylmer Rd. N2 —3C 42
Aylmer Rd. W12 —3D 72
Aylmer Rd. Dag —8J 49
Ayloffe Rd. Dag —2K 65
Ayloffs Clo. Horn —2H 51
Ayloffs Wlk. Horn —3H 51
Aylsham Dri. Uxb —7A 36
Aylsham La. Romf —4G 35
Aylton Est. SE16 —3G 77
Aylward Ho. E14 —8J 61
(off Dupont St.)
Aylward Rd. SE23 —8H 93
Aylward Rd. SW20 —6K 105
Aylwards Ri. Stan —4E 22
Aylward St. E1 —9G 61
(in two parts)
Aylwin Est. SE1 —4C 76
Aynhoe Mans. W14 —5H 73
(off Aynhoe Rd.)
Aynhoe Rd. W14 —5H 73
Aynho St. Wat —7F 8
Aynscombe Angle. Orp —2E 128
Aynscombe Path. SW14 —1A 88
Ayot Path. Borwd —1L 11
Ayr Ct. W3 —9L 55
Ayres Clo. E13 —6E 62
Ayres Cres. NW10 —3B 56
Ayres St. SE1 —3A 76
Ayr Grn. Romf —8C 34
Ayrsome Rd. N16 —8C 44
Ayrton Gould Ho. E2 —6H 61
(off Roman Rd.)
Ayrton Rd. SW7 —4B 74
Ayr Way. Romf —8C 34
Aysgarth Ct. Sutt —5M 121
Aysgarth Rd. SE21 —6C 92
Ayshford Ho. E2 —6F 60
(off Viaduct St.)
Ayston Ho. SE16 —5H 77
(off Plough Way)
Ayton Ho. SE5 —8B 76
(off Edmund St.)
Aytoun Pl. SW9 —1K 91
Aytoun Rd. SW9 —1K 91
Azalea Clo. W7 —2D 70
Azalea Clo. Ilf —1M 63
Azalea Ct. W7 —2D 70
Azalea Ct. Wfd G —6C 30
Azalea Dri. Swan —8B 114
Azalea Ho. SE14 —8K 77
(off Achilles St.)
Azalea Wlk. Pinn —3F 36
Azania M. NW5 —2F 58
Azenby Rd. SE15 —1D 92
Azof St. SE10 —5C 78
Azov Ho. E1 —7J 61
(off Commodore St.)

Baalbec Rd. N5 —1M 59
Babbacombe Clo. Chess —7H 119
Babbacombe Gdns. Ilf —2J 47
Babbacombe Rd. Brom —5E 110
Baber Bri. Cvn. Site. Felt —4G 85
Baber Dri. Felt —5G 85
Babington Ct. WC1 —8J 59
(off Orde Hall St.)
Babington Ho. SE1 —3A 76
(off Disney St.)
Babington Ri. Wemb —2L 55
Babington Rd. NW4 —2F 40
Babington Rd. SW16 —2H 107
Babington Rd. Dag —1G 65
Babington Rd. Horn —6F 50
Babmaes St. SW1 —1H 75
Bacchus Wlk. N1 —5C 60
(off Regan Way)
Bache's St. N1 —6B 60
Back All. EC3 —9C 60
(off Northumberland All.)
Bk. Church La. E1 —9E 60
Back Grn. W on T —8G 117
Back Hill. EC1 —7L 59
Backhouse Pl. SE17 —5C 76
(off Surrey Sq.)
Back La. N8 —3J 43
Back La. NW3 —9A 42
Back La. Bark —4A 64
Back La. Bex —6L 97
Back La. Bren —7H 71
Back La. Edgw —8A 24
Back La. Let H —3C 10
Back La. Rich —8G 87
(in two parts)
Back La. Romf —5H 49
Backley Gdns. SE25 —1E 124
Back Rd. Sidc —1E 112
Back Rd. Tedd —4C 102
Bacon Gro. SE1 —4D 76
Bacon La. NW9 —2M 39
Bacon La. Edgw —8L 23
Bacon Link. Romf —6M 33
Bacons La. N6 —6E 42
Bacon St. E1 & E2 —7D 60
Bacon Ter. Dag —1F 64
Bacton St. E2 —6G 61
Badburgham Ct. Wal A —6M 7
Baddeley Clo. Enf —1L 17
Baddesley Ho. SE11 —6K 75
(off Jonathan St.)
Baddow Clo. Dag —4L 65
Baddow Clo. Wfd G —6H 31
Baddow Wlk. N1 —4A 60
(off New N. Rd.)
Baden Pl. SE1 —3B 76
Baden Powell Clo. Dag —4J 65
Baden Powell Clo. Surb —4K 119
Baden Powell Ho. SW7 —5A 74
(off Queens Ga.)
Baden Powell Ho. Belv —4L 81
Baden Rd. N8 —2H 43
Baden Rd. Ilf —1M 63
Bader Clo. Kenl —7B 138
Bader Way. Rain —2E 66
Badger Clo. Felt —9F 84
Badger Clo. Houn —2G 85
Badger Clo. Ilf —4A 48
Badger Ct. NW2 —8G 41
Badgers Clo. Borwd —4K 11
Badgers Clo. Enf —5M 15
Badgers Clo. Harr —4B 38
Badgers Clo. Hay —1C 68
Badgers Copse. Orp —4D 128
Badgers Copse. Wor Pk —4D 120
Badger's Ct. Eps —5C 134
Badgers Cft. N20 —9J 13
Badgers Cft. SE9 —9L 95
Badgers Hole. Croy —6H 125
Badgers Wlk. N Mald —6C 104
Badgers Wlk. Purl —3G 137
Badlis Rd. E17 —1L 45
Badlow Clo. Eri —8C 82
Badminton Clo. Borwd —4L 11
Badminton Clo. Harr —2C 38
Badminton Clo. N'holt —2L 53
Badminton Ho. Wat —4G 9
(off Anglian Clo.)
Badminton M. E16 —2E 78
Badminton Rd. SW12 —5E 90
Badsworth Rd. SE5 —9A 76
Baffin Way. E14 —2A 78
(off Blackwall Way)
Bagley Clo. W Dray —3J 143
Bagley's La. SW6 —9M 73
Bagleys Spring. Romf —2J 49
Bagnigge Ho. WC1 —6L 59
(off Margery St.)
Bagot Clo. Asht —8K 133
Bagshot Ct. SE18 —9L 79
Bagshot Ho. NW1 —6F 58
(off Redhill St.)
Bagshot Rd. Enf —9D 16
Bagshot St. SE17 —6C 76
Bahram Rd. Eps —2B 134
Baildon. E2 —5G 61
(off Cyprus St.)
Baildon St. SE8 —8K 77
Bailey Clo. E4 —4A 30
Bailey Clo. N11 —7H 27
Bailey M. W4 —7M 71
(off Hervert Gdns.)
Bailey Pl. SE26 —3H 109
Baillie Clo. Rain —7F 66
Baillies Wlk. W5 —3H 71
Bainbridge Clo. Rich —2J 103
Bainbridge Rd. Dag —9K 49
Bainbridge St. WC1 —9H 59
Baines Clo. S Croy —7B 124
Baird Av. S'hall —1M 69
Baird Clo. E10 —6L 45
Baird Clo. NW9 —4A 40
Baird Clo. Bush —8M 9
Baird Gdns. SE19 —1C 108
Baird Ho. W12 —1F 72
(off White City Est.)
Baird Memorial Cotts. N14 —2H 27
(off Balaams La.)
Baird Rd. Enf —5F 16
Baird St. EC1 —7A 60
Bairstow Clo. Borwd —3J 11
Baisley Ho. Chesh —1A 6
Baizdon Rd. SE3 —1C 94
Baker Beal Ct. Bexh —2M 97
Baker Boy La. New Ad —5J 139
Baker Ct. Borwd —4M 11
Baker Ho. W7 —2D 70
Baker La. Mitc —6E 106
Baker Pass. NW10 —4C 56
Baker Rd. NW10 —4C 56
Baker Rd. SE18 —8J 79
Bakers Av. E17 —4M 45
Bakers Ct. SE25 —7C 108
Bakers Ct. Uxb —3B 142
Bakerscroft. Chesh —1E 6
Bakers End. SW20 —6J 105
Baker's Fld. N7 —9J 43
Bakers Gdns. Cars —4C 122
Bakers Hall Ct. EC3 —1C 76
(off Cross La.)
Bakers Hill. E5 —6G 45
Bakers Hill. New Bar —4M 13
Bakers Ho. W5 —2H 71
(off Grove, The)
Bakers La. N6 —4D 42
Baker's M. W1 —9E 58
Bakers M. Grn St —8D 128
Bakers Pas. NW3 —9A 42
(off Heath St.)
Baker's Rents. E2 —6D 60
Bakers Rd. Chesh —3B 6
Bakers Rd. Uxb —3B 142
Baker's Row. E15 —5C 62
Baker's Row. EC1 —7L 59
Baker Street. (Junct.) —8D 58
Baker St. NW1 & W1 —7D 58
Baker St. Enf —5B 16
Baker St. Wey —6A 116
Baker's Yd. EC1 —7L 59
(off Bakers Rd.)
Bakers Yd. Uxb —3B 142
Bakery Clo. SW9 —8K 75
Bakery M. Surb —3L 119
Bakery Path. Edgw —6M 23
(off St Margaret's Rd.)
Bakery Pl. SW11 —3D 90
Bakewell Way. N Mald —6C 104
Balaam Ho. Sutt —6L 121
Balaams La. N14 —2H 27
Balaam St. E13 —7E 62
Balaclava Rd. SE1 —5D 76
Balaclava Rd. Surb —2G 119
Balcaskie Rd. SE9 —4K 95
Balchen Rd. SE3 —1H 95
Balchier Rd. SE22 —5F 92
Balcombe Clo. Bexh —3H 97
Balcombe Ho. NW1 —7C 58
(off Taunton Pl.)
Balcombe St. NW1 —7D 58
Balcon Ct. W5 —9K 55
Balcon Way. Borwd —3A 12
Balcorne St. E9 —3G 61
Balder Ri. SE12 —8F 94
Balderton Flats. W1 —9E 58
(off Balderton St.)
Balderton St. W1 —9E 58
Baldewyne Ct. N17 —8E 28
Baldock St. E3 —5M 61
Baldock Way. Borwd —3K 11
Baldrey Ho. SE10 —6D 78
(off Blackwall La.)
Baldry Gdns. SW16 —3J 107
Baldwin Cres. SE5 —9A 76
Baldwin Gdns. Houn —9A 70
Baldwin Ho. SW2 —7L 91
Baldwins Gdns. WC1 —8L 59
Baldwins Hill. Lou —4K 19
Baldwin's La. Crox G —6A 8
Baldwin St. EC1 —6B 60
Baldwin Ter. N1 —5A 60
Baldwyn Gdns. W3 —1B 72
Baldwyn's Pk. Bex —8B 98
Baldwyn's Rd. Bex —8B 98
Bale Rd. E1 —8J 61
Bales Ter. N9 —3D 28
Balfern Gro. W4 —6C 72
Balfern St. SW11 —1C 90
Balfe St. N1 —5J 59
Balfont Clo. S Croy —5E 138
Balforn Tower. E14 —9A 62
Balfour Av. W7 —2D 70
Balfour Bus. Cen. S'hall —4G 69
Balfour Gro. N20 —3D 26
Balfour Ho. W10 —8H 57
(off St Charles Sq.)
Balfour M. N9 —3E 28
Balfour M. W1 —2E 74
Balfour Pl. SW15 —3F 88
Balfour Pl. W1 —1E 74
Balfour Rd. N5 —9A 44
Balfour Rd. SE25 —9E 108
Balfour Rd. SW19 —4M 105
Balfour Rd. W3 —8A 56
Balfour Rd. W13 —3E 70
Balfour Rd. Brom —9H 111
Balfour Rd. Cars —9D 122
Balfour Rd. Harr —3B 38
Balfour Rd. Houn —2M 85
Balfour Rd. Ilf —7M 47
Balfour Rd. S'hall —4H 69
Balfour St. SE17 —5B 76
Balfour Ter. N3 —9M 25
Balfron Tower. E14 —9A 62
Balgonie Rd. E4 —1B 30
Balgores Cres. Romf —1F 50
Balgores La. Romf —1F 50
Balgores Sq. Romf —2F 50
Balgowan Clo. N Mald —9C 104
Balgowan Rd. Beck —7J 109
Balgowan St. SE18 —5D 80
Balham. —7F 90
Balham Continental Mkt. SW12
(off Shipka Rd.) —7F 90
Balham Gro. SW12 —6E 90
Balham High Rd. SW17 & SW12 —9E 90
Balham Hill. SW12 —6F 90
Balham New Rd. SW12 —6F 90
Balham Pk. Rd. SW12 —7D 90
Balham Rd. N9 —2E 28
Balham Sta. Rd. SW12 —7F 90
Balin Ho. SE1 —3B 76
(off Long La.)
Balkan Wlk. E1 —1F 76
Balladier Wlk. E14 —8M 61
Ballamore Rd. Brom —9E 94
Ballance Rd. E9 —2H 61
Ballantine St. SW18 —3A 90
Ballantrae Ho. NW2 —9K 41
Ballard Clo. King T —4B 104
Ballard Ho. SE10 —7M 77
(off Thames St.)
Ballards Clo. Dag —4M 65
Ballards Farm Rd. S Croy & Croy —8E 124
(in two parts)
Ballards La. N3 & N12 —8L 25
Ballards M. Edgw —6L 23
Ballards Ri. S Croy —8E 124
Ballards Rd. NW2 —7E 40
Ballards Rd. Dag —5M 65
Ballards Way. S Croy & Croy —8E 124
Ballast Quay. SE10 —6B 78
Ballater Clo. Wat —4G 21
Ballater Rd. SW2 —3J 91
Ballater Rd. S Croy —7D 124
Ball Ct. EC3 —9B 60
(off Cornhill)
Ballina St. SE23 —6H 93
Ballin Ct. E14 —3A 78
(off Stewart St.)
Ballingdon Rd. SW11 —5E 90
Ballinger Ct. Wat —5F 8
Balliol Av. E4 —4C 30
Balliol Rd. N17 —8C 28
Balliol Rd. W10 —9G 57
Balliol Rd. Well —1F 96
Balloch Rd. SE6 —7B 94
Ballogie Av. NW10 —9C 40
Ballow Clo. SE5 —8C 76
Ball's Pond Pl. N1 —2B 60
Balls Pond Rd. N1 —2B 60
Balmain Clo. W5 —2H 71
Balmain Ct. Houn —9M 69
Balmain Lodge. Surb —8J 103
(off Cranes Pk. Av.)
Balman Ho. SE16 —5H 77
(off Rotherhithe New Rd.)
Balmer Rd. E3 —5K 61
Balmes Rd. N1 —4B 60
Balmoral Av. N11 —6E 26
Balmoral Av. Beck —8J 109
Balmoral Clo. SW15 —5H 89
Balmoral Clo. Park —1M 5
Balmoral Ct. SE12 —1F 110
Balmoral Ct. SE16 —2H 77
(off King & Queen Wharf)
Balmoral Ct. SE27 —1A 108
Balmoral Ct. Sutt —9L 121
Balmoral Ct. Wemb —8K 39
Balmoral Ct. Wor Pk —4F 120
Balmoral Cres. W Mol —7L 101
Balmoral Dri. Borwd —7B 12
Balmoral Dri. Hay —7C 52
Balmoral Dri. S'hall —7K 53
Balmoral Gdns. W13 —4E 70
Balmoral Gdns. Bex —6K 97
Balmoral Gdns. Ilf —6D 48
Balmoral Gdns. S Croy —2B 138
Balmoral Gro. N7 —2K 59
Balmoral Ho. E14 —4M 77
(off Lanark Sq.)
Balmoral Ho. W14 —5J 73
(off Windsor Way)
Balmoral M. W12 —4D 72
Balmoral Rd. E7 —9G 47
Balmoral Rd. E10 —7M 45
Balmoral Rd. NW2 —2F 56
Balmoral Rd. Ab L —5E 4
Balmoral Rd. Enf —9D 6
Balmoral Rd. Harr —9L 37

Begonia Clo.—Berkeley Av.

Begonia Clo. E6 —8K 63
Begonia Pl. Hamp —3L 101
Begonia Wlk. W12 —9D 56
Beira St. SW12 —6F 90
Beken Ct. Wat —8G 5
Bekesbourne St. E14 —9J 61
Belcroft Clo. Brom —4D 110
Beldanes Lodge. NW10 —3E 56
Beldham Gdns. W Mol —6M 101
Belfairs Dri. Romf —5G 49
Belfairs Grn. Wat —5H 21
Belfast Rd. N16 —7D 44
Belfast Rd. SE25 —8F 108
Belfield Rd. Eps —1B 134
Belfont Wlk. N7 —9J 43
(in two parts)
Belford Gro. SE18 —5L 79
Belford Ho. E8 —4D 60
Belford Rd. Borwd —2K 11
Belfort Rd. SE15 —1G 93
Belfry Clo. SE16 —6F 76
Belgrade Rd. N16 —9C 44
Belgrade Rd. Hamp —5M 101
Belgrave Av. Romf —1G 51
Belgrave Av. Wat —7D 8
Belgrave Clo. N14 —7G 15
Belgrave Clo. NW7 —5B 24
Belgrave Clo. W3 —3M 71
Belgrave Clo. Orp —8G 113
Belgrave Clo. W on T —6F 116
Belgrave Ct. E13 —7G 63
Belgrave Ct. SW8 —8G 75
(off Ascalon St.)
Belgrave Ct. W4 —6A 72
Belgrave Cres. Sun —5F 100
Belgrave Dri. K Lan —1A 4
Belgrave Gdns. N14 —6H 15
Belgrave Gdns. NW8 —4M 57
Belgrave Gdns. Stan —5G 23
Belgrave Heights. E11 —6E 46
Belgrave Ho. SW9 —8L 75
Belgrave M. Uxb —7B 142
Belgrave M. N. SW1 —3E 74
Belgrave M. S. SW1 —4E 74
Belgrave M. W. SW1 —4E 74
Belgrave Pl. SW1 —4E 74
Belgrave Rd. E10 —6A 46
Belgrave Rd. E11 —7E 46
Belgrave Rd. E13 —7G 63
Belgrave Rd. E17 —3L 45
Belgrave Rd. SE25 —8D 108
Belgrave Rd. SW1 —5F 74
Belgrave Rd. SW13 —8D 72
Belgrave Rd. Houn —2K 85
Belgrave Rd. Ilf —6K 47
Belgrave Rd. Mitc —7B 106
Belgrave Rd. Sun —5F 100
Belgrave Sq. SW1 —4E 74
Belgrave St. E1 —8H 61
Belgrave Ter. Wfd G —3E 30
Belgrave Wlk. Mitc —7B 106
Belgrave Yd. SW1 —4F 74
(off Lwr. Belgrave St.)
Belgravia. —4E 74
Belgravia Clo. Barn —5K 13
Belgravia Ct. SW1 —4F 74
(off Ebury St.)
Belgravia Gdns. Brom —3C 110
Belgravia Ho. SW1 —4E 74
(off Halkin Pl.)
Belgravia Ho. SW4 —5H 91
Belgravia M. King T —8H 103
Belgravia Workshops. N19 —7J 43
(off Marlborough Rd.)
Belgrove St. NW1 —6J 59
Belham Wlk. SE5 —9B 76
Belhaven Ct. Borwd —3K 11
Belinda Rd. SW9 —2M 91
Belitha Vs. N1 —3K 59
Bellamy Clo. E14 —3L 77
Bellamy Clo. W14 —6K 73
Bellamy Clo. Edgw —2A 24
Bellamy Clo. Wat —3E 8
Bellamy Ct. Stan —8F 22
Bellamy Dri. Stan —8F 22
Bellamy Ho. Houn —7L 69
Bellamy Rd. E4 —6M 29
Bellamy Rd. Chesh —2E 6
Bellamy Rd. Enf —4B 16
Bellamy's Ct. SE16 —2H 77
(off Abbotshade Rd.)
Bellamy St. SW12 —6F 90
Bellasis Av. SW2 —8J 91
Bell Av. Romf —8F 34
Bell Av. W Dray —5K 143
Bell Clo. Bedm —1D 4
Bell Clo. Pinn —9G 21
Bell Clo. Ruis —8D 36
Bellclose Rd. W Dray —3J 143
Bell Corner. Upm —7M 51
Bell Ct. NW4 —2G 41
Bell Dri. SW18 —6J 89
Bellefield Rd. Orp —9F 112
Bellefields Rd. SW9 —2K 91
Bellegrove Clo. Well —1D 96
Bellegrove Pde. Well —2D 96
Bellegrove Rd. Well —1C 96
Bellenden Rd. SE15 —9D 76
Bellestaines Pleasaunce. E4 —2L 29
Belleville Rd. SW11 —4C 90
Belle Vue. Gnfd —4B 54
Belle Vue Est. NW4 —2H 41
Bellevue La. Bus H —1B 22
Bellevue M. N11 —5E 26
Bellevue Pk. T Hth —7A 108
Bellevue Pl. E1 —7G 61
Belle Vue Rd. E17 —9B 30
Bellevue Rd. N11 —4E 26
Belle Vue Rd. NW4 —2H 41
Bellevue Rd. SW13 —1E 88
Bellevue Rd. SW17 —7C 90
Bellevue Rd. W13 —7F 54
Bellevue Rd. Bexh —4K 97
Bellevue Rd. Horn —6K 51
Bellevue Rd. King T —7J 103
(in two parts)
Belle Vue Rd. Orp —2L 141
Belle Vue Rd. Romf —6A 34
Bellew St. SW17 —9A 90
Bell Farm Av. Dag —8A 50
Bellfield. Croy —1J 139
Bellfield Av. Harr —6B 22
Bellflower Clo. E6 —8J 63
Bellflower Path. Romf —7G 35
Bell Gdns. E10 —6L 45
(off Church Rd.)
Bell Gdns. Orp —9G 113
Bellgate M. NW5 —9F 42
Bell Green. —1J 109
Bell Grn. SE26 —1K 109
Bell Grn. La. SE26 —2K 109
Bell Hill. Croy —4A 124
Bell Ho. SE10 —7A 78
(off Haddo St.)
Bellhouse Cotts. Hay —1C 68
Bell Ho. Rd. Romf —6A 50
Bellina M. NW5 —9F 42
Bell Ind. Est. W4 —5A 72
Bellingham. —9M 93
Bellingham. N17 —7F 28
(off Park La.)
Bellingham Ct. Bark —6F 64
Bellingham Grn. SE6 —9L 93
Bellingham Rd. SE6 —9M 93
Bellingham Trad. Est. SE6 —9M 93
Bell Inn Yd. EC3 —9B 60
Bell Junct. Houn —2M 85
Bell La. E1 —8D 60
Bell La. E16 —2D 78
Bell La. NW4 & NW11 —2H 41
Bell La. Bedm —1D 4
Bell La. Enf —2H 17
Bell La. Twic —7E 86
Bell La. Wemb —8H 39
Bell Mdw. SE19 —2C 108
Bell Moor. NW3 —8A 42
(off E. Heath Rd.)
Bellmount Wood Av. Wat —3C 8
Bello Clo. SE24 —6M 91
Bellot Gdns. SE10 —6C 78
(off Bellot St.)
Bellot St. SE10 —6C 78
Bellring Clo. Belv —7L 81
Bell Rd. E Mol —9B 102
Bell Rd. Enf —3B 16
Bell Rd. Houn —2M 85
Bells All. SW6 —1L 89
Bells Hill. Barn —7H 13
Bell St. NW1 —8C 58
Bell St. SE18 —9J 79
Bell, The. (Junct.) —1L 45
Belltrees Gro. SW16 —2K 107
Bell Vw. Mnr. Ruis —5B 36
Bell Water Ga. SE18 —4L 79
Bell Wharf La. EC4 —1A 76
Bellwood Rd. SE15 —3H 93
Bell Yd. WC2 —9L 59
Belmarsh Rd. SE28 —3C 80
Belmont. —9E 22
(Harrow)
Belmont. —2L 135
(Sutton)
Belmont. Wey —8A 116
Belmont Av. N9 —1E 28
Belmont Av. N13 —5K 27
Belmont Av. N17 —1A 44
Belmont Av. Barn —7D 14
Belmont Av. N Mald —8E 104
Belmont Av. S'hall —4J 69
Belmont Av. Upm —7K 51
Belmont Av. Well —1C 96
Belmont Av. Wemb —4K 55
Belmont Circ. Harr —8F 22
Belmont Clo. E4 —5B 30
Belmont Clo. N20 —1M 25
Belmont Clo. SW4 —2G 91
Belmont Clo. Cockf —6D 14
Belmont Clo. Uxb —2B 142
Belmont Clo. Wfd G —4F 30
Belmont Ct. N5 —9A 44
Belmont Ct. NW11 —3K 41
Belmont Gro. SE13 —2B 94
Belmont Gro. W4 —5B 72
Belmont Hall Ct. SE13 —2B 94
Belmont Hill. SE13 —2A 94
Belmont La. Chst —2M 111
(in two parts)
Belmont La. Stan —8G 23
Belmont Lodge. Har W —7B 22
Belmont M. SW19 —8H 89
Belmont Pde. Chst —2A 112
Belmont Pk. SE13 —3B 94
Belmont Pk. Clo. SE13 —3C 94
Belmont Pk. Rd. E10 —4M 45
Belmont Ri. Sutt —8K 121
Belmont Rd. N15 & N17 —2A 44
Belmont Rd. SE25 —9F 108
Belmont Rd. SW4 —2G 91
Belmont Rd. W4 —5B 72
Belmont Rd. Beck —6J 109
Belmont Rd. Bush —7J 9
Belmont Rd. Chst —2M 111
Belmont Rd. Eri —8L 81
Belmont Rd. Harr —1D 38
Belmont Rd. Horn —8H 51
Belmont Rd. Ilf —8A 48
Belmont Rd. Sutt —2L 135
Belmont Rd. Twic —8B 86
Belmont Rd. Uxb —3B 142
Belmont Rd. Wall —7F 122
Belmont St. NW1 —3E 58
Belmont Ter. W4 —5B 72
Belmor. Els —8L 11
Belmore Av. Hay —9E 52
Belmore La. N7 —1H 59
Belmore St. SW8 —9H 75
Beloe Clo. SW15 —3E 88
Belsham St. E9 —2G 61
Belsize Av. N13 —6K 27
Belsize Av. NW3 —2B 58
Belsize Av. W13 —4F 70
Belsize Ct. NW3 —1B 58
Belsize Ct. Garages. NW3 —1B 58
(off Belsize La.)
Belsize Cres. NW3 —1B 58
Belsize Gdns. Sutt —6M 121
Belsize Gro. NW3 —2C 58
Belsize La. NW3 —2B 58
Belsize M. NW3 —2B 58
Belsize Pk. NW3 —2B 58
Belsize Pk. Gdns. NW3 —2B 58
Belsize Pk. M. NW3 —2B 58
Belsize Pl. NW3 —1B 58
Belsize Rd. NW6 —4L 57
Belsize Rd. Harr —7B 22
Belsize Sq. NW3 —2B 58
Belsize Ter. NW3 —2B 58
Belson Rd. SE18 —5K 79
Beltane Dri. SW19 —9H 89
Belthorn Cres. SW12 —6G 91
Beltinge Rd. Romf —9K 35
Beltona Gdns. Chesh —1D 6
Belton Rd. E7 —3F 62
Belton Rd. E11 —9C 46
Belton Rd. N17 —1C 44
Belton Rd. NW2 —2E 56
Belton Rd. Sidc —1E 112
Belton Way. E3 —8L 61
Beltran Rd. SW6 —1M 89
Beltwood Rd. Belv —5A 82
Belvedere. —4M 81
Belvedere Av. SW19 —2J 105
Belvedere Av. Ilf —9M 31
Belvedere Bldgs. SE1 —3M 75
Belvedere Clo. Esh —7M 117
Belvedere Clo. Tedd —2C 102
Belvedere Ct. SW15 —3G 89
Belvedere Ct. Belv —4K 81
Belvedere Dri. SW19 —2J 105
Belvedere Gdns. W Mol —9K 101
Belvedere Gro. SW19 —2J 105
Belvedere M. SE15 —2G 93
Belvedere Pl. SE1 —3M 75
Belvedere Pl. SW2 —3K 91
Belvedere Rd. E10 —6J 45
Belvedere Rd. SE1 —2K 75
Belvedere Rd. SE2 —2G 81
Belvedere Rd. SE19 —4D 108
Belvedere Rd. W7 —4D 70
Belvedere Rd. Bexh —2K 97
Belvedere Rd. Big H —9K 141
Belvedere Sq. SW19 —2J 105
Belvedere Strand. NW9 —9D 24
Belvedere, The. SW10 —9A 74
(off Chelsea Harbour)
Belvedere Way. Harr —4J 39
Belvoir Clo. SE9 —9J 95
Belvoir Rd. SE22 —6E 92
Belvue Bus. Cen. N'holt —3M 53
Belvue Clo. N'holt —3L 53
Belvue Rd. N'holt —3L 53
Bembridge Clo. NW6 —3J 57
Bembridge Gdns. Ruis —7B 36
Bembridge Ho. SE8 —5K 77
(off Longshore)
Bembridge Pl. Wat —6E 4
Bemersyde Point. E13 —6F 62
(off Dongola Rd. W.)
Bemerton Est. N1 —3J 59
Bemerton St. N1 —4K 59
Bemish Rd. SW15 —2H 89
Bempton Dri. Ruis —7F 36
Bemsted Rd. E17 —1K 45
Benares Rd. SE18 —5D 80
Benbow Ct. W6 —4G 73
(off Benbow Rd.)
Benbow Ho. SE8 —7L 77
(off Benbow St.)
Benbow Moorings. Uxb —8A 142
Benbow Rd. W6 —4F 72
Benbow St. SE8 —7L 77
Benbow Waye. Uxb —8A 142
Benbury Clo. Brom —2A 110
Bence Ho. SE8 —6J 77
Bench Fld. S Croy —8D 124
Bench, The. Rich —9G 87
Bencombe Rd. Purl —6L 137
Bencroft Rd. SW16 —4G 107
Bencurtis Pk. W W'ck —5B 126
Bendall M. NW1 —8C 58
(off Bell St.)
Bendemeer Rd. SW15 —2H 89
Benden Ho. SE13 —4A 94
(off Monument Gdns.)
Bendish Rd. E6 —3J 63
Bendmore Av. SE2 —6E 80
Bendon Valley. SW18 —6M 89
Bendysh Rd. Bush —5J 9
Benedict Clo. Belv —4J 81
Benedict Clo. Orp —5C 128
Benedict Ct. Romf —4K 49
Benedict Dri. Felt —6B 84
Benedict Rd. SW9 —2K 91
Benedict Rd. Mitc —7B 106
Benedict Way. N2 —1A 42
Benedict Wharf. Mitc —7B 106
Benenden Grn. Brom —9E 110
Benets Rd. Horn —6L 51
Benett Gdns. SW16 —6J 107
Ben Ezra Ct. SE17 —5A 76
(off Asolando Dri.)
Benfleet Clo. Sutt —5A 122
Benfleet Ct. E8 —4D 60
Benfleet Way. N11 —2E 26
Bengal Ct. EC3 —9B 60
(off Birchin La.)
Bengal Ho. E1 —8H 61
(off Duckett St.)
Bengal Rd. Ilf —9M 47
Bengarth Dri. Harr —9B 22
Bengarth Rd. N'holt —4J 53
Bengeworth Rd. SE5 —2A 92
Bengeworth Rd. Harr —7E 38
Ben Hale Clo. Stan —5F 22
Benham Clo. SW11 —2B 90
Benham Clo. Chess —8G 119
Benham Gdns. Houn —4K 85
Benham Rd. W7 —8C 54
Benham's Pl. NW3 —9A 42
Benhill Av. Sutt —6M 121
Benhill Rd. SE5 —8B 76
Benhill Rd. Sutt —5A 122
Benhill Wood Rd. Sutt —5A 122
Benhilton. —4M 121
Benhilton Gdns. Sutt —5M 121
Benhurst Av. Horn —9F 50
Benhurst Clo. S Croy —2H 139
Benhurst Ct. SW16 —2L 107
Benhurst Gdns. S Croy —2G 139
Benhurst La. SW16 —2L 107
Benin St. SE13 —6B 94
Benjafield Clo. N18 —4F 28
Benjamin Clo. E8 —4E 60
Benjamin Clo. Horn —4E 50
Benjamin Ct. Belv —7K 81
Benjamin St. EC1 —8M 59
Ben Jonson Ct. N1 —5C 60
Ben Jonson Ho. EC2 —8A 60
(off Beech St.)
Ben Jonson Pl. EC2 —8A 60
(off Beech St.)
Ben Jonson Rd. E1 —8H 61
Benledi St. E14 —9B 62
Benneck Ho. Wat —8C 8
Bennelong Clo. W12 —1F 72
Bennerley Rd. SW11 —4C 90
Bennets Fld. Rd. Uxb —2M 143
Bennet's Hill. EC4 —1A 76
Bennet St. SW1 —2G 75
Bennett Clo. Hamp W —5G 103
Bennett Clo. N'wd —7D 20
Bennett Clo. Well —1E 96
Bennett Ct. N7 —8K 43
Bennett Gro. SE13 —9M 77
Bennett Ho. SW1 —5H 75
(off Page St.)
Bennett Pk. SE3 —2D 94
Bennett Rd. E13 —7G 63
Bennett Rd. N16 —9C 44
Bennett Rd. Romf —4J 49
Bennetts Av. Croy —4J 125
Bennetts Av. Gnfd —4C 54
Bennett's Castle La. Dag —7G 49
Bennetts Clo. N17 —6D 28
Bennetts Clo. Mitc —5F 106
Bennetts Copse. Chst —3J 111
Bennett St. W4 —7C 72
Bennetts Way. Croy —4J 125
Bennett's Yd. SW1 —4H 75
Bennett's Yd. Uxb —3A 142
Benningholme Rd. Edgw —6C 24
Bennington Rd. E4 —7C 30
Bennington Rd. N17 —8C 28
Bennions Clo. Horn —2G 67
Bennison Dri. H Wood —9H 35
Benn's All. Hamp —6M 101
Benn St. E9 —2J 61
Benns Wlk. Rich —3J 87
(off Michelsdale Dri.)
Benrek Clo. Ilf —7A 32
Bensbury Clo. SW15 —6F 88
Bensham Clo. T Hth —8A 108
Bensham Gro. T Hth —6A 108
Bensham La. T Hth & Croy —8M 107
Bensham Mnr. Rd. T Hth —8A 108
Benskin Rd. Wat —7E 8
Benskins La. Noak H —1H 35
Bensley Clo. N11 —5D 26
Ben Smith Way. SE16 —4E 76
Benson Av. E6 —5G 63
Benson Clo. Houn —3L 85
Benson Clo. Uxb —8C 142
Benson Ho. E2 —7D 60
(off Ligonier St.)
Benson Ho. SE1 —2M 75
(off Hatfields)
Benson Quay. E1 —1G 77
Benson Rd. SE23 —7G 93
Benson Rd. Croy —5L 123
Bentalls Cen., The. King T —6H 103
Bentfield Gdns. SE9 —9H 95
Benthall Gdns. Kenl —9A 138
Benthal Rd. N16 —8E 44
Bentham Ct. N1 —3A 60
(off Ecclesbourne Rd.)
Bentham Ct. SE1 —4B 76
(off Falmouth Rd.)
Bentham Rd. E9 —2H 61
Bentham Rd. SE28 —1F 80
Bentham Wlk. NW10 —1A 56
Ben Tillet Clo. E16 —2K 79
Ben Tillet Clo. Bark —3E 64
Ben Tillet Ho. N15 —1M 43
Bentinck Clo. NW8 —5C 58
Bentinck Ho. W12 —1F 72
(off White City Est.)
Bentinck M. W1 —9E 58
Bentinck Rd. W Dray —2H 143
Bentinck St. W1 —9E 58
Bentley Dri. NW2 —8K 41
Bentley Dri. Ilf —4A 48
Bentley Ho. SE5 —9C 76
(off Peckham Rd.)
Bentley Rd. N1 —2C 60
Bentley Way. Stan —5E 22
Bentley Way. Wfd G —3E 30
Benton Rd. Ilf —6B 48
Benton Rd. Wat —5H 21
Bentons La. SE27 —1A 108
Benton's Ri. SE27 —2B 108
Bentry Clo. Dag —7J 49
Bentry Rd. Dag —7J 49
Bentworth Ct. E2 —7E 60
(off Granby St.)
Bentworth Rd. W12 —9F 56
Benville Ho. SW8 —8K 75
(off Oval Pl.)
Benwell Ct. Sun —5E 100
Benwell Rd. N7 —9L 43
Benwick Clo. SE16 —5F 76
Benwood Ct. Sutt —5A 122
Benworth St. E3 —6K 61
Benyon Ct. N1 —4C 60
(off De Beauvoir Est.)
Benyon Ho. EC1 —6L 59
(off Myddelton Pas.)
Benyon Rd. N1 —4B 60
Berberis Ct. Ilf —2M 63
Berberis Ho. E3 —8L 61
(off Gale St.)
Berberis Wlk. W Dray —5J 143
Berber Pl. E14 —1L 77
Berber Rd. SW11 —4D 90
Berberry Clo. Edgw —4A 24
Berceau Wlk. Wat —3C 8
Bercta Rd. SE9 —8A 96
Berenger Tower. SW10 —8B 74
(off Worlds End Est.)
Berenger Wlk. SW10 —8B 74
(off Worlds End Est.)
Berens Ct. Sidc —1D 112
Berens Rd. NW10 —6H 57
Berens Rd. Orp —9H 113
Berens Way. Chst —7D 112
Beresford Av. N20 —2D 26
Beresford Av. W7 —8B 54
Beresford Av. Surb —3M 119
Beresford Av. Twic —5G 87
Beresford Av. Wemb —4K 55
Beresford Dri. Brom —7H 111
Beresford Dri. Wfd G —4G 31
Beresford Gdns. Enf —6C 16
Beresford Gdns. Houn —4K 85
Beresford Gdns. Romf —3J 49
Beresford Rd. E4 —1C 30
Beresford Rd. E17 —8M 29
Beresford Rd. N2 —1C 42
Beresford Rd. N5 —1B 60
Beresford Rd. N8 —3L 43
Beresford Rd. Harr —3B 38
Beresford Rd. King T —5K 103
Beresford Rd. N Mald —8A 104
Beresford Rd. S'hall —2H 69
Beresford Rd. Sutt —9K 121
Beresford Sq. SE18 —5M 79
Beresford St. SE18 —4M 79
Beresford Ter. N5 —1A 60
Berestede Rd. W4 —6D 72
Bere St. E1 —1H 77
Bergen Ho. SE5 —1A 92
(off Carew St.)
Bergen Sq. SE16 —4J 77
Berger Clo. Orp —1B 128
Berger Rd. E9 —2H 61
Berghem M. W14 —4H 73
Bergholt Av. Ilf —3J 47
Bergholt Cres. N16 —5C 44
Bergholt M. NW1 —3G 59
Berglen Ct. E14 —9J 61
Berglen Ho. E14 —9J 61
Bering Sq. E14 —6L 77
Bering Wlk. E16 —9H 63
Berisford M. SW18 —5A 90
Berkeley Av. Bexh —9H 81

Berkeley Av.—Birch Av.

Berkeley Av. Gnfd —2C 54
Berkeley Av. Houn —9E 68
Berkeley Av. Ilf —9L 31
Berkeley Av. Romf —7A 34
Berkeley Clo. Ab L —5D 4
Berkeley Clo. Bren —7E 70
Berkeley Clo. Els —7L 11
Berkeley Clo. Horn —7M 51
Berkeley Clo. King T —4J 103
Berkeley Clo. Orp —2C 128
Berkeley Clo. Ruis —8E 36
Berkeley Clo. Twic —9C 86
(off Wellesley Rd.)
Berkeley Ct. N3 —8M 25
Berkeley Ct. N14 —8G 15
Berkeley Ct. NW1 —7D 58
(off Marylebone Rd.)
Berkeley Ct. NW10 —9C 40
Berkeley Ct. NW11 —5K 41
(off Ravenscroft Av.)
Berkeley Ct. W5 —1G 71
(off Gordon Rd.)
Berkeley Ct. Crox G —7B 8
Berkeley Ct. Croy —6B 124
(off Coombe Rd.)
Berkeley Ct. Surb —2H 119
Berkeley Ct. Swan —7C 114
Berkeley Ct. Wall —5G 123
Berkeley Ct. Wey —4B 116
Berkeley Cres. Barn —7B 14
Berkeley Cres. Dart —7K 99
Berkeley Dri. Horn —6L 51
Berkeley Dri. W Mol —7K 101
Berkeley Gdns. N21 —9B 16
Berkeley Gdns. W8 —2L 73
Berkeley Gdns. Clay —8E 118
Berkeley Gdns. W on T —2D 116
Berkeley Ho. SE8 —6K 77
(off Grove St.)
Berkeley Ho. Bren —7H 71
(off Albany Rd.)
Berkeley M. W1 —9D 58
Berkeley Pl. SW19 —3H 105
Berkeley Pl. Eps —8B 134
Berkeley Rd. E12 —1J 63
Berkeley Rd. N8 —3H 43
Berkeley Rd. N15 —4B 44
Berkeley Rd. NW9 —2L 39
Berkeley Rd. SW13 —9E 72
Berkeley Rd. Uxb —3A 52
Berkeley Sq. W1 —1F 74
Berkeley St. W1 —1F 74
Berkeley Wlk. N4 —7K 43
(off Durham Rd.)
Berkeley Waye. Houn —7H 69
Berkely Clo. Sun —7G 101
Berkhampstead Rd. Belv —6L 81
Berkhamsted Av. Wemb —2K 55
Berkley Av. Wal X —7D 6
Berkley Gro. NW1 —3E 58
Berkley Pl. Wal X —7D 6
Berkley Rd. NW1 —3D 58
Berkshire Ct. W7 —7D 54
(off Copley Clo.)
Berkshire Gdns. N13 —6L 27
Berkshire Gdns. N18 —5F 28
Berkshire Ho. SE6 —1L 109
Berkshire Rd. E9 —2K 61
Berkshire Sq. Mitc —8J 107
Berkshire Way. Horn —3L 51
Berkshire Way. Mitc —8J 107
Bermans Way. NW10 —9C 40
Bermer Rd. Wat —3G 9
Bermondsey. —3E 76
Bermondsey Sq. SE1 —4C 76
Bermondsey St. SE1 —2C 76
Bermondsey Trad. Est. SE16 —6G 77
Bermondsey Wall E. SE16 —3E 76
Bermondsey Wall W. SE16 —3E 76
Bernal Clo. SE28 —1H 81
Bernard Angell Ho. SE10 —7B 78
(off Trafalgar Rd.)
Bernard Ashley Dri. SE7 —6F 78
Bernard Av. W13 —4F 70
Bernard Cassidy St. E16 —8D 62
Bernard Gdns. SW19 —2K 105
Bernard Gro. Wal A —6H 7
Bernard Mans. WC1 —7J 59
Bernard Rd. N15 —3D 44
Bernard Rd. Romf —5A 50
Bernard Rd. Wall —6F 122
Bernards Clo. Ilf —7B 32
Bernard Shaw Ct. NW1 —3G 59
(off St Pancras Way)
Bernard St. WC1 —7J 59
Bernard Sunley Ho. SW9 —8L 75
(off S. Island Pl.)
Bernays Clo. Stan —6G 23
Bernays Gro. SW9 —3K 91
Bernel Dri. Croy —5K 125
Berne Rd. T Hth —9A 108
Berners Dri. W13 —1E 70
Berners Ho. N1 —5L 59
(off Barnsbury Est.)
Berners M. W1 —8G 59
Berners Pl. W1 —9G 59
Berners Rd. N1 —4M 59
Berners Rd. N22 —8L 27
Berners St. W1 —8G 59
Berner Ter. E1 —9E 60
(off Fairclough St.)
Berney Ho. Beck —9J 109
Berney Rd. Croy —2B 124
Bernhart Clo. Edgw —7A 24
Bernice Clo. Rain —7G 67
Bernville Way. Harr —3K 39
Bernwell Rd. E4 —3C 30
Berridge Grn. Edgw —7L 23
Berridge M. NW6 —1L 57
Berridge Rd. SE19 —2B 108
Berriman Rd. N7 —8K 43
Berriton Rd. Harr —8K 37
Berry Av. Wat —9F 4
Berrybank Clo. E4 —2A 30
Berry Clo. N21 —1M 27
Berry Clo. NW10 —3C 56
Berry Clo. Horn —1G 67
Berry Ct. Houn —4K 85
Berrydale Rd. Hay —7J 53
Berryfield Clo. E17 —2M 45
Berryfield Clo. Brom —5J 111
Berryfield Rd. SE17 —6M 75
Berrygrove. (Junct.) —2K 9
Berry Gro. La. Wat —2J 9
(in two parts)
Berryhill. SE9 —3M 95
Berry Hill. Stan —4H 23
Berryhill Gdns. SE9 —3M 95
Berry Ho. E1 —7F 60
(off Headlam St.)
Berrylands. —1L 119
Berrylands. SW20 —7G 105
Berrylands. Orp —5G 129
Berrylands. Surb —1K 119
Berrylands Rd. Surb —1K 119
Berry La. SE21 —1B 108
Berry La. W on T —7H 117
Berryman Clo. Dag —8G 49
Berryman's La. SE26 —1H 109
Berry Meade. Asht —9K 133
Berrymead Gdns. W3 —2A 72
Berrymede Rd. W4 —4B 72
Berry Pl. EC1 —6M 59
Berry's Green. —8M 141
Berry's Grn. Rd. Berr G —8M 141
Berry's Hill. Berr G —7M 141
Berry St. EC1 —7M 59
Berry Way. W5 —4J 71
Bertal Rd. SW17 —1B 106
Bertha Hollamby Ct. Sidc —2G 113
(off Sidcup Hill)
Bertha James Ct. Brom —8F 110
Berther Rd. Horn —5H 51
Berthold M. Wal A —6H 7
Berthons Gdns. E17 —3B 46
(off Wood St.)
Berthon St. SE8 —8L 77
Bertie Rd. NW10 —2E 56
Bertie Rd. SE26 —3H 109
Bertram Cotts. SW19 —4L 105
Bertram Rd. NW4 —4E 40
Bertram Rd. Enf —6E 16
Bertram Rd. King T —4L 103
Bertram St. N19 —7F 42
Bertrand Ho. SW16 —9J 91
(off Leigham Av.)
Bertrand St. SE13 —2M 93
Bertrand Way. SE28 —1F 80
Bert Rd. T Hth —9A 108
Bert Way. Enf —6D 16
Berwick Av. Hay —9H 53
Berwick Clo. Stan —6D 22
Berwick Clo. Wal X —7G 7
Berwick Cres. Sidc —6C 96
Berwick Ho. N2 —9B 26
Berwick Pond Clo. Rain —5H 67
Berwick Pond Rd. Rain & Upm —5K 67
Berwick Rd. E16 —9F 62
Berwick Rd. N22 —8M 27
Berwick Rd. Borwd —2K 11
Berwick Rd. Rain —5H 67
Berwick Rd. Well —9F 80
Berwick St. W1 —9G 59
Berwick Way. Orp —3E 128
Berwyn Av. Houn —9M 69
Berwyn Rd. SE24 —7M 91
Berwyn Rd. Rich —3M 87
Beryl Av. E6 —8J 63
Beryl Rd. W6 —6H 73
Berystede. King T —4M 103
Besant Clo. NW2 —8J 41
Besant Ct. N1 —1B 60
Besant Ho. NW8 —4A 58
(off Boundary Rd.)
Besant Ho. Wat —4H 9
Besant Rd. NW2 —9J 41
Besant Wlk. N7 —7K 43
Besant Way. NW10 —1A 56
Besford Ho. E2 —5E 60
(off Pritchard's Rd.)
Besley St. SW16 —3G 107
Bessant Dri. Rich —9L 71
Bessborough Gdns. SW1 —6H 75
Bessborough Pl. SW1 —6H 75
Bessborough Rd. SW15 —7E 88
Bessborough Rd. Harr —6B 38
Bessborough St. SW1 —6H 75
Bessemer Ct. NW1 —3G 59
(off Rochester Sq.)
Bessemer Rd. SE5 —1A 92
Bessie Lansbury Clo. E6 —9L 63
Bessingby Rd. Ruis —7F 36
Bessingham Wlk. SE4 —3H 93
(off Aldersford Clo.)
Besson St. SE14 —9G 77
Bessy St. E2 —6G 61
Best Ter. Swan —1A 130
Bestwood St. SE8 —5H 77
Beswick M. NW6 —2M 57
Betam Rd. Hay —3B 68
Beta Pl. SW9 —3K 91
Betchworth Clo. Sutt —7B 122
Betchworth Rd. Ilf —7C 48
Betchworth Way. New Ad —1A 140
Bethal Est. SE1 —2C 76
(off Tooley St.)
Betham Rd. Gnfd —7B 54
Bethany Waye. Felt —6C 84
Bethecar Rd. Harr —3C 38
Bethell Av. E16 —7D 62
Bethell Av. Ilf —5L 47
Bethel Rd. Well —2G 97
Bethersden Clo. Beck —4K 109
Bethersden Ho. SE17 —6C 76
(off Kinglake St.)
Bethlehem Ho. E14 —1K 77
(off Limehouse Causeway)
Bethnal Green. —6F 60
Bethnal Green Mus. of Childhood. —6G 61
Bethnal Grn. Rd. E1 & E2 —7D 60
Bethune Av. N11 —4D 26
Bethune Clo. N16 —6C 44
Bethune Rd. N16 —5B 44
Bethune Rd. NW10 —7B 56
Bethwin Rd. SE5 —8M 75
Betjeman Clo. Chesh —1A 6
Betjeman Clo. Coul —9K 137
Betjeman Clo. Pinn —2L 37
Betjeman Ct. W Dray —2H 143
Betley Ct. W on T —5F 116
Betony Clo. Croy —3H 125
Betony Rd. Romf —6G 35
Betoyne Av. E4 —4C 30
Betsham Ho. SE1 —3B 76
(off Newcomen St.)
Betsham Rd. Eri —8D 82
Betstyle Cir. N11 —4F 26
Betstyle Ho. N10 —7E 26
Betstyle Rd. N11 —4F 26
Betterton Dri. Sidc —8J 97
Betterton Ho. WC2 —9J 59
(off Betterton St.)
Betterton Rd. Rain —6C 66
Betterton St. WC2 —9J 59
Bettles Clo. Uxb —5A 142
Bettons Pk. E15 —4C 62
Bettridge Rd. SW6 —1K 89
Betts Clo. Beck —6J 109
Betts Ho. E1 —1F 76
(off Betts St.)
Betts M. E17 —4K 45
Betts Rd. E16 —1F 78
Betts St. E1 —1F 76
Betts Way. SE20 —5F 108
Betts Way. Surb —3F 118
Betty Brooks Ho. E11 —8B 46
Betty May Gray Ho. E14 —5A 78
(off Pier St.)
Betula Clo. Kenl —7B 138
Betula Wlk. Rain —6H 67
Beulah Av. T Hth —6A 108
Beulah Clo. Edgw —3M 23
Beulah Cres. T Hth —6A 108
Beulah Gro. Croy —1A 124
Beulah Hill. SE19 —3M 107
Beulah Path. E17 —3A 46
Beulah Rd. E17 —3M 45
Beulah Rd. SW19 —4K 105
Beulah Rd. Horn —8G 51
Beulah Rd. Sutt —6L 121
Beulah Rd. T Hth —7A 108
Beult Rd. Dart —3E 98
Bevan Av. Bark —3E 64
Bevan Ct. Croy —7L 123
Bevan Ho. WC1 —8J 59
(off Boswell St.)
Bevan Ho. Twic —5H 87
Bevan Ho. Wat —4H 9
Bevan Pk. Eps —2D 134
Bevan Pl. Swan —8D 114
Bevan Rd. SE2 —6F 80
Bevan Rd. Barn —6D 14
Bevan St. N1 —4A 60
Bevan Way. Horn —9K 51
Bev Callender Clo. SW8 —2F 90
Bevenden St. N1 —6B 60
Bevercote Wlk. Belv —7K 81
Beverley Av. SW20 —5D 104
Beverley Av. Houn —3K 85
Beverley Av. Sidc —6D 96
Beverley Clo. N21 —1A 28
Beverley Clo. SW11 —3B 90
Beverley Clo. SW13 —1E 88
Beverley Clo. Chess —6G 119
Beverley Clo. Enf —6C 16
Beverley Clo. Eps —3G 135
Beverley Clo. Horn —5K 51
Beverley Clo. Wey —4C 116
Beverley Cotts. SW15 —9C 88
Beverley Ct. N2 —2D 42
(off Western Rd.)
Beverley Ct. N14 —9G 15
Beverley Ct. SE4 —2K 93
Beverley Ct. W4 —6A 72
Beverley Ct. Harr —1B 38
Beverley Ct. Houn —3K 85
Beverley Ct. Kent —2G 39
Beverley Cres. Wfd G —8F 30
Beverley Dri. Edgw —1L 39
Beverley Gdns. NW11 —5J 41
Beverley Gdns. SW13 —2D 88
Beverley Gdns. Chesh —3A 6
Beverley Gdns. Horn —5K 51
Beverley Gdns. Stan —8E 22
Beverley Gdns. Wemb —6K 39
Beverley Gdns. Wor Pk —3E 120
Beverley Ho. Brom —2B 110
(off Brangbourne Rd.)
Beverley La. SW15 —9D 88
Beverley La. King T —4C 104
Beverley M. E4 —6B 30
Beverley Path. SW13 —1D 88
Beverley Rd. E4 —6B 30
Beverley Rd. E6 —6H 63
Beverley Rd. SE20 —6F 108
Beverley Rd. SW13 —2D 88
Beverley Rd. W4 —6D 72
Beverley Rd. Bexh —1A 98
Beverley Rd. Brom —4J 127
Beverley Rd. Dag —9J 49
Beverley Rd. King T —5G 103
Beverley Rd. Mitc —8H 107
Beverley Rd. N Mald —8E 104
Beverley Rd. Ruis —7E 36
Beverley Rd. S'hall —5J 69
Beverley Rd. Sun —5D 100
Beverley Rd. Whyt —8C 138
Beverley Rd. Wor Pk —4G 121
Beverley Trad. Est. Mord —2H 121
Beverley Way. SW20 & N Mald —5D 104
Beversbrook Rd. N19 —8H 43
Beverstone Rd. SW2 —4K 91
Beverstone Rd. T Hth —8L 107
Beverston M. W1 —8D 58
(off Up. Montagu St.)
Bevill Allen Clo. SW17 —2D 106
Bevill Clo. SE25 —7E 108
Bevin Clo. SE16 —2J 77
Bevin Ct. WC1 —6K 59
Bevington Rd. W10 —8J 57
Bevington Rd. Beck —6M 109
Bevington St. SE16 —3E 76
Bevin Ho. E2 —6G 61
(off Butler St.)
Bevin Rd. Hay —6E 52
Bevin Sq. SW17 —9D 90
Bevin Way. WC1 —5L 59
Bevis Marks. EC3 —9C 60
Bewcastle Gdns. Enf —6J 15
Bew Ct. SE22 —6E 92
Bewdley St. N1 —3L 59
Bewick St. SW8 —1F 90
Bewley Clo. Chesh —4D 6
Bewley Ho. E1 —1F 76
(off Bewley St.)
Bewley St. E1 —1G 77
Bewlys Rd. SE27 —2M 107
Bexhill Clo. Felt —8J 85
Bexhill Rd. N11 —5H 27
Bexhill Rd. SE4 —5K 93
Bexhill Rd. SW14 —2A 88
Bexhill Wlk. E15 —4C 62
Bexley. —6L 97
Bexley Clo. Dart —4C 98
Bexley Cotts. Hort K —8M 115
Bexley Gdns. N9 —3B 28
Bexley Gdns. Chad H —3F 48
Bexley Hall Place Vis. Cen. —5A 98
Bexleyheath. —3L 97
Bexley High St. Bex —6L 97
Bexley Ho. SE4 —3J 93
Bexley La. Dart —4C 98
Bexley La. Sidc —1G 113
Bexley Local Studies & Archive Cen. —5A 98
Bexley Rd. SE9 —4M 95
Bexley Rd. Eri —9A 82
(in two parts)
Beynon Rd. Cars —7D 122
Bianca Rd. SE15 —7E 76
Bibsworth Rd. N3 —9K 25
Bibury Clo. SE15 —7C 76
(in two parts)
Bicester Rd. Rich —2L 87
Bickenhall Mans. NW1 —8D 58
(off Bickenhall St., in two parts)
Bickenhall St. W1 —8D 58
Bickersteth Rd. SW17 —3D 106
Bickerton Rd. N19 —7G 43
Bickley. —7J 111
Bickley Cres. Brom —8J 111
Bickley Pk. Rd. Brom —7J 111
Bickley Rd. E10 —5M 45
Bickley Rd. Brom —6H 111
Bickley St. SW17 —2C 106
Bicknell Ho. E1 —9E 60
(off Ellen St.)
Bicknell Rd. SE5 —2A 92
Bicknoller Clo. Sutt —2M 135
Bicknoller Rd. Enf —3C 16
Bicknor Rd. Orp —2C 128
Bidborough Clo. Brom —9D 110
Bidborough St. WC1 —6J 59
Biddenden Way. SE9 —1L 111
Biddenham Ho. SE16 —5H 77
(off Plough Way)
Biddenham Turn. Wat —8G 5
Bidder St. E16 —8C 62
(in two parts)
Biddesden Ho. SW3 —5D 74
(off Cadogan St.)
Biddestone Rd. N7 —9K 43
Biddulph Ho. SE18 —5K 79
Biddulph Mans. W9 —6M 57
(off Elgin Av.)
Biddulph Rd. W9 —6M 57
Biddulph Rd. S Croy —2A 138
Bideford Av. Gnfd —5F 54
Bideford Clo. Edgw —8L 23
Bideford Clo. Felt —9K 85
Bideford Clo. Romf —8G 35
Bideford Gdns. Enf —9C 16
Bideford Rd. Brom —9D 94
Bideford Rd. Enf —2K 17
Bideford Rd. Ruis —8F 36
Bideford Rd. Well —8F 80
Bidwell Gdns. N11 —7G 27
Bidwell St. SE15 —9F 76
Big Ben. —3J 75
Bigbury Clo. N17 —7B 28
Biggerstaff Rd. E15 —4A 62
Biggerstaff St. N4 —7L 43
Biggin Av. Mitc —5D 106
Biggin Hill. —9H 141
Biggin Hill. SE19 —5M 107
Biggin Hill Bus. Pk. Big H —7H 141
Biggin Hill Clo. King T —2G 103
Biggin Way. SE19 —4M 107
Bigginwood Rd. SW16 —4M 107
Biggs Row. SW15 —2H 89
Big Hill. E5 —6F 44
Bigland St. E1 —9F 60
Bignell Rd. SE18 —6M 79
Bignold Rd. E7 —9E 46
Bigwood Ct. NW11 —3M 41
Bigwood Rd. NW11 —3M 41
Biko Clo. Uxb —9A 142
Bilberry Ho. E3 —8L 61
(off Watts Gro.)
Billet Clo. Romf —1H 49
Billet La. Horn —6H 51
Billet Rd. E17 —8H 29
Billet Rd. Romf —1F 48
Billets Hart Clo. W7 —3C 70
Bill Hamling Clo. SE9 —8K 95
Billing Clo. Dag —3G 65
Billingford Clo. SE4 —3H 93
Billing Ho. E1 —9H 61
(off Bower St.)
Billingley. NW1 —4G 59
(off Pratt St.)
Billing Pl. SW10 —8M 73
Billing Rd. SW10 —8M 73
Billingsgate Fish Market. —2M 77
Billingsgate Rd. E14 —1L 77
Billing St. SW6 —8M 73
Billington Rd. SE14 —8H 77
Billinton Hill. Croy —4B 124
Billiter Sq. EC3 —9C 60
(off Fenchurch Av.)
Billiter St. EC3 —9C 60
Bill Nicholson Way. N17 —7D 28
(off High Rd.)
Billockby Clo. Chess —8K 119
Billson St. E14 —5A 78
Bilsby Gro. SE9 —1H 111
Bilsby Lodge. Wemb —8A 40
(off Chalklands)
Bilton Cen., The. Gnfd —4F 54
Bilton Rd. Eri —8E 82
Bilton Rd. Gnfd —4E 54
Bilton Towers. W1 —9D 58
(off Gt. Cumberland Pl.)
Bilton Way. Enf —3J 17
Bilton Way. Hay —3F 68
Bina Gdns. SW5 —5A 74
Binbrook Ho. W10 —8G 57
(off Sutton Way)
Bincote Rd. Enf —5K 15
Binden Rd. W12 —4D 72
Bindon Grn. Mord —8M 105
Binfield Rd. SW8 —9J 75
Binfield Rd. S Croy —7D 124
Bingfield St. N1 —4J 59
(in two parts)
Bingham Ct. N1 —3M 59
(off Halton Rd.)
Bingham Pl. W1 —8E 58
Bingham Rd. Croy —3E 124
Bingham St. N1 —2B 60
Bingley Rd. E16 —9G 63
Bingley Rd. Gnfd —7A 54
Bingley Rd. Sun —4E 100
Binley Ho. SW15 —5D 88
Binney St. W1 —9E 58
Binnie Ct. SE10 —8M 77
(off Greenwich High Rd.)
Binnie Ho. SE1 —4A 76
(off Bath Ter.)
Binns Rd. W4 —6C 72
Binns Ter. W4 —6C 72
Binsey Wlk. SE2 —3G 81
Binstead Clo. Hay —8J 53
Binyon Cres. Stan —5D 22
Birbetts Rd. SE9 —8K 95
Bircham Path. SE4 —3H 93
(off Aldersford Clo.)
Birchanger Rd. SE25 —9E 108
Birch Av. N13 —3A 28
Birch Av. W Dray —9D 142

Birch Clo.—Blantyre Wlk.

Birch Clo. E16 —8C 62
Birch Clo. N19 —7G 43
Birch Clo. SE15 —1E 92
(off Bournemouth Clo.)
Birch Clo. Bren —8F 70
Birch Clo. Buck H —3H 31
Birch Clo. Eyns —5H 131
Birch Clo. Houn —1B 86
Birch Clo. Romf —1M 49
Birch Clo. Shep —6C 100
Birch Clo. Tedd —2E 102
Birch Copse. Brick W —3J 5
Birch Ct. N'wd —6A 20
Birch Ct. Wall —6F 122
Birch Cres. Horn —2J 51
Birch Cres. Uxb —4D 142
Birchdale Gdns. Romf —5H 49
Birchdale Rd. E7 —1G 63
Birchdene Dri. SE28 —2E 80
Birchen Clo. NW9 —7B 40
Birchend Clo. S Croy —8B 124
Birchen Gro. NW9 —7B 40
Birches Clo. Eps —7C 134
Birches Clo. Mitc —7D 106
Birches Clo. Pinn —3J 37
Birches, The. E12 —9J 47
Birches, The. N21 —8K 15
Birches, The. SE7 —7F 78
Birches, The. Brom —8D 110
(off Durham Rd.)
Birches, The. Bush —7A 10
Birches, The. Houn —6K 85
Birches, The. Orp —6L 127
Birches, The. Swan —6C 114
Birchfield Clo. Coul —8K 137
Birchfield Gro. Eps —2G 135
Birchfield Ho. E14 —1L 77
(off Birchfield St.)
Birchfield Rd. Chesh —2B 6
Birchfield St. E14 —1L 77
Birch Gdns. Dag —8A 50
Birch Grn. NW9 —7C 24
Birch Gro. E11 —9C 46
Birch Gro. SE12 —6D 94
Birch Gro. W3 —2L 71
Birch Gro. Shep —6C 100
Birch Gro. Well —3E 96
Birch Hill. Croy —7H 125
Birch Ho. N22 —8L 27
(off Acacia Rd.)
Birch Ho. SE14 —9K 77
Birch Ho. SW2 —5L 91
(off Tulse Hill)
Birch Ho. W10 —7J 57
(off Droop St.)
Birchington Clo. Bexh —9M 81
Birchington Clo. Orp —3G 129
Birchington Ct. NW6 —4M 57
(off W. End La.)
Birchington Ho. E5 —1F 60
Birchington Rd. N8 —4H 43
Birchington Rd. NW6 —4L 57
Birchington Rd. Surb —2K 119
Birchin La. EC3 —9B 60
Birchlands Av. SW12 —6D 90
Birch La. Purl —3J 137
Birchmead. Orp —4L 127
Birchmead. Wat —2D 8
Birchmead Av. Pinn —2G 37
Birchmere Bus. Site. SE28 —3E 80
Birchmere Lodge. SE16 —6F 76
(off Sherwood Gdns.)
Birchmere Row. SE3 —1D 94
Birchmore Hall. N5 —8A 44
Birchmore Wlk. N5 —8A 44
Birch Pk. Harr —7A 22
Birch Rd. Felt —2H 101
Birch Rd. Romf —1M 49
Birch Row. Brom —2L 127
Birch Tree Av. W W'ck —7D 126
Birch Tree Wlk. Wat —1D 8
Birch Tree Way. Croy —4F 124
Birch Va. Ct. NW8 —7B 58
(off Pollitt Dri.)
Birchville Ct. Bus H —1C 22
Birch Wlk. Borwd —3L 11
Birch Wlk. Eri —7A 82
Birch Wlk. Mitc —5F 106
Birchway. Hay —2E 68
Birch Way. Warl —9J 139
Birchwood. Wal A —7L 7
Birchwood Av. N10 —1E 42
Birchwood Av. Beck —8K 109
Birchwood Av. Sidc —8F 96
Birchwood Av. Wall —5E 122
Birchwood Clo. Mord —8M 105
Birchwood Ct. N13 —5M 27
Birchwood Ct. Edgw —9A 24
Birchwood Dri. NW3 —8M 41
Birchwood Dri. Dart —1C 114
Birchwood Gro. Hamp —3L 101
Birchwood La. Esh & Oxs —1B 132
Birchwood Pde. Dart —1C 114
Birchwood Pk. Av. Swan —7C 114
Birchwood Rd. SW17 —2F 106
Birchwood Rd. Orp —8B 112
Birchwood Rd. Swan & Dart —5A 114
Birchwood Way. Park —1M 5
Birdbrook Clo. Dag —3A 66
Birdbrook Ho. N1 —3A 60
(off Popham Rd.)
Birdbrook Rd. SE3 —3G 95
Birdcage Wlk. SW1 —3G 75
Birdham Clo. Brom —9J 111
Birdhouse La. Orp —7K 141
Birdhurst Av. S Croy —6B 124
Birdhurst Gdns. S Croy —6B 124
Birdhurst Ri. S Croy —7C 124
Birdhurst Rd. SW18 —4A 90
Birdhurst Rd. SW19 —3C 106
Birdhurst Rd. S Croy —7C 124
Bird in Bush Rd. SE15 —8E 76
Bird in Hand La. Brom —6H 111
Bird-in-Hand Pas. SE23 —8G 93
Bird in Hand Yd. NW3 —9A 42
Birdlip Clo. SE15 —7C 76
Birdsall Ho. SE5 —2C 92
Birds Farm Av. Romf —7M 33
Birdsfield La. E3 —4K 61
Birds Hill Dri. Oxs —5B 132
Birds Hill Ri. Oxs —5B 132
Birds Hill Rd. Oxs —4B 132
Bird St. W1 —9E 58
Bird Wlk. Twic —7K 85
Birdwood Clo. S Croy —3G 139
Birdwood Clo. Tedd —1C 102
Birkbeck Av. W3 —1A 72
Birkbeck Av. Gnfd —4A 54
Birkbeck Ct. W3 —2B 72
Birkbeck Gdns. Wfd G —2E 30
Birkbeck Gro. W3 —3B 72
Birkbeck Hill. SE21 —7M 91
Birkbeck M. E8 —1D 60
Birkbeck M. W3 —2B 72
Birkbeck Pl. SE21 —8A 92
Birkbeck Rd. E8 —1D 60
Birkbeck Rd. N8 —2J 43
Birkbeck Rd. N12 —5A 26
Birkbeck Rd. N17 —8D 28
Birkbeck Rd. NW7 —5D 24
Birkbeck Rd. SW19 —2M 105
Birkbeck Rd. W3 —2B 72
Birkbeck Rd. W5 —5G 71
Birkbeck Rd. Beck —6G 109
Birkbeck Rd. Enf —3B 16
Birkbeck Rd. Ilf —3B 48
Birkbeck Rd. Romf —6B 50
Birkbeck Rd. Sidc —9E 96
Birkbeck St. E2 —6F 60
Birkbeck Way. Gnfd —4B 54
Birkdale Av. Pinn —1L 37
Birkdale Av. Romf —7K 35
Birkdale Clo. SE16 —6F 76
Birkdale Clo. Orp —2B 128
Birkdale Ct. S'hall —9A 54
(off Redcroft Rd.)
Birkdale Gdns. Croy —6H 125
Birkdale Gdns. Wat —3H 21
Birkdale Rd. SE2 —5E 80
Birkdale Rd. W5 —7J 55
Birkenhead Av. King T —6K 103
Birkenhead St. WC1 —6J 59
Birken M. N'wd —5A 20
Birkhall Rd. SE6 —7B 94
Birkwood Clo. SW12 —6H 91
Birley Lodge. NW8 —5B 58
(off Acacia Rd.)
Birley Rd. N20 —2A 26
Birley St. SW11 —1E 90
Birling Rd. Eri —8D 82
Birnam Rd. N4 —7K 43
Birnbeck Ct. NW11 —3K 41
Birnbeck Ct. Barn —6H 13
Birrell Ho. SW9 —1K 91
(off Stockwell Rd.)
Birse Cres. NW10 —8C 40
Birstall Grn. Wat —4H 21
Birstall Rd. N15 —3C 44
Biscay Ho. E1 —7H 61
(off Mile End Rd.)
Biscay Rd. W6 —6H 73
Biscoe Clo. Houn —7L 69
Biscoe Way. SE13 —2B 94
Biscott Ho. E3 —7M 61
Bisenden Rd. Croy —4C 124
Bisham Clo. Cars —3D 122
Bisham Gdns. N6 —6E 42
Bishop Butt Clo. Orp —5D 128
Bishop Ct. N12 —4M 25
Bishop Ct. Rich —2J 87
Bishop Duppas Pk. Shep —2C 116
Bishop Fox Way. W Mol —8K 101
Bishop Ken Rd. Harr —9D 22
Bishop King's Rd. W14 —5J 73
Bishop Rd. N14 —9F 14
Bishop's Av. E13 —4F 62
Bishop's Av. SW6 —1H 89
Bishops Av. Brom —6G 111
Bishops Av. Els —7K 11
Bishops Av. N'wd —4C 20
Bishops Av. Romf —4G 49
Bishops Av., The. N2 —4B 42
Bishop's Bri. Rd. W2 —9M 57
Bishops Clo. E17 —2M 45
Bishop's Clo. N19 —8G 43
Bishop's Clo. SE9 —8A 96
Bishops Clo. W4 —6A 72
Bishops Clo. Barn —8B 13
Bishop's Clo. Coul —9L 137
Bishops Clo. Enf —4F 16
Bishops Clo. Rich —9H 87
Bishop's Clo. Sutt —5L 121
Bishops Clo. Uxb —5E 142
Bishop's Ct. EC4 —9M 59
(off Old Bailey)
Bishops Ct. W2 —9M 57
(off Bishop's Bri. Rd.)
Bishop's Ct. WC2 —9L 59
(off Star Yd.)
Bishops Ct. Chesh —3B 6
Bishopsdale Ho. NW6 —4L 57
(off Kilburn Va.)
Bishop's Dri. Felt —5B 84
Bishops Dri. N'holt —4J 53
Bishopsford Rd. Mord —2A 122
Bishopsgate. EC2 —9C 60
Bishopsgate Arc. EC2 —8C 60
(off Bishopsgate)
Bishopsgate Chu. Yd. EC2 —8C 60
Bishopsgate Institute & Libraries.
(off Bishopsgate) —8C 60
Bishops Grn. Brom —5F 110
(off Up. Park Rd.)
Bishops Gro. N2 —4C 42
Bishop's Gro. Hamp —1K 101
Bishops Gro. Cvn. Site. Hamp —1L 101
Bishop's Hall. King T —6H 103
Bishops Hill. W on T —2E 116
Bishops Ho. SW8 —8J 75
Bishop's Mans. SW6 —1H 89
(in two parts)
Bishops Mead. SE5 —8A 76
(off Camberwell Rd.)
Bishopsmead Clo. Eps —2B 134
Bishop's Pk. Rd. SW6 —1H 89
Bishops Pk. Rd. SW16 —5J 107
Bishops Rd. N6 —4E 42
Bishops Rd. SW6 —9J 73
Bishop's Rd. SW11 —8C 74
Bishops Rd. W7 —3C 70
Bishop's Rd. Croy —2M 123
Bishop's Rd. Hay —9A 52
Bishop's Ter. SE11 —5L 75
Bishopsthorpe Rd. SE26 —1H 109
Bishop St. N1 —4A 60
Bishops Vw. Ct. N10 —2F 42
Bishops Wlk. Chst —5A 112
Bishops Wlk. Croy —7H 125
Bishops Wlk. Pinn —1J 37
Bishop's Way. E2 —5F 60
Bishopswood Rd. N6 —5D 42
Bishop Way. NW10 —3C 56
Bishop Wilfred Wood Clo. SE15 —1E 92
Bishop Wilfred Wood Ct. E13 —5G 63
(off Pragel St.)
Biskra. Wat —3E 8
Bisley Clo. Wal X —6D 6
Bisley Clo. Wor Pk —3G 121
Bison Ct. Felt —6F 84
Bispham Rd. NW10 —6K 55
Bissextile Ho. SE8 —1M 93
Bisson Rd. E15 —5A 62
Bisterne Av. E17 —1B 46
Bittacy Bus. Cen. NW7 —6J 25
Bittacy Clo. NW7 —6H 25
Bittacy Ct. NW7 —7J 25
Bittacy Hill. NW7 —6H 25
Bittacy Pk. Av. NW7 —5H 25
Bittacy Ri. NW7 —6G 25
Bittacy Rd. NW7 —6H 25
Bittern Clo. Hay —8H 53
Bittern Ct. NW9 —9C 24
Bittern Ct. SE8 —7L 77
Bittern Ho. SE1 —3A 76
(off Gt. Suffolk St.)
Bittern Pl. N22 —9K 27
Bittern St. SE1 —3A 76
Bittoms Ct. King T —7H 103
Bittoms, The. King T —7H 103
(in two parts)
Bixley Clo. S'hall —5K 69
Blackall St. EC2 —7C 60
Blackberry Clo. Shep —8C 100
Blackberry Farm Clo. Houn —8J 69
Blackberry Fld. Orp —5E 112
Blackbird Ct. NW9 —7B 40
Blackbird Hill. NW9 —7A 40
Blackbirds La. A'ham —7M 5
Blackbird Yd. E2 —6D 60
Blackborne Rd. Dag —2L 65
Black Boy La. N15 —3A 44
Black Boy Wood. Brick W —3L 5
Blackbrook La. Brom —9L 111
Blackburn. NW9 —9D 24
Blackburne's M. W1 —1E 74
Blackburn Rd. NW6 —2M 57
Blackbush Av. Romf —3H 49
Blackbush Clo. Sutt —9M 121
Blackdown Clo. N2 —9A 26
Blackett St. SW15 —2H 89
Black Fan Clo. Enf —3A 16
Blackfen. —5E 96
Blackfen Pde. Sidc —5E 96
Blackfen Rd. Sidc —5C 96
Blackford Clo. S Croy —1M 137
Blackford Rd. Wat —5H 21
Blackford's Path. SW15 —6E 88
Blackfriars Bri. SE1 & EC4 —1M 75
Blackfriars Ct. EC4 —1M 75
(off New Bri. St.)
Black Friars La. EC4 —9M 59
(in two parts)
Blackfriars Pas. EC4 —1M 75
Blackfriars Rd. SE1 —3M 75
Blackfriars Underpass. EC4 —1L 75
Black Gates. Pinn —1K 37
Blackheath. —1D 94
Blackheath Av. SE10 —8B 78
Blackheath Bus. Est. SE10 —9A 78
(off Blackheath Hill)
Blackheath Gro. SE3 —1D 94
Blackheath Hill. SE10 —9A 78
Blackheath Park. —3E 94
Blackheath Pk. SE3 —2D 94
Blackheath Ri. SE13 —1A 94
Blackheath Rd. SE10 —9M 77
Blackheath Vale. —1D 94
Blackheath Va. SE3 —1C 94
Blackheath Village. SE3 —1D 94
Blackhills. Esh —9L 117
Black Horse Ct. SE1 —4B 76
(off Gt. Dover St.)
Blackhorse La. E17 —9H 29
Black Horse La. Croy —2E 124
Blackhorse M. E17 —1H 45
Black Horse Pde. Eastc —3F 36
Blackhorse Pl. Uxb —4A 142
Blackhorse Road. (Junct.) —2H 45
Blackhorse Rd. E17 —2H 45
Blackhorse Rd. SE8 —7J 77
Blackhorse Rd. Sidc —1E 112
Black Horse Yd. Uxb —4A 142
Blacklands Dri. Hay —7A 52
Blacklands Rd. SE6 —1A 110
Blacklands Ter. SW3 —5D 74
Blackley Clo. Wat —1D 8
Black Lion La. W6 —5E 72
Black Lion M. W6 —5E 72
Blackmans Clo. Dart —7G 99
Blackman's La. Warl —6C 140
Blackmans Yd. E2 —7E 60
(off Grimsby St.)
Blackmoor La. Wat —7B 8
Blackmore Av. S'hall —2B 70
Blackmore Ho. N1 —4K 59
(off Barnsbury Est.)
Blackmore Rd. Buck H —9J 19
Blackmore's Gro. Tedd —3E 102
Blackmore Tower. W3 —4A 72
(off Stanley Rd.)
Blackmore Way. Uxb —2B 142
Blackness La. Kes —1H 141
Black Path. E10 —5J 45
Blackpool Gdns. Hay —7C 52
Blackpool Rd. SE15 —1F 92
Black Prince Interchange. (Junct.) —5M 97
Black Prince Rd. SE1 & SE11 —5K 75
Black Rod Clo. Hay —4D 68
Blackshaw Rd. SW17 —1A 106
Blacksmiths Clo. Romf —4G 49
Blacksmiths Hill. S Croy —5E 138
Blacksmiths Ho. E17 —2L 45
(off Gillards M.)
Blacksmith's La. Orp —9G 113
Blacksmith's La. Rain —4D 66
Blacks Rd. W6 —6G 73
Blackstock M. N4 —7M 43
Blackstock Rd. N4 & N5 —7M 43
Blackstone Est. E8 —3F 60
Blackstone Ho. SW1 —6G 75
(off Churchill Gdns.)
Blackstone Rd. NW2 —1G 57
Black Swan Yd. SE1 —3C 76
Blackthorn Av. W Dray —5L 143
Blackthorn Clo. Wat —5F 4
Blackthorn Ct. Houn —8J 69
Blackthorne Av. Croy —3G 125
Blackthorne Ct. SE15 —8D 76
(off Cator St.)
Blackthorne Ct. S'hall —2M 69
(off Dormers Wells La.)
Blackthorne Dri. E4 —4B 30
Blackthorn Gro. Bexh —2J 97
Blackthorn Rd. Big H —8H 141
Blackthorn St. E3 —7L 61
Blacktree M. SW9 —2L 91
Blackwall. —1A 78
Blackwall La. SE10 —6C 78
(in two parts)
Blackwall Trad. Est. E14 —8B 62
Blackwall Tunnel. E14 & SE10 —2B 78
(in two parts)
Blackwall Tunnel App. E14 —1A 78
Blackwall Tunnel Northern App. E3 & E14 —5M 61
Blackwall Tunnel Southern App. SE10 —4C 78
Blackwall Way. E14 —1A 78
Blackwater Clo. E7 —9D 46
Blackwater Clo. Rain —8B 66
Blackwater Ho. NW8 —8B 58
(off Church St.)
Blackwater St. SE22 —4D 92
Blackwell Clo. E5 —9H 45
Blackwell Clo. Harr —7B 22
Blackwell Dri. Wat —8G 9
Blackwell Gdns. Edgw —4L 23
Blackwell Ho. SW4 —5H 91
Blackwood Ho. E1 —7F 60
(off Collingwood St.)
Blackwood St. SE17 —6B 76
Blade M. SW15 —3K 89
Bladen Ho. E1 —9H 61
(off Dunelm St.)
Blades Ct. SW15 —3K 89
Blades Ho. SE11 —7L 75
(off Kennington Oval)
Bladindon Dri. Bex —6G 97
Bladon Clo. Wey —8B 116
Bladon Ct. SW16 —3J 107
Bladon Gdns. Harr —4M 37
Blagdens Clo. N14 —2H 27
Blagdens La. N14 —2H 27
Blagdon Ct. W7 —1C 70
Blagdon Rd. SE13 —5M 93
Blagdon Rd. N Mald —8D 104
Blagdon Wlk. Tedd —3G 103
Blagrove Rd. W10 —8J 57
Blair Av. NW9 —5C 40
Blair Av. Esh —4A 118
Blair Clo. N1 —2A 60
Blair Clo. Hay —5E 68
Blair Clo. Sidc —4C 96
Blair Ct. NW8 —4B 58
Blair Ct. SE6 —7D 94
Blair Ct. Beck —5M 109
Blairderry Rd. SW2 —8J 91
Blairhead Dri. Wat —3F 20
Blair Ho. SW9 —1K 91
Blair St. E14 —9A 62
Blake Av. Bark —4C 64
Blakeborough Dri. H Wood —9J 35
Blake Clo. Cars —3C 122
Blake Clo. Rain —4D 66
Blake Clo. Well —9C 80
Blake Ct. NW6 —6L 57
(off Stafford Clo.)
Blake Ct. SE16 —6F 76
(off Stubbs Dri.)
Blakeden Dri. Clay —8D 118
Blake Gdns. SW6 —9M 73
Blake Gdns. Dart —3K 99
Blake Hall Cres. E11 —6E 46
Blake Hall Rd. E11 —5E 46
Blakehall Rd. Cars —8D 122
Blake Ho. E14 —3L 77
(off Admirals Way)
Blake Ho. SE1 —4L 75
Blake Ho. SE8 —7L 77
(off New King St.)
Blakeley Cotts. SE10 —3B 78
Blakemore Rd. SW16 —9J 91
Blakemore Rd. T Hth —9K 107
Blakemore Way. Belv —4J 81
Blakeney Av. Beck —5K 109
Blakeney Clo. E8 —1E 60
Blakeney Clo. N20 —1A 26
Blakeney Clo. NW1 —3H 59
Blakeney Clo. Eps —3B 134
Blakeney Rd. Beck —4K 109
Blakenham Rd. SW17 —1D 106
Blaker Ct. SE7 —8G 79
(in two parts)
Blake Rd. E16 —7D 62
Blake Rd. N11 —7G 27
Blake Rd. Croy —4C 124
Blake Rd. Mitc —7C 106
Blaker Rd. E15 —4A 62
Blakes Av. N Mald —9D 104
Blakes Clo. W10 —8G 57
Blake's Grn. W W'ck —3A 126
Blakes La. N Mald —9D 104
Blakesley Av. W5 —9G 55
Blakesley Wlk. SW20 —6K 105
Blake's Rd. SE15 —8C 76
Blakes Ter. N Mald —9E 104
Blakesware Gdns. N9 —9B 16
Blakewood Clo. Felt —1G 101
Blanchard Clo. SE9 —9J 95
Blanchard Gro. Enf —2M 17
Blanchard Ho. Twic —5H 87
(off Clevedon Rd.)
Blanchard M. Romf —7K 35
Blanchard Way. E8 —2E 60
Blanch Clo. SE15 —8G 77
Blanchedowne. SE5 —3B 92
Blanche St. E16 —7D 62
Blanchland Rd. Mord —9M 105
Blandfield Rd. SW12 —6E 90
Blandford Av. Beck —6J 109
Blandford Av. Twic —7M 85
Blandford Clo. N2 —2A 42
Blandford Clo. Croy —5J 123
Blandford Clo. Romf —2L 49
Blandford Ct. E8 —3C 60
(off St Peter's Way)
Blandford Ct. NW6 —3H 57
Blandford Cres. E4 —9A 18
Blandford Ho. SW8 —8K 75
(off Richborne Ter.)
Blandford Rd. W4 —4C 72
Blandford Rd. W5 —3H 71
Blandford Rd. Beck —7G 109
Blandford Rd. S'hall —5L 69
Blandford Rd. Tedd —2B 102
Blandford Sq. NW1 —7C 58
Blandford St. W1 —9D 58
Blandford Waye. Hay —9G 53
Bland Ho. SE11 —6K 75
(off Vauxhall St.)
Bland St. SE9 —3H 95
Blaney Cres. E6 —6M 63
Blanmerle Rd. SE9 —7M 95
Blann Clo. SE9 —5H 95
Blantyre St. SW10 —8B 74
Blantyre Tower. SW10 —8B 74
(off Blantyre St.)
Blantyre Wlk. SW10 —8B 74
(off Worlds End Est.)

Blashford—Boswell Clo.

Blashford. NW3 —3D 58
(off Adelaide Rd.)
Blashford St. SE13 —6B 94
Blasker Wlk. E14 —6M 77
Blattner Clo. Els —6J 11
Blawith Rd. Harr —2C 38
Blaxland Ho. W12 —1F 72
(off White City Est.)
Blaxland Ter. Chesh —1D 6
(off Davison Dri.)
Blaydon Clo. N17 —7F 28
Blaydon Clo. Ruis —5C 36
Blaydon Ct. N'holt —2L 53
Blazer Ct. NW8 —6B 58
(off St John's Wood Rd.)
Bleak Hill La. SE18 —7D 80
Blean Gro. SE20 —4G 109
Blear Ho. Eps —3D 134
Bleasdale Av. Gnfd —5E 54
Blechynden St. W10 —1H 73
Bleddyn Clo. Sidc —5G 97
Bledlow Clo. SE28 —1G 81
Bledlow Ho. NW8 —7B 58
(off Capland St.)
Bledlow Ri. Gnfd —5A 54
Bleeding Heart Yd. EC1 —8L 59
(off Greville St.)
Blegborough Rd. SW16 —3G 107
Blendon. —5H 97
Blendon Dri. Bex —5H 97
Blendon Path. Brom —4D 110
Blendon Rd. Bex —5H 97
Blendon Row. SE17 —5B 76
(off Townley St.)
Blendon Ter. SE18 —6A 80
Blendworth Way. SE15 —8C 76
(off Clanfield Way)
Blenheim Av. Ilf —4L 47
Blenheim Clo. N21 —1A 28
Blenheim Clo. SW20 —7G 105
Blenheim Clo. Dart —5G 99
Blenheim Clo. Gnfd —5B 54
Blenheim Clo. Romf —2A 50
Blenheim Clo. Wall —9G 123
Blenheim Clo. Wat —9G 9
Blenheim Ct. N19 —7J 43
Blenheim Ct. SE16 —2H 77
(off King & Queen Wharf)
Blenheim Ct. Brom —8D 110
Blenheim Ct. Horn —1G 67
Blenheim Ct. Kent —4E 38
Blenheim Ct. Sidc —9B 96
Blenheim Ct. Sutt —8A 122
Blenheim Cres. W11 —1J 73
Blenheim Cres. Ruis —7B 36
Blenheim Cres. S Croy —9A 124
Blenheim Dri. Well —9D 80
Blenheim Gdns. NW2 —2G 57
Blenheim Gdns. SW2 —5K 91
Blenheim Gdns. Ave —2M 83
Blenheim Gdns. King T —4M 103
Blenheim Gdns. S Croy —4E 138
Blenheim Gdns. Wall —8G 123
Blenheim Gdns. Wemb —8J 39
Blenheim Gro. SE15 —1E 92
Blenheim Ho. Houn —2L 85
Blenheim Pde. Uxb —7F 142
Blenheim Pk. Rd. S Croy —1A 138
Blenheim Pas. NW8 —5A 58
(in two parts)
Blenheim Ri. N15 —2D 44
Blenheim Rd. E6 —6H 63
Blenheim Rd. E15 —9C 46
Blenheim Rd. E17 —1H 45
Blenheim Rd. NW8 —5A 58
Blenheim Rd. SE20 —4G 109
Blenheim Rd. SW20 —7G 105
Blenheim Rd. W4 —4C 72
Blenheim Rd. Ab L —5E 4
Blenheim Rd. Barn —5H 13
Blenheim Rd. Brom —8J 111
Blenheim Rd. Dart —5G 99
Blenheim Rd. Eps —3B 134
Blenheim Rd. Harr —4M 37
Blenheim Rd. N'holt —2M 53
Blenheim Rd. Orp —4G 129
Blenheim Rd. Sidc —7G 97
Blenheim Rd. Sutt —5L 121
Blenheim Shop. Cen. SE20 —4G 109
Blenheim St. W1 —9F 58
Blenheim Ter. NW8 —5A 58
Blenheim Way. Iswth —9E 70
Blenkarne Rd. SW11 —5D 90
Bleriot. NW9 —9D 24
(off Belvedere Strand)
Bleriot Rd. Houn —8G 69
Blessbury Rd. Edgw —8A 24
Blessington Clo. SE13 —2B 94
Blessington Rd. SE13 —2B 94
Blessing Way. Bark —6G 65
Bletchingley Clo. T Hth —8M 107
Bletchley Ct. N1 —5B 60
(off Bletchley St., in two parts)
Bletchley St. N1 —5B 60
Bletchmore Clo. Hay —6B 68
Bletsoe Wlk. N1 —5A 60
Blewbury Ho. SE2 —3H 81
Blewetts Cotts. Rain —6D 66
(off New Rd.)
Blick Ho. SE16 —4G 77
(off Neptune St.)
Blincoe Clo. SW19 —8H 89
Blind La. Bans —7C 136
Blind La. Lou —4C 18
Blindman's La. Chesh —3D 6
Bliss Cres. SE13 —1M 93
Blissett St. SE10 —9A 78
Blisworth Clo. Hay —7J 53
Blisworth Ho. E2 —4E 60
(off Whiston Rd.)
Blithbury Rd. Dag —2F 64
Blithdale Rd. SE2 —5E 80
Blithfield St. W8 —4M 73
Blockley Rd. Wemb —7F 38
Bloemfontein Av. W12 —2F 72
Bloemfontein Rd. W12 —1F 72
Bloemfontein Way. W12 —2F 72
Blomfield Ct. W9 —7A 58
(off Lanark Pl.)
Blomfield Rd. W9 —8M 57
Blomfield St. EC2 —8B 60
Blomfield Vs. W2 —8M 57
Blomville Rd. Dag —8J 49
Blondell Clo. W Dray —7H 143
Blondel St. SW11 —1E 90
Blondin Av. W5 —5G 71
Blondin St. E3 —5L 61
Bloomburg St. SW1 —5H 75
Bloomfield Ct. N6 —4E 42
Bloomfield Cres. Ilf —4M 47
Bloomfield Ho. E1 —8E 60
(off Old Montague St.)
Bloomfield Pl. W1 —1F 74
(off Grosvenor Hill)
Bloomfield Rd. N6 —4E 42
Bloomfield Rd. SE18 —7M 79
Bloomfield Rd. Brom —9H 111
Bloomfield Rd. King T —8J 103
Bloomfields, The. Bark —2A 64
Bloomfield Ter. SW1 —6E 74
Bloom Gro. SE27 —9M 91
Bloomhall Rd. SE19 —2B 108
Bloom Pk. Rd. SW6 —8K 73
Bloomsbury. —8J 59
Bloomsbury Clo. W5 —1K 71
Bloomsbury Clo. Eps —2B 134
Bloomsbury Ct. WC1 —8J 59
(off Barter St.)
Bloomsbury Ct. Houn —9F 68
Bloomsbury Ct. Pinn —1K 37
Bloomsbury Ho. SW4 —5H 91
Bloomsbury Pl. SW18 —4A 90
Bloomsbury Pl. WC1 —8J 59
Bloomsbury Sq. WC1 —8J 59
Bloomsbury St. WC1 —8H 59
Bloomsbury Theatre. —7H 59
(off Gordon St.)
Bloomsbury Way. WC1 —8J 59
Blore Clo. SW8 —9H 75
Blore Ct. W1 —9H 59
(off Berwick St.)
Blossom Clo. W5 —3J 71
Blossom Clo. Dag —4K 65
Blossom Clo. S Croy —7D 124
Blossom La. Enf —3A 16
Blossom St. E1 —7C 60
Blossom Way. Uxb —3D 142
Blossom Way. W Dray —5L 143
Blossom Waye. Houn —7J 69
Blount Ho. E14 —8J 61
Blount St. E14 —8J 61
Bloxam Gdns. SE9 —4J 95
Bloxhall Rd. E10 —6K 45
Bloxham Cres. Hamp —4K 101
Bloxworth Clo. Wall —5G 123
Blucher Rd. SE5 —8A 76
Blue Anchor All. Rich —3J 87
Blue Anchor La. SE16 —5E 76
Blue Anchor Yd. E1 —1E 76
Blue Ball Yd. SW1 —2G 75
Bluebell Av. E12 —1H 63
Bluebell Clo. E9 —4G 61
Bluebell Clo. SE26 —1D 108
Bluebell Clo. Orp —4A 128
Bluebell Clo. Rush G —7C 50
Bluebell Clo. Wall —3F 122
Bluebell Dri. Bedm —1D 4
Bluebell Way. Ilf —2M 63
Blueberry Clo. Wfd G —6E 30
Blueberry Gdns. Coul —8K 137
Bluebird La. Dag —3L 65
Bluebird Wlk. Wemb —8M 39
Bluebird Way. SE28 —3B 80
Bluebird Way. Brick W —3K 5
Blue Cedars. Bans —6H 135
Bluefield Clo. Hamp —2L 101
Bluegates. Ewe —9E 120
Bluehouse Rd. E4 —2C 30
Blue Riband Ind. Est. Croy —4M 123
Blue Water. SW18 —3M 89
Blundell Ho. SE14 —8J 77
(off Goodwood Rd.)
Blundell Rd. Edgw —8B 24
Blundell St. N7 —3J 59
Blunden Clo. Dag —6G 49
Blunt Rd. S Croy —7B 124
Blunts Av. W Dray —8L 143
Blunts Rd. SE9 —4L 95
Blurton Rd. E5 —9G 45
Blydon Ct. N21 —7K 15
(off Chaseville Pk. Rd.)
Blyth Clo. E14 —5B 78
Blyth Clo. Borwd —3K 11
Blyth Clo. Twic —5D 86
Blyth Ct. Brom —5D 110
(off Blyth Rd.)
Blythe Clo. SE6 —6K 93
Blythe Hill. —6K 93
Blythe Hill. SE6 —6K 93
Blythe Hill. Orp —5D 112
Blythe Hill La. SE6 —6K 93
Blythe Ho. SE11 —7L 75
Blythe M. W14 —4H 73
Blythendale Ho. E2 —5E 60
(off Mansford St.)
Blythe Rd. W14 —4H 73
Blythe St. E2 —6F 60
Blythe Va. SE6 —7K 93
Blyth Hill Pl. SE6 —6M 93
Blyth Rd. E17 —5K 45
Blyth Rd. SE28 —1G 81
Blyth Rd. Brom —5D 110
Blyth Rd. Hay —3C 68
Blythswood Rd. Ilf —6E 48
Blyth Wood Pk. Brom —5D 110
Blythwood Rd. N4 —5J 43
Blythwood Rd. Pinn —8H 21
Boades M. NW3 —9B 42
Boadicea St. N1 —4K 59
Boakes Clo. NW9 —2A 40
Boar Clo. Chig —5E 32
Boardman Av. E4 —7M 17
Boardman Clo. Barn —7J 13
Boardwalk Pl. E14 —2A 78
Boarhound. NW9 —9D 24
(off Further Acre)
Boarley Ho. SE17 —5C 76
(off Massinger St.)
Boars Head Yd. Bren —8H 71
Boathouse Wlk. SE15 —8D 76
(in two parts)
Boat Lifter Way. SE16 —5J 77
Bob Anker Clo. E13 —6E 62
Bobbin Clo. SW4 —2G 91
Bobby Moore Way. N12 —7D 26
Bob Marley Way. SE24 —3L 91
Bobs La. Romf —7E 34
Bockhampton Rd. King T —4K 103
Bocking St. E8 —4F 60
Boddicott Clo. SW19 —8J 89
Boddington Ho. SE14 —9G 77
(off Pomeroy St.)
Bodeney Ho. SE5 —9C 76
(off Peckham Rd.)
Boden Ho. E1 —8E 60
(off Woodseer St.)
Bodiam Clo. Enf —4C 16
Bodiam Rd. SW16 —4H 107
Bodington Ct. W12 —3H 73
Bodley Clo. N Mald —9C 104
Bodley Mnr. Way. SW2 —6L 91
Bodley Rd. N Mald —1B 120
Bodmin. NW9 —9D 24
(off Further Acre)
Bodmin Clo. Harr —8K 37
Bodmin Clo. Orp —3G 129
Bodmin Gro. Mord —9M 105
Bodmin Pl. SE27 —1M 107
Bodmin St. SW18 —7L 89
Bodnant Gdns. SW20 —7E 104
Bodney Rd. E8 —1F 60
Boeing Way. S'hall —4F 68
Boevey Path. Belv —6K 81
Bogey La. Orp —9L 127
Bognor Gdns. Wat —5G 21
Bognor Rd. Well —9H 81
Bohemia Pl. E8 —2G 61
Bohn Rd. E1 —8J 61
Bohun Gro. Barn —8C 14
Boileau Pde. W5 —9K 55
(off Boileau Rd.)
Boileau Rd. SW13 —8E 72
Boileau Rd. W5 —9K 55
Boisseau Ho. E1 —8G 61
(off Stepney Way)
Bolden St. SE8 —1M 93
Boldero Pl. NW8 —7C 58
(off Gateforth St.)
Bolderwood Way. W W'ck —4M 125
Boldmere Rd. Pinn —5G 37
Boleyn Av. Enf —3F 16
Boleyn Av. Eps —2F 134
Boleyn Clo. E17 —2L 45
Boleyn Clo. Lou —8J 19
Boleyn Ct. Buck H —1E 30
Boleyn Dri. Ruis —7H 37
Boleyn Dri. W Mol —7K 101
Boleyn Gdns. Dag —3A 66
Boleyn Gdns. W W'ck —4M 125
Boleyn Gro. W W'ck —4A 126
Boleyn Rd. E6 —5H 63
Boleyn Rd. E7 —3E 62
Boleyn Rd. N16 —1C 60
Boleyn Way. Barn —5A 14
Boleyn Way. Ilf —6A 32
Bolina Rd. SE16 —6G 77
Bolingbroke Gro. SW11 —3C 90
Bolingbroke Rd. W14 —4H 73
Bolingbroke Wlk. SW11 —9B 74
Bolingbroke Way. Hay —2B 68
Bolliger Ct. NW10 —7A 56
Bollo Bri. Rd. W3 —4M 71
Bollo Ct. W3 —4A 72
(off Bollo Bri. Rd.)
Bollo La. W3 & W4 —3M 71
Bolney Ga. SW7 —3C 74
Bolney St. SW8 —8K 75
Bolney Way. Felt —9J 85
Bolsover St. W1 —7F 58
Bolstead Rd. Mitc —5F 106
Bolster Gro. N22 —7H 27
Bolt Ct. EC4 —9L 59
Bolters La. Bans —6K 135
Boltmore Clo. NW4 —1H 41
Bolton Clo. SE20 —6E 108
Bolton Clo. Chess —8H 119
Bolton Cres. SE5 —8M 75
Bolton Gdns. NW10 —5H 57
Bolton Gdns. SW5 —6M 73
Bolton Gdns. Brom —3D 110
Bolton Gdns. Tedd —3E 102
Bolton Gdns. M. SW10 —6A 74
Bolton Ho. SE10 —6C 78
(off Trafalgar Rd.)
Bolton Pl. NW8 —4M 57
(off Bolton Rd.)
Bolton Rd. E15 —2D 62
Bolton Rd. N18 —5D 28
Bolton Rd. NW8 —4M 57
Bolton Rd. NW10 —4C 56
Bolton Rd. W4 —8A 72
Bolton Rd. Chess —8H 119
Bolton Rd. Harr —2A 38
Boltons Ct. SW5 —6M 73
(off Old Brompton Rd.)
Bolton's La. Hay —8M 143
Boltons Pl. SW5 —6A 74
Boltons, The. SW10 —6A 74
Boltons, The. Wemb —9D 38
Bolton St. W1 —2F 74
Bolton Studios. SW10 —6A 74
Bolton Wlk. N4 —7K 43
(off Durham Rd.)
Bombay St. SE16 —5F 76
Bomer Clo. W Dray —8L 143
Bomore Rd. W11 —1J 73
Bonar Pl. Chst —4J 111
Bonar Rd. SE15 —8E 76
Bonchester Clo. Chst —4L 111
Bonchurch Clo. Sutt —9M 121
Bonchurch Ct. Purf —6M 83
Bonchurch Rd. W10 —8J 57
Bonchurch Rd. W13 —2F 70
Bond Clo. W Dray —9D 142
Bond Ct. EC4 —1B 76
Bondfield Av. Hay —6E 52
Bondfield Rd. E6 —8K 63
Bondfield Wlk. Dart —3K 99
Bond Gdns. Wall —6G 123
Bond Ho. NW6 —5K 57
(off Rupert Rd.)
Bond Ho. SE14 —8J 77
(off Goodwood Rd.)
Bonding Yd. Wlk. SE16 —4J 77
Bond Rd. Mitc —6C 106
Bond Rd. Surb —4K 119
Bond Rd. Warl —9H 139
Bond St. E15 —1C 62
Bond St. W4 —5B 72
Bond St. W5 —1H 71
Bondway. SW8 —7J 75
Boneta Rd. SE18 —4K 79
Bonfield Rd. SE13 —3A 94
Bonham Gdns. Dag —7H 49
Bonham Rd. SW2 —4K 91
Bonham Rd. Dag —7H 49
Bonheur Rd. W4 —3B 72
Bonhill St. EC2 —7B 60
Boniface Gdns. Harr —7M 21
Boniface Rd. Uxb —8A 36
Boniface Wlk. Harr —7M 21
Bonington Rd. Horn —1H 67
Bon Marche Ter. M. SE27 —1C 108
Bonner Ct. Chesh —1D 6
(off Coopers Wlk.)
Bonner Hill Rd. King T —6K 103
(in two parts)
Bonner Rd. E2 —5G 61
Bonnersfield Clo. Harr —4D 38
Bonnersfield La. Harr —4D 38
Bonner St. E2 —5G 61
Bonnett M. Horn —6J 51
Bonneville Gdns. SW4 —5G 91
Bonney Gro. G Oak —3A 6
Bonney Way. Swan —6C 114
Bonnington Ct. N'holt —5H 53
(off Gallery Gdns.)
Bonnington Ho. N1 —5K 59
Bonnington Sq. SW8 —7K 75
Bonny St. NW1 —3G 59
Bonser Rd. Twic —8D 86
Bonsey's Yd. Uxb —3B 142
Bonsor Ho. SW8 —9G 75
Bonsor St. SE5 —8C 76
Bonville Gdns. NW4 —2F 40
Bonville Rd. Brom —2D 110
Bookbinders Cottage Homes. N20 —3D 26
Booker Clo. E14 —8K 61
Booker Rd. N18 —5E 28
Bookham Ct. SW19 —7B 106
Boomes Ind. Est. Rain —7D 66
Boone Ct. N9 —3G 29
Boones Rd. SE13 —3C 94
Boone St. SE13 —3C 94
Boord St. SE10 —4C 78
Boothby Ct. E4 —3A 30
Boothby Rd. N19 —7H 43
Booth Clo. E9 —4F 60
Booth Clo. SE28 —2F 80
Booth La. EC4 —1A 76
(off Baynard St.)
Boothman Ho. Kent —1H 39
Booth Rd. NW9 —9B 24
Booth Rd. Croy —4M 123
Booth's Pl. W1 —8G 59
Boot Pde. Edgw —6L 23
(off High St.)
Boot St. N1 —6C 60
Bordars Rd. W7 —8C 54
Bordars Wlk. W7 —8C 54
Borden Av. Enf —8B 16
Border Cres. SE26 —2F 108
Border Gdns. Croy —6M 125
Bordergate. Mitc —5C 106
Border Rd. SE26 —2F 108
Border's La. Lou —6L 19
Bordesley Rd. Mord —9M 105
Bordeston Ct. Bren —8G 71
(off Augustus Clo.)
Bordon Wlk. SW15 —6E 88
Boreas Wlk. N1 —5M 59
(off Nelson Pl.)
Boreham Av. E16 —9E 62
Boreham Clo. E10 —6A 46
Boreham Holt. Els —6K 11
Boreham Rd. N22 —9A 28
Borehamwood. —5L 11
Borehamwood Enterprise Cen. Borwd —5K 11
Borehamwood F.C. —4M 11
Borehamwood Ind. Pk. Borwd —4B 12
Boreman Ho. SE10 —7A 78
(off Thames St.)
Borgard Rd. SE18 —5K 79
Borkwood Pk. Orp —6D 128
Borkwood Way. Orp —6C 128
Borland Rd. SE15 —3G 93
Borland Rd. Tedd —4F 102
Borneo St. SW15 —2G 89
Borough High St. SE1 —3A 76
Borough Hill. Croy —5M 123
Borough Rd. SE1 —4M 75
Borough Rd. Iswth —9C 70
Borough Rd. King T —5L 103
Borough Rd. Mitc —6C 106
Borough Sq. SE1 —3A 76
(off McCoid Way)
Borough, The. —3B 76
Borrett Clo. SE17 —6A 76
Borrodaile Rd. SW18 —5M 89
Borrowdale. NW1 —6G 59
(off Robert St.)
Borrowdale Av. Harr —9E 22
Borrowdale Clo. Ilf —2J 47
Borrowdale Clo. S Croy —5D 138
Borrowdale Ct. Enf —3A 16
Borrowdale Dri. S Croy —4D 138
Borthwick M. E15 —9C 46
Borthwick Rd. E15 —9C 46
Borthwick Rd. NW9 —4D 40
Borthwick St. SE8 —6L 77
Borwick Av. E17 —1K 45
Bosanquet Clo. Uxb —7B 142
Bosbury Rd. SE6 —9A 94
Boscastle Rd. NW5 —8F 42
Boscobel Ho. E8 —2F 60
Boscobel Pl. SW1 —5E 74
Boscobel St. W2 —7B 58
Bosco Clo. Orp —6D 128
Boscombe Av. E10 —5B 46
Boscombe Av. Horn —5H 51
Boscombe Clo. E5 —1J 61
Boscombe Gdns. SW16 —3J 107
Boscombe Ho. Croy —3B 124
(off Sydenham Rd.)
Boscombe Rd. SW17 —3E 106
Boscombe Rd. SW19 —5M 105
Boscombe Rd. W12 —2E 72
Boscombe Rd. Wor Pk —3G 121
Bose Clo. N3 —8J 25
Bosgrove. E4 —2A 30
Boss Ho. SE1 —3D 76
(off Boss St.)
Boss St. SE1 —3D 76
Bostall Hill. SE2 —6E 80
Bostall La. SE2 —6F 80
Bostall Mnr. Way. SE2 —5F 80
Bostall Pk. Av. Bexh —8J 81
Bostall Rd. Orp —4F 112
Bostock Ho. Houn —7L 69
Boston Bus. Pk. W7 —4C 70
Boston Gdns. W4 —7C 72
Boston Gdns. W7 —5E 70
Boston Gdns. Bren —5E 70
Boston Gro. Ruis —4A 36
Boston Manor. —5E 70
Boston Manor House. —6F 70
Boston Mnr. Rd. Bren —5F 70
Boston Pde. W7 —4E 70
Boston Pk. Rd. Bren —6G 71
Boston Pl. NW1 —7D 58
Boston Rd. E6 —6J 63
Boston Rd. E17 —4L 45
Boston Rd. W7 —2C 70
Boston Rd. Croy —1K 123
Boston Rd. Edgw —7A 24
Bostonthorpe Rd. W7 —3C 70
Boston Va. W7 —5E 70
Bosun Clo. E14 —3L 77
Boswell Clo. Orp —1G 129

Boswell Ct.—Braemar Rd.

Boswell Ct. W14 —4H 73
(off Blythe Rd.)
Boswell Ct. WC1 —8J 59
Boswell Ct. King T —5K 103
(off Clifton Rd.)
Boswell Ho. WC1 —8J 59
(off Boswell St.)
Boswell Path. Hay —5D 68
Boswell Rd. T Hth —8A 108
Boswell St. WC1 —8J 59
Bosworth Clo. E17 —8K 29
Bosworth Cres. Romf —6G 35
Bosworth Ho. W10 —7J 57
(off Bosworth Rd.)
Bosworth Ho. Eri —6C 82
(off Saltford Clo.)
Bosworth Rd. N11 —6H 27
Bosworth Rd. W10 —7J 57
Bosworth Rd. Barn —5L 13
Bosworth Rd. Dag —8L 49
Botany Bay. —1H 15
Botany Bay La. Chst —7A 112
Botany Clo. Barn —6C 14
Botany Way. Purf —6M 83
Boteley Clo. E4 —2B 30
Botham Clo. Edgw —7A 24
Botha Rd. E13 —8F 62
Bothwell Clo. E16 —8D 62
Bothwell Rd. New Ad —2A 140
Bothwell St. SW6 —7H 73
Botolph All. EC3 —1C 76
(off Botolph La.)
Botolph La. EC3 —1C 76
Botsford Rd. SW20 —6J 105
Bott Rd. Dart —1K 115
Botts M. W2 —9L 57
Botwell Comn. Rd. Hay —1B 68
Botwell Cres. Hay —9C 52
Botwell La. Hay —1C 68
Boucher Clo. Tedd —2D 102
Bouchier Ho. N2 —9B 26
Bouchier Wlk. Rain —2E 66
Bough Beech Ct. Enf —1H 17
Boughton Av. Brom —2D 126
Boughton Ho. SE1 —3B 76
(off Tennis St.)
Boughton Rd. SE28 —4C 80
Boulcott St. E1 —9H 61
Boulevard Cen., The. Borwd —5L 11
Boulevard, The. SW17 —8E 90
Boulevard, The. SW18 —3M 89
Boulevard, The. Pinn —2L 37
(in two parts)
Boulevard, The. Wat —7B 8
Boulevard, The. Wfd G —6L 31
Boulevard 25. Borwd —5L 11
Boulmer Rd. Uxb —6A 142
Boulogne Ho. SE1 —4D 76
(off Abbey St.)
Boulogne Rd. Croy —1A 124
Boulter Gdns. Rain —2E 66
Boulter Ho. SE14 —9G 77
(off Kender St.)
Boulton Ho. Bren —6J 71
Boulton Rd. Dag —7J 49
Boultwood Rd. E6 —9K 63
Bounces La. N9 —2F 28
Bounces Rd. N9 —2F 28
Boundaries Rd. SW12 —8D 90
Boundaries Rd. Felt —7G 85
Boundary Av. E17 —5K 45
Boundary Bus. Ct. Mitc —7B 106
Boundary Clo. SE25 —6E 108
Boundary Clo. Barn —3K 13
Boundary Clo. Ilf —9C 48
Boundary Clo. King T —7M 103
Boundary Clo. S'hall —6L 69
Boundary Ct. N18 —6D 28
(off Snells Pk.)
Boundary Ho. SE5 —8A 76
Boundary La. E13 —6H 63
Boundary La. SE5 —7A 76
Boundary M. NW8 —4A 58
(off Boundary Rd.)
Boundary Pas. E1 —7D 60
Boundary Rd. E13 —5G 63
Boundary Rd. E17 —5K 45
Boundary Rd. N2 —8B 26
Boundary Rd. N9 —8G 17
Boundary Rd. N22 —1M 43
Boundary Rd. NW8 —4M 57
Boundary Rd. SW19 —3B 106
Boundary Rd. Bark —5A 64
(in two parts)
Boundary Rd. Cars & Wall —8F 122
Boundary Rd. Pinn —5H 37
Boundary Rd. Romf —4E 50
Boundary Rd. Sidc —4C 96
Boundary Rd. Upm —8L 51
Boundary Rd. Wemb —8J 39
Boundary Row. SE1 —3M 75
Boundary St. E2 —6D 60
(in two parts)
Boundary St. Eri —8D 82
Boundary Way. Croy —7L 125
Boundary Way. Wat —5F 4
Boundfield Rd. SE6 —9C 94
Bounds Green. —6H 27
Bounds Grn. Ct. N11 —6H 27
(off Bounds Grn. Rd.)
Bounds Grn. Ind. Est. N11 —6G 27
Bounds Grn. Rd. N11 & N22 —6G 27
Bourbon Ho. SE6 —2A 110
Bourchier St. W1 —1H 75
(in two parts)
Bourdon Pl. W1 —1F 74
(off Bourdon St.)
Bourdon Rd. SE20 —6G 109
Bourdon St. W1 —1F 74
Bourke Clo. NW10 —2C 56
Bourke Clo. SW4 —5J 91
Bourlet Clo. W1 —8G 59
Bourn Av. N15 —2B 44
Bourn Av. Uxb —7E 142
Bournbrook Rd. SE3 —2H 95
Bourne Av. N14 —2J 27
Bourne Av. Barn —7B 14
Bourne Av. Hay —4A 68
Bourne Av. Ruis —1G 53
Bournebridge. —1M 33
Bournebridge La. Stap A —1M 33
Bourne Cir. Hay —4A 68
Bourne Clo. Th Dit —4D 118
Bourne Ct. W4 —7A 72
Bourne Ct. S Ruis —1F 52
Bourne Ct. Wfd G —1H 47
Bourne Dri. Mitc —6B 106
Bourne End. Horn —5L 51
Bourne End Rd. N'wd —4C 20
Bourne Est. EC1 —8L 59
Bourne Gdns. E4 —4M 29
Bournehall. Bush —8L 9
Bournehall Av. Bush —7L 9
Bournehall La. Bush —8L 9
Bourne Hall Mus. —1D 134
Bournehall Rd. Bush —8L 9
Bourne Hill. N14 —1J 27
Bourne Hill Clo. N13 —2K 27
Bourne Ind. Pk., The. Dart —4C 98
Bourne Mead. Bex —4A 98
Bournemead Av. N'holt —5E 52
Bournemead Clo. N'holt —6E 52
Bournemead Way. N'holt —5F 52
Bourne M. W1 —9E 58
Bournemouth Clo. SE15 —1E 92
Bournemouth Rd. SE15 —1E 92
Bournemouth Rd. SW19 —5L 105
Bourne Pde. Bex —6M 97
Bourne Pk. Clo. Kenl —8C 138
Bourne Pl. W4 —6B 72
Bourne Rd. E7 —8D 46
Bourne Rd. N8 —4J 43
Bourne Rd. Bex & Dart —6M 97
Bourne Rd. Brom —8H 111
Bourne Rd. Bush —7L 9
Bournes Ho. N15 —4C 44
(off Chisley Rd.)
Bourneside Cres. N14 —1H 27
Bourneside Gdns. SE6 —2A 110
Bourne St. SW1 —5E 74
Bourne St. Croy —4M 123
Bourne Ter. W2 —8M 57
Bourne, The. N14 —1H 27
Bourne Va. Brom —3D 126
Bournevale Rd. SW16 —1J 107
Bourne Vw. Gnfd —2D 54
Bourne Vw. Kenl —7B 138
Bourne Way. Brom —4D 126
Bourne Way. Eps —6A 120
Bourne Way. Sutt —7K 121
Bourne Way. Swan —7A 114
Bournewood Rd. SE18 —8E 80
Bournewood Rd. Orp —2F 128
Bournville Rd. SE6 —6L 93
Bournwell Clo. Barn —5D 14
Bourton Clo. Hay —2E 68
Bousfield Rd. SE14 —1H 93
Boutflower Rd. SW11 —3C 90
Boutique Hall. SE13 —3A 94
Bouverie Gdns. Harr —4H 39
Bouverie Gdns. Purl —6K 137
Bouverie M. N16 —7C 44
Bouverie Pl. W2 —9B 58
Bouverie Rd. N16 —7C 44
Bouverie Rd. Harr —4A 38
Bouverie St. EC4 —9L 59
Bouvier Rd. Enf —2G 17
Boveney Rd. SE23 —6H 93
Bovill Rd. SE23 —6H 93
Bovingdon Av. Wemb —2L 55
Bovingdon Clo. N19 —7G 43
Bovingdon Cres. Wat —7H 5
Bovingdon La. NW9 —8C 24
Bovingdon Rd. SW6 —9M 73
Bovingdon Sq. Mitc —8J 107
Bow. —6L 61
Bow Arrow La. Dart —5L 99
Bowater Clo. NW9 —3B 40
Bowater Clo. SW2 —5J 91
Bowater Ho. EC1 —7A 60
(off Golden La. Est.)
Bowater Pl. SE3 —8F 78
Bowater Rd. SE18 —4H 79
Bow Bri. Est. E3 —6M 61
Bow Brook, The. E2 —5H 61
(off Mace St.)
Bow Chyd. EC4 —9A 60
(off Cheapside)
Bow Common. —8L 61
Bow Comn. La. E3 —7K 61
Bowden Clo. Felt —7C 84
Bowden Dri. Horn —6J 51
Bowden St. SE11 —6L 75
Bowditch. SE8 —5K 77
(in two parts)
Bowdon Rd. E17 —5L 45
Bowen Dri. SE21 —9C 92
Bowen Rd. Harr —5A 38
Bowen St. E14 —9M 61
Bowens Wood. Croy —1K 139
Bower Av. SE10 —9C 78
Bower Clo. N'holt —5G 53
Bower Clo. Romf —7B 34
Bower Ct. E4 —1A 30
(off Ridgeway, The)
Bowerdean St. SW6 —9M 73
Bower Farm Rd. Hav —3A 34
Bower Ho. SE14 —9H 77
(off Besson St.)
Bower La. Eyns & Knat —4J 131
Bowerman Av. SE14 —7J 77
Bowerman Ct. N19 —7H 43
(off St John's Way)
Bower Rd. Swan —4E 114
Bower St. E1 —9H 61
Bowers Wlk. E6 —9K 63
Bowes Clo. Sidc —5F 96
Bowes Ct. Dart —5M 99
(off Osbourne Rd.)
Bowe's Ho. Bark —3M 63
Bowes-Lyon Hall. E16 —2E 78
(off Wesley Av., in two parts)
Bowes Park. —7J 27
Bowes Rd. N11 & N13 —5G 27
Bowes Rd. W3 —1C 72
Bowes Rd. Dag —9G 49
Bowes Rd. W on T —4F 116
Bowfell Rd. W6 —7G 73
Bowford Av. Bexh —9J 81
Bowhill Clo. SW9 —8L 75
Bowie Clo. SW4 —6H 91
Bow Ind. Pk. E15 —3L 61
Bow Interchange. (Junct.) —5M 61
Bowland Rd. SW4 —3H 91
Bowland Rd. Wfd G —5G 31
Bowland Yd. SW1 —3D 74
(off Kinnerton St.)
Bow La. EC4 —9A 60
Bow La. N12 —7A 26
Bow La. Mord —1J 121
Bowl Ct. EC2 —7C 60
Bowles Grn. Enf —9B 6
Bowles Rd. SE1 —7E 76
Bowley Clo. SE19 —3D 108
Bowley Ho. SE16 —4E 76
Bowley La. SE19 —2D 108
Bowling Clo. Uxb —4D 142
Bowling Ct. Wat —6E 8
Bowling Grn. Clo. SW15 —6F 88
Bowling Grn. Ct. Wemb —7K 39
Bowling Grn. La. EC1 —7L 59
Bowling Grn. Pl. SE1 —3B 76
Bowling Grn. Row. SE18 —4K 79
Bowling Grn. St. SE11 —7L 75
Bowling Grn. Wlk. N1 —6C 60
Bowls Clo. Stan —5F 22
Bowls, The. Chig —3C 32
Bowman Av. E16 —1D 78
Bowman M. SW18 —7K 89
Bowmans. —6D 98
Bowman's Bldgs. NW1 —8C 58
(off Penfold Pl.)
Bowmans Clo. W13 —2F 70
Bowmans Grn. Wat —9J 5
Bowmans Lea. SE23 —6G 93
Bowmans Mdw. Wall —5F 122
Bowman's M. E1 —1E 76
Bowman's M. N7 —8J 43
Bowman's Pl. N7 —8J 43
Bowman's Rd. Dart —6D 98
Bowman Trad. Est. NW9 —2L 39
Bowmead. SE9 —8K 95
Bowmore Wlk. NW1 —3H 59
Bowness Clo. E8 —2D 60
(off Beechwood Rd.)
Bowness Cres. SW15 —2C 104
Bowness Dri. Houn —3J 85
Bowness Ho. SE15 —8G 77
(off Hillbeck Clo.)
Bowness Rd. SE6 —6M 93
Bowness Rd. Bexh —1M 97
Bowness Way. Horn —1E 66
Bowood Rd. SW11 —4E 90
Bowood Rd. Enf —4H 17
Bowring Grn. Wat —5G 21
Bow Rd. E3 —6K 61
Bowrons Av. Wemb —3H 55
Bowry Ho. E14 —8K 61
(off Wallwood St.)
Bowsley Ct. Felt —8E 84
Bowsprit Point. E14 —4L 77
(off Westferry Rd.)
Bow St. E15 —1C 62
Bow St. WC2 —9J 59
Bow Triangle Bus. Cen. E3 —7L 61
Bowyer Clo. E6 —8K 63
Bowyer Ho. N1 —4C 60
(off Whitmore Est.)
Bowyer Pl. SE5 —8A 76
Bowyers Clo. Asht —9K 133
Bowyer St. SE5 —8A 76
Boxall Rd. SE21 —5C 92
Boxelder Clo. Edgw —5A 24
Boxford Clo. S Croy —4H 139
Boxgrove Rd. SE2 —3F 80
Box La. Bark —5F 64
Boxley Rd. Mord —8A 106
Boxley St. E16 —2F 78
Boxmoor Ho. W11 —2H 73
(off Queensdale Cres.)
Boxmoor Ho. W11 —2H 73
(off Queensdale Cres.)
Boxmoor Rd. Harr —2F 38
Boxmoor Rd. Romf —5A 34
Boxoll Rd. Dag —9K 49
Box Ridge Av. Purl —4K 137
Boxted Clo. Buck H —1J 31
Box Tree Ho. SE8 —7J 77
Boxtree La. Harr —8A 22
Boxtree Rd. Harr —7B 22
Box Tree Wlk. Orp —3H 129
Boxwood Clo. W Dray —3K 143
Boxwood Way. Warl —9H 139
Boxworth Clo. N12 —5B 26
Boxworth Gro. N1 —4K 59
Boyard Rd. SE18 —6M 79
Boyce Clo. Borwd —3J 11
Boyce Ho. W10 —6K 57
(off Bruckner St.)
Boyce Way. E13 —7E 62
Boycroft Av. NW9 —4A 40
Boyd Av. S'hall —2K 69
Boyd Clo. King T —4L 103
Boydell Ct. NW8 —3B 58
Boyden Ho. E17 —1A 46
Boyd Rd. SW19 —3B 106
Boyd St. E1 —9E 60
Boyfield St. SE1 —3M 75
Boyland Rd. Brom —2D 110
Boyle Av. Stan —6E 22
Boyle Clo. Uxb —5D 142
Boyle Farm Rd. Th Dit —1E 118
Boyle St. W1 —1G 75
Boyne Av. NW4 —2H 41
Boyne Rd. SE13 —2A 94
Boyne Rd. Dag —8L 49
Boyne Ter. M. W11 —2K 73
Boyseland Ct. Edgw —2A 24
Boyson Rd. SE5 —7A 76
(in two parts)
Boyson Wlk. SE17 —7B 76
Boyton Clo. E1 —7G 61
Boyton Clo. N8 —1J 43
Boyton Ho. NW8 —5B 58
(off Wellington Rd.)
Boyton Rd. N8 —1J 43
Brabant Ct. EC3 —1C 76
(off Philpot La.)
Brabant Rd. N22 —9K 27
Brabazon Av. Wall —9J 123
Brabazon Rd. Houn —8G 69
Brabazon Rd. N'holt —5L 53
Brabazon St. E14 —9M 61
Brabner Ho. E2 —6E 60
(off Wellington Row)
Brabourne Clo. SE19 —2C 108
Brabourne Cres. Bexh —7K 81
Brabourne Heights. NW7 —3C 24
Brabourne Ri. Beck —9A 110
Brabourn Gro. SE15 —1G 93
Brabrook Ct. Wall —6F 122
Brabstone Ho. Gnfd —5D 54
Bracer Ho. N1 —5C 60
(off Whitmore Est.)
Bracewell Av. Gnfd —1D 54
Bracewell Rd. W10 —8G 57
Bracewood Gdns. Croy —5D 124
Bracey M. N19 —7J 43
Bracey St. N4 —7J 43
Bracken Av. SW12 —5E 90
Bracken Av. Croy —5L 125
Brackenbridge Dri. Ruis —8H 37
Brackenbury. N4 —6L 43
(off Osborne Rd.)
Brackenbury Gdns. W6 —4F 72
Brackenbury Rd. N2 —1A 42
Brackenbury Rd. W6 —4F 72
Bracken Clo. E6 —8K 63
Bracken Clo. Borwd —3M 11
Bracken Clo. Sun —3D 100
Bracken Clo. Twic —6L 85
Brackendale. N21 —2K 27
Brackendale Clo. Houn —9M 69
Brackendale Gdns. Upm —9M 51
Brackendene. Brick W —3K 5
Brackendene. Dart —1C 114
Bracken Dri. Chig —6M 31
Bracken End. Iswth —4B 86
Brackenfield Clo. E5 —8F 44
Bracken Gdns. SW13 —1E 88
Brackenhill. Ruis —9J 37
Bracken Hill Clo. Brom —5D 110
Bracken Hill La. Brom —5D 110
Bracken Ho. E3 —8L 61
(off Devons Rd.)
Bracken Ind. Est. Ilf —7D 32
Bracken M. E4 —1A 30
Bracken M. Romf —4M 49
Bracken Path. Eps —5M 133
Brackens. Beck —4L 109
Brackens, The. Enf —9C 16
Brackens, The. Orp —7E 128
Bracken, The. E4 —2A 30
Brackenwood. Sun —5E 100
Brackenwood Lodge. Barn —6L 13
(off Prospect Rd.)
Brackley. Wey —7B 116
Brackley Clo. Wall —9J 123
Brackley Ct. NW8 —7B 58
(off Henderson Dri.)
Brackley Rd. W4 —6C 72
Brackley Rd. Beck —4K 109
Brackley Sq. Wfd G —7H 31
Brackley St. EC1 —7A 60
Brackley Ter. W4 —6C 72
Bracklyn Ct. N1 —5B 60
(in three parts)
Bracklyn St. N1 —5B 60
Bracknell Clo. N22 —8L 27
Bracknell Gdns. NW3 —9M 41
Bracknell Ga. NW3 —1M 57
Bracknell Way. NW3 —9M 41
Bracondale. Esh —7A 118
Bracondale Rd. SE2 —5E 80
Bradbeer Ho. E2 —6G 61
(off Cornwall Av.)
Bradbourne Rd. Bex —6L 97
Bradbourne St. SW6 —1L 89
Bradbury Clo. Borwd —3M 11
Bradbury Clo. S'hall —5K 69
Bradbury M. N16 —1C 60
(off Bradbury St.)
Bradbury St. N16 —1C 60
Braddock Clo. Iswth —1D 86
Braddon Ct. Barn —5J 13
Braddon Rd. Rich —2K 87
Braddyll St. SE10 —6C 78
Bradenham. SE17 —7B 76
(off Bradenham Clo.)
Bradenham Av. Well —3E 96
Bradenham Clo. SE17 —7B 76
Bradenham Rd. Harr —2F 38
Bradenham Rd. Hay —6C 52
Braden St. W9 —7M 57
Bradfield Ct. NW1 —3F 58
(off Hawley Rd.)
Bradfield Dri. Bark —1E 64
Bradfield Rd. E16 —3E 78
Bradfield Rd. Ruis —1J 53
Bradford Clo. N17 —6D 28
Bradford Clo. SE26 —1F 108
Bradford Clo. Brom —3K 127
Bradford Dri. Eps —8D 120
Bradford Ho. W14 —4H 73
(off Spring Va. Ter.)
Bradford Rd. W3 —3C 72
Bradford Rd. Ilf —6B 48
Bradgate Rd. SE6 —5M 93
Brading Cres. E11 —7F 46
Brading Rd. SW2 —6K 91
Brading Rd. Croy —1K 123
Brading Ter. W12 —4E 72
Bradiston Rd. W9 —6K 57
Bradley Clo. N7 —2J 59
Bradley Clo. Belm —2M 135
Bradley Ct. Enf —2J 17
(off Bradley Rd.)
Bradley Gdns. W13 —9F 54
Bradley Ho. E2 —5E 60
(off Claredale St.)
Bradley Ho. SE16 —5G 77
(off Raymouth Rd.)
Bradley M. SW17 —7D 90
Bradley Rd. N22 —9K 27
Bradley Rd. SE19 —3A 108
Bradley Rd. Enf —2J 17
Bradley Rd. Wal A —8J 7
Bradley's Clo. N1 —5L 59
Bradley Stone Rd. E6 —8K 63
Bradman Row. Edgw —7A 24
Bradmead. SW8 —8F 74
Bradmore Ho. E1 —8G 61
(off Jamaica St.)
Bradmore Pk. Rd. W6 —5F 72
Bradmore Way. Coul —9J 137
Bradshaw Clo. SW19 —3L 105
Bradshawe Waye. Uxb —8D 142
Bradshaw Rd. Wat —3G 9
Bradshaws Clo. SE25 —7E 108
Bradstock Ho. E9 —3H 61
Bradstock Rd. E9 —2H 61
Bradstock Rd. Eps —7E 120
Brad St. SE1 —2L 75
Bradwell Av. Dag —7L 49
Bradwell Clo. E18 —2D 46
Bradwell Clo. Horn —2F 66
Bradwell Ho. NW6 —4M 57
(off Mortimer Cres.)
Bradwell M. N18 —4E 28
Bradwell Rd. Buck H —9J 19
Brady Ct. Dag —6H 49
Brady Ho. SW8 —9G 75
(off Corunna Rd.)
Bradymead. E6 —9L 63
Brady St. E1 —7F 60
Braeburn Ct. Barn —6B 14
Braemar Av. N22 —8J 27
Braemar Av. NW10 —8B 40
Braemar Av. SW19 —8L 89
Braemar Av. Bexh —3A 98
Braemar Av. S Croy —2A 138
Braemar Av. T Hth —7L 107
Braemar Av. Wemb —3H 55
Braemar Ct. SE6 —7D 94
Braemar Gdns. NW9 —8B 24
Braemar Gdns. Horn —4L 51
Braemar Gdns. Sidc —9B 96
Braemar Gdns. W W'ck —3A 126
Braemar Ho. W9 —6A 58
(off Maida Va.)
Braemar Rd. E13 —7D 62
Braemar Rd. N15 —3C 44
Braemar Rd. Bren —7H 71
Braemar Rd. Wor Pk —5F 120

Braemer Clo.—Briar Clo.

Braemer Clo. SE16 —6F 76
(off Masters Dri.)
Braeside. Beck —2L 109
Braeside Av. SW19 —5J 105
Braeside Clo. Pinn —7L 21
Braeside Cres. Bexh —3A 98
Braeside Rd. SW16 —4G 107
Braes St. N1 —3M 59
Braesyde Clo. Belv —5K 81
Brafferton Rd. Croy —6A 124
Braganza St. SE17 —6M 75
Bragg Clo. Dag —2F 64
Bragg Rd. Tedd —3C 102
Braham Ho. SE11 —6K 75
Braham St. E1 —9D 60
Braid Av. W3 —9C 56
Braid Clo. Felt —8K 85
Braid Ho. SE10 —9A 78
(off Blackheath Hill)
Braidwood Pas. EC1 —8A 60
(off Aldersgate St.)
Braidwood Rd. SE6 —7B 94
Brailsford Clo. SW19 —4C 106
Brailsford Rd. SW2 —4L 91
Brainton Av. Felt —6F 84
Braintree Av. Ilf —2J 47
Braintree Ho. E1 —7G 61
(off Malcolm Rd.)
Braintree Rd. Dag —8L 49
Braintree Rd. Ruis —9F 36
Braintree St. E2 —6G 61
Braithwaite Av. Romf —5L 49
Braithwaite Gdns. Stan —8G 23
Braithwaite Ho. E14 —9B 62
Braithwaite Ho. EC1 —7B 60
(off Bunhill Row)
Braithwaite Rd. Enf —5K 17
Braithwaite Tower. W2 —8B 58
(off Hall Pl.)
Bramah Grn. SW9 —9L 75
Bramah Tea & Coffee Mus.
(off Maguire St.) —3D 76
Bramalea Clo. N6 —4E 42
Bramall Clo. E15 —1D 62
Bramall Ct. N7 —1K 59
(off George's Rd.)
Bramber. WC1 —6J 59
(off Cromer St.)
Bramber Ct. W5 —5J 71
Bramber Ct. Dart —5M 99
(off Bow Arrow La.)
Bramber Rd. N12 —5C 26
Bramber Rd. W14 —7K 73
Brambleacres Clo. Sutt —9L 121
Bramble Banks. Cars —1E 136
Bramblebury Rd. SE18 —6A 80
Bramble Clo. N15 —2E 44
Bramble Clo. Beck —9A 110
Bramble Clo. Croy —6L 125
Bramble Clo. Shep —7B 100
Bramble Clo. Stan —7H 23
Bramble Clo. Uxb —9D 142
Bramble Clo. Wat —7E 4
Bramble Cft. Eri —5A 82
Brambledown Clo. W W'ck —9C 110
Brambledown Rd. Cars & Wall —9E 122
Brambledown Rd. S Croy —9C 124
Bramble Gdns. W12 —1D 72
Bramble Ho. E3 —8L 61
(off Devons Rd.)
Bramble La. Hamp —3K 101
Brambles Clo. Iswth —8F 70
Brambles Farm Dri. Uxb —6E 142
Brambles, The. SW19 —2K 105
(off Woodside)
Brambles, The. Chesh —4D 6
Brambles, The. Chig —5A 32
Brambles, The. W Dray —5J 143
Bramble Wlk. Eps —6M 133
Bramblewood Clo. Cars —3C 122
Brambling Clo. Bush —6J 9
Brambling Ct. SE8 —7K 77
(off Abinger Gro.)
Bramblings, The. E4 —4B 30
Bramcote Av. Mitc —8D 106
Bramcote Gro. SE16 —6G 77
Bramcote Rd. SW15 —3F 88
Bramdean Cres. SE12 —7E 94
Bramdean Gdns. SE12 —7E 94
Bramerton Rd. Beck —7K 109
Bramerton St. SW3 —7C 74
Bramfield. Wat —7J 5
Bramfield Ct. N4 —8A 44
(off Queens Dri.)
Bramfield Rd. SW11 —5C 90
Bramford Ct. N14 —2H 27
Bramford Rd. SW18 —3A 90
Bramham Ct. N'wd —6C 20
Bramham Gdns. SW5 —6M 73
Bramham Gdns. Chess —6H 119
Bramham Ho. SE15 —2D 92
Bramhope La. SE7 —7F 78
Bramlands Clo. SW11 —2C 90
Bramleas. Wat —7D 8
Bramley Av. Coul —7G 137
Bramley Av. Shep —7C 100
Bramley Clo. E17 —9J 29
Bramley Clo. N14 —7F 14
Bramley Clo. Eastc —1D 36
Bramley Clo. Hay —1E 68
Bramley Clo. Orp —3M 127
Bramley Clo. S Croy —7A 124
Bramley Clo. Swan —8C 114
Bramley Clo. Twic —5A 86
Bramley Ct. E4 —1A 30
(off Ridgeway, The)
Bramley Ct. Barn —6C 14
Bramley Ct. Mitc —6B 106
Bramley Ct. S'hall —1A 70
(off Baird Av.)
Bramley Ct. Wat —5F 4
Bramley Ct. Well —9F 80
Bramley Cres. SW8 —8H 75
Bramley Cres. Ilf —4L 47
Bramley Gdns. Wat —5G 21
Bramley Hill. S Croy —7M 123
Bramley Ho. SW15 —5D 88
(off Tunworth Cres.)
Bramley Ho. W10 —9H 57
Bramley Ho. Houn —3K 85
Bramley Ho. Ct. Enf —1B 16
Bramleyhyrst. S Croy —6A 124
(off Bramley Hill)
Bramley Pde. N14 —6G 15
Bramley Pl. Dart —3E 98
Bramley Rd. N14 —7F 14
Bramley Rd. W5 —4G 71
Bramley Rd. W10 —9H 57
Bramley Rd. Cheam —1H 135
Bramley Rd. Sutt —7B 122
Bramley Shaw. Wal A —6M 7
Bramley Way. Asht —9K 133
Bramley Way. Houn —4K 85
Bramley Way. W W'ck —4M 125
Brampton. WC1 —8K 59
(off Red Lion Sq.)
Brampton Clo. E5 —7F 44
Brampton Clo. Chesh —1A 6
Brampton Ct. NW4 —2F 40
Brampton Gdns. N15 —3A 44
Brampton Gdns. W on T —7G 117
Brampton Gro. NW4 —2F 40
Brampton Gro. Harr —2E 38
Brampton Gro. Wemb —6L 39
Brampton La. NW4 —2G 41
Brampton Pk. Rd. N8 —1L 43
Brampton Rd. E6 —6H 63
Brampton Rd. N15 —3A 44
Brampton Rd. NW9 —2L 39
Brampton Rd. SE2 & Bexh —7G 81
Brampton Rd. Croy —2D 124
Brampton Rd. Uxb —5F 142
Brampton Rd. Wat —3E 20
Brampton Ter. Borwd —2L 11
(off Stapleton Rd.)
Bramshaw Gdns. Wat —5H 21
Bramshaw Ri. N Mald —1C 120
Bramshaw Rd. E9 —2H 61
Bramshill Clo. Chig —5C 32
Bramshill Gdns. NW5 —8F 42
Bramshill Rd. NW10 —5D 56
Bramshot Av. SE7 —7E 78
Bramshot Way. Wat —2E 20
Bramshurst. NW8 —4M 57
(off Abbey Rd.)
Bramston Clo. Ilf —6D 32
Bramston Rd. NW10 —5E 56
Bramston Rd. SW17 —9A 90
Bramwell Clo. Sun —6H 101
Bramwell Ho. SE1 —4A 76
Bramwell Ho. SW1 —6G 75
(off Churchill Gdns.)
Bramwell M. N1 —4K 59
Brancaster Dri. NW7 —7E 24
Brancaster Ho. E1 —6H 61
(off Moody St.)
Brancaster La. Purl —2A 138
Brancaster Pl. Lou —5K 19
Brancaster Rd. E12 —9K 47
Brancaster Rd. SW16 —9J 91
Brancaster Rd. Ilf —4C 48
Brancepeth Gdns. Buck H —2E 30
Branch Hill. NW3 —8A 42
Branch Hill Ho. NW3 —8M 41
Branch Pl. N1 —4B 60
Branch Rd. E14 —1J 77
Branch Rd. Ilf —5F 32
Branch St. SE5 —8C 76
Brancker Clo. Wall —9J 123
Brancker Rd. Harr —1H 39
Brancroft Way. Enf —3J 17
Brand Clo. N4 —6M 43
Brandesbury Sq. Wfd G —7L 31
Brandlehow Rd. SW15 —3K 89
Brandon. NW9 —9D 24
(off Further Acre)
Brandon Est. SE17 —7M 75
Brandon Ho. Beck —2M 109
(off Beckenham Hill Rd.)
Brandon Mans. W14 —7J 73
(off Queen's Club Gdns.)
Brandon M. EC2 —8B 60
(off Silk St.)
Brandon Rd. E17 —2A 46
Brandon Rd. N7 —3J 59
Brandon Rd. Dart —6L 99
Brandon Rd. S'hall —6K 69
Brandon Rd. Sutt —6M 121
Brandon St. SE17 —5A 76
(in three parts)
Brandram M. SE13 —3C 94
(off Brandram Rd.)
Brandram Rd. SE13 —2C 94
Brandreth Ct. Harr —4D 38
Brandreth Rd. E6 —9K 63
Brandreth Rd. SW17 —8F 90
Brandries, The. Wall —5H 123
Brand St. SE10 —8A 78
Brandt Ct. Borwd —4B 12
(off Elstree Way)
Brandville Gdns. Ilf —2M 47
Brandville Rd. W Dray —3J 143
Brandy Way. Sutt —9L 121
Branfill Rd. Upm —7M 51
Brangbourne Rd. Brom —2A 110
Brangton Rd. SE11 —6K 75
Brangwyn Ct. W14 —4J 73
(off Blythe Rd.)
Brangwyn Cres. SW19 —5A 106
Branham Ho. SE18 —6M 79
Branksea St. SW6 —8J 73
Branksome Av. N18 —6D 28
Branksome Clo. Tedd —1B 102
Branksome Clo. W on T —4H 117
Branksome Ho. SW8 —8K 75
(off Meadow Rd.)
Branksome Rd. SW2 —4J 91
Branksome Rd. SW19 —5L 105
Branksome Way. Harr —4K 39
Branksome Way. N Mald —5A 104
Branksone Ct. N2 —1A 42
Bransby Rd. Chess —8J 119
Branscombe. NW1 —4G 59
(off Plender St.)
Branscombe Ct. Brom —9D 110
Branscombe Gdns. N21 —9L 15
Branscombe St. SE13 —2M 93
Bransdale Clo. NW6 —4L 57
Bransell Clo. Swan —1A 130
Bransgrove Rd. Edgw —8K 23
Branston Cres. Orp —3B 128
Branstone Ct. Purf —6M 83
Branstone Rd. Rich —9K 71
Brants Wlk. W7 —7C 54
Brantwood Av. Eri —8A 82
Brantwood Av. Iswth —3E 86
Brantwood Clo. E17 —1M 45
Brantwood Gdns. Enf —6J 15
Brantwood Gdns. Ilf —2J 47
Brantwood Ho. SE5 —8A 76
(off Wyndam Est.)
Brantwood Rd. N17 —6E 28
Brantwood Rd. SE24 —4A 92
Brantwood Rd. Bexh —1M 97
Brantwood Rd. S Croy —1A 138
Brantwood Way. Orp —7G 113
Branxholme Ct. Brom —5D 110
(off Highland Rd.)
Brasenose Dri. SW13 —7G 73
Brasher Clo. Gnfd —1B 54
Brassett Point. E15 —4C 62
(off Abbey Rd.)
Brassey Clo. Felt —7E 84
Brassey Ho. E14 —5M 77
(off Cahir St.)
Brassey Rd. NW6 —2K 57
Brassey Sq. SW11 —2E 90
Brassie Av. W3 —9C 56
Brass Talley All. SE16 —3H 77
Brasted Clo. SE26 —1G 109
Brasted Clo. Bexh —4H 97
Brasted Clo. Orp —4D 128
Brasted Clo. Sutt —2L 135
Brasted Lodge. SE20 —4L 109
Brasted Rd. Eri —8C 82
Brathay. NW1 —5G 59
(off Ampthill Est.)
Brathway Rd. SW18 —6L 89
Bratley St. E1 —7E 60
Bratten Ct. Croy —1B 124
Braund Av. Gnfd —7M 53
Braundton Av. Sidc —7D 96
Braunston Dri. Hay —7J 53
Bravington Pl. W9 —7K 57
Bravington Rd. W9 —5K 57
Brawne Ho. SE17 —7M 75
(off Brandon Est.)
Braxfield Rd. SE4 —3J 93
Braxted Pk. SW16 —3K 107
Bray. NW3 —3C 58
Brayards Rd. SE15 —1F 92
Brayards Rd. Est. SE15 —1G 93
(off Brayards Rd.)
Braybourne Clo. Uxb —2A 142
Braybourne Dri. Iswth —8D 70
Braybrooke Gdns. SE19 —4C 108
Braybrook St. W12 —8D 56
Brayburne Av. SW4 —1G 91
Bray Clo. Borwd —3A 12
Bray Ct. SW16 —2J 107
Braycourt Av. W on T —2F 116
Bray Cres. SE16 —3H 77
Braydon Rd. N16 —6E 44
Bray Dri. E16 —1D 78
Brayfield Ter. N1 —3L 59
Brayford Sq. E1 —9G 61
Bray Lodge. Chesh —1E 6
(off High St.)
Bray Pas. E16 —1E 78
Bray Pl. SW3 —5D 74
Bray Rd. NW7 —6H 25
Brays Springs. Wal A —7L 7
Brayton Gdns. Enf —6H 15
Braywood Rd. SE9 —3B 96
Brazil Clo. Bedd —2J 123
Breach La. Dag —6L 65
Bread St. EC4 —9A 60
(in two parts)
Breakfield. Coul —8J 137
Breakspear Ct. Ab L —3D 4
Breakspear Crematorium. Ruis —3A 36
Breakspeare Clo. Wat —2F 8
Breakspeare Rd. Ab L —4C 4
Breakspear Ho. Ruis —3B 36
Breakspear Rd. Ruis —5A 36
Breakspears Dri. Orp —5E 112
Breakspears M. SE4 —1K 93
Breakspears Rd. SE4 —3K 93
Bream Clo. N17 —2F 44
Bream Gdns. E6 —6L 63
Breamore Clo. SW15 —7E 88
Breamore Ho. SE15 —8E 76
(off Friary Est.)
Breamore Rd. Ilf —7D 48
Bream's Bldgs. EC4 —9L 59
Bream St. E3 —3L 61
Breamwater Gdns. Rich —9F 86
Brearley Clo. Edgw —7A 24
Brearley Clo. Uxb —2C 142
Breasley Clo. SW15 —3F 88
Breasy Pl. NW4 —2F 40
(off Burroughs Gdns.)
Brechin Pl. SW7 —5A 74
Brecknock Rd. N19 & N7 —9G 43
Brecknock Rd. Est. N19 —9G 43
Breckonmead. Brom —6G 111
Brecon Clo. Mitc —7J 107
Brecon Clo. Wor Pk —4G 121
Brecon Grn. NW9 —4C 40
Brecon Ho. W2 —9A 58
(off Hallfield Est.)
Brecon M. NW5 —1H 59
Brecon Rd. W6 —7J 73
Brecon Rd. Enf —6G 17
Brecons, The. Wey —6B 116
Brede Clo. E6 —6L 63
Bredel Ho. E14 —8L 61
(off St Paul's Way)
Bredgar Rd. N19 —7G 43
Bredhurst Clo. SE20 —3G 109
Bredo Ho. Bark —6F 64
Bredon Rd. Croy —2D 124
Bredune. Kenl —7B 138
Breer St. SW6 —2M 89
Breezers Ct. E1 —1E 76
(off Highway, The)
Breezer's Hill. E1 —1E 76
Breeze Ter. Chesh —1D 6
Brember Rd. Harr —7A 38
Bremer M. E17 —2M 45
Bremner Clo. Swan —8E 114
Bremner Rd. SW7 —4A 74
Brenchley Clo. Brom —1D 126
Brenchley Clo. Chst —5L 111
Brenchley Gdns. SE23 —5G 93
Brenchley Rd. Orp —6D 112
Brendans Clo. Horn —6J 51
Brenda Rd. SW17 —8D 90
Brende Gdns. W Mol —8M 101
Brendon Av. NW10 —9C 40
Brendon Clo. Eri —9C 82
Brendon Clo. Esh —8A 118
Brendon Clo. Hay —8A 68
Brendon Ct. S'hall —5M 69
Brendon Dri. Esh —8A 118
Brendon Gdns. Harr —9M 37
Brendon Gdns. Ilf —3C 48
Brendon Gro. N2 —9A 26
Brendon Rd. SE9 —8B 96
Brendon Rd. Dag —6K 49
Brendon St. W1 —9C 58
Brendon Vs. N21 —1A 28
Brendon Way. Enf —9C 16
Brenley Clo. Mitc —7E 106
Brenley Gdns. SE9 —3H 95
Brenley Ho. SE1 —3B 76
(off Tennis St.)
Brennand Ct. N19 —8G 43
Brent Clo. Bex —7J 97
Brent Clo. Dart —5M 99
Brentcot Clo. W13 —7F 54
Brent Ct. NW11 —5H 41
Brent Ct. W7 —1B 70
Brent Cres. NW10 —5K 55
Brent Cross. —5G 41
Brent Cross Fly-Over. NW2 —5H 41
Brent Cross Gdns. NW4 —4H 41
Brent Cross Interchange. (Junct.) —5H 41
Brent Cross Shop. Cen. NW4 —5G 41
Brentfield. NW10 —3M 55
Brentfield Clo. NW10 —2B 56
Brentfield Gdns. NW2 —5H 41
Brentfield Ho. NW10 —3B 56
Brentfield Rd. NW10 —2B 56
Brentfield Rd. Dart —5L 99
Brentford. —7H 71
Brentford Bus. Cen. Bren —8G 71
Brentford Clo. Hay —7H 53
Brentford End. —8F 70
Brentford F.C. —7H 71
Brentford Ho. Twic —6F 86
Brentford Musical Mus. —7J 71
Brent Grn. NW4 —3G 41
Brent Grn. Wlk. Wemb —8A 40
Brentham Way. W5 —7H 55
Brenthouse Rd. E9 —3G 61
Brenthurst Rd. NW10 —2D 56
Brentlands Dri. Dart —7L 99
Brent La. Dart —6K 99
Brent Lea. Bren —8G 71
Brentmead Clo. W7 —1C 70
Brentmead Gdns. NW10 —5K 55
Brentmead Pl. NW11 —4H 41
Brent New Enterprise Cen. NW10 —2D 56
Brenton St. E14 —9J 61
Brent Pk. Ind. Est. W7 —4F 68
Brent Pk. Rd. NW9 & NW4 —5F 40
(in two parts)
Brent Pl. Barn —7K 13
Brent Rd. E16 —9E 62
Brent Rd. SE18 —8M 79
Brent Rd. Bren —7G 71
Brent Rd. S'hall —4G 69
Brent Rd. S Croy —1F 138
Brent Side. Bren —7G 71
Brentside Clo. W13 —7E 54
Brentside Executive Cen. Bren —7F 70
Brent St. NW4 —2G 41
Brent Ter. NW2 —6G 41
(in two parts)
Brent, The. Dart —6L 99
Brent Trad. Cen. NW10 —1C 56
Brentvale Av. S'hall —2B 70
Brentvale Av. Wemb —4K 55
Brent Vw. Rd. NW9 —4E 40
Brentwaters Bus. Pk. Bren —8G 71
Brent Way. N3 —6L 25
Brent Way. Bren —8H 71
Brent Way. Dart —5M 99
Brent Way. Wemb —2M 55
Brentwick Gdns. Bren —5J 71
Brentwood Clo. SE9 —7A 96
Brentwood Ho. SE18 —8H 79
(off Portway Gdns.)
Brentwood Lodge. NW4 —3H 41
(off Holmdale Gdns.)
Brentwood Rd. Romf —4D 50
Brereton Rd. N17 —7D 28
Bressenden Pl. SW1 —4F 74
Bressey Av. Enf —3E 16
Bressey Gro. E18 —9D 30
Breton Highwalk. EC2 —8A 60
(off Golden La.)
Breton Ho. EC1 —8A 60
(off Beech St.)
Breton Ho. SE1 —4D 76
(off Abbey St.)
Brett Clo. N16 —7C 44
Brett Clo. N'holt —6H 53
Brett Ct. N9 —2G 29
Brett Cres. NW10 —4B 56
Brettell St. SE17 —6B 76
Brettenham Av. E17 —8L 29
Brettenham Rd. E17 —9L 29
Brettenham Rd. N18 —4E 28
Brett Gdns. Dag —3J 65
Brettgrave. Eps —2A 134
Brett Ho. Chesh —1D 6
Brett Ho. Clo. SW15 —6H 89
Brettinghurst. SE1 —6E 76
(off Avondale Sq.)
Brett Pas. E8 —1F 60
Brett Pl. Wat —1E 8
Brett Rd. E8 —1F 60
Brett Rd. Barn —7G 13
Brewer's Fld. Dart —1G 115
Brewer's Grn. SW1 —4H 75
(off Buckingham Ga.)
Brewer's Hall Garden. EC2 —8A 60
(off London Wall)
Brewers La. Rich —4H 87
Brewer St. W1 —1G 75
Brewery Clo. Wemb —1E 54
Brewery Ind. Est., The. N1 —5A 60
(off Wenlock Rd.)
Brewery La. Twic —6D 86
Brewery M. Cen. Iswth —2E 86
Brewery Rd. N7 —3J 59
Brewery Rd. SE18 —6B 80
Brewery Rd. Brom —3J 127
Brewery Sq. SE1 —3D 76
(off Horselydown La.)
Brewhouse La. E1 —2F 76
Brewhouse Rd. SE18 —5K 79
Brewhouse St. SW15 —2J 89
Brewhouse Wlk. SE16 —2J 77
Brewhouse Yd. EC1 —7M 59
Brewood Rd. Dag —2F 64
Brewster Gdns. W10 —8G 57
Brewster Ho. E14 —1K 77
(off Three Colt St.)
Brewster Ho. SE1 —5D 76
(off Dunton Rd.)
Brewster Rd. E10 —6M 45
Brian Av. S Croy —4C 138
Brian Clo. Horn —9F 50
Briane Rd. Eps —2A 134
Brian Rd. Romf —3G 49
Briant Ho. SE1 —4K 75
(off Hercules Rd.)
Briants Clo. Pinn —9K 21
Briant St. SE14 —9H 77
Briar Av. SW16 —4K 107
Briarbank Rd. W13 —9E 54
Briar Banks. Cars —1E 136
Briar Clo. N2 —1M 41
Briar Clo. N13 —3A 28

Briar Clo.—Broad Mead

Briar Clo. Buck H —2H 31
Briar Clo. Chesh —2C 6
Briar Clo. Hamp —2K 101
Briar Clo. Iswth —4D 86
Briar Ct. SW15 —3F 88
Briar Ct. Sutt —6G 121
Briar Cres. N'holt —2M 53
Briardale Gdns. NW3 —8L 41
Briarfield Av. N2 —1M 41
Briarfield Av. N3 —9M 25
Briar Gdns. Brom —3D 126
Briar Gro. S Croy —5E 138
Briar Hill. Purl —3J 137
Briaris Clo. N17 —7F 28
Briar La. Cars —1E 136
Briar La. Croy —6M 125
Briar Rd. NW2 —9G 41
Briar Rd. SW16 —7J 107
Briar Rd. Bex —9B 98
Briar Rd. Harr —3G 39
Briar Rd. Romf —7G 35
Briar Rd. Twic —7C 86
Briar Rd. Wat —7E 4
Briars Ct. Oxs —6B 132
Briars, The. Bush —9C 10
Briars, The. Chesh —4E 6
Briars Wlk. Romf —9J 35
Briarswood Way. Orp —7D 128
Briar Wlk. SW15 —3F 88
Briar Wlk. W10 —7J 57
Briar Wlk. Edgw —7A 24
Briar Way. W Dray —3L 143
Briarwood Clo. NW9 —4A 40
Briarwood Clo. Felt —1C 100
Briarwood Ct. Wor Pk —3E 120
(off Avenue, The)
Briarwood Dri. N'wd —9E 20
Briarwood Rd. SW4 —4H 91
Briarwood Rd. Eps —8E 120
Briary Clo. NW3 —3C 58
Briary Ct. Sidc —2F 112
Briary Gdns. Brom —2F 110
Briary Gro. Edgw —9M 23
Briary La. N9 —3D 28
Briary Lodge. Beck —5A 110
Briavels Ct. Eps —7C 134
Brickbarn Clo. SW10 —8A 74
(off King's Barn)
Brick Clo. Eri —7C 82
Brick Ct. EC4 —9L 59
Brickenden Ct. Wal A —6M 7
Brickett Clo. Ruis —3A 36
Bricket Wood. —3K 5
Brick Farm Clo. Rich —9M 71
Brickfield Clo. Bren —8G 71
Brickfield Cotts. SE18 —8D 80
Brickfield Farm Gdns. Orp —6A 128
Brickfield La. Ark —8D 12
Brickfield La. Hay —7B 68
Brickfield Rd. SW19 —1M 105
Brickfield Rd. T Hth —5M 107
Brickfields. Harr —7B 38
(in two parts)
Brickfields Cotts. Borwd —5K 11
Brickfields Way. W Dray —4K 143
Brick Kiln Clo. Wat —8J 9
Brick La. E2 & E1 —6D 60
Brick La. Enf —4F 16
Brick La. Stan —7H 23
Brick Lane Music Hall. —6C 60
(off Curtain Rd.)
Bricklayers Arms. (Junct.) —4B 76
Bricklayers Arms Bus. Cen. SE1 —5C 76
Brick St. W1 —2F 74
Brickwall La. Ruis —6C 36
Brickwood Clo. SE26 —9F 92
Brickwood Rd. Croy —4C 124
Brideale Clo. SE15 —7D 76
Bride Ct. EC4 —9M 59
(off Bride La.)
Bride La. EC4 —9M 59
Bridel M. N1 —4M 59
(off Colebrook Row)
Bride St. N7 —2K 59
Bridewain St. SE1 —4D 76
(in two parts)
Bridewell Pl. E1 —2F 76
Bridewell Pl. EC4 —9M 59
Bridewell, The. —9M 59
(off Bridewell Pl.)
Bridford M. W1 —8F 58
Bridge App. NW1 —3E 58
Bridge Av. W6 —5G 73
Bridge Av. W7 —8B 54
Bridge Av. Upm —8L 51
Bridge Clo. W10 —9H 57
Bridge Clo. Enf —4F 16
Bridge Clo. Romf —4C 50
Bridge Clo. Tedd —1D 102
Bridge Clo. W on T —2D 116
Bridge Ct. E10 —6K 45
Bridge Dri. N13 —4K 27
Bridge End. E17 —8A 30
Bridgefield Clo. Bans —7G 135
Bridgefield Rd. Sutt —8L 121
Bridgefoot. SE1 —6J 75
Bridgefoot. Sun —5D 100
Bridgeford Ho. Wat —5F 8
Bridge Gdns. Ashf —4A 100
Bridge Gdns. E Mol —8B 102
Bridge Ga. N21 —9A 16
Bridge Ho. E9 —2H 61
(off Shepherds La.)
Bridge Ho. NW3 —3E 58
(off Adelaide Rd.)
Bridge Ho. SE4 —3K 93
Bridge Ho. SW1 —6F 74
Bridge Ho. Dart —6J 99
Bridge Ho. Sutt —8M 121
(off Bridge Rd.)
Bridgehouse Ct. SE1 —3M 75
Bridge Ho. Quay. E14 —2A 78
Bridgeland Rd. E16 —1E 78
Bridge La. NW11 —2J 41
Bridge La. SW11 —9C 74
Bridgeman Rd. N1 —3K 59
Bridgeman Rd. Tedd —3E 102
Bridgeman St. NW8 —5C 58
Bridge Meadows. SE14 —7H 77
Bridgen. —6J 97
Bridgend Rd. SW18 —3A 90
Bridgend Rd. Enf —8C 6
Bridgenhall Rd. Enf —3D 16
Bridgen Ho. E1 —9F 60
(off Nelson St.)
Bridgen Rd. Bex —6J 97
Bridge Pde. N21 —9A 16
(off Ridge Av.)
Bridgepark. SW18 —4L 89
Bridge Pl. SW1 —5F 74
Bridge Pl. Croy —3B 124
Bridge Pl. Wat —7H 9
Bridgeport Pl. E1 —2E 76
Bridger Clo. Wat —6H 5
Bridge Rd. E6 —3K 63
Bridge Rd. E15 —3B 62
Bridge Rd. E17 —5K 45
Bridge Rd. N9 —3E 28
Bridge Rd. N22 —8J 27
Bridge Rd. NW10 —2C 56
Bridge Rd. Beck —4K 109
Bridge Rd. Bexh —1J 97
Bridge Rd. Chess —7J 119
Bridge Rd. E Mol —8B 102
Bridge Rd. Eps —4D 134
Bridge Rd. Eri —1D 98
Bridge Rd. Houn & Iswth —2B 86
Bridge Rd. K Lan —6A 4
Bridge Rd. Orp —1F 128
Bridge Rd. Rain —7E 66
Bridge Rd. S'hall —3K 69
Bridge Rd. Sutt —8M 121
Bridge Rd. Twic —5F 86
Bridge Rd. Uxb —5A 142
Bridge Rd. Wall —7F 122
Bridge Rd. Wemb —8L 39
Bridge Row. Croy —3B 124
Bridges Ct. SW11 —2B 90
(in two parts)
Bridges Dri. Dart —4M 99
Bridges Ho. SE5 —8B 76
(off Elmington Est.)
Bridgeside Ho. N1 —5A 60
(off Wharf Rd.)
Bridges La. Croy —6J 123
Bridges Pl. SW6 —9K 73
Bridges Rd. SW19 —3M 105
Bridges Rd. Stan —5D 22
Bridges Rd. M. SW19 —3M 105
Bridge St. SW1 —3J 75
Bridge St. W4 —5B 72
Bridge St. Pinn —1J 37
Bridge St. Rich —4H 87
Bridge St. W on T —3C 116
Bridge Ter. E15 —3B 62
(in two parts)
Bridge, The. Harr —2D 38
Bridgetown Clo. SE19 —2C 108
Bridge Vw. W6 —6G 73
Bridgeview Ct. Ilf —6B 32
Bridgewalk Heights. SE1 —3B 76
(off Weston St.)
Bridgewater Clo. Chst —7C 112
Bridgewater Gdns. Edgw —9K 23
Bridgewater Highwalk. EC2 —8A 60
(off Beech St.)
Bridgewater Rd. E15 —4A 62
Bridgewater Rd. Ruis —9E 36
Bridgewater Rd. Wemb —2G 55
Bridgewater Rd. Wey —8B 116
Bridgewater Sq. EC2 —8A 60
Bridgewater St. EC2 —8A 60
Bridgewater Way. Bush —8M 9
Bridge Way. N11 —3G 27
Bridge Way. NW11 —3K 41
Bridgeway. Bark —3D 64
Bridge Way. Twic —6A 86
Bridge Way. Uxb —1F 142
Bridgeway. Wemb —3J 55
Bridgeway St. NW1 —5G 59
Bridge Wharf. E2 —5H 61
Bridge Wharf Rd. Iswth —2F 86
Bridgewood Clo. SE20 —4F 108
Bridgewood Rd. SW16 —4H 107
Bridgewood Rd. Wor Pk —6E 120
Bridge Works. Uxb —7A 142
Bridge Yd. SE1 —2B 76
Bridgford St. SW18 —9A 90
Bridgman Rd. W4 —4A 72
Bridgnorth Ho. SE15 —7E 76
(off Friary Est.)
Bridgwater Clo. Romf —5H 35
Bridgwater Ho. W2 —9A 58
(off Hallfield Est.)
Bridgwater Rd. Romf —5G 35
Bridgwater Wlk. Romf —5H 35
Bridle Clo. Enf —1K 17
Bridle Clo. Eps —7B 120
Bridle Clo. King T —8H 103
Bridle Clo. Sun —7E 100
Bridle End. Eps —5D 134
Bridle La. W1 —1G 75
Bridle La. Stoke D & Oxs —7A 132
Bridle La. Twic —5F 86
Bridle Path. Croy —5J 123
(in two parts)
Bridle Path. Wat —4F 8
Bridle Path, The. E4 —7C 30
Bridle Path, The. Eps —2G 135
Bridlepath Way. Felt —7C 84
Bridle Rd. Clay —8F 118
Bridle Rd. Croy —5L 125
(in two parts)
Bridle Rd. Eps —5D 134
Bridle Rd. Pinn —4F 36
Bridle Rd. S Croy —1E 138
Bridle Rd., The. Purl —2J 137
Bridle Way. Croy —6L 125
Bridle Way. Orp —6A 128
Bridleway Clo. Eps —2G 135
Bridle Way, The. Croy —2J 139
Bridleway, The. Wall —7G 123
Bridlington Rd. N9 —9F 16
Bridlington Rd. Wat —3H 21
Bridport. SE17 —6B 76
(off Date St.)
Bridport Av. Romf —4M 49
Bridport Ho. N1 —4B 60
(off Bridport Pl.)
Bridport Pl. N1 —4B 60
(in two parts)
Bridport Rd. N18 —5C 28
Bridport Rd. Gnfd —4M 53
Bridport Rd. T Hth —7L 107
Bridstow Pl. W2 —9L 57
Brief St. SE5 —9M 75
Brierfield. NW1 —4G 59
(off Arlington Rd.)
Brierley. New Ad —8M 125
(in two parts)
Brierley Av. N9 —1G 29
Brierley Clo. SE25 —8E 108
Brierley Clo. Horn —4G 51
Brierley Ct. W7 —1C 70
Brierley Rd. E11 —9B 46
Brierley Rd. SW12 —8G 91
Brierly Gdns. E2 —5G 61
Brigade Clo. Harr —7B 38
Brigade St. SE3 —1D 94
Brigadier Av. Enf —2A 16
Brigadier Hill. Enf —2A 16
Briggeford Clo. E5 —7E 44
Briggs Clo. Mitc —5F 106
Briggs Ho. E2 —6D 60
(off Chambord St.)
Brighstone Ct. Purf —6M 83
Bright Clo. Belv —5H 81
Brightfield Rd. SE12 —4C 94
Brightling Rd. SE4 —5K 93
Brightlingsea Pl. E14 —1K 77
Brightman Rd. SW18 —7B 90
Brighton Av. E17 —3K 45
Brighton Bldgs. SE1 —4C 76
(off Tower Bri. Rd.)
Brighton Clo. Uxb —3F 142
Brighton Dri. N'holt —2L 53
Brighton Gro. SE14 —9J 77
Brighton Rd. E6 —6L 63
(in two parts)
Brighton Rd. N2 —9A 26
Brighton Rd. N16 —9C 44
Brighton Rd. Coul & Purl —9G 137
Brighton Rd. Purl & S Croy —3L 137
Brighton Rd. S Croy —7A 124
Brighton Rd. Surb —1G 119
Brighton Rd. Sutt —3L 135
Brighton Rd. Wat —2E 8
Brighton Ter. SW9 —3K 91
Brights Av. Rain —7F 66
Brightside Rd. SE13 —5B 94
Brightside, The. Enf —3H 17
Bright St. E14 —9M 61
Brightview Clo. Brick W —2J 5
Brightwell Clo. Croy —3L 123
Brightwell Cres. SW17 —2D 106
Brightwell Rd. Wat —7E 8
Brig M. SE8 —7L 77
Brigstock Ho. SE5 —1A 92
Brigstock Rd. Belv —5M 81
Brigstock Rd. Coul —7F 136
Brigstock Rd. T Hth —9L 107
Brill Pl. NW1 —5H 59
Brim Hill. N2 —2A 42
Brimpsfield Clo. SE2 —4F 80
Brimsdown. —4J 17
Brimsdown Av. Enf —4J 17
Brimsdown Ho. E3 —7M 61
Brimsdown Ind. Est. Brim —4K 17
Brimsdown Ind. Est. Enf —3K 17
Brimstone Clo. Orp —9G 129
Brimstone Ho. E15 —3C 62
(off Victoria St.)
Brindle Ga. Sidc —7C 96
Brindles. Horn —2J 51
Brindles, The. Bans —9K 135
Brindley Clo. Bexh —2L 97
Brindley Clo. Gnfd —4H 55
Brindley St. SE14 —9K 77
Brindley Way. Brom —2E 110
Brindley Way. S'hall —1M 69
Brindwood Rd. E4 —3K 29
Brinkburn Clo. SE2 —5E 80
Brinkburn Clo. Edgw —1M 39
Brinkburn Gdns. Edgw —1L 39
Brinkley Rd. Wor Pk —4F 120
Brinklow Cres. SE18 —8M 79
Brinklow Ho. W2 —8M 57
(off Torquay St.)
Brinkworth Rd. Ilf —1J 47
Brinkworth Way. E9 —2K 61
Brinley Clo. Chesh —4D 6
Brinsdale Rd. NW4 —1H 41
Brinsley Ho. E1 —9G 61
(off Tarling St.)
Brinsley Rd. Harr —9B 22
Brinsley St. E1 —9F 60
Brinsmead Rd. Romf —9L 35
Brinsworth Clo. Twic —7B 86
Brinsworth Ho. Twic —8B 86
Brinton Wlk. SE1 —2M 75
(off Chancel St.)
Brion Pl. E14 —8A 62
Brisbane Av. SW19 —5M 105
Brisbane Ho. W12 —1F 72
(off White City Est.)
Brisbane Rd. E10 —7M 45
Brisbane Rd. W13 —3E 70
Brisbane Rd. Ilf —5M 47
Brisbane St. SE5 —8B 76
Briscoe Clo. E11 —7D 46
Briscoe Rd. SW19 —3B 106
Briscoe Rd. Rain —5G 67
Briset Rd. SE9 —2H 95
Briset St. EC1 —8M 59
Briset Way. N7 —7K 43
Brisson Clo. Esh —7K 117
Bristol Clo. Stanw —5C 144
Bristol Clo. Wall —9J 123
Bristol Ct. Stanw —5C 144
Bristol Gdns. SW15 —6G 89
Bristol Gdns. W9 —7M 57
Bristol Ho. SE11 —4L 75
(off Lambeth Wlk.)
Bristol Ho. Bark —3E 64
(off Margaret Bondfield Av.)
Bristol Ho. Borwd —4L 11
(off Eldon Av.)
Bristol M. W9 —7M 57
Bristol Pk. Rd. E17 —2J 45
Bristol Rd. E7 —2G 63
Bristol Rd. Gnfd —4M 53
Bristol Rd. Mord —9A 106
Briston Gro. N8 —4J 43
Briston M. NW7 —7E 24
Bristow Rd. SE19 —2C 108
Bristow Rd. Bexh —9J 81
Bristow Rd. Croy —6J 123
Bristow Rd. Houn —2A 86
Britain Vis. Cen. —2H 75
(off Regent St.)
Britania Bus. Cen. NW2 —9H 41
Britannia Bri. E14 —9K 61
Britannia Bus. Pk. Wal X —7F 6
Britannia Clo. SW4 —3H 91
Britannia Clo. N'holt —6H 53
Britannia Ct. W Dray —4H 143
Britannia Ga. E16 —2E 78
Britannia Junction. (Junct.) —4F 58
Britannia La. Twic —6A 86
Britannia Rd. E14 —5L 77
Britannia Rd. N12 —3A 26
Britannia Rd. SW6 —8M 73
(in two parts)
Britannia Rd. Ilf —8M 47
Britannia Rd. Surb —2K 119
Britannia Rd. Wal X —7F 6
Britannia Row. N1 —4M 59
Britannia St. WC1 —6K 59
Britannia Wlk. N1 —5B 60
(in two parts)
Britannia Way. NW10 —7M 55
Britannia Way. SW6 —8M 73
(off Britannia Rd.)
Britannia Way. Stanw —6B 144
Britannic Highwalk. EC2 —8B 60
(off Moor La.)
Britannic Tower. EC2 —8B 60
(off Ropemaker St.)
British Gro. W4 —6D 72
British Gro. Pas. W4 —6D 72
British Gro. S. W4 —6D 72
British Legion Rd. E4 —2D 30
British Library. —6H 59
British Mus. —8J 59
British St. E3 —6K 61
British Telecom Cen. EC1 —9A 60
(off Newgate St.)
British Wharf Ind. Est. SE14 —6H 77
Britley Ho. E14 —9K 61
(off Copenhagen Pl.)
Briton Clo. S Croy —3C 138
Briton Cres. S Croy —3C 138
Briton Hill Rd. S Croy —2C 138
Brittain Ho. SE9 —7J 95
Brittain Rd. Dag —8J 49
Brittain Rd. W on T —7H 117
Brittany Point. SE11 —5L 75
Britten Clo. NW11 —6M 41
Britten Clo. Els —8H 11
Britten Ct. E15 —5B 62
Brittenden Clo. Orp —8D 128
Brittenden Pde. Grn St —8D 128
Britten Dri. S'hall —9L 53
Britten St. SW3 —6C 74
Britton Clo. SE6 —6B 94
Britton St. EC1 —7M 59
Brixham Cres. Ruis —6E 36
Brixham Gdns. Ilf —1C 64
Brixham Rd. Well —9H 81
Brixham St. E16 —2L 79
Brixton. —3K 91
Brixton Est. Edgw —9M 23
Brixton Hill. SW2 —6J 91
Brixton Hill Ct. SW2 —4K 91
Brixton Hill Pl. SW2 —6J 91
Brixton Oval. SW9 —3L 91
Brixton Rd. SW9 & SE11 —3L 91
Brixton Rd. Wat —3F 8
Brixton Sta. Rd. SW9 —2L 91
Brixton Water La. SW2 —4K 91
Broad Acre. Brick W —3J 5
Broadbent Clo. N6 —6F 42
Broadbent St. W1 —1F 74
Broadbridge Clo. SE3 —8E 78
Broadbury Ct. N18 —6F 28
Broad Clo. W on T —5H 117
Broad Comn. Est. N16 —6E 44
(off Osbaldeston Rd.)
Broadcoombe. S Croy —9G 125
Broad Ct. WC2 —9J 59
Broadcroft Av. Stan —9H 23
Broadcroft Rd. Orp —2B 128
Broadeaves Clo. S Croy —7C 124
Broadfield. NW6 —2M 57
Broadfield Clo. NW2 —8G 41
Broadfield Clo. Croy —4K 123
Broadfield Clo. Romf —3D 50
Broadfield Ct. Bus H —2C 22
Broadfield Ct. N Har —8M 21
(off Broadfields)
Broadfield Heights. NW7 —4M 23
Broadfield La. NW1 —3J 59
Broadfield Rd. SE6 —6C 94
Broadfields. E Mol —1C 118
Broadfields. Harr —9M 21
Broadfields Av. N21 —8L 15
Broadfields Av. Edgw —4M 23
Broadfields Cen. Edgw —1M 23
Broadfields La. Wat —1F 20
Broadfield Sq. Enf —4F 16
Broadfields Way. NW10 —1D 56
Broadfield Way. Buck H —3G 31
Broadford Ho. E1 —7J 61
(off Commodore St.)
Broadgate. EC2 —8C 60
(off Broadgate Cir.)
Broadgate. Wal A —6M 7
Broadgate Circ. EC2 —8C 60
(off Broadgate)
Broadgate Rd. E16 —9H 63
Broadgates Av. Barn —3M 13
Broadgates Ct. SE11 —6L 75
(off Cleaver St.)
Broadgates Rd. SW18 —7B 90
Broad Green. —2M 123
Broad Grn. Av. Croy —2M 123
Broadhead Strand. NW9 —9D 24
Broadheath Dri. Chst —2K 111
Broadhinton Rd. SW4 —2F 90
Broadhurst. Asht —8J 133
Broadhurst Av. Edgw —4M 23
Broadhurst Av. Ilf —9D 48
Broadhurst Clo. NW6 —2A 58
Broadhurst Clo. Rich —4K 87
Broadhurst Gdns. NW6 —2M 57
Broadhurst Gdns. Chig —4A 32
(in two parts)
Broadhurst Gdns. Ruis —7G 37
Broadhurst Wlk. Rain —2E 66
Broadlands. E17 —1J 45
Broadlands. Hanw —9L 85
Broadlands Av. SW16 —8J 91
Broadlands Av. Enf —5F 16
Broadlands Av. Shep —1A 116
Broadlands Clo. N6 —5E 42
Broadlands Clo. SW16 —8J 91
Broadlands Clo. Enf —5G 17
Broadlands Clo. Wal X —7C 6
Broadlands Ct. Rich —8L 71
(off Kew Gdns. Rd.)
Broadlands Lodge. N6 —5D 42
Broadlands Rd. N6 —5D 42
Broadlands Rd. Brom —1F 110
Broadlands Way. N Mald —1D 120
Broad La. EC2 —8C 60
(in two parts)
Broad La. N8 —3K 43
Broad La. N15 —2D 44
Broad La. Dart —1E 114
Broad La. Hamp —4K 101
Broad Lawn. SE9 —8L 95
Broadlawns Ct. Harr —8D 22
Broadley St. NW8 —8B 58
Broadley Ter. NW1 —7C 58
Broadmayne. SE17 —6B 76
(off Portland St.)
Broadmead. SE6 —9L 93
Broadmead. W14 —5J 73
Broad Mead. Asht —9K 133

Broadmead Av.—Broomcroft Av.

Broadmead Av. Wor Pk —2E 120
Broadmead Clo. Hamp —3L 101
Broadmead Clo. Pinn —7J 21
Broadmead Ct. Wfd G —6E 30
Broadmead Rd. Hay & N'holt —7J 53
Broadmead Rd. Wfd G —6E 30
Broadoak. Sun —3D 100
Broad Oak. Wfd G —5F 30
Broadoak Av. Enf —8D 6
Broad Oak Clo. E4 —5L 29
Broad Oak Clo. Orp —6E 112
Broadoak Clo. S at H —3L 115
Broadoak Ct. SW9 —2L 91
Broadoak Ho. NW6 —4M 57
(off Mortimer Cres.)
Broadoak Rd. Eri —8B 82
Broadoaks. Surb —4M 119
Broadoaks Way. Brom —9D 110
Broad Sanctuary. SW1 —3H 75
Broadstone Ho. SW8 —8K 75
(off Dorset Rd.)
Broadstone Pl. W1 —8E 58
Broadstone Rd. Horn —7E 50
Broad St. Dag —3L 65
Broad St. Tedd —3D 102
Broad St. Av. EC2 —8C 60
Broad St. Mkt. Dag —3L 65
Broad St. Pl. EC2 —8B 60
(off Blomfield St.)
Broadstrood. Lou —2L 19
Broad Vw. NW9 —4L 39
Broadview Rd. SW16 —4H 107
Broadwalk. E18 —1D 46
Broad Wlk. N21 —2K 27
Broad Wlk. NW1 —4E 58
Broad Wlk. SE3 —1G 95
Broad Wlk. W1 —1D 74
Broadwalk. Harr —3L 37
Broad Wlk. Houn —9H 69
Broad Wlk. Orp —5H 129
Broad Wlk. Rich —8K 71
Broadwalk Ct. W8 —2L 73
(off Palace Gdns. Ter.)
Broadwalk Ho. EC2 —7C 60
Broadwalk Ho. SW7 —3A 74
(off Broadwalk Ho.)
Broad Wlk. La. NW11 —5K 41
Broadwalk Shop. Cen. Edgw —6M 23
Broad Wlk., The. W8 —2M 73
Broad Wlk., The. E Mol —8D 102
Broadwalk, The. N'wd —9A 20
Broadwall. SE1 —2L 75
Broadwater Clo. W on T —7E 116
Broadwater Farm Est. N17 —9B 28
Broadwater Gdns. Orp —6M 127
Broadwater Pl. Wey —4C 116
Broadwater Rd. N17 —8C 28
Broadwater Rd. SE28 —4B 80
Broadwater Rd. SW17 —1C 106
Broadwater Rd. N. W on T —7D 116
Broadwater Rd. S. W on T —7D 116
Broadway. E13 —5F 62
Broadway. E15 —3B 62
(in two parts)
Broadway. SW1 —4H 75
Broadway. W7 —2C 70
Broadway. W13 —2E 70
Broadway. Bark —4A 64
Broadway. Bexh —3J 97
Broadway. Rain —7E 66
Broadway. Romf —9E 34
Broadway. Surb —3M 119
Broadway. Swan —1A 130
Broadway Arc. W6 —5G 73
(off Hammersmith B'way.)
Broadway Av. Croy —9B 108
Broadway Av. Twic —5F 86
Broadway Cen., The. W6 —5G 73
Broadway Clo. S Croy —6F 138
Broadway Clo. Wfd G —6F 30
Broadway Ct. SW19 —3L 105
Broadway Ct. Beck —7A 110
Broadway Gdns. Mitc —8C 106
Broadway Gdns. Wfd G —6F 30
Broadway Ho. E8 —4F 60
Broadway Ho. Brom —2B 110
(off Bromley Rd.)
Broadway Mkt. E8 —4F 60
Broadway Mkt. SW17 —1D 106
Broadway Mkt. Ilf —9B 32
(in two parts)
Broadway Mkt. M. E8 —4E 60
Broadway M. N13 —5K 27
Broadway M. N16 —5D 44
Broadway M. N21 —1M 27
Broadway Pde. E4 —6A 30
Broadway Pde. N8 —4J 43
Broadway Pde. Harr —3M 37
Broadway Pde. Hay —2E 68
Broadway Pde. Horn —9F 50
(off Broadway, The)
Broadway Pl. SW19 —3K 105
Broadway Shop. Cen. Bexh —3L 97
Broadway Shop. Mall. SW1 —4H 75
Broadway, The. E4 —6B 30
Broadway, The. N8 —4J 43
Broadway, The. N9 —3E 28
Broadway, The. N11 —5E 26
(off Stanford Rd.)
Broadway, The. N14 —1H 27
(off Southgate Cir.)
Broadway, The. N22 —9L 27
Broadway, The. NW7 —7E 24
(off Colenso Dri.)
Broadway, The. NW7 —5C 24
(Watford Way)
Broadway, The. NW9 —4D 40
Broadway, The. SW14 —1C 88
Broadway, The. SW19 —3K 105
Broadway, The. W3 —3L 71
Broadway, The. W5 —1H 71
Broadway, The. Cheam —8J 121
Broadway, The. Croy —6J 123
Broadway, The. Dag —7K 49
Broadway, The. Gnfd —7A 54
Broadway, The. Horn —9F 50
Broadway, The. N'wd —9E 20
Broadway, The. S'hall —1H 69
Broadway, The. Stan —5G 23
Broadway, The. Sutt —7A 122
Broadway, The. Th Dit —3C 118
Broadway, The. Wat —5G 9
Broadway, The. W'stone —9C 22
Broadway, The. Wemb —8J 39
Broadway, The. Wfd G —6F 30
Broadwell Ct. Houn —9H 69
(off Springwell Rd.)
Broadwick St. W1 —1G 75
Broadwood Av. Ruis —4C 36
Broadwood Ter. W14 —5K 73
(off Warwick Rd.)
Broad Yd. EC1 —7M 59
Brocas Clo. NW3 —3C 58
Brockbridge Ho. SW15 —5D 88
Brockdene Dri. Kes —6H 127
Brockdish Av. Bark —1D 64
Brockenhurst. W Mol —9K 101
Brockenhurst Av. Wor Pk —3C 120
Brockenhurst Gdns. NW7 —5C 24
Brockenhurst Gdns. Ilf —1A 64
Brockenhurst M. N18 —4E 28
Brockenhurst Rd. Croy —2F 124
Brockenhurst Way. SW16 —6H 107
Brocket Clo. Chig —4D 32
Brocket Ho. SW8 —1H 91
Brocket Way. Chig —5C 32
Brockham Clo. SW19 —2K 105
Brockham Cres. New Ad —9B 126
Brockham Dri. SW2 —6K 91
Brockham Dri. Ilf —4M 47
Brockham Ho. NW1 —4G 59
(off Bayham Pl.)
Brockham Ho. SW2 —6K 91
(off Brockham Dri.)
Brockham St. SE1 —4A 76
Brockhurst Clo. Stan —6D 22
Brockill Cres. SE4 —3J 93
Brocklebank Ho. E16 —2L 79
(off Glenister St.)
Brocklebank Ind. Est. SE7 —5E 78
Brocklebank Rd. SE7 —5F 78
Brocklebank Rd. SW18 —6A 90
Brocklehurst St. SE14 —8H 77
Brocklesbury Clo. Wat —4H 9
Brocklesby Rd. SE25 —8F 108
Brockley. —3K 93
Brockley Av. Stan —3J 23
Brockley Clo. Stan —4J 23
Brockley Combe. Wey —6B 116
Brockley Cres. Romf —7A 34
Brockley Cross. SE4 —2J 93
Brockley Cross Bus. Cen. SE4 —2J 93
Brockley Footpath. SE4 —4J 93
(in two parts)
Brockley Footpath. SE15 —3G 93
Brockley Gdns. SE4 —1K 93
Brockley Gro. SE4 —4K 93
Brockley Hall Rd. SE4 —4J 93
Brockley Hill. Stan —1G 23
Brockley M. SE4 —4J 93
Brockley Pk. SE23 —6J 93
Brockley Ri. SE23 —7J 93
Brockley Rd. SE4 —2K 93
Brockley Side. Stan —4J 23
Brockley Vw. SE23 —6J 93
Brockley Way. SE4 —4H 93
Brockman Ri. Brom —1B 110
Brockmer Ho. E1 —1F 76
(off Crowder St.)
Brock Pl. E3 —7M 61
Brock Rd. E13 —8F 62
Brocks Dri. Sutt —5J 121
Brockshot Clo. Bren —6H 71
Brock St. SE15 —2G 93
Brockton Clo. Romf —2D 50
Brockway Clo. E11 —7C 46
Brockweir. E2 —5G 61
(off Cyprus St.)
Brockwell Clo. Orp —9D 112
Brockwell Ct. SW2 —4L 91
Brockwell Ho. SE11 —7K 75
(off Vauxhall St.)
Brockwell Pk. Gdns. SE24 —6L 91
Brodewater Rd. Borwd —4M 11
Brodia Rd. N16 —8C 44
Brodie Ho. SE1 —6D 76
(off Cooper's Rd.)
Brodie Rd. E4 —1A 30
Brodie Rd. Enf —2A 16
Brodie St. SE1 —6D 76
Brodlove La. E1 —1H 77
Brodrick Gro. SE2 —5F 80
Brodrick Rd. SW17 —8C 90
Brograve Gdns. Beck —6M 109
Broken Wharf. EC4 —1A 76
Brokesley St. E3 —6K 61
Broke Wlk. E8 —4D 60
Bromar Rd. SE5 —2C 92
Bromborough Grn. Wat —5G 21
Bromefield. Stan —8G 23
Bromefield Ct. Wal A —6M 7
Bromell's Rd. SW4 —3G 91
Brome Rd. SE9 —2K 95
Bromet Clo. Wat —2D 8
(in two parts)
Bromfelde Rd. SW4 —2H 91
Bromfelde Wlk. SW4 —1H 91
Bromfield St. N1 —4L 59
Bromhall Rd. Dag —2F 64
Bromhead Rd. E1 —9G 61
(off Jubilee St.)
Bromhead St. E1 —9G 61
Bromhedge. SE9 —9K 95
Bromholm Rd. SE2 —4F 80
Bromleigh Clo. Chesh —1E 6
Bromleigh Ct. SE23 —8E 92
Bromleigh Ho. SE1 —4D 76
(off Abbey St.)
Bromley. —6M 61
(Bow)
Bromley. —6E 110
(Chislehurst)
Bromley Av. Brom —4C 110
Bromley Common. —3J 127
Bromley Comn. Brom —8G 111
Bromley Cres. Brom —7D 110
Bromley Cres. Ruis —9D 36
Bromley F.C. —9F 110
Bromley Gdns. Brom —7D 110
Bromley Gro. Brom —6B 110
Bromley Hall Rd. E14 —8A 62
Bromley High St. E3 —6M 61
Bromley Hill. Brom —3C 110
Bromley Ind. Cen. Brom —7H 111
(off Waldo Rd.)
Bromley La. Chst —4A 112
Bromley Mus. —2F 128
Bromley Park. —5C 110
Bromley Pk. Brom —5D 110
Bromley Pl. W1 —8G 59
Bromley Rd. E10 —4M 45
Bromley Rd. E17 —1L 45
Bromley Rd. N17 —8D 28
Bromley Rd. N18 —3B 28
Bromley Rd. SE6 & Brom —7M 93
Bromley Rd. Beck & Short —5M 109
Bromley Rd. Chst —5M 111
Bromley St. E1 —8H 61
Brompton. —4C 74
Brompton Arc. SW1 —3D 74
(off Brompton Rd.)
Brompton Clo. SE20 —6E 108
Brompton Clo. Houn —4K 85
Brompton Dri. Eri —8F 82
Brompton Gro. N2 —2C 42
Brompton Pk. Cres. SW6 —7M 73
Brompton Pl. SW3 —4C 74
Brompton Rd. SW3 & SW1 —5C 74
Brompton Sq. SW3 —4C 74
Brompton Ter. SE18 —9K 79
Bromwich Av. N6 —7E 42
Bromyard Av. W3 —1C 72
Bromyard Ho. SE15 —8F 76
(off Commercial Way)
Bron Ct. NW6 —4L 57
Brondesbury. —3K 57
Brondesbury Ct. NW2 —2H 57
Brondesbury M. NW6 —3L 57
Brondesbury Park. —4J 57
Brondesbury Pk. NW2 & NW6 —2F 56
Brondesbury Rd. NW6 —5K 57
Brondesbury Vs. NW6 —5K 57
Bronhill Ter. N17 —8E 28
Bronsart Rd. SW6 —8J 73
Bronson Rd. SW20 —6H 105
Bronte Clo. E7 —9E 46
Bronte Clo. Eri —8M 81
Bronte Clo. Ilf —2L 47
Bronte Gro. Dart —3K 99
Bronte Ho. N16 —1C 60
Bronte Ho. NW6 —6L 57
(off Cambridge Rd.)
Bronte Ho. SW4 —6G 91
Bronti Clo. SE17 —6A 76
Bronwen Ct. NW8 —6B 58
(off Grove End Rd.)
Bronze Age Way. Belv & Eri —3M 81
Bronze St. SE8 —8L 77
Brook Av. Dag —3M 65
Brook Av. Edgw —6M 23
Brook Av. Wemb —8L 39
Brook Bank. Enf —1F 16
Brookbank Av. W7 —8B 54
Brookbank Rd. SE13 —2L 93
Brook Clo. NW7 —7J 25
Brook Clo. SW17 —8E 90
Brook Clo. SW20 —7F 104
Brook Clo. W5 —2L 71
Brook Clo. Borwd —4M 11
Brook Clo. Eps —1C 134
Brook Clo. Romf —8D 34
Brook Clo. Ruis —5C 36
Brook Clo. Stanw —6D 144
Brook Ct. E11 —8C 46
Brook Ct. E15 —1M 61
(off Clays La.)
Brook Ct. E17 —1J 45
Brook Ct. SE12 —9G 95
Brook Ct. Beck —5K 109
Brook Ct. Edgw —5M 23
Brook Cres. E4 —4L 29
Brook Cres. N9 —4F 28
Brookdale. N11 —4G 27
Brookdale Av. Upm —8L 51
Brookdale Clo. Upm —8M 51
Brookdale Rd. E17 —1L 45
Brookdale Rd. SE6 —6M 93
(in two parts)
Brookdale Rd. Bex —5J 97
Brookdales. NW4 —2J 41
Brookdene Av. Wat —9F 8
Brookdene Dri. N'wd —7D 20
Brookdene Rd. SE18 —5C 80
Brook Dri. SE11 —4L 75
Brook Dri. Harr —2A 38
Brook Dri. Ruis —5C 36
Brooke Av. Harr —8A 38
Brooke Clo. Bush —9A 10
Brooke Ho. SE14 —9J 77
Brookehowse Rd. SE6 —8L 93
Brookend Rd. Sidc —7C 96
Brooke Rd. E5 —8E 44
Brooke Rd. E17 —2A 46
Brooke Rd. N16 —8D 44
Brooker Rd. Wal A —7J 7
(in two parts)
Brookers Clo. Asht —9G 133
Brooke's Ct. WC1 —8L 59
Brooke's Mkt. EC1 —8L 59
(off Dorrington St.)
Brooke St. EC1 —8L 59
Brooke Trad. Est. Horn —5D 50
Brooke Way. Bush —9A 10
Brookfield. N6 —8E 42
Brookfield Av. E17 —2A 46
Brookfield Av. NW7 —6F 24
Brookfield Av. W5 —7H 55
Brookfield Av. Sutt —6C 122
Brookfield Clo. NW7 —6F 24
Brookfield Ct. Chesh —1D 6
Brookfield Ct. Gnfd —6A 54
Brookfield Cres. NW7 —6F 24
Brookfield Cres. Harr —3J 39
Brookfield Gdns. Chesh —1D 6
Brookfield Gdns. Clay —8D 118
Brookfield La. E. Chesh —1D 6
Brookfield La. W. Chesh —1B 6
(in two parts)
Brookfield Pk. NW5 —8F 42
Brookfield Path. Wfd G —6C 30
Brookfield Rd. E9 —2J 61
Brookfield Rd. N9 —3E 28
Brookfield Rd. W4 —3B 72
Brookfields. Enf —6H 17
Brookfields Av. Mitc —9C 106
Brook Gdns. E4 —4M 29
Brook Gdns. SW13 —2D 88
Brook Gdns. King T —5A 104
Brook Ga. W1 —1D 74
Brook Green. —5H 73
Brook Grn. W6 —4H 73
Brookhill Clo. SE18 —6M 79
Brookhill Clo. E Barn —7C 14
Brookhill Rd. SE18 —7M 79
Brookhill Rd. Barn & E Barn —7C 14
Brook Ho. W6 —5G 73
(off Shepherd's Bush Rd.)
Brookhouse Gdns. E4 —4C 30
Brook Houses. NW1 —5G 59
(off Cranleigh St.)
Brook Ind. Est. Hay —2H 69
Brooking Rd. E7 —1E 62
Brookland Clo. NW11 —2L 41
Brookland Gth. NW11 —2L 41
Brookland Hill. NW11 —2M 41
Brookland Ri. NW11 —2L 41
Brooklands. Dart —7J 99
Brooklands App. Romf —2B 50
Brooklands Av. SW19 —8M 89
Brooklands Av. Sidc —8B 96
Brooklands Clo. Romf —2B 50
Brooklands Clo. Sun —5C 100
Brooklands Ct. N21 —7B 16
Brooklands Ct. NW6 —3K 57
Brooklands Ct. King T —8H 103
(off Surbiton Rd.)
Brooklands Ct. Mitc —6B 106
Brooklands Dri. Gnfd —4G 55
Brooklands Gdns. Horn —4G 51
Brooklands La. Romf —2B 50
Brooklands Pk. SE3 —2E 94
Brooklands Pas. SW8 —9H 75
Brooklands Rd. Romf —2B 50
Brooklands Rd. Th Dit —3D 118
Brooklands, The. Iswth —9B 70
Brook La. SE3 —1F 94
Brook La. Bex —5H 97
Brook La. Brom —3E 110
Brook La. Bus. Cen. Bren —6H 71
Brook La. N. Bren —6H 71
(in two parts)
Brooklea Clo. NW9 —8C 24
Brook Lodge. Romf —2B 50
(off Brooklands Rd.)
Brooklyn Av. SE25 —8F 108
Brooklyn Av. Lou —6J 19
Brooklyn Clo. Cars —4C 122
Brooklyn Gro. SE25 —8F 108
Brooklyn Rd. SE25 —8F 108
Brooklyn Rd. Brom —9H 111
Brooklyn Way. W Dray —4H 143
Brookmarsh Ind. Est. SE8 —8M 77
Brook Mead. Eps —8C 120
Brookmead Av. Brom —9K 111
Brookmead Clo. Orp —2F 128
Brookmead Ind. Est. Croy —1G 123
Brook Mdw. N12 —3M 25
Brook Mdw. Clo. Wfd G —6C 30
Brookmead Rd. Croy —1G 123
Brookmead Way. Orp —1F 128
Brook M. WC2 —9H 59
Brook M. N. W2 —1A 74
Brookmill Clo. Wat —9F 8
Brookmill Rd. SE8 —9L 77
Brook Pde. Chig —3M 31
Brook Pk. Dart —8L 99
Brook Pk. Clo. N21 —7M 15
Brook Path. Lou —6J 19
Brook Pl. Barn —7L 13
Brook Ri. Chig —3L 31
Brook Rd. N2 —7C 26
Brook Rd. N8 —2J 43
Brook Rd. N22 —1K 43
Brook Rd. NW2 —7D 40
Brook Rd. Borwd —3L 11
Brook Rd. Buck H —2E 30
Brook Rd. Ilf —4C 48
Brook Rd. Lou —6J 19
Brook Rd. Romf —9D 34
Brook Rd. Surb —4J 119
Brook Rd. Swan —7B 114
Brook Rd. T Hth —8A 108
Brook Rd. Twic —5E 86
Brook Rd. Wal X —7F 6
Brook Rd. S. Bren —7H 71
Brooks Av. E6 —7K 63
Brooksbank St. E9 —2G 61
Brooksby M. N1 —3L 59
Brooksby St. N1 —3L 59
Brooksby's Wlk. E9 —1H 61
Brooks Clo. SE9 —8L 95
Brooks Ct. SW8 —8G 75
Brookscroft. E17 —1M 45
(off Forest Rd.)
Brookscroft. Croy —2K 139
Brookscroft Rd. E17 —8M 29
(in two parts)
Brookshill. Harr —5B 22
Brookshill Av. Harr —5B 22
Brookshill Dri. Harr —5B 22
Brookside. N21 —8K 15
Brookside. Cars —7E 122
Brookside. E Barn —8C 14
Brookside. Horn —3J 51
Brookside. Ilf —6A 32
Brookside. Orp —2D 128
Brookside. Uxb —3D 142
Brookside. Wal A —5L 7
Brookside. Wat —1H 9
Brookside Caravans. Wat —9F 8
Brookside Clo. Barn —8J 13
Brookside Clo. Felt —9E 84
Brookside Clo. Kent —3H 39
Brookside Clo. S Harr —9J 37
Brookside Cres. Wor Pk —3E 120
Brookside Gdns. Enf —1G 17
Brookside Rd. N9 —4F 28
(in two parts)
Brookside Rd. N19 —7G 43
Brookside Rd. NW11 —4J 41
Brookside Rd. Hay —1G 69
Brookside Rd. Wat —9F 8
Brookside S. E Barn —9E 14
Brookside Wlk. N12 —6L 25
Brookside Wlk. NW11 —2J 41
Brookside Way. Croy —1H 125
Brooks La. W4 —7L 71
Brooks M. W1 —1F 74
Brooks Rd. E13 —4E 62
Brooks Rd. W4 —6L 71
Brookstone Ct. SE15 —3F 92
Brook St. N17 —9D 28
Brook St. W1 —1F 74
Brook St. W2 —1B 74
Brook St. Belv & Eri —6M 81
Brook St. King T —6J 103
Brooksville Av. NW6 —4J 57
Brooks Wlk. N3 —1J 41
Brooks Way. St P —6G 113
Brook Va. Eri —9M 81
Brookview Ct. Enf —7C 16
Brookview Rd. SW16 —2G 107
Brookville Rd. SW6 —8K 73
Brook Wlk. N2 —8B 26
Brook Wlk. Edgw —6B 24
Brookway. SE3 —2E 94
Brook Way. Chig —3L 31
Brook Way. Rain —8F 66
Brookwood Av. SW13 —1D 88
Brookwood Clo. Brom —8D 110
Brookwood Ho. SE1 —3M 75
(off Webber St.)
Brookwood Rd. SW18 —7K 89
Brookwood Rd. Houn —1M 85
Broom Av. Orp —6F 112
Broom Clo. Brom —1J 127
Broom Clo. Esh —7M 117
Broom Clo. Tedd —4H 103
Broomcroft Av. N'holt —6G 53

Broome Rd. Hamp —4K 101
Broomer Pl. Chesh —2C 6
Broome Way. SE5 —8B 76
Broomfield. E17 —5K 45
Broomfield. NW1 —3E 58
(off Ferdinand St.)
Broomfield. Sun —5E 100
Broomfield Av. N13 —5K 27
Broomfield Av. Lou —8K 19
Broomfield Clo. Romf —7B 34
Broomfield Ct. SE16 —4E 76
(off Ben Smith Way)
Broomfield Ho. SE17 —5C 76
(off Massinger St.)
Broomfield Ho. Stan —3E 22
(off Stanmore Hill)
Broomfield House Mus. —4J 27
Broomfield La. N13 —4J 27
Broomfield Pl. W13 —2F 70
Broomfield Ride. Oxs —4B 132
Broomfield Ri. Ab L —5B 4
Broomfield Rd. N13 —5J 27
Broomfield Rd. W13 —2F 70
Broomfield Rd. Beck —7J 109
Broomfield Rd. Bexh —4L 97
Broomfield Rd. Rich —9K 71
Broomfield Rd. Romf —5H 49
Broomfield Rd. Surb —3K 119
Broomfield Rd. Tedd —3G 103
Broomfields. Esh —7A 118
Broomfield St. E14 —8L 61
Broom Gdns. Croy —5L 125
Broom Gro. Wat —2E 8
Broomgrove Gdns. Edgw —8L 23
Broomgrove Rd. SW9 —1K 91
Broom Hall. Oxs —6B 132
Broomhall Rd. S Croy —1B 138
Broom Hill. —2D 128
Broomhill Ct. Wfd G —6E 30
Broom Hill Ri. Bexh —4L 97
Broomhill Rd. SW18 —4L 89
Broomhill Rd. Dart —5F 98
Broomhill Rd. Ilf —7E 48
Broomhill Rd. Orp —2E 128
Broomhill Rd. Wfd G —6E 30
(in two parts)
Broomhill Wlk. Wfd G —6D 30
Broomhouse La. SW6 —1L 89
Broomhouse Rd. SW6 —1L 89
Broomleigh. Brom —5E 110
(off Tweedy Rd.)
Broomloan La. Sutt —4L 121
Broom Lock. Tedd —3G 103
Broom Mead. Bexh —5L 97
Broom Pk. Tedd —4H 103
Broom Rd. Croy —5L 125
Broom Rd. Tedd —2F 102
Broomsleigh Bus. Pk. SE26 —2K 109
Broomsleigh St. NW6 —1K 57
Broomstick Hall Rd. Wal A —6L 7
Broom Water. Tedd —3G 103
Broom Water W. Tedd —2G 103
Broom Way. Wey —6C 116
Broomwood Clo. Bex —8B 98
Broomwood Clo. Croy —9H 109
Broomwood Rd. SW11 —5D 90
Broomwood Rd. Orp —6F 112
Broseley Gdns. Romf —4J 35
Broseley Gro. SE26 —2J 109
Broseley Rd. Romf —4J 35
Broster Gdns. SE25 —7D 108
Brougham Ct. Dart —5M 99
(off Hardwick Cres.)
Brougham Rd. E8 —4E 60
Brougham Rd. W3 —9A 56
Brougham St. SW11 —1D 90
Brough Clo. SW8 —8J 75
Brough Clo. King T —2H 103
Broughinge Rd. Borwd —4M 11
Broughton Av. N3 —1J 41
Broughton Av. Rich —9F 86
Broughton Ct. W13 —1F 70
Broughton Dri. SW9 —3L 91
Broughton Gdns. N6 —4G 43
Broughton Rd. SW6 —1M 89
Broughton Rd. W13 —1F 70
Broughton Rd. Orp —4B 128
Broughton Rd. T Hth —1L 123
Broughton St. SW8 —1E 90
Broughton St. Ind. Est. SW11 —1E 90
Brouncker Rd. W3 —3A 72
Brow Clo. Orp —2H 129
Brow Cres. Orp —3G 129
Browells La. Felt —8F 84
Brown Bear Ct. Felt —1H 101
Brown Clo. Wall —9J 123
Browne Clo. Romf —5M 33
Browne Ho. SE8 —8L 77
(off Deptford Chu. St.)
Brownfield Area. E14 —9A 62
(off Brownfield St.)
Brownfield St. E14 —9M 61
Browngraves Rd. Hay —8A 68
Brown Hart Gdns. W1 —1E 74
Brownhill Rd. SE6 —6M 93
Browning Av. W7 —9D 54
Browning Av. Sutt —6C 122
Browning Av. Wor Pk —3F 120
Browning Clo. E17 —2A 46
Browning Clo. W9 —7A 58
Browning Clo. Col R —7K 33
Browning Clo. Hamp —1K 101
Browning Clo. Well —9C 80
Browning M. W1 —8F 58
Browning Rd. E11 —5D 46
Browning Rd. E12 —1K 63
Browning Rd. Dart —3K 99
Browning Rd. Enf —1B 16
Browning St. SE17 —6A 76
Browning Way. Houn —9H 69
Brownlea Gdns. Ilf —7E 48
Brownlow Ct. N2 —3A 42
Brownlow Ct. N11 —6J 27
(off Brownlow Rd.)
Brownlow Ho. SE16 —3E 76
(off George Row)
Brownlow M. WC1 —7K 59
Brownlow Rd. E7 —9E 46
Brownlow Rd. E8 —4D 60
Brownlow Rd. N3 —7M 25
Brownlow Rd. N11 —6J 27
Brownlow Rd. NW10 —3C 56
Brownlow Rd. W13 —2E 70
Brownlow Rd. Borwd —6L 11
Brownlow Rd. Croy —6C 124
Brownlow St. WC1 —8K 59
Browns Arc. W1 —1G 75
(off Regent St.)
Brown's Bldgs. EC3 —9C 60
Browns La. NW5 —1F 58
Brownspring Dri. SE9 —1M 111
Browns Rd. E17 —1L 45
Brown's Rd. Surb —2K 119
Brown St. W1 —9D 58
Brownswell Rd. N2 —9B 26
Brownswood Park. —7M 43
Brownswood Rd. N4 —8M 43
Brow, The. Wat —6F 4
Broxash Rd. SW11 —5E 90
Broxbourne Av. E18 —2F 46
Broxbourne Rd. E7 —8E 46
Broxbourne Rd. Orp —3D 128
Broxhill Cen. Romf —4F 34
Broxhill Rd. Hav —3C 34
Broxholme Ho. SW6 —9M 73
(off Harwood Rd.)
Broxholm Rd. SW16 —9L 91
Broxted Rd. SE23 —8K 93
Broxwood Way. NW8 —4C 58
Bruce Av. Horn —7G 51
Bruce Av. Shep —1A 116
Bruce Castle Ct. N17 —8D 28
(off Lordship La.)
Bruce Castle Mus. —8C 28
Bruce Castle Rd. N17 —8D 28
Bruce Clo. W10 —8H 57
Bruce Clo. Well —9F 80
Bruce Ct. Sidc —1D 112
Bruce Dri. S Croy —1H 139
Bruce Gdns. N20 —3D 26
Bruce Gro. N17 —8C 28
Bruce Gro. Orp —3E 128
Bruce Gro. Wat —2G 9
Bruce Hall M. SW17 —1E 106
Bruce Ho. W10 —8H 57
Bruce Rd. E3 —6M 61
Bruce Rd. NW10 —3B 56
Bruce Rd. SE25 —8B 108
Bruce Rd. Barn —5J 13
Bruce Rd. Harr —9C 22
Bruce Rd. Mitc —4E 106
Bruce Way. Wal X —6D 6
Bruckner St. W10 —6J 57
Brudenell Rd. SW17 —9D 90
Bruffs Mdw. N'holt —2J 53
Bruges Pl. NW1 —3G 59
(off Randolph St.)
Brumfield Rd. Eps —7A 120
Brummel Clo. Bexh —2A 98
Brune Ho. E1 —8D 60
(off Bell La.)
Brunei Gallery. —8H 59
Brunel Clo. SE19 —3D 108
Brunel Clo. Houn —8F 68
Brunel Clo. N'holt —6K 53
Brunel Clo. Romf —2C 50
Brunel Est. W2 —8L 57
Brunel Ho. E14 —6M 77
(off Ship Yd.)
Brunel Pl. S'hall —9M 53
Brunel Rd. E17 —4J 45
Brunel Rd. SE16 —3G 77
Brunel Rd. W3 —8C 56
Brunel Rd. Wfd G —5K 31
Brunel Science Pk. Uxb —6C 142
Brunel St. E16 —9D 62
Brunel Wlk. N15 —2C 44
Brunel Wlk. Twic —6L 85
Brune St. E1 —8D 60
Brunlees Ho. SE1 —4A 76
(off Bath Ter.)
Brunner Clo. NW11 —3M 41
Brunner Ho. SE6 —1A 110
Brunner Rd. E17 —3J 45
Brunner Rd. W5 —7H 55
Bruno Pl. NW9 —7A 40
Brunswick Av. N11 —3E 26
(in two parts)
Brunswick Cen. WC1 —7J 59
Brunswick Clo. Bexh —3H 97
Brunswick Clo. Pinn —4J 37
Brunswick Clo. T Dit —3D 118
Brunswick Clo. Twic —9B 86
Brunswick Clo. W on T —4G 117
Brunswick Clo. Est. EC1 —6M 59
Brunswick Ct. EC1 —6M 59
(off Tompion St.)
Brunswick Ct. SE1 —3C 76
Brunswick Ct. SW1 —5H 75
(off Regency St.)
Brunswick Ct. Barn —7B 14
Brunswick Ct. Sutt —6M 121
Brunswick Cres. N11 —3E 26
Brunswick Gdns. W5 —7J 55
Brunswick Gdns. W8 —2L 73
Brunswick Gdns. Ilf —7A 32
Brunswick Gro. N11 —3E 26
Brunswick Ho. E2 —5D 60
(off Thurtle Rd.)
Brunswick Ho. N3 —8K 25
Brunswick Ind. Pk. N11 —4F 26
Brunswick Mans. WC1 —7J 59
(off Handel St.)
Brunswick M. SW16 —3H 107
Brunswick M. W1 —9D 58
Brunswick Park. —3E 26
Brunswick Pk. SE5 —9C 76
Brunswick Pk. Gdns. N11 —2E 26
Brunswick Pk. Rd. N11 —2E 26
Brunswick Pl. N1 —6B 60
Brunswick Pl. NW1 —7E 58
Brunswick Pl. SE19 —4E 108
Brunswick Quay. SE16 —4H 77
Brunswick Rd. E10 —6A 46
Brunswick Rd. E14 —9A 62
Brunswick Rd. N15 —2C 44
(in two parts)
Brunswick Rd. W5 —7H 55
Brunswick Rd. Bexh —3H 97
Brunswick Rd. Enf —2L 17
Brunswick Rd. King T —5L 103
Brunswick Rd. Sutt —6M 121
Brunswick Sq. N17 —6D 28
Brunswick Sq. WC1 —7J 59
Brunswick St. E17 —3A 46
Brunswick Vs. SE5 —9C 76
Brunswick Way. N11 —4F 26
Brunton Pl. E14 —9J 61
Brushfield St. EC2 —8C 60
(in two parts)
Brushrise. Wat —9F 4
Brussels Rd. SW11 —3B 90
Bruton Clo. Chst —4K 111
Bruton La. W1 —1F 74
Bruton Pl. W1 —1F 74
Bruton Rd. Mord —8A 106
Bruton St. W1 —1F 74
Bruton Way. W13 —8E 54
Brutus Ct. SE11 —5M 75
(off Kennington La.)
Bryan Av. NW10 —3F 56
Bryan Clo. Sun —4E 100
Bryan Ho. SE16 —3K 77
Bryan Rd. SE16 —3K 77
Bryan's All. SW6 —1M 89
Bryanston Av. Twic —7M 85
Bryanston Clo. S'hall —5K 69
Bryanston Ct. W1 —9D 58
(off Seymour Pl., in two parts)
Bryanstone Ct. Sutt —5A 122
Bryanstone Rd. N8 —4H 43
Bryanstone Rd. Wal X —7F 6
Bryanston Mans. W1 —8D 58
(off York St.)
Bryanston M. E. W1 —8D 58
Bryanston M. W. W1 —8D 58
Bryanston Pl. W1 —8D 58
Bryanston Sq. W1 —9D 58
Bryanston St. W1 —9D 58
Bryant Av. Romf —8H 35
Bryant Clo. Barn —7K 13
Bryant Ct. E2 —5D 60
(off Whiston Rd., in two parts)
Bryant Rd. N'holt —6G 53
Bryant Row. Noak H —2G 35
Bryant St. E15 —3B 62
Bryantwood Rd. N7 —1L 59
Brycedale Cres. N14 —4G 27
Bryce Ho. SE14 —7H 77
(off John Williams Clo.)
Bryce Rd. Dag —9G 49
Brydale Ho. SE16 —5H 77
(off Rotherhithe New Rd.)
Bryden Clo. SE26 —2J 109
Brydges Pl. WC2 —1J 75
Brydges Rd. E15 —1B 62
Brydon Wlk. N1 —4J 59
Bryer Ct. EC2 —8A 60
(off Beech St.)
Bryet Rd. N7 —8J 43
Bryher Ct. SE11 —6L 75
(off Sancroft St.)
Brymay Clo. E3 —5L 61
Brynmaer Rd. SW11 —9D 74
Brynmawr Rd. Enf —6D 16
Bryony Clo. Lou —6M 19
Bryony Clo. Uxb —8D 142
Bryony Rd. W12 —1E 72
Bryony Way. Sun —3E 100
Buccleugh Ho. E5 —5E 44
Buchanan Clo. N21 —7K 15
Buchanan Clo. Ave —2M 83
Buchanan Clo. Borwd —4A 12
Buchanan Ct. SE16 —5H 77
(off Worgan St.)
Buchanan Gdns. NW10 —5F 56
Buchan Clo. Uxb —7A 142
Buchan Rd. SE15 —2G 93
Bucharest Rd. SW18 —6A 90
Buckbean Path. Romf —7G 35
Buckden Clo. N2 —2D 42
Buckden Clo. SE12 —5E 94
Buckettsland La. Borwd —2B 12
Buckfast Ct. W13 —1E 70
Buckfast Rd. Mord —8M 105
Buckfast St. E2 —6E 60
Buck Hill Wlk. W2 —1B 74
Buckhold Rd. SW18 —5L 89
Buckhurst Av. Cars —3C 122
Buckhurst Ct. Buck H —2H 31
(off Albert Rd.)
Buckhurst Hill. —2H 31
Buckhurst Hill Ho. Buck H —2F 30
Buckhurst Ho. N7 —1H 59
Buckhurst St. E1 —7F 60
Buckhurst Ter. Buck H —1H 31
Buckhurst Way. Buck H —4H 31
Buckingham Arc. WC2 —1J 75
(off Strand)
Buckingham Av. N20 —9A 14
Buckingham Av. Felt —5F 84
Buckingham Av. Gnfd —4E 54
Buckingham Av. T Hth —5L 107
Buckingham Av. Well —3C 96
Buckingham Av. W Mol —6M 101
Buckingham Chambers. SW1 —5G 75
(off Greencoat Pl.)
Buckingham Clo. W5 —8G 55
Buckingham Clo. Enf —4C 16
Buckingham Clo. Hamp —2K 101
Buckingham Clo. Horn —4H 51
Buckingham Clo. Orp —2C 128
Buckingham Ct. NW4 —1E 40
Buckingham Ct. W7 —7D 54
(off Copley Clo.)
Buckingham Ct. N'holt —5J 53
Buckingham Ct. Sutt —1L 135
Buckingham Dri. Chst —1A 112
Buckingham Gdns. Edgw —7K 23
Buckingham Gdns. T Hth —6L 107
Buckingham Gdns. W Mol —6M 101
Buckingham Ga. SW1 —4G 75
Buckingham Gro. Borwd —6B 12
Buckingham Gro. Uxb —5E 142
Buckingham La. SE23 —6J 93
Buckingham Mans. NW6 —1M 57
(off W. End La.)
Buckingham M. N1 —2C 60
Buckingham M. NW10 —5D 56
Buckingham M. SW1 —4G 75
(off Stafford Pl.)
Buckingham Palace. —3F 74
Buckingham Pal. Rd. SW1 —5F 74
Buckingham Pde. Stan —5G 23
Buckingham Pl. SW1 —4G 75
Buckingham Rd. E10 —8M 45
Buckingham Rd. E11 —3G 47
Buckingham Rd. E15 —1D 62
Buckingham Rd. E18 —8D 30
Buckingham Rd. N1 —2C 60
Buckingham Rd. N22 —8J 27
Buckingham Rd. NW10 —5D 56
Buckingham Rd. Borwd —6B 12
Buckingham Rd. Edgw —7K 23
Buckingham Rd. Hamp —1K 101
Buckingham Rd. Harr —3B 38
Buckingham Rd. Ilf —7B 48
Buckingham Rd. King T —8K 103
Buckingham Rd. Mitc —8J 107
Buckingham Rd. Rich —8H 87
Buckingham Rd. Wat —1G 9
Buckingham St. WC2 —1J 75
Buckingham Way. Wall —1G 137
Buckland Ct. N1 —5C 60
(off St Johns Est.)
Buckland Ct. Ick —7A 36
Buckland Cres. NW3 —3B 58
Buckland Ri. Pinn —8G 21
Buckland Rd. E10 —7A 46
Buckland Rd. Chess —7K 119
Buckland Rd. Orp —6C 128
Buckland Rd. Sutt —2G 135
Bucklands Rd. Tedd —3G 103
Buckland St. N1 —5B 60
Buckland's Wharf. King T —6H 103
Buckland Wlk. W3 —3A 72
Buckland Wlk. Mord —8A 106
Buckland Way. Wor Pk —3G 121
Buck La. NW9 —3B 40
Bucklebury. NW1 —7G 59
(off Stanhope St.)
Buckleigh Av. SW20 —7J 105
Buckleigh Rd. SW16 —3H 107
Buckleigh Way. SE19 —4D 108
Buckler Gdns. SE9 —9K 95
Bucklers All. SW6 —7K 73
(in two parts)
Bucklersbury. EC2 —9B 60
(off Queen Victoria St.)
Bucklersbury Pas. EC2 —9B 60
Buckler's Way. Cars —5D 122
Buckles Ct. Belv —5H 81
Buckle St. E1 —9D 60
Buckles Way. Bans —8J 135
Buckley Clo. Dart —1D 98
Buckley Ct. NW6 —3K 57
Buckley Rd. NW6 —3K 57
Buckmaster Clo. SW9 —2L 91
(off Stockwell Pk. Rd.)
Buckmaster Ho. N7 —9K 43
Buckmaster Rd. SW11 —3C 90
Bucknalls Clo. Wat —5J 5
Bucknalls Dri. Brick W —4K 5
Bucknalls La. Wat —5H 5
Bucknall St. WC1 —9J 59
Bucknall Way. Beck —8M 109
Bucknell Clo. SW9 —3K 91
Buckner Rd. SW2 —3K 91
Bucknill Ho. SW1 —6F 74
(off Ebury Bri. Rd.)
Bucknills Clo. Eps —6A 134
Buckrell Rd. E4 —2B 30
Buckridge Ho. EC1 —8L 59
(off Portpool La.)
Buck's Av. Wat —9J 9
Bucks Cross Rd. Orp —7J 129
Buckstone Clo. SE23 —5G 93
Buckstone Rd. N18 —5E 28
Buck St. NW1 —3F 58
Buckters Rents. SE16 —2J 77
Buckthorne Rd. SE4 —4J 93
Buckthorn Ho. Sidc —9D 96
(off Longlands Rd.)
Buckton Rd. Borwd —2K 11
Buck Wlk. E17 —2B 46
Buckwheat Ct. Eri —4H 81
Budd Clo. N12 —4M 25
Buddings Circ. Wemb —8A 40
Budd's All. Twic —4G 87
Bude Clo. E17 —3K 45
Budge La. Mitc —2D 122
Budge Row. EC4 —1B 76
Budge's Wlk. W2 —2A 74
(off Broad Wlk., The)
Budleigh Cres. Well —9G 81
Budleigh Ho. SE15 —8E 76
(off Bird in Bush Rd.)
Budoch Ct. Ilf —7E 48
Budoch Dri. Ilf —7E 48
Buer Rd. SW6 —1J 89
Buff Av. Bans —6M 135
Bugsby's Way. SE10 & SE7 —5D 78
Bulbarrow. NW8 —4M 57
(off Abbey Rd.)
Bulganak Rd. T Hth —8A 108
Bullace La. Dart —5J 99
Bullace Row. SE5 —9B 76
Bull All. Well —2F 96
Bullard Rd. Tedd —3C 102
Bullard's Pl. E2 —6H 61
Bullbanks Rd. Belv —5A 82
Bulleid Way. SW1 —5F 74
Bullen Ho. E1 —7F 60
(off Collingwood St.)
Bullen St. SW11 —1C 90
Buller Clo. SE15 —8E 76
Buller Rd. N17 —9E 28
Buller Rd. N22 —9L 27
Buller Rd. NW10 —6H 57
Buller Rd. Bark —3C 64
Buller Rd. T Hth —6B 108
Bullers Clo. Sidc —2J 113
Bullers Wood Dri. Chst —4K 111
Bullescroft Rd. Edgw —3L 23
Bullfinch Rd. S Croy —2H 139
Bullhead Rd. Borwd —5A 12
Bull Hill. Hort K —8M 115
Bullingham Mans. W8 —3L 73
(off Pitt St. La.)
Bull Inn Ct. WC2 —1J 75
(off Strand)
Bullivant St. E14 —1A 78
Bull La. N18 —5C 28
Bull La. Chst —4B 112
Bull La. Dag —8M 49
Bull Rd. E15 —5D 62
Bullrush Clo. Croy —1C 124
Bullrush Gro. Uxb —7A 142
Bull's All. SW14 —1B 88
Bull's Bri. Cen. Hay —4F 68
Bull's Bri. Ind. Est. Hay —4E 68
Bullsbridge Rd. S'hall —5G 69
Bullsbrook Rd. Hay —2G 69
Bulls Cross. —8A 6
Bull's Cross. Enf —8A 6
Bulls Cross Ride. Wal X —6A 6
Bulls Gdns. SW3 —5C 74
(in two parts)
Bulls Head Pas. EC3 —9C 60
(off Gracechurch St.)
Bulls Head Yd. Dart —5J 99
(off High St.)
Bullsmoor. —9C 6
Bullsmoor Clo. Wal X —8C 6
Bullsmoor Gdns. Wal X —8B 6
Bullsmoor La. Enf —8A 6
Bullsmoor Ride. Wal X —8C 6
Bullsmoor Way. Wal X —8C 6
Bullwell Cres. Chesh —2E 6
Bull Wharf La. EC4 —1A 76
Bull Yd. SE15 —9E 76
Bulmer Gdns. Harr —5H 39
Bulmer M. W11 —1L 73
Bulmer Pl. W11 —2L 73
Bulmer Wlk. Rain —5G 67
Bulow Est. SW6 —9M 73
(off Pearscroft Rd.)
Bulstrode Av. Houn —1K 85
Bulstrode Gdns. Houn —2L 85
Bulstrode Pl. W1 —8E 58
Bulstrode Rd. Houn —2L 85
Bulstrode St. W1 —9E 58

Bulwer Ct.—Buttercup Clo.

Bulwer Ct. E11 —6B 46
Bulwer Ct. Rd. E11 —6B 46
Bulwer Gdns. Barn —6A 14
Bulwer Rd. E11 —5B 46
Bulwer Rd. N18 —4C 28
Bulwer Rd. Barn —6M 13
Bulwer St. W12 —2G 73
Bunbury Ho. SE15 —8E 76
(off Fenham Rd.)
Bunbury Way. Eps —8F 134
Bunce's La. Wfd G —7D 30
Bungalow Rd. SE25 —8C 108
Bungalows, The. E10 —4A 46
Bungalows, The. SW16 —4F 106
Bungalows, The. Ilf —8C 32
Bungalows, The. Wall —7F 122
Bunhill Row. EC1 —7B 60
Bunhouse Pl. SW1 —6E 74
Bunkers Hill. NW11 —5A 42
Bunkers Hill. Belv —5L 81
Bunkers Hill. Sidc —9K 97
Bunning Way. N7 —3J 59
Bunns La. NW7 —6C 24
(in two parts)
Bunsen Ho. E3 —5J 61
(off Grove Rd.)
Bunsen St. E3 —5J 61
Buntingbridge Rd. Ilf —3B 48
Bunting Clo. N9 —1H 29
Bunting Clo. Mitc —9D 106
Bunting Ct. NW9 —9C 24
Bunton St. SE18 —4L 79
Bunyan Ct. EC2 —8A 60
(off Beech St.)
Bunyan Rd. E17 —1J 45
Buonaparte M. SW1 —6H 75
Burbage Clo. SE1 —4B 76
Burbage Clo. Chesh —4F 6
Burbage Clo. Hay —9B 52
Burbage Ho. N1 —4B 60
(off Poole St.)
Burbage Ho. SE14 —7H 77
(off Samuel Clo.)
Burbage Rd. SE24 & SE21 —5A 92
Burberry Clo. N Mald —6C 104
Burbridge Way. N17 —9E 28
Burcham St. E14 —9M 61
Burcharbro Rd. SE2 —7H 81
Burchell Ct. Bush —9A 10
Burchell Ho. SE11 —6K 75
(off Jonathan St.)
Burchell Rd. E10 —6M 45
Burchell Rd. SE15 —9F 76
Burchetts Way. Shep —1A 116
Burchett Way. Romf —4K 49
Burchwall Clo. Romf —7A 34
Burcote. Wey —8B 116
Burcote Rd. SW18 —6B 90
Burcott Rd. Purl —6L 137
Burden Clo. Bren —6G 71
Burden Ho. SW8 —8J 75
(off Thorncroft St.)
Burdenshott Av. Rich —3M 87
Burden Way. E11 —7F 46
Burder Clo. N1 —2C 60
Burder Rd. N1 —2C 60
Burdett Av. SW20 —5E 104
Burdett Clo. W7 —2D 70
Burdett Clo. Sidc —2J 113
Burdett M. NW3 —2B 58
Burdett M. W2 —9M 57
Burdett Rd. E3 & E14 —7J 61
Burdett Rd. Croy —1B 124
Burdett Rd. Rich —1K 87
Burdetts Rd. Dag —4K 65
Burdock Clo. Croy —3H 125
Burdock Rd. N17 —1E 44
Burdon La. Sutt —9J 121
Burdon Pk. Sutt —1K 135
Bure Ct. New Bar —7M 13
Burfield Clo. SW17 —1B 106
Burford Clo. Dag —8G 49
Burford Clo. Ilf —2A 48
Burford Gdns. N13 —3K 27
Burford Ho. Bren —6H 71
Burford Ho. Eps —3G 135
Burford La. Eps —3G 135
Burford Rd. E6 —6J 63
Burford Rd. E15 —4B 62
Burford Rd. SE6 —8K 93
Burford Rd. Bren —6J 71
Burford Rd. Brom —8J 111
Burford Rd. Sutt —4L 121
Burford Rd. Wor Pk —2D 120
Burford Wlk. SW6 —8A 74
Burford Way. New Ad —8A 126
Burgate Clo. Dart —2D 98
Burge Rd. E7 —9H 47
Burges Clo. Horn —4K 51
Burges Gro. SW13 —8F 72
Burges Rd. E6 —3J 63
Burgess Av. NW9 —4B 40
Burgess Clo. Felt —1J 101
Burgess Ct. E6 —3L 63
Burgess Ct. Borwd —2K 11
Burgess Ct. S'hall —9M 53
(off Fleming Rd.)
Burgess Hill. NW2 —9L 41
Burgess Ind. Pk. SE5 —8B 76
Burgess M. SW19 —3M 105
Burgess Pk. —7C 76
Burgess Rd. E6 —3L 63
Burgess Rd. E15 —9C 46
Burgess Rd. Sutt —6M 121
Burgess St. E14 —8L 61
Burge St. SE1 —4B 76
Burgh Cft. Eps —7D 134
Burghfield. Eps —7D 134
Burgh Heath Rd. Eps —6D 134
Burghill Rd. SE26 —1J 109
Burghley Av. Borwd —7A 12
Burghley Av. N Mald —7H 104
Burghley Hall Clo. SW19 —7J 89
Burghley Pl. Mitc —9D 106
Burghley Rd. E11 —6C 46
Burghley Rd. N8 —1L 43
Burghley Rd. NW5 —9F 42
Burghley Rd. SW19 —1H 105
Burghley Tower. W3 —1D 72
Burgh Mt. Bans —7K 135
Burgh St. N1 —5M 59
Burgh Wood. Bans —7J 135
Burgoine Quay. King T —5H 103
Burgon St. EC4 —9M 59
Burgos Clo. Croy —8L 123
Burgos Gro. SE10 —9M 77
Burgoyne Rd. N4 —4M 43
Burgoyne Rd. SE25 —8D 108
Burgoyne Rd. SW9 —2K 91
Burgoyne Rd. Sun —3D 100
Burham Clo. SE20 —4G 109
Burhill Gro. Pinn —9J 21
Burhill Rd. W on T —9F 116
Burke Clo. SW15 —3C 88
Burke Lodge. E13 —6F 62
Burke St. E16 —8D 62
Burket Clo. S'hall —5J 69
Burland Rd. SW11 —4D 90
Burland Rd. Romf —6A 34
Burlea Clo. W on T —7F 116
Burleigh Av. Sidc —4D 96
Burleigh Av. Wall —5E 122
Burleigh Gdns. N14 —1G 27
Burleigh Gdns. Ashf —2A 100
Burleigh Ho. SW3 —7B 74
(off Beaufort St.)
Burleigh Ho. W10 —8J 57
(off St Charles Sq.)
Burleigh Pde. N14 —1H 27
Burleigh Pl. SW15 —4H 89
Burleigh Rd. Chesh —5E 6
Burleigh Rd. Enf —6C 16
Burleigh Rd. Sutt —3J 121
Burleigh Rd. Uxb —4F 142
Burleigh St. WC2 —1K 75
Burleigh Wlk. SE6 —7A 94
Burleigh Way. Enf —5B 16
Burley Clo. E4 —5L 29
Burley Clo. SW16 —6H 107
Burley Ho. E1 —9H 61
(off Chudleigh St.)
Burley Rd. E16 —9G 63
Burlington Arc. W1 —1G 75
Burlington Av. Rich —9L 71
Burlington Av. Romf —4M 49
Burlington Clo. E6 —9J 63
Burlington Clo. W9 —7L 57
Burlington Clo. Felt —6B 84
Burlington Clo. Orp —4M 127
Burlington Clo. Pinn —1F 36
Burlington Gdns. SW6 —1J 89
Burlington Gdns. W1 —1G 75
Burlington Gdns. W3 —2A 72
Burlington Gdns. W4 —6A 72
Burlington Gdns. Romf —5J 49
Burlington La. W4 —8A 72
Burlington M. SW15 —4K 89
Burlington M. W3 —2A 72
Burlington Pl. SW6 —1J 89
Burlington Pl. Wfd G —3F 30
Burlington Ri. E Barn —1C 26
Burlington Rd. N10 —1E 42
Burlington Rd. N17 —8E 28
Burlington Rd. SW6 —1J 89
Burlington Rd. W4 —6A 72
Burlington Rd. Enf —3B 16
Burlington Rd. Iswth —9B 70
Burlington Rd. N Mald —8D 104
Burlington Rd. T Hth —6A 108
Burma M. N16 —9B 44
Burman Clo. Dart —6M 99
Burma Rd. N16 —9B 44
Burmarsh Ct. SE20 —5G 109
Burma Ter. SE19 —2C 108
Burmester Rd. SW17 —9A 90
Burnaby Cres. W4 —7A 72
Burnaby Gdns. W4 —7M 71
Burnaby St. SW10 —8A 74
Burnand Ho. W14 —4H 73
(off Redan St.)
Burnard Pl. N7 —1K 59
Burnaston Ho. E5 —8E 44
Burnbrae Clo. N12 —6M 25
Burnbury Rd. SW12 —7G 91
Burn Clo. Bush —5B 10
Burn Clo. Oxs —7B 132
Burncroft Av. Enf —4G 17
Burndell Way. Hay —8H 53
Burne Jones Ho. W14 —5J 73
(off N. End Rd.)
Burnell Av. Rich —2G 103
Burnell Av. Well —1E 96
Burnell Gdns. Stan —9H 23
Burnell Rd. Sutt —6M 121
Burnell Wlk. SE1 —6D 76
(off Abingdon Clo.)
Burnels Av. E6 —6L 63
Burness Clo. N7 —2K 59
Burness Clo. Uxb —5B 142
Burne St. NW1 —8C 58
Burnet Gro. Eps —5A 134
Burnett Clo. E9 —1G 61
Burnett Ho. SE13 —1A 94
(off Lewisham Hill)
Burnett Rd. Eri —7H 83
Burney Av. Surb —9K 103
Burney Dri. Lou —4M 19
(in two parts)
Burney St. SE10 —8A 78
Burnfoot Av. SW6 —9J 73
Burnham. NW3 —3C 58
Burnham Av. Uxb —9A 36
Burnham Clo. NW7 —7E 24
Burnham Clo. SE1 —5D 76
Burnham Clo. Enf —2C 16
Burnham Clo. W'stone —2E 38
Burnham Ct. W2 —1M 73
(off Moscow Rd.)
Burnham Cres. E11 —2G 47
Burnham Cres. Dart —3G 99
Burnham Dri. Wor Pk —4H 121
Burnham Est. E2 —6G 61
(off Burnham St.)
Burnham Gdns. Croy —2D 124
Burnham Gdns. Hay —4B 68
Burnham Gdns. Houn —9F 68
Burnham Rd. E4 —5K 29
Burnham Rd. Dag —3F 64
Burnham Rd. Dart —3G 99
Burnham Rd. Mord —8M 105
Burnham Rd. Romf —1B 50
Burnham Rd. Sidc —8J 97
Burnham St. E2 —6G 61
Burnham St. King T —5L 103
Burnham Ter. Dart —4H 99
Burnham Trad. Est. Dart —3H 99
Burnham Way. SE26 —2K 109
Burnham Way. W13 —5F 70
Burnhill Rd. Beck —6L 109
Burnley Clo. Wat —5G 21
Burnley Rd. NW10 —1D 56
Burnley Rd. SW9 —1K 91
Burnsall St. SW3 —6C 74
Burns Av. Chad H —5G 49
Burns Av. Felt —5E 84
Burns Av. Sidc —5F 96
Burns Av. S'hall —1L 69
Burns Clo. E17 —2A 46
Burns Clo. SW19 —3B 106
Burns Clo. Cars —1E 136
Burns Clo. Eri —9D 82
Burns Clo. Hay —8D 52
Burns Clo. Well —9D 80
Burns Dri. Bans —6J 135
Burns Ho. E2 —6G 61
(off Cornwall Av.)
Burns Ho. SE17 —6M 75
(off Doddington Gro.)
Burn Side. N9 —3G 29
Burnside. Asht —9K 133
Burnside Av. E4 —6K 29
Burnside Clo. SE16 —2H 77
Burnside Clo. Barn —5L 13
Burnside Clo. Twic —5E 86
Burnside Cres. Wemb —4H 55
Burnside Ind. Est. Ilf —5F 32
Burnside Rd. Dag —7G 49
Burns Rd. NW10 —4D 56
Burns Rd. SW11 —1D 90
Burns Rd. W13 —3F 70
Burns Rd. Wemb —5J 55
Burns Way. Houn —1H 85
Burnt Ash Hill. SE12 —5D 94
(in two parts)
Burnt Ash La. Brom —4E 110
Burnt Ash Rd. SE12 —4D 94
Burnt Ho. La. Dart —1J 115
(in two parts)
Burnthwaite Rd. SW6 —8K 73
Burnt Oak. —8A 24
Burnt Oak B'way. Edgw —7M 23
Burnt Oak Fields. Edgw —8A 24
Burnt Oak La. Sidc —5E 96
Burntwood Av. Horn —4H 51
Burntwood Clo. SW18 —7C 90
Burntwood Grange Rd. SW18 —7B 90
Burntwood La. SW17 —9A 90
Burntwood Vw. SE19 —2D 108
Burnway. Horn —5J 51
Buross St. E1 —9F 60
Burpham Clo. Hay —8H 53
Burrage Ct. SE16 —5H 77
(off Worgan St.)
Burrage Gro. SE18 —5A 80
Burrage Pl. SE18 —6M 79
Burrage Rd. SE18 —7A 80
Burrard Rd. E16 —9F 62
Burrard Rd. NW6 —1L 57
Burr Bank Ter. Wilm —1G 115
Burr Clo. E1 —2E 76
Burr Clo. Bexh —2K 97
Burrell Clo. Croy —1J 125
Burrell Clo. Edgw —2M 23
Burrell Row. Beck —6L 109
Burrell St. SE1 —2M 75
Burrells Wharf Sq. E14 —6M 77
Burrell Towers. E10 —5L 45
Burrfield Dri. Orp —9H 113
Burrhill Ct. SE16 —4H 77
(off Worgan St.)
Burritt Rd. King T —6L 103
Burroughs Cotts. E14 —8J 61
(off Halley St.)
Burroughs Gdns. NW4 —2F 40
Burroughs Pde. NW4 —2F 40
Burroughs, The. NW4 —2F 40
Burrow Clo. Chig —5D 32
Burrow Grn. Chig —5D 32
Burrow Ho. SW9 —1L 91
(off Stockwell Pk. Rd.)
Burrow Rd. SE22 —3C 92
Burrow Rd. Chig —5D 32
Burrows Hill Clo. H'row —2A 144
Burrows Hill La. H'row A —3A 144
Burrows M. SE1 —3M 75
Burrows Rd. NW10 —6G 57
Burrow Wlk. SE21 —6A 92
Burr Rd. SW18 —7L 89
Bursar St. SE1 —2C 76
(off Tooley St.)
Bursdon Clo. Sidc —8D 96
Bursland Rd. Enf —6H 17
Burslem Av. Ilf —6E 32
Burslem St. E1 —9E 60
Burstock Rd. SW15 —3J 89
Burston Dri. Park —1M 5
Burston Rd. SW15 —4H 89
Burstow Rd. SW20 —5J 105
Burtenshaw Rd. Th Dit —2E 118
Burtley Clo. N4 —6A 44
Burton Av. Wat —6E 8
Burton Bank. N1 —3B 60
(off Yeate St.)
Burton Clo. Chess —9H 119
Burton Clo. T Hth —7B 108
Burton Ct. SE20 —6G 109
Burton Ct. SW3 —6D 74
(off Turks Row, in two parts)
Burton Dri. Enf —1L 17
Burton Gdns. Houn —9K 69
Burton Gro. SE17 —6B 76
Burtonhole Clo. NW7 —4H 25
Burtonhole La. NW7 —5G 25
(in two parts)
Burton Ho. SE16 —3F 76
(off Cherry Garden St.)
Burton La. SW9 —1L 91
(in two parts)
Burton M. SW1 —5E 74
Burton Pl. WC1 —7H 59
Burton Rd. E18 —1F 46
Burton Rd. NW6 —3K 57
Burton Rd. SW9 —1M 91
(Akerman Rd.)
Burton Rd. SW9 —1L 91
(Brixton Rd.)
Burton Rd. King T —4J 103
Burton's Rd. Hamp H —1M 101
Burton St. WC1 —6H 59
Burtonwood Ho. N4 —5B 44
Burt Rd. E16 —2G 79
Burtt Ho. N1 —6C 60
(off Aske St.)
Burtwell La. SE27 —1B 108
Burvale Ct. Wat —5F 8
Burwash Ct. St M —9G 113
Burwash Ho. SE1 —3B 76
(off Kipling Est.)
Burwash Rd. SE18 —6B 80
Burwell. King T —6L 103
(off Excelsior Rd.)
Burwell Av. Gnfd —2C 54
Burwell Clo. E1 —9F 60
Burwell Rd. E10 —6J 45
Burwell Rd. Ind. Est. E10 —6J 45
Burwell Wlk. E3 —7L 61
Burwood Av. Brom —4F 126
Burwood Av. Kenl —6M 137
Burwood Av. Pinn —3F 36
Burwood Clo. Surb —3L 119
Burwood Clo. W on T —8G 117
Burwood Gdns. Rain —6D 66
Burwood Ho. SW9 —3M 91
Burwood Park. —7D 116
Burwood Pk. Rd. W on T —6F 116
Burwood Pl. W2 —9C 58
Burwood Rd. W on T —9C 116
Bury Av. Hay —5C 52
Bury Av. Ruis —4A 36
Bury Clo. SE16 —2H 77
Bury Ct. EC3 —9C 60
Bury Green. —4A 6
Bury Grn. Rd. Chesh —4A 6
(in two parts)
Bury Gro. Mord —9M 105
Bury Hall Vs. N9 —9D 16
Bury Pl. WC1 —8J 59
Bury Rd. E4 —5B 18
Bury Rd. N22 —9L 27
Bury Rd. Dag —1M 65
Bury St. EC3 —9C 60
Bury St. N9 —9D 16
Bury St. SW1 —2G 75
Bury St. Ruis —3A 36
Bury St. W. N9 —9B 16
Bury Wlk. SW3 —5C 74
Busbridge Ho. E14 —8L 61
(off Brabazon St.)
Busby M. NW5 —2H 59
Busby Pl. NW5 —2H 59
Busch Clo. Iswth —9F 70
Bushbaby Clo. SE1 —4C 76
Bushbarns. Chesh —2A 6
Bushberry Rd. E9 —2J 61
Bush Clo. Ilf —3B 48
Bush Cotts. SW18 —4L 89
Bush Ct. N14 —1H 27
Bush Ct. W12 —3H 73
Bushell Clo. SW2 —8K 91
Bushell Grn. Bus H —2B 22
Bushell St. E1 —2E 76
Bushell Way. Chst —2L 111
Bush Elms Rd. Horn —5E 50
Bushey. —9M 9
Bushey Av. E18 —1D 46
Bushey Av. Orp —2B 128
Bushey Clo. E4 —3A 30
Bushey Clo. Kenl —8D 138
Bushey Ct. SW20 —7F 104
Bushey Down. SW12 —8F 90
Bushey Gro. Rd. Bush —6H 9
Bushey Hall Dri. Bush —6J 9
Bushey Hall Mobile Home Pk. Bush —5J 9
Bushey Hall Rd. Bush —6H 9
Bushey Heath. —1B 22
Bushey Hill Rd. SE5 —9C 76
Bushey La. Sutt —6L 121
Bushey Mead. —6H 105
Bushey Mill Cres. Wat —1G 9
Bushey Mill La. Wat —1G 9
Bushey Rd. E13 —5G 63
Bushey Rd. N15 —4C 44
Bushey Rd. SW20 —7F 104
Bushey Rd. Croy —4L 125
Bushey Rd. Hay —5C 68
Bushey Rd. Sutt —6L 121
Bushey Shaw. Asht —9F 132
Bushey Vw. Wlk. Wat —4H 9
Bushey Way. Beck —1B 126
Bush Fair Ct. N14 —8F 14
Bushfield Clo. Edgw —2M 23
Bushfield Cres. Edgw —2M 23
Bushfields. Lou —7L 19
Bush Gro. NW9 —5A 40
Bush Gro. Stan —8H 23
Bushgrove Rd. Dag —9H 49
Bush Hill. N21 —9A 16
Bush Hill Pde. N9 —9B 16
Bush Hill Park. —8D 16
Bush Hill Rd. N21 —8B 16
Bush Hill Rd. Harr —4K 39
Bush Ind. Est. N19 —8G 43
Bush Ind. Est. NW10 —7B 56
Bush La. EC4 —1B 76
Bushmead Clo. N15 —2D 44
Bushmoor Cres. SE18 —8M 79
Bushnell Rd. SW17 —8F 90
Bush Rd. E8 —4F 60
Bush Rd. E11 —5D 46
Bush Rd. SE8 —5H 77
Bush Rd. Buck H —4H 31
Bush Rd. Rich —7K 71
Bushway. Dag —9H 49
Bushwood. E11 —6D 46
Bushwood Dri. SE1 —5D 76
Bushwood Rd. Rich —7L 71
Bushy Ct. King T —5G 103
(off Up. Teddington Rd.)
Bushy Lees. Sidc —5D 96
Bushy Pk. Gdns. Tedd —2B 102
Bushy Pk. Rd. Tedd —4F 102
(in two parts)
Bushy Rd. Tedd —3D 102
Business Cen., The. Romf —7H 35
Business Innovation Cen. Enf —9F 6
Butcher Row. E14 & E1 —1H 77
Butchers Rd. E16 —9E 62
Bute Av. Rich —8J 87
Bute Ct. Wall —7G 123
Bute Gdns. W6 —5H 73
Bute Gdns. Rich —7J 87
Bute Gdns. Wall —7G 123
Bute Gdns. W. Wall —7G 123
Bute Rd. Croy —3L 123
Bute Rd. Ilf —3M 47
Bute Rd. Wall —6G 123
Bute St. SW7 —5B 74
Bute Wlk. N1 —2B 60
Butfield Ho. E9 —2G 61
(off Stevens Av.)
Butler Av. Harr —5B 38
Butler Ct. Wemb —9E 38
Butler Ho. E2 —6G 61
(off Bacton St.)
Butler Ho. E14 —9K 61
(off Burdett St.)
Butler Ho. SW9 —9M 75
(off Lothian Rd.)
Butler Pl. SW1 —4H 75
(off Palmer St.)
Butler Rd. NW10 —3D 56
Butler Rd. Dag —9F 48
Butler Rd. Harr —5A 38
Butlers & Colonial Wharf. SE1 —3D 76
(off Shad Thames)
Butlers Dri. E4 —2A 18
Butler St. E2 —6G 61
Butler St. Uxb —7F 142
Butlers Wharf. SE1 —2D 76
(off Gainsford St.)
Butley Ct. E3 —5J 61
(off Ford St.)
Buttercup Clo. Romf —8H 35

Buttercup Sq. Stanw —7B 144
Butterfield Clo. N17 —6A 28
Butterfield Clo. SE16 —3F 76
Butterfield Clo. Twic —5D 86
Butterfields. E17 —3A 46
Butterfield Sq. E6 —9K 63
Butterfly La. SE9 —5M 95
Butterfly La. Els —5E 10
Butterfly Wlk. SE5 —1B 92
(off Denmark Hill)
Butter Hill. Cars —5E 122
Butteridges Clo. Dag —4K 65
Butterly Av. Dart —8K 99
Buttermere. NW1 —6F 58
(off Augustus St.)
Buttermere Clo. E15 —9B 46
Buttermere Clo. SE1 —5D 76
Buttermere Clo. Felt —7D 84
Buttermere Clo. Mord —1H 121
Buttermere Ct. NW8 —4B 58
(off Boundary Rd.)
Buttermere Dri. SW15 —4J 89
Buttermere Gdns. Purl —5B 138
Buttermere Pl. Wat —6E 4
Buttermere Rd. Orp —8H 113
Buttermere Wlk. E8 —2D 60
Butterwick. W6 —5H 73
Butterwick. Wat —9J 5
Butterworth Gdns. Wfd G —6E 30
Buttesland St. N1 —6B 60
Buttfield Clo. Dag —2M 65
Buttmarsh Clo. SE18 —6M 79
Button St. Swan —6G 115
Buttsbury Rd. Ilf —1A 64
(in two parts)
Butts Cotts. Felt —9J 85
Butts Cres. Hanw —9L 85
Butts Grn. Rd. Horn —4H 51
Buttsmead. N'wd —7A 20
Butts Piece. N'holt —5F 52
Butts Rd. Brom —2C 110
Butts, The. Bren —7G 71
Butts, The. Sun —7G 101
Buxhall Cres. E9 —2K 61
Buxted Rd. E8 —3D 60
Buxted Rd. N12 —5C 26
Buxted Rd. SE22 —3C 92
Buxton Clo. Wfd G —6H 31
Buxton Ct. N1 —6A 60
(off Thoresby St.)
Buxton Cres. Sutt —6J 121
Buxton Dri. E11 —2C 46
Buxton Dri. N Mald —6B 104
Buxton Gdns. W3 —1M 71
Buxton Ho. E11 —2C 46
Buxton Path. Wat —3G 21
Buxton Rd. E4 —9B 18
Buxton Rd. E6 —6J 63
Buxton Rd. E15 —1C 62
Buxton Rd. E17 —2J 45
Buxton Rd. N19 —6H 43
Buxton Rd. NW2 —2F 56
Buxton Rd. SW14 —2C 88
Buxton Rd. Eri —8B 82
Buxton Rd. Ilf —4C 48
Buxton Rd. T Hth —9M 107
Buxton St. E1 —7D 60
Buzzard Creek Ind. Est. Bark —8E 64
Byam St. SW6 —1A 90
Byards Ct. SE16 —5H 77
(off Worgan St.)
Byards Cft. SW16 —5H 107
Byatt Wlk. Hamp —3J 101
Bychurch End. Tedd —2D 102
Bycroft Rd. S'hall —7L 53
Bycroft St. SE20 —4H 109
Bycullah Av. Enf —5M 15
Bycullah Rd. Enf —4M 15
Byegrove Rd. SW19 —3B 106
Byelands Clo. SE16 —2H 77
Bye, The. W3 —9C 56
Byewaters. Wat —8A 8
Byeways. Twic —9M 85
Byeways, The. Surb —9L 103
Byeway, The. SW14 —2A 88
Bye Way, The. Harr —8C 22
Byfeld Gdns. SW13 —9E 72
Byfield Clo. SE16 —3K 77
Byfield Pas. Iswth —2E 86
Byfield Rd. Iswth —2E 86
Byfleet Ind. Est. Crox G —1A 20
Byford Clo. E15 —3C 62
Byford Ho. Barn —6H 13
Bygrove. New Ad —8L 125
Bygrove St. E14 —9M 61
(in two parts)
Byland Clo. N21 —9K 15
Bylands Clo. SE2 —4F 80
Byne Rd. SE26 —3G 109
Byne Rd. Cars —4C 122
Bynes Rd. S Croy —9B 124
Byng Pl. WC1 —7H 59
Byng Rd. Barn —4H 13
Byng St. E14 —3L 77
Byron Av. Bexh —2K 97
Byre Rd. N14 —8F 14
Byrne Rd. SW12 —7F 90
Byron Av. E12 —2J 63
Byron Av. E18 —1D 46
Byron Av. NW9 —2M 39
Byron Av. Borwd —7L 11
Byron Av. Coul —7J 137
Byron Av. Houn —1E 84
Byron Av. N Mald —9E 104
Byron Av. Sutt —6B 122
Byron Av. Wat —3H 9
Byron Av. E. Sutt —6B 122
Byron Clo. E8 —4E 60
Byron Clo. SE20 —7F 108
Byron Clo. SE26 —1J 109
Byron Clo. SE28 —2G 81
Byron Clo. SW16 —3J 107
Byron Clo. Hamp —1K 101
Byron Clo. W on T —3J 117
Byron Ct. E11 —2F 46
(off Makepeace Rd.)
Byron Ct. NW6 —3A 58
(off Fairfax Rd.)
Byron Ct. W7 —5E 70
(off Boston Rd.)
Byron Ct. W9 —7L 57
(off Lanhill Rd.)
Byron Ct. WC1 —7K 59
(off Mecklenburgh Sq.)
Byron Ct. Chesh —1B 6
Byron Ct. Enf —4M 15
Byron Ct. Harr —4C 38
Byron Dri. N2 —4B 42
Byron Dri. Eri —8M 81
Byron Gdns. Sutt —6B 122
Byron Hill Rd. Harr —6B 38
Byron Ho. Dart —4C 98
Byron Mans. Upm —8M 51
Byron M. NW3 —1D 58
Byron M. W9 —7L 57
Byron Pde. Uxb —7A 52
Byron Rd. E10 —6M 45
Byron Rd. E17 —1L 45
Byron Rd. NW2 —7F 40
Byron Rd. NW7 —5E 24
Byron Rd. W5 —2K 71
Byron Rd. Dart —3M 99
Byron Rd. Harr —4C 38
Byron Rd. S Croy —2F 138
Byron Rd. W'stone —9D 22
Byron Rd. Wemb —7G 39
Byron St. E14 —9A 62
Byron Ter. N9 —8G 17
Byron Way. Hay —7D 52
Byron Way. N'holt —6J 53
Byron Way. Romf —8G 35
Byron Way. W Dray —5K 143
Bysouth Clo. N15 —2B 44
Bysouth Clo. Ilf —8M 31
By the Wood. Wat —2H 21
Bythorn St. SW9 —2K 91
Byton Rd. SW17 —3D 106
Byward Av. Felt —5G 85
Byward St. EC3 —1C 76
Bywater Ho. SE18 —4J 79
Bywater Pl. SE16 —2J 77
Bywater St. SW3 —6D 74
Byway. E11 —3G 47
Byway, The. Eps —6D 120
Byway, The. Sutt —1B 136
Bywell Pl. W1 —8G 59
(off Wells St.)
Bywood Av. Croy —1G 125
Bywood Clo. Kenl —7M 137
Byworth Wlk. N19 —6J 43

Cabbell St. NW1 —8C 58
Cabinet War Rooms. —3H 75
Cabinet Way. E4 —6K 29
Cable Ho. WC1 —6L 59
(off Gt. Percy St.)
Cable Pl. SE10 —9A 78
Cables Clo. Belv —4A 82
Cable St. E1 —1E 76
Cable Trade Pk. SE7 —5G 79
Cabot Ct. SE16 —5H 77
(off Worgan St.)
Cabot Sq. E14 —2L 77
Cabot Way. E6 —4H 63
Cab Rd. SE1 —3L 75
(off West Rd.)
Cabul Rd. SW11 —1C 90
Caci Ho. W14 —5K 73
(off Avonmore Rd.)
Cactus Clo. SE15 —1C 92
Cactus Wlk. W12 —9D 56
Cadbury Clo. Iswth —9E 70
Cadbury Clo. Sun —4C 100
Cadbury Rd. Sun —4C 100
Cadbury Way. SE16 —4D 76
(in two parts)
Caddington Clo. Barn —7C 14
Caddington Rd. NW2 —8J 41
Caddis Clo. Stan —7D 22
Cadell Clo. E2 —5D 60
Cade Rd. SE10 —9B 78
Cader Rd. SW18 —5A 90
Cadet Dri. SE1 —5D 76
Cadet Pl. SE10 —6C 78
Cadiz Ct. Dag —3B 66
(off Rainham Rd. S.)
Cadiz Rd. Dag —3A 66
Cadiz St. SE17 —6A 76
Cadley Ter. SE23 —8G 93
Cadman Clo. SW9 —8M 75
Cadman Ct. W4 —6M 71
(off Chaseley Dri.)
Cadmer Clo. N Mald —8C 104
Cadmore Ct. Chesh —1D 6
Cadmore Ho. N1 —3M 59
(off Sutton Est., The)
Cadmore La. Chesh —1D 6
Cadmus Clo. SW4 —2H 91
Cadmus Ct. SW9 —9L 75
(off Southey Rd.)
Cadnam Lodge. E14 —4A 78
(off Schooner Clo.)
Cadogan Clo. E9 —3K 61
Cadogan Clo. Beck —5B 110
Cadogan Clo. Harr —9M 37
Cadogan Clo. Tedd —2C 102
Cadogan Ct. SW3 —5D 74
(off Draycott Av.)
Cadogan Ct. Sutt —8M 121
Cadogan Gdns. E18 —1F 46
Cadogan Gdns. N3 —8M 25
Cadogan Gdns. N21 —7L 15
Cadogan Gdns. SW3 —5D 74
Cadogan Ga. SW1 —5D 74
Cadogan Ho. SW3 —7B 74
(off Beaufort St.)
Cadogan La. SW1 —4E 74
Cadogan Pl. SW1 —4D 74
Cadogan Rd. Surb —9H 103
Cadogan Sq. SW1 —4D 74
Cadogan St. SW3 —5D 74
Cadogan Ter. E9 —2K 61
Cadoxton Av. N15 —4D 44
Cadwallon Rd. SE9 —8M 95
Caedmon Rd. N7 —9K 43
Caerleon Clo. Sidc —2G 113
Caerleon Ter. SE2 —5F 80
Caernarvon Clo. Horn —6L 51
Caernarvon Clo. Mitc —7J 107
Caernarvon Dri. Ilf —8L 31
Caernarvon Ho. W2 —9A 58
(off Hallfield Est.)
Caesars Wlk. Mitc —9D 106
Caesars Way. Shep —1B 116
Cahill St. EC1 —7A 60
Cahir St. E14 —5M 77
Cain Ct. W5 —8G 55
(off Castlebar M.)
Caine Ho. W3 —3M 71
(off Hanbury Rd.)
Cain's La. Felt —4C 84
Caird St. W10 —6J 57
Cairn Av. W5 —2H 71
Cairn Ct. Eps —2D 134
Cairndale Clo. Brom —4D 110
Cairnfield Av. NW2 —8C 40
Cairngorm Clo. Tedd —2E 102
Cairns Av. Wfd G —6J 31
Cairns Clo. Dart —4H 99
Cairns Rd. SW11 —4C 90
Cairn Way. Stan —6D 22
Cairo New Rd. Croy —4M 123
Cairo Rd. E17 —2L 45
Caishowe Rd. Borwd —3M 11
Caister Ho. N7 —2K 59
Caistor Ho. E15 —4D 62
(off Caistor Pk. Rd.)
Caistor M. SW12 —6F 90
Caistor Pk. Rd. E15 —4D 62
Caistor Rd. SW12 —6F 90
Caithness Dri. Eps —6B 134
Caithness Gdns. Sidc —5D 96
Caithness Ho. N1 —4K 59
(off Twyford St.)
Caithness Rd. W14 —4H 73
Caithness Rd. Mitc —4F 106
Calabria Rd. N5 —2M 59
Calais Ga. SE5 —9M 75
Calais St. SE5 —9M 75
Calbourne Av. Horn —1F 66
Calbourne Rd. SW12 —6D 90
Calcott Ct. W14 —4J 73
(off Blythe Rd.)
Calcott Wlk. SE9 —1J 111
Calcraft Ho. E2 —5G 61
(off Bonner Rd.)
Caldbeck. Wal A —7K 7
Caldbeck Av. Wor Pk —4E 120
Caldecote. King T —6L 103
(off Excelsior Clo.)
Caldecote Gdns. Bush —9C 10
Caldecote Hill. —9C 10
Caldecote La. Bush —8D 10
Caldecote Towers. Bush —9C 10
Caldecot Rd. SE5 —1A 92
Caldecott Way. E5 —8H 45
Calder Av. Gnfd —5D 54
Calder Clo. Enf —5C 16
Calder Ct. SE16 —2K 77
Calder Gdns. Edgw —1L 39
Calderon Ho. NW8 —5C 58
(off Townshend Est.)
Calderon Pl. W10 —8G 57
Calderon Rd. E11 —9A 46
Calder Rd. Mord —9A 106
Caldervale Rd. SW4 —4H 91
Calderwood St. SE18 —5L 79
Caldew Ct. NW7 —7E 24
Caldew St. SE5 —8B 76
Caldicot Grn. NW9 —4C 40
Caldwell Rd. Wat —4H 21
Caldwell St. SW9 —8K 75
Caldy Rd. Belv —4M 81
Caldy Wlk. N1 —3A 60
Caleb St. SE1 —3A 76
Caledonia Ct. Bark —5G 65
(off Keel Clo.)
Caledonia Ho. E14 —9J 61
Caledonian Clo. Ilf —6F 48
Caledonian Ct. Wat —4F 8
Caledonian Rd. N7 & N1 —9K 43
Caledonian Wharf. E14 —5B 78
Caledonia Rd. Stai —7C 144
Caledonia St. N1 —5J 59
Caledon Rd. E6 —4K 63
Caledon Rd. Wall —6E 122
Cale St. SW3 —6C 74
Caletock Way. SE10 —6D 78
Calfstock La. F'ham —8K 115
Calgarth. NW1 —5G 59
(off Ampthill Est.)
Calgary Ct. SE16 —3G 77
(off Canada Est.)
Caliban Tower. N1 —5C 60
(off Arden Est.)
Calico Row. SW11 —2A 90
Calidore Clo. SW2 —5K 91
California La. Bus H & Bush —1B 22
California Pl. Bush —1B 22
(off High Rd.)
California Rd. N Mald —8M 103
Callaby Ter. N1 —2B 60
Callaghan Clo. SE13 —3C 94
Callaghan Cotts. E1 —8G 61
(off Lindley St.)
Callander Rd. SE6 —8M 93
Callanders, The. Bush —1C 22
Callard Av. N13 —4M 27
Callcott Ct. NW6 —3K 57
Callcott Rd. NW6 —3K 57
Callcott St. W8 —2L 73
Callendar Rd. SW7 —4B 74
Callenders Cotts. Belv —3B 82
Calley Down Cres. New Ad —2B 140
Callingham Clo. E14 —8K 61
Callis Farm Clo. Stanw —5C 144
Callis Rd. E17 —4K 45
Callonfield. E17 —2H 45
Callow Fld. Purl —5L 137
Callowland Clo. Wat —2F 8
Callow St. SW3 —7B 74
Callum Welch Ho. EC1 —7A 60
(off Goswell Rd.)
Calmington Rd. SE5 —7C 76
Calmont Rd. Brom —3B 110
Calmore Clo. Horn —1G 67
Calne Av. Ilf —8M 31
Calonne Rd. SW19 —1H 105
Calshot Ct. Dart —5M 99
(off Osbourne Rd.)
Calshot Ho. N1 —5K 59
(off Priory Grn. Est.)
Calshot Rd. H'row A —1E 144
(in two parts)
Calshot St. N1 —5K 59
Calshot Way. Enf —5M 15
Calshot Way. H'row A —1E 144
(in two parts)
Calstock. NW1 —4H 59
(off Royal College St.)
Calstock Ho. SE11 —6L 75
(off Kennings Way)
Calthorpe Gdns. Edgw —5J 23
Calthorpe Gdns. Sutt —5A 122
Calthorpe St. WC1 —7K 59
Calton Av. SE21 —5C 92
Calton Rd. New Bar —8A 14
Calverley Clo. Beck —3M 109
Calverley Cres. Dag —7L 49
Calverley Gdns. Harr —5H 39
Calverley Gro. N19 —6H 43
Calverley Rd. Eps —8E 120
Calvert Av. E1 —6C 60
Calvert Clo. Belv —5L 81
Calvert Clo. Sidc —3J 113
Calvert Ho. W12 —1F 72
(off White City Est.)
Calverton. SE17 —7C 76
(off Albany Rd.)
Calverton Rd. E6 —4L 63
Calvert Rd. SE10 —6D 78
Calvert Rd. Barn —4H 13
Calvert's Bldgs. SE1 —2B 76
Calvert St. NW1 —4E 58
Calvin Clo. Orp —7H 113
Calvin St. E1 —7D 60
Calydon Rd. SE7 —6F 78
Calypso Way. SE16 —4K 77
Camac Rd. Twic —7B 86
Cambalt Rd. SW15 —4H 89
Cambay Ho. E1 —7J 61
(off Harford St.)
Camber Ho. SE15 —7G 77
Camberley Av. SW20 —6F 104
Camberley Av. Enf —6C 16
Camberley Clo. Sutt —5H 121
Camberley Ho. NW1 —5F 58
(off Redhill St.)
Camberley Rd. H'row A —2E 144
Cambert Way. SE3 —3F 94
Camberwell. —9B 76
Camberwell Chu. St. SE5 —9B 76
Camberwell Glebe. SE5 —9C 76
Camberwell Green. (Junct.) —9B 76
Camberwell Grn. SE5 —9B 76
Camberwell Gro. SE5 —9B 76
Camberwell New Rd. SE5 —7L 75
Camberwell Pl. SE5 —9A 76
Camberwell Rd. SE17 & SE5 —7A 76
Camberwell Sta. Rd. SE5 —9A 76
Camberwell Trad. Est. SE5 —9M 75
Cambeys Rd. Dag —1M 65
Camborne Av. W13 —3F 70
Camborne Av. Romf —7J 35
Camborne Clo. H'row A —2E 144
Camborne Rd. SW18 —6L 89
Camborne Rd. Croy —2E 124
Camborne Rd. Mord —9H 105
Camborne Rd. Sidc —9G 97
Camborne Rd. Sutt —9L 121
Camborne Rd. Well —1C 96
Camborne Way. Houn —9L 69
Camborne Way. Romf —7J 35
Cambourne Av. N9 —9H 17
Cambourne M. W11 —9J 57
(off St Mark's Rd.)
Cambourne Rd. H'row A —2E 144
Cambourne Wlk. Rich —5H 87
Cambrai Ct. N13 —3J 27
Cambray Rd. SW12 —7G 91
Cambray Rd. Orp —2D 128
Cambria Clo. Houn —3L 85
Cambria Clo. Sidc —7B 96
Cambria Ct. Felt —6F 84
Cambria Gdns. Stai —6C 144
(in two parts)
Cambria Ho. E14 —9J 61
Cambria Ho. SE26 —1E 108
(off High Level Dri.)
Cambria Ho. Eri —8C 82
(off Larner Rd.)
Cambrian Av. Ilf —3C 48
Cambrian Clo. SE27 —9M 91
Cambrian Grn. NW9 —3C 40
(off Snowden Dri.)
Cambrian Rd. E10 —5L 45
Cambrian Rd. Rich —5K 87
Cambria Rd. SE5 —2A 92
Cambria St. SW6 —8M 73
Cambridge Av. NW6 —5L 57
Cambridge Av. NW10 —6G 57
Cambridge Av. Gnfd —1D 54
Cambridge Av. N Mald —7C 104
(in two parts)
Cambridge Av. Romf —1G 51
Cambridge Av. Well —3D 96
Cambridge Barracks Rd. SE18 —5K 79
Cambridge Cir. WC2 —9H 59
Cambridge Clo. E17 —4K 45
Cambridge Clo. N22 —8L 27
Cambridge Clo. NW10 —8A 40
Cambridge Clo. SW20 —5F 104
Cambridge Clo. Chesh —2C 6
Cambridge Clo. Houn —3J 85
Cambridge Clo. W Dray —7H 143
Cambridge Cotts. Kew & Rich —7L 71
Cambridge Ct. E2 —5F 60
(off Cambridge Heath Rd.)
Cambridge Ct. N15 —5C 44
(off Amhurst Pk.)
Cambridge Ct. NW6 —5L 57
(in three parts)
Cambridge Ct. W2 —8C 58
(off Edgware Rd.)
Cambridge Ct. W6 —5G 73
(off Shepherd's Bush Rd.)
Cambridge Cres. E2 —5F 60
Cambridge Cres. Tedd —2E 102
Cambridge Dri. SE12 —4E 94
Cambridge Dri. Ruis —7G 37
Cambridge Gdns. N10 —8E 26
Cambridge Gdns. N17 —7B 28
Cambridge Gdns. N21 —9B 16
Cambridge Gdns. NW6 —5L 57
Cambridge Gdns. W10 —9H 57
Cambridge Gdns. Enf —4E 16
Cambridge Gdns. King T —6L 103
Cambridge Ga. NW1 —7F 58
Cambridge Ga. M. NW1 —7F 58
Cambridge Grn. SE9 —7M 95
Cambridge Gro. SE20 —5F 108
Cambridge Gro. W6 —5F 72
Cambridge Gro. Rd. King T —7L 103
(in two parts)
Cambridge Heath Rd. E1 & E2 —8F 60
Cambridge Ho. W6 —5F 72
(off Cambridge Gro.)
Cambridge Ho. W13 —9E 54
Cambridge Lodge Vs. E8 —4F 60
Cambridge Pde. Enf —3E 16
Cambridge Pk. E11 —5E 46
Cambridge Pk. Twic —5G 87
Cambridge Pk. Ct. Twic —6H 87
Cambridge Pk. Rd. E11 —5D 46
Cambridge Pl. W8 —3M 73
Cambridge Rd. E4 —1B 30
Cambridge Rd. E11 —4D 46
Cambridge Rd. NW6 —5L 57
(in two parts)
Cambridge Rd. SE20 —7F 108
Cambridge Rd. SW11 —9D 74
Cambridge Rd. SW13 —1D 88
Cambridge Rd. SW20 —5E 104
Cambridge Rd. W7 —3D 70
Cambridge Rd. Ashf —4A 100
Cambridge Rd. Bark —3A 64
Cambridge Rd. Brom —4E 110
Cambridge Rd. Cars —8C 122
Cambridge Rd. Hamp —4K 101

Cambridge Rd.—Cardine M.

Cambridge Rd. Harr —3L 37
Cambridge Rd. Houn —3J 85
Cambridge Rd. Ilf —6C 48
Cambridge Rd. King T —6K 103
Cambridge Rd. Mitc —7G 107
Cambridge Rd. N Mald —8C 104
Cambridge Rd. Rich —8L 71
Cambridge Rd. Sidc —1C 112
Cambridge Rd. S'hall —2K 69
Cambridge Rd. Tedd —1D 102
Cambridge Rd. Twic —5H 87
Cambridge Rd. Uxb —2B 142
Cambridge Rd. W on T —1F 116
Cambridge Rd. Wat —6G 9
Cambridge Rd. W Mol —8K 101
Cambridge Rd. N. W4 —6M 71
Cambridge Rd. S. W4 —6M 71
Cambridge Row. SE18 —6M 79
Cambridge Sq. W2 —9C 58
Cambridge St. SW1 —5F 74
Cambridge Ter. N9 —9C 16
Cambridge Ter. NW1 —6F 58
Cambridge Ter. M. NW1 —6F 58
Cambridge Theatre. —9J 59
(off Earlham St.)
Cambridge Yd. W7 —3D 70
Cambstone Clo. N11 —2E 26
Cambus Clo. Hay —8J 53
Cambus Rd. E16 —8E 62
Cam Ct. SE15 —7D 76
Camdale Rd. SE18 —8D 80
Camden Arts Cen. —1A 58
Camden Av. Felt —7G 85
Camden Av. Hay —1H 69
Camden Clo. Chst —5A 112
Camden Ct. NW1 —3G 59
(off Rousden St.)
Camden Ct. Belv —6L 81
Camden Gdns. NW1 —3F 58
Camden Gdns. Sutt —7M 121
Camden Gdns. T Hth —7M 107
Camden Gro. Chst —3M 111
Camden High St. NW1 —3F 58
Camden Hill Rd. SE19 —3C 108
Camden Ho. SE8 —6K 77
Camdenhurst St. E14 —9J 61
Camden La. N7 —1H 59
Camden Lock Market. —3F 58
Camden Lock Pl. NW1 —3F 58
Camden M. NW1 —3G 59
Camden Pk. Rd. NW1 —2H 59
Camden Pk. Rd. Chst —4K 111
Camden Passage. —5M 59
Camden Pas. N1 —4M 59
(in two parts)
Camden Peoples Theatre. —7G 59
(off Hampstead Rd.)
Camden Rd. E11 —4F 46
Camden Rd. E17 —4K 45
Camden Rd. NW1 & N7 —3G 59
Camden Rd. Bex —7K 97
Camden Rd. Cars —6D 122
Camden Rd. Sutt —7M 121
Camden Row. SE3 —1C 94
Camden Row. Pinn —1G 37
Camden Sq. NW1 —3H 59
Camden Sq. SE15 —9D 76
Camden St. NW1 —3G 59
Camden Studios. NW1 —4G 59
(off Camden St.)
Camden Ter. NW1 —2H 59
Camden Town. —4F 58
Camden Wlk. N1 —4M 59
(in two parts)
Camden Way. Chst —4K 111
Camden Way. T Hth —7M 107
Cameford Ct. SW12 —6J 91
Camelford. NW1 —4G 59
(off Royal College St.)
Camelford Ct. W11 —9J 57
Camelford Ho. SE1 —6J 75
Camelford Ho. Romf —4J 35
(off Chudleigh Rd.)
Camelford Wlk. W11 —9J 57
Camel Gro. King T —2H 103
Camellia Clo. Romf —8J 35
Camellia Ho. SE8 —8K 77
(off Idonia St.)
Camellia Pl. Twic —6M 85
Camellia St. SW8 —8J 75
Camelot Clo. SE28 —3B 80
Camelot Clo. SW19 —1K 105
Camelot Clo. Big H —8G 141
Camelot Ho. NW1 —2H 59
Camel Rd. E16 —2H 79
Camera Pl. SW10 —7B 74
Cameret Ct. W14 —3H 73
(off Holland Rd.)
Cameron Clo. N18 —4F 28
Cameron Clo. N20 —2B 26
Cameron Clo. Bex —9C 98
Cameron Dri. Wal X —7D 6
Cameron Ho. NW8 —5C 58
(off St John's Wood Ter.)
Cameron Ho. SE5 —8A 76
Cameron Pl. E1 —9F 60
Cameron Rd. SE6 —8K 93
Cameron Rd. Brom —9E 110
Cameron Rd. Croy —1M 123
Cameron Rd. Ilf —6C 48
Cameron Sq. Mitc —5C 106
Cameron Ter. SE12 —9F 94
Camerton Clo. E8 —2D 60
Camilla Clo. Sun —3D 100
Camilla Rd. SE16 —5F 76
Camille Clo. SE25 —7E 108
Camlan Rd. Brom —1D 110
Camlet St. E2 —7D 60
Camlet Way. Barn —4L 13
Camley St. NW1 —3H 59
Camm Gdns. King T —6K 103
Camm Gdns. Th Dit —2D 118
Camomile Av. Mitc —5D 106
Camomile Rd. Rush G —7B 50
Camomile St. EC2 —9C 60
Camomile Way. W Dray —9C 142
Campana Rd. SW6 —9L 73
Campania Building. E1 —1H 77
(off Jardine Rd.)
Campbell Av. Ilf —2M 47
Campbell Clo. SE18 —9L 79
Campbell Clo. SW16 —1H 107
Campbell Clo. Romf —6C 34
Campbell Clo. Ruis —4E 36
Campbell Clo. Twic —8B 86
Campbell Ct. N17 —8D 28
Campbell Ct. SE21 —6E 92
Campbell Ct. SW7 —4A 74
(off Gloucester Rd.)
Campbell Cft. Edgw —5L 23
Campbell Gordon Way. NW2 —9F 40
Campbell Ho. SW1 —6G 75
(off Churchill Gdns.)
Campbell Ho. W12 —1F 72
(off White City Est.)
Campbell Rd. E3 —6L 61
Campbell Rd. E6 —4J 63
Campbell Rd. E15 —9D 46
Campbell Rd. E17 —2K 45
Campbell Rd. N17 —8E 28
Campbell Rd. W7 —1C 70
Campbell Rd. Croy —2M 123
Campbell Rd. E Mol —7C 102
Campbell Rd. Twic —8B 86
Campbell Wlk. N1 —4J 59
(off Outram Pl.)
Campdale Rd. N7 —8H 43
Campden Cres. Dag —9F 48
Campden Cres. Wemb —8F 38
Campden Gro. W8 —3L 73
Campden Hill. W8 —3L 73
Campden Hill Ct. W8 —3L 73
Campden Hill Gdns. W8 —2L 73
Campden Hill Ga. W8 —3L 73
Campden Hill Mans. W8 —2L 73
(off Kensington Church St.)
Campden Hill Pl. W11 —2K 73
Campden Hill Rd. W11 —2L 73
Campden Hill Sq. W11 —2K 73
Campden Ho. NW6 —3B 58
Campden Ho. W8 —2L 73
Campden Ho. Clo. W8 —3L 73
Campden Houses. W8 —2L 73
(off Peel St.)
Campden Rd. S Croy —7C 124
Campden St. W8 —2L 73
Campe Ho. N10 —7E 26
Campen Clo. SW19 —8J 89
Camperdown Ho. Wall —8F 122
(off Stanley Pk. Rd.)
Camperdown St. E1 —9D 60
Campfield Rd. SE9 —6H 95
Campine Clo. Chesh —1D 6
Campion Clo. E6 —1K 79
Campion Clo. Croy —6C 124
Campion Clo. Harr —4K 39
Campion Clo. Rush G —7B 50
Campion Clo. Uxb —8D 142
Campion Clo. Wat —6E 4
Campion Ct. Wemb —5J 55
Campion Gdns. Wfd G —5E 30
Campion Pl. SE28 —2E 80
Campion Rd. SW15 —3G 89
Campion Rd. Iswth —9D 70
Campions. Lou —2L 19
Campions Clo. Borwd —1L 11
Campions, The. Borwd —2K 11
Campion Ter. NW2 —8H 41
Campion Way. Edgw —4A 24
Camplin Rd. Harr —3J 39
Camplin St. SE14 —8H 77
Camp Rd. SW19 —2F 104
(in two parts)
Campsbourne Rd. N8 —1J 43
(in two parts)
Campsbourne, The. N8 —2J 43
Campsey Gdns. Dag —3F 64
Campsey Rd. Dag —3F 64
Campsfield Rd. N8 —1J 43
Campshill Pl. SE13 —4A 94
Campshill Rd. SE13 —4A 94
Campus Rd. E17 —4K 45
Campus Way. NW4 —1F 40
Camp Vw. SW19 —2F 104
Cam Rd. E15 —4B 62
Camrose Av. Edgw —9K 23
Camrose Av. Eri —7M 81
Camrose Av. Felt —1G 101
Camrose Clo. Croy —2J 125
Camrose Clo. Mord —8L 105
Camrose St. SE2 —6E 80
Canada Av. N18 —6A 28
Canada Cres. W3 —8A 56
Canada Est. SE16 —4G 77
Canada Gdns. SE13 —4A 94
Canada Rd. W3 —8A 56
Canada Rd. Eri —8F 82
Canada Sq. E14 —2M 77
Canada St. SE16 —3H 77
Canada Way. W12 —1F 72
Canada Wharf. SE16 —2K 77
Canadian Av. SE6 —7M 93
Canal App. SE8 —6J 77
Canal Bridge. (Junct.) —7E 76
Canal Building. N1 —5A 60
(off Shepherdess Wlk.)
Canal Clo. E1 —7J 61
Canal Clo. W10 —7H 57
Canal Gro. SE15 —7F 76
Canal Path. E2 —4D 60
Canal Rd. E3 —7J 61
Canalside. SE28 —1H 81
Canal St. SE5 —7B 76
Canal Wlk. N1 —4B 60
Canal Wlk. SE25 —1C 124
Canal Wlk. SE26 —2G 109
Canal Way. W10 —7H 57
Canary Wharf. —2M 77
Canberra Clo. NW4 —1E 40
Canberra Clo. Dag —3B 66
Canberra Clo. Horn —9G 51
Canberra Cres. Dag —3B 66
Canberra Dri. N'holt —6G 53
Canberra Rd. E6 —4K 63
Canberra Rd. SE7 —7G 79
Canberra Rd. Bexh —7H 81
Canberra Rd. H'row A —2E 144
Canbury Av. King T —5K 103
Canbury Bus. Cen. King T —5J 103
Canbury Bus. Pk. King T —5J 103
Canbury M. SE26 —9E 92
Canbury Pk. Rd. King T —5J 103
Canbury Pas. King T —5H 103
Canbury Path. Orp —8E 112
Cancell Rd. SW9 —9L 75
Candahar Rd. SW11 —1C 90
Candida Ct. NW1 —3F 58
Candler M. Twic —6E 86
Candler St. N15 —4B 44
Candover Clo. W Dray —8H 143
Candover Rd. Horn —6F 50
Candover St. W1 —8G 59
Candy St. E3 —4K 61
Cane Clo. Wall —9J 123
(in two parts)
Cane Hill. H Wood —9J 35
Caneland Ct. Wal A —7M 7
Caney M. NW2 —7H 41
Canfield Dri. Ruis —1F 52
Canfield Gdns. NW6 —3M 57
Canfield Ho. N15 —4C 44
(off Albert Rd.)
Canfield Pl. NW6 —2A 58
Canfield Rd. Rain —4D 66
Canfield Rd. Wfd G —7J 31
Canford Av. N'holt —4K 53
Canford Clo. Enf —4L 15
Canford Gdns. N Mald —1C 120
Canford Pl. Tedd —3G 103
Canford Rd. SW11 —4E 90
Canham Rd. SE25 —7C 108
Canham Rd. W3 —3C 72
Canmore Gdns. SW16 —4G 107
Cann Hall. —9C 46
Cann Hall Rd. E11 —9C 46
Cann Ho. W14 —4J 73
(off Russell Rd.)
Canning Cres. N22 —8K 27
Canning Cross. SE5 —1C 92
Canning Ho. W12 —1F 72
(off White City Est.)
Canning Pas. W8 —4A 74
(in two parts)
Canning Pl. W8 —4A 74
Canning Pl. M. W8 —4A 74
(off Canning Pl.)
Canning Rd. E15 —5B 62
Canning Rd. E17 —2J 45
Canning Rd. N5 —8M 43
Canning Rd. Croy —4D 124
Canning Rd. Harr —1C 38
Cannington Rd. Dag —2G 65
Canning Town. —9D 62
Canning Town. (Junct.) —8C 62
Cannizaro Rd. SW19 —3G 105
Cannock Ho. N4 —5A 44
Cannonbury Av. Pinn —4H 37
Cannon Clo. SW20 —7G 105
Cannon Clo. Hamp —3M 101
Cannon Dri. E14 —1L 77
Cannon Hill. N14 —3J 27
Cannon Hill. NW6 —1L 57
Cannon Hill La. SW20 —9H 105
Cannon Hill M. N14 —3J 27
Cannon Ho. SE11 —5K 75
(off Beaufoy Wlk.)
Cannon La. NW3 —8B 42
Cannon La. Pinn —3J 37
Cannon M. Wal A —6H 7
Cannon Pl. NW3 —8B 42
Cannon Pl. SE7 —6J 79
Cannon Retail Pk. SE28 —1E 80
Cannon Rd. N14 —3J 27
Cannon Rd. Bexh —9J 81
Cannon Rd. Wat —7G 9
Cannon St. EC4 —9A 60
Cannon St. Rd. E1 —9F 60
Cannon Trad. Est. Wemb —9M 39
Cannon Way. W Mol —8L 101
Cannon Wharf Bus. Cen. SE8 —5J 77
Cannon Workshops. E14 —1L 77
(off Cannon Dri.)
Canon Av. Romf —3G 49
Canon Beck Rd. SE16 —3G 77
Canonbie Rd. SE23 —6G 93
Canonbury. —2A 60
Canonbury Bus. Cen. N1 —4B 60
Canonbury Ct. N1 —3M 59
(off Hawes St.)
Canonbury Cres. N1 —3A 60
Canonbury Gro. N1 —3A 60
Canonbury La. N1 —3M 59
Canonbury Pk. N. N1 —2A 60
Canonbury Pk. S. N1 —2A 60
Canonbury Pl. N1 —2M 59
(in two parts)
Canonbury Rd. N1 —2M 59
Canonbury Rd. Enf —3C 16
Canonbury Sq. N1 —3M 59
Canonbury St. N1 —3A 60
Canonbury Vs. N1 —3M 59
Canon Mohan Clo. N14 —8E 14
Canon Rd. Brom —7G 111
Canon Row. SW1 —3J 75
(in two parts)
Canon's Clo. N2 —5B 42
Canons Clo. Edgw —6K 23
Canons Corner. Edgw —4J 23
Canons Ct. Edgw —6K 23
Canons Dri. Edgw —6J 23
Canons Hill. Coul —9L 137
(in two parts)
Canonsleigh Rd. Dag —3F 64
Canons Park. —6J 23
Canons Pk. Stan —6H 23
Canons Pk. Clo. Edgw —7J 23
Canon St. N1 —4A 60
Canon's Wlk. Croy —5H 125
Canopus Way. N'wd —4E 20
Canopus Way. Stai —6C 144
Canrobert St. E2 —5F 60
Cantelowes Rd. NW1 —2H 59
Canterbury Av. Ilf —5J 47
Canterbury Av. Sidc —8F 96
Canterbury Clo. E6 —9K 63
Canterbury Clo. SE5 —1A 92
(off Lilford Rd.)
Canterbury Clo. Beck —5M 109
Canterbury Clo. Chig —3D 32
Canterbury Clo. Dart —6L 99
Canterbury Clo. Gnfd —8M 53
Canterbury Clo. N'wd —6D 20
Canterbury Ct. NW6 —5L 57
Canterbury Ct. NW9 —9C 24
Canterbury Ct. SE12 —9F 94
Canterbury Cres. SW9 —2L 91
Canterbury Gro. SE27 —1L 107
Canterbury Ho. SE1 —4K 75
Canterbury Ho. SW9 —8L 75
Canterbury Ho. Bark —3E 64
(off Margaret Bondfield Av.)
Canterbury Ho. Borwd —4L 11
(off Stratfield Rd.)
Canterbury Ho. Eri —8D 82
Canterbury Ho. Wat —4G 9
(off Anglian Clo.)
Canterbury Ind. Pk. SE15 —7G 77
Canterbury M. Oxs —5A 132
Canterbury Pl. SE17 —6M 75
Canterbury Rd. E10 —5A 46
Canterbury Rd. NW6 —5K 57
(in two parts)
Canterbury Rd. Borwd —4L 11
Canterbury Rd. Croy —2K 123
Canterbury Rd. Felt —8J 85
Canterbury Rd. Harr —3M 37
Canterbury Rd. Mord —2M 121
Canterbury Rd. Wat —4F 8
Canterbury Ter. NW6 —5L 57
Canterbury Way. Crox G —5A 8
Cantium Retail Pk. SE1 —7E 76
Cantley Gdns. SE19 —5D 108
Cantley Gdns. Ilf —4A 48
Cantley Rd. W7 —4E 70
Canton St. E14 —9L 61
Cantrel Lodge. Enf —9D 6
Cantrell Rd. E3 —7K 61
Cantwell Rd. SE18 —8M 79
Canute Gdns. SE16 —5H 77
Canvey St. SE1 —2A 76
Cape Clo. Bark —3M 63
Cape Henry Ct. E14 —1B 78
(off Jamestown Way)
Cape Ho. E8 —2D 60
(off Dalston La.)
Capel Av. Wall —7K 123
Capel Clo. N20 —3A 26
Capel Clo. Brom —3J 127
Capel Ct. EC2 —9B 60
(off Bartholomew La.)
Capel Ct. SE20 —5G 109
Capel Gdns. Ilf —9D 48
Capel Gdns. Pinn —2K 37
Capella Rd. N'wd —4D 20
Capel Manor Gardens. —8A 6
Capel Pl. Dart —1G 115
Capel Rd. E7 & E12 —9F 46
Capel Rd. Barn —8C 14
Capel Rd. Enf —9B 6
Capel Rd. Wat —8J 9
Capelvere Wlk. Wat —3C 8
Capener's Clo. SW1 —3E 74
(off Kinnerton St.)
Capern Rd. SW18 —7A 90
Cape Rd. N17 —1E 44
Cape Yd. E1 —1E 76
(off Kennet St.)
Capital Bus. Cen. Wat —9H 5
Capital Bus. Cen. Wemb —5H 55
Capital Ind. Est. Belv —4M 81
Capital Ind. Est. Mitc —9D 106
Capital Interchange Way. Bren —6L 71
Capital Pl. Croy —7K 123
Capital Wharf. E1 —2E 76
Capitol Ind. Pk. NW9 —1A 40
Capitol Way. NW9 —1A 40
Capland Ho. NW8 —7B 58
(off Capland St.)
Capland St. NW8 —7B 58
Caple Ho. SW10 —8A 74
(off King's Rd.)
Caple Rd. NW10 —5D 56
Capper St. W1 —7G 59
Caprea Clo. Hay —8H 53
Capricorn Cen. Dag —5K 49
Capri Ho. E17 —9K 29
Capri Rd. Croy —3D 124
Capstan Clo. Romf —4F 48
Capstan Ct. Dart —3M 99
Capstan Ho. E14 —1B 78
(off Clove Cres.)
Capstan Ho. E14 —5A 78
(off Stebondale St.)
Capstan Ride. Enf —4L 15
Capstan Rd. SE8 —5K 77
Capstan Sq. E14 —3A 78
Capstan Way. SE16 —2J 77
Capstone Rd. Brom —1D 110
Capthorne Av. Harr —6J 37
Capuchin Clo. Stan —6F 22
Capulet M. E16 —2E 78
Capworth St. E10 —6L 45
Caractacus Cottage Vw. Wat —9E 8
Caractacus Grn. Wat —8D 8
Caradoc Clo. W2 —9L 57
Caradoc Evans Clo. N11 —5F 26
(off Springfield Rd.)
Caradoc St. SE10 —6C 78
Caradon Clo. E11 —6C 46
Caradon Way. N15 —2B 44
Caravel Clo. E14 —4L 77
Caravelle Gdns. N'holt —6H 53
Caravel M. SE8 —7L 77
Caraway Clo. E13 —8F 62
Caraway Heights. E14 —1A 78
(off Poplar High St.)
Caraway Pl. Wall —5F 122
Carberry Rd. SE19 —3C 108
Carbery Av. W3 —3K 71
Carbis Clo. E4 —1B 30
Carbis Rd. E14 —9K 61
Carbuncle Pas. Way. N17 —9E 28
Carburton St. W1 —8F 58
Carbury Clo. Horn —2G 67
Cardale St. E14 —4A 78
Carden Rd. SE15 —2F 92
Cardiff Ho. SE15 —7E 76
(off Friary Est.)
Cardiff Rd. W7 —4E 70
Cardiff Rd. Enf —6F 16
Cardiff Rd. Wat —8F 8
(in two parts)
Cardiff Rd. Ind. Est. Wat —8F 8
Cardiff St. SE18 —8C 80
Cardiff Way. Ab L —5E 4
Cardigan Ct. W7 —7D 54
(off Copley Clo.)
Cardigan Gdns. Ilf —7E 48
Cardigan Ho. Romf —5H 35
(off Bridgwater Wlk.)
Cardigan Pl. SE3 —1B 94
Cardigan Rd. E3 —5K 61
Cardigan Rd. SW13 —1E 88
Cardigan Rd. SW19 —3A 106
Cardigan Rd. Rich —5J 87
Cardigan St. SE11 —6L 75
Cardigan Wlk. N1 —3A 60
(off Ashby Gro.)
Cardinal Av. Borwd —5M 11
Cardinal Av. King T —2J 103
Cardinal Av. Mord —1J 121
Cardinal Bourne St. SE1 —4B 76
Cardinal Cap All. SE1 —2A 76
Cardinal Clo. Chst —5B 112
Cardinal Clo. Edgw —7B 24
Cardinal Clo. Mord —1J 121
Cardinal Clo. S Croy —5E 138
Cardinal Clo. Wor Pk —6E 120
Cardinal Ct. E1 —1E 76
(off Thomas More St.)
Cardinal Cres. N Mald —6A 104
Cardinal Dri. Ilf —6A 32
Cardinal Dri. W on T —3H 117
Cardinal Pl. SW15 —3H 89
Cardinal Rd. Felt —7F 84
Cardinal Rd. Ruis —6H 37
Cardinals Wlk. Hamp —4A 102
Cardinals Wlk. Sun —3C 100
Cardinals Way. N19 —6H 43
Cardinal Way. Harr —1C 38
Cardinal Way. Rain —5H 67
Cardine M. SE15 —8F 76

Castle St.—Century M.

Castle St. King T —6J 103
Castleton. Cars —3B 136
Castleton Av. Bexh —9B 82
Castleton Av. Wemb —9J 39
Castleton Clo. Bans —7L 135
Castleton Clo. Croy —1J 125
Castleton Dri. Bans —7L 135
Castleton Gdns. Wemb —8J 39
Castleton Ho. E14 —5A 78
(off Pier St.)
Castleton Rd. E17 —9B 30
Castleton Rd. SE9 —1H 111
Castleton Rd. Ilf —6E 48
Castleton Rd. Mitc —8H 107
(in two parts)
Castleton Rd. Ruis —6H 37
Castletown Rd. W14 —6J 73
Castle Vw. Eps —6M 133
Castleview Clo. N4 —7A 44
Castleview Gdns. Ilf —4J 47
Castle Vw. Rd. Wey —6A 116
Castle Wlk. Sun —7G 101
Castle Way. SW19 —9H 89
Castle Way. Eps —2E 134
Castle Way. Felt —1G 101
Castle Wharf. E14 —1C 78
(off Orchard Pl.)
Castlewood Dri. SE9 —1K 95
Castlewood Rd. N15 & N16 —4E 44
Castlewood Rd. Cockf —5B 14
Castle Yd. N6 —5E 42
Castle Yd. SE1 —2M 75
Castle Yd. Rich —4H 87
Castor La. E14 —1M 77
Catalina Rd. H'row A —1F 144
Catalin Ct. Wal A —6K 7
(off Howard Clo.)
Caterham Av. Ilf —9K 31
Caterham Ct. Wal A —7M 7
Caterham Rd. SE13 —2B 94
Catesby St. SE17 —5B 76
Catford. —6M 93
Catford B'way. SE6 —6M 93
Catford Greyhound Stadium. —5L 93
Catford Gyratory. (Junct.) —6M 93
Catford Hill. SE6 —7K 93
Catford Island. SE6 —6M 93
Catford M. SE6 —6M 93
Catford Rd. SE6 —6L 93
Catford Trad. Est. SE6 —8M 93
Cathall Rd. E11 —7B 46
Cathay Ho. SE16 —3F 76
Cathay St. SE16 —3F 76
Cathay Wlk. N'holt —5L 53
(off Brabazon Rd.)
Cathcart Dri. Orp —4C 128
Cathcart Hill. N19 —8G 43
Cathcart Rd. SW10 —7M 73
Cathcart St. NW5 —2F 58
Cathedral Lodge. EC1 —8A 60
(off Aldersgate St.)
Cathedral Mans. SW1 —5G 75
(off Vauxhall Bri. Rd.)
Cathedral Piazza. SW1 —4G 75
Cathedral Pl. EC4 —9A 60
(off Paternoster Row)
Cathedral St. SE1 —2B 76
Catherall Rd. N5 —8A 44
Catherine Clo. Lou —8J 19
Catherine Ct. N14 —7G 15
Catherine Ct. SW19 —2K 105
Catherine Ct. Ilf —4A 48
Catherine Dri. Rich —3J 87
Catherine Dri. Sun —3D 100
Catherine Gdns. Houn —3B 86
Catherine Griffiths Ct. EC1 —7L 59
(off Pine St.)
Catherine Gro. SE10 —9M 77
Catherine Ho. N1 —4C 60
(off Whitmore Est.)
Catherine Howard Ct. SE9 —5B 96
Catherine Howard Ct. Wey
(off Old Palace Rd.) —5A 116
Catherine of Aragon Ct. SE9 —5B 96
Catherine Parr Ct. SE9 —5B 96
Catherine Pl. SW1 —4G 75
Catherine Pl. Harr —3D 38
Catherine Rd. Enf —1J 17
Catherine Rd. Romf —3F 50
Catherine Rd. Surb —9H 103
Catherines Clo. W Dray —3H 143
Catherine St. WC2 —1K 75
Catherine Wheel All. EC2 —8C 60
(in two parts)
Catherine Wheel Rd. Bren —8H 71
Catherine Wheel Yd. SW1 —2G 75
(off Lit. St James's St.)
Catherwood Ct. N1 —5B 60
(off Murray Gro.)
Cat Hill. Barn —8C 14
Cathles Rd. SW12 —5F 90
Cathnor Rd. W12 —3F 72
Catinthia Ct. SE16 —5J 77
(off Plough Way)
Catisfield Rd. Enf —1J 17
Catlin Cres. Shep —9B 100
Catling Clo. SE23 —9G 93
Catlin's La. Pinn —1F 36
Catlin St. SE16 —6E 76
Cator Clo. New Ad —3C 140
Cator Cres. New Ad —3C 140
Cator La. Beck —5K 109
Cato Rd. SW4 —2H 91
Cator Rd. SE26 —3H 109
Cator Rd. Cars —7D 122
Cator St. SE15 —8D 76
(Commercial Way)
Cator St. SE15 —7D 76
(St George's Way)
Cato's Hill. Esh —6M 117
Cato St. W1 —8C 58
Catsey La. Bush —9A 10
Catsey Wood. Bush —9A 10
Catterick Clo. N11 —6E 26
Catterick Way. Borwd —3K 11
Cattistock Rd. SE9 —2J 111
Cattley Clo. Barn —6J 13
Catton St. WC1 —8K 59
Caudwell Ter. SW18 —5B 90
Caughley Ho. SE11 —4L 75
(off Lambeth Wlk.)
Caulfield Rd. E6 —4J 63
Caulfield Rd. SE15 —1F 92
Causeway, The. N2 —2C 42
Causeway, The. SW18 —4M 89
(in two parts)
Causeway, The. SW19 —2G 105
Causeway, The. Cars —5E 122
Causeway, The. Chess —6J 119
Causeway, The. Clay —9D 118
Causeway, The. Felt & Houn —3E 84
Causeway, The. Sutt —1A 136
Causeway, The. Tedd —3D 102
Causeyware Rd. N9 —9G 17
Causton Cotts. E14 —8J 61
Causton Ho. SE5 —8A 76
Causton Rd. N6 —5F 42
Causton Sq. Dag —3L 65
Causton St. SW1 —5H 75
Cautley Av. SW4 —4G 91
Cavalier Clo. Romf —2H 49
Cavalier Ct. Surb —1K 119
Cavalier Gdns. Hay —9B 52
Cavalry Cres. Houn —3H 85
Cavalry Gdns. SW15 —4K 89
Cavan Pl. Pinn —8K 21
Cavaye Pl. SW10 —6A 74
Cavell Cres. Dart —3L 99
Cavell Cres. H Wood —9J 35
Cavell Dri. Enf —4L 15
Cavell Ho. N1 —4C 60
(off Colville Est.)
Cavell Rd. N17 —7B 28
Cavell Rd. Chesh —1A 6
Cavell St. E1 —8F 60
Cavell Way. Eps —3L 133
Cavendish Av. N3 —9L 25
Cavendish Av. NW8 —5B 58
Cavendish Av. W13 —8E 54
Cavendish Av. Eri —7A 82
Cavendish Av. Harr —9B 38
Cavendish Av. Horn —2F 66
Cavendish Av. N Mald —9E 104
Cavendish Av. Ruis —1F 52
Cavendish Av. Sidc —6E 96
Cavendish Av. Well —2D 96
Cavendish Av. Wfd G —8F 30
Cavendish Clo. N18 —5F 28
Cavendish Clo. NW6 —2K 57
Cavendish Clo. NW8 —6B 58
Cavendish Clo. Hay —8C 52
Cavendish Clo. Sun —3D 100
Cavendish Ct. EC3 —9C 60
(off Devonshire Row)
Cavendish Ct. Sun —3D 100
Cavendish Cres. Els —6L 11
Cavendish Cres. Horn —2F 66
Cavendish Dri. E11 —6B 46
Cavendish Dri. Clay —7C 118
Cavendish Dri. Edgw —6K 23
Cavendish Gdns. SW4 —5G 91
Cavendish Gdns. Bark —1C 64
Cavendish Gdns. Ilf —6L 47
Cavendish Gdns. Romf —3J 49
Cavendish Ho. NW8 —5B 58
(off Cavendish Av.)
Cavendish Mans. EC1 —7L 59
(off Rosebery Av.)
Cavendish Mans. NW6 —1L 57
Cavendish M. N. W1 —8F 58
Cavendish M. S. W1 —8F 58
Cavendish Pde. SW12 —5F 90
(off Clapham Comn. S. Side)
Cavendish Pde. Houn —1J 85
Cavendish Pl. SW4 —4H 91
Cavendish Pl. W1 —9F 58
Cavendish Rd. E4 —6A 30
Cavendish Rd. N4 —4M 43
Cavendish Rd. N18 —5F 28
Cavendish Rd. NW6 —3J 57
Cavendish Rd. SW12 —5F 90
Cavendish Rd. SW19 —4B 106
Cavendish Rd. W4 —9A 72
Cavendish Rd. Barn —5G 13
Cavendish Rd. Croy —3M 123
Cavendish Rd. N Mald —8D 104
Cavendish Rd. Sun —3D 100
Cavendish Rd. Sutt —9A 122
Cavendish Rd. Wey —9A 116
Cavendish Sq. W1 —9F 58
Cavendish St. N1 —5B 60
Cavendish Ter. Felt —8E 84
Cavendish Way. W W'ck —3M 125
Cavenham Gdns. Horn —3G 51
Cavenham Gdns. Ilf —8B 48
Caverleigh Way. Wor Pk —3E 120
Cave Rd. E13 —6F 62
Cave Rd. Rich —1G 103
Caversham Av. N13 —3L 27
Caversham Av. Sutt —4J 121
Caversham Ct. N11 —2E 26
Caversham Ho. N15 —2A 44
(off Caversham Rd.)
Caversham Ho. SE15 —7E 76
(off Haymerle Rd.)
Caversham Ho. King T —6J 103
(off Lady Booth Rd.)
Caversham Rd. N15 —2A 44
Caversham Rd. NW5 —2G 59
Caversham Rd. King T —6K 103
Caversham St. SW3 —7D 74
Caverswall St. W12 —9G 57
Caveside Clo. Chst —5L 111
Cavour Ho. SE17 —6M 75
(off Alberta Est.)
Cawdor Cres. W7 —5E 70
Cawnpore St. SE19 —2C 108
Caxton Ct. SW11 —1C 90
Caxton Dri. Uxb —5B 142
Caxton Gro. E3 —6L 61
Caxton M. Bren —7H 71
Caxton Pl. Ilf —8L 47
Caxton Rd. N22 —9K 27
Caxton Rd. SW19 —2A 106
Caxton Rd. W12 —3H 73
Caxton Rd. S'hall —4H 69
Caxton St. SW1 —4G 75
Caxton St. N. E16 —9D 62
Caxton St. S. E16 —1E 78
Caxton Trad. Est. Hay —3C 68
Caxton Wlk. WC2 —9H 59
Caxton Way. Romf —2C 50
Caxton Way. Wat —9B 8
Caygill Clo. Brom —8D 110
Cayley Clo. Wall —9J 123
Cayley Rd. S'hall —4M 69
Cayton Pl. EC1 —6B 60
(off Cayton St.)
Cayton Rd. Gnfd —5C 54
Cayton St. EC1 —6B 60
Cazenove Rd. E17 —8L 29
Cazenove Rd. N16 —7D 44
Cearns Ho. E6 —4H 63
Cearn Way. Coul —7K 137
Cecil Av. Bark —3B 64
Cecil Av. Enf —6D 16
Cecil Av. Horn —1J 51
Cecil Av. Wemb —1K 55
Cecil Clo. W5 —8H 55
Cecil Clo. Ashf —4A 100
Cecil Clo. Chess —6H 119
Cecil Ct. NW6 —3M 57
Cecil Ct. SW10 —7A 74
(off Hollywood Rd.)
Cecil Ct. WC2 —1J 75
Cecil Ct. Barn —5H 13
Cecil Ct. Enf —6B 16
Cecile Pk. N8 —4J 43
Cecil Ho. E17 —8L 29
Cecilia Clo. N2 —1A 42
Cecilia Rd. E8 —1D 60
Cecil Pk. Pinn —2J 37
Cecil Pl. Mitc —9D 106
Cecil Rhodes Ho. NW1 —5H 59
(off Goldington St.)
Cecil Rd. E11 —8D 46
Cecil Rd. E13 —4E 62
Cecil Rd. E17 —8L 29
Cecil Rd. N10 —9F 26
Cecil Rd. N14 —1G 27
Cecil Rd. NW9 —1C 40
Cecil Rd. NW10 —4C 56
Cecil Rd. SW19 —4M 105
Cecil Rd. W3 —8A 56
Cecil Rd. Ashf —4A 100
Cecil Rd. Chesh —5E 6
Cecil Rd. Croy —1J 123
Cecil Rd. Enf —5A 16
Cecil Rd. Harr —1C 38
Cecil Rd. Houn —1A 86
Cecil Rd. Ilf —9M 47
Cecil Rd. Romf —5H 49
Cecil Rd. Sutt —8K 121
Cecil Rosen Ct. Wemb —8F 38
Cecil St. Wat —2F 8
Cecil Way. Brom —3E 126
Cedar Av. Barn —9C 14
Cedar Av. Enf —4G 17
Cedar Av. Hay —9E 52
Cedar Av. Romf —3J 49
Cedar Av. Ruis —1G 53
Cedar Av. Sidc —6E 96
Cedar Av. Twic —5M 85
Cedar Av. Upm —9L 51
Cedar Av. Wal X —6D 6
Cedar Av. W Dray —1K 143
Cedar Clo. SE21 —7A 92
Cedar Clo. SW15 —1B 104
Cedar Clo. Brom —5J 127
Cedar Clo. Buck H —2H 31
Cedar Clo. Cars —8D 122
Cedar Clo. E Mol —8C 102
Cedar Clo. Eps —6D 134
Cedar Clo. Esh —8K 117
Cedar Clo. Romf —2A 50
Cedar Clo. Swan —6A 114
Cedar Copse. Brom —6K 111
Cedar Ct. E18 —8E 30
Cedar Ct. N1 —3A 60
Cedar Ct. N10 —9E 26
Cedar Ct. N11 —5G 27
Cedar Ct. N20 —1B 26
Cedar Ct. SE7 —7G 79
Cedar Ct. SW19 —9H 89
Cedar Ct. W1 —9C 58
(off Harrowby St.)
Cedar Ct. Bren —7G 71
Cedar Ct. Sutt —8A 122
Cedar Cres. Brom —5J 127
Cedarcroft Rd. Chess —6K 119
Cedar Dri. N2 —2C 42
Cedar Dri. Pinn —6L 21
Cedar Dri. S at H —6M 115
Cedar Gdns. Sutt —8A 122
Cedar Grange. Enf —7C 16
Cedar Gro. W5 —4J 71
Cedar Gro. Bex —5H 97
Cedar Gro. S'hall —8L 53
Cedar Gro. Wey —6A 116
Cedar Heights. NW2 —2K 57
Cedar Heights. Rich —7J 87
Cedar Hill. Eps —8A 134
Cedar Ho. E14 —3A 78
(off Manchester Rd.)
Cedar Ho. N22 —8L 27
(off Acacia Rd.)
Cedar Ho. SE14 —9H 77
Cedar Ho. SE16 —3H 77
(off Woodland Cres.)
Cedar Ho. W8 —4M 73
(off Marloes Rd.)
Cedar Ho. Hay —7G 53
Cedarhurst. Brom —4C 110
Cedarhurst Cotts. Bex —6L 97
Cedarhurst Dri. SE9 —4G 95
Cedarland Ter. SW20 —4F 104
Cedar Lawn Av. Barn —7J 13
Cedar Lodge. Chesh —1D 6
Cedar Mt. SE9 —7H 95
Cedarne Rd. SW6 —8M 73
Cedar Pk. Gdns. Romf —5H 49
Cedar Pk. Rd. Enf —2A 16
Cedar Pl. SE7 —6G 79
Cedar Pl. N'wd —6A 20
Cedar Ri. N14 —9E 14
Cedar Rd. N17 —8D 28
Cedar Rd. NW2 —9G 41
Cedar Rd. Brom —6G 111
Cedar Rd. Croy —4B 124
Cedar Rd. Dart —7H 99
Cedar Rd. E Mol —8C 102
Cedar Rd. Enf —2M 15
Cedar Rd. Eri —9E 82
Cedar Rd. Felt —7B 84
Cedar Rd. Horn —8G 51
Cedar Rd. Houn —1G 85
Cedar Rd. Romf —2A 50
Cedar Rd. Sutt —8A 122
Cedar Rd. Tedd —2E 102
Cedar Rd. Wat —8G 9
Cedars. Bans —6D 136
Cedars Av. E17 —3L 45
Cedars Av. Mitc —8E 106
Cedars Clo. NW4 —1H 41
Cedars Clo. SE13 —2B 94
Cedars Clo. Borwd —6M 11
Cedars Ct. N9 —2C 28
Cedars Dri. Uxb —5D 142
Cedars Ho. E17 —1M 45
Cedars M. SW4 —3F 90
(in two parts)
Cedars Rd. E15 —2C 62
Cedars Rd. N9 —2E 28
Cedars Rd. N21 —2M 27
Cedars Rd. SW4 —2F 90
Cedars Rd. SW13 —1E 88
Cedars Rd. W4 —7A 72
Cedars Rd. Beck —6J 109
Cedars Rd. Croy —5J 123
Cedars Rd. Hamp W —5G 103
Cedars Rd. Mord —8L 105
Cedars, The. E15 —3D 62
Cedars, The. W13 —9G 55
Cedars, The. Buck H —1E 30
Cedars, The. Tedd —3D 102
Cedars, The. Wall —6G 123
Cedar Ter. Rich —3J 87
Cedar Tree Gro. SE27 —2M 107
Cedarville Gdns. SW16 —3K 107
Cedar Wlk. Clay —8D 118
Cedar Wlk. Kenl —8A 138
Cedar Wlk. Wal A —7K 7
Cedar Way. NW1 —3H 59
Cedar Way. Sun —4C 100
Cedar Way Ind. Est. NW1 —3H 59
Cedar Wood Dri. Wat —8F 4
Cedra Ct. N16 —6E 44
Cedric Av. Romf —1C 50
Cedric Rd. SE9 —9A 96
Celadon Clo. Enf —5J 17
Celandine Clo. E3 —8L 61
Celandine Ct. E4 —3M 29
Celandine Dri. E8 —3D 60
Celandine Dri. SE28 —2F 80
Celandine Rd. W on T —6J 117
Celandine Way. E15 —6C 62
Celbridge M. W2 —9M 57
Celestial Gdns. SE13 —3B 94
Celia Ho. N1 —5C 60
(off Arden Est.)
Celia Johnson Ct. Borwd —3A 12
Celia Rd. N19 —9G 43
Celtic Av. Brom —7C 110
Celtic St. E14 —8M 61
Cemetery La. SE7 —7J 79
Cemetery Rd. E7 —1D 62
Cemetery Rd. N17 —7C 28
Cemetery Rd. SE2 —8F 80
Cenacle Clo. NW3 —8L 41
Cenotaph. —3J 75
Centaur Ct. Bren —6J 71
Centaurs Bus. Cen. Iswth —7E 70
Centaur St. SE1 —4K 75
Centenary Ct. F'ham —2L 131
Centenary Rd. Enf —6K 17
Centenary Trad. Est. Enf —5K 17
Centennial Av. Borwd & Els —9G 11
Centennial Pk. Els —9G 11
Central Av. E11 —7B 46
Central Av. N2 —9B 26
(East Finchley)
Central Av. N2 —2M 41
(St Marylebone Cemetery)
Central Av. N9 —3C 28
Central Av. SW11 —8D 74
Central Av. Ave —3M 83
Central Av. Enf —4F 16
Central Av. Hay —2D 68
Central Av. Houn —3A 86
Central Av. Pinn —4K 37
Central Av. Wall —7J 123
Central Av. Wal X —6E 6
Central Av. Well —1D 96
Central Av. W Mol —8K 101
Central Bus. Cen. NW10 —1C 56
Central Cir. NW4 —4G 41
Central Criminal Court. —9M 59
(Old Bailey)
Central Dri. Horn —8J 51
Central Gdns. Mord —9M 105
Central Hill. SE19 —2A 108
Central Ho. E15 —5A 62
Central Mans. NW4 —3F 40
(off Watford Way)
Central Markets (Smithfield).
(off Charterhouse St.) —8M 59
Central Pde. E17 —2L 45
Central Pde. SE20 —4H 109
(off High St.)
Central Pde. W3 —3M 71
Central Pde. Enf —4G 17
Central Pde. Felt —6G 85
Central Pde. Gnfd —6E 54
Central Pde. Harr —3D 38
Central Pde. Houn —8K 69
Central Pde. Ilf —4B 48
Central Pde. New Ad —2A 140
Central Pde. Sidc —9E 96
Central Pde. Surb —1J 119
Central Pde. W Mol —8K 101
Central Pk. Av. Dag —8M 49
Central Pk. Est. Houn —4H 85
Central Pk. Rd. E6 —5H 63
Central Pl. SE25 —9E 108
Central Rd. Dart —3J 99
Central Rd. Mord —1L 121
Central Rd. Wemb —1F 54
Central Rd. Wor Pk —3E 120
Central School Path. SW14 —2A 88
Central Sq. NW11 —4M 41
Central Sq. Wemb —1J 55
Central St. EC1 —6A 60
Central Ter. Beck —7H 109
Central Way. NW10 —6A 56
Central Way. SE28 —2E 80
Central Way. Cars —9C 122
Central Way. Felt —4E 84
Central Way. N'wd —7C 20
Centre Av. N2 —9C 26
Centre Av. NW10 —6G 57
Centre Av. W3 —2B 72
Centre Comn. Rd. Chst —3A 112
Centre Ct. Shop. Cen. SW19 —3K 105
Centre Dri. E7 —9G 47
Centre Heights. NW3 —3B 58
Centre Point. SE1 —6E 76
Centrepoint. WC1 —9H 59
(off St Giles High St.)
Centre Point Ho. WC2 —9H 59
Centre Rd. E11 & E7 —7E 46
Centre Rd. Dag —5M 65
Centre St. E2 —5F 60
Centre, The. Felt —8E 84
Centre, The. Houn —2M 85
Centre, The. W on T —3D 116
Centre Way. E17 —7A 30
Centre Way. N9 —2G 29
Centre Way. Ilf —7A 48
Centric Clo. NW1 —4E 58
Centro Ct. E6 —7K 63
Centurion Clo. N7 —3K 59
Centurion Ct. Hack —4F 122
Centurion La. E3 —4K 61
Centurion Way. Eri —4M 81
Centurion Way. Purf —5K 83
Centuryan Pl. Dart —3F 98
Century Clo. NW4 —3H 41
Century Ct. Wat —9A 8
Century Ho. SW15 —3H 89
Century M. E5 —9G 45

Charlton Rd. SE3 & SE7 —8E 78
Charlton Rd. Harr —2H 39
Charlton Rd. Shep —7A 100
Charlton Rd. Wemb —6K 39
Charlton Way. SE3 —9C 78
Charlwood. Croy —1K 139
Charlwood Clo. Harr —6C 22
Charlwood Dri. Oxs —7B 132
Charlwood Ho. SW1 —5H 75
(off Vauxhall Bri. Rd.)
Charlwood Houses. WC1 —6J 59
(off Midhope St.)
Charlwood Pl. SW1 —5G 75
Charlwood Rd. SW15 —3H 89
Charlwood Sq. Mitc —7B 106
Charlwood St. SW1 —6G 75
(in two parts)
Charlwood Ter. SW15 —3H 89
Charmans Ho. SW8 —8J 75
(off Wamdsworth Rd.)
Charmian Av. Stan —1H 39
Charminster Av. SW19 —6L 105
Charminster Ct. Surb —2H 119
Charminster Rd. SE9 —1H 111
Charminster Rd. Wor Pk —3H 121
Charmouth Ct. Rich —4K 87
Charmouth Ho. SW8 —8K 75
Charmouth Rd. Well —9G 81
Charnock. Swan —8C 114
(in two parts)
Charnock Ho. W12 —1F 72
(off White City Est.)
Charnock Rd. E5 —8F 44
Charnwood Av. SW19 —6L 105
Charnwood Clo. N Mald —8C 104
Charnwood Dri. E18 —1F 46
Charnwood Gdns. E14 —5L 77
Charnwood Pl. N20 —3A 26
Charnwood Rd. SE25 —9B 108
Charnwood Rd. Enf —9B 6
Charnwood Rd. Uxb —5E 142
Charnwood St. E5 —7F 44
Charrington Rd. Croy —4A 124
Charrington St. NW1 —5H 59
Charsley Rd. SE6 —8M 93
Chart Clo. Brom —5C 110
Chart Clo. Croy —1G 125
Chart Clo. Mitc —8D 106
Charter Av. Ilf —6B 48
Charter Ct. N4 —6L 43
Charter Ct. N22 —8H 27
Charter Ct. N Mald —7C 104
Charter Ct. S'hall —2L 69
Charter Cres. Houn —3J 85
Charter Dri. Bex —6J 97
Charter Ho. WC2 —9J 59
(off Crown Ct.)
Charter Ho. Sutt —8M 121
(off Mulgrave Rd.)
Charterhouse Av. Wemb —9G 39
Charterhouse Bldgs. EC1 —7A 60
Charterhouse M. EC1 —8M 59
Charterhouse Rd. Orp —5E 128
Charterhouse Sq. EC1 —8M 59
Charterhouse St. EC1 —8L 59
Charteris Rd. N4 —6L 43
Charteris Rd. NW6 —4K 57
Charteris Rd. Wfd G —7F 30
Charter Pl. Uxb —3B 142
Charter Pl. Wat —5G 9
Charter Rd. King T —7M 103
Charter Rd., The. Wfd G —6C 30
Charters Clo. SE19 —2C 108
Charter Sq. King T —6M 103
Charter Way. N3 —2K 41
Charter Way. N14 —8G 15
Chartes Ho. SE1 —4C 76
(off Stevens St.)
Chartfield Av. SW15 —4F 88
Chartfield Sq. SW15 —4H 89
Chartham Ct. SW9 —2L 91
(off Canterbury Cres.)
Chartham Gro. SE27 —9M 91
Chartham Ho. SE1 —4B 76
(off Weston St.)
Chartham Rd. SE25 —7F 108
Chart Hills Clo. SE28 —9J 65
Chart Ho. E14 —6M 77
(off Burrells Wharf Sq.)
Chartley Av. NW2 —8C 40
Chartley Av. Stan —6D 22
Charton Clo. Belv —7K 81
Chartres Ct. Gnfd —5B 54
Chartridge. SE17 —7B 76
(off Westmoreland Rd.)
Chartridge. Wat —2H 21
Chartridge Clo. Barn —7E 12
Chartridge Clo. Bush —8A 10
Chart St. N1 —6B 60
Chartwell Clo. SE9 —8B 96
Chartwell Clo. Croy —3B 124
Chartwell Clo. Gnfd —4M 53
Chartwell Clo. Wal A —6L 7
Chartwell Ct. Barn —6J 13
Chartwell Ct. Hay —1D 68
Chartwell Ct. Wfd G —7D 30
Chartwell Dri. Orp —7B 128
Chartwell Gdns. Sutt —5J 121
Chartwell Lodge. Beck —4L 109
Chartwell Pl. Eps —6C 134
Chartwell Pl. Harr —7B 38
Chartwell Pl. Sutt —5K 121
Chartwell Rd. N'wd —6D 20
Chartwell Way. SE20 —5F 108
Charville Ct. Harr —4D 38
Charville La. Hay —6A 52
Charville La. W. Uxb —6F 142
Char Wood. SW16 —1L 107
Chase Bank Ct. N14 —8G 15
(off Avenue Rd.)
Chase Cen., The. NW10 —6B 56
Chase Ct. Iswth —1E 86
Chase Ct. Gdns. Enf —5A 16
Chase Cross. —6C 34
Chase Cross Rd. Romf —7A 34
Chase End. Eps —4B 134
Chasefield Rd. SW17 —1D 106
Chase Gdns. E4 —4L 29
Chase Gdns. Twic —6B 86
Chase Grn. Enf —5A 16
Chase Grn. Av. Enf —4M 15
Chase Hill. Enf —5A 16
Chase Ho. Gdns. Horn —3K 51
Chase La. Chig —3D 32
Chase La. Ilf —3B 48
(in two parts)
Chaseley Dri. W4 —6M 71
Chaseley Dri. S Croy —2B 138
Chaseley St. E14 —9J 61
Chasemore Clo. Mitc —2D 122
Chasemore Gdns. Croy —7L 123
Chasemore Ho. SW6 —8J 73
Chase Ridings. Enf —4L 15
Chase Rd. N14 —7G 15
Chase Rd. NW10 —7B 56
Chase Rd. Eps —4B 134
Chase Rd. Trad. Est. NW10 —7B 56
Chase Side. —4A 16
Chase Side. N14 —8E 14
Chase Side. Enf —5A 16
Chaseside Av. SW20 —5J 105
Chase Side Av. Enf —4A 16
Chaseside Clo. Romf —6C 34
Chase Side Cres. Enf —3A 16
Chase Side Pl. Enf —4A 16
Chase Side Works Ind. Est. N14 —9H 15
Chase, The. E12 —9H 47
Chase, The. SW4 —2F 90
Chase, The. SW16 —4K 107
Chase, The. SW20 —5J 105
Chase, The. Asht —9G 133
Chase, The. Bexh —2M 97
Chase, The. Brom —7F 110
Chase, The. Chad H —4J 49
Chase, The. Chig —4A 32
Chase, The. Coul —6G 137
Chase, The. Eastc —4G 37
Chase, The. Edgw —8M 23
Chase, The. Lou —9H 19
Chase, The. Oxs —7A 132
Chase, The. Pinn —2K 37
Chase, The. Rain —4F 66
Chase, The. Romf —1C 50
Chase, The. Rush G —8C 50
Chase, The. Stan —6E 22
Chase, The. Sun —5F 100
Chase, The. Uxb —1E 142
Chase, The. Wall —7J 123
Chase, The. Wat —6C 8
Chaseville Pde. N21 —7K 15
Chaseville Pk. Rd. N21 —7J 15
Chase Way. N14 —2F 26
Chaseways Vs. Romf —8K 33
Chasewood Av. Enf —4M 15
Chasewood Ct. NW7 —5B 24
Chasewood Pk. Harr —8D 38
Chastilian Rd. Dart —6D 98
Chaston St. NW5 —1E 58
(off Grafton Ter.)
Chater Ho. E2 —6H 61
(off Roman Rd.)
Chatfield Rd. SW11 —2A 90
Chatfield Rd. Croy —3M 123
Chatham Av. Brom —2D 126
Chatham Clo. NW11 —3L 41
Chatham Clo. Sutt —2K 121
Chatham Pl. E9 —2G 61
Chatham Rd. E17 —1J 45
Chatham Rd. E18 —9D 30
Chatham Rd. SW11 —5D 90
Chatham Rd. King T —6L 103
Chatham St. SE17 —5B 76
Chatsfield. Eps —2E 134
Chatsfield Pl. W5 —9J 55
Chatsworth Av. NW4 —9G 25
Chatsworth Av. SW20 —5J 105
Chatsworth Av. Brom —1F 110
Chatsworth Av. Sidc —7E 96
Chatsworth Av. Wemb —1K 55
Chatsworth Clo. NW4 —9G 25
Chatsworth Clo. W4 —7A 72
Chatsworth Clo. Borwd —5L 11
Chatsworth Clo. W W'ck —4D 126
Chatsworth Ct. W8 —5L 73
(off Pembroke Rd.)
Chatsworth Ct. Stan —5G 23
Chatsworth Cres. Houn —3B 86
Chatsworth Dri. Enf —9E 16
Chatsworth Est. E5 —9H 45
Chatsworth Gdns. W3 —2M 71
Chatsworth Gdns. Harr —6M 37
Chatsworth Gdns. N Mald —9D 104
Chatsworth Ho. Brom —8E 110
(off Westmoreland Rd.)
Chatsworth Lodge. W4 —6B 72
(off Bourne Pl.)
Chatsworth Pde. Orp —9A 112
Chatsworth Pl. Mitc —7D 106
Chatsworth Pl. Oxs —5B 132
Chatsworth Pl. Tedd —1E 102
Chatsworth Ri. W5 —7K 55
Chatsworth Rd. E5 —8G 45
Chatsworth Rd. E15 —1D 62
Chatsworth Rd. NW2 —2G 57
(in two parts)
Chatsworth Rd. W4 —7A 72
Chatsworth Rd. W5 —7K 55
Chatsworth Rd. Croy —6B 124
Chatsworth Rd. Dart —4G 99
Chatsworth Rd. Hay —7F 52
Chatsworth Rd. Sutt —7H 121
Chatsworth Way. SE27 —9M 91
Chatteris Av. Romf —6G 35
Chattern Hill. Ashf —1A 100
Chattern Rd. Ashf —1A 100
Chatterton Ct. Rich —1K 87
Chatterton M. N4 —8M 43
(off Chatterton Rd.)
Chatterton Rd. N4 —8M 43
Chatterton Rd. Brom —8H 111
Chatto Rd. SW11 —4D 90
Chaucer Av. Hay —8E 52
Chaucer Av. Houn —1F 84
Chaucer Av. Rich —2L 87
Chaucer Clo. N11 —5G 27
Chaucer Clo. Bans —6J 135
Chaucer Ct. New Bar —7M 13
Chaucer Dri. SE1 —5D 76
Chaucer Gdns. Sutt —5L 121
(in two parts)
Chaucer Grn. Croy —2F 124
Chaucer Ho. SW1 —6G 75
(off Churchill Gdns.)
Chaucer Ho. Barn —6H 13
Chaucer Ho. Sutt —5L 121
(off Chaucer Gdns.)
Chaucer Mans. W14 —7J 73
(off Queen's Club Gdns.)
Chaucer Pk. Dart —6K 99
Chaucer Rd. E7 —2E 62
Chaucer Rd. E11 —4E 46
Chaucer Rd. E17 —9A 30
Chaucer Rd. SE24 —4L 91
Chaucer Rd. W3 —2A 72
Chaucer Rd. Romf —7F 34
Chaucer Rd. Sidc —7G 97
Chaucer Rd. Sutt —6L 121
Chaucer Rd. Well —9C 80
Chaucer Theatre. —9D 60
(off Braham St.)
Chaucer Way. SW19 —3A 106
Chaucer Way. Dart —3L 99
(in two parts)
Chaulden Ho. EC1 —6B 60
(off Cranwood St.)
Chauncey Clo. N9 —3E 28
Chauncey Ho. Wat —8C 8
Chaundrye Clo. SE9 —5K 95
Chauntler Clo. E16 —9F 62
Chave Rd. Dart —9J 99
Chaville Ho. N11 —4E 26
Cheadle Ct. NW8 —7B 58
Cheadle Ho. E14 —9K 61
(off Copenhagen Pl.)
Cheam. —8J 121
Cheam Comn. Rd. Wor Pk —4F 120
Cheam Mans. Sutt —9J 121
Cheam Pk. Way. Sutt —8J 121
Cheam Rd. Eps & Ewe —2E 134
Cheam Rd. Sutt —8K 121
Cheam St. SE15 —2G 93
Cheam Village. (Junct.) —8J 121
Cheapside. EC2 —9A 60
Cheapside. N13 —4B 28
Cheapside. N22 —1L 43
Chearsley. SE17 —5A 76
(off Deacon Way)
Cheddar Clo. N11 —6D 26
Cheddar Waye. Hay —9F 52
Cheddington Ho. E2 —4E 60
(off Whiston Rd.)
Cheddington Rd. N18 —3C 28
Chedworth Clo. E16 —9D 62
Cheeseman Clo. Hamp —3J 101
Cheesemans Ter. W14 —6K 73
(in two parts)
Chelford Rd. Brom —2B 110
Chelmer Cres. Bark —5F 64
Chelmer Rd. E9 —1H 61
Chelmsford Av. Romf —7B 34
Chelmsford Clo. E6 —9K 63
Chelmsford Clo. W6 —7H 73
Chelmsford Clo. Sutt —1L 135
Chelmsford Ct. N14 —9H 15
(off Chelmsford Rd.)
Chelmsford Dri. Upm —8K 51
Chelmsford Gdns. Ilf —5J 47
Chelmsford Ho. N7 —9K 43
(off Holloway Rd.)
Chelmsford Rd. E11 —6B 46
Chelmsford Rd. E17 —4L 45
Chelmsford Rd. E18 —8D 30
Chelmsford Rd. N14 —9G 15
Chelmsford Sq. NW10 —4G 57
Chelmsine Ct. Ruis —3A 36
Chelsea. —6C 74
Chelsea Bri. SW1 & SW8 —7F 74
Chelsea Bri. Bus. Cen. SW8 —8F 74
Chelsea Bri. Rd. SW1 —6E 74
Chelsea Bri. Wharf. SW8 —7F 74
Chelsea Cloisters. SW3 —5C 74
Chelsea Clo. NW10 —4B 56
Chelsea Clo. Edgw —9L 23
Chelsea Clo. Hamp H —2A 102
Chelsea Clo. Wor Pk —2E 120
Chelsea Ct. Brom —7J 111
Chelsea Cres. NW2 —2K 57
Chelsea Cres. SW10 —9A 74
Chelsea Embkmt. SW3 —7C 74
Chelsea Farm Ho. Studios. SW10 —7B 74
(off Milman's St.)
Chelsea F.C. —8M 73
Chelsea Gdns. SW1 —6E 74
Chelsea Gdns. Sutt —6J 121
Chelsea Ga. SW1 —6E 74
(off Ebury Bri. Rd.)
Chelsea Harbour Design Cen. SW10 —9A 74
Chelsea Harbour Dri. SW10 —9A 74
Chelsea Lodge. SW3 —7D 74
(off Tite St.)
Chelsea Mnr. Ct. SW3 —7C 74
Chelsea Mnr. Gdns. SW3 —6C 74
Chelsea Mnr. St. SW3 —6C 74
Chelsea M. Horn —6F 50
Chelsea Pk. Gdns. SW3 —7B 74
Chelsea Physic Garden. —7D 74
Chelsea Reach Tower. SW10 —8B 74
(off Worlds End Est.)
Chelsea Sq. SW3 —6B 74
Chelsea Studios. SW6 —8M 73
(off Fulham Rd.)
Chelsea Towers. SW3 —7C 74
(off Chelsea Mnr. Gdns.)
Chelsea Village. SW6 —8M 73
(off Fulham Rd.)
Chelsea Wharf. SW10 —8B 74
(off Lots Rd.)
Chelsfield. —7F 128
Chelsfield Av. N9 —9H 17
Chelsfield Gdns. SE26 —9G 93
Chelsfield Grn. N9 —9H 17
Chelsfield Hill. Orp —9G 129
Chelsfield Ho. SE17 —5C 76
(off Massinger St.)
Chelsfield La. Orp —2H 129
(BR5)
Chelsfield La. Orp —9L 129
(BR6)
Chelsfield Rd. Orp —1G 129
Chelsfield Village. —7J 129
Chelsham. —9L 139
Chelsham Common. —8L 139
Chelsham Comn. Rd. Warl —9L 139
Chelsham Ct. Rd. Warl —9B 140
Chelsham Rd. SW4 —2H 91
Chelsham Rd. S Croy —9B 124
Chelsham Rd. Warl —9K 139
Chelsiter Ct. Sidc —1D 112
Chelston App. Ruis —7E 36
Chelston Rd. Ruis —6E 36
Chelsworth Clo. Romf —7K 35
Chelsworth Dri. SE18 —7B 80
Chelsworth Dri. Romf —8J 35
Cheltenham Av. Twic —6E 86
Cheltenham Clo. N Mald —7A 104
Cheltenham Clo. N'holt —2M 53
Cheltenham Ct. Stan —5G 23
(off Marsh La.)
Cheltenham Gdns. E6 —5J 63
Cheltenham Gdns. Lou —8J 19
Cheltenham Ho. Wat —4G 9
(off Exeter Clo.)
Cheltenham Pl. W3 —2M 71
Cheltenham Pl. Harr —2J 39
Cheltenham Rd. E10 —4A 46
Cheltenham Rd. SE15 —3G 93
Cheltenham Rd. Orp —5E 128
Cheltenham Ter. SW3 —6D 74
Chelverton Rd. SW15 —3H 89
Chelwood. N20 —2B 26
Chelwood Clo. E4 —8M 17
Chelwood Clo. Eps —4D 134
Chelwood Clo. N'wd —7A 20
Chelwood Gdns. Rich —1L 87
Chelwood Gdns. Pas. Rich —1L 87
Chelwood Ho. W2 —9B 58
(off Gloucester Sq.)
Chelwood Wlk. SE4 —3J 93
Chenappa Clo. E13 —6E 62
Chenduit Way. Stan —5D 22
Cheney Ct. SE23 —7H 93
Cheney Rd. NW1 —5J 59
Cheney Row. E17 —8K 29
Cheneys Rd. E11 —8C 46
Cheney St. Pinn —2G 37
Chenies Ho. W4 —8D 72
(off Corney Reach Way)
Chenies M. WC1 —7H 59
Chenies Pl. NW1 —5H 59
Chenies St. WC1 —8H 59
Chenies, The. NW1 —5H 59
(off Pancras Rd.)
Chenies, The. Orp —1C 128
Chenies, The. Wilm —1C 114
Chenies Way. Wat —9C 8
Cheniston Gdns. W8 —4M 73
Chepstow Av. Horn —8J 51
Chepstow Clo. SW15 —5J 89
Chepstow Corner. W2 —9L 57
(off Pembridge Vs.)
Chepstow Ct. W2 —1L 73
(off Chepstow Vs.)
Chepstow Cres. W11 —1L 73
Chepstow Cres. Ilf —4C 48
Chepstow Gdns. S'hall —9K 53
Chepstow Ho. Romf —5L 35
(off Leamington Av.)
Chepstow Pl. W2 —9L 57
Chepstow Ri. Croy —5C 124
Chepstow Rd. W2 —9L 57
Chepstow Rd. W7 —4E 70
Chepstow Rd. Croy —5C 124
Chepstow Vs. W11 —1K 73
Chepstow Way. SE15 —8D 76
Chequers. Buck H —1F 30
Chequers Clo. NW9 —1C 40
Chequers Clo. Orp —8D 112
Chequers Ct. EC1 —7B 60
(off Chequer St.)
Chequers Ho. NW8 —7C 58
(off Jerome Cres.)
Chequers La. Dag —8K 65
Chequers La. Wat —3F 4
Chequers Pde. N13 —5A 28
Chequers Pde. SE9 —5K 95
(off Eltham High St.)
Chequers Pde. Dag —4K 65
Chequers Rd. Lou —7L 19
Chequers Rd. Romf & S Wea —2J 35
Chequers Sq. Uxb —3A 142
Chequers, The. Pinn —1H 37
Chequer St. EC1 —7A 60
(in two parts)
Chequers Wlk. Wal A —6M 7
Chequers Way. N13 —5M 27
Cherbury Clo. SE28 —9H 65
Cherbury Ct. N1 —5B 60
(off St John's Est.)
Cherbury St. N1 —5B 60
Cherchefelle M. Stan —5F 22
Cherimoya Gdns. W Mol —7M 101
Cherington Rd. W7 —2C 70
Cheriton Av. Brom —9D 110
Cheriton Av. Ilf —9K 31
Cheriton Clo. W5 —8G 55
Cheriton Clo. Barn —5D 14
Cheriton Ct. SE12 —6E 94
Cheriton Ct. W on T —3G 117
Cheriton Dri. SE18 —8B 80
Cheriton Sq. SW17 —8E 90
Cherry Av. S'hall —2H 69
Cherry Av. Swan —8B 114
Cherry Blossom Clo. N13 —5M 27
Cherry Clo. E17 —3M 45
Cherry Clo. SW2 —6L 91
Cherry Clo. W5 —4H 71
Cherry Clo. Bans —6H 135
Cherry Clo. Cars —4D 122
Cherry Clo. Mord —8J 105
Cherry Clo. Ruis —8D 36
Cherrycot Hill. Orp —6A 128
Cherrycot Ri. Orp —6A 128
Cherry Ct. W3 —2C 72
Cherry Ct. Pinn —9H 21
Cherry Cres. Bren —8F 70
Cherrycroft Gdns. Pinn —7K 21
Cherrydale. Wat —6D 8
Cherrydown Av. E4 —3K 29
Cherrydown Clo. E4 —3L 29
Cherrydown Rd. Sidc —8H 97
Cherrydown Wlk. Romf —9M 33
Cherry Garden Ho. SE16 —3F 76
(off Cherry Garden St.)
Cherry Gdns. Dag —1K 65
Cherry Gdns. N'holt —3M 53
Cherry Garden St. SE16 —3F 76
Cherry Gth. Bren —6H 71
Cherry Gro. Hay —2F 68
Cherry Gro. Uxb —8A 52
Cherry Hill. Harr —6D 22
Cherry Hill. New Bar —8M 13
Cherry Hill Gdns. Croy —6K 123
Cherry Hills. Wat —5J 21
Cherry Hollow. Ab L —4D 4
Cherrylands Clo. NW9 —7A 40
Cherry La. W Dray —5K 143
Cherry Laurel Wlk. SW2 —5K 91
Cherry Orchard. SE7 —7G 79
Cherry Orchard. W Dray —3J 143
Cherry Orchard Clo. Orp —9G 113
Cherry Orchard Gdns. Croy —3B 124
Cherry Orchard Gdns. W Mol —7K 101
Cherry Orchard Rd. Brom —4J 127
Cherry Orchard Rd. Croy —4B 124
Cherry Orchard Rd. W Mol —7L 101
Cherry Rd. Enf —2G 17
Cherry St. Romf —3B 50
Cherry Tree Av. W Dray —9D 142
Cherry Tree Clo. E9 —4G 61
Cherry Tree Clo. Rain —5E 66
Cherry Tree Clo. Wemb —9E 38
Cherry Tree Ct. NW1 —3G 59
(off Camden Rd.)
Cherry Tree Ct. NW9 —2A 40
Cherry Tree Ct. SE7 —7G 79
Cherry Tree Ct. Coul —9K 137
Cherrytree Dri. SW16 —9J 91
Cherry Tree Grn. S Croy —6F 138

Chingley Clo.—Church Wlk.

Chingley Clo. Brom —3C 110
Ching Way. E4 —6K 29
(in two parts)
Chinnery Clo. Enf —3D 16
Chinnock's Wharf. E14 —1J 77
Chinnor Cres. Gnfd —5M 53
Chipka St. E14 —3A 78
(in two parts)
Chipley St. SE14 —7J 77
Chipmunk Gro. N'holt —6J 53
Chippendale All. Uxb —3B 142
Chippendale Ho. SW1 —6F 74
(off Churchill Gdns.)
Chippendale St. E5 —8H 45
Chippendale Waye. Uxb —3B 142
Chippenham. King T —6K 103
(off Excelsior Clo.)
Chippenham Av. Wemb —1M 55
Chippenham Clo. Pinn —2D 36
Chippenham Clo. Romf —5H 35
Chippenham Gdns. NW6 —6L 57
Chippenham Gdns. Romf —5H 35
Chippenham M. W9 —7L 57
Chippenham Rd. W9 —7L 57
Chippenham Rd. H Hill & Romf —6H 35
Chippenham Wlk. Romf —6H 35
Chipperfield Ho. SW3 —6C 74
(off Ixworth Pl.)
Chipperfield Rd. Orp & St P —5E 112
Chipping Barnet. —6J 13
Chipping Clo. Barn —5J 13
Chipstead. —9D 136
Chipstead Av. T Hth —8M 107
Chipstead Clo. SE19 —4D 108
Chipstead Clo. Coul —8E 136
Chipstead Clo. Sutt —1M 135
Chipstead Gdns. NW2 —7F 40
Chipstead Rd. Bans —9K 135
Chipstead Rd. Eri —8C 82
Chipstead Rd. H'row A —2E 144
Chipstead St. SW6 —9L 73
Chipstead Valley Rd. Coul —8E 136
Chipstead Way. Bans —8D 136
Chip St. SW4 —2H 91
Chirdland Ho. Wat —8C 8
Chirk Clo. Hay —7J 53
Chisenhale Rd. E3 —5J 61
Chisholm Ct. W6 —6E 72
Chisholm Rd. Croy —4C 124
Chisholm Rd. Rich —5K 87
Chisledon Wlk. E9 —2K 61
(off Osborne Rd.)
Chislehurst. —3M 111
Chislehurst Av. N12 —7A 26
Chislehurst Caves. —5L 111
Chislehurst Rd. Brom & Chst —6H 111
Chislehurst Rd. Orp —8C 112
Chislehurst Rd. Rich —4J 87
Chislehurst Rd. Sidc —2E 112
Chislehurst West. —2L 111
Chislet Clo. Beck —4L 109
Chisley Rd. N15 —4C 44
Chiswell Ct. Wat —2G 9
Chiswell Sq. SE3 —1F 94
Chiswell St. EC1 —8A 60
Chiswick. —7B 72
Chiswick Bri. SW14 & W4 —1A 88
Chiswick Clo. Croy —5K 123
Chiswick Comn. Rd. W4 —5B 72
Chiswick Ct. W4 —5M 71
Chiswick Ct. Pinn —1K 37
Chiswick High Rd. Bren & W4 (in two parts) —6L 71
Chiswick House. —7C 72
Chiswick La. W4 —6C 72
Chiswick La. S. W4 —7D 72
Chiswick Mall. W4 & W6 —7D 72
Chiswick Pk. W4 —5M 71
Chiswick Plaza. W4 —7A 72
Chiswick Quay. W4 —9A 72
Chiswick Rd. N9 —2E 28
Chiswick Rd. W4 —5A 72
Chiswick Roundabout. (Junct.) —6L 71
Chiswick Sq. W4 —7C 72
Chiswick Staithe. W4 —9A 72
Chiswick Ter. W4 —5A 72
Chiswick Village. W4 —7L 71
Chiswick Wharf. W4 —7D 72
Chitterfield Ga. W Dray —8L 143
Chitty's La. Dag —7H 49
Chitty St. W1 —8G 59
Chivalry Rd. SW11 —4C 90
Chive Clo. Croy —3H 125
Chivenor Gro. King T —2H 103
Chivers Rd. E4 —3M 29
Choats Rd. Bark & Dag —5G 65
Chobham Gdns. SW19 —8H 89
Chobham Rd. E15 —1B 62
Cholmeley Cres. N6 —5F 42
Cholmeley Lodge. N6 —6F 42
Cholmeley Pk. N6 —6F 42
Cholmley Gdns. NW6 —1L 57
Cholmley Rd. Th Dit —1F 118
Cholmondeley Av. NW10 —5E 56
Cholmondeley Wlk. Rich —4G 87
(in two parts)
Choppin's Ct. E1 —2F 76
Chopwell Clo. E15 —3B 62
Chorleywood Cres. Orp —6D 112
Choumert Gro. SE15 —1E 92
Choumert Rd. SE15 —2D 92
Choumert Sq. SE15 —1E 92
Chow Sq. E8 —1D 60
Chrislaine Clo. Stanw —5B 144
Chrisp Ho. SE10 —7C 78
(off Maze Hill)
Chrisp St. E14 —8M 61
(in two parts)
Christabel Clo. Iswth —2C 86
Christchurch Av. N12 —6A 26
Christchurch Av. NW6 —4H 57
Christchurch Av. Eri —7B 82
Christchurch Av. Harr —2D 38
Christchurch Av. Rain —5D 66
Christchurch Av. Tedd —2E 102
Christchurch Av. Wemb —2J 55
Christchurch Clo. N12 —7B 26
Christchurch Clo. SW19 —4B 106
Christchurch Ct. NW10 —4C 56
Christchurch Ct. Hay —7G 53
(off Dunedin Way)
Christchurch Cres. Rad —1E 10
Christchurch Flats. Rich —2J 87
Christchurch Gdns. Eps —3M 133
Christchurch Gdns. Harr —2E 38
Christchurch Grn. Wemb —2J 55
Christchurch Hill. NW3 —8B 42
Christchurch Ho. SW2 —7K 91
(off Christchurch Rd.)
Christchurch La. Barn —4J 13
Christchurch Lodge. Barn —6D 14
Christ Chu. Mt. Eps —4M 133
(in two parts)
Christchurch Pk. Sutt —9A 122
Christchurch Pas. NW3 —8A 42
Christchurch Pas. High Bar —4J 13
Christchurch Path. Hay —4A 68
Christchurch Pl. SW8 —1H 91
Christchurch Pl. Eps —3M 133
Christchurch Rd. N8 —4J 43
Christchurch Rd. SW2 —7K 91
Christ Chu. Rd. SW14 —4M 87
Christchurch Rd. SW19 —4B 106
Christ Chu. Rd. Beck —6L 109
Christchurch Rd. Dart —6G 99
Christ Chu. Rd. Eps —4J 133
Christchurch Rd. Ilf —6M 47
Christchurch Rd. H'row A —2E 144
Christchurch Rd. Purl —3M 137
Christchurch Rd. Sidc —1D 112
Christchurch Rd. Surb —1K 119
Christchurch Sq. E9 —4G 61
Christchurch St. SW3 —7D 74
Christchurch Ter. SW3 —7D 74
(off Christchurch St.)
Christchurch Way. SE10 —6C 78
Christian Ct. SE16 —2K 77
Christian Fields. SW16 —4L 107
Christian Pl. E1 —9E 60
(off Burslem St.)
Christian St. E1 —9E 60
Christie Ct. N19 —7J 43
Christie Dri. Croy —9E 108
Christie Gdns. Romf —4F 48
Christie Ho. SE10 —6D 78
(off Blackwall La.)
Christie Rd. E9 —2J 61
Christie Rd. Wal A —8H 7
Christina Sq. N4 —6M 43
Christina St. EC2 —7C 60
Christine Ct. Rain —8E 66
Christine Worsley Clo. N21 —1M 27
Christopher Av. W7 —4E 70
Christopher Clo. SE16 —3H 77
Christopher Clo. Horn —9H 51
Christopher Clo. Sidc —4D 96
Christopher Gdns. Dag —1H 65
Christopher Ho. Sidc —8E 96
(off Station Rd.)
Christopher Pl. NW1 —6H 59
Christopher Rd. S'hall —5F 68
Christophers M. W11 —2J 73
Christopher St. EC2 —7B 60
Christy Rd. Big H —7G 141
Chryssell Rd. SW9 —8L 75
Chubworthy St. SE14 —7J 77
Chudleigh. Sidc —1F 112
Chudleigh Cres. Ilf —9C 48
Chudleigh Gdns. Sutt —5A 122
Chudleigh Rd. NW6 —3H 57
Chudleigh Rd. SE4 —4K 93
Chudleigh Rd. Romf —4J 35
Chudleigh Rd. Twic —5C 86
(in two parts)
Chudleigh St. E1 —9H 61
Chudleigh Way. Ruis —6E 36
Chulsa Rd. SE26 —2F 108
Chumleigh St. SE5 —7C 76
Chumleigh Wlk. Surb —8K 103
Church All. A'ham —2A 10
Church All. Croy —3L 123
Church App. SE21 —9B 92
Church App. Stanw —5B 144
Church Av. E4 —6B 30
Church Av. N2 —9B 26
Church Av. NW1 —2F 58
Church Av. SW14 —2B 88
Church Av. Beck —5L 109
Church Av. N'holt —3K 53
Church Av. Pinn —4J 37
Church Av. Ruis —6B 36
Church Av. Sidc —2E 112
Church Av. S'hall —4J 69
Churchbank. E17 —2L 45
(off Teresa M.)
Churchbury Clo. Enf —4C 16
Churchbury La. Enf —5B 16
Churchbury Rd. SE9 —6G 95
Churchbury Rd. Enf —4C 16
Church Cloisters. EC3 —1C 76
(off Lovat La.)
Church Clo. N20 —3C 26
Church Clo. W8 —3M 73
Church Clo. Edgw —5A 24
Church Clo. Eps —5C 134
Church Clo. Hay —8B 52
Church Clo. Houn —1J 85
Church Clo. Lou —4K 19
Church Clo. N'wd —7D 20
Church Clo. Rad —1E 10
Church Clo. Uxb —5A 142
Church Clo. W Dray —4J 143
Church Ct. SE16 —3K 77
(off Rotherhithe St.)
Church Ct. Rich —4H 87
Church Ct. Wfd G —6G 31
Church Cres. E9 —3H 61
Church Cres. N3 —8K 25
Church Cres. N10 —2F 42
Church Cres. N20 —3C 26
Churchcroft Clo. SW12 —6E 90
Churchdown. Brom —1C 110
Church Dri. NW9 —6B 40
Church Dri. Harr —4L 37
Church Dri. W W'ck —5C 126
Church Elm La. Dag —2L 65
Church End. —8K 25
(Finchley)
Church End. —2C 56
(Willesden)
Church End. E17 —2M 45
Church End. NW4 —1F 40
Church Entry. EC4 —9M 59
(off Carter La.)
Church Est. Almshouses. Rich
(off Sheen Rd.) —3K 87
Church Farm Clo. Swan —1A 130
Church Farm House Mus. —1F 40
Church Farm La. Sutt —8J 121
Church Farm Way. A'ham —2M 9
Church Fld. Dart —8H 99
Churchfield Av. N12 —6B 26
Churchfield Clo. Harr —2A 38
Churchfield Clo. Hay —1D 68
Churchfield Mans. SW6 —1K 89
(off New King's Rd.)
Church Fld. Path. Chesh —2C 6
(in two parts)
Churchfield Rd. W3 —2A 72
Churchfield Rd. W7 —3C 70
Churchfield Rd. W13 —2F 70
Churchfield Rd. W on T —3E 116
Churchfield Rd. Well —2E 96
Churchfields. E18 —8E 30
Churchfields. SE10 —7A 78
Churchfields. Lou —6J 19
Churchfields. W Mol —7L 101
Churchfields Av. Felt —9K 85
Churchfields Av. Wey —7A 116
Churchfields Rd. Beck —6H 109
Churchfields Rd. Wat —9D 4
Churchfield Way. N12 —6A 26
Church Gdns. W5 —3H 71
Church Gdns. Wemb —9E 38
Church Gth. N19 —7H 43
(off St John's Gro.)
Churchgate. —3A 6
Church Ga. SW6 —2J 89
Churchgate. Chesh —2B 6
Churchgate Rd. Chesh —2B 6
Church Grn. SW9 —9L 75
Church Grn. Hay —9D 52
Church Grn. W on T —8G 117
Church Gro. SE13 —4M 93
Church Gro. King T —5G 103
Church Hill. E17 —2L 45
Church Hill. N21 —9K 15
Church Hill. SE18 —4K 79
Church Hill. SW19 —2K 105
Church Hill. Cars —7D 122
Church Hill. Cray —3C 98
Church Hill. Cud —7M 141
Church Hill. Dart —8H 99
Church Hill. Harr —6C 38
Church Hill. Lou —5J 19
Church Hill. Orp —2E 128
Church Hill. Purl —2J 137
Church Hill Rd. E17 —2M 45
Church Hill Rd. Barn & E Barn —8C 14
Church Hill Rd. Surb —9J 103
Church Hill Rd. Sutt —5H 121
Church Hill Wood. Orp —9D 112
Church Hollow. Purf —6L 83
Church Ho. SW1 —4H 75
(off Gt. Smith St.)
Church Hyde. SE18 —7C 80
Churchill Av. Harr —4F 38
Churchill Av. Uxb —6F 142
Churchill Clo. Dart —7M 99
Churchill Clo. Felt —7D 84
Churchill Clo. Uxb —6F 142
Churchill Clo. Warl —9G 139
Churchill Ct. N4 —5L 43
Churchill Ct. W5 —7K 55
Churchill Ct. Farnb —7A 128
Churchill Ct. N'holt —1L 53
Churchill Ct. N'wd —6B 20
Churchill Ct. Pinn —8J 21
Churchill Ct. S Harr —3M 37
Churchill Dri. Wey —6A 116
Churchill Gdns. SW1 —6G 75
(off Churchill Gdns., in three parts)
Churchill Gdns. W3 —9L 55
Churchill Gdns. Rd. SW1 —6F 74
Churchill Pk. Dart —4L 99
Churchill Pl. E14 —2M 77
Churchill Pl. Harr —2C 38
Churchill Rd. E16 —9G 63
Churchill Rd. NW2 —2F 56
Churchill Rd. NW5 —9F 42
Churchill Rd. Edgw —6K 23
Churchill Rd. Eps —3L 133
Churchill Rd. S Croy —1A 138
Churchills M. Wfd G —6D 30
Churchill Ter. E4 —4L 29
Churchill Theatre. —6E 110
Churchill Wlk. E9 —1G 61
Churchill Way. Big H —5H 141
Churchill Way. Brom —6E 110
Churchill Way. Sun —2E 100
Church La. E11 —6C 46
Church La. E17 —2M 45
Church La. N2 —1B 42
Church La. N8 —2K 43
Church La. N9 —2E 28
Church La. N17 —8C 28
Church La. NW9 —4A 40
Church La. SW17 —2D 106
Church La. SW19 —5K 105
Church La. W5 —3G 71
Church La. A'ham —2M 9
Church La. Brom —3J 127
Church La. Chel —8M 139
Church La. Chesh —2B 6
Church La. Chess —8K 119
Church La. Chst —5A 112
Church La. Dag —3A 66
Church La. Enf —5B 16
Church La. Eps —9H 135
Church La. Harr —8D 22
Church La. Lou —5K 19
Church La. Pinn —1J 37
Church La. Purf —6L 83
Church La. Rich —7J 87
Church La. Romf —2C 50
Church La. Tedd —2D 102
Church La. Th Dit —1D 118
Church La. Twic —7E 86
Church La. Uxb —5A 142
Church La. Wall —5H 123
Church La. Warl —9H 139
Church La. Wen —9H 67
Churchley Rd. SE26 —1F 108
Church Manorway. SE2 —6E 80
Church Manorway. Eri —4B 82
Church Mead. SE5 —8A 76
(off Camberwell Rd.)
Churchmead Clo. E Barn —8C 14
Church Mdw. Surb —4G 119
Churchmead Rd. NW10 —2E 56
Churchmore Rd. SW16 —5G 107
Chu. Mt. N2 —3B 42
Chu. Paddock Ct. Wall —5H 123
Church Pas. EC2 —9A 60
(off Guildhall Yd.)
Church Pas. Barn —5J 13
Church Pas. Surb —9J 103
Church Pas. Twic —7F 86
Church Path. E11 —3E 46
Church Path. E17 —2M 45
Church Path. N5 —1M 59
Church Path. N12 —4A 26
Church Path. N17 —8C 28
Church Path. NW10 —3C 56
Church Path. SW14 —3B 88
(in two parts)
Church Path. SW19 —6K 105
Church Path. W3 & W4 —3A 72
(in two parts)
Church Path. W7 —2C 70
Church Path. Bark —4A 64
Church Path. Barn —6J 13
Church Path. Croy —4A 124
(in two parts)
Church Path. Mitc —7C 106
(in two parts)
Church Path. Romf —3C 50
Church Path. S'hall —2L 69
(UB1)
Church Path. S'hall —4K 69
(UB2)
Church Path. Swan —5F 114
Church Pl. W1 —1G 75
Church Pl. W5 —3H 71
Church Pl. Ick —8A 36
Church Pl. Mitc —7C 106
Church Ri. SE23 —8H 93
Church Ri. Chess —8K 119
Church Rd. E10 —6L 45
Church Rd. E12 —1J 63
Church Rd. E17 —9J 29
Church Rd. N6 —4E 42
Church Rd. N17 —8C 28
(in two parts)
Church Rd. NW4 —2F 40
Church Rd. NW10 —3C 56
Church Rd. SE19 —5C 108
Church Rd. SW13 —1D 88
Church Rd. SW19 —2J 105
Church Rd. SW19 & Mitc —5B 106
Church Rd. W3 —2A 72
Church Rd. W7 —1B 70
Church Rd. Ashf —9D 144
Church Rd. Asht —9H 133
Church Rd. Bark —2A 64
Church Rd. Bexh —1K 97
Church Rd. Big H —9H 141
Church Rd. Brom —6E 110
Church Rd. Buck H —1F 30
Church Rd. Cat —9D 138
Church Rd. Clay —8D 118
Church Rd. Cran —6F 68
Church Rd. Croy —5A 124
(in two parts)
Church Rd. E Mol —8B 102
Church Rd. Enf —8G 17
Church Rd. Eps —4C 134
Church Rd. Eri —6B 82
Church Rd. Farnb —7A 128
Church Rd. Felt —2H 101
Church Rd. Ham & Rich —1H 103
Church Rd. H Wood —8K 35
Church Rd. Hay —2D 68
Church Rd. H Bee —5E 18
Church Rd. Houn —8L 69
Church Rd. Ilf —4C 48
Church Rd. Iswth —9B 70
Church Rd. Kenl —7B 138
Church Rd. Kes —9H 127
Church Rd. King T —6K 103
Church Rd. Noak H —1G 35
Church Rd. N'holt —5H 53
Church Rd. N'wd —7D 20
Church Rd. Orp —9G 129
Church Rd. Purl —2J 137
Church Rd. Rich —3J 87
Church Rd. Shep —2A 116
Church Rd. Short —7C 110
Church Rd. Sidc —1E 112
Church Rd. S'hall —4K 69
Church Rd. Stan —5F 22
Church Rd. Surb —3G 119
Church Rd. Sutt —8J 121
Church Rd. S at H —3K 115
Church Rd. Swan —2B 130
(Crockenhill)
Church Rd. Swan —5H 115
(Swanley Village)
Church Rd. Tedd —1C 102
Church Rd. Uxb —7B 142
Church Rd. Wall —5G 123
Church Rd. Warl —9H 139
Church Rd. Wat —3E 8
Church Rd. Well —1F 96
Church Rd. W Dray —4H 143
Church Rd. W Ewe —9B 120
Church Rd. Whyt —9D 138
Church Rd. Wor Pk —3C 120
Church Rd. Almshouses. E10
(off Church Rd.) —7M 45
Church Rd. Ind. Est. E10 —6L 45
Church Rd. N. N2 —9B 26
Church Rd. S. N2 —9B 26
Church Row. NW3 —9A 42
Church Row. Chst —5A 112
Church Row M. Chst —4A 112
Church Side. Eps —5M 133
Churchside Clo. Big H —9G 141
Church St. E15 —4C 62
Church St. E16 —2M 79
Church St. N9 —9B 16
Church St. W2 & NW8 —8B 58
Church St. W4 —7D 72
Church St. Croy —5M 123
Church St. Dag —2M 65
Church St. Enf —5A 16
Church St. Eps —1E 134
Church St. Esh —6M 117
Church St. Ewe —5C 134
Church St. Hamp —5A 102
Church St. Iswth —2F 86
Church St. King T —6H 103
Church St. Sun —7F 100
Church St. Sutt —7M 121
Church St. Twic —7E 86
Church St. Wal A —6J 7
Church St. W on T —3E 116
Church St. Wat —6G 9
Church St. Est. NW8 —7B 58
(in two parts)
Church St. N. E15 —4C 62
Church St. Pas. E15 —4C 62
Church Stretton Rd. Houn —4A 86
Church Ter. NW4 —1F 40
Church Ter. SE13 —2C 94
Church Ter. Rich —4H 87
Church Va. N2 —1D 42
Church Va. SE23 —8H 93
Church Vw. Rich —4J 87
Church Vw. Swan —7B 114
Church Vw. Upm —7M 51
Churchview Rd. Twic —7B 86
Church Wlk. N6 —8E 42
Church Wlk. N16 —8B 44
(in three parts)
Church Wlk. NW2 —8K 41
Church Wlk. NW4 —1G 41
Church Wlk. NW9 —7B 40
Church Wlk. SW13 —9E 72

Church Wlk.—Clementina Rd.

Church Wlk. SW15 —4F 88
Church Wlk. SW16 —6G 107
Church Wlk. SW20 —7G 105
Church Wlk. Bren —7G 71
(in two parts)
Church Wlk. Bush —8L 9
Church Wlk. Dart —9H 99
Church Wlk. Enf —5B 16
Church Wlk. Eyns —5J 131
Church Wlk. Hay —9C 52
(in three parts)
Church Wlk. Rich —4H 87
Church Wlk. Th Dit —1D 118
Church Wlk. W on T —3E 116
Churchward Ho. W14 —6K 73
(off Ivatt Pl.)
Church Way. N20 —3C 26
Churchway. NW1 —6H 59
(in two parts)
Church Way. Barn —6D 14
Church Way. Edgw —6L 23
Church Way. S Croy —2D 138
Churchwell Path. E9 —1G 61
Churchwood Gdns. Wfd G —4E 30
Churchyard Pas. SE5 —1B 92
Churchyard Row. SE11 —5M 75
Churnfield. N4 —7L 43
Churston Av. E13 —4F 62
Churston Clo. SW2 —7L 91
Churston Dri. Mord —9H 105
Churston Gdns. N11 —6G 27
Churton Pl. SW1 —5G 75
Churton St. SW1 —5G 75
Chusan Pl. E14 —9K 61
Chute Ho. SW9 —1L 91
(off Stockwell Pk. Rd.)
Chuters Gro. Eps —4D 134
Chyngton Clo. Sidc —9D 96
Cibber Rd. SE23 —8H 93
Cicada Rd. SW18 —5A 90
Cicely Ho. NW8 —5B 58
(off Cochrane St.)
Cicely Rd. SE15 —9E 76
Cinderford Way. Brom —1C 110
Cinnamon Clo. Croy —2J 123
Cinnamon Row. SW11 —2A 90
Cinnamon St. E1 —2F 76
Cinnamon Wharf. SE1 —3D 76
(off Shad Thames)
Cintra Pk. SE19 —4D 108
Circle Gdns. SW19 —6L 105
Circle, The. NW2 —8C 40
Circle, The. NW7 —6B 24
Circle, The. SE1 —3D 76
(off Queen Elizabeth St.)
Circuits, The. Pinn —2G 37
Circular Rd. N2 —9B 26
Circular Rd. N17 —1D 44
Circular Way. SE18 —7K 79
Circus Lodge. NW8 —6B 58
(off Circus Rd.)
Circus M. W1 —8D 58
(off Enford St.)
Circus Pl. EC2 —8B 60
Circus Rd. NW8 —6B 58
Circus St. SE10 —8A 78
Cirencester St. W2 —8M 57
Cissbury Ho. SE26 —9E 92
Cissbury Ring N. N12 —5K 25
Cissbury Ring S. N12 —5K 25
Cissbury Rd. N15 —3B 44
Citadel Pl. SE11 —6K 75
Citizen Rd. N7 —9L 43
Citrus Ho. SE8 —6K 77
(off Alverton St.)
City Bus. Cen. SE16 —4G 77
City Central Est. EC1 —6A 60
(off Seward St.)
City Garden Row. N1 —5M 59
City Harbour. E14 —4M 77
(off Selsdon Way)
City Heights. SE1 —2C 76
(off Weavers La.)
City Ho. Wall —3E 122
(off Corbet Clo.)
City of London. —9B 60
City of London Almshouses. SW9 —3K 91
City of London Crematorium. E12 —8J 47
City Pavilion. EC1 —8M 59
(off Britton St.)
City Rd. EC1 —5M 59
City Tower. EC2 —8B 60
(off Basinghall St.)
City Vw. Ct. SE22 —6E 92
Civic Way. B'side & Ilf —2A 48
Civic Way. Ruis —1H 53
Clabon M. SW1 —4D 74
Clack La. Ruis —6A 36
Clack St. SE16 —3G 77
Clacton Rd. E13 —6H 63
Clacton Rd. E17 —4J 45
Clacton Rd. N17 —9D 28
Claigmar Gdns. N3 —8M 25
Claire Ct. N12 —4A 26
Claire Ct. NW2 —2J 57
Claire Ct. Bush —1B 22
Claire Ct. Chesh —5E 6
Claire Ct. Pinn —7K 21
Claire Gdns. Stan —5G 23
Claire Ho. Edgw —9A 24
(off Burnt Oak B'way.)
Claire Pl. E14 —4L 77
Clairvale. Horn —5J 51
Clairvale Rd. Houn —9H 69
Clairview Rd. SW16 —2F 106
Clairville Gdns. W7 —2C 70
Clairville Point. SE23 —9H 93
(off Dacres Rd.)
Clammas Way. Uxb —8A 142
Clamp Hill. Stan —4B 22
Clancarty Rd. SW6 —1L 89
Clandeboye Ho. E15 —4D 62
(off John St.)
Clandon Clo. W3 —3M 71
Clandon Clo. Eps —8D 120
Clandon Gdns. N3 —1L 41
Clandon Ho. SE1 —3M 75
(off Webber St.)
Clandon Rd. Ilf —7C 48
Clandon St. SE8 —1L 93
Clandon Ter. SW20 —6H 105
Clanfield Way. SE15 —8C 76
Clanricarde Gdns. W2 —1L 73
Clapgate Rd. Bush —8M 9
Clapham. —3G 91
Clapham Common. (Junct.) —3H 91
Clapham Comn. N. Side. SW4 —3D 90
Clapham Comn. S. Side. SW4 —5F 90
Clapham Comn. W. Side. SW4 —3D 90
(in two parts)
Clapham Cres. SW4 —3H 91
Clapham High St. SW4 —3H 91
Clapham Junction. —2C 90
Clapham Junct. App. SW11 —2C 90
Clapham Mnr. Ct. SW4 —2G 91
Clapham Mnr. St. SW4 —2G 91
Clapham Park. —5H 91
Clapham Pk. Est. SW4 —5H 91
Clapham Pk. Rd. SW4 —3G 91
Clapham Pk. Ter. SW4 —4J 91
(off Kings Av.)
Clapham Rd. SW4 & SW9 —2J 91
Clapham Rd. Est. SW4 —2J 91
Clap La. Dag —7M 49
Claps Ga. La. E6 —7L 63
Clapton Comn. E5 —5D 44
Clapton Park. —9H 45
Clapton Pk. Est. E5 —9H 45
Clapton Pas. E5 —1G 61
Clapton Sq. E5 —1G 61
Clapton Ter. N16 —6E 44
Clapton Way. E5 —9E 44
Clara Grant Ho. E14 —4L 77
(off Mellish St.)
Clara Nehab Ho. NW11 —3K 41
(off Leeside Cres.)
Clara Pl. SE18 —5L 79
Clare Clo. N2 —1A 42
Clare Clo. Els —8K 11
Clare Corner. SE9 —6M 95
Clare Ct. WC1 —6J 59
(off Judd St.)
Clare Ct. Enf —8E 6
Claredale Ho. E2 —5F 60
(off Claredale St.)
Claredale St. E2 —5E 60
Clare Gdns. E7 —9E 46
Clare Gdns. W11 —9J 57
Clare Gdns. Bark —2D 64
Clare Hill. Esh —8M 117
Clare Ho. E16 —1L 79
(off University Way)
Clare La. N1 —3A 60
Clare Lawn Av. SW14 —4A 88
Clare Mkt. WC2 —9K 59
Clare M. SW6 —8M 73
Claremont. Brick W —4L 5
Claremont. Chesh —2A 6
Claremont. Shep —1A 116
Claremont Av. Esh —8K 117
Claremont Av. Harr —3J 39
Claremont Av. N Mald —9E 104
Claremont Av. Sun —5F 100
Claremont Av. W on T —6H 117
Claremont Clo. E16 —2L 79
Claremont Clo. N1 —5L 59
Claremont Clo. SW2 —7J 91
Claremont Clo. Orp —6L 127
Claremont Clo. S Croy —7F 138
Claremont Clo. W on T —7G 117
Claremont Cres. Crox G —7A 8
Claremont Cres. Dart —3C 98
Claremont Dri. Esh —8M 117
Claremont End. Esh —8M 117
Claremont Gdns. Ilf —7C 48
Claremont Gdns. Surb —9J 103
Claremont Gro. W4 —8C 72
Claremont Gro. Wfd G —6G 31
Claremont Ho. Wat —8B 8
Claremont Landscape Garden. —9L 117
Claremont La. Esh —7M 117
Claremont Park. —9L 117
Claremont Pk. N3 —8J 25
Claremont Pk. Rd. Esh —8M 117
Claremont Rd. E7 —1F 62
Claremont Rd. E11 —8B 46
Claremont Rd. E17 —9J 29
Claremont Rd. N6 —5G 43
Claremont Rd. NW2 —5H 41
Claremont Rd. W9 —5J 57
Claremont Rd. W13 —8E 54
Claremont Rd. Barn —2A 14
Claremont Rd. Brom —8J 111
Claremont Rd. Clay —9C 118
Claremont Rd. Croy —3E 124
Claremont Rd. Harr —9C 22
Claremont Rd. Horn —4E 50
Claremont Rd. Surb —9J 103
Claremont Rd. Swan —4C 114
Claremont Rd. Tedd —2D 102
Claremont Rd. Twic —6F 86
Claremont Sq. N1 —5L 59
Claremont St. E16 —3L 79
Claremont St. N18 —6E 28
Claremont St. SE10 —7M 77
Claremont Ter. Surb —2F 118
Claremont Way. NW2 —6G 41
(in two parts)
Claremont Way Ind. Est. NW2 —6G 41
Claremount Clo. Eps —9G 135
Claremount Gdns. Eps —9G 135
Clarence Av. SW4 —6H 91
Clarence Av. Brom —8J 111
Clarence Av. Ilf —4L 47
Clarence Av. N Mald —6A 104
Clarence Av. Upm —7L 51
Clarence Clo. Barn —7B 14
Clarence Clo. Bus H —9D 10
Clarence Clo. W on T —6F 116
Clarence Ct. NW7 —5C 24
Clarence Ct. W6 —5F 72
(off Cambridge Gro.)
Clarence Cres. SW4 —5H 91
Clarence Cres. Sidc —9F 96
Clarence Gdns. NW1 —6F 58
Clarence Ga. Wfd G —6K 31
(in four parts)
Clarence Ga. Gdns. NW1 —7D 58
(off Glentworth St.)
Clarence House. —3G 75
(off St James's Pal.)
Clarence La. SW15 —5C 88
Clarence M. E5 —1F 60
Clarence M. SE16 —2H 77
Clarence M. SW12 —6F 90
Clarence Pas. NW1 —5J 59
Clarence Pl. E5 —1F 60
Clarence Rd. E5 —9F 44
Clarence Rd. E12 —9H 47
Clarence Rd. E16 —7C 62
Clarence Rd. E17 —9H 29
Clarence Rd. N15 —3A 44
Clarence Rd. N22 —7J 27
Clarence Rd. NW6 —3K 57
Clarence Rd. SE9 —8J 95
Clarence Rd. SW19 —3M 105
Clarence Rd. W4 —6L 71
Clarence Rd. Bexh —3J 97
Clarence Rd. Brom —7H 111
Clarence Rd. Croy —2B 124
Clarence Rd. Enf —7G 17
Clarence Rd. Rich —9K 71
Clarence Rd. Sidc —9F 96
Clarence Rd. Sutt —7M 121
Clarence Rd. Tedd —3D 102
Clarence Rd. Wall —7F 122
Clarence Rd. W on T —6F 116
Clarence St. King T —6H 103
(in three parts)
Clarence St. Rich —3J 87
Clarence St. S'hall —4H 69
Clarence Ter. NW1 —7D 58
Clarence Ter. Houn —3M 85
Clarence Wlk. SW4 —1J 91
Clarence Way. NW1 —3F 58
Clarenden Pl. Dart —2C 114
Clarendon Clo. E9 —3G 61
Clarendon Clo. W2 —1C 74
Clarendon Clo. Orp —7E 112
Clarendon Ct. NW2 —3G 57
Clarendon Ct. NW11 —2K 41
Clarendon Ct. Beck —5M 109
(off Albemarle Rd.)
Clarendon Ct. Houn —9E 68
Clarendon Ct. Rich —9K 71
Clarendon Cres. Twic —9B 86
Clarendon Cross. W11 —1J 73
Clarendon Dri. SW15 —3G 89
Clarendon Flats. W1 —9E 58
(off Balderton St.)
Clarendon Gdns. NW4 —1E 40
Clarendon Gdns. W9 —7A 58
Clarendon Gdns. Ilf —5K 47
Clarendon Gdns. Wemb —8H 39
Clarendon Grn. Orp —8E 112
Clarendon Gro. NW1 —6H 59
Clarendon Gro. Mitc —7D 106
Clarendon Gro. Orp —8E 112
Clarendon Ho. NW1 —5G 59
(off Werrington St.)
Clarendon M. W2 —1C 74
Clarendon M. Bex —7M 97
Clarendon M. Borwd —5L 11
Clarendon Pde. Chesh —2D 6
Clarendon Path. Orp —8E 112
(in two parts)
Clarendon Pl. W2 —1C 74
Clarendon Ri. SE13 —3A 94
Clarendon Rd. E11 —6B 46
Clarendon Rd. E17 —4M 45
Clarendon Rd. E18 —1E 46
Clarendon Rd. N8 —1K 43
Clarendon Rd. N15 —2A 44
Clarendon Rd. N18 —6E 28
Clarendon Rd. N22 —9K 27
Clarendon Rd. SW19 —4C 106
Clarendon Rd. W5 —7J 55
Clarendon Rd. W11 —1J 73
Clarendon Rd. Ashf —9D 144
Clarendon Rd. Borwd —5L 11
Clarendon Rd. Chesh —2D 6
Clarendon Rd. Croy —4M 123
Clarendon Rd. Harr —4C 38
Clarendon Rd. Hay —3D 68
Clarendon Rd. Wall —8G 123
Clarendon Rd. Wat —4F 8
Clarendon St. SW1 —6F 74
Clarendon Ter. W9 —7A 58
Clarendon Wlk. W11 —9J 57
Clarendon Way. N21 —8A 16
Clarendon Way. Chst & St M —7D 112
Clarens St. SE6 —8K 93
Clare Pl. SW15 —6D 88
Clare Rd. E11 —4B 46
Clare Rd. NW10 —3E 56
Clare Rd. SE14 —9K 77
Clare Rd. Gnfd —2B 54
Clare Rd. Houn —2K 85
Clare Rd. Stai & Stanw —7B 144
Clare St. E2 —5F 60
Claret Gdns. SE25 —7C 108
Clareville Gro. SW7 —5A 74
Clareville Gro. M. SW7 —5A 74
(off Clareville St.)
Clareville Rd. Orp —4A 128
Clareville St. SW7 —5A 74
Clare Way. Bexh —9J 81
Clarewood Ct. W1 —8D 58
(off Seymour Pl.)
Clarewood Wlk. SW9 —3L 91
Clarges M. W1 —2F 74
Clarges St. W1 —2F 74
Claribel Rd. SW9 —1M 91
Clarice Way. Wall —1J 137
Claridge Ct. SW6 —1K 89
Claridge Rd. Dag —6H 49
Clarion Ho. SW1 —6G 75
(off Moreton Pl.)
Clarion Ho. W1 —9H 59
(off St Anne's Ct.)
Clarissa Ho. E14 —9M 61
(off Cordela St.)
Clarissa Rd. Romf —5H 49
Clarissa St. E8 —4D 60
Clark Clo. Eri —9E 82
Clark Ct. NW10 —3A 56
Clarke Grn. Wat —8E 4
Clarke Mans. Bark —3D 64
(off Upney La.)
Clarke Path. N16 —6E 44
Clarkes Av. Wor Pk —3H 121
Clarkes Dri. Uxb —8C 142
Clarke's M. W1 —8E 58
Clarke Way. Wat —8E 4
Clarks Mead. Bush —9A 10
Clarkson Rd. E16 —9D 62
Clarkson Row. NW1 —5G 59
(off Mornington Ter.)
Clarksons, The. Bark —5A 64
Clarkson St. E2 —6F 60
Clark's Pl. EC2 —9C 60
Clarks Rd. Ilf —7B 48
Clark St. E1 —8F 60
Clark Way. Houn —8H 69
Classon Clo. W Dray —3J 143
Claston Clo. Dart —3C 98
Claude Rd. E10 —7A 46
Claude Rd. E13 —4F 62
Claude Rd. SE15 —1F 92
Claude St. E14 —5L 77
Claudia Jones Ho. N17 —8A 28
Claudia Jones Way. SW2 —5J 91
Claudia Pl. SW19 —7J 89
Claughton Rd. E13 —5G 63
Clauson Av. N'holt —1M 53
Clavell St. SE10 —7A 78
Claverdale Rd. SW2 —6K 91
Claverhambury Rd. Wal A —1M 7
Clavering Av. SW13 —7F 72
Clavering Clo. Twic —1E 102
Clavering Ho. SE13 —3B 94
(off Blessington Rd.)
Clavering Ind. Est. N9 —2G 29
(off Montagu Rd.)
Clavering Rd. E12 —6H 47
Claverley Gro. N3 —8M 25
Claverley Vs. N3 —7M 25
Claverton. Asht —9J 133
Claverton St. SW1 —6G 75
Clave St. E1 —2G 77
Claxton Gro. W6 —6H 73
Claxton Path. SE4 —3H 93
(off Coston Wlk.)
Clay Av. Mitc —6F 106
Claybank Gro. SE13 —2M 93
Claybourne M. SE19 —4C 108
Claybridge Rd. SE12 —1G 111
Claybrook Clo. N2 —1B 42
Claybrook Rd. W6 —7H 73
Claybury. Bush —9M 9
Claybury B'way. Ilf —1J 47
Claybury Rd. Wfd G —7J 31
Clay Ct. E17 —1B 46
Claydon. SE17 —5A 76
(off Deacon Way)
Claydon Dri. Croy —6J 123
Claydon Ho. NW4 —9H 25
(off Holders Hill Rd.)
Claydon Ho. SE28 —9H 65
(off St Georges Clo.)
Claydown M. SE18 —6L 79
Clay Farm Rd. SE9 —8A 96
Claygate. —8D 118
Claygate Clo. Horn —9E 50
Claygate Cres. New Ad —8A 126
Claygate La. Esh —4E 118
(in two parts)
Claygate La. Th Dit —3E 118
Claygate La. Wal A —3L 7
(in two parts)
Claygate Lodge Clo. Clay —9C 118
Claygate Rd. W13 —4F 70
Clayhall. —9K 31
Clayhall Av. Ilf —1J 47
Clay Hill. —1A 16
Clay Hill. Enf —1A 16
Clayhill. Surb —9L 103
Clayhill Cres. SE9 —1H 111
Claylands Pl. SW8 —8L 75
Claylands Rd. SW8 —7K 75
Clay La. Bus H —9C 10
Clay La. Edgw —2L 23
Clay La. Stanw —6D 144
Claymore Clo. Mord —2L 121
Claypit Hill. Wal A —1G 19
Claypole Ct. E17 —3L 45
(off Yunus Khan Clo.)
Claypole Dri. Houn —9J 69
Claypole Rd. E15 —5A 62
Clayponds Av. W5 & Bren —5H 71
Clayponds Gdns. W5 —5H 71
(in two parts)
Clayponds La. Bren —6J 71
Clay Ride. Lou —3H 19
Clayside. Chig —5A 32
Clays La. E15 —1M 61
Clay's La. Lou —3L 19
Clays La. Clo. E15 —1M 61
Clay St. W1 —8D 58
Clayton Av. Upm —1M 67
Clayton Av. Wemb —3J 55
Clayton Clo. E6 —9K 63
Clayton Ct. E17 —9J 29
Clayton Cres. Bren —6H 71
Clayton Cft. Rd. Dart —8E 98
Clayton Fld. NW9 —7C 24
Clayton M. SE10 —9B 78
Clayton Pde. Chesh —3D 6
Clayton Rd. SE15 —9E 76
Clayton Rd. Chess —6G 119
Clayton Rd. Eps —4C 134
Clayton Rd. Hay —3C 68
Clayton Rd. Iswth —2C 86
Clayton Rd. Romf —6A 50
Clayton St. SE11 —7L 75
Clayton Ter. Hay —8J 53
Clayton Way. Uxb —7B 142
Claywood Clo. Orp —2C 128
Clayworth Clo. Sidc —5F 96
Cleall Av. Wal A —7J 7
Cleanthus Clo. SE18 —9M 79
Cleanthus Rd. SE18 —1M 95
(in two parts)
Clearbrook Way. E1 —9G 61
Clearwater Pl. Surb —1G 119
Clearwater Ter. W11 —3J 73
(off Lorne Gdns.)
Clearwell Dri. W9 —7M 57
Cleave Av. Hay —5C 68
Cleave Av. Orp —8C 128
Cleaveland Rd. Surb —9H 103
Cleaverholme Clo. SE25 —1F 124
Cleaver Ho. NW3 —3D 58
(off Adelaide Rd.)
Cleaver Sq. SE11 —6L 75
Cleaver St. SE11 —6L 75
Cleaves Almshouses. King T —6J 103
(off London Rd.)
Cleeve Ct. Felt —7C 84
Cleeve Hill. SE23 —7F 92
Cleeve Pk. Gdns. Sidc —8F 96
Cleeves Vw. Dart —5H 99
(off Priory Pl.)
Cleeve Way. SW15 —6D 88
Cleeve Workshops. E1 —6C 60
(off Boundary Rd.)
Clegg Ho. SE3 —3F 94
Clegg St. E1 —2F 76
Clegg St. E13 —5E 62
Cleland Path. Lou —3M 19
Clematis Clo. Romf —7G 35
Clematis Gdns. Wfd G —5E 30
Clematis St. W12 —1E 72
Clem Attlee Ct. SW6 —7K 73
Clem Attlee Pde. SW6 —7K 73
(off N. End Rd.)
Clemence Rd. Dag —4A 66
Clemence St. E14 —8K 61
Clement Av. SW4 —3H 91
Clement Clo. NW6 —3G 57
Clement Clo. W4 —5B 72
Clement Clo. Purl —8M 137
Clement Gdns. Hay —5C 68
Clementhorpe Rd. Dag —2G 65
Clement Ho. SE8 —5J 77
Clement Ho. W10 —8G 57
(off Dalgarno Gdns.)
Clementina Rd. E10 —6K 45

Clementine Clo.—Cobham Ct.

Clementine Clo. W13 —3F 70
Clement Rd. SW19 —2J 105
Clement Rd. Beck —6H 109
Clement Rd. Chesh —1E 6
Clement's Av. E16 —1E 78
Clements Ct. Houn —3H 85
Clements Ct. Ilf —8M 47
Clement's Inn. WC2 —9K 59
Clement's Inn Pas. WC2 —9K 59
(off Grange Ct.)
Clements La. EC4 —1B 76
Clements La. Ilf —8M 47
Clements Pl. Bren —6H 71
Clements Rd. E6 —3J 63
Clement's Rd. SE16 —4E 76
Clements Rd. Ilf —8M 47
Clements Rd. W on T —4F 116
Clement Street. —3H 115
Clement St. Swan & S at H —3H 115
Clement Way. Upm —8K 51
Clemson Ho. E8 —4D 60
Clendon Way. SE18 —5A 80
Clennam St. SE1 —3A 76
Clensham Ct. Sutt —4L 121
Clensham La. Sutt —4L 121
Clenston M. W1 —9D 58
Cleopatra's Needle. —1K 75
Clephane Rd. N1 —2A 60
Clephane Rd. N. N1 —2A 60
Clere Pl. EC2 —7B 60
Clere St. EC2 —7B 60
Clerics Wlk. Shep —2B 116
Clerkenwell. —7L 59
Clerkenwell Clo. EC1 —7L 59
(in two parts)
Clerkenwell Grn. EC1 —7L 59
Clerkenwell Rd. EC1 —7L 59
Clerk's Piece. Lou —5K 19
Clermont Rd. E9 —4G 61
Cleveden Ct. S Croy —7C 124
Clevedon. Wey —7B 116
Clevedon Clo. N16 —8D 44
Clevedon Gdns. Hay —4B 68
Clevedon Gdns. Houn —9F 68
Clevedon Mans. NW5 —9E 42
Clevedon Pas. N16 —7D 44
Clevedon Rd. SE20 —5H 109
Clevedon Rd. King T —6L 103
Clevedon Rd. Twic —5H 87
(in two parts)
Cleve Ho. NW6 —3M 57
Cleveland Av. SW20 —6K 105
Cleveland Av. W4 —5D 72
Cleveland Av. Hamp —4K 101
Cleveland Clo. W on T —5F 116
Cleveland Ct. W13 —8F 54
Cleveland Cres. Borwd —7A 12
Cleveland Gdns. N4 —3A 44
Cleveland Gdns. NW2 —7H 41
Cleveland Gdns. SW13 —1D 88
Cleveland Gdns. W2 —9A 58
Cleveland Gdns. Wor Pk —4C 120
Cleveland Gro. E1 —7G 61
Cleveland Ho. N2 —9B 26
(off Grange, The)
Cleveland La. N9 —9F 16
Cleveland Mans. SW9 —8L 75
(off Mowll St.)
Cleveland Mans. W9 —7L 57
Cleveland M. W1 —8G 59
Cleveland Pk. Stai —5C 144
Cleveland Pk. Av. E17 —2L 45
Cleveland Pk. Cres. E17 —2L 45
Cleveland Pl. SW1 —2G 75
Cleveland Ri. Mord —2H 121
Cleveland Rd. E18 —1E 46
Cleveland Rd. N1 —3B 60
Cleveland Rd. SW13 —1D 88
Cleveland Rd. W4 —4A 72
Cleveland Rd. W13 —8E 54
Cleveland Rd. Ilf —8M 47
Cleveland Rd. Iswth —3E 86
Cleveland Rd. N Mald —8C 104
Cleveland Rd. Uxb —7B 142
Cleveland Rd. Well —1D 96
Cleveland Rd. Wor Pk —4C 120
Cleveland Row. SW1 —2G 75
Cleveland Sq. W2 —9A 58
Clevelands, The. Bark —2A 64
Cleveland St. W1 —7F 58
Cleveland Ter. W2 —9A 58
Cleveland Way. E1 —7G 61
Cleveley Clo. SE7 —5H 79
Cleveley Cres. W5 —5J 55
Cleveleys Rd. E5 —8F 44
Cleverly Est. W12 —2E 72
Cleve Rd. NW6 —3M 57
Cleve Rd. Sidc —9H 97
Cleves Av. Eps —1F 134
Cleves Clo. Lou —8J 19
Cleves Ct. Dart —6J 99
Cleves Ct. Eps —4D 134
Cleves Cres. New Ad —3A 140
Cleves Rd. E6 —4H 63
Cleves Rd. Rich —9G 87
Cleves Wlk. Ilf —7A 32
Cleves Way. Hamp —4K 101
Cleves Way. Ruis —6H 37
Cleves Way. Sun —3D 100
Cleves Wood. Wey —6C 116
Clewer Ct. E10 —6L 45
(off Leyton Grange Est.)
Clewer Cres. Harr —8B 22
Clewer Ho. SE2 —3H 81
(off Wolvercote Rd.)
Cley Ho. SE4 —3H 93
Clichy Est. E1 —8G 61
Clichy Ho. E1 —8G 61
(off Stepney Way)
Clifden Rd. E5 —1G 61
Clifden Rd. Bren —7H 71
Clifden Rd. Twic —7D 86
Cliffe Ho. SE10 —6D 78
(off Blackwall La.)
Cliff End. Purl —4M 137
Cliffe Rd. S Croy —7B 124
Cliffe Wlk. Sutt —7A 122
(off Greyhound Rd.)
Clifford Av. SW14 —2M 87
(in two parts)
Clifford Av. Chst —3K 111
Clifford Av. Ilf —8M 31
Clifford Av. Wall —6G 123
Clifford Clo. N'holt —4J 53
Clifford Ct. W2 —8M 57
(off Westbourne Pk. Vs.)
Clifford Dri. SW9 —3M 91
Clifford Gdns. NW10 —5G 57
Clifford Gdns. Hay —5C 68
Clifford Gro. Ashf —9E 144
Clifford Haigh Ho. SW6 —8H 73
Clifford Ho. W14 —5K 73
(off Edith Vs.)
Clifford Rd. E16 —7D 62
Clifford Rd. E17 —9A 30
Clifford Rd. N1 —4C 60
Clifford Rd. N9 —8G 17
Clifford Rd. SE25 —8E 108
Clifford Rd. Barn —5M 13
Clifford Rd. Houn —2H 85
Clifford Rd. Rich —8H 87
Clifford Rd. Wemb —3H 55
Clifford's Inn Pas. WC2 —9L 59
Clifford St. W1 —1G 75
Clifford Way. NW10 —9D 40
Cliff Rd. NW1 —2H 59
Cliffsend Ho. SW9 —9L 75
(off Cowley Rd.)
Cliff Ter. SE8 —1L 93
Cliffview Rd. SE13 —2L 93
Cliff Vs. NW1 —2H 59
Cliff Wlk. E16 —8D 62
(in two parts)
Clifton Av. E17 —1H 45
Clifton Av. N3 —8K 25
Clifton Av. W12 —2D 72
Clifton Av. Felt —9G 85
Clifton Av. Stan —9F 22
Clifton Av. Sutt —3M 135
Clifton Av. Wemb —2K 55
Clifton Clo. Chesh —2E 6
Clifton Clo. Orp —7A 128
Clifton Ct. N4 —7L 43
Clifton Ct. NW8 —7B 58
(off Maida Va.)
Clifton Ct. SE15 —8F 76
Clifton Ct. Beck —5M 109
Clifton Ct. Stanw —5C 144
Clifton Ct. Wfd G —6E 30
Clifton Cres. SE15 —8F 76
Clifton Est. SE15 —9F 76
Clifton Gdns. N15 —4D 44
Clifton Gdns. NW11 —4K 41
Clifton Gdns. W4 —5B 72
(in two parts)
Clifton Gdns. W9 —7A 58
Clifton Gdns. Enf —6J 15
Clifton Gdns. Uxb —5F 142
Clifton Gro. E8 —2E 60
Clifton Hill. NW6 —5M 57
Clifton Ho. E2 —7D 60
(off Club Row)
Clifton Ho. E11 —7C 46
Clifton Pde. Felt —1G 101
Clifton Pk. Av. SW20 —6G 105
Clifton Pl. SE16 —3G 77
Clifton Pl. W2 —9B 58
Clifton Pl. Bans —7L 135
Clifton Ri. SE14 —8J 77
(in two parts)
Clifton Rd. E7 —2H 63
Clifton Rd. E16 —8C 62
Clifton Rd. N3 —8A 26
Clifton Rd. N8 —4H 43
Clifton Rd. N22 —8G 27
Clifton Rd. NW10 —5E 56
Clifton Rd. SE25 —8C 108
Clifton Rd. SW19 —3H 105
Clifton Rd. W9 —7A 58
Clifton Rd. Coul —7F 136
Clifton Rd. Gnfd —7A 54
Clifton Rd. Harr —2K 39
Clifton Rd. Horn —4E 50
Clifton Rd. Ilf —4B 48
Clifton Rd. Iswth —1C 86
Clifton Rd. King T —4K 103
Clifton Rd. Lou —6J 19
Clifton Rd. Sidc —1C 112
Clifton Rd. S'hall —5J 69
Clifton Rd. Tedd —1C 102
Clifton Rd. Wall —7F 122
Clifton Rd. Wat —7F 8
Clifton Rd. Well —2G 97
Clifton St. EC2 —8C 60
Clifton Ter. N4 —7L 43
Clifton Vs. W9 —8A 58
Cliftonville Ct. SE12 —7E 94
Clifton Wlk. W6 —5F 72
(off King St.)
Clifton Wlk. Dart —5M 99
Clifton Way. SE15 —8F 76
Clifton Way. Borwd —3L 11
Clifton Way. H'row A —2F 144
Clifton Way. Wemb —4J 55
Climsland Ho. SE1 —2L 75
Clinch Ct. E16 —8E 62
(off Plymouth Rd., in two parts)
Cline Rd. N11 —6G 27
Clinger Ct. N1 —4C 60
Clink Exhibition, The. —2B 76
(off Clink St.)
Clink St. SE1 —2B 76
Clink Wharf. SE1 —2B 76
(off Clink St.)
Clinton Av. E Mol —8A 102
Clinton Av. Well —3E 96
Clinton Cres. Ilf —6C 32
Clinton Rd. E3 —6J 61
Clinton Rd. E7 —9E 46
Clinton Rd. N15 —2B 44
Clipper Clo. SE16 —3H 77
Clipper Ho. E14 —6A 78
(off Manchester Rd.)
Clipper Way. SE13 —3A 94
Clippesby Clo. Chess —8K 119
Clipstone M. W1 —8G 59
Clipstone Rd. Houn —2L 85
Clipstone St. W1 —8F 58
Clissold Clo. N2 —1D 42
Clissold Ct. N4 —7A 44
Clissold Cres. N16 —8B 44
Clissold Rd. N16 —8B 44
Clitheroe Av. Harr —6L 37
Clitheroe Gdns. Wat —3H 21
Clitheroe Rd. SW9 —1J 91
Clitheroe Rd. Romf —5A 34
Clitherow Av. W7 —4E 70
Clitherow Ct. Bren —6G 71
Clitherow Pas. Bren —6G 71
Clitherow Rd. Bren —6F 70
Clitterhouse Cres. NW2 —6G 41
Clitterhouse Rd. NW2 —6G 41
Clive Av. N18 —6E 28
Clive Av. Dart —5D 98
Clive Ct. W9 —7A 58
(off Maida Va.)
Cliveden Clo. N12 —4A 26
Cliveden Pl. SW1 —5E 74
Cliveden Pl. Shep —1A 116
Cliveden Rd. SW19 —5K 105
Clivedon Ct. W13 —8F 54
Clivedon Rd. E4 —5C 30
Clive Ho. SE10 —7A 78
(off Haddo St.)
Clive Lloyd Ho. N15 —3A 44
(off Woodlands Pk. Rd.)
Clive Lodge. NW4 —4H 41
Clive Pde. N'wd —7C 20
Clive Pas. SE21 —9B 92
Clive Rd. SE21 —9B 92
Clive Rd. SW19 —3C 106
Clive Rd. Belv —5L 81
Clive Rd. Enf —6E 16
Clive Rd. Esh —6M 117
Clive Rd. Felt —5E 84
Clive Rd. Romf —3F 50
Clive Rd. Twic —1D 102
Clivesdale Dri. Hay —2F 68
Clive Way. Enf —6E 16
Clive Way. Wat —3G 9
Cloak La. EC4 —1A 76
Clochar Ct. NW10 —4D 56
Clock House. —6F 136
Clock Ho. E3 —6A 62
Clock Ho. E17 —2B 46
(off Wood St.)
Clockhouse Av. Bark —4A 64
Clockhouse Clo. SW19 —8G 89
Clockhouse Ct. Beck —6J 109
Clockhouse La. Ashf & Felt —9E 144
Clockhouse La. Romf —7M 33
Clock Ho. Mead. Oxs —6A 132
Clock House Pde. E11 —3F 46
Clockhouse Pde. N13 —5L 27
Clockhouse Pl. SW15 —5J 89
Clock Ho. Rd. Beck —7J 109
Clockhouse Roundabout. (Junct.) —7F 144
Clock Mus., The. —9A 60
(off Aldermanbury)
Clock Pde. Enf —7B 16
Clock Pl. SE11 —5M 75
(off Newington Butts)
Clock Tower Ind. Est. Iswth —2D 86
Clock Tower M. N1 —4A 60
Clock Tower M. SE28 —1F 80
Clock Tower Pl. N7 —2J 59
Clock Tower Rd. Iswth —2D 86
Cloister Clo. Rain —7F 66
Cloister Clo. Tedd —2F 102
Cloister Gdns. SE25 —1F 124
Cloister Gdns. Edgw —5A 24
Cloister Rd. NW2 —8K 41
Cloister Rd. W3 —8A 56
Cloisters Av. Brom —9K 111
Cloisters Bus. Cen. SW8 —8F 74
(off Battersea Pk. Rd.)
Cloisters Ct. Bexh —2M 97
Cloisters Mall. King T —6J 103
Cloisters, The. E1 —8D 60
(off Commercial St.)
Cloisters, The. SW9 —9L 75
Cloisters, The. Bush —8M 9
Cloisters, The. Dart —5J 99
(off Orchard St.)
Cloisters, The. Wat —6G 9
Clonard Way. Pinn —6L 21
Clonbrock Rd. N16 —9C 44
Cloncurry St. SW6 —1H 89
Clonmel Clo. Harr —7B 38
Clonmell Rd. N17 —1B 44
Clonmel Rd. SW6 —8K 73
Clonmel Rd. Tedd —1B 102
Clonmore St. SW18 —7K 89
Cloonmore Av. Orp —6D 128
Clorane Gdns. NW3 —8L 41
Closemead Clo. N'wd —6A 20
Close, The. E4 —7A 30
Close, The. N10 —9F 26
Close, The. N14 —2H 27
Close, The. N20 —2K 25
Close, The. SE3 —1B 94
Close, The. SE25 —1E 124
Close, The. Beck —8J 109
Close, The. Berr G —8M 141
Close, The. Bex —5L 97
Close, The. Bush —8M 9
Close, The. Cars —1C 136
Close, The. E Barn —8D 14
Close, The. Eastc —5G 37
Close, The. Harr —9A 22
Close, The. Ilf —4C 48
Close, The. Iswth —1B 86
Close, The. Mitc —8D 106
Close, The. N Mald —6A 104
Close, The. Orp —1C 128
Close, The. Pinn —5K 37
Close, The. Purl —2M 137
(Pampisford Rd.)
Close, The. Purl —2K 137
(Russell Hill)
Close, The. Rich —2M 87
Close, The. Romf —4J 49
Close, The. Sidc —1F 112
Close, The. Surb —1J 119
Close, The. Sutt —2K 121
Close, The. Uxb —4E 142
Close, The. Wemb —2J 55
(HA0)
Close, The. Wemb —8A 40
(HA9)
Close, The. Wilm —9G 99
Cloth Ct. EC1 —8M 59
(off Cloth Fair)
Cloth Fair. EC1 —8M 59
Clothier St. E1 —9C 60
Cloth St. EC1 —8A 60
Clothworkers Rd. SE18 —8B 80
Cloudberry Rd. Romf —6H 35
Cloudesdale Rd. SW17 —8F 90
Cloudesley Pl. N1 —4L 59
Cloudesley Rd. N1 —4L 59
(in two parts)
Cloudesley Rd. Bexh —9K 81
Cloudesley Rd. Eri —9D 82
Cloudesley Sq. N1 —4L 59
Cloudesley St. N1 —4L 59
Clouston Clo. Wall —7J 123
Clova Rd. E7 —2D 62
Clove Cres. E14 —1B 78
Clove Hitch Quay. SW11 —2A 90
Clovelly Av. NW9 —2D 40
Clovelly Av. Uxb —9A 36
Clovelly Clo. Pinn —1F 36
Clovelly Clo. Uxb —9A 36
Clovelly Ct. Horn —7L 51
Clovelly Gdns. SE19 —5D 108
Clovelly Gdns. Enf —9C 16
Clovelly Gdns. Romf —8M 33
Clovelly Ho. W2 —9A 58
(off Hallfield Est.)
Clovelly Rd. N8 —2H 43
Clovelly Rd. W4 —3B 72
Clovelly Rd. W5 —3G 71
Clovelly Rd. Bexh —7J 81
Clovelly Rd. Houn —1L 85
Clovelly Way. E1 —9G 61
Clovelly Way. Orp —1D 128
Clovelly Way. S Harr —7K 37
Clover Clo. E11 —7B 46
Cloverdale Gdns. Sidc —5D 96
Clover Fld., The. Bush —8K 9
Cloverleys. Lou —7H 19
Clover M. SW3 —7D 74
Clover Way. Wall —3E 122
Clove St. E13 —7E 62
Clowders Rd. SE6 —9K 93
Clowser Clo. Sutt —7A 122
Cloysters Grn. E1 —2E 76
Cloyster Wood. Edgw —7H 23
Club Gdns. Rd. Hayes —2E 126
Club Row. E2 & E1 —7D 60
Clumps, The. Ashf —1B 100
Clunas Gdns. Romf —1H 51
Clunbury Av. S'hall —6K 69
Clunbury St. N1 —5B 60
Cluny Est. SE1 —4C 76
Cluny M. SW5 —5L 73
Cluny Pl. SE1 —4C 76
Cluse Ct. N1 —5A 60
(off St Peters St., in two parts)
Clutton St. E14 —8M 61
Clydach Rd. Enf —6D 16
Clyde Av. S Croy —7F 138
Clyde Cir. N15 —2C 44
Clyde Ct. NW1 —5H 59
(off Hampden Clo.)
Clyde Flats. SW6 —8K 73
(off Rhylston Rd.)
Clyde Ho. King T —5H 103
Clyde Pl. E10 —5M 45
Clyde Rd. N15 —2C 44
Clyde Rd. N22 —8H 27
Clyde Rd. Croy —4D 124
Clyde Rd. Stai & Stanw —7B 144
Clyde Rd. Sutt —7L 121
Clyde Rd. Wall —8G 123
Clydesdale. Enf —6H 17
Clydesdale Av. Stan —1H 39
Clydesdale Clo. Borwd —7B 12
Clydesdale Clo. Iswth —2D 86
Clydesdale Ct. N20 —1B 26
Clydesdale Gdns. Rich —3M 87
Clydesdale Ho. W11 —9K 57
(off Clydesdale Rd.)
Clydesdale Ho. Eri —3J 81
(off Kale Rd.)
Clydesdale Path. Borwd —7B 12
(off Clydesdale Clo.)
Clydesdale Rd. W11 —9K 57
Clydesdale Rd. Horn —5D 50
Clyde St. SE8 —7K 77
Clyde Ter. SE23 —8G 93
Clyde Va. SE23 —8G 93
Clyde Way. Romf —7C 34
Clyde Wharf. E16 —2E 78
Clydon Clo. Eri —7C 82
Clyfford Rd. Ruis —9D 36
Clymping Dene. Felt —6F 84
Clynes Ho. E2 —6H 61
(off Knottisford St.)
Clynes Ho. Dag —8L 49
(off Uvedale Rd.)
Clyston Rd. Wat —8D 8
Clyston St. SW8 —1G 91
Coach & Horses Yd. W1 —1G 75
Coach Ho. La. N5 —9M 43
Coach Ho. La. SW19 —1H 105
Coach Ho. M. SE1 —3C 76
Coach Ho. M. SE20 —4F 108
Coach Ho. M. SE23 —5H 93
Coach Ho. Yd. NW3 —9A 42
(off Hampstead High St.)
Coach Ho. Yd. SW18 —3M 89
Coach Yd. M. N19 —6J 43
Coaldale Wlk. SE21 —6A 92
Coalecroft Rd. SW15 —3G 89
Coalport Ho. SE11 —5L 75
(off Walnut Tree Wlk.)
Coates Av. SW18 —5C 90
Coates Dell. Wat —6J 5
Coates Hill Rd. Brom —6L 111
Coates Rd. Els —9H 11
Coate St. E2 —5E 60
Coates Wlk. Bren —7J 71
Coates Way. Wat —6H 5
Cobalt Sq. SW8 —7K 75
(off S. Lambeth Rd.)
Cobbett Clo. Enf —9C 6
Cobbett Rd. SE9 —2J 95
Cobbett Rd. Twic —7L 85
Cobbetts Av. Ilf —3H 47
Cobbetts Hill. Wey —9A 116
Cobbett St. SW8 —8K 75
Cobb Grn. Wat —5F 4
Cobbinsbank. Wal A —6K 7
Cobbins, The. Wal A —6L 7
Cobble La. N1 —3M 59
Cobble M. N4 —8A 44
Cobblers Wlk. Hamp & Tedd —5A 102
(in two parts)
Cobblestone Pl. Croy —3A 124
Cobbold Ct. SW1 —5H 75
(off Elverton St.)
Cobbold Ind. Est. NW10 —2D 56
Cobbold M. W12 —3D 72
Cobbold Rd. E11 —8D 46
Cobbold Rd. NW10 —2D 56
Cobbold Rd. W12 —3C 72
Cobb's Ct. EC4 —9M 59
(off Carter La.)
Cobb's Rd. Houn —3K 85
Cobb St. E1 —8D 60
Cob Clo. Borwd —7B 12
Cobden Clo. Uxb —4A 142
Cobden Ct. Brom —8G 111
Cobden Hill. Rad —1F 10
Cobden Ho. E2 —6E 60
(off Nelson Gdns.)
Cobden Ho. NW1 —5G 59
(off Arlington Rd.)
Cobden M. SE26 —2F 108
Cobden Rd. E11 —8C 46
Cobden Rd. SE25 —9E 108
Cobden Rd. Orp —6B 128
Cobham Av. N Mald —9E 104
Cobham Clo. SW11 —5C 90
Cobham Clo. Brom —2J 127
Cobham Clo. Edgw —9M 23
Cobham Clo. Enf —5E 16
Cobham Clo. Sidc —5F 96
Cobham Clo. Wall —8J 123
Cobham Ct. Mitc —6B 106

Colva Wlk.—Coombe Ri.

Colva Wlk. N19 —7F 42
Colverson Ho. E1 —8G 61
(off Lindley St.)
Colvestone Cres. E8 —1D 60
Colview Ct. SE9 —7H 95
Colville Est. N1 —4C 60
Colville Est. W. E2 —6D 60
(off Turin St.)
Colville Gdns. W11 —9K 57
(in two parts)
Colville Houses. W11 —9K 57
Colville M. W11 —9K 57
Colville Pl. W1 —8G 59
Colville Rd. E11 —8A 46
Colville Rd. E17 —9J 29
Colville Rd. N9 —1F 28
Colville Rd. W3 —4M 71
Colville Rd. W11 —9K 57
Colville Sq. W11 —9K 57
Colville Sq. M. W11 —9K 57
Colville Ter. W11 —9K 57
Colvin Clo. SE26 —2G 109
Colvin Gdns. E4 —3A 30
Colvin Gdns. E18 —2F 46
Colvin Gdns. Ilf —8A 32
Colvin Gdns. Wal X —8D 6
Colvin Rd. E6 —3J 63
Colvin Rd. T Hth —9L 107
Colwall Gdns. Wfd G —5E 30
Colwell Rd. SE22 —4D 92
Colwick Clo. N6 —5H 43
Colwith Rd. W6 —7G 73
Colwood Gdns. SW19 —4B 106
Colworth Gro. SE17 —5A 76
Colworth Rd. E11 —4C 46
Colworth Rd. Croy —3E 124
Colwyn Av. Gnfd —5D 54
Colwyn Clo. SW16 —2G 107
Colwyn Cres. Houn —9A 70
Colwyn Grn. NW9 —4C 40
(off Snowden Dri.)
Colwyn Ho. SE1 —4L 75
Colwyn Rd. NW2 —8F 40
Colwyn Way. N18 —5E 28
Colyer Clo. N1 —5K 59
Colyer Clo. SE9 —8M 95
Colyers Clo. Eri —9B 82
Colyers La. Eri —9A 82
Colyers Wlk. Eri —9C 82
Colyton Clo. Well —9H 81
Colyton Clo. Wemb —2G 55
Colyton Rd. SE22 —4F 92
Combe Av. SE3 —8D 78
Combedale Rd. SE10 —6E 78
Combe Dene. Brom —8D 110
(off Cumberland Rd.)
Combe Ho. Wat —8C 8
Combemartin Rd. SW18 —6J 89
Combe M. SE3 —8D 78
Comber Clo. NW2 —8F 40
Comber Gro. SE5 —8A 76
Comber Ho. SE5 —8A 76
Combermere Rd. SW9 —2K 91
Combermere Rd. Mord —1M 121
Combe Rd. Wat —8D 8
Comberton. King T —6L 103
(off Eureka Rd.)
Comberton Rd. E5 —7F 44
Combeside. SE18 —8D 80
Combe, The. NW1 —6F 58
(in two parts)
Combwell Cres. SE2 —4E 80
Comedy Store. —1H 75
(off Oxendon St.)
Comedy Theatre. —1H 75
(off Panton St.)
Comely Bank Rd. E17 —3A 46
Comeragh M. W14 —6J 73
Comeragh Rd. W14 —6J 73
Comer Cres. S'hall —3A 70
(off Windmill Av.)
Comerell Pl. SE10 —6D 78
Comerford Rd. SE4 —3J 93
Comet Clo. E12 —9H 47
Comet Clo. Purf —5L 83
Comet Clo. Wat —7D 4
Comet Pl. SE8 —8L 77
(in two parts)
Comet Rd. Stanw —6B 144
Comet St. SE8 —8L 77
Commerce Rd. N22 —8K 27
Commerce Rd. Bren —7G 71
Commerce Way. Croy —4K 123
Commercial Rd. E1 —9E 60
Commercial Rd. N18 —5C 28
Commercial Rd. Ind. Est. N18 —6D 28
Commercial St. E1 —7D 60
Commercial Way. NW10 —5M 55
Commercial Way. SE15 —8D 76
Commercial Wharf. E1 —6J 61
Commerell St. SE10 —6C 78
Commodity Quay. E1 —1D 76
Commodore Ct. SE8 —9L 77
(off Albyn Rd.)
Commodore Ho. E14 —1A 78
(off Poplar High St.)
Commodore Sq. SW10 —9A 74
Commodore St. E1 —7J 61
Commondale. SW15 —2G 89
Commonfield La. SW17 —2C 106
Commonfield Rd. Bans —6L 135
Common La. Clay —9E 118
Common La. Dart —8E 98
Common La. Let H & Rad —3C 10
Commonmeadow La. Wat —7M 5
Common Rd. SW13 —2F 88
Common Rd. Clay —8E 118
Common Rd. Stan —4B 22
Common Side. Eps —7L 133
Commonside. Kes —6G 127
Commonside Clo. Sutt —3M 135
Commonside E. Mitc —7E 106
(in two parts)
Commonside W. Mitc —7D 106
Common, The. W5 —1J 71
(in two parts)
Common, The. Asht —8H 133
Common, The. S'hall —5G 69
Common, The. Stan —2C 22
Common, The. W Dray —5G 143
Commonwealth Av. W12 —1F 72
(in three parts)
Commonwealth Av. Hay —9B 52
Commonwealth Rd. N17 —7E 28
Commonwealth Way. SE2 —6F 80
Community Clo. Houn —9F 68
Community Clo. Uxb —8A 36
Community La. N7 —1H 59
Community Rd. E15 —1B 62
Community Rd. Gnfd —4A 54
Community Way. Esh —6A 118
Como Rd. SE23 —8J 93
Como St. Romf —3B 50
Compass Ct. SE1 —2D 76
(off Shad Thames)
Compass Hill. Rich —5H 87
Compass Ho. SW18 —3M 89
Compass Point. E14 —1K 77
(off Grenade St.)
Compayne Gdns. NW6 —3M 57
Comport Grn. New Ad —4C 140
Compton Av. E6 —5H 63
Compton Av. N1 —2M 59
Compton Av. N6 —5C 42
Compton Av. Romf —1G 51
Compton Clo. E3 —8L 61
Compton Clo. NW1 —6F 58
(off Robert St.)
Compton Clo. NW11 —8H 41
Compton Clo. W13 —9E 54
Compton Clo. Edgw —7A 24
Compton Clo. Esh —8B 118
Compton Ct. SE19 —3C 108
Compton Ct. Sutt —6A 122
Compton Cres. N17 —7A 28
Compton Cres. W4 —7A 72
Compton Cres. Chess —7J 119
Compton Cres. N'holt —4H 53
Compton Pas. EC1 —7M 59
Compton Pl. WC1 —7J 59
Compton Pl. Eri —7D 82
Compton Pl. Wat —3J 21
Compton Ri. Pinn —3J 37
Compton Rd. N1 —2M 59
Compton Rd. N21 —1L 27
Compton Rd. NW10 —6H 57
Compton Rd. SW19 —3K 105
Compton Rd. Croy —3F 124
Compton Rd. Hay —1C 68
Compton St. EC1 —7M 59
Compton Ter. N1 —2M 59
Compton Ter. N21 —1L 27
Comreddy Clo. Enf —3M 15
Comus Ho. SE17 —5C 76
(off Comus Pl.)
Comus Pl. SE17 —5C 76
Comyne Rd. Wat —9D 4
Comyn Rd. SW11 —3C 90
Comyns Clo. E16 —8D 62
Comyns Rd. Dag —3L 65
Comyns, The. Bush —1A 22
Conant Ho. SE11 —7M 75
(off St Agnes Pl.)
Conant M. E1 —1E 76
Conaways Clo. Eps —2E 134
Concanon Rd. SW2 —3K 91
Concert Hall App. SE1 —2K 75
Concord Bus. Cen. W3 —7M 55
Concord Cen., The. W12 —3H 73
Concord Clo. N'holt —6H 53
Concord Ct. King T —7K 103
(off Winery La.)
Concorde Bus. Pk. Big H —7H 141
Concorde Clo. Houn —1M 85
Concorde Clo. Uxb —5C 142
Concorde Dri. E6 —8K 63
Concorde Ho. Horn —2F 66
(off Astra Clo.)
Concord Ho. N17 —7D 28
(off Park La.)
Concordia Wharf. E14 —2A 78
(off Coldharbour)
Concord Rd. W3 —7M 55
Concord Rd. Enf —7G 17
Concourse, The. N9 —2F 28
(off Plevna Rd.)
Concourse, The. NW9 —8C 24
Condell Rd. SW8 —9G 75
Conder St. E14 —9J 61
Condor Path. N'holt —5L 53
(off Union Rd.)
Condor Wlk. Horn —3F 66
Condover Cres. SE18 —8M 79
Condray Pl. SW11 —8C 74
Conduit Av. SE10 —9B 78
Conduit Ct. WC2 —1J 75
(off Floral St.)
Conduit La. N18 —5G 29
Conduit La. Enf —8J 17
Conduit La. S Croy & Croy —7E 124
(in two parts)
Conduit M. W2 —9B 58
Conduit Pas. W2 —9B 58
(off Conduit Pl.)
Conduit Pl. W2 —9B 58
Conduit Rd. SE18 —6M 79
Conduit St. W1 —1F 74
Conduit Way. NW10 —3A 56
Conewood St. N5 —8M 43
Coney Acre. SE21 —7A 92
Coney Burrows. E4 —2C 30
Coney Gro. Uxb —6E 142
Coneygrove Path. N'holt —2J 53
(off Arnold Rd.)
Coney Hall. —5C 126
Coney Hall Pde. W W'ck —5C 126
Coney Hill Rd. W W'ck —4C 126
Coney Way. SW8 —7K 75
Conference Clo. E4 —2A 30
Conference Rd. SE2 —5G 81
Congers Ho. SE8 —8L 77
Congleton Gro. SE18 —6A 80
Congo Rd. SE18 —6B 80
Congress Rd. SE2 —5G 81
Congreve Ho. N16 —1C 60
Congreve Rd. SE9 —2K 95
Congreve Rd. Wal A —6L 7
Congreve St. SE17 —5C 76
Congreve Wlk. E16 —8H 63
(off Stansfield Rd.)
Conical Corner. Enf —4A 16
Conifer Av. Romf —5M 33
Conifer Clo. Orp —6B 128
Conifer Clo. Wal X —2A 6
Conifer Gdns. SW16 —9J 91
Conifer Gdns. Enf —8C 16
Conifer Gdns. Sutt —4M 121
Conifer Ho. SE4 —3K 93
(off Brockley Rd.)
Conifer Pk. Eps —3C 134
Conifers. Wey —6C 116
Conifers Clo. Tedd —4F 102
Conifers, The. Wat —8G 5
Conifer Way. Hay —1E 68
Conifer Way. Swan —5A 114
Conifer Way. Wemb —8G 39
Coniffe Ct. SE9 —4M 95
Coniger Rd. SW6 —1L 89
Coningesby Dri. Wat —3C 8
Coningham Ct. SW10 —8A 74
(off King's Rd.)
Coningham M. W12 —2E 72
Coningham Rd. W12 —3F 72
Coningsby Cotts. W5 —3H 71
Coningsby Gdns. E4 —6M 29
Coningsby Rd. N4 —5M 43
Coningsby Rd. W5 —3H 71
Coningsby Rd. S Croy —1A 138
Conington Rd. SE13 —1M 93
Conisbee Ct. N14 —7G 15
Conisborough Ct. Dart —5M 99
(off Osbourne Rd.)
Conisborough Cres. SE6 —9A 94
Conisbrough. NW1 —4G 59
(off Bayham St.)
Coniscliffe Clo. Chst —5L 111
Coniscliffe Rd. N13 —3A 28
Coniston. NW1 —6G 59
(off Harrington St.)
Coniston Av. Bark —3C 64
Coniston Av. Gnfd —6F 54
Coniston Av. Upm —9M 51
Coniston Av. Well —2C 96
Coniston Clo. N20 —3A 26
Coniston Clo. SW13 —8D 72
Coniston Clo. SW20 —1H 121
Coniston Clo. W4 —8A 72
Coniston Clo. Bark —3C 64
Coniston Clo. Bexh —9A 82
Coniston Clo. Dart —7F 98
Coniston Clo. Eri —8C 82
Coniston Ct. SE16 —3H 77
(off Eleanor Clo.)
Coniston Ct. W2 —9C 58
(off Kendal St.)
Conistone Way. N7 —3J 59
Coniston Gdns. N9 —1G 29
Coniston Gdns. NW9 —3B 40
Coniston Gdns. Ilf —2J 47
Coniston Gdns. Pinn —2E 36
Coniston Gdns. Sutt —8B 122
Coniston Gdns. Wemb —6G 39
Coniston Ho. E3 —7K 61
(off Southern Gro.)
Coniston Ho. SE5 —8A 76
(off Wyndham Rd.)
Coniston Rd. N10 —9F 26
Coniston Rd. N17 —6E 28
Coniston Rd. Bexh —9A 82
Coniston Rd. Brom —3C 110
Coniston Rd. Coul —8G 137
Coniston Rd. Croy —2E 124
Coniston Rd. Twic —5M 85
Coniston Wlk. E9 —1G 61
Coniston Way. Chess —5J 119
Coniston Way. Horn —1E 66
Conlan St. W10 —7J 57
Conley Rd. NW10 —2C 56
Conley St. SE10 —6C 78
Connaught Av. E4 —9B 18
Connaught Av. SW14 —2A 88
Connaught Av. Ashf —9C 144
Connaught Av. E Barn —1D 26
Connaught Av. Enf —4C 16
Connaught Av. Houn —3J 85
Connaught Av. Lou —6H 19
Connaught Bri. E16 —2H 79
Connaught Bus. Cen. NW9 —3D 40
Connaught Bus. Cen. Mitc —9D 106
Connaught Clo. E10 —7H 45
Connaught Clo. W2 —9C 58
(off Connaught St.)
Connaught Clo. Enf —4C 16
Connaught Clo. Sutt —4B 122
Connaught Clo. Uxb —7A 52
Connaught Ct. E17 —2M 45
(off Orford Rd.)
Connaught Dri. NW11 —2L 41
Connaught Gdns. N10 —3F 42
Connaught Gdns. N13 —4M 27
Connaught Gdns. Mord —8A 106
Connaught Hill. Lou —6H 19
Connaught Ho. W1 —1F 74
(off Davies St.)
Connaught La. Ilf —7A 48
Connaught Lodge. N4 —5L 43
(off Connaught Rd.)
Connaught M. SE18 —6L 79
Connaught M. SW6 —9J 73
Connaught Pl. W2 —1D 74
Connaught Rd. E4 —9C 18
Connaught Rd. E11 —6B 46
Connaught Rd. E16 —1G 79
(in two parts)
Connaught Rd. E17 —3L 45
Connaught Rd. N4 —5L 43
Connaught Rd. NW10 —4C 56
Connaught Rd. SE18 —6L 79
Connaught Rd. W13 —1F 70
Connaught Rd. Barn —8H 13
Connaught Rd. Harr —8D 22
Connaught Rd. Horn —8H 51
Connaught Rd. Ilf —7B 48
Connaught Rd. N Mald —8C 104
Connaught Rd. Rich —4K 87
Connaught Rd. Sutt —4B 122
Connaught Rd. Tedd —2B 102
Connaught Sq. W2 —9D 58
Connaught St. W2 —9C 58
Connaught Way. N13 —4M 27
Connell Ct. SE14 —7H 77
(off Myers La.)
Connell Cres. W5 —7K 55
Connemara Clo. Borwd —8B 12
Connett Ho. E2 —5E 60
(off Mansford St.)
Connington Cres. E4 —3B 30
Connolly Pl. SW19 —3A 106
Connop Rd. Enf —2H 17
Connor Clo. E11 —5C 46
Connor Clo. Ilf —8A 32
Connor Ct. SW11 —9F 74
Connor Rd. Dag —9K 49
Connor St. E9 —4H 61
Conolly Rd. W7 —2C 70
Conqueror Ct. H Hill —7H 35
Conrad Dri. Wor Pk —3G 121
Conrad Ho. N16 —1C 60
(off Matthias Rd.)
Conrad Ho. SW8 —8J 75
(off Wyvil Rd.)
Conrad Tower. W3 —4M 71
(off Bollo La.)
Consec Farriers M. SE15 —2G 93
Consfield Av. N Mald —8E 104
Consort Ho. E14 —6M 77
(off St Davids Sq.)
Consort Ho. W2 —1M 73
(off Queensway)
Consort Lodge. NW8 —4D 58
(off Prince Albert Rd.)
Consort M. Iswth —4B 86
Consort Rd. SE15 —9F 76
Cons St. SE1 —3L 75
Constable Av. E16 —2F 78
Constable Clo. NW11 —4M 41
Constable Clo. Hay —5A 52
Constable Ct. SE16 —6F 76
(off Stubbs Dri.)
Constable Ct. W4 —6M 71
(off Chaseley Dri.)
Constable Cres. N15 —3E 44
Constable Gdns. Edgw —8L 23
Constable Gdns. Iswth —4B 86
Constable Ho. NW3 —3D 58
Constable Ho. N'holt —5H 53
(off Gallery Gdns.)
Constable M. Dag —9F 48
Constable Wlk. SE21 —9C 92
Constance Cres. Brom —2D 126
Constance Rd. Croy —2M 123
Constance Rd. Enf —8C 16
Constance Rd. Sutt —6A 122
Constance Rd. Twic —6M 85
Constance St. E16 —2J 79
Constant Ho. E14 —1M 77
(off Harrow La.)
Constantine Pl. Hil —4D 142
Constantine Rd. NW3 —9C 42
Constitution Hill. SW1 —3F 74
Constitution Ri. SE18 —9L 79
Consul Gdns. Swan —4E 114
Content St. SE17 —5B 76
Contessa Clo. Orp —7C 128
Control Tower Rd. H'row A —2E 144
Convair Wlk. N'holt —6H 53
Convent Clo. Beck —4A 110
Convent Gdns. W5 —5G 71
Convent Gdns. W11 —9J 57
Convent Hill. SE19 —3A 108
Convent Way. S'hall —5G 69
Conway Clo. Rain —3E 66
Conway Clo. Stan —6E 22
Conway Cres. Gnfd —5C 54
Conway Cres. Romf —4G 49
Conway Dri. Ashf —3A 100
Conway Dri. Hay —4A 68
Conway Dri. Sutt —8M 121
Conway Gdns. Enf —2C 16
Conway Gdns. Mitc —8J 107
Conway Gdns. Wemb —5G 39
Conway Gro. W3 —8B 56
Conway Ho. E14 —5L 77
(off Cahir St.)
Conway Ho. E17 —3J 45
(off Mission Gro.)
Conway Ho. Borwd —6A 12
Conway M. W1 —7G 59
(off Conway St.)
Conway Rd. N14 —3J 27
Conway Rd. N15 —3M 43
Conway Rd. NW2 —7G 41
Conway Rd. SE18 —5B 80
Conway Rd. SW20 —5G 105
Conway Rd. Felt —2H 101
Conway Rd. Houn —6K 85
Conway Rd. H'row A —2F 144
Conway St. W1 —7G 59
(in two parts)
Conway Wlk. Hamp —3K 101
Conybeare. NW3 —3C 58
Conyers Clo. W on T —7H 117
Conyers Clo. Wfd G —6C 30
Conyer's Rd. SW16 —2H 107
Conyer St. E3 —5J 61
Conyers Way. Lou —5M 19
Cooden Clo. Brom —4F 110
Cook Ct. SE16 —2G 77
(off Rotherhithe St.)
Cook Ct. Eri —8D 82
Cookes Clo. E11 —7D 46
Cookes La. Sutt —8J 121
Cookham Clo. S'hall —4M 69
Cookham Cres. SE16 —3H 77
Cookham Dene Clo. Chst —5B 112
Cookham Hill. Orp —5L 129
Cookham Ho. E2 —7D 60
(off Montclare St.)
Cookham Rd. Swan —5K 113
Cookhill Rd. SE2 —3F 80
Cook Rd. Dag —4J 65
Cook's Clo. Romf —8A 34
Cooks Hole Rd. Enf —2M 15
Cooks Mead. Bush —8M 9
Cookson Gro. Eri —8M 81
Cook Sq. Eri —8D 82
Cook's Rd. E15 —5M 61
Cook's Rd. SE17 —7M 75
Coolfin Rd. E16 —9E 62
Coolgardie Av. E4 —5B 30
Coolgardie Av. Chig —3L 31
Coolgardie Rd. Ashf —2A 100
Coolhurst Rd. N8 —4H 43
Cool Oak La. NW9 —6C 40
Coomassie Rd. W9 —7K 57
Coombe. —4B 104
Coombe Av. Croy —6C 124
Coombe Bank. King T —5C 104
Coombe Clo. Edgw —9K 23
Coombe Clo. Houn —3L 85
Coombe Corner. N21 —1M 27
Coombe Ct. Croy —6B 124
(off St Peter's Rd.)
Coombe Cres. Hamp —4J 101
Coombe Dri. Ruis —6F 36
Coombe End. King T —4B 104
Coombefield Clo. N Mald —9C 104
Coombe Gdns. SW20 —6E 104
Coombe Gdns. N Mald —8D 104
Coombe Hill Glade. King T —4C 104
Coombe Hill Rd. King T —4C 104
Coombe Ho. E4 —6K 29
Coombe Ho. N7 —1H 59
Coombe Ho. Chase. N Mald —5B 104
Coombehurst Clo. Barn —4D 14
Coombe Lane. (Junct.) —5D 104
Coombe La. SW20 —5D 104
Coombe La. Croy —7F 124
Coombe La. W Vill —9D 116
Coombe La. Flyover. King T —5D 104
Coombe La. W. King T —5M 103
Coombe Lea. Brom —7J 111
Coombe Lodge. SE7 —7G 79
Coombe Neville. King T —8J 104
Coombe Pk. King T —2A 104
Coomber Ho. SW6 —2M 89
(off Wandsworth Bri. Rd.)
Coombe Ridings. King T —2A 104
Coombe Ri. King T —5A 104

Coombe Rd.—Cottenham Pl.

Coombe Rd. N22 —9L 27
Coombe Rd. NW10 —8B 40
Coombe Rd. SE26 —1F 108
Coombe Rd. W4 —6C 72
Coombe Rd. W13 —4F 70
Coombe Rd. Bush —9B 10
Coombe Rd. Croy —6B 124
Coombe Rd. Hamp —3K 101
Coombe Rd. King T —5L 103
Coombe Rd. N Mald —6C 104
Coombe Rd. Romf —1K 51
Coomber Way. Croy —2H 123
(in two parts)
Coombes Rd. Dag —4K 65
Coombe Wlk. Sutt —5M 121
Coombe Wood Dri. Romf —4K 49
Coombe Wood Hill. Purl —5A 138
Coombewood Rd. King T —2A 104
Coombs St. N1 —5M 59
Coomer M. SW6 —7K 73
Coomer Pl. SW6 —7K 73
Coomer Rd. SW6 —7K 73
Cooms Wlk. Edgw —8A 24
Cooperage Clo. N17 —6D 28
Cooper Av. E17 —8J 29
Cooper Clo. SE1 —3L 75
Cooper Ct. E15 —1M 61
Cooper Ct. SE18 —7M 79
Cooper Cres. Cars —5D 122
Cooper Ho. NW8 —7B 58
(off Lyons Pl.)
Cooper Ho. Houn —2K 85
Cooper Rd. NW4 —4H 41
Cooper Rd. NW10 —1D 56
Cooper Rd. Croy —7L 123
Coopersale Clo. Wfd G —7G 31
Coopersale Rd. E9 —1H 61
Coopers Clo. E1 —7G 61
Coopers Clo. Chig —2F 32
Coopers Clo. Dag —2M 65
Coopers Ct. W3 —2A 72
(off Church Rd.)
Coopers Ct. Iswth —1D 86
(off Woodlands Rd.)
Coopers Cres. Borwd —3A 12
Coopers La. E10 —6M 45
Coopers La. NW1 —5H 59
Cooper's La. SE12 —8F 94
Cooper's Rd. SE1 —6D 76
Coopers Row. EC3 —1D 76
Cooper St. E16 —8D 62
Coopers Wlk. E15 —1C 62
Coopers Wlk. Chesh —1D 6
Cooper's Yd. SE19 —3C 108
Coote Gdns. Dag —8K 49
Coote Rd. Bexh —9K 81
Coote Rd. Dag —8K 49
Cope Ho. EC1 —6A 60
(off Bath St.)
Copeland Dri. E14 —5L 77
Copeland Ho. SE11 —4L 75
(off Lambeth Wlk.)
Copeland Rd. E17 —4M 45
Copeland Rd. SE15 —1E 92
Copeman Clo. SE26 —2G 109
Copenhagen Gdns. W4 —3B 72
Copenhagen Ho. N1 —4K 59
(off Barnsbury Est.)
Copenhagen Pl. E14 —9K 61
(in two parts)
Copenhagen St. N1 —4J 59
Copenhagen Way. W on T —5F 116
Cope Pl. W8 —4L 73
Copers Cope Rd. Beck —4K 109
Cope St. SE16 —5H 77
Copford Clo. Wfd G —6J 31
Copford Wlk. N1 —4A 60
(off Popham St.)
Copgate Path. SW16 —3K 107
Copinger Wlk. Edgw —8M 23
Copland Av. Wemb —1H 55
Copland Clo. Wemb —1G 55
Copland M. Wemb —2J 55
Copland Rd. Wemb —2J 55
Copleston M. SE15 —1D 92
Copleston Pas. SE5 —1D 92
Copleston Rd. SE15 —2D 92
Copley Clo. SE17 —7A 76
Copley Clo. W7 —7D 54
Copley Dene. Brom —5H 111
Copley Pk. SW16 —3K 107
Copley Rd. Stan —5G 23
Copley St. E1 —8H 61
Copnor Way. SE15 —8C 76
Coppard Gdns. Chess —8G 119
Coppelia Rd. SE3 —3D 94
Coppen Rd. Dag —5K 49
Copperas St. SE8 —7M 77
Copperbeech Clo. NW3 —1B 58
Copper Beech Clo. Ilf —8K 31
Copper Beech Clo. Orp —9G 113
Copper Beech Ct. Lou —3L 19
Copper Beeches Ct. Iswth —9B 70
Copper Clo. SE19 —4D 108
Copperdale Rd. Hay —3E 68
Copperfield. Chig —5B 32
Copperfield App. Chig —6B 32
Copperfield Av. Uxb —8E 142
Copperfield Clo. S Croy —3A 138
Copperfield Dri. N15 —2D 44
Copperfield Ho. SE1 —3E 76
(off Wolseley St.)
Copperfield Ho. W1 —8E 58
(off Marylebone High St.)
Copperfield Ho. W11 —2H 73
(off St Ann's Rd.)
Copperfield M. N18 —4C 28
Copperfield Rd. E3 —7J 61
Copperfield Rd. SE28 —9G 65
Copperfields. Beck —5A 110
Copperfields. Dart —5J 99
Copperfields. Harr —5C 38
Copperfields Ct. W3 —3L 71
Copperfield St. SE1 —3M 75
Copperfields Way. Romf —8H 35
Copperfield Way. Chst —3A 112
Copperfield Way. Pinn —2K 37
Coppergate Clo. Brom —5F 110
Copper Mead Clo. NW2 —8G 41
Copper Mill Dri. Iswth —1D 86
Coppermill La. E17 —4G 45
Copper Mill La. SW17 —1A 106
Copper Row. SE1 —2D 76
(off Horselydown La.)
Coppetts Cen. N11 —7D 26
Coppetts Clo. N12 —7C 26
Coppetts Rd. N10 —7D 26
Coppice Clo. SW20 —7G 105
Coppice Clo. Beck —8M 109
Coppice Clo. Ruis —4B 36
Coppice Clo. Stan —6D 22
Coppice Dri. SW15 —5F 88
Coppice Path. Chig —4F 32
Coppice, The. Ashf —3A 100
Coppice, The. Bex —9B 98
Coppice, The. Enf —6M 15
Coppice, The. New Bar —8M 13
(off Gt. North Rd.)
Coppice, The. Wat —8G 9
Coppice, The. W Dray —9C 142
Coppice Wlk. N20 —3L 25
Coppice Way. E18 —2D 46
Coppies Gro. N11 —4F 26
Copping Clo. Croy —6C 124
Coppins, The. Harr —6C 22
Coppins, The. New Ad —8M 125
Coppock Clo. SW11 —1C 90
Coppsfield. W Mol —7L 101
Copse Av. W W'ck —5M 125
Copse Clo. SE7 —7F 78
Copse Clo. N'wd —9A 20
Copse Clo. W Dray —4H 143
Copse Edge Av. Eps —5D 134
Copse Glade. Surb —2H 119
Copse Hill. —4F 104
Copse Hill. SW20 —5E 104
Copse Hill. Purl —5J 137
Copse Hill. Sutt —9M 121
Copsem Dri. Esh —8M 117
Copsem La. Esh & Oxs —8M 117
Copsem Way. Esh —9A 118
Copsem Wood. Oxs —3A 132
Copse, The. E4 —1D 30
Copse, The. N2 —1D 42
Copse, The. Wat —5J 5
Copse Vw. S Croy —1H 139
Copsewood Clo. Sidc —5C 96
Copsewood Rd. Wat —3F 8
Copse Wood Way. N'wd —8A 20
Coptefield Dri. Belv —4H 81
Copthall Av. EC2 —9B 60
(in three parts)
Copthall Bldgs. EC2 —9B 60
(off Copthall Av.)
Copthall Clo. EC2 —9B 60
Copthall Dri. NW7 —7E 24
Copthall Gdns. NW7 —7E 24
Copthall Gdns. Twic —7D 86
Copthorne Av. SW12 —6H 91
Copthorne Av. Brom —4K 127
Copthorne Av. Ilf —6M 31
Copthorne Clo. Shep —1A 116
Copthorne Gdns. Horn —3L 51
Copthorne M. Hay —5C 68
Copthorne Ri. S Croy —5B 138
Coptic St. WC1 —8J 59
Copwood Clo. N12 —4B 26
Coral Clo. Romf —2G 49
Coral Ho. E1 —7J 61
(off Harford St.)
Coraline Clo. S'hall —6K 53
Coralline Wlk. SE2 —3G 81
Coral Row. SW11 —2A 90
Coral St. SE1 —3L 75
Coram Ho. W4 —6C 72
(off Wood St.)
Coram Ho. WC1 —7J 59
(off Herbrand St.)
Coram St. WC1 —7J 59
Coran Clo. N9 —9H 17
Corban Rd. Houn —2L 85
Corbar Clo. Barn —3B 14
Corbden Clo. SE15 —9D 76
Corbet Clo. Wall —3E 122
Corbet Ct. EC3 —9B 60
Corbet Ho. N1 —5L 59
(off Barnsbury Est.)
Corbet Pl. E1 —8D 60
Corbet Rd. Eps —2C 134
Corbets Av. Upm —1M 67
Corbets Tey. —1M 67
Corbets Tey Rd. Upm —9M 51
Corbett Clo. Croy —4B 140
Corbett Ct. SE26 —1K 109
Corbett Gro. N22 —7J 27
Corbett Ho. SW10 —7A 74
(off Cathcart Rd.)
Corbett Rd. E11 —4G 47
Corbett Rd. E17 —1A 46
Corbetts La. SE16 —5G 77
(in two parts)
Corbetts Pas. SE16 —5G 77
(off Corbetts La.)
Corbetts Wharf. SE16 —3F 76
(off Bermondsey Wall E.)
Corbicum. E11 —5C 46
Corbidge Ct. SE8 —7M 77
Corbiere Ct. SW19 —3H 105
Corbiere Ho. N1 —4C 60
(off De Beauvoir Est.)
Corbins La. Harr —8M 37
Corbridge. N17 —7F 28
Corbridge Cres. E2 —5F 60
Corby Cres. Enf —6J 15
Corbylands Rd. Sidc —6C 96
Corbyn St. N4 —6J 43
Corby Rd. NW10 —5B 56
Corby Way. E3 —7L 61
Cordelia Clo. SE24 —3M 91
Cordelia Gdns. Stai —6C 144
Cordelia Ho. N1 —5C 60
(off Arden Est.)
Cordelia Rd. Stai —6C 144
Cordelia St. E14 —9M 61
Cordell Clo. Chesh —1E 6
Cordell Ho. N15 —3E 44
(off Newton Rd.)
Cordingley Rd. Ruis —7B 36
Cording St. E14 —8M 61
Cordrey Gdns. Coul —7J 137
(in two parts)
Cordwainers Wlk. E13 —5E 62
Cord Way. E14 —4L 77
Cordwell Rd. SE13 —4C 94
Corefield Clo. N11 —2E 26
Corelli Ct. SW5 —5L 73
(off W. Cromwell Rd.)
Corelli Rd. SE3 —1J 95
Corfe Av. Harr —9L 37
Corfe Clo. Asht —9G 133
Corfe Clo. Borwd —5B 12
Corfe Clo. Hay —9G 53
Corfe Ho. SW8 —8K 75
(off Dorset Rd.)
Corfe Tower. W3 —3M 71
Corfield Rd. N21 —7K 15
Corfield St. E2 —6F 60
Corfton Lodge. W5 —8J 55
Corfton Rd. W5 —9J 55
Corhaven Ho. Eri —8C 82
Coriander Av. E14 —9B 62
Cories Clo. Dag —7H 49
Corinium Clo. Wemb —9K 39
Corinne Rd. N19 —9G 43
Corinthian Manorway. Eri —5B 82
Corinthian Rd. Eri —5B 82
Corinthian Way. Stanw —6B 144
Corkers Path. Ilf —7A 48
Corker Wlk. N7 —7K 43
Corkran Rd. Surb —2H 119
Corkscrew Hill. W W'ck —4A 126
Cork Sq. E1 —2F 76
Cork St. W1 —1G 75
Cork St. M. W1 —1G 75
(off Cork St.)
Cork Tree Est., The. E4 —5J 29
Cork Tree Ho. SE27 —2M 107
(off Lakeview Rd.)
Cork Tree Way. E4 —5J 29
Corlett St. NW1 —8C 58
Cormont Rd. SE5 —9M 75
Cormorant Clo. E17 —7J 29
Cormorant Ct. SE8 —7K 77
(off Pilot Clo.)
Cormorant Pl. Sutt —7K 121
Cormorant Rd. E7 —1D 62
Cormorant Wlk. Horn —2F 66
Cornbury Ho. SE8 —7K 77
(off Evelyn St.)
Cornbury Rd. Edgw —7H 23
Cornel Ho. Sidc —9E 96
Cornelia Ho. Twic —5H 87
(off Denton Rd.)
Cornelia Pl. Eri —7C 82
Cornelia St. N7 —2K 59
Cornell Building. E1 —9E 60
(off Coke St.)
Cornell Clo. Sidc —3J 113
Cornell Ho. S Harr —8K 37
Cornell Way. Romf —5L 33
Cornercroft. Sutt —7H 121
(off Wickham Av.)
Corner Fielde. SW2 —7K 91
Corner Grn. SE3 —1E 94
Corner Ho. St. WC2 —2J 75
(off Northumberland St.)
Corner Mead. NW9 —7D 24
Cornerside. Ashf —4A 100
Cornerstone Ho. Croy —2A 124
Corner, The. W5 —2J 71
Corney Reach Way. W4 —8C 72
Corney Rd. W4 —7C 72
Cornfield Clo. Uxb —5B 142
Cornfield Rd. Bush —6M 9
Cornflower La. Croy —3H 125
Cornflower Ter. SE22 —5F 92
Cornflower Way. Romf —8J 35
Cornford Clo. Brom —9E 110
Cornford Gro. SW12 —8F 90
Cornhill. EC3 —9B 60
Cornhill Dri. Enf —1J 17
(off Ordnance Rd.)
Cornick Ho. SE16 —4F 76
(off Slippers Pl.)
Cornish Ct. N9 —9F 16
Cornish Gro. SE20 —5F 108
Cornish Ho. SE17 —7M 75
(off Brandon Est.)
Cornish Ho. Bren —6K 71
Cornmill. Wal A —6H 7
Corn Mill Dri. Orp —2E 128
Cornmill La. SE13 —2A 94
Cornmow Dri. NW10 —1D 56
Cornshaw Rd. Dag —6H 49
Cornthwaite Rd. E5 —8G 45
Cornwall Av. E2 —6G 61
Cornwall Av. N3 —7L 25
Cornwall Av. N22 —8J 27
Cornwall Av. Clay —9D 118
Cornwall Av. S'hall —8K 53
Cornwall Av. Well —2C 96
Cornwall Clo. Bark —2D 64
Cornwall Clo. Horn —2L 51
Cornwall Clo. Wal X —6E 6
Cornwall Ct. W7 —7D 54
(off Copley Clo.)
Cornwall Ct. Pinn —7K 21
Cornwall Cres. W11 —9J 57
Cornwall Dri. Orp —4G 113
Cornwall Gdns. NW10 —2F 56
Cornwall Gdns. SE25 —8D 108
Cornwall Gdns. SW7 —4M 73
Cornwall Gdns. Wlk. SW7 —4M 73
Cornwall Gro. W4 —6C 72
Cornwallis Av. N9 —2F 28
Cornwallis Av. SE9 —8B 96
Cornwallis Clo. Eri —7D 82
Cornwallis Ct. SW8 —9J 75
(off Lansdowne Grn.)
Cornwallis Gro. N9 —2F 28
Cornwallis Ho. W12 —1F 72
(off India Way)
Cornwallis Rd. E17 —2H 45
Cornwallis Rd. N9 —2F 28
Cornwallis Rd. N19 —7J 43
Cornwallis Rd. Dag —9H 49
Cornwallis Sq. N19 —7J 43
Cornwallis Wlk. SE9 —2K 95
Cornwall Mans. SW10 —8A 74
(off Cremorne Rd.)
Cornwall M. S. SW7 —4A 74
Cornwall M. W. SW7 —4M 73
Cornwall Rd. N4 —5L 43
Cornwall Rd. N15 —3B 44
Cornwall Rd. N18 —5E 28
Cornwall Rd. SE1 —2L 75
Cornwall Rd. Croy —4M 123
Cornwall Rd. Dart —2K 99
Cornwall Rd. Harr —4A 38
Cornwall Rd. Pinn —7K 21
Cornwall Rd. Ruis —8D 36
Cornwall Rd. Sutt —9K 121
Cornwall Rd. Twic —6E 86
Cornwall Rd. Uxb —2B 142
Cornwall Sq. SE11 —6M 75
(off Seaton Clo.)
Cornwall St. E1 —1F 76
Cornwall Ter. NW1 —7D 58
Cornwall Ter. M. NW1 —7D 58
(off Allsop Pl.)
Corn Way. E11 —8B 46
Cornwell Cres. E7 —9G 47
Cornwood Clo. N2 —3B 42
Cornwood Dri. E1 —9G 61
Cornworthy Rd. Dag —1G 65
Corona Rd. SE12 —6E 94
Coronation Av. N16 —9D 44
Coronation Clo. Bex —5H 97
Coronation Clo. Ilf —2A 48
Coronation Ct. E15 —2D 62
Coronation Ct. W10 —8G 57
(off Brewster Gdns.)
Coronation Ct. Eri —8B 82
Coronation Dri. Horn —1F 66
Coronation Rd. E13 —6G 63
Coronation Rd. NW10 —6K 55
Coronation Rd. Hay —5D 68
Coronation Wlk. Twic —7L 85
Coronet Pde. Wemb —2J 55
Coronet St. N1 —6C 60
Corporate Dri. Felt —9F 84
Corporate Ho. Har W —8B 22
Corporation Av. Houn —3J 85
Corporation Row. EC1 —7L 59
Corporation St. E15 —5C 62
Corporation St. N7 —1J 59
Corrance Rd. SW2 —3J 91
Corri Av. N14 —4H 27
Corrib Ct. N13 —3K 27
Corrib Dri. Sutt —7C 122
Corrigan Av. Coul —7E 136
Corrigan Clo. NW4 —1G 41
Corringham Ct. NW11 —5L 41
Corringham Ho. E1 —9H 61
(off Pitsea St.)
Corringham Rd. NW11 —5L 41
Corringham Rd. Wemb —7L 39
Corringway. NW11 —5M 41
Corringway. W5 —7L 55
Corris Grn. NW9 —3C 40
Corry Ho. E14 —1M 77
(off Wade's Pl.)
Corsair Clo. Stai —6B 144
Corsair Rd. Stai —6C 144
Corscombe Clo. King T —2A 104
Corsehill St. SW16 —3G 107
Corsham St. N1 —6B 60
Corsica St. N1 —2M 59
Corsley Way. E9 —2K 61
(off Osborne Rd.)
Cortayne Ct. Twic —8C 86
Cortayne Rd. SW6 —1K 89
Cortis Rd. SW15 —5F 88
Cortis Ter. SW15 —5F 88
Corunna Rd. SW8 —9G 75
Corunna Ter. SW8 —9G 75
Corvette Sq. SE10 —7B 78
Corwell Gdns. Uxb —9A 52
Corwell La. Uxb —9A 52
(in two parts)
Coryton Path. W9 —7K 57
(off Ashmore Rd.)
Cosbycote Av. SE24 —4A 92
Cosdach Av. Wall —9H 123
Cosedge Cres. Croy —7L 123
Cosgrove Clo. N21 —2A 28
Cosgrove Clo. Hay —7J 53
Cosgrove Ho. E2 —4E 60
(off Whiston Rd.)
Cosmo Pl. WC1 —8J 59
Cosmur Clo. W12 —4D 72
Cossall Wlk. SE15 —1F 92
Cosser St. SE1 —4L 75
Costa St. SE15 —1E 92
Costons Av. Gnfd —6B 54
Costons La. Gnfd —6B 54
Coston Wlk. SE4 —3H 93
Cosway Mans. NW1 —8C 58
(off Shroton St.)
Cosway St. NW1 —8C 58
Cotall St. E14 —8L 61
Coteford Clo. Lou —4M 19
Coteford Clo. Pinn —3E 36
Coteford St. SW17 —1D 106
Cotelands. Croy —5C 124
Cotesbach Rd. E5 —8G 45
Cotes Ho. NW8 —7C 58
(off Broadley St.)
Cotesmore Gdns. Dag —9G 49
Cotford Rd. T Hth —8A 108
Cotham St. SE17 —5A 76
Cotherstone. Eps —2B 134
Cotherstone Rd. SW2 —7K 91
Cotleigh Av. Bex —8H 97
Cotleigh Rd. NW6 —3L 57
Cotleigh Rd. Romf —4B 50
Cotman Clo. NW11 —4A 42
Cotman Clo. SW15 —5H 89
Cotmandene Cres. Orp —6E 112
Cotman Gdns. Edgw —9L 23
Cotman Ho. NW8 —5C 58
(off Townshend Est.)
Cotman Ho. N'holt —5H 53
(off Academy Gdns.)
Cotman M. Dag —1G 65
(off Highgrove Rd.)
Cotmans Clo. Hay —2E 68
Coton Rd. Well —2E 96
Cotsford Av. N Mald —9A 104
Cotswold Av. Bush —8A 10
Cotswold Clo. N11 —4E 26
Cotswold Clo. Bexh —1C 98
Cotswold Clo. Hin W —4D 118
Cotswold Clo. King T —3A 104
Cotswold Clo. Uxb —4A 142
Cotswold Ct. EC1 —7A 60
(off Gee St.)
Cotswold Ct. Gnfd —5D 54
(off Hodder Dri.)
Cotswold Gdns. E6 —6H 63
Cotswold Gdns. NW2 —7H 41
Cotswold Gdns. Ilf —5B 48
Cotswold Ga. NW2 —6J 41
Cotswold Grn. Enf —6K 15
Cotswold M. SW11 —9B 74
Cotswold Ri. Orp —1D 128
Cotswold Rd. Hamp —3L 101
Cotswold Rd. Romf —9K 35
Cotswold Rd. Sutt —2M 135
Cotswold St. SE27 —1M 107
Cotswold Way. Enf —5K 15
Cotswold Way. Wor Pk —4G 121
Cottage Av. Brom —3J 127
Cottage Clo. E1 —7G 61
(off Mile End Rd.)
Cottage Clo. Ruis —6B 36
Cottage Clo. Wat —4D 8
Cottage Fld. Clo. Sidc —7G 97
Cottage Gdns. Chesh —2D 6
Cottage Grn. SE5 —8B 76
Cottage Gro. SW9 —2J 91
Cottage Gro. Surb —1H 119
Cottage M. Horn —2G 51
Cottage Pl. SW3 —4C 74
Cottage Rd. Eps —9B 120
Cottage St. E14 —1M 77
Cottage Wlk. N16 —8D 44
Cottenham Dri. SW20 —4F 104
Cottenham Pde. SW20 —6F 104
Cottenham Park. —5F 104
Cottenham Pk. Rd. SW20
(in two parts) —5E 104
Cottenham Pl. SW20 —4F 104

Cottenham Rd.—Cranleigh Rd.

Cottenham Rd. E17 —2K 45
Cotterill Rd. Surb —4J 119
Cottesbrook St. SE14 —8J 77
Cottesloe Ho. NW8 —7C 58
(off Jerome Cres.)
Cottesloe M. SE1 —4L 75
(off Emery St.)
Cottesloe Theatre. —2L 75
(off Royal National Theatre)
Cottesmore Av. Ilf —9L 31
Cottesmore Ct. W8 —4M 73
(off Stanford Rd.)
Cottesmore Gdns. W8 —4M 73
Cottimore Av. W on T —3F 116
Cottimore Cres. W on T —2F 116
Cottimore La. W on T —2F 116
Cottimore Ter. W on T —2F 116
Cottingham Chase. Ruis —8E 36
Cottingham Rd. SE20 —4H 109
Cottingham Rd. SW8 —8K 75
Cottington Rd. Felt —1H 101
Cottington St. SE11 —6L 75
Cottle Way. SE16 —3F 76
(off Paradise St.)
Cotton Av. W3 —9B 56
Cotton Clo. Dag —3G 65
Cottongrass Clo. Croy —3H 125
Cotton Hill. Brom —1A 110
Cotton Ho. SW2 —6J 91
Cotton La. Dart & Grnh —5M 99
Cotton Row. SW11 —2A 90
Cottons App. Romf —3B 50
Cottons Cen. SE1 —2C 76
Cottons Ct. Romf —3B 50
Cotton's Gdns. E2 —6C 60
Cottons La. SE1 —2B 76
Cotton St. E14 —1A 78
Cotts Clo. W7 —8D 54
Couchmore Av. Esh —4C 118
Couchmore Av. Ilf —9K 31
Coulgate St. SE4 —2J 93
Coulsdon. —8H 137
Coulsdon Ct. Rd. Coul —8K 137
Coulsdon Ri. Coul —9J 137
Coulsdon Rd. Coul & Cat —7K 137
Coulson Clo. Dag —6G 49
Coulson St. SW3 —6D 74
Coulter Clo. Hay —7J 53
Coulter Rd. W6 —4F 72
Coulthurst Ct. SW16 —4J 107
(off Heybridge Av.)
Councillor St. SE5 —8A 76
Counter Ct. SE1 —2B 76
(off Borough High St.)
Counter St. SE1 —2C 76
(off Hays La.)
Countess Rd. NW5 —1G 59
Countisbury Av. Enf —9D 16
Country Way. Hanw —3F 100
County Gdns. Bark —5C 64
County Ga. SE9 —9A 96
County Ga. New Bar —8M 13
County Gro. SE5 —9A 76
County Hall Apartments. SE1 —3K 75
(off Westminster Bri. Rd.)
County Pde. Bren —8H 71
County Rd. E6 —8M 63
County Rd. T Hth —6M 107
County St. SE1 —4A 76
Coupland Pl. SE18 —6A 80
Courage Clo. Horn —4G 51
Courcy Rd. N8 —1L 43
Courland Gro. SW8 —9H 75
Courland St. SW8 —9H 75
(in two parts)
Course, The. SE9 —9L 95
Courtauld Clo. SE28 —2E 80
Courtauld Ho. E2 —4E 60
(off Goldsmiths Row)
Courtauld Institute Galleries. —1K 75
(off Strand)
Courtauld Rd. N19 —6J 43
Court Av. Belv —6K 81
Court Av. Romf —7L 35
Court Clo. Harr —1J 39
Court Clo. Twic —9M 85
Court Clo. Wall —9H 123
Court Clo. Av. Twic —9M 85
Court Cres. Chess —7H 119
Court Cres. Swan —8C 114
Court Downs Rd. Beck —6M 109
Court Dri. Croy —6K 123
Court Dri. Stan —4J 23
Court Dri. Sutt —6C 122
Court Dri. Uxb —4D 142
Courtenay Av. N6 —5C 42
Courtenay Av. Harr —7A 22
Courtenay Av. Sutt —1L 135
Courtenay Dri. Beck —6B 110
Courtenay Gdns. Harr —9A 22
Courtenay M. E17 —3J 45
Courtenay Pl. E17 —3J 45
Courtenay Rd. E11 —8D 46
Courtenay Rd. E17 —2H 45
Courtenay Rd. SE20 —3H 109
Courtenay Rd. Wemb —8H 39
Courtenay Rd. Wor Pk —5G 121
Courtenay Sq. SE11 —6L 75
Courtenay St. SE11 —6L 75
Courtens M. Stan —7G 23
Court Farm Av. Eps —7B 120
Court Farm Gdns. Eps —3A 134
Court Farm La. N'holt —3L 53
Court Farm Pk. War —8E 138
Court Farm Rd. SE9 —8H 95
Court Farm Rd. N'holt —3L 53
Court Farm Rd. Warl —9E 138
Courtfield. W5 —8G 55
Courtfield Av. Harr —3D 38
Courtfield Cres. Harr —3D 38
Courtfield Gdns. SW5 —5M 73
Courtfield Gdns. W13 —9E 54
Courtfield Gdns. Ruis —7D 36
Courtfield Ho. WC1 —8L 59
(off Baldwins Gdns.)
Courtfield M. SW5 —5A 74
Courtfield Ri. W W'ck —5B 126
Courtfield Rd. SW7 —5A 74
Courtfield Rd. Ashf —3A 100
Court Gdns. N7 —2L 59
(in two parts)
Court Gdns. Romf —6L 35
Court Haw. Bans —7C 136
Court Hill. Coul —9C 136
Court Hill. S Croy —4C 138
Courthill Rd. SE13 —3A 94
Courthope Ho. SE16 —4G 77
(off Lower Rd.)
Courthope Ho. SW8 —8J 75
(off Hartington Rd.)
Courthope Rd. NW3 —9D 42
Courthope Rd. SW19 —2J 105
Courthope Rd. Gnfd —5B 54
Courthope Vs. SW19 —4J 105
Court Ho. Gdns. N3 —6L 25
Court Ho. Mans. Eps —4B 134
Courthouse Rd. N12 —6M 25
Courtland Av. E4 —2D 30
Courtland Av. NW7 —3B 24
Courtland Av. SW16 —4K 107
Courtland Av. Ilf —7K 47
Courtland Dri. Chig —3M 31
Courtland Gro. SE28 —1H 81
Courtland Rd. E6 —4J 63
Courtlands. Rich —4L 87
Courtlands. W on T —2E 116
Courtlands Av. SE12 —4F 94
Courtlands Av. Brom —3C 126
Courtlands Av. Esh —8K 117
Courtlands Av. Hamp —3K 101
Courtlands Av. Rich —1M 87
Courtlands Clo. Ruis —5D 36
Courtlands Clo. S Croy —2D 138
Courtlands Clo. Wat —8C 4
Courtlands Cres. Bans —7L 135
Courtlands Dri. Eps —8C 120
Courtlands Dri. Wat —1C 8
Courtlands Rd. Surb —2L 119
Court La. SE21 —5C 92
Court La. Eps —5A 134
Court La. Gdns. SE21 —6C 92
Courtleet Dri. Eri —9M 81
Courtleigh. NW11 —3K 41
Courtleigh Av. Barn —2A 14
Courtleigh Gdns. NW11 —2J 41
Court Lodge. Belv —6L 81
Courtman Rd. N17 —7A 28
Court Mead. N'holt —6K 53
Courtmead Clo. SE24 —5A 92
Courtnell St. W2 —9L 57
Courtney Clo. SE19 —3C 108
Courtney Ct. N7 —1L 59
Courtney Cres. Cars —9D 122
Courtney Ho. NW4 —1G 41
(off Mulberry Clo.)
Courtney Ho. W14 —4J 73
(off Russell Rd.)
Courtney Pl. Croy —5L 123
Courtney Rd. N7 —1L 59
Courtney Rd. SW19 —4C 106
Courtney Rd. Croy —5L 123
Courtney Rd. H'row A —2E 144
Court Pde. Wemb —8F 38
(in two parts)
Courtrai Rd. SE23 —5J 93
Court Rd. SE9 —5K 95
Court Rd. SE25 —6D 108
Court Rd. Bans —8L 135
Court Rd. Orp —2F 128
Court Rd. S'hall —5K 69
Court Rd. Uxb —1F 142 & 9A 36
Courtside. N8 —4H 43
Courtside. SE26 —9F 92
Court St. E1 —8F 60
Court St. Brom —6E 110
Court, The. Ruis —9J 37
Courtville Ho. W10 —6J 57
(off Third Av.)
Court Way. NW9 —2C 40
Court Way. W3 —8A 56
Court Way. Ilf —1A 48
Court Way. Romf —9J 35
Court Way. Twic —6D 86
Court Way. Wfd G —5G 31
Courtway, The. Wat —2J 21
Court Wood La. Croy —3K 139
Court Yd. SE9 —5J 95
Courtyards, The. Wat —9B 8
Courtyard, The. N1 —3K 59
Courtyard, The. NW1 —3E 58
Courtyard Theatre. —5J 59
(off York Way)
Cousin La. EC4 —1B 76
Cousins Clo. W Dray —1J 143
Couthurst Rd. SE3 —7F 78
Coutts Av. Chess —7J 119
Coutt's Cres. NW5 —8E 42
Coutts Ho. SE7 —6G 79
Couzens Ho. E3 —8K 61
(off Weatherley Clo.)
Coval Gdns. SW14 —3M 87
Coval La. SW14 —3M 87
Coval Pas. SW14 —3A 88
Coval Rd. SW14 —3M 87
Covelees Wall. E6 —9L 63
Covell Ct. SE8 —8L 77
Covell Ct. Enf —2K 15
(off Ridgeway, The)
Covent Garden. —1J 75
Covent Garden. —1J 75
Covent Garden. WC2 —1J 75
Coventry Clo. E6 —9K 63
Coventry Clo. NW6 —5L 57
Coventry Cross. E3 —7A 62
Coventry Hall. SW16 —2J 107
Coventry Rd. E1 & E2 —7F 60
Coventry Rd. SE25 —8E 108
Coventry Rd. Ilf —7M 47
Coventry St. W1 —1H 75
Coverack Clo. N14 —8G 15
Coverack Clo. Croy —2J 125
Coverdale Clo. Stan —5F 22
Coverdale Ct. Enf —1J 17
Coverdale Gdns. Croy —5D 124
Coverdale Rd. N11 —6E 26
Coverdale Rd. NW2 —3H 57
Coverdale Rd. W12 —3F 72
Coverdales, The. Bark —5B 64
Coverley Clo. E1 —8E 60
Coverley Point. SE11 —5K 75
(off Tyers St.)
Coverton Rd. SW17 —2C 106
Covert Rd. Ilf —5D 32
Coverts Rd. Clay —9D 118
Covert, The. SE19 —4D 108
(off Fox Hill)
Covert, The. N'wd —8A 20
Covert, The. Orp —1C 128
Covert Way. Barn —4A 14
Covet Wood Clo. Orp —1D 128
Covey Clo. SW19 —6M 105
Covington Gdns. SW16 —4M 107
Covington Way. SW16 —3K 107
(in two parts)
Cowan Clo. E6 —8J 63
Cowan Ct. NW10 —3B 56
Cowbridge La. Bark —3M 63
Cowbridge Rd. Harr —2K 39
Cowcross St. EC1 —8M 59
Cowdenbeath Path. N1 —4K 59
Cowden Rd. Orp —2D 128
Cowden St. SE6 —1L 109
Cowdray Rd. Uxb —4A 52
Cowdray Way. Horn —9D 50
Cowdrey Clo. Enf —4C 16
Cowdrey Ct. Dart —6F 98
Cowdrey Rd. SW19 —2M 105
Cowdry Rd. E9 —2J 61
Cowen Av. Harr —7B 38
Cowgate Rd. Gnfd —6B 54
Cowick Rd. SW17 —1D 106
Cowings Mead. N'holt —2J 53
Cowland Av. Enf —6G 17
Cow La. Bush —8L 9
Cow La. Gnfd —5B 54
Cow La. Wat —9G 5
Cow Leaze. E6 —9L 63
Cowleaze Rd. King T —5J 103
Cowles. Chesh —1A 6
Cowley. —7A 142
Cowley Bus. Pk. Cow —6A 142
Cowley Clo. S Croy —1G 139
Cowley Cres. Uxb —8A 142
Cowley Cres. W on T —6G 117
Cowley Hill. Borwd —1L 11
Cowley La. E11 —8C 46
Cowley Mill Rd. Cow & Uxb —5A 142
Cowley Peachey. —9B 142
Cowley Pl. NW4 —3G 41
Cowley Rd. E11 —3F 46
Cowley Rd. SW9 —9L 75
Cowley Rd. SW14 —2C 88
Cowley Rd. W3 —2D 72
Cowley Rd. Ilf —5K 47
Cowley Rd. Romf —7F 34
Cowley Rd. Uxb —5A 142
Cowley St. SW1 —4J 75
Cowling Clo. W11 —2J 73
Cowper Av. E6 —3J 63
Cowper Av. Sutt —6B 122
Cowper Clo. Brom —8H 111
Cowper Clo. Well —4E 96
Cowper Ct. Wat —1E 8
Cowper Gdns. N14 —8F 14
Cowper Gdns. Wall —8G 123
Cowper Ho. SE17 —6A 76
(off Browning St.)
Cowper Ho. SW1 —6H 75
(off Aylesford St.)
Cowper Rd. N14 —1F 26
Cowper Rd. N16 —1C 60
Cowper Rd. N18 —5E 28
Cowper Rd. SW19 —3A 106
Cowper Rd. W3 —2B 72
Cowper Rd. W7 —1D 70
Cowper Rd. Belv —5K 81
Cowper Rd. Brom —8H 111
Cowper Rd. King T —2K 103
Cowper Rd. Rain —7E 66
Cowper's Ct. EC3 —9B 60
(off Birchin La.)
Cowper St. EC2 —7B 60
Cowper Ter. W10 —8H 57
Cowslip Clo. Uxb —3C 142
Cowslip Rd. E18 —9F 30
Cowthorpe Rd. SW8 —9H 75
Cox Ct. Barn —6C 14
Coxe Pl. W'stone —2E 38
Cox Ho. W6 —7J 73
(off Field Rd.)
Cox La. Chess —6K 119
Cox La. Eps —7M 119
Coxley Ri. Purl —5A 138
Coxmount Rd. SE7 —6H 79
Coxs Av. Shep —7C 100
Cox's Ct. E1 —8D 60
(off Bell La.)
Coxson Way. SE1 —3D 76
Cox's Wlk. SE21 & SE26 —7E 92
Coxtie Grn. Rd. Pil H & S Wea —1L 35
Coxwell Rd. SE18 —6B 80
Coxwell Rd. SE19 —4C 108
Coxwold Path. Chess —9J 119
Crabbs Cft. Clo. Orp —7A 128
Crab Hill. Beck —4B 110
Crab La. A'ham —8M 5
Crabtree Av. Romf —2H 49
Crabtree Av. Wemb —5J 55
Crabtree Clo. E2 —5D 60
Crabtree Clo. Bush —7M 9
Crabtree Ct. E15 —1M 61
Crabtree Ct. New Bar —6M 13
Crabtree Hill. —1K 33
Crabtree La. SW6 —8G 73
(in two parts)
Crabtree Manorway N. Belv —3A 82
Crabtree Manorway S. Belv —4A 82
Crabtree Wlk. SE15 —9D 76
(off Peckham Rd.)
Crabtree Wlk. Croy —3E 124
Craddock Rd. Enf —5D 16
Craddocks Av. Asht —9J 133
Craddocks Pde. Asht —9J 133
(in two parts)
Craddock St. NW5 —2E 58
Cradley Rd. SE9 —7B 96
Crafts Council & Gallery. —5L 59
Cragg Av. Rad —1D 10
Cragie Ho. SE1 —5D 76
(off Balaclava Rd.)
Craigdale Rd. Horn —4D 50
Craig Dri. Uxb —9F 142
Craigen Av. Croy —3F 124
Craigerne Rd. SE3 —8F 78
Craig Gdns. E18 —9D 30
Craigholm. SE18 —1L 95
Craigmore Ct. N'wd —7C 20
Craigmuir Pk. Wemb —4K 55
Craignair Rd. SW2 —6L 91
Craignish Av. SW16 —6K 107
Craig Pk. Rd. N18 —4F 28
Craig Rd. Rich —1G 103
Craig's Ct. SW1 —2J 75
Craigs Wlk. Chesh —1D 6
Craigton Rd. SE9 —3K 95
Craigweil Clo. Stan —5H 23
Craigweil Dri. Stan —5H 23
Craigwell Av. Felt —9E 84
Craik Ct. NW6 —5K 57
(off Carlton Va.)
Crail Row. SE17 —5B 76
Crakers Mead. Wat —5F 8
Crales Ho. SE18 —4J 79
Cramer St. W1 —8E 58
Crammerville Wlk. Rain —7F 66
Crammond Clo. W6 —7J 73
Cramond Ct. Felt —7C 84
Cramonde Ct. Well —1E 96
Crampton Ho. SW8 —9G 75
Crampton Rd. SE20 —3G 109
Crampton St. SE17 —5A 76
Cranberry Clo. N'holt —5H 53
Cranberry La. E16 —7C 62
Cranborne Av. S'hall —5L 69
Cranborne Av. Surb —5L 119
Cranborne Ct. Enf —9D 6
Cranborne Gdns. Upm —7M 51
Cranborne Rd. Bark —4B 64
Cranborne Rd. Chesh —5D 6
Cranborne Waye. Hay —9F 52
(in two parts)
Cranbourn All. WC2 —1H 75
(off Cranbourn St.)
Cranbourne Av. E11 —2F 46
Cranbourne Clo. SW16 —7J 107
Cranbourne Dri. Pinn —3H 37
Cranbourne Gdns. NW11 —3J 41
Cranbourne Gdns. Ilf —1A 48
Cranbourne Pas. SE16 —3F 76
Cranbourne Rd. E12 —1J 63
Cranbourne Rd. E15 —9A 46
Cranbourne Rd. N10 —9F 26
Cranbourne Rd. N'wd —1D 36
Cranbourn Ho. SE16 —3F 76
(off Marigold St.)
Cranbourn St. WC2 —1H 75
Cranbrook. —6K 47
Cranbrook. NW1 —4G 59
(off Camden St.)
Cranbrook Clo. Brom —1E 126
Cranbrook Ct. Bren —7G 71
Cranbrook Dri. Esh —3A 118
Cranbrook Dri. Romf —2G 51
Cranbrook Dri. Twic —7M 85
Cranbrook Est. E2 —5H 61
Cranbrook Ho. Eri —8D 82
(off Boundary St.)
Cranbrook M. E17 —3K 45
Cranbrook Pk. N22 —8L 27
Cranbrook Ri. Ilf —4K 47
Cranbrook Rd. SE8 —9L 77
Cranbrook Rd. SW19 —4J 105
Cranbrook Rd. W4 —6C 72
Cranbrook Rd. Barn —8B 14
Cranbrook Rd. Bexh —9K 81
Cranbrook Rd. Houn —3K 85
Cranbrook Rd. Ilf —5L 47
Cranbrook Rd. T Hth —6A 108
Cranbrook St. E2 —5H 61
Cranbury Rd. SW6 —1M 89
Crandley Ct. SE8 —5J 77
Crane Av. W3 —1A 72
Crane Av. Isl'wth —4E 86
Cranebank M. Twic —3E 86
Cranebrook. Twic —8A 86
Crane Clo. Dag —2L 65
Crane Clo. Harr —8A 38
Crane Ct. EC4 —9L 59
Crane Ct. Eps —6A 120
Cranefield Dri. Wat —5J 5
Craneford Clo. Twic —6D 86
Craneford Way. Twic —6C 86
Crane Gdns. Hay —5D 68
Crane Gro. N7 —2L 59
Crane Ho. E3 —5J 61
(off Roman Rd.)
Crane Ho. SE15 —9D 76
Crane Ho. Felt —9L 85
Crane Lodge Rd. Houn —7F 68
Crane Mead. SE16 —5H 77
Crane Mead Ct. Twic —6D 86
Crane Pk. Rd. Twic —8M 85
Crane Rd. Twic —7C 86
Cranesbill Clo. NW9 —1B 40
Cranes Dri. Surb —8J 103
Cranes Pk. Surb —8J 103
Cranes Pk. Av. Surb —8J 103
Cranes Pk. Cres. Surb —8K 103
Crane St. SE10 —6B 78
Crane St. SE15 —9D 76
Craneswater. Hay —8D 68
Craneswater Pk. S'hall —6K 69
Cranes Way. Borwd —7A 12
Crane Way. Twic —6A 86
Cranfield Clo. SE27 —9A 92
Cranfield Ct. W1 —8C 58
(off Homer St.)
Cranfield Dri. NW9 —7C 24
Cranfield Ho. WC1 —8J 59
(off Southampton Row)
Cranfield Rd. SE4 —2K 93
Cranfield Rd. E. Cars —1E 136
Cranfield Rd. W. Cars —1D 136
Cranfield Row. SE1 —4L 75
(off Gerridge St.)
Cranford. —9E 68
Cranford Av. N13 —5J 27
Cranford Av. Stai —6C 144
Cranford Clo. SW20 —4F 104
Cranford Clo. Purl —5A 138
Cranford Clo. Stai —6C 144
Cranford Cotts. E1 —1H 77
(off Cranford St.)
Cranford Dri. Hay —5D 68
Cranford La. Hay —7B 68
Cranford La. H'row —9D 68
(in two parts)
Cranford La. Houn —8F 68
Cranford Pk. Rd. Hay —5D 68
Cranford Ri. Esh —7A 118
Cranford Rd. Dart —7J 99
Cranford St. E1 —1H 77
Cranford Way. N8 —2K 43
Cranham Rd. Horn —4F 50
Cranhurst Rd. NW2 —1G 57
Cranleigh Clo. SE20 —6F 108
Cranleigh Clo. Bex —5M 97
Cranleigh Clo. Chesh —1A 6
Cranleigh Clo. Orp —5E 128
Cranleigh Clo. S Croy —4E 138
Cranleigh Ct. Mitc —7B 106
Cranleigh Ct. Rich —2L 87
Cranleigh Ct. S'hall —9K 53
Cranleigh Dri. Swan —8C 114
Cranleigh Gdns. N21 —7L 15
Cranleigh Gdns. SE25 —7C 108
Cranleigh Gdns. Bark —3B 64
Cranleigh Gdns. Harr —3J 39
Cranleigh Gdns. King T —3K 103
Cranleigh Gdns. Lou —8K 19
Cranleigh Gdns. S'hall —9K 53
Cranleigh Gdns. S Croy —4E 138
Cranleigh Gdns. Sutt —4M 121
Cranleigh Gdns. Ind. Est. S'hall —8K 53
Cranleigh Houses. NW1 —5G 59
(off Cranleigh St.)
Cranleigh M. SW11 —1C 90
Cranleigh Rd. N15 —3A 44

Cromwell Clo.—Cumberland Rd.

Cromwell Clo. Brom —8F 110
Cromwell Clo. W on T —3F 116
Cromwell Ct. Enf —7H 17
Cromwell Cres. W8 —5L 73
Cromwell Gdns. SW7 —4B 74
Cromwell Gro. W6 —4G 73
Cromwell Highwalk. EC2 —8A 60
(off Beech St.)
Cromwell Ho. Croy —5M 123
Cromwell Ind. Est. E10 —6J 45
Cromwell Lodge. E1 —7G 61
(off Cleveland Gro.)
Cromwell Lodge. Bexh —4J 97
Cromwell M. SW7 —5B 74
Cromwell Pl. EC2 —8A 60
(off Beech St.)
Cromwell Pl. N6 —6F 42
Cromwell Pl. SW7 —5B 74
Cromwell Pl. SW14 —2A 88
Cromwell Rd. E7 —3G 63
Cromwell Rd. E17 —3A 46
Cromwell Rd. N3 —8A 26
Cromwell Rd. N10 —7E 26
(in two parts)
Cromwell Rd. SW5 & SW7 —5L 73
Cromwell Rd. SW9 —9M 75
Cromwell Rd. SW19 —2L 105
Cromwell Rd. Beck —6J 109
Cromwell Rd. Borwd —3J 11
Cromwell Rd. Chesh —1B 6
Cromwell Rd. Croy —2B 124
Cromwell Rd. Felt —7F 84
Cromwell Rd. Hay —9B 52
Cromwell Rd. Houn —3L 85
Cromwell Rd. King T —5J 103
Cromwell Rd. Tedd —3E 102
Cromwell Rd. W on T —3F 116
Cromwell Rd. Wemb —5J 55
Cromwell Rd. Wor Pk —5B 120
Cromwells Mere. Romf —6B 34
Cromwell St. Houn —3L 85
Cromwell Tower. EC2 —8A 60
(off Beech St.)
Crondace Rd. SW6 —9L 73
Crondall Ct. N1 —5C 60
(off St John's Est.)
Crondall St. N1 —5B 60
Crone Ct. NW6 —5K 57
(off Denmark Rd.)
Cronin St. SE15 —8D 76
Crooked Billet. (Junct.) —8L 29
Crooked Billet. SW19 —3G 105
Crooked Billet Yd. E2 —6C 60
Crooked Mile. Wal A —2J 7
Crooked Usage. N3 —1J 41
Crooke Rd. SE8 —6J 77
Crookham Rd. SW6 —9K 73
Crook Log. Bexh —2H 97
Crookston Rd. SE9 —2L 95
Croombs Rd. E16 —8G 63
Croom's Hill. SE10 —8A 78
Croom's Hill Gro. SE10 —8A 78
Cropley Ct. N1 —5B 60
(off Cropley St., in two parts)
Cropley St. N1 —5B 60
Croppath Rd. Dag —9L 49
Cropthorne Ct. W9 —6A 58
Crosbie. NW9 —9D 24
Crosbie Ho. E17 —1A 46
(off Prospect Hill)
Crosby Clo. Felt —9J 85
Crosby Ct. SE1 —3B 76
(off Crosby Row)
Crosby Ct. Chig —3E 32
Crosby Ho. E7 —2E 62
Crosby Ho. E14 —4A 78
(off Manchester Rd.)
Crosby Rd. E7 —2E 62
Crosby Rd. Dag —5M 65
Crosby Row. SE1 —3B 76
Crosby Sq. EC3 —9C 60
Crosby Wlk. E8 —2D 60
Crosby Wlk. SW2 —6L 91
Crosby Way. SW2 —6L 91
Crosfield Ct. Wat —7G 9
Crosier Clo. SE3 —9J 79
Crosier Rd. Ick —9A 36
Crosier Way. Ruis —8C 36
Crosland Pl. SW11 —2E 90
Cross Av. SE10 —7B 78
Crossbow Ho. W13 —2F 70
(off Sherwood Clo.)
Crossbow Rd. Chig —5D 32
Crossbrook Rd. SE3 —1J 95
Crossbrook St. Chesh —4D 6
Cross Clo. SE15 —1F 92
Cross Deep. Twic —8D 86
Cross Deep Gdns. Twic —8D 86
Crossfield Ho. W11 —1J 73
(off Mary Pl.)
Crossfield Rd. N17 —1A 44
Crossfield Rd. NW3 —2B 58
Crossfields. Lou —7M 19
Crossfield St. SE8 —8L 77
Crossford St. SW9 —1K 91
Cross Ga. Edgw —3L 23
Crossgate. Gnfd —2F 54
Cross Keys Clo. N9 —2E 28
(off Green, The)
Cross Keys Clo. N9 —2E 28
(off Lacey Clo.)
Cross Keys Clo. W1 —8E 58
Cross Keys Sq. EC1 —8A 60
(off Little Britain)
Cross Lances Rd. Houn —3M 85
Crossland Rd. T Hth —1M 123
Crosslands Av. W5 —2K 71
Crosslands Av. S'hall —6K 69
Crosslands Rd. Eps —8B 120
Cross La. EC3 —1C 76
Cross La. N8 —1K 43
(in two parts)
Cross La. Bex —6K 97
Crossleigh Ct. SE14 —8K 77
(off New Cross Rd.)
Crosslet St. SE17 —5B 76
Crosslet Va. SE10 —9M 77
Crossley Clo. Big H —7H 141
Crossley St. N7 —2L 59
Crossmead. SE9 —7K 95
Crossmead. Wat —8F 8
Crossmead Av. Gnfd —6L 53
Crossmount Ho. SE5 —8A 76
(off Bowyer St.)
Crossness Footpath. Eri —2K 81
Crossness La. SE28 —1H 81
Crossness Rd. Bark —6D 64
Cross Rd. E4 —1B 30
Cross Rd. N11 —5F 26
Cross Rd. N22 —7L 27
Cross Rd. SW19 —4L 105
Cross Rd. Belm —2L 135
Cross Rd. Brom —4J 127
Cross Rd. Chad H —5G 49
Cross Rd. Croy —3B 124
Cross Rd. Dart —5G 99
Cross Rd. Enf —6C 16
Cross Rd. Felt —1J 101
Cross Rd. Harr —2B 38
Cross Rd. Hawl —1K 115
Cross Rd. King T —4K 103
Cross Rd. Mawn & Romf —2L 49
Cross Rd. Orp —9F 112
Cross Rd. Purl —5M 137
Cross Rd. Sidc —1F 112
Cross Rd. S Harr —8M 37
Cross Rd. Sutt —7B 122
Cross Rd. Uxb —3A 142
Cross Rd. Wal X —6E 6
Cross Rd. Wat —8J 9
Cross Rd. W'stone —9E 22
Cross Rd. Wey —5B 116
Cross Rd. Wfd G —6K 31
Cross Roads. H Bee —4F 18
Cross St. N1 —4M 59
Cross St. N18 —5E 28
Cross St. SE5 —2B 92
Cross St. SW13 —1C 88
Cross St. Eri —7C 82
Cross St. Hamp H —2A 102
Cross St. Uxb —3A 142
Cross St. Wat —5G 9
Cross Ter. Wal A —7L 7
(off Stonyshotts)
Crossthwaite Av. SE5 —3B 92
Crosswall. EC3 —1D 76
Crossway. N12 —6B 26
Crossway. N16 —1C 60
Crossway. NW9 —2D 40
Crossway. SE28 —1F 80
Crossway. SW20 —8G 105
Crossway. W13 —7E 54
Crossway. Dag —8G 49
Crossway. Enf —9C 16
Crossway. Hay —2E 68
Crossway. Orp —8B 112
Cross Way. Pinn —9F 20
Crossway. Ruis —9G 37
Crossway. W on T —4F 116
Cross Way. Wfd G —4G 31
Crossway Ct. SE4 —1J 93
Crossways. N21 —8A 16
Crossways. Lou —7L 19
Crossways. Romf —1F 50
Crossways. S Croy —9J 125
Crossways. Sun —4D 100
Crossways. Sutt —1B 136
Crossways Boulevd. Dart —3M 99
Crossways Rd. Beck —8L 109
Crossways Rd. Mitc —7F 106
Crossways Ter. E5 —9G 45
Crossways, The. Houn —8K 69
Crossways, The. Surb —3M 119
Crossways, The. Wemb —7L 39
Crossway, The. N22 —7M 27
Crossway, The. SE9 —8H 95
Cross Way, The. Harr —9C 22
Crossway, The. Uxb —5D 142
Crosswell Clo. Shep —6A 100
Croston St. E8 —4E 60
Crothall Clo. N13 —3K 27
Crouch Av. Bark —5F 64
Crouch Clo. Beck —3L 109
Crouch Cft. SE9 —9L 95
Crouch End. —5H 43
Crouch End Hill. N8 —5H 43
Crouch Hall Ct. N19 —6J 43
Crouch Hall Rd. N8 —4H 43
Crouch Hill. N8 & N4 —4J 43
Crouchman's Clo. SE26 —9D 92
Crouch Rd. NW10 —3B 56
Crowborough Clo. Warl —9J 139
Crowborough Dri. Warl —9J 139
Crowborough Path. Wat —4H 21
Crowborough Rd. SW17 —3E 106
Crowden Way. SE28 —1G 81
Crowder St. E1 —1F 76
Crowfield Ho. N5 —9A 44
Crowfoot Clo. E9 —1K 61
Crowhill. Orp —2L 141
Crowhurst Clo. SW9 —1L 91
Crowhurst Ho. SW9 —1K 91
(off Aytoun Rd.)
Crowhurst Way. Orp —9G 113
Crowland Av. Hay —5C 68
Crowland Gdns. N14 —9J 15
Crowland Ho. NW8 —4A 58
(off Springfield Rd.)
Crowland Rd. N15 —3D 44
Crowland Rd. T Hth —8B 108
Crowlands Av. Romf —4M 49
Crowland Ter. N1 —3B 60
Crowland Wlk. Mord —1M 121
Crow La. Romf —5K 49
Crowley Cres. Croy —7L 123
Crowline Wlk. N1 —2A 60
Crowmarsh Gdns. SE23 —6G 93
Crown Arc. King T —6H 103
Crown Ash Hill. W'ham —6F 140
Crown Ash La. Warl & Big H —8E 140
Crownbourne Ct. Sutt —6M 121
(off St Nicholas Way)
Crown Bldgs. E4 —1B 30
Crown Clo. E3 —4L 61
Crown Clo. NW6 —2M 57
Crown Clo. NW7 —2D 24
Crown Clo. Hay —3D 68
Crown Clo. Orp —7E 128
Crown Clo. W on T —2G 117
Crown Clo. Bus. Cen. E3 —4L 61
(off Crown Clo.)
Crown Cotts. Romf —8L 33
Crown Ct. EC4 —9A 60
(off Cheapside)
Crown Ct. N10 —7E 26
Crown Ct. SE12 —5F 94
Crown Dale. SE19 —3M 107
Crowndale Ct. NW1 —5H 59
(off Crowndale Ct.)
Crowndale Rd. NW1 —5G 59
Crownfield Av. Ilf —4C 48
Crownfield Rd. E15 —9B 46
Crown Hill. Croy —4A 124
Crown Hill Rd. NW10 —4D 56
Crownhill Rd. Wfd G —7J 31
Crown Ho. Ruis —6E 36
Crown La. N14 —1G 27
Crown La. SW16 —2L 107
Crown La. Brom —9H 111
Crown La. Chst —5A 112
Crown La. Mord —8L 105
Crown La. Gdns. SW16 —2L 107
Crown La. Spur. Brom —1H 127
Crown Lodge. SW3 —5C 74
Crownmead Way. Romf —2M 49
Crown M. E13 —4G 63
Crown M. W6 —5E 72
Crown Office Row. EC4 —1L 75
Crown Pde. N14 —1G 27
Crown Pde. SE19 —3M 107
Crown Pde. Mord —7L 105
Crown Pas. SW1 —2G 75
Crown Pas. King T —6H 103
Crown Pas. Wat —6G 9
Crown Pl. EC2 —8C 60
Crown Pl. NW5 —2F 58
Crown Reach. SW1 —6H 75
Crown Ri. Wat —7G 5
Crown Rd. N10 —7E 26
Crown Rd. Borwd —3L 11
Crown Rd. Enf —6F 16
Crown Rd. Ilf —2B 48
Crown Rd. Mord —8M 105
Crown Rd. N Mald —5A 104
Crown Rd. Orp —7E 128
Crown Rd. Ruis —1H 53
Crown Rd. Sutt —6M 121
Crown Rd. Twic —5F 86
Crownstone Ct. SW2 —4L 91
Crownstone Rd. SW2 —4L 91
Crown St. SE5 —8A 76
Crown St. W3 —2M 71
Crown St. Dag —2A 66
(in two parts)
Crown St. Harr —6B 38
Crown Ter. N14 —1H 27
(off Crown La.)
Crown Ter. Rich —3K 87
Crown Trad. Cen. Hay —3C 68
Crowntree Clo. Iswth —7D 70
Crown Wlk. Uxb —3A 142
Crown Wlk. Wemb —8K 39
Crown Way. W Dray —2K 143
Crown Wharf. E14 —2A 78
(off Coldharbour)
Crown Wharf. SE8 —6K 77
(off Grove St.)
Crown Woods. SE18 —1M 95
Crown Woods Way. SE9 —4B 96
Crown Yd. Houn —2A 86
Crowshott Av. Stan —9G 23
Crows Rd. E15 —6B 62
Crows Rd. Bark —2M 63
Crowther Av. Bren —5J 71
Crowther Rd. SE25 —9E 108
Crowthorne Clo. SW18 —6K 89
Crowthorne Rd. W10 —9H 57
Croxall Ho. W on T —1G 117
Croxdale Rd. Borwd —4K 11
Croxden Clo. Edgw —1L 39
Croxden Wlk. Mord —1A 122
Croxford Gdns. N22 —7M 27
Croxford Way. Romf —6B 50
Croxley Centre. —8B 8
Croxley Clo. Orp —6F 112
Croxley Grn. Orp —5F 112
Croxley Rd. W9 —6K 57
Croxley Vw. Wat —8C 8
Croxted Clo. SE21 —6A 92
Croxted M. SE24 —5A 92
Croxted Rd. SE24 & SE21 —5A 92
Croxteth Ho. SW8 —1H 91
Croyde Av. Gnfd —6A 54
Croyde Av. Hay —5C 68
Croyde Clo. Sidc —6B 96
Croydon. —4A 124
Croydon. N17 —9B 28
(off Gloucester Rd.)
Croydon Crematorium. Croy —9K 107
Croydon Flyover, The. Croy —5A 124
Croydon Gro. Croy —3M 123
Croydon Ho. SE1 —2L 75
(off Wootton St.)
Croydon La. Bans —6M 135
Croydon La. S. Bans —6M 135
Croydon Rd. E13 —7D 62
Croydon Rd. SE20 —6F 108
Croydon Rd. Beck —9H 109
Croydon Rd. Brom & Kes —5G 127
Croydon Rd. H'row A —1F 144
Croydon Rd. Mitc & Bedd —8E 106
Croydon Rd. Wall & Croy —6F 122
Croydon Rd. W W'ck & Brom —5C 126
Croydon Rd. Ind. Est. Beck —8H 109
Croyland Rd. N9 —1E 28
Croylands Dri. Surb —2J 119
Croysdale Av. Sun —7E 100
Crozier Dri. S Croy —2F 138
Crozier Ho. SE3 —2F 94
Crozier Ho. SW8 —8K 75
(off Wilkinson St.)
Crozier Ter. E9 —1H 61
Crucible Clo. Romf —4F 48
Crucifix La. SE1 —3C 76
Cruden Ho. SE5 —7M 75
(off Brandon Est.)
Cruden St. N1 —4M 59
Cruikshank Ho. NW8 —5C 58
(off Townshend Rd.)
Cruikshank Rd. E15 —9C 46
Cruikshank St. WC1 —6L 59
Crummock Gdns. NW9 —3C 40
Crumpsall St. SE2 —5G 81
Crundale Av. NW9 —3L 39
Crunden Rd. S Croy —9B 124
Crusader Clo. Purf —5L 83
Crusader Ct. Dart —4K 99
Crusader Gdns. Croy —5C 124
Crusader Way. Wat —8D 8
Crusoe M. N16 —7B 44
Crusoe Rd. Eri —6B 82
Crusoe Rd. Mitc —4D 106
Crutched Friars. EC3 —1C 76
Crutchfield La. W on T —4F 116
Crutchley Rd. SE6 —8C 94
Crystal Av. Horn —9J 51
Crystal Palace. —3D 108
Crystal Palace F.C. —8C 108
Crystal Palace Mus. —3D 108
Crystal Palace National Sports Centre. —3E 108
Crystal Pal. Pde. SE19 —3D 108
Crystal Pal. Pk. Rd. SE26 —2E 108
Crystal Pal. Rd. SE22 —5D 92
Crystal Pal. Sta. Rd. SE19 —3E 108
Crystal Ter. SE19 —3B 108
Crystal Vw. Ct. Brom —1B 110
Crystal Way. Dag —6G 49
Crystal Way. Harr —3D 38
Cuba Dri. Enf —4G 17
Cuba St. E14 —3L 77
Cubitt Ho. SW4 —5G 91
Cubitt Sq. S'hall —2A 70
Cubitt Steps. E14 —2L 77
Cubitt St. WC1 —6K 59
Cubitt St. Croy —7K 123
Cubitt's Yd. WC2 —1J 75
(off James St.)
Cubitt Ter. SW4 —2G 91
Cubitt Town. —5A 78
Cuckoo Av. W7 —7C 54
Cuckoo Dene. W7 —8B 54
Cuckoo Hall La. N9 —9G 17
Cuckoo Hall Rd. N9 —9G 17
Cuckoo Hill. Pinn —1G 37
Cuckoo Hill Dri. Pinn —1G 37
Cuckoo Hill Rd. Pinn —2G 37
Cuckoo La. W7 —1C 70
Cuckoo Pound. Shep —9C 100
Cudas Clo. Eps —6D 120
Cuddington. SE17 —5A 76
(off Deacon Way)
Cuddington Av. Wor Pk —5D 120
Cuddington Ct. Sutt —1H 135
Cuddington Glade. Eps —4L 133
Cuddington Pk. Clo. Bans —5K 135
Cuddington Way. Sutt —4H 135
Cudham Clo. Belm —2L 135
Cudham Dri. New Ad —2A 140
Cudham La. N. Cud & Orp —9C 128
Cudham Rd. Orp —3L 141
Cudham St. SE6 —6A 94
Cudworth Ho. SW8 —9G 75
Cudworth St. E1 —7F 60
Cuff Cres. SE9 —5H 95
Cuffley Av. Wat —7H 5
Cuff Point. E2 —6D 60
(off Columbia Rd.)
Cugley Rd. Dart —6M 99
Culford Gdns. SW3 —5D 74
Culford Gro. N1 —2C 60
Culford Mans. SW3 —5D 74
Culford M. N1 —2C 60
Culford Rd. N1 —3C 60
(in two parts)
Culgaith Gdns. Enf —6J 15
Culham Ho. E2 —6D 60
(off Palissy St.)
Cullen Way. NW10 —7A 56
Cullera Clo. N'wd —6D 20
Cullerne Clo. Ewe —2D 134
Cullesden Rd. Kenl —7M 137
Cullinet Ho. Borwd —4B 12
Culling Rd. SE16 —4G 77
Cullings Ct. Wal A —6M 7
Cullington Clo. Harr —2E 38
Cullingworth Rd. NW10 —1E 56
Culloden Clo. SE1 —6E 76
Culloden Rd. Enf —4M 15
Culloden St. E14 —9A 62
Cullum St. EC3 —1C 76
Cullum Welch Ct. N1 —6B 60
(off Haberdasher St.)
Culmington Pde. W13 —2G 71
(off Culmington Rd.)
Culmington Rd. W13 —2G 71
Culmington Rd. S Croy —1A 138
Culmore Rd. SE15 —8F 76
Culmstock Rd. SW11 —4E 90
Culpeper Clo. Ilf —6M 31
Culpeper Ho. E14 —9J 61
Culpepper Ct. SE11 —5L 75
(off Kennington Rd.)
Culross Bldgs. N1 —5J 59
(off Battle Bri. Rd.)
Culross Clo. N15 —2A 44
Culross St. W1 —1E 74
Culsac Rd. Surb —4J 119
Culverden Rd. SW12 —8G 91
Culverden Rd. Wat —3F 20
Culver Gro. Stan —9G 23
Culverhay. Asht —8J 133
Culverhouse. WC1 —8K 59
(off Red Lion Sq.)
Culverhouse Gdns. SW16 —9K 91
Culverlands Clo. Stan —4F 22
Culverley Rd. SE6 —7M 93
Culvers Av. Cars —4D 122
Culvers Retreat. Cars —3D 122
Culverstone Clo. Hayes —1D 126
Culvers Way. Cars —4D 122
Culvert La. Uxb —5A 142
Culvert Pl. SW11 —1E 90
Culvert Rd. N15 —3C 44
Culvert Rd. SW11 —1D 90
Culworth Ho. NW8 —5C 58
(off Allitsen Rd.)
Culworth St. NW8 —5C 58
Culzean Clo. SE27 —9M 91
Cumberland Av. NW10 —6M 55
Cumberland Av. Horn —8J 51
Cumberland Av. Well —2C 96
Cumberland Bus. Pk. NW10 —6M 55
Cumberland Clo. E8 —2D 60
Cumberland Clo. SW20 —4H 105
Cumberland Clo. Eps —2C 134
Cumberland Clo. Horn —8J 51
Cumberland Clo. Ilf —8A 32
Cumberland Clo. Twic —5F 86
Cumberland Ct. SW1 —6F 74
(off Cumberland St.)
Cumberland Ct. Croy —3B 124
Cumberland Ct. Harr —1C 38
(off Princes Dri.)
Cumberland Ct. Well —1C 96
Cumberland Cres. W14 —5J 73
(in two parts)
Cumberland Dri. Bexh —8J 81
Cumberland Dri. Chess —5K 119
Cumberland Dri. Dart —6K 99
Cumberland Dri. Esh —4E 118
Cumberland Gdns. NW4 —9J 25
Cumberland Gdns. WC1 —6L 59
Cumberland Ga. W1 —1D 74
Cumberland Ho. N9 —1G 29
(off Cumberland Rd.)
Cumberland Ho. King T —4M 103
Cumberland Mans. W1 —9D 58
(off George St.)
Cumberland Mkt. NW1 —6F 58
Cumberland Mills Sq. E14 —6B 78
Cumberland Pk. W3 —1A 72
Cumberland Pk. Ind. Est. NW10 —6E 56
Cumberland Pl. NW1 —6F 58
Cumberland Pl. SE6 —7D 94
Cumberland Pl. Sun —8E 100
Cumberland Rd. E12 —9H 47

Cumberland Rd.—Danson Interchange. (Junct.)

Cumberland Rd. E13 —8F 62
Cumberland Rd. E17 —9J 29
Cumberland Rd. N9 —1G 29
Cumberland Rd. N22 —9K 27
Cumberland Rd. SE25 —1F 124
Cumberland Rd. SW13 —9D 72
Cumberland Rd. W3 —1A 72
Cumberland Rd. W7 —3D 70
Cumberland Rd. Ashf —9B 144
Cumberland Rd. Brom —8C 110
Cumberland Rd. Harr —3M 37
Cumberland Rd. Rich —8L 71
Cumberland Rd. Stan —1K 39
Cumberlands. Kenl —7B 138
Cumberland St. SW1 —6F 74
Cumberland Ter. NW1 —5F 58
Cumberland Ter. M. NW1 —5F 58
(off Cumberland Ter.)
Cumberland Vs. W3 —1A 72
(off Cumberland Rd.)
Cumberlow Av. SE25 —7D 108
Cumbernauld Gdns. Sun —2D 100
Cumberton Rd. N17 —8B 28
Cumbrae Gdns. Surb —4H 119
Cumbrian Av. Bexh —1C 98
Cumbrian Gdns. NW2 —7H 41
Cumbrian Way. Uxb —3B 142
Cuming Mus. —5A 76
(off Walworth Rd.)
Cummings Hall La. Noak H —3G 35
Cumming St. N1 —5K 59
Cumnor Clo. SW9 —1K 91
(off Robsart St.)
Cumnor Gdns. Eps —8E 120
Cumnor Ri. Kenl —9A 138
Cumnor Rd. Sutt —8A 122
Cunard Cres. N21 —8B 16
Cunard Pl. EC3 —9C 60
Cunard Rd. NW10 —6B 56
Cunard Wlk. SE16 —5H 77
Cundy Rd. E16 —9G 63
Cundy St. SW1 —5E 74
Cunliffe Pde. Eps —6D 120
Cunliffe Rd. Eps —6D 120
Cunliffe St. SW16 —3G 107
Cunningham Av. Enf —9E 6
Cunningham Clo. Romf —3G 49
Cunningham Clo. W W'ck —4M 125
Cunningham Ct. Chesh —1E 6
Cunningham Ho. SE5 —8B 76
(off Elmington Est.)
Cunningham Pk. Harr —3A 38
Cunningham Pl. NW8 —7B 58
Cunningham Rd. N15 —2E 44
Cunningham Rd. Bans —7B 136
Cunningham Rd. Chesh —1E 6
Cunnington St. W4 —4A 72
Cupar Rd. SW11 —9E 74
Cupola Clo. Brom —2F 110
Curates Wlk. Dart —9H 99
Cureton St. SW1 —5H 75
Curfew Ho. Bark —4A 64
Curie Ct. Harr —5F 38
Curie Gdns. NW9 —9C 24
Curlew Clo. SE28 —1H 81
Curlew Clo. Ilf —1L 47
Curlew Clo. S Croy —3H 139
Curlew Ct. W13 —7D 54
Curlew Ct. Surb —5L 119
Curlew Ho. SE4 —3J 93
(off St Norbert Rd.)
Curlew Ho. SE15 —9D 76
Curlew St. SE1 —3D 76
Curlew Way. Hay —8H 53
Curnick's La. SE27 —1A 108
Curran Av. Sidc —4D 96
Curran Av. Wall —5E 122
Curran Clo. Uxb —7A 142
Curran Ho. SW3 —5C 74
(off Lucan Pl.)
Currey Rd. Gnfd —2B 54
Curricle St. W3 —2C 72
Currie Hill Clo. SW19 —1K 105
Currie Ho. E14 —9B 62
(off Abbott Rd.)
Curry Ri. NW7 —6H 25
Cursitor St. WC2 —9L 59
Curtain Pl. EC2 —6C 60
(off Curtain Rd.)
Curtain Rd. EC2 —7C 60
(in two parts)
Curthwaite Gdns. Enf —6H 15
Curtis Dri. W3 —9B 56
Curtis Fld. Rd. SW16 —1K 107
Curtis Ho. SE17 —6B 76
(off Morecambe St.)
Curtis La. Wemb —1J 55
Curtismill Clo. Orp —7F 112
Curtismill Way. Orp —7F 112
Curtis Rd. Eps —6A 120
Curtis Rd. Horn —6K 51
Curtis Rd. Houn —6K 85
Curtiss Dri. Leav —7D 4
Curtis St. SE1 —5D 76
Curtis Way. SE1 —5D 76
Curtis Way. SE28 —1F 80
Curtlington Ho. Edgw —9A 24
(off Burnt Oak B'way.)
Curvan Clo. Eps —2D 134
Curve, The. W12 —1E 72
Curwen Av. E7 —9F 46
Curwen Rd. W12 —3E 72
Curzon Av. Enf —7H 17
Curzon Av. Stan —8E 22
Curzon Clo. Orp —6B 128
Curzon Ct. SW6 —9M 73
(off Maltings Pl.)
Curzon Cres. NW10 —3C 56
Curzon Cres. Bark —5D 64
Curzon Ga. W1 —2E 74
Curzon Ga. Ct. Wat —3E 8
Curzon Pl. W1 —2E 74
Curzon Pl. Pinn —3G 37
Curzon Rd. N10 —9F 26
Curzon Rd. W5 —7F 54
Curzon Rd. T Hth —1L 123
Curzon St. W1 —2E 74
Cusack Clo. Twic —1D 102
Cussans Ho. Wat —8C 8
Cussons Clo. Chesh —2A 6
Custance Ho. N1 —5B 60
(off Provost Est.)
Custance St. N1 —6B 60
Custom House. —9G 63
Custom House. —1C 76
Custom Ho. Reach. SE16 —3K 77
Custom Ho. Wlk. EC3 —1C 76
Cutbush Ho. N7 —1H 59
Cutcombe Rd. SE5 —1A 92
Cuthberga St. Bark —3A 64
(off George St.)
Cuthbert Gdns. SE25 —7C 108
Cuthbert Harrowing Ho. EC1 —7A 60
(off Golden La. Est.)
Cuthbert Ho. W2 —8B 58
(off Hall Pl.)
Cuthbert Rd. E17 —1A 46
Cuthbert Rd. N18 —5E 28
Cuthbert Rd. Croy —4M 123
Cuthbert St. W2 —8B 58
Cuthill Wlk. SE5 —9B 76
Cutlers Gdns. E1 —9C 60
(off Cutlers St.)
Cutlers Sq. E14 —5L 77
Cutler St. E1 —9C 60
Cut, The. SE1 —3L 75
Cutthroat All. Rich —8G 87
Cutty Sark Clipper Ship. —7A 78
Cuxton. Pet W —9A 112
Cuxton Clo. Bexh —4J 97
Cyclamen Clo. Hamp —3L 101
Cyclamen Rd. Swan —8B 114
Cyclamen Way. Eps —7A 120
Cyclops M. E14 —5L 77
Cygnet Av. Felt —6G 85
Cygnet Clo. NW10 —1B 56
Cygnet Clo. Borwd —3A 12
Cygnet Clo. N'wd —6A 20
Cygnets, The. Felt —1J 101
Cygnet St. E1 —7D 60
Cygnet Way. Hay —8H 53
Cygnus Bus. Cen. NW10 —1D 56
Cymbeline Ct. Harr —4D 38
(off Gayton Rd.)
Cynthia St. N1 —5K 59
Cyntra Pl. E8 —3F 60
Cypress Av. Twic —6A 86
Cypress Clo. Wal A —7K 7
Cypress Gdns. SE4 —4J 93
Cypress Gro. Ilf —6C 32
Cypress Ho. SE14 —9H 77
Cypress Path. Romf —7H 35
Cypress Pl. W1 —7G 59
Cypress Rd. SE25 —6C 108
Cypress Rd. Harr —9B 22
Cypress Tree Clo. Sidc —7D 96
Cypress Wlk. Wat —8F 4
Cypress Way. Bans —6H 135
Cyprus. —1L 79
Cyprus Av. N3 —9J 25
Cyprus Clo. N4 —4M 43
Cyprus Gdns. N3 —9J 25
Cyprus Pl. E2 —5G 61
Cyprus Pl. E6 —1L 79
Cyprus Rd. N3 —9K 25
Cyprus Rd. N9 —2D 28
Cyprus St. E2 —5G 61
(in two parts)
Cyrena Rd. SE22 —5D 92
Cyril Lodge. Sidc —1E 112
Cyril Mans. SW11 —9D 74
Cyril Rd. Bexh —1J 97
Cyril Rd. Orp —2E 128
Cyrus Ho. EC1 —7M 59
(off Cyrus St.)
Cyrus St. EC1 —7M 59
(off Cyrus St.)
Czar St. SE8 —7L 77

Dabbling Clo. Eri —7F 82
Dabbs Hill La. N'holt —2K 53
(in two parts)
Dabbs La. EC1 —7L 59
(off Farringdon Rd.)
D'Abernon Chase. Lea —6E 132
D'Abernon Clo. Esh —6L 117
Dabin Cres. SE10 —9A 78
Dacca St. SE8 —7K 77
Dace Rd. E3 —4L 61
Dacre Av. Ilf —9L 31
Dacre Clo. Chig —4A 32
Dacre Clo. Gnfd —5M 53
Dacre Gdns. SE13 —3C 94
Dacre Gdns. Borwd —7B 12
Dacre Gdns. Chig —4A 32
Dacre Ho. SW3 —7B 74
(off Beaufort St.)
Dacre Ind. Est. Chesh —2F 6
Dacre Pk. SE13 —2C 94
Dacre Pl. SE13 —2C 94
Dacre Rd. E11 —6D 46
Dacre Rd. E13 —4F 62
Dacre Rd. Croy —2J 123
Dacres Ho. SW4 —2F 90
Dacres Rd. SE23 —8H 93
Dacre St. SW1 —4H 75
Dade Way. S'hall —6K 69
Daerwood Clo. Brom —3K 127
Daffodil Clo. Croy —3H 125
Daffodil Gdns. Ilf —1M 63
Daffodil Pl. Hamp —3L 101
Daffodil St. W12 —1D 72
Dafforne Rd. SW17 —9E 90
Dagenham. —2L 65
Dagenham & Redbridge F.C. —1M 65
Dagenham Av. Dag —4J 65
(in two parts)
Dagenham Leisure Pk. Dag —4J 65
Dagenham Rd. E10 —6K 45
Dagenham Rd. Dag & Romf —9M 49
Dagenham Rd. Rain —3B 66
Dagenham Rd. Romf & Rush G —5B 50
Dagger La. Els —8E 10
Dagmar Av. Wemb —9K 39
Dagmar Ct. E14 —4A 78
Dagmar Gdns. NW10 —5H 57
Dagmar M. S'hall —4J 69
(off Dagmar Rd.)
Dagmar Pas. N1 —4M 59
(off Cross St.)
Dagmar Rd. N4 —5L 43
Dagmar Rd. N15 —2B 44
Dagmar Rd. N22 —8H 27
Dagmar Rd. SE5 —9C 76
Dagmar Rd. SE25 —9C 108
Dagmar Rd. Dag —3A 66
Dagmar Rd. King T —5K 103
Dagmar Rd. S'hall —4J 69
Dagmar Ter. N1 —4M 59
Dagnall Cres. Uxb —8A 142
Dagnall Pk. SE25 —1C 124
Dagnall Rd. SE25 —9C 108
Dagnall St. SW11 —1D 90
Dagnam Pk. Clo. Romf —5L 35
Dagnam Pk. Dri. Romf —5J 35
Dagnam Pk. Gdns. Romf —6L 35
(in two parts)
Dagnam Pk. Sq. Romf —6M 35
Dagnan Rd. SW12 —6F 90
Dagobert Ho. E1 —8G 61
(off Smithy St.)
Dagonet Gdns. Brom —9E 94
Dagonet Rd. Brom —9E 94
Dahlia Dri. Swan —6D 114
Dahlia Gdns. Ilf —2M 63
Dahlia Gdns. Mitc —8H 107
Dahlia Rd. SE2 —5F 80
Dahomey Rd. SW16 —3G 107
Daimler Way. Wall —9J 123
Dain Ct. W8 —5L 73
(off Lexham Gdns.)
Daines Clo. E12 —8K 47
Dainford Clo. Brom —2B 110
Dainton Clo. Brom —5F 110
Daintry Clo. Harr —2E 38
Daintry Lodge. N'wd —7D 20
Daintry Way. E9 —2K 61
Dairsie Ct. Brom —6G 111
Dairsie Rd. SE9 —2L 95
Dairy Clo. NW10 —4E 56
Dairy Clo. Brom —4F 110
Dairy Clo. S at H —4M 115
Dairy Clo. T Hth —6A 108
Dairyglen Av. Chesh —4E 6
Dairy La. SE18 —5K 79
Dairyman Clo. NW2 —8H 41
Dairy M. SW9 —2J 91
Dairy M. Wat —7E 8
Dairy Wlk. SW19 —1J 105
Dairy Way. Ab L —2D 4
Daisy Clo. Croy —3H 125
Daisy Dobbings Wlk. N19 —5J 43
(off Jessie Blythe La.)
Daisy La. SW6 —2L 89
Daisy Rd. E16 —7C 62
Daisy Rd. E18 —9F 30
Dakota Clo. Wall —9K 123
Dakota Gdns. E6 —7J 63
Dakota Gdns. N'holt —6J 53
Dalberg Rd. SW2 —3L 91
(in two parts)
Dalberg Way. SE2 —4H 81
Dalby Rd. SW18 —3A 90
Dalbys Cres. N17 —6C 28
Dalby St. NW5 —2F 58
Dalcross Rd. Houn —1J 85
Dale Av. Edgw —8K 23
Dale Av. Houn —2J 85
Dalebury Rd. SW17 —8D 90
Dale Clo. SE3 —2E 94
Dale Clo. Dart —5D 98
Dale Clo. New Bar —8M 13
Dale Clo. Pinn —8F 20
Dale Ct. King T —4K 103
(off York Rd.)
Dale Ct. Wat —7E 4
Dale Dri. Hay —7D 52
Dale End. Dart —5D 98
Dale Gdns. Wfd G —4F 30
Dalegarth Gdns. Purl —5B 138
Dale Grn. Rd. N11 —3F 26
Dale Gro. N12 —5A 26
Daleham Dri. Uxb —9F 142
Daleham Gdns. NW3 —1B 58
Daleham M. NW3 —2B 58
Dalehead. NW1 —5G 59
(off Harrington Sq.)
Dale Ho. NW8 —4A 58
(off Boundary Rd.)
Dale Ho. SE4 —3J 93
Dale Lodge. N6 —4G 43
Dalemain M. E16 —2E 78
Dale Pk. Av. Cars —4D 122
Dale Pk. Rd. SE19 —5A 108
Dale Rd. NW5 —1E 58
Dale Rd. SE17 —7M 75
Dale Rd. Dart —5D 98
Dale Rd. Gnfd —8M 53
Dale Rd. Purl —4L 137
Dale Rd. Sun —4D 100
Dale Rd. Sutt —6K 121
Dale Rd. Swan —6A 114
Dale Rd. W on T —2D 116
Dale Row. W11 —9J 57
Daleside. Orp —7E 128
Daleside Clo. Orp —8E 128
Daleside Gdns. Chig —3A 32
Daleside Rd. SW16 —2F 106
Daleside Rd. Eps —8B 120
Dales Path. Borwd —7B 12
Dales Rd. Borwd —7B 12
Dalestone M. Romf —6F 34
Dale St. W4 —6C 72
Dale, The. Kes —6H 127
Dale, The. Wal A —7L 7
Dale Vw. Eri —1D 98
Dale Vw. Av. E4 —2A 30
Dale Vw. Cres. E4 —2A 30
Dale Vw. Gdns. E4 —3B 30
Daleview Rd. N15 —4C 44
Dale Wlk. Dart —7M 99
Dalewood Clo. Horn —5K 51
Dalewood Gdns. Wor Pk —4F 120
Dale Wood Rd. Orp —2C 128
Daley Ho. W12 —9F 56
Daley St. E9 —2H 61
Daley Thompson Way. SW8 —1F 90
Dalgarno Gdns. W10 —8F 56
Dalgarno Way. W10 —7G 57
Dalgleish St. E14 —9J 61
Daling Way. E3 —4J 61
Dali Universe. —3K 75
Dalkeith Ct. SW1 —5H 75
(off Vincent St.)
Dalkeith Gro. Stan —5H 23
Dalkeith Ho. SW9 —9M 75
(off Lothian Rd.)
Dalkeith Rd. SE21 —7A 92
Dalkeith Rd. Ilf —8A 48
Dallas Rd. NW4 —5E 40
Dallas Rd. SE26 —9F 92
Dallas Rd. W5 —8K 55
Dallas Rd. Sutt —8J 121
Dallas Ter. Hay —4D 68
Dallega Clo. Hay —1B 68
Dallinger Rd. SE12 —5D 94
Dalling Rd. W6 —5F 72
Dallington Clo. W on T —8G 117
Dallington St. EC1 —7M 59
Dallin Rd. SE18 —8M 79
Dallin Rd. Bexh —3H 97
Dalmain Rd. SE23 —7H 93
Dalmally Rd. Croy —2D 124
Dalmeny Av. N7 —9H 43
Dalmeny Av. SW16 —6L 107
Dalmeny Clo. Wemb —2G 55
Dalmeny Cres. Houn —3B 86
Dalmeny Rd. N7 —8H 43
(in three parts)
Dalmeny Rd. Cars —9E 122
Dalmeny Rd. Eri —9M 81
Dalmeny Rd. New Bar —8A 14
Dalmeny Rd. Wor Pk —5F 120
Dalmeyer Rd. NW10 —2D 56
Dalmore Av. Clay —8D 118
Dalmore Rd. SE21 —8A 92
Dalo Lodge. E3 —8L 61
(off Gale St.)
Dalrymple Clo. N14 —9H 15
Dalrymple Rd. SE4 —3J 93
Dalston. —2D 60
Dalston Gdns. Stan —8J 23
Dalston La. E8 —2D 60
Dalton Av. Mitc —6C 106
Dalton Clo. Hay —7B 52
Dalton Clo. Orp —5C 128
Dalton Clo. Purl —4A 138
Dalton Ho. SE14 —7H 77
(off John Williams Clo.)
Dalton Ho. SW1 —6F 74
(off Ebury Bri. Rd.)
Dalton Rd. W'stone —9B 22
Daltons Rd. Orp & Swan —6M 129
Dalton St. SE27 —8M 91
Dalwood St. SE5 —9C 76
Daly Ct. E15 —1M 61
Dalyell Rd. SW9 —2K 91
Damascene Wlk. SE21 —7A 92
Damask Cres. E16 —7C 62
Damer Ter. SW10 —8A 74
Dames Rd. E7 —8E 46
Dame St. N1 —5A 60
Damien Ct. E1 —9F 60
(off Damien St.)
Damien St. E1 —9F 60
Damon Clo. Sidc —9F 96
Damory Ho. SE16 —5F 76
(off Abbeyfield Est.)
Damson Ct. Swan —8B 114
Damson Dri. Hay —1E 68
Damsonwood Rd. S'hall —4L 69
Danbrook Rd. SW16 —5J 107
Danbury Clo. Romf —1H 49
Danbury Mans. Bark —3M 63
(off Whiting Av.)
Danbury M. Wall —6F 122
Danbury Rd. Lou —9J 19
Danbury Rd. Rain —4D 66
Danbury St. N1 —5M 59
Danbury Way. Wfd G —6G 31
Danby Ct. Enf —5A 16
(off Horseshoe La.)
Danby St. SE15 —2D 92
Dancer Rd. SW6 —9K 73
Dancer Rd. Rich —2L 87
Dancers Hill Rd. Barn —1G 13
Dandelion Clo. Rush G —7C 50
Dando Cres. SE3 —2F 94
Dandridge Clo. SE10 —6D 78
Dandridge Ho. E1 —8D 60
(off Lamb St.)
Danebury. New Ad —8A 126
Danebury Av. SW15 —5C 88
(in two parts)
Daneby Rd. SE6 —9M 93
Dane Clo. Bex —6L 97
Dane Clo. Orp —7B 128
Danecourt Gdns. Croy —5D 124
Danecroft Rd. SE24 —4A 92
Danehill Wlk. Sidc —9E 96
Dane Ho. N14 —9H 15
Danehurst Ct. Eps —5D 134
Danehurst Gdns. Ilf —3J 47
Danehurst St. SW6 —9J 73
Daneland. Barn —8D 14
Danemead Gro. N'holt —1M 53
Danemere St. SW15 —2G 89
Dane Pl. E3 —5K 61
Dane Rd. N18 —3G 29
Dane Rd. SW19 —5A 106
Dane Rd. W13 —2G 71
Dane Rd. Ashf —3A 100
Dane Rd. Ilf —1A 64
Dane Rd. S'hall —1J 69
Dane Rd. Warl —9H 139
Danesbury Rd. Felt —7F 84
Danes Clo. Oxs —6A 132
Danescombe. SE12 —7E 94
Danes Ct. NW8 —4D 58
(off St Edmund's Ter.)
Danes Ct. Wemb —8M 39
Danescourt Cres. Sutt —4A 122
Danescroft. NW4 —3H 41
Danescroft Av. NW4 —3H 41
Danescroft Gdns. NW4 —3H 41
Danesdale Rd. E9 —2J 61
Danesfield. SE17 —7C 76
(off Albany Rd.)
Danesfield Clo. W on T —5F 116
Danes Ga. Harr —1C 38
Daneshill Dri. Oxs —6B 132
Danes Ho. W10 —8G 57
(off Sutton Way)
Danes Rd. Romf —5A 50
Danes, The. Park —1M 5
Dane St. WC1 —8K 59
Danes Way. Oxs —6B 132
Daneswood Av. SE6 —9A 94
Daneswood Clo. Wey —7A 116
Danethorpe Rd. Wemb —2H 55
Danetree Clo. Eps —9A 120
Danetree Rd. Eps —9A 120
Danette Gdns. Dag —7L 49
Daneville Rd. SE5 —9B 76
Dangan Rd. E11 —4F 46
Daniel Bolt Clo. E14 —8M 61
Daniel Clo. N18 —4G 29
Daniel Clo. SW17 —3C 106
Daniel Clo. Houn —6K 85
Daniel Ct. NW9 —8C 24
Daniel Gdns. SE15 —8D 76
Daniel Ho. N1 —5B 60
(off Cranston Est.)
Daniell Way. Croy —3J 123
Daniel Pl. NW4 —5F 40
Daniel Rd. W5 —1K 71
Daniels La. Warl —8K 139
Daniels Rd. SE15 —2G 93
Daniel Way. Bans —6M 135
Danleigh Ct. N14 —9H 15
Dan Leno Wlk. SW6 —8M 73
Dansey Pl. W1 —1H 75
(off Wardour St.)
Dansington Rd. Well —3E 96
Danson Cres. Well —2E 96
Danson Interchange. (Junct.) —5G 97

Devon Rd.—Dorchester Rd.

Devon Rd. S Dar —5M 115
Devon Rd. Sutt —1J 135
Devon Rd. W on T —6G 117
Devon Rd. Wat —3H 9
Devons Est. E3 —6M 61
Devonshire Av. Dart —5F 98
Devonshire Av. Sutt —9A 122
Devonshire Clo. E15 —9C 46
Devonshire Clo. N13 —3L 27
Devonshire Clo. W1 —8F 58
Devonshire Ct. E1 —6G 61
(off Bancroft Rd.)
Devonshire Ct. WC1 —8J 59
(off Boswell St.)
Devonshire Ct. Pinn —8K 21
(off Devonshire Rd.)
Devonshire Cres. NW7 —7H 25
Devonshire Dri. SE10 —8M 77
Devonshire Dri. Surb —3H 119
Devonshire Gdns. N17 —6A 28
Devonshire Gdns. N21 —9A 16
Devonshire Gdns. W4 —8A 72
Devonshire Gro. SE15 —7F 76
Devonshire Hill La. N17 —6M 27
(in two parts)
Devonshire Ho. NW6 —2K 57
(off Kilburn High Rd.)
Devonshire Ho. SE1 —4A 76
(off Bath Ter.)
Devonshire Ho. SW1 —6H 75
(off Lindsay Sq.)
Devonshire Ho. Sutt —9A 122
Devonshire Ho. Bus. Cen. Brom
(off Devonshire Sq.) —8F 110
Devonshire M. N13 —4L 27
Devonshire M. W4 —6C 72
Devonshire M. N. W1 —8F 58
Devonshire M. S. W1 —8F 58
Devonshire M. W. W1 —7E 58
Devonshire Pas. W4 —6C 72
Devonshire Pl. NW1 —7E 58
Devonshire Pl. NW2 —8L 41
Devonshire Pl. W8 —4M 73
Devonshire Pl. M. W1 —8E 58
Devonshire Rd. E16 —9F 62
Devonshire Rd. E17 —4L 45
Devonshire Rd. N9 —1G 29
Devonshire Rd. N13 —4K 27
Devonshire Rd. N17 —6A 28
Devonshire Rd. NW7 —7H 25
Devonshire Rd. SE9 —8J 95
Devonshire Rd. SE23 —7G 93
Devonshire Rd. SW19 —4C 106
Devonshire Rd. W4 —6C 72
Devonshire Rd. W5 —4G 71
Devonshire Rd. Bexh —3J 97
Devonshire Rd. Cars —6E 122
Devonshire Rd. Croy —2B 124
Devonshire Rd. Eastc —4G 37
Devonshire Rd. Felt —9J 85
Devonshire Rd. Harr —4B 38
Devonshire Rd. Horn —7G 51
Devonshire Rd. Ilf —5C 48
Devonshire Rd. Orp —2E 128
Devonshire Rd. Pinn —8K 21
Devonshire Rd. S'hall —8L 53
Devonshire Rd. Sutt —9A 122
Devonshire Row. EC2 —8C 60
Devonshire Row M. W1 —7F 58
(off Devonshire St.)
Devonshire Sq. EC2 —9C 60
Devonshire Sq. Brom —8F 110
Devonshire St. W1 —8E 58
Devonshire St. W4 —6C 72
Devonshire Ter. W2 —9A 58
Devonshire Way. Croy —4J 125
Devonshire Way. Hay —9F 52
Devons Rd. E3 —8L 61
(in two parts)
Devon St. SE15 —7F 76
Devon Way. Chess —7G 119
Devon Way. Eps —7M 119
Devon Way. Uxb —5D 142
Devon Waye. Houn —8K 69
Devon Wharf. E14 —8A 62
(off Leven Rd.)
De Walden Ho. NW8 —5C 58
(off Allitsen Rd.)
De Walden St. W1 —8E 58
Dewar St. SE15 —2E 92
Dewberry Gdns. E6 —8J 63
Dewberry St. E14 —8A 62
Dewey Path. Horn —2G 67
Dewey Rd. N1 —5L 59
Dewey Rd. Dag —2M 65
Dewey St. SW17 —2D 106
Dewgrass Gro. Wal X —8D 6
Dewhurst Rd. W14 —4H 73
Dewhurst Rd. Chesh —2B 6
Dewlands Av. Dart —6M 99
Dewsbury Clo. Pinn —4J 37
Dewsbury Clo. Romf —6J 35
Dewsbury Ct. W4 —5A 72
Dewsbury Gdns. Romf —6H 35
Dewsbury Gdns. Wor Pk —5E 120
Dewsbury Rd. NW10 —1E 56
Dewsbury Rd. Romf —6H 35
Dewsbury Ter. NW1 —4F 58
Dexter Ho. Eri —4J 81
(off Kale Rd.)
Dexter Rd. Barn —8H 13
Deyncourt Gdns. Upm —7M 51
Deyncourt Rd. N17 —8A 28
Deynecourt Gdns. E11 —2G 47
D'Eynsford Rd. SE5 —9B 76
Dhonau Ho. SE1 —5D 76
(off Longfield Est.)
Diadem Ct. W1 —9H 59
(off Dean St.)
Dial Wlk., The. W8 —3M 73
(off Broad Wlk., The)
Diamedes Av. Stanw —6B 144
Diameter Rd. Orp —2M 127
Diamond Clo. Dag —6G 49
Diamond Ct. Horn —6E 50
Diamond Est. SW17 —9C 90
Diamond Ho. E3 —5J 61
(off Roman Rd.)
Diamond Rd. Ruis —9H 37
Diamond Rd. Wat —2E 8
Diamond St. NW10 —3B 56
Diamond St. SE5 —8C 76
Diamond Ter. SE10 —9A 78
Diamond Way. SE8 —7L 77
Diana Clo. E18 —8F 30
Diana Clo. SE8 —7K 77
Diana Ct. Eri —7C 82
Diana Gdns. Surb —4K 119
Diana Ho. SW13 —9D 72
Diana Rd. E17 —1K 45
Dianne Way. Barn —6C 14
Dianthus Clo. SE2 —6F 80
Diban Av. Horn —9F 50
Diban Ct. Horn —9F 50
(off Diban Av.)
Dibden Ho. SE5 —8C 76
Dibden St. N1 —4A 60
Dibdin Clo. Sutt —5L 121
Dibdin Ho. NW6 —5M 57
Dibdin Rd. Sutt —5L 121
Diceland Rd. Bans —8K 135
Dicey Av. NW2 —9G 41
Dickens Av. N3 —8A 26
Dickens Av. Dart —3L 99
Dickens Av. Uxb —9F 142
Dickens Clo. Eri —8M 81
Dickens Clo. Hay —5C 68
Dickens Clo. Rich —8J 87
Dickens Ct. E11 —2E 46
(off Makepeace Rd.)
Dickens Dri. Chst —3A 112
Dickens Est. SE1 —3E 76
Dickens Est. SE16 —4E 76
Dickens' House. —7K 59
(off Doughty St.)
Dickens Ho. NW6 —6L 57
(off Malvern Rd.)
Dickens Ho. NW8 —7B 58
(off Fisherton St.)
Dickens Ho. SE17 —6M 75
(off Doddington Gro.)
Dickens Ho. W9 —7L 57
(off Malvern Rd.)
Dickens Ho. WC1 —7J 59
(off Herbrand St.)
Dickens La. N18 —5C 28
Dickens M. EC1 —8M 59
(off Turnmill St.)
Dickenson Clo. N9 —1E 28
Dickenson Ho. N8 —4K 43
Dickenson Rd. N8 —5J 43
Dickenson Rd. Felt —2G 101
Dickensons La. SE25 —9E 108
(in two parts)
Dickensons Pl. SE25 —1E 124
Dickens Ri. Chig —3M 31
Dickens Rd. E6 —5H 63
Dickens Sq. SE1 —4A 76
Dickens St. SW8 —1F 90
Dickens Way. Romf —2C 50
Dickenswood Clo. SE19 —4M 107
Dickerage La. N Mald —7A 104
Dickerage Rd. King T & N Mald —5A 104
Dicksee Ho. NW8 —7B 58
(off Lyons Pl.)
Dickson. Chesh —1A 6
Dickson Fold. Pinn —2H 37
Dickson Ho. E1 —9F 60
(off Philpot St.)
Dickson Rd. SE9 —2J 95
Dick Turpin Way. Felt —3D 84
Didsbury Clo. E6 —4K 63
Digby Bus. Cen. E9 —2H 61
(off Digby Rd.)
Digby Cres. N4 —7A 44
Digby Gdns. Dag —4L 65
Digby Mans. W6 —6F 72
(off Hammersmith Bri. Rd.)
Digby Pl. Croy —5D 124
Digby Rd. E9 —2H 61
Digby Rd. Bark —3D 64
Digby St. E2 —6G 61
Digby Wlk. Horn —2G 67
Digdens Ri. Eps —7A 134
Diggens Ct. Lou —5J 19
Diggon St. E1 —8H 61
Dighton Ct. SE17 —7A 76
(off John Ruskin St.)
Dighton Rd. SW18 —4A 90
Dignum St. N1 —5L 59
Digswell Clo. Borwd —2L 11
Digswell St. N7 —2L 59
Dilhorne Clo. SE12 —9F 94
Dilke St. SW3 —7D 74
Dilloway La. S'hall —3J 69
Dillwyn Clo. SE26 —1J 109
Dilston Clo. N'holt —6G 53
Dilston Gro. SE16 —5G 77
Dilton Gdns. SW15 —7E 88
Dilwyn Ct. E17 —9J 29
Dimes Pl. W6 —5F 72
Dimmock Dri. Gnfd —1B 54
Dimond Clo. E7 —9E 46
Dimsdale Dri. NW9 —6A 40
Dimsdale Dri. Enf —9E 16
Dimsdale Wlk. E13 —5E 62
Dimson Cres. E3 —6L 61
Dingle Clo. Barn —8D 12
Dingle Gdns. E14 —1L 77
Dingle Rd. Ashf —2A 100
Dingles Ct. Pinn —8H 21
Dingle, The. Uxb —6F 142
Dingley La. SW16 —8H 91
Dingley Pl. EC1 —6A 60
Dingley Rd. EC1 —6A 60
Dingwall Av. Croy & New Ad —4A 124
Dingwall Gdns. NW11 —4L 41
Dingwall Rd. SW18 —6A 90
Dingwall Rd. Cars —1D 136
Dingwall Rd. Croy —3B 124
Dinmont Est. E2 —5E 60
Dinmont Ho. E2 —5E 60
(off Pritchard's Rd.)
Dinmont St. E2 —5F 60
Dinnington Ho. E1 —7F 60
(off Coventry Rd.)
Dinsdale Gdns. SE25 —9C 108
Dinsdale Gdns. New Bar —7M 13
Dinsdale Rd. SE3 —7D 78
Dinsmore Rd. SW12 —6F 90
Dinton Ho. NW8 —7C 58
(off Lilestone St.)
Dinton Rd. SW19 —3B 106
Dinton Rd. King T —4K 103
Diploma Av. N2 —2C 42
Diploma Ct. N2 —2C 42
Dirdene Clo. Eps —4D 134
Dirdene Gdns. Eps —4D 134
Dirdene Gro. Eps —4C 134
Dirleton Rd. E15 —4D 62
Disbrowe Rd. W6 —7J 73
Discovery Bus. Pk. SE16 —4E 76
(off St James's Rd.)
Discovery Ho. E14 —1A 78
(off Newby Pl.)
Discovery Wlk. E1 —2F 76
Dishforth La. NW9 —7C 24
Disley Ct. S'hall —9M 53
(off Howard Rd.)
Disney Pl. SE1 —3A 76
Disney St. SE1 —3A 76
Dison Clo. Enf —3H 17
Disraeli Clo. SE28 —2G 81
Disraeli Clo. W4 —4B 72
Disraeli Gdns. SW15 —3K 89
Disraeli Rd. E7 —2E 62
Disraeli Rd. NW10 —5B 56
Disraeli Rd. SW15 —3J 89
Disraeli Rd. W5 —2H 71
Diss St. E2 —6D 60
Distaff La. EC4 —1A 76
Distillery La. W6 —6G 73
Distillery Rd. W6 —6G 73
Distillery Wlk. Bren —7J 71
Distin St. SE11 —5L 75
District Rd. Wemb —1F 54
Ditch All. SE10 —9M 77
Ditchburn St. E14 —1A 78
Ditches Ride, The. Lou & Epp —1L 19
Ditchfield Rd. Hay —7J 53
Ditchley Ct. W7 —8D 54
(off Templeman Rd.)
Dittisham Rd. SE9 —1J 111
Ditton Clo. Th Dit —2E 118
Dittoncroft Clo. Croy —6C 124
Ditton Grange Clo. Surb —3H 119
Ditton Grange Dri. Surb —3H 119
Ditton Hill. Surb —3G 119
Ditton Hill Rd. Surb —3G 119
Ditton Lawn. Th Dit —3E 118
Ditton Pl. SE20 —5F 108
Ditton Reach. Th Dit —1F 118
Ditton Rd. Bexh —4H 97
Ditton Rd. S'hall —6K 69
Ditton Rd. Surb —4H 119
Divis Way. SW15 —5F 88
(off Dover Pk. Dri.)
Dixon Clark Ct. N1 —2M 59
Dixon Clo. E6 —9K 63
Dixon Ho. W10 —9H 57
(off Darfield Way)
Dixon Pl. W W'ck —3M 125
Dixon Rd. SE14 —9J 77
Dixon Rd. SE25 —7C 108
Dixon's All. SE16 —3F 76
Dobbin Clo. Harr —9E 22
Dobell Rd. SE9 —4K 95
Doble Ct. S Croy —4E 138
Dobree Av. NW10 —3F 56
Dobson Clo. NW6 —3B 58
Dobson Ho. SE5 —8B 76
(off Edmund St.)
Dobson Ho. SE14 —7H 77
(off John Williams Clo.)
Doby Ct. EC4 —1A 76
(off Skinners La.)
Dockers Tanner Rd. E14 —5L 77
Dockhead. SE1 —3D 76
Dockhead Wharf. SE1 —3D 76
(off Shad Thames)
Dock Hill Av. SE16 —2H 77
Dockland St. E16 —2L 79
(in two parts)
Dockley Rd. SE16 —4E 76
Dockley Rd. Ind. Est. SE16 —4E 76
(off Dockley Rd.)
Dock Offices. SE16 —4G 77
(off Surrey Quays Rd.)
Dock Rd. E16 —1D 78
Dock Rd. Bren —8H 71
Dockside Rd. E16 —1H 79
Dock St. E1 —1E 76
Dockwell Clo. Felt —3E 84
Doctor Johnson Av. SW17 —9F 90
Doctors Clo. SE26 —2G 109
Docwra's Bldgs. N1 —2C 60
Dodbrooke Rd. SE27 —9L 91
Dodd Ho. SE16 —5F 76
(off Rennie Est.)
Doddington Gro. SE17 —7M 75
Doddington Pl. SE17 —7M 75
Dodsley Pl. N9 —3G 29
Dodson St. SE1 —3L 75
Dod St. E14 —9K 61
Doebury Wlk. SE18 —7E 80
(off Prestwood Clo.)
Doel Clo. SW19 —4A 106
Dog and Duck Yd. WC1 —8K 59
(off Princeton St.)
Doggett Rd. SE6 —6L 93
Doggett's Corner. Horn —7K 51
Doggetts Courts. Barn —7C 14
Doghurst Av. Hay —8M 143
Doghurst Dri. W Dray —8M 143
Dog Kennel Hill. SE5 —2C 92
Dog Kennel Hill Est. SE22 —2C 92
(off Albrighton Rd.)
Dog La. NW10 —9C 40
Doherty Rd. E13 —7E 62
Dokal Ind. Est. S'hall —4J 69
Dolben Ct. SE8 —5K 77
Dolben St. SE1 —2M 75
(in two parts)
Dolby Rd. SW6 —1K 89
Dolland Ho. SE11 —6K 75
(off Newburn St.)
Dolland St. SE11 —6K 75
Dollar Bay. E14 —3A 78
(off Lawn Ho. Clo.)
Dollary Pde. King T —7M 103
(off Kingston Rd.)
Dollis Av. N3 —8K 25
Dollis Brook Wlk. Barn —8J 13
Dollis Cres. Ruis —6G 37
Dolliscroft. NW7 —7J 25
Dollis Hill. —7F 40
Dollis Hill Av. NW2 —8F 40
Dollis Hill Est. NW2 —8E 40
Dollis Hill La. NW2 —9D 40
Dollis M. N3 —8L 25
Dollis Pk. N3 —8K 25
Dollis Rd. NW7 & N3 —7J 25
Dollis Valley Way. Barn —8K 13
Dolman Clo. N3 —8A 26
Dolman Rd. W4 —5B 72
Dolman St. SW4 —3K 91
Dolphin App. Romf —2D 50
Dolphin Clo. SE16 —3H 77
Dolphin Clo. SE28 —9H 65
Dolphin Clo. Surb —9H 103
Dolphin Ct. NW11 —4J 41
Dolphin Ct. Chig —3M 31
Dolphin Est. Sun —5C 100
Dolphin Ho. SW18 —3M 89
Dolphin La. E14 —1M 77
Dolphin Rd. N'holt —5K 53
Dolphin Rd. Sun —5C 100
Dolphin Rd. N. Sun —5C 100
Dolphin Rd. S. Sun —5C 100
Dolphin Rd. W. Sun —5C 100
Dolphin Sq. SW1 —6G 75
Dolphin Sq. W4 —8C 72
Dolphin St. King T —6J 103
Dolphin Tower. SE8 —7K 77
(off Abinger Gro.)
Dombey Ho. SE1 —3E 76
(off Wolseley St.)
Dombey Ho. W11 —2H 73
(off St Ann's Rd.)
Dombey St. WC1 —8K 59
(in two parts)
Dome Hill Pk. SE26 —1D 108
Dome, The. (Junct.) —9G 5
Domett Clo. SE5 —3B 92
Domfe Pl. E5 —9G 45
Domingo St. EC1 —7A 60
Dominica Clo. E13 —6G 63
Dominic Ct. Wal A —6H 7
Dominion Bus. Pk. N9 —2H 29
Dominion Cen., The. S'hall —3J 69
Dominion Dri. Romf —6M 33
Dominion Ho. E14 —6M 77
(off St Davids Sq.)
Dominion Pde. Harr —3D 38
Dominion Rd. Croy —2D 124
Dominion Rd. S'hall —3J 69
Dominion St. EC2 —8B 60
Dominion Theatre. —9H 59
(off Tottenham Ct. Rd.)
Dominion Way. Rain —6E 66
Domitian Pl. Enf —7D 16
Domonic Dri. SE9 —1M 111
Domville Clo. N20 —2B 26
Donald Dri. Romf —3G 49
Donald Hunter Ho. E7 —1F 62
(off Post Office App., in two parts)
Donald Rd. E13 —4F 62
Donald Rd. Croy —2K 123
Donaldson Rd. NW6 —4K 57
Donaldson Rd. SE18 —9L 79
Donald Woods Gdns. Surb —4M 119
Doncaster Dri. N'holt —1K 53
Doncaster Gdns. N4 —4A 44
Doncaster Gdns. N'holt —1K 53
Doncaster Grn. Wat —5G 21
Doncaster Rd. N9 —9F 16
Doncaster Way. Upm —8K 51
Doncel Ct. E4 —9B 18
Donegal Ho. E1 —7F 60
(off Cambridge Heath Rd.)
Donegal St. N1 —5K 59
Doneraile Ho. SW1 —6F 74
(off Ebury Bri. Rd.)
Doneraile St. SW6 —1H 89
Dongola Rd. E1 —8J 61
Dongola Rd. E13 —6F 62
Dongola Rd. N17 —1C 44
Dongola Rd. W. E13 —6F 62
Donington Av. Ilf —3A 48
Donkey All. SE22 —6E 92
Donkey La. Enf —4E 16
Donkey La. F'ham —4M 131
Donkey La. W Dray —5G 143
Donkin Ho. SE16 —5F 76
(off Rennie Est.)
Donmar Warehouse Theatre.
(off Earlham St.) —9J 59
Donnatt's Rd. SE14 —9K 77
Donne Ct. SE24 —5A 92
Donnefield Av. Edgw —7J 23
Donne Ho. E14 —9L 61
(off Dod St.)
Donne Ho. SE14 —7H 77
(off Samuel Clo.)
Donnelly Ct. SW6 —8J 73
(off Dawes Rd.)
Donne Pl. SW3 —5C 74
Donne Pl. Mitc —8F 106
Donne Rd. Dag —7G 49
Donnington Ct. NW1 —3F 58
(off Castlehaven Rd.)
Donnington Ct. NW10 —3F 56
Donnington Ct. Dart —5M 99
(off Bow Arrow La.)
Donnington Rd. NW10 —3F 56
Donnington Rd. Harr —3H 39
Donnington Rd. Wor Pk —4E 120
Donnybrook Rd. SW16 —4G 107
Donoghue Cotts. E14 —8J 61
(off Maroon St.)
Donovan Av. N10 —9F 26
Donovan Clo. Eps —2B 134
Donovan Ct. NW10 —3A 56
Donovan Ct. SW10 —6B 74
(off Drayton Gdns.)
Donovan Ho. E1 —1G 77
(off Cable St.)
Don Phelan Clo. SE5 —9B 76
Don Way. Romf —7C 34
Doone Clo. Tedd —3E 102
Doon St. SE1 —2L 75
Dorado Gdns. Orp —5H 129
Dora Ho. E14 —9K 61
(off Rhodeswell Rd.)
Dora Ho. W11 —1H 73
(off St Ann's Rd.)
Doral Way. Cars —7D 122
Doran Ct. E6 —5K 63
Dorando Clo. W12 —1F 72
Doran Gro. SE18 —8C 80
Doran Mnr. N2 —3D 42
(off Gt. North Rd.)
Doran Wlk. E15 —3A 62
Dora Rd. SW19 —2L 105
Dora St. E14 —9K 61
Dorchester Av. N13 —4A 28
Dorchester Av. Bex —7H 97
Dorchester Av. Harr —4A 38
Dorchester Clo. Dart —6K 99
Dorchester Clo. N'holt —1M 53
Dorchester Clo. Orp —4F 112
Dorchester Ct. E18 —8D 30
(off Buckingham Rd.)
Dorchester Ct. N1 —3C 60
(off Englefield Rd.)
Dorchester Ct. N10 —1F 42
Dorchester Ct. N14 —9F 14
Dorchester Ct. NW2 —8H 41
Dorchester Ct. SE24 —4A 92
Dorchester Ct. Wat —8J 9
(off Chalk Hill)
Dorchester Dri. SE24 —4A 92
Dorchester Dri. Felt —5C 84
Dorchester Gdns. E4 —4L 29
Dorchester Gdns. NW11 —2L 41
Dorchester Gro. W4 —6C 72
Dorchester M. N Mald —8B 104
Dorchester M. Twic —5G 87
Dorchester Rd. Mord —2M 121
Dorchester Rd. N'holt —1M 53
Dorchester Rd. Wor Pk —3G 121

Drive, The—Durnsford Av.

Drive, The. Eps —8D 120
Drive, The. Eri —8M 81
Drive, The. Esh —3A 118
Drive, The. Felt —6G 85
Drive, The. H Wood —8J 35
Drive, The. Harr —5L 37
Drive, The. High Bar —5J 13
Drive, The. Houn & Iswth —1B 86
Drive, The. Ilf —4J 47
Drive, The. King T —4A 104
Drive, The. Lou —5J 19
(in two parts)
Drive, The. Mord —9A 106
Drive, The. New Bar —8A 14
Drive, The. N'wd —9C 20
Drive, The. Orp —4D 128
Drive, The. Sidc —9F 96
Drive, The. Surb —2J 119
Drive, The. Sutt —4K 135
Drive, The. T Hth —8B 108
Drive, The. Uxb —1C 142
Drive, The. Wall —2G 137
Drive, The. Wat —1B 8
Drive, The. Wemb —7A 40
Drive, The. W W'ck —2B 126
Driveway, The. E17 —4M 45
(off Hoe St.)
Dr Johnson's House. —9L 59
(off Pemberton Row)
Droitwich Clo. SE26 —9E 92
Dromey Gdns. Harr —7D 22
Dromore Rd. SW15 —5J 89
Dronfield Gdns. Dag —1G 65
Dron Ho. E1 —8G 61
(off Adelina Gro.)
Droop St. W10 —6H 57
Drop La. Brick W —3M 5
Drovers Ct. King T —6J 103
(off Fairfield E.)
Drovers Pl. SE15 —8G 77
Drovers Rd. S Croy —7B 124
Droveway. Lou —4M 19
Druce Rd. SE21 —5C 92
Druid St. SE1 —3C 76
Druids Way. Brom —8B 110
Drumaline Ridge. Wor Pk —4C 120
Drummond Av. Romf —2B 50
Drummond Cen. Croy —4A 124
Drummond Clo. Eri —9C 82
Drummond Cres. NW1 —6H 59
Drummond Dri. Stan —7D 22
Drummond Gdns. Eps —3A 134
Drummond Ga. SW1 —6H 75
Drummond Ho. E2 —5E 60
(off Goldsmiths Row)
Drummond Pl. Twic —6F 86
Drummond Rd. E11 —4G 47
Drummond Rd. SE16 —4F 76
Drummond Rd. Croy —4A 124
(in two parts)
Drummond Rd. Romf —2B 50
Drummonds, The. Buck H —2F 30
Drummond St. NW1 —7G 59
Drum St. E1 —9D 60
Drury Cres. Croy —4L 123
Drury Ho. SW8 —9G 75
Drury La. WC2 —9J 59
Drury Lane Theatre. —1K 75
(off Catherine St.)
Drury Rd. Harr —5A 38
Drury Way. NW10 —1B 56
Drury Way Ind. Est. NW10 —1A 56
Dryad St. SW15 —2H 89
Dryburgh Gdns. NW9 —1L 39
Dryburgh Ho. SW1 —6F 74
(off Abbots Mnr.)
Dryburgh Rd. SW15 —2F 88
Dryden Av. W7 —9D 54
Dryden Clo. Ilf —6D 32
Dryden Ct. SE11 —5M 75
Dryden Mans. W14 —7J 73
(off Queen's Club Gdns.)
Dryden Rd. SW19 —3A 106
Dryden Rd. Enf —8C 16
Dryden Rd. Harr —8D 22
Dryden Rd. Well —9D 80
Dryden St. WC2 —9J 59
Dryden Way. Orp —3E 128
Dryfield Clo. NW10 —2A 56
Dryfield Rd. Edgw —6A 24
Dryfield Wlk. SE8 —7L 77
Dryhill Rd. Belv —7K 81
Dryland Av. Orp —6D 128
Drylands Rd. N8 —4J 43
Drynham Pk. Wey —5C 116
Drysdale Av. E4 —9M 17
Drysdale Clo. N'wd —7C 20
Drysdale Ho. N1 —6C 60
(off Drysdale St.)
Drysdale Pl. N1 —6C 60
Drysdale St. N1 —6C 60
Dublin Av. E8 —4E 60
Dublin Ct. S Harr —7B 38
(off Northolt Rd.)
Du Burstow Ter. W7 —3C 70
Ducal St. E2 —6D 60
Du Cane Clo. W12 —9G 57
Du Cane Ct. SW17 —7E 90
Du Cane Rd. W12 —9D 56
Ducavel Ho. SW2 —7K 91
Duchess Clo. N11 —5F 26
Duchess Clo. Sutt —6A 122
Duchess Gro. Buck H —2F 30
Duchess M. W1 —8F 58
Duchess of Bedford Ho. W8 —3L 73
(off Duchess of Bedford's Wlk.)
Duchess of Bedford's Wlk. W8 —3L 73
Duchess St. W1 —8F 58
Duchess Theatre. —1K 75
(off Catherine St.)
Duchy Rd. Barn —2B 14
Duchy St. SE1 —2L 75
(in two parts)
Ducie St. SW4 —3K 91
Duckett M. N4 —4M 43
Duckett Rd. N4 —4M 43
Ducketts Rd. Dart —4D 98
Duckett St. E1 —7H 61
Ducking Stool Ct. Romf —2C 50
Duck La. W1 —9H 59
(off Broadwick St.)
Duck Lees La. Enf —6J 17
Duck's Hill Rd. N'wd & Ruis
(in two parts) —8A 20
Ducks Island. —8H 13
Ducks Wlk. Twic —4G 87
Du Cros Dri. Stan —6H 23
Du Cros Rd. W3 —2C 72
Dudden Hill. —1F 56
Dudden Hill La. NW10 —9D 40
Dudden Hill Pde. NW10 —9D 40
Duddington Clo. SE9 —1H 111
Dudley Av. Harr —1G 39
Dudley Av. Wal X —5D 6
Dudley Ct. NW11 —2K 41
Dudley Ct. W1 —9D 58
(off Up. Berkeley St.)
Dudley Ct. WC2 —9J 59
Dudley Dri. Mord —3J 121
Dudley Dri. Ruis —1F 52
Dudley Gdns. W13 —3F 70
Dudley Gdns. Harr —6B 38
Dudley Gdns. Romf —6H 35
Dudley Gro. Eps —6A 134
Dudley Ho. W2 —8B 58
(off N. Wharf Rd.)
Dudley Rd. E17 —9L 29
Dudley Rd. N3 —9M 25
Dudley Rd. NW6 —5J 57
Dudley Rd. SW19 —3L 105
Dudley Rd. Felt —7A 84
Dudley Rd. Harr —7A 38
Dudley Rd. Ilf —9M 47
Dudley Rd. King T —7K 103
Dudley Rd. Rich —1K 87
Dudley Rd. Romf —6H 35
Dudley Rd. S'hall —3H 69
Dudley Rd. W on T —1E 116
Dudley St. W2 —8B 58
Dudlington Rd. E5 —7G 45
Dudmaston M. SW3 —6B 74
(off Fulham Rd.)
Dudsbury Rd. Dart —5F 98
Dudsbury Rd. Sidc —3F 112
Dudset La. Houn —9E 68
Duffell Ho. SE11 —6K 75
(off Loughborough St.)
Dufferin Av. EC1 —7B 60
(off Loughborough St.)
Dufferin Ct. EC1 —7B 60
(off Dufferin St.)
Dufferin St. EC1 —7A 60
Duffield Clo. Harr —3D 38
Duffield Dri. N15 —2D 44
Duff St. E14 —9M 61
Dufour's Pl. W1 —9G 59
Dugard Way. SE11 —5M 75
Duke Gdns. Ilf —2B 48
Duke Humphrey Rd. SE3 —9C 78
(in two parts)
Duke of Cambridge Clo. Twic —5B 86
Duke of Edinburgh Rd. Sutt —4B 122
Duke of Wellington Pl. SW1 —3E 74
Duke of York Memorial. —2H 75
(off Carlton Ho. Ter.)
Duke of York's Theatre. —1J 75
(off St Martin's La.)
Duke of York St. SW1 —2G 75
Duke Rd. W4 —6B 72
Duke Rd. Ilf —2B 48
Dukes Av. N3 —8M 25
Duke's Av. N10 —1F 42
Duke's Av. W4 —6B 72
Duke's Av. Edgw —6K 23
Dukes Av. Harr —2C 38
Dukes Av. Houn —3J 85
Dukes Av. N Mald —7D 104
Dukes Av. N Har —4K 37
Dukes Av. N'holt —3J 53
Dukes Av. Rich & King T —1G 103
Dukes Clo. Ashf —1A 100
Dukes Clo. Hamp —2K 101
Dukes Ct. E6 —4L 63
Dukes Ct. SE13 —1A 94
Dukes Ga. W4 —5A 72
Dukes Grn. Av. Felt —4E 84
Dukes Head Pas. Hamp —4A 102
Duke's Head Yd. N6 —6F 42
Duke Shore Pl. E14 —1K 77
Duke Shore Wharf. E14 —1K 77
Duke's Ho. SW1 —5H 75
(off Vincent St.)
Dukes La. W8 —3M 73
Dukes M. N10 —1F 42
Duke's M. W1 —9E 58
(off Duke St.)
Dukes Orchard. Bex —7A 98
Duke's Pas. E17 —2A 46
Duke's Pl. EC3 —9C 60
Dukes Rd. E6 —4L 63
Duke's Rd. NW1 —6H 59
Dukes Rd. W3 —7L 55
Dukes Rd. W on T —7H 117
Dukesthorpe Rd. SE26 —1H 109
Duke St. SW1 —2G 75
Duke St. W1 —9E 58
Duke St. Rich —3H 87
Duke St. Sutt —6B 122
Duke St. Wat —5G 9
Duke St. Hill. SE1 —2B 76
Duke St. Mans. W1 —9E 58
(off Duke St.)
Dukes Way. Uxb —4A 142
Dukes Way. W W'ck —5C 126
Duke's Yd. W1 —1E 74
Dulas St. N4 —6K 43
Dulford St. W11 —1J 73
Dulka Rd. SW11 —4D 90
Dulverton. NW1 —4G 59
(off Royal College St.)
Dulverton Mans. WC1 —7K 59
(off Gray's Inn Rd.)
Dulverton Rd. SE9 —8A 96
Dulverton Rd. Romf —6H 35
Dulverton Rd. Ruis —6E 36
Dulverton Rd. S Croy —2G 139
Dulwich. —8C 92
Dulwich Comn. SE21 & SE22 —7C 92
Dulwich Hamlet F.C. —3C 92
Dulwich Lawn Clo. SE22 —4D 92
Dulwich Oaks Pl. SE21 —9C 92
Dulwich Picture Gallery. —6C 92
Dulwich Ri. Gdns. SE22 —4D 92
Dulwich Rd. SE24 —4L 91
Dulwich Village. —6C 92
Dulwich Village. SE21 —5B 92
Dulwich Wood Av. SE19 —1C 108
Dulwich Wood Pk. SE19 —1C 108
Dumain Ct. SE11 —5M 75
(off Opal St.)
Dumbarton Av. Wal X —7D 6
Dumbarton Ct. SW2 —5J 91
Dumbarton Rd. SW2 —5J 91
Dumbleton Clo. King T —5M 103
Dumbreck Rd. SE9 —3K 95
Dumfries Clo. Wat —3D 20
Dumont Rd. N16 —8C 44
Dumpton Pl. NW1 —3E 58
Dunally Pk. Shep —2B 116
Dunbar Av. SW16 —6L 107
Dunbar Av. Beck —8J 109
Dunbar Av. Dag —8L 49
Dunbar Clo. Hay —9F 52
Dunbar Ct. Brom —8E 110
(off Durham Rd.)
Dunbar Ct. W on T —3G 117
Dunbar Gdns. Dag —1L 65
Dunbar Rd. E7 —2E 62
Dunbar Rd. N22 —8L 27
Dunbar Rd. N Mald —8A 104
Dunbar St. SE27 —9A 92
Dunbar Wharf. E14 —1K 77
(off Narrow St.)
Dunblane Clo. Edgw —2M 23
Dunblane Rd. SE9 —2J 95
Dunboe Pl. Shep —2A 116
Dunboyne Rd. NW3 —1D 58
Dunbridge Ho. SW15 —5D 88
(off Highcliffe Dri.)
Dunbridge St. E2 —7E 60
Duncan Clo. Barn —6A 14
Duncan Ct. N21 —1M 27
Duncan Gro. W3 —9C 56
Duncan Ho. NW3 —3D 58
(off Fellows Rd.)
Duncan Ho. SW1 —6G 75
(off Dolphin Sq.)
Duncannon Ho. SW1 —6H 75
(off Lindsay Sq.)
Duncannon St. WC2 —1J 75
Duncan Rd. E8 —4F 60
Duncan Rd. Rich —3J 87
Duncan St. N1 —5M 59
Duncan Ter. N1 —5M 59
(in two parts)
Duncan Way. Bush —4K 9
Dunch St. E1 —9F 60
Duncombe Hill. SE23 —6J 93
Duncombe Rd. N19 —6H 43
Duncrievie Rd. SE13 —5B 94
Duncroft. SE18 —8C 80
Dundalk Ho. E1 —9G 61
(off Clark St.)
Dundalk Rd. SE4 —2J 93
Dundas Gdns. W Mol —7M 101
Dundas Rd. SE15 —1G 93
Dundee Ct. E1 —2F 76
(off Wapping High St.)
Dundee Ho. W9 —6A 58
(off Maida Va.)
Dundee Rd. E13 —5F 62
Dundee Rd. SE25 —9F 108
Dundee St. E1 —2F 76
Dundee Way. Enf —5J 17
Dundee Wharf. E14 —1K 77
Dundela Gdns. Wor Pk —6F 120
Dundonald Clo. E6 —9J 63
Dundonald Ho. E14 —3M 77
(off Admirals Way)
Dundonald Rd. NW10 —4H 57
Dundonald Rd. SW19 —4J 105
Dundry Ho. SE26 —9E 92
Dunedin Ho. E16 —2K 79
(off Manwood St.)
Dunedin Rd. E10 —8M 45
Dunedin Rd. Ilf —6A 48
Dunedin Rd. Rain —6D 66
Dunedin Way. Hay —7G 53
Dunelm Gro. SE27 —9A 92
Dunelm St. E1 —9H 61
Dunfield Gdns. SE6 —2M 109
Dunfield Rd. SE6 —2M 109
(in two parts)
Dunford Ct. Pinn —7K 21
Dunford Rd. N7 —9K 43
Dungarvan Av. SW15 —3E 88
Dunheved Clo. T Hth —1L 123
Dunheved Rd. N. T Hth —1L 123
Dunheved Rd. S. T Hth —1L 123
Dunheved Rd. W. T Hth —1L 123
Dunholme Grn. N9 —3D 28
Dunholme La. N9 —3D 28
Dunholme Rd. N9 —3D 28
Dunkeld Ho. E14 —9B 62
(off Abbott Rd.)
Dunkeld Rd. SE25 —8B 108
Dunkeld Rd. Dag —7F 48
Dunkery Rd. SE9 —1H 111
Dunkin Rd. Dart —3L 99
Dunkirk St. SE27 —1A 108
Dunlace Rd. E5 —9G 45
Dunleary Clo. Houn —6K 85
Dunley Dri. New Ad —9M 125
Dunlin Ho. SE16 —5H 77
(off Tawny Way)
Dunloe Av. N17 —1B 44
Dunloe Ct. E2 —5D 60
(off Dawson St.)
Dunloe St. E2 —5D 60
Dunlop Pl. SE16 —4D 76
Dunmall Dri. Purl —6C 138
Dunmore Point. E2 —6D 60
(off Gascoigne Pl.)
Dunmore Rd. NW6 —4J 57
Dunmore Rd. SW20 —5G 105
Dunmow Clo. Felt —9J 85
Dunmow Clo. Lou —8J 19
Dunmow Clo. Romf —3G 49
Dunmow Dri. Rain —4D 66
Dunmow Ho. SE11 —6K 75
(off Newburn St.)
Dunmow Rd. E15 —9B 46
Dunmow Wlk. N1 —4A 60
(off Popham St.)
Dunnage Cres. SE16 —5J 77
Dunnico Ho. SE17 —6C 76
(off East St.)
Dunningford Clo. Horn —1D 66
Dunn Mead. NW9 —7D 24
Dunnock Clo. E6 —9J 63
Dunnock Clo. N9 —1H 29
Dunnock Clo. Borwd —6L 11
Dunn's Pas. WC1 —9J 59
(off High Holborn)
Dunn St. E8 —1D 60
Dunnymans Rd. Bans —7K 135
Dunollie Pl. NW5 —1G 59
Dunollie Rd. NW5 —1G 59
Dunoon Gdns. SE23 —6H 93
Dunoon Ho. N1 —4K 59
(off Bemerton Est.)
Dunoon Rd. SE23 —6G 93
Dunoran Home. Brom —5J 111
Dunraven Dri. Enf —4L 15
Dunraven Rd. W12 —2E 72
Dunraven St. W1 —1D 74
Dunsany Rd. W14 —4H 73
Dunsbury Clo. Sutt —1M 135
Dunsfold Ri. Coul —5H 137
Dunsfold Way. New Ad —1M 139
Dunsford Way. SW15 —5F 88
Dunsmore Clo. Bush —8B 10
Dunsmore Clo. Hay —7J 53
Dunsmore Rd. W on T —1F 116
Dunsmore Way. Bush —8B 10
Dunsmure Rd. N16 —6C 44
Dunspring La. Ilf —9M 31
Dunstable Clo. Romf —6H 35
Dunstable M. W1 —8E 58
Dunstable Rd. Rich —3J 87
Dunstable Rd. Romf —6H 35
Dunstable Rd. W Mol —8K 101
Dunstall Rd. SW20 —3F 104
Dunstall Way. W Mol —7M 101
Dunstall Welling Est. Well —1F 96
Dunstan Clo. N2 —1A 42
Dunstan Glade. Orp —1B 128
Dunstan Houses. E1 —8G 61
(off Stepney Grn.)
Dunstan Rd. NW11 —6K 41
Dunstan Rd. Coul —9H 137
Dunstan's Gro. SE22 —5F 92
Dunstan's Rd. SE22 —6E 92
Dunster Av. Mord —3H 121
Dunster Clo. Barn —6H 13
Dunster Clo. Romf —9A 34
Dunster Ct. EC3 —1C 76
Dunster Ct. Borwd —5B 12
Dunster Cres. Horn —7L 51
Dunster Dri. NW9 —6A 40
Dunster Gdns. NW6 —3K 57
Dunster Ho. SE6 —9A 94
Dunsterville Way. SE1 —3B 76
Dunster Way. Harr —8J 37
Dunston Rd. E8 —4D 60
Dunston Rd. SW11 —1E 90
Dunston St. E8 —4C 60
Dunton Clo. Surb —3J 119
Dunton Ct. SE23 —8F 92
Dunton Rd. E10 —5M 45
Dunton Rd. SE1 —6D 76
Dunton Rd. Romf —2C 50
Duntshill Rd. SW18 —7M 89
Dunvegan Clo. W Mol —8M 101
Dunvegan Rd. SE9 —3K 95
Dunwich Rd. Bexh —9K 81
Dunworth M. W11 —9K 57
Duplex Ride. SW1 —3D 74
Dupont Rd. SW20 —6H 105
Dupont St. E14 —9J 61
Duppas Av. Croy —6M 123
Duppas Clo. Shep —9B 100
Duppas Ct. Croy —5M 123
(off Duppas Hill Ter.)
Duppas Hill La. Croy —6M 123
Duppas Hill Rd. Croy —6L 123
Duppas Hill Ter. Croy —5M 123
Duppas Rd. Croy —5L 123
Dupree Rd. SE7 —6F 78
Duraden Clo. Beck —4M 109
Durand Clo. Cars —3D 122
Durand Gdns. SW9 —9K 75
Durands Wlk. SE16 —3K 77
Durand Way. NW10 —3A 56
Durant Rd. Swan —3E 114
Durants Pk. Av. Enf —6H 17
Durants Rd. Enf —6G 17
Durant St. E2 —5E 60
Durban Ct. E7 —3H 63
Durban Gdns. Dag —3A 66
Durban Ho. W12 —1F 72
(off White City Est.)
Durban Rd. E15 —6C 62
Durban Rd. E17 —8K 29
Durban Rd. N17 —6C 28
Durban Rd. SE27 —1A 108
Durban Rd. Beck —6K 109
Durban Rd. Ilf —6C 48
Durban Rd. E. Wat —6E 8
Durban Rd. W. Wat —6E 8
Durbin Rd. Chess —6J 119
Durdan Cotts. S'hall —9K 53
(off Denbigh Rd.)
Durdans Rd. S'hall —9K 53
Durell Gdns. Dag —1H 65
Durell Rd. Dag —1H 65
Durfey Ho. SE5 —8B 76
(off Edmund St.)
Durford Cres. SW15 —7F 88
Durham Av. Brom —8D 110
Durham Av. Houn —6K 69
Durham Av. Romf —2G 51
Durham Av. Wfd G —5H 31
Durham Clo. SW20 —6F 104
Durham Ct. NW6 —5L 57
(off Kilburn Pk. Rd., in two parts)
Durham Ct. Tedd —1C 102
Durham Hill. Brom —1D 110
Durham Ho. Bark —3E 64
(off Margaret Bondfield Av.)
Durham Ho. Borwd —4L 11
(off Canterbury Rd.)
Durham Ho. Brom —8C 110
Durham Ho. Dag —1A 66
Durham Ho. St. WC2 —1J 75
(off John Adam St.)
Durham Pl. SW3 —6D 74
Durham Pl. Ilf —9A 48
Durham Ri. SE18 —6A 80
Durham Rd. E12 —9H 47
Durham Rd. E16 —7C 62
Durham Rd. N2 —1C 42
Durham Rd. N7 —7K 43
Durham Rd. N9 —2E 28
Durham Rd. SW20 —5F 104
Durham Rd. W5 —4H 71
Durham Rd. Borwd —5A 12
Durham Rd. Brom —7D 110
Durham Rd. Dag —1A 66
Durham Rd. Felt —6G 85
Durham Rd. Harr —3M 37
Durham Rd. Sidc —2F 112
Durham Row. E1 —8H 61
Durham St. SE11 —7K 75
Durham Ter. W2 —9M 57
Durham Wharf. Bren —8G 71
Durham Yd. E2 —6F 60
Duriun Way. Eri —8F 82
Durley Av. Pinn —5J 37
Durley Gdns. Orp —5F 128
Durley Rd. N16 —5C 44
Durlston Rd. E5 —7E 44
Durlston Rd. King T —3J 103
Durnell Way. Lou —5L 19
Durnford Ho. SE6 —9A 94
Durnford St. N15 —3C 44
Durnford St. SE10 —7A 78
Durning Rd. SE19 —2B 108
Durnsford Av. SW19 —8L 89

Durnsford Rd.—Eccleston Sq. M.

Durnsford Rd. N11 —8H 27
Durnsford Rd. SW19 —8L 89
Durrant Ct. Har W —9C 22
Durrants Clo. Rain —5G 67
Durrants Dri. Crox G —5A 8
Durrant Way. Orp —7B 128
Durrell Rd. SW6 —9K 73
Durrell Way. Shep —1B 116
Durrels Ho. W14 —5K 73
(off Warwick Rd.)
Durrington Av. SW20 —4G 105
Durrington Pk. Rd. SW20 —5G 105
Durrington Rd. E5 —9J 45
Durrington Tower. SW8 —1G 91
Durrisdeer Ho. NW2 —9K 41
(off Lyndale)
Dursley Clo. SE3 —1G 95
Dursley Ct. SE15 —8C 76
(off Lydney Clo.)
Dursley Gdns. SE3 —9H 79
Dursley Rd. SE3 —1G 95
Durward St. E1 —8F 60
Durweston M. W1 —8D 58
(off Crawford St.)
Durweston St. W1 —8D 58
Dury Falls Clo. Horn —6L 51
Dury Falls Ct. Romf —9A 34
Dury Rd. Barn —3K 13
Dutch Barn Clo. Stanw —5B 144
Dutch Gdns. King T —3M 103
Dutch Yd. SW18 —4L 89
Duthie St. E14 —1A 78
Dutton Bus. Pk. SE9 —8L 95
Dutton St. SE10 —9A 78
Duxberry Av. Felt —9G 85
Duxberry Clo. Brom —9J 111
Duxford Clo. Horn —2G 67
Duxford Ho. SE2 —3H 81
(off Wolvercote Rd.)
Dwight Rd. Wat —9B 8
Dye Ho. La. E3 —4L 61
Dyer Ho. Hamp —5M 101
Dyer's Bldgs. EC1 —8L 59
Dyers Hall Rd. E11 —6C 46
Dyers Hill Rd. E11 —7B 46
Dyers La. SW15 —3F 88
Dyers Way. Romf —7F 34
Dyke Dri. Orp —3G 129
Dykes Way. Brom —7D 110
Dykewood Clo. Bex —9B 98
Dylan Clo. Els —9H 11
Dylan Rd. SE24 —3M 91
Dylan Rd. Belv —4L 81
Dylan Thomas Ho. N8 —2K 43
Dylways. SE5 —3B 92
Dymchurch Clo. Ilf —9L 31
Dymchurch Clo. Orp —6C 128
Dymes Path. SW19 —8H 89
Dymock Ct. SE15 —8C 76
(off Lydney Clo.)
Dymock St. SW6 —2M 89
Dymoke Rd. Horn —5D 50
Dyneley Rd. SE12 —9G 95
Dyne Rd. NW6 —3J 57
Dynevor Rd. N16 —8C 44
Dynevor Rd. Rich —4J 87
Dynham Rd. NW6 —3L 57
Dyott St. WC1 —9H 59
Dyrham La. Barn —1E 12
Dysart Av. King T —2G 103
Dysart St. EC2 —7B 60
Dyson Ct. NW2 —6G 41
Dyson Ct. W7 —7G 9
Dyson Ct. Wemb —9E 38
Dyson Ho. SE10 —6D 78
(off Blackwall La.)
Dyson Rd. E11 —4C 46
Dyson Rd. E15 —2D 62
Dysons Clo. Wal X —6D 6
Dysons Rd. N18 —5F 28

Eade Rd. N4 —5A 44
Eagans Clo. N2 —1B 42
Eagle Av. Romf —4J 49
Eagle Clo. SE16 —6G 77
Eagle Clo. Enf —6G 17
Eagle Clo. Horn —2F 66
Eagle Clo. Wall —8J 123
Eagle Clo. Wal A —7M 7
Eagle Ct. E11 —2E 46
Eagle Ct. EC1 —8M 59
Eagle Dri. NW9 —9C 24
Eagle Heights. —4F 130
Eagle Hill. SE19 —3B 108
Eagle Ho. E1 —7F 60
(off Headlam St.)
Eagle La. E11 —2E 46
Eagle Lodge. NW11 —5K 41
Eagle M. N1 —2C 60
Eagle Pl. SW10 —6A 74
(off Rolandway)
Eagle Pl. W1 —1G 75
(off Piccadilly)
Eagle Rd. Wemb —3H 55
Eagles Dri. Tats —9H 141
(in two parts)
Eaglesfield Rd. SE18 —9M 79
Eagle St. WC1 —8K 59
Eagle Ter. Wfd G —7F 30
Eagle Trad. Est. Mitc —1D 122
Eagle Wharf Ct. SE1 —2D 76
(off Lafone St.)
Eagle Wharf E. E14 —1J 77
(off Narrow St.)
Eagle Wharf Rd. N1 —5A 60
Eagle Wharf W. E14 —1J 77
(off Narrow St.)
Ealdham Sq. SE9 —3G 95
Ealing. —1H 71
Ealing B'way. Cen. W5 —1H 71
Ealing Clo. Borwd —3B 12
Ealing Common. (Junct.) —1K 71
Ealing Downs Ct. Gnfd —6E 54
Ealing Grn. W5 —2H 71
Ealing Pk. Gdns. W5 —5G 71
Ealing Rd. Bren —5H 71
Ealing Rd. N'holt —4L 53
Ealing Rd. Wemb —2J 55
Ealing Rd. Trad. Est. Bren —6H 71
Ealing Village. W5 —9J 55
Eamont Clo. Ruis —5A 36
Eamont Ct. NW8 —5C 58
(off Eamont St.)
Eamont St. NW8 —5C 58
Eardemont Clo. Dart —3D 98
Eardley Cres. SW5 —6L 73
Eardley Rd. SW16 —2G 107
Eardley Rd. Belv —6L 81
Earl Clo. N11 —5F 26
Earldom Rd. SW15 —3G 89
Earle Gdns. King T —4J 103
Earlham Gro. E7 —1D 62
Earlham Gro. N22 —7K 27
Earlham St. WC2 —9J 59
Earl Ho. NW8 —7C 58
(off Lisson Gro.)
Earlom Ho. WC1 —6L 59
(off Margery St.)
Earl Ri. SE18 —6B 80
Earl Rd. SW14 —3A 88
Earls Court. —6L 73
Earl's Court Exhibition Building. —6L 73
Earls Ct. Gdns. SW5 —5M 73
Earl's Ct. Rd. W8 & SW5 —4L 73
Earl's Ct. Sq. SW5 —6M 73
Earls Cres. Harr —2C 38
Earlsdown Ho. Bark —5B 64
Earlsferry Way. N1 —3J 59
(in two parts)
Earlsfield. —7A 90
Earlsfield Rd. SW18 —7A 90
Earlshall Rd. SE9 —3K 95
Earlsmead. Harr —9K 37
Earlsmead Rd. N15 —3D 44
Earlsmead Rd. NW10 —6G 57
Earl's Path. Lou —4G 19
Earls Ter. W8 —4K 73
Earlsthorpe M. SW12 —5E 90
Earlsthorpe Rd. SE26 —1H 109
Earlstoke St. EC1 —6M 59
Earlston Gro. E9 —4F 60
Earl St. EC2 —8B 60
Earl St. Wat —5G 9
Earls Wlk. W8 —4L 73
Earl's Wlk. Dag —9F 48
Earls Way. Orp —4E 128
Earlswood Av. T Hth —9L 107
Earlswood Clo. SE10 —7C 78
Earlswood Gdns. Ilf —1L 47
Earlswood St. SE10 —6C 78
Early M. NW1 —4F 58
Earnshaw St. WC2 —9H 59
Earsby St. W14 —5J 73
(in three parts)
Easby Cres. Mord —1M 121
Easebourne Rd. Dag —1G 65
Easedale Dri. Horn —1E 66
Easley's M. W1 —9E 58
(off Wigmore St.)
East Acton. —1C 72
E. Acton Arc. W3 —9C 56
E. Acton Ct. W3 —1C 72
E. Acton La. W3 —2C 72
E. Arbour St. E1 —9H 61
East Av. E12 —3J 63
East Av. E17 —2M 45
East Av. N2 —2M 41
East Av. Hay —3D 68
East Av. S'hall —1K 69
East Av. Wall —7K 123
East Bank. N16 —5C 44
Eastbank Rd. Hamp H —2A 102
East Barnet. —8C 14
E. Barnet Rd. Barn —6B 14
E. Beckton District Cen. E6 —8K 63
East Bedfont. —6B 84
East Block. SE1 —3K 75
(off York Rd.)
E. Boundary Rd. E12 —8K 47
Eastbourne Av. W3 —9B 56
Eastbourne Gdns. SW14 —2A 88
Eastbourne M. W2 —9A 58
Eastbourne Rd. E6 —6L 63
(in two parts)
Eastbourne Rd. E15 —4C 62
Eastbourne Rd. N15 —4C 44
Eastbourne Rd. SW17 —3E 106
Eastbourne Rd. W4 —7A 72
Eastbourne Rd. Bren —6G 71
Eastbourne Rd. Felt —8H 85
Eastbourne Ter. W2 —9A 58
Eastbournia Av. N9 —3F 28
Eastbrook Av. N9 —9G 17
Eastbrook Av. Dag —9A 50
Eastbrook Dri. Romf —8C 50
Eastbrook Rd. SE3 —9F 78
Eastbrook Rd. Wal A —6L 7
Eastbury. —4D 20
Eastbury Av. Bark —4C 64
Eastbury Av. Enf —3D 16
Eastbury Av. N'wd —5C 20
Eastbury Ct. Bark —4C 64
Eastbury Ct. New Bar —7A 14
(off Lyonsdown Rd.)
Eastbury Ct. Wat —9G 9
Eastbury Gro. W4 —6C 72
Eastbury Pl. N'wd —5D 20
Eastbury Rd. E6 —7L 63
Eastbury Rd. King T —4J 103
Eastbury Rd. N'wd —6C 20
Eastbury Rd. Orp —1B 128
Eastbury Rd. Romf —4B 50
Eastbury Rd. Wat —9F 8
Eastbury Sq. Bark —4D 64
Eastbury Ter. E1 —7H 61
Eastcastle St. W1 —9G 59
Eastcheap. EC3 —1C 76
E. Churchfield Rd. W3 —2B 72
Eastchurch Rd. H'row A —1C 84
East Clo. W5 —7L 55
East Clo. Barn —6E 14
East Clo. Gnfd —5A 54
East Clo. Rain —7F 66
Eastcombe Av. SE7 —7F 78
Eastcote. —5F 36
Eastcote. Orp —3D 128
Eastcote Av. Gnfd —1E 54
Eastcote Av. Harr —7M 37
Eastcote Av. W Mol —9K 101
Eastcote Ho. Eps —4C 134
Eastcote Ind. Est. Ruis —5G 37
Eastcote La. Harr —9J 37
Eastcote La. N'holt —1K 53
(in two parts)
Eastcote La. N. N'holt —2K 53
Eastcote Rd. Harr —8A 38
Eastcote Rd. Pinn —3H 37
Eastcote Rd. Ruis —5C 36
Eastcote Rd. Well —1B 96
Eastcote St. SW9 —1K 91
Eastcote Vw. Pinn —2G 37
Eastcote Village. —3F 36
East Ct. Wemb —7G 39
East Cres. N11 —4D 26
East Cres. Enf —7D 16
Eastcroft Rd. Eps —9C 120
E. Cross Cen. E15 —2L 61
E. Cross Route. E9 & E3 —3K 61
Eastdean Av. Eps —5M 133
E. Dene Dri. H Hill —5H 35
Eastdown Ct. SE13 —3B 94
Eastdown Ho. E8 —9E 44
Eastdown Pk. SE13 —3B 94
East Dri. Cars —1C 136
East Dri. N'wd —2C 20
East Dri. Orp —1F 128
East Dri. Wat —9F 4
E. Duck Lees La. Enf —6J 17
East Dulwich. —3D 92
E. Dulwich Gro. SE22 —4C 92
E. Dulwich Rd. SE22 & SE15 —3D 92
E. End Farm. Pinn —1K 37
E. End Rd. N3 & N2 —9L 25
E. End Way. Pinn —1J 37
East Entrance. Dag —5M 65
Eastern Av. E11 & Ilf —4F 46
Eastern Av. Pinn —5H 37
Eastern Av. Wal X —6E 6
Eastern Av. E. Romf —1B 50
Eastern Av. W. Romf —2J 49
(in two parts)
Eastern Ind. Est. Eri —3L 81
Eastern Path. Horn —4J 67
Eastern Perimeter Rd. H'row A —1D 84
Eastern Rd. E13 —5F 62
Eastern Rd. E17 —3A 46
Eastern Rd. N2 —1D 42
Eastern Rd. N22 —8J 27
Eastern Rd. SE4 —3L 93
Eastern Rd. Romf —3C 50
Eastern Vw. Big H —9G 141
Easternville Gdns. Ilf —4A 48
Eastern Way. SE28 —3E 80
East Ewell. —2G 135
E. Ferry Rd. E14 —5M 77
Eastfield Av. Wat —3H 9
Eastfield Gdns. Dag —9L 49
Eastfield Rd. E17 —2L 45
Eastfield Rd. N8 —1J 43
Eastfield Rd. Dag —9K 49
Eastfield Rd. Enf —2H 17
Eastfield Rd. Wal X —4F 6
Eastfields. Pinn —3G 37
Eastfields Rd. W3 —8A 56
Eastfields Rd. Mitc —6E 106
Eastfield St. E14 —8J 61
East Finchley. —2C 42
East Gdns. SW17 —3C 106
Eastgate. Bans —6K 135
Eastgate Clo. SE28 —9H 65
Eastglade. N'wd —5D 20
Eastglade. Pinn —1K 37
E. Hall La. Wen —9H 67
E. Hall Rd. Orp —2J 129
East Ham. —4K 63
E. Ham and Barking By-Pass. Bark —5C 64
Eastham Clo. Barn —7K 13
E. Ham Ind. Est. E6 —7J 63
E. Ham Mnr. Way. E6 —9L 63
E. Harding St. EC4 —9L 59
E. Heath Rd. NW3 —8A 42
East Hill. SW18 —4M 89
East Hill. Dart —6K 99
East Hill. S Croy —2C 138
East Hill. Wemb —7L 39
E. Hill Dri. Dart —6K 99
Eastholm. NW11 —2M 41
East Holme. Eri —9B 82
East Holme. Hay —2E 68
E. India Bldgs. E14 —1L 77
(off Saltwell St.)
E. India Dock Ho. E14 —9A 62
E. India Dock Rd. E14 —9L 61
E. India Dock Wall Rd. E14 —1B 78
Eastlake Ho. NW8 —7B 58
(off Frampton St.)
Eastlake Rd. SE5 —1A 92
Eastlands Cres. SE21 —5D 92
East La. SE16 —3E 76
(Chambers St.)
East La. SE16 —3E 76
(Scott Lidgett Cres., in two parts)
East La. Ab L & Bedm —1D 4
(in two parts)
East La. King T —7H 103
East La. Wemb —8F 38
Eastlea Av. Wat —1J 9
Eastlea M. E16 —7C 62
Eastleigh Av. Harr —7M 37
Eastleigh Clo. NW2 —8C 40
Eastleigh Clo. Sutt —9M 121
Eastleigh Rd. E17 —9K 29
Eastleigh Rd. Bexh —2A 98
Eastleigh Rd. H'row A —2D 84
Eastleigh Wlk. SW15 —6E 88
Eastleigh Way. Felt —7E 84
E. Lodge La. Enf —1H 15
East London Crematorium. E13 —6D 62
Eastman Ho. SW4 —5G 91
Eastman Rd. W3 —3B 72
East Mascalls. SE7 —7G 79
East Mead. Ruis —8H 37
Eastmead Av. Gnfd —6M 53
Eastmead Clo. Brom —6J 111
Eastmearn Rd. SE27 —8A 92
East Molesey. —8B 102
Eastmont Rd. Esh —4C 118
Eastmoor Pl. SE7 —4H 79
Eastmoor St. SE7 —4H 79
E. Mount St. E1 —8F 60
Eastney Rd. Croy —3M 123
Eastney St. SE10 —6B 78
Eastnor Rd. SE9 —7A 96
Easton Gdns. Borwd —6C 12
Easton St. WC1 —7L 59
East Pk. Clo. Romf —3H 49
East Parkside. SE10 —3C 78
East Pas. EC1 —8A 60
(off Cloth St.)
East Pier. E1 —2F 76
East Pl. SE27 —1A 108
East Point. SE1 —6E 76
E. Poultry Av. EC1 —8M 59
East Ramp. H'row A —9M 143
East Rd. E15 —4E 62
East Rd. EC1 —6B 60
East Rd. N2 —8C 26
East Rd. SW19 —3A 106
East Rd. Barn —1E 26
East Rd. Chad H —3J 49
East Rd. Edgw —8M 23
East Rd. Enf —2G 17
East Rd. Felt —6B 84
East Rd. Harr —5F 38
East Rd. King T —5J 103
East Rd. Rush G —5B 50
East Rd. Well —1F 96
East Rd. W Dray —5K 143
East Rd. Wey —9B 116
E. Rochester Way. Sidc & Bex —3C 96
East Row. E11 —4E 46
East Row. W10 —7J 57
Eastry Av. Brom —1D 126
Eastry Ho. SW8 —8J 75
(off Hartington Rd.)
Eastry Rd. Eri —8L 81
East Sheen. —3A 88
E. Sheen Av. SW14 —4B 88
Eastside Rd. NW11 —2K 41
East Smithfield. E1 —1D 76
East St. SE17 —6A 76
East St. Bark —4A 64
East St. Bexh —3L 97
East St. Bren —8G 71
East St. Brom —6E 110
East St. Eps —5C 134
E. Surrey Gro. SE15 —8D 76
E. Tenter St. E1 —9D 60
East Ter. Sidc —7C 96
East Towers. Pinn —3H 37
East Va. W3 —2D 72
East Vw. E4 —5A 30
East Vw. Barn —4K 13
Eastview Av. SE18 —8C 80
Eastville Av. NW11 —4K 41
East Wlk. E Barn —9E 14
East Wlk. Hay —2E 68
Eastway. E9 —2K 61
(in two parts)
East Way. E11 —3F 46
East Way. Brom —2F 126
East Way. Croy —4J 125
Eastway. Eps —4A 134
East Way. Hay —2E 68
Eastway. Mord —9H 105
East Way. Ruis —6E 36
Eastway. Wall —6G 123
Eastway Commercial Cen. E15 —1L 61
Eastwell Clo. Beck —4J 109
Eastwell Ho. SE1 —4B 76
(off Weston St.)
East Wickham. —9G 81
Eastwick Rd. W on T —8F 116
Eastwood Clo. E18 —9E 30
Eastwood Clo. N17 —7F 28
Eastwood Dri. Rain —9F 66
Eastwood Rd. E18 —9E 30
Eastwood Rd. N10 —9E 26
Eastwood Rd. Ilf —5E 48
Eastwood Rd. W Dray —3L 143
East Woodside. Bex —7J 97
Eastwood St. SW16 —3G 107
Eatington Rd. E10 —3B 46
Eaton Clo. SW1 —5E 74
Eaton Clo. Stan —4F 22
Eaton Dri. SW9 —3M 91
Eaton Dri. King T —4L 103
Eaton Dri. Romf —7M 33
Eaton Garages. NW3 —2C 58
Eaton Gdns. Dag —3J 65
Eaton Ga. SW1 —5E 74
Eaton Ga. N'wd —6A 20
Eaton Gro. N19 —8H 43
Eaton Ho. SW11 —9B 74
Eaton La. SW1 —4F 74
Eaton Mans. SW1 —5E 74
(off Bourne St.)
Eaton M. N. SW1 —5E 74
Eaton M. S. SW1 —5E 74
Eaton M. W. SW1 —5E 74
Eaton Pk. Rd. N13 —2L 27
Eaton Pl. SW1 —5E 74
Eaton Ri. E11 —3G 47
Eaton Ri. W5 —8H 55
Eaton Rd. NW4 —3G 41
Eaton Rd. Enf —5C 16
Eaton Rd. Houn —3B 86
Eaton Rd. Sidc —8H 97
Eaton Rd. Sutt —8A 122
Eaton Row. SW1 —4F 74
Eatons Mead. E4 —2L 29
Eaton Sq. SW1 —5E 74
Eaton Ter. E3 —6J 61
Eaton Ter. SW1 —5E 74
Eaton Ter. M. SW1 —5E 74
(off Eaton Ter.)
Eatonville Rd. SW17 —8D 90
Eatonville Vs. SW17 —8D 90
Ebbas Way. Eps —7M 133
Ebbisham Dri. SW8 —7K 75
Ebbisham Rd. Eps —6M 133
Ebbisham Rd. Wor Pk —4G 121
Ebbsfleet Rd. NW2 —1J 57
Ebdon Way. SE3 —2F 94
Ebenezer Ho. SE11 —5M 75
Ebenezer Mussel Ho. E2 —5G 61
(off Patriot Sq.)
Ebenezer St. N1 —6B 60
Ebenezer Wlk. SW16 —5G 107
Ebley Clo. SE15 —7D 76
Ebner St. SW18 —4M 89
Ebor Cotts. SW15 —9C 88
Ebor St. E2 —7D 60
Ebrington Rd. Harr —4H 39
Ebsworth St. SE23 —6H 93
Eburne Rd. N7 —8J 43
Ebury Bri. SW1 —6F 74
Ebury Bri. Est. SW1 —6F 74
Ebury Bri. Rd. SW1 —6E 74
Ebury Clo. Kes —5J 127
Ebury Clo. N'wd —5A 20
Ebury M. SE27 —9M 91
Ebury M. SW1 —5F 74
Ebury M. E. SW1 —4F 74
Ebury Rd. Wat —5G 9
Ebury Sq. SW1 —5E 74
Ebury St. SW1 —5E 74
Ecclesbourne Clo. N13 —5L 27
Ecclesbourne Gdns. N13 —5L 27
Ecclesbourne Rd. N1 —3A 60
Ecclesbourne Rd. T Hth —9A 108
Eccleshill. Brom —8D 110
(off Durham Rd.)
Eccles Rd. SW11 —3D 90
Eccleston Bri. SW1 —5F 74
Eccleston Clo. Cockf —6D 14
Eccleston Clo. Orp —3B 128
Eccleston Cres. Romf —5F 48
Ecclestone Ct. Wemb —1J 55
Ecclestone M. Wemb —1J 55
Ecclestone Pl. Wemb —1K 55
Eccleston Ho. SW2 —5L 91
Eccleston M. SW1 —4E 74
Eccleston Pl. SW1 —5F 74
Eccleston Rd. W13 —1E 70
Eccleston Sq. SW1 —5F 74
Eccleston Sq. M. SW1 —5F 74

Eccleston St.—Elgood Av.

Eccleston St. SW1 —4F 74
Echo Heights. E4 —1M 29
Eckford St. N1 —5L 59
Eckington Ho. N15 —4B 44
(off Fladbury Rd.)
Eckstein Rd. SW11 —3C 90
Eclipse Rd. E13 —8F 62
Ector Rd. SE6 —8C 94
Edam Ct. Sidc —9E 96
Edans Ct. W12 —3D 72
Edbrooke Rd. W9 —7L 57
Eddington St. N4 —6L 43
Eddisbury Ho. SE26 —9E 92
Eddiscombe Rd. SW6 —1K 89
Eddy Clo. Romf —4M 49
Eddystone. Cars —3B 136
Eddystone Rd. SE4 —4J 93
Eddystone Tower. SE8 —6J 77
Eddystone Wlk. Stai —6C 144
Ede Clo. Houn —2K 85
Edenbridge Clo. SE16 —6F 76
(off Masters Dri.)
Edenbridge Clo. Orp —8H 113
Edenbridge Rd. E9 —3H 61
Edenbridge Rd. Enf —8C 16
Eden Clo. NW3 —7L 41
Eden Clo. W8 —4L 73
Eden Clo. Bex —1B 114
Eden Clo. Enf —1L 17
Eden Clo. Wemb —4H 55
Edencourt Rd. SW16 —3F 106
Edendale. W3 —1M 71
Edendale Rd. Bexh —9B 82
Edenfield Gdns. Wor Pk —5D 120
Eden Gro. E17 —3M 45
Eden Gro. N7 —1K 59
Edenhall Clo. Romf —5G 35
Edenhall Glen. Romf —5G 35
Edenhall Rd. Romf —5G 35
Edenham Way. W10 —7K 57
Eden Ho. NW8 —7C 58
(off Church St.)
Edenhurst Av. SW6 —2K 89
Eden M. SW17 —9A 90
Eden Park. —9L 109
Eden Pk. Av. Beck —8J 109
(in two parts)
Eden Rd. E17 —3M 45
Eden Rd. SE27 —1M 107
Eden Rd. Beck —8J 109
Eden Rd. Bex —1A 114
Eden Rd. Croy —6B 124
Edensor Gdns. W4 —8C 72
Edensor Rd. W4 —8C 72
Eden St. King T —6H 103
Edenvale Clo. Mitc —4E 106
Edenvale Rd. Mitc —4E 106
Edenvale St. SW6 —1M 89
Eden Wlk. King T —6J 103
Eden Way. Beck —9K 109
Ederline Av. SW16 —7K 107
Edgar Clo. Swan —7D 114
Edgar Ct. N Mald —6C 104
Edgar Ho. E9 —1J 61
(off Homerton Rd.)
Edgar Ho. E11 —5E 46
Edgar Ho. SW8 —8J 75
(off Wyvil Rd.)
Edgar Kail Way. SE22 —3C 92
Edgarley Ter. SW6 —9J 73
Edgar Rd. E3 —6M 61
Edgar Rd. Houn —6K 85
Edgar Rd. Romf —5H 49
Edgar Rd. S Croy —1B 138
Edgar Rd. W Dray —1J 143
Edgbaston Rd. Wat —3F 20
Edgeborough Way. Brom —4H 111
Edgebury. Chst —1M 111
Edgebury Wlk. Chst —1A 112
Edge Bus. Cen., The. NW2 —7F 40
Edgecombe Ho. SE5 —1C 92
Edgecoombe. S Croy —9G 125
Edgecoombe Clo. King T —4B 104
Edgecote Clo. W3 —2A 72
Edgecot Gro. N15 —3C 44
Edgefield Av. Bark —3D 64
Edgefield Clo. Dart —7M 99
Edgefield Ct. Bark —3D 64
(off Edgefield Av.)
Edgefoot Gro. N15 —3C 44
Edge Hill. SE18 —7M 79
Edge Hill. SW19 —4H 105
Edge Hill Av. N3 —2L 41
Edge Hill Ct. SW19 —4H 105
Edge Hill Ct. Sidc —1D 112
Edgehill Ct. W on T —3G 117
Edgehill Gdns. Dag —9L 49
Edgehill Ho. SW9 —1M 91
Edgehill Rd. W13 —8G 55
Edgehill Rd. Chst —9A 96
Edgehill Rd. Mitc —5F 106
Edgehill Rd. Purl —2L 137
Edgeley La. SW4 —2H 91
Edgeley Rd. SW4 —2H 91
Edgel St. SW18 —3M 89
Edgepoint Clo. SE27 —2M 107
Edge St. W8 —2L 73
Edgewood Dri. Orp —7D 128
Edgewood Grn. Croy —3H 125
Edgeworth Av. NW4 —3E 40
Edgeworth Clo. NW4 —3E 40
Edgeworth Ct. Barn —6C 14
(off Fordham Rd.)
Edgeworth Cres. NW4 —3E 40
Edgeworth Ho. NW8 —4A 58
(off Boundary Rd.)
Edgeworth Rd. SE9 —3G 95
Edgeworth Rd. Cockf —6C 14
Edgington Rd. SW16 —3H 107
Edgington Way. Sidc —4G 113
Edgson Ho. SW1 —6F 74
(off Ebury Bri. Rd.)
Edgware. —6L 23
Edgware Bury. —1K 23
Edgwarebury Gdns. Edgw —5L 23
Edgwarebury La. Els & Edgw
(in three parts) —9J 11
Edgware Ct. Edgw —6L 23
Edgware Rd. NW2 —6F 40
Edgware Rd. NW9 —9A 24
Edgware Rd. W2 —7B 58
Edgware Way. Edgw —4K 23
Edgware Way. Els —1H 23
Edinburgh Clo. E2 —5G 61
Edinburgh Clo. Pinn —5H 37
Edinburgh Clo. Uxb —9A 36
Edinburgh Ct. SE16 —2H 77
(off Rotherhithe St.)
Edinburgh Ct. SW20 —9H 105
Edinburgh Ct. Eri —8B 82
Edinburgh Ct. King T —7J 103
(off Watersplash Clo.)
Edinburgh Cres. Wal X —6E 6
Edinburgh Dri. Ab L —5E 4
Edinburgh Dri. Romf —2A 50
Edinburgh Dri. Uxb
—9A 36 & 1F 142
Edinburgh Ga. SW1 —3D 74
Edinburgh Ho. NW4 —1G 41
Edinburgh Ho. W9 —6M 57
(off Maida Va.)
Edinburgh Rd. E13 —5F 62
Edinburgh Rd. E17 —3L 45
Edinburgh Rd. N18 —5E 28
Edinburgh Rd. W7 —3D 70
Edinburgh Rd. Sutt —4A 122
Edington. NW5 —2E 58
Edington Rd. SE2 —4F 80
Edington Rd. Enf —4G 17
Edison Av. Horn —6D 50
Edison Building. E14 —3L 77
Edison Clo. E17 —3L 45
Edison Clo. Horn —6C 50
Edison Dri. S'hall —9M 53
Edison Dri. Wemb —8J 39
Edison Gro. SE18 —8D 80
Edison Ho. Wemb —8A 40
(off Barnhill Rd.)
Edison Rd. N8 —4H 43
Edison Rd. Brom —6E 110
Edison Rd. Enf —4K 17
Edison Rd. Well —9D 80
Edis St. NW1 —4E 58
Edith Brinson Ho. E14 —9B 62
(off Oban St.)
Edith Cavell Clo. N19 —5J 43
Edith Gdns. Surb —2M 119
Edith Gro. SW10 —7A 74
Edith Ho. W6 —6G 73
(off Queen Caroline St.)
Edithna St. SW9 —2J 91
Edith Neville Cotts. NW1 —6H 59
Edith Ramsay Ho. E1 —8J 61
(off Duckett St.)
Edith Rd. E6 —3H 63
Edith Rd. E15 —1B 62
Edith Rd. N11 —7H 27
Edith Rd. SE25 —9B 108
Edith Rd. SW19 —3M 105
Edith Rd. W14 —5J 73
Edith Rd. Orp —7E 128
Edith Rd. Romf —5H 49
Edith Row. SW6 —9M 73
Edith St. E2 —5E 60
Edith Summerskill Ho. SW6
(off Clem Attlee Est.) —8K 73
Edith Ter. SW10 —8A 74
Edith Vs. W14 —5K 73
Edith Yd. SW10 —8A 74
Edmansons Clo. N17 —8D 28
Edmeston Clo. E9 —2J 61
Edmond Ct. SE14 —9G 77
Edmond Halley Way. SE10 —3C 78
Edmonscote. W13 —8E 54
Edmonton. —4E 28
Edmonton Ct. SE16 —4G 77
(off Canada Est.)
Edmonton Grn. Shop. Cen. N9
—2E 28
Edmund Ho. SE17 —7M 75
Edmund Hurst Dri. E6 —8M 63
Edmund Rd. Mitc —7C 106
Edmund Rd. Orp —1G 129
Edmund Rd. Rain —5C 66
Edmund Rd. Well —2E 96
Edmunds Av. Orp —7H 113
Edmundsbury Ct. Est. SW9 —3K 91
Edmunds Clo. Hay —8G 53
Edmund St. SE5 —8B 76
Edmunds Wlk. N2 —2C 42
Ednam Ho. SE15 —7E 76
(off Haymerle Rd.)
Edna Rd. SW20 —6H 105
Edna St. SW11 —9C 74
Edred Ho. E9 —9J 45
(off Lindisfarne Way)
Edrich Ho. SW4 —9J 75
Edric Ho. SW1 —5H 75
(off Page St.)
Edrick Rd. Edgw —6A 24
Edrick Wlk. Edgw —6A 24
Edric Rd. SE14 —8H 77
Edridge Clo. Bush —7A 10
Edridge Clo. Horn —1H 67
Edridge Rd. Croy —5A 124
Edulf Rd. Borwd —3M 11
Edward Amey Clo. Wat —9G 5
Edward Av. E4 —6M 29
Edward Av. Mord —9B 106
Edward Bond Ho. WC1 —6J 59
(off Cromer St.)
Edward Clo. N9 —9D 16
Edward Clo. NW2 —9H 41
Edward Clo. Ab L —5D 4
Edward Clo. Hamp H —2A 102
Edward Clo. N'holt —6G 53
Edward Clo. Romf —1B 51
Edward Ct. E16 —8E 62
Edward Ct. Chesh —3E 6
Edward Ct. Wal A —6M 7
Edward Dodd Ct. N1 —6B 60
(off Haberdasher St.)
Edward Edward's Ho. SE1 —2M 75
(off Nicholson St.)
Edwardes Pl. W8 —4K 73
Edwardes Sq. W8 —4K 73
Edward Gro. Barn —7B 14
Edward Ho. SE11 —6K 75
(off Newburn St.)
Edward Mann Clo. E1 —9H 61
(off Caroline St.)
Edward Mans. Bark —3D 64
(off Upney La.)
Edward M. NW1 —6F 58
Edward Pl. SE8 —7K 77
Edward Rd. E17 —2H 45
Edward Rd. SE20 —4H 109
Edward Rd. Barn —7B 14
Edward Rd. Big H —9J 141
Edward Rd. Brom —4F 110
Edward Rd. Chst —2M 111
Edward Rd. Coul —7H 137
Edward Rd. Croy —2C 124
Edward Rd. Felt —4B 84
Edward Rd. Hamp H —2A 102
Edward Rd. Harr —1A 38
Edward Rd. N'holt —5G 53
Edward Rd. Romf —4J 49
Edward Robinson Ho. SE14
(off Reaston St.) —8H 77
Edward's Av. Ruis —2F 52
Edwards Clo. Wor Pk —4H 121
Edward's Cotts. N1 —2M 59
Edwards Ct. S Croy —6B 124
(off South Pk. Hill Rd.)
Edwards Dri. N11 —7H 27
Edwards Gdns. Swan —8B 114
Edward's La. N16 —7B 44
Edwards M. N1 —3M 59
Edwards M. W1 —9E 58
Edward Sq. N1 —4K 59
Edward Sq. SE16 —2J 77
Edwards Rd. Belv —5L 81
Edward St. E16 —7E 62
Edward St. SE14 —8J 77
Edwards Yd. Wemb —4J 55
Edward Temme Av. E15 —3D 62
Edward Tyler Rd. SE12 —8G 95
Edward Way. Ashf —8D 144
Edwick Ct. Chesh —2D 6
Edwina Gdns. Ilf —3J 47
Edwin Arnold Ct. Sidc —1D 112
Edwin Av. E6 —5L 63
(in two parts)
Edwin Clo. Bexh —7K 81
Edwin Clo. Rain —6D 66
Edwin Ho. SE15 —8E 76
Edwin Pl. Croy —3C 124
Edwin Rd. Dart —9F 98
Edwin Rd. Edgw —6B 24
Edwin Rd. Twic —7C 86
(in two parts)
Edwin's Mead. E9 —9J 45
Edwinstray Ho. Felt —8L 85
Edwin St. E1 —7G 61
Edwin St. E16 —8E 62
Edwin Ware Ct. Pinn —9G 21
Edwyn Clo. Barn —8G 13
Effie Pl. SW6 —8L 73
Effie Rd. SW6 —8L 73
Effingham Clo. Sutt —9M 121
Effingham Lodge. King T —8H 103
Effingham Rd. N8 —3L 43
Effingham Rd. SE12 —4C 94
Effingham Rd. Croy —2K 123
Effingham Rd. Surb —2F 118
Effort St. SW17 —2C 106
Effra Ct. SW2 —4K 91
(off Brixton Hill)
Effra Pde. SW2 —4L 91
Effra Rd. SW2 —3L 91
Effra Rd. SW19 —3M 105
Effra Rd. Retail Pk. SW2 —4L 91
Egan Way. Hay —1C 68
Egbert St. NW1 —4E 58
Egbury Ho. SW15 —5D 88
(off Tangley Gro.)
Egerton Av. Swan —4D 114
Egerton Clo. Dart —7F 98
Egerton Clo. Pinn —2E 36
Egerton Ct. E11 —5B 46
Egerton Cres. SW3 —5C 74
Egerton Dri. SE10 —9M 77
Egerton Gdns. NW4 —2F 40
Egerton Gdns. NW10 —4G 57
Egerton Gdns. SW3 —5C 74
Egerton Gdns. W13 —9F 54
Egerton Gdns. Ilf —8D 48
Egerton Gdns. M. SW3 —4C 74
Egerton Pl. SW3 —4C 74
Egerton Pl. Wey —8A 116
Egerton Rd. N16 —5D 44
Egerton Rd. SE25 —7C 108
Egerton Rd. N Mald —8D 104
Egerton Rd. Twic —6C 86
Egerton Rd. Wemb —3K 55
Egerton Rd. Wey —8A 116
Egerton Ter. SW3 —4C 74
Egerton Way. Hay —8M 143
Eggardon Ct. N'holt —2M 53
Egham Clo. SW19 —8J 89
Egham Clo. Sutt —4J 121
Egham Cres. Sutt —5J 121
Egham Rd. E13 —8F 62
Eglantine La. F'ham & Hort K
—2L 131
Eglantine Rd. SW18 —4A 90
Egleston Rd. Mord —1M 121
Eglington Ct. SE17 —7A 76
Eglington Rd. E4 —9B 18
Eglinton Hill. SE18 —7M 79
Eglinton Rd. SE18 —7L 79
Eglise Rd. Warl —9J 139
Egliston M. SW15 —2G 89
Egliston Rd. SW15 —2G 89
Eglon M. NW1 —3D 58
Egmont Av. Surb —3K 119
Egmont Rd. N Mald —8D 104
Egmont Rd. Surb —3K 119
Egmont Rd. Sutt —9A 122
Egmont Rd. W on T —2F 116
Egmont St. SE14 —8H 77
Egremont Ho. SE13 —1M 93
(off Russett Way)
Egremont Rd. SE27 —9L 91
Egret Ho. SE16 —5H 77
(off Tawny Way)
Egret Way. Hay —8H 53
Eider Clo. E7 —1D 62
Eider Clo. Hay —8H 53
Eider Ct. SE8 —7K 77
(off Pilot Clo.)
Eighteenth Rd. Mitc —8J 107
Eighth Av. E12 —9K 47
Eighth Av. Hay —2E 68
Eileen Rd. SE25 —9B 108
Eileen Wilkinson Ho. SW6 —7K 73
(off Clem Attlee Ct.)
Eindhoven Clo. Cars —3E 122
Einstein Ho. Wemb —8A 40
Eisenhower Dri. E6 —8J 63
Elaine Gro. NW5 —1E 58
Elam Clo. SE5 —1M 91
Elam St. SE5 —1M 91
Elan Ct. E1 —8F 60
Eland Pl. Croy —5M 123
Eland Rd. SW11 —2D 90
Eland Rd. Croy —5M 123
Elba Pl. SE17 —5A 76
Elberon Av. Croy —1G 123
Elbe St. SW6 —1A 90
Elborough Rd. SE25 —9E 108
Elborough St. SW18 —7L 89
Elbourne Ct. SE16 —4H 77
(off Worgan St.)
Elbourne Trad. Est. Belv —4M 81
Elbourn Ho. SW3 —6C 74
(off Cale St.)
Elbury Dri. E16 —9E 62
Elcho St. SW11 —8C 74
Elcot Av. SE15 —8F 76
Eldenwall Ind. Est. Dag —6J 49
Elder Av. N8 —3J 43
Elderbek Clo. Chesh —1A 6
Elderberry Gro. SE27 —1A 108
Elderberry Rd. W5 —3J 71
Elderberry Way. Wat —8F 4
Elder Clo. N20 —2M 25
Elder Clo. Sidc —7D 96
Elder Clo. W Dray —1J 143
Elder Ct. Bush —2C 22
Elderfield Ho. E14 —1L 77
Elderfield Pl. SW17 —1F 106
Elderfield Rd. E5 —9H 45
Elderfield Wlk. E11 —3F 46
Elderflower Way. E15 —3C 62
Elder Gdns. SE27 —2A 108
Elder Oak Clo. SE20 —5F 108
Elder Oak Ct. SE20 —5F 108
(off Anerley Ct.)
Elder Rd. SE27 —1A 108
Elderslie Clo. Beck —9L 109
Elderslie Rd. SE9 —4L 95
Elder St. E1 —7D 60
(in two parts)
Elderton Rd. SE26 —1J 109
Eldertree Pl. Mitc —5G 107
Eldertree Way. Mitc —5G 107
Elder Wlk. N1 —4M 59
(off Popham St.)
Elder Way. Rain —6H 67
Elderwood Pl. SE27 —2A 108
Eldon Av. Borwd —4L 11
Eldon Av. Croy —4G 125
Eldon Av. Houn —8L 69
Eldon Ct. NW6 —4L 57
Eldon Gro. NW3 —1B 58
Eldon Pk. SE25 —8F 108
Eldon Rd. E17 —2K 45
Eldon Rd. N9 —1G 29
Eldon Rd. N22 —8M 27
Eldon Rd. W8 —4M 73
Eldon St. EC2 —8B 60
Eldon Way. NW10 —6M 55
Eldred Dri. Orp —3G 129
Eldred Rd. Bark —4C 64
Eldrick Ct. Felt —7B 84
Eldridge Clo. Felt —7E 84
Eldridge Ct. SE16 —4E 76
Eleanora Ter. Sutt —7A 122
(off Lind Rd.)
Eleanor Av. Eps —2B 134
Eleanor Clo. N15 —1D 44
Eleanor Clo. SE16 —3H 77
Eleanor Cres. NW7 —5H 25
Eleanor Cross Rd. Wal X —7E 6
(in two parts)
Eleanor Gdns. Barn —7H 13
Eleanor Gdns. Dag —7K 49
Eleanor Gro. SW13 —2C 88
Eleanor Gro. Ick & Uxb —7A 36
Eleanor Ho. W6 —6G 73
(off Queen Caroline St.)
Eleanor Rd. E8 —2F 60
Eleanor Rd. E15 —2D 62
Eleanor Rd. N11 —6J 27
Eleanor Rd. Wal X —6E 6
Eleanor St. E3 —6L 61
Eleanor Wlk. SE18 —5J 79
Eleanor Way. Wal X —7F 6
Electric Av. SW9 —3L 91
Electric Av. Enf —9F 6
Electric La. SW9 & SW2 —3L 91
(in two parts)
Electric Pde. E18 —9E 30
(off George La.)
Electric Pde. Ilf —7C 48
Electric Pde. Surb —1H 119
Elephant & Castle. (Junct.) —4M 75
Elephant & Castle. SE1 —5M 75
Elephant La. SE16 —3G 77
Elephant Rd. SE17 —5A 76
Elers Rd. W13 —3G 71
Elers Rd. Hay —5B 68
Eleven Acre Ri. Lou —5K 19
Eley Rd. N18 —4G 29
Eleys Est. N9 —3H 29
Eleys Est. N18 —5H 29
(Advent Way)
Eleys Est. N18 —4H 29
(Kynoch Rd.)
Elfindale Rd. SE24 —4A 92
Elfin Gro. Tedd —2D 102
Elford Clo. SE3 —3F 94
Elford M. SW4 —4G 91
Elfort Rd. N5 —9L 43
Elfrida Cres. SE6 —1L 109
Elfrida Rd. Wat —7G 9
Elf Row. E1 —1G 77
Elfwine Rd. W7 —8C 54
Elgal Clo. Orp —7M 127
Elgar. N8 —1J 43
(off Boyton Clo.)
Elgar Av. NW10 —2B 56
(in two parts)
Elgar Av. SW16 —7J 107
Elgar Av. W5 —3J 71
Elgar Av. Surb —3L 119
Elgar Clo. E13 —5G 63
Elgar Clo. SE8 —8L 77
Elgar Clo. Buck H —2H 31
Elgar Clo. Els —9H 11
Elgar Ct. W14 —4J 73
(off Blythe Rd.)
Elgar Ho. NW6 —3A 58
Elgar Ho. SW1 —6F 74
(off Churchill Gdns.)
Elgar St. SE16 —4J 77
Elgin Av. W9 —7K 57
Elgin Av. W12 —3F 72
Elgin Av. Ashf —3A 100
Elgin Av. Harr —9F 22
Elgin Av. Romf —7M 35
Elgin Ct. W9 —7M 57
Elgin Ct. S Croy —6A 124
(off Bramley Hill)
Elgin Cres. W11 —1J 73
Elgin Cres. H'row A —1C 84
Elgin Dri. N'wd —7C 20
Elgin Est. W9 —7L 57
(off Elgin Av.)
Elgin Ho. E14 —9M 61
(off Ricardo St.)
Elgin Mans. W9 —6M 57
Elgin M. W11 —9J 57
Elgin M. N. W9 —6M 57
Elgin M. S. W9 —6M 57
Elgin Pl. Wey —8A 116
Elgin Rd. N22 —9G 27
Elgin Rd. Chesh —3C 6
Elgin Rd. Croy —4D 124
Elgin Rd. Ilf —6C 48
Elgin Rd. Sutt —5A 122
Elgin Rd. Wall —8G 123
Elgood Av. N'wd —6D 20

Elgood Clo.—Elsham Rd.

Elgood Clo. W11 —1J 73
Elgood Ho. NW8 —5B 58
(off Wellington Rd.)
Elham Clo. Brom —4H 111
Elham Ho. E5 —1F 60
Elia M. N1 —5M 59
Elias Pl. SW8 —7L 75
Elia St. N1 —5M 59
Elibank Rd. SE9 —3K 95
Elim Est. SE1 —4C 76
Elim St. SE1 —4B 76
(in two parts)
Elim Way. E13 —6D 62
Eliot Bank. SE23 —8F 92
Eliot Cotts. SE3 —1C 94
Eliot Dri. Harr —7M 37
Eliot Gdns. SW15 —3E 88
Eliot Hill. SE13 —1A 94
Eliot M. NW8 —5A 58
Eliot Pk. SE13 —1A 94
Eliot Pl. SE3 —1C 94
Eliot Rd. Dag —9H 49
Eliot Rd. Dart —4M 99
Eliot Va. SE3 —1B 94
Elis David Almshouses. Croy —5M 123
Elizabethan Clo. Stanw —6B 144
Elizabethan Way. Stanw —6B 144
Elizabeth Av. N1 —4A 60
Elizabeth Av. Enf —5M 15
Elizabeth Av. Ilf —7B 48
Elizabeth Barnes Ct. SW6 —1M 89
Elizabeth Blackwell Ho. N22 —8L 27
(off Progress Way)
Elizabeth Bri. SW1 —5F 74
Elizabeth Clo. E14 —9M 61
Elizabeth Clo. W9 —7A 58
Elizabeth Clo. Barn —5H 13
Elizabeth Clo. Romf —8M 33
Elizabeth Clo. Sutt —6K 121
Elizabeth Clyde Clo. N15 —2C 44
Elizabeth Cotts. Kew —9K 71
Elizabeth Ct. E4 —5K 29
Elizabeth Ct. SW1 —4H 75
(off Milmans Ct.)
Elizabeth Ct. SW10 —7B 74
Elizabeth Ct. Brom —5D 110
(off Highland Rd.)
Elizabeth Ct. Tedd —2C 102
Elizabeth Ct. Wat —2D 8
Elizabeth Ct. Whyt —9D 138
Elizabeth Ct. Wfd G —7G 31
Elizabeth Fry Ho. Hay —5D 68
Elizabeth Fry Rd. E8 —3F 60
Elizabeth Gdns. W3 —2D 72
Elizabeth Gdns. Stan —6G 23
Elizabeth Gdns. Sun —7G 101
Elizabeth Garrett Anderson Ho. Belv
(off Ambrook Rd.) —4L 81
Elizabeth Ho. SE11 —5L 75
(off Reedworth St.)
Elizabeth Ho. W6 —6G 73
(off Queen Caroline St.)
Elizabeth Ho. Wat —4G 9
Elizabeth Ind. Est. SE14 —7H 77
Elizabeth M. NW3 —2C 58
Elizabeth M. Harr —4C 38
Elizabeth Newcomen Ho. SE1
(off Newcomen St.) —3B 76
Elizabeth Pl. N15 —2B 44
Elizabeth Pl. F'ham —1K 131
Elizabeth Ride. N9 —9F 16
Elizabeth Rd. E6 —4H 63
Elizabeth Rd. N15 —3C 44
Elizabeth Rd. Rain —8F 66
Elizabeth Sq. SE16 —1J 77
(off Sovereign Cres.)
Elizabeth St. SW1 —5E 74
Elizabeth Ter. SE9 —5K 95
Elizabeth Way. SE19 —4B 108
Elizabeth Way. Felt —1G 101
Elizabeth Way. Orp —9G 113
Elkanet M. N20 —2A 26
Elkington Point. SE11 —5L 75
(off Lollard St.)
Elkington Rd. E13 —7F 62
Elkins, The. Romf —9C 34
Elkstone Ct. SE15 —7C 76
(off Birdlip Clo.)
Elkstone Rd. W10 —8K 57
Ellaline Rd. W6 —7H 73
Ella M. NW3 —9D 42
Ellanby Cres. N18 —4F 28
Elland Ho. E14 —9K 61
(off Copenhagen Pl.)
Elland Rd. SE15 —3G 93
Elland Rd. W on T —4H 117
Ella Rd. N8 —5J 43
Ellement Clo. Pinn —3H 37
Ellena Ct. N14 —3J 27
(off Conway Rd.)
Ellenborough Ho. W12 —1F 72
(off White City Est.)
Ellenborough Pl. SW15 —3E 88
Ellenborough Rd. N22 —8A 28
Ellenborough Rd. Sidc —2H 113
Ellenbridge Way. S Croy —1C 138
Ellenbrook Clo. Wat —3G 9
Ellen Clo. Brom —7H 111
Ellen Ct. E4 —1A 30
(off Ridgeway, The)
Ellen Ct. N9 —2G 29
Ellen St. E1 —9E 60
Ellen Webb Dri. W'stone —1C 38
Ellen Wilkinson Ho. E2 —6H 61
(off Usk St.)
Ellen Wilkinson Ho. Dag —8L 49
Elleray Rd. Tedd —3D 102
Ellerby St. SW6 —9H 73
Ellerdale Clo. NW3 —9A 42
Ellerdale Rd. NW3 —1A 58
Ellerdale St. SE13 —3M 93
Ellerdine Rd. Houn —3A 86
Ellerker Gdns. Rich —5J 87
Ellerman Av. Twic —7K 85
Ellerslie Gdns. NW10 —4E 56
Ellerslie Rd. W12 —2F 72
Ellerslie Sq. Ind. Est. SW2 —4J 91
Ellerton Gdns. Dag —3G 65
Ellerton Lodge. N3 —9L 25
Ellerton Rd. SW13 —9E 72
Ellerton Rd. SW18 —7B 90
Ellerton Rd. SW20 —4E 104
Ellerton Rd. Dag —3G 65
Ellerton Rd. Surb —4K 119
Ellery Ho. SE17 —5B 76
Ellery Rd. SE19 —4B 108
Ellery St. SE15 —1F 92
Ellesborough Clo. Wat —5G 21
Ellesmere Av. NW7 —3B 24
Ellesmere Av. Beck —6M 109
Ellesmere Clo. E11 —3D 46
Ellesmere Clo. Ruis —5A 36
Ellesmere Ct. W4 —6B 72
Ellesmere Dri. S Croy —6F 138
Ellesmere Gdns. Ilf —3J 47
Ellesmere Gro. Barn —7K 13
Ellesmere Pl. W on T —7C 116
Ellesmere Rd. E3 —5J 61
Ellesmere Rd. NW10 —1E 56
Ellesmere Rd. W4 —7A 72
Ellesmere Rd. Gnfd —7A 54
Ellesmere Rd. Twic —5G 87
Ellesmere Rd. Wey —9C 116
Ellesmere St. E14 —9M 61
Elleswood Ct. Surb —2H 119
Ellie M. Ashf —8C 144
Ellingfort Rd. E8 —3F 60
Ellingham Rd. E15 —9B 46
Ellingham Rd. W12 —3E 72
Ellingham Rd. Chess —8H 119
Ellington Ct. N14 —2H 27
Ellington Ho. SE1 —4A 76
Ellington Rd. N10 —2F 42
Ellington Rd. Felt —1D 100
Ellington Rd. Houn —1M 85
Ellington St. N7 —2L 59
Ellington Way. Eps —9F 134
Elliot Clo. E15 —3C 62
Elliot Ho. W1 —8C 58
(off Cato St.)
Elliot Rd. NW4 —4F 40
Elliots Clo. Cow —8A 142
Elliott Av. Ruis —7F 36
Elliott Clo. Wemb —8L 39
Elliott Gdns. Romf —8F 34
Elliott Rd. SW9 —9M 75
Elliott Rd. W4 —5C 72
Elliott Rd. Brom —8H 111
Elliott Rd. Stan —6E 22
Elliott Rd. T Hth —8M 107
Elliott's Pl. N1 —4M 59
Elliott Sq. NW3 —3C 58
Elliotts Row. SE11 —5M 75
Ellis Av. Rain —8E 66
Ellis Clo. NW10 —2F 56
Ellis Clo. SE9 —8A 96
Ellis Clo. Edgw —6C 24
Ellis Clo. Swan —8B 114
Elliscombe Mt. SE7 —7G 79
Elliscombe Rd. SE7 —6G 79
Ellis Ct. W7 —8D 54
Ellisfield Dri. SW15 —6E 88
Ellis Franklin Ct. NW8 —5A 58
(off Abbey Rd.)
Ellis Ho. SE17 —6B 76
(off Brandon St.)
Ellison Gdns. S'hall —5K 69
Ellison Ho. SE13 —1M 93
(off Lewisham Rd.)
Ellison Rd. SW13 —1D 88
Ellison Rd. SW16 —4H 107
Ellison Rd. Sidc —7B 96
Ellis Rd. Mitc —1D 122
Ellis Rd. S'hall —2A 70
Ellis St. SW1 —5E 74
Ellis Way. Dart —8K 99
Ellmore Clo. Romf —8F 34
Ellora Rd. SW16 —2H 107
Ellsworth St. E2 —6F 60
Ellwood Ct. W9 —7M 57
(off Clearwell Dri.)
Ellwood Ct. Wat —7F 4
Ellwood Gdns. Wat —7G 5
Elmar Rd. N15 —2B 44
Elm Av. W5 —2J 71
Elm Av. Ashf —8C 144
Elm Av. Ruis —6E 36
Elm Av. Upm —8M 51
Elm Av. Wat —9J 9
Elm Bank. N14 —9J 15
Elmbank Av. Barn —6G 13
Elm Bank Dri. Brom —6H 111
Elm Bank Gdns. SW13 —1C 88
Elmbank Way. W7 —8B 54
Elmbourne Dri. Belv —5M 81
Elmbourne Rd. SW17 —9E 90
Elmbridge Av. Surb —9M 103
Elmbridge Clo. Ruis —4E 36
Elmbridge Dri. Ruis —3D 36
Elmbridge Rd. Ilf —6E 32
Elmbridge Wlk. E8 —3E 60
Elmbrook Clo. Sun —5F 100
Elmbrook Gdns. SE9 —3J 95
Elmbrook Rd. Sutt —6K 121
Elm Clo. E11 —4F 46
Elm Clo. N19 —7G 43
Elm Clo. NW4 —3H 41
Elm Clo. SW20 —8G 105
Elm Clo. Buck H —2H 31
Elm Clo. Cars —3D 122
Elm Clo. Dart —7G 99
Elm Clo. Harr —4M 37
Elm Clo. Hay —9E 52
Elm Clo. Romf —8M 33
Elm Clo. S Croy —8C 124
Elm Clo. Stanw —7B 144
Elm Clo. Surb —2A 120
Elm Clo. Twic —8M 85
Elm Clo. Wal A —7K 7
Elm Clo. Warl —9H 139
Elmcote. Pinn —9H 21
Elm Cotts. Mitc —6D 106
Elm Ct. EC4 —9L 59
(off Terrace, The)
Elm Ct. SE13 —2B 94
Elm Ct. Wat —5F 8
Elm Ct. W Mol —8M 101
Elmcourt Rd. SE27 —8M 91
Elm Cres. W5 —3J 71
Elm Cres. King T —5J 103
Elmcroft. N6 —5G 43
Elmcroft Av. E11 —3F 46
Elmcroft Av. N9 —8F 16
Elmcroft Av. NW11 —5K 41
Elmcroft Av. Sidc —6D 96
Elmcroft Clo. E11 —2F 46
Elmcroft Clo. N8 —3K 43
Elmcroft Clo. W5 —9H 55
Elmcroft Clo. Chess —5J 119
Elmcroft Clo. Felt —5D 84
Elmcroft Cres. NW11 —5J 41
Elmcroft Cres. Harr —1L 37
Elmcroft Dri. Chess —5J 119
Elmcroft Gdns. NW9 —2L 39
Elmcroft Rd. Orp —2E 128
Elmcroft St. E5 —9G 45
Elmcroft Ter. Uxb —9E 142
Elmdale Rd. N13 —5K 27
Elmdene. Surb —3A 120
Elmdene Av. Horn —3K 51
Elmdene Clo. Beck —1K 125
Elmdene Rd. SE18 —6M 79
Elmdon Rd. Houn —1H 85
Elmdon Rd. H'row A —2D 84
Elm Dri. Chesh —1E 6
Elm Dri. Harr —4M 37
Elm Dri. Sun —6G 101
Elm Dri. Swan —6B 114
Elmer Av. Hav —3C 34
Elmer Clo. Enf —5K 15
Elmer Clo. Rain —3E 66
Elmer Gdns. Edgw —7M 23
Elmer Gdns. Iswth —2B 86
Elmer Gdns. Rain —3E 66
Elmer Ho. NW1 —8C 58
(off Broadley St.)
Elmer Rd. SE6 —6A 94
Elmers Dri. Tedd —3F 102
Elmers End. —8J 109
Elmers End Rd. SE20 & Beck —6G 109
Elmerside Rd. Beck —8J 109
Elmers Rd. SE25 —2E 124
Elmfield Av. N8 —3J 43
Elmfield Av. Mitc —5E 106
Elmfield Av. Tedd —2D 102
Elmfield Clo. Harr —7C 38
Elmfield Ct. Well —9F 80
Elmfield Ho. N2 —9B 26
(off Grange, The)
Elmfield Pk. Brom —7E 110
Elmfield Rd. E4 —2A 30
Elmfield Rd. E17 —4H 45
Elmfield Rd. N2 —1B 42
Elmfield Rd. SW17 —8E 90
Elmfield Rd. Brom —6E 110
Elmfield Rd. S'hall —4J 69
Elmfield Way. W9 —8L 57
Elmfield Way. S Croy —1D 138
Elm Friars Wlk. NW1 —3H 59
Elm Gdns. N2 —1A 42
Elm Gdns. Clay —8D 118
Elm Gdns. Enf —2B 16
Elm Gdns. Mitc —8H 107
Elmgate Av. Felt —9F 84
Elmgate Gdns. Edgw —5A 24
Elm Grn. W3 —9C 56
Elm Gro. N8 —4J 43
Elm Gro. NW2 —9H 41
Elm Gro. SE15 —1D 92
Elm Gro. SW19 —4J 105
Elm Gro. Eps —6A 134
Elm Gro. Eri —8B 82
Elm Gro. Harr —5L 37
Elm Gro. Horn —4J 51
Elm Gro. King T —5J 103
Elm Gro. Orp —3D 128
Elm Gro. Sutt —6M 121
Elm Gro. Wat —1E 8
Elm Gro. W Dray —1K 143
Elm Gro. Wfd G —5D 30
Elmgrove Cres. Harr —3D 38
Elmgrove Gdns. Harr —3E 38
Elm Gro. Pde. Wall —5E 122
Elm Gro. Rd. SW13 —9E 72
Elm Gro. Rd. W5 —3J 71
Elmgrove Rd. Croy —2F 124
Elmgrove Rd. Harr —3D 38
Elmgrove Rd. Kent —3E 38
Elm Hall Gdns. E11 —3F 46
(in two parts)
Elm Hatch. Pinn —7K 21
(off Westfield Pk.)
Elm Ho. E14 —3A 78
(off E. Ferry Rd.)
Elm Ho. W10 —7J 57
(off Briar Wlk.)
Elm Ho. King T —4K 103
(off Elm Rd.)
Elmhurst. Belv —7J 81
Elmhurst Av. N2 —1B 42
Elmhurst Av. Mitc —4F 106
Elmhurst Clo. Bush —6J 9
Elmhurst Ct. Croy —6B 124
Elmhurst Dri. E18 —9E 30
Elmhurst Dri. Horn —6G 51
Elmhurst Lodge. Sutt —9A 122
Elmhurst Mans. SW4 —2H 91
Elmhurst Rd. E7 —3F 62
Elmhurst Rd. N17 —9D 28
Elmhurst Rd. SE9 —8J 95
Elmhurst Rd. Enf —1G 17
Elmhurst St. SW4 —2H 91
Elmhurst Way. Lou —9K 19
Elmington Clo. Bex —5M 97
Elmington Est. SE5 —8B 76
Elmington Rd. SE5 —8B 76
Elmira St. SE13 —2M 93
Elm La. SE6 —8K 93
Elm Lawn Clo. Uxb —3C 142
Elmlea Dri. Hay —8C 52
Elm Lea Trad. Est. N17 —6F 28
Elmlee Clo. Chst —3K 111
Elmley Clo. E6 —8J 63
Elmley St. SE18 —6B 80
(in two parts)
Elm Lodge. SW6 —9G 73
Elmore Clo. Wemb —5J 55
Elmore Ho. SW9 —1M 91
Elmore Rd. E11 —8A 46
Elmore Rd. Enf —2H 17
Elmores. Lou —6L 19
Elmore St. N1 —3A 60
Elm Pde. Horn —9F 50
Elm Pde. Sidc —1E 112
Elm Park. —9F 50
Elm Pk. SW2 —5K 91
Elm Pk. Stan —5F 22
Elm Pk. Av. N15 —3D 44
Elm Pk. Av. Horn —9E 50
Elm Pk. Chambers. SW10 —6B 74
Elm Pk. Ct. Pinn —1G 37
Elm Pk. Gdns. NW4 —3H 41
Elm Pk. Gdns. SW10 —6B 74
Elm Pk. Gdns. S Croy —2G 139
Elm Pk. Ho. SW10 —6B 74
Elm Pk. La. SW3 —6B 74
Elm Pk. Mans. SW10 —7A 74
(off Park Wlk.)
Elm Pk. Rd. E10 —6J 45
Elm Pk. Rd. N3 —7K 25
Elm Pk. Rd. N21 —9A 16
Elm Pk. Rd. SE25 —7D 108
Elm Pk. Rd. SW3 —7B 74
Elm Pk. Rd. Pinn —9G 21
Elm Pas. Barn —6K 13
Elm Pl. SW7 —6B 74
Elm Quay Ct. SW8 —7H 75
Elm Rd. E7 —2D 62
Elm Rd. E11 —7B 46
Elm Rd. E17 —3A 46
Elm Rd. N22 —8M 27
Elm Rd. SW14 —2A 88
Elm Rd. Barn —6K 13
Elm Rd. Beck —6K 109
Elm Rd. Chess —6J 119
Elm Rd. Clay —8D 118
Elm Rd. Dart —7H 99
Elm Rd. Eps —8D 120
Elm Rd. Eri —9E 82
Elm Rd. Felt —7B 84
Elm Rd. King T —5K 103
Elm Rd. N Mald —6B 104
Elm Rd. Orp —9E 128
Elm Rd. Purl —5M 137
Elm Rd. Romf —9M 33
Elm Rd. Sidc —1E 112
Elm Rd. T Hth —8B 108
Elm Rd. Wall —3E 122
Elm Rd. Warl —9H 139
Elm Rd. Wemb —1J 55
Elm Rd. W. Sutt —2K 121
Elm Row. NW3 —8A 42
Elms Av. N10 —1F 42
Elms Av. NW4 —3H 41
Elmscott Gdns. N21 —8A 16
Elmscott Rd. Brom —2C 110
Elms Ct. Wemb —9E 38
Elms Cres. SW4 —5G 91
Elmsdale Rd. E17 —2K 45
Elms Farm Rd. Horn —1G 67
Elms Gdns. Dag —9K 49
Elms Gdns. Wemb —9E 38
Elmshaw Rd. SW15 —4E 88
Elmshorn. Eps —8G 135
Elmshurst Cres. N2 —2B 42
Elmside. New Ad —8M 125
Elmside Rd. Wemb —8L 39
Elms Ind. Est. H Wood —7M 35
Elms La. Wemb —8E 38
Elmsleigh Av. Harr —2F 38
Elmsleigh Ct. Sutt —5M 121
Elmsleigh Ho. Twic —8B 86
(off Staines Rd.)
Elmsleigh Rd. Twic —8B 86
Elmslie Clo. Eps —6A 134
Elmslie Clo. Wfd G —6K 31
Elmslie Point. E3 —8K 61
(off Leopold St.)
Elms M. W2 —1B 74
Elms Pk. Av. Wemb —9E 38
Elms Rd. SW4 —4G 91
Elms Rd. Harr —7C 22
Elmstead. —3K 111
Elmstead Av. Chst —2K 111
Elmstead Av. Wemb —6J 39
Elmstead Clo. N20 —2L 25
Elmstead Clo. Eps —7C 120
Elmstead Gdns. Wor Pk —5E 120
Elmstead Glade. Chst —3K 111
Elmstead La. Chst —4J 111
Elmstead Rd. Eri —9C 82
Elmstead Rd. Ilf —7C 48
Elmsted Cres. Well —7G 81
Elms, The. E12 —2H 63
Elms, The. SW13 —2D 88
Elms, The. Clay —9D 118
Elms, The. Croy —3A 124
(off Tavistock Rd.)
Elms, The. Lou —4D 18
Elmstone Rd. SW6 —9L 73
Elmstone Ter. St M —8G 113
Elm St. WC1 —7K 59
Elmswood. Chig —6B 32
Elmsworth Av. Houn —1M 85
Elm Ter. NW2 —8L 41
Elm Ter. NW3 —9C 42
Elm Ter. SE9 —5L 95
Elm Ter. Harr —8B 22
Elm Ter. Stan —5G 23
Elmton Ct. NW8 —7B 58
(off Cunningham Pl.)
Elmton Way. E5 —8E 44
Elm Tree Av. Esh —2B 118
Elm Tree Clo. NW8 —6B 58
Elm Tree Clo. N'holt —5K 53
Elm Tree Ct. NW8 —6B 58
(off Elm Tree Rd.)
Elm Tree Ct. SE7 —7G 79
Elm Tree Rd. NW8 —6B 58
Elmtree Rd. Tedd —1C 102
Elm Vw. Ct. S'hall —5L 69
Elm Vw. Ho. Hay —5C 68
Elm Wlk. NW3 —7L 41
Elm Wlk. SW20 —8G 105
Elm Wlk. Orp —5K 127
Elm Wlk. Rad —1D 10
Elm Wlk. Romf —1E 50
Elm Way. N11 —6E 26
Elm Way. NW10 —9C 40
Elm Way. Eps —7B 120
Elm Way. Wor Pk —5G 121
Elmwood Av. N13 —5J 27
Elmwood Av. Borwd —6M 11
Elmwood Av. Felt —8E 84
Elmwood Av. Harr —3E 38
Elmwood Clo. Asht —9H 133
Elmwood Clo. Eps —9E 120
Elmwood Clo. Wall —4F 122
Elmwood Ct. E10 —6L 45
(off Goldsmith Rd.)
Elmwood Ct. SW11 —9F 74
Elmwood Ct. Asht —9H 133
Elmwood Ct. Wemb —8E 38
Elmwood Cres. NW9 —2A 40
Elmwood Dri. Bex —6J 97
Elmwood Dri. Eps —8E 120
Elmwood Gdns. W7 —9C 54
Elmwood Rd. SE24 —4B 92
Elmwood Rd. W4 —7A 72
Elmwood Rd. Croy —2M 123
Elmwood Rd. Mitc —7D 106
Elmworth Gro. SE21 —8B 92
Elnathan M. W9 —7M 57
Elphinstone Ct. SW16 —3J 107
Elphinstone Rd. E17 —9K 29
Elphinstone St. N5 —9M 43
Elrick Clo. Eri —7C 82
Elrington Rd. E8 —2E 60
Elrington Rd. Wfd G —5E 30
Elruge Clo. W Dray —4H 143
Elsa Cotts. E14 —8J 61
(off Halley St.)
Elsa Ct. Beck —5K 109
Elsa Rd. Well —1F 96
Elsa St. E1 —8J 61
Elsdale St. E9 —2G 61
Elsden M. E2 —5G 61
Elsden Rd. N17 —8D 28
Elsenham Rd. E12 —1L 63
Elsenham St. SW18 —7K 89
Elsham Rd. E11 —8C 46
Elsham Rd. W14 —3J 73

Elsham Ter.—Essex Clo.

Elsham Ter. W14 —4J 73
(off Elsham Rd.)
Elsiedene Rd. N21 —9A 16
Elsie La. Ct. W2 —8L 57
(off Westbourne Pk. Vs.)
Elsiemaud Rd. SE4 —4K 93
Elsie Rd. SE22 —3D 92
Elsinge Rd. Enf —9B 6
Elsinore Av. Stai —6C 144
Elsinore Gdns. NW2 —8J 41
Elsinore Ho. N1 —4L 59
(off Denmark Gro.)
Elsinore Ho. W6 —6G 73
(off Fulham Pal. Rd.)
Elsinore Rd. SE23 —7J 93
Elsinore Way. Rich —2M 87
Elsley Rd. SW11 —2D 90
Elsmore Ho. SE5 —1A 92
(off Denmark Rd.)
Elspeth Rd. SW11 —3D 90
Elspeth Rd. Wemb —1J 55
Elsrick Av. Mord —9L 105
Elstan Way. Croy —2J 125
Elstead Ct. Sutt —3J 121
Elstead Ho. SW2 —6K 91
(off Redlands Way)
Elsted St. SE17 —5B 76
Elstow Clo. SE9 —4K 95
(in two parts)
Elstow Clo. Ruis —5H 37
Elstow Gdns. Dag —4J 65
Elstow Rd. Dag —3J 65
Elstree. —8H 11
Elstree Aerodrome. —6E 10
Elstree Distribution Pk. Borwd —5B 12
Elstree Gdns. N9 —1F 28
Elstree Gdns. Belv —5J 81
Elstree Gdns. Ilf —1A 64
Elstree Hill. Brom —4C 110
Elstree Hill N. Els —7H 11
Elstree Hill S. Els —9H 11
Elstree Ho. Borwd —4B 12
(off Elstree Way)
Elstree Pk. Mobile Homes. Barn —8B 12
Elstree Rd. Bus H & Bush —9B 10
Elstree Studios. Borwd —5M 11
Elstree Tower. Borwd —4B 12
(off Elstree Way)
Elstree Way. Borwd —5M 11
Elswick Rd. SE13 —1M 93
Elswick St. SW6 —1A 90
Elsworth Clo. Felt —7C 84
Elsworthy. Th Dit —1C 118
Elsworthy Ri. NW3 —3C 58
Elsworthy Rd. NW3 —4C 58
Elsworthy Ter. NW3 —3C 58
Elsynge Rd. SW18 —4B 90
Eltham. —5K 95
Eltham Crematorium. SE9 —3B 96
Eltham Grn. SE9 —4H 95
Eltham Grn. Rd. SE9 —3G 95
Eltham High St. SE9 —5K 95
Eltham Hill. SE9 —4H 95
Eltham Palace. —6J 95
Eltham Pal. Rd. SE9 —5G 95
Eltham Park. —3L 95
Eltham Pk. Gdns. SE9 —3L 95
Eltham Rd. SE12 & SE9 —4D 94
Elthiron Rd. SW6 —9L 73
Elthorne Av. W7 —3D 70
Elthorne Ct. Felt —7G 85
Elthorne Heights. —8B 54
Elthorne Pk. Rd. W7 —3D 70
Elthorne Rd. N19 —7H 43
Elthorne Rd. NW9 —5B 40
Elthorne Rd. Uxb —5B 142
Elthorne Way. NW9 —4B 40
Elthruda Rd. SE13 —5B 94
Eltisley Rd. Ilf —9M 47
Elton Av. Barn —7K 13
Elton Av. Gnfd —2C 54
Elton Av. Wemb —1F 54
Elton Clo. King T —4G 103
Elton Ho. E3 —4K 61
(off Candy St.)
Elton Pk. Wat —4E 8
Elton Pl. N16 —1C 60
Elton Rd. King T —5K 103
Elton Rd. Purl —4G 137
Elton Way. Wat —3L 9
Eltringham St. SW18 —3A 90
Elvaston M. SW7 —4A 74
Elvaston Pl. SW7 —4A 74
Elveden Ho. SE24 —4M 91
Elveden Pl. NW10 —5L 55
Elveden Rd. NW10 —5L 55
Elvendon Rd. N13 —6J 27
Elver Gdns. E2 —6E 60
(off St Peter's Clo.)
Elverson Rd. SE8 —1M 93
Elverton St. SW1 —5H 75
Elvet Av. Romf —2G 51
Elvington Grn. Brom —9D 110
Elvington La. NW9 —8C 24
Elvino Rd. SE26 —2J 109
Elvis Rd. NW2 —2G 57
Elwick Ct. Dart —3E 98
Elwill Way. Beck —8A 110
Elwin St. E2 —6E 60
Elwood St. N5 —8M 43
Elworth Ho. SW8 —8K 75
(off Oval Pl.)
Elwyn Gdns. SE12 —6E 94
Ely Clo. Eri —1D 98
Ely Clo. N Mald —6D 104
Ely Cotts. SW8 —8K 75
Ely Ct. EC1 —8L 59
(off Ely Pl.)
Ely Ct. NW6 —5L 57
(off Chichester Rd., in two parts)
Ely Gdns. Borwd —7B 12
Ely Gdns. Dag —8A 50
Ely Gdns. Ilf —5J 47
Ely Ho. SE15 —8E 76
(off Friary Est.)
Elyne Rd. N4 —4L 43
Ely Pl. EC1 —8L 59
Ely Pl. Wfd G —6L 31
Ely Rd. E10 —4A 46
Ely Rd. Croy —9B 108
Ely Rd. Houn —2G 85
Ely Rd. H'row A —1D 84
Elysian Av. Orp —1D 128
Elysium Pl. SW6 —1K 89
(off Elysium St.)
Elysium St. SW6 —1K 89
Elystan Bus. Cen. Hay —1G 69
Elystan Clo. Wall —9G 123
Elystan Pl. SW3 —6C 74
Elystan St. SW3 —5C 74
Elystan Wlk. N1 —4L 59
Emanuel Av. W3 —9A 56
Emanuel Dri. Hamp —2K 101
Embankment. SW15 —1H 89
Embankment Gdns. SW3 —7D 74
Embankment Pl. WC2 —2J 75
Embankment, The. Twic —7E 86
Embassy Ct. N11 —6H 27
(off Bounds Grn. Rd.)
Embassy Ct. NW8 —5B 58
(off Wellington Rd.)
Embassy Ct. W5 —1K 71
Embassy Ct. Sidc —9F 96
Embassy Ct. Wall —8F 122
Embassy Ct. Well —2F 96
Embassy Gdns. Beck —5K 109
Embassy Ho. NW6 —3M 57
Emba St. SE16 —3E 76
Ember Cen. W on T —4J 117
Ember Clo. Orp —2A 128
Ember Ct. NW9 —9C 24
Embercourt Rd. Th Dit —1C 118
Ember Farm Av. E Mol —1B 118
Ember Farm Way. E Mol —1B 118
Ember Gdns. Th Dit —2C 118
Ember La. Esh & E Mol —2B 118
Emberton. SE17 —7C 76
(off Albany Rd.)
Emberton Ct. EC1 —6M 59
(off Tompion St.)
Embleton Rd. SE13 —3M 93
Embleton Rd. Wat —3E 20
Embleton Wlk. Hamp —2K 101
Embley Point. E5 —9F 44
(off Tiger Way)
Embroidery Bus. Cen. Wfd G —9H 31
(off Southend Rd.)
Embry Clo. Stan —4E 22
Embry Dri. Stan —6E 22
Embry Way. Stan —5E 22
Emden Clo. W Dray —3L 143
Emden St. SW6 —9M 73
Emerald Clo. E16 —9H 63
Emerald Ct. Borwd —3K 11
(off Aycliffe Rd.)
Emerald Ct. Coul —7H 137
Emerald Gdns. Dag —6L 49
Emerald Sq. S'hall —4H 69
Emerald St. WC1 —8K 59
Emerson Dri. Horn —5H 51
Emerson Gdns. Harr —4K 39
Emerson Park. —5H 51
Emerson Pk. Ct. Horn —5H 51
Emerson Rd. Ilf —5L 47
Emersons Av. Swan —4D 114
Emerson St. SE1 —2A 76
Emerton Clo. Bexh —3J 97
Emery Hill St. SW1 —4G 75
Emery St. SE1 —4L 75
Emes Rd. Eri —8A 82
Emilia Clo. Enf —7F 16
Emily Pl. N7 —9L 43
Emily St. E16 —9D 62
(off Jude St.)
Emlyn Gdns. W12 —3C 72
Emlyn Rd. W12 —3C 72
Emmanuel Ct. E10 —5M 45
Emmanuel Ho. SE11 —5L 75
Emmanuel Lodge. Chesh —3C 6
Emmanuel Rd. SW12 —7G 91
Emmanuel Rd. N'wd —7D 20
Emma Rd. E13 —5D 62
Emma St. E2 —5F 60
Emmaus Way. Chig —5L 31
Emminster. NW6 —4M 57
(off Abbey Rd.)
Emmott Av. Ilf —3A 48
Emmott Clo. E1 —7J 61
Emmott Clo. NW11 —4A 42
Emms Pas. King T —6H 103
Emperor's Ga. SW7 —4A 74
Empingham Ho. SE8 —5H 77
(off Chilton Ho.)
Empire Av. N18 —5A 28
Empire Cen. Wat —3G 9
Empire Ct. Wemb —8M 39
Empire Pde. N18 —6B 28
Empire Pde. Wemb —8L 39
Empire Rd. Gnfd —4F 54
Empire Sq. N7 —8J 43
Empire Sq. SE20 —4H 109
(off High St.)
Empire Way. Wemb —9K 39
Empire Wharf. E3 —4J 61
(off Old Ford Rd.)
Empire Wharf Rd. E14 —5B 78
Empress Av. E4 —7M 29
Empress Av. E12 —7G 47
Empress Av. Ilf —7K 47
Empress Av. Wfd G —7D 30
Empress Dri. Chst —3M 111
Empress Pde. E4 —7L 29
Empress Pl. SW6 —6L 73
Empress St. SE17 —7A 76
Empson St. E3 —7M 61
Emsworth Clo. N9 —1G 29
Emsworth Ct. SW16 —9J 91
Emsworth Rd. Ilf —9M 31
Emsworth St. SW2 —8K 91
Emu Rd. SW8 —1F 90
Ena Rd. SW16 —7J 107
Enbrook St. W10 —6J 57
Endale Clo. Cars —4D 122
Endeavour Rd. Chesh —1E 6
Endeavour Way. SW19 —1M 105
Endeavour Way. Bark —5E 64
Endeavour Way. Croy —2J 123
Endell St. WC2 —9J 59
Enderby St. SE10 —6B 78
Enderley Clo. Harr —9C 22
Enderley Rd. Harr —8C 22
Endersby Rd. Barn —7G 13
Endersleigh Gdns. NW4 —2E 40
Endlebury Rd. E4 —2A 30
Endlesham Rd. SW12 —6E 90
Endsleigh Clo. S Croy —2G 139
Endsleigh Gdns. WC1 —7H 59
Endsleigh Gdns. Ilf —7K 47
Endsleigh Gdns. Surb —1G 119
Endsleigh Gdns. W on T —7G 117
Endsleigh Ind. Est. S'hall —5J 69
Endsleigh Pl. WC1 —7H 59
Endsleigh Rd. W13 —1E 70
Endsleigh Rd. S'hall —5J 69
Endsleigh St. WC1 —7H 59
End Way. Surb —2L 119
Endwell Rd. SE4 —1J 93
Endymion Rd. N4 —5L 43
Endymion Rd. SW2 —5K 91
Energen Clo. NW10 —2C 56
Enfield. —5B 16
Enfield Bus. Cen. Enf —4G 17
Enfield Cloisters. N1 —6C 60
(off Fanshaw St.)
Enfield Clo. Uxb —5B 142
Enfield Crematorium. Enf —1F 16
Enfield Highway. —4H 17
Enfield Ho. SW9 —1J 91
(off Stockwell Rd.)
Enfield Ho. Romf —7J 35
(off Leyburn Cres.)
Enfield Island Village. —2L 17
Enfield Lock. —1K 17
Enfield Retail Pk. Enf —5F 16
Enfield Rd. N1 —3C 60
Enfield Rd. W3 —3M 71
Enfield Rd. Bren —6H 71
Enfield Rd. Enf —6H 15
Enfield Rd. H'row A —1C 84
Enfield Town. —5B 16
Enfield Wlk. Bren —6H 71
Enfield Wash. —1H 17
Enford St. W1 —8D 58
Engadine Clo. Croy —5D 124
Engadine St. SW18 —7K 89
Engate St. SE13 —3A 94
Engayne Gdns. Upm —6M 51
Engel Pk. NW7 —6G 25
Engine Ct. SW1 —2G 75
(off St James' Pal.)
Engineer Clo. SE18 —7L 79
Engineers Way. Wemb —9L 39
England's La. NW3 —2D 58
Englands La. Lou —4L 19
England Way. N Mald —8M 103
Englefield. NW1 —6G 59
(off Clarence Gdns.)
Englefield Clo. Croy —1A 124
Englefield Clo. Enf —4L 15
Englefield Clo. Orp —9D 112
Englefield Cres. Orp —8D 112
Englefield Path. Orp —8E 112
Englefield Rd. N1 —3B 60
Engleheart Dri. Felt —5D 84
Engleheart Rd. SE6 —6M 93
Englemere Pk. Oxs —5A 132
Englewood Rd. SW12 —5F 90
English Grounds. SE1 —2C 76
English St. E3 —7K 61
Enid Clo. Brick W —4K 5
Enid St. SE16 —4D 76
Enmore Av. SE25 —9E 108
Enmore Gdns. SW14 —4B 88
Enmore Rd. SE25 —9E 108
Enmore Rd. SW15 —3G 89
Enmore Rd. S'hall —7L 53
Ennerdale. NW1 —6G 59
(off Ennerdale)
Ennerdale Av. Horn —1E 66
Ennerdale Av. Stan —1G 39
Ennerdale Clo. Felt —7D 84
Ennerdale Clo. Sutt —6K 121
Ennerdale Dri. NW9 —3C 40
Ennerdale Gdns. Wemb —6G 39
Ennerdale Ho. E3 —7K 61
Ennerdale Rd. Bexh —9L 81
Ennerdale Rd. Rich —1K 87
Ennersdale Rd. SE13 —4B 94
Ennis Ho. E14 —9M 61
(off Vesey Path)
Ennismore Av. W4 —5D 72
Ennismore Av. Gnfd —2C 54
Ennismore Gdns. SW7 —3C 74
Ennismore Gdns. Th Dit —1C 118
Ennismore Gdns. M. SW7 —4C 74
Ennismore M. SW7 —4C 74
Ennismore St. SW7 —4C 74
Ennis Rd. N4 —6L 43
Ennis Rd. SE18 —7A 80
Ennor Ct. Sutt —6G 121
Ensbury Ho. SW8 —8K 75
(off Carroun Rd.)
Ensign Clo. Purl —2L 137
Ensign Clo. Stanw —7B 144
Ensign Dri. N13 —3A 28
Ensign Ho. E14 —3L 77
(off Admirals Way)
Ensign Ind. Cen. E1 —1E 76
(off Ensign St.)
Ensign St. E1 —1E 76
Ensign Way. Stanw —7B 144
Enslin Rd. SE9 —6L 95
Ensor M. SW7 —6B 74
Enstone Rd. Enf —5J 17
Enterprise Bus. Pk. E14 —3M 77
Enterprise Cen., The. Beck —2J 109
(off Cricket La.)
Enterprise Clo. Croy —3L 123
Enterprise Ho. E14 —6M 77
(off St Davids Sq.)
Enterprise Ho. Bark —6D 64
Enterprise Ind. Est. SE16 —6G 77
Enterprise Way. NW10 —6D 56
Enterprise Way. SW18 —3L 89
Enterprise Way. Tedd —3D 102
Enterprize Way. SE8 —5K 77
Epcot M. NW10 —6H 57
Epirus M. SW6 —8L 73
Epirus Rd. SW6 —8K 73
Epping Clo. E14 —5L 77
Epping Clo. Romf —1M 49
Epping Forest. —1J 19
Epping Forest. —3H 19
Epping Forest District Mus. —6J 7
Epping Glade. E4 —8A 18
Epping New Rd. Buck H & Lou —2F 30
Epping Pl. N1 —2L 59
Epping Way. E4 —8M 17
Epple Rd. SW6 —9K 73
Epsom. —5B 134
Epsom Bus. Pk. Eps —3C 134
Epsom Clo. Bexh —2M 97
Epsom Clo. N'holt —1K 53
Epsom Gap. Lea —7F 132
Epsom Ho. Romf —5J 35
(off Dagnam Pk. Dri.)
Epsom Rd. E10 —4A 46
Epsom Rd. Asht —9K 133
Epsom Rd. Croy —6L 123
Epsom Rd. Eps —3D 134
Epsom Rd. Ilf —4D 48
Epsom Rd. Sutt & Mord —2K 121
Epsom Sq. H'row A —1D 84
Epsom Way. Horn —9K 51
Epstein Rd. SE28 —2E 80
Epworth Rd. Iswth —8F 70
Epworth St. EC1 —7B 60
Equity Sq. E2 —6D 60
(off Shacklewell St.)
Erasmus St. SW1 —5H 75
Erconwald St. W12 —9D 56
Eresby Dri. Beck —3L 125
Eresby Ho. SW7 —3C 74
(off Rutland Ga.)
Eresby Pl. NW6 —3L 57
Erica Ct. Swan —8C 114
Erica Gdns. Croy —5M 125
Erica Ho. N22 —8L 27
(off Acacia Rd.)
Erica Ho. SE4 —2K 93
Erica St. W12 —1E 72
Eric Clarke La. Bark —7M 63
Eric Clo. E7 —9E 46
Ericcson Clo. SW18 —4L 89
Eric Fletcher Ct. N1 —3A 60
(off Essex Rd.)
Eric Rd. E7 —9E 46
Eric Rd. NW10 —2D 56
Eric Rd. Romf —5H 49
Ericson Ho. SE13 —3B 94
(off Blessington Rd.)
Eric St. E3 —7K 61
(in two parts)
Eric Wilkins Ho. SE1 —6E 76
(off Old Kent Rd.)
Eridge Grn. Clo. Orp —3G 129
Eridge Rd. NW10 —3C 56
Eridge Rd. W4 —4B 72
Erin Clo. Brom —4C 110
Erin Clo. Ilf —4E 48
Erindale. SE18 —7B 80
Erindale Ter. SE18 —7B 80
Eriswell Cres. W on T —8C 116
Eriswell Rd. W on T —6D 116
Erith. —6C 82
Erith Ct. Purf —5L 83
Erith Cres. Romf —8A 34
Erith High St. Eri —6C 82
Erith Mus. —6C 82
Erith Rd. Belv & Eri —6L 81
Erith Rd. Bexh & N Hth —3M 97
Erith Small Bus. Cen. Eri —7D 82
Erlanger Rd. SE14 —9H 77
Erlesmere Gdns. W7 —4E 70
Erlich Cotts. E1 —8G 61
(off Sidney St.)
Ermine Clo. Chesh —4B 6
Ermine Clo. Houn —1G 85
Ermine Rd. N15 —4D 44
Ermine Rd. SE13 —3M 93
Ermine Side. Enf —7E 16
Ermington Rd. SE9 —8A 96
Ernald Av. E6 —5J 63
Erncroft Way. Twic —5D 86
Ernest Av. SE27 —1M 107
Ernest Clo. Beck —9L 109
Ernest Cotts. Eps —9D 120
Ernest Gdns. W4 —7M 71
Ernest Gro. Beck —9K 109
Ernest Harriss Ho. W9 —7L 57
(off Elgin Av.)
Ernest Rd. Horn —4J 51
Ernest Rd. King T —6M 103
Ernest Sq. King T —6M 103
Ernest St. E1 —7H 61
Ernle Rd. SW20 —4F 104
Ernshaw Pl. SW15 —4J 89
Eros. —1H 75
Eros Ho. Shops. SE23 —6J 93
(off Brockley Pk.)
Erpingham Rd. SW15 —2G 89
Erridge Rd. SW19 —6L 105
Errington Rd. W9 —7K 57
Errol Gdns. Hay —7F 52
Errol Gdns. N Mald —8E 104
Erroll Rd. Romf —2D 50
Errol St. EC1 —7A 60
Erskine Clo. Sutt —5C 122
Erskine Cres. N17 —2F 44
Erskine Hill. NW11 —2L 41
Erskine Ho. SW1 —6G 75
(off Churchill Gdns.)
Erskine M. NW3 —3D 58
(off Erskine Rd.)
Erskine Rd. E17 —2K 45
Erskine Rd. NW3 —3D 58
Erskine Rd. Sutt —6B 122
Erwood Rd. SE7 —6J 79
Esam Way. SW16 —2L 107
Escot Rd. Sun —4D 100
Escott Gdns. SE9 —1J 111
Escot Way. Barn —7G 13
Escreet Gro. SE18 —5L 79
Esher. —6M 117
Esher Av. Romf —4A 50
Esher Av. Sutt —5H 121
Esher Av. W on T —2E 116
Esher By-Pass. Clay —1F 132
Esher By-Pass. Cob & Esh —2A 132
Esher Clo. Bex —7J 97
Esher Clo. Esh —7M 117
Esher Common. (Junct.) —2A 132
Esher Cres. H'row A —1D 84
Esher Gdns. SW19 —8H 89
Esher Grn. Esh —6M 117
Esher Green Dri. Esh —5M 117
Esher M. Mitc —7E 106
Esher Pk. Av. Esh —6M 117
Esher Pl. Av. Esh —6L 117
Esher Rd. E Mol —1B 118
Esher Rd. Ilf —8C 48
Esher Rd. W on T —7H 117
Eskdale. NW1 —5G 59
(off Stanhope St.)
Eskdale Av. N'holt —4K 53
Eskdale Clo. Wemb —7H 39
Eskdale Gdns. Purl —6B 138
Eskdale Rd. Bexh —1L 97
Eskmont Ridge. SE19 —4B 108
Esk Rd. E13 —7E 62
Esk Way. Romf —7B 34
Esmar Cres. NW9 —5E 40
Esmeralda Rd. SE1 —5E 76
Esmond Clo. Rain —3F 66
Esmond Ct. W8 —4M 73
(off Ansdell St.)
Esmond Gdns. W4 —5B 72
Esmond Rd. NW6 —4K 57
Esmond Rd. W4 —5B 72
Esmond St. SW15 —3J 89
Esparto St. SW18 —6M 89
Essan Ho. W5 —8F 54
Essenden Rd. Belv —6L 81
Essenden Rd. S Croy —9C 124
Essendine Rd. W9 —6L 57
Essex Av. Iswth —2C 86
Essex Clo. E17 —2J 45
Essex Clo. Mord —2H 121
Essex Clo. Romf —2M 49

Farrant Way—Filston Rd.

Farrant Way. Borwd —3J 11
Farr Av. Bark —5E 64
Farrell Ho. E1 —9G 61
(off Ronald St.)
Farren Rd. SE23 —8J 93
Farrer Ct. Twic —6H 87
Farrer Ho. SE8 —8L 77
Farrer M. N8 —2G 43
Farrer Rd. N8 —2G 43
Farrer Rd. Harr —3J 39
Farrer's Pl. Croy —6H 125
Farrier Clo. Brom —7H 111
Farrier Clo. Sun —7E 100
Farrier Clo. Uxb —9E 142
Farrier Rd. N'holt —5L 53
Farriers Clo. Eps —4C 134
Farriers Ct. Leav —5F 4
Farriers Ho. EC1 —7A 60
(off Errol St.)
Farriers Rd. Eps —4C 134
Farrier St. NW1 —3F 58
Farriers Way. Borwd —7B 12
Farrier Wlk. SW10 —7A 74
Farringdon La. EC1 —7L 59
Farringdon Rd. EC1 —7L 59
Farringdon St. EC4 —8M 59
Farrington Av. Orp —7F 112
Farrington Pl. Chst —4B 112
Farrington Pl. N'wd —4D 20
Farrins Rents. SE16 —2J 77
Farrow La. SE14 —8G 77
Farrow Pl. SE16 —4J 77
Farr Rd. Enf —3B 16
Farthingale Ct. Wal A —7M 7
Farthingale La. Wal A —7M 7
(in two parts)
Farthingale Wlk. E15 —3B 62
Farthing All. SE1 —3E 76
Farthing Barn La. Orp —1L 141
Farthing Clo. Dart —3K 99
Farthing Fields. E1 —2F 76
Farthings Clo. E4 —3C 30
Farthings Clo. Pinn —4F 36
Farthings, The. King T —5L 103
Farthing Street. —1K 141
Farthing St. Orp —9K 127
Farwell Rd. Sidc —1F 112
Farwig La. Brom —5D 110
Fashion St. E1 —8D 60
Fashoda Rd. Brom —8H 111
Fassett Rd. E8 —2E 60
Fassett Rd. King T —8J 103
Fassett Sq. E8 —2E 60
Fassnidge Vw. Uxb —3A 142
Fauconberg Ct. W4 —7A 72
(off Fauconberg Rd.)
Fauconberg Rd. W4 —7A 72
Faulkner Clo. Dag —5H 49
Faulkners All. EC1 —8M 59
Faulkners Rd. W on T —7G 117
Faulkner St. SE14 —9G 77
Fauna Clo. Romf —4G 49
Faunce Ho. SE17 —7M 75
(off Doddington Gro.)
Faunce St. SE17 —6M 75
Favart Rd. SW6 —9L 73
Faverolle Grn. Chesh —1C 6
Faversham Av. E4 —1C 30
Faversham Av. Enf —8B 16
Faversham Clo. Chig —2F 32
Faversham Ho. NW1 —4G 59
(off Bayham Pl.)
Faversham Ho. SE17 —6C 76
(off Kinglake St.)
Faversham Rd. SE6 —6K 93
Faversham Rd. Beck —6K 109
Faversham Rd. Mord —1M 121
Fawcett Clo. SW11 —1B 90
Fawcett Clo. SW16 —2L 107
Fawcett Est. E5 —6E 44
Fawcett Rd. NW10 —3D 56
Fawcett Rd. Croy —5A 124
Fawcett St. SW10 —7A 74
Fawcus Clo. Clay —8C 118
Fawe Pk. Rd. SW15 —3K 89
Fawe St. E14 —8M 61
Fawkes Av. Dart —8K 99
Fawkham Ho. SE1 —5D 76
(off Longfield Est.)
Fawley Lodge. E14 —5B 78
(off Millennium Dri.)
Fawley Rd. NW6 —1M 57
Fawnbrake Av. SE24 —4M 91
Fawn Rd. E13 —5G 63
Fawn Rd. Chig —5D 32
Fawns Mnr. Clo. Felt —7A 84
Fawns Mnr. Rd. Felt —7B 84
Fawood Av. NW10 —3A 56
Faygate Cres. Bexh —4L 97
Faygate Rd. SW2 —8K 91
Fay Grn. Ab L —6B 4
Fayland Av. SW16 —2G 107
Fearnley Cres. Hamp —2J 101
Fearnley Ho. SE5 —1C 92
Fearnley St. Wat —6F 8
Fearon St. SE10 —6E 78
Featherbed La. Croy & Warl —9K 125
Featherbed La. Romf —1J 33
Feathers Pl. SE10 —7B 78
Featherstone Av. SE23 —8F 92
Featherstone Gdns. Borwd —6B 12
Featherstone Ho. Hay —8G 53
Featherstone Ind. Est. S'hall —3J 69
(off Straight, The)
Featherstone Rd. NW7 —6F 24
Featherstone Rd. S'hall —4J 69
Featherstone St. EC1 —7B 60
Featherstone Ter. S'hall —4J 69
Featley Rd. SW9 —2M 91
Federal Rd. Gnfd —4G 55
Federal Way. Wat —3G 9
Federation Rd. SE2 —5F 80
Fee Farm Rd. Clay —9D 118
Felbridge Av. Stan —8E 22
Felbridge Clo. SW16 —1L 107
Felbridge Clo. Sutt —1M 135
Felbridge Ct. Felt —7F 84
(off High St.)
Felbridge Ct. Hay —7B 68
Felbridge Ho. SE22 —2C 92
Felbrigge Rd. Ilf —7D 48
Felcott Clo. W on T —5G 117
Felcott Rd. W on T —5G 117
Felday Rd. SE13 —5M 93
Felden Clo. Pinn —7J 21
Felden Clo. Wat —7H 5
Felden St. SW6 —9K 73
Feldman Clo. N16 —6E 44
Felgate M. W6 —5F 72
Felhampton Rd. SE9 —8M 95
Felhurst Cres. Dag —9M 49
Feline Ct. Barn —8C 14
Felix Av. N8 —4J 43
Felix Ct. E17 —3M 45
Felix Ho. E16 —1L 79
(off University Way)
Felix La. Shep —1C 116
Felix Mnr. Chst —3C 112
Felix Rd. W13 —1E 70
Felix Rd. W on T —1E 116
Felixstowe Ct. E16 —2M 79
Felixstowe Rd. N9 —3E 28
Felixstowe Rd. N17 —1D 44
Felixstowe Rd. NW10 —6F 56
Felixstowe Rd. SE2 —4F 80
Felix St. E2 —5F 60
Fellbrigg Rd. SE22 —4D 92
Fellbrigg St. E1 —7F 60
Fellbrook. Rich —9F 86
Fellmongers Path. SE1 —3D 76
(off Tower Bri. Rd.)
Fellmongers Yd. Croy —5A 124
(off Surrey St.)
Fellowes Clo. Hay —7H 53
Fellowes Rd. Cars —5C 122
Fellows Ct. E2 —5D 60
(in four parts)
Fellows Rd. NW3 —3B 58
Fell Path. Borwd —7B 12
(off Clydesdale Clo.)
Fell Rd. Croy —5A 124
(in two parts)
Felltram Way. SE7 —6E 78
Fell Wlk. Edgw —8A 24
Felmersham Clo. SW4 —3J 91
Felmingham Rd. SE20 —6G 109
Felnex Trad. Est. NW10 —5B 56
Felsberg Rd. SW2 —5J 91
Fels Clo. Dag —8M 49
Fels Farm Av. Dag —8A 50
Felsham Rd. SW15 —2G 89
Felspar Clo. SE18 —6D 80
Felstead Av. Ilf —8L 31
Felstead Gdns. E14 —6A 78
Felstead Rd. E9 —2K 61
Felstead Rd. E11 —5E 46
Felstead Rd. Eps —3B 134
Felstead Rd. Lou —9J 19
Felstead Rd. Orp —4E 128
Felstead Rd. Romf —7A 34
Felstead Rd. Wal X —5E 6
Felstead St. E9 —2K 61
Felstead Wharf. E14 —6A 78
Felsted Rd. E16 —9H 63
Feltham. —8E 84
Feltham Av. E Mol —8C 102
Felthambrook Ind. Est. Felt —9F 84
Felthambrook Way. Felt —9F 84
Feltham Bus. Complex. Felt —8F 84
Felthamhill. —2D 100
Feltham Hill Rd. Ashf —2A 100
Felthamhill Rd. Felt —1E 100
Feltham Rd. Mitc —6D 106
Felton Clo. Borwd —2J 11
Felton Clo. Orp —1M 127
Felton Gdns. Bark —4C 64
Felton Ho. N1 —4B 60
(off Colville Est.)
Felton Ho. SE3 —3F 94
Felton Lea. Sidc —2D 112
Felton Rd. W13 —3G 71
Felton Rd. Bark —5C 64
Felton St. N1 —4B 60
Fencepiece Rd. Chig —5A 32
Fenchurch Av. EC3 —9C 60
Fenchurch Bldgs. EC3 —9C 60
Fenchurch Pl. EC3 —9C 60
Fenchurch St. EC3 —1C 76
Fen Ct. EC3 —9C 60
Fendall Rd. Eps —7A 120
Fendall St. SE1 —4C 76
(in two parts)
Fendt Clo. E16 —9D 62
Fendyke Rd. Belv —5H 81
Fenelon Pl. W14 —5K 73
Fen Gro. Sidc —4D 96
Fenham Rd. SE15 —8E 76
Fenman Ct. N17 —8F 28
Fenman Gdns. Ilf —6F 48
Fenn Clo. Brom —3E 110
Fennel Clo. E16 —7C 62
Fennel Clo. Croy —3H 125
Fennells Mead. Eps —1D 134
Fennell St. SE18 —7L 79
Fenner Clo. SE16 —5F 76
Fenner Ho. E1 —2F 76
(off Watts St.)
Fenner Sq. SW11 —2B 90
Fenn Ho. Iswth —9F 70
Fenning St. SE1 —3C 76
Fenn St. E9 —1G 61
Fenstanton. N4 —6K 43
(off Marquis Rd.)
Fenstanton Av. N12 —6B 26
Fen St. E16 —1D 78
Fens Way. Swan —3E 114
Fenswood Clo. Bex —5L 97
Fentiman Rd. SW8 —7J 75
Fentiman Way. Horn —6J 51
Fenton Clo. E8 —2D 60
Fenton Clo. SW9 —1K 91
Fenton Clo. Chst —2K 111
Fenton House. —9A 42
(off Windmill Hill)
Fenton Ho. SE14 —8J 77
Fenton Ho. Houn —7L 69
Fenton Rd. N17 —7A 28
Fentons Av. E13 —6F 62
Fenton St. E1 —9F 60
Fenwick Clo. SE18 —7L 79
Fenwick Gro. SE15 —2E 92
Fenwick Path. Borwd —2K 11
Fenwick Pl. SW9 —2J 91
Fenwick Pl. S Croy —9M 123
Fenwick Rd. SE15 —2E 92
Ferby Ct. SE9 —9B 96
(off Main Rd.)
Ferdinand Pl. NW1 —3E 58
Ferdinand St. NW1 —3E 58
Ferguson Av. Romf —9G 35
Ferguson Av. Surb —9K 103
Ferguson Cen., The. E17 —4J 45
Ferguson Clo. E14 —5L 77
Ferguson Clo. Brom —7B 110
Ferguson Ct. Romf —9H 35
Ferguson Dri. W3 —9B 56
Ferguson Gro. Chesh —2D 6
Ferguson Ho. SE10 —9A 78
Fergus Rd. N5 —1M 59
Fermain Ct. E. N1 —4C 60
(off De Beauvoir Est.)
Fermain Ct. N. N1 —4C 60
(off De Beauvoir Est.)
Fermain Ct. W. N1 —4C 60
(off De Beauvoir Est.)
Ferme Pk. Rd. N8 & N4 —3J 43
Fermor Rd. SE23 —7J 93
Fermoy Rd. W9 —7K 57
Fermoy Rd. Gnfd —7M 53
Fern Av. Mitc —8H 107
Fernbank. Buck H —1F 30
Fern Bank. Eyns —4K 131
Fernbank Av. Horn —9G 51
Fernbank Av. W on T —2J 117
Fernbank Av. Wemb —9D 38
Fernbank M. SW12 —5F 90
Fernbrook Av. Sidc —4C 96
Fernbrook Cres. SE13 —5C 94
(off Fernbrook Rd.)
Fernbrook Dri. Harr —5M 37
Fernbrook Rd. SE13 —5C 94
Ferncliff Rd. E8 —1E 60
Fern Clo. N1 —5C 60
Fern Clo. Eri —9F 82
Fern Clo. Warl —9J 139
Fern Ct. SE14 —1H 93
Fern Ct. Bexh —3L 97
Ferncroft Av. N12 —6D 26
Ferncroft Av. NW3 —8L 41
Ferncroft Av. Ruis —7G 37
Ferndale. Brom —6G 111
Ferndale Av. E17 —3B 46
Ferndale Av. Houn —2J 85
Ferndale Clo. Bexh —9J 81
Ferndale Cres. Uxb —6A 142
Ferndale Rd. E7 —3F 62
Ferndale Rd. E11 —7C 46
Ferndale Rd. N15 —4D 44
Ferndale Rd. SE25 —9F 108
Ferndale Rd. SW4 & SW9 —3J 91
Ferndale Rd. Bans —8K 135
Ferndale Rd. Enf —1J 17
Ferndale Rd. Romf —9A 34
Ferndale St. E6 —1M 79
Ferndale Ter. Harr —2D 38
Ferndale Way. Orp —7B 128
Ferndell Av. Bex —9B 98
Fern Dene. W13 —8F 54
Ferndene. Brick W —4K 5
Ferndene Rd. SE24 —3A 92
Fernden Way. Romf —4M 49
Ferndown. Horn —4K 51
Ferndown. N'wd —9E 20
Ferndown Av. Orp —3B 128
Ferndown Clo. Pinn —7J 21
Ferndown Clo. Sutt —8B 122
Ferndown Ct. S'hall —9A 54
(off Haldane Rd.)
Ferndown Lodge. E14 —4A 78
(off Manchester Rd.)
Ferndown Rd. SE9 —6H 95
Ferndown Rd. Wat —4G 21
Fernes Clo. Uxb —9A 142
Ferney Meade Way. Iswth —1E 86
Ferney Rd. E Barn —9E 14
Fern Gro. Felt —6F 84
Fernhall Dri. Ilf —3H 47
Fernham Rd. T Hth —7A 108
Fernhead Rd. W9 —5K 57
Fernheath Way. Dart —2B 114
Fern Hill. Oxs —6B 132
Fernhill Ct. E17 —9B 30
Fernhill Gdns. King T —2H 103
Fern Hill Pl. Farnb —7A 128
Fernhills. K Lan —7B 4
Fernhill St. E16 —2K 79
Fernholme Rd. SE15 —4H 93
Fernhurst Gdns. Edgw —6L 23
Fernhurst Rd. SW6 —9J 73
Fernhurst Rd. Ashf —1A 100
Fernhurst Rd. Croy —2F 124
Fernie Clo. Chig —5E 32
Fernie Way. Chig —5E 32
Fern La. Houn —6K 69
Fernlea Rd. SW12 —7F 90
Fernlea Rd. Mitc —6E 106
Fernleigh Clo. Croy —6L 123
Fernleigh Clo. W on T —5F 116
Fernleigh Ct. Harr —9M 21
Fernleigh Ct. Romf —3A 50
Fernleigh Ct. Wemb —7J 39
Fernleigh Rd. N21 —2L 27
Fernsbury St. WC1 —6L 59
Ferns Clo. Enf —9E 6
Ferns Clo. S Croy —2F 138
Fernshaw Clo. SW10 —7A 74
Fernshaw Rd. SW10 —7A 74
Fernside. NW11 —7L 41
Fernside. Buck H —1F 30
Fernside Av. NW7 —3B 24
Fernside Av. Felt —1F 100
Fernside Ct. NW4 —9H 25
(off Holders Hill Rd.)
Fernside Rd. SW12 —7D 90
Ferns Rd. E15 —2D 62
Fern St. E3 —7L 61
Fernthorpe Rd. SW16 —3G 107
Ferntower Rd. N5 —1B 60
Fern Wlk. SE1 —6E 76
(off Argyle Way)
Fern Way. Wat —8F 4
Fernways. Ilf —9M 47
Fernwood. Croy —1J 139
Fernwood Av. SW16 —1H 107
Fernwood Av. Wemb —2G 55
Fernwood Clo. Brom —6G 111
Fernwood Cres. N20 —3D 26
Ferny Hill. Barn —2D 14
Ferranti Clo. SE18 —4H 79
Ferraro Clo. Houn —7L 69
Ferrers Av. Wall —6H 123
Ferrers Av. W Dray —3H 143
Ferrers Rd. SW16 —2H 107
Ferrestone Rd. N8 —2K 43
Ferriby Clo. N1 —3L 59
Ferrier Ind. Est. SW18 —3M 89
(off Ferrier St.)
Ferrier Point. E16 —8E 62
(off Forty Acre La.)
Ferrier St. SW18 —3M 89
Ferring Clo. Harr —6A 38
Ferrings. SE21 —9C 92
Ferris Av. Croy —5K 125
Ferris Rd. SE22 —3E 92
Ferron Rd. E5 —8F 44
Ferro Rd. Rain —7E 66
Ferry App. SE18 —4L 79
Ferrybridge Ho. SE11 —4L 75
(off Lambeth Wlk.)
Ferrydale Lodge. NW4 —2G 41
(off Church Rd.)
Ferryhills Clo. Wat —3G 21
Ferry Ho. E5 —6F 44
(off High Hill Ferry)
Ferry Island Retail Pk. N17 —1E 44
Ferry La. N17 —2E 44
Ferry La. SW13 —7D 72
Ferry La. Bren —7J 71
Ferry La. Rain —9C 66
Ferry La. Rich —7K 71
Ferry La. Ind. Est. E17 —2H 45
Ferry La. Ind. Est. Rain —8D 66
Ferrymead Av. Gnfd —6L 53
Ferrymead Dri. Gnfd —5L 53
Ferrymead Gdns. Gnfd —5M 53
Ferrymoor. Rich —9F 86
Ferry Pl. SE18 —4L 79
Ferry Quays. Bren —8H 71
(in two parts)
Ferry Rd. SW13 —8E 72
Ferry Rd. Tedd —2F 102
Ferry Rd. Th Dit —1F 118
Ferry Rd. Twic —7F 86
Ferry Rd. W Mol —7L 101
Ferry Sq. Bren —8J 71
Ferry Sq. Shep —2A 116
Ferry St. E14 —6A 78
Festing Rd. SW15 —2H 89
Festival Clo. Bex —7H 97
Festival Clo. Eri —8D 82
Festival Clo. Uxb —4F 142
Festival Wlk. Cars —7D 122
Fetter La. EC4 —9L 59
(in two parts)
Fettes Ho. NW8 —5B 58
(off Cochrane St.)
Ffinch St. SE8 —8L 77
Fickleshole. —6B 140
Fiddicroft Av. Bans —6M 135
Fidler Pl. Bush —8M 9
Field Clo. E4 —6M 29
Field Clo. Brom —6G 111
Field Clo. Buck H —3G 31
Field Clo. Chess —7G 119
Field Clo. Hay —8A 68
Field Clo. Houn —9F 68
Field Clo. Ruis —6A 36
Field Clo. S Croy —6F 138
Field Clo. W Mol —9M 101
Fieldcommon. —2K 117
Fieldcommon La. W on T —3J 117
Field Ct. SW19 —9L 89
Field Ct. WC1 —8K 59
Field End. Barn —6F 12
Field End. Coul —6H 137
Field End. N'holt —2J 53
Field End. Ruis —2G 53
Field End. Twic —1D 102
Field End Clo. Wat —9J 9
Fieldend Rd. SW16 —5G 107
Field End Rd. Eastc & Pinn —3F 36
Fielders Clo. Enf —6C 16
Fielders Clo. Harr —6A 38
Fieldfare Rd. SE28 —1G 81
Fieldgate La. Mitc —6C 106
Fieldgate Mans. E1 —8E 60
(off Fieldgate St., in two parts)
Fieldgate St. E1 —8E 60
Fieldhouse Clo. E18 —8F 30
Fieldhouse Rd. SW12 —7G 91
Fieldhouse Vs. Bans —7C 136
Fielding Av. Twic —9A 86
Fielding Ho. NW6 —6L 57
(off Cambridge Rd.)
Fielding Ho. W4 —7C 72
(off Devonshire Rd.)
Fielding M. SW13 —7F 72
(off Jenner Pl.)
Fielding Rd. W4 —4B 72
Fielding Rd. W14 —4H 73
Fieldings Rd. Chesh —2F 6
Fieldings, The. SE23 —7G 93
Fielding St. SE17 —7A 76
Fielding Ter. W5 —1K 71
Field La. Bren —8G 71
Field La. Tedd —2E 102
Field Mead. NW7 —7C 24
Field Pl. N Mald —1D 120
Field Point. E7 —9E 46
Field Rd. E7 —9D 46
Field Rd. N17 —1B 44
Field Rd. W6 —6J 73
Field Rd. Felt —5F 84
Field Rd. Wat —8J 9
Fieldsend Rd. Sutt —7J 121
Fields Est. E8 —3E 60
Fieldside Clo. Orp —6A 128
Fieldside Rd. Brom —2B 110
Fields Pk. Cres. Romf —3H 49
Field St. WC1 —6K 59
Fieldsway Ho. N5 —1L 59
Fieldview. SW18 —7B 90
Field Vw. Felt —1B 100
Fieldview Cotts. N14 —2H 27
(off Balaams La.)
Field Vw. Ri. Brick W —2J 5
Field Way. NW10 —3A 56
Fieldway. Dag —8G 49
Field Way. Gnfd —4M 53
Fieldway. New Ad —9M 125
Fieldway. Orp —1B 128
Field Way. Ruis —6A 36
Field Way. Uxb —7B 142
Fieldway Cres. N5 —1L 59
Fiennes Clo. Dag —6G 49
Fife Rd. E16 —8E 62
Fife Rd. N22 —7M 27
Fife Rd. SW14 —4A 88
Fife Rd. King T —6J 103
(in two parts)
Fife Ter. N1 —5K 59
Fifield Path. SE23 —9H 93
Fifth Av. E12 —9K 47
Fifth Av. W10 —6J 57
Fifth Av. Hay —2D 68
Fifth Av. Wat —8H 5
Fifth Cross Rd. Twic —8B 86
Fifth Way. Wemb —9M 39
Figges Rd. Mitc —4E 106
Fig Tree Clo. NW10 —4C 56
Figure Ct. SW3 —6D 74
(off Royal Hospital Rd.)
Filanco Ct. W7 —2D 70
(off Uxbridge Rd.)
Filby Rd. Chess —8K 119
Filey Av. N16 —6E 44
Filey Clo. Sutt —9A 122
Filey Waye. Ruis —7E 36
Filigree Ct. SE16 —2K 77
Fillebrook Av. Enf —4C 16
Fillebrook Rd. E11 —6B 46
Filmer Rd. SW6 —9J 73
Filston Rd. Eri —6A 82

Filton Ct.—Floriston Av.

Filton Ct. SE14 —8G 77
(off Farrow La.)
Finborough Ho. SW10 —7A 74
(off Fawcett St.)
Finborough Rd. SW10 —6M 73
Finborough Rd. SW17 —3D 106
Finborough Theatre, The. —7M 73
(off Finborough Rd.)
Finchale Rd. SE2 —4E 80
Fincham Clo. Uxb —8A 36
Finch Av. SE27 —1B 108
Finch Clo. NW10 —2B 56
Finch Clo. Barn —7L 13
Finch Ct. Sidc —9F 96
Finchdean Ho. SW15 —6D 88
Finch Dri. Felt —6H 85
Finch Gdns. E4 —5L 29
Finch Ho. SE8 —8M 77
(off Bronze St.)
Finchingfield Av. Wfd G —7G 31
Finch La. EC3 —9B 60
Finch La. Bush —5K 9
Finchley. —8L 25
Finchley Clo. Dart —5L 99
Finchley Ct. N3 —6M 25
Finchley Ind. Est. N12 —4A 26
Finchley La. NW4 —2G 41
Finchley Pk. N12 —4A 26
Finchley Pl. NW8 —5B 58
Finchley Rd. NW3 —1L 57
Finchley Rd. NW8 —4B 58
Finchley Rd. NW11 & NW2 —2K 41
Finchley Way. N3 —7L 25
Finch Lodge. W2 —8L 57
(off Admiral Wlk.)
Finch M. SE15 —9D 76
Finch's Ct. E14 —1M 77
Finden Rd. E7 —1G 63
Findhorn Av. Hay —8F 52
Findhorn St. E14 —9A 62
Findon Clo. SW18 —5L 89
Findon Clo. Harr —8M 37
Findon Gdns. Rain —8E 66
Findon Rd. N9 —1F 28
Findon Rd. W12 —3E 72
Fine Bush La. Hare —4A 36
Fingal St. SE10 —6D 78
Fingest Ho. NW8 —7C 58
(off Lilestone St.)
Finglesham Clo. Orp —3H 129
Finians Clo. Uxb —3D 142
Finland Rd. SE4 —2J 93
Finland St. SE16 —4J 77
Finlays Clo. Chess —7L 119
Finlay St. SW6 —9H 73
Finmere Ho. N4 —5A 44
Finnart Clo. Wey —6A 116
Finnart Ho. Dri. Wey —6A 116
Finnemore Ho. N1 —4A 60
(off Britannia Row)
Finney La. Iswth —9E 70
Finn Ho. N1 —6B 60
(off Bevenden St.)
Finnis St. E2 —6F 60
Finnymore Rd. Dag —3J 65
Finsbury. —6L 59
Finsbury Av. EC2 —8B 60
(in two parts)
Finsbury Av. Sq. EC2 —8C 60
(off Finsbury Av.)
Finsbury Cir. EC2 —8B 60
Finsbury Cotts. N22 —7J 27
Finsbury Ct. Wal X —7E 6
Finsbury Est. EC1 —6L 59
Finsbury Ho. N22 —8J 27
Finsbury Mkt. EC2 —7C 60
(in two parts)
Finsbury Park. —6L 43
Finsbury Pk. Av. N4 —4A 44
Finsbury Pk. Rd. N4 —7M 43
Finsbury Pavement. EC2 —8B 60
Finsbury Rd. N22 —7K 27
Finsbury Sq. EC2 —8B 60
Finsbury St. EC2 —8B 60
Finsbury Way. Bex —5K 97
Finsen Rd. SE5 —3A 92
Finstock Rd. W10 —9H 57
Finucane Dri. Orp —2G 129
Finucane Gdns. Rain —2E 66
Finucane Ri. Bus H —2A 22
Finway Ct. Wat —7D 8
Finwhale Ho. E14 —4M 77
(off Glengall Gro.)
Fiona Ct. NW6 —5L 57
Fiona Ct. Enf —5M 15
Firbank Clo. E16 —8H 63
Firbank Clo. Enf —6A 16
Firbank Dri. Wat —9J 9
Firbank Rd. SE15 —1F 92
Firbank Rd. Romf —5M 33
Fir Clo. W on T —2E 116
Fircroft Gdns. Harr —8C 38
Fircroft Rd. SW17 —8D 90
Fircroft Rd. Chess —6K 119
Fir Dene. Orp —5K 127
Firdene. Surb —3A 120
Fire Bell La. Surb —1J 119
Firecrest Dri. NW3 —8M 41
Firefly Clo. Wall —9J 123
Firefly Gdns. E6 —7J 63
Firemans Flats. N22 —7J 27
Fire Sta. All. High Bar —5J 13
Fire Sta. M. Beck —5L 109
Firethorn Clo. Edgw —4A 24
Firfields. Wey —8A 116
Fir Grange Av. Wey —7A 116
Fir Gro. N Mald —1D 120
Firham Pk. Av. Romf —7L 35
Firhill Rd. SE6 —1L 109
Fir Ho. W10 —7J 57
(off Droop St.)
Firlands. Wey —8C 116
Firle Ct. Eps —4D 134
Firle Ho. W10 —8G 57
(off Sutton Way)
Firmingers Rd. Orp —7M 129
Firmin Rd. Dart —4G 99
Fir Rd. Felt —2H 101
Fir Rd. Sutt —3K 121
Firs Av. N10 —1E 42
Firs Av. N11 —6D 26
Firs Av. SW14 —3A 88
Firsby Av. Croy —3H 125
Firsby Rd. N16 —6E 44
Firs Clo. N10 —2E 42
Firs Clo. SE23 —6J 93
Firs Clo. Clay —8C 118
Firs Clo. Mitc —5F 106
Firscroft. N13 —3A 28
Firs Dri. Houn —8F 68
Firs Dri. Lou —3L 19
Firs Ho. N22 —8L 27
(off Acacia Rd.)
Firside Gro. Sidc —7D 96
Firs La. N13 & N21 —3A 28
Firs La. N21 —9A 16
Firs Pk. Av. N21 —1A 28
Firs Pk. Gdns. N21 —1A 28
Firs Rd. Kenl —7M 137
First Av. E12 —9J 47
First Av. E13 —6E 62
First Av. E17 —3L 45
First Av. N18 —4G 29
First Av. NW4 —2G 41
First Av. SW14 —2C 88
First Av. W3 —2D 72
First Av. W10 —7K 57
First Av. Bexh —8G 81
First Av. Dag —5M 65
First Av. Enf —7D 16
First Av. Eps —1C 134
First Av. Hay —2D 68
First Av. Romf —3G 49
First Av. W on T —1F 116
First Av. Wat —8G 5
First Av. Wemb —7H 39
First Av. W Mol —8K 101
First Clo. W Mol —7A 102
First Cross Rd. Twic —8C 86
First Dri. NW10 —3A 56
Firs, The. E6 —3J 63
Firs, The. N20 —1B 26
Firs, The. SE26 —2F 108
(Lawrie Pk. Gdns.)
Firs, The. SE26 —2G 109
(Venner Rd.)
Firs, The. W5 —8H 55
Firs, The. Bex —7B 98
Firs, The. Sidc —9D 96
First Quarter Ind. Pk. Eps —3C 134
First Slip. Lea —9E 132
First St. SW3 —5C 74
Firstway. SW20 —6G 105
First Way. Wemb —9M 39
Firs Wlk. N'wd —6B 20
Firs Wlk. Wfd G —5E 30
Firswood Av. Eps —7C 120
Firth Gdns. SW6 —9J 73
Firth Ho. E2 —6E 60
(off Barnet Gro.)
Firtree Av. Mitc —6E 106
Fir Tree Av. W Dray —4L 143
Firtree Clo. SW16 —2G 107
Fir Tree Clo. W5 —9J 55
Fir Tree Clo. Eps —7G 135
Fir Tree Clo. Esh —7A 118
Firtree Clo. Ewe —6D 120
Fir Tree Clo. Orp —7D 128
Fir Tree Clo. Romf —1B 50
Firtree Ct. Borwd —6K 11
Firtree Gdns. Croy —6L 125
Fir Tree Gro. Cars —9D 122
Fir Tree Ho. SE14 —8G 77
(off Avonley Rd.)
Fir Tree Rd. Bans —6G 135
Fir Tree Rd. Eps —8F 134
Fir Tree Rd. Houn —3J 85
Fir Trees Clo. SE16 —2J 77
Fir Tree Wlk. Dag —8A 50
Fir Tree Wlk. Enf —5B 16
Fir Wlk. Sutt —8H 121
Fisher Athletic F.C. —2H 77
Fisher Clo. Croy —3D 124
Fisher Clo. Enf —1L 17
Fisher Clo. Gnfd —6L 53
Fisher Clo. W on T —6F 116
Fisher Ho. E1 —1G 77
(off Cable St.)
Fisher Ho. N1 —4L 59
(off Barnsbury Est.)
Fisherman Clo. Rich —1F 102
Fishermans Dri. SE16 —3H 77
Fisherman's Pl. W4 —7D 72
Fisherman's Wlk. E14 —2L 77
Fishermans Wlk. E14 —2L 77
Fishermans Wlk. SE28 —3C 80
Fisher Rd. Harr —9D 22
Fisher's Clo. SW16 —9H 91
Fishers Clo. Bush —5J 9
Fishers Clo. Wal X —7G 7
Fishers Ct. SE14 —9H 77
Fishers Dene. Clay —9E 118
Fishers Green. —2H 7
Fishers Grn. La. Wal A —2H 7
Fisher's Ind. Est. Wat —7G 9
Fisher's La. W4 —5B 72
Fisher St. E16 —8E 62
Fisher St. WC1 —8K 59
Fishers Way. Belv —2A 82
Fisherton St. NW8 —7B 58
Fishguard Way. E16 —2M 79
(in two parts)
Fishmongers Hall Wharf. EC4
(off Swan La.) —1B 76
Fishponds Rd. SW17 —1C 106
Fishponds Rd. Kes —7H 127
Fish St. Hill. EC3 —1B 76
Fish Wharf. EC3 —1B 76
(off Lwr. Thames St.)
Fiske Ct. N17 —8E 28
Fiske Ct. Bark —5B 64
Fisons Rd. E16 —2E 78
Fitzalan Ho. Ewe —2D 134
Fitzalan Rd. N3 —1J 41
Fitzalan Rd. Clay —9C 118
Fitzalan St. SE11 —5L 75
Fitzgeorge Av. W14 —5J 73
Fitzgeorge Av. N Mald —5B 104
Fitzgerald Av. SW14 —2C 88
Fitzgerald Ct. E10 —6M 45
(off Leyton Grange Est.)
Fitzgerald Ho. E14 —9M 61
(off E. India Dock Rd.)
Fitzgerald Ho. SW9 —1L 91
Fitzgerald Rd. E11 —3E 46
Fitzgerald Rd. SW14 —2B 88
Fitzgerald Rd. Th Dit —1E 118
Fitzhardinge Ho. W1 —9E 58
(off Portman Sq.)
Fitzhardinge St. W1 —9E 58
Fitzhugh Gro. SW18 —5B 90
Fitzilian Av. Romf —8K 35
Fitzjames Av. W14 —5J 73
Fitzjames Av. Croy —4E 124
Fitzjohn Av. Barn —7J 13
Fitzjohn's Av. NW3 —9A 42
Fitzmaurice Ho. SE16 —5F 76
(off Rennie Est.)
Fitzmaurice Pl. W1 —2F 74
Fitzneal St. W3 —9D 56
Fitzroy Clo. N6 —6D 42
Fitzroy Ct. N6 —4G 43
Fitzroy Ct. W1 —7G 59
(off Tottenham Ct. Rd.)
Fitzroy Ct. Croy —2B 124
Fitzroy Ct. Dart —7M 99
(off Churchill Clo.)
Fitzroy Cres. W4 —8B 72
Fitzroy Gdns. SE19 —4C 108
Fitzroy Ho. E14 —8K 61
(off Wallwood St.)
Fitzroy Ho. SE1 —6D 76
(off Coopers La.)
Fitzroy M. W1 —7G 59
(off Cleveland St.)
Fitzroy Pk. N6 —6D 42
Fitzroy Rd. NW1 —4E 58
Fitzroy Sq. W1 —7G 59
Fitzroy St. W1 —7G 59
(in two parts)
Fitzroy Yd. NW1 —4E 58
Fitzsimmons Ct. NW10 —4B 56
Fitzstephen Rd. Dag —1F 64
Fitzwarren Gdns. N19 —6G 43
Fitzwilliam Av. Rich —1K 87
Fitzwilliam Heights. SE23 —8G 93
Fitzwilliam Ho. Rich —3H 87
Fitzwilliam M. E16 —2E 78
Fitzwilliam Rd. SW4 —2G 91
Fitzwygram Clo. Hamp H —2A 102
Five Acre. NW9 —9D 24
Fiveacre Clo. T Hth —1L 123
Five Acres Av. Brick W —2K 5
Five Bell All. E14 —9K 61
(off Three Colt St.)
Five Elms Rd. Brom —4F 126
Five Elms Rd. Dag —8K 49
Five Fields Clo. Wat —2K 21
Five Oaks La. Chig —6J 33
Fives Ct. SE11 —4M 75
Fiveways. (Junct.) —8M 95
Fiveways. SE9 —8M 95
Five Ways Bus. Cen. Felt —9F 84
Fiveways Corner. (Junct.) —8F 24
(Hendon)
Fiveways Corner. (Junct.) —6L 123
(Waddon)
Fiveways Rd. SW9 —1L 91
Five Wents. Swan —6E 114
Flack Ct. E10 —5M 45
Fladbury Rd. N15 —4B 44
Fladgate Rd. E11 —4C 46
Flag Clo. Croy —3H 125
Flagstaff Clo. Wal A —6H 7
Flagstaff Rd. Wal A —6H 7
Flag Wlk. Pinn —4E 36
Flambard Rd. Harr —4E 38
Flamborough Ho. SE15 —9E 76
(off Clayton Rd.)
Flamborough Rd. Ruis —8E 36
Flamborough St. E14 —9J 61
Flamborough Wlk. E14 —9J 61
Flamingo Ct. SE8 —8L 77
(off Hamilton St.)
Flamingo Gdns. N'holt —6J 53
Flamingo Wlk. Horn —2E 66
Flamstead End. —1B 6
Flamstead End Rd. Chesh —1B 6
Flamstead Gdns. Dag —3G 65
Flamstead Ho. SW3 —6C 74
(off Cale St.)
Flamstead Rd. Dag —3G 65
Flamsted Av. Wemb —2L 55
Flamsteed Rd. SE7 —6J 79
Flanchford Rd. W12 —4D 72
Flanders Ct. E17 —5J 45
Flanders Cres. SW17 —4D 106
Flanders Mans. W4 —5D 72
Flanders Rd. E6 —5K 63
Flanders Rd. W4 —5C 72
Flanders Way. E9 —2H 61
Flank St. E1 —1E 76
Flansham Ho. E14 —9K 61
(off Clemence St.)
Flash La. Enf —1M 15
Flask Wlk. NW3 —9A 42
Flatford Ho. SE6 —1A 110
Flatiron Yd. SE1 —2A 76
(off Union St.)
Flaunden Ho. Wat —8C 8
Flavell M. SE10 —6C 78
Flaxen Clo. E4 —3M 29
Flaxen Rd. E4 —3M 29
Flaxley Rd. Mord —1M 121
Flaxman Ct. W1 —9H 59
(off Wardour St.)
Flaxman Ct. WC1 —6H 59
Flaxman Ct. Belv —6L 81
(off Hoddesdon Rd.)
Flaxman Ho. W4 —6C 72
(off Devonshire St.)
Flaxman Rd. SE5 —2M 91
Flaxman Ter. WC1 —6H 59
Flaxmore Pl. Beck —1B 126
Flaxton Rd. SE18 —9B 80
Flecker Clo. Stan —5D 22
Flecker Ho. SE5 —8B 76
(off Lomond Gro.)
Fleece Dri. N9 —4E 28
Fleece Rd. Surb —3G 119
Fleece Wlk. N7 —2J 59
Fleeming Clo. E17 —9K 29
Fleeming Rd. E17 —9K 29
Fleet Av. Dart —7M 99
Fleetbank Ho. EC4 —9L 59
(off Salisbury Sq.)
Fleet Building. EC4 —9M 59
(off Shoe La.)
Fleet Clo. Ruis —4A 36
Fleet Clo. W Mol —9K 101
Fleetdale Pde. Dart —7M 99
Fleet Downs. —7M 99
Fleetfield. WC1 —6J 59
(off Birkenhead St.)
Fleet La. W Mol —1K 117
Fleet Pl. EC4 —9M 59
(off Limeburner La., in two parts)
Fleet Rd. NW3 —1C 58
Fleet Rd. Dart —7M 99
Fleetside. W Mol —9K 101
Fleet Sq. WC1 —6K 59
Fleet St. EC4 —9L 59
Fleet St. Hill. E1 —7E 60
Fleetway. WC1 —6J 59
(off Birkenhead St.)
Fleetway Bus. Cen. NW2 —6D 40
Fleetway W. Bus. Pk. Gnfd —5F 54
Fleetwood Clo. E16 —8H 63
Fleetwood Clo. Chess —9H 119
Fleetwood Clo. Croy —5D 124
Fleetwood Ct. E6 —8K 63
(off Evelyn Dennington Rd.,
in three parts)
Fleetwood Ct. Stanw —5B 144
Fleetwood Rd. NW10 —1E 56
Fleetwood Rd. King T —7M 103
Fleetwood Sq. King T —7M 103
Fleetwood St. N16 —7C 44
Fleetwood Way. Wat —4G 21
Fleming. N8 —1J 43
(off Boyton Clo.)
Fleming Clo. W9 —7L 57
Fleming Ct. W2 —8B 58
(off St Marys Sq.)
Fleming Ct. Croy —7L 123
Fleming Dri. N21 —7K 15
Fleming Gdns. H Wood —9H 35
Fleming Ho. N4 —6A 44
Fleming Ho. SE16 —3E 76
(off George Row)
Fleming Ho. Wemb —8A 40
(off Barnhill Rd.)
Fleming Lodge. W2 —8L 57
(off Admiral Wlk.)
Fleming Mead. Mitc —4C 106
Fleming Rd. SE17 —7M 75
Fleming Rd. S'hall —9M 53
Fleming Wlk. NW9 —1C 40
Fleming Way. SE28 —1H 81
Fleming Way. Iswth —3D 86
Flemming Av. Ruis —6F 36
Flempton Rd. E10 —6J 45
Fletcher Bldgs. WC2 —9J 59
(off Martlett Ct.)
Fletcher Clo. E6 —9M 63
Fletcher La. E10 —5A 46
Fletcher Path. SE8 —8L 77
Fletcher Rd. W4 —4A 72
Fletcher Rd. Chig —5D 32
Fletchers Clo. Brom —8F 110
Fletcher St. E1 —1E 76
Fletching Rd. E5 —8G 45
Fletching Rd. SE7 —7G 79
Flete Ho. Wat —8C 8
Fletton Rd. N11 —7J 27
Fleur-de-Lis St. E1 —7D 60
(in two parts)
Fleur Gates. SW19 —6H 89
Flexmere Rd. N17 —8B 28
Flight App. NW9 —9D 24
Flimwell Clo. Brom —2C 110
Flinders Ho. E1 —2F 76
(off Green Bank)
Flint Clo. Bans —6M 135
Flint Clo. Grn St —8D 128
Flint Down Clo. Orp —5E 112
Flintmill Cres. SE3 —1J 95
(in three parts)
Flinton St. SE17 —6C 76
Flint St. SE17 —5B 76
Flitcroft St. WC2 —9H 59
Flitton Ho. N1 —3M 59
(off Sutton Est., The)
Flock Mill Pl. SW18 —7M 89
Flockton St. SE16 —3E 76
Flodden Rd. SE5 —9A 76
Flood La. Twic —7E 86
Flood Pas. SE18 —4J 79
Flood St. SW3 —6C 74
Flood Wlk. SW3 —7C 74
Flora Clo. E14 —9M 61
Flora Gdns. W6 —5F 72
(off Albion Gdns.)
Flora Gdns. Croy —3A 140
Flora Gdns. Romf —4G 49
Floral Ct. Asht —9G 133
Floral Pl. N1 —1B 60
Floral St. WC2 —1J 75
Flora St. Belv —6K 81
Florence Av. Enf —5A 16
Florence Av. Mord —9A 106
Florence Clo. Horn —7J 51
Florence Clo. W on T —2F 116
Florence Clo. Wat —8E 4
Florence Ct. E5 —8E 44
Florence Ct. E11 —2F 46
Florence Ct. N1 —3M 59
(off Florence St.)
Florence Ct. SW19 —3J 105
Florence Ct. W9 —6A 58
(off Maida Va.)
Florence Dri. Enf —5A 16
Florence Elson Clo. E12 —8L 47
(off Grantham Rd.)
Florence Gdns. W4 —7A 72
Florence Ho. SE16 —6F 76
(off Rotherhithe New Rd.)
Florence Ho. W11 —1H 73
Florence Ho. King T —4K 103
(off Floerence Rd)
Florence Mans. NW4 —3F 40
(off Vivian Av.)
Florence Nightingale Mus. —3K 75
Florence Rd. E6 —4G 63
Florence Rd. E13 —5D 62
Florence Rd. N4 —5K 43
(in two parts)
Florence Rd. SE2 —5G 81
Florence Rd. SE14 —9K 77
Florence Rd. SW19 —3M 105
Florence Rd. W4 —4B 72
Florence Rd. W5 —1J 71
Florence Rd. Beck —6J 109
Florence Rd. Brom —5E 110
Florence Rd. Felt —7F 84
Florence Rd. King T —4K 103
Florence Rd. S'hall —5H 69
Florence Rd. S Croy —1B 138
Florence Rd. W on T —2F 116
Florence St. E16 —7D 62
Florence St. N1 —3M 59
Florence St. NW4 —2G 41
Florence Ter. SE14 —9K 77
Florence Ter. SW15 —9C 88
Florence Way. SW12 —7D 90
Flores Ho. E1 —8H 61
(off Shandy St.)
Florey Lodge. W9 —8L 57
(off Admiral Wlk.)
Florfield Pas. E8 —2F 60
(off Florfield Rd.)
Florfield Rd. E8 —2F 60
Florian. SE5 —9C 76
Florian Av. Sutt —6B 122
Florian Rd. SW15 —3J 89
Florida Clo. Bus H —2B 22
Florida Ct. Brom —8D 110
(off Westmoreland Rd.)
Florida Rd. T Hth —5M 107
Florida St. E2 —6E 60
Florin Ct. N18 —4C 28
Florin Ct. SE1 —3D 76
(off Tanner St.)
Floris Pl. SW4 —2G 91
Floriston Av. Uxb —3A 52

Floriston Clo.—Frampton Ct.

Floriston Clo. Stan —8F 22
Floriston Ct. N'holt —1M 53
Floriston Gdns. Stan —8F 22
Floss St. SW15 —1G 89
Flower & Dean Wlk. E1 —8D 60
(in two parts)
Flower La. NW7 —5D 24
Flowerpot Clo. N15 —4D 44
Flowers Clo. NW2 —8E 40
Flowersmead. SW17 —8E 90
Flowers M. N19 —7G 43
Flower Wlk., The. SW7 —3A 74
Floyd Rd. SE7 —6G 79
Fludyer St. SE13 —3C 94
Fogerty Clo. Enf —1M 17
Foley Ct. Dart —7M 99
(off Churchill Clo.)
Foley Ho. E1 —9G 61
(off Tarling St.)
Foley M. Clay —8C 118
Foley Rd. Big H —9H 141
Foley Rd. Clay —9C 118
Foley St. W1 —8G 59
Folgate St. E1 —8C 60
(in two parts)
Foliot Ho. N1 —5K 59
(off Priory Grn. Est.)
Foliot St. W3 —9D 56
Folkestone Ct. N'holt —1M 53
(off Newmarket Av.)
Folkestone Rd. E6 —5L 63
Folkestone Rd. E17 —2M 45
Folkestone Rd. N18 —4E 28
Folkingham La. NW9 —8B 24
Folkington Corner. N12 —5K 25
Folland. NW9 —9D 24
(off Hundred Acre)
Follet Dri. Ab L —4D 4
Follett Ho. SW10 —8B 74
(off Worlds End Est.)
Follett St. E14 —9A 62
Follingham Ct. N1 —6C 60
(off Drysdale Pl.)
Follyfield Rd. Bans —6L 135
Folly La. E17 —8J 29
(in two parts)
Folly M. W11 —9K 57
Folly Wall. E14 —3A 78
Fontaine Rd. SW16 —4K 107
Fontarabia Rd. SW11 —3E 90
Fontayne Av. Chig —4A 32
Fontayne Av. Rain —3C 66
Fontayne Av. Romf —9C 34
Fontenelle Gdns. SE5 —9C 76
Fontenoy Ho. SE11 —5M 75
(off Kennington La.)
Fontenoy Rd. SW12 —8F 90
Fonteyne Gdns. Wfd G —9H 31
Fonthill Clo. SE20 —6E 108
Fonthill M. N4 —7K 43
Fonthill Rd. N4 —6K 43
Font Hills. N2 —9A 26
Fontley Way. SW15 —6E 88
Fontwell Clo. Harr —7C 22
Fontwell Clo. N'holt —2L 53
Fontwell Dri. Brom —9L 111
Fontwell Pk. Gdns. Horn —9J 51
Football La. Harr —6D 38
Footbury Hill Rd. Orp —1E 128
Footpath, The. SW15 —5E 88
Foots Cray. —3G 113
Foots Cray High St. Sidc —3G 113
Foots Cray La. Sidc —7G 97
Footscray Rd. SE9 —5L 95
Forber Ho. E2 —6G 61
(off Cornwall Av.)
Forbes Clo. NW2 —8E 40
Forbes Clo. Horn —6F 50
Forbes St. E1 —9E 60
Forbes Way. Ruis —7F 36
Forburg Rd. N16 —6E 44
Fordbridge Cvn. Pk. Sun —1D 116
Fordbridge Rd. Sun —1C 116
Ford Clo. E3 —5J 61
Ford Clo. Bush —6A 10
Ford Clo. Harr —5B 38
Ford Clo. Rain —3D 66
Ford Clo. T Hth —9M 107
Fordcroft Rd. Orp —9F 112
Forde Av. Brom —7G 111
Fordel Rd. SE6 —7B 94
Ford End. Wfd G —6F 30
Fordham. King T —6L 103
(off Excelsior Clo.)
Fordham Clo. Barn —5C 14
Fordham Clo. Horn —5L 51
Fordham Rd. Barn —5B 14
Fordham St. E1 —9E 60
Fordhook Av. W5 —2K 71
Ford Ho. Barn —7M 13
Ford Ind. Pk. Dag —7M 65
Fordingley Rd. W9 —6K 57
Fordington Ho. SE26 —9E 92
Fordington Rd. N6 —3D 42
Ford La. Rain —3D 66
Fordmill Rd. SE6 —8L 93
Ford Rd. E3 —5K 61
Ford Rd. Dag —3K 65
Fords Gro. N21 —1A 28
Fords Pk. Rd. E16 —8E 62
Ford Sq. E1 —8F 60
Ford St. E3 —4J 61
Ford St. E16 —9D 62
Fordwich Clo. Orp —2D 128
Fordwych Rd. NW2 —9J 41
Fordyce Clo. Horn —5K 51
Fordyce Rd. SE13 —5A 94
Fordyke Rd. Dag —7K 49
Foreign St. SE5 —1M 91
Foreland Ct. NW4 —8H 25
Foreland Ho. W11 —1J 73
(off Walmer Rd.)
Foreland St. SE18 —5B 80
Foreman Ct. Twic —7D 86
Foremark Clo. Ilf —5D 32
Foreshore. SE8 —5K 77
Forest App. E4 —9C 18
Forest App. Wfd G —7E 30
Forest Av. E4 —9C 18
Forest Av. Chig —5L 31
Forest Bus. Pk. E17 —5J 45
Forest Clo. E11 —3E 46
Forest Clo. Chst —5L 111
Forest Clo. Wal A —1F 18
Forest Clo. Wfd G —3F 30
Forest Ct. E4 —1D 30
Forest Ct. N12 —5M 25
Forest Cres. Asht —8L 133
Forest Cft. SE23 —8F 92
Forestdale. —1K 139
Forestdale. N14 —4H 27
Forestdale Cen., The. Croy —9K 125
Forest Dene Ct. Sutt —8A 122
Forest Dri. E12 —8H 47
Forest Dri. Kes —6J 127
Forest Dri. Sun —4D 100
Forest Dri. Wfd G —7B 30
Forest Dri. E. E11 —5B 46
Forest Dri. W. E11 —5A 46
Forest Edge. Buck H —4G 31
Forester Rd. SE15 —2F 92
Foresters Clo. Wall —9H 123
Foresters Cres. Bexh —3M 97
Foresters Dri. E17 —2B 46
Foresters Dri. Wall —9H 123
Forest Gdns. N17 —9D 28
Forest Gate. —1F 62
Forest Ga. NW9 —2C 40
Forest Glade. E4 —4C 30
Forest Glade. E11 —4C 46
Forest Gro. E8 —2D 60
Forest Hill. —8G 93
Forest Hill Bus. Cen. SE23 —8G 93
(off Clyde Va.)
Forest Hill Ind. Est. SE23 —8G 93
Forest Hill Rd. SE22 & SE23 —4F 92
Forestholme Clo. SE23 —8G 93
Forest Ind. Pk. Ilf —8C 32
Forest La. E15 & E7 —1C 62
Forest La. Chig —5L 31
Forest Lodge. SE26 —9G 93
(off Dartmouth Rd.)
Forest Mt. Rd. E4 —7B 30
Forest Point. E7 —1F 62
(off Windsor Rd.)
Fore St. EC2 —8A 60
Fore St. N18 & N9 —6D 28
Fore St. Pinn —1D 36
Fore St. Av. EC2 —8B 60
Forest Ridge. Beck —7L 109
Forest Ridge. Kes —6J 127
Forest Ri. E17 —1B 46
(in two parts)
Forest Rd. E7 —9E 46
Forest Rd. E8 —2D 60
Forest Rd. E11 —5B 46
Forest Rd. N9 —1F 28
Forest Rd. N17 & E17 —2G 45
Forest Rd. Chesh —2D 6
Forest Rd. Enf —9E 6
Forest Rd. Eri —9E 82
Forest Rd. Felt —8G 85
Forest Rd. Ilf —9B 32
Forest Rd. Lou —5H 19
Forest Rd. Rich —8L 71
Forest Rd. Romf —1M 49
Forest Rd. Sutt —3L 121
Forest Rd. Wat —6F 4
Forest Rd. Wfd G —3E 30
Forest Side. E4 —9D 18
Forest Side. E7 —9F 46
Forest Side. Buck H —1G 31
Forest Side. Wal A —1G 19
Forest Side. Wor Pk —3D 120
Forest St. E7 —1E 62
Forest Ter. Chig —5L 31
Forest, The. E11 —2C 46
Forest Trad. Est. E17 —1H 45
Forest Vw. E4 —9B 18
Forest Vw. E11 —5D 46
Forest Vw. Av. E10 —3B 46
Forest Vw. Rd. E12 —9J 47
Forest Vw. Rd. E17 —8A 30
Forest Vw. Rd. Lou —6H 19
Forest Wlk. Bush —3K 9
Forest Way. N19 —7G 43
Forest Way. Asht —9K 133
Forest Way. Lou —5J 19
Forest Way. Orp —9D 112
Forest Way. Sidc —6B 96
Forest Way. Wfd G —4F 30
Forest Works Ind. Est. E17 —1H 45
Forfar Rd. N22 —8M 27
Forfar Rd. SW11 —9E 74
Forge Clo. Brom —3E 126
Forge Clo. Hay —7B 68
Forge Cotts. W5 —2H 71
Forge Dri. Clay —9E 118
Forge Fld. Big H —8H 141
Forge La. Felt —2J 101
Forge La. N'wd —7C 20
Forge La. Sun —7E 100
Forge La. Sutt —9J 121
Forge Pl. NW1 —2E 58
Forge Steading. Bans —7M 135
Forman Pl. N16 —9D 44
Formby Av. Stan —1G 39
Formby Ct. N7 —1L 59
(off Morgan Rd.)
Former County Hall. —3K 75
Formosa Ho. E1 —7J 61
(off Ernest St.)
Formosa St. W9 —7M 57
Formunt Clo. E16 —8D 62
Forres Gdns. NW11 —4L 41
Forrester Path. SE26 —1G 109
Forrest Gdns. SW16 —7K 107
Forris Av. Hay —2D 68
Forset Ct. W2 —9C 58
(off Harrowby St.)
Forset St. W1 —9C 58
Forstal Clo. Brom —7E 110
Forster Clo. E4 —7B 30
Forster Ho. Brom —1B 110
Forster Rd. E17 —4J 45
Forster Rd. N17 —1D 44
Forster Rd. SW12 —6J 91
Forster Rd. Beck —7J 109
Forsters Clo. Romf —4K 49
Forsters Way. Hay —9F 52
Forston St. N1 —5A 60
Forsyte Cres. SE19 —5C 108
Forsythe Shades Ct. Beck —5A 110
Forsyth Gdns. SE17 —7M 75
Forsyth Ho. SW1 —6G 75
(off Tachbrook St.)
Forsythia Clo. Ilf —1M 63
Forsyth Pl. Enf —7C 16
Forterie Gdns. Ilf —8E 48
Fortescue Av. E8 —3F 60
Fortescue Av. Twic —9A 86
Fortescue Rd. SW19 —4B 106
Fortescue Rd. Edgw —8B 24
Fortess Gro. NW5 —1G 59
Fortess Rd. NW5 —1F 58
Fortess Wlk. NW5 —1F 58
Fortess Yd. NW5 —9F 42
Forthbridge Rd. SW11 —3E 90
Fortis Clo. E16 —9G 63
Fortis Ct. N10 —1E 42
Fortis Green. —2D 42
Fortis Grn. N2 & N10 —2C 42
Fortis Grn. Av. N2 —1D 42
Fortis Grn. Rd. N10 —1E 42
Fortismere Av. N10 —1E 42
Fortnam Rd. N19 —7H 43
Fortnum's Acre. Stan —6D 22
Fort Rd. SE1 —5D 76
Fort Rd. N'holt —3L 53
Fortrose Gdns. SW2 —7J 91
Fort St. E1 —8C 60
Fort St. E16 —2F 78
Fortuna Clo. N7 —2K 59
Fortune Ct. Bark —5G 65
Fortunegate Rd. NW10 —4C 56
Fortune Green. —9L 41
Fortune Grn. Rd. NW6 —9L 41
Fortune Ho. EC1 —7A 60
(off Fortune St.)
Fortune Ho. SE11 —5L 75
(off Marylee Way)
Fortune La. Els —8H 11
Fortunes Mead. N'holt —2J 53
Fortune St. EC1 —7A 60
Fortune Theatre. —9J 59
(off Russell St.)
Fortune Wlk. SE28 —4B 80
(off Broadwater Rd.)
Fortune Way. NW10 —6E 56
Forty Acre La. E16 —8E 62
Forty Av. Wemb —8K 39
Forty Clo. Wemb —8K 39
Forty Footpath. SW14 —2A 88
Forty Foot Way. SE9 —6A 96
Forty Hall. —1D 16
Forty Hall Mus. —1D 16
Forty Hill. —2C 16
Forty Hill. Enf —2C 16
Forty La. Wemb —7M 39
Forum Magnus Sq. SE1 —3K 75
(off York Rd.)
Forumside. Edgw —6L 23
Forum, The. W Mol —8M 101
Forum Way. Edgw —6L 23
Forval Clo. Mitc —9D 106
Forward Bus. Cen. E16 —7B 62
Forward Dri. Harr —2D 38
Fosbrooke Ho. SW8 —8J 75
(off Davidson Gdns.)
Fosbury M. W2 —1M 73
Foscote M. W9 —7L 57
Foscote Rd. NW4 —4F 40
Foskett Rd. SW6 —1K 89
Foss Av. Croy —7L 123
Fossdene Rd. SE7 —6F 78
Fossdyke Clo. Hay —8J 53
Fosset Lodge. Bexh —9A 82
Fosse Way. W13 —8E 54
Fossil Rd. SE13 —2L 93
Fossington Rd. Belv —5H 81
Foss Rd. SW17 —1B 106
Fossway. Dag —7G 49
Foster Ct. NW1 —3G 59
(off Royal College St.)
Foster Ct. NW4 —2G 41
Foster Ho. SE14 —9K 77
Foster La. EC2 —9A 60
Foster Rd. E13 —7E 62
Foster Rd. W3 —1C 72
Foster Rd. W4 —6B 72
Fosters Clo. E18 —8F 30
Fosters Clo. Chesh —3D 6
Fosters Clo. Chst —2K 111
Foster St. NW4 —2G 41
Foster's Way. SW18 —7M 89
Foster Wlk. NW4 —2G 41
Fothergill Clo. E13 —5E 62
Fothergill Dri. N21 —7J 15
Fotheringham Rd. Enf —6D 16
Foubert's Pl. W1 —9G 59
Foulden Rd. N16 —9D 44
Foulden Ter. N16 —9D 44
Foulis Ter. SW7 —6B 74
Foulser Rd. SW17 —9D 90
Foulsham Rd. T Hth —7A 108
Founder Clo. E6 —9M 63
Founders Ct. EC2 —9B 60
(off Lothbury)
Founders Gdns. SE19 —4A 108
Founders Ho. SW1 —6H 75
(off Aylesford St.)
Foundling Ct. WC1 —7J 59
(off Brunswick Cen.)
Foundry Clo. SE16 —2J 77
Foundry Ho. E14 —8M 61
(off Morris Rd.)
Foundry M. NW1 —7G 59
(off Drummond St.)
Foundry Pl. SW18 —6M 89
Fountain Clo. Uxb —8A 52
Fountain Ct. EC4 —1L 75
Fountain Ct. SE23 —8H 93
Fountain Ct. SW1 —5F 74
(off Buckingham Pal. Rd.)
Fountain Ct. Eyns —4J 131
Fountain Ct. Sidc —5F 96
Fountain Dri. SE19 —1D 108
Fountain Dri. Cars —9D 122
Fountain Grn. Sq. SE16 —3E 76
Fountain Ho. NW6 —3J 57
Fountain Ho. W1 —2E 74
(off Park St.)
Fountain M. N5 —9A 44
(off Highbury Grange)
Fountain M. NW3 —2D 58
Fountain Pl. SW9 —9L 75
Fountain Pl. Wal A —7J 7
Fountain Rd. SW17 —2B 106
Fountain Rd. T Hth —7A 108
Fountain Roundabout. N Mald —8C 104
Fountains Av. Felt —9K 85
Fountains Clo. Felt —8K 85
(in two parts)
Fountains Cres. N14 —9J 15
Fountain Sq. SW1 —5F 74
Fountains, The. N3 —7M 25
(off Ballards La.)
Fountains, The. Lou —9H 19
Fountayne Bus. Cen. N15 —2E 44
Fountayne Rd. N15 —2E 44
Fountayne Rd. N16 —7E 44
Fount St. SW8 —8H 75
Fouracres. Enf —3J 17
Fourland Wlk. Edgw —6A 24
Fournier St. E1 —8D 60
Four Seasons Clo. E3 —5L 61
Four Seasons Cres. Sutt —4K 121
Four Sq. Ct. Houn —5L 85
Fourth Av. E12 —9K 47
Fourth Av. W10 —7J 57
Fourth Av. Hay —2D 68
Fourth Av. Romf —6B 50
Fourth Av. Wat —8H 5
Fourth Cross Rd. Twic —8B 86
Fourth Dri. Coul —8G 137
Fourth Way. Wemb —9M 39
Four Tubs, The. Bush —9B 10
Four Wents, The. E4 —1B 30
Fovant Ct. SW8 —1G 91
Fowey Av. Ilf —3H 47
Fowey Clo. E1 —2F 76
Fowey Ho. SE11 —6L 75
(off Kennings Way)
Fowler Clo. SW11 —2B 90
Fowler Ho. N15 —3B 44
(off South Gro.)
Fowler Rd. E7 —9E 46
Fowler Rd. N1 —4M 59
Fowler Rd. Ilf —6F 32
Fowler Rd. Mitc —6E 106
Fowlers Clo. Sidc —2J 113
Fowler's Wlk. W5 —7H 55
Fowley Clo. Wal X —7F 6
Fowley Mead Pk. Wal X —7G 7
Fownes St. SW11 —2C 90
Fox All. Wat —7G 9
Fox & Knot St. EC1 —8M 59
(off Charterhouse Sq.)
Foxberry Rd. SE4 —2J 93
Foxborough Gdns. SE4 —4L 93
Foxbourne Rd. SW17 —8E 90
Fox Burrow Rd. Chig —4H 33
Foxbury Av. Chst —3B 112
Foxbury Clo. Brom —3F 110
Foxbury Clo. Orp —7E 128
Foxbury Dri. Orp —8E 128
Foxbury Rd. Brom —3E 110
Fox Clo. E1 —7G 61
Fox Clo. E16 —8E 62
Fox Clo. Bush —7M 9
Fox Clo. Els —8H 11
Fox Clo. Orp —7E 128
Fox Clo. Romf —5M 33
Fox Clo. Wey —7B 116
Foxcombe. New Ad —8M 125
(in two parts)
Foxcombe Clo. E6 —5H 63
Foxcombe Rd. SW15 —7E 88
Foxcote. SE5 —6C 76
Foxcroft. WC1 —5K 59
(off Penton Ri.)
Foxcroft Rd. SE18 —9M 79
Foxdell. N'wd —6B 20
Foxearth Rd. S Croy —2F 138
Foxearth Spur. S Croy —1G 139
Foxes Dale. SE3 —2E 94
Foxes Dale. Brom —7B 110
Foxes Dri. Wal X —2A 6
Foxfield. NW1 —4F 58
(off Arlington Rd.)
Foxfield Clo. N'wd —6D 20
Foxfield Rd. Orp —4B 128
Foxglove Clo. S'hall —1J 69
Foxglove Clo. Stanw —7B 144
Foxglove Ct. Wemb —5J 55
Foxglove Gdns. E11 —2G 47
Foxglove Gdns. Purl —3J 137
Foxglove La. Chess —6L 119
Foxglove Rd. Rush G —7C 50
Foxglove St. W12 —1D 72
Foxglove Way. Wall —3F 122
Foxgrove. N14 —3J 27
Fox Gro. W on T —2F 116
Foxgrove Av. Beck —4M 109
Foxgrove Path. Wat —5H 21
Foxgrove Rd. Beck —4M 109
Foxhall Rd. Upm —1M 67
Foxham Rd. N19 —8H 43
Fox Hill. SE19 —4D 108
Fox Hill. Kes —7G 127
Foxhill. Wat —9E 4
Fox Hill Gdns. SE19 —4D 108
Foxhole Rd. SE9 —4J 95
Foxholes. Wey —7B 116
Fox Hollow Clo. SE18 —6C 80
Fox Hollow Dri. Bexh —2H 97
Foxholt Gdns. NW10 —3A 56
Foxhome Clo. Chst —3L 111
Fox Ho. Rd. Belv —5M 81
(in two parts)
Foxlands Clo. Leav & Wat —7E 4
Foxlands Cres. Dag —1A 66
Foxlands La. Dag —1B 66
Foxlands Rd. Dag —1A 66
Fox La. N13 —2K 27
Fox La. W5 —7J 55
(in two parts)
Fox La. Kes —7F 126
Foxleas Ct. Brom —4C 110
Foxlees. Wemb —9E 38
Foxley Clo. E8 —1E 60
Foxley Clo. Lou —4M 19
Foxley Ct. Sutt —9A 122
Foxley Gdns. Purl —5M 137
Foxley Hall. Purl —5L 137
Foxley Hill Rd. Purl —4L 137
Foxley La. Purl —3G 137
Foxley Rd. SW9 —8L 75
Foxley Rd. Kenl —6M 137
Foxley Rd. T Hth —8M 107
Foxleys. Wat —3J 21
Foxley Sq. SW9 —9M 75
Foxmead Clo. Enf —5K 15
Foxmore St. SW11 —9D 74
Fox Rd. E16 —8D 62
Fox's Path. Mitc —6C 106
Foxton Gro. Mitc —6B 106
Foxton Ho. E16 —3L 79
(off Albert Rd.)
Foxtree Ho. Wat —9J 5
Foxwarren. Clay —1D 132
Foxwell M. SE4 —2J 93
Foxwell St. SE4 —2J 93
Foxwood Chase. Wal A —8J 7
Foxwood Clo. NW7 —4C 24
Foxwood Clo. Felt —9F 84
Foxwood Grn. Clo. Enf —8C 16
Foxwood Rd. SE3 —3D 94
Foyle Rd. N17 —8E 28
Foyle Rd. SE3 —7D 78
Framfield Clo. N12 —3L 25
Framfield Ct. Enf —8C 16
(off Queen Annes Gdns.)
Framfield Rd. N5 —1M 59
Framfield Rd. W7 —9C 54
Framfield Rd. Mitc —4E 106
Framlingham Clo. E5 —7G 45
Framlingham Cres. SE9 —1J 111
Frampton. NW1 —3H 59
(off Wrotham Rd.)
Frampton Clo. Sutt —9L 121
Frampton Ct. W3 —3A 72
(off Cheltenham Pl.)

Frampton Ho.—Fursby Av.

Frampton Ho. NW8 —7B 58
(off Frampton St.)
Frampton Pk. Est. E9 —3G 61
Frampton Pk. Rd. E9 —2G 61
Frampton Rd. Houn —4J 85
Frampton St. W2 —7B 58
Francemary Rd. SE4 —4L 93
Frances Ct. E17 —4L 45
Frances Gray Ho. E1 —8H 61
(off Tralagar Gdns.)
Frances Rd. E4 —6L 29
Frances St. SE18 —4K 79
Franche Ct. Rd. SW17 —9A 90
Francis Av. Bexh —1L 97
Francis Av. Felt —9E 84
Francis Av. Ilf —7B 48
Francis Barber Clo. SW16 —2K 107
Franciscan Rd. SW17 —2D 106
Francis Chichester Way. SW11 —9E 74
Francis Clo. E14 —5B 78
Francis Clo. Eps —6B 120
Francis Ct. EC1 —8M 59
(off Briset St.)
Francis Ct. NW7 —5D 24
(off Watford Way)
Francis Ct. SE14 —7H 77
(off Myers La.)
Francis Ct. Surb —8J 103
(off Cranes Pk. Av.)
Francis Greene Ho. Wal A —6H 7
(off Grove Ct.)
Francis Gro. SW19 —3K 105
(in two parts)
Francis Ho. E17 —4K 45
Francis Ho. N1 —4C 60
(off Colville Est.)
Francis M. SE12 —6E 94
Francis Rd. E10 —6A 46
Francis Rd. N2 —2D 42
Francis Rd. Croy —2M 123
Francis Rd. Dart —4H 99
Francis Rd. Gnfd —5F 54
Francis Rd. Harr —3E 38
Francis Rd. Houn —1H 85
Francis Rd. Ilf —7B 48
Francis Rd. Orp —7H 113
Francis Rd. Pinn —3G 37
Francis Rd. Wall —8G 123
Francis Rd. Wat —6F 8
Francis St. E15 —1C 62
Francis St. SW1 —5G 75
Francis St. Ilf —7B 48
Francis Ter. N19 —8G 43
Francis Wlk. N1 —4K 59
Francklyn Gdns. Edgw —3L 23
Francombe Gdns. Romf —3E 50
Franconia Rd. SW4 —4H 91
Frank Bailey Wlk. E12 —1L 63
Frank Beswick Ho. SW6 —7K 73
(off Clem Attlee Ct.)
Frank Burton Clo. SE7 —6F 78
Frank Dixon Clo. SE21 —6C 92
Frank Dixon Way. SE21 —7C 92
Frankfurt Rd. SE24 —4A 92
Frankham Ho. SE8 —8L 77
(off Frankham St.)
Frankham St. SE8 —8L 77
Frank Ho. SW8 —8J 75
(off Wyvil Rd.)
Frankland Clo. SE16 —4F 76
Frankland Clo. Wfd G —5G 31
Frankland Rd. E4 —5L 29
Frankland Rd. SW7 —4B 74
Frankland Rd. Crox G —8A 8
Franklin Av. Chesh —3B 6
Franklin Building. E14 —3L 77
Franklin Clo. N20 —9A 14
Franklin Clo. SE13 —9M 77
Franklin Clo. SE27 —9M 91
Franklin Clo. King T —7L 103
Franklin Cotts. Stan —4F 22
Franklin Cres. Mitc —8G 107
Franklin Ho. E1 —2F 76
(off Watts St.)
Franklin Pas. SE9 —2J 95
Franklin Rd. SE20 —4G 109
Franklin Rd. Bexh —9J 81
Franklin Rd. Horn —2G 67
Franklin Rd. Wat —4F 8
Franklins M. Harr —7A 38
Franklin Sq. W14 —6K 73
Franklin's Row. SW3 —6D 74
Franklin St. E3 —6M 61
Franklin St. N15 —4C 44
Franklin Way. Croy —2J 123
Franklyn Gdns. Ilf —6B 32
Franklyn Rd. NW10 —2D 56
Franklyn Rd. W on T —1E 116
Frank Martin Ct. Chesh —3B 6
Franks Av. N Mald —8A 104
Franks La. Hort K —9M 115
Frank Soskice Ho. SW6 —7K 73
(off Clem Attlee Ct.)
Frank St. E13 —7E 62
Franks Wood Av. Orp —9M 111
Frankswood Av. W Dray —9D 142
Frank Towell Ct. Felt —6E 84
Frank Welsh Ct. Pinn —2G 37
Frank Whymark Ho. SE16 —3G 77
(off Rupack St.)
Franlaw Cres. N13 —4A 28
Franmil Rd. Horn —6E 50
Fransfield Gro. SE26 —9F 92
Frans Hals Ct. E14 —4A 78
Frant Clo. SE20 —4G 109
Franthorne Way. SE6 —8M 93
Frant Rd. T Hth —9M 107
Fraser Clo. E6 —9J 63
Fraser Clo. Bex —7A 98
Fraser Ct. E14 —6A 78
(off Ferry St.)
Fraser Ho. Bren —6K 71
Fraser Rd. E17 —3M 45
Fraser Rd. N9 —3F 28
Fraser Rd. Chesh —1E 6
Fraser Rd. Eri —6A 82
Fraser Rd. Gnfd —4F 54
Fraser St. W4 —6C 72
Frating Cres. Wfd G —6F 30
Frays Av. W Dray —3H 143
Frays Clo. W Dray —4H 143
Frayslea. Uxb —5A 142
Frays Waye. Uxb —4A 142
Frazer Av. Ruis —1G 53
Frazer Clo. Romf —5D 50
Frazier St. SE1 —3L 75
Frean St. SE16 —4E 76
Frearson Ho. WC1 —6K 59
(off Penton Ri.)
Freda Corbett Clo. SE15 —8E 76
Frederica Rd. E4 —9B 18
Frederica St. N7 —3K 59
Frederick Charrington Ho. E1 —7G 61
(off Wickford St.)
Frederick Clo. W2 —1D 74
Frederick Clo. Sutt —6K 121
Frederick Cres. SW9 —8M 75
Frederick Cres. Enf —4G 17
Frederick Gdns. Croy —1M 123
Frederick Gdns. Sutt —6K 121
Frederick Pl. SE18 —6M 79
Frederick Rd. SE17 —7M 75
Frederick Rd. Rain —5B 66
Frederick Rd. Sutt —7K 121
Frederick's Pl. EC2 —9B 60
Fredericks Pl. N12 —4A 26
Frederick Sq. SE16 —1J 77
(off Sovereign Cres.)
Frederick's Row. EC1 —6M 59
Frederick St. WC1 —6K 59
Frederick Ter. E8 —3D 60
Frederic M. SW1 —3D 74
(off Kinnerton St.)
Frederic St. E17 —3J 45
Fredora Av. Hay —7D 52
Fred Styles Ho. SE7 —7G 79
Fred White Wlk. N7 —2J 59
Freeborne Gdns. Rain —2E 66
Freedom Clo. E17 —2H 45
Freedom Rd. N17 —9B 28
Freedom St. SW11 —1D 90
Freedown La. Sutt —5M 135
Freegrove Rd. N7 —1J 59
(in two parts)
Freehold Ind. Cen. Houn —4G 85
Freeland Ct. Sidc —9E 96
Freeland Pk. NW4 —9J 25
Freeland Rd. W5 —1K 71
Freelands Av. S Croy —1H 139
Freelands Gro. Brom —5F 110
Freelands Rd. Brom —5F 110
Freeland Way. Eri —9E 82
Freeling Ho. NW8 —4B 58
(off Dorman Way)
Freeling St. N1 —3J 59
(in two parts)
Freeman Clo. N'holt —3J 53
Freeman Clo. Shep —8C 100
Freeman Dri. W Mol —8K 101
Freeman Rd. Mord —9B 106
Freemans La. Hay —1C 68
Freemantle Av. Enf —7H 17
Freemantle Ho. E1 —7F 60
(off Somerford St.)
Freemantle St. SE17 —6C 76
Freeman Way. Horn —4K 51
Freemasons Rd. E16 —8F 62
Freemasons Rd. Croy —3C 124
Freesia Clo. Orp —7D 128
Freethorpe Clo. SE19 —4B 108
Free Trade Wharf. E1 —1H 77
Freezeland Way. Hil & Uxb —2F 142
Freezy Water. —9D 6
Freightmaster Est. Rain —9C 66
Freke Rd. SW11 —2E 90
Fremantle Rd. Belv —5L 81
Fremantle Rd. Ilf —9M 31
Fremont St. E9 —4F 60
French Apartments, The. Purl —4L 137
French Ordinary Ct. EC3 —1C 76
(off Crutched Friars)
French Pl. E1 —6C 60
French St. Sun —6G 101
Frendsbury Rd. SE4 —3J 93
Frensham. Chesh —1A 6
Frensham Clo. S'hall —7K 53
Frensham Dri. SW15 —9D 88
Frensham Dri. New Ad —9A 126
Frensham Rd. SE9 —8B 96
Frensham Rd. Kenl —6M 137
Frensham St. SE15 —7E 76
Frensham Way. Eps —8G 135
Frere St. SW11 —1C 90
Fresham Ho. Brom —7D 110
(off Durham Rd.)
Freshfield Av. E8 —3D 60
Freshfield Clo. SE13 —3B 94
Freshfield Dri. N14 —9F 14
Freshfields. Croy —3K 125
Freshfields Av. Upm —1M 67
Freshford St. SW17 —9A 90
Freshmount Gdns. Eps —3M 133
Freshwater Clo. SW17 —3E 106
Freshwater Ct. W1 —8C 58
(off Crawford St.)
Freshwater Ct. S'hall —6L 53
Freshwater Rd. SW17 —3E 106
Freshwater Rd. Dag —6H 49
Freshwell Av. Romf —2G 49
Fresh Wharf Rd. Bark —4M 63
Freshwood Clo. Beck —5M 109
Freshwood Way. Wall —1F 136
Freston Gdns. Barn —7E 14
Freston Pk. N3 —9K 25
Freston Rd. W10 & W11 —1H 73
Freswick Ho. SE8 —5H 77
(off Chilton Gro.)
Freta Rd. Bexh —4K 97
Freud Mus., The. —2A 58
(off Maresfield Gdns.)
Frewell Ho. EC1 —8L 59
(off Bourne Est.)
Frewing Clo. Chst —3K 111
Frewin Rd. SW18 —7B 90
Friar M. SE27 —9M 91
Friar Rd. Hay —7H 53
Friar Rd. Orp —9E 112
Friars Av. N20 —3C 26
Friars Av. SW15 —9D 88
Friars Clo. E4 —3A 30
Friars Clo. SE1 —2M 75
(off Bear La.)
Friars Clo. N'holt —6H 53
Friars Ct. E17 —8L 29
Friars Gdns. W3 —9B 56
Friars Ga. Clo. Wfd G —4E 30
Friars La. Rich —4H 87
Friars Mead. E14 —4A 78
Friars M. SE9 —4L 95
Friars Pl. La. W3 —1B 72
Friars Rd. E6 —4H 63
Friars Stile Pl. Rich —5J 87
Friars Stile Rd. Rich —5J 87
Friars, The. Chig —4C 32
Friar St. EC4 —9M 59
Friars Wlk. N14 —9F 14
Friars Wlk. SE2 —6H 81
Friars Way. W3 —9B 56
Friars Way. Bush —3K 9
Friarswood. Croy —1J 139
Friary Clo. N12 —5C 26
Friary Ct. SW1 —2G 75
(off St James' Pal.)
Friary Est. SE15 —7E 76
(in two parts)
Friary La. Wfd G —4E 30
Friary Pk. Ct. W3 —9A 56
Friary Rd. N12 —4B 26
Friary Rd. SE15 —8E 76
Friary Rd. W3 —9A 56
Friary, The. Wal X —6F 6
Friary Way. N12 —4C 26
Friday Hill. —2C 30
Friday Hill. E4 —2C 30
Friday Hill E. E4 —3C 30
Friday Hill W. E4 —2C 30
Friday Rd. Eri —6B 82
Friday Rd. Mitc —4D 106
Friday St. EC4 —1A 76
Frideswide Pl. NW5 —1G 59
Friendly Pl. SE13 —9M 77
Friendly St. SE8 —1L 93
Friendly St. M. SE8 —1L 93
Friends Av. Chesh —5D 6
Friendship Wlk. N'holt —6H 53
Friends Rd. Croy —5B 124
Friends Rd. Purl —4M 137
Friend St. EC1 —6M 59
Friends Wlk. Uxb —3B 142
Friern Barnet. —5D 26
Friern Barnet La. N20 & N11 —2B 26
Friern Barnet Rd. N11 —5D 26
Friern Bri. Retail Pk. N11 —6F 26
Friern Ct. N20 —3B 26
Friern Mt. Dri. N20 —9A 14
Friern Pk. N12 —5A 26
Friern Rd. SE22 —6E 92
Friern Watch Av. N12 —4A 26
Frigate Ho. E14 —5A 78
(off Stebondale St.)
Frigate M. SE8 —7L 77
Frimley Av. Horn —6L 51
Frimley Av. Wall —7J 123
Frimley Clo. SW19 —8J 89
Frimley Clo. New Ad —9A 126
Frimley Ct. Sidc —2G 113
Frimley Cres. New Ad —9A 126
Frimley Gdns. Mitc —7C 106
Frimley Rd. Chess —7H 119
Frimley Rd. Ilf —8C 48
Frimley St. E1 —7H 61
(off Frimley Way)
Frimley Way. E1 —7H 61
Fringewood Clo. N'wd —8A 20
Frinstead Ho. W10 —1H 73
(off Freston Rd.)
Frinsted Gro. Orp —8H 113
Frinsted Rd. Eri —8B 82
Frinton Clo. Wat —2F 20
Frinton Ct. W13 —8F 54
(off Hardwick Grn.)
Frinton Dri. Wfd G —7B 30
Frinton M. Ilf —4L 47
Frinton Rd. E6 —6H 63
Frinton Rd. N15 —4C 44
Frinton Rd. SW17 —3E 106
Frinton Rd. Romf —7K 33
Frinton Rd. Sidc —8J 97
Friston Path. Chig —5C 32
Friston St. SW6 —1M 89
Friswell Pl. Bexh —3L 97
Fritham Clo. N Mald —1C 120
Frith Ct. NW7 —7J 25
Frith Ho. NW8 —7B 58
(off Frampton St.)
Frith Knowle. W on T —8F 116
Frith La. NW7 —7J 25
Frith Rd. E11 —9A 46
Frith Rd. Croy —4A 124
Frith St. W1 —9H 59
Frithville Gdns. W12 —2G 73
Frithwood Av. N'wd —6C 20
Frizlands La. Dag —7M 49
Frobisher Clo. Bush —8L 9
Frobisher Clo. Kenl —9A 138
Frobisher Clo. Pinn —5H 37
Frobisher Ct. NW9 —9C 24
Frobisher Ct. SE10 —7B 78
(off Old Woolwich Rd.)
Frobisher Ct. SE23 —8F 92
Frobisher Ct. W12 —3G 73
(off Lime Gro.)
Frobisher Ct. Sutt —9J 121
Frobisher Cres. EC2 —8A 60
(off Beech St.)
Frobisher Cres. Stai —6C 144
Frobisher Gdns. E10 —5M 45
Frobisher Gdns. Stai —6C 144
Frobisher Ho. E1 —2F 76
(off Watts St.)
Frobisher Ho. SW1 —7H 75
(off Dolphin Sq.)
Frobisher Pas. E14 —2L 77
Frobisher Rd. E6 —9K 63
Frobisher Rd. N8 —2L 43
Frobisher Rd. Eri —8D 82
Frobisher St. SE10 —7C 78
Froghall La. Chig —4B 32
Frog La. Frog —8B 66
Frogley Rd. SE22 —3D 92
Frogmore. SW18 —4L 89
Frogmore Av. Hay —7C 52
Frogmore Clo. Sutt —5H 121
Frogmore Cotts. Wat —7H 9
Frogmore Ct. S'hall —5K 69
Frogmore Gdns. Hay —7C 52
Frogmore Gdns. Sutt —6J 121
Frogmore Ind. Est. N5 —1A 60
Frogmore Ind. Est. NW10 —6A 56
Frogmore Ind. Est. Hay —3C 68
Frognal. NW3 —9A 42
Frognal Av. Harr —2D 38
Frognal Av. Sidc —3E 112
Frognal Clo. NW3 —1A 58
Frognal Corner. (Junct.) —3D 112
Frognal Ct. NW3 —2A 58
Frognal Gdns. NW3 —9A 42
Frognal La. NW3 —1M 57
Frognal Pde. NW3 —2A 58
Frognal Pl. Sidc —3E 112
Frognal Ri. NW3 —8A 42
Frognal Way. NW3 —9A 42
Froissart Rd. SE9 —4H 95
Frome Ho. SE15 —3F 92
Frome Rd. N15 —1M 43
Frome St. N1 —5A 60
Fromondes Rd. Sutt —7J 121
Frontenac. NW10 —3F 56
Frostic Wlk. E1 —8E 60
(off Hopetown St.)
Froude St. SW8 —1F 90
Fruen Rd. Felt —6D 84
Fruiterers Pas. EC4 —1A 76
(off Queen St. Pl.)
Fryatt Rd. N17 —7B 28
(in two parts)
Fryatt St. E14 —9C 62
Fry Clo. Romf —5L 33
Fryent Clo. NW9 —4L 39
Fryent Country Pk. —5M 39
Fryent Cres. NW9 —4C 40
Fryent Fields. NW9 —4C 40
Fryent Gro. NW9 —4C 40
Fryent Way. NW9 —3L 39
Fry Ho. E7 —3G 63
Frying Pan All. E1 —8D 60
(off Bell La.)
Frylands Ct. New Ad —3A 140
Fry Rd. E6 —3H 63
Fry Rd. NW10 —4D 56
Fryston Av. Coul —6F 136
Fryston Av. Croy —4E 124
Fuchsia Clo. Rush G —7C 50
Fuchsia St. SE2 —6F 80
Fulbeck Dri. NW9 —8C 24
Fulbeck Ho. N7 —2K 59
(off Sutterton St.)
Fulbeck Rd. N19 —9G 43
Fulbeck Wlk. Edgw —2M 23
Fulbeck Way. Harr —9A 22
Fulbourn. King T —6L 103
(off Eureka Rd.)
Fulbourne Rd. E17 —8A 30
Fulbourne St. E1 —8F 60
Fulbrook M. N19 —9G 43
Fulcher Ho. N1 —4C 60
(off Colville Ho.)
Fulcher Ho. SE8 —6K 77
Fulford Gro. Wat —2F 20
Fulford Ho. Eps —9B 120
Fulford Rd. Eps —9B 120
Fulford St. SE16 —3F 76
Fulham. —1J 89
Fulham Broadway. (Junct.) —8L 73
Fulham B'way. SW6 —8L 73
Fulham Clo. Uxb —7A 52
Fulham Ct. SW6 —9L 73
Fulham F.C. —9H 73
Fulham High St. SW6 —1J 89
Fulham Pal. Rd. W6 & SW6 —6G 73
Fulham Pk. Gdns. SW6 —1K 89
Fulham Pk. Rd. SW6 —1K 89
Fulham Rd. SW6 —1J 89
Fulham Rd. SW10 & SW3 —7A 74
Fullbrooks Av. Wor Pk —3D 120
Fuller Clo. E2 —7E 60
(off Cheshire St.)
Fuller Clo. Orp —7D 128
Fuller Gdns. Wat —1F 8
Fuller Rd. Dag —8F 48
Fuller Rd. Wat —1F 8
Fullers Av. E18 —7D 30
Fullers Av. Surb —4K 119
Fullers Clo. Romf —7A 34
Fullers Clo. Wal A —6M 7
Fuller's Griffin Brewery & Vis. Cen. —7D 72
Fullers La. Romf —7A 34
Fullers Rd. E18 —7D 30
Fuller St. NW4 —2G 41
Fullers Way N. Surb —5K 119
Fullers Way S. Chess —6J 119
Fuller's Wood. Croy —7L 125
Fullerton Ct. Tedd —3E 102
Fullerton Rd. SW18 —4M 89
Fullerton Rd. Cars —1C 136
Fullerton Rd. Croy —2D 124
Fuller Way. Hay —6D 68
Fullwell Av. Ilf —8K 31
Fullwell Cross. Ilf —9B 32
Fullwell Pde. Ilf —8L 31
Fullwood's M. N1 —6B 60
Fulmar Ct. Surb —1K 119
Fulmar Ho. SE16 —5H 77
(off Tawny Way)
Fulmar Rd. Horn —3E 66
Fulmead St. SW6 —9M 73
Fulmer Clo. Hamp —2J 101
Fulmer Ho. NW1 —7C 58
(off Rossmore Rd.)
Fulmer Rd. E16 —8H 63
Fulmer Way. W13 —4F 70
Fulneck. E1 —8G 61
(off Mile End Rd.)
Fulready Rd. E10 —3B 46
Fulstone Clo. Houn —3K 85
Fulthorp Rd. SE3 —1D 94
Fulton Ct. Borwd —2K 11
(off Aycliffe Rd.)
Fulton M. W2 —1A 74
(off Porchester Ter.)
Fulton Rd. Wemb —8L 39
Fulwell. —1B 102
Fulwell Ct. S'hall —1A 70
(off Baird Av.)
Fulwell Cross. —9A 32
Fulwell Pk. Av. Twic —8M 85
Fulwell Rd. Tedd —1B 102
Fulwich Rd. Dart —5K 99
Fulwood Av. Wemb —5K 55
Fulwood Clo. Hay —9D 52
Fulwood Ct. Kent —4E 38
Fulwood Gdns. Twic —5D 86
Fulwood Pl. WC1 —8K 59
Fulwood Wlk. SW19 —7J 89
Furber St. W6 —4F 72
Furham Fld. Pinn —7L 21
Furley Ho. SE15 —8E 76
(off Peckham Pk. Rd.)
Furley Rd. SE15 —8E 76
Furlong Clo. Wall —3F 122
Furlong Path. N'holt —2J 53
(off Arnold Rd.)
Furlong Rd. N7 —2L 59
Furmage St. SW18 —6M 89
Furneaux Av. SE27 —2M 107
Furner Clo. Dart —2D 98
Furness Ho. SW1 —6F 74
(off Abbots Mnr.)
Furness Rd. NW10 —5E 56
Furness Rd. SW6 —1M 89
Furness Rd. Harr —5M 37
Furness Rd. Mord —1M 121
Furness Way. Horn —1E 66
Furnival Mans. W1 —8G 59
(off Wells St.)
Furnival St. EC4 —9L 59
Furrow La. E9 —1G 61
Furrows, The. W on T —4G 117
Fursby Av. N3 —6L 25

Fursecroft—Gateway

Fursecroft. W1 —9D 58
(off George St.)
Further Acre. NW9 —9D 24
Furtherfield. Ab L —5C 4
Furtherfield Clo. Croy —1L 123
Further Grn. Rd. SE6 —6C 94
Furze Clo. Wat —5G 21
Furzedown. —2F 106
Furzedown Dri. SW17 —2F 106
Furzedown Rd. SW17 —2F 106
Furzedown Rd. Sutt —3A 136
Furze Farm Clo. Romf —9J 33
Furzefield. Chesh —1B 6
Furze Fld. Oxs —5B 132
Furzefield Clo. Chst —3M 111
Furzefield Rd. SE3 —7F 78
Furzeground Way. Uxb —2A 68
Furzeham Rd. W Dray —3J 143
Furze Hill. Purl —3J 137
Furzehill Pde. Borwd —5L 11
Furzehill Rd. Borwd —6L 11
(in two parts)
Furzehill Sq. St M —8F 112
Furze La. Purl —3J 137
Furze Rd. T Hth —7A 108
Furze St. E3 —8L 61
Furzewood. Sun —5E 100
Fye Foot La. EC4 —1A 76
(off Queen Victoria St., in two parts)
Fyfe Way. Brom —6E 110
Fyfield. N4 —7L 43
(off Six Acres Est.)
Fyfield Clo. Brom —8B 110
Fyfield Ct. E7 —2E 62
Fyfield Ho. E6 —4J 63
(off Ron Leighton Way)
Fyfield Rd. E17 —1B 46
Fyfield Rd. SW9 —2L 91
Fyfield Rd. Enf —5C 16
Fyfield Rd. Rain —4D 66
Fyfield Rd. Wfd G —7G 31
Fynes St. SW1 —5H 75

Gable Clo. Ab L —5C 4
Gable Clo. Dart —4E 98
Gable Clo. Pinn —7L 21
Gable Ct. SE26 —1F 108
Gables Av. Borwd —5K 11
Gables Clo. SE5 —9C 76
Gables Clo. SE12 —7E 94
Gables Lodge. Barn —2A 14
Gables, The. N10 —1E 42
(off Fortis Grn.)
Gables, The. Bans —9K 135
Gables, The. Bark —2A 64
Gables, The. Brom —4F 110
Gables, The. Leav —6H 5
Gables, The. Oxs —4A 132
Gables, The. Wat —9G 9
Gables, The. Wemb —8L 39
Gabriel Clo. Felt —1J 101
Gabriel Clo. Romf —7A 34
Gabriel Ho. SE11 —5K 75
Gabrielle Clo. Wemb —8K 39
Gabrielle Ct. NW3 —2B 58
Gabriel St. SE23 —6H 93
Gabriels Wharf. SE1 —2L 75
Gad Clo. E13 —6F 62
Gaddesden Av. Wemb —2K 55
Gaddesden Cres. Wat —7H 5
Gaddesden Ho. EC1 —6B 60
(off Cranwood St.)
Gade Av. Wat —6C 8
Gade Bank. Wat —6B 8
Gadebridge Ho. SW3 —6C 74
(off Cale St.)
Gade Clo. Hay —2F 68
Gade Clo. Wat —6C 8
Gadesden Rd. Eps —8A 120
(in two parts)
Gade Side. Wat —8C 4
Gade Vw. Gdns. K Lan —5A 4
Gadsbury Clo. NW9 —4D 40
Gadsden Ho. W10 —7J 57
(off Hazlewood Cres.)
Gadswell Clo. Wat —9H 5
Gadwall Clo. E16 —9F 62
Gadwall Way. SE28 —3B 80
Gage Rd. E16 —8C 62
Gage St. WC1 —8J 59
Gainford Ho. E2 —6F 60
(off Ellsworth St.)
Gainford St. N1 —4L 59
Gainsboro Gdns. Gnfd —1C 54
Gainsborough Av. E12 —1L 63
Gainsborough Av. Dart —4G 99
Gainsborough Clo. Beck —4L 109
Gainsborough Clo. Esh —3C 118
Gainsborough Ct. N12 —5M 25
Gainsborough Ct. SE16 —6F 76
(off Stubbs Dri.)
Gainsborough Ct. SE21 —8C 92
Gainsborough Ct. W4 —6M 71
(off Chaseley Dri.)
Gainsborough Ct. W12 —3G 73
Gainsborough Ct. W on T —6E 116
Gainsborough Dri. S Croy —5E 138
Gainsborough Gdns. NW3 —8B 42
Gainsborough Gdns. NW11 —5K 41
Gainsborough Gdns. Edgw —9K 23
Gainsborough Gdns. Iswth —4B 86
Gainsborough Ho. SW1 —5H 75
(off Erasmus St.)
Gainsborough Ho. Dag —9F 48
(off Gainsborough Rd.)
Gainsborough Lodge. Harr —3D 38
(off Hindes Rd.)
Gainsborough Mans. W14 —7J 73
(off Queen's Club Gdns.)
Gainsborough M. SE26 —9F 92
Gainsborough Pl. Chig —3D 32
Gainsborough Rd. E11 —5C 46
Gainsborough Rd. E15 —6C 62
Gainsborough Rd. N12 —5M 25
Gainsborough Rd. W4 —5D 72
Gainsborough Rd. Dag —9F 48
Gainsborough Rd. Eps —2A 134
Gainsborough Rd. Hay —5A 52
Gainsborough Rd. N Mald —1B 120
Gainsborough Rd. Rain —4E 66
Gainsborough Rd. Rich —1K 87
Gainsborough Rd. Wfd G —6J 31
Gainsborough Sq. Bexh —2H 97
Gainsborough Ter. Sutt —9K 121
(off Belmont Ri.)
Gainsborough Tower. N'holt —5H 53
(off Academy Gdns.)
Gainsfield Ct. E11 —8C 46
Gainsford Rd. E17 —2K 45
Gainsford St. SE1 —3D 76
Gairloch Ho. NW1 —3H 59
(off Stratford Vs.)
Gairloch Rd. SE5 —1C 92
Gaisford St. NW5 —2G 59
Gaitskell Ct. SW11 —1C 90
Gaitskell Ho. E6 —4H 63
Gaitskell Ho. E17 —1M 45
Gaitskell Ho. SE17 —7C 76
(off Villa St.)
Gaitskell Rd. SE9 —7A 96
Galahad Rd. Brom —1E 110
Galata Rd. SW13 —8E 72
Galatea Sq. SE15 —2F 92
Galba Ct. Bren —8H 71
Galbraith St. E14 —4A 78
Galdana Av. Barn —5A 14
Galeborough Av. Wfd G —7B 30
Gale Clo. Hamp —3J 101
Gale Clo. Mitc —7B 106
Gale Cres. Bans —9L 135
Galena Ho. W6 —5F 72
(off Galena Rd.)
Galena Rd. W6 —5F 72
Galen Clo. Eps —3L 133
Galen Pl. WC1 —8J 59
Galesbury Rd. SW18 —5A 90
Gales Gdns. E2 —6F 60
Gale St. E3 —8L 61
Gale St. Dag —1G 65
Gales Way. Wfd G —7J 31
Galgate Clo. SW19 —7H 89
Gallants Farm Rd. E Barn —9C 14
Galleon Clo. SE16 —3H 77
Galleon Clo. Eri —5B 82
Galleon Ho. E14 —5A 78
(off Glengarnock Av.)
Gallery Ct. SE1 —3B 76
(off Pilgrimage St.)
Gallery Ct. SW10 —7A 74
Gallery Gdns. N'holt —5H 53
Gallery Rd. SE21 —7B 92
Galley Hill. Wal A —3M 7
Galleyhill Rd. Wal A —6L 7
Galley La. Barn —2E 12
Galleywall Rd. SE16 —5F 76
Galleywall Rd. Trad. Est. SE16 —5F 76
(off Galleywall Rd.)
Galleywood Cres. Romf —6B 34
Galliard Clo. N9 —8G 17
Galliard Ct. N9 —8E 16
Galliard Rd. N9 —9E 16
Gallia Rd. N5 —1M 59
Gallions Clo. Bark —6E 64
Gallions Entrance. E16 —2A 80
Gallions Rd. SE7 —5F 78
(in two parts)
Gallions Vw. Rd. SE28 —3C 80
Galliver Pl. E5 —9F 44
Gallon Clo. SE7 —5G 79
Gallop, The. S Croy —9F 124
Gallop, The. Sutt —1B 136
Gallosson Rd. SE18 —5C 80
Galloway Path. Croy —6B 124
Galloway Rd. W12 —2E 72
Gallows Corner. —9G 35
Gallows Corner. (Junct.) —8G 35
Gallows Hill. K Lan —5A 4
Gallows Hill La. Ab L —5A 4
Gallus Clo. N21 —8K 15
Gallus Sq. SE3 —2F 94
Galpins Rd. T Hth —9J 107
Galsworthy Av. E14 —8J 61
Galsworthy Av. Romf —5F 48
Galsworthy Clo. NW2 —9J 41
Galsworthy Clo. SE28 —2F 80
Galsworthy Ct. W3 —4M 71
(off Bollo Bri. Rd.)
Galsworthy Cres. SE3 —9G 79
Galsworthy Ho. W11 —9J 57
Galsworthy Rd. NW2 —9J 41
Galsworthy Rd. King T —4M 103
Galsworthy Ter. N16 —8C 44
Galton St. W10 —6J 57
Galva Clo. Barn —6E 14
Galvani Way. Croy —3K 123
Galveston Ho. E1 —7J 61
(off Harford St.)
Galveston Rd. SW15 —4K 89
Galway Clo. SE16 —6F 76
(off Masters Dri.)
Galway Ho. E1 —8H 61
(off White Horse La.)
Galway Ho. EC1 —6A 60
(off Radnor St.)
Galway St. EC1 —6A 60
Galy. NW9 —9D 24
Gambetta St. SW8 —1F 90
Gambia St. SE1 —2M 75
Gambier Ho. EC1 —6A 60
(off Mora St.)
Gambole Rd. SW17 —1C 106
Games Rd. Barn —5D 14
Gamlen Rd. SW15 —3H 89
Gammons Farm Clo. Wat —9D 4
Gammons La. Wat —9C 4
(in two parts)
Gamuel Clo. E17 —4L 45
Gander Grn. Cres. Hamp —5L 101
Gander Grn. La. Sutt —4J 121
Ganders Ash. Wat —6E 4
Gandhi Clo. E17 —4L 45
Gandhi Ct. Wat —4H 9
Gandolfi St. SE15 —7C 76
Gant Ct. Wal A —7M 7
Ganton St. W1 —1G 75
Ganton Wlk. Wat —4H 21
Gants Hill. —4L 47
Gants Hill. (Junct.) —4L 47
Gantshill Cres. Ilf —3L 47
Gants Hill Cross. Ilf —4L 47
Gap Rd. SW19 —2L 105
Garage Rd. W3 —9L 55
Garbett Ho. SE17 —7M 75
(off Doddington Gro.)
Garbrand Wlk. Eps —1D 134
Garbutt Pl. W1 —8E 58
Garden Av. Bexh —2L 97
Garden Av. Mitc —4F 106
Garden City. Edgw —6L 23
Garden Clo. E4 —5L 29
Garden Clo. SE12 —9F 94
Garden Clo. SW15 —6G 89
Garden Clo. Ark —6G 13
Garden Clo. Ashf —3A 100
Garden Clo. Bans —7L 135
Garden Clo. Hamp —2K 101
Garden Clo. N'holt —4J 53
Garden Clo. Ruis —7C 36
Garden Clo. Wall —7J 123
Garden Clo. Wat —4D 8
Garden Cotts. St P —6G 113
Garden Ct. W4 —4A 72
Garden Ct. WC2 —1L 75
(off Temple)
Garden Ct. Croy —4D 124
Garden Ct. Hamp —2K 101
Garden Ct. Rich —9K 71
Garden Ct. Stan —5G 23
Gardener Gro. Felt —8K 85
Gardeners Clo. N11 —2E 26
Gardeners Rd. Croy —3M 123
Garden Ho. N2 —9B 26
(off Grange, The)
Gardenia Rd. Enf —8C 16
Gardenia Way. Wfd G —6E 30
Garden La. SW2 —7K 91
Garden La. Brom —3F 110
Garden M. W2 —1L 73
Garden Pl. E8 —4D 60
Garden Pl. Dart —9H 99
Garden Rd. NW8 —6A 58
Garden Rd. SE20 —5G 109
Garden Rd. Ab L —4C 4
Garden Rd. Brom —4F 110
Garden Rd. Rich —2L 87
Garden Rd. W on T —1F 116
Garden Row. SE1 —4M 75
Gardens, The. N8 —2J 43
(in two parts)
Gardens, The. SE22 —3E 92
Gardens, The. Beck —5A 110
Gardens, The. Esh —6L 117
Gardens, The. Felt —4B 84
Gardens, The. Harr —4A 38
Gardens, The. Pinn —4K 37
Gardens, The. Wat —4D 8
Garden St. E1 —8H 61
Garden Ter. SW1 —6H 75
Garden Ter. SW7 —3C 74
(off Trevor Pl.)
Garden Vw. E7 —9G 47
Garden Wlk. EC2 —6C 60
Garden Wlk. Beck —5K 109
Garden Way. NW10 —2A 56
Garden Way. Lou —2L 19
Gardiner Av. NW2 —1G 57
Gardiner Clo. Enf —8H 17
Gardiner Clo. Orp —6G 113
Gardiner Ct. NW10 —4B 56
Gardiner Ct. S Croy —8A 124
Gardiners Clo. Dag —9H 49
Gardner Clo. E11 —4F 46
Gardner Ho. Felt —8K 85
Gardner Ho. S'hall —1H 69
(off Broadway, The)
Gardner Ind. Est. SE26 —2K 109
Gardner Rd. E13 —7F 62
Gardners La. EC4 —1A 76
Gardnor Rd. NW3 —9B 42
Gard St. EC1 —6M 59
Garendon Gdns. Mord —2M 121
Garendon Rd. Mord —2M 121
Garenne Ct. E4 —1A 30
Gareth Clo. Wor Pk —4H 121
Gareth Ct. SW16 —9H 91
Gareth Ct. Borwd —2K 11
(off Aycliffe Rd.)
Gareth Gro. Brom —1E 110
Garfield. Enf —7B 16
(off Private Rd.)
Garfield M. SW11 —2E 90
Garfield Rd. E4 —1B 30
Garfield Rd. E13 —7D 62
Garfield Rd. SW11 —2E 90
Garfield Rd. SW19 —2A 106
Garfield Rd. Enf —6G 17
Garfield Rd. Twic —7E 86
Garfield St. Wat —2F 8
Garford St. E14 —1L 77
Garganey Ct. NW10 —2B 56
(off Elgar Av.)
Garganey Wlk. SE28 —1G 81
Garibaldi St. SE18 —5C 80
Garland Clo. Chesh —4E 6
Garland Rd. SE18 —8B 80
Garland Rd. Stan —8J 23
Garlands Ct. Croy —6B 124
(off Chatsworth Rd.)
Garland Way. Horn —2J 51
Garlichill Rd. Eps —9F 134
Garlick Hill. EC4 —1A 76
Garlies Rd. SE23 —9J 93
Garlinge Rd. NW2 —2K 57
Garman Clo. N18 —5B 28
Garman Rd. N17 —7G 29
Garnault M. EC1 —6L 59
(off Rosebery Av.)
Garnault Pl. EC1 —6L 59
Garnault Rd. Enf —2D 16
Garner Clo. Dag —6H 49
Garner Rd. E17 —8A 30
Garner St. E2 —5E 60
Garnet Ho. E1 —2G 77
(off Garnet St.)
Garnet Rd. NW10 —2C 56
Garnet Rd. T Hth —8A 108
Garnet St. E1 —1G 77
Garnett Clo. SE9 —2K 95
Garnett Clo. Wat —1H 9
Garnett Dri. Brick W —2K 5
Garnett Rd. NW3 —1D 58
Garnett Way. E17 —8J 29
(off Swansland Gdns.)
Garnet Wlk. E6 —8J 63
Garnham Clo. N16 —7D 44
Garnham St. N16 —7D 44
Garnies Clo. SE15 —8D 76
Garrad's Rd. SW16 —9H 91
Garrard Clo. Bexh —2L 97
Garrard Clo. Chst —2M 111
Garrard Rd. Bans —8L 135
Garrard Wlk. NW10 —2C 56
Garratt Clo. Croy —6J 123
Garratt Ct. SW18 —6M 89
Garratt La. SW18 & SW17 —5M 89
Garratt Rd. Edgw —7L 23
Garratts La. Bans —8K 135
Garratts Rd. Bush —9A 10
Garratt Ter. SW17 —1C 106
Garrett Clo. W3 —8B 56
Garrett St. EC1 —7A 60
Garrick Av. NW11 —4J 41
Garrick Clo. SW18 —3A 90
Garrick Clo. W5 —7J 55
Garrick Clo. Rich —4H 87
Garrick Clo. W on T —6F 116
Garrick Cres. Croy —4C 124
Garrick Dri. NW4 —9G 25
Garrick Dri. SE28 —4B 80
Garrick Gdns. W Mol —7L 101
Garrick Ho. W1 —2F 74
Garrick Ho. W4 —7C 72
Garrick Ho. King T —8J 103
(off Surbiton Rd.)
Garrick Ind. Est. NW9 —3D 40
Garrick Pk. NW4 —9H 25
Garrick Rd. NW9 —4D 40
Garrick Rd. Gnfd —7M 53
Garrick Rd. Rich —1L 87
Garrick St. WC2 —1J 75
Garrick Theatre. —1H 75
(off Charing Cross Rd.)
Garrick Way. NW4 —2H 41
Garrick Yd. WC2 —1J 75
(off St Martin's La.)
Garrison Clo. SE18 —8L 79
Garrison Clo. Houn —4K 85
Garrison La. Chess —9H 119
Garrison Pde. Purf —5L 83
Garrolds Clo. Swan —6B 114
Garrowsfield. Barn —8K 13
Garry Clo. Romf —7C 34
Garry Way. Romf —7C 34
Garsdale Clo. N11 —6E 26
Garsdale Ter. W14 —6K 73
(off Aisgill Av.)
Garside Clo. SE28 —4B 80
Garside Clo. Hamp —3M 101
Garsington M. SE4 —2K 93
Garsmouth Way. Wat —9H 5
Garson Clo. Esh —8K 117
Garson Ho. W2 —1B 74
(off Gloucester Ter.)
Garston. —8G 5
Garston Cres. Wat —7G 5
Garston Dri. Wat —7G 5
Garston Gdns. Kenl —7B 138
Garston Ho. N1 —3M 59
(off Sutton Est., The)
Garston La. Kenl —6B 138
Garston La. Wat —7H 5
Garston Pk. Pde. Wat —7H 5
Garter Way. SE16 —3H 77
Garth Clo. W4 —6B 72
Garth Clo. King T —2K 103
Garth Clo. Mord —2H 121
Garth Clo. Ruis —6H 37
Garth Ct. W4 —6B 72
Garth Ct. Harr —4D 38
(off Northwick Pk. Rd.)
Garthland Dri. Barn —7F 12
Garth M. W5 —7J 55
Garthorne Rd. SE23 —6H 93
Garth Rd. NW2 —7K 41
Garth Rd. W4 —6B 72
Garth Rd. King T —2K 103
Garth Rd. Mord —1G 121
Garth Rd. Ind. Est. Mord —3H 121
Garthside. Ham —2J 103
Garth, The. Ab L —6B 4
Garth, The. Hamp —3M 101
Garth, The. Harr —4K 39
Garthway. N12 —6C 26
Gartlet Rd. Wat —5G 9
Gartmoor Gdns. SW19 —7K 89
Gartmore Rd. Ilf —7D 48
Garton Pl. SW18 —5A 90
Gartons Clo. Enf —6G 17
Gartons Way. SW11 —2A 90
Garvary Rd. E16 —9F 62
Garway Rd. W2 —9M 57
Garwood Clo. N17 —8F 28
Gascoigne Gdns. Wfd G —7C 30
Gascoigne Pl. E2 —6D 60
(in two parts)
Gascoigne Rd. Bark —4A 64
Gascoigne Rd. New Ad —2A 140
Gascony Av. NW6 —3L 57
Gascoyne Clo. Romf —7H 35
Gascoyne Dri. Dart —2D 98
Gascoyne Ho. E9 —3J 61
Gascoyne Rd. E9 —3H 61
Gaselee St. E14 —1A 78
Gaskarth Rd. SW12 —5F 90
Gaskarth Rd. Edgw —8A 24
Gaskell Rd. N6 —4D 42
Gaskell St. SW4 —1J 91
Gaskin St. N1 —4M 59
Gaspar Clo. SW5 —5M 73
(off Courtfield Gdns.)
Gaspar M. SW5 —5M 73
Gassiot Rd. SW17 —1D 106
Gassiot Way. Sutt —5B 122
Gasson Ho. SE14 —7H 77
(off John Williams Clo.)
Gastein Rd. W6 —7H 73
Gastigny Ho. EC1 —6A 60
(off Lever St.)
Gaston Bell Clo. Rich —2K 87
Gaston Bri. Rd. Shep —1B 116
Gaston Rd. Mitc —7E 106
Gaston Way. Shep —9B 100
Gataker Ho. SE16 —4F 76
(off Slippers Pl.)
Gataker St. SE16 —4F 76
Gatcombe Ct. Beck —4L 109
Gatcombe Ho. SE22 —2C 92
Gatcombe M. W5 —1K 71
Gatcombe Rd. E16 —2E 78
Gatcombe Rd. N19 —8H 43
Gatcombe Way. Barn —5D 14
Gateacre Ct. Sidc —1F 112
Gate Cen., The. Bren —8E 70
Gate Clo. Borwd —3A 12
Gate End. N'wd —7E 20
Gateforth St. NW8 —7C 58
Gate Hill Ct. W11 —2K 73
(off Ladbroke Ter.)
Gatehill Rd. N'wd —7D 20
Gatehouse Clo. King T —4A 104
Gatehouse Sq. SE1 —2A 76
(off Porter St.)
Gateley Ho. SE4 —3H 93
(off Coston Wlk.)
Gateley Rd. SW9 —2K 91
Gate Lodge. W9 —8L 57
Gate M. SW7 —3C 74
(off Rutland Ga.)
Gater Dri. Enf —3B 16
Gates. NW9 —9D 24
Gatesborough St. EC2 —7C 60
Gates Ct. SE17 —6A 76
Gatesden. WC1 —6J 59
Gates Grn. Rd. W W'ck —5D 126
Gateshead Rd. Borwd —3K 11
Gateside Rd. SW17 —9D 90
Gatestone Rd. SE19 —3C 108
Gate St. WC2 —9K 59
Gate Theatre, The. —2L 73
(off Pembridge Rd.)
Gateway. SE17 —7A 76
Gateway. Wey —5A 116

Gladsmuir Rd. Barn —4J 13
Gladstone Av. E12 —3J 63
Gladstone Av. N22 —9L 27
Gladstone Av. Felt —5E 84
Gladstone Av. Twic —7B 86
Gladstone Ct. SW1 —5H 75
(off Regency St.)
Gladstone Gdns. Houn —9A 70
Gladstone Ho. E14 —9L 61
(off E. India Dock Rd.)
Gladstone M. N22 —9L 27
Gladstone M. NW6 —3K 57
Gladstone M. SE20 —4G 109
Gladstone Pde. NW2 —7G 41
Gladstone Pk. Gdns. NW2 —8F 40
Gladstone Pl. E3 —5K 61
Gladstone Pl. Barn —6H 13
Gladstone Pl. E Mol —9C 102
Gladstone Rd. SW19 —4L 105
Gladstone Rd. W4 —4B 72
Gladstone Rd. Buck H —1G 31
Gladstone Rd. Croy —2B 124
Gladstone Rd. Dart —5K 99
Gladstone Rd. King T —7L 103
Gladstone Rd. Orp —7A 128
Gladstone Rd. S'hall —3J 69
Gladstone Rd. Surb —4H 119
Gladstone Rd. Wat —5G 9
Gladstone St. SE1 —4M 75
Gladstone Ter. SE27 —2A 108
(off Bentons La.)
Gladstone Ter. SW8 —9F 74
Gladstone Way. Harr —1C 38
Gladwell Rd. N8 —4K 43
Gladwell Rd. Brom —3E 110
Gladwin Ho. NW1 —5G 59
(off Cranleigh St.)
Gladwyn Rd. SW15 —2H 89
Gladys Dimson Ho. E7 —1D 62
Gladys Rd. NW6 —3L 57
Glaisher St. SE8 —7L 77
Glamis Clo. Chesh —2A 6
Glamis Ct. W3 —3M 71
Glamis Cres. Hay —4A 68
Glamis Dri. Horn —6J 51
Glamis Pl. E1 —1G 77
Glamis Rd. E1 —1G 77
Glamis Way. N'holt —2A 54
Glamorgan Clo. Mitc —7J 107
Glamorgan Ct. W7 —8D 54
(off Copley Clo.)
Glamorgan Rd. King T —4G 103
Glanfield Rd. Beck —8K 109
Glanleam Rd. Stan —4H 23
Glanville Dri. Horn —6K 51
Glanville Rd. SW2 —4J 91
Glanville Rd. Brom —7F 110
Glasbrook Av. Twic —7K 85
Glasbrook Rd. SE9 —6H 95
Glaserton Rd. N16 —5C 44
Glasford St. SW17 —3D 106
Glasfryn Ct. Harr —7B 38
(off Roxeth Hill)
Glasfryn Ho. Harr —7B 38
(off Roxeth Hill)
Glasgow Ho. W9 —5M 57
(off Maida Va.)
Glasgow Rd. E13 —5F 62
Glasgow Rd. N18 —5F 28
Glasgow Ter. SW1 —6G 75
Glasier Ct. E15 —3C 62
Glasse Clo. W13 —1E 70
Glasshill St. SE1 —3M 75
Glasshouse Fields. E1 —1H 77
Glasshouse St. W1 —1G 75
Glasshouse Wlk. SE1 —6J 75
Glasshouse Yd. EC1 —7A 60
Glasslyn Rd. N8 —3H 43
Glassmill La. Brom —6D 110
(in two parts)
Glass St. E2 —7F 60
Glass Yd. SE18 —4L 79
Glastonbury Av. Wfd G —7H 31
Glastonbury Clo. Orp —3G 129
Glastonbury Ct. SE14 —8G 77
(off Farrow La.)
Glastonbury Ct. W13 —2E 70
(off Talbot Rd.)
Glastonbury Ho. SE12 —4D 94
(off Wantage Rd.)
Glastonbury Ho. SW1 —6F 74
(off Abbots Mnr.)
Glastonbury Pl. E1 —9G 61
Glastonbury Rd. N9 —1E 28
Glastonbury Rd. Mord —2L 121
Glastonbury St. NW6 —1K 57
Glaston Ct. W5 —2H 71
(off Grange Rd.)
Glaucus St. E3 —8M 61
Glazbury Rd. W14 —5J 73
Glazebrook Clo. SE21 —8B 92
Glazebrook Rd. Tedd —4D 102
Glebe Av. Enf —5M 15
Glebe Av. Harr —2J 39
Glebe Av. Mitc —6C 106
Glebe Av. Ruis —2F 52
Glebe Av. Uxb —8A 36
Glebe Av. Wfd G —6E 30
Glebe Clo. W4 —6C 72
Glebe Clo. S Croy —3D 138
Glebe Clo. Uxb —9A 36
Glebe Cotts. Felt —9L 85
Glebe Ct. N13 —3L 27
Glebe Ct. SE3 —2C 94
(off Glebe, The)
Glebe Ct. W5 —2H 71
Glebe Ct. W7 —1B 70
Glebe Ct. Mitc —7D 106
Glebe Ct. Stan —5G 23
Glebe Cres. NW4 —2G 41
Glebe Cres. Harr —1J 39
Glebe Gdns. N Mald —2C 120
Glebe Ho. SE16 —4F 76
(off Slippers Pl.)
Glebe Ho. Dri. Brom —3F 126
Glebe Hyrst. SE19 —1C 108
Glebe Hyrst. S Croy —4D 138
Glebeland Gdns. Shep —1A 116
Glebelands. E10 —7M 45
Glebelands. Chig —3F 32
Glebelands. Clay —1D 132
Glebelands. Dart —3D 98
Glebelands. W Mol —9M 101
Glebelands Av. E18 —9E 30
Glebelands Av. Ilf —5B 48
Glebelands Clo. SE5 —2C 92
Glebelands Rd. Felt —7E 84
Glebe La. Barn —7E 12
Glebe La. Harr —2J 39
Glebe Path. Mitc —7D 106
Glebe Pl. SW3 —7C 74
Glebe Rd. E8 —3D 60
Glebe Rd. N3 —8A 26
Glebe Rd. N8 —2K 43
Glebe Rd. NW10 —2E 56
Glebe Rd. SW13 —1E 88
Glebe Rd. Asht —9H 133
Glebe Rd. Brom —5E 110
Glebe Rd. Cars —8D 122
Glebe Rd. Dag —2M 65
Glebe Rd. Hay —2D 68
Glebe Rd. Rain —6G 67
Glebe Rd. Stan —5G 23
Glebe Rd. Sutt —1J 135
Glebe Rd. Uxb —5A 142
Glebe Rd. Warl —9H 139
Glebe Side. Twic —5D 86
Glebe Sq. Mitc —7D 106
Glebe St. W4 —6C 72
Glebe Ter. E3 —6M 61
Glebe Ter. W4 —6C 72
Glebe, The. SE3 —2C 94
Glebe, The. SW16 —1H 107
Glebe, The. Chst —5A 112
Glebe, The. Wat —6H 5
Glebe, The. W Dray —5K 143
Glebe, The. Wor Pk —3D 120
Glebe Way. Eri —7C 82
Glebe Way. Hanw —9L 85
Glebe Way. Horn —5J 51
Glebe Way. S Croy —4D 138
Glebe Way. W W'ck —4A 126
Glebe Way. Wfd G —5G 31
Gledhow Gdns. SW5 —5A 74
Gledstanes Rd. W14 —6J 73
Gledwood Av. Hay —8D 52
Gledwood Cres. Hay —8D 52
Gledwood Dri. Hay —8D 52
Gledwood Gdns. Hay —8D 52
Gleed Av. Bus H —2B 22
Gleeson Dri. Orp —7D 128
Glegg Pl. SW15 —3H 89
Glenaffric Av. E14 —5B 78
Glen Albyn Rd. SW19 —8H 89
Glenallan Ho. W14 —5K 73
(off N. End Cres.)
Glenalla Rd. Ruis —5D 36
Glenalmond Rd. Harr —2J 39
Glenalvon Way. SE18 —5J 79
Glena Mt. Sutt —6A 122
Glenarm Rd. E5 —9G 45
Glen Av. Ashf —9E 144
Glenavon Clo. Clay —8E 118
Glenavon Ct. Wor Pk —4F 120
Glenavon Lodge. Beck —4L 109
Glenavon Rd. E15 —3C 62
Glenbarr Clo. SE9 —2M 95
Glenbow Rd. Brom —3C 110
Glenbrook N. Enf —6K 15
Glenbrook Rd. NW6 —1L 57
Glenbrook S. Enf —6K 15
Glenbuck Rd. Surb —1H 119
Glenburnie Rd. SW17 —9D 90
Glencairn Dri. W5 —7G 55
Glencairne Clo. E16 —8H 63
Glencairn Rd. SW16 —5J 107
Glencoe Av. Ilf —5B 48
Glencoe Dri. Dag —9L 49
Glencoe Mans. SW9 —8L 75
(off Mowll St.)
Glencoe Rd. Bush —8L 9
Glencoe Rd. Hay —8H 53
Glencourse Grn. Wat —4H 21
Glen Ct. Sidc —1E 112
Glen Cres. Wfd G —6F 30
Glendale. Swan —9D 114
Glendale Av. N22 —7L 27
Glendale Av. Edgw —4K 23
Glendale Av. Romf —5G 49
Glendale Clo. SE9 —2L 95
Glendale Dri. SW19 —2K 105
Glendale Gdns. Wemb —6H 39
Glendale M. Beck —5M 109
Glendale Ri. Kenl —7M 137
Glendale Rd. Eri —5A 82
Glendale Wlk. Chesh —3E 6
Glendale Way. SE28 —1G 81
Glendall St. SW9 —3K 91
Glendarvon St. SW15 —2H 89
Glendean Ct. Enf —9E 6
Glendevon Clo. Edgw —3M 23
Glendish Rd. N17 —8F 28
Glendor Gdns. NW7 —4B 24
Glendower Cres. Orp —1E 128
Glendower Gdns. SW14 —2B 88
Glendower Pl. SW7 —5B 74
Glendower Rd. E4 —1B 30
Glendower Rd. SW14 —2B 88
Glendown Ho. E8 —1E 60
Glendown Rd. SE2 —6E 80
Glendun Ct. W3 —1C 72
Glendun Rd. W3 —1C 72
Gleneagle M. SW16 —2H 107
Gleneagle Rd. SW16 —2H 107
Gleneagles. W13 —8F 54
(off Malvern Way)
Gleneagles. Stan —7F 22
Gleneagles Clo. SE16 —6F 76
(off Ryder Dri.)
Gleneagles Clo. Orp —3B 128
Gleneagles Clo. Romf —7K 35
Gleneagles Clo. Stanw —5A 144
Gleneagles Clo. Wat —4H 21
Gleneagles Grn. Orp —3B 128
Gleneagles Tower. S'hall —9A 54
(off Fleming Rd.)
Gleneldon M. SW16 —1J 107
Gleneldon Rd. SW16 —1J 107
Glenelg Rd. SW2 —4J 91
Glenesk Rd. SE9 —2L 95
Glenfarg Rd. SE6 —7A 94
Glenfield Cres. Ruis —5B 36
Glenfield Rd. SW12 —7G 91
Glenfield Rd. W13 —3F 70
Glenfield Rd. Ashf —3A 100
Glenfield Rd. Bans —7M 135
Glenfield Ter. W13 —3F 70
Glenfinlas Way. SE5 —8M 75
Glenforth St. SE10 —6D 78
Glengall Gro. E14 —4M 77
Glengall Pas. NW6 —4L 57
(off Priory Pk. Rd., in two parts)
Glengall Rd. NW6 —4K 57
Glengall Rd. SE15 —6D 76
Glengall Rd. Bexh —2J 97
Glengall Rd. Edgw —3M 23
Glengall Rd. Wfd G —6E 30
Glengall Ter. SE15 —7D 76
Glen Gdns. Croy —5L 123
Glengarnock Av. E14 —5A 78
Glengarry Rd. SE22 —4C 92
Glenham Dri. Ilf —3M 47
Glenhaven Av. Borwd —5L 11
Glenhead Clo. SE9 —2M 95
Glenhill Clo. N3 —9L 25
Glen Ho. E16 —2L 79
(off Storey St.)
Glenhouse Rd. SE9 —4L 95
Glenhurst. Beck —5A 110
Glenhurst Av. NW5 —9E 42
Glenhurst Av. Bex —7K 97
Glenhurst Av. Ruis —5A 36
Glenhurst Ri. SE19 —4A 108
Glenhurst Rd. N12 —5B 26
Glenhurst Rd. Bren —7G 71
Glenilla Rd. NW3 —2C 58
Glenister Pk. Rd. SW16 —4H 107
Glenister Rd. SE10 —6D 78
Glenister St. E16 —2L 79
Glenkerry Ho. E14 —9A 62
(off Burcham St.)
Glenlea Rd. SE9 —4K 95
Glenloch Rd. NW3 —2C 58
Glenloch Rd. Enf —4G 17
Glenluce Rd. SE3 —7E 78
Glenlyon Rd. SE9 —4L 95
Glenmead. Buck H —1G 31
Glenmere Av. NW7 —7E 24
Glenmill. Hamp —2K 101
Glenmore Gdns. Ab L —5E 4
Glenmore Lawns. W13 —9E 54
Glenmore Lodge. Beck —5M 109
Glenmore Pde. Wemb —4J 55
Glenmore Rd. NW3 —2C 58
Glenmore Rd. Well —8D 80
Glenmore Way. Bark —5E 64
Glenmount Path. SE18 —6A 80
Glenn Av. Purl —3M 137
Glennie Ho. SE10 —9A 78
(off Blackheath Hill)
Glennie Rd. SE27 —9L 91
Glenny Rd. Bark —2A 64
Glenorchy Clo. Hay —8J 53
Glenparke Rd. E7 —2F 62
Glenridding. NW1 —5G 59
(off Ampthill Est.)
Glen Ri. Wfd G —6F 30
Glen Rd. E13 —7G 63
Glen Rd. E17 —3K 45
Glen Rd. Chess —6K 119
Glen Rd. End. Wall —1F 136
Glenrosa St. SW6 —1A 90
Glenrose Ct. Sidc —2F 112
Glenroy St. W12 —9G 57
Glensdale Rd. SE4 —2K 93
Glenshaw Mans. SW9 —8L 75
(off Brixton Rd.)
Glenshee Clo. N'wd —6A 20
Glenshiel Rd. SE9 —4L 95
Glenside. Chig —6M 31
Glentanner Way. SW17 —9B 90
Glen Ter. E14 —3A 78
(off Manchester Rd.)
Glentham Gdns. SW13 —7F 72
Glentham Rd. SW13 —7E 72
Glen, The. Brom —6C 110
Glen, The. Croy —5H 125
Glen, The. Eastc —3F 36
Glen, The. Enf —6M 15
Glen, The. N'wd —7B 20
Glen, The. Orp —5K 127
Glen, The. Pinn —5J 37
Glen, The. Rain —7G 67
Glen, The. S'hall —6K 69
Glen, The. Wemb —9J 39
Glenthorne Av. Croy —3F 124
Glenthorne Clo. Sutt —3L 121
Glenthorne Clo. Uxb —6E 142
Glenthorne Gdns. Ilf —1L 47
Glenthorne Gdns. Sutt —3L 121
Glenthorne M. W6 —5F 72
Glenthorne Rd. E17 —3J 45
Glenthorne Rd. N11 —5D 26
Glenthorne Rd. W6 —5F 72
Glenthorne Rd. King T —8K 103
Glenthorpe Av. SW15 —3E 88
Glenthorpe Rd. Mord —9H 105
Glenton Clo. Romf —7C 34
Glenton Rd. SE13 —3C 94
Glenton Way. Romf —7C 34
Glentrammon Av. Orp —8D 128
Glentrammon Clo. Orp —7D 128
Glentrammon Gdns. Orp —8D 128
Glentrammon Rd. Orp —8D 128
Glentworth St. NW1 —7D 58
Glenure Rd. SE9 —4L 95
Glenview. SE2 —7H 81
Glenview Rd. Brom —6H 111
Glenville Av. Enf —2A 16
Glenville Gro. SE8 —8K 77
Glenville M. SW18 —6M 89
Glenville Rd. King T —5L 103
Glen Wlk. Iswth —4B 86
Glen Way. Wat —2C 8
Glenwood Av. NW9 —6C 40
Glenwood Av. Rain —7E 66
Glenwood Clo. Harr —3D 38
Glenwood Ct. E18 —1E 46
Glenwood Ct. Sidc —1E 112
Glenwood Dri. Romf —3E 50
Glenwood Gdns. Ilf —3L 47
Glenwood Gro. NW9 —6A 40
Glenwood Rd. N15 —3M 43
Glenwood Rd. NW7 —3C 24
Glenwood Rd. SE6 —7K 93
Glenwood Rd. Eps —8E 120
Glenwood Rd. Houn —2B 86
Glenwood Way. Croy —1H 125
Glenworth Av. E14 —5B 78
Gliddon Rd. W14 —5J 73
Glimpsing Grn. Eri —4J 81
Glisson Rd. Uxb —5E 142
Gload Cres. Orp —4H 129
Global App. E3 —5M 61
Globe Pond Rd. SE16 —2J 77
Globe Rd. E2 & E1 —6G 61
(in two parts)
Globe Rd. E15 —1D 62
Globe Rd. Horn —4E 50
Globe Rd. Wfd G —6G 31
Globe Rope Wlk. E14 —5M 77
(off E. Ferry Rd.)
Globe St. SE1 —4B 76
Globe Ter. E2 —6G 61
Globe Town. —6H 61
Globe Town Mkt. E2 —6H 61
Globe Wharf. SE16 —1H 77
Globe Yd. W1 —9F 58
(off S. Molton St.)
Glossop Ho. Romf —5J 35
(off Lindfield Rd.)
Glossop Rd. S Croy —1B 138
Gloster Rd. N Mald —8C 104
Gloucester Arc. SW7 —5A 74
Gloucester Av. NW1 —3E 58
Gloucester Av. Horn —2L 51
Gloucester Av. Sidc —8C 96
Gloucester Av. Wal X —6E 6
Gloucester Av. Well —3D 96
Gloucester Cir. SE10 —8A 78
Gloucester Clo. NW10 —3B 56
Gloucester Clo. Th Dit —3E 118
Gloucester Ct. EC3 —1C 76
Gloucester Ct. NW11 —5K 41
(off Golders Grn. Rd.)
Gloucester Ct. W7 —8D 54
(off Copley Clo.)
Gloucester Ct. Harr —1C 38
Gloucester Ct. Mitc —9J 107
Gloucester Ct. Rich —8L 71
Gloucester Cres. NW1 —4F 58
Gloucester Dri. N4 —7M 43
Gloucester Dri. NW11 —2L 41
Gloucester Gdns. NW11 —5K 41
Gloucester Gdns. W2 —9A 58
Gloucester Gdns. Cockf —6E 14
Gloucester Gdns. Ilf —5J 47
Gloucester Gdns. Sutt —4M 121
Gloucester Ga. NW1 —5F 58
(in two parts)
Gloucester Ga. M. NW1 —5F 58
Gloucester Gro. Edgw —8B 24
Gloucester Ho. NW6 —5L 57
(off Cambridge Rd.)
Gloucester Ho. SE5 —8L 75
Gloucester Ho. Borwd —4L 11
Gloucester Ho. Rich —4L 87
Gloucester M. E10 —5L 45
Gloucester M. W2 —9A 58
Gloucester M. W. W2 —9A 58
Gloucester Pde. Hay —4A 68
Gloucester Pde. Sidc —4E 96
Gloucester Pl. NW1 & W1 —7D 58
Gloucester Pl. M. W1 —8D 58
Gloucester Rd. E10 —5L 45
Gloucester Rd. E11 —3F 46
Gloucester Rd. E12 —8K 47
Gloucester Rd. E17 —9H 29
Gloucester Rd. N17 —9B 28
Gloucester Rd. N18 —5D 28
Gloucester Rd. SW7 —4A 74
Gloucester Rd. W3 —3A 72
Gloucester Rd. W5 —3G 71
Gloucester Rd. Barn —7M 13
Gloucester Rd. Belv —6K 81
Gloucester Rd. Croy —3B 124
Gloucester Rd. Dart —6F 98
Gloucester Rd. Enf —2A 16
Gloucester Rd. Felt —7G 85
Gloucester Rd. Hamp —4M 101
Gloucester Rd. Harr —3M 37
Gloucester Rd. Houn —3J 85
Gloucester Rd. King T —6L 103
Gloucester Rd. Rich —8L 71
Gloucester Rd. Romf —4C 50
Gloucester Rd. Tedd —2C 102
Gloucester Rd. Twic —7A 86
Gloucester Sq. E2 —4E 60
Gloucester Sq. W2 —9B 58
Gloucester St. SW1 —6G 75
Gloucester Ter. N14 —1H 27
(off Crown La.)
Gloucester Ter. W2 —9M 57
Gloucester Wlk. W8 —3L 73
Gloucester Way. EC1 —6L 59
Glover Clo. SE2 —5G 81
Glover Dri. N18 —6G 29
Glover Ho. NW6 —3A 58
Glover Ho. SE15 —3F 92
Glover Rd. Pinn —4H 37
Glovers Gro. Ruis —5A 36
Gloxinia Wlk. Hamp —3L 101
Glycena Rd. SW11 —2D 90
Glyn Av. Barn —6B 14
Glyn Clo. SE25 —6C 108
Glyn Clo. Eps —1E 134
Glyn Ct. SW16 —9L 91
Glyndale Grange. Sutt —8M 121
Glyndebourne Ct. N'holt —6G 53
(off Canberra Dri.)
Glyndebourne Pk. Orp —4M 127
Glynde M. SW3 —4C 74
(off Walton St.)
Glynde Reach. WC1 —6J 59
(off Harrison St.)
Glynde Rd. Bexh —2H 97
Glynde St. SE4 —5K 93
Glyndon Rd. SE18 —5A 80
Glyn Dri. Sidc —1F 112
Glynfield Rd. NW10 —3C 56
Glynne Rd. N22 —9L 27
Glyn Rd. E5 —8H 45
Glyn Rd. Enf —6G 17
Glyn Rd. Wor Pk —4H 121
Glyn St. SE11 —6K 75
Glynwood Ct. SE23 —8G 93
Goater's All. SW6 —8K 73
(off Dawes Rd.)
Goat Ho. Bri. SE25 —7E 108
Goat La. Enf —2D 16
Goat Rd. Mitc —2E 122
Goatswood La. Nave —1F 34
Goat Wharf. Bren —7J 71
Gobions Av. Romf —7B 34
Godalming Av. Wall —7J 123
Godalming Rd. E14 —8M 61
Godbold Rd. E15 —7C 62
Goddard Ct. W'stone —9E 22
Goddard Pl. N19 —8G 43
Goddard Rd. Beck —8H 109
Goddards Way. Ilf —6B 48
Goddarts Ho. E17 —1L 45
Goddington. —4H 129
Goddington Chase. Orp —6F 128
Goddington La. Orp —5E 128
Godfrey Av. N'holt —4J 53
Godfrey Av. Twic —6B 86
Godfrey Hill. SE18 —5J 79
Godfrey Ho. EC1 —6B 60
(off St Luke's Est.)
Godfrey Rd. SE18 —5K 79
Godfrey St. E15 —5A 62
Godfrey St. SW3 —6C 74
Godfrey Way. Houn —6J 85
Goding St. SE11 —6J 75
Godley Rd. SW18 —7B 90
Godliman St. EC4 —9M 59
Godman Rd. SE15 —1F 92
Godolphin Clo. N13 —6M 27
Godolphin Clo. Sutt —3K 135
Godolphin Ho. NW3 —3C 58
(off Fellows Rd.)
Godolphin Pl. W3 —1B 72
Godolphin Rd. W12 —2F 72
(in two parts)

Godolphin Rd.—Grand Arc.

Godolphin Rd. Wey —8B 116
Godric Cres. New Ad —2B 140
Godson Rd. Croy —5L 123
Godstone Ho. SE1 —4B 76
(off Pardoner St.)
Godstone Mt. Purl —4M 137
Godstone Rd. Kenl & Purl —4L 137
Godstone Rd. Sutt —6A 122
Godstone Rd. Twic —5F 86
Godstow Rd. SE2 —3F 80
Godwin Clo. E4 —3A 18
Godwin Clo. N1 —5A 60
Godwin Clo. Eps —8A 120
Godwin Ct. NW1 —5G 59
(off Chalton St.)
Godwin Ho. NW6 —5M 57
(off Tollgate Gdns., in three parts)
Godwin Rd. E7 —9F 46
Godwin Rd. Brom —7G 111
Goffers Rd. SE3 —9C 78
Goff's La. Chesh & G Oak —2A 6
Goffs Rd. Ashf —3B 100
Goidel Clo. Wall —6H 123
Golborne Gdns. W10 —7J 57
Golborne Ho. W10 —7J 57
(off Adair Rd.)
Golborne M. W10 —8J 57
Golborne Rd. W10 —8J 57
Golda Clo. Barn —8H 13
Goldbeaters Gro. Edgw —6C 24
Goldcliff Clo. Mord —2L 121
Goldcrest Clo. E16 —8H 63
Goldcrest Clo. SE28 —1G 81
Goldcrest M. W5 —8H 55
Goldcrest Way. Bush —1A 22
Goldcrest Way. New Ad —1B 140
Goldcrest Way. Purl —2H 137
Golden Ct. Barn —6C 14
Golden Ct. Rich —4H 87
Golden Cres. Hay —2D 68
Golden Cross M. W11 —9K 57
(off Portobello Rd.)
Golden Hinde Educational Mus. —2B 76
Golden Hind Pl. SE8 —5K 77
(off Grove St.)
Golden La. EC1 —7A 60
Golden La. Est. EC1 —7A 60
Golden Mnr. W7 —1C 70
Golden M. SE20 —5G 109
Golden Pde. E17 —1A 46
(off Wood St.)
Golden Plover Clo. E16 —9E 62
Golden Sq. W1 —1G 75
Golden Yd. NW3 —9A 42
(off Holly Mt.)
Golders Clo. Edgw —5M 23
Golders Ct. NW11 —5K 41
Golders Gdns. NW11 —5J 41
Golders Green. —4J 41
Golders Green Crematorium. NW11 —5L 41
Golders Grn. Cres. NW11 —5K 41
Golders Grn. Rd. NW11 —4J 41
Golders Mnr. Dri. NW11 —4H 41
Golders Pk. Clo. NW11 —6L 41
Golders Ri. NW4 —3H 41
Golders Way. NW11 —5K 41
Golderton. NW4 —2F 40
(off Prince of Wales Clo.)
Goldeslea. NW11 —6L 41
Goldfinch Clo. Orp —7E 128
Goldfinch Rd. SE28 —4B 80
Goldfinch Rd. S Croy —2J 139
Goldfinch Way. Borwd —6L 11
Goldhawk Ind. Est. W6 —4F 72
Goldhawk M. W12 —3F 72
Goldhawk Rd. W6 & W12 —5D 72
Goldhaze Clo. Wfd G —7H 31
Gold Hill. Edgw —6B 24
Goldhurst Gdns. NW6 —3A 58
Goldhurst Ter. NW6 —3M 57
Goldie Ho. N19 —5H 43
Golding Clo. Chess —8G 119
Golding Ct. Ilf —8L 47
Goldings Hill. Lou —1K 19
Goldings Ri. Lou —3L 19
Goldings Rd. Lou —3L 19
Golding St. E1 —9E 60
Golding Ter. E1 —9E 60
Golding Ter. SW11 —1E 90
Goldington Ct. NW1 —4H 59
(off Royal College St.)
Goldington Cres. NW1 —5H 59
Goldington St. NW1 —5H 59
Gold La. Edgw —6B 24
Goldman Clo. E2 —7E 60
Goldmark Ho. SE3 —2F 94
Goldney Rd. W9 —7L 57
Goldrill Dri. N11 —2E 26
Goldrings Rd. Oxs —5A 132
Goldsboro' Rd. SW8 —9H 75
Goldsborough Cres. E4 —2M 29
Goldsborough Ho. E14 —6M 77
(off St Davids Sq.)
Goldsdown Clo. Enf —4J 17
Goldsdown Rd. Enf —4H 17
Goldsel Rd. Swan —9B 114
Goldsmere Ct. Horn —6J 51
Goldsmid St. SE18 —6C 80
Goldsmith Av. E12 —2J 63
Goldsmith Av. NW9 —3C 40
Goldsmith Av. W3 —1B 72
Goldsmith Av. Romf —5L 49
Goldsmith Clo. Harr —6M 37
Goldsmith Ct. WC2 —9J 59
(off Stukeley St.)
Goldsmith La. NW9 —2M 39
Goldsmith Rd. E10 —6L 45
Goldsmith Rd. E17 —9H 29
Goldsmith Rd. N11 —5D 26
Goldsmith Rd. SE15 —9E 76
Goldsmith Rd. W3 —2B 72
Goldsmith's Bldgs. W3 —2B 72
Goldsmiths Clo. W3 —2B 72
Goldsmith's Pl. NW6 —4M 57
(off Springfield La.)
Goldsmith's Row. E2 —5E 60
Goldsmith's Sq. E2 —5E 60
Goldsmith St. EC2 —9A 60
Goldsworthy Gdns. SE16 —6G 77
Goldthorpe. NW1 —4G 59
(off Camden St.)
Goldwell Ho. SE22 —2C 92
Goldwell Rd. T Hth —8K 107
Goldwin Clo. SE14 —9G 77
Goldwing Clo. E16 —9E 62
Golf Clo. Bush —5H 9
Golf Clo. Stan —7G 23
Golf Clo. T Hth —5L 107
Golf Club Dri. King T —4B 104
Golfe Rd. Ilf —8B 48
Golf Rd. W5 —9K 55
Golf Rd. Brom —7L 111
Golf Rd. Kenl —9B 138
Golf Side. Sutt —3J 135
Golf Side. Twic —4E 86
Golfside Clo. N20 —3C 26
Golfside Clo. N Mald —6C 104
Goliath Clo. Wall —9J 123
Gollogly Ter. SE7 —6G 79
Gomer Gdns. Tedd —3E 102
Gomer Pl. Tedd —3E 102
Gomm Rd. SE16 —4G 77
Gomshall Av. Wall —7J 123
Gomshall Gdns. Kenl —7C 138
Gomshall Rd. Sutt —2G 135
Gondar Gdns. NW6 —1K 57
Gonson St. SE8 —7M 77
Gonston Clo. SW19 —8J 89
Gonville Cres. N'holt —2M 53
Gonville Rd. T Hth —9K 107
Gonville St. SW6 —2J 89
Gooch Ho. E5 —8F 44
Gooch Ho. WC1 —8L 59
(off Portpool La.)
Goodall Ho. SE4 —3H 93
Goodall Rd. E11 —8A 46
Gooden Ct. Harr —8C 38
Goodenough Rd. SW19 —4K 105
Goodey Rd. Bark —3C 64
Goodge Pl. W1 —8G 59
Goodge St. W1 —8G 59
Goodhall St. NW10 —6D 56
(in two parts)
Goodhart Pl. E14 —1J 77
Good Hart Pl. E14 —1J 77
Goodhart Way. W W'ck —2C 126
Goodhew Rd. Croy —1E 124
Gooding Clo. N Mald —8A 104
Goodinge Clo. N7 —2J 59
Gooding Ho. SE7 —6G 79
Goodman Cres. SW2 —8J 91
Goodman Rd. E10 —5A 46
Goodman's Ct. E1 —1D 76
(off Goodman's Yd.)
Goodmans Ct. Wemb —9H 39
Goodman's Stile. E1 —9E 60
Goodmans Yd. EC3 —1D 76
Goodmayes. —6E 48
Goodmayes Av. Ilf —6E 48
Goodmayes La. Ilf —9E 48
Goodmayes Rd. Ilf —6E 48
Goodmead Rd. Orp —2E 128
Goodrich Clo. Wat —8E 4
Goodrich Ct. W10 —9H 57
Goodrich Rd. SE22 —5D 92
Goodson Rd. NW10 —3C 56
Goodson St. N1 —5L 59
Goods Way. NW1 —5J 59
Goodway Gdns. E14 —9B 62
Goodwill Ho. E14 —1M 77
(off Simpson's Rd.)
Goodwin Clo. SE16 —4D 76
Goodwin Clo. Mitc —7B 106
Goodwin Ct. N8 —1J 43
(off Campsbourne Rd.)
Goodwin Ct. SW19 —4C 106
Goodwin Ct. Barn —8C 14
Goodwin Ct. Chesh —1E 6
Goodwin Dri. Sidc —9H 97
Goodwin Gdns. Croy —8M 123
Goodwin Ho. N9 —1G 29
Goodwin Ho. Wat —8C 8
Goodwin Rd. N9 —1H 29
Goodwin Rd. W12 —3E 72
Goodwin Rd. Croy —7M 123
Goodwins Ct. WC2 —1J 75
Goodwin St. N4 —7L 43
Goodwood Av. Enf —1G 17
Goodwood Av. Horn —9J 51
Goodwood Av. Wat —8C 4
Goodwood Clo. Mord —8L 105
Goodwood Clo. Stan —5G 23
Goodwood Ct. W1 —8F 58
(off Devonshire St.)
Goodwood Dri. N'holt —2L 53
Goodwood Ho. SE14 —9J 77
(off Goodwood St.)
Goodwood Pde. Beck —8J 109
Goodwood Pde. Wat —9C 4
Goodwood Path. Borwd —4L 11
Goodwood Rd. SE14 —8J 77
Goodwyn Av. NW7 —5C 24
Goodwyns Va. N10 —8E 26
Goodyear Ho. N2 —9B 26
(off Grange, The)
Goodyear Pl. SE5 —7A 76
Goodyer Ho. SW1 —6H 75
(off Tachbrook St.)
Goodyers Gdns. NW4 —3H 41
Goosander Way. SE28 —4B 80
Gooseacre La. Harr —3H 39
Goose Grn. Clo. Orp —6E 112
Goose Grn. Trad. Est. SE22 —3D 92
Gooseley La. E6 —6L 63
(in two parts)
Goosens Clo. Sutt —7A 122
Goose Sq. E6 —9K 63
Gooshays Dri. Romf —5J 35
Gooshays Gdns. Romf —6J 35
Gophir La. EC4 —1B 76
Gopsall St. N1 —4B 60
Gordon Av. E4 —6C 30
Gordon Av. SW14 —3C 88
Gordon Av. Horn —7D 50
Gordon Av. S Croy —2A 138
Gordon Av. Stan —7D 22
Gordon Av. Twic —4E 86
Gordonbrock Rd. SE4 —4L 93
Gordon Clo. E17 —4L 45
Gordon Clo. N19 —6G 43
Gordon Ct. W12 —9G 57
Gordon Ct. Edgw —5J 23
Gordon Cres. Croy —3C 124
Gordon Cres. Hay —4E 68
Gordondale Rd. SW19 —8L 89
Gordon Dri. Shep —2B 116
Gordon Gdns. Edgw —9M 23
Gordon Gro. SE5 —1M 91
Gordon Hill. Enf —3A 16
Gordon Ho. E1 —1G 77
(off Glamis Rd.)
Gordon Ho. SE10 —8M 77
(off Tarves Way)
Gordon Ho. W5 —6J 55
Gordon Ho. Rd. NW5 —9E 42
Gordon Mans. WC1 —7H 59
(off Torrington Pl.)
Gordon Pl. W8 —3L 73
Gordon Rd. E4 —9C 18
Gordon Rd. E11 —4E 46
Gordon Rd. E15 —9A 46
Gordon Rd. E18 —8F 30
Gordon Rd. N3 —7K 25
Gordon Rd. N9 —2F 28
Gordon Rd. N11 —7H 27
Gordon Rd. SE15 —1F 92
Gordon Rd. W4 —7M 71
Gordon Rd. W13 & W5 —1F 70
Gordon Rd. Ashf —9C 144
Gordon Rd. Bark —4C 64
Gordon Rd. Beck —7K 109
Gordon Rd. Belv —5A 82
Gordon Rd. Cars —8D 122
Gordon Rd. Chad H & Romf —4K 49
Gordon Rd. Clay —9C 118
Gordon Rd. Dart —6H 99
Gordon Rd. Enf —3A 16
Gordon Rd. Harr —1C 38
Gordon Rd. Houn —3A 86
Gordon Rd. Ilf —8B 48
Gordon Rd. King T —5K 103
Gordon Rd. Rich —1K 87
Gordon Rd. Shep —1B 116
Gordon Rd. Sidc —4C 96
Gordon Rd. S'hall —5J 69
Gordon Rd. Surb —2K 119
Gordon Rd. Wal A —7G 7
Gordon Rd. W Dray —1J 143
Gordon Sq. WC1 —7H 59
Gordon St. E13 —6E 62
Gordon St. WC1 —7H 59
Gordon Way. Barn —6K 13
Gordon Way. Brom —5E 110
Gore Ct. NW9 —3L 39
Gorefield Ho. NW6 —5L 57
(off Canterbury Rd.)
Gorefield Pl. NW6 —5L 57
Gore Rd. E9 —4G 61
Gore Rd. SW20 —6G 105
Goresbrook Interchange. (Junct.) —5K 65
Goresbrook Rd. Dag —4F 64
Gore St. SW7 —4A 74
Gorham Pl. W11 —1J 73
Goring Clo. Romf —8A 34
Goring Gdns. Dag —9G 49
Goring Rd. N11 —6J 27
Goring Rd. Dag —2B 66
Goring St. EC3 —9C 60
(off Houndsditch)
Goring Way. Gnfd —5A 54
Gorle Clo. Wat —8E 4
Gorleston Rd. N15 —3B 44
Gorleston St. W14 —5J 73
(in two parts)
Gorman Rd. SE18 —5K 79
Gorringe Pk. Av. Mitc —4D 106
Gorse Clo. E16 —9E 62
Gorsefield Ho. E14 —1L 77
(off E. India Dock Rd.)
Gorse Hill. F'ham —2L 131
Gorse Ri. SW17 —2E 106
Gorse Rd. Croy —6L 125
Gorse Rd. Orp —3K 129
Gorse Wlk. W Dray —9C 142
Gorseway. Romf —6C 50
Gorst Rd. NW10 —7A 56
Gorst Rd. SW11 —5D 90
Gorsuch Pl. E2 —6D 60
Gorsuch St. E2 —5D 60
Gosberton Rd. SW12 —7D 90
Gosbury Hill. Chess —6L 119
Gosfield Rd. Dag —7L 49
Gosfield Rd. Eps —4B 134
Gosfield St. W1 —8G 59
Gosford Gdns. Ilf —3K 47
Gosford Ho. Wat —8C 8
Gosforth La. Wat —3E 20
Gosforth Path. Wat —3E 20
Goshawk Gdns. Hay —6C 52
Goslett Yd. WC2 —9H 59
Gosling Clo. Gnfd —6L 53
Gosling Ho. E1 —1G 77
(off Sutton St.)
Gosling Way. SW9 —9L 75
Gospatrick Rd. N17 —7A 28
Gospel Oak. —9E 42
Gospel Oak Est. NW5 —1D 58
Gosport Dri. Horn —2G 67
Gosport Rd. E17 —3K 45
Gosport Wlk. N17 —2F 44
Gosport Way. SE15 —8D 76
Gossage Rd. SE18 —6B 80
Gossage Rd. Uxb —3D 142
Gossamers, The. Wat —7J 5
Gosset St. E2 —6D 60
Goss Hill. Swan —3G 115
Gosshill Rd. Chst —6L 111
Gossington Clo. Chst —1M 111
Gosterwood St. SE8 —7J 77
Gostling Rd. Twic —7L 85
Goston Gdns. T Hth —7L 107
Goswell Pl. EC1 —6M 59
(off Goswell Rd.)
Goswell Rd. EC1 —5M 59
Gothic Clo. Dart —9H 99
Gothic Cotts. Enf —4A 16
(off Chase Grn. Av.)
Gothic Ct. SE5 —8A 76
(off Wyndham Rd.)
Gothic Ct. Hay —7B 68
Gothic Rd. Twic —8B 86
Gottfried M. NW5 —9G 43
Goudhurst Rd. Brom —2C 110
Gough Ho. N1 —4M 59
(off Windsor St.)
Gough Ho. King T —6J 103
(off Eden St.)
Gough Rd. E15 —9D 46
Gough Rd. Enf —4F 16
Gough Sq. EC4 —9L 59
Gough St. WC1 —7K 59
Gough Wlk. E14 —9L 61
Goulden Ho. SW11 —1C 90
Goulding Gdns. T Hth —6A 108
Gouldman Ho. E1 —7G 61
(off Wyllen Clo.)
Gould Rd. Felt —6C 84
Gould Rd. Twic —7C 86
Goulds Green. —9F 142
Gould's Grn. Uxb —1M 143
Gould Ter. E8 —1F 60
Goulston St. E1 —9D 60
Goulton Rd. E5 —9F 44
Gourley Pl. N15 —3C 44
Gourley St. N15 —3C 44
Gourock Rd. SE9 —4L 95
Govan St. E2 —4E 60
Gover Ct. SW4 —1J 91
Government Row. Enf —2L 17
Govett Av. Shep —9A 100
Govier Clo. E15 —3C 62
Gowan Av. SW6 —9J 73
Gowan Ho. E2 —6D 60
(off Chambord St.)
Gowan Rd. NW10 —2F 56
Gower Clo. SW4 —5G 91
Gower Ct. WC1 —7H 59
Gower Ho. E17 —1M 45
Gower Ho. SE17 —6A 76
Gower M. WC1 —8H 59
Gower M. Mans. WC1 —8H 59
(off Gower M.)
Gower Pl. WC1 —7H 59
Gower Rd. E7 —2E 62
Gower Rd. Iswth —7D 70
Gower Rd. Wey —8B 116
Gower St. WC1 —7G 59
Gower's Wlk. E1 —9E 60
Gowland Pl. Beck —6K 109
Gowlett Rd. SE15 —2E 92
Gowrie Rd. SW11 —2E 90
Graburn Way. E Mol —7B 102
Grace Av. Bexh —1K 97
Gracechurch St. EC3 —1B 76
Grace Clo. SE9 —9H 95
Grace Clo. Borwd —3B 12
Grace Clo. Edgw —7A 24
Grace Clo. Ilf —6D 32
Grace Ct. Croy —5M 123
(off Waddon Rd.)
Gracedale Rd. SW16 —2F 106
Gracefield Gdns. SW16 —9J 91
Gracehill. E1 —8G 61
(off Hannibal Rd.)
Grace Ho. SE11 —7K 75
(off Vauxhall St.)
Grace Jones Clo. E8 —2E 60
Grace Path. SE26 —1G 109
Grace Pl. E3 —6M 61
Grace Rd. Croy —1A 124
Graces All. E1 —1E 76
Graces M. NW8 —5A 58
Grace's M. SE5 —1B 92
Grace's Rd. SE5 —1C 92
Grace St. E3 —6M 61
Gradient, The. SE26 —1E 108
Graeme Rd. Enf —4B 16
Graemesdyke Av. SW14 —2M 87
Grafely Way. SE15 —8D 76
Grafton Clo. W13 —9E 54
Grafton Clo. Houn —7J 85
Grafton Clo. Wor Pk —5C 120
Grafton Ct. Felt —7B 84
Grafton Cres. NW1 —2F 58
Grafton Gdns. N4 —4A 44
Grafton Gdns. Dag —7J 49
Grafton Ho. SE8 —6K 77
Grafton M. N1 —5A 60
(off Frome St.)
Grafton M. W1 —7G 59
Grafton Pk. Rd. Wor Pk —4C 120
Grafton Pl. NW1 —6H 59
Grafton Rd. NW5 —1E 58
Grafton Rd. W3 —1A 72
Grafton Rd. Croy —3L 123
Grafton Rd. Dag —6J 49
Grafton Rd. Enf —5K 15
Grafton Rd. Harr —3A 38
Grafton Rd. N Mald —7C 104
Grafton Rd. Wor Pk —5B 120
Grafton Sq. SW4 —2G 91
Graftons, The. NW2 —8L 41
Grafton St. W1 —1F 74
Grafton Ter. NW5 —1D 58
Grafton Way. W1 & WC1 —7G 59
Grafton Way. W Mol —8K 101
Grafton Yd. NW5 —2F 58
Graham Av. W13 —3F 70
Graham Av. Mitc —5E 106
Graham Clo. Croy —4L 125
Graham Ct. SE14 —7H 77
(off Myers La.)
Graham Ct. N'holt —1K 53
Grahame Park. —8D 24
Grahame Pk. Est. NW9 —8C 24
Grahame Pk. Way. NW7 & NW9 —7D 24
Grahame White Ho. Kent —1H 39
Graham Gdns. Surb —3J 119
Graham Ho. N9 —1G 29
(off Cumberland Rd.)
Graham Lodge. NW4 —4F 40
Graham Mans. Bark —3E 64
(off Lansbury Av.)
Graham Rd. E8 —2E 60
Graham Rd. E13 —6E 62
Graham Rd. N15 —1M 43
Graham Rd. NW4 —4F 40
Graham Rd. SW19 —4K 105
Graham Rd. W4 —4B 72
Graham Rd. Bexh —3L 97
Graham Rd. Hamp —1L 101
Graham Rd. Harr —1C 38
Graham Rd. Mitc —5E 106
Graham Rd. Purl —5L 137
Graham St. N1 —5M 59
Graham Ter. SW1 —5E 74
Graham Ter. Sidc —5F 96
(off Westerham Dri.)
Grainger Clo. N'holt —1M 53
Grainger Ct. SE5 —8A 76
Grainger Rd. N22 —8A 28
Grainger Rd. Iswth —1D 86
Grainges Yd. Uxb —3A 142
Gramer Clo. E11 —7B 46
Gramophone La. Hay —3C 68
Grampian Clo. Hay —8B 68
Grampian Clo. Orp —1D 128
Grampian Gdns. NW2 —6J 41
Grampians, The. W12 —3H 73
(off Shepherd's Bush Rd.)
Grampion Clo. Sutt —9A 122
Granada St. SW17 —2C 106
Granard Av. SW15 —4F 88
Granard Bus. Cen. NW7 —6C 24
Granard Ho. E9 —2H 61
Granard Rd. SW12 —6D 90
Granaries, The. Wal A —7L 7
Granary Clo. N9 —9G 17
Granary Rd. E1 —7F 60
Granary Sq. N1 —2L 59
Granary St. NW1 —4H 59
Granby Pk. Rd. Chesh —1A 6
Granby Pl. SE1 —3L 75
(off Station App. Rd.)
Granby Rd. SE9 —1K 95
Granby St. E2 —7E 60
(in two parts)
Granby Ter. NW1 —5G 59
Grand Arc. N12 —5A 26

Grand Av.—Greencroft Gdns.

Grand Av. EC1 —8M 59
(in two parts)
Grand Av. N10 —2E 42
Grand Av. Surb —9M 103
Grand Av. Wemb —1L 55
Grand Av. E. Wemb —1M 55
Grand Depot Rd. SE18 —6L 79
Grand Dri. SW20 —6G 105
Grand Dri. S'hall —3A 70
Granden Rd. SW16 —6J 107
Grandfield Av. Wat —3D 8
Grandfield Ct. W4 —7B 72
Grandison Rd. SW11 —4D 90
Grandison Rd. Wor Pk —4G 121
Grand Junct. Wharf. N1 —5A 60
Grand Pde. N4 —3M 43
Grand Pde. SW14 —3A 88
(off Up. Richmond Rd. W.)
Grand Pde. Surb —3L 119
Grand Pde. Wemb —7L 39
Grand Pde. M. SW15 —4J 89
Grandstand Rd. Eps —9D 134
Grand Union Cen. W10 —7H 57
(off West Row)
Grand Union Clo. W9 —8K 57
Grand Union Cres. E8 —4E 60
Grand Union Ind. Est. NW10 —5M 55
Grand Union Office Pk., The. Uxb —9A 142
Grand Union Wlk. NW1 —3F 58
(off Kentish Town Rd.)
Grand Vw. Av. Big H —9G 141
Grand Vitesse Ind. Cen. SE1 —2M 75
(off Dolben St.)
Grand Wlk. E1 —7J 61
Granfield St. SW11 —9B 74
Grange Av. N12 —5A 26
Grange Av. N20 —9J 13
Grange Av. SE25 —6C 108
Grange Av. E Barn —1C 26
Grange Av. Stan —9F 22
Grange Av. Twic —8C 86
Grange Av. Wfd G —6E 30
Grangecliffe Gdns. SE25 —6C 108
Grange Clo. Edgw —5A 24
Grange Clo. Hay —8C 52
Grange Clo. Houn —7K 69
Grange Clo. Sidc —9E 96
Grange Clo. Wat —3E 8
Grange Clo. W Mol —8M 101
Grange Clo. Wfd G —7E 30
Grange Ct. NW10 —8C 40
(off Neasden La.)
Grange Ct. WC2 —9K 59
Grange Ct. Harr —8D 38
Grange Ct. Lou —7H 19
Grange Ct. N'holt —5G 53
Grange Ct. Pinn —1J 37
Grange Ct. Sutt —9M 121
Grange Ct. Wal A —7J 7
Grange Ct. W on T —4E 116
Grangecourt Rd. N16 —6C 44
Grange Cres. SE28 —9G 65
Grange Cres. Chig —5B 32
Grange Cres. Dart —5M 99
Grangedale Clo. N'wd —8C 20
Grange Dri. Chst —3J 111
Grange Farm Clo. Harr —7A 38
Grangefield. NW1 —3H 59
(off Marquis Rd.)
Grange Gdns. N14 —1H 27
Grange Gdns. NW3 —8M 41
Grange Gdns. SE25 —6C 108
Grange Gdns. Bans —5M 135
Grange Gdns. Pinn —1J 37
Grange Gro. N1 —2A 60
Grange Hill. —5B 32
Grange Hill. SE25 —6C 108
Grange Hill. Edgw —5A 24
Grangehill Pl. SE9 —2K 95
Grangehill Rd. SE9 —3K 95
Grange Ho. SE1 —4D 76
Grange Ho. Eri —1E 98
Grange La. SE21 —8D 92
Grange La. Let H —3B 10
Grange Lodge. SW19 —3H 105
Grange Mans. Eps —9D 120
Grange Mdw. Bans —5M 135
Grange M. Felt —1E 100
Grangemill Rd. SE6 —9L 93
Grangemill Way. SE6 —8L 93
Grange Mus. of Community History. —9C 40
Grange Park. —8M 15
Grange Pk. W5 —2J 71
Grange Pk. Av. N21 —8A 16
Grange Pk. Pl. SW20 —4F 104
Grange Pk. Rd. E10 —6M 45
Grange Pk. Rd. T Hth —8B 108
Grange Pl. NW6 —3L 57
Grange Rd. E10 —6L 45
Grange Rd. E13 —6D 62
Grange Rd. E17 —3J 45
(in two parts)
Grange Rd. N6 —4E 42
Grange Rd. N17 & N18 —6E 28
Grange Rd. NW10 —2F 56
Grange Rd. SE1 —4C 76
Grange Rd. SW13 —9E 72
Grange Rd. W4 —6M 71
Grange Rd. W5 —2H 71
Grange Rd. Ave —2M 83
Grange Rd. Bush —7J 9
Grange Rd. Chess —6J 119
Grange Rd. Edgw —6B 24
Grange Rd. Els —7K 11
Grange Rd. Harr —3E 38
Grange Rd. Hay —9C 52
Grange Rd. Ilf —9M 47
Grange Rd. King T —7J 103
Grange Rd. Orp —4B 128
Grange Rd. Romf —6F 34
Grange Rd. S'hall —3J 69
Grange Rd. S Croy —2A 138
Grange Rd. S Harr —7B 38
Grange Rd. Sutt —9L 121
Grange Rd. T Hth & SE25 —8B 108
Grange Rd. W on T —6J 117
Grange Rd. W Mol —8M 101
Granger Way. Romf —4E 50
Grange St. N1 —4B 60
Grange, The. E17 —3J 45
(off Grange Rd.)
Grange, The. N2 —9B 26
Grange, The. N20 —1B 26
(Athenaeum Rd.)
Grange, The. N20 —1A 26
(Chandos Av.)
Grange, The. SE1 —4D 76
Grange, The. SW19 —3H 105
Grange, The. W3 —3M 71
Grange, The. W4 —6M 71
Grange, The. W13 —8G 55
Grange, The. W14 —5K 73
Grange, The. Ab L —4C 4
Grange, The. Croy —4K 125
Grange, The. N Mald —9D 104
Grange, The. W on T —4F 116
Grange, The. Wemb —3L 55
Grange, The. Wor Pk —5B 120
Grange Va. Sutt —9M 121
Grangeview Rd. N20 —1A 26
Grange Wlk. SE1 —4C 76
Grange Wlk. M. SE1 —4C 76
(off Grange Wlk.)
Grange Way. N12 —4M 25
Grange Way. NW6 —3L 57
Grange Way. Eri —8F 82
Grange Way. Wfd G —4G 31
Grangeway Gdns. Ilf —3J 47
Grangeway, The. N21 —8M 15
Grangewood. Bex —7K 97
Grangewood Av. Rain —7G 67
Grangewood Clo. Pinn —3E 36
Grangewood Dri. Sun —4D 100
Grangewood La. Beck —3K 109
Grangewood St. E6 —4H 63
Grangewood Ter. SE25 —6B 108
Grange Yd. SE1 —4D 76
Granham Gdns. N9 —2D 28
Granite St. SE18 —6D 80
Granleigh Rd. E11 —7C 46
Gransden Av. E8 —3F 60
Gransden Ho. SE8 —6K 77
Gransden Rd. W12 —3D 72
Grantbridge St. N1 —5M 59
Grantchester. King T —6L 103
(off St Peters Rd.)
Grantchester Clo. Harr —8D 38
Grant Clo. N14 —9G 15
Grant Clo. Shep —1A 116
Grant Ct. E4 —1A 30
(off Ridgeway, The)
Grantham Clo. Edgw —3J 23
Grantham Ct. SE16 —3H 77
(off Eleanor Clo.)
Grantham Ct. Romf —5K 49
Grantham Gdns. Romf —4K 49
Grantham Grn. Borwd —7A 12
Grantham Ho. SE15 —7E 76
(off Friary Est.)
Grantham Pl. W1 —2F 74
Grantham Rd. E12 —9L 47
Grantham Rd. SW9 —1J 91
Grantham Rd. W4 —8C 72
Grantley Ho. SE14 —7H 77
(off Myers La.)
Grantley Rd. Houn —1G 85
Grantley St. E1 —6H 61
Grantock Rd. E17 —8B 30
Granton Av. Upm —8K 51
Granton Rd. SW16 —5G 107
Granton Rd. Ilf —6E 48
Granton Rd. Sidc —3G 113
Grant Pl. Croy —3D 124
Grant Rd. SW11 —3B 90
Grant Rd. Croy —3D 124
Grant Rd. Harr —1D 38
Grants Clo. NW7 —7G 25
Grants Quay Wharf. EC3 —1B 76
Grant St. E13 —6E 62
Grant St. N1 —5L 59
Grantully Rd. W9 —6M 57
Grant Way. Iswth —7E 70
Granville Arc. SW9 —3L 91
Granville Av. N9 —3G 29
Granville Av. Felt —8E 84
Granville Av. Houn —4L 85
Granville Clo. Croy —4C 124
Granville Clo. Wey —8A 116
Granville Ct. N1 —4C 60
(off Colville Est.)
Granville Ct. SE14 —8J 77
(off Nynehead St.)
Granville Gdns. SW16 —5K 107
Granville Gdns. W5 —2K 71
Granville Gro. SE13 —2A 94
Granville Ho. E14 —9L 61
(off E. India Dock Rd.)
Granville Mans. W12 —3G 73
(off Shepherd's Bush Grn.)
Granville M. Sidc —1E 112
Granville Pk. SE13 —2A 94
Granville Pl. N12 —7A 26
Granville Pl. SW6 —8M 73
Granville Pl. W1 —9E 58
Granville Pl. Pinn —1H 37
Granville Point. NW2 —7K 41
Granville Rd. E17 —4M 45
Granville Rd. E18 —9F 30
Granville Rd. N4 —4K 43
Granville Rd. N12 —7A 26
Granville Rd. N13 —6K 27
Granville Rd. N22 —8M 27
Granville Rd. NW2 —7K 41
Granville Rd. NW6 —5L 57
(in two parts)
Granville Rd. SW18 —6K 89
Granville Rd. SW19 —4L 105
Granville Rd. Barn —6G 13
Granville Rd. Hay —5D 68
Granville Rd. Ilf —6M 47
Granville Rd. Sidc —1E 112
Granville Rd. Uxb —2F 142
Granville Rd. Wat —6G 9
Granville Rd. Well —2G 97
Granville Rd. Wey —9A 116
Granville Sq. SE15 —8C 76
Granville Sq. WC1 —6K 59
Granville St. WC1 —6K 59
Granwood Ct. Iswth —9C 70
Grape St. WC2 —9J 59
Graphite Sq. SE11 —6K 75
Grapsome Clo. Chess —9G 119
Grasdene Rd. SE18 —8E 80
Grasmere. NW1 —6F 58
(off Osnaburgh St.)
Grasmere Av. SW15 —1B 104
Grasmere Av. SW19 —7L 105
Grasmere Av. W3 —1B 72
Grasmere Av. Houn —5M 85
Grasmere Av. Orp —5M 127
Grasmere Av. Ruis —5A 36
Grasmere Av. Wemb —5G 39
Grasmere Clo. Felt —7D 84
Grasmere Clo. Lou —4K 19
Grasmere Clo. Wat —5F 4
Grasmere Ct. N22 —6K 27
Grasmere Ct. SE26 —2E 108
Grasmere Ct. Sutt —8A 122
Grasmere Gdns. Harr —9E 22
Grasmere Gdns. Ilf —3K 47
Grasmere Gdns. Orp —5M 127
Grasmere Point. SE15 —8G 77
(off Old Kent Rd.)
Grasmere Rd. E13 —5E 62
Grasmere Rd. N10 —8F 26
Grasmere Rd. N17 —6E 28
Grasmere Rd. SE25 —1F 124
Grasmere Rd. SW16 —2K 107
Grasmere Rd. Bexh —1A 98
Grasmere Rd. Brom —5D 110
Grasmere Rd. Orp —5M 127
Grasmere Rd. Purl —3M 137
Grasshaven Way. SE28 —2D 80
(in two parts)
Grassington Clo. N11 —6E 26
Grassington Clo. Brick W —3L 5
Grassington Rd. Sidc —1E 112
Grassmere Rd. Horn —2K 51
Grassmount. SE23 —8F 92
Grassmount. Purl —2G 137
Grass Pk. N3 —8K 25
Grass Way. Wall —6G 123
Grasvenor Av. Barn —7L 13
Gratton Rd. W14 —4J 73
Gratton Ter. NW2 —8H 41
Gravel Clo. Chig —2E 32
Graveley Av. Borwd —7A 12
Gravel Hill. N3 —9K 25
Gravel Hill. Bexh —4M 97
Gravel Hill. Croy —8H 125
Gravel Hill. Lou —2E 18
Gravel Hill. Uxb —1B 142
Gravel Hill Clo. Bexh —4M 97
Gravel La. E1 —9D 60
Gravel La. Chig —1E 32
Gravel Pit La. SE9 —4M 95
Gravel Pit Way. Orp —4E 128
Gravel Rd. Brom —5J 127
Gravel Rd. S at H —4M 115
Gravel Rd. Twic —7C 86
Gravelwood Clo. Chst —9A 96
Gravely Ho. SE8 —5J 77
(off Chilton Gro.)
Gravenel Gdns. SW17 —2C 106
(off Nutwell St.)
Graveney Gro. SE20 —4G 109
Graveney Rd. SW17 —1C 106
Gravesend Rd. W12 —1E 72
Gray Av. Dag —6K 49
Gray Gdns. Rain —2E 66
Grayham Cres. N Mald —8B 104
Grayham Rd. N Mald —8B 104
Gray Ho. SE17 —6A 76
Grayland Clo. Brom —5H 111
Grayling Clo. E16 —7C 62
Grayling Ct. W5 —2H 71
(off Grange Rd.)
Grayling Rd. N16 —7B 44
Grayling Sq. E2 —6E 60
(off Nelson Gdns.)
Graylings, The. Ab L —6B 4
Grays Ct. Dag —3M 65
Grayscroft Rd. SW16 —4H 107
Grays Farm Rd. Orp —5F 112
Grayshott Rd. SW11 —1E 90
Gray's Inn. —8K 59
Gray's Inn Bldgs. EC1 —7L 59
(off Rosebery Av.)
Gray's Inn Pl. WC1 —8K 59
Gray's Inn Rd. WC1 —6J 59
Gray's Inn Sq. WC1 —8K 59
Grays La. Ashf —9F 144
Grayson Ho. EC1 —6A 60
(off Pleydell Est.)
Grays Rd. Uxb —5C 142
Gray St. SE1 —3L 75
Grayswood Gdns. SW20 —6F 104
Gray's Yd. W1 —9E 58
(off James St.)
Graywood Ct. N12 —7A 26
Grazebrook Rd. N16 —7B 44
Grazeley Clo. Bexh —4A 98
Grazeley Ct. SE19 —2C 108
Gt. Acre Ct. SW4 —3H 91
Gt. Arthur Ho. EC1 —7A 60
(off Golden La. Est.)
Gt. Bell All. EC2 —9B 60
Great Benty. W Dray —5J 143
Great Brownings. SE21 —1D 108
Great Burgh. —9G 135
Gt. Bushey Dri. N20 —1M 25
Gt. Cambridge Ind. Est. Enf —7F 16
Great Cambridge Junction. (Junct.) —5B 28
Gt. Cambridge Rd. N18 & Enf —4B 28
Gt. Cambridge Rd. Chesh & Wal X —7C 6
Gt. Castle St. W1 —9F 58
Gt. Central Av. Ruis —1G 53
Gt. Central St. NW1 —8D 58
Gt. Central Way. NW10 —1C 56
Gt. Central Way. Wemb & NW10 —9A 40
Gt. Chapel St. W1 —9H 59
Gt. Chertsey Rd. W4 —1A 88
Gt. Chertsey Rd. Felt —9K 85
Gt. Church La. W6 —5H 73
Gt. College St. SW1 —4J 75
Great Cft. WC1 —6J 59
(off Cromer St.)
Gt. Cross Av. SE10 —8B 78
(in three parts)
Great Cullings. Romf —7C 50
Gt. Cumberland M. W1 —9D 58
Gt. Cumberland Pl. W1 —9D 58
Gt. Dover St. SE1 —3A 76
Greatdown Rd. W7 —7D 54
Gt. Eastern Bldgs. E1 —8E 60
(off Fieldgate St.)
Gt. Eastern Enterprise Cen. E14 —3M 77
Gt. Eastern Rd. E15 —3B 62
Gt. Eastern St. EC2 —6C 60
Gt. Eastern Wlk. EC2 —8C 60
(off Bishopsgate)
Gt. Eastern Wharf. SW11 —8C 74
Great Ellshams. Bans —8L 135
Gt. Elms Rd. Brom —8G 111
Great Fld. NW9 —8C 24
Greatfield Av. E6 —7K 63
Greatfield Clo. N19 —9G 43
Greatfield Clo. SE4 —3L 93
Greatfields Dri. Uxb —8E 142
Greatfields Rd. Bark —4B 64
Gt. Fleete Way. Bark —5G 65
Gt. Galley Clo. Bark —6F 64
Gt. Gardens Rd. Horn —4F 50
Gt. Gatton Clo. Croy —2J 125
Gt. George St. SW1 —3H 75
Great Gro. Bush —6M 9
Gt. Guildford Bus. Sq. SE1 —2A 76
(off Gt. Guildford St.)
Gt. Guildford St. SE1 —2A 76
Greatham Rd. Bush —5H 9
Greatham Wlk. SW15 —7E 88
Gt. Harry Dri. SE9 —9L 95
Gt. James St. WC1 —8K 59
Gt. Marlborough St. W1 —9G 59
Gt. Maze Pond. SE1 —3B 76
(in two parts)
Gt. Nelmes Chase. Horn —3K 51
Gt. Newport St. WC2 —1J 75
Gt. New St. EC4 —9L 59
Gt. N. Leisure Pk. N12 —7B 26
Gt. North Rd. N2 & N6 —3C 42
Gt. North Rd. Barn —4K 13
Gt. North Rd. New Bar —7L 13
Gt. North Way. NW4 —9F 24
Great Oaks. Chig —4A 32
Greatorex Ho. E1 —8E 60
(off Greatorex St.)
Greatorex St. E1 —8E 60
Gt. Ormond St. WC1 —8J 59
Gt. Owl Rd. Chig —3L 31
Gt. Percy St. WC1 —6K 59
Gt. Peter St. SW1 —4H 75
Gt. Portland St. W1 —7F 58
Gt. Pulteney St. W1 —1G 75
Gt. Queen St. WC2 —9J 59
Gt. Queen St. Dart —6K 99
Gt. Russell St. WC1 —9H 59
Gt. St Helen's. EC2 —9C 60
Gt. St Thomas Apostle. EC4 —1A 76
Gt. Scotland Yd. SW1 —2J 75
Gt. Smith St. SW1 —4H 75
Gt. South W. Rd. Bedf & Felt —6A 84
Great Spilmans. SE22 —4C 92
Great Strand. NW9 —8D 24
Gt. Suffolk St. SE1 —2M 75
Gt. Sutton St. EC1 —7M 59
Gt. Swan All. EC2 —9B 60
(in two parts)
Gt. Tattenhams. Eps —9H 135
Great Thrift. Orp —8A 112
Gt. Titchfield St. W1 —7F 58
Gt. Tower St. EC3 —1C 76
Gt. Trinity La. EC4 —1A 76
Great Turnstile. WC1 —8K 59
Gt. Western Ind. Pk. S'hall —3M 69
Gt. Western Rd. W9 & W11 —8K 57
Gt. West Rd. W4 & W6 —6D 72
Gt. West Rd. Houn & Iswth —1H 85
Gt. West Rd. Iswth —8E 70
Gt. West Trad. Est. Bren —7F 70
Gt. Winchester St. EC2 —9B 60
Gt. Windmill St. W1 —1H 75
Greatwood. Chst —4L 111
Gt. Woodcote Dri. Purl —2H 137
Gt. Woodcote Pk. Purl —2H 137
Great Yd. SE1 —3C 76
(off Crucifix La.)
Greaves Clo. Bark —3B 64
Greaves Cotts. E14 —8J 61
Greaves Pl. SW17 —1C 106
Greaves Tower. SW10 —8A 74
(off Worlds End Est.)
Grebe Av. Hay —9H 53
Grebe Clo. E7 —1D 62
Grebe Clo. E17 —7J 29
Grebe Ct. E14 —3A 78
(off River Barge Clo.)
Grebe Ct. SE8 —7K 77
(off Dorking Clo.)
Grebe Ct. Sutt —7K 121
Grebe Ter. King T —7J 103
Grecian Cres. SE19 —3M 107
Greek Ct. W1 —9H 59
Greek St. W1 —9H 59
Greenacre. Dart —8H 99
Greenacre Clo. Barn —2K 13
Greenacre Clo. N'holt —1K 53
Greenacre Clo. Swan —8C 114
Greenacre Gdns. E17 —2A 46
Greenacre Pl. Hack —4F 122
Greenacres. N3 —9K 25
Greenacres. SE9 —5L 95
Greenacres. Bus H —2B 22
Green Acres. Croy —5D 124
Greenacres. Sidc —1E 112
Greenacres Clo. Orp —6A 128
Greenacres Clo. Rain —6J 67
Greenacres Dri. Stan —6F 22
Greenacres Sq. SE16 —3H 77
Greenacre Wlk. N14 —3H 27
Greenall Clo. Chesh —3E 6
Grn. Arbour Ct. EC4 —9M 59
(off Old Bailey)
Green Av. NW7 —4B 24
Green Av. W13 —4F 70
Greenaway Gdns. NW3 —9M 41
Greenaway Ho. NW8 —4A 58
(off Boundary Rd.)
Greenaway Ho. WC1 —6L 59
(off Fernsbury St.)
Green Bank. E1 —2F 76
Greenbank. N12 —4M 25
Greenbank. Chesh —1B 6
Greenbank Av. Wemb —1E 54
Green Bank Clo. E4 —2A 30
Greenbank Clo. Romf —3H 35
Greenbank Cres. NW4 —2J 41
Greenbank Rd. Wat —9B 4
Greenbanks. Dart —8J 99
Greenbanks. Harr —9C 38
Greenbay Rd. SE7 —8H 79
Greenberry St. NW8 —5C 58
Greenbrook Av. Barn —3A 14
Green Clo. E15 —4C 62
Green Clo. NW9 —4A 40
Green Clo. NW11 —5A 42
Green Clo. Brom —7C 110
Green Clo. Cars —4D 122
Green Clo. Chesh —4E 6
Green Clo. Felt —2J 101
Greencoat Mans. SW1 —4G 75
(off Greencoat Row)
Greencoat Pl. SW1 —5G 75
Greencoat Row. SW1 —4G 75
Greencourt Av. Croy —4F 124
Greencourt Av. Edgw —8M 23
Greencourt Gdns. Croy —3F 124
Greencourt Rd. Orp —9B 112
Green Ct. Rd. Swan —1B 130
Greencrest Pl. NW2 —8E 40
Greencroft. Edgw —5A 24
Greencroft Av. Ruis —7G 37
Greencroft Clo. E6 —8H 63
Greencroft Gdns. NW6 —3M 57
Greencroft Gdns. Enf —5C 16

Greencroft Rd.—Griffin Ct.

Greencroft Rd. Houn —9K 69
Green Curve. Bans —6K 135
Greendale. NW7 —4C 24
Green Dale. SE5 —3B 92
Green Dale. SE22 —4C 92
Grn. Dale Clo. SE22 —4C 92
Grn. Dragon Ct. SE1 —2B 76
(off Bedale St.)
Grn. Dragon La. N21 —8L 15
Grn. Dragon La. Bren —6J 71
Grn. Dragon Yd. E1 —8E 60
Green Dri. S'hall —2L 69
Greene Ct. SE14 —7H 77
(off Samuel Clo.)
Green Edge. Wat —8E 4
Greene Ho. SE1 —4B 76
(off Burbage Clo.)
Green End. N21 —2M 27
Green End. Chess —6J 119
Greenend Rd. W4 —3C 72
Greener Ho. SW4 —2H 91
Green Farm Clo. Orp —8D 128
Greenfell Mans. SE8 —7M 77
Greenfield Av. Surb —2M 119
Greenfield Av. Wat —2H 21
Greenfield Dri. N2 —2D 42
Greenfield Dri. Brom —6G 111
Greenfield Gdns. NW2 —7J 41
Greenfield Gdns. Dag —4H 65
Greenfield Gdns. Orp —2B 128
Greenfield Link. Coul —7J 137
Greenfield Rd. E1 —8E 60
Greenfield Rd. N15 —3C 44
Greenfield Rd. Dag —3G 65
Greenfield Rd. Dart —2B 114
Greenfields. Lou —6L 19
Greenfields. S'hall —9L 53
Greenfields Clo. Lou —6L 19
Greenfield St. Wal A —7J 7
Greenfield Way. Harr —1M 37
Greenford. —6A 54
Greenford Av. W7 —7C 54
Greenford Av. S'hall —1K 69
Greenford Bus. Cen. Gnfd —3B 54
Greenford Gdns. Gnfd —6M 53
Greenford Green. —2C 54
Greenford Ind. Est. N'holt —3M 53
Greenford Rd. S'hall & Gnfd —2A 70
Greenford Rd. Sutt —6M 121
(in two parts)
Greenford Roundabout. (Junct.) —5B 54
Green Gdns. Orp —7A 128
Greengate. Gnfd —2F 54
Greengate Lodge. E13 —5F 62
(off Hollybush St.)
Greengate St. E13 —5F 62
Green Glades. Horn —4K 51
Greenhalgh Wlk. N2 —2A 42
Greenham Clo. SE1 —3L 75
Greenham Cres. E4 —6K 29
Greenham Ho. Houn —2B 86
Greenham Rd. N10 —9E 26
Greenhaven Dri. SE28 —9F 64
Greenhayes Av. Bans —6L 135
Greenhayes Gdns. Bans —7L 135
Greenheath Bus. Cen. E2 —7F 60
(off Three Colts La.)
Green Hedge. Twic —4G 87
Greenheys Clo. N'wd —8C 20
Greenheys Dri. E18 —1D 46
Greenhill. —3C 38
Greenhill. NW3 —9B 42
Green Hill. SE18 —6K 79
Greenhill. Buck H —1G 31
Green Hill. Orp —4K 141
Greenhill. Sutt —4A 122
Greenhill. Wemb —7M 39
Greenhill Ct. SE18 —6K 79
Greenhill Ct. New Bar —7M 13
Greenhill Cres. Wat —8B 8
Greenhill Gdns. N'holt —5K 53
Greenhill Gro. E12 —9J 47
Green Hill La. Warl —9J 139
Greenhill Pde. New Bar —7M 13
Greenhill Pk. NW10 —4C 56
Greenhill Pk. New Bar —7M 13
Greenhill Rd. NW10 —4C 56
Greenhill Rd. Harr —4C 38
Greenhill Rd. Wat —8C 8
Greenhill's Rents. EC1 —8M 59
Greenhills Ter. N1 —2B 60
Greenhill Ter. SE18 —6K 79
Greenhill Ter. N'holt —5K 53
Greenhill Way. Harr —4C 38
Greenhill Way. Wemb —7M 39
Greenhithe Clo. Sidc —6C 96
Greenholm Rd. SE9 —4M 95
Grn. Hundred Rd. SE15 —7E 76
Greenhurst Rd. SE27 —2L 107
Greening St. SE2 —5G 81
Greenland Cres. S'hall —4G 69
Greenland Ho. E1 —7J 61
(off Ernest St.)
Greenland M. SE8 —6H 77
Greenland Pl. NW1 —4F 58
Greenland Quay. SE16 —5H 77
Greenland Rd. NW1 —4G 59
Greenland Rd. Barn —8G 13
Greenlands Rd. Wey —5A 116
Greenland St. NW1 —4F 58
Green La. E4 —3C 18
Green La. NW4 —2H 41
Green La. SE9 & Chst —7M 95
Green La. SE20 —4H 109
Green La. SW16 & T Hth —4K 107
Green La. W7 —3C 70
Green La. Asht —9G 133
Green La. Chess —1H 133
(in two parts)
Green La. Chig —1A 32
Green La. Edgw —4K 23
Green La. Felt —2J 101
Green La. Harr —8C 38
Green La. Houn —2F 84
Green La. Ilf & Dag —7B 48
Green La. Mord —2G 121
(Battersea Cemetery)
Green La. Mord —1L 121
(Morden)
Green La. N Mald —9A 104
Green La. N'wd —6B 20
Green La. Purl —3G 137
Green La. Shep —1A 116
Green La. Stan —4F 22
Green La. Sun —4D 100
Green La. Uxb —8A 52
Green La. W on T —8F 116
Green La. Warl —8J 139
Green La. Wat —9G 9
Green La. W Mol —9M 101
Green La. Wor Pk —3E 120
Green La. Av. W on T —7G 117
Green La. Cotts. Stan —4F 22
Green La. Gdns. T Hth —6A 108
Green Lanes. N8 & N4 —1M 43
Green Lanes. N13 & N21 —3L 27
Green Lanes. Eps —1C 134
(in two parts)
Greenlaw Ct. W5 —9H 55
(off Mount Pk. Rd.)
Greenlaw Gdns. N Mald —2D 120
Greenlawns. N12 —6M 25
Green Lawns. Ruis —6G 37
Greenlaw St. SE18 —4L 79
Green Leaf Av. Wall —6H 123
Greenleaf Clo. SW2 —6L 91
Greenleafe Dri. Ilf —1M 47
Greenleaf Rd. E6 —4G 63
Greenleaf Rd. E17 —1K 45
Green Leas. King T —7J 103
(off Mill St.)
Green Leas. Sun —3D 100
Greenleas. Wal A —7L 7
Green Leas Clo. Sun —3D 100
Greenleaves Ct. Ashf —3A 100
Greenleigh Av. St P —8F 112
Green Man Gdns. W13 —1E 70
Green Man La. W13 —1E 70
Green Man La. Felt —3E 84
Green Man Pas. W13 —1E 70
(in two parts)
Green Man Roundabout. (Junct.) —5D 46
Greenman St. N1 —3A 60
Greenmead. Eri —4J 81
Green Mead. Esh —8K 117
Greenmead Clo. SE25 —9E 108
Green Moor Link. N21 —9M 15
Greenmoor Rd. Enf —4G 17
Greenoak Clo. Cockf —4D 14
Green Oaks. S'hall —5H 69
Greenoak Way. SW19 —1H 105
Greenock Rd. SW16 —5H 107
Greenock Rd. W3 —4M 71
Greenock Way. Romf —7C 34
Green Pde. Houn —4M 85
Green Pk. —3F 74
Greenpark Ct. Wemb —3G 55
Grn. Park Way. Gnfd —3C 54
Green Pl. Dart —4C 98
Green Point. E15 —2C 62
Grn. Pond Clo. E17 —1J 45
Grn. Pond Rd. E17 —1J 45
Green Ride. Lou —6G 19
Greenrigg Wlk. Wemb —8M 39
Green Rd. N14 —8F 14
Green Rd. N20 —3A 26
Greens Clo., The. Lou —4L 19
Green's Ct. W1 —1H 75
(off Brewer St.)
Green's End. SE18 —5M 79
Greenshank Clo. E17 —7J 29
Greenshields Ind. Est. E16 —3E 78
Greenside. Bex —7J 97
Greenside. Borwd —2L 11
Green Side. Dag —6G 49
Greenside. Swan —6B 114
Greenside Clo. N20 —2B 26
Greenside Clo. SE6 —8B 94
Greenside Rd. W12 —4E 72
Greenside Rd. Croy —2L 123
Greenslade Rd. Bark —3B 64
Greenstead Av. Wfd G —7G 31
Greenstead Clo. Wfd G —6G 31
Greenstead Gdns. SW15 —4F 88
Greenstead Gdns. Wfd G —6G 31
Greensted Rd. Lou —9J 19
Greenstone M. E11 —4E 46
Green St. E7 & E13 —2F 62
Green St. W1 —1E 74
Green St. Enf —4G 17
Green St. Shenl & Borwd —1L 11
Green St. Sun —5E 100
Green Street Green. —8D 128
Green St. Grn. Rd. Dart —7M 99
Greenstreet Hill. SE14 —1H 93
Greensward. Bush —8M 9
Green Ter. EC1 —6L 59
Green, The. E4 —1A 30
Green, The. E11 —4F 46
Green, The. E15 —2C 62
Green, The. N9 —2E 28
Green, The. N14 —2H 27
Green, The. N17 —6A 28
Green, The. N21 —9L 15
Green, The. SW19 —2H 105
Green, The. W3 —9C 56
Green, The. W5 —2H 71
Green, The. Bexh —9L 81
Green, The. Brom —9E 94
(in two parts)
Green, The. Buck H —1F 30
Green, The. Cars —6E 122
Green, The. Chesh —1C 6
Green, The. Clay —8D 118
Green, The. Croy —1K 139
Green, The. Eps —3E 134
Green, The. Felt —8F 84
Green, The. Hav —3C 34
Green, The. Hayes —2E 126
Green, The. Hers —7G 117
Green, The. Houn —7L 69
Green, The. Ick —7A 36
Green, The. Let H —3C 10
Green, The. Mord —8J 105
Green, The. N Mald —7B 104
Green, The. Noak H —2G 35
Green, The. Orp —6M 127
Green, The. Rich —4H 87
Green, The. St P —4F 112
Green, The. Shep —8C 100
Green, The. Sidc —1E 112
Green, The. S'hall —4J 69
Green, The. Sutt —5M 121
Green, The. Twic —7C 86
Green, The. Wal A —7J 7
Green, The. Warl —9H 139
Green, The. Well —3C 96
Green, The. Wemb —7E 38
Green, The. Wen —1J 83
Green, The. W Dray —4H 143
Green, The. Wfd G —5E 30
Green Va. W5 —9K 55
Green Va. Bexh —4H 97
Greenvale Rd. SE9 —3K 95
Green Verges. Stan —7H 23
Green Vw. Chess —9K 119
Greenview Av. Beck —1J 125
Greenview Av. Croy —1J 125
Greenview Clo. W3 —2C 72
Greenview Ct. Ashf —9D 144
Green Wlk. NW4 —3H 41
Green Wlk. SE1 —4C 76
Green Wlk. Dart —4D 98
Green Wlk. Hamp —3K 101
Green Wlk. Lou —9J 19
Green Wlk. Ruis —6D 36
Green Wlk. S'hall —6L 69
Green Wlk. Wfd G —6J 31
Green Wlk., The. E4 —1B 30
Greenway. N14 —2J 27
Greenway. N20 —2L 25
Green Way. SE9 —4H 95
Greenway. SW20 —8G 105
Green Way. Brom —1J 127
Greenway. Chst —2L 111
Greenway. Dag —7G 49
Greenway. Hay —6E 52
Greenway. Kent —3J 39
Greenway. Pinn —9F 20
Greenway. Romf —6M 35
Green Way. Sun —8E 100
Greenway. Wall —6G 123
Green Way. Wfd G —5G 31
Greenway Av. E17 —2B 46
Greenway Clo. N4 —7A 44
Greenway Clo. N11 —6E 26
Greenway Clo. N15 —2D 44
Greenway Clo. N20 —2L 25
Greenway Clo. NW9 —9B 24
Greenway Gdns. NW9 —9B 24
Greenway Gdns. Croy —5K 125
Greenway Gdns. Gnfd —6L 53
Greenway Gdns. Harr —9C 22
Greenways. Ab L —5C 4
Greenways. Beck —1L 109
Greenways. Esh —6C 118
Greenways Ct. Horn —4H 51
Greenways, The. Twic —5E 86
Greenway, The. NW9 —9B 24
Greenway, The. Enf —8D 6
Greenway, The. Eps —6L 133
Greenway, The. Houn —3K 85
Greenway, The. Ick —7A 36
Greenway, The. Orp —1F 128
Green Way, The. Pinn —4K 37
Greenway, The. Uxb —5B 142
Green Way, The. W'stone —8C 22
Greenwell St. W1 —7F 58
Greenwich. —8A 78
Greenwich Bus. Cen. SE10 —8M 77
(off Greenwich High Rd.)
Greenwich Bus. Pk. SE10 —8M 77
Greenwich Chu. St. SE10 —7A 78
Greenwich Ct. E1 —9F 60
(off Cavell St.)
Greenwich Ct. Wal X —7E 6
Greenwich Cres. E6 —8J 63
Greenwich Gateway Vis. Cen. —7A 78
Greenwich High Rd. SE10 —9M 77
Greenwich Ind. Est. SE7 —5F 78
Greenwich Ind. Est. SE10 —8M 77
Greenwich Mkt. SE10 —7A 78
Greenwich Pk. —8C 78
Greenwich Pk. St. SE10 —7B 78
Greenwich S. St. SE10 —9M 77
Greenwich Vw. Pl. E14 —4M 77
Greenwich Way. Wal A —9J 7
Greenwood Av. Chesh —4B 6
Greenwood Av. Dag —9M 49
Greenwood Av. Enf —4J 17
Greenwood Bus. Cen. Croy —2D 124
Greenwood Clo. Bus H —9C 10
Greenwood Clo. Chesh —4B 6
Greenwood Clo. Mord —8J 105
Greenwood Clo. Orp —1C 128
Greenwood Clo. Sidc —8E 96
Greenwood Clo. Th Dit —3E 118
Greenwood Dri. E4 —5B 30
Greenwood Dri. Wat —7F 4
Greenwood Gdns. N13 —3M 27
Greenwood Gdns. Ilf —7A 32
Greenwood Ho. N22 —8L 27
Greenwood Ho. SE4 —3H 93
Greenwood La. Hamp H —2M 101
Greenwood Mans. Bark —3E 64
(off Lansbury Av.)
Greenwood Pk. King T —4C 104
Greenwood Pl. NW5 —1F 58
Greenwood Rd. E8 —2E 60
Greenwood Rd. E13 —5D 62
Greenwood Rd. Bex —1B 114
Greenwood Rd. Chig —4F 32
Greenwood Rd. Croy —2M 123
Greenwood Rd. Iswth —2D 86
Greenwood Rd. Mitc —7H 107
Greenwood Rd. Th Dit —3E 118
Greenwoods, The. S Harr —8A 38
Greenwood Ter. NW10 —4B 56
Green Wrythe Cres. Cars —3C 122
Green Wrythe La. Cars —1B 122
Green Yd. WC1 —7K 59
(off Gough St.)
Greenyard. Wal A —6J 7
Green Yd., The. EC3 —9C 60
(off Leadenhall St.)
Greer Rd. Harr —8A 22
Greet Ho. SE1 —3L 75
(off Frazier St.)
Greet St. SE1 —2L 75
Greg Clo. E10 —4A 46
Gregory Clo. Brom —8C 110
Gregory Cres. SE9 —6H 95
Gregory M. Wal A —5H 7
Gregory Pl. W8 —3M 73
Gregory Rd. Romf —2H 49
Gregory Rd. S'hall —4L 69
Gregson Clo. Borwd —3A 12
Gregson's Ride. Lou —2L 19
Greig Clo. N8 —3J 43
Greig Ter. SE17 —7M 75
Grenaby Av. Croy —2B 124
Grenaby Rd. Croy —2B 124
Grenada Ho. E14 —1K 77
(off Limehouse Causeway)
Grenada Rd. SE7 —8G 79
Grenade St. E14 —1K 77
Grenadier St. E16 —2L 79
Grena Gdns. Rich —3K 87
Grena Rd. Rich —3K 87
Grendon Gdns. Wemb —7L 39
Grendon Ho. E9 —3G 61
(off Shore Pl.)
Grendon Ho. N1 —5K 59
(off Priory Grn. Est.)
Grendon Lodge. Edgw —2A 24
Grendon St. NW8 —7C 58
Grenfell Av. Horn —6D 50
Grenfell Clo. Borwd —3A 12
Grenfell Ct. NW7 —6F 24
Grenfell Gdns. Harr —5J 39
Grenfell Gdns. Ilf —3D 48
Grenfell Ho. SE5 —8A 76
Grenfell Rd. SW17 —3D 106
Grenfell Rd. W11 —1H 73
Grenfell Tower. W11 —1H 73
Grenfell Wlk. W11 —1H 73
Grennell Clo. Sutt —4B 122
Grennell Rd. Sutt —4A 122
Grenoble Gdns. N13 —6L 27
Grenside Rd. Wey —5A 116
Grenville Clo. N3 —8J 25
Grenville Clo. Surb —3A 120
Grenville Clo. Wal X —5D 6
Grenville Ct. W13 —8F 54
Grenville Gdns. Wfd G —8G 31
Grenville Ho. E3 —5J 61
(off Arbery Rd.)
Grenville Ho. SE8 —7L 77
(off New King St.)
Grenville Ho. SW1 —7H 75
(off Dolphin Sq.)
Grenville M. SW7 —5A 74
(off Harrington Gdns.)
Grenville M. Hamp —2M 101
Grenville Pl. NW7 —5B 24
Grenville Pl. SW7 —4A 74
Grenville Rd. N19 —6J 43
Grenville Rd. New Ad —1A 140
Grenville St. WC1 —7J 59
Gresham Av. N20 —4D 26
Gresham Clo. Bex —5J 97
Gresham Clo. Enf —5A 16
Gresham Ct. Purl —3L 137
Gresham Dri. Romf —3F 48
Gresham Gdns. NW11 —6J 41
Gresham Lodge. E17 —3M 45
Gresham M. W4 —4A 72
Gresham Rd. E6 —5K 63
Gresham Rd. E16 —9F 62
Gresham Rd. NW10 —1B 56
Gresham Rd. SE25 —8E 108
Gresham Rd. SW9 —2L 91
Gresham Rd. Beck —6J 109
Gresham Rd. Edgw —6K 23
Gresham Rd. Hamp —3L 101
Gresham Rd. Houn —9A 70
Gresham Rd. Uxb —5E 142
Gresham St. EC2 —9A 60
Gresham Way. SW19 —9M 89
Gresley Clo. E17 —4J 45
Gresley Clo. N15 —2B 44
Gresley Ct. Enf —8C 6
Gresley Rd. N19 —6G 43
Gressenhall Rd. SW18 —5K 89
Gresse St. W1 —9H 59
Gresswell Clo. Sidc —9E 96
Greswell St. SW6 —9H 73
Gretton Ho. E2 —6G 61
(off Globe Rd.)
Gretton Rd. N17 —7D 28
Greville Av. S Croy —2H 139
Greville Clo. Twic —6F 86
Greville Ct. Harr —9C 38
Greville Hall. NW6 —5M 57
Greville Lodge. E13 —4F 62
Greville Lodge. N12 —5M 25
Greville Lodge. Edgw —4M 23
(off Broadhurst Av.)
Greville M. NW6 —4M 57
(off Greville Rd.)
Greville Pk. Av. Asht —9J 133
Greville Pk. Rd. Asht —9J 133
Greville Pl. NW6 —5M 57
Greville Rd. E17 —2A 46
Greville Rd. NW6 —5M 57
Greville Rd. Rich —5K 87
Greville St. EC1 —8L 59
(in two parts)
Grey Alders. Bans —6G 135
Greycaine Rd. Wat —1H 9
Greycaine Trad. Est. Wat —1H 9
Grey Clo. NW11 —4A 42
Greycoat Gdns. SW1 —4H 75
(off Greycoat St.)
Greycoat Pl. SW1 —4H 75
Greycoat St. SW1 —4H 75
Greycot Rd. Beck —2L 109
Grey Eagle St. E1 —7D 60
Greyfell Clo. Stan —5G 23
Greyfields Clo. Purl —5M 137
Greyfriars. SE26 —9E 92
(off Wells Pk. Rd.)
Greyfriars Pas. EC1 —9M 59
Greyhound Commercial Cen., The. Dart —4C 98
Greyhound Ct. WC2 —1K 75
Greyhound Hill. NW4 —1E 40
Greyhound La. SW16 —3H 107
Greyhound Mans. W6 —7J 73
(off Greyhound Rd.)
Greyhound Rd. N15 —1C 44
Greyhound Rd. NW10 —6F 56
Greyhound Rd. W6 & W14 —7H 73
Greyhound Rd. Sutt —7A 122
Greyhound Ter. SW16 —5G 107
Greyhound Way. Dart —4C 98
Grey Ho. W12 —1F 72
(off White City Est.)
Grey Ho., The. Wat —4E 8
Greyladies Gdns. SE10 —1A 94
Greys Pk. Clo. Kes —7H 127
Greystead Rd. SE23 —6G 93
Greystoke Av. Pinn —1L 37
Greystoke Ct. W5 —7J 55
Greystoke Dri. Ruis —5A 36
Greystoke Gdns. W5 —7J 55
Greystoke Gdns. Enf —6H 15
Greystoke Ho. SE15 —7E 76
(off Peckham Pk. Rd.)
Greystoke Lodge. W5 —7K 55
(off Hanger La.)
Greystoke Pk. Ter. W5 —6H 55
Greystoke Pl. EC4 —9L 59
Greystone Clo. S Croy —3G 139
Greystone Gdns. Harr —4G 39
Greystone Gdns. Ilf —9A 32
Greystone Path. E11 —5D 46
(off Mornington Rd.)
Greyswood St. SW16 —3F 106
Grey Towers Av. Horn —5H 51
Grey Towers Gdns. Horn —5G 51
Grey Turner Ho. W12 —9E 56
Grice Av. Big H —5F 140
Gridiron Pl. Upm —8M 51
Grierson Rd. SE23 —6H 93
Griffin Cen. Felt —4F 84
Griffin Cen., The. King T —6H 103
(off Market Pl.)
Griffin Clo. NW10 —1F 56
Griffin Ct. W4 —6D 72

Gypsy Corner. (Junct.)—Hammersmith Flyover. (Junct.)

Gypsy Corner. (Junct.) —8B 56
Gypsy La. K Lan —8B 4

Haarlem Rd. W14 —4H 73
Haberdasher Est. N1 —6B 60
Haberdasher Pl. N1 —6B 60
Haberdashers Ct. SE14 —2H 93
Haberdasher St. N1 —6B 60
Habgood Rd. Lou —5J 19
Habington Ho. SE5 —8B 76 (off Notley St.)
Haccombe Rd. SW19 —3A 106
Hackbridge. —4E 122
Hackbridge Grn. Wall —4E 122
Hackbridge Pk. Gdns. Cars —4D 122
Hackbridge Rd. Wall —4E 122
Hackford Rd. SW9 —9K 75
Hackford Wlk. SW9 —9K 75
Hackforth Clo. Barn —7F 12
Hackington Cres. Beck —3L 109
Hacklington Ct. New Bar —6M 13
Hackney. —2F 60
Hackney Clo. Borwd —7B 12
Hackney Gro. E8 —2F 60
Hackney Rd. E2 —6C 60
Hackney Wick. —2L 61
Hackney Wick. (Junct.) —2K 61
Hacton. —1K 67
Hacton Dri. Horn —9H 51
Hacton La. Horn & Upm —7K 51
Hacton Pde. Horn —8K 51
Hadar Clo. N20 —1L 25
Haddenham Ct. Wat —3H 21
Hadden Rd. SE28 —4C 80
Hadden Way. Gnfd —2B 54
Haddington Ct. SE10 —8M 77 (off Tarves Way)
Haddington Rd. Brom —9B 94
Haddo Ho. SE10 —7M 77 (off Haddo St.)
Haddon Clo. Borwd —4L 11
Haddon Clo. Enf —8E 16
Haddon Clo. N Mald —9D 104
Haddon Clo. Wey —5C 116
Haddon Ct. NW4 —1G 41
Haddon Ct. W3 —1D 72
Haddonfield. SE8 —5H 77
Haddon Gro. Sidc —6D 96
Haddon Rd. Orp —9G 113
Haddon Rd. Sutt —6M 121
Haddo St. SE10 —7M 77
Haden Ct. N4 —7L 43
Hadfield Clo. S'hall —6K 53
Hadfield Ho. E1 —9E 60 (off Ellen St.)
Hadfield Rd. Stanw —5B 144
Hadleigh Clo. E1 —7G 61
Hadleigh Clo. SW20 —6K 105
Hadleigh Ct. E4 —9C 18
Hadleigh Dri. Sutt —1L 135
Hadleigh Ho. E1 —7G 61 (off Hadleigh Clo.)
Hadleigh Rd. N9 —9F 16
Hadleigh St. E2 —6G 61
Hadleigh Wlk. E6 —9J 63
Hadley. —5K 13
Hadley Clo. N21 —8L 15
Hadley Clo. Els —8K 11
Hadley Comn. Barn —4L 13
Hadley Ct. N16 —6E 44
Hadley Ct. New Bar —5M 13
Hadley Gdns. W4 —6B 72
Hadley Gdns. S'hall —6K 69
Hadley Grn. Rd. Barn —4K 13
Hadley Grn. W. Barn —4K 13
Hadley Gro. Barn —4J 13
Hadley Highstone. Barn —3K 13
Hadley Mnr. Trad. Est. Barn —5K 13
Hadley M. Barn —5K 13
Hadley Pde. Barn —5J 13 (off High St.)
Hadley Ridge. Barn —5K 13
Hadley Rd. Barn —4M 13
Hadley Rd. Barn & Enf —2E 14
Hadley Rd. Belv —5K 81
Hadley Rd. Mitc —8H 107
Hadley St. NW1 —2F 58 (in two parts)
Hadley Way. N21 —8L 15
Hadley Wood. —2A 14
Hadley Wood Ri. Kenl —7M 137
Hadley Wood Rd. Barn —4A 14
Hadlow Ho. SE17 —6C 76 (off Kinglake Est.)
Hadlow Pl. SE19 —4E 108
Hadlow Rd. Sidc —1E 112
Hadlow Rd. Well —8G 81
Hadrian Clo. Stai —6C 144
Hadrian Clo. Wall —9J 123
Hadrian Ct. Sutt —9M 121
Hadrian Est. E2 —5E 60 (off Hackney Rd.)
Hadrians Ride. Enf —7D 16
Hadrian St. SE10 —6C 78
Hadrian Way. Stai & Stanw (in two parts) —6B 144
Hadstock Ho. NW1 —6H 59 (off Ossulston St.)
Hadyn Pk. Ct. W12 —3E 72 (off Curwen Rd.)
Hadyn Pk. Rd. W12 —3E 72
Hafer Rd. SW11 —3D 90
Hafton Rd. SE6 —7C 94
Hagden La. Wat —6D 8
Haggard Rd. Twic —6F 86
Hagger Ct. E17 —1B 46
Haggerston. —5D 60
Haggerston Rd. E8 & E2 —3D 60
Haggerston Rd. Borwd —2J 11
Hague St. E2 —6E 60
Ha Ha Rd. SE18 —7K 79
Haig Ho. E2 —5E 60 (off Shipton St.)
Haig Pl. Mord —1L 121
Haig Rd. Big H —9J 141
Haig Rd. Stan —5G 23
Haig Rd. Uxb —8F 142
Haig Rd. E. E13 —6G 63
Haig Rd. W. E13 —6G 63
Haigville Gdns. Ilf —2M 47
Hailes Clo. SW19 —3A 106
Haileybury Av. Enf —8D 16
Haileybury Rd. Orp —6E 128
Hailey Rd. Eri —3L 81
Hailsham Av. SW2 —8K 91
Hailsham Clo. Romf —5G 35
Hailsham Clo. Surb —2H 119
Hailsham Cres. Bark —2D 64
Hailsham Dri. Harr —1B 38
Hailsham Gdns. Romf —5G 35
Hailsham Rd. SW17 —3E 106
Hailsham Rd. Romf —5G 35
Hailsham Ter. N18 —5B 28
Haimo Rd. SE9 —4H 95
Hainault. —5E 32
Hainault Bus. Pk. Ilf —5G 33
Hainault Ct. E17 —2B 46
Hainault Forest Country Pk. —3H 33
Hainault Gore. Romf —3J 49
Hainault Gro. Chig —4A 32
Hainault Ind. Est. Ilf —5G 33
Hainault Rd. E11 —6A 46
Hainault Rd. Chad H —4K 49
Hainault Rd. Chig —3M 31
Hainault Rd. Col R & Romf —9A 34
Hainault Rd. Romf —7F 32
Hainault St. SE9 —7M 95
Hainault St. Ilf —7A 48
Haines Ct. Wey —7B 116
Haines St. SW8 —8G 75
Haines Wlk. Mord —2M 121
Haines Way. Wat —7E 4
Hainford Clo. SE4 —3H 93
Haining Clo. W4 —6L 71
Hainthorpe Rd. SE27 —9M 91
Hainton Clo. E1 —9F 60
Halberd M. E5 —7F 44
Halbutt Gdns. Dag —8K 49
Halbutt St. Dag —9K 49
Halcomb St. N1 —4C 60
Halcot Av. Bexh —4M 97
Halcrow St. E1 —8F 60
Halcyon. Enf —7C 16 (off Private Rd.)
Halcyon Way. Horn —6K 51
Halcyon Wharf. E1 —2E 76 (off Hermitage Wall)
Haldane Clo. N10 —7F 26
Haldane Clo. Enf —2M 17
Haldane Pl. SW18 —7M 89
Haldane Rd. E6 —6H 63
Haldane Rd. SE28 —1H 81
Haldane Rd. SW6 —8K 73
Haldane Rd. S'hall —1A 70
Haldan Rd. E4 —6A 30
Haldon Clo. Chig —5C 32
Haldon Rd. SW18 —5K 89
Hale Clo. E4 —3A 30
Hale Clo. Edgw —5A 24
Hale Clo. Orp —6A 128
Hale Ct. Edgw —5A 24
Hale Dri. NW7 —6A 24
Hale End. —6B 30
Hale End. Romf —6F 34
Hale End Clo. Ruis —4E 36
Hale End Rd. E4 —6B 30
Halefield Rd. N17 —8F 28
Hale Gdns. N17 —2E 44
Hale Gdns. W3 —2L 71
Hale Gro. Gdns. NW7 —5C 24
Hale Ho. SW1 —6H 75 (off Lindsay Sq.)
Hale Ho. Horn —4E 50 (off Benjamin Clo.)
Hale La. NW7 —5B 24
Hale La. Edgw —5M 23
Hale Path. SE27 —1M 107
Hale Rd. E6 —7J 63
Hale Rd. N17 —1E 44
Halesowen Rd. Mord —2M 121
Hales Prior. N1 —5K 59 (off Calshot St.)
Hales St. SE8 —8L 77
Hale St. E14 —1M 77
Halesworth Clo. E5 —7G 45
Halesworth Clo. Romf —7J 35
Halesworth Rd. SE13 —2M 93
Halesworth Rd. Romf —6J 35
Hale, The. —5B 24
Hale, The. E4 —7B 30
Hale, The. N17 —1E 44
Hale Wlk. W7 —8C 54
Haley Rd. NW4 —4G 41
Half Acre. Bren —7H 71
Half Acre. Stan —6G 23
Half Acre Rd. W7 —2C 70
Halfhides. Wal A —6K 7
Half Moon Ct. EC1 —8A 60 (off Bartholomew Clo.)
Half Moon Cres. N1 —5K 59 (in two parts)
Half Moon La. SE24 —5A 92
Half Moon Pas. E1 —9D 60 (in two parts)
Half Moon St. W1 —2F 74
Halford Clo. Edgw —9M 23
Halford Rd. E10 —3B 46
Halford Rd. SW6 —7L 73
Halford Rd. Rich —4J 87
Halford Rd. Uxb —1E 142
Halfway Ct. Purf —5L 83
Halfway Grn. W on T —5F 116
Halfway St. Sidc —6B 96
Haliburton Rd. Twic —4E 86
Haliday Ho. N1 —2B 60 (off Mildmay St.)
Haliday Wlk. N1 —2B 60
Halidon Clo. E9 —1G 61
Halidon Ri. Romf —6M 35
Halifax. NW9 —9D 24
Halifax Clo. Leav —7D 4
Halifax Clo. Tedd —3C 102
Halifax Ho. Romf —5J 35 (off Lindfield Rd.)
Halifax Rd. Enf —4A 16
Halifax Rd. Gnfd —4M 53
Halifax St. SE26 —9F 92
Halifield Dri. Belv —4J 81
Haling Down Pas. Purl —2M 137 (in two parts)
Haling Gro. S Croy —9A 124
Haling Pk. Gdns. S Croy —8M 123
Haling Pk. Rd. S Croy —7M 123
Haling Rd. S Croy —8B 124
Haliwell Ho. NW6 —4M 57 (off Mortimer Cres.)
Halkin Arc. SW1 —4D 74 (in two parts)
Halkin M. SW1 —4E 74
Halkin Pl. SW1 —4E 74
Halkin St. SW1 —3E 74
Hallam Clo. Chst —2K 111
Hallam Clo. Wat —4G 9
Hallam Ct. W1 —8F 58 (off Hallam St.)
Hallam Gdns. Pinn —7J 21
Hallam Ho. SW1 —6G 75 (off Churchill Gdns.)
Hallam M. W1 —8F 58
Hallam Rd. N15 —2M 43
Hallam Rd. SW13 —2F 88
Hallam St. W1 —7F 58
Halland Way. N'wd —6B 20
Hallane Ho. SE27 —2A 108
Hall Clo. W5 —8J 55
Hall Ct. Tedd —2D 102
Hall Cres. Ave —3M 83
Hall Dri. SE26 —2G 109
Hall Dri. W7 —9C 54
Halley Gdns. SE13 —3B 94
Halley Ho. E2 —5E 60 (off Pritchards Rd.)
Halley Ho. SE10 —6D 78 (off Armitage Rd.)
Halley Rd. E7 & E12 —2G 63
Halley Rd. Wal A —9H 7
Halley St. E14 —8J 61
Hall Farm Clo. Stan —4F 22
Hall Farm Dri. Twic —6B 86
Hallfield Est. W2 —9A 58 (in two parts)
Hallford Way. Dart —5G 99
Hall Gdns. E4 —4K 29
Hall Ga. NW8 —6B 58
Halliards, The. W on T —1E 116
Halliday Sq. S'hall —2B 70
Halliford Clo. Shep —8B 100
Halliford Rd. Shep & Sun —9C 100
Halliford St. N1 —3A 60
Hallingbury Ct. E17 —1M 45
Halliwell Ct. SE22 —4E 92
Halliwell Rd. SW2 —5K 91
Halliwick Ct. Pde. N12 —6D 26 (off Woodhouse Rd.)
Halliwick Rd. N10 —8E 26
Hall Lane. (Junct.) —5H 29
Hall La. E4 —5J 29
Hall La. NW4 —8E 24
Hall La. Hay —8B 68
Hall La. Upm —9M 35 & 6M 51
Hallmark Trad. Cen. Wemb —9A 40
Hallmead Rd. Sutt —5M 121
Hall Oak Wlk. NW6 —2K 57
Hallowell Av. Croy —6J 123
Hallowell Clo. Mitc —7E 106
Hallowell Rd. N'wd —7C 20
Hallowes Cres. Wat —3E 20
Hallowfield Way. Mitc —7C 106
Hall Pk. Rd. Upm —1M 67
Hall Place. —5A 98
Hall Pl. W2 —7B 58 (in two parts)
Hall Pl. Cres. Bex —4A 98
Hall Pl. Dri. Wey —7C 116
Hall Place Mus. —5A 98
Hall Rd. E6 —4K 63
Hall Rd. E15 —9B 46
Hall Rd. NW8 —6A 58
Hall Rd. Ave —3M 83
Hall Rd. Chad H —4G 49
Hall Rd. Dart —3K 99
Hall Rd. Gid P —1F 50
Hall Rd. Iswth —4B 86
Hall Rd. Wall —1F 136
Hallside Rd. Enf —2D 16
Hall St. EC1 —6M 59
Hall St. N12 —5A 26
Hallsville Rd. E16 —9D 62
Hallswelle Pde. NW11 —3K 41
Hallswelle Rd. NW11 —3K 41
Hall Ter. Romf —7L 35
Hall, The. SE3 —2E 94
Hall Tower. W2 —8B 58 (off Hall Pl.)
Hall Vw. SE9 —8H 95
Hall Way. Purl —5M 137
Hallywell Cres. E6 —8K 63
Halons Rd. SE9 —6L 95
Halpin Pl. SE17 —5B 76
Halsbrook Rd. SE3 —2G 95
Halsbury Clo. Stan —4F 22
Halsbury Ct. Stan —5F 22
Halsbury Rd. W12 —2F 72
Halsbury Rd. E. N'holt —9A 38
Halsbury Rd. W. N'holt —1M 53
Halsend. Hay —2F 68
Halsey M. SW3 —5D 74
Halsey Pl. Wat —2F 8
Halsey Rd. Wat —5F 8
Halsey St. SW3 —5D 74
Halsmere Rd. SE5 —9M 75
Halstead Clo. Croy —5A 124
Halstead Ct. E17 —5K 45
Halstead Ct. N1 —5B 60 (off Fairbank Est.)
Halstead Gdns. N21 —1B 28
Halstead Ho. Romf —6H 35 (off Dartfields)
Halstead Rd. E11 —3E 46
Halstead Rd. N21 —1B 28
Halstead Rd. Enf —6C 16
Halstead Rd. Eri —9C 82
Halston Clo. SW11 —5D 90
Halstow Rd. NW10 —6H 57
Halstow Rd. SE10 —6E 78
Halsway. Hay —2E 68
Halter Clo. Borwd —7B 12
Halton Clo. N11 —6D 26
Halton Clo. Park —1M 5
Halton Cross St. N1 —4M 59
Halton Mans. N1 —3M 59
Halton Pl. N1 —4A 60
Halton Rd. N1 —3M 59
Halt Robin La. Belv —5M 81
Halt Robin Rd. Belv —5L 81 (in two parts)
Halyard Ho. E14 —4A 78
Ham. —9G 87
Hamara Ghar. E13 —4G 63
Hambalt Rd. SW4 —4G 91
Hamble Clo. Ruis —7C 36
Hamble Ct. Wat —6E 8
Hambleden Pl. SE21 —7C 92
Hambledon. SE17 —7B 76 (off Villa St.)
Hambledon Clo. Uxb —7F 142
Hambledon Ct. SE22 —3C 92
Hambledon Ct. W5 —1J 71
Hambledon Gdns. SE25 —7D 108
Hambledon Hill. Eps —8A 134
Hambledon Rd. SW18 —6K 89
Hambledon Va. Eps —8A 134
Hambledown Rd. Sidc —6B 96
Hamblehyrst. Beck —6M 109
Hamble St. SW6 —2M 89
Hambleton Clo. Wor Pk —4G 121
Hamble Wlk. N'holt —5L 53 (off Brabazon Rd.)
Hambley Ho. SE16 —5F 76 (off Camilla Rd.)
Hamblin Ho. S'hall —1J 69 (off Broadway, The)
Hambridge Way. SW2 —6L 91
Hambro Av. Brom —3E 126
Hambrook Rd. SE25 —7F 108
Hambro Rd. SW16 —3H 107
Hambrough Ho. Hay —8G 53
Hambrough Rd. S'hall —2J 69
Hamburgh Ct. Chesh —1D 6
Ham Clo. Rich —9G 87 (in two parts)
Ham Comn. Rich —9H 87
Hamden Cres. Dag —8M 49
Hamel Clo. Harr —2H 39
Hame Way. E6 —7L 63
Ham Farm Rd. Rich —1H 103
Hamfrith Rd. E15 —2D 62
Ham Ga. Av. Rich —9H 87
Ham House. —7G 87
Hamilton Av. N9 —9E 16
Hamilton Av. Ilf —2M 47
Hamilton Av. Romf —9B 34
Hamilton Av. Surb —4L 119
Hamilton Av. Sutt —4J 121
Hamilton Bldgs. EC2 —7C 60 (off Gt. Eastern St.)
Hamilton Clo. N17 —1D 44
Hamilton Clo. NW8 —6B 58
Hamilton Clo. SE16 —3J 77
Hamilton Clo. Brick W —4L 5
Hamilton Clo. Cockf —6C 14
Hamilton Clo. Eps —4A 134
Hamilton Clo. Felt —2D 100
Hamilton Clo. Purl —4M 137
Hamilton Clo. Stan —2C 22
Hamilton Ct. SE6 —7D 94
Hamilton Ct. SW15 —2J 89
Hamilton Ct. W5 —1J 71
Hamilton Ct. W9 —6A 58 (off Maida Va.)
Hamilton Ct. Croy —3E 124
Hamilton Ct. Eri —8D 82 (off Frobisher Rd.)
Hamilton Cres. N13 —4L 27
Hamilton Cres. Harr —8K 37
Hamilton Cres. Houn —4M 85
Hamilton Dri. Romf —9J 35
Hamilton Gdns. NW8 —6A 58
Hamilton Ho. E14 —6M 77 (off St Davids Sq.)
Hamilton Ho. NW8 —6B 58 (off Hall Rd.)
Hamilton Ho. W4 —7C 72
Hamilton La. N5 —9M 43
Hamilton Lodge. E1 —7G 61 (off Cleveland Gro.)
Hamilton M. SW18 —7L 89
Hamilton M. SW19 —4L 105
Hamilton M. W1 —3F 74
Hamilton Pde. Felt —1D 100
Hamilton Pk. N5 —9M 43
Hamilton Pk. W. N5 —9M 43
Hamilton Pl. W1 —2E 74
Hamilton Pl. Sun —4F 100
Hamilton Rd. E15 —6C 62
Hamilton Rd. E17 —9J 29
Hamilton Rd. N2 —1A 42
Hamilton Rd. N9 —9E 16
Hamilton Rd. NW10 —1E 56
Hamilton Rd. NW11 —5H 41
Hamilton Rd. SE27 —1B 108
Hamilton Rd. SW19 —4M 105
Hamilton Rd. W4 —3C 72
Hamilton Rd. W5 —1J 71
Hamilton Rd. Bexh —1J 97
Hamilton Rd. Bren —7H 71
Hamilton Rd. Cockf —6C 14
Hamilton Rd. Felt —1D 100
Hamilton Rd. Harr —3C 38
Hamilton Rd. Hay —1F 68
Hamilton Rd. Ilf —9M 47
Hamilton Rd. K Lan —6A 4
Hamilton Rd. Romf —3F 50
Hamilton Rd. Sidc —1E 112
Hamilton Rd. S'hall —2K 69
Hamilton Rd. T Hth —7B 108
Hamilton Rd. Twic —7C 86
Hamilton Rd. Uxb —7B 142
Hamilton Rd. Wat —3F 20
Hamilton Rd. Ind. Est. SE27 (off Hamilton Rd.) —1B 108
Hamilton Rd. M. SW19 —4M 105
Hamilton Sq. N12 —6B 26
Hamilton Sq. SE1 —3B 76 (off Kipling St.)
Hamilton St. SE8 —7L 77
Hamilton St. Wat —7G 9
Hamilton Ter. NW8 —5M 57
Hamilton Wlk. Eri —8D 82
Hamilton Way. N3 —6L 25
Hamilton Way. N13 —4M 27
Hamilton Way. Wall —1H 137
Hamlea Clo. SE12 —4E 94
Hamlet Clo. SE13 —3C 94
Hamlet Clo. Brick W —3K 5
Hamlet Clo. Romf —7L 33
Hamlet Ct. SE11 —6M 75 (off Opal St.)
Hamlet Ct. W6 —5E 72
Hamlet Ct. Enf —7C 16
Hamlet Gdns. W6 —5E 72
Hamlet Ho. Eri —8C 82
Hamlet Ind. Est. E9 —3L 61
Hamlet Rd. SE19 —4D 108
Hamlet Rd. Romf —7L 33
Hamlet Sq. NW2 —8J 41
Hamlets Way. E3 —7K 61 (in two parts)
Hamlet, The. SE5 —2B 92
Hamlet Way. SE1 —3B 76
Hamlin Cres. Pinn —3G 37
Hamlyn Clo. Edgw —3J 23
Hamlyn Gdns. SE19 —4C 108
Hammelton Ct. Brom —5D 110 (off London Rd.)
Hammelton Grn. SW9 —9M 75
Hammelton Rd. Brom —5D 110
Hammerfield Ho. SW3 —6C 74 (off Marlborough St.)
Hammers La. NW7 —5E 24
Hammersley Ho. SE14 —8G 77 (off Pomeroy St.)
Hammersmith. —5G 73
Hammersmith Bri. SW13 & W6 —7F 72
Hammersmith Bri. Rd. W6 —6G 73 (in two parts)
Hammersmith Broadway. (Junct.) —5G 73
Hammersmith B'way. W6 —5G 73
Hammersmith Flyover. (Junct.) —6G 73

Hatherley Cres.—Headlam Rd.

Hatherley Cres. Sidc —8E 96
Hatherley Gdns. E6 —6H 63
Hatherley Gdns. N8 —4J 43
Hatherley Gro. W2 —9M 57
Hatherley Ho. E17 —2L 45
Hatherley M. E17 —2L 45
Hatherley Rd. E17 —2K 45
Hatherley Rd. Rich —9K 71
Hatherley Rd. Sidc —1E 112
Hatherley St. SW1 —5G 75
Hathern Gdns. SE9 —1L 111
Hatherop Rd. Hamp —4K 101
Hathersage Ct. N1 —1B 60
Hathorne Clo. SE15 —1F 92
Hathway St. SE15 —1H 93
Hathway Ter. SE15 —1H 93
(off Hathway St.)
Hatley Av. Ilf —2A 48
Hatley Clo. N11 —5D 26
Hatley Rd. N7 —7K 43
Hatteraick St. SE16 —3G 77
Hattersfield Clo. Belv —5K 81
Hatters La. Wat —8B 8
Hatton. —3D 84
Hatton Clo. SE18 —8B 80
Hatton Cross. (Junct.) —3D 84
Hatton Garden. EC1 —8L 59
Hatton Gdns. Mitc —9D 106
Hatton Grn. Felt —3E 84
Hatton Gro. W Dray —3H 143
Hatton Ho. King T —6K 103
(off Victoria Rd.)
Hatton Pl. EC1 —8L 59
Hatton Rd. Bedf & Felt —6A 84
Hatton Rd. Chesh —2D 6
Hatton Rd. Croy —3L 123
Hatton Rd. S. Felt —3D 84
Hatton Row. NW8 —7B 58
(off Hatton St.)
Hatton St. NW8 —7B 58
Hatton Wall. EC1 —8L 59
Haughmond. N12 —4M 25
Haunch of Venison Yd. W1 —9F 58
Hauteville Ct. Gdns. W6 —4D 72
(off South Side)
Havana Clo. Romf —3C 50
Havana Rd. SW19 —8L 89
Havannah St. E14 —3L 77
Havant Rd. E17 —1A 46
Havelock Clo. W12 —1F 72
Havelock Ct. S'hall —4K 69
(off Havelock Rd.)
Havelock Ho. SE23 —7G 93
Havelock Pl. Harr —4C 38
Havelock Rd. N17 —9E 28
Havelock Rd. SW19 —2A 106
Havelock Rd. Belv —5K 81
Havelock Rd. Brom —8G 111
Havelock Rd. Croy —4D 124
Havelock Rd. Dart —6F 98
Havelock Rd. Harr —1C 38
Havelock Rd. S'hall —4J 69
Havelock St. N1 —4J 59
Havelock St. Ilf —7M 47
Havelock Ter. SW8 —9F 74
Havelock Wlk. SE23 —7G 93
Haven Clo. SE9 —9K 95
Haven Clo. SW19 —9H 89
Haven Clo. Hay —7C 52
Haven Clo. Sidc —3G 113
Haven Clo. Swan —6D 114
Haven Ct. Beck —6A 110
Haven Ct. Surb —1K 119
Haven Grn. W5 —9H 55
Haven Grn. Ct. W5 —9H 55
Havenhurst Ri. Enf —4L 15
Haven La. W5 —9J 55
Haven Lodge. Enf —8C 16
(off Village Rd.)
Haven M. E3 —8K 61
Haven Pl. W5 —1H 71
Havenpool. NW8 —4M 57
(off Abbey Rd.)
Haven Rd. Ashf —9F 144
Haven St. NW1 —3F 58
Haven, The. N14 —8F 14
Haven, The. Rich —2L 87
Haven, The. Sun —4E 100
Havent Ho. Romf —7J 35
(off Kingsbridge Cir.)
Haven Wood. Wemb —8M 39
Haverfield Gdns. Rich —8L 71
Haverfield Rd. E3 —6J 61
Haverford Way. Edgw —8K 23
Haverhill Rd. E4 —1A 30
Haverhill Rd. SW12 —7G 91
Havering. NW1 —3F 58
(off Castlehaven Rd.)
Havering-Atte-Bower. —3C 34
Havering Country Pk. —4A 34
Havering Dri. Romf —2C 50
Havering Gdns. Romf —3G 49
Havering Park. —5M 33
Havering Rd. Romf —5B 34
Havering St. E1 —9H 61
Havering Way. Bark —6F 64
Havers Av. W on T —7H 117
Haversham Clo. Twic —5H 87
Haversham Ct. Gnfd —2D 54
Haversham Pl. N6 —7D 42
Haverstock Ct. Orp —6F 112
(off Cotmandene Cres.)
Haverstock Hill. NW3 —1C 58
Haverstock Pl. EC1 —6M 59
(off Haverstock St.)
Haverstock Rd. NW5 —1E 58
Haverstock St. N1 —5M 59
Haverthwaite Rd. Orp —4B 128
Havil St. SE5 —8C 76
Havisham Ho. SE16 —3E 76
Havisham Pl. SE19 —4M 107
Hawarden Gro. SE24 —6A 92
Hawarden Hill. NW2 —8E 40
Hawarden Rd. E17 —2H 45
Hawbridge Rd. E11 —6B 46
Hawes Clo. N'wd —7D 20
Hawes Ho. E17 —2H 45
Hawes La. E4 —2A 18
Hawes La. W W'ck —3A 126
Hawes Rd. N18 —6F 28
Hawes Rd. Brom —5F 110
(in two parts)
Hawes St. N1 —3M 59
Haweswater Dri. Wat —6G 5
Hawfield Bank. Orp —5H 129
Hawgood St. E3 —8L 61
Hawk Clo. Wal A —7M 7
Hawkdene. E4 —8M 17
Hawke Ct. Hay —7G 53
(off Perth Av.)
Hawke Ho. E1 —7H 61
(off Ernest St.)
Hawke Pk. Rd. N22 —1M 43
Hawke Pl. SE16 —3H 77
Hawker Clo. Wall —9J 123
Hawker Ct. King T —6K 103
(off Church Rd.)
Hawke Rd. SE19 —3B 108
Hawkesbury Rd. SW15 —4F 88
Hawkesfield Rd. SE23 —8J 93
Hawkesley Clo. Twic —1E 102
Hawkes Rd. Felt —6E 84
Hawkes Rd. Mitc —5D 106
Hawkesworth Clo. N'wd —7C 20
Hawke Tower. SE14 —7J 77
Hawkewood Rd. Sun —7E 100
Hawkfield Ct. Iswth —1C 86
Hawkhirst Rd. Kenl —7B 138
Hawkhurst Gdns. Chess —6J 119
Hawkhurst Gdns. Romf —6B 34
Hawkhurst Rd. SW16 —5H 107
Hawkhurst Rd. Kenl —9C 138
Hawkhurst Way. N Mald —9B 104
Hawkhurst Way. W W'ck —4M 125
Hawkinge. N17 —9B 28
(off Gloucester Rd.)
Hawkinge Wlk. Orp —7F 112
Hawkinge Way. Horn —2G 67
Hawkins Clo. NW7 —5B 24
Hawkins Clo. Borwd —4A 12
Hawkins Clo. Harr —5B 38
Hawkins Ct. SE18 —5J 79
Hawkins Ho. SE8 —7L 77
(off New King St.)
Hawkins Ho. SW1 —7G 75
(off Dolphin Sq.)
Hawkins Rd. Tedd —3F 102
Hawkins Way. SE6 —2L 109
Hawkley Gdns. SE27 —8M 91
Hawkridge Clo. Romf —4G 49
Hawksbrook La. Beck —1M 125
(in two parts)
Hawkshaw Clo. SW2 —6J 91
Hawkshead. NW1 —6G 59
(off Stanhope St.)
Hawkshead Clo. Brom —4C 110
Hawkshead Rd. NW10 —3D 56
Hawkshead Rd. W4 —3C 72
Hawkshill Clo. Esh —8L 117
Hawkshill Pl. Esh —8L 117
Hawkshill Way. Esh —8K 117
Hawkslade Rd. SE15 —4H 93
Hawksley Rd. N16 —8C 44
Hawksmead Clo. Enf —9D 6
Hawks M. SE10 —8A 78
Hawksmoor Clo. E6 —9J 63
Hawksmoor Clo. SE18 —6C 80
Hawksmoor Ho. E14 —8J 61
(off Aston St.)
Hawksmoor M. E1 —1F 76
Hawksmoor Pl. E2 —7E 60
(off Cheshire St.)
Hawksmoor St. W6 —7H 73
Hawksmouth. E4 —9A 18
Hawks Pas. King T —6K 103
(off Fairfield Rd.)
Hawks Rd. King T —6K 103
Hawkstone Rd. SE16 —5G 77
Hawkwell Ct. E4 —3A 30
Hawkwell Wlk. N1 —4A 60
(off Maldon Rd.)
Hawkwood Cres. E4 —8M 17
Hawkwood La. Chst —5A 112
Hawkwood Mt. E5 —6F 44
Hawlands Dri. Pinn —5J 37
Hawley. —1K 115
Hawley Clo. Hamp —3K 101
Hawley Cres. NW1 —3F 58
Hawley M. NW1 —3F 58
Hawley Rd. N18 —5H 29
Hawley Rd. NW1 —3F 58
(in three parts)
Hawley Rd. Dart & S at H —8J 99
Hawley St. NW1 —3F 58
Hawley Ter. Dart —1L 115
Hawley Va. Dart —2L 115
Hawstead La. Orp —7K 129
Hawstead Rd. SE6 —5M 93
Hawsted. Buck H —9F 18
Hawtter. NW9 —8D 24
Hawthorn Av. E3 —4K 61
Hawthorn Av. N13 —5J 27
Hawthorn Av. Big H —7H 141
Hawthorn Av. Rain —7F 66
Hawthorn Cen. Harr —3D 38
Hawthorn Clo. Ab L —5E 4
Hawthorn Clo. Bans —6J 135
Hawthorn Clo. Hamp —2L 101
Hawthorn Clo. Houn —8F 68
Hawthorn Clo. Orp —1B 128
Hawthorn Clo. Wat —2D 8
Hawthorn Cotts. Well —2E 96
(off Hook La.)
Hawthorn Ct. Pinn —9G 21
(off Rickmansworth Rd.)
Hawthorn Ct. Rich —9M 71
Hawthorn Cres. SW17 —2E 106
Hawthorn Cres. S Croy —3G 139
Hawthornden Clo. N12 —6C 26
Hawthorndene Clo. Brom —4D 126
Hawthorndene Rd. Brom —4D 126
Hawthorn Dri. Den —2A 142
Hawthorn Dri. Harr —4L 37
Hawthorn Dri. W W'ck —6C 126
Hawthorne Av. Cars —9E 122
Hawthorne Av. Chesh —4B 6
Hawthorne Av. Harr —4E 38
Hawthorne Av. Mitc —6B 106
Hawthorne Av. Ruis —4F 36
Hawthorne Av. T Hth —5M 107
Hawthorne Clo. N1 —2C 60
Hawthorne Clo. Brom —7K 111
Hawthorne Clo. Chesh —4B 6
Hawthorne Clo. Sutt —4A 122
Hawthorne Ct. W5 —2J 71
Hawthorne Ct. N'wd —9E 20
Hawthorne Ct. Stanw —6B 144
(off Hawthorne Way)
Hawthorne Cres. W Dray —3K 143
Hawthorne Farm Av. N'holt —4J 53
Hawthorne Gro. NW9 —5A 40
Hawthorne Ho. SW1 —6G 75
(off Churchill Gdns.)
Hawthorne M. Gnfd —9A 54
Hawthorne Pl. Eps —4C 134
Hawthorne Pl. Hay —1D 68
Hawthorne Rd. E17 —1L 45
Hawthorne Rd. Brom —7J 111
Hawthorne Way. Stanw —6B 144
Hawthorn Gdns. W5 —4H 71
Hawthorn Gro. SE20 —4F 108
Hawthorn Gro. Barn —8D 12
Hawthorn Gro. Enf —2B 16
Hawthorn Hatch. Bren —8F 70
Hawthorn M. NW7 —8J 25
Hawthorn Pl. Eri —6A 82
Hawthorn Rd. N8 —1H 43
Hawthorn Rd. N18 —6D 28
Hawthorn Rd. NW10 —3E 56
Hawthorn Rd. Bexh —3K 97
Hawthorn Rd. Bren —8F 70
Hawthorn Rd. Buck H —4H 31
Hawthorn Rd. Dart —8H 99
Hawthorn Rd. Sutt —8C 122
Hawthorn Rd. Wall —9F 122
Hawthorns. S Croy —6M 123
(off Bramley Hill)
Hawthorns. Wfd G —3E 30
Hawthorns, The. Eps —9D 120
Hawthorns, The. Lou —6L 19
Hawthorn Wlk. W10 —7J 57
Hawthorn Way. N9 —2C 28
Hawthorn Way. Shep —8B 100
Hawtrey Av. N'holt —5H 53
Hawtrey Dri. Ruis —5E 36
Hawtrey Rd. NW3 —3C 58
Haxted Rd. Brom —5F 110
Hayburn Way. Horn —6D 50
Hay Clo. E15 —3C 62
Hay Clo. Borwd —4A 12
Haycroft Gdns. NW10 —4E 56
Haycroft Rd. SW2 —4J 91
Haycroft Rd. Surb —4H 119
Hay Currie St. E14 —9M 61
Hayday Rd. E16 —8E 62
Hayden Rd. Wal A —8J 7
Haydens Clo. Orp —1G 129
Haydens M. W3 —9A 56
Hayden's Pl. W11 —9K 57
Hayden Way. Romf —9A 34
Haydn Av. Purl —6L 137
Haydock Av. N'holt —2L 53
Haydock Clo. Horn —9K 51
Haydock Grn. N'holt —2L 53
Haydock Grn. Flats. N'holt —2L 53
(off Haydock Grn.)
Haydon Clo. NW9 —2A 40
Haydon Clo. Enf —8C 16
Haydon Dri. Pinn —2E 36
Haydon Pk. Rd. SW19 —2L 105
Haydon Rd. Dag —7G 49
Haydon Rd. Wat —8J 9
Haydons Rd. SW19 —2M 105
Haydon St. EC3 —1D 76
Haydon Wlk. E1 —9D 60
Haydon Way. SW11 —3B 90
Hayes. —3E 126
(Bromley)
Hayes. —9C 52
(Hillingdon)
Hayes Bri. Retail Cen. Hay —1G 69
Hayes Chase. W W'ck —1B 126
Hayes Clo. Brom —4E 126
Hayes Ct. SE5 —8A 76
(off Camberwell New Rd.)
Hayes Ct. SW2 —7J 91
Hayes Cres. NW11 —3K 41
Hayes Cres. Sutt —6H 121
Hayes Dri. Rain —3F 66
Hayes End. —8B 52
Hayes End Clo. Hay —8B 52
Hayes End Dri. Hay —7B 52
Hayes End Rd. Hay —7B 52
Hayes F.C. —1D 68
Hayesford Pk. Dri. Brom —9D 110
Hayes Garden. Brom —4E 126
Hayes Hill. Brom —3C 126
Hayes Hill Farm. —1J 7
Hayes Hill Rd. Brom —3D 126
Hayes La. Beck —7A 110
Hayes La. Brom —9E 110
Hayes La. Kenl —8M 137
Hayes Mead Rd. Brom —3C 126
Hayes Metro Cen. Hay —1G 69
Hayes Pl. NW1 —7C 58
Hayes Rd. Brom —8E 110
Hayes Rd. S'hall —5F 68
Hayes St. Brom —3F 126
Hayes Town. —3D 68
Hayes Way. Beck —8A 110
Hayes Wood Av. Brom & Hayes —3F 126
Hayfield Clo. Bush —6M 9
Hayfield Pas. E1 —7G 61
Hayfield Rd. Orp —9E 112
Hayfield Yd. E1 —7G 61
Haygarth Pl. SW19 —2H 105
Haygreen Clo. King T —3M 103
Hay Hill. W1 —1F 74
Hayland Clo. NW9 —2B 40
Hay La. NW9 —2A 40
Hayles Bldgs. SE11 —5M 75
(off Elliotts Row)
Hayles St. SE11 —5M 75
Haylett Gdns. King T —8H 103
Hayling Av. Felt —9E 84
Hayling Clo. N16 —1C 60
Hayling Ct. Sutt —6G 121
Hayling Rd. Wat —3E 20
Haymaker Clo. Uxb —3D 142
Hayman Cres. Hay —5B 52
Haymans Point. SE11 —5K 75
Hayman St. N1 —3M 59
Haymarket. SW1 —1H 75
Haymarket Arc. SW1 —1H 75
(off Haymarket)
Haymarket Theatre Royal. —1H 75
(off Haymarket)
Haymeads Dri. Esh —8A 118
Haymer Gdns. Wor Pk —5E 120
Haymerle Ho. SE15 —7E 76
(off Haymerle Rd.)
Haymerle Rd. SE15 —7E 76
Haymill Clo. Gnfd —6D 54
Hayne Ho. W11 —2J 73
(off Penzance Pl.)
Hayne Rd. Beck —6K 109
Haynes Clo. N11 —3E 26
Haynes Clo. N17 —7F 28
Haynes Clo. SE3 —2C 94
Haynes La. SE19 —3C 108
Haynes Rd. Horn —2H 51
Haynes Rd. Wemb —3J 55
Hayne St. EC1 —8M 59
Haynt Wlk. SW20 —7J 105
Hay's Galleria. SE1 —2C 76
Hays La. SE1 —2C 76
Haysleigh Gdns. SE20 —6E 108
Hay's M. W1 —2F 74
Haysoms Clo. Romf —2C 50
Haystall Clo. Hay —5C 52
Hay St. E2 —4E 60
Hays Wlk. Sutt —2H 135
Hayter Ct. E11 —7F 46
Hayter Rd. SW2 —4J 91
Hayton Clo. E8 —2D 60
Hayward Clo. SW19 —4M 105
Hayward Clo. Dart —4B 98
Hayward Ct. SW9 —1J 91
(off Clapham Rd.)
Hayward Dri. Dart —8K 99
Hayward Gallery. —2K 75
(off Belvedere Rd.)
Hayward Gdns. SW15 —5G 89
Hayward Rd. N20 —2A 26
Hayward Rd. Th Dit —3D 118
Haywards Clo. Chad H —3F 48
Hayward's Pl. EC1 —7M 59
Haywards Yd. SE4 —4K 93
(off Lindal Rd.)
Haywood Clo. Pinn —9H 21
Haywood Ct. Wal A —7M 7
Haywood Lodge. N11 —6J 27
(off Oak La.)
Haywood Ri. Orp —7C 128
Haywood Rd. Brom —8H 111
Hayworth Clo. Enf —4J 17
Hazel Av. W Dray —1L 143
Hazel Bank. SE25 —6C 108
Hazel Bank. Surb —3A 120
Hazelbank Rd. SE6 —8B 94
Hazelbourne Rd. SW12 —5F 90
Hazelbrouck Gdns. Ilf —7B 32
Hazelbury Av. Ab L —5A 4
Hazelbury Clo. SW19 —6L 105
Hazelbury Grn. N9 —3C 28
Hazelbury La. N9 —3C 28
Hazel Clo. N13 —3B 28
Hazel Clo. N19 —7G 43
Hazel Clo. SE15 —1E 92
Hazel Clo. Bren —8F 70
Hazel Clo. Croy —2H 125
Hazel Clo. Horn —8F 50
Hazel Clo. Mitc —8H 107
Hazel Clo. Twic —6A 86
Hazel Ct. W5 —1J 71
Hazel Ct. Lou —5K 19
Hazel Cres. Romf —8M 33
Hazel Cft. Pinn —6M 21
Hazelcroft Clo. Uxb —3D 142
Hazeldean Rd. NW10 —3B 56
Hazeldene. Wal X —5E 6
Hazeldene Ct. Kenl —7B 138
Hazeldene Dri. Pinn —1G 37
Hazeldene Gdns. Uxb —4A 52
Hazeldene Rd. Ilf —7F 48
Hazeldene Rd. Well —1G 97
Hazeldon Rd. SE4 —4J 93
Hazel Dri. Eri —9E 82
Hazeleigh Gdns. Wfd G —5J 31
Hazel End. Swan —9C 114
Hazel Gdns. Edgw —4M 23
Hazelgreen Clo. N21 —1M 27
Hazel Gro. SE26 —1H 109
Hazel Gro. Orp —4M 127
Hazel Gro. Romf —1J 49
Hazel Gro. Wat —8F 4
Hazel Gro. Wemb —4J 55
Hazelhurst. Beck —5B 110
Hazelhurst Ct. SE6 —2A 110
(off Beckenham Hill Rd.)
Hazelhurst Rd. SW17 —1A 106
Hazel La. Rich —8J 87
Hazellville Rd. N19 —5H 43
Hazel Mead. Barn —7F 12
Hazel Mead. Eps —2E 134
Hazelmere Clo. Felt —5C 84
Hazelmere Clo. N'holt —5K 53
Hazelmere Ct. SW2 —7K 91
Hazelmere Dri. N'holt —5K 53
Hazelmere Gdns. Horn —3G 51
Hazelmere Rd. NW6 —4K 57
Hazelmere Rd. N'holt —5K 53
Hazelmere Rd. Orp —8A 112
Hazelmere Wlk. N'holt —5K 53
Hazelmere Way. Brom —1E 126
Hazel Ri. Horn —4G 51
Hazel Rd. E15 —1C 62
Hazel Rd. NW10 —6F 56
(in two parts)
Hazel Rd. Dart —8H 99
Hazel Rd. Eri —9E 82
Hazel Rd. Park —1M 5
Hazeltree La. N'holt —6J 53
Hazel Tree Rd. Wat —1F 8
Hazel Wlk. Brom —1L 127
Hazel Way. E4 —6K 29
Hazel Way. SE1 —5D 76
Hazelwood. Lou —7H 19
Hazelwood Av. Mord —8M 105
Hazelwood Clo. W5 —3J 71
Hazelwood Clo. Harr —2M 37
Hazelwood Ct. N13 —4L 27
(off Hazelwood La.)
Hazelwood Ct. NW10 —8C 40
Hazelwood Ct. Surb —1J 119
Hazelwood Cres. N13 —4L 27
Hazelwood Dri. Pinn —9F 20
Hazelwood Gro. S Croy —5F 138
Hazelwood Ho. SE8 —5J 77
Hazelwood Houses. Short —7C 110
Hazelwood La. N13 —4L 27
Hazelwood La. Ab L —5A 4
Hazelwood Pk. Clo. Chig —5C 32
Hazelwood Rd. E17 —3J 45
Hazelwood Rd. Crox G —8A 8
Hazelwood Rd. Enf —8D 16
Hazlebury Rd. SW6 —1M 89
Hazledean Rd. Croy —4B 124
Hazledene Rd. W4 —7A 72
Hazlemere Gdns. Wor Pk —3E 120
Hazlewell Rd. SW15 —4G 89
Hazlewood Clo. E5 —8J 45
Hazlewood Cres. W10 —7J 57
Hazlewood Tower. W10 —7J 57
(off Golborne Gdns.)
Hazlitt Clo. Felt —1J 101
Hazlitt M. W14 —4J 73
Hazlitt Rd. W14 —4J 73
Hazon Way. Eps —4A 134
Heacham Av. Uxb —8A 36
Headbourne Ho. SE1 —4B 76
(off Law St.)
Headcorn Pl. T Hth —8K 107
Headcorn Rd. N17 —7D 28
Headcorn Rd. Brom —2D 110
Headcorn Rd. T Hth —8K 107
Headfort Pl. SW1 —3E 74
Headingley Clo. Ilf —6D 32
Headington Ct. Croy —6A 124
(off Tanfield Rd.)
Headington Rd. SW18 —8A 90
Headlam Rd. SW4 —5H 91
(in two parts)

Henry Ho.—Highfield

Henry Ho. SW8 —8J 75
(off Wyvil Rd.)
Henry Jackson Rd. SW15 —2H 89
Henry Macaulay Av. King T —5H 103
Henry Peters Dri. Tedd —2C 102
Henry Rd. E6 —5J 63
Henry Rd. N4 —6A 44
Henry Rd. Barn —7B 14
Henrys Av. Wfd G —5D 30
Henryson Rd. SE4 —4L 93
Henry St. Brom —5F 110
Henry's Wlk. Ilf —7B 32
Henry Wise Ho. SW1 —5G 75
(off Vauxhall Bri. Rd.)
Hensford Gdns. SE26 —1F 108
Henshall St. N1 —2B 60
Henshawe Rd. Dag —8H 49
Henshaw St. SE17 —5B 76
Henslowe Rd. SE22 —4E 92
Henslow Ho. SE15 —8E 76
(off Peckham Pk. Rd.)
Henson Av. NW2 —1G 57
Henson Clo. Orp —4M 127
Henson Path. Harr —1H 39
Henson Pl. N'holt —4G 53
Henstridge Pl. NW8 —4C 58
Henty Clo. SW11 —8C 74
Henty Wlk. SW15 —4F 88
Henville Rd. Brom —5F 110
Henwick Rd. SE9 —2H 95
Henwood Side. Wfd G —6K 31
Hepburn Gdns. Brom —3C 126
Hepburn M. SW11 —4D 90
Hepple Clo. Iswth —1F 86
Hepplestone Clo. SW15 —5F 88
Hepscott Rd. E9 —2L 61
Hepworth Ct. N1 —4M 59
(off Gaskin St.)
Hepworth Ct. NW3 —1C 58
Hepworth Gdns. Bark —1E 64
Hepworth Rd. SW16 —4J 107
Hepworth Way. W on T —3D 116
Heracles. NW9 —8D 24
(off Five Acre)
Heracles Clo. Wall —9J 123
Hera Ct. E14 —5L 77
(off Homer Dri.)
Herald Gdns. Wall —4F 122
Herald's Pl. SE11 —5M 75
Herald St. E2 —7F 60
Herald Wlk. Dart —4K 99
Herbal Hill. EC1 —7L 59
Herbal Hill Gdns. EC1 —7L 59
Herbal Pl. EC1 —7L 59
(off Herbal Hill)
Herbert Cres. SW1 —4D 74
Herbert Gdns. NW10 —5F 56
Herbert Gdns. W4 —7M 71
Herbert Gdns. Romf —5H 49
Herbert Ho. E1 —9D 60
(off Old Castle St.)
Herbert Morrison Ho. SW6 —7K 73
(off Clem Attlee Ct.)
Herbert Pl. SE18 —7M 79
Herbert Rd. E12 —9J 47
Herbert Rd. E17 —5K 45
Herbert Rd. N11 —7J 27
Herbert Rd. N15 —3D 44
Herbert Rd. NW9 —4E 40
Herbert Rd. SE18 —8L 79
(in two parts)
Herbert Rd. SW19 —4K 105
(in two parts)
Herbert Rd. Bexh —1J 97
Herbert Rd. Brom —9H 111
Herbert Rd. Horn —5J 51
Herbert Rd. Ilf —7C 48
Herbert Rd. King T —7K 103
Herbert Rd. S'hall —2K 69
Herbert Rd. Swan —3F 114
Herbert St. E13 —5E 62
Herbert St. NW5 —2E 58
Herbrand Est. WC1 —7J 59
Herbrand St. WC1 —7J 59
Hercies Rd. Uxb —3D 142
Hercules Pl. N7 —8J 43
(in two parts)
Hercules Rd. SE1 —4K 75
Hercules St. N7 —8J 43
Hercules Tower. SE14 —7J 77
Hercules Wharf. E14 —1C 78
(off Orchard Pl.)
Hercules Yd. N7 —8J 43
Hereford Av. Barn —1D 26
Hereford Bldgs. SW3 —7B 74
Hereford Clo. Eps —5B 134
Hereford Ct. W7 —8D 54
(off Copley Clo.)
Hereford Ct. Harr —2C 38
Hereford Ct. Sutt —9L 121
Hereford Gdns. SE13 —4C 94
Hereford Gdns. Ilf —5J 47
Hereford Gdns. Pinn —3J 37
Hereford Gdns. Twic —7A 86
Hereford Ho. NW6 —5L 57
(off Carlton Va.)
Hereford Ho. SW3 —4C 74
(off Old Brompton Rd.)
Hereford Ho. SW10 —8M 73
(off Fulham Rd.)
Hereford M. W2 —9L 57
Hereford Pl. SE14 —8K 77
Hereford Retreat. SE15 —8E 76
Hereford Rd. E11 —3F 46
Hereford Rd. W2 —9L 57
Hereford Rd. W3 —1M 71
Hereford Rd. W5 —4G 71
Hereford Rd. Felt —7G 85
Hereford Sq. SW7 —5A 74
Hereford St. E2 —7E 60
Hereford Way. Chess —7G 119
Herent Dri. Ilf —2J 47
Hereward Av. Purl —3L 137
Hereward Clo. Wal A —5K 7
Hereward Gdns. N13 —5L 27
Hereward Rd. SW17 —1D 106
Herga Ct. Harr —8C 38
Herga Ct. Wat —4E 8
Herga Rd. Harr —2D 38
Heriot Av. E4 —2L 29
Heriot Rd. NW4 —3G 41
Heriots Clo. Stan —4E 22
Heritage Clo. SW9 —2M 91
Heritage Clo. Uxb —7A 142
Heritage Ct. SE8 —6H 77
(off Trundley's Rd.)
Heritage Hill. Kes —7G 127
Heritage Vw. Harr —8D 38
Herkomer Clo. Bush —8M 9
Herkomer Rd. Bush —7L 9
Herlwyn Av. Ruis —7C 36
Herlwyn Gdns. SW17 —1D 106
Her Majesty's Theatre. —2H 75
(off Haymarket)
Herm Clo. Iswth —8A 70
Hermes Clo. W9 —7L 57
Hermes Ct. SW9 —9L 75
(off Southey Rd.)
Hermes St. N1 —5L 59
Hermes Wlk. N'holt —5L 53
Hermes Way. Wall —9H 123
Herm Ho. N1 —2A 60
Herm Ho. Enf —2H 17
Hermiston Av. N8 —3J 43
Hermitage Clo. E18 —2D 46
Hermitage Clo. Clay —8E 118
Hermitage Clo. Enf —4M 15
Hermitage Ct. E1 —2E 76
(off Knighten St.)
Hermitage Ct. E18 —2E 46
Hermitage Ct. NW2 —8L 41
Hermitage Gdns. NW2 —8L 41
Hermitage Gdns. SE19 —4A 108
Hermitage Grn. SW16 —5J 107
Hermitage La. N18 —5B 28
Hermitage La. NW2 —8L 41
Hermitage La. SE25 —1E 124
(in two parts)
Hermitage La. SW16 —4K 107
Hermitage La. Croy & SE25 —2E 124
Hermitage Path. SW16 —5J 107
Hermitage Rd. N4 & N15 —5M 43
Hermitage Rd. SE19 —4A 108
Hermitage Rd. Kenl —7A 138
Hermitage Rooms. —1K 75
(off Embankment)
Hermitage Row. E8 —1E 60
Hermitage St. W2 —8B 58
Hermitage, The. SE13 —1A 94
Hermitage, The. SE23 —7G 93
Hermitage, The. SW13 —9D 72
Hermitage, The. Felt —9D 84
Hermitage, The. King T —8H 103
Hermitage, The. Rich —4J 87
Hermitage, The. Uxb —2B 142
Hermitage Wlk. E18 —2D 46
Hermitage Wall. E1 —2E 76
Hermitage Way. Stan —8E 22
Hermit Pl. NW6 —4M 57
Hermit Rd. E16 —8D 62
Hermit St. EC1 —6M 59
Hermon Gro. Hay —2E 68
Hermon Hill. E11 & E18 —3E 46
Herndon Rd. SW18 —4A 90
Herne Clo. NW10 —1B 56
Herne Ct. Bush —9A 10
Herne Hill. —4A 92
Herne Hill. SE24 —5A 92
Herne Hill Ho. SE24 —5M 91
(off Railton Rd.)
Herne Hill Rd. SE24 —2A 92
Herne Hill Stadium. —3B 92
Herne M. N18 —4E 28
Herne Pl. SE24 —4M 91
Herne Rd. Bush —8M 9
Herne Rd. Surb —4H 119
Heron Clo. E17 —9K 29
Heron Clo. NW10 —2C 56
Heron Clo. Buck H —1E 30
Heron Clo. Sutt —7K 121
Heron Clo. Uxb —2B 142
Heron Ct. E14 —4A 78
(off New Union Clo.)
Heron Ct. Brom —8G 111
Heron Ct. Eps —6E 134
Heron Ct. King T —7J 103
Heron Ct. Ruis —7B 36
Heron Cres. Sidc —9C 96
Herondale. S Croy —1H 139
Herondale Av. SW18 —7B 90
Heron Dri. N4 —7A 44
Heron Flight Av. Horn —3E 66
Herongate Clo. Enf —4D 16
Herongate Rd. E12 —7G 47
Herongate Rd. Swan —3C 114
Heron Hill. Belv —6K 81
Heron Ho. E6 —3J 63
Heron Ho. NW8 —5C 58
(off Barrow Hill Est.)
Heron Ho. SW11 —8C 74
(off Searles Clo.)
Heron Ho. W13 —7E 54
Heron Ho. Sidc —9F 96
Heron Ind. Est. E15 —5M 61
Heron M. Ilf —7M 47
Heron Pl. SE16 —2J 77
Heron Pl. W1 —9E 58
(off Thayer St.)
Heron Quay. E14 —2L 77
Heron Rd. SE24 —3A 92
Heron Rd. Croy —4C 124
Heron Rd. Twic —3E 86
Heronry, The. W on T —8E 116
Herons Cft. Wey —8A 116
Heronsforde. W13 —9G 55
Herons Ga. Edgw —5L 23
Heron's Lea. N6 —4D 42
Herons Lea. Wat —9G 5
Heronslea Dri. Stan —5J 23
Heron's Pl. Iswth —2F 86
Heron Sq. Rich —4H 87
Herons Ri. New Bar —6C 14
Herons, The. E11 —4D 46
Herons, The. Horn —6H 51
Heronswood. Wal A —7L 7
Heron Trad. Est. W3 —8M 55
Heron Wlk. N'wd —4C 20
Heron Way. Wfd G —4G 31
Herrick Ho. SE5 —8B 76
(off Elmington Est.)
Herrick Rd. N5 —8A 44
Herrick St. SW1 —5H 75
Herries St. W10 —5J 57
Herringham Rd. SE7 —4G 79
Herron Ct. Short —8D 110
Hersant Clo. NW10 —4E 56
Herschell M. SE5 —2A 92
Herschell Rd. SE23 —6J 93
Hersham. —7H 117
Hersham By-Pass. W on T —7F 116
Hersham Clo. SW15 —6E 88
Hersham Gdns. W on T —6F 116
Hersham Green. —8H 117
Hersham Grn. Cen. W on T —7H 117
Hersham Pl. W on T —7H 117
Hersham Rd. W on T —3E 116
Hersham Trad. Est. W on T —4J 117
Hershell Ct. SW14 —3M 87
Hertford Av. SW14 —4B 88
Hertford Clo. Barn —5B 14
Hertford Ct. E6 —6K 63
(off Vicarage La.)
Hertford Ct. N13 —3L 27
Hertford Pl. W1 —7G 59
Hertford Rd. N1 —4C 60
(in two parts)
Hertford Rd. N2 —1C 42
Hertford Rd. N9 & Wal X —2F 28
Hertford Rd. Bark —3L 63
Hertford Rd. Barn —5A 14
Hertford Rd. Ilf —4C 48
Hertford Sq. Mitc —8J 107
Hertford St. W1 —2F 74
Hertford Wlk. Belv —6L 81
Hertford Way. Mitc —8J 107
Hertslet Rd. N7 —8K 43
Hertsmere Ho. E14 —1L 77
(off Hertsmere Rd.)
Hertsmere Ind. Pk. Borwd —5B 12
Hertsmere Rd. E14 —2L 77
Hertswood Ct. Barn —6J 13
Hervey Clo. N3 —8L 25
Hervey Pk. Rd. E17 —2J 45
Hervey Rd. SE3 —9F 78
Hervey Way. N3 —8L 25
Hesa Rd. Hay —9E 52
Hesewall Clo. SW4 —1G 91
Hesiers Hill. Warl —9C 140
Hesiers Rd. Warl —8C 140
Hesketh Av. Dart —7M 99
Hesketh Pl. W11 —1J 73
Hesketh Rd. E7 —8E 46
Heslop Rd. SW12 —7D 90
Hesper M. SW5 —5M 73
Hesperus Clo. E14 —5M 77
Hesperus Cres. E14 —5M 77
Hessel Rd. W13 —3E 70
Hessel St. E1 —9F 60
Hesselyn Dri. Rain —3F 66
Hessle Gro. Eps —3D 134
Hestercombe Av. SW6 —1J 89
Hesterman Way. Croy —3K 123
Hester Rd. N18 —5E 28
Hester Rd. SW11 —8C 74
Hester Ter. Rich —2L 87
Heston. —8L 69
Heston Av. Houn —7J 69
Heston Cen., The. Houn —6G 69
Heston Grange. Houn —7K 69
Heston Grange La. Houn —7K 69
Heston Ho. SE8 —9L 77
Heston Ind. Cen. Houn —7G 69
Heston Ind. Mall. Houn —8K 69
Heston Rd. Houn —8L 69
Heston St. SE14 —9L 77
Heswell Grn. Wat —3E 20
Hetherington Rd. SW4 —3J 91
Hetherington Rd. Shep —6A 100
Hethpool Ho. W2 —7B 58
(off Hall Pl.)
Hetley Gdns. SE19 —4D 108
Hetley Rd. W12 —2F 72
Heton Gdns. NW4 —2F 40
Hevelius Clo. SE10 —6D 78
Hever Cft. SE9 —1L 111
Hever Gdns. Brom —6L 111
Heverham Rd. SE18 —5C 80
Hever Ho. SE15 —7H 77
(off Lovelinch Clo.)
Heversham Ho. SE15 —7G 77
Heversham Rd. Bexh —1L 97
Hewens Rd. Uxb —7A 52
Hewer St. W10 —8H 57
Hewett Clo. Stan —4F 22
Hewett Pl. Swan —8B 114
Hewett Rd. Dag —1H 65
Hewett St. EC2 —7C 60
Hewins Clo. Wal A —5L 7
Hewish Rd. N18 —4C 28
Hewison St. E3 —5K 61
Hewitt Av. N22 —9M 27
Hewitt Clo. Croy —5L 125
Hewitt Rd. N8 —3L 43
Hewitts Rd. Orp —9K 129
Hewitts Roundabout. (Junct.) —9K 129
Hewlett Ho. SW8 —8F 74
(off Havelock Ter.)
Hewlett Rd. E3 —5J 61
Hexagon Ho. Romf —3D 50
(off Mercury Gdns.)
Hexagon, The. N6 —6D 42
Hexal Rd. SE6 —9C 94
Hexham Gdns. Iswth —8E 70
Hexham Rd. SE27 —8A 92
Hexham Rd. Barn —6M 13
Hexham Rd. Mord —3M 121
Hextable. —4D 114
Heybourne Rd. N17 —7F 28
Heybridge. NW1 —2F 58
(off Lewis St.)
Heybridge Av. SW16 —4J 107
Heybridge Dri. Ilf —9B 32
Heybridge Way. E10 —5J 45
Heydon Ho. SE14 —9G 77
(off Kender St.)
Heyford Av. SW8 —8J 75
Heyford Av. SW20 —7K 105
Heyford Rd. Mitc —6C 106
Heyford Rd. Rad —1D 10
Heyford Ter. SW8 —8J 75
Heygate St. SE17 —5A 76
Heylyn Sq. E3 —6K 61
Heynes Rd. Dag —9G 49
Heysham Dri. Wat —5G 21
Heysham La. NW3 —8M 41
Heysham Rd. N15 —4B 44
Heythorp St. SW18 —7K 89
Heywood Av. NW9 —8C 24
Heywood Ct. Stan —5G 23
Heywood Ho. SE14 —7H 77
(off Myers La.)
Heyworth Rd. E5 —9F 44
Heyworth Rd. E15 —1D 62
Hibbert Av. Wat —2H 9
Hibbert Rd. E17 —5K 45
Hibbert Rd. Harr & W'stone —9D 22
Hibbert St. SW11 —2B 90
Hibbs Clo. Swan —6B 114
Hibernia Gdns. Houn —3L 85
Hibernia Point. SE2 —3H 81
(off Wolvercote Rd.)
Hibernia Rd. Houn —3L 85
Hibiscus Clo. Edgw —4A 24
Hichisson Rd. SE15 —4G 93
Hickes Ho. NW6 —3B 58
Hickey's Almshouses. Rich —3K 87
Hickin Clo. SE7 —5H 79
Hickin St. E14 —4A 78
Hickleton. NW1 —4G 59
(off Camden St.)
Hickling Ho. SE16 —4F 76
(off Slippers Pl.)
Hickling Rd. Ilf —1M 63
Hickman Av. E4 —6A 30
Hickman Clo. E16 —8H 63
Hickman Rd. Romf —5G 49
Hickmore Wlk. SW4 —2H 91
Hickory Clo. N9 —9E 16
Hicks Av. Gnfd —6B 54
Hicks Clo. SW11 —2C 90
Hicks Ct. Dag —8M 49
Hicks St. SE8 —6J 77
Hidcote Gdns. SW20 —7F 104
Hide. E6 —9L 63
Hideaway, The. Ab L —4D 4
Hide Pl. SW1 —5H 75
Hider Ct. SE3 —8G 79
Hide Rd. Harr —2A 38
Hides St. N7 —2K 59
Hide Tower. SW1 —5H 75
(off Regency St.)
Higgins Ho. N1 —4C 60
(off Colville Est.)
Higginson Ho. NW3 —3D 58
(off Fellows Rd.)
Higgins Wlk. Hamp —3J 101
(off Abbott Clo.)
Higgs Ind. Est. SE24 —2M 91
High Acres. Ab L —5B 4
High Acres. Enf —5M 15
Higham Hill. —9J 29
Higham Hill Rd. E17 —8J 29
Higham Path. E17 —1J 45
Higham Pl. E17 —1J 45
Higham Rd. N17 —1B 44
Higham Rd. Wfd G —6E 30
Highams Ct. E4 —3B 30
Highams Hill. Warl —4E 140
Highams Lodge Bus. Cen. E17 —1H 45
Highams Park. —6B 30
Highams Pk. Ind. Est. E4 —6A 30
Higham Sta. Av. E4 —6L 29
Highams, The. E17 —8A 30
Higham St. E17 —1J 45
Highbanks Clo. Well —8F 80
Highbanks Rd. Pinn —6M 21
Highbank Way. N8 —4L 43
High Barnet. —4H 13
Highbarrow Rd. Croy —3E 124
High Beech. —2F 18
High Beech. N21 —8K 15
High Beech. S Croy —9C 124
High Beeches. Bans —6G 135
High Beeches. Orp —8E 128
High Beeches. Sidc —2J 113
High Beeches Clo. Purl —2H 137
High Beech Rd. Lou —6H 19
High Birch Ct. New Bar —6C 14
(off Park Rd.)
High Bri. SE10 —6B 78
Highbridge Ct. SE14 —8G 77
(off Farrow La.)
Highbridge Ind. Est. Uxb —3A 142
Highbridge Retail Pk. Wal A —7H 7
Highbridge Rd. Bark —4M 63
Highbridge St. Wal A —6H 7
(in two parts)
High Bri. Wharf. SE10 —6B 78
(off High Bri.)
Highbrook Rd. SE3 —2H 95
High Broom Cres. W W'ck —2M 125
Highbury. —9M 43
Highbury Av. T Hth —6L 107
Highbury Barn. N5 —9A 44
Highbury Clo. N Mald —8A 104
Highbury Clo. W W'ck —4M 125
Highbury Corner. (Junct.) —2M 59
Highbury Cres. N5 —1M 59
Highbury Est. N5 —1A 60
Highbury Gdns. Ilf —7C 48
Highbury Grange. N5 —9A 44
Highbury Gro. N5 —1M 59
Highbury Hill. N5 —8L 43
Highbury M. N7 —2L 59
Highbury New Pk. N5 —1A 60
Highbury Pk. N5 —8M 43
Highbury Pk. M. N5 —9A 44
Highbury Pl. N5 —2M 59
Highbury Quad. N5 —8A 44
Highbury Rd. SW19 —2J 105
Highbury Sta. Rd. N1 —2L 59
Highbury Ter. N5 —1M 59
Highbury Ter. M. N5 —1M 59
High Canons. Borwd —1A 12
High Cedar Dri. SW20 —4G 105
Highclere Clo. Kenl —7A 138
Highclere Rd. N Mald —7B 104
Highclere St. SE26 —1J 109
Highcliffe. W13 —8F 54
(off Clivedon Ct.)
Highcliffe Dri. SW15 —5D 88
Highcliffe Gdns. Ilf —3J 47
Highcombe. SE7 —7F 78
Highcombe Clo. SE9 —7H 95
High Coombe Pl. King T —3B 104
High Cft. NW9 —3C 40
Highcroft Av. Wemb —3L 55
High Cft. Cotts. Swan —8E 114
Highcroft Est. N19 —5J 43
Highcroft Gdns. NW11 —4K 41
Highcroft Rd. N19 —5J 43
High Cross. —1B 10
High Cross. A'ham —1B 10
High Cross Cen., The. N15 —2E 44
High Cross Rd. N17 —1E 44
Highcross Way. SW15 —7E 88
Highdaun Dri. SW16 —8K 107
Highdown. Wor Pk —4C 120
Highdown La. Sutt —3M 135
Highdown Rd. SW15 —5F 88
High Dri. N Mald —5A 104
High Dri. Oxs —6B 132
High Elms. Chig —4C 32
High Elms. Wfd G —5E 30
High Elms Clo. N'wd —6A 20
High Elms La. Wat —4F 4
High Elms Rd. Dow & Orp —3L 141 & 9A 128
Higher Dri. Bans —4H 135
Higher Dri. Purl —5L 137
Higher Grn. Eps —5E 134
Highfield. Bans —9C 136
Highfield. Bus H —2C 22
Highfield. Felt —7E 84
Highfield. Wat —3K 21

Highfield Av.—Hillrise Mans.

Highfield Av. NW9 —3A 40
Highfield Av. NW11 —5H 41
Highfield Av. Eri —7M 81
Highfield Av. Gnfd —1C 54
Highfield Av. Orp —8D 128
Highfield Av. Pinn —3K 37
Highfield Av. Wemb —8K 39
Highfield Clo. N22 —8L 27
Highfield Clo. NW9 —3A 40
Highfield Clo. SE13 —5B 94
Highfield Clo. N'wd —8C 20
Highfield Clo. Oxs —3B 132
Highfield Clo. Romf —6A 34
Highfield Clo. Surb —3G 119
Highfield Cotts. Dart —3F 114
Highfield Ct. N14 —8G 15
Highfield Ct. NW11 —4J 41
Highfield Cres. Horn —7K 51
Highfield Cres. N'wd —8C 20
Highfield Dri. Brom —8C 110
Highfield Dri. Eps —8D 120
Highfield Dri. W W'ck —4M 125
Highfield Gdns. NW11 —4J 41
Highfield Hill. SE19 —4B 108
Highfield Link. Romf —6A 34
Highfield Rd. N21 —2M 27
Highfield Rd. NW11 —4J 41
Highfield Rd. W3 —8M 55
Highfield Rd. Bexh —4K 97
Highfield Rd. Big H —9G 141
Highfield Rd. Brom —8K 111
Highfield Rd. Bush —7J 9
Highfield Rd. Chst —7D 112
Highfield Rd. Dart —6H 99
Highfield Rd. Felt —8E 84
Highfield Rd. Horn —7K 51
Highfield Rd. Iswth —9D 70
Highfield Rd. N'wd —8C 20
Highfield Rd. Purl —2K 137
Highfield Rd. Romf —7A 34
Highfield Rd. Sun —9D 100
Highfield Rd. Surb —2A 120
Highfield Rd. Sutt —7C 122
Highfield Rd. W on T —3E 116
Highfield Rd. Wfd G —7J 31
Highfield Rd. N. Dart —5H 99
Highfield Rd. S. Dart —6H 99
Highfields. Sutt —4L 121
Highfields Gro. N6 —6D 42
Highfield Towers. Romf —5B 34
Highfield Way. Horn —7K 51
High Firs. Swan —8C 114
High Foleys. Clay —9F 118
High Gables. Brom —6C 110
High Gables. Lou —7H 19
High Garth. Esh —8A 118
Highgate. —6F 42
Highgate Av. N6 —5F 42
Highgate Cemetery. —7F 42
Highgate Clo. N6 —5E 42
Highgate Edge. N2 —3C 42
Highgate Heights. N6 —4G 43
Highgate High St. N6 —6E 42
Highgate Hill. N6 & N19 —6F 42
Highgate Ho. SE26 —9E 92
Highgate Rd. N6 —8E 42
Highgate Spinney. N8 —4H 43
Highgate Wlk. SE23 —8G 93
Highgate W. Hill. N6 —7E 42
High Gro. SE18 —8B 80
High Gro. Brom —5H 111
Highgrove Clo. N11 —5E 26
Highgrove Clo. Chst —5J 111
Highgrove Ct. Beck —4L 109
Highgrove Ct. Sutt —8L 121
Highgrove Ct. Wal X —7C 6
Highgrove M. Cars —5D 122
Highgrove Rd. Dag —1G 65
Highgrove Way. Ruis —4E 36
High Hill Est. E5 —6F 44
High Hill Ferry. E5 —6F 44
High Hill Rd. Warl —7A 140
High Holborn. WC1 —9J 59
Highland Av. W7 —9C 54
Highland Av. Dag —8A 50
Highland Av. Lou —8J 19
Highland Cotts. Wall —6G 123
Highland Ct. E18 —8F 30
Highland Cft. Beck —2M 109
Highland Dri. Bush —9M 9
Highland Pk. Felt —1D 100
Highland Rd. SE19 —3C 108
Highland Rd. Bexh —4L 97
Highland Rd. Brom —5D 110
Highland Rd. N'wd —9D 20
Highland Rd. Purl —6L 137
Highlands. N20 —2C 26
Highlands. Wat —1G 21
Highlands Av. N21 —7K 15
Highlands Av. W3 —1A 72
Highlands Clo. N4 —5J 43
Highlands Clo. Houn —9M 69
Highlands Ct. SE19 —3C 108
Highlands Gdns. Ilf —6K 47
Highlands Heath. SW15 —6G 89
Highlands Hill. Swan —5E 114
Highlands Rd. Barn —7L 13
Highlands Rd. Orp —2F 128
Highlands, The. Barn —6L 13
Highlands, The. Edgw —9M 23
Highlands Village. —7K 15
Highland Ter. SE13 —2M 93
(off Claybank Gro.)
High La. W7 —8B 54
(in two parts)
Highlawn Hall. Harr —8C 38
Highlea Clo. NW9 —7C 24
High Level Dri. SE26 —1E 108
Highlever Rd. W10 —8G 57
Highmead. N18 —5E 28
(off Alpha Rd.)
Highmead. SE18 —8D 80
High Mead. Cars —3B 136
(off Pine Cres.)
High Mead. Chig —2A 32
High Mead. Harr —3C 38
High Mead. W W'ck —4B 126
Highmead Cres. Wemb —3K 55
High Mdw. Clo. Pinn —2G 37
High Mdw. Cres. NW9 —3B 40
High Meadows. Chig —5B 32
High Meads Rd. E16 —9H 63
Highmore Rd. SE3 —8C 78
High Mt. NW4 —4E 40
High Oaks. Enf —2K 15
High Oaks. N'wd —5D 20
High Pde., The. SW16 —9J 91
High Pk. Av. Rich —9L 71
High Pk. Rd. Rich —9L 71
High Path. SW19 —5M 105
High Pine Clo. Wey —7A 116
Highpoint. N6 —5E 42
High Point. SE9 —9M 95
High Ridge. N10 —8F 26
Highridge Clo. Eps —6C 134
High Ridge Pl. Enf —2K 15
(off Oak Av.)
High Rd. E18 —8E 30
High Rd. N11 —5F 26
High Rd. N15 & N17 —3D 44
High Rd. N22 —8K 27
High Rd. NW10 —2C 56
High Rd. Buck H & Lou —2F 30
High Rd. Bus H & Bush —1B 22
High Rd. Chig —5L 31
High Rd. Cow & Uxb —8A 142
High Rd. Dart —9G 99
High Rd. Eastc —4E 36
High Rd. Harr —7C 22
High Rd. Hay —8C 52
High Rd. Ick —8A 36
High Rd. Ilf & Romf —8M 47
(in five parts)
High Rd. Leav —8D 4
High Rd. Romf —5H 49
High Rd. Wemb —1H 55
High Rd. E. Finchley. N2 —8B 26
High Rd. Leyton. E10 & E15 —4M 45
High Rd. Leytonstone. E11 & E15 —9C 46
High Rd. N. Finchley. N12 —3A 26
High Rd. Whetstone. N20 —9A 14
High Rd. Woodford Grn. Wfd G —6D 30
High St. Bans —7L 135
High Sheldon. N6 —4D 42
Highshore Rd. SE15 —1D 92
(in two parts)
High Silver. Lou —6H 19
Highstead Cres. Eri —9C 82
Highstone Av. E11 —4E 46
Highstone Ct. E11 —4D 46
(off New Wanstead)
Highstone Mans. NW1 —3G 59
(off Camden Rd.)
High St. E11 —3E 46
High St. E13 —5E 62
High St. E15 —5A 62
High St. E17 —3J 45
High St. N8 —2J 43
High St. N14 —1H 27
High St. NW7 —5F 24
High St. SE20 —3G 109
High St. SE25 —8D 108
High St. SW19 —2H 105
High St. W3 —2M 71
High St. W5 —2H 71
High St. Ab L —4C 4
High St. B'side —1A 48
High St. Barn —5J 13
High St. Beck —6L 109
High St. Bedm —1D 4
High St. Bren —8G 71
High St. Brom —6E 110
High St. Bush —3K 9
High St. Cars —7E 122
High St. Cheam —8J 121
High St. Chesh —2D 6
High St. Chst —3M 111
High St. Clay —8D 118
High St. Cow —7A 142
High St. Cran —9E 68
High St. Croy —4A 124
(in two parts)
High St. Dart —5J 99
High St. Dow —3L 141
High St. Edgw —6L 23
High St. Els —8H 11
High St. Enf —7G 17
High St. Eps —5B 134
High St. Esh —6M 117
High St. Ewe —1D 134
High St. Eyns —4J 131
High St. Farnb —7M 127
High St. F'ham —1J 131
High St. Felt —9D 84
High St. Grn St —9D 128
High St. Hamp —5A 102
High St. Hamp H —3A 102
High St. Hamp W —5G 103
High St. Harm —7H 143
High St. Harr —6C 38
(HA1)
High St. Harr —9C 22
(HA3)
High St. Hay —7B 68
High St. Horn —6H 51
High St. Houn —2M 85
High St. King T —7H 103
High St. N Mald —8C 104
High St. N'wd —8D 20
High St. Orp —4E 128
High St. Oxs —5B 132
High St. Pinn —1J 37
High St. Purf —6L 83
High St. Purl —3L 137
High St. Romf —3C 50
High St. Ruis —5C 36
High St. St M —1G 129
High St. Shep —1A 116
High St. S'hall —2K 69
High St. Stanw —5B 144
High St. Sutt —6M 121
High St. Swan —7D 114
High St. Tedd —2D 102
High St. Th Dit —1E 118
High St. T Hth —8A 108
High St. Uxb —3A 142
(in two parts)
High St. Wal X —6E 6
(in two parts)
High St. W on T —3E 116
High St. Wat —5F 8
(in four parts)
High St. W'stone —9C 22
High St. Wemb —9K 39
High St. W Dray —1H 143
High St. W Mol —8L 101
High St. W W'ck —3M 125
High St. Whit —6A 86
High St. Colliers Wood. SW19 —4B 106
High St. Harlesden. NW10 —5D 56
High St. M. SW19 —2J 105
High St. N. E12 & E6 —1J 63
High St. S. E6 —5K 63
High Timber St. EC4 —1A 76
High Tor Clo. Brom —4F 110
High Trees. N20 —3A 26
High Trees. SW2 —7L 91
High Trees. Barn —7C 14
High Trees. Croy —3J 125
Hightrees Ct. W7 —1C 70
Highview. N6 —4G 43
Highview. NW7 —3B 24
Highview. N'holt —6J 53
High Vw. Pinn —2G 37
High Vw. Sutt —3K 135
High Vw. Wat —8D 8
Highview Av. Edgw —4A 24
Highview Av. Wall —7K 123
High Vw. Clo. SE19 —6D 108
High Vw. Clo. Lou —7G 19
High Vw. Ct. Har W —7C 22
Highview Ct. Lou —7H 19
Highview Gdns. N3 —1J 41
Highview Gdns. N11 —5G 27
Highview Gdns. Edgw —4A 24
Highview Gdns. Upm —7M 51
Highview Ho. Romf —2J 49
High Vw. Pde. Ilf —3K 47
Highview Path. Bans —7L 135
High Vw. Rd. E18 —9D 30
High Vw. Rd. N2 —8D 26
Highview Rd. SE19 —3B 108
Highview Rd. W13 —8E 54
High Vw. Rd. Dow —2L 141
High Vw. Rd. Sidc —1F 112
Highway, The. E1 & E14 —1E 76
Highway, The. Orp —7F 128
Highway, The. Stan —8D 22
Highway, The. Sutt —1A 136
Highway Trad. Cen., The. E1
(off Heckford St.) —1H 77
Highwold. Coul —9E 136
Highwood. Short —7C 110
Highwood Av. N12 —4A 26
Highwood Av. Bush —3K 9
Highwood Clo. Kenl —9A 138
Highwood Clo. Orp —4A 128
Highwood Ct. N12 —3A 26
Highwood Ct. Barn —7L 13
Highwood Dri. Orp —4A 128
Highwood Gdns. Ilf —3K 47
Highwood Gro. NW7 —5B 24
Highwood Hill. —3D 24
Highwood Hill. NW7 —2D 24
Highwood La. Lou —7L 19
Highwood Rd. N19 —8J 43
High Worple. Harr —5K 37
Highworth Rd. N11 —6H 27
Highworth St. NW1 —8C 58
(off Daventry St.)
Hilary Av. Mitc —7E 106
Hilary Clo. E11 —3E 46
Hilary Clo. SW6 —8M 73
Hilary Clo. Eri —9M 81
Hilary Clo. Horn —1H 67
Hilary Dennis Ct. E11 —2E 46
Hilary Rd. W12 —9D 56
(in two parts)
Hilbert Rd. Sutt —5H 121
Hilborough Ct. E8 —3D 60
Hilborough Way. Orp —7B 128
Hilda Ct. Surb —2H 119
Hilda May Av. Swan —7C 114
Hilda Rd. E6 —3H 63
Hilda Rd. E16 —7C 62
Hilda Ter. SW9 —1L 91
Hilda Va. Clo. Orp —6M 127
Hilda Va. Rd. Orp —6L 127
Hildenborough Gdns. Brom —3C 110
Hildenborough Ho. Beck —4K 109
(off Bethersden Clo.)
Hilden Dri. Eri —8F 82
Hildenlea Pl. Brom —6B 110
Hilderley Ho. King T —7K 103
(off Winery La.)
Hilders, The. Asht —9M 133
Hildreth St. SW12 —7F 90
Hildyard Rd. SW6 —7L 73
Hiley Rd. NW10 —6G 57
Hilfield La. A'ham —3M 9
Hilfield La. S. Bush —8D 10
Hilgrove Rd. NW6 —3A 58
Hiliary Gdns. Stan —9G 23
Hillars Heath Rd. Coul —7J 137
Hillary. N8 —1J 43
(off Boyton Clo.)
Hillary Ct. W12 —3G 73
(off Titmuss St.)
Hillary Cres. W on T —3G 117
Hillary Ho. Borwd —5M 11
(off Eldon Av.)
Hillary Ri. Barn —6L 13
Hillary Rd. S'hall —4L 69
Hill Barn. S Croy —3C 138
Hillbeck Clo. SE15 —8G 77
Hillbeck Way. Gnfd —4B 54
Hillborne Clo. Hay —6E 68
Hillboro Ct. E11 —5B 46
Hillborough Clo. SW19 —4A 106
Hillbrook Rd. SW17 —9D 90
Hill Brow. Brom —5H 111
Hill Brow. Dart —5D 98
Hillbrow. N Mald —7D 104
Hill Brow Clo. Bex —1B 114
Hillbrow Rd. Brom —4C 110
Hillbrow Rd. Esh —6A 118
Hillbury Av. Harr —3F 38
Hillbury Clo. Warl —9F 138
Hillbury Rd. SW17 —9F 90
Hillbury Rd. Warl —9E 138 & 9G 139
Hill Clo. NW2 —8F 40
Hill Clo. NW11 —4L 41
Hill Clo. Barn —7G 13
Hill Clo. Chst —2M 111
Hill Clo. Harr —8C 38
Hill Clo. Purl —5A 138
Hill Clo. Stan —4F 22
Hillcote Av. SW16 —4L 107
Hill Ct. W5 —7K 55
Hill Ct. Barn —6C 14
Hill Ct. N'holt —1L 53
Hill Ct. Romf —2D 50
Hillcourt Av. N12 —6M 25
Hillcourt Est. N16 —6B 44
Hillcourt Rd. SE22 —5F 92
Hill Cres. N20 —2M 25
Hill Cres. Bex —7A 98
Hill Cres. Harr —3E 38
Hill Cres. Horn —4G 51
Hill Cres. Surb —9K 103
Hill Cres. Wor Pk —4G 121
Hillcrest. N6 —5E 42
Hillcrest. N21 —9L 15
Hillcrest. SE5 —3B 92
Hillcrest. Sidc —6E 96
Hill Crest. Surb —2J 119
Hillcrest. Wey —6A 116
Hillcrest Av. NW11 —3K 41
Hillcrest Av. Edgw —4M 23
Hillcrest Av. Pinn —2H 37
Hillcrest Clo. SE26 —1E 108
Hillcrest Clo. Beck —1K 125
Hillcrest Clo. Eps —7D 134
Hillcrest Ct. Romf —8B 34
Hillcrest Ct. Sutt —8B 122
Hillcrest Gdns. N3 —2J 41
Hillcrest Gdns. NW2 —8E 40
Hillcrest Gdns. Esh —5D 118
Hillcrest Pde. Coul —6F 136
Hillcrest Rd. E17 —9B 30
Hillcrest Rd. E18 —9E 30
Hillcrest Rd. W3 —2L 71
Hillcrest Rd. W5 —8J 55
Hillcrest Rd. Big H —8H 141
Hillcrest Rd. Brom —2E 110
Hillcrest Rd. Dart —6C 98
Hillcrest Rd. Horn —5E 50
Hillcrest Rd. Lou —8H 19
Hillcrest Rd. Orp —4E 128
Hillcrest Rd. Purl —2K 137
Hillcrest Rd. Whyt —9D 138
Hillcrest Vw. Beck —1K 125
Hillcroft. Lou —4L 19
Hillcroft Av. Pinn —4K 37
Hillcroft Av. Purl —5G 137
Hillcroft Cres. W5 —9J 55
Hillcroft Cres. Ruis —8H 37
Hillcroft Cres. Wat —1F 20
Hillcroft Cres. Wemb —9K 39
Hillcroft Rd. E6 —8M 63
Hillcroome Rd. Sutt —8B 122
Hillcross Av. Mord —1H 121
Hilldale Rd. Sutt —6K 121
Hilldeane Rd. Purl —1L 137
Hilldene Av. Romf —6G 35
Hilldene Clo. H Hill —5H 35
Hilldown Ct. SW16 —4J 107
Hilldown Rd. SW16 —4J 107
Hilldown Rd. Brom —3C 126
Hill Dri. NW9 —6A 40
Hill Dri. SW16 —7K 107
Hilldrop Cres. N7 —1H 59
Hilldrop Est. N7 —9H 43
Hilldrop La. N7 —1H 59
Hilldrop Rd. N7 —1H 59
Hilldrop Rd. Brom —3F 110
Hille Bus. Cen. Wat —3F 8
Hillend. SE18 —9L 79
Hill End. Orp —4D 128
Hiller Ho. NW1 —3H 59
(off Camden Sq.)
Hillersden Ho. SW1 —6F 74
(off Ebury Bri. Rd.)
Hillersdon Av. SW13 —1E 88
Hillersdon Av. Edgw —5K 23
Hillery Clo. SE17 —5B 76
Hill Farm Av. Wat —5E 4
Hill Farm Clo. Wat —6E 4
Hill Farm Cotts. Ruis —5A 36
Hill Farm Rd. W10 —8G 57
Hill Farm Rd. Uxb —9B 36
Hillfield Av. N8 —3J 43
Hillfield Av. NW9 —3C 40
Hillfield Av. Mord —1C 122
Hillfield Av. Wemb —3J 55
Hillfield Clo. Harr —2A 38
Hillfield Ct. NW3 —1C 58
Hillfield Ct. Esh —7M 117
Hillfield Ho. N5 —1A 60
Hillfield Pk. N10 —2F 42
Hillfield Pk. N21 —2L 27
Hillfield Pk. M. N10 —2F 42
Hillfield Rd. NW6 —1K 57
Hill Fld. Rd. Hamp —4K 101
Hillfoot Av. Romf —8A 34
Hillfoot Rd. Romf —8A 34
Hillgate Pl. SW12 —6F 90
Hillgate Pl. W8 —2L 73
Hillgate St. W11 —2L 73
Hill Gro. Felt —8K 85
Hill Gro. Romf —1C 50
Hill Ho. E5 —6F 44
(off Harrington Hill)
Hill Ho. Brom —6D 110
Hillhouse. Wal A —6M 7
Hillhouse Av. Stan —7D 22
Hill Ho. Clo. N21 —9L 15
Hill Ho. Dri. Hamp —5L 101
Hill Ho. Rd. SW16 —2K 107
Hilliard Ho. E1 —2F 76
(off Prusom St.)
Hilliard Rd. N'wd —8D 20
Hilliards Ct. E1 —2G 77
Hilliards Rd. Uxb —9B 142
Hillier Clo. New Bar —8M 13
Hillier Gdns. Croy —7L 123
Hillier Lodge. Tedd —2B 102
Hillier Pl. Chess —8H 119
Hillier Rd. SW11 —5D 90
Hilliers Av. Uxb —6E 142
Hilliers La. Croy —5J 123
Hillingdale. Big H —9F 140
Hillingdon. —6E 142
Hillingdon Av. Stai —7C 144
Hillingdon Cir. Hil —2F 142
Hillingdon Ct. Harr —2H 39
Hillingdon Heath. —7F 142
Hillingdon Hill. Uxb —5C 142
Hillingdon Rd. Bexh —1A 98
Hillingdon Rd. Uxb —4B 142
Hillingdon Rd. Wat —7E 4
Hillingdon St. SE5 & SE17 —7M 75
(in two parts)
Hillington Gdns. Wfd G —9H 31
Hill La. Ruis —6A 36
Hillman Clo. Horn —1H 51
Hillman Clo. Uxb —1C 142
Hillman Dri. W10 —7G 57
Hillman St. E8 —2F 60
Hillmarton Rd. N7 —1J 59
Hillmead Dri. SW9 —3M 91
Hillmont Rd. Esh —5C 118
Hillmore Ct. SE13 —2B 94
(off Belmont Hill)
Hillmore Gro. SE26 —2J 109
Hill Path. SW16 —2K 107
Hillreach. SE18 —6K 79
Hill Ri. N9 —8F 16
Hill Ri. NW11 —2M 41
Hill Ri. SE23 —7F 92
Hill Ri. Esh —4F 118
Hill Ri. Gnfd —3A 54
Hill Ri. Rich —4H 87
Hill Ri. Ruis —6A 36
Hill Ri. Upm —7L 51
Hill Ri. W on T —2D 116
Hillrise Av. Wat —2H 9
Hillrise Mans. N19 —5J 43
(off Warltersville Rd.)

Hillrise Rd.—Holly Farm Rd.

Hillrise Rd. N19 —5J 43
Hillrise Rd. Romf —6A 34
Hill Rd. N10 —8D 26
Hill Rd. NW8 —6A 58
Hill Rd. Cars —8C 122
Hill Rd. Dart —8J 99
Hill Rd. Harr —3E 38
Hill Rd. Mitc —5F 106
Hill Rd. N'wd —6B 20
Hill Rd. Pinn —3J 37
Hill Rd. Purl —4K 137
Hill Rd. Sutt —7M 121
Hill Rd. Wemb —8F 38
Hillsboro' Rd. SE22 —4C 92
Hillsborough Ct. NW6 —4M 57
(off Mortimer Cres.)
Hillsborough Grn. Wat —3E 20
Hillsgrove Clo. Well —8G 81
Hillside. —5A 82
Hillside. N8 —4H 43
Hillside. NW5 —8E 42
Hillside. NW9 —2B 40
Hillside. NW10 —3A 56
Hillside. SW19 —3H 105
Hillside. Bans —7J 135
Hillside. Eri —5A 82
Hillside. Esh —7M 117
Hillside. F'ham —2K 131
Hillside. H Hill —4H 35
Hillside. New Bar —7A 14
Hillside Av. N11 —6D 26
Hillside Av. Borwd —6M 11
Hillside Av. Chesh —4D 6
Hillside Av. Purl —5M 137
Hillside Av. Wemb —9K 39
Hillside Av. Wfd G —6G 31
Hillside Clo. NW8 —5M 57
Hillside Clo. Ab L —5C 4
Hillside Clo. Bans —8J 135
Hillside Clo. Mord —8J 105
Hillside Clo. Wfd G —5G 31
Hillside Ct. Chesh —4D 6
Hillside Ct. Swan —8E 114
Hillside Cres. Chesh —4D 6
Hillside Cres. Enf —2B 16
Hillside Cres. Harr —6A 38
Hillside Cres. N'wd —8E 20
Hillside Cres. Wat —8J 9
Hillside Dri. Edgw —6L 23
Hillside Est. N15 —4D 44
Hillside Gdns. E17 —1B 46
Hillside Gdns. N6 —4F 42
Hillside Gdns. N11 —6G 27
Hillside Gdns. SW2 —8L 91
Hillside Gdns. Barn —6J 13
Hillside Gdns. Edgw —4K 23
Hillside Gdns. Harr —5J 39
Hillside Gdns. N'wd —7E 20
Hillside Gdns. Wall —9G 123
Hillside Gro. N14 —9H 15
Hillside Gro. NW7 —7E 24
Hillside Ho. Croy —6M 123
(off Violet La.)
Hillside La. Brom —4D 126
(in two parts)
Hillside Mans. Barn —6K 13
Hillside Pas. SW16 —8K 91
Hillside Ri. N'wd —7E 20
Hillside Rd. N16 —5C 44
Hillside Rd. SW2 —8K 91
Hillside Rd. W5 —8J 55
Hillside Rd. Asht —9K 133
Hillside Rd. Brom —7D 110
Hillside Rd. Bush —7J 9
Hillside Rd. Coul —9J 137
Hillside Rd. Croy —7M 123
Hillside Rd. Dart —5E 98
Hillside Rd. Eps —2G 135
Hillside Rd. N'wd —7E 20
Hillside Rd. Pinn —7F 20
Hillside Rd. S'hall —7L 53
Hillside Rd. Surb —8K 103
Hillside Rd. Sutt —9K 121
Hillside, The. Orp —9F 128
Hills La. N'wd —8C 20
Hillsleigh Rd. W8 —2K 73
Hillsmead Way. S Croy —5E 138
Hills M. W5 —1J 71
Hills Pl. W1 —9G 59
Hills Rd. Buck H —1F 30
Hillstowe St. E5 —8G 45
Hill St. W1 —2E 74
Hill St. Rich —4H 87
Hilltop. E17 —1M 45
Hilltop. NW11 —2M 41
Hill Top. Lou —4L 19
Hill Top. Mord —1L 121
Hill Top. Sutt —2K 121
Hill Top Clo. Lou —5L 19
Hilltop Ct. NW8 —3A 58
(off Alexandra Rd.)
Hill Top Clo. Wfd G —6K 31
Hilltop Gdns. NW4 —9F 24
Hilltop Gdns. Dart —4K 99
Hilltop Gdns. Orp —4C 128
Hill Top Pl. Lou —5L 19
Hilltop Rd. NW6 —3L 57
Hilltop Rd. K Lan —1B 4
Hilltop Rd. Whyt —9C 138
Hill Top Vw. Wfd G —6K 31
Hilltop Way. Stan —3E 22
Hillview. SW20 —4F 104
Hillview Av. Harr —3J 39
Hillview Av. Horn —4G 51
Hillview Clo. Pinn —6K 21
Hillview Clo. Purl —3M 137
Hillview Clo. Wemb —7K 39
Hill Vw. Cres. Ilf —4K 47
Hill Vw. Cres. Orp —3C 128
Hill Vw. Dri. Well —1C 96
Hillview Gdns. NW4 —2H 41
Hill Vw. Gdns. NW9 —3B 40
Hillview Gdns. Harr —1L 37
Hillview Rd. NW7 —4H 25
Hillview Rd. Chst —2L 111
Hill Vw. Rd. Clay —9E 118
Hill Vw. Rd. Orp —3D 128
Hillview Rd. Pinn —7K 21
Hillview Rd. Sutt —5A 122
Hill Vw. Rd. Twic —5E 86
Hillway. N6 —7E 42
Hillway. NW9 —6C 40
Hillwood Ho. NW1 —5G 59
(off Polygon Rd.)
Hillworth. Beck —6M 109
Hillworth Rd. SW2 —6L 91
Hillyard Ho. SW9 —9L 75
Hillyard Rd. W7 —8C 54
Hillyard St. SW9 —9L 75
Hillyfield. E17 —9J 29
Hillyfields. Lou —4L 19
Hilly Fields Cres. SE4 —2L 93
Hilsea St. E5 —9G 45
Hilton Av. N12 —5B 26
Hilton Clo. Uxb —5A 142
Hilton Ho. SE4 —3H 93
Hilton's Wharf. SE10 —7M 77
(off Norman Rd.)
Hilton Way. S Croy —7F 138
Hilversum Cres. SE22 —4C 92
Himalayan Way. Wat —8D 8
Himley Rd. SW17 —2C 106
Hinchinbrook Ho. NW6 —4M 57
(off Mortimer Cres.)
Hinchley Clo. Esh —6D 118
Hinchley Dri. Esh —5D 118
Hinchley Way. Esh —5E 118
Hinchley Wood. —5D 118
Hinckley Rd. SE15 —3E 92
Hind Clo. Chig —5D 32
Hind Ct. EC4 —9L 59
Hind Cres. Eri & N Hth —7B 82
Hinde Ho. W1 —9E 58
(off Hinde St.)
Hinde M. W1 —9E 58
(off Marlebone La.)
Hindes Rd. Harr —3B 38
Hinde St. W1 —9E 58
Hind Gro. E14 —9L 61
Hindhead Clo. N16 —6C 44
Hindhead Clo. Uxb —8F 142
Hindhead Gdns. N'holt —4J 53
Hindhead Grn. Wat —5G 21
Hindhead Way. Wall —7J 123
Hind Ho. SE14 —7H 77
(off Myers La.)
Hindlip Ho. SW8 —9H 75
Hindmans Rd. SE22 —4E 92
Hindmans Way. Dag —7K 65
Hindmarsh Clo. E1 —1E 76
Hindrey Rd. E5 —1F 60
Hindsley's Pl. SE23 —8G 93
Hinkler Clo. Wall —9J 123
(in two parts)
Hinkler Rd. Harr —1H 39
Hinksey Path. SE2 —3H 81
Hinstock. NW6 —4M 57
(off Belsize Rd.)
Hinstock Rd. SE18 —7A 80
Hinton Av. Houn —3H 85
Hinton Clo. SE9 —7J 95
Hinton Ct. E10 —7M 45
(off Leyton Grange Est.)
Hinton Ho. W5 —9G 55
Hinton Rd. N18 —4C 28
Hinton Rd. SW9 —2M 91
Hinton Rd. Uxb —4A 142
Hinton Rd. Wall —8G 123
Hippodrome M. W11 —1J 73
Hippodrome Pl. W11 —1J 73
Hiroshima Promenade. SE7 —4G 79
Hissocks Ho. NW10 —3A 56
(off Stilton Cres.)
Hitcham Rd. E17 —5K 45
Hitchin Clo. Romf —4G 35
Hitchin Sq. E3 —5J 61
Hitherbroom Rd. Hay —2E 68
Hither Farm Rd. SE3 —2G 95
Hitherfield Rd. SW16 —8K 91
Hitherfield Rd. Dag —7J 49
Hither Green. —5C 94
Hither Grn. La. SE13 —4A 94
Hitherwell Dri. Harr —8B 22
Hitherwood Clo. Horn —9H 51
Hitherwood Dri. SE19 —1D 108
Hive Clo. Bus H —2B 22
Hive Rd. Bus H —2B 22
(in two parts)
HMS Belfast. —2C 76
Hoadly Rd. SW16 —9H 91
Hobart Clo. N20 —2C 26
Hobart Clo. Hay —7H 53
Hobart Ct. S Croy —7B 124
(off South Pk. Hill Rd.)
Hobart Dri. Hay —7H 53
Hobart Gdns. T Hth —7B 108
Hobart La. Hay —7H 53
Hobart Pl. SW1 —4F 74
Hobart Pl. Rich —6K 87
Hobart Rd. Dag —9H 49
Hobart Rd. Hay —7H 53
Hobart Rd. Ilf —9A 32
Hobart Rd. Wor Pk —5F 120
Hobbayne Rd. W7 —9B 54
Hobbes Wlk. SW15 —4F 88
Hobbs Clo. Chesh —2D 6
Hobbs Ct. SE1 —3D 76
(off Mill St.)
Hobbs Grn. N2 —1A 42
Hobbs M. Ilf —7D 48
Hobbs Pl. N1 —4C 60
Hobbs Pl. Est. N1 —4C 60
(off Hobbs Pl.)
Hobbs Rd. SE27 —1A 108
Hobday St. E14 —9M 61
Hobill Wlk. Surb —1K 119
Hoblands End. Chst —3C 112
Hobson's Pl. E1 —8E 60
Hobury St. SW10 —7A 74
Hockenden. —7L 113
Hockenden La. Swan —7L 113
Hocker St. E2 —6D 60
Hockett Clo. SE8 —5J 77
Hockley Av. E6 —5J 63
Hockley Ct. E18 —8E 30
Hockley Dri. Romf —9F 34
Hockley M. Bark —6C 64
Hockliffe Ho. W10 —8G 57
(off Sutton Way)
Hockney Ct. SE16 —6F 76
(off Rossetti Rd.)
Hocroft Av. NW2 —8K 41
Hocroft Ct. NW2 —8K 41
Hocroft Rd. NW2 —8K 41
Hocroft Wlk. NW2 —8K 41
Hodder Dri. Gnfd —5D 54
Hoddesdon Rd. Belv —6L 81
Hodes Row. NW3 —9E 42
Hodford Rd. NW11 —6K 41
Hodges Way. Wat —8E 8
Hodgkin Clo. SE28 —1H 81
Hodister Clo. SE5 —8A 76
Hodnet Gro. SE16 —5H 77
Hodsoll Ct. Orp —9H 113
Hodson Clo. Harr —8K 37
Hodson Cres. Orp —9H 113
Hodson Pl. Enf —2L 17
Hoecroft Ct. Enf —2G 17
(off Hoe La.)
Hoe La. Abr —1H 33
Hoe La. Enf —2E 16
Hoe St. E17 —2L 45
Hoe, The. Wat —2H 21
Hoever Ho. SE6 —1A 110
Hofland Rd. W14 —4J 73
Hogan M. W2 —8A 58
Hogan Way. E5 —7E 44
Hogarth Av. Ashf —3A 100
Hogarth Bus. Cen. W4 —7C 72
Hogarth Clo. E16 —8H 63
Hogarth Clo. W5 —8J 55
Hogarth Ct. E1 —9E 60
(off Batty St.)
Hogarth Ct. EC3 —9C 60
Hogarth Ct. NW1 —3G 59
(off St Pancras Way)
Hogarth Ct. SE19 —1D 108
Hogarth Ct. Bush —9M 9
Hogarth Ct. Houn —8J 69
Hogarth Cres. SW19 —5B 106
Hogarth Cres. Croy —2A 124
Hogarth Gdns. Houn —8L 69
Hogarth Hill. NW11 —2K 41
Hogarth Ho. SW1 —5H 75
(off Erasmus St.)
Hogarth Ho. N'holt —5H 53
(off Gallery Gdns.)
Hogarth Ind. Est. NW10 —7E 56
Hogarth La. W4 —7C 72
Hogarth Pl. SW5 —5M 73
(off Hogarth Rd.)
Hogarth Reach. Lou —7K 19
Hogarth Rd. SW5 —5M 73
Hogarth Rd. Dag —1F 64
Hogarth Rd. Edgw —9L 23
Hogarth Roundabout. (Junct.) —7C 72
Hogarth's House. —7C 72
Hogarth Ter. W4 —7C 72
Hogarth Way. Hamp —5A 102
Hog Hill Rd. Romf —7K 33
Hog La. Els —6E 10
Hogshead Pas. E1 —1F 76
(off Pennington St.)
Hogsmill Ho. King T —7K 103
(off Vineyard Clo.)
Hogsmill Wlk. King T —7J 103
(off Penrhyn Rd.)
Hogsmill Way. Eps —7A 120
Hogs Orchard. Swan —5F 114
Holbeach Gdns. Sidc —5C 96
Holbeach M. SW12 —7F 90
Holbeach Rd. SE6 —6L 93
Holbeck Row. SE15 —8E 76
Holbein Ga. N'wd —5C 20
Holbein Ho. SW1 —6E 74
(off Holbein M.)
Holbein M. SW1 —6E 74
Holbein Pl. SW1 —5E 74
Holbein Ter. Dag —9G 49
(off Marlborough Rd.)
Holberton Gdns. NW10 —6F 56
Holborn. —8L 59
Holborn. WC1 —8L 59
Holborn Cir. EC1 —8L 59
Holborn Pl. WC2 —8K 59
(off High Holborn)
Holborn Rd. E13 —8F 62
Holborn Viaduct. EC4 —8L 59
Holborn Way. Mitc —6D 106
Holbrook Clo. N19 —6F 42
Holbrook Clo. Enf —3D 16
Holbrooke Ct. N7 —8J 43
Holbrooke Pl. Rich —4H 87
Holbrook Ho. Chst —5B 112
Holbrook La. Chst —4B 112
Holbrook Rd. E15 —5D 62
Holbrook Way. Brom —1K 127
Holburne Clo. SE3 —9G 79
Holburne Gdns. SE3 —9H 79
Holburne Rd. SE3 —9G 79
Holcombe Hill. NW7 —3E 24
Holcombe Ho. SW9 —2J 91
(off Landor Rd.)
Holcombe Pl. SE4 —2J 93
(off S. Asaph Rd.)
Holcombe Rd. N17 —1D 44
(in two parts)
Holcombe Rd. Ilf —5L 47
Holcombe St. W6 —5F 72
Holcote Clo. Belv —4J 81
Holcroft Ct. W1 —8G 59
(off Clipstone St.)
Holcroft Ho. SW11 —2B 90
Holcroft Rd. E9 —3G 61
Holdbrook. —7F 6
Holdbrook N. Wal X —6F 6
Holdbrook S. Wal X —7F 6
Holdbrook Way. Romf —9K 35
Holden Av. N12 —5M 25
Holden Av. NW9 —6A 40
Holdenby Rd. SE4 —4J 93
Holden Clo. Dag —8F 48
Holden Ho. N1 —4A 60
(off Prebend St.)
Holden Ho. SE8 —8L 77
Holdenhurst Av. N12 —7A 26
Holden Rd. N12 —5M 25
Holden St. SW11 —1E 90
Holder Clo. N3 —7M 25
Holdernesse Clo. Iswth —9E 70
Holdernesse Rd. SW17 —9D 90
Holderness Ho. SE5 —2C 92
Holderness Way. SE27 —2M 107
Holders Hill. —9H 25
Holder's Hill Av. NW4 —9H 25
Holders Hill Cir. NW7 —7J 25
Holders Hill Cres. NW4 —9H 25
Holders Hill Dri. NW4 —1H 41
Holder's Hill Gdns. NW4 —9J 25
Holders Hill Rd. NW4 & NW7 —9H 25
Holecroft. Wal A —7L 7
Holford Ho. SE16 —5F 76
(off Camilla Rd.)
Holford M. WC1 —6L 59
(off Cruikshank St.)
Holford Pl. WC1 —6K 59
Holford Rd. NW3 —8A 42
Holford St. WC1 —6K 59
Holford Yd. WC1 —5L 59
Holgate Av. SW11 —2B 90
Holgate Ct. Romf —3C 50
(off Western Rd.)
Holgate Gdns. Dag —2L 65
Holgate Rd. Dag —1L 65
Holgate St. SE7 —4H 79
Hollam Ho. N8 —2K 43
Holland Av. SW20 —5D 104
Holland Av. Sutt —1L 135
Holland Clo. Brom —4D 126
Holland Clo. New Bar —9B 14
Holland Clo. Romf —3A 50
Holland Clo. Stan —5F 22
Holland Ct. E17 —2A 46
(off Evelyn Rd.)
Holland Ct. NW7 —6E 24
Holland Ct. Surb —2H 119
Holland Dri. SE23 —9J 93
Holland Gdns. W14 —4J 73
Holland Gdns. Wat —8G 5
Holland Gro. SW9 —8L 75
Holland Ho. E4 —4B 30
Holland Park. —2K 73
Holland Park. (Junct.) —3H 73
Holland Pk. —3K 73
Holland Pk. W11 —2J 73
Holland Pk. Av. W11 —3J 73
Holland Pk. Av. Ilf —4C 48
Holland Pk. Gdns. W14 —3J 73
Holland Pk. M. W11 —2J 73
Holland Pk. Rd. W14 —4K 73
Holland Pk. Theatre. —3K 73
(off Holland Pk.)
Holland Pas. N1 —4A 60
(off Basire St.)
Holland Pl. W8 —3M 73
(off Kensington Chu. St.)
Holland Pl. Chambers. W8 —3M 73
(off Pitt St. La.)
Holland Ri. Ho. SW9 —8K 75
(off Clapham Rd.)
Holland Rd. E6 —4K 63
Holland Rd. E15 —6C 62
Holland Rd. NW10 —4E 56
Holland Rd. SE25 —9E 108
Holland Rd. W14 —3H 73
Holland Rd. Wemb —2H 55
Hollands, The. Felt —1H 101
Hollands, The. Wor Pk —3D 120
Holland St. SE1 —2M 75
Holland St. W8 —3L 73
Holland Vs. Rd. W14 —3J 73
Holland Wlk. N19 —6H 43
Holland Wlk. W8 —2K 73
(off Holland Pk. Av.)
Holland Wlk. Stan —5E 22
Holland Way. Brom —4D 126
Hollar Rd. N16 —8D 44
Hollen St. W1 —9H 59
Holles Clo. Hamp —3L 101
Holles Ho. SW9 —1L 91
Holles St. W1 —9F 58
Holley Rd. W3 —3C 72
Hollick Wood Av. N12 —6D 26
Holliday Sq. SW11 —2B 90
(off Fowler Clo.)
Hollidge Way. Dag —3M 65
Hollies Av. Sidc —8D 96
Hollies Clo. SW16 —3L 107
Hollies Clo. Twic —8D 86
Hollies End. NW7 —5F 24
Hollies Rd. W5 —5G 71
Hollies, The. E11 —3E 46
(off New Wanstead)
Hollies, The. N20 —1B 26
Hollies, The. Harr —2E 38
Hollies Way. SW12 —6E 90
Holligrave Rd. Brom —5E 110
Hollingbourne Av. Bexh —9K 81
Hollingbourne Gdns. W13 —8F 54
Hollingbourne Rd. SE24 —4A 92
Hollingsworth Ct. Surb —2H 119
Hollingsworth Rd. Croy —8F 124
Hollington Ct. Chst —3M 111
Hollington Cres. N Mald —1D 120
Hollington Rd. E6 —6K 63
Hollington Rd. N17 —9E 28
Hollingworth Clo. W Mol —8K 101
Hollingworth Rd. Orp —1M 127
Hollins Ho. N7 —9J 43
Hollisfield. WC1 —6J 59
(off Cromer St.)
Hollman Gdns. SW16 —3M 107
Holloway. —8J 43
Holloway Clo. W Dray —6J 143
Holloway Ho. NW2 —8G 41
Holloway La. W Dray —7H 143
Holloway Rd. E6 —6K 63
Holloway Rd. E11 —8B 46
Holloway Rd. N19 & N7 —7H 43
Holloway St. Houn —2M 85
Hollow Cotts. Purf —6L 83
Hollowfield Wlk. N'holt —3J 53
Hollows, The. Bren —7K 71
Hollows Wood. —9M 129
Hollow, The. Wfd G —4D 30
Holly Av. Stan —9J 23
Holly Av. W on T —3H 117
Hollybank Clo. Hamp —2L 101
Hollyberry La. NW3 —9A 42
Hollybrake Clo. Chst —4B 112
Hollybush Clo. E11 —3E 46
Hollybush Clo. Harr —8C 22
Hollybush Clo. Wat —9G 9
Hollybush Gdns. E2 —6F 60
Hollybush Hill. E11 —4D 46
Hollybush Hill. NW3 —9A 42
Hollybush Ho. E2 —6F 60
Holly Bush La. Hamp —4K 101
Holly Bush La. Orp —8L 129
Hollybush Pl. E2 —6F 60
Hollybush Rd. King T —2J 103
Hollybush Steps. NW3 —9A 42
(off Holly Mt.)
Hollybush St. E13 —6F 62
Holly Bush Va. NW3 —9A 42
Hollybush Wlk. SW9 —3M 91
Hollybush Way. Chesh —1A 6
Holly Clo. NW10 —3C 56
Holly Clo. Beck —8A 110
Holly Clo. Buck H —3H 31
Holly Clo. Felt —2J 101
Holly Clo. Wall —9F 122
Holly Cottage M. Uxb —8E 142
Holly Ct. N15 —2C 44
Holly Ct. Sidc —1F 112
(off Sidcup Hill)
Holly Ct. Sutt —9L 121
Holly Cres. Beck —9K 109
Holly Cres. Wfd G —7B 30
Hollycroft Av. NW3 —8L 41
Hollycroft Av. Wemb —7K 39
Hollycroft Clo. S Croy —7C 124
Hollycroft Clo. W Dray —7L 143
Hollycroft Gdns. W Dray —7L 143
Hollydale Clo. N'holt —9M 37
Hollydale Dri. Brom —5K 127
Hollydale Rd. SE15 —9G 77
Holly Dene. SE15 —9F 76
Hollydene. Brom —5D 110
(off Beckenham Rd.)
Hollydown Way. E11 —8B 46
Holly Dri. E4 —9M 17
Holly Farm Rd. S'hall —6J 69

Hollyfield Av.—Hornbuckle Clo.

Hollyfield Av. N11 —5D 26
Hollyfield Rd. Surb —2K 119
Holly Gdns. W Dray —3K 143
Holly Grn. Wey —6B 116
Holly Gro. NW9 —5A 40
Holly Gro. SE15 —1D 92
Hollygrove. Bush —9B 10
Holly Gro. Pinn —8J 21
Hollygrove Clo. Houn —3K 85
Holly Hedge Ter. SE13 —4B 94
Holly Hill. N21 —8K 15
Holly Hill. NW3 —9A 42
Holly Hill Dri. Bans —9L 135
Holly Hill Rd. Belv & Eri —6M 81
Holly Ho. W10 —7J 57
(off Hawthorn Wlk.)
Holly Ho. Iswth —7G 71
Holly Ind. Pk. Wat —3G 9
Holly La. Bans —8L 135
Holly La. E. Bans —8M 135
Holly La. W. Bans —9L 135
Holly Lodge. Harr —3B 38
Holly Lodge Gdns. N6 —7E 42
Holly Lodge Mans. N6 —7E 42
Hollymead. Cars —5D 122
Holly M. SW10 —6A 74
(off Drayton Gdns.)
Hollymoor La. Eps —2B 134
Holly Mt. NW3 —9A 42
Hollymount Clo. SE10 —9A 78
Holly Pk. N3 —1K 41
Holly Pk. N4 —5J 43
(in two parts)
Holly Pk. Est. N4 —5K 43
Holly Pk. Gdns. N3 —1L 41
Holly Pk. Rd. N11 —5E 26
Holly Pk. Rd. W7 —2D 70
Holly Pl. NW3 —9A 42
(off Holly Berry La.)
Holly Rd. E11 —5D 46
Holly Rd. W4 —5B 72
Holly Rd. Dart —7H 99
Holly Rd. Enf —9D 6
Holly Rd. Hamp & Hamp H —3A 102
Holly Rd. Houn —3M 85
Holly Rd. Orp —9E 128
Holly Rd. Twic —7D 86
Holly St. E8 —3D 60
Holly Ter. N6 —6E 42
Holly Ter. N20 —2A 26
Hollytree Av. Swan —6C 114
Holly Tree Clo. SW19 —7H 89
Holly Tree Ho. SE4 —2K 93
(off Brockley Rd.)
Hollytree Ho. Wat —9C 4
Hollytree Pde. Sidc —3G 113
(off Sidcup Hill)
Holly Vw. Clo. NW4 —4E 40
Holly Village. N6 —7F 42
Holly Wlk. NW3 —9A 42
Holly Wlk. Enf —5A 16
Holly Way. Mitc —8H 107
Hollywood Ct. W5 —1K 71
Hollywood Ct. Borwd —6L 11
Hollywood Gdns. Hay —9F 52
Hollywood M. SW10 —7A 74
Hollywood Rd. E4 —5J 29
Hollywood Rd. SW10 —7A 74
Hollywoods. Croy —1K 139
Hollywood Way. Eri —8F 82
Hollywood Way. Wfd G —7B 30
Holman Ct. Ewe —1E 134
Holman Ho. E2 —6H 61
(off Roman Rd.)
Holman Hunt Ho. W6 —6J 73
(off Field Rd.)
Holman Rd. SW11 —1B 90
Holman Rd. Eps —7A 120
Holmbank Dri. Shep —8C 100
Holmbridge Gdns. Enf —6H 17
Holmbrook. NW1 —5G 59
(off Eversholt St.)
Holmbrook Dri. NW4 —3H 41
Holmbury Ct. SW17 —9D 90
Holmbury Ct. S Croy —7C 124
Holmbury Gdns. Hay —2D 68
Holmbury Gro. Croy —9K 125
Holmbury Ho. SE24 —4M 91
Holmbury Mnr. Sidc —1E 112
Holmbury Pk. Brom —4J 111
Holmbury Vw. E5 —6F 44
Holmbush Rd. SW15 —5J 89
Holmcote Gdns. N5 —1A 60
Holm Ct. SE12 —9F 94
Holmcroft Ho. E17 —2M 45
Holmcroft Way. Brom —9K 111
Holmdale Clo. Borwd —4K 11
Holmdale Gdns. NW4 —3H 41
Holmdale Rd. NW6 —1L 57
Holmdale Rd. Chst —2A 112
Holmdale Ter. N15 —5C 44
Holmdene. N12 —5M 25
Holmdene Av. NW7 —6E 24
Holmdene Av. SE24 —4A 92
Holmdene Av. Harr —1M 37
Holmdene Clo. Beck —6A 110
Holmead Rd. SW6 —8M 73
Holmebury Clo. Bush —2C 22
Holme Chase. Wey —8A 116
Holme Clo. Chesh —4E 6
Holme Lacey Rd. SE12 —5D 94
Holme Lea. Wat —7G 5
Holme Pk. Borwd —4K 11
Holme Rd. E6 —4J 63
Holme Rd. Horn —6L 51
Holmes Av. E17 —1K 45
Holmes Av. NW7 —5J 25
Holmesdale. Wal X —8C 6
Holmesdale Av. SW14 —2M 87
Holmesdale Clo. SE25 —7D 108
Holmesdale Ho. NW6 —4L 57
(off Kilburn Va.)
Holmesdale Rd. N6 —5F 42
Holmesdale Rd. Bexh —1H 97
Holmesdale Rd. Croy & SE25 —9B 108
Holmesdale Rd. Rich —9K 71
Holmesdale Rd. Tedd —4G 103
Holmesdale Tunnel. Wal X —7D 6
Holmesley Rd. SE23 —5J 93
Holmes Pl. SW10 —7A 74
Holmes Rd. NW5 —1F 58
Holmes Rd. SW19 —4A 106
Holmes Rd. Twic —8D 86
Holmes Ter. SE1 —3L 75
(off Waterloo Rd.)
Holmeswood Ct. N22 —9L 27
Holme Way. Stan —6D 22
Holmewood Gdns. SW2 —6K 91
Holmewood Rd. SE25 —7C 108
Holmewood Rd. SW2 —6J 91
Holmfield Av. NW4 —3H 41
Holmfield Ct. NW3 —1C 58
Holm Gro. Uxb —3E 142
Holmhurst Rd. Belv —6M 81
Holmlea Ct. Croy —6B 124
(off Chatsworth Rd.)
Holmleigh Av. Dart —4G 99
Holmleigh Ct. Enf —6G 17
Holmleigh Rd. N16 —6C 44
Holmleigh Rd. Est. N16 —6C 44
Holmoak Clo. SW15 —5K 89
Holm Oak M. SW4 —4J 91
Holm Oak Pk. Wat —7D 8
Holmoaks Ho. Beck —6A 110
Holmsdale Gro. Bexh —1C 98
Holmsdale Ho. E14 —1M 77
(off Poplar High St.)
Holmsdale Ho. N11 —4F 26
(off Coppies Gro.)
Holmshaw Clo. SE26 —1J 109
Holmshill La. Borwd —1C 12
Holmside Ri. Wat —3F 20
Holmside Rd. SW12 —5E 90
Holmsley Clo. N Mald —1D 120
Holmsley Ho. SW15 —6D 88
(off Tangley Gro.)
Holmstall Av. Edgw —1A 40
Holmstall Pde. Edgw —9A 24
Holm Wlk. SE3 —1E 94
Holmwood Av. S Croy —5D 138
Holmwood Clo. Harr —1A 38
Holmwood Clo. N'holt —2M 53
Holmwood Clo. Sutt —1H 135
Holmwood Gdns. N3 —9L 25
Holmwood Gdns. Wall —8F 122
Holmwood Gro. NW7 —5B 24
Holmwood Rd. Chess —7H 119
Holmwood Rd. Enf —9D 6
Holmwood Rd. Ilf —7C 48
Holmwood Rd. Sutt —1G 135
Holmwood Vs. SE7 —6E 78
Holne Chase. N2 —4A 42
Holne Chase. Mord —1K 121
Holness Rd. E15 —2D 62
Holroyd Clo. Clay —1D 132
Holroyd Rd. SW15 —3G 89
Holroyd Rd. Clay —1D 132
Holst Ct. SE1 —4L 75
(off Westminster Bri. Rd.)
Holstein Way. Eri —4H 81
Holst Mans. SW13 —7G 73
Holstock Rd. Ilf —7A 48
Holsworth Clo. Harr —3A 38
Holsworthy Ho. H Hill —8H 35
Holsworthy Sq. WC1 —7K 59
(off Elm St.)
Holsworthy Way. Chess —7G 119
Holt Clo. N10 —2E 42
Holt Clo. SE28 —1F 80
Holt Clo. Chig —5D 32
Holt Clo. Els —6K 11
Holt Ct. E15 —1A 62
Holt Ho. SW2 —5L 91
Holton St. E1 —7H 61
Holt Rd. E16 —2J 79
Holt Rd. Wemb —8F 38
Holtsmere Clo. Wat —8G 5
Holt, The. Ilf —6A 32
Holt, The. Mord —8L 105
Holt, The. Wall —6G 123
Holt Way. Chig —5D 32
Holtwhites Av. Enf —4A 16
Holtwhite's Hill. Enf —3M 15
Holtwood Rd. Oxs —5A 132
Holwell Pl. Pinn —2J 37
Holwood Clo. W on T —4G 117
Holwood Pk. Av. Orp —6K 127
Holwood Pl. SW4 —3H 91
Holybourne Av. SW15 —6E 88
Holybush. Chesh —1B 6
Holyfield. —2K 7
Holyfield Rd. Wal A —2J 7
Holyhead Clo. E3 —6L 61
Holyhead Clo. E6 —8K 63
Holyhead Ct. King T —8H 103
(off Anglesea Rd.)
Holyoake Ct. SE16 —3K 77
Holyoake Ho. W5 —7G 55
Holyoake Wlk. N2 —1A 42
Holyoake Wlk. W5 —7G 55
Holyoak Rd. SE11 —5M 75
Holyport Rd. SW6 —8H 73
Holyrood Av. Harr —9J 37
Holy Rood. Ct. Wat —6F 8
Holyrood Gdns. Edgw —1M 39
Holyrood M. E16 —2E 78
(off Badminton M.)
Holyrood Rd. New Bar —8A 14
Holyrood St. SE1 —2C 76
Holywell. —8D 8
Holywell Clo. SE3 —7E 78
Holywell Clo. SE16 —6F 76
Holywell Clo. Orp —6E 128
Holywell Clo. Stai —7C 144
Holywell La. EC2 —7C 60
Holywell Rd. Wat —7E 8
Holywell Row. EC2 —7C 60
Holywell Way. Stai —7C 144
Homan Ct. N12 —4B 26
Homebush Ho. E4 —9M 17
Home Clo. Cars —4D 122
Home Clo. N'holt —6K 53
Home Ct. Felt —7E 84
Home Ct. Surb —9H 103
Homecroft Gdns. Lou —6M 19
Homecroft Rd. N22 —8A 28
Homecroft Rd. SE26 —2G 109
Home Farm Clo. Eps —9H 135
Home Farm Clo. Esh —8M 117
Home Farm Clo. Shep —8C 100
Home Farm Clo. Th Dit —2D 118
Home Farm Gdns. W on T —4G 117
Homefarm Rd. W7 —9C 54
Home Fld. Barn —7K 13
Homefield. Mord —8L 105
Homefield. Wal A —5M 7
Homefield Av. Ilf —3C 48
Homefield Av. W on T —6H 117
Homefield Clo. NW10 —2A 56
Homefield Clo. Hay —7H 53
Homefield Clo. St P —8F 112
Homefield Clo. Swan —7D 114
Homefield Ct. SW16 —9J 91
Homefield Gdns. N2 —1B 42
Homefield Gdns. Mitc —6A 106
Homefield Ho. SE23 —9H 93
Homefield M. Beck —5L 109
Homefield Pk. Sutt —8M 121
Homefield Ri. Orp —3E 128
Homefield Rd. SW19 —3H 105
Homefield Rd. W4 —5D 72
Homefield Rd. Brom —5G 111
Homefield Rd. Bush —6L 9
Homefield Rd. Edgw —6B 24
Homefield Rd. Rad —1D 10
Homefield Rd. S at H —5L 115
Homefield Rd. W on T —2J 117
Homefield Rd. Wemb —9E 38
Homefield St. N1 —5C 60
Homefirs Ho. Wemb —8K 39
Home Gdns. Dag —8A 50
Home Gdns. Dart —5J 99
Home Hill. Swan —4D 114
Homeland Dri. Sutt —1M 135
Homelands Dri. SE19 —4C 108
Home Lea. Orp —7D 128
Homeleigh Ct. Chesh —2B 6
Homeleigh Rd. SE15 —4H 93
Homeleigh St. Chesh —3B 6
Homemanor Ho. Wat —5F 8
(off Cassio Rd.)
Home Mead. Stan —8G 23
Home Mdw. Bans —8L 135
Homemead Rd. Brom —9K 111
Homemead Rd. Croy —1G 123
Home Orchard. Dart —5J 99
(in two parts)
Home Pk. Cotts. K Lan —3A 4
Home Pk. Ct. King T —8H 103
(off Palace Rd.)
Home Pk. Ind. Est. K Lan —4A 4
Home Pk. Mill Link Rd. K Lan —3A 4
Home Pk. Pde. King T —6H 103
(off High St.)
Home Pk. Rd. SW19 —1K 105
Home Pk. Ter. King T —6H 103
(off Hampton Ct. Rd.)
Home Pk. Wlk. King T —8H 103
Homer Clo. Bexh —9A 82
Homer Dri. E14 —5L 77
Home Rd. SW11 —1C 90
Homer Rd. E9 —2J 61
Homer Rd. Croy —1H 125
Homer Row. W1 —8C 58
Homersham Rd. King T —6L 103
Homer St. NW1 —8C 58
Homerton. —1H 61
Homerton Gro. E9 —1H 61
Homerton High St. E9 —1H 61
Homerton Rd. E9 —1J 61
Homerton Row. E9 —1G 61
Homerton Ter. E9 —2G 61
(in two parts)
Homesdale Clo. E11 —3E 46
Homesdale Rd. Brom —8G 111
Homesdale Rd. Orp —2C 128
Homesfield. NW11 —3L 41
Homestall Rd. SE22 —4G 93
Homestead Ct. Barn —7L 13
Homestead Gdns. Clay —7C 118
Homestead Paddock. N14 —7F 14
Homestead Pk. NW2 —8D 40
Homestead Rd. SW6 —8K 73
Homestead Rd. Dag —7K 49
Homestead Rd. Orp —9F 128
Homesteads, The. N11 —4F 26
Homestead, The. Dart —4C 98
(off Crayford High St.)
Homestead, The. Dart —5G 99
(West Hill Dri.)
Homestead Way. New Ad —3A 140
Homewater Ho. Eps —5C 134
Homewaters Av. Sun —5D 100
Homeway. Romf —6M 35
Homewillow Clo. N21 —8M 15
Homewood Clo. Hamp —3K 101
Homewood Cres. Chst —3C 112
Homewoods. SW12 —6G 91
Homildon Ho. SE26 —9E 92
Honduras St. EC1 —7A 60
Honeybourne Rd. NW6 —1M 57
Honeybourne Way. Orp —3B 128
Honey Brook. Wal A —6L 7
Honeybrook Rd. SW12 —6G 91
Honey Clo. Dag —2M 65
Honeycroft. Lou —6L 19
Honeycroft Hill. Uxb —3C 142
Honeyden Rd. Sidc —3J 113
Honey Hill. Uxb —3D 142
Honey La. EC2 —9A 60
(off Trump St.)
Honey La. Wal A —6L 7
Honey La. Ho. Wal A —7M 7
Honeyman Clo. NW6 —3H 57
(in two parts)
Honeymead. N8 —1J 43
(off Campsfield Rd.)
Honeypot Bus. Cen. Stan —8J 23
Honeypot Clo. NW9 —2K 39
Honeypot La. Stan & NW9 —7H 23
Honeysett Rd. N17 —9D 28
Honeysuckle Clo. Romf —6G 35
Honeysuckle Clo. S'hall —1J 69
Honeysuckle Ct. E12 —2M 63
Honeysuckle Gdns. Croy —2H 125
Honeysuckle La. N22 —9A 28
Honeytree Ct. Lou —4M 19
Honeywell Rd. SW11 —5D 90
Honeywood Heritage Cen. —6D 122
Honeywood Rd. NW10 —5D 56
Honeywood Rd. Iswth —3E 86
Honeywood Wlk. Cars —6D 122
Honister Clo. Stan —8F 22
Honister Gdns. Stan —7F 22
Honister Heights. Purl —6B 138
Honister Pl. Stan —8F 22
Honiton Gdns. SE15 —1G 93
(off Gibbon Rd.)
Honiton Rd. NW6 —5K 57
Honiton Rd. Romf —4B 50
Honiton Rd. Well —1D 96
Honley Rd. SE6 —6M 93
Honnor Gdns. Iswth —1B 86
Honor Oak. —5G 93
Honor Oak Crematorium. SE23 —4J 93
Honor Oak Park. —6J 93
Honor Oak Pk. SE23 —5G 93
Honor Oak Ri. SE23 —5G 93
Honor Oak Rd. SE23 —7G 93
Hood Av. N14 —8F 14
Hood Av. SW14 —4A 88
Hood Av. Orp —9F 112
Hood Clo. Croy —3M 123
Hoodcote Gdns. N21 —9M 15
Hood Ct. EC4 —9L 59
(off Fleet St.)
Hood Ho. SE5 —8B 76
(off Elmington Est.)
Hood Ho. SW1 —6H 75
(off Dolphin Sq.)
Hood Rd. SW20 —4D 104
Hood Rd. Rain —5D 66
Hood Wlk. Romf —8M 33
Hook. —6H 119
Hooke Ho. E3 —5J 61
(off Gernon Rd.)
Hookers Rd. E17 —1H 45
Hook Farm Rd. Brom —9H 111
Hookfield. Eps —5A 134
Hookfield M. Eps —5A 134
Hook Ga. Enf —9B 6
Hook Green. —1E 114
Hook Grn. La. Dart —9D 98
Hookham Ct. SW8 —9H 75
Hook Hill. S Croy —2C 138
(in two parts)
Hooking Grn. Harr —3M 37
Hook Junction. (Junct.) —5J 119
Hook La. Well —4D 96
Hook Ri. Bus. Cen. Chess —5L 119
Hook Ri. N. Surb —5J 119
Hook Ri. S. Surb —5J 119
Hook Ri. S. Ind. Pk. Chess —5K 119
Hook Rd. Chess & Surb —7H 119
Hook Rd. Eps —9A 120
Hooks Clo. SE15 —9F 76
Hookshall Dri. Dag —8A 50
Hookstone Way. Wfd G —7H 31
Hooks Way. SE22 —7E 92
Hook, The. New Bar —8B 14
Hook Wlk. Edgw —6A 24
Hooper Rd. E16 —9E 62
Hooper's Ct. SW3 —3D 74
Hooper's M. W3 —2A 72
Hooper Sq. E1 —9E 60
(off Hooper St.)
Hooper St. E1 —9E 60
Hoop La. NW11 —5K 41
(in two parts)
Hope Clo. N1 —2A 60
Hope Clo. SE12 —9F 94
Hope Clo. Bren —6J 71
Hope Clo. Chad H —2H 49
Hope Clo. Sutt —7A 122
Hope Clo. Wfd G —6G 31
Hopedale Rd. SE7 —7F 78
Hopefield Av. NW6 —5J 57
Hope Grn. Wat —6E 4
Hope Ho. Croy —6C 124
(off Steep Hill)
Hope Pk. Brom —4D 110
Hopes Clo. Houn —7L 69
Hope St. SW11 —2B 90
Hopetown St. E1 —8D 60
Hopewell St. SE5 —8B 76
Hope Wharf. SE16 —3G 77
Hop Gdns. WC2 —1J 75
Hop Garden Way. Wat —4G 5
Hopgood St. W12 —2G 73
Hopkins Clo. N10 —7E 26
Hopkins Clo. Romf —1G 51
Hopkins Ho. E14 —9L 61
(off Canton St.)
Hopkins M. E15 —4D 62
Hopkinsons Pl. NW1 —4E 58
Hopkins St. W1 —9G 59
Hoppers Rd. N13 & N21 —2L 27
Hoppett Rd. E4 —2C 30
Hopping La. N1 —2M 59
Hoppingwood Av. N Mald —7C 104
Hoppner Rd. Hay —5B 52
Hopton Ct. Hayes —3F 126
Hopton Gdns. N Mald —1E 120
Hopton Rd. SW16 —2J 107
Hopton's Gdns. SE1 —2M 75
(off Hopton St.)
Hopton St. SE1 —2M 75
Hopwood Clo. SW17 —9A 90
Hopwood Clo. Wat —9C 4
Hopwood Rd. SE17 —7B 76
Hopwood Wlk. E8 —3E 60
Horace Av. Romf —6A 50
Horace Rd. E7 —9F 46
Horace Rd. Ilf —1A 48
Horace Rd. King T —7K 103
Horatio Ct. SE16 —2G 77
(off Rotherhithe St.)
Horatio Ho. E2 —5D 60
(off Horatio St.)
Horatio Ho. W6 —6H 73
(off Fulham Pal. Rd.)
Horatio Pl. E14 —3A 78
(off Preston's Rd.)
Horatio Pl. SW19 —5L 105
Horatio St. E2 —5D 60
(in two parts)
Horatius Way. Croy —7K 123
Horbury Cres. W11 —1L 73
Horbury M. W11 —1K 73
Horder Rd. SW6 —9J 73
Hordle Promenade E. SE15 —8D 76
Hordle Promenade N. SE15 —8D 76
Hordle Promenade S. SE15 —8D 76
(off Quarley Way)
Hordle Promenade W. SE15
(off Clanfield Way) —8C 76
Horizon Building. E14 —1L 77
(off Hertsmere Rd.)
Horizon Ho. Eps —5C 134
Horizon Ho. Swan —8C 114
Horizon Way. SE7 —5F 78
Horle Wlk. SW9 —1M 91
Horley Clo. Bexh —4L 97
Horley Rd. SE9 —1J 111
Hormead Rd. W9 —7K 57
Hornbeam Av. Upm —9L 51
Hornbeam Clo. NW7 —3D 24
Hornbeam Clo. SE11 —5L 75
Hornbeam Clo. Borwd —3L 11
Hornbeam Clo. Buck H —3H 31
Hornbeam Clo. Ilf —1B 64
Hornbeam Clo. N'holt —1K 53
Hornbeam Cres. Bren —8F 70
Hornbeam Gro. E4 —3C 30
Hornbeam Ho. Buck H —3H 31
Hornbeam La. E4 —7C 18
Hornbeam La. Bexh —1A 98
Hornbeam Rd. Buck H —3H 31
Hornbeam Rd. Hay —8G 53
Hornbeams. Brick W —3K 5
Hornbeams Av. Enf —8C 6
Hornbeams Ri. N11 —6E 26
Hornbeam Ter. Cars —3C 122
Hornbeam Wlk. Rich —8K 87
Hornbeam Way. Brom —1L 127
Hornbeam Way. Wal X —2A 6
Hornbill Clo. Uxb —9B 142
Hornblower Clo. SE16 —4J 77
Hornbuckle Clo. Harr —7B 38

Hornby Clo.—Hurn Ct. Rd.

Hornby Clo. NW3 —3B 58
Hornby Ho. SE11 —7L 75
(off Clayton St.)
Horncastle Clo. SE12 —6E 94
Horncastle Rd. SE12 —6E 94
Hornchurch. —6J 51
Hornchurch. N17 —9B 28
(off Gloucester Rd.)
Hornchurch Clo. King T —1H 103
Hornchurch Country Pk. —3G 67
Hornchurch Hill. Whyt —9D 138
Hornchurch Rd. Horn —6E 50
Horndean Clo. SW15 —7E 88
Horndon Clo. Romf —8A 34
Horndon Grn. Romf —8A 34
Horndon Rd. Romf —8A 34
Horner Ho. N1 —4C 60
(off Whitmore Est.)
Horner La. Mitc —6B 106
Hornets, The. Wat —6F 8
Horne Way. SW15 —1G 89
Hornfair Rd. SE7 —7G 79
Hornford Way. Romf —5C 50
Horniman Dri. SE23 —7F 92
Horniman Mus. —7F 92
Horning Clo. SE9 —1J 111
Horn La. SE10 —6E 78
(in three parts)
Horn La. W3 —1A 72
(in two parts)
Horn La. Wfd G —6E 30
Hornminster Glen. Horn —7L 51
Horn Park. —4F 94
Horn Pk. Clo. SE12 —4F 94
Hornpark La. SE12 —4F 94
Horns End Pl. Pinn —2G 37
Hornsey. —2J 43
Hornsey La. N6 —6F 42
Hornsey La. Est. N19 —5H 43
Hornsey La. Gdns. N6 —5G 43
Hornsey Pk. Rd. N8 —1K 43
Hornsey Ri. N19 —5H 43
Hornsey Ri. Gdns. N19 —5H 43
Hornsey Rd. N19 & N7 —6J 43
Hornsey St. N7 —1K 59
Hornsey Vale. —3K 43
Hornshay St. SE15 —7G 77
Horns Rd. Ilf —2B 48
Hornton Ct. W8 —3L 73
(off Kensington High St.)
Hornton Pl. W8 —3M 73
Hornton St. W8 —3L 73
Horsa Clo. Wall —9J 123
Horsa Rd. SE12 —6G 95
Horsa Rd. Eri —8M 81
Horse & Dolphin Yd. W1 —1H 75
(off Macclesfield St.)
Horsebridge Clo. Dag —4J 65
Horsecroft. Bans —9K 135
Horsecroft Clo. Orp —3F 128
Horsecroft Rd. Edgw —7B 24
Horse Fair. King T —6H 103
Horseferry Pl. SE10 —7A 78
Horseferry Rd. E14 —1J 77
Horseferry Rd. SW1 —4H 75
Horseferry Rd. Est. SW1 —4H 75
(off Horseferry Rd.)
Horseguards Av. SW1 —2J 75
Horse Guards Rd. SW1 —2H 75
Horse Leaze. E6 —9L 63
Horsell Rd. N5 —1L 59
(in two parts)
Horsell Rd. Orp —5F 112
Horselydown La. SE1 —3D 76
Horselydown Mans. SE1 —3D 76
(off Lafone St.)
Horsemongers M. SE1 —3A 76
(off Cole St.)
Horsenden Av. Gnfd —1D 54
Horsenden Cres. Gnfd —1D 54
Horsenden La. Gnfd —2C 54
Horsenden La. N. Gnfd —2D 54
Horsenden La. S. Gnfd —4E 54
Horse Ride. SW1 —2G 75
(off Mall, The)
Horse Ride. Cars —2C 136
Horseshoe Clo. E14 —6A 78
Horseshoe Clo. NW2 —7F 40
Horse Shoe Cres. N'holt —5L 53
Horseshoe Dri. Uxb —9E 142
Horse Shoe Grn. Sutt —4M 121
Horseshoe La. N20 —1H 25
Horseshoe La. Enf —5A 16
Horseshoe La. Wat —5F 4
Horseshoe, The. Bans —7K 135
Horseshoe, The. Coul —5H 137
Horseshoe Wharf. SE1 —2B 76
(off Clink St.)
Horse Yd. N1 —4M 59
(off Essex Rd.)
Horsfeld Gdns. SE9 —4J 95
Horsfeld Rd. SE9 —4H 95
Horsfield Clo. Dart —6M 99
Horsfield Ho. N1 —3A 60
(off Northampton St.)
Horsford Rd. SW2 —4K 91
Horsham Av. N12 —5C 26
Horsham Ct. N17 —8E 28
(off Lansdowne Rd.)
Horsham Rd. Bexh —4L 97
Horsham Rd. Felt —5A 84
Horsley Clo. Eps —5B 134
Horsley Dri. King T —2H 103
Horsley Dri. New Ad —9A 126
Horsley Rd. E4 —2A 30
Horsley Rd. Brom —5F 110
Horsley St. SE17 —7B 76
Horsman Ho. SE5 —7A 76
(off Bethwin Rd.)
Horsman St. SE5 —7A 76
Horsmonden Clo. Orp —2D 128
Horsmonden Rd. SE4 —4K 93
Hortensia Ho. SW10 —8A 74
(off Hortensia Rd.)
Hortensia Rd. SW10 —8A 74
Horticultural Pl. W4 —6B 72
Horton. —2A 134
Horton Av. NW2 —9J 41
Horton Bri. Rd. W Dray —2K 143
Horton Clo. W Dray —2L 143
Horton Country Pk. —9M 119
Horton Footpath. Eps —3A 134
Horton Gdns. Eps —3A 134
Horton Hill. Eps —3A 134
Horton Ho. SE15 —7G 77
Horton Ho. SW8 —8K 75
Horton Ho. W6 —6J 73
(off Field Rd.)
Horton Ind. Pk. W Dray —2K 143
Horton Kirby. —8M 115
Horton Kirby Trad. Est. S Dar —5M 115
Horton La. Eps —3L 133
Horton Pde. W Dray —2J 143
Horton Pk. Children's Farm. —2L 133
Horton Rd. E8 —2F 60
Horton Rd. Hort K & S Dar —8M 115
Horton Rd. W Dray —2J 143
Horton Rd. Ind. Est. W Dray —2K 143
Horton St. SE13 —2M 93
Horton Way. Croy —9H 109
Horton Way. F'ham —2K 131
Hortus Rd. E4 —2A 30
Hortus Rd. S'hall —3K 69
Horvath Clo. Wey —6B 116
Horwood Ct. Wat —1H 9
Horwood Ho. NW8 —7C 58
(off Paveley St.)
Hosack Rd. SW17 —8E 90
Hoser Av. SE12 —8E 94
Hosier La. EC1 —8M 59
Hoskins Clo. E16 —9G 63
Hoskins Clo. Hay —6D 68
Hoskins St. SE10 —6B 78
Hospital Bri. Rd. Twic —6M 85
Hospital Bridge Roundabout. (Junct.) —8M 85
Hospital Cres. Romf —8K 35
Hospital Rd. E9 —1H 61
Hospital Rd. Houn —2L 85
Hospital Way. SE13 —6B 94
Hotham Clo. S at H —4M 115
Hotham Clo. Swan —5F 114
Hotham Clo. W Mol —7L 101
Hotham Rd. SW15 —2G 89
Hotham Rd. SW19 —4A 106
Hotham Rd. M. SW19 —4A 106
Hotham St. E15 —4C 62
Hothfield Pl. SE16 —4G 77
Hotspur Ind. Est. N17 —6F 28
Hotspur Rd. N'holt —5L 53
Hotspur St. SE11 —5L 75
Houblon Rd. Rich —4J 87
Houghton Clo. E8 —2D 60
Houghton Clo. Hamp —3J 101
Houghton Rd. N15 —2D 44
Houghton St. WC2 —9K 59
(in two parts)
Houlder Cres. Croy —8M 123
Houndsden Rd. N21 —8K 15
Houndsditch. EC3 —9C 60
Houndsfield Rd. N9 —9F 16
Hounslow. —2M 85
Hounslow Av. Houn —4M 85
Hounslow Bus. Pk. Houn —3M 85
Hounslow Cen. Houn —2M 85
Hounslow Gdns. Houn —4M 85
Hounslow Rd. Felt —7F 84
Hounslow Rd. Hanw —1H 101
Hounslow Rd. Twic —5M 85
Hounslow Urban Farm. —4E 84
(off Fagg's Rd.)
Hounslow West. —1J 85
Houseman Way. SE5 —8B 76
Houses of Parliament. —4J 75
Houston Bus. Pk. Hay —2G 69
Houston Pl. Esh —3B 118
Houston Rd. SE23 —8J 93
Houstoun Ct. Houn —8K 69
Hove Av. E17 —3K 45
Hoveden Rd. NW2 —1J 57
Hove Gdns. Sutt —3M 121
Hoveton Rd. SE28 —9G 65
Hoveton Way. Ilf —7M 31
Howard Av. Bex —7G 97
Howard Av. Eps —2E 134
Howard Bus. Pk. Wal A —7K 7
Howard Clo. N11 —2E 26
Howard Clo. NW2 —9J 41
Howard Clo. W3 —9M 55
Howard Clo. Bus H —9C 10
Howard Clo. Hamp —4A 102
Howard Clo. Lou —8J 19
Howard Clo. Sun —3D 100
Howard Clo. Wal A —7K 7
Howard Clo. Wat —1E 8
Howard Ct. Bark —4B 64
Howard Dri. Borwd —6B 12
Howard Ho. SE8 —7K 77
(off Evelyn St.)
Howard Ho. SW1 —6G 75
(off Dolphin Sq.)
Howard Ho. SW9 —2M 91
(off Barrington Rd.)
Howard Ho. W1 —7F 58
(off Cleveland St.)
Howard M. N5 —9M 43
Howard Rd. E6 —5K 63
Howard Rd. E11 —8C 46
Howard Rd. E17 —1L 45
Howard Rd. N15 —4C 44
Howard Rd. N16 —9B 44
Howard Rd. NW2 —9H 41
Howard Rd. SE20 —5G 109
Howard Rd. SE25 —9E 108
Howard Rd. Bark —4B 64
Howard Rd. Brom —4E 110
Howard Rd. Coul —7G 137
Howard Rd. Dart —5L 99
Howard Rd. Ilf —9M 47
Howard Rd. Iswth —2D 86
Howard Rd. N Mald —7C 104
Howard Rd. S'hall —9M 53
Howard Rd. Surb —1K 119
Howard Rd. Upm —7M 51
Howards Clo. Pinn —4G 37
Howards Crest Clo. Beck —6A 110
Howard's La. SW15 —3F 88
Howards Rd. E13 —6E 62
Howard St. Th Dit —2F 118
Howard Wlk. N2 —2A 42
Howard Way. SE22 —6E 92
Howard Way. Barn —7H 13
Howarth Ct. E15 —1M 61
Howarth Rd. SE2 —6E 80
Howberry Clo. Edgw —6H 23
Howberry Rd. Stan & Edgw —6H 23
Howberry Rd. T Hth —5B 108
Howbury La. Eri —1E 98
Howbury Rd. SE15 —2G 93
Howcroft Cres. N3 —7L 25
Howcroft La. Gnfd —6B 54
Howden Clo. SE28 —1H 81
Howden Ho. Houn —6J 85
Howden Rd. SE25 —6D 108
Howden St. SE15 —2E 92
Howe Clo. Romf —8L 33
Howell Clo. Romf —3H 49
Howell Ct. E10 —5M 45
Howell Hill Clo. Eps —3G 135
Howell Hill Gro. Eps —2G 135
Howell Wlk. SE17 —5M 75
Howerd Way. SE18 —9J 79
(in two parts)
Howes Clo. N3 —1L 41
Howeth Ct. N11 —6D 26
(off Ribblesdale Av.)
Howfield Pl. N17 —1D 44
Howgate Rd. SW14 —2B 88
Howick Pl. SW1 —4G 75
Howie St. SW11 —8C 74
Howitt Clo. N16 —9C 44
Howitt Clo. NW3 —2C 58
Howitt Rd. NW3 —2C 58
Howitts Clo. Esh —8L 117
Howland Est. SE16 —4G 77
Howland Ho. SW16 —9J 91
Howland M. E. W1 —8G 59
Howland St. W1 —8G 59
Howland Way. SE16 —3J 77
How La. Coul —9E 136
Howletts La. Ruis —3A 36
Howlett's Rd. SE24 —5A 92
Howley Pl. W2 —8A 58
Howley Rd. Croy —5M 123
Hows Clo. Uxb —4A 142
Howse Rd. Wal A —8H 7
Howsman Rd. SW13 —7E 72
Howson Rd. SE4 —3J 93
Howson Ter. Rich —5J 87
Hows Rd. Uxb —4A 142
How's St. E2 —5D 60
Howton Pl. Bus H —1B 22
How Wood. —1M 5
How Wood. Park —1M 5
Hoxton. —5C 60
Hoxton Hall Theatre. —5C 60
(off Hoxton Rd.)
Hoxton Mkt. N1 —6C 60
(off Coronet St.)
Hoxton Sq. N1 —6C 60
Hoxton St. N1 —4C 60
Hoylake Gdns. Mitc —7G 107
Hoylake Gdns. Romf —7L 35
Hoylake Gdns. Ruis —6F 36
Hoylake Gdns. Wat —4H 21
Hoylake Rd. W3 —9C 56
Hoyland Clo. SE15 —8F 76
Hoyle Rd. SW17 —2C 106
Hoy St. E16 —9D 62
Hubbard Dri. Chess —8H 119
Hubbard Rd. SE27 —1A 108
Hubbards Chase. Horn —3L 51
Hubbards Clo. Horn —3L 51
Hubbard St. E15 —4C 62
Huberd Ho. SE1 —4B 76
(off Manciple St.)
Hubert Clo. SW19 —5A 106
(off Nelson Gro. Rd.)
Hubert Gro. SW9 —2J 91
Hubert Ho. NW8 —7C 58
Hubert Rd. E6 —6H 63
Hubert Rd. Rain —6D 66
Hucknall Clo. Romf —6K 35
Hucknall Ct. NW8 —7B 58
(off Cunningham Pl.)
Huddart St. E3 —8K 61
(in two parts)
Huddleston Clo. E2 —5G 61
Huddlestone Rd. E7 —9D 46
Huddlestone Rd. NW2 —2F 56
Huddleston Rd. N7 —8G 43
Hudson. NW9 —8D 24
(off Near Acre)
Hudson Clo. W12 —1F 72
Hudson Clo. Wat —9D 4
Hudson Ct. E14 —6L 77
(off Maritime Quay)
Hudson Gdns. Grn St —8D 128
Hudson Pl. SE18 —6A 80
Hudson Rd. Bexh —1K 97
Hudson Rd. Hay —7B 68
Hudson's Pl. SW1 —5F 74
(off Bridge Pl.)
Huggin Ct. EC4 —1A 76
(off Huggin Hill)
Huggin Hill. EC4 —1A 76
Huggins Pl. SW2 —7K 91
Hughan Rd. E15 —1B 62
Hugh Astor Ct. SE1 —4M 75
(off Keyworth St.)
Hugh Clark Ho. W13 —2E 70
(off Singapore Rd.)
Hugh Dalton Av. SW6 —7K 73
Hughenden Av. Harr —3F 38
Hughenden Gdns. N'holt —6G 53
(in two parts)
Hughenden Ho. NW8 —7C 58
(off Jerome Cres.)
Hughenden Rd. Wor Pk —2E 120
Hughendon. New Bar —6M 13
Hughendon Ter. E15 —9A 46
Hughes Ct. N7 —1H 59
Hughes Ho. E2 —6G 61
(off Sceptre Ho.)
Hughes Ho. SE8 —7L 77
(off Benbow St.)
Hughes Ho. SE17 —5M 75
(off Peacock St.)
Hughes Mans. E1 —7E 60
Hughes M. SW11 —4D 90
Hughes Rd. Ashf —3A 100
Hughes Rd. Hay —1F 68
Hughes Ter. E16 —8D 62
(off Clarkson Rd.)
Hughes Wlk. Croy —2A 124
Hugh Gaitskell Clo. SW6 —7K 73
Hugh Gaitskell Ho. N16 —7D 44
Hugh Herland Ho. King T —7J 103
Hugh M. SW1 —5F 74
Hugh Platt Ho. E2 —5F 60
(off Patriot Sq.)
Hugh St. SW1 —5F 74
Hugo Gdns. Rain —2E 66
Hugon Rd. SW6 —2M 89
Hugo Rd. N19 —9G 43
Huguenot Pl. E1 —8D 60
Huguenot Pl. SW18 —4A 90
Huguenot Sq. SE15 —2F 92
Hulberry. —4E 130
Hullbridge M. N1 —4B 60
Hull Clo. SE16 —3H 77
Hull Pl. E16 —2A 80
Hull St. EC1 —6A 60
Hulme Pl. SE1 —3A 76
Hulse Av. Bark —2B 64
Hulse Av. Romf —8M 33
Hulsewood Clo. Dart —9F 98
Hulverston Clo. Sutt —2M 135
Humber Clo. W Dray —2H 143
Humber Ct. W7 —9B 54
(off Hobbayne Rd.)
Humber Dri. W10 —7H 57
Humber Rd. NW2 —7F 40
Humber Rd. SE3 —7D 78
Humber Rd. Dart —4H 99
Humberstone Rd. E13 —6G 63
Humberton Clo. E9 —1J 61
Humbolt Rd. W6 —7J 73
Hume Ct. N1 —3M 59
(off Hawes St.)
Hume Ho. W11 —2H 73
(off Queensdale Cres.)
Humes Av. W7 —4C 70
Hume Ter. E16 —8F 62
Hume Way. Ruis —4E 36
Humphrey Clo. Ilf —8K 31
Humphrey St. SE1 —6D 76
Humphries Clo. Dag —9K 49
Hundred Acre. NW9 —9D 24
Hundred Acres. Wal X —7G 7
Hungerdown. E4 —1A 30
Hungerford Ho. SW1 —7G 75
(off Churchill Gdns.)
Hungerford La. WC2 —2J 75
(off Craven St., in two parts)
Hungerford Rd. N7 —2H 59
Hungerford Sq. Wey —6B 116
Hungerford St. E1 —9F 60
Hunsdon Clo. Dag —2J 65
Hunsdon Rd. SE14 —8H 77
Hunslett St. E2 —6G 61
Hunstanton Ho. NW1 —8C 58
(off Cosway St.)
Hunston Rd. Mord —3M 121
Hunt Ct. N14 —9F 14
Hunt Ct. N'holt —5H 53
(off Gallery Gdns.)
Hunter Clo. SE1 —4B 76
Hunter Clo. Borwd —7A 12
Hunter Ct. Eps —2L 133
Huntercrombe Gdns. Wat —4G 21
Hunter Dri. Horn —9G 51
Hunter Ho. SE1 —3M 75
(off Lancaster St.)
Hunter Ho. SW5 —6L 73
(off Old Brompton Rd.)
Hunter Ho. SW8 —8H 75
Hunter Ho. WC1 —7J 59
(off Hunter St.)
Hunterian Mus., The. —9K 59
(off Portugal St.)
Hunter Lodge. W9 —8L 57
(off Admiral Wlk.)
Hunter Rd. SW20 —5G 105
Hunter Rd. Ilf —1M 63
Hunter Rd. T Hth —7B 108
Hunters Clo. SW12 —7E 90
Hunters Clo. Bex —9C 98
Hunters Clo. Eps —5A 134
Hunters Ct. Rich —4H 87
Hunters Gro. Harr —2G 39
Hunters Gro. Hay —2E 68
Hunters Gro. Orp —6M 127
Hunters Gro. Romf —5M 33
Hunters Hall Rd. Dag —9L 49
Hunters Hill. Ruis —8G 37
Hunter's La. Leav & Wat —6D 4
Hunters Mdw. SE19 —1C 108
Hunters Reach. Wal X —2A 6
Hunters Ride. Brick W —4L 5
Hunter's Rd. Chess —5J 119
Hunters Sq. Dag —9L 49
Hunter St. WC1 —7J 59
Hunter's Way. Croy —6C 124
Hunters Way. Enf —3L 15
Hunter Wlk. E13 —5E 62
Hunter Wlk. Borwd —7B 12
Hunting Clo. Esh —6L 117
Huntingdon Clo. Mitc —7J 107
Huntingdon Gdns. W4 —8A 72
Huntingdon Gdns. Wor Pk —5G 121
Huntingdon Rd. N2 —1C 42
Huntingdon Rd. N9 —1G 29
Huntingdon St. E16 —9D 62
Huntingdon St. N1 —3K 59
Huntingfield. Croy —9K 125
Huntingfield Rd. SW15 —3E 88
Hunting Ga. Clo. Enf —5L 15
Hunting Ga. Dri. Chess —9J 119
Hunting Ga. M. Sutt —5M 121
Hunting Ga. M. Twic —7C 86
Huntings Farm. Ilf —7C 48
Huntings Rd. Dag —2L 65
Huntland Clo. Rain —8F 66
Huntley Dri. N3 —6L 25
Huntley St. WC1 —7G 59
Huntley Way. SW20 —6E 104
Huntly Rd. SE25 —8C 108
Hunton Bridge. —6A 4
Hunton Bridge. (Junct.) —8B 4
Hunton Bri. Hill. K Lan —6A 4
Hunton Bri. Ind. Est. K Lan —6A 4
Hunton St. E1 —8E 60
Hunt Rd. S'hall —4L 69
Hunt's Clo. SE3 —1E 94
Hunt's Ct. WC2 —1H 75
Hunts La. E15 —5A 62
Huntsman Rd. Ilf —5F 32
Huntsmans Clo. Felt —1F 100
Huntsman St. SE17 —5C 76
Hunts Mead. Enf —5H 17
Huntsmead Clo. Chst —4K 111
Huntsmoor Rd. Eps —7B 120
Huntspill St. SW17 —9A 90
Hunts Slip Rd. SE21 —9C 92
Hunt St. W11 —2H 73
Huntsworth M. NW1 —7D 58
Hunt Way. SE22 —7E 92
Hurdwick Pl. NW1 —5G 59
(off Hampstead Rd.)
Hurleston Ho. SE8 —6K 77
Hurley Clo. W on T —4F 116
Hurley Ct. W5 —9G 55
Hurley Cres. SE16 —3H 77
Hurley Ho. SE11 —5M 75
Hurley Rd. Gnfd —9M 53
Hurlfield. Dart —9G 99
Hurlingham. —2M 89
Hurlingham Bus. Pk. SW6 —2L 89
Hurlingham Ct. SW6 —2K 89
Hurlingham Gdns. SW6 —2K 89
Hurlingham Retail Pk. SW6 —2M 89
Hurlingham Rd. SW6 —1K 89
Hurlingham Rd. Bexh —8K 81
Hurlingham Sq. SW6 —2L 89
Hurlock St. N5 —8M 43
Hurlstone Rd. SE25 —9C 108
Hurn Ct. Houn —1H 85
Hurn Ct. Rd. Houn —1H 85

Kelsey Pk. Av.—Kestrel Clo.

Kelsey Pk. Av. Beck —6M 109
Kelsey Pk. Rd. Beck —6L 109
Kelsey Rd. Orp —6F 112
Kelsey Sq. Beck —6L 109
Kelsey St. E2 —7E 60
Kelsey Way. Beck —7L 109
Kelshall. Wat —9J 5
Kelsie Way. Ilf —6C 32
Kelson Ho. E14 —4A 78
Kelso Pl. W8 —4M 73
Kelso Rd. Cars —2A 122
Kelston Rd. Ilf —9M 31
Kelvedon Av. W on T —9C 116
Kelvedon Clo. King T —3L 103
Kelvedon Ho. SW8 —9J 75
Kelvedon Rd. SW6 —8K 73
Kelvedon Wlk. Rain —4D 66
Kelvedon Way. Wfd G —6K 31
Kelvin Av. N13 —6K 27
Kelvin Av. Tedd —3C 102
Kelvinbrook. W Mol —7M 101
Kelvin Clo. Eps —8L 119
Kelvin Ct. SE20 —5F 108
Kelvin Ct. W11 —1L 73
Kelvin Ct. Iswth —1C 86
Kelvin Cres. Harr —7C 22
Kelvin Dri. Twic —5F 86
Kelvin Gdns. Croy —2J 123
Kelvin Gdns. S'hall —9L 53
Kelvin Gro. SE26 —9F 92
Kelvin Gro. Chess —5H 119
Kelvington Clo. Croy —2J 125
Kelvington Rd. SE15 —4H 93
Kelvin Pde. Orp —3C 128
Kelvin Rd. N5 —9A 44
Kelvin Rd. Well —2E 96
Kember St. N1 —3K 59
Kemble Clo. Wey —6B 116
Kemble Ct. SE15 —8C 76
(off Lydney Clo.)
Kemble Dri. Brom —5J 127
Kemble Ho. SW9 —2M 91
(off Barrington Rd.)
Kemble Rd. N17 —8E 28
Kemble Rd. SE23 —7H 93
Kemble Rd. Croy —5M 123
Kembleside Rd. Big H —9G 141
Kemble St. WC2 —9K 59
Kemerton Rd. SE5 —2A 92
Kemerton Rd. Beck —6M 109
Kemerton Rd. Croy —2D 124
Kemeys St. E9 —1J 61
Kemnal Rd. Chst —4A 112
(in two parts)
Kemp. NW9 —8D 24
(off Concourse, The)
Kemp Ct. SW8 —8J 75
(off Hartington Rd.)
Kempe Ho. SE1 —4B 76
(off Burge St.)
Kempe Rd. NW6 —5H 57
Kempe Rd. Enf —9B 6
(in two parts)
Kemp Gdns. Croy —1A 124
Kemp Ho. E6 —2L 63
Kemp Ho. W1 —1H 75
(off Berwick St.)
Kempis Way. SE22 —4C 92
Kemplay Rd. NW3 —9B 42
Kemp Pl. Bush —8L 9
Kemp Rd. Dag —6H 49
Kemprow. —1B 10
Kemprow. A'ham —1B 10
Kemps Ct. W1 —9H 59
(off Hopkins St.)
Kemps Dri. E14 —1L 77
Kemp's Dri. E14 —1L 77
Kemps Dri. N'wd —7D 20
Kempsford Gdns. SW5 —6L 73
Kempsford Rd. SE11 —5L 75
(in two parts)
Kemps Gdns. SE13 —4A 94
Kempshott Rd. SW16 —4H 107
Kempson Rd. SW6 —9L 73
Kempthorne Rd. SE8 —5K 77
Kempton Av. Horn —9K 51
Kempton Av. N'holt —2L 53
Kempton Av. Sun —5F 100
Kempton Clo. Eri —7A 82
Kempton Clo. Uxb —9A 36
Kempton Ct. E1 —8F 60
Kempton Ct. Sun —5F 100
Kempton Pk. Racecourse. —4G 101
Kempton Rd. E6 —4K 63
Kempton Rd. Hamp —6K 101
(in three parts)
Kempton Wlk. Croy —1J 125
Kempt St. SE18 —7L 79
Kemsing Clo. Bex —6J 97
Kemsing Clo. Brom —4D 126
Kemsing Clo. T Hth —8A 108
Kemsing Ho. SE1 —3B 76
(off Long La.)
Kemsing Rd. SE10 —6E 78
Kemsley Ct. W13 —2G 71
Kenbrook Ho. W14 —4K 73
Kenbury Gdns. SE5 —1A 92
Kenbury Mans. SE5 —1A 92
(off Kenbury St.)
Kenbury St. SE5 —1A 92
Kenchester Clo. SW8 —8J 75
Kencot Way. Eri —3K 81
Kendal. NW1 —6F 58
(off Augustus St.)
Kendal Av. N18 —4B 28
Kendal Av. W3 —7L 55
(in two parts)
Kendal Av. Bark —4C 64
Kendal Clo. SW9 —8M 75
Kendal Clo. Felt —7D 84
Kendal Clo. Hay —5C 52
Kendal Clo. Wfd G —2D 30
Kendal Ct. W3 —8L 55
Kendal Ct. Borwd —4A 12
Kendal Cft. Horn —1E 66
Kendale Rd. Brom —2C 110
Kendal Gdns. N18 —4B 28
Kendal Gdns. Sutt —4A 122
Kendal Ho. E9 —4G 61
Kendal Ho. N1 —5K 59
(off Priory Grn. Est.)
Kendal Ho. SE20 —6E 108
(off Derwent Rd.)
Kendall Av. Beck —6J 109
Kendall Av. S Croy —1B 138
Kendall Av. S. S Croy —2A 138
Kendall Ct. SW19 —3B 106
Kendall Ct. Sidc —9E 96
Kendall Lodge. Brom —5F 110
(off Willow Tree Wlk.)
Kendall Pl. W1 —8E 58
Kendall Rd. SE18 —9J 79
Kendall Rd. Beck —6J 109
Kendall Rd. Iswth —1E 86
Kendalmere Clo. N10 —8F 26
Kendal Pde. N18 —4B 28
Kendal Pl. SW15 —4K 89
Kendal Rd. NW10 —9E 40
Kendal Rd. Wal A —8J 7
Kendals Clo. Rad —1C 10
Kendal Steps. W2 —9C 58
(off St George's Fields)
Kendal St. W2 —9C 58
Kender St. SE14 —8G 77
Kendoa Rd. SW4 —3H 91
Kendon Clo. E11 —3F 46
Kendor Av. Eps —3A 134
Kendra Hall Rd. S Croy —9M 123
Kendrey Gdns. Twic —6C 86
Kendrick Ct. SE15 —9F 76
(off Woods Rd.)
Kendrick M. SW7 —5B 74
Kendrick Pl. SW7 —5B 74
Kenelm Clo. Harr —8E 38
Kenerne Dri. Barn —7J 13
Kenford Clo. Wat —5F 4
Kenilford Rd. SW12 —6F 90
Kenilworth Av. E17 —1L 45
Kenilworth Av. SW19 —2L 105
Kenilworth Av. Harr —9K 37
Kenilworth Av. Romf —6M 35
Kenilworth Av. Stoke D —6A 132
Kenilworth Clo. Bans —8M 135
Kenilworth Clo. Borwd —5A 12
Kenilworth Ct. Dart —5M 99
(off Bow Arrow La.)
Kenilworth Ct. Wat —3E 8
Kenilworth Cres. Enf —3C 16
Kenilworth Dri. Borwd —5A 12
Kenilworth Dri. Crox G —6A 8
Kenilworth Dri. W on T —5H 117
Kenilworth Gdns. SE18 —1M 95
Kenilworth Gdns. Hay —8D 52
Kenilworth Gdns. Horn —8G 51
Kenilworth Gdns. Ilf —7D 48
Kenilworth Gdns. Lou —8K 19
Kenilworth Gdns. S'hall —6K 53
Kenilworth Gdns. Wat —5G 21
Kenilworth Rd. E3 —5J 61
Kenilworth Rd. NW6 —4K 57
Kenilworth Rd. SE20 —5H 109
Kenilworth Rd. W5 —2J 71
Kenilworth Rd. Ashf —9B 144
Kenilworth Rd. Edgw —3A 24
Kenilworth Rd. Eps —7E 120
Kenilworth Rd. Orp —1A 128
Kenley. —6A 138
Kenley Av. NW9 —8C 24
Kenley Clo. Barn —6C 14
Kenley Clo. Bex —6L 97
Kenley Clo. Chst —7C 112
Kenley Ct. Kenl —7M 137
Kenley Gdns. Horn —7K 51
Kenley Gdns. T Hth —8M 107
Kenley La. Kenl —6A 138
Kenley Rd. SW19 —6L 105
Kenley Rd. King T —6M 103
Kenley Rd. Twic —5F 86
Kenley Wlk. W11 —1J 73
Kenley Wlk. Sutt —6H 121
Kenlor Rd. SW17 —2B 106
Kenmare Dri. Mitc —4D 106
Kenmare Gdns. N13 —4A 28
Kenmare Rd. T Hth —1L 123
Kenmere Gdns. Wemb —4L 55
Kenmere Rd. Well —1G 97
Kenmont Gdns. NW10 —6F 56
Kenmore Av. Harr —2E 38
Kenmore Clo. Rich —8L 71
Kenmore Cres. Hay —6D 52
Kenmore Gdns. Edgw —9M 23
Kenmore Rd. Harr —1H 39
Kenmore Rd. Kenl —6M 137
Kenmure Rd. E8 —1F 60
Kenmure Yd. E8 —1F 60
Kennacraig Clo. E16 —2E 78
Kennard Ho. SW11 —1E 90
Kennard Rd. E15 —3B 62
Kennard Rd. N11 —5D 26
Kennard St. E16 —2K 79
Kennard St. SW11 —9E 74
Kennedy Av. Enf —8G 17
Kennedy Clo. E13 —5E 62
Kennedy Clo. Chesh —1E 6
Kennedy Clo. Mitc —5E 106
Kennedy Clo. Orp —3B 128
Kennedy Clo. Pinn —6K 21
Kennedy Ct. Bush —2B 22
Kennedy Ct. Croy —1K 125
Kennedy Cox Ho. E16 —8D 62
(off Burke St.)
Kennedy Ho. SE11 —6K 75
(off Vauxhall Wlk.)
Kennedy Path. W7 —7D 54
Kennedy Rd. W7 —8C 54
Kennedy Rd. Bark —4C 64
Kennedy Wlk. SE17 —5B 76
(off Elsted St.)
Kennel Wood Cres. New Ad —3B 140
Kennet Clo. SW11 —3B 90
Kenneth Av. Ilf —9M 47
Kenneth Campbell Ho. NW8 —7B 58
(off Orchardson St.)
Kenneth Ct. SE11 —5L 75
Kenneth Cres. NW2 —1F 56
Kenneth Gdns. Stan —6E 22
Kenneth More Rd. Ilf —8M 47
Kenneth More Theatre. —8M 47
Kennet Ho. NW8 —7B 58
(off Church St. Est.)
Kenneth Rd. Bans —7B 136
Kenneth Rd. Romf —5H 49
Kenneth Robbins Ho. N17 —7F 28
Kenneth Younger Ho. SW6 —7K 73
(off Clem Attlee Ct.)
Kennet Rd. W9 —7K 57
Kennet Rd. Dart —2E 98
Kennet Rd. Iswth —2D 86
Kennet Sq. SW19 —5B 106
Kennet St. E1 —2E 76
Kennett Ct. W4 —8M 71
Kennett Ct. Swan —7C 114
(off Oakleigh Clo.)
Kennett Ct. Wat —6F 8
(off Whippendell Rd.)
Kennett Dri. Hay —8J 53
Kennett Wharf La. EC4 —1A 76
Kenninghall. (Junct.) —5G 29
Kenninghall Rd. E5 —8E 44
Kenninghall Rd. N18 —5G 29
Kenning Ho. N1 —4C 60
(off Colville Est.)
Kenning St. SE16 —3G 77
Kennings Way. SE11 —6L 75
Kennington. —7L 75
Kennington Grn. SE11 —6L 75
Kennington Gro. SE11 —7K 75
Kennington La. SE11 —6K 75
Kennington Oval. (Junct.) —7L 75
Kennington Oval. SE11 —7K 75
Kennington Pal. Ct. SE11 —6L 75
(off Sancroft St.)
Kennington Pk. Gdns. SE11 —7M 75
Kennington Pk. Ho. SE11 —6L 75
(off Kennington Pk. Pl.)
Kennington Pk. Pl. SE11 —7L 75
Kennington Pk. Rd. SE11 —7L 75
Kennington Rd. SE1 & SE11 —4L 75
Kennistoun Ho. NW5 —1G 59
Kenny Dri. Cars —1E 136
Kennyland Ct. NW4 —4F 40
(off Hendon Way)
Kennylands Rd. Ilf —7E 32
Kenny Rd. NW7 —6J 25
Kenrick Pl. W1 —8E 58
Kensal Green. —6G 57
Kensal Ho. W10 —7H 57
(off Ladbroke Gro.)
Kensal Rise. —5H 57
Kensal Rd. W10 —7J 57
Kensal Town. —7J 57
Kensington. —3M 73
Kensington Arc. W8 —3M 73
(off Kensington High St.)
Kensington Av. E12 —2J 63
Kensington Av. T Hth —5L 107
Kensington Av. Wat —6D 8
Kensington Cen. W14 —5J 73
(in two parts)
Kensington Chu. Ct. W8 —3M 73
Kensington Chu. St. W8 —2L 73
Kensington Chu. Wlk. W8 —3M 73
(in two parts)
Kensington Clo. N11 —6E 26
Kensington Ct. SE16 —2H 77
(off King & Queen Wharf)
Kensington Ct. W8 —3M 73
Kensington Ct. Gdns. W8 —4M 73
(off Kensington Ct. Pl.)
Kensington Ct. M. W8 —4M 73
(off Kensington Ct. Pl.)
Kensington Ct. Pl. W8 —4M 73
Kensington Dri. Wfd G —9H 31
Kensington Gardens. —2A 74
Kensington Gdns. Ilf —6K 47
Kensington Gdns. King T —7H 103
(in two parts)
Kensington Gdns. Sq. W2 —9M 57
Kensington Ga. W8 —4A 74
Kensington Gore. SW7 —3A 74
Kensington Hall Gdns. W14 —6K 73
Kensington Heights. W8 —2L 73
Kensington High St. W14 & W8 —4K 73
Kensington Ho. W14 —3H 73
Kensington Mall. W8 —2L 73
Kensington Mans. SW5 —6L 73
(off Trebovir Rd., in two parts)
Kensington Palace. —2M 73
Kensington Pal. Gdns. W8 —2M 73
Kensington Pk. Gdns. W11 —1K 73
Kensington Pk. M. W11 —9K 57
Kensington Pk. Rd. W11 —9K 57
Kensington Pl. W8 —2L 73
Kensington Rd. W8 & SW7 —3A 74
Kensington Rd. N'holt —6L 53
Kensington Rd. Romf —4A 50
Kensington Sq. W8 —4M 73
Kensington Ter. S Croy —9B 124
Kensington Village. W14 —5K 73
Kensington Way. Borwd —5B 12
Kensington W. W14 —5J 73
Kenswick Ct. SE13 —4M 93
Kensworth Ho. EC1 —6B 60
(off Cranwood St.)
Kent Av. W13 —8F 54
Kent Av. Dag —7L 65
Kent Av. Well —4D 96
Kent Clo. Borwd —2B 12
Kent Clo. Mitc —8J 107
Kent Clo. Orp —8C 128
Kent Clo. Uxb —2A 142
Kent Ct. E2 —5D 60
Kent Ct. NW9 —9C 24
Kent Dri. Cockf —6E 14
Kent Dri. Horn —9H 51
Kent Dri. Tedd —2C 102
Kentford Way. N'holt —4J 53
Kent Gdns. W13 —8F 54
Kent Gdns. Ruis —4E 36
Kent Ga. Way. Croy —8K 125
Kent Ho. SE1 —6D 76
Kent Ho. SW1 —6H 75
(off Aylesford St.)
Kent Ho. W4 —6C 72
(off Devonshire St.)
Kent Ho. La. Beck —3J 109
Kent Ho. Rd. SE26 & Beck —2J 109
Kentish Bldgs. SE1 —3B 76
(off Borough High St.)
Kentish Rd. Belv —5L 81
Kentish Town. —1F 58
Kentish Town Ind. Est. NW5 —1F 58
Kentish Town Rd. NW1 & NW5 —3F 58
Kentish Way. Brom —6E 110
Kentlea Rd. SE28 —3C 80
Kentmere Ho. SE15 —7G 77
Kentmere Mans. W5 —7F 54
Kentmere Rd. SE18 —5C 80
Kenton. —3G 39
Kenton Av. Harr —5D 38
Kenton Av. S'hall —1L 69
Kenton Av. Sun —6H 101
Kenton Ct. SE26 —1J 109
(off Adamsrill Rd.)
Kenton Ct. W14 —4K 73
Kenton Ct. Kent —4F 38
Kenton Ct. Twic —5H 87
Kentone Ct. SE25 —8F 108
Kenton Gdns. Harr —3G 39
Kenton Ho. E1 —7G 61
(off Mantus Clo.)
Kenton La. Harr —6D 22
Kenton Pk. Av. Harr —2H 39
Kenton Pk. Clo. Harr —2G 39
Kenton Pk. Cres. Harr —2H 39
Kenton Pk. Mans. Kent —3G 39
(off Kenton Rd.)
Kenton Pk. Pde. Harr —3G 39
Kenton Pk. Rd. Harr —2G 39
Kenton Rd. E9 —2H 61
Kenton Rd. Harr —5D 38
Kenton St. WC1 —7J 59
Kenton Way. Hay —6C 52
Kent Pk. Ind. Est. SE15 —7F 76
Kent Pas. NW1 —7D 58
Kent Rd. N21 —1B 28
Kent Rd. W4 —4A 72
Kent Rd. Dag —1M 65
Kent Rd. Dart —5H 99
Kent Rd. E Mol —8A 102
Kent Rd. King T —7H 103
Kent Rd. Orp & St M —1F 128
Kent Rd. Rich —8L 71
Kent Rd. W W'ck —3M 125
Kent's Pas. Hamp —5K 101
Kent St. E2 —5D 60
Kent St. E13 —6F 62
Kent Ter. NW1 —6C 58
Kent Vw. Ave —3M 83
Kent Vw. Wen —1H 83
Kent Vw. Gdns. Ilf —7C 48
Kent Wlk. SW9 —3M 91
Kent Way. Surb —5J 119
Kentwell Clo. SE4 —3J 93
Kent Wharf. SE8 —8M 77
(off Creekside)
Kentwode Grn. SW13 —8E 72
Kent Yd. SW7 —3C 74
Kenver Av. N12 —6B 26
Kenward Rd. SE9 —4G 95
Kenway. Rain —6H 67
Kenway. Romf —9A 34
Ken Way. Wemb —8A 40
Kenway Clo. Rain —6G 67
Kenway Rd. SW5 —5M 73
Kenway Wlk. Rain —6H 67
Ken Wilson Ho. E2 —5E 60
(off Pritchards Rd.)
Kenwood Av. N14 —7H 15
Kenwood Clo. NW3 —6B 42
Kenwood Clo. W Dray —7L 143
Kenwood Dri. Beck —7A 110
Kenwood Dri. W on T —8F 116
Kenwood Gdns. E18 —1F 46
Kenwood Gdns. Ilf —2L 47
Kenwood House. —6C 42
Kenwood Ho. SW9 —3M 91
Kenwood Ho. Wat —9B 8
Kenwood Pk. Wey —8B 116
Kenwood Ridge. Kenl —9M 137
Kenwood Rd. N6 —4D 42
Kenwood Rd. N9 —1E 28
Kenworth Clo. Wal X —6D 6
Kenworthy Rd. E9 —1J 61
Kenwrick Ho. N1 —4K 59
(off Barnsbury Est.)
Kenwyn Dri. NW2 —7C 40
Kenwyn Lodge. N2 —2D 42
Kenwyn Rd. SW4 —3H 91
Kenwyn Rd. SW20 —5G 105
Kenwyn Rd. Dart —4H 99
Kenya Rd. SE7 —8H 79
Kenyngton Ct. Sun —2E 100
Kenyngton Dri. Sun —2E 100
Kenyngton Pl. Harr —3G 39
Kenyon Mans. W14 —7J 73
(off Queen's Club Gdns.)
Kenyon St. SW6 —9H 73
Keogh Rd. E15 —2C 62
Keple Pl. SW13 —7F 72
Kepler Ho. SE10 —6D 78
(off Armitage Rd.)
Kepler Rd. SW4 —3J 91
Keppel Ho. SE8 —6K 77
Keppel Rd. E6 —3K 63
Keppel Rd. Dag —9J 49
Keppel Row. SE1 —2A 76
Keppel St. WC1 —8H 59
Kerbela St. E2 —7E 60
Kerbey St. E14 —9M 61
Kerfield Cres. SE5 —9B 76
Kerfield Pl. SE5 —9B 76
Kernow Clo. Horn —7J 51
Kerri Clo. Barn —6G 13
Kerridge Ct. N1 —2C 60
(off Balls Pond Rd.)
Kerrington Ct. W12 —3G 73
(off Uxbridge Rd.)
Kerrison Pl. W5 —2H 71
Kerrison Rd. E15 —4B 62
Kerrison Rd. SW11 —2C 90
Kerrison Rd. W5 —2H 71
Kerrison Vs. W5 —2H 71
Kerry. N7 —2J 59
Kerry Av. Ave —4L 83
Kerry Av. Stan —4G 23
Kerry Clo. E16 —9F 62
Kerry Clo. N13 —2K 27
Kerry Ct. Stan —4H 23
Kerry Ho. E1 —9G 61
(off Sidney St.)
Kerry Path. SE14 —7K 77
Kerry Rd. SE14 —7K 77
Kersey Dri. S Croy —4G 139
Kersey Gdns. SE9 —1J 111
Kersey Gdns. Romf —7J 35
Kersfield Rd. SW15 —5H 89
Kershaw Clo. SW18 —5B 90
Kershaw Clo. Horn —5J 51
Kershaw Rd. Dag —8L 49
Kersley M. SW11 —9D 74
Kersley Rd. N16 —7C 44
Kersley St. SW11 —1D 90
Kerstin Clo. Hay —1D 68
Kerswell Clo. N15 —3C 44
Kerwick Clo. N7 —3J 59
Keslake Mans. NW10 —5H 57
(off Station Ter.)
Keslake Rd. NW6 —5H 57
Kessock Clo. N17 —3F 44
Kesteven Clo. Ilf —6D 32
Kestlake Rd. Bex —5G 97
Keston. —7G 127
Keston Av. Kes —7G 127
Keston Clo. N18 —3B 28
Keston Clo. Well —8G 81
Keston Ct. Bex —6K 97
Keston Ct. Surb —9K 103
(off Cranes Pk.)
Keston Gdns. Kes —6G 127
Keston Ho. SE17 —6C 76
(off Kinglake St.)
Keston Mark. —6J 127
Keston Mark. (Junct.) —5J 127
Keston M. Wat —4F 8
Keston Pk. Clo. Kes —5K 127
Keston Rd. N17 —1B 44
Keston Rd. SE15 —2E 92
Keston Rd. T Hth —1L 123
Kestral Clo. Wat —7J 5
Kestrel Av. E6 —8J 63
Kestrel Av. SE24 —4M 91
Kestrel Clo. NW9 —9C 24
Kestrel Clo. NW10 —1B 56
Kestrel Clo. Eps —3M 133

Kingsland High St.—Knole Ct.

Kingsland High St. E8 —2D 60
Kingsland Pas. E8 —2C 60
Kingsland Rd. E2 & E8 —6C 60
Kingsland Rd. E13 —6G 63
Kingsland Shop. Cen. E8 —2D 60
Kings La. Sutt —8B 122
Kingslawn Clo. SW15 —4F 88
Kingsleigh Pl. Mitc —7D 106
Kingsleigh Wlk. Brom —8D 110
Kingsley Av. W13 —8E 54
Kingsley Av. Bans —7L 135
Kingsley Av. Borwd —4K 11
Kingsley Av. Chesh —2B 6
Kingsley Av. Dart —4L 99
Kingsley Av. Houn —1A 86
Kingsley Av. S'hall —1L 69
Kingsley Av. Sutt —6B 122
Kingsley Clo. N2 —3A 42
Kingsley Clo. Dag —9M 49
Kingsley Ct. NW10 —2F 56
Kingsley Ct. Bexh —4L 97
Kingsley Ct. Edgw —3M 23
Kingsley Ct. Romf —4F 50
Kingsley Ct. Sutt —9M 121
Kingsley Ct. Wor Pk —4D 120
(off Avenue, The)
Kingsley Dri. Wor Pk —4D 120
Kingsley Flats. SE1 —5C 76
(off Old Kent Rd.)
Kingsley Gdns. E4 —5L 29
Kingsley Gdns. Horn —2H 51
Kingsley Ho. SW3 —7B 74
(off Beaufort St.)
Kingsley Mans. W14 —7J 73
(off Greyhound Rd.)
Kingsley M. E1 —1F 76
Kingsley M. W8 —4M 73
Kingsley M. Chst —3M 111
Kingsley Pl. N6 —5E 42
Kingsley Rd. E7 —3E 62
Kingsley Rd. E17 —9A 30
Kingsley Rd. N13 —4L 27
Kingsley Rd. NW6 —4K 57
Kingsley Rd. SW19 —2M 105
Kingsley Rd. Croy —3L 123
Kingsley Rd. Harr —9A 38
Kingsley Rd. Houn —9M 69
Kingsley Rd. Ilf —8A 32
Kingsley Rd. Orp —9D 128
Kingsley Rd. Pinn —2K 37
Kingsley St. SW11 —2D 90
Kingsley Way. NW11 —4A 42
Kingsley Wood Dri. SE9 —9K 95
Kingslyn Cres. SE19 —5C 108
Kings Lynn Clo. H Hill —6H 35
Kings Lynn Dri. Romf —6H 35
Kings Lynn Path. H Hill —6H 35
Kings Mall. W6 —5G 73
Kingsman Pde. SE18 —4K 79
Kingsman St. SE18 —4K 79
Kingsmead. Barn —6L 13
Kingsmead. Big H —8H 141
Kings Mead. Rich —5K 87
Kingsmead. Wal X —1D 6
Kingsmead Av. N9 —1F 28
Kingsmead Av. NW9 —5B 40
Kingsmead Av. Mitc —7G 107
Kingsmead Av. Romf —4C 50
Kingsmead Av. Sun —6G 101
Kingsmead Av. Surb —4L 119
Kingsmead Av. Wor Pk —4F 120
Kingsmead Clo. Eps —9B 120
Kingsmead Clo. Sidc —8E 96
Kingsmead Clo. Tedd —3F 102
Kingsmead Cotts. Brom —3J 127
Kingsmead Ct. N6 —5H 43
Kingsmead Dri. N'holt —3K 53
Kingsmead Ho. E9 —9J 45
Kingsmead Mans. Romf —4D 50
(off Kingsmead Av.)
Kingsmeadow. King T —7M 103
Kings Mead Pk. Clay —9C 118
Kingsmead Rd. SW2 —8L 91
King's Mead Way. E9 —9J 45
Kingsmere Clo. SW15 —2H 89
Kingsmere Pk. NW9 —6M 39
Kingsmere Pl. N16 —6B 44
Kingsmere Rd. SW19 —8H 89
King's M. SW4 —4J 91
King's M. WC1 —7K 59
Kings M. Chig —2A 32
Kingsmill. NW8 —5B 58
(off Kingsmill Ter.)
Kingsmill Gdns. Dag —1K 65
Kingsmill Ho. SW3 —6C 74
(off Marlborough St.)
Kingsmill Rd. Dag —1K 65
Kingsmill Ter. NW8 —5B 58
Kingsnorth Ho. W10 —9H 57
Kingsnympton Pk. King T —4M 103
King's Orchard. SE9 —5J 95
King's Paddock. Hamp —5A 102
Kings Pde. N17 —1D 44
King's Pde. NW10 —4G 57
Kings Pde. W12 —4E 72
King's Pde. Cars —5D 122
(off Wrythe La.)
King's Pde. Edgw —5L 23
(off Edgwarebury La.)
Kingspark Ct. E18 —1E 46
Kings Pas. E11 —5C 46
Kings Pas. King T —6H 103
King's Pas. King T —5H 103
King's Pl. SE1 —3A 76
King's Pl. W4 —6A 72
Kings Pl. Buck H —2G 31
Kings Pl. Lou —9H 19
King Sq. EC1 —6A 60
King's Quay. SW10 —9A 74
(off Chelsea Harbour)
Kings Reach Tower. SE1 —2L 75
(off Hatfields)
Kings Ride Ga. Rich —3L 87
Kingsridge. SW19 —8J 89
Kingsridge Gdns. Dart —5H 99
Kings Rd. E4 —1B 30
King's Rd. E6 —4G 63
Kings Rd. E11 —5C 46
King's Rd. N17 —8D 28
Kings Rd. N18 —5E 28
Kings Rd. N22 —8K 27
King's Rd. NW10 —3F 56
Kings Rd. SE25 —7E 108
King's Rd. SW6, SW10 & SW3 —8M 73
Kings Rd. SW14 —2B 88
Kings Rd. SW19 —3L 105
Kings Rd. W5 —8H 55
Kings Rd. Bark —3A 64
Kings Rd. Barn —5G 13
Kings Rd. Big H —8G 141
Kings Rd. Felt —7G 85
Kings Rd. Harr —7K 37
King's Rd. King T —5J 103
King's Rd. Mitc —7E 106
King's Rd. Orp —6D 128
Kings Rd. Rich —5K 87
King's Rd. Romf —3E 50
King's Rd. Surb —3G 119
King's Rd. Sutt —2L 135
King's Rd. Tedd —2B 102
Kings Rd. Twic —5F 86
King's Rd. Uxb —5B 142
Kings Rd. Wal X —6E 6
Kings Rd. W on T —4F 116
King's Rd. W Dray —3K 143
Kings Rd. Bungalows. S Harr —9K 37
King's Scholars' Pas. SW1 —4G 75
(off Carlisle Pl.)
King's Shade Wlk. Eps —5B 134
King Stairs Clo. SE16 —3F 76
King's Ter. NW1 —4G 59
King's Ter. Iswth —3E 86
Kingsthorpe Rd. SE26 —1H 109
Kingston Av. Felt —5C 84
Kingston Av. Sutt —5J 121
Kingston Av. W Dray —1K 143
(in two parts)
Kingston Bri. King T —6H 103
Kingston Bus. Cen. Chess —5J 119
Kingston By-Pass. SW15 & SW20 —1C 104
Kingston By-Pass. Surb & N Mald —5H 119
Kingston By-Pass Rd. Esh & Surb —4C 118
Kingston Clo. N'holt —4K 53
Kingston Clo. Romf —1J 49
(in two parts)
Kingston Clo. Tedd —3F 102
Kingston Cres. Beck —5K 109
Kingston Gdns. Croy —5J 123
Kingston Hall Rd. King T —7H 103
Kingston Hill. King T —5L 103
Kingston Hill Av. Romf —1J 49
Kingston Hill Pl. King T —1A 104
Kingston Ho. NW6 —3J 57
Kingston Ho. King T —8H 103
(off Surbiton Rd.)
Kingston Ho. E. SW7 —3C 74
(off Prince's Ga.)
Kingston Ho. Est. Surb —1F 118
Kingston Ho. N. SW7 —3C 74
(off Prince's Ga.)
Kingston Ho. S. SW7 —3C 74
(off Ennismore Gdns.)
Kingstonian F.C. —7L 103
Kingston La. Tedd —2E 102
Kingston La. Uxb —6C 142
Kingston La. W Dray —3K 143
Kingston Mus. —6J 103
Kingston Pl. Harr —7D 22
Kingston Rd. N9 —2E 28
Kingston Rd. SW15 & SW19 —8E 88
Kingston Rd. SW20 & SW19 —6H 105
Kingston Rd. Barn —7B 14
Kingston Rd. Eps —1D 134
Kingston Rd. Ilf —9M 47
Kingston Rd. King T & N Mald —7M 103
Kingston Rd. Lea —9E 132
Kingston Rd. Romf —2D 50
Kingston Rd. S'hall —3K 69
Kingston Rd. Surb & Eps —4M 119
Kingston Rd. Tedd —2F 102
Kingston Sq. SE19 —2B 108
Kingston Upon Thames. —6J 103
Kingston upon Thames Crematorium. King T —7L 103
Kingston Vale. —1C 104
Kingston Va. SW15 —1B 104
Kingstown St. NW1 —4E 58
(in two parts)
King St. E13 —7E 62
King St. EC2 —9A 60
King St. N2 —1B 42
King St. N17 —8D 28
King St. SW1 —2G 75
King St. W3 —2A 72
King St. W6 —5E 72
King St. WC2 —1J 75
King St. Rich —4H 87
King St. S'hall —4J 69
King St. Twic —7E 86
King St. Wat —6G 9
King St. Pde. Twic —7E 86
(off King St.)
Kingsvale Ct. W Dray —1H 143
Kings Wlk. S Croy —6F 138
Kings Wlk. Shop. Cen. SW3 —6D 74
Kings Warren. Oxs —3A 132
Kingswater Pl. SW11 —8C 74
Kingsway. N12 —6A 26
Kingsway. SW14 —2M 87
Kingsway. WC2 —9K 59
King's Way. Croy —7K 123
Kingsway. Enf —7F 16
Kings Way. Harr —2C 38
Kingsway. Hay —8A 52
Kingsway. N Mald —8G 105
Kingsway. Orp —9B 112
Kingsway. Stai —7B 144
Kingsway. Wemb —9J 39
Kingsway. W W'ck —5C 126
Kings Way. Wfd G —5G 31
Kingsway Av. S Croy —1G 139
Kingsway Bus. Pk. Hamp —5K 101
Kingsway Cres. Harr —2A 38
Kingsway Est. N18 —6H 29
Kingsway Mans. WC1 —8K 59
(off Red Lion Sq.)
Kingsway N. Orbital Rd. Wat —8D 4
Kingsway Pl. EC1 —7L 59
(off Corporation Row)
Kingsway Rd. Sutt —9J 121
Kingsway, The. Eps —3C 134
Kingswear Rd. NW5 —8F 42
Kingswear Rd. Ruis —7E 36
Kingswood. —7F 4
Kingswood. E2 —5G 61
(off Cyprus St.)
Kingswood Av. NW6 —4J 57
Kingswood Av. Belv —5K 81
Kingswood Av. Brom —7C 110
Kingswood Av. Hamp —3M 101
Kingswood Av. Houn —9K 69
Kingswood Av. S Croy —7F 138
Kingswood Av. Swan —8D 114
Kingswood Av. T Hth —9L 107
Kingswood Clo. N20 —9A 14
Kingswood Clo. SW8 —8J 75
Kingswood Clo. Dart —5G 99
Kingswood Clo. Enf —7C 16
Kingswood Clo. N Mald —1D 120
Kingswood Clo. Orp —2C 128
Kingswood Clo. Surb —2J 119
Kingswood Ct. E4 —5L 29
Kingswood Ct. NW6 —3L 57
(off W. End La.)
Kingswood Dri. SE19 —1C 108
Kingswood Dri. Cars —3D 122
Kingswood Dri. Sutt —1M 135
Kingswood Est. SE21 —1C 108
Kingswood La. Warl —7G 139
(in two parts)
Kingswood Pk. N3 —8K 25
Kingswood Pl. SE13 —3C 94
Kingswood Rd. E11 —5C 46
Kingswood Rd. SE20 —3G 109
Kingswood Rd. SW2 —5J 91
Kingswood Rd. SW19 —4K 105
Kingswood Rd. W4 —4A 72
Kingswood Rd. Brom & Short —8B 110
Kingswood Rd. Ilf —6E 48
Kingswood Rd. Wat —7F 4
Kingswood Rd. Wemb —8L 39
Kingswood Ter. W4 —4A 72
Kingswood Way. S Croy —5G 139
(in two parts)
Kingswood Way. Wall —7J 123
Kingsworth Clo. Beck —9J 109
Kingsworthy Clo. King T —7K 103
Kings Yd. E9 —2L 61
Kings Yd. SW15 —2G 89
(off Lwr. Richmond Rd.)
Kingthorpe Rd. NW10 —3B 56
Kingthorpe Ter. NW10 —2B 56
Kington Ho. NW6 —4M 57
(off Mortimer Cres.)
Kingward Ho. E1 —8E 60
(off Hanbury St.)
Kingwell Rd. Barn —2B 14
King William IV Gdns. SE20 —3G 109
King William La. SE10 —6C 78
King William's Ct. SE10 —7B 78
(off Park Row)
King William St. EC4 —9B 60
King William Wlk. SE10 —7A 78
(in two parts)
Kingwood Rd. SW6 —9J 73
Kinlet Rd. SE18 —9A 80
Kinloch Dri. NW9 —5B 40
Kinloch St. N7 —8K 43
Kinloss Ct. N3 —2K 41
Kinloss Gdns. N3 —1K 41
Kinloss Rd. Cars —2A 122
Kinnaird Av. W4 —8A 72
Kinnaird Av. Brom —3D 110
Kinnaird Clo. Brom —3D 110
Kinnaird Way. Wfd G —6K 31
Kinnear Rd. W12 —3D 72
Kinnerton Pl. N. SW1 —3D 74
(off Kinnerton St.)
Kinnerton Pl. S. SW1 —3D 74
(off Kinnerton St.)
Kinnerton St. SW1 —3E 74
Kinnerton Yd. SW1 —3E 74
(off Kinnerton St.)
Kinnoul Rd. W6 —7J 73
Kinross Av. Wor Pk —4E 120
Kinross Clo. Edgw —2M 23
Kinross Clo. Harr —3K 39
Kinross Clo. Sun —2D 100
Kinross Ct. SE6 —7D 94
Kinross Ct. Brom —5D 110
(off Highland Rd.)
Kinross Dri. Sun —2D 100
Kinross Ter. E17 —9K 29
Kinsale Rd. SE15 —2E 92
Kinsella Gdns. SW19 —2F 104
Kinsham Ho. E2 —7E 60
(off Ramsey St.)
Kintore Way. SE1 —5D 76
Kintyre Clo. SW16 —6K 107
Kintyre Ct. SW2 —6J 91
Kintyre Ho. E14 —2A 78
(off Coldharbour)
Kinveachy Gdns. SE7 —6J 79
Kinver Rd. SE26 —1G 109
Kipling Ct. W7 —1D 70
Kipling Dri. SW19 —3B 106
Kipling Est. SE1 —3B 76
Kipling Ho. SE5 —8B 76
(off Elmington Est.)
Kipling Pl. Stan —6D 22
Kipling Rd. Bexh —9J 81
Kipling Rd. Dart —4M 99
Kipling St. SE1 —3B 76
Kipling Ter. N9 —3B 28
Kipling Tower. W3 —4A 72
(off Palmerston Rd.)
Kippington Dri. SE9 —7H 95
Kirby Clo. Eps —7D 120
Kirby Clo. Ilf —6C 32
Kirby Clo. Lou —9J 19
Kirby Clo. N'wd —6D 20
Kirby Clo. Romf —5L 35
Kirby Est. SE16 —4F 76
Kirby Est. W Dray —1H 143
Kirby Gro. SE1 —3C 76
Kirby St. EC1 —8L 59
Kirby Way. W on T —1G 117
Kirchen Rd. W13 —1F 70
Kirkby Clo. N11 —6E 26
Kirkcaldy Grn. Wat —3G 21
Kirkdale. SE26 —8F 92
Kirkdale Corner. SE26 —1G 109
Kirkdale Rd. E11 —6C 46
Kirkeby Ho. EC1 —8L 59
(off Leather La.)
Kirkfield Clo. W13 —2F 70
Kirkgate, The. Eps —5C 134
Kirkham Ho. Romf —5H 35
(off Montgomery Cres.)
Kirkham Rd. E6 —9J 63
Kirkham St. SE18 —7C 80
Kirkland Av. Ilf —9L 31
Kirkland Clo. Sidc —5C 96
Kirkland Ho. E14 —6M 77
(off Westferry Rd.)
Kirkland Ho. E14 —6M 77
(off St Davids Sq.)
Kirkland Wlk. E8 —2D 60
Kirk La. SE18 —7A 80
Kirkleas Rd. Surb —3J 119
Kirklees Rd. Dag —1G 65
Kirklees Rd. T Hth —9L 107
Kirkley Rd. SW19 —5L 105
Kirkly Clo. S Croy —1C 138
Kirkman Pl. W1 —8H 59
(off Tottenham Ct. Rd.)
Kirkmichael Rd. E14 —9A 62
Kirk Ri. Sutt —5M 121
Kirk Rd. E17 —4K 45
Kirkside Rd. SE3 —7E 78
Kirkstall Av. N17 —2B 44
Kirkstall Gdns. SW2 —7J 91
Kirkstall Rd. SW2 —7H 91
Kirksted Rd. Mord —3M 121
Kirkstone. NW1 —6G 59
(off Harrington St.)
Kirkstone Way. Brom —4C 110
Kirk St. WC1 —7K 59
(off Northington St.)
Kirkton Rd. N15 —2C 44
Kirkwall Pl. E2 —6G 61
Kirkwood La. NW1 —3E 58
Kirkwood Rd. SE15 —1F 92
Kirn Rd. W13 —1F 70
Kirrane Clo. N Mald —9D 104
Kirtley Ho. SW8 —9G 75
Kirtley Rd. SE26 —1J 109
Kirtling St. SW8 —8G 75
Kirton Clo. W4 —5B 72
Kirton Clo. Horn —2G 67
Kirton Gdns. E2 —6D 60
(in two parts)
Kirton Lodge. SW18 —5M 89
Kirton Rd. E13 —5G 63
Kirton Wlk. Edgw —7A 24
Kirwyn Way. SE5 —8M 75
Kitcat Ter. E3 —6L 61
Kitchener Rd. E7 —2F 62
Kitchener Rd. E17 —8M 29
Kitchener Rd. N2 —1C 42
Kitchener Rd. N17 —1C 44
Kitchener Rd. Dag —2M 65
Kitchener Rd. T Hth —7B 108
Kite Pl. E2 —6E 60
(off Lampern St.)
Kite Yd. SW11 —9D 74
(off Cambridge Rd.)
Kitley Gdns. SE19 —5D 108
Kitson Rd. SE5 —8B 76
Kitson Rd. SW13 —9E 72
Kitters Grn. Ab L —4C 4
Kittiwake Clo. S Croy —2J 139
Kittiwake Ct. SE8 —7K 77
(off Abinger Gro.)
Kittiwake Pl. Sutt —7K 121
Kittiwake Rd. N'holt —6H 53
Kittiwake Way. Hay —8H 53
Kitto Rd. SE14 —1H 93
Kitt's End. —1J 13
Kitts End Rd. Barn —1J 13
Kiver Rd. N19 —7H 43
Klea Av. SW4 —5G 91
Klein's Wharf. E14 —4L 77
(off Westferry Rd.)
Knapdale Clo. SE23 —8F 92
Knapmill Rd. SE6 —8L 93
Knapmill Way. SE6 —8M 93
Knapp Clo. NW10 —2C 56
Knapp Rd. E3 —7L 61
Knapp Rd. Ashf —9D 144
Knapton M. SW17 —3E 106
Knaresborough Dri. SW18 —7M 89
Knaresborough Pl. SW5 —5M 73
Knatchbull Rd. NW10 —4B 56
Knatchbull Rd. SE5 —1M 91
Knebworth Av. E17 —8L 29
Knebworth Ho. SW8 —1H 91
Knebworth Path. Borwd —6B 12
Knebworth Rd. N16 —9C 44
Knee Hill. SE2 —5G 81
Kneehill Cres. SE2 —5G 81
Kneller Gdns. Iswth —5B 86
Kneller Ho. N'holt —5H 53
(off Academy Gdns.)
Kneller Rd. SE4 —3J 93
Kneller Rd. N Mald —2C 120
Kneller Rd. Twic —5A 86
Knight Clo. Dag —7G 49
Knight Ct. E4 —1A 30
(off Ridgeway, The)
Knight Ct. N15 —3C 44
Knighten St. E1 —2F 76
Knighthead Point. E14 —3L 77
Knight Ho. SE17 —5C 76
(off Tatum St.)
Knightland Rd. E5 —7F 44
Knightleas Ct. NW2 —2G 57
Knighton Clo. Romf —4B 50
Knighton Clo. S Croy —1M 137
Knighton Clo. Wfd G —4F 30
Knighton Dri. Wfd G —4F 30
Knighton Grn. Buck H —2F 30
Knighton La. Buck H —2F 30
Knighton Pk. Rd. SE26 —2H 109
Knighton Rd. E7 —8E 46
Knighton Rd. Romf —4A 50
Knightrider Ct. EC4 —1A 76
(off Knightrider St.)
Knightrider St. EC4 —9M 59
Knights Arc. SW1 —3D 74
(off Knightsbridge)
Knights Av. W5 —3J 71
Knightsbridge. —3C 74
Knightsbridge. SW7 & SW1 —3D 74
Knightsbridge Ct. SW1 —3D 74
(off Sloane St.)
Knightsbridge Gdns. Romf —3B 50
Knightsbridge Grn. SW1 —3D 74
(in two parts)
Knights Clo. E9 —1G 61
Knights Ct. Brom —9D 94
Knights Ct. King T —7J 103
Knights Hill. SE27 —2M 107
Knight's Hill Sq. SE27 —1M 107
Knights Ho. SW8 —8J 75
(off S. Lambeth Rd.)
Knights La. N9 —3E 28
Knights Mnr. Way. Dart —4K 99
Knight's Pk. King T —7J 103
Knights Ridge. Orp —7F 128
Knight's Rd. E16 —3E 78
Knights Rd. Stan —4G 23
Knight's Wlk. SE11 —5M 75
(in two parts)
Knights Way. Ilf —6A 32
Knightswood Clo. Edgw —2A 24
Knightswood Ct. N6 —5H 43
Knightswood Ho. N12 —6A 26
Knightswood Rd. Rain —5E 66
Knightwood Cres. N Mald —1C 120
Knivet Rd. SW6 —7L 73
Knobs Hill Rd. E15 —4M 61
Knockholt Clo. Sutt —2M 135
Knockholt Rd. SE9 —4H 95
Knole Clo. Croy —1G 125
Knole Ct. N'holt —6G 53
(off Broomcroft Av.)

Knole Ga.—Lancelot Cres.

Knole Ga. Sidc —9C 96
Knole Rd. Dart —6E 98
Knole, The. SE9 —1L 111
Knoll Cres. N'wd —8C 20
(in two parts)
Knoll Dri. N14 —9E 14
Knoll Ho. NW8 —5A 58
(off Carlton Hill)
Knoll Ho. Pinn —9H 21
Knollmead. Surb —3A 120
Knoll Ri. Orp —3D 128
Knoll Rd. SW18 —4A 90
Knoll Rd. Bex —6L 97
Knoll Rd. Sidc —2F 112
Knolls Clo. Wor Pk —5F 120
Knolls, The. Eps —8G 135
Knoll, The. W13 —8G 55
Knoll, The. Beck —5M 109
Knoll, The. Brom —4E 126
Knollys Clo. SW16 —9L 91
Knolly's Ho. WC1 —7J 59
(off Tavistock Pl.)
Knollys Rd. SW16 —9K 91
Knottisford St. E2 —6G 61
Knotts Grn. M. E10 —4M 45
Knotts Grn. Rd. E10 —4M 45
Knowlden Ho. E1 —1G 77
(off Cable St.)
Knowle Av. Bexh —8J 81
Knowle Clo. SW9 —2L 91
Knowle Rd. Brom —4K 127
Knowle Rd. Twic —7C 86
Knowles Clo. W Dray —2J 143
Knowles Ct. Harr —4D 38
(off Gayton Rd.)
Knowles Hill Cres. SE13 —4B 94
Knowles Wlk. SW4 —2G 91
Knowl Pk. Els —7J 11
Knowlton Grn. Brom —9D 110
Knowlton Ho. SW9 —9L 75
(off Cowley Rd.)
Knowl Way. Els —7K 11
Knowsley Av. S'hall —2M 69
Knowsley Rd. SW11 —1D 90
Knox Ct. SW4 —1J 91
Knox Rd. E7 —2D 62
Knox St. W1 —8D 58
Knoyle St. SE14 —7J 77
Knutsford Av. Wat —2H 9
Koblenz Ho. N8 —1J 43
(off Newland Rd.)
Kohat Rd. SW19 —2M 105
Koh-I-Nor Av. Bush —8L 9
Komeheather Ho. Ilf —3K 47
Koonowla Clo. Big H —7H 141
Kossuth St. SE10 —6C 78
Kotree Way. SE1 —5E 76
Kramer M. SW5 —6L 73
Kreedman Wlk. E8 —1E 60
Kreisel Wlk. Rich —7K 71
Kristina Ct. Sutt —8L 121
(off Overton Rd.)
Krupnik Pl. EC2 —7C 60
(off Bateman's Row)
Kuala Gdns. SW16 —5K 107
Kubrick Bus. Est. E7 —9F 46
(off Station App.)
Kuhn Way. E7 —1E 62
Kwame Ho. E16 —1M 79
(off University Way)
Kydbrook Clo. Orp —2A 128
Kylemore Clo. E6 —5H 63
Kylemore Rd. NW6 —3L 57
Kylestrome Ho. SW1 —5E 74
(off Cundy St.)
Kymberley Rd. Harr —4C 38
Kyme Rd. Horn —4D 50
Kymes Ct. S Harr —7B 38
Kynance Clo. Romf —3G 35
Kynance Gdns. Stan —8G 23
Kynance M. SW7 —4M 73
Kynance Pl. W8 —4A 74
Kynaston Av. N16 —8D 44
Kynaston Av. T Hth —9A 108
Kynaston Clo. Harr —7B 22
Kynaston Cres. T Hth —9A 108
Kynaston Rd. N16 —8C 44
Kynaston Rd. Brom —2E 110
Kynaston Rd. Enf —3B 16
Kynaston Rd. Orp —2F 128
Kynaston Rd. T Hth —9A 108
Kynaston Wood. Harr —7B 22
Kynnersley Clo. Cars —5D 122
Kynoch Rd. N18 —4G 29
Kyrle Rd. SW11 —5E 90
Kytes Dri. Wat —6H 5
Kytes Est. Wat —6H 5
Kyverdale Rd. N16 —6D 44

Laburnum Av. N9 —2D 28
Laburnum Av. N17 —7B 28
Laburnum Av. Dart —7G 99
Laburnum Av. Horn —7E 50
Laburnum Av. Sutt —5C 122
Laburnum Av. Swan —7B 114
Laburnum Av. W Dray —1K 143
Laburnum Clo. E4 —6K 29
Laburnum Clo. N11 —6E 26
Laburnum Clo. SE15 —8G 77
Laburnum Clo. Chesh —4D 6
Laburnum Ct. E2 —4D 60
(in two parts)
Laburnum Ct. SE16 —3G 77
(off Albion St.)
Laburnum Ct. SE19 —5D 108
Laburnum Ct. Harr —4M 37
Laburnum Ct. Stan —4G 23
Laburnum Cres. Sun —5F 100
Laburnum Gdns. N21 —2A 28
Laburnum Gdns. Croy —2H 125
Laburnum Gro. N21 —2A 28
Laburnum Gro. NW9 —5A 40
Laburnum Gro. Houn —3K 85
Laburnum Gro. N Mald —6B 104
Laburnum Gro. Ruis —4B 36
Laburnum Gro. S'hall —7K 53
Laburnum Ho. Brom —5B 110
Laburnum Lodge. N3 —9K 25
Laburnum Pl. SE9 —4L 95
Laburnum Rd. SW19 —4A 106
Laburnum Rd. Eps —5C 134
Laburnum Rd. Hay —5D 68
Laburnum Rd. Mitc —6E 106
Laburnums, The. E6 —7J 63
Laburnum St. E2 —4D 60
Laburnum Wlk. Horn —1G 67
Laburnum Way. Brom —2L 127
Laburnum Way. Stai —7D 144
Lacebark Clo. Sidc —6D 96
Lacey Clo. N9 —2E 28
Lacey Dri. Edgw —4K 23
Lacey Dri. Hamp —5K 101
Lacey Wlk. E3 —5L 61
Lacine Ct. SE16 —3H 77
(off Christopher Clo.)
Lackford Rd. Coul —9D 136
Lackington St. EC2 —8B 60
Lackland Ho. SE1 —6D 76
(off Rowcross St.)
Lackmore Rd. Enf —8C 6
Lacland Ho. SW10 —8B 74
(off Worlds End Est.)
Lacock Clo. SW19 —3A 106
Lacock Ct. W13 —2E 70
(off Singapore Rd.)
Lacon Ho. WC1 —8K 59
(off Theobalds Rd.)
Lacon Rd. SE22 —3E 92
Lacrosse Way. SW16 —5H 107
Lacy Dri. Dag —8G 49
Lacy Rd. SW15 —3H 89
Ladas Rd. SE27 —1A 108
Ladbroke Cres. W11 —9J 57
Ladbroke Gdns. W11 —1K 73
Ladbroke Gro. W10 & W11 —7H 57
Ladbroke Gro. Ho. W11 —1K 73
Ladbroke M. W11 —2J 73
Ladbroke Rd. W11 —2K 73
Ladbroke Rd. Enf —8D 16
Ladbroke Rd. Eps —6B 134
Ladbroke Sq. W11 —1K 73
Ladbroke Ter. W11 —1K 73
Ladbroke Wlk. W11 —2K 73
Ladbrook Clo. Pinn —3K 37
Ladbrooke Cres. Sidc —9H 97
Ladbrook Rd. SE25 —8B 108
Ladderstile Ride. King T —2M 103
Ladderswood Way. N11 —5G 27
Ladds Way. Swan —8B 114
Ladlands. SE22 —6E 92
Lady Booth Rd. King T —6J 103
Ladycroft Gdns. Orp —7A 128
Ladycroft Rd. SE13 —2M 93
Ladycroft Wlk. Stan —8H 23
Ladycroft Way. Orp —7A 128
Lady Dock Wlk. SE16 —3J 77
Lady Elizabeth Ho. SW14 —2A 88
Ladyfields Clo. Lou —6M 19
Lady Forsdyke Way. Eps —1L 133
Ladygate La. Ruis —4A 36
Ladygrove. Croy —1J 139
Lady Harewood Way. Eps —1L 133
Lady Hay. Wor Pk —4D 120
Lady Margaret Rd. NW5 & N19 —1G 59
Lady Margaret Rd. S'hall —1K 69
Lady Micos Almshouses. E1
(off Aylward St.) —9G 61
Lady Sarah Ho. N11 —6D 26
(off Asher Loftus Way)
Lady's Clo. Wat —6G 9
Lady Shaw Ct. N13 —2K 27
Ladyship Ter. SE22 —6E 92
Ladysmith Av. E6 —5J 63
Ladysmith Av. Ilf —5C 48
Ladysmith Clo. NW7 —7E 24
Ladysmith Rd. E16 —6D 62
Ladysmith Rd. N17 —9E 28
Ladysmith Rd. N18 —5F 28
Ladysmith Rd. SE9 —5L 95
Ladysmith Rd. Enf —5C 16
(in two parts)
Ladysmith Rd. Harr —9C 22
Lady Somerset Rd. NW5 —9F 42
Ladywell. —4M 93
Ladywell Clo. SE4 —4L 93
Ladywell Heights. SE4 —5K 93
Ladywell Rd. SE13 —4L 93
Ladywell St. E15 —4D 62
Ladywood Av. Orp —9C 112
Ladywood Rd. Surb —4L 119
Lafone Av. Felt —8G 85
Lafone St. SE1 —3D 76
Lagado M. SE16 —2H 77
Lagonda Av. Ilf —6D 32
Lagonda Way. Dart —3G 99
Lagoon Rd. Orp —9G 113
Laidlaw Dri. N21 —7K 15
Laing Clo. Ilf —6B 32
Laing Dean. N'holt —4G 53
Laing Ho. SE5 —8A 76
Laings Av. Mitc —6D 106
Lainlock Pl. Houn —9M 69
Lainson St. SW18 —6L 89
Lairdale Clo. SE21 —7A 92
Laird Ho. SE5 —8A 76
(off Redcar St.)
Lairs Clo. N7 —1J 59
Laitwood Rd. SW12 —7F 90
Lakanal. SE5 —9C 76
(off Dalwood St.)
Lake Av. Brom —3E 110
Lake Av. Rain —5H 67
Lake Bus. Cen. N17 —7E 28
Lake Clo. SW19 —2K 105
Lakedale Rd. SE18 —7C 80
Lake Dri. Bush —2B 22
Lakefield Clo. SE20 —4F 108
Lakefield Rd. N22 —9M 27
Lakefields Clo. Rain —5H 67
Lake Footpath. SE2 —3H 81
Lake Gdns. Dag —1L 65
Lake Gdns. Rich —8F 86
Lake Gdns. Wall —5F 122
Lakehall Gdns. T Hth —9M 107
Lakehall Rd. T Hth —9M 107
Lake Ho. SE1 —3A 76
(off Southwark Bri. Rd.)
Lake Ho. Rd. E11 —8E 46
Lakehurst Rd. Eps —7C 120
Lakeland Clo. Chig —4F 32
Lakeland Clo. Harr —6B 22
Lakenheath. N14 —7H 15
Laker Ct. SW4 —9J 75
Laker Ind. Est. SE26 —2J 109
(off Kent Ho. La.)
Lake Ri. Romf —9D 34
Lake Rd. SW19 —2K 105
Lake Rd. Croy —4K 125
Lake Rd. Romf —2H 49
Laker Pl. SW15 —5J 89
Lakers Ri. Bans —8C 136
Lakeside. N3 —9M 25
Lakeside. W13 —9G 55
Lakeside. Beck —7M 109
Lakeside. Enf —6H 15
Lakeside. Eps —8C 120
Lakeside. Rain —5J 67
Lakeside. Wall —6F 122
Lakeside. Wey —4C 116
Lakeside Av. SE28 —3E 80
Lakeside Av. Ilf —2H 47
Lakeside Clo. SE25 —6E 108
Lakeside Clo. Ruis —2A 36
Lakeside Clo. Sidc —4G 97
Lakeside Ct. N4 —7A 44
Lakeside Ct. Els —7L 11
Lakeside Cres. Barn —7D 14
Lakeside Dri. Brom —5J 127
Lakeside Dri. Esh —8A 118
Lakeside Grange. Wey —5A 116
Lakeside Rd. N13 —4K 27
Lakeside Rd. W14 —4H 73
Lakeside Rd. Chesh —1C 6
Lakeside Ter. EC2 —8A 60
(off Beech St.)
Lakeside Way. SE2 —4H 81
Lakeside Way. Wemb —9L 39
Lakes Rd. Kes —7G 127
Lakeswood Rd. Orp —1M 127
Lake, The. Bush —1B 22
Lake Vw. Edgw —5K 23
Lake Vw. Ct. SW1 —4F 74
(off Bressenden Pl.)
Lake Vw. Est. E3 —5J 61
Lakeview Pk. Noak H —3G 35
Lakeview Rd. SE27 —2L 107
Lakeview Rd. Well —3F 96
Lake Vw. Ter. N18 —4D 28
(off Sweet Briar Wlk.)
Lakis Clo. NW3 —9A 42
Laleham Av. NW7 —3B 24
Laleham Ho. E2 —7D 60
(off Camlet St.)
Laleham Rd. SE6 —6A 94
Laleham Rd. Shep —9A 100
Lalor St. SW6 —1J 89
Lambarde Av. SE9 —1L 111
Lambard Ho. SE10 —8A 78
(off Langdale Rd.)
Lamb Clo. Wat —7G 5
Lamb Ct. E14 —1J 77
(off Narrow St.)
Lamberhurst Clo. Orp —3H 129
Lamberhurst Ho. SE15 —7G 77
Lamberhurst Rd. SE27 —1L 107
Lamberhurst Rd. Dag —6K 49
Lambert Av. Rich —2L 87
Lambert Clo. Big H —8H 141
Lambert Ct. Eri —7A 82
(off Park Cres.)
Lambert Ct. Wat —6H 9
Lambert Jones M. EC2 —8A 60
(off Beech St.)
Lambert Lodge. Bren —6H 71
(off Layton Rd.)
Lamberton Ct. Borwd —3L 11
(off Gateshead Rd.)
Lambert Rd. E16 —9F 62
Lambert Rd. N12 —5B 26
Lambert Rd. SW2 —4J 91
Lambert Rd. Bans —6L 135
Lambert's Pl. Croy —3B 124
Lamberts Rd. Surb —9J 103
Lambert St. N1 —3L 59
Lambert Wlk. Wemb —8H 39
Lambert Way. N12 —5A 26
Lambeth. —4K 75
Lambeth Bri. SW1 & SE1 —5J 75
Lambeth Crematorium. SW17 —1A 106
Lambeth High St. SE1 —5K 75
Lambeth Hill. EC4 —1A 76
Lambeth Pal. Rd. SE1 —4K 75
Lambeth Rd. SE1 & SE11 —5K 75
Lambeth Rd. Croy —2L 123
Lambeth Towers. SE1 —4L 75
(off Kennington Rd.)
Lambeth Wlk. SE11 —5K 75
(in two parts)
Lambfold Ho. N7 —2J 59
Lamb Ho. SE5 —8A 76
(off Elmington Est.)
Lamb Ho. SE10 —7A 78
(off Haddo St.)
Lamb La. E8 —3F 60
Lamble St. NW5 —1E 58
Lambley Rd. Dag —2F 64
Lambolle Pl. NW3 —2C 58
Lambolle Rd. NW3 —2C 58
Lambourn Chase. Rad —1D 10
Lambourn Clo. NW5 —9G 43
Lambourn Clo. W7 —3D 70
Lambourne Av. SW19 —1K 105
Lambourne Clo. Chig —3F 32
Lambourne Ct. Uxb —4A 142
Lambourne Ct. Wfd G —7G 31
Lambourne Cres. Chig —2F 32
Lambourne End. —1J 33
Lambourne Gdns. E4 —2L 29
Lambourne Gdns. Bark —3D 64
Lambourne Gdns. Enf —4D 16
Lambourne Gdns. Horn —7H 51
Lambourne Ho. NW8 —8B 58
(off Broadley St.)
Lambourne Ho. SE16 —5H 77
Lambourne Pl. SE3 —9F 78
Lambourne Rd. E11 —5A 46
Lambourne Rd. Bark —3C 64
Lambourne Rd. Chig —4D 32
Lambourne Rd. Ilf —7C 48
Lambourne Sq. Abr —1G 33
Lambourn Gro. King T —6M 103
Lambourn Rd. SW8 —2F 90
Lamb Pas. Bren —7K 71
Lambrook Ho. SE15 —9E 76
Lambrook Ter. SW6 —9J 73
Lamb's Bldgs. EC1 —7B 60
Lamb's Clo. N9 —2E 28
Lamb's Conduit Pas. WC1 —8K 59
(off Red Lion St.)
Lamb's Conduit St. WC1 —7K 59
(in three parts)
Lambscroft Av. SE9 —9G 95
Lambs La. Ind. Est. Rain —7G 67
Lamb's La. N. Rain —7G 67
Lamb's La. S. Rain —8F 66
Lambs Mdw. Wfd G —9H 31
Lamb's M. N1 —4M 59
Lamb's Pas. EC1 —7B 60
Lambs Ter. N9 —2B 28
Lamb St. E1 —8C 60
Lamb's Wlk. Enf —4A 16
Lambton Av. Wal X —5D 6
Lambton Pl. W11 —1K 73
Lambton Rd. N19 —6J 43
Lambton Rd. SW20 —5G 105
Lamb Wlk. SE1 —3C 76
LAMDA Theatre. —5L 73
(off Logan Pl.)
Lamerock Rd. Brom —1D 110
Lamerton Rd. Ilf —9M 31
Lamerton St. SE8 —7L 77
Lamford Clo. N17 —7B 28
Lamington St. W6 —5F 72
Lamlash St. SE11 —5M 75
Lamley Ho. SE10 —8M 77
(off Ashburnham Pl.)
Lammas Av. Mitc —6E 106
Lammas Grn. SE26 —9F 92
Lammas Hill. Esh —6M 117
Lammas La. Esh —7L 117
Lammas Pk. Gdns. W5 —2G 71
Lammas Pk. Rd. W5 —3H 71
Lammas Rd. E9 —3H 61
Lammas Rd. E10 —7J 45
Lammas Rd. Rich —1G 103
Lammas Rd. Wat —7G 9
Lammermoor Rd. SW12 —6F 90
Lamont Rd. SW10 —7B 74
Lamont Rd. Pas. SW10 —7B 74
(off Lamont Rd.)
Lamorbey. —7D 96
Lamorbey Clo. Sidc —7D 96
Lamorna Clo. E17 —9A 30
Lamorna Clo. Orp —2E 128
Lamorna Gro. Stan —8H 23
Lampard Gro. N16 —6D 44
Lampern Sq. E2 —6E 60
Lampeter Ho. Romf —7J 35
(off Kingsbridge Cir.)
Lampeter Sq. W6 —7J 73
Lamplighter Clo. E1 —7G 61
Lamplighters Clo. Dart —5K 99
Lampmead Rd. SE12 —4D 94
Lamp Office Ct. WC1 —7K 59
(off Conduit St.)
Lamport Clo. SE18 —5K 79
Lamps Ct. SE5 —8A 76
Lampton. —9M 69
Lampton Av. Houn —9M 69
Lampton Ct. Houn —9M 69
Lampton Ho. Clo. SW19 —1H 105
Lampton Pk. Rd. Houn —1M 85
Lampton Rd. Houn —1M 85
Lamson Rd. Rain —7D 66
Lanacre Av. NW9 —8B 24
Lanain Ct. SE12 —6D 94
Lanark Clo. W5 —8G 55
Lanark Ct. N'holt —1L 53
(off Newmarket Av.)
Lanark Ho. SE1 —6E 76
(off Old Kent Rd.)
Lanark Mans. W9 —7A 58
(off Lanark Rd.)
Lanark M. W9 —6A 58
Lanark Pl. W9 —7A 58
Lanark Rd. W9 —5M 57
Lanark Sq. E14 —4M 77
Lanata Wlk. Hay —7H 53
(off Alba Clo.)
Lanbury Rd. SE15 —3H 93
Lancashire Ct. W1 —1F 74
(off New Bond St.)
Lancaster Av. E18 —2F 46
Lancaster Av. SE27 —8M 91
Lancaster Av. SW19 —2H 105
Lancaster Av. Bark —3C 64
Lancaster Av. Barn —2B 14
Lancaster Av. Mitc —9J 107
Lancaster Clo. N1 —3C 60
Lancaster Clo. N17 —7E 28
Lancaster Clo. NW9 —7D 24
Lancaster Clo. SE27 —8M 91
Lancaster Clo. W2 —1M 73
(off St Petersburgh Pl.)
Lancaster Clo. Brom —8D 110
Lancaster Clo. Croy —4J 123
Lancaster Clo. King T —2H 103
Lancaster Clo. Stanw —5C 144
Lancaster Cotts. Rich —5J 87
Lancaster Ct. SE27 —8M 91
Lancaster Ct. SW6 —8K 73
Lancaster Ct. W2 —1A 74
(off Lancaster Ga.)
Lancaster Ct. Bans —6K 135
Lancaster Ct. Eps —2B 134
Lancaster Ct. Sutt —9L 121
(off Mulgrave Rd.)
Lancaster Ct. W on T —2E 116
Lancaster Dri. E14 —2A 78
Lancaster Dri. NW3 —2C 58
Lancaster Dri. Horn —1F 66
Lancaster Dri. Lou —8J 19
Lancaster Gdns. SW19 —2J 105
Lancaster Gdns. W13 —3F 70
Lancaster Gdns. King T —2H 103
Lancaster Ga. W2 —1A 74
Lancaster Gro. NW3 —2B 58
Lancaster Hall. E16 —2E 78
(off Wesley Av., in two parts)
Lancaster Ho. Enf —3B 16
Lancaster Lodge. W11 —9J 57
(off Lancaster Rd.)
Lancaster M. SW18 —4M 89
Lancaster M. W2 —1A 74
Lancaster M. Rich —5J 87
Lancaster Pk. Rich —4J 87
Lancaster Pl. SW19 —2H 105
Lancaster Pl. WC2 —1K 75
Lancaster Pl. Houn —1G 85
Lancaster Pl. Ilf —1A 64
Lancaster Pl. Twic —5E 86
Lancaster Rd. E7 —3E 62
Lancaster Rd. E11 —7C 46
Lancaster Rd. E17 —9H 29
Lancaster Rd. N4 —5K 43
Lancaster Rd. N11 —6H 27
Lancaster Rd. N18 —5D 28
Lancaster Rd. NW10 —1E 56
Lancaster Rd. SE25 —6D 108
Lancaster Rd. SW19 —2H 105
Lancaster Rd. W11 —9J 57
Lancaster Rd. Barn —6B 14
(in two parts)
Lancaster Rd. Enf —3B 16
Lancaster Rd. Harr —3L 37
Lancaster Rd. N'holt —2A 54
Lancaster Rd. S'hall —1J 69
Lancaster Rd. Uxb —2B 142
Lancaster Stables. NW3 —2C 58
Lancaster St. SE1 —3M 75
Lancaster Ter. W2 —1B 74
Lancaster Wlk. W2 —2A 74
Lancaster Wlk. Hay —9A 52
Lancaster Way. Ab L —4D 4
Lancastrian Rd. Wall —9K 123
Lancefield Ct. W10 —5J 57
Lancefield Ho. SE15 —2F 92
Lancefield St. W10 —6K 57
Lancell St. N16 —7C 44
Lancelot Av. Wemb —9H 39
Lancelot Ct. Orp —4F 128
Lancelot Cres. Wemb —9H 39

Lancelot Gdns.—Lauderdale Ho.

Lancelot Gdns. E Barn —9E 14
Lancelot Pl. SW7 —3D 74
Lancelot Rd. Ilf —6C 32
Lancelot Rd. Well —3E 96
Lancelot Rd. Wemb —9H 39
Lance Rd. Harr —5A 38
Lancer Sq. W8 —3M 73
Lancey Clo. SE7 —5J 79
Lanchester Ct. W2 —9D 58
(off Seymour St.)
Lanchester Rd. N6 —3D 42
Lancing Gdns. N9 —1D 28
Lancing Ho. Croy —6B 124
(off Coombe Rd.)
Lancing Ho. Wat —4G 9
(off Hallam Clo.)
Lancing Rd. W13 —1F 70
Lancing Rd. Croy —2K 123
Lancing Rd. Felt —8D 84
Lancing Rd. Ilf —4B 48
Lancing Rd. Orp —4E 128
Lancing Rd. Romf —7J 35
Lancing St. NW1 —6H 59
Lancing Way. Crox G —7A 8
Lancresse Clo. Uxb —2B 142
Lancresse Ct. N1 —4C 60
(off De Beauvoir Est.)
Landale Gdns. Dart —6G 99
Landale Ho. SE16 —4G 77
(off Lower Rd.)
Landau Ct. S Croy —7A 124
(off Warham Rd.)
Landau Way. Eri —6H 83
Landcroft Rd. SE22 —4D 92
Landells Rd. SE22 —5D 92
Landford Rd. SW15 —2G 89
Landgrove Rd. SW19 —2L 105
Landin Ho. E14 —9L 61
(off Thomas Rd.)
Landleys Fld. NW5 —1H 59
(off Long Mdw.)
Landmann Ho. SE16 —5F 76
(off Rennie Est.)
Landmann Way. SE14 —6H 77
Landmark Commercial Cen. N18 —6C 28
Landmark Ho. W6 —6G 73
(off Hammersmith Bri. Rd.)
Landmead Rd. Chesh —2E 6
Landon Pl. SW1 —4D 74
Landon's Clo. E14 —2A 78
Landon Wlk. E14 —1M 77
Landon Way. Ashf —3A 100
Landor Ho. SE5 —8B 76
(off Elmington Est.)
Landor Rd. SW4 —2J 91
Landor Wlk. W12 —3E 72
Landra Gdns. N21 —8M 15
Landrake. NW1 —4G 59
(off Plender St.)
Landridge Dri. Enf —2F 16
Landridge Rd. SW6 —1K 89
Landrock Rd. N8 —4J 43
Landscape Rd. Wfd G —7F 30
Landseer Av. E12 —1L 63
Landseer Clo. SW19 —5A 106
Landseer Clo. Edgw —9L 23
Landseer Clo. Horn —6F 50
Landseer Ct. Hay —5B 52
Landseer Ho. NW8 —7B 58
(off Frampton St.)
Landseer Ho. SW1 —5H 75
(off Herrick St.)
Landseer Ho. SW11 —9E 74
Landseer Ho. N'holt —5H 53
(off Parkfield Dri.)
Landseer Rd. N19 —8J 43
(in two parts)
Landseer Rd. Enf —7E 16
Landseer Rd. N Mald —2B 120
Landseer Rd. Sutt —8L 121
Lands End. Els —8H 11
Landstead Rd. SE18 —8B 80
Landulph Ho. SE11 —6L 75
(off Kennings Way)
Landward Ct. W1 —9C 58
(off Harrowby St.)
Landway, The. Orp —7G 113
Lane App. NW7 —5J 25
Lane Clo. NW2 —8F 40
Lane End. SW15 —5H 89
Lane End. Bexh —2M 97
Lane End. Eps —6M 133
Lane Gdns. Bus H —9C 10
Lane M. E12 —8K 47
Lanercost Clo. SW2 —8L 91
Lanercost Gdns. N14 —9J 15
Lanercost Rd. SW2 —8L 91
Lanesborough Pl. SW1 —3E 74
(off Grosvenor Pl.)
Laneside. Chst —2M 111
Laneside. Edgw —5A 24
Laneside Av. Dag —5K 49
Lane, The. NW8 —5A 58
Lane, The. SE3 —2E 94
Laneway. SW15 —4F 88
Laney Ho. EC1 —8L 59
(off Leather La.)
Lanfranc Ct. Harr —8D 38
Lanfranc Rd. E3 —5J 61
Lanfrey Pl. W14 —6K 73
Langbourne Av. N6 —7E 42
Langbourne Ct. E17 —4J 45
Langbourne Mans. N6 —7E 42
Langbourne Pl. E14 —6M 77
Langbourne Way. Clay —8E 118
Langbrook Rd. SE3 —2H 95
Langcroft Clo. Cars —5D 122
Langdale. NW1 —6G 59
(off Stanhope St.)
Langdale Av. Mitc —7D 106
Langdale Clo. SE17 —7A 76
Langdale Clo. SW14 —3M 87
Langdale Clo. Dag —6G 49
Langdale Clo. Orp —5M 127
Langdale Cres. Bexh —8L 81
Langdale Dri. Hay —5C 52
Langdale Gdns. Gnfd —6F 54
Langdale Gdns. Horn —1E 66
Langdale Gdns. Wal X —8D 6
Langdale Ho. SW1 —6G 75
(off Churchill Gdns.)
Langdale Pde. Mitc —7D 106
Langdale Rd. SE10 —8A 78
Langdale Rd. T Hth —8L 107
Langdale St. E1 —9F 60
Langdon Ct. EC1 —5M 59
(off City Rd.)
Langdon Ct. NW10 —4C 56
Langdon Cres. E6 —5L 63
Langdon Dri. NW9 —6A 40
Langdon Ho. E14 —9A 62
Langdon Pk. Rd. N6 —5G 43
Langdon Pl. SW14 —2A 88
Langdon Rd. E6 —4L 63
Langdon Rd. Brom —7F 110
Langdon Rd. Mord —9A 106
Langdons Ct. S'hall —4L 69
Langdon Shaw. Sidc —2D 112
Langdon Wlk. Mord —9A 106
Langdon Way. SE1 —5E 76
Langford Clo. E8 —1E 60
Langford Clo. N15 —4C 44
Langford Clo. NW8 —5A 58
Langford Clo. W3 —3M 71
Langford Ct. NW8 —5A 58
(off Abbey Rd.)
Langford Cres. Cockf —6D 14
Langford Grn. SE5 —2C 92
Langford Ho. SE8 —7L 77
Langford Pl. NW8 —5A 58
Langford Pl. Sidc —9E 96
Langford Rd. SW6 —1M 89
Langford Rd. Cockf —6D 14
Langford Rd. Wfd G —6G 31
Langfords. Buck H —2H 31
Langham Clo. N15 —1M 43
(off Langham Rd.)
Langham Ct. NW4 —3H 41
Langham Ct. Horn —5H 51
Langham Ct. Ruis —1F 52
Langham Dene. Kenl —7M 137
Langham Dri. Romf —4F 48
Langham Gdns. N21 —7L 15
Langham Gdns. W13 —1F 70
Langham Gdns. Edgw —7A 24
Langham Gdns. Rich —1G 103
Langham Gdns. Wemb —7G 39
Langham Ho. Clo. Rich —1H 103
Langham Mans. SW5 —6M 73
(off Earl's Ct. Sq.)
Langham Pl. N15 —1M 43
Langham Pl. W1 —8F 58
Langham Pl. W4 —7C 72
Langham Rd. N15 —1M 43
Langham Rd. SW20 —5G 105
Langham Rd. Edgw —6A 24
Langham Rd. Tedd —2F 102
Langham St. W1 —8F 58
Langhedge Clo. N18 —6D 28
Langhedge La. N18 —6D 28
Langhedge La. Ind. Est. N18 —6D 28
Langholm Clo. SW12 —6H 91
Langholme. Bush —1A 22
Langhorn Dri. Twic —6C 86
Langhorne Ct. NW8 —3B 58
(off Dorman Way)
Langhorne Rd. Dag —3L 65
Lang Ho. SW8 —8J 75
(off Hartington Rd.)
Langland Ct. N'wd —7A 20
Langland Cres. Stan —9H 23
Langland Dri. Pinn —7J 21
Langland Gdns. NW3 —1M 57
Langland Gdns. Croy —4K 125
Langland Ho. SE5 —8B 76
(off Edmund St.)
Langlands Ri. Eps —5A 134
Langler Rd. NW10 —5G 57
Langley Av. Ruis —7F 36
Langley Av. Surb —3H 119
Langley Av. Wor Pk —3H 121
Langleybury La. Wat & K Lan (in two parts) —7A 4
Langley Clo. Romf —7H 35
Langley Ct. WC2 —1J 75
Langley Cres. E11 —5G 47
Langley Cres. Dag —3G 65
Langley Cres. Edgw —3A 24
Langley Cres. Hay —8D 68
Langley Dri. E11 —5F 46
Langley Dri. W3 —3M 71
Langley Gdns. Brom —8G 111
Langley Gdns. Dag —3H 65
Langley Gdns. Orp —1M 127
Langley Gro. N Mald —6C 104
Langley La. SW8 —7J 75
Langley La. Ab L —4D 4
Langley Mans. SW8 —7K 75
(off Langley La.)
Langley Oaks Av. S Croy —2E 138
Langley Pk. NW7 —6C 24
Langley Pk. Rd. Sutt —7A 122
Langley Rd. SW19 —5K 105
Langley Rd. Ab L —4C 4
Langley Rd. Beck —8J 109
Langley Rd. Iswth —1D 86
Langley Rd. S Croy —1H 139
Langley Rd. Surb —2J 119
Langley Rd. Wat —3D 8
Langley Rd. Well —7G 81
Langley Row. Barn —3K 13
Langley St. WC2 —9J 59
Langley Va. Rd. Eps —9C 134
Langley Way. Wat —4C 8
Langley Way. W W'ck —3B 126
Langmead Dri. Bus H —1C 22
Langmead St. SE27 —1M 107
Langmore Ct. Bexh —2H 97
Langmore Ho. E1 —9E 60
(off Stutfield St.)
Langport Ct. W on T —3G 117
Langport Ho. SW9 —1M 91
Langport Ho. Romf —7J 35
(off Leyburn Rd.)
Langridge M. Hamp —3K 101
Langroyd Rd. SW17 —8D 90
Langside Av. SW15 —3E 88
Langside Cres. N14 —3H 27
Langston Hughes Clo. SE24 —3M 91
Lang St. E1 —7G 61
Langthorn Ct. EC2 —9B 60
Langthorne Ct. SE6 —1A 110
Langthorne Ho. Hay —5C 68
Langthorne Rd. E11 —8A 46
Langthorne St. SW6 —8H 73
Langton Av. E6 —6L 63
Langton Av. N20 —9A 14
Langton Av. Eps —3D 134
Langton Clo. WC1 —7K 59
Langton Gro. N'wd —5A 20
Langton Ho. SE11 —5K 75
(off Lambeth Wlk.)
Langton Pl. SW18 —7L 89
Langton Ri. SE23 —6F 92
Langton Rd. NW2 —8G 41
Langton Rd. SW9 —8M 75
Langton Rd. Harr —7A 22
Langton Rd. W Mol —8A 102
Langton St. SW10 —7A 74
Langton Way. SE3 —9D 78
Langton Way. Croy —5C 124
Langtry Pl. SW6 —7L 73
Langtry Rd. NW8 —4M 57
Langtry Rd. N'holt —5H 53
Langtry Wlk. NW8 —4M 57
Langwood Chase. Tedd —3G 103
Langwood Clo. Asht —9L 133
Langwood Gdns. Wat —3E 8
Langworth Clo. Dart —9H 99
Langworth Dri. Hay —9E 52
Langworthy. Pinn —6L 21
Lanhill Rd. W9 —7L 57
Lanier Rd. SE13 —5B 94
Lanigan Dri. Houn —4M 85
Lankaster Gdns. N2 —8B 26
Lankers Dri. Harr —4K 37
Lankton Clo. Beck —5A 110
Lannock Rd. Hay —2D 68
Lannoy Point. SW6 —8J 73
(off Pellant Rd.)
Lannoy Rd. SE9 —7A 96
Lanrick Ho. E14 —9B 62
(off Lanrick Rd.)
Lanrick Rd. E14 —9B 62
Lanridge Rd. SE2 —4H 81
Lansbury Av. N18 —5B 28
Lansbury Av. Bark —3E 64
Lansbury Av. Felt —5F 84
Lansbury Av. Romf —3J 49
Lansbury Clo. NW10 —1A 56
Lansbury Cres. Dart —4L 99
Lansbury Dri. Hay —5C 52
Lansbury Est. E14 —9M 61
Lansbury Gdns. E14 —9B 62
Lansbury Rd. Enf —3H 17
Lansbury Way. N18 —5C 28
Lanscombe Wlk. SW8 —9J 75
Lansdell Ho. SW2 —5L 91
(off Tulse Hill)
Lansdell Rd. Mitc —6E 106
Lansdown Clo. W on T —3G 117
Lansdowne Av. Bexh —8H 81
Lansdowne Av. Orp —3M 127
Lansdowne Clo. SW20 —4H 105
Lansdowne Clo. Surb —4M 119
Lansdowne Clo. Twic —7D 86
Lansdowne Clo. Wat —8H 5
Lansdowne Ct. W11 —1J 73
(off Lansdowne Ri.)
Lansdowne Ct. Ilf —1J 47
Lansdowne Ct. Purl —2M 137
Lansdowne Ct. Wor Pk —4E 120
Lansdowne Cres. W11 —1J 73
Lansdowne Dri. E8 —2E 60
Lansdowne Gdns. SW8 —9J 75
Lansdowne Grn. Est. SW8 —9J 75
Lansdowne Gro. NW10 —9C 40
Lansdowne Hill. SE27 —9M 91
Lansdowne La. SE7 —7H 79
Lansdowne M. SE7 —6H 79
Lansdowne M. W11 —2K 73
Lansdowne Pl. SE1 —4B 76
Lansdowne Pl. SE19 —4D 108
Lansdowne Ri. W11 —1J 73
Lansdowne Rd. E4 —2L 29
Lansdowne Rd. E11 —7D 46
Lansdowne Rd. E17 —4L 45
Lansdowne Rd. E18 —1E 46
Lansdowne Rd. N3 —7L 25
Lansdowne Rd. N10 —9G 27
Lansdowne Rd. N17 —8D 28
Lansdowne Rd. SW19 —4G 105
Lansdowne Rd. W11 —1J 73
Lansdowne Rd. Brom —4E 110
Lansdowne Rd. Croy —4A 124
Lansdowne Rd. Eps —9A 120
Lansdowne Rd. Harr —5C 38
Lansdowne Rd. Houn —2M 85
Lansdowne Rd. Ilf —6D 48
Lansdowne Rd. Purl —4L 137
Lansdowne Rd. Stan —6G 23
Lansdowne Rd. Uxb —9A 52
Lansdowne Row. W1 —2F 74
Lansdowne Ter. WC1 —7J 59
Lansdowne Wlk. W11 —2K 73
Lansdowne Way. SW8 —9H 75
Lansdowne Wood Clo. SE27 —9M 91
Lansdowne Workshops. SE7 —6G 79
Lansdown Rd. E7 —3G 63
Lansdown Rd. Sidc —9F 96
Lansfield Av. N18 —4E 28
Lantern Clo. SW15 —3E 88
Lantern Clo. Wemb —1H 55
Lanterns Ct. E14 —3M 77
Lantern Way. W Dray —3J 143
Lant Ho. SE1 —3A 76
(off Toulmin St.)
Lant St. SE1 —3A 76
Lanvanor Rd. SE15 —1G 93
Lanyard Ho. SE8 —5K 77
Lapford Clo. W9 —7K 57
Lapponum Wlk. Hay —7H 53
Lapse Wood Wlk. SE23 —7F 92
Lapstone Gdns. Harr —4G 39
Lapwing Clo. Eri —8F 82
Lapwing Clo. S Croy —2J 139
Lapwing Ct. Surb —5L 119
Lapwing Pl. Wat —5G 5
Lapwing Tower. SE8 —7K 77
(off Abinger Gro., in two parts)
Lapwing Way. Ab L —4E 4
Lapwing Way. Hay —9H 53
Lapworth. N11 —4F 26
(off Coppies Gro.)
Lapworth Clo. Orp —4G 129
Lapworth Ct. W2 —8M 57
(off Chichester Rd.)
Lara Clo. SE13 —5A 94
Lara Clo. Chess —9J 119
Larbert Rd. SW16 —4G 107
Larby Pl. Eps —2C 134
Larch Av. W3 —2C 72
Larch Av. Brick W —3J 5
Larch Clo. E13 —7F 62
Larch Clo. N11 —7E 26
Larch Clo. N19 —7G 43
Larch Clo. SE8 —7K 77
Larch Clo. SW12 —8F 90
Larch Cres. Eps —8M 119
Larch Cres. Hay —8G 53
Larch Dene. Orp —4L 127
Larch Dri. W4 —6L 71
Larches Av. SW14 —3B 88
Larches Av. Enf —8C 6
Larches, The. N13 —3A 28
Larches, The. Bush —7H 9
Larches, The. N'wd —6A 20
Larches, The. Uxb —6F 142
Larch Grn. NW9 —8C 24
Larch Gro. Sidc —7D 96
Larch Ho. SE16 —3G 77
(off Ainsty Est.)
Larch Ho. W10 —7J 57
(off Rowan Wlk.)
Larch Ho. Brom —5C 110
Larch Ho. Hay —8G 53
Larch Rd. E10 —7L 45
Larch Rd. NW2 —9G 41
Larch Rd. Dart —6H 99
Larch Tree Way. Croy —5L 125
Larchvale Ct. Sutt —9M 121
Larch Wlk. Swan —6B 114
Larch Way. Brom —2L 127
Larchwood Av. Romf —6M 33
Larchwood Clo. Bans —7J 135
Larchwood Clo. Romf —6A 34
Larchwood Rd. SE9 —8M 95
Larcombe Clo. Croy —6D 124
Larcombe Ct. Sutt —9M 121
(off Worcester Rd.)
Larcom St. SE17 —5A 76
Larden Rd. W3 —2C 72
Largewood Av. Surb —4L 119
Largo Wlk. Eri —9C 82
Larissa St. SE17 —6B 76
Larkbere Rd. SE26 —1J 109
Larken Clo. Bush —1A 22
Larken Dri. Bush —1A 22
Larkfield Av. Harr —1F 38
Larkfield Clo. Brom —4D 126
Larkfield Rd. Rich —3J 87
Larkfield Rd. Sidc —9D 96
Larkhall Clo. W on T —8G 117
Larkhall La. SW4 —1H 91
Larkhall Ri. SW4 —2G 91
Larkham Clo. Felt —9C 84
Larkin Clo. Coul —9K 137
Lark Row. E2 —4G 61
Larksfield Gro. Enf —3F 16
Larks Gro. Bark —3C 64
Larkshall Ct. Romf —9A 34
Larkshall Cres. E4 —4A 30
Larkshall Rd. E4 —5A 30
Larkspur Clo. E6 —8J 63
Larkspur Clo. N17 —7B 28
Larkspur Clo. NW9 —3M 39
Larkspur Clo. Orp —4G 129
Larkspur Clo. Ruis —5A 36
Larkspur Gro. Edgw —4A 24
Larkspur Lodge. Sidc —9F 96
Larkspur Way. Eps —7A 120
Larkswood Clo. Eri —9E 82
Larkswood Ct. E4 —5B 30
Larkswood Ri. Pinn —2G 37
Larkswood Rd. E4 —4L 29
Lark Way. Cars —2C 122
Larkway Clo. NW9 —2B 40
Larmans Rd. Enf —9C 6
Larnach Rd. W6 —7H 73
Larne Rd. Ruis —5D 36
Larner Rd. Eri —8C 82
Larpent Av. SW15 —4G 89
Larsen Dri. Wal A —7K 7
Larwood Clo. Gnfd —1B 54
Lascelles Av. Harr —5B 38
Lascelles Clo. E11 —7B 46
Lascelles Ho. NW1 —7C 58
(off Harewood Av.)
Lascotts Rd. N22 —6K 27
Laseron Ho. N15 —2D 44
(off Tottenham Grn. E.)
Lassa Rd. SE9 —4J 95
Lassell St. SE10 —6B 78
Lasseter Pl. SE3 —7C 78
Latchett Rd. E18 —8F 30
Latchford Pl. Chig —4F 32
Latching Clo. Romf —4H 35
Latchingdon Ct. E17 —2H 45
Latchingdon Gdns. Wfd G —6J 31
Latchmere Clo. Rich —2J 103
Latchmere La. King T —3K 103
Latchmere Pas. SW11 —1C 90
Latchmere Rd. SW11 —1D 90
Latchmere Rd. King T —4J 103
Latchmere St. SW11 —1D 90
Lateward Rd. Bren —7H 71
Latham Clo. E6 —8J 63
Latham Clo. Big H —8G 141
Latham Clo. Twic —6E 86
Latham Ct. W14 —5L 73
(off W. Cromwell Rd.)
Latham Ct. N'holt —6H 53
(off Seasprite Clo.)
Latham Ho. E1 —9H 61
(off Chudleigh St.)
Latham Rd. Bexh —4L 97
Latham Rd. Twic —6D 86
Latham's Way. Croy —3K 123
Lathkill Clo. Enf —9E 16
Lathkill Ct. Beck —5K 109
Lathom Rd. E6 —3J 63
Latimer Av. E6 —4K 63
Latimer Clo. Pinn —8G 21
Latimer Clo. Wat —9C 8
Latimer Clo. Wor Pk —6F 120
Latimer Ct. Brom —8D 110
(off Durham Rd.)
Latimer Ct. Wal X —7F 6
Latimer Dri. Horn —8H 51
Latimer Gdns. Pinn —8G 21
Latimer Ho. E9 —2H 61
Latimer Ho. W11 —1K 73
(off Kensington Pk. Rd.)
Latimer Pl. W10 —9G 57
Latimer Rd. E7 —9F 46
Latimer Rd. N15 —4C 44
Latimer Rd. SW19 —3M 105
Latimer Rd. W10 —8G 57
(in two parts)
Latimer Rd. Barn —5M 13
Latimer Rd. Croy —5M 123
Latimer Rd. Tedd —2D 102
Latona Ct. SW9 —8L 75
(off Caldwell St.)
Latona Rd. SE15 —7E 76
La Tourne Gdns. Orp —5A 128
Lattimer Pl. W4 —8C 72
Latton Clo. Esh —6M 117
Latton Clo. W on T —2J 117
Latymer Clo. Wey —6A 116
Latymer Ct. W6 —5H 73
Latymer Gdns. N3 —9J 25
Latymer Rd. N9 —1D 28
Latymer Way. N9 —2C 28
Lauder Clo. N'holt —5H 53
Lauder Ct. N14 —9J 15
Lauderdale Dri. Rich —9H 87
Lauderdale Ho. SW9 —9L 75
(off Gosling Way)

Lee St.—Lillechurch Rd.

Lee St. E8—4D 60
Lee Ter. SE3—2C 94
Lee, The. N'wd—5D 20
Lee Valley Ice Centre. —7H 45
Lee Valley Leisure Centre. —1J 29
Lee Valley Pk. —1G 7
Lee Valley Technopark. N17—1E 44
Lee Vw. Enf—3M 15
Leeward Ct. E1—1E 76
Leeward Gdns. SW19—2J 105
Leeway. SE8—6K 77
Leeway Clo. H End—7K 21
Leeways, The. Sutt—8J 121
Leewood Clo. SE12—5E 94
Leewood Pl. Swan—8B 114
Lefa Bus. & Ind. Est. Sidc—3H 113
Lefevre Wlk. E3—4K 61
Leff Ho. NW6—4J 57
Lefroy Ho. SE1—3A 76
(off Southwark Bri. Rd.)
Lefroy Rd. W12—3D 72
Legard Rd. N5—8M 43
Legatt Rd. SE9—4H 95
Leggatt Rd. E15—5A 62
Leggatts Clo. Wat—9D 4
Leggatts Ri. Wat—8E 4
Leggatts Way. Wat—9D 4
Leggatts Wood Av. Wat—9F 4
Legge St. SE13—4A 94
Leghorn Rd. NW10—5D 56
Leghorn Rd. SE18—6B 80
Legion Clo. N1—3L 59
Legion Ct. Mord—1L 121
Legion Rd. Gnfd—4A 54
Legion Ter. E3—4K 61
Legion Way. N12—7C 26
Legon Av. Romf—6A 50
Legrace Av. Houn—1H 85
Leicester Av. Mitc—8J 107
Leicester Clo. Wor Pk—6G 121
Leicester Ct. WC2—1H 75
(off Lisle St.)
Leicester Ct. Twic—5H 87
(off Clevedon Rd.)
Leicester Fields. WC2—1H 75
(off Leicester Sq.)
Leicester Gdns. Ilf—5C 48
Leicester Ho. SW9—2M 91
(off Loughborough Rd.)
Leicester M. N2—1C 42
Leicester Pl. WC2—1H 75
Leicester Rd. E11—3F 46
Leicester Rd. N2—1C 42
Leicester Rd. NW10—3B 56
Leicester Rd. Barn & New Bar—7M 13
Leicester Rd. Croy—2C 124
Leicester Sq. WC2—1H 75
Leicester St. WC2—1H 75
Leigham Av. SW16—9J 91
Leigham Clo. SW16—9K 91
Leigham Ct. Rd. SW16—8J 91
Leigham Dri. Iswth—8C 70
Leigham Hall Pde. SW16—9J 91
(off Streatham High Rd.)
Leigham Va. SW16 & SW2—9K 91
Leigh Av. Ilf—2H 47
Leigh Clo. N Mald—8A 104
Leigh Clo. Ind. Est. N Mald—8B 104
Leigh Ct. Borwd—4B 12
Leigh Ct. Harr—6C 38
Leigh Cres. New Ad—9M 125
Leigh Dri. Romf—4H 35
Leigh Gdns. NW10—5G 57
Leigh Hunt Dri. N14—1H 27
Leigh Orchard Clo. SW16—9K 91
Leigh Pl. EC1—8L 59
Leigh Pl. Dart—1L 115
Leigh Pl. Well—1E 96
Leigh Rd. E6—2L 63
Leigh Rd. E10—5A 46
Leigh Rd. N5—9M 43
Leigh Rd. Houn—3B 86
Leigh Rodd. Wat—3K 21
Leigh St. WC1—6J 59
Leigh Ter. Orp—7F 112
Leighton Av. E12—1L 63
Leighton Av. Pinn—1J 37
Leighton Clo. Edgw—9L 23
Leighton Ct. Chesh—2D 6
Leighton Cres. NW5—1G 59
Leighton Gdns. NW10—5F 56
Leighton Gdns. Croy—3M 123
Leighton Gdns. S Croy—5F 138
Leighton Gro. NW5—1G 59
Leighton Ho. SW1—5H 75
(off Herrick St.)
Leighton House Art Gallery. —4K 73
Leighton House Mus. —4K 73
Leighton Mans. W14—7J 73
(off Greyhound Rd.)
Leighton Pl. NW5—1G 59
Leighton Rd. NW5—1G 59
Leighton Rd. W13—3E 70
Leighton Rd. Enf—7D 16
Leighton Rd. Har W—9B 22
Leighton St. Croy—3M 123
Leighton Way. Eps—6B 134
Leila Parnell Pl. SE7—7G 79
Leinster Av. SW14—2A 88
Leinster Ct. NW6—6L 57
Leinster Gdns. W2—9A 58
Leinster M. W2—1A 74
Leinster Pl. W2—9A 58
Leinster Rd. N10—2F 42
Leinster Sq. W2—9L 57
Leinster Ter. W2—1A 74
Leisure Way. N12—7B 26
Leisure West. Felt—8F 84
Leith Clo. NW9—6B 40
Leithcote Gdns. SW16—1K 107
Leithcote Path. SW16—9K 91
Leith Hill. Orp—5E 112
Leith Hill Grn. Orp—5E 112
Leith Mans. W9—6M 57
(off Grantully Rd.)
Leith Rd. N22—8M 27
Leith Rd. Eps—4C 134
Leith Towers. Sutt—9M 121
Lela Av. Houn—1G 85
Lelita Clo. E8—4E 60
Lely Ho. N'holt—5H 53
(off Academy Gdns.)
Leman Pas. E1—9E 60
(off Leman St.)
Leman St. E1—9D 60
Lemark Clo. Stan—6G 23
Le May Av. SE12—9F 94
Lemmon Rd. SE10—7C 78
Lemna Rd. E11—5D 46
Le Moal Ho. E1—8G 61
(off Stepney Way)
Lemon Fld. Dri. Wat—5J 5
Lemonwell Dri. SE9—5A 96
Lemsford Clo. N15—4E 44
Lemsford Ct. N4—7A 44
Lemsford Ct. Borwd—6A 12
Lemuel St. SW18—5A 90
Lena Gdns. W6—4G 73
Lena Kennedy Clo. E4—6A 30
Lenanton Steps. E14—3L 77
(off Manilla St.)
Len Clifton Ho. SE18—5K 79
(off Cambridge Barracks Rd.)
Lendal Ter. SW4—2H 91
Lenderyou Ct. Dart—6H 99
(off Phoenix Pl.)
Lenelby Rd. Surb—3L 119
Len Freeman Pl. SW6—7K 73
Lenham Ho. SE1—4B 76
(off Long La.)
Lenham Rd. SE12—3D 94
Lenham Rd. Bexh—7K 81
Lenham Rd. Sutt—6M 121
Lenham Rd. T Hth—6B 108
Lennard Av. W W'ck—4C 126
Lennard Clo. W W'ck—4C 126
Lennard Rd. SE20 & Beck—3H 109
Lennard Rd. Brom—3K 127
Lennard Rd. Croy—3A 124
Lennon Rd. NW2—1G 57
Lennox Clo. Romf—4D 50
Lennox Gdns. NW10—9D 40
Lennox Gdns. SW1—4D 74
Lennox Gdns. Croy—6M 123
Lennox Gdns. Ilf—6K 47
Lennox Gdns. M. SW1—4D 74
Lennox Ho. Belv—4L 81
(off Picardy St.)
Lennox Ho. Twic—5H 87
(off Clevedon Rd.)
Lennox Rd. E17—4K 45
Lennox Rd. N4—7K 43
Lenor Clo. Bexh—3J 97
Lensbury Clo. Chesh—1E 6
Lensbury Way. SE2—4G 81
Lens Rd. E7—3G 63
Lenthall Ho. SW1—6G 75
(off Churchill Gdns.)
Lenthall Rd. E8—3E 60
Lenthorp Rd. SE10—5D 78
Lentmead Rd. Brom—9D 94
Lenton Path. SE18—7B 80
Lenton Ri. Rich—2J 87
Lenton Rd. SE18—5B 80
Len Williams Ct. NW6—5L 57
Leo Ct. Bren—8H 71
Leof Cres. SE6—2M 109
Leominster Rd. Mord—1A 122
Leominster Wlk. Mord—1A 122
Leonard Av. Mord—9A 106
Leonard Av. Romf—6B 50
Leonard Ct. WC1—7H 59
Leonard Ct. Har W—8C 22
Leonard Rd. E4—6L 29
Leonard Rd. E7—9E 46
Leonard Rd. N9—3D 28
Leonard Rd. SW16—5G 107
Leonard Rd. S'hall—4H 69
Leonard Robbins Path. SE28—1F 80
(off Tawney Rd.)
Leonard's Rd. E14—8A 62
Leonard St. E16—2J 79
Leonard St. EC1—7B 60
Leonora Ho. W9—7A 58
(off Lanark Rd.)
Leontine Clo. SE15—8E 76
Leopards Ct. EC1—8L 59
(off Baldwins Gdns.)
Leopold Av. SW19—2K 105
Leopold Bldgs. E2—6D 60
(off Columbia Rd.)
Leopold M. E9—4G 61
Leopold Rd. E17—3L 45
Leopold Rd. N2—1B 42
Leopold Rd. N18—5F 28
Leopold Rd. NW10—3C 56
Leopold Rd. SW19—1K 105
Leopold Rd. W5—2K 71
Leopold St. E3—8K 61
Leopold Ter. SW19—2K 105
Leo St. SE15—8F 76
Leo Yd. EC1—7M 59
(off St John St.)
Leppoc Rd. SW4—4H 91
Leroy St. SE1—5C 76
Lerry Clo. W14—7K 73
Lerwick Ct. Enf—7C 16
Lescombe Clo. SE23—9J 93
Lescombe Rd. SE23—9J 93
Lesley Clo. Bex—6M 97
Lesley Clo. Swan—7B 114
Leslie Gdns. Sutt—8L 121
Leslie Gro. Croy—3C 124
Leslie Gro. Pl. Croy—3C 124
Leslie Pk. Rd. Croy—3C 124
Leslie Prince Ct. SE5—8B 76
Leslie Rd. E11—9A 46
Leslie Rd. E16—9F 62
Leslie Rd. N2—1B 42
Leslie Smith Sq. SE18—7L 79
Lesnes Abbey. —5H 81
Lesney Farm Est. Eri—8B 82
Lesney Pk. Eri—7B 82
Lesney Pk. Rd. Eri—7B 82
Lessar Av. SW4—5G 91
Lessingham Av. SW17—1D 106
Lessingham Av. Ilf—1L 47
Lessing St. SE23—6J 93
Lessington Av. Romf—4A 50
Lessness Av. Bexh—8H 81
Lessness Heath. —6L 81
Lessness Pk. Belv—6K 81
Lessness Rd. Belv—7L 81
Lessness Rd. Mord—1A 122
Lester Av. E15—7C 62
Lester Ct. Wat—1G 9
Leston Clo. Rain—6F 66
Leswin Pl. N16—8D 44
Leswin Rd. N16—8D 44
Letchford Gdns. NW10—6E 56
Letchford M. NW10—6E 56
Letchford Ter. Harr—8M 21
Letchmore Heath. —3C 10
Letchworth Av. Felt—6D 84
Letchworth Clo. Brom—9E 110
Letchworth Clo. Wat—5H 21
Letchworth Dri. Brom—9E 110
Letchworth St. SW17—1D 106
Lethbridge Clo. SE13—9A 78
Letterstone Rd. SW6—8K 73
Lettice St. SW6—9K 73
Lett Rd. E15—3B 62
Lettsom St. SE5—1C 92
Lettsom Wlk. E13—5E 62
Leucha Rd. E17—3J 45
Levana Clo. SW19—7J 89
Levant Ho. E1—7H 61
(off Ernest St.)
Levehurst Ho. SE27—2A 108
Leven Clo. Wal X—6D 6
Leven Clo. Wat—5H 21
Levendale Rd. SE23—8J 93
Leven Dri. Wal X—6D 6
Levenhurst Way. SW4—1J 91
Leven Rd. E14—8A 62
Leven Way. Hay—9C 52
Leveret Clo. New Ad—3B 140
Leveret Clo. Wat—7E 4
Leverett St. SW3—5C 74
Leverholme Gdns. SE9—9L 95
Leverington Pl. N1—6B 60
(off Charles Sq.)
Leverson St. SW16—3G 107
Leverstock Ho. SW3—6C 74
(off Cale St.)
Lever St. EC1—6M 59
Leverton Pl. NW5—1G 59
Leverton St. NW5—1G 59
Leverton Way. Wal A—6J 7
Levett Gdns. Ilf—9D 48
Levett Rd. Bark—2C 64
Levine Gdns. Bark—5H 65
Levison Way. N19—6H 43
Levita Ho. NW1—6H 59
(off Ossulston St., in two parts)
Lewes Clo. N'holt—2L 53
Lewesdon Clo. SW19—7H 89
Lewes Ho. SE1—3C 76
Lewes Ho. SE15—7E 76
(off Friary Est.)
Lewes Rd. N12—5C 26
Lewes Rd. Brom—6H 111
Lewes Rd. Romf—4H 35
Leweston Pl. N16—5D 44
Lewes Way. Crox G—6A 8
Lewey Ho. E3—7K 61
(off Joseph St.)
Lewgars Av. NW9—4A 40
Lewing Clo. Orp—3C 128
Lewin Rd. SW14—2B 88
Lewin Rd. SW16—3H 107
Lewin Rd. Bexh—4J 97
Lewins Rd. Eps—6M 133
Lewis Av. E17—8L 29
Lewis Clo. N14—9G 15
Lewis Ct. SE16—6F 76
(off Stubbs Dri.)
Lewis Cres. NW10—1B 56
Lewis Gdns. N2—9B 26
Lewis Gro. SE13—3A 94
Lewisham. —2A 94
Lewisham Bus. Cen. SE14—7H 77
Lewisham Cen. SE13—3A 94
Lewisham Crematorium. SE6—8D 94
Lewisham Heights. SE23—7G 93
Lewisham High St. SE13—5M 93
Lewisham Hill. SE13—1A 94
Lewisham Model Mkt. SE13—3A 94
(off Lewisham High St.)
Lewisham Pk. SE13—4A 94
Lewisham Rd. SE13—9M 77
Lewisham St. SW1—3H 75
(in two parts)
Lewisham Way. SE14 & SE4—9K 77
Lewis Ho. E14—2A 78
(off Coldharbour)
Lewis Rd. Horn—4G 51
Lewis Rd. Mitc—6B 106
(in two parts)
Lewis Rd. Rich—4H 87
Lewis Rd. Sidc—9G 97
Lewis Rd. S'hall—3J 69
Lewis Rd. Sutt—6M 121
Lewis Rd. Well—2G 97
Lewis Silkin Ho. SE15—7G 77
(off Lovelinch Clo.)
Lewis St. NW1—2F 58
(in two parts)
Lewis Way. Dag—2M 65
Lexden Dri. Romf—4F 48
Lexden Rd. W3—1M 71
Lexden Rd. Mitc—8H 107
Lexden Ter. Wal A—7J 7
(off Sewardstone Rd.)
Lexham Gdns. W8—5L 73
Lexham Gdns. M. W8—4M 73
Lexham Ho. Bark—4B 64
(off St Margarets)
Lexham M. W8—5L 73
Lexham Wlk. W8—4M 73
Lexington Apartments. EC1—7B 60
Lexington Clo. Borwd—5K 11
Lexington Ct. Purl—2A 138
Lexington St. W1—1G 75
Lexington Way. Barn—6H 13
Lexton Gdns. SW12—7H 91
Leybourne Av. W13—3F 70
Leybourne Pk. Rich—9L 71
Leybourne Clo. Brom—1E 126
Leybourne Ho. E14—9K 61
Leybourne Ho. SE15—7G 77
Leybourne Rd. E11—6D 46
Leybourne Rd. NW1—3F 58
Leybourne Rd. NW9—3L 39
Leybourne Rd. Uxb—4A 52
Leybourne St. NW1—3F 58
Leybridge Ct. SE12—4E 94
Leyburn Clo. E17—2M 45
Leyburn Cres. Romf—7J 35
Leyburn Gdns. Croy—4C 124
Leyburn Gro. N18—6E 28
Leyburn Rd. N18—6E 28
Leyburn Rd. Romf—7J 35
Leycroft Clo. Lou—7L 19
Leycroft Gdns. Eri—9F 82
Leydenhatch La. Swan—5A 114
Leyden Mans. N19—5J 43
Leyden St. E1—8D 60
Leydon Clo. SE16—2H 77
Leyes Rd. E16—9H 63
Leyfield. Wor Pk—3C 120
Leyhill Clo. Swan—9C 114
Leyland Av. Enf—4J 17
Leyland Clo. Chesh—1C 6
Leyland Gdns. Wfd G—5G 31
Leyland Ho. E14—1M 77
(off Hale St.)
Leyland Rd. SE12—4E 94
Leylang Rd. SE14—8H 77
Leys Av. Dag—4A 66
Leys Clo. Dag—3B 66
(in two parts)
Leys Clo. Harr—3B 38
Leys Ct. SW9—1L 91
Leysdown Av. Bexh—3A 98
Leysdown Ho. SE17—6C 76
(off Madron St.)
Leysdown Rd. SE9—8J 95
Leysfield Rd. W12—4E 72
Leys Gdns. Barn—7E 14
Leyspring Rd. E11—6D 46
Leys Rd. Oxs—4B 132
Leys Rd. E. Enf—3J 17
Leys Rd. W. Enf—3J 17
Leys Sq. N3—8M 25
Leys, The. N2—2A 42
Leys, The. Harr—4K 39
Leys, The. W on T—6K 117
Ley St. Ilf—7M 47
Leyswood Dri. Ilf—3C 48
Leythe Rd. W3—3A 72
Leyton. —8A 46
Leyton Bus. Cen. E10—7L 45
Leyton Ct. SE23—7G 93
Leyton Cross. —8E 98
Leyton Cross Rd. Dart—9D 98
Leyton Grange Est. E10—7L 45
Leyton Grn. Rd. E10—4A 46
Leyton Ind. Village. E17—5H 45
Leyton Orient F.C. —8M 45
Leyton Pk. Rd. E10—8A 46
Leyton Rd. E15—1A 62
Leyton Rd. SW19—4A 106
Leytonstone. —6C 46
Leytonstone Rd. E15—9C 46
Leyton Way. E11—5C 46
Leywick St. E15—5C 62
Lezayre Rd. Orp—8D 128
Liardet St. SE14—7J 77
Liberia Rd. N5—2M 59
Liberty Av. SW19—5A 106
Liberty Ct. Bark—5F 64
Liberty M. N22—8M 27
Liberty M. SW12—5F 90
Liberty St. SW9—9K 75
Liberty, The. Romf—3C 50
Liberty 2 Cen. Romf—2D 50
Libra Ct. E4—4L 29
Libra Rd. E13—5E 62
Library Ct. N17—1D 44
Library Pde. NW10—4C 56
(off Craven Pk. Rd.)
Library Pl. E1—1F 76
Library St. SE1—3M 75
Library Way. Twic—6A 86
Lichfield Clo. Barn—5D 14
Lichfield Ct. Rich—3J 87
Lichfield Ct. Surb—9J 103
(off Claremont Rd.)
Lichfield Gdns. Rich—3J 87
Lichfield Gro. N3—8L 25
Lichfield Rd. E3—6J 61
Lichfield Rd. E6—6H 63
Lichfield Rd. N9—2E 28
Lichfield Rd. NW2—9J 41
Lichfield Rd. Dag—9F 48
Lichfield Rd. Houn—2G 85
Lichfield Rd. N'wd—1E 36
Lichfield Rd. Rich—9K 71
Lichfield Rd. Wfd G—4C 30
Lichfield Ter. Rich—4J 87
Lichfield Way. S Croy—2H 139
Lichlade Clo. Orp—6D 128
Lickey Ho. W14—7K 73
(off N. End Rd.)
Lidbury Rd. NW7—6J 25
Lidcote Gdns. SW9—1K 91
Liddall Way. W Dray—2K 143
Liddell Clo. Harr—1H 39
Liddell Gdns. NW10—5G 57
Liddell Rd. NW6—2L 57
Lidding Rd. Harr—3H 39
Liddington Rd. E15—4D 62
Liddon Rd. E13—6F 62
Liddon Rd. Brom—7G 111
Liden Clo. E17—5K 45
Lidfield Rd. N16—9B 44
Lidgate Rd. SE15—8D 76
Lidiard Rd. SW18—8A 90
Lidlington Pl. NW1—5G 59
Lido Sq. N17—9B 28
Lidyard Rd. N19—6G 43
Lieutenant Ellis Way. Chesh & Wal X—3A 6
Lifetimes. —5A 124
(off Katharine St.)
Liffler Rd. SE18—6C 80
Liffords Pl. SW13—1D 88
Lifford St. SW15—3H 89
Light App. NW9—9D 24
Lightcliffe Rd. N13—4L 27
Lighter Clo. SE16—5J 77
Lighterman Ho. E14—1A 78
Lighterman M. E1—9H 61
Lightermans Rd. E14—3L 77
Lightermans Wlk. SW18—3L 89
Lightfoot Rd. N8—3J 43
Light Horse Ct. SW3—6E 74
(off Royal Hospital Rd.)
Lightley Clo. Wemb—4J 55
Ligonier St. E2—7D 60
Lilac Clo. E4—6K 29
Lilac Clo. Chesh—4B 6
Lilac Ct. E13—4G 63
Lilac Ct. Tedd—1D 102
Lilac Gdns. W5—4H 71
Lilac Gdns. Croy—5L 125
Lilac Gdns. Hay—9C 52
Lilac Gdns. Romf—6C 50
Lilac Gdns. Swan—7B 114
Lilac Ho. SE4—2L 93
Lilac Pl. SE11—5K 75
Lilac Pl. W Dray—1K 143
Lilacs Av. Enf—9C 6
Lilac St. W12—1E 72
Lila Pl. Swan—8C 114
Lilburne Gdns. SE9—4J 95
Lilburne Rd. SE9—4J 95
Lilburne Wlk. NW10—2A 56
Lile Cres. W7—8C 54
Lilestone Ho. NW8—7B 58
(off Frampton St.)
Lilestone St. NW8—7C 58
Lilford Ho. SE5—1A 92
Lilford Rd. SE5—1M 91
Lilian Barker Clo. SE12—4E 94
Lilian Board Way. Gnfd—1B 54
Lilian Clo. N16—8C 44
Lilian Gdns. Wfd G—8F 30
Lilian Rd. SW16—5G 107
Lillechurch Rd. Dag—2F 64

Lilleshall Rd.—Lister Wlk.

Lilleshall Rd. Mord —1B 122
Lilley Clo. E1 —2E 76
Lilley La. NW7 —5B 24
Lillian Av. W3 —3L 71
Lillian Rd. SW13 —7E 72
Lillie Mans. W14 —7J 73
(off Lillie Rd.)
Lillie Rd. SW6 —7H 73
Lillie Rd. Big H —9H 141
Lillieshall Rd. SW4 —2F 90
Lillie Yd. SW6 —7L 73
Lillington Gdns. Est. SW1 —5G 75
(off Vauxhall Bri. Rd.)
Lilliput Av. N'holt —4J 53
Lilliput Ct. SE12 —4F 94
Lilliput Rd. Romf —5B 50
Lily Clo. W14 —5H 73
(in two parts)
Lily Dri. W Dray —5G 143
Lily Gdns. Wemb —5G 55
Lily Pl. EC1 —8L 59
Lily Rd. E17 —4L 45
Lilyville Rd. SW6 —9K 73
Limberg Ho. SE8 —5K 77
Limborough Ho. E14 —8L 61
(off Thomas Rd.)
Limbourne Av. Dag —5K 49
Limburg Rd. SW11 —3C 90
Lime Av. Upm —9L 51
Lime Av. W Dray —1K 143
Limeburner La. EC4 —9M 59
Lime Clo. E1 —2E 76
Lime Clo. Brom —8J 111
Lime Clo. Buck H —2H 31
Lime Clo. Cars —4D 122
Lime Clo. Harr —9E 22
Lime Clo. Pinn —1D 36
Lime Clo. Romf —2A 50
Lime Clo. Wat —9H 9
Lime Ct. E11 —7C 46
(off Trinity Clo.)
Lime Ct. E17 —3A 46
Lime Ct. SE9 —8M 95
Lime Ct. Harr —4D 38
Lime Ct. Mitc —6B 106
Lime Cres. Sun —6G 101
Limecroft Clo. Eps —9B 120
Limedene Clo. Pinn —8H 21
Lime Gro. E4 —6K 29
Lime Gro. N20 —1K 25
Lime Gro. W12 —3G 73
Lime Gro. Hay —1B 68
Lime Gro. Ilf —6D 32
Lime Gro. N Mald —7B 104
Lime Gro. Orp —4M 127
Lime Gro. Ruis —4F 36
Lime Gro. Sidc —5D 96
Lime Gro. Twic —5D 86
Limeharbour. E14 —4M 77
Limeharbour Ct. E14 —4M 77
Limehouse. —9K 61
Limehouse Causeway. E14 —1K 77
Limehouse Cut. E14 —8M 61
(off Morris Rd.)
Limehouse Fields Est. E1 —8J 61
Limehouse Link. E14 —9J 61
Lime Kiln Dri. SE7 —7F 78
Limekiln Pl. SE19 —4D 108
Lime Mdw. Av. S Croy —5E 138
Limerick Clo. SW12 —6G 91
Lime Rd. Eri —4K 81
Lime Rd. Rich —3K 87
Lime Rd. Swan —7B 114
Lime Row. Eri —4K 81
Limerston St. SW10 —7A 74
Limes Av. E11 —2F 46
Limes Av. E12 —8J 47
Limes Av. N12 —4A 26
Limes Av. NW7 —6C 24
Limes Av. NW11 —5J 41
Limes Av. SE20 —4F 108
Limes Av. SW13 —1D 88
Limes Av. Cars —3D 122
Limes Av. Chig —5A 32
Limes Av. Croy —5L 123
Limes Av., The. N11 —5F 26
Limes Clo. N11 —5G 27
Limesdale Gdns. Edgw —9A 24
Limes Fld. Rd. SW14 —2C 88
Limesford Rd. SE15 —3H 93
Limes Gdns. SW18 —5L 89
Limes Gro. SE13 —3A 94
Limes Pl. Croy —2B 124
Limes Rd. Beck —6M 109
Limes Rd. Chesh —5E 6
Limes Rd. Croy —1B 124
Limes Row. Farnb —7M 127
Limes, The. SW18 —5L 89
Limes, The. W2 —1L 73
(off Linden Gdns.)
Limes, The. Dart —6K 99
Limes, The. Kes —4J 127
Limes, The. Purf —6L 83
Limes, The. W Mol —8M 101
Limestone Wlk. Eri —3H 81
Lime St. E17 —2J 45
Lime St. EC3 —1C 76
Lime St. Pas. EC3 —9C 60
Limes Wlk. SE15 —3G 93
Limes Wlk. W5 —3H 71
Lime Ter. W7 —1C 70
Lime Tree Av. Esh & Th Dit —3B 118
Limetree Clo. SW2 —7K 91
Limetree Ct. Pinn —7L 21
(off Avenue, The)
Lime Tree Ct. S Croy —8A 124
Lime Tree Gro. Croy —5K 125
Lime Tree Pl. Mitc —5F 106
Lime Tree Rd. Houn —9M 69
Limetree Ter. SE6 —7K 93
Limetree Ter. Well —2E 96
Limetree Wlk. SW17 —2E 106
Lime Tree Wlk. Bush —1C 22
Lime Tree Wlk. Enf —2A 16
Lime Tree Wlk. W W'ck —6D 126
Lime Wlk. E15 —4C 62
Lime Wlk. Den —1A 142
Limewood Clo. E17 —2K 45
Limewood Clo. W13 —9F 54
Limewood Clo. Beck —9A 110
Limewood Ct. Ilf —3K 47
Limewood Rd. Eri —8A 82
Limpsfield Av. SW19 —8H 89
Limpsfield Av. T Hth —9K 107
Limpsfield Rd. S Croy & Warl —4E 138
Linacre Clo. SE15 —2F 92
Linacre Ct. W6 —6H 73
(off Talgarth Rd.)
Linacre Rd. NW2 —2F 56
Linale Ho. N1 —5B 60
(off Murray Gro.)
Linberry Wlk. SE8 —5K 77
Linchmere Rd. SE12 —6D 94
Lincoln Av. N14 —3G 27
Lincoln Av. SW19 —9H 89
Lincoln Av. Romf —7B 50
Lincoln Av. Twic —8A 86
Lincoln Clo. SE25 —1E 124
Lincoln Clo. Eri —1D 98
Lincoln Clo. Gnfd —4A 54
Lincoln Clo. Harr —3K 37
Lincoln Clo. Horn —3L 51
Lincoln Ct. N16 —5B 44
Lincoln Ct. SE12 —9G 95
Lincoln Ct. Borwd —7B 12
Lincoln Ct. S Croy —7A 124
(off Warham Rd.)
Lincoln Cres. Enf —7C 16
Lincoln Dri. Wat —3G 21
Lincoln Gdns. Ilf —5J 47
Lincoln Grn. Rd. Orp —9D 112
Lincoln Ho. SW3 —3D 74
Lincoln Ho. SW9 & SE5 —8L 75
Lincoln M. NW6 —4K 57
Lincoln M. SE21 —8B 92
Lincoln Rd. E7 —2H 63
Lincoln Rd. E13 —7F 62
Lincoln Rd. E18 —8D 30
Lincoln Rd. N2 —1C 42
Lincoln Rd. SE25 —7F 108
Lincoln Rd. Enf —6C 16
Lincoln Rd. Eri —1D 98
(in two parts)
Lincoln Rd. Felt —9K 85
Lincoln Rd. Harr —3K 37
Lincoln Rd. Mitc —9J 107
Lincoln Rd. N Mald —7A 104
Lincoln Rd. N'wd —1D 36
Lincoln Rd. Sidc —2F 112
Lincoln Rd. Wemb —2H 55
Lincoln Rd. Wor Pk —3F 120
Lincolnsfield Cen., The. Bush —6K 9
Lincoln's Inn. —9K 59
Lincolns Inn Fields. WC2 —9K 59
Lincolns, The. NW7 —3D 24
Lincoln St. E11 —7C 46
Lincoln St. SW3 —5D 74
Lincoln Wlk. Eps —2B 134
(in two parts)
Lincoln Way. Enf —7F 16
Lincoln Way. Sun —5C 100
Lincombe Rd. Brom —9D 94
Lindal Cres. Enf —6J 15
Lindal Rd. SE4 —4K 93
Lindbergh Rd. Wall —9J 123
Linden Av. NW10 —5H 57
Linden Av. Coul —8F 136
Linden Av. Dart —7G 99
Linden Av. Enf —3E 16
Linden Av. Houn —4M 85
Linden Av. Ruis —6E 36
Linden Av. T Hth —8M 107
Linden Av. Wemb —1K 55
Linden Clo. N14 —8G 15
Linden Clo. Orp —7E 128
Linden Clo. Ruis —6E 36
Linden Clo. Stan —5F 22
Linden Clo. Th Dit —2D 118
Linden Clo. Wal X —3B 6
Linden Ct. W12 —2G 73
Linden Ct. Sidc —1C 112
Linden Cres. Gnfd —2D 54
Linden Cres. King T —6K 103
Linden Cres. Wfd G —6F 30
Lindenfield. Chst —6M 111
Linden Gdns. W2 —1L 73
Linden Gdns. W4 —6C 72
Linden Gdns. Enf —3E 16
Linden Gro. SE15 —2F 92
Linden Gro. SE26 —3G 109
Linden Gro. N Mald —7C 104
Linden Gro. Tedd —2D 102
Linden Gro. W on T —4D 116
Linden Gro. Warl —9J 139
Linden Ho. SE15 —2F 92
Linden Ho. Hamp —3L 101
Linden Lawns. Wemb —9K 39
Linden Lea. N2 —3A 42
Linden Lea. Pinn —7K 21
Linden Lea. Wat —6E 4
Linden Leas. W W'ck —4B 126
Linden M. N1 —1B 60
Linden M. W2 —1L 73
Linden Pl. Eps —4C 134
Linden Pl. Mitc —8C 106
Linden Rd. N10 —2F 42
Linden Rd. N11 —2D 26
Linden Rd. N15 —2A 44
Linden Rd. Hamp —4L 101
Lindens, The. E17 —2M 45
(off Prospect Hill)
Lindens, The. N12 —5B 26
Lindens, The. W4 —9A 72
Lindens, The. Lou —7K 19
Lindens, The. New Ad —8A 126
Linden St. Romf —2B 50
Linden Wlk. N19 —7G 43
Linden Way. N14 —8G 15
Linden Way. Purl —2G 137
Linden Way. Shep —9A 100
Lindeth Clo. Stan —6F 22
Lindfield Gdns. NW3 —1M 57
Lindfield Rd. W5 —7G 55
Lindfield Rd. Croy —1D 124
Lindfield Rd. Romf —5J 35
Lindfield St. E14 —9L 61
Lindhill Clo. Enf —4H 17
Lindholme Ct. NW9 —8C 24
(off Pageant Av.)
Lindisfarne Rd. SW20 —4E 104
Lindisfarne Rd. Dag —8G 49
Lindisfarne Way. E9 —9J 45
Lindley Ct. King T —5G 103
Lindley Est. SE15 —8E 76
Lindley Ho. E1 —8G 61
(off Lindley St.)
Lindley Ho. SE15 —8E 76
(off Peckham Pk. Rd.)
Lindley Pl. Kew —9L 71
Lindley Rd. E10 —7A 46
Lindley Rd. W on T —5H 117
Lindley St. E1 —8G 61
Lindop Ho. E1 —7J 61
(off Mile End Rd.)
Lindore Rd. SW11 —3D 90
Lindores Rd. Cars —2A 122
Lindo St. SE15 —1G 93
Lind Rd. Sutt —7A 122
Lindrop St. SW6 —1A 90
Lindsay Clo. Chess —9J 119
Lindsay Clo. Eps —5A 134
Lindsay Clo. Stanw —4B 144
Lindsay Ct. Croy —6B 124
(off Eden Rd.)
Lindsay Dri. Harr —4J 39
Lindsay Dri. Shep —1B 116
Lindsay Pl. Chesh —3B 6
Lindsay Rd. Hamp H —1M 101
Lindsay Rd. Wor Pk —4F 120
Lindsay Sq. SW1 —6H 75
Lindsell St. SE10 —9A 78
Lindsey Clo. Brom —7H 111
Lindsey Clo. Mitc —8J 107
Lindsey Ct. N13 —3L 27
(off Green Lanes)
Lindsey Gdns. Felt —6B 84
Lindsey Ho. W5 —5H 71
Lindsey M. N1 —3A 60
Lindsey Rd. Dag —9G 49
Lindsey St. EC1 —8M 59
Lindsey Way. Horn —3G 51
Lind St. SE8 —1L 93
Lindum Rd. Tedd —4G 103
Lindway. SE27 —2M 107
Lindwood Clo. E6 —9K 63
Linfield. WC1 —6K 59
(off Sidmouth St.)
Linfield Clo. NW4 —2G 41
Linfield Clo. W on T —7F 116
Linford Christie Stadium. —9E 56
Linford Rd. E17 —1A 46
Linford St. SW8 —9G 75
Lingard Ho. E14 —4A 78
(off Marshfield St.)
Lingards Rd. SE13 —3A 94
Lingey Clo. Sidc —8D 96
Lingfield Av. Dart —6M 99
Lingfield Av. King T —8J 103
Lingfield Av. Upm —8K 51
Lingfield Clo. Enf —8C 16
Lingfield Clo. N'wd —7C 20
Lingfield Ct. N'holt —5L 53
Lingfield Cres. SE9 —3B 96
Lingfield Gdns. N9 —9F 16
Lingfield Ho. SE1 —3M 75
(off Lancaster St.)
Lingfield Rd. SW19 —2H 105
Lingfield Rd. Wor Pk —5G 121
Lingfield Way. Wat —2D 8
Lingham St. SW9 —1J 91
Lingholm Way. Barn —7H 13
Lingmere Clo. Chig —2A 32
Lingmoor Dri. Wat —6G 5
Ling Rd. E16 —8E 62
Ling Rd. Eri —7A 82
Lingrove Gdns. Buck H —2F 30
Lings Coppice. SE21 —8B 92
Lingwell Rd. SW17 —9C 90
Lingwood. Bexh —1M 97
Lingwood Gdns. Iswth —8C 70
Lingwood Rd. E5 —5E 44
Linhope St. NW1 —7D 58
Linkenholt Mans. W6 —5D 72
(off Stamford Brook Av.)
Linkfield. Hayes —1E 126
Linkfield. W Mol —7M 101
Linkfield Rd. Iswth —1D 86
Link Ho. E3 —5M 61
Link La. Wall —8H 123
Linklea Clo. NW9 —7C 24
Link Pl. Ilf —6D 32
Link Rd. E1 —1E 76
Link Rd. N8 —1L 43
(in two parts)
Link Rd. N11 —4E 26
Link Rd. Dag —5M 65
Link Rd. Felt —6D 84
Link Rd. Wall —3E 122
Link Rd. Wat —4H 9
Links Av. Mord —8L 105
(in two parts)
Links Av. Romf —9F 34
Links Clo. Asht —9G 133
Links Dri. N20 —1L 25
Links Dri. Els —5K 11
Links Gdns. SW16 —4L 107
Linkside. N12 —6L 25
Linkside. Chig —5A 32
Linkside. N Mald —6C 104
Linkside Clo. Enf —5K 15
Linkside Gdns. Enf —5K 15
Links Pl. Asht —9H 133
Links Rd. NW2 —7D 40
Links Rd. SW17 —3E 106
Links Rd. W3 —9L 55
Links Rd. Asht —9G 133
Links Rd. Eps —5E 134
Links Rd. W W'ck —3A 126
Links Rd. Wfd G —5E 30
Links Side. Enf —5K 15
Links, The. E17 —2J 45
Links, The. W on T —4E 116
Link St. E9 —2G 61
Linksview. N2 —3D 42
(off Gt. North Rd.)
Links Vw. N3 —7K 25
Links Vw. Dart —7F 98
Links Vw. Clo. Stan —7E 22
Links Vw. Ct. Hamp —1B 102
Links Vw. Rd. Croy —5L 125
Links Vw. Rd. Hamp H —2A 102
Linksway. NW4 —9H 25
Links Way. Beck —1L 125
Links Way. Crox G —5A 8
Links Way. N'wd —7A 20
Links Yd. E1 —8E 60
(off Spelman St.)
Link, The. SE9 —9L 95
(off William Barefoot Dri.)
Link, The. W3 —9M 55
Link, The. Enf —3J 17
Link, The. N'holt —1K 53
Link, The. Pinn —5G 37
Link, The. Tedd —3D 102
Link, The. Wemb —6G 39
Linkway. N4 —5A 44
Linkway. SW20 —8F 104
Link Way. Brom —2J 127
Linkway. Dag —9G 49
Link Way. Horn —6J 51
Link Way. Pinn —8H 21
Linkway. Rich —8F 86
Linkway, The. Barn —8M 13
Linkway, The. Sutt —1A 136
Linkwood Wlk. NW1 —3H 59
Linley Ct. Sutt —6A 122
Linley Cres. Romf —1M 49
Linley Rd. N17 —9C 28
Linley Sambourne House. —4L 73
(off Stafford Ter.)
Linnell Clo. NW11 —4M 41
Linnell Dri. NW11 —4M 41
Linnell Ho. E1 —8D 60
(off Folgate St.)
Linnell Rd. N18 —5E 28
Linnell Rd. SE5 —1C 92
Linnet Clo. N9 —1H 29
Linnet Clo. SE28 —1G 81
Linnet Clo. Bush —9A 10
Linnet Clo. S Croy —2H 139
Linnet M. SW12 —6E 90
Linnet Rd. Ab L —4E 4
Linnett Clo. E4 —4A 30
Linnet Way. Purf —6M 83
Linom Rd. SW4 —3J 91
Linscott Rd. E5 —9G 45
Linsdell Rd. Bark —4A 64
Linsey Ct. E10 —6L 45
(off Grange Rd.)
Linsey St. SE16 —5E 76
(in two parts)
Linslade Clo. Houn —4J 85
Linslade Clo. Pinn —1F 36
Linslade Ho. E2 —4E 60
Linslade Ho. NW8 —7C 58
(off Paveley St.)
Linslade Rd. Orp —8E 128
Linstead St. NW6 —3L 57
Linstead Way. SW18 —6J 89
Linster Gro. Borwd —7A 12
Lintaine Clo. SW6 —7J 73
Linthorpe Av. Wemb —2G 55
Linthorpe Rd. N16 —5C 44
Linthorpe Rd. Cockf —5C 14
Linton Av. Borwd —3K 11
Linton Clo. SE7 —6G 79
Linton Clo. Mitc —2D 122
Linton Clo. Well —9F 80
Linton Ct. Romf —9C 34
Linton Gdns. E6 —9J 63
Linton Glade. Croy —1J 139
(in two parts)
Linton Gro. SE27 —2M 107
Linton Ho. E14 —8L 61
(off St Paul's Way)
Linton Rd. Bark —3A 64
Lintons La. Eps —4C 134
Lintons, The. Bark —3A 64
Linton St. N1 —4A 60
(in two parts)
Lintott Ct. Stanw —5B 144
Linver Rd. SW6 —1L 89
Linwood Clo. SE5 —1D 92
Linwood Cres. Enf —3E 16
Linzee Rd. N8 —2J 43
Lion Av. Twic —7D 86
Lion Clo. SE4 —5L 93
Lion Ct. E1 —1H 77
(off Highway, The)
Lion Ct. N1 —4K 59
(off Copenhagen St.)
Lion Ct. SE1 —2C 76
(off Magdalen St.)
Lion Ct. Borwd —3A 12
Lionel Gdns. SE9 —4H 95
Lionel Mans. W14 —4H 73
(off Haarlem Rd.)
Lionel M. W10 —8J 57
Lionel Rd. SE9 —4H 95
Lionel Rd. N. Bren —4J 71
Lionel Rd. S. Bren —6K 71
Lion Ga. Gdns. Rich —2K 87
Liongate M. E Mol —7D 102
Lion Grn. Rd. Coul —8H 137
Lion Mills. E2 —5E 60
Lion Pk. Av. Chess —6L 119
Lion Rd. E6 —8K 63
Lion Rd. N9 —2E 28
Lion Rd. Bexh —3J 97
Lion Rd. Croy —9A 108
Lion Rd. Twic —7D 86
Lions Clo. SE9 —9H 95
Lion Way. Bren —8H 71
Lion Wharf Rd. Iswth —2F 86
Lion Yd. SW4 —3H 91
Liphook Clo. Horn —9D 50
Liphook Cres. SE23 —6G 93
Liphook Rd. Wat —4H 21
Lippitts Hill. Lou —3C 18
Lipsham Clo. Bans —5B 136
Lipton Clo. SE28 —1G 81
Lipton Rd. E1 —9H 61
Lisbon Av. Twic —8A 86
Lisbon Clo. E17 —9K 29
Lisburne Rd. NW3 —9D 42
Lisford St. SE15 —9D 76
Lisgar Ter. W14 —5K 73
Liskeard Clo. Chst —3A 112
Liskeard Gdns. SE3 —9E 78
Liskeard Ho. SE11 —6L 75
(off Kennings Way)
Lisle Clo. SW17 —1F 106
Lisle Ct. NW2 —8J 41
Lisle St. WC2 —1H 75
Lismirrane Ind. Pk. Els —8F 10
Lismore. SW19 —2K 105
(off Woodside)
Lismore Cir. NW5 —1E 58
Lismore Clo. Iswth —1E 86
Lismore Ho. SE15 —2F 92
Lismore Rd. N17 —1B 44
Lismore Rd. S Croy —8C 124
Lismore Wlk. N1 —2A 60
(off Clephane Rd.)
Lisselton Ho. NW4 —2H 41
(off Belle Vue Est.)
Lissenden Gdns. NW5 —9E 42
(in two parts)
Lissenden Mans. NW5 —9E 42
Lisson Grn. Est. NW8 —7C 58
Lisson Grove. —8C 58
Lisson Gro. NW8 & NW1 —7B 58
Lisson Ho. NW1 —8C 58
(off Lisson St.)
Lisson St. NW1 —8C 58
Lister Av. H Wood —9H 35
Lister Clo. W3 —8B 56
Lister Clo. Mitc —5C 106
Lister Cotts. Els —7E 10
Lister Ct. Harr —5F 38
Lister Gdns. N18 —5A 28
Listergate Ct. SW15 —3G 89
Lister Ho. E1 —8E 60
Lister Ho. SE3 —7C 78
(off Restell Clo.)
Lister Ho. Hay —5C 68
Lister Ho. Wemb —8A 40
(off Barnhill Rd.)
Lister Lodge. W2 —8L 57
(off Admiral Wlk.)
Lister M. N7 —9K 43
Lister Rd. E11 —6C 46
Lister Wlk. SE28 —1H 81

Longfield Av.—Loxton Rd.

Longfield Av. *NW7* —7E 24
Longfield Av. *W5* —1G 71
Longfield Av. *Enf* —1G 17
Longfield Av. *Horn* —5D 50
Longfield Av. *Wall* —3E 122
Longfield Av. *Wemb* —6J 39
Longfield Cres. *SE26* —9G 93
Longfield Dri. *SW14* —4M 87
Longfield Dri. *Mitc* —4C 106
Longfield Est. *SE1* —5D 76
Longfield La. *Chesh* —1A 6
Longfield Rd. *W5* —9G 55
Longfield St. *SW18* —6L 89
Longfield Wlk. *W5* —9G 55
Longford Av. *Felt* —5C 84
Longford Av. *S'hall* —1M 69
Longford Av. *Stai* —7C 144
Longford Clo. *Hamp H* —1L 101
Longford Clo. *Hanw* —9J 85
Longford Clo. *Hay* —1H 69
Longford Ct. *NW4* —2H 41
Longford Ct. *Eps* —6A 120
Longford Ct. S'hall —2L 69
(off Uxbridge Rd.)
Longford Gdns. *Hay* —1H 69
Longford Gdns. *Sutt* —5A 122
Longford Ho. E1 —9G 61
(off Jubilee St.)
Longford Ho. Brom —2B 110
(off Brangbourne Rd.)
Longford Ho. *Hamp* —1L 101
Longford Rd. *Twic* —7L 85
Longford St. *NW1* —7F 58
Longford Wlk. *SW2* —6L 91
Longford Way. *Stai* —7C 144
Long Grn. *Chig* —4C 32
Long Gro. *H Wood* —9J 35
Long Gro. Rd. *Eps* —2M 133
Longhayes Av. *Romf* —2H 49
Longhayes Ct. *Romf* —2H 49
Longheath Gdns. *Croy* —9G 109
Longhedge Ho. SE26 —1E 108
(off High Level Dri.)
Long Hedges. *Houn* —1L 85
Longhedge St. *SW11* —1E 90
Longhill Rd. *SE6* —8B 94
Longhook Gdns. *N'holt* —6F 52
Longhope Clo. *SE15* —7C 76
Longhurst Rd. *SE13* —4B 94
Longhurst Rd. *Croy* —1F 124
Longland Ct. *SE1* —6E 76
Longland Dri. *N20* —3M 25
Longlands. —9B 96
Longlands Av. *Coul* —6E 136
Longlands Clo. *Chesh* —5D 6
Longlands Ct. W11 —1K 73
(off Westbourne Gro.)
Longlands Ct. *Sidc* —9D 96
Longlands Pk. Cres. *Sidc* —9C 96
Longlands Rd. *Sidc* —9C 96
Long La. *EC1* —8M 59
Long La. *N3 & N2* —8M 25
Long La. *SE1* —3B 76
Long La. *Bexh* —8H 81
Long La. *Croy* —1F 124
Long La. *Hil* —2F 142
Long La. *Stai & Stanw* —8D 144
Long La. *Uxb* —6E 142
Longleat Ho. SW1 —6H 75
(off Rampayne St.)
Longleat M. *St M* —8G 113
Longleat Rd. *Enf* —7C 16
Longleat Way. *Felt* —6B 84
Longleigh Ho. SE5 —9C 76
(off Peckham Rd.)
Longleigh La. *SE2 & Bexh* —7G 81
Long Lents Ho. *NW10* —4B 56
Longley Av. *Wemb* —4K 55
Longley Ct. *SW8* —9J 75
Longley Rd. *SW17* —3C 106
Longley Rd. *Croy* —2M 123
Longley Rd. *Harr* —3A 38
Long Leys. *E4* —6M 29
Longley St. *SE1* —5E 76
Longley Way. *NW2* —8G 41
Long Lodge Dri. *W on T* —5G 117
Longman Ho. E2 —5H 61
(off Mace St.)
Longman Ho. E8 —4D 60
(off Haggerston Rd.)
Longmans. *Wat* —8A 8
Long Mark Rd. *E16* —8H 63
Longmarsh Vw. *S at H* —5M 115
Long Mead. *NW9* —8D 24
Longmead. *Chst* —6L 111
Longmead Bus. Cen. *Eps* —3B 134
Longmead Dri. *Sidc* —8H 97
Longmead Ho. *SE27* —2A 108
Long Mdw. *NW5* —1H 59
Long Mdw. *Noak H* —2G 35
Long Mdw. Clo. *W W'ck* —2A 126
Longmeadow Rd. *Sidc* —7C 96
Longmead Rd. *SW17* —2D 106
Longmead Rd. *Eps* —3B 134
Longmead Rd. *Hay* —1D 68
Longmead Rd. *Th Dit* —2C 118
Long Moor. *Chesh* —2E 6
Longmoore St. *SW1* —5G 75
Longmore Av. *Barn* —8A 14
Longmore Rd. *W on T* —6J 117
Longnor Est. *E1* —6H 61
Longnor Rd. *E1* —6H 61
Long Pond Rd. *SE3* —9C 78
Longport Clo. *Ilf* —6E 32
Longreach Ct. *Bark* —5B 64
Long Reach Rd. *Bark* —7D 64
Longreach Rd. *Eri* —8F 82
Longridge Ho. *SE1* —4A 76
Longridge La. *S'hall* —9M 53
Longridge Rd. *SW5* —5L 73
Longridge Rd. *Bark & Dag* —3A 64
Longridge Rd. *Rich* —5K 87
Long Ridges. N10 —1E 42
(off Fortis Grn.)
Long Rd. *SW4* —3F 90
Long's Ct. WC2 —1H 75
(off Orange St.)
Longs Ct. *Rich* —3K 87
Longshaw Rd. *E4* —3B 30
Longshore. *SE8* —5K 77
Longshott Ct. SW5 —5L 73
(off W. Cromwell Rd.)
Longspring. *Wat* —2F 8
Longstaff Cres. *SW18* —5L 89
Longstaff Rd. *SW18* —5L 89
Longstone Av. *NW10* —3D 56
Longstone Rd. *SW17* —2F 106
Long St. *E2* —6D 60
Longthornton Rd. *SW16* —6G 107
Longton Av. *SE26* —1E 108
Longton Gro. *SE26* —1F 108
Longtown Clo. *Romf* —5G 35
Longtown Ct. Dart —5M 99
(off Osbourne Rd.)
Longtown Rd. *Romf* —5G 35
Longview Vs. *Romf* —8K 33
Longview Way. *Romf* —8B 34
Longville Rd. *SE11* —5M 75
Long Wlk. *SE1* —4C 76
Long Wlk. *SE18* —7M 79
Long Wlk. *SW13* —1C 88
Long Wlk. *N Mald* —7A 104
Long Wlk. *Wal A* —3G 7
Longwalk Rd. *Uxb* —2M 143
Long Wall. *E15* —6B 62
Longwater Ho. King T —7H 103
(off Portsmouth Rd.)
Longwood Clo. *Upm* —1M 67
Longwood Ct. Upm —1M 67
(off Corbets Tey Rd.)
Longwood Dri. *SW15* —5E 88
Longwood Gdns. *Ilf* —2K 47
Longwood Rd. *Kenl* —8B 138
(in two parts)
Longworth Clo. *SE28* —9H 65
Long Yd. *WC1* —7K 59
Loning, The. *NW9* —2D 40
Loning, The. *Enf* —2G 17
Lonsdale Av. *E6* —7H 63
Lonsdale Av. *Romf* —4A 50
Lonsdale Av. *Wemb* —1J 55
Lonsdale Clo. *E6* —7J 63
Lonsdale Clo. *SE9* —9H 95
Lonsdale Clo. *Edgw* —5K 23
Lonsdale Clo. *Pinn* —7J 21
Lonsdale Clo. *Uxb* —8A 52
Lonsdale Ct. *Surb* —2H 119
Lonsdale Cres. *Ilf* —4M 47
Lonsdale Dri. *Enf* —6H 15
Lonsdale Gdns. *SW16* —8K 107
Lonsdale Ho. *W11* —9K 57
Lonsdale M. W11 —9K 57
(off Lonsdale Rd.)
Lonsdale M. *Rich* —9L 71
Lonsdale Pl. *N1* —3L 59
Lonsdale Rd. *E11* —4D 46
Lonsdale Rd. *NW6* —4K 57
Lonsdale Rd. *SE25* —8F 108
Lonsdale Rd. *SW13* —9D 72
Lonsdale Rd. *W4* —5D 72
Lonsdale Rd. *W11* —9K 57
Lonsdale Rd. *Bexh* —1K 97
Lonsdale Rd. *S'hall* —4H 69
Lonsdale Sq. *N1* —3L 59
Lonsdale Yd. *W11* —1L 73
Loobert Rd. *N15* —1C 44
Looe Gdns. *Ilf* —1M 47
Loom La. *Rad* —1D 10
Loom Pl. *Rad* —1E 10
Loop Rd. *Chst* —3A 112
Loop Rd. *Eps* —8A 134
Lopen Rd. *N18* —4C 28
Lopez Ho. *SW9* —2J 91
Lorac Ct. *Sutt* —9L 121
Lorain Clo. *N12* —4M 25
Loraine Clo. *Enf* —7G 17
Loraine Ct. *Chst* —2M 111
Loraine Gdns. *Asht* —9J 133
Loraine Ho. *Wall* —6F 122
Loraine Rd. *N7* —9K 43
Loraine Rd. *W4* —7M 71
Lorane Ct. *Wat* —4E 8
Lord Amory Way. *E14* —3A 78
Lord Av. *Ilf* —2K 47
Lord Chancellor Wlk. *King T* —5A 104
Lordell Pl. *SW19* —3G 105
Lorden Wlk. *E2* —6E 60
Lord Gdns. *Ilf* —2J 47
Lord Hills Bri. *W2* —8M 57
Lord Hills Rd. *W2* —8M 57
Lord Holland La. *SW9* —1L 91
Lord Knyvett Clo. *Stanw* —5B 144
Lord Knyvetts Ct. *Stanw* —5B 144
Lord Napier Pl. *W6* —6E 72
Lord N. St. *SW1* —4J 75
Lord Roberts M. *SW6* —8M 73
Lord Robert's Ter. *SE18* —6L 79
Lordsbury Fld. *Wall* —2G 137
Lords Clo. *SE21* —8A 92
Lords Clo. *Felt* —8J 85
Lord's Cricket Ground. —6B 58
Lordship Gro. *N16* —7B 44
Lordship La. *N22 & N17* —9L 27
Lordship La. *SE22* —3D 92
Lordship La. Est. *SE21* —6E 92
Lordship Pk. *N16* —7A 44
Lordship Pk. M. *N16* —7A 44
Lordship Pl. *SW3* —7C 74
Lordship Rd. *N16* —6B 44
Lordship Rd. *Chesh* —3B 6
Lordship Rd. *N'holt* —3J 53
Lordship Ter. *N16* —7B 44
Lordsmead Rd. *N17* —8C 28
Lord St. *E16* —2J 79
Lord St. *Wat* —5G 9
Lords Vw. *NW8* —6B 58
Lord Warwick St. *SE18* —4K 79
Loreburn Ho. *N7* —9K 43
Lorenzo St. *WC1* —6K 59
Loretto Gdns. *Harr* —2J 39
Loring Rd. *N20* —2C 26
Loring Rd. *SE14* —9J 77
Loring Rd. *Iswth* —1D 86
Loris Rd. *W6* —4G 73
Lorn Ct. *SW9* —1L 91
Lorne Av. *Croy* —2H 125
Lorne Clo. *NW8* —6C 58
Lorne Gdns. *E11* —2G 47
Lorne Gdns. *W11* —3H 73
Lorne Gdns. *Croy* —2H 125
Lorne Ho. E1 —8J 61
(off Ben Jonson Rd.)
Lorne Rd. *E7* —9F 46
Lorne Rd. *E17* —3L 45
Lorne Rd. *N4* —6K 43
Lorne Rd. *Harr* —9D 22
Lorne Rd. *Rich* —4K 87
Lorne Ter. *N3* —9K 25
Lorn Rd. *SW9* —1K 91
Lorraine Clo. *S Ock* —3K 83
Lorraine Ct. *NW1* —3F 58
Lorraine Pk. *Harr* —7C 22
Lorrimore Rd. *SE17* —7M 75
Lorrimore Sq. *SE17* —7M 75
Lorton Ho. NW6 —4L 57
(off Kilburn Va.)
Loseberry Rd. *Clay* —7B 118
Lothair Rd. *W5* —3H 71
Lothair Rd. N. *N4* —4M 43
Lothair Rd. S. *N4* —5L 43
Lothbury. *EC2* —9B 60
Lothian Av. *Hay* —8F 52
Lothian Clo. *Wemb* —9E 38
Lothian Rd. *SW9* —9M 75
Lothrop St. *W10* —6J 57
Lots Rd. *SW10* —8A 74
Lotus Clo. *SE21* —9B 92
Lotus Rd. *Big H* —9K 141
Loubet St. *SW17* —3D 106
Loudoun Av. *Ilf* —3M 47
Loudoun Rd. *NW8* —4A 58
Loudwater Clo. *Sun* —8E 100
Loudwater Rd. *Sun* —8E 100
Loughborough Est. *SW9* —2M 91
Loughborough Pk. *SW9* —3M 91
Loughborough Rd. *SW9* —1L 91
Loughborough St. *SE11* —6K 75
Lough Rd. *N7* —1K 59
Loughton. —6J 19
Loughton Way. *Buck H* —1H 31
Louisa Ct. *Twic* —8C 86
Louisa Gdns. *E1* —7H 61
Louisa St. *E1* —7H 61
Louise Bennett Clo. *SE24* —3M 91
Louise Ct. *N22* —8L 27
Louise De Marillac Ho. E1 —8G 61
(off Smithy St.)
Louise Gdns. *Rain* —6C 66
Louise Rd. *E15* —2C 62
Louise White Ho. *N19* —6H 43
Louis M. *N10* —8F 26
Louisville Rd. *SW17* —9E 90
Lousada Lodge. N14 —8G 15
(off Avenue Rd.)
Louvaine Rd. *SW11* —3B 90
Louvain Way. *Wat* —5F 4
Lovage App. *E6* —8J 63
Lovat Clo. *NW2* —8D 40
Lovat La. *EC3* —1C 76
(in two parts)
Lovatt Clo. *Edgw* —6M 23
Lovatt Ct. *SW12* —7F 90
Lovatt Dri. *Ruis* —3E 36
Lovat Wlk. *Houn* —8J 69
Loveday Rd. *W13* —3F 70
Lovegrove St. *SE1* —6E 76
Lovegrove Wlk. *E14* —2A 78
Lovekyn Clo. *King T* —6J 103
Lovelace Av. *Brom* —1L 127
Lovelace Gdns. *Bark* —9E 48
Lovelace Gdns. *Surb* —2H 119
Lovelace Gdns. *W on T* —7G 117
Lovelace Grn. *SE9* —2K 95
Lovelace Ho. E8 —4D 60
(off Haggerston Rd.)
Lovelace Rd. *SE21* —8A 92
Lovelace Rd. *Barn* —9C 14
Lovelace Rd. *Surb* —2G 119
Loveland Mans. Bark —3D 64
(off Upney La.)
Love La. *EC2* —9A 60
Love La. *N17* —7D 28
Love La. *SE18* —5L 79
Love La. *SE25* —7F 108
(in two parts)
Love La. *Ab L* —3D 4
Love La. *Ave* —3M 83
Love La. *Bex* —5K 97
Love La. Brom —7F 110
(off Elmfield Rd.)
Love La. *Mitc* —7C 106
(in two parts)
Love La. *Mord* —2L 121
Love La. *Pinn* —9H 21
Love La. *Surb* —4G 119
Love La. *Sutt* —8J 121
Love La. *Wfd G* —6K 31
Lovel Av. *Well* —1E 96
Lovelinch Clo. *SE15* —7G 77
Lovell Ho. E8 —4E 60
(off Shrubland Rd.)
Lovell Pl. *SE16* —4J 77
Lovell Rd. *Enf* —8B 6
Lovell Rd. *Rich* —9G 87
Lovell Rd. *S'hall* —9M 53
Lovell Wlk. *Rain* —2E 66
Lovelock Clo. *Kenl* —9A 138
Loveridge M. *NW6* —2K 57
Loveridge Rd. *NW6* —2K 57
Lovers Wlk. *NW7 & N3* —6K 25
Lovers Wlk. *SE10* —7B 78
Lovers' Wlk. *W1* —2E 74
Lovers Wlk. *Romf* —5B 34
Lovett Dri. *Cars* —2A 122
Lovett Way. *NW10* —1A 56
Love Wlk. *SE5* —1B 92
Lovibonds Av. *Orp* —6M 127
Lovibonds Av. *W Dray* —9D 142
Lowbrook Rd. *Ilf* —9M 47
Low Cross Wood La. *SE21* —9D 92
Lowdell Clo. *W Dray* —9C 142
Lowden Rd. *N9* —1F 28
Lowden Rd. *SE24* —3M 91
Lowden Rd. *S'hall* —1J 69
Lowder Ho. E1 —2F 76
(off Wapping La.)
Lowe Av. *E16* —8E 62
Lowe Clo. *Chig* —5E 32
Lowell Ho. SE5 —8A 76
(off Wyndham Est.)
Lowell St. *E14* —9J 61
Lowen Rd. *Rain* —5B 66
Lwr. Addiscombe Rd. *Croy* —3C 124
Lwr. Addison Gdns. *W14* —3J 73
Lwr. Alderton Hall La. *Lou* —7L 19
Lwr. Barn Rd. *Purl* —4A 138
Lwr. Bedfords Rd. *Romf* —6C 34
Lwr. Belgrave St. *SW1* —4F 74
Lwr. Boston Rd. *W7* —2C 70
Lwr. Broad St. *Dag* —4L 65
Lower Camden. *Chst* —4K 111
Lwr. Church St. *Croy* —4M 123
Lower Clapton. —9F 44
Lwr. Clapton Rd. *E5* —8F 44
Lwr. Clarendon Wlk. W11 —9J 57
(off Clarendon Rd.)
Lwr. Common S. *SW15* —2F 88
Lwr. Coombe St. *Croy* —6A 124
Lwr. Court Rd. *Eps* —3A 134
Lower Cft. *Swan* —8D 114
Lwr. Derby Rd. *Wat* —6G 9
Lwr. Downs Rd. *SW20* —5H 105
Lwr. Drayton Pl. *Croy* —4M 123
Lwr. Dunnymans. *Bans* —6K 135
Lower Edmonton. —3E 28
Lower Feltham. —9D 84
Lower Fosters. NW4 —3G 41
(off New Brent St.)
Lwr. George St. *Rich* —4H 87
Lwr. Gravel Rd. *Brom* —3J 127
Lower Green. —4M 117
Lwr. Green Rd. *Esh* —4M 117
Lwr. Green W. *Mitc* —7C 106
Lwr. Grosvenor Pl. *SW1* —4F 74
Lwr. Grove Rd. *Rich* —5K 87
Lower Halliford. —2C 116
Lwr. Hall La. *E4* —5J 29
(in two parts)
Lwr. Hampton Rd. *Sun* —7G 101
Lwr. Ham Rd. *King T* —2H 103
Lwr. High St. *Wat* —6G 9
Lwr. Hill Rd. *Eps* —4M 133
Lower Holloway. —1K 59
Lwr. Island Way. *Wal A* —8J 7
Lwr. James St. *W1* —1G 75
Lwr. John St. *W1* —1G 75
Lwr. Kenwood Av. *Enf* —7J 15
Lwr. Lea Crossing. *E14* —1C 78
Lwr. Maidstone Rd. *N11* —6G 27
Lower Mall. *W6* —6F 72
Lwr. Mardyke Av. *Rain* —5A 66
Lower Marsh. *SE1* —3L 75
Lwr. Marsh La. *King T* —8K 103
(in two parts)
Lower Mdw. *Chesh* —1D 6
Lwr. Merton Ri. *NW3* —3C 58
Lower Mill. *Eps* —9D 120
Lwr. Morden La. *Mord* —1G 121
Lwr. Mortlake Rd. *Rich* —3J 87
Lwr. Noke Clo. *Brtwd* —2J 35
Lwr. Northfield. *Bans* —6K 135
Lwr. Paddock Rd. *Wat* —8J 9
Lwr. Park Rd. *N11* —5G 27
Lwr. Park Rd. *Belv* —5L 81
Lwr. Park Rd. *Coul* —9C 136
Lwr. Park Rd. *Lou* —7H 19
Lower Pk. Trad. Est. *W3* —7A 56
Lwr. Pillory Downs. *Cars* —5F 136
Lower Place. —5A 56
Lwr. Place Bus. Cen. *NW10* —5B 56
Lwr. Queen's Rd. *Buck H* —2H 31
Lwr. Richmond Rd. *SW15* —2F 88
Lwr. Richmond Rd. *Rich & SW14* —2L 87
Lower Rd. *SE1* —3L 75
Lower Rd. *SE16 & SE8* —3G 77
(in two parts)
Lower Rd. *Belv & Eri* —4M 81
Lower Rd. *Harr* —6B 38
Lower Rd. *Kenl* —5M 137
Lower Rd. *Lou* —3L 19
Lower Rd. *Orp* —1F 128
Lower Rd. *Sutt* —6A 122
Lower Rd. *Swan* —4D 114
Lower Sawleywood. *Bans* —6K 135
Lwr. Sloane St. *SW1* —5E 74
Lower Sq. *Iswth* —2F 86
Lower Sq., The. *Sutt* —7M 121
Lwr. Station Rd. *Cray* —5C 98
Lower Strand. *NW9* —9D 24
Lwr. Sunbury Rd. *Hamp* —6K 101
Lower Sydenham. —1H 109
Lwr. Sydenham Ind. Est. *SE26* —2K 109
Lower Tail. *Wat* —3J 21
Lwr. Teddington Rd. *King T* —5H 103
Lower Ter. *NW3* —8A 42
Lwr. Thames St. *EC3* —1B 76
Lower Tub. *Bush* —9B 10
Lowerwood Ct. W11 —9J 57
(off Westbourne Pk. Rd.)
Lwr. Wood Rd. *Clay* —8F 118
Lowestoft Clo. E5 —7G 45
(off Mt. Pleasant Hill)
Lowestoft M. *E16* —3M 79
Lowestoft Rd. *Wat* —3F 8
Loweswater Clo. *Wat* —6G 5
Loweswater Clo. *Wemb* —7H 39
Loweswater Ho. *E3* —7K 61
Lowe, The. *Chig* —5E 32
Lowfield Rd. *NW6* —3L 57
Lowfield Rd. *W3* —9M 55
Lowfield St. *Dart* —6J 99
Low Hall Clo. *E4* —9M 17
Low Hall La. *E17* —4J 45
Low Hall Mnr. Bus. Cen. *E17* —4J 45
Lowick Rd. *Harr* —2C 38
Lowlands Dri. *Stanw* —4B 144
Lowlands Gdns. *Romf* —3M 49
Lowlands Rd. *Ave* —2M 83
Lowlands Rd. *Harr* —4C 38
Lowlands Rd. *Pinn* —5G 37
Lowman Rd. *N7* —9K 43
Lowndes Clo. *SW1* —4E 74
Lowndes Ct. *SW1* —4D 74
Lowndes Ct. W1 —9G 59
(off Kingly St.)
Lowndes Pl. *SW1* —4E 74
Lowndes Sq. *SW1* —3D 74
Lowndes St. *SW1* —4E 74
Lownds Ct. *Brom* —6E 110
Lowood Ho. E1 —1G 77
(off Bewley St.)
Lowood St. *E1* —1F 76
Lowry Clo. *Eri* —5B 82
Lowry Ct. SE16 —6F 76
(off Stubbs Dri.)
Lowry Cres. *Mitc* —6C 106
Lowry Ho. N17 —8D 28
(off Pembury Rd.)
Lowry Rd. *Dag* —1F 64
Lowshoe La. *Romf* —8L 33
Lowson Gro. *Wat* —9J 9
Lowswood Clo. *N'wd* —8A 20
Lowther Clo. *Els* —7K 11
Lowther Dri. *Enf* —6J 15
Lowther Gdns. *SW7* —3B 74
Lowther Hill. *SE23* —6J 93
Lowther Ho. E8 —4D 60
(off Clarissa St.)
Lowther Ho. SW1 —6G 75
(off Churchill Gdns.)
Lowther Rd. *E17* —9J 29
Lowther Rd. *N7* —1L 59
Lowther Rd. *SW13* —9D 72
Lowther Rd. *King T* —5K 103
Lowther Rd. *Stan* —1K 39
Lowth Rd. *SE5* —9A 76
Loxford. —1A 64
Loxford Av. *E6* —5H 63
Loxford La. *Ilf* —1A 64
Loxford Rd. *Bark* —2M 63
Loxford Ter. *Bark* —2A 64
Loxham Rd. *E4* —7M 29
Loxham St. *WC1* —6J 59
Loxley Clo. *SE26* —2H 109
Loxley Rd. *SW18* —7B 90
Loxley Rd. *Hamp* —1K 101
Loxton Rd. *SE23* —7H 93

Loxwood Clo.—Macdonald Way

Loxwood Clo. Felt —7B 84
Loxwood Clo. Orp —4H 129
Loxwood Rd. N17 —1C 44
Lubbock Ho. E14 —1M 77
(off Poplar High St.)
Lubbock Rd. Chst —4K 111
Lubbock St. SE14 —8G 77
Lucan Ho. N1 —4B 60
(off Colville Est.)
Lucan Pl. SW3 —5C 74
Lucan Rd. Barn —5J 13
Lucas Av. E13 —4F 62
Lucas Av. Harr —7L 37
Lucas Ct. SE26 —2J 109
Lucas Ct. SW11 —9E 74
Lucas Ct. Wal A —6M 7
Lucas Rd. NW10 —3E 56
Lucas Rd. SE20 —3G 109
Lucas Sq. NW11 —4L 41
Lucas St. SE8 —9L 77
Lucerne Clo. N13 —3J 27
Lucerne Ct. Eri —4J 81
Lucerne Gro. E17 —2B 46
Lucerne M. W8 —2L 73
Lucerne Rd. N5 —9M 43
Lucerne Rd. Orp —3D 128
Lucerne Rd. T Hth —9M 107
Lucerne Way. Romf —6H 35
Lucey Rd. SE16 —4E 76
Lucey Way. SE16 —4E 76
(in two parts)
Lucien Rd. SW17 —1E 106
Lucien Rd. SW19 —8M 89
Lucinda Ct. Enf —7C 16
Lucknow St. SE18 —8C 80
Lucorn Clo. SE12 —5D 94
Lucton M. Lou —6M 19
Luctons Av. Buck H —1G 31
Lucy Brown Ho. SE1 —2A 76
(off Park St.)
Lucy Cres. W3 —8A 56
Lucy Gdns. Dag —8J 49
Luddesdon Rd. Eri —8L 81
Ludford Clo. NW9 —9C 24
Ludford Clo. Croy —5M 123
Ludgate B'way. EC4 —9M 59
Ludgate Cir. EC4 —9M 59
Ludgate Hill. EC4 —9M 59
Ludgate Sq. EC4 —9M 59
Ludham Clo. SE28 —9G 65
Ludlow Clo. Brom —7E 110
Ludlow Clo. Harr —9K 37
Ludlow Ct. W3 —3A 72
Ludlow Mead. Wat —3F 20
Ludlow Rd. W5 —7G 55
Ludlow Rd. Felt —1E 100
Ludlow St. EC1 —7A 60
Ludlow Way. N2 —2A 42
Ludlow Way. Crox G —6A 8
Ludovick Wlk. SW15 —3C 88
Ludwick M. SE14 —8J 77
Luffield Rd. SE2 —4F 80
Luffman Rd. SE12 —9F 94
Lugard Ho. W12 —2F 72
Lugard Rd. SE15 —1F 92
Lugg App. E12 —8L 47
Luke Ho. E1 —9F 60
(off Tillman St.)
Luke St. EC2 —7C 60
Lukin Cres. E4 —3B 30
Lukin St. E1 —9G 61
Lukintone Clo. Lou —8J 19
Lullarook Clo. Big H —8G 141
Lullingstone. —6G 131
Lullingstone Av. Swan —7D 114
Lullingstone Castle. —7G 131
Lullingstone Clo. Orp —4F 112
Lullingstone Cres. Orp —4E 112
Lullingstone Ho. SE15 —7G 77
(off Lovelinch Clo.)
Lullingstone La. SE13 —5B 94
Lullingstone La. Eyns —5G 131
Lullingstone Pk. Vis. Cen. —8F 130
Lullingstone Rd. Belv —7K 81
Lullingstone Roman Villa. —5F 130
Lullington Gth. N12 —5K 25
Lullington Gth. Borwd —7M 11
Lullington Gth. Brom —4C 110
Lullington Rd. SE20 —4E 108
Lullington Rd. Dag —3J 65
Lulot Gdns. N19 —7F 42
Lulworth. NW1 —3H 59
(off Wrotham Rd.)
Lulworth. SE17 —6B 76
(off Portland St.)
Lulworth Av. Houn —9M 69
Lulworth Av. Wemb —5G 39
Lulworth Clo. Harr —8K 37
Lulworth Cres. Mitc —6C 106
Lulworth Dri. Pinn —4H 37
Lulworth Dri. Romf —5M 33
Lulworth Gdns. Harr —7J 37
Lulworth Ho. SW8 —8K 75
Lulworth Rd. SE9 —8J 95
Lulworth Rd. SE15 —1F 92
Lulworth Rd. Well —1D 96
Lulworth Waye. Hay —9F 52
Lumen Rd. Wemb —7H 39
Lumiere Building, The. E7 —1H 63
(off Romford Rd.)
Lumley Clo. Belv —6L 81
Lumley Ct. WC2 —1J 75
Lumley Flats. SW1 —6E 74
(off Holbein Pl.)
Lumley Gdns. Sutt —7J 121
Lumley Rd. Sutt —7J 121
Lumley St. W1 —9E 58
Lumsdon. NW8 —4M 57
(off Abbey Rd.)
Lunar Clo. Big H —8H 141
Luna Rd. T Hth —7A 108
Lundin Wlk. Wat —4H 21
Lund Point. E15 —4A 62
Lundy Dri. Hay —5C 68
Lundy Wlk. N1 —2A 60
Lunedale Rd. Dart —8M 99
Lunham Rd. SE19 —3C 108
Luntley Pl. E1 —8E 60
Lupin Clo. SW2 —8M 91
Lupin Clo. Croy —3H 125
Lupin Clo. Rush G —7B 50
Lupin Clo. W Dray —6H 143
Lupin Cres. Ilf —2M 63
Lupin Point. SE1 —3D 76
(off Abbey St.)
Lupton Clo. SE12 —9F 94
Lupton St. NW5 —9G 43
(in two parts)
Lupus St. SW1 —6F 74
Luralda Gdns. E14 —6A 78
Lurgan Av. W6 —7H 73
Lurline Gdns. SW11 —9E 74
Luscombe Ct. Short —6C 110
Luscombe Way. SW8 —8J 75
Lushes Ct. Lou —7M 19
Lushes Rd. Lou —7M 19
Lushington Ho. W on T —1G 117
Lushington Rd. NW10 —5F 56
Lushington Rd. SE6 —1M 109
Lushington Ter. E8 —1E 60
(off Wayland Av.)
Lusted Hall La. Tats —9H 141
Lutea Ho. Sutt —9A 122
(off Walnut M.)
Luther Clo. Edgw —2A 24
Luther King Clo. E17 —4K 45
Luther Rd. Tedd —2D 102
Luton Ho. E13 —7E 62
(off Luton Rd.)
Luton Ho. Romf —5J 35
(off Linfield Rd.)
Luton Pl. SE10 —8A 78
Luton Rd. E13 —7E 62
Luton Rd. E17 —1K 45
Luton Rd. Sidc —9G 97
Luton St. NW8 —7B 58
Lutton Ter. NW3 —9A 42
(off Heath St.)
Luttrell Av. SW15 —4F 88
Lutwyche Rd. SE6 —8K 93
Lutyens Ho. SW1 —6G 75
(off Churchill Gdns.)
Luxborough Ho. W1 —8E 58
(off Luxborough St.)
Luxborough La. Chig —3J 31
Luxborough St. W1 —8E 58
Luxborough Tower. W1 —8E 58
(off Luxborough St.)
Luxemburg Gdns. W6 —5H 73
Luxfield Rd. SE9 —7J 95
Luxford St. SE16 —5H 77
Luxmore St. SE4 —9K 77
Luxor St. SE5 —2A 92
Luxted. —6L 141
Luxted Rd. Dow & Orp —4L 141
Lyall Av. SE21 —1C 108
Lyall M. SW1 —4E 74
Lyall M. W. SW1 —4E 74
Lyall St. SW1 —4E 74
Lyal Rd. E3 —5J 61
Lycett Pl. W12 —3E 72
Lyceum Theatre. —1K 75
(off Strand)
Lych Ga. Wat —6H 5
Lychgate Mnr. Harr —5C 38
Lych Ga. Rd. Orp —3E 128
Lych Ga. Wlk. Hay —1D 68
(in two parts)
Lyconby Gdns. Croy —2J 125
Lydd Clo. Sidc —9C 96
Lydden Gro. SW18 —6M 89
Lydden Rd. SW18 —6M 89
Lydd Rd. Bexh —8K 81
Lydeard Rd. E6 —3K 63
Lydford. NW1 —4G 59
(off Royal College St.)
Lydford Clo. N16 —1C 60
(off Pellerin Rd.)
Lydford Ct. Dart —5M 99
(off Clifton Wlk.)
Lydford Rd. N15 —3B 44
Lydford Rd. NW2 —2G 57
Lydford Rd. W9 —7K 57
Lydhurst Av. SW2 —8K 91
Lydia Ct. N12 —6A 26
Lydia Rd. Eri —7D 82
Lydney Clo. SE15 —8C 76
Lydney Clo. SW19 —8J 89
Lydon Rd. SW4 —2G 91
Lydstep Rd. Chst —1L 111
Lye La. Brick W —1L 5
Lyfield. Oxs —6A 132
Lyford Rd. SW18 —6B 90
Lyford St. SE7 —5J 79
Lygon Ho. E2 —6D 60
(off Gosset St.)
Lygon Ho. SW6 —9J 73
(off Fulham Pal. Rd.)
Lygon Pl. SW1 —4F 74
Lyham Clo. SW2 —5J 91
Lyham Rd. SW2 —4J 91
Lyle Clo. Mitc —2E 122
Lyly Ho. SE1 —4B 76
(off Burbage Clo.)
Lymbourne Clo. Sutt —2L 135
Lyme Farm Rd. SE12 —3E 94
Lyme Gro. E9 —3G 61
Lymer Av. SE19 —2D 108
Lyme Regis Rd. Bans —9K 135
Lyme Rd. Well —9F 80
Lymescote Gdns. Sutt —4L 121
Lyme St. NW1 —3G 59
Lyme Ter. NW1 —3G 59
Lyminge Clo. Sidc —1D 112
Lyminge Gdns. SW18 —7C 90
Lymington Av. N22 —9L 27
Lymington Clo. E6 —8K 63
Lymington Clo. SW16 —6H 107
Lymington Ct. Sutt —5M 121
Lymington Ct. Wat —7E 4
Lymington Dri. Ruis —7B 36
Lymington Gdns. Eps —7D 120
Lymington Rd. NW6 —2M 57
Lymington Rd. Dag —6H 49
Lyminster Clo. Hay —8J 53
Lympne. N17 —9B 28
(off Gloucester Rd.)
Lympstone Gdns. SE15 —8E 76
Lynbridge Gdns. N13 —4M 27
Lynbrook Clo. SE15 —8C 76
Lynbrook Clo. Rain —5B 66
Lynbury Ct. Wat —5E 8
Lynch Clo. Uxb —3A 142
Lynchen Clo. Houn —9F 68
Lynch, The. Uxb —3A 142
Lynch Wlk. SE8 —7K 77
Lyncott Cres. SW4 —3F 90
Lyncourt. SE3 —1B 94
Lyncroft Av. Pinn —3J 37
Lyncroft Gdns. NW6 —1L 57
Lyncroft Gdns. W13 —3G 71
Lyncroft Gdns. Eps —1D 134
Lyncroft Gdns. Houn —4A 86
Lyncroft Mans. NW6 —1L 57
Lyndale. NW2 —9K 41
Lyndale. Th Dit —2C 118
Lyndale Av. NW2 —8K 41
Lyndale Clo. SE3 —7D 78
Lynde Ho. SW4 —2H 91
Lynde Ho. W on T —1G 117
Lynden Hyrst. Croy —4D 124
Lynden Way. Swan —7A 114
Lyndhurst Av. N12 —6D 26
Lyndhurst Av. NW7 —6C 24
Lyndhurst Av. SW16 —6H 107
Lyndhurst Av. Pinn —8F 20
Lyndhurst Av. S'hall —2M 69
Lyndhurst Av. Sun —7E 100
Lyndhurst Av. Surb —3M 119
Lyndhurst Av. Twic —7K 85
Lyndhurst Clo. NW10 —8B 40
Lyndhurst Clo. Bexh —2M 97
Lyndhurst Clo. Croy —5D 124
Lyndhurst Clo. Orp —6M 127
Lyndhurst Ct. E18 —8E 30
Lyndhurst Ct. NW8 —4B 58
(off Finchley Rd.)
Lyndhurst Ct. Sutt —9L 121
(off Grange Rd.)
Lyndhurst Dri. E10 —5A 46
Lyndhurst Dri. Horn —6G 51
Lyndhurst Dri. N Mald —2C 120
Lyndhurst Gdns. N3 —8J 25
Lyndhurst Gdns. NW3 —1B 58
Lyndhurst Gdns. Bark —2C 64
Lyndhurst Gdns. Enf —6C 16
Lyndhurst Gdns. Ilf —4B 48
Lyndhurst Gdns. Pinn —8F 20
Lyndhurst Gro. SE15 —1C 92
Lyndhurst Lodge. E14 —5B 78
(off Millennium Dri.)
Lyndhurst Ri. Chig —4L 31
Lyndhurst Rd. E4 —7A 30
Lyndhurst Rd. N18 —4E 28
Lyndhurst Rd. N22 —6L 27
Lyndhurst Rd. NW3 —1B 58
Lyndhurst Rd. Bexh —2M 97
Lyndhurst Rd. Coul —8E 136
Lyndhurst Rd. Gnfd —7M 53
Lyndhurst Rd. T Hth —8L 107
Lyndhurst Sq. SE15 —9D 76
Lyndhurst Ter. NW3 —1B 58
Lyndhurst Way. SE15 —9D 76
Lyndhurst Way. Sutt —1L 135
Lyndon Av. Pinn —6J 21
Lyndon Av. Sidc —4D 96
Lyndon Av. Wall —5E 122
Lyndon Rd. Belv —5L 81
Lyne Cres. E17 —8K 29
Lynegrove Av. Ashf —2A 100
Lyneham Wlk. E5 —1J 61
Lyneham Wlk. Pinn —1D 36
Lynette Av. SW4 —5F 90
Lynford Clo. Barn —7D 12
Lynford Clo. Edgw —8A 24
Lynford Ct. Croy —6C 124
(off Coombe Rd.)
Lynford Gdns. Edgw —3M 23
Lynford Gdns. Ilf —7D 48
Lynford Ter. N9 —1D 28
Lynhurst Cres. Uxb —3A 52
Lynhurst Rd. Uxb —3A 52
Lynmere Rd. Well —1F 96
Lyn M. E3 —6K 61
Lyn M. N16 —9C 44
Lynmouth Av. Enf —8D 16
Lynmouth Av. Mord —1H 121
Lynmouth Dri. Ruis —7F 36
Lynmouth Gdns. Gnfd —4F 54
Lynmouth Gdns. Houn —8H 69
Lynmouth Ho. Romf —5J 35
(off Dagnam Pk. Dri.)
Lynmouth Ri. Orp —8F 112
Lynmouth Rd. E17 —4J 45
Lynmouth Rd. N2 —1D 42
Lynmouth Rd. N16 —6D 44
Lynmouth Rd. Gnfd —4F 54
Lynn Clo. Ashf —2B 100
Lynn Clo. Harr —9B 22
Lynn Ct. Whyt —9D 138
Lynne Clo. SE23 —6K 93
Lynne Clo. Orp —8D 128
Lynne Clo. S Croy —3G 139
Lynne Ct. S Croy —6C 124
(off Birdhurst Rd.)
Lynnett Rd. Dag —7H 49
Lynne Wlk. Esh —7A 118
Lynne Way. NW10 —2C 56
Lynne Way. N'holt —5H 53
Lynn Ho. SE15 —7F 76
(off Friary Est.)
Lynn M. E11 —7C 46
Lynn Rd. E11 —7C 46
Lynn Rd. SW12 —6F 90
Lynn Rd. Ilf —5B 48
Lynn St. Enf —3B 16
Lynross Clo. Romf —9K 35
Lynscott Way. S Croy —1M 137
Lynstead Ct. Beck —6J 109
Lynsted Clo. Bexh —4M 97
Lynsted Clo. Brom —6G 111
Lynsted Gdns. SE9 —2H 95
Lynton Av. N12 —4B 26
Lynton Av. NW9 —2D 40
Lynton Av. W13 —9E 54
Lynton Av. Orp —8F 112
Lynton Av. Romf —8L 33
Lynton Clo. NW10 —1C 56
Lynton Clo. Chess —6J 119
Lynton Clo. Iswth —3D 86
Lynton Cres. Ilf —4M 47
Lynton Est. SE1 —5E 76
Lynton Gdns. N11 —6H 27
Lynton Gdns. Enf —9C 16
Lynton Grange. N2 —1D 42
Lynton Ho. W2 —9A 58
(off Hallfield Est.)
Lynton Ho. Ilf —7A 48
Lynton Mans. SE1 —4L 75
(off Kennington Rd.)
Lynton Mead. N20 —3L 25
Lynton Pde. Chesh —3E 6
Lynton Rd. E4 —5M 29
Lynton Rd. N8 —3H 43
(in two parts)
Lynton Rd. NW6 —5K 57
Lynton Rd. SE1 —5D 76
Lynton Rd. W3 —1L 71
Lynton Rd. Croy —1L 123
Lynton Rd. Harr —7J 37
Lynton Rd. N Mald —9B 104
Lynton Ter. W3 —9A 56
Lynton Wlk. Hay —6C 52
Lynwood Av. Coul —7F 136
Lynwood Av. Eps —6D 134
Lynwood Clo. E18 —8G 31
Lynwood Clo. Harr —8J 37
Lynwood Clo. Romf —6M 33
Lynwood Ct. Eps —5D 134
Lynwood Ct. King T —6M 103
Lynwood Dri. N'wd —8D 20
Lynwood Dri. Romf —6M 33
Lynwood Dri. Wor Pk —4E 120
Lynwood Gdns. Croy —6K 123
Lynwood Gdns. S'hall —9K 53
Lynwood Gro. N21 —1L 27
Lynwood Gro. Orp —2C 128
Lynwood Rd. SW17 —9D 90
Lynwood Rd. W5 —6H 55
Lynwood Rd. Eps —6D 134
Lynwood Rd. Th Dit —4D 118
Lyon Bus. Pk. Bark —5C 64
Lyon Ct. Ruis —6H 36
Lyon Ho. NW8 —7C 58
Lyon Ind. Est. NW2 —7F 40
Lyon Meade. Stan —8G 23
Lyon Pk. Av. Wemb —2J 55
(in two parts)
Lyon Rd. SW19 —5A 106
Lyon Rd. Harr —4D 38
Lyon Rd. Romf —5D 50
Lyon Rd. W on T —4J 117
Lyonsdown. —7A 14
Lyonsdown Av. New Bar —8A 14
Lyonsdown Rd. Barn & New Bar —8A 14
Lyons Ind. Est. Uxb —1H 143
Lyons Pl. NW8 —7B 58
Lyon St. N1 —3K 59
Lyons Wlk. W14 —5J 73
Lyon Way. Gnfd —4C 54
Lyoth Rd. Orp —4A 128
Lyric Dri. Gnfd —7M 53
Lyric M. SE26 —1G 109
Lyric Rd. SW13 —9D 72
Lyric Theatre. —5G 73
(Hammersmith)
Lyric Theatre. —1H 75
(off Shaftesbury Av., Westminster)
Lysander Gdns. Surb —1K 119
Lysander Gro. N19 —6H 43
Lysander Ho. E2 —5F 60
(off Temple St.)
Lysander M. N19 —6G 43
Lysander Rd. Croy —8K 123
Lysander Rd. Ruis —7B 36
Lysander Way. Ab L —5E 4
Lysander Way. Orp —5A 128
Lysias Rd. SW12 —5F 90
Lysia St. SW6 —8H 73
Lysons Wlk. SW15 —3E 88
Lytchet Rd. Brom —4E 110
Lytchet Way. Enf —3G 17
Lytchgate Clo. S Croy —9C 124
Lytcott Dri. W Mol —7K 101
Lytcott Gro. SE22 —4C 92
Lytham Av. Wat —5H 21
Lytham Clo. SE28 —9J 65
Lytham Ct. S'hall —9M 53
(off Whitecote Rd.)
Lytham Gro. W5 —6K 55
Lytham St. SE17 —6B 76
Lyttelton Clo. NW3 —3C 58
Lyttelton Ct. N2 —3A 42
Lyttelton Rd. E10 —8M 45
Lyttelton Rd. N2 —3A 42
Lyttelton Theatre. —2L 75
(off Royal National Theatre)
Lyttleton Ct. Hay —7G 53
(off Dunedin Way)
Lyttleton Rd. N8 —1L 43
Lytton Av. N13 —2L 27
Lytton Av. Enf —2J 17
Lytton Clo. N2 —3B 42
Lytton Clo. N'holt —3K 53
Lytton Gdns. Wall —6H 123
Lytton Gro. SW15 —4H 89
Lytton Rd. E11 —5C 46
Lytton Rd. Barn & New Bar —6A 14
Lytton Rd. Pinn —7J 21
Lytton Rd. Romf —3F 50
Lytton Strachey Path. SE28 —1F 80
Lyveden Rd. SE3 —8F 78
Lyveden Rd. SW17 —3D 106

Mabbett Ho. SE18 —7L 79
(off Nightingale Pl.)
Mabbutt Clo. Brick W —3J 5
Mabel Evetts Ct. Hay —1F 68
Mabel Rd. Swan —3E 114
Maberley Cres. SE19 —4E 108
Maberley Rd. SE19 —5D 108
Maberley Rd. Beck —7H 109
Mabledon Ct. WC1 —6H 59
(off Mabledon Pl.)
Mabledon Pl. NW1 —6H 59
Mablethorpe Rd. SW6 —8J 73
Mabley St. E9 —1J 61
Mablin Lodge. Buck H —1G 31
Macaret Clo. N20 —9M 13
Macarthur Clo. E7 —2E 62
Macarthur Ter. SE7 —7H 79
Macartney Ho. SW9 —9L 75
(off Gosling Way)
Macaulay Av. Esh —4D 118
Macaulay Ct. SW4 —2F 90
Macaulay Rd. E6 —5H 63
Macaulay Rd. SW4 —2F 90
Macaulay Sq. SW4 —3F 90
Macaulay Way. SE28 —2F 80
McAuley Clo. SE1 —4L 75
McAuley Clo. SE9 —4M 95
Macauley M. SE13 —9A 78
Macbean St. SE18 —4M 79
Macbeth Ho. N1 —5C 60
Macbeth St. W6 —6F 72
McCall Clo. SW4 —1J 91
McCall Cres. SE7 —6J 79
McCall Ho. N7 —9J 43
McCarthy Rd. Felt —2H 101
Macclesfield Ho. EC1 —6A 60
(off Central St.)
Macclesfield Ho. Romf —5J 35
(off Dagnam Pk. Dri.)
Macclesfield Rd. EC1 —6A 60
Macclesfield Rd. SE25 —9F 108
Macclesfield St. W1 —1H 75
McClintock Pl. Enf —1M 17
McCoid Way. SE1 —3A 76
McCrone M. NW3 —2B 58
McCudden Rd. Dart —2K 99
McCullum Rd. E3 —4K 61
McDermott Clo. SW11 —2C 90
McDermott Rd. SE15 —2E 92
Macdonald Av. Dag —8M 49
Macdonald Av. Horn —1J 51
Macdonald Rd. E7 —9E 46
Macdonald Rd. E17 —9A 30
Macdonald Rd. N11 —5D 26
Macdonald Rd. N19 —7G 43
Macdonald Way. Horn —2J 51

Macdonnell Gdns.—Manilla St.

Macdonnell Gdns. Wat —8D 4
McDonough Clo. Chess —6J 119
McDowall Clo. E16 —8D 62
McDowall Rd. SE5 —9A 76
Macduff Rd. SW11 —9E 74
Mace Clo. E1 —2F 76
Mace Gateway. E16 —1E 78
McEntee Av. E17 —8J 29
Mace St. E2 —5H 61
McEwen Way. E15 —4B 62
Macey St. SE10 —7A 78
(off Thames St.)
Macfarlane La. Iswth —7D 70
Macfarlane Rd. W12 —2G 73
Macfarren Pl. NW1 —7E 58
McGlashon Ho. E1 —7E 60
(off Hunton St.)
McGrath Rd. E15 —1D 62
McGredy. Chesh —2B 6
McGregor Ct. N1 —6C 60
(off Hoxton St.)
MacGregor Rd. E16 —8G 63
McGregor Rd. W11 —9K 57
Machell Rd. SE15 —2G 93
McIndoe Ct. N1 —4B 60
(off Sherborne St.)
McIntosh Clo. Romf —1C 50
McIntosh Clo. Wall —9J 123
McIntosh Ho. SE16 —5G 77
(off Millender Wlk.)
Macintosh Ho. W1 —8E 58
(off Beaumont St.)
McIntosh Rd. Romf —1C 50
McIntyre Ct. SE18 —5J 79
(off Prospect Va.)
Mackay Ho. W12 —1F 72
(off White City Est.)
Mackay Rd. SW8 —2F 90
McKay Rd. SW20 —4F 104
McKay Trad. Est. W10 —7J 57
McKellar Clo. Bus H —2A 22
Mackennal St. NW8 —5C 58
Mackenzie Clo. W12 —1F 72
Mackenzie Ho. NW2 —8E 40
Mackenzie Rd. N7 —2K 59
Mackenzie Rd. Beck —6G 109
Mackenzie Wlk. E14 —2L 77
McKenzie Way. Eps —1L 133
McKerrell Rd. SE15 —9E 76
Mackeson Rd. NW3 —9D 42
Mackie Rd. SW2 —6L 91
McKillop Way. Sidc —4G 113
Mackintosh La. E9 —1H 61
Macklin St. WC2 —9J 59
Mackonochie Ho. EC1 —8L 59
(off Baldwins Gdns.)
Mackrow Wlk. E14 —1A 78
Mack's Rd. SE16 —5E 76
Mackworth Ho. NW1 —6G 59
(off Augustus St.)
Mackworth St. NW1 —6G 59
Maclaren M. SW15 —3G 89
Maclean Rd. SE23 —5J 93
Maclennan Av. Rain —6H 67
Macleod Rd. N21 —7J 15
McLeod Rd. SE2 —5F 80
McLeod's M. SW7 —5M 73
Macleod St. SE17 —6A 76
Maclise Ho. SW1 —5J 75
(off Marsham St.)
Maclise Rd. W14 —4J 73
Macmillan Ct. S Harr —6L 37
Macmillan Gdns. Dart —3L 99
McMillan Ho. SE4 —2J 93
(off Arica Rd.)
McMillan St. SE8 —7L 77
McNair Rd. S'hall —4M 69
Macnamara Ho. SW10 —8B 74
(off Worlds End Est.)
McNeil Rd. SE5 —1C 92
McNicol Dri. NW10 —5A 56
Macoma Rd. SE18 —7B 80
Macoma Ter. SE18 —7B 80
Maconochies Rd. E14 —6M 77
Macquarie Way. E14 —5M 77
McRae La. Mitc —2D 122
Macready Ho. W1 —8C 58
(off Crawford St.)
Macready Pl. N7 —9J 43
Macroom Rd. W9 —6K 57
Macs Ho. E17 —1M 45
Mac's Pl. EC4 —9L 59
(off Greystoke Pl.)
Madame Tussaud's. —7E 58
Madans Wlk. Eps —7B 134
(in two parts)
Mada Rd. Orp —5M 127
Maddams St. E3 —7M 61
Maddison Clo. Tedd —3D 102
Maddocks Clo. Sidc —2J 113
Maddocks Ho. E1 —1F 76
(off Cornwall St.)
Maddock Way. SE17 —7M 75
Maddox St. W1 —1F 74
Madeira Av. Brom —4C 110
Madeira Gro. Wfd G —6G 31
Madeira Rd. E11 —6B 46
Madeira Rd. N13 —4M 27
Madeira Rd. SW16 —2J 107
Madeira Rd. Mitc —8D 106
Madeley Rd. W5 —9H 55
Madeline Gro. Ilf —1B 64
Madeline Rd. SE20 —4E 108
Madge Gill Way. E6 —4J 63
(off High St. N.)
Madinah Rd. E8 —2E 60
Madison Cres. Bexh —8G 81
Madison Gdns. Bexh —8G 81
Madison Gdns. Brom —7D 110
Madras Pl. N7 —2L 59
Madras Rd. Ilf —9M 47
Madrid Rd. SW13 —9E 72
Madrigal La. SE5 —8M 75
Madron St. SE17 —6C 76
Mafeking Av. E6 —5J 63
Mafeking Av. Bren —7J 71
Mafeking Av. Ilf —5B 48
Mafeking Rd. E16 —7D 62
Mafeking Rd. N17 —9E 28
Mafeking Rd. Enf —5D 16
Magdala Av. N19 —7G 43
Magdala Rd. Iswth —2E 86
Magdala Rd. S Croy —9B 124
Magdalene Clo. SE15 —1F 92
Magdalene Gdns. E6 —7L 63
Magdalen Gro. Orp —6F 128
Magdalen Pas. E1 —1D 76
Magdalen Rd. SW18 —7A 90
Magdalen St. SE1 —2C 76
Magee St. SE11 —7L 75
Magellan Ct. NW10 —3B 56
(off Stonebridge Pk.)
Magellan Ho. E1 —7H 61
(off Ernest St.)
Magellan Pl. E14 —5L 77
Magnaville Rd. Bus H —9C 10
Magnet Rd. Wemb —7H 39
Magnin Clo. E8 —4E 60
Magnolia Av. Ab L —5E 4
Magnolia Clo. E10 —7L 45
Magnolia Clo. King T —3M 103
Magnolia Ct. N'holt —7J 53
Magnolia Ct. Rich —9M 71
Magnolia Ct. Sutt —9L 121
(off Grange Rd.)
Magnolia Ct. Uxb —2F 142
Magnolia Ct. Wall —7F 122
Magnolia Dri. Big H —8H 141
Magnolia Gdns. E10 —7L 45
Magnolia Gdns. Edgw —4A 24
Magnolia Ho. SE8 —7K 77
Magnolia Lodge. E4 —3M 29
Magnolia Lodge. W8 —4M 73
Magnolia Pl. SW4 —4J 91
Magnolia Pl. W5 —8H 55
Magnolia Pl. Harr —5K 39
Magnolia Rd. W4 —7M 71
Magnolia St. W Dray —6H 143
Magnolia Way. Eps —7A 120
Magnum Clo. Rain —7F 66
Magpie All. EC4 —9L 59
Magpie Clo. E7 —1D 62
Magpie Clo. NW9 —9C 24
Magpie Clo. Enf —3E 16
Magpie Hall Clo. Brom —1J 127
Magpie Hall La. Brom —2J 127
Magpie Hall Rd. Bus H —2C 22
Magpie Pl. SE14 —7J 77
Magpie Pl. Wat —5G 5
Magri Wlk. E1 —8G 61
Maguire Dri. Rich —1G 103
Maguire St. SE1 —3D 76
Mahatma Gandhi Ind. Est. SE24 —3M 91
Mahlon Av. Ruis —1F 52
Mahogany Clo. SE16 —2J 77
Mahon Clo. Enf —3D 16
Maida Av. E4 —9M 17
Maida Av. W2 —8A 58
Maida Hill. —7K 57
Maida Rd. Belv —4L 81
Maida Vale. —6M 57
Maida Va. W9 —5M 57
Maida Va. Rd. Dart —4E 98
Maida Way. E4 —9M 17
Maiden Erlegh Av. Bex —7J 97
Maiden La. NW1 —3H 59
Maiden La. SE1 —2A 76
Maiden La. WC2 —1J 75
Maiden La. Dart —2E 98
Maiden Pl. N19 —8G 43
Maiden Rd. E15 —3C 62
Maidenshaw Rd. Eps —4B 134
Maidenstone Hill. SE10 —9A 78
Maids of Honour Row. Rich —4H 87
Maidstone Av. Romf —9A 34
Maidstone Bldgs. SE1 —2A 76
Maidstone Ho. E14 —9M 61
(off Carmen St.)
Maidstone Rd. N11 —6H 27
Maidstone Rd. Sidc —3H 113
Mail Coach Yd. E2 —6C 60
Main Av. Enf —7D 16
Main Av. N'wd —3A 20
Main Dri. Wemb —8H 39
Mainridge Rd. Chst —1L 111
Main Rd. Big H & W'ham —5G 141
Main Rd. Crock —1B 130
Main Rd. Eyns —1J 131
Main Rd. F'ham —4M 131
Main Rd. Hex —4D 114
Main Rd. Orp —7G 113
Main Rd. Romf —2D 50
Main Rd. Sidc —9B 96
Main Rd. S at H —3M 115
Main St. Felt —2H 101
Mais Ho. SE26 —8F 92
Maisie Webster Clo. Stanw —6A 144
Maismore St. SE15 —7E 76
Maisonettes, The. Sutt —7K 121
Maitland Clo. SE10 —8M 77
Maitland Clo. Houn —2K 85
Maitland Clo. W on T —4J 117
Maitland Ct. W2 —1B 74
(off Lancaster Ter.)
Maitland Ho. SW1 —7G 75
(off Churchill Gdns.)
Maitland Pk. Est. NW3 —2D 58
Maitland Pk. Rd. NW3 —2D 58
Maitland Pk. Vs. NW3 —2D 58
Maitland Pl. E5 —9F 44
Maitland Rd. E15 —2D 62
Maitland Rd. SE26 —3H 109
Maitlands. Lou —5K 19
Maitland Yd. W13 —2E 70
Maize Row. E14 —1K 77
Majendie Rd. SE18 —6B 80
Majestic Way. Mitc —6D 106
Major Rd. E15 —1B 62
Major Rd. SE16 —4E 76
Makepeace Av. N6 —7E 42
Makepeace Mans. N6 —7E 42
Makepeace Rd. E11 —2E 46
Makepeace Rd. N'holt —5J 53
Makinen Ho. Buck H —1G 31
Makins St. SW3 —5C 74
Malabar Ct. W12 —1F 72
(off India Way)
Malabar St. E14 —3L 77
Malam Ct. SE11 —5L 75
Malam Gdns. E14 —1M 77
Malan Clo. Big H —9J 141
Malan Sq. Rain —2F 66
Malbrook Rd. SW15 —3F 88
Malcolm Ct. E7 —2D 62
Malcolm Ct. NW4 —4E 40
Malcolm Ct. Stan —5G 23
Malcolm Cres. NW4 —4E 40
Malcolm Dri. Surb —3H 119
Malcolm Gavin Clo. SW17 —8C 90
Malcolm Ho. N1 —5C 60
(off Arden Est.)
Malcolm Pl. E2 —7G 61
Malcolm Rd. E1 —7G 61
Malcolm Rd. SE20 —4G 109
Malcolm Rd. SE25 —1E 124
Malcolm Rd. SW19 —3J 105
Malcolm Rd. Coul —7H 137
Malcolmson Ho. SW1 —6H 75
(off Aylesford St.)
Malcolm Way. E11 —3E 46
Malcombs Way. N14 —7G 15
Malden Av. SE25 —8F 108
Malden Av. Gnfd —1C 54
Malden Ct. N4 —4A 44
Malden Ct. N Mald —7F 104
Malden Cres. NW1 —2E 58
Malden Fields. Bush —7H 9
Malden Green. —3E 120
Malden Grn. Av. Wor Pk —3D 120
Malden Hill. N Mald —7D 104
Malden Hill Gdns. N Mald —7D 104
Malden Junction . (Junct) —9D 104
Malden Pk. N Mald —1D 120
Malden Pl. NW5 —1E 58
Malden Rd. NW5 —1D 58
Malden Rd. Borwd —5L 11
Malden Rd. N Mald & Wor Pk —9C 104
Malden Rd. Sutt —6G 121
Malden Rd. Wat —4F 8
Malden Rushett. —3G 133
Malden Way. N Mald —1B 120
Maldon Clo. E15 —1C 62
Maldon Clo. N1 —4A 60
Maldon Clo. SE5 —2C 92
Maldon Ct. E6 —4L 63
Maldon Ct. Wall —7G 123
Maldon Rd. N9 —3D 28
Maldon Rd. W3 —1A 72
Maldon Rd. Romf —5A 50
Maldon Rd. Wall —7F 122
Maldon Wlk. Wfd G —6G 31
Malet Pl. WC1 —7H 59
Malet St. WC1 —7H 59
Maley Av. SE27 —8M 91
Malford Ct. E18 —9E 30
Malford Gro. E18 —2D 46
Malfort Rd. SE5 —2C 92
Malham Clo. N11 —6E 26
Malham Rd. SE23 —7H 93
Malham Ter. N18 —6F 28
(off Dysons Rd.)
Malibu Ct. SE26 —9F 92
Malins Clo. Barn —7F 12
Mallams M. SW9 —2M 91
Mallard Clo. E9 —2K 61
Mallard Clo. NW6 —5L 57
Mallard Clo. W7 —3C 70
Mallard Clo. Dart —4K 99
Mallard Clo. New Bar —8B 14
Mallard Clo. Twic —6L 85
Mallard Ct. E17 —1B 46
Mallard Ho. NW8 —5C 58
(off Barrow Hill Est.)
Mallard Path. SE28 —4B 80
(off Goosander Way)
Mallard Pl. N22 —9K 27
Mallard Pl. Twic —9E 86
Mallard Rd. Ab L —4E 4
Mallard Rd. S Croy —2H 139
Mallards. E11 —5E 46
(off Blake Hall Rd.)
Mallards Ct. Wat —3K 21
(off Hangar Ruding)
Mallards Reach. Wey —4B 116
Mallards Rd. Wfd G —7F 30
Mallard Wlk. Beck —9H 109
Mallard Wlk. Sidc —3G 113
Mallard Way. NW9 —5A 40
Mallard Way. N'wd —7A 20
Mallard Way. Wall —1G 137
Mallard Way. Wat —1J 9
Mall Chambers. W8 —2L 73
(off Kensington Mall)
Mallet Dri. N'holt —1K 53
Mallet Rd. SE13 —5B 94
Mall Galleries. —2H 75
(off Carlton Ho. Ter.)
Mall Gallery. WC2 —9J 59
(off Thomas Neals Shop. Mall)
Malling Clo. Croy —1G 125
Malling Gdns. Mord —1A 122
Malling Way. Brom —2D 126
Mallinson Clo. Horn —1G 67
Mallinson Rd. SW11 —4C 90
Mallinson Rd. Croy —5H 123
Mallion Ct. Wal A —6M 7
Mallon Gdns. E1 —9D 60
(off Commercial St.)
Mallord St. SW3 —7B 74
Mallory Clo. SE4 —3J 93
Mallory Gdns. E Barn —9E 14
Mallory Ho. E14 —8M 61
(off Teviot St.)
Mallory St. NW8 —7C 58
Mallow Clo. Croy —3H 125
Mallow Mead. NW7 —7J 25
Mallows, The. Uxb —8A 36
Mallow St. EC1 —7B 60
Mall Rd. W6 —6F 72
Mall, The. E15 —3B 62
Mall, The. N14 —3J 27
Mall, The. SW1 —3G 75
Mall, The. SW14 —4A 88
Mall, The. W5 —1J 71
Mall, The. Bexh —3L 97
Mall, The. Bren —7H 71
Mall, The. Brom —7E 110
Mall, The. Croy —4A 124
Mall, The. Dag —2L 65
Mall, The. Harr —4K 39
Mall, The. Horn —6F 50
Mall, The. Park —1M 5
Mall, The. Surb —9H 103
Mall, The. Swan —7C 114
Mall, The. W on T —7H 117
Malmains Clo. Beck —8B 110
Malmains Way. Beck —8A 110
Malmesbury. E2 —5G 61
(off Cyprus St.)
Malmesbury Clo. Pinn —2D 36
Malmesbury Rd. E3 —6K 61
Malmesbury Rd. E16 —8C 62
Malmesbury Rd. E18 —8D 30
Malmesbury Rd. Mord —2A 122
Malmesbury Ter. E16 —8D 62
Malmsey Ho. SE11 —6K 75
Malpas Dri. Pinn —3H 37
Malpas Rd. E8 —1F 60
Malpas Rd. SE4 —1K 93
Malpas Rd. Dag —2H 65
Malsmead Ho. E9 —1K 61
(off Homerton Rd.)
Malta Rd. E10 —6L 45
Malta St. EC1 —7M 59
Maltby Clo. Orp —3E 128
Maltby Dri. Enf —2F 16
Maltby Rd. Chess —8L 119
Maltby St. SE1 —3D 76
Malthouse Dri. W4 —7D 72
Malthouse Dri. Felt —2H 101
Malthouse Pas. SW13 —1D 88
(off Maltings Clo.)
Malthus Path. SE28 —2G 81
Malting Ho. E14 —1K 77
(off Oak La.)
Maltings. W4 —6L 71
Maltings Clo. SW13 —1D 88
Maltings Lodge. W4 —7C 72
(off Corney Reach Way)
Maltings M. Sidc —9E 96
Maltings Pl. SE1 —3C 76
(off Tower Bri. Rd.)
Maltings Pl. SW6 —9M 73
Maltings, The. K Lan —7A 4
Maltings, The. Orp —3D 128
Maltings, The. Romf —5D 50
Malting Way. Iswth —2D 86
Malton M. SE18 —7C 80
Malton M. W10 —9J 57
Malton Rd. W10 —9J 57
Malton St. SE18 —7C 80
Maltravers St. WC2 —1K 75
Malt Shovel Cotts. Eyns —5H 131
Malt St. SE1 —7E 76
Malva Clo. SW18 —4M 89
Malvern Av. E4 —7B 30
Malvern Av. Bexh —8J 81
Malvern Av. Harr —8J 37
Malvern Clo. SE20 —6E 108
Malvern Clo. W10 —8K 57
Malvern Clo. Bush —8A 10
Malvern Clo. Mitc —7G 107
Malvern Clo. Surb —3J 119
Malvern Ct. SW7 —5B 74
(off Onslow Sq.)
Malvern Ct. W12 —3E 72
(off Hadyn Pk. Rd.)
Malvern Ct. Eps —6B 134
Malvern Ct. Sutt —9L 121
Malvern Dri. Felt —2H 101
Malvern Dri. Ilf —9D 48
Malvern Dri. Wfd G —5G 31
Malvern Gdns. NW2 —7J 41
Malvern Gdns. Harr —2J 39
Malvern Gdns. Lou —8K 19
Malvern Ho. N16 —6D 44
Malvern Ho. Wat —8B 8
Malvern M. NW6 —6L 57
Malvern Pl. NW6 —6K 57
Malvern Rd. E6 —4J 63
Malvern Rd. E8 —3E 60
Malvern Rd. E11 —7C 46
Malvern Rd. N8 —1L 43
Malvern Rd. N17 —1E 44
Malvern Rd. NW6 —6L 57
(in two parts)
Malvern Rd. Enf —1J 17
Malvern Rd. Hamp —4L 101
Malvern Rd. Hay —8C 68
Malvern Rd. Horn —4E 50
Malvern Rd. Orp —6F 128
Malvern Rd. Surb —4J 119
Malvern Rd. T Hth —8L 107
Malvern Ter. N1 —4L 59
Malvern Ter. N9 —1D 28
Malvern Way. W13 —8F 54
Malvern Way. Crox G —7A 8
Malwood Rd. SW12 —5F 90
Malyons Rd. SE13 —5M 93
Malyons Rd. Swan —4D 114
Malyons Ter. SE13 —4M 93
Malyons, The. Shep —1B 116
Managers St. E14 —2A 78
Manatee Pl. Wall —5H 123
Manaton Clo. SE15 —2F 92
Manaton Cres. S'hall —9L 53
Manbey Gro. E15 —2C 62
Manbey Pk. Rd. E15 —2C 62
Manbey Rd. E15 —2C 62
Manbey St. E15 —2C 62
Manbre Rd. W6 —7G 73
Manbrough Av. E6 —6L 63
Manchester Dri. W10 —7J 57
Manchester Gro. E14 —6A 78
Manchester Ho. SE17 —6A 76
Manchester M. W1 —8E 58
(off Manchester St.)
Manchester Rd. E14 —3A 78
Manchester Rd. N15 —4B 44
Manchester Rd. T Hth —7A 108
Manchester Sq. W1 —9E 58
Manchester St. W1 —8E 58
Manchester Way. Dag —9M 49
Manchuria Rd. SW11 —5E 90
Manciple St. SE1 —3B 76
Mandalay Rd. SW4 —4G 91
Mandarin Ct. NW10 —2B 56
(off Mitchellbrook Way)
Mandarin Ct. SE8 —7L 77
(off Edward St.)
Mandarin St. E14 —1L 77
Mandarin Way. Hay —9J 53
Mandela Clo. NW10 —3A 56
Mandela Clo. W12 —1F 72
Mandela Ct. Uxb —8A 142
Mandela Ho. E2 —6D 60
(off Virginia Rd.)
Mandela Ho. SE5 —1M 91
Mandela Pl. Wat —4H 9
Mandela Rd. E16 —9E 62
Mandela St. NW1 —4G 59
Mandela St. SW9 —8L 75
(in two parts)
Mandela Way. SE1 —5C 76
Mandeville Clo. SE3 —8D 78
Mandeville Clo. SW19 —4J 105
Mandeville Clo. Wat —2D 8
Mandeville Ct. E4 —5J 29
Mandeville Dri. Surb —3H 119
Mandeville Ho. SE1 —6D 76
(off Rolls Rd.)
Mandeville Ho. SW4 —4G 91
Mandeville M. SW4 —3H 91
Mandeville Pl. W1 —9E 58
Mandeville Rd. N14 —2F 26
Mandeville Rd. Enf —9D 6
Mandeville Rd. Iswth —1E 86
Mandeville Rd. N'holt —3L 53
Mandeville St. E5 —8J 45
Mandrake Rd. SW17 —9D 90
Mandrake Way. E15 —3C 62
Mandrell Rd. SW2 —4J 91
Manesty Ct. N14 —9H 15
(off Ivy Rd.)
Manette St. W1 —9H 59
Manford Clo. Chig —4E 32
Manford Cross. Chig —5E 32
Manford Ind. Est. Eri —7F 82
Manford Way. Chig —5C 32
Manfred Rd. SW15 —4K 89
Manger Rd. N7 —2J 59
Mangold Way. Eri —4H 81
Manilla St. E14 —3L 77

Margery Pk. Rd.—Mary Flux Ct.

Margery Pk. Rd. E7 —2E 62
Margery Rd. Dag —8H 49
Margery St. WC1 —6L 59
Margherita Pl. Wal A —7M 7
Margherita Rd. Wal A —7M 7
Margin Dri. SW19 —2H 105
Margravine Gdns. W6 —6H 73
Margravine Rd. W6 —6H 73
Marham Gdns. SW18 —7C 90
Marham Gdns. Mord —1A 122
Maria Clo. SE1 —5F 76
Mariam Gdns. Horn —7K 51
Marian Clo. Hay —7H 53
Marian Ct. E9 —1G 61
Marian Ct. Sutt —7M 121
Marian Gdns. Leav —6F 4
Marian Pl. E2 —5F 60
Marian Rd. SW16 —5G 107
Marian Sq. E2 —5F 60
Marian St. E2 —5F 60
Marian Way. NW10 —3D 56
Maria Ter. E1 —8H 61
Maria Theresa Clo. N Mald —9B 104
Maribor. SE10 —8A 78
(off Burney St.)
Maricas Av. Harr —8B 22
Marie Lloyd Gdns. N19 —5J 43
Marie Lloyd Ho. N1 —5B 60
(off Murray Gro.)
Marie Lloyd Wlk. E8 —2D 60
Mariette Way. Wall —1J 137
Marigold All. SE1 —1M 75
(off Up. Ground)
Marigold Clo. S'hall —1J 69
Marigold Rd. N17 —7G 29
Marigold St. SE16 —3F 76
Marigold Way. Croy —3H 125
Marina App. Hay —8J 53
Marina Av. N Mald —9F 104
Marina Clo. Brom —7E 110
Marina Dri. Dart —7L 99
Marina Dri. Well —1C 96
Marina Gdns. Chesh —3C 6
Marina Gdns. Romf —3M 49
Marina Way. Tedd —4H 103
Marine Ct. Eri —8D 82
Marine Dri. SE18 —5K 79
Marinefield Rd. SW6 —1M 89
Marinel Ho. SE5 —8A 76
Mariner Gdns. Rich —9G 87
Mariner Rd. E12 —9L 47
Mariners M. E14 —5B 78
Mariners Wlk. Eri —7D 82
Marine St. SE16 —4E 76
Marine Tower. SE8 —7K 77
(off Abinger Gro.)
Marion Av. Shep —9A 100
Marion Clo. Bush —3K 9
Marion Clo. Ilf —7B 32
Marion Cres. Orp —9E 112
Marion Gro. Wfd G —5C 30
Marion Rd. NW7 —5E 24
Marion Rd. T Hth —9A 108
Marischal Rd. SE13 —2B 94
Maritime Ind. Est. SE7 —5F 78
Maritime Quay. E14 —6L 77
Maritime St. E3 —7K 61
Marius Pas. SW17 —8E 90
Marius Rd. SW17 —8E 90
Marjorams Av. Lou —4K 19
Marjorie Gro. SW11 —3D 90
Marjorie M. E1 —9H 61
Markab Rd. N'wd —5D 20
Mark Av. E4 —8M 17
Mark Clo. Bexh —9J 81
Mark Clo. S'hall —1M 69
Marke Clo. Kes —6J 127
Markeston Grn. Wat —4H 21
Market Cen., The. S'hall —5F 68
Market Chambers. Enf —5B 16
(off Church St.)
Market Ct. W1 —9G 59
(off Market Pl.)
Market Entrance. SW8 —8G 75
Market Est. N7 —2J 59
Market Hill. SE18 —4L 79
Market La. Edgw —8A 24
Market Link. Romf —2C 50
Market Mdw. Orp —8G 113
Market M. W1 —2F 74
Market Pde. E10 —4A 46
(off High Rd. Leyton)
Market Pde. E17 —1K 45
(off Forest Rd.)
Market Pde. N9 —2E 28
(off Winchester Rd.)
Market Pde. Brom —5E 110
(off East St.)
Market Pde. Felt —9J 85
Market Pde. Sidc —1F 112
Market Pavilion. E10 —8L 45
Market Pl. N2 —1C 42
Market Pl. NW11 —2M 41
Market Pl. SE16 —5E 76
(in two parts)
Market Pl. W1 —9G 59
Market Pl. W3 —2A 72
Market Pl. Bexh —3L 97
Market Pl. Bren —8G 71
Market Pl. Dart —6J 99
Market Pl. Enf —5B 16
Market Pl. King T —6H 103
Market Pl. Romf —3C 50
Market Pl. S'hall —2K 69
Market Rd. N7 —2J 59
Market Rd. Rich —2L 87
Market Row. SW9 —3L 91
Market Sq. Felt —8H 85
Market Sq. E14 —9M 61
Market Sq. Brom —6E 110
Market Sq. Uxb —3A 142
Market Sq. Wal A —6J 7
Market Sq., The. N9 —2F 28
(off Plevna Rd.)
Market St. E6 —5K 63
Market St. SE18 —5L 79
Market St. Dart —6J 99
Market St. Wat —6F 8
Market Ter. Bren —7J 71
(off Albany Rd.)
Market, The. Sutt —3A 122
Market Way. E14 —9M 61
Market Way. Wemb —1J 55
Market Yd. M. SE1 —4C 76
(off Bermondsey St.)
Markfield. Croy —2K 139
(in three parts)
Markfield Gdns. E4 —9M 17
Markfield Rd. N15 —2E 44
Markham Clo. Borwd —4K 11
Markham Ho. Dag —8L 49
(off Uvedale Rd.)
Markham Pl. SW3 —6D 74
Markham Sq. SW3 —6D 74
Markham St. SW3 —6C 74
Markhole Clo. Hamp —4K 101
Mark Ho. E2 —5H 61
(off Sewardstone Rd.)
Markhouse Av. E17 —4J 45
Markhouse Pas. E17 —4K 45
(off Markhouse Rd.)
Markhouse Rd. E17 —4K 45
Markland Ho. W10 —1H 73
(off Darfield Way)
Mark La. EC3 —1C 76
Mark Lodge. Cockf —6C 14
(off Edgeworth Rd.)
Markmanor Av. E17 —5J 45
Mark Rd. N22 —8M 27
Marksbury Av. Rich —2L 87
Marks Gate. —8J 33
Marks Lodge. Romf —3B 50
Mark Sq. EC2 —7C 60
Marks Rd. Romf —3A 50
Marks Rd. Warl —9J 139
Markstone Ho. SE1 —3M 75
(off Lancaster St.)
Mark St. E15 —3C 62
Mark St. EC2 —7C 60
Markway. Sun —6G 101
Mark Way. Swan —9E 114
Markwell Clo. SE26 —1F 108
Markyate Rd. Dag —1F 64
Marlands Rd. Ilf —1J 47
Marlborough Av. E8 —4E 60
(in three parts)
Marlborough Av. N14 —3G 27
Marlborough Av. Edgw —3M 23
Marlborough Av. Ruis —4A 36
Marlborough Clo. N20 —3D 26
Marlborough Clo. SE17 —5A 76
Marlborough Clo. SW19 —3C 106
Marlborough Clo. Orp —1D 128
Marlborough Clo. W on T —5H 117
Marlborough Ct. W1 —1G 75
(off Kingly St.)
Marlborough Ct. W8 —5L 73
(off Pembroke Rd.)
Marlborough Ct. Buck H —2G 31
Marlborough Ct. Enf —7C 16
Marlborough Ct. Harr —2B 38
Marlborough Ct. N'wd —7D 20
Marlborough Ct. S Croy —6C 124
(off Birdhurst Rd.)
Marlborough Ct. Wall —9G 123
Marlborough Cres. W4 —4B 72
Marlborough Dri. Ilf —1J 47
Marlborough Dri. Wey —5A 116
Marlborough Flats. SW3 —5C 74
(off Walton St.)
Marlborough Gdns. N20 —3D 26
Marlborough Gdns. Surb —2H 119
Marlborough Gro. SE1 —6E 76
Marlborough Hill. NW8 —5A 58
Marlborough Hill. Harr —2B 38
Marlborough House. —2G 75
Marlborough Ho. NW1 —7F 58
(off Osnaburgh St.)
Marlborough La. SE7 —7G 79
Marlborough Mans. NW6 —1M 57
(off Canon Hill)
Marlborough M. SW2 —3K 91
Marlborough Pde. Uxb —7F 142
Marlborough Pk. Av. Sidc —6E 96
Marlborough Pl. NW8 —5A 58
Marlborough Rd. E4 —6M 29
Marlborough Rd. E7 —3G 63
Marlborough Rd. E15 —9C 46
Marlborough Rd. E18 —9E 30
Marlborough Rd. N9 —1D 28
Marlborough Rd. N19 —7H 43
(in two parts)
Marlborough Rd. N22 —7J 27
Marlborough Rd. SW1 —2G 75
Marlborough Rd. SW19 —3C 106
Marlborough Rd. W4 —6A 72
Marlborough Rd. W5 —3H 71
Marlborough Rd. Bexh —2H 97
Marlborough Rd. Brom —8G 111
Marlborough Rd. Dag —9F 48
Marlborough Rd. Dart —5G 99
Marlborough Rd. Felt —8H 85
Marlborough Rd. Hamp —3L 101
Marlborough Rd. Iswth —9F 70
Marlborough Rd. Rich —5K 87
Marlborough Rd. Romf —2L 49
Marlborough Rd. S'hall —4G 69
Marlborough Rd. S Croy —9A 124
Marlborough Rd. Sutt —5L 121
Marlborough Rd. Uxb —7F 142
Marlborough Rd. Wat —6F 8
Marlborough St. SW3 —5C 74
Marlborough Yd. N19 —7H 43
Marlbury. NW8 —4M 57
(off Abbey Rd.)
Marld, The. Asht —9K 133
Marle Gdns. Wal A —5J 7
Marler Ho. Eri —1D 98
Marler Rd. SE23 —7J 93
Marlescroft Way. Lou —7M 19
Marley Av. Bexh —7H 81
Marley Clo. N15 —2M 43
Marley Clo. Gnfd —6L 53
Marley Ho. W11 —1H 73
(off St Ann's Rd.)
Marley Wlk. NW2 —1G 57
Marlin Clo. Sun —3C 100
Marlingdene Clo. Hamp —3L 101
Marlings Clo. Chst —8C 112
Marlings Clo. Whyt —9C 138
Marlings Pk. Av. Chst —8C 112
Marlin Ho. Wat —8B 8
Marlins Clo. Sutt —7A 122
Marlins Mdw. Wat —8B 8
Marlin Sq. Ab L —4D 4
Marlins, The. N'wd —5D 20
Marloes Clo. Wemb —9H 39
Marloes Rd. W8 —4M 73
Marlow Av. Purf —5L 83
Marlow Clo. SE20 —7F 108
Marlow Ct. N14 —9G 15
Marlow Ct. NW6 —3H 57
Marlow Ct. NW9 —1D 40
Marlow Ct. W2 —9M 57
Marlow Cres. Twic —5D 86
Marlow Dri. Sutt —4H 121
Marlowe Bus. Cen. SE14 —8J 77
(off Batavia Rd.)
Marlowe Clo. Chst —3B 112
Marlowe Clo. Ilf —8A 32
Marlowe Ct. SW3 —5C 74
Marlowe Gdns. SE9 —5L 95
Marlowe Gdns. Romf —8G 35
Marlowe Ho. SE8 —6K 77
(off Bowditch)
Marlowe Ho. King T —8H 103
(off Portsmouth Rd.)
Marlowe Rd. E17 —2A 46
Marlowe Sq. Mitc —8G 107
Marlowes, The. NW8 —4B 58
Marlowes, The. Dart —3B 98
Marlowe Way. Croy —4J 123
Marlow Gdns. Hay —4B 68
Marlow Ho. E2 —6D 60
(off Calvert Av.)
Marlow Ho. SE1 —4D 76
(off Maltby St.)
Marlow Ho. Surb —9J 103
(off Cranes Pk.)
Marlow Ho. Tedd —1E 102
Marlow Rd. E6 —6K 63
Marlow Rd. SE20 —7F 108
Marlow Rd. S'hall —4K 69
Marlow Way. SE16 —3H 77
Marlpit Av. Coul —9J 137
Marlpit La. Coul —8H 137
Marl Rd. SW18 —3A 90
Marlton St. SE10 —6D 78
Marlwood Clo. Sidc —8C 96
Marlyon Rd. Ilf —5F 32
Marmadon Rd. SE18 —5D 80
Marmion App. E4 —4L 29
Marmion Av. E4 —4K 29
Marmion Clo. E4 —4K 29
Marmion M. SW11 —2E 90
Marmion Rd. SW11 —3E 90
Marmont Rd. SE15 —9E 76
Marmora Ho. E1 —8J 61
(off Ben Jonson Rd.)
Marmora Rd. SE22 —5G 93
Marmot Rd. Houn —2H 85
Marne Av. N11 —4F 26
Marne Av. Well —2E 96
Marnell Way. Houn —2H 85
Marne St. W10 —6J 57
Marney Rd. SW11 —3E 90
Marneys Clo. Eps —7L 133
Marnfield Cres. SW2 —7L 91
Marnham Av. NW2 —9J 41
Marnham Ct. Wemb —1G 55
Marnham Cres. Gnfd —6M 53
Marnock Ho. SE17 —6B 76
(off Brandon St.)
Marnock Rd. SE4 —4K 93
Maroon Ho. E14 —8J 61
Maroon St. E14 —8J 61
Maroons Way. SE6 —1L 109
Marqueen Towers. SW16 —4J 107
Marquess Rd. N1 —2B 60
Marquess Rd. N. N1 —2A 60
Marquess Rd. S. N1 —2A 60
Marquis Clo. Wemb —3K 55
Marquis Ct. N4 —6K 43
(off Marquis Rd.)
Marquis Ct. Bark —1C 64
Marquis Ct. King T —8H 103
(off Anglesea Rd.)
Marquis Rd. N4 —6K 43
Marquis Rd. N22 —6K 27
Marquis Rd. NW1 —2H 59
Marrabon Clo. Sidc —7E 96
Marrick Clo. SW15 —3E 88
Marrick Ho. NW6 —4M 57
(off Mortimer Cres.)
Marriett Ho. SE6 —1A 110
Marrilyne Av. Enf —2K 17
Marriner Ct. Hay —1C 68
(off Barra Hall Rd.)
Marriott Clo. Felt —5B 84
Marriott Rd. E15 —4C 62
Marriott Rd. N4 —6K 43
Marriott Rd. N10 —8D 26
Marriott Rd. Barn —5H 13
Marriott Rd. Dart —6K 99
Marriotts Clo. NW9 —4D 40
Marrowells. Wey —5D 116
Marryat Ho. SW1 —6G 75
(off Churchill Gdns.)
Marryat Pl. SW19 —1J 105
Marryat Rd. SW19 —2H 105
Marryat Rd. Enf —8B 6
Marryat Sq. SW6 —9J 73
Marsala Rd. SE13 —3M 93
Marsden Rd. N9 —2F 28
Marsden Rd. SE15 —2D 92
Marsden St. NW5 —2E 58
(in two parts)
Marsden Way. Orp —5D 128
Marshall Clo. SW18 —5A 90
Marshall Clo. Harr —5B 38
Marshall Clo. Houn —4K 85
Marshall Clo. S Croy —5E 138
Marshall Dri. Hay —8D 52
Marshall Est. NW7 —4E 24
Marshall Ho. N1 —5B 60
(off Cranston Est.)
Marshall Ho. NW6 —5K 57
(off Albert Rd.)
Marshall Ho. SE1 —4C 76
(off Page's Wlk.)
Marshall Ho. SE17 —6B 76
Marshall Path. SE28 —1F 80
Marshall Rd. N17 —8B 28
Marshalls Clo. N11 —4F 26
Marshalls Clo. Eps —5A 134
Marshalls Dri. Romf —1C 50
Marshalls Gro. SE18 —5J 79
Marshall's Pl. SE16 —4D 76
Marshalls Rd. Romf —2B 50
Marshall's Rd. Sutt —6M 121
Marshall St. W1 —9G 59
Marshall Way. E10 —8M 45
Marshalsea Rd. SE1 —3A 76
Marsham Clo. Chst —2M 111
Marsham Ct. SW1 —5H 75
(off Marsham St.)
Marsham Ho. Eri —3H 81
Marsham St. SW1 —4H 75
Marsh Av. Eps —2C 134
Marsh Av. Mitc —6D 106
Marshbrook Clo. SE3 —2H 95
Marsh Cen., The. E1 —9D 60
(off Whitechapel High St.)
Marsh Clo. NW7 —3D 24
Marsh Clo. Wal X —6E 6
Marsh Ct. E8 —3D 60
(off St Philip's Rd.)
Marshcroft Dri. Chesh —3E 6
Marsh Dri. NW9 —4D 40
Marsh Farm Rd. Twic —7D 86
Marshfield St. E14 —4A 78
Marsh Ga. Bus. Cen. E15 —4A 62
Marshgate La. E15 —3M 61
Marshgate Path. SE28 —4A 80
Marshgate Trad. Est. E15 —3M 61
Marsh Grn. Rd. Dag —4L 65
Marsh Hall. Wemb —8K 39
Marsh Hill. E9 —1J 61
Marsh Hill. Wal A —1L 7
Marsh Ho. SW1 —6H 75
(off Aylesford St.)
Marsh Ho. SW8 —9G 75
Marsh La. E10 —7K 45
Marsh La. N17 —8F 28
Marsh La. NW7 —3C 24
Marsh La. Stan —5G 23
Marsh Rd. Pinn —2J 37
Marsh Rd. Wemb —6H 55
Marshside Clo. N9 —1G 29
Marsh St. E14 —5M 77
Marsh St. Dart —1L 99
(in two parts)
Marsh Wall. E14 —2L 77
Marsh Way. Rain —6B 66
(in two parts)
Marshwood Ho. NW6 —4L 57
(off Kilburn Va.)
Marsland Clo. SE17 —6M 75
Marsom Ho. N1 —5B 60
(off Provost Est.)
Marston. Eps —3A 134
Marston Av. Chess —8J 119
Marston Av. Dag —7L 49
Marston Clo. NW6 —3A 58
Marston Clo. Dag —8L 49
Marston Ct. W on T —3G 117
Marston Dri. Warl —9J 139
Marston Ho. SW9 —1L 91
Marston Rd. Ilf —8J 31
Marston Rd. Tedd —2F 102
Marston Way. SE19 —4M 107
Marsworth Av. Pinn —8H 21
Marsworth Clo. Hay —8J 53
Marsworth Clo. Wat —9C 8
Marsworth Ho. E2 —4E 60
(off Whiston Rd.)
Martaban Rd. N16 —7D 44
Martello St. E8 —3F 60
Martello Ter. E8 —3F 60
Martell Rd. SE21 —9B 92
Martel Pl. E8 —2D 60
Marten Rd. E17 —9L 29
Martens Av. Bexh —3M 97
Martens Clo. Bexh —3A 98
Martha Ct. E2 —5F 60
Martham Clo. SE28 —1H 81
Martha Rd. E15 —2C 62
Martha St. E1 —9G 61
Marthorne Cres. Harr —9B 22
Martina Ter. Chig —5C 32
Martin Bowes Rd. SE9 —2K 95
Martinbridge Trad. Est. Enf —7E 16
Martin Clo. N9 —1H 29
Martin Clo. S Croy —3H 139
Martin Clo. Uxb —5C 142
Martin Clo. Warl —8F 138
Martin Ct. E14 —3A 78
(off River Barge Clo.)
Martin Ct. S Croy —7B 124
(off Birdhurst Rd.)
Martin Cres. Croy —3L 123
Martindale. SW14 —4A 88
Martindale Av. E16 —1E 78
Martindale Av. Orp —7E 128
Martindale Ho. E14 —1M 77
(off Poplar High St.)
Martin Dale Ind. Est. Enf —5F 16
Martindale Rd. SW12 —6F 90
Martindale Rd. Houn —2J 85
Martin Dene. Bexh —4K 97
Martin Dri. Enf —1L 17
Martin Dri. N'holt —1K 53
Martin Dri. Rain —7F 66
Martin Dri. Stne —6M 99
Martineau Clo. Esh —6B 118
Martineau Est. E1 —1G 77
Martineau Ho. SW1 —6G 75
(off Churchill Gdns.)
Martineau M. N5 —9M 43
Martineau Rd. N5 —9M 43
Martingale Clo. Sun —8E 100
Martingales Clo. Rich —9H 87
Martin Gdns. Dag —9G 49
Martin Gro. Mord —7L 105
Martin Ho. SE1 —4A 76
Martin Ho. SW8 —8J 75
(off Wyvil Rd.)
Martin La. EC4 —1B 76
(in two parts)
Martin Ri. Bexh —4K 97
Martin Rd. Dag —9G 49
Martin Rd. Dart —9G 99
Martins Clo. Orp —7H 113
Martins Clo. W W'ck —3B 126
Martins Dri. Chesh —1E 6
Martinsfield Clo. Chig —4C 32
Martins Mt. New Bar —6L 13
Martin's Rd. Brom —6C 110
Martins, The. Wemb —8K 39
Martinstown Clo. Horn —4L 51
Martin St. SE28 —2C 80
Martins Wlk. N10 —8E 26
Martins Wlk. Borwd —6L 11
Martin Way. SW20 & Mord —6H 105
Martlesham. N17 —9C 28
(off Adams Rd.)
Martlesham Clo. Horn —1G 67
Martlet Gro. N'holt —6H 53
Martlett Ct. WC2 —9J 59
Martley Dri. Ilf —3M 47
Martock Clo. Harr —2E 38
Martock Gdns. N11 —5D 26
Marton Clo. SE6 —9L 93
Marton Rd. N16 —7C 44
Martynside. NW9 —8D 24
Martys Yd. NW3 —9B 42
Marvell Av. Hay —8E 52
Marvell Ho. SE5 —8B 76
(off Camberwell Rd.)
Marvels Clo. SE12 —8F 94
Marvels La. SE12 —8F 94
Marville Rd. SW6 —8K 73
Marvin St. E8 —2F 60
Marwell Clo. Romf —3E 50
Marwell Clo. W W'ck —4D 126
Marwood Clo. Well —2F 96
Mary Adelaide Clo. SW15 —1C 104
Mary Ann Gdns. SE8 —7L 77
Maryatt Av. Harr —7M 37
Mary Bank. SE18 —5K 79
Mary Clo. Stan —2K 39
Mary Datchelor Clo. SE5 —9B 76
Maryfield Clo. Bex —9C 98
Mary Flux Ct. SW5 —6M 73
(off Bramham Gdns.)

Meadow Clo.—Merlin Gro.

Meadow Clo. Ruis —4D 36
Meadow Clo. Sutt —4A 122
Meadow Clo. W on T —6K 117
Meadow Ct. N1 —5C 60
Meadow Ct. Eps —5A 134
Meadow Ct. Houn —5M 85
Meadowcourt Rd. SE3 —3D 94
Meadowcroft. W4 —6L 71
(off Brooks Rd.)
Meadowcroft. Brom —7K 111
Meadowcroft. Bush —8M 9
(off High St.)
Meadowcroft Clo. N13 —2L 27
Meadowcroft Rd. N13 —2L 27
Meadowcross. Wal A —7L 7
Meadow Dri. N10 —1F 42
Meadow Dri. NW4 —9G 25
Meadow Gdns. Edgw —6M 23
Meadow Gth. NW10 —2A 56
Meadow Hill. Coul —6G 137
Meadow Hill. N Mald —1C 120
Meadowlands. Horn —5J 51
Meadow La. SE12 —9F 94
Meadowlea Clo. Harm —7H 143
Meadow M. SW8 —7K 75
Meadow Pl. SW8 —8J 75
Meadow Pl. W4 —8C 72
Meadow Ri. Coul —5H 137
Meadow Rd. SW8 —8K 75
Meadow Rd. SW19 —4A 106
Meadow Rd. Ashf —2B 100
Meadow Rd. Asht —9J 133
Meadow Rd. Bark —3D 64
Meadow Rd. Borwd —4M 11
Meadow Rd. Brom —6C 110
Meadow Rd. Bush —7M 9
Meadow Rd. Clay —8C 118
Meadow Rd. Dag —2K 65
Meadow Rd. Felt —8J 85
Meadow Rd. Lou —7J 19
Meadow Rd. Pinn —2H 37
Meadow Rd. Romf —6A 50
Meadow Rd. S'hall —1K 69
Meadow Rd. Sutt —6C 122
Meadow Rd. Wat —7E 4
Meadow Row. SE1 —4A 76
Meadows Clo. E10 —7L 45
Meadows Ct. Sidc —3F 112
Meadows End. Sun —5E 100
Meadowside. SE9 —3G 95
Meadowside. Dart —7H 99
Meadowside. Twic —6H 87
Meadowside. W on T —4G 117
Meadowside Rd. Sutt —1J 135
Meadowside Rd. Upm —1M 67
Meadows Leigh Clo. Wey —5A 116
Meadows, The. Orp —8G 129
Meadows, The. Warl —9H 139
Meadow Stile. Croy —5A 124
Meadowsweet Clo. E16 —8H 63
Meadowsweet Clo. SW20 —8G 105
Meadow, The. N10 —1F 42
Meadow, The. Chst —3A 112
Meadow Vw. Cow —8A 142
(in three parts)
Meadow Vw. Harr —6C 38
Meadow Vw. Orp —7G 113
Meadow Vw. Sidc —6F 96
Meadowview Rd. SE6 —2K 109
Meadowview Rd. Bex —5J 97
Meadowview Rd. Eps —1C 134
Meadow Vw. Rd. Hay —7B 52
Meadow Vw. Rd. T Hth —9M 107
Meadow Wlk. E18 —2E 46
Meadow Wlk. Dag —2K 65
Meadow Wlk. Dart —1G 115
(in two parts)
Meadow Wlk. Eps —8C 120
(in two parts)
Meadow Wlk. Wall —5F 122
Meadow Way. NW9 —3B 40
Meadow Way. Bedm —1D 4
Meadow Way. Chess —7J 119
Meadow Way. Chig —3A 32
Meadow Way. Dart —6M 99
Meadow Way. Orp —5L 127
Meadow Way. Ruis —4F 36
Meadow Way. Tad —9J 135
Meadow Way. Upm —8M 51
Meadow Way. Wemb —9H 39
Meadow Waye. Houn —7J 69
Meadow Way, The. Harr —8C 22
Mead Path. SW17 —1A 106
Mead Pl. E9 —2G 61
Mead Pl. Croy —3A 124
Mead Plat. NW10 —2A 56
Mead Rd. Chst —3A 112
Mead Rd. Dart —7H 99
Mead Rd. Edgw —6L 23
Mead Rd. Rich —9G 87
Mead Rd. Uxb —3B 142
Mead Rd. W on T —6J 117
Mead Row. SE1 —4L 75
Meads Ct. E15 —2D 62
Meadside Clo. Beck —5J 109
Meads La. Ilf —5C 48
Meads Rd. N22 —9M 27
Meads Rd. Enf —3J 17
Meads, The. Brick W —2K 5
Meads, The. Edgw —6B 24
Meads, The. Mord —9C 106
Meads, The. Sutt —5J 121
Meads, The. Uxb —7C 142
Mead Ter. Wemb —9H 39
Mead, The. N2 —9A 26
Mead, The. W13 —8F 54
Mead, The. Beck —5A 110
Mead, The. Chesh —2C 6
Mead, The. Wall —8H 123
Mead, The. Wat —3J 21
Mead, The. W W'ck —3B 126
Meadvale Rd. W5 —7F 54
Meadvale Rd. Croy —2D 124
Meadway. N14 —2H 27
Meadway. NW11 —4L 41
Mead Way. SW20 —8G 105
Meadway. Ashf —9E 144
Meadway. Barn & New Bar —6L 13
Meadway. Beck —5A 110
Mead Way. Brom —1D 126
Mead Way. Bush —4J 9
Mead Way. Coul —9J 137
Mead Way. Croy —4J 125
Meadway. Enf —9C 6
Meadway. Eps —4A 134
Meadway. Esh —9M 117 & 1A 132
Meadway. Ilf —9C 48
Meadway. Oxs —6C 132
Meadway. Romf —9E 34
Mead Way. Ruis —4B 36
Meadway. Surb —3A 120
Meadway. Twic —7B 86
Meadway. Warl —8G 139
Mead Way. Wfd G —5G 31
Meadway Clo. NW11 —4M 41
Meadway Clo. Barn —6L 13
Meadway Clo. Pinn —6M 21
Meadway Ct. NW11 —4M 41
Meadway Ct. W5 —7K 55
Meadway Ct. Dag —7K 49
Meadway Ct. Tedd —2G 103
Meadway Gdns. Ruis —4B 36
Meadway Ga. NW11 —4L 41
Meadway, The. SE3 —1B 94
Meadway, The. Buck H —1H 31
Meadway, The. Lou —8K 19
Meadway, The. Orp —8F 128
Meaford Way. SE20 —4F 108
Meakin Est. SE1 —4C 76
Meanley Rd. E12 —9J 47
Meard St. W1 —9H 59
(in two parts)
Meath Clo. Orp —9F 112
Meath Rd. E15 —5D 62
Meath Rd. Ilf —8A 48
Meath St. SW11 —9F 74
Mechanic's Path. SE8 —8L 77
Mecklenburgh Pl. WC1 —7K 59
Mecklenburgh Sq. WC1 —7K 59
Mecklenburgh St. WC1 —7K 59
Medburn St. NW1 —5H 59
Medcalf Rd. Enf —1K 17
Medcroft Gdns. SW14 —3A 88
Medebourne Clo. SE3 —2E 94
Mede Ho. Brom —2F 110
(off Pike Clo.)
Medesenge Way. N13 —6M 27
Medfield St. SW15 —6E 88
Medhurst Clo. E3 —5J 61
Median Rd. E5 —1G 61
Medina Av. Esh —5C 118
Medina Gro. N7 —8L 43
Medina Ho. Eri —8C 82
Medina Rd. N7 —8L 43
Medina Sq. Eps —1L 133
Medland Clo. Wall —3E 122
Medland Ho. E14 —1J 77
Medlar Clo. N'holt —5H 53
Medlar Ho. Sidc —9E 96
Medlar St. SE5 —9A 76
Medley Rd. NW6 —2L 57
Medman Clo. Uxb —5A 142
Medmenham. Cars —3B 136
(off Pine Cres.)
Medora Rd. SW2 —6K 91
Medora Rd. Romf —2B 50
Medusa Rd. SE6 —5M 93
Medway Bldgs. E3 —5J 61
(off Medway Rd.)
Medway Clo. Croy —1G 125
Medway Clo. Ilf —1A 64
Medway Clo. Wat —7G 5
Medway Ct. WC1 —6J 59
(off Judd St.)
Medway Dri. Gnfd —5D 54
Medway Gdns. Wemb —9E 38
Medway Ho. NW8 —7C 58
(off Penfold St.)
Medway Ho. SE1 —3B 76
(off Hankey Pl.)
Medway Ho. King T —5H 103
Medway M. E3 —5J 61
Medway Pde. Gnfd —5D 54
Medway Rd. E3 —5J 61
Medway Rd. Dart —2E 98
Medway St. SW1 —4H 75
Medwin St. SW4 —3K 91
Meek Rd. SW10 —8A 74
Meerbrook Rd. SE3 —2G 95
Meeson Rd. E15 —3D 62
Meeson St. E5 —9J 45
Meeting All. Wat —6G 9
Meeting Fld. Path. E9 —2G 61
Meetinghouse All. E1 —2F 76
Meeting Ho. La. SE15 —9F 76
Mehetabel Rd. E9 —1G 61
Meister Clo. Ilf —6B 48
Melancholy Wlk. Rich —8G 87
Melanda Clo. Chst —2K 111
Melanie Clo. Bexh —9J 81
Melba Way. SE13 —9M 77
Melbourne Av. N13 —6K 27
Melbourne Av. W13 —2E 70
Melbourne Av. Pinn —1M 37
Melbourne Clo. SE20 —4E 108
Melbourne Clo. Orp —2C 128
Melbourne Clo. Wall —7G 123
Melbourne Ct. N10 —7F 26
Melbourne Ct. W9 —7A 58
(off Clifton Rd.)
Melbourne Gdns. Romf —3J 49
Melbourne Gro. SE22 —3C 92
Melbourne Ho. W8 —2L 73
(off Kensington Pl.)
Melbourne Ho. Hay —7G 53
Melbourne Mans. W14 —7J 73
(off Musard Rd.)
Melbourne M. SE6 —6A 94
Melbourne M. SW9 —9L 75
Melbourne Pl. WC2 —9K 59
Melbourne Rd. E6 —5K 63
Melbourne Rd. E10 —5M 45
Melbourne Rd. E17 —2J 45
Melbourne Rd. SW19 —5L 105
Melbourne Rd. Bush —7M 9
Melbourne Rd. Ilf —6M 47
Melbourne Rd. Tedd —3G 103
Melbourne Rd. Wall —7F 122
Melbourne Sq. SW9 —9L 75
Melbourne Way. Enf —8D 16
Melbray M. SW6 —1K 89
Melbreak Ho. SE22 —2C 92
Melbury Av. S'hall —4M 69
Melbury Clo. Chst —3J 111
Melbury Clo. Clay —8F 118
Melbury Ct. W8 —4K 73
Melbury Dri. SE5 —8C 76
Melbury Gdns. SW20 —5F 104
Melbury Ho. SW8 —8K 75
(off Richborne Ter.)
Melbury Rd. W14 —4K 73
Melbury Rd. Harr —3K 39
Melbury Ter. NW1 —7C 58
Melchester. W11 —9K 57
(off Ledbury Rd.)
Melchester Ho. N19 —8H 43
(off Wedmore St.)
Melcombe Ct. NW1 —8D 58
(off Melcombe Pl.)
Melcombe Gdns. Harr —4K 39
Melcombe Ho. SW8 —8K 75
(off Dorset Rd.)
Melcombe Pl. NW1 —8D 58
Melcombe Regis Ct. W1 —8E 58
(off Weymouth St.)
Melcombe St. NW1 —7D 58
Meldex Clo. NW7 —6G 25
(off Prince of Wales Clo.)
Meldon Clo. SW6 —9M 73
Meldone Clo. Surb —2M 119
Meldrum Clo. Orp —1G 129
Meldrum Rd. Ilf —7E 48
Melfield Gdns. SE6 —1A 110
Melford Av. Bark —2C 64
Melford Clo. Chess —7K 119
Melford Ct. SE1 —4C 76
(off Fendall St.)
Melford Ct. SE22 —7E 92
Melford Pas. SE22 —6E 92
Melford Rd. E6 —7K 63
Melford Rd. E11 —7C 46
Melford Rd. E17 —2J 45
Melford Rd. SE22 —6E 92
Melford Rd. Ilf —7B 48
Melfort Av. T Hth —7M 107
Melfort Rd. T Hth —7M 107
Melgund Rd. N5 —1L 59
Melina Clo. Hay —8B 52
Melina Ct. SW15 —2E 88
Melina Pl. NW8 —6B 58
Melina Rd. W12 —3F 72
Melior Ct. N6 —4G 43
Melior Pl. SE1 —3C 76
Melior St. SE1 —3C 76
Meliot Rd. SE6 —8B 94
Melksham Clo. Romf —7K 35
Melksham Dri. Romf —7K 35
Melksham Gdns. Romf —7J 35
Melksham Grn. Romf —7K 35
Meller Clo. Croy —5J 123
Melling Dri. Enf —3E 16
Melling St. SE18 —7C 80
Mellish Clo. Bark —4D 64
Mellish Flats. E10 —5L 45
Mellish Gdns. Wfd G —5E 30
Mellish Ho. E1 —9F 60
(off Varden St.)
Mellish Ind. Est. SE18 —4H 79
Mellish St. E14 —4L 77
Mellish Way. Horn —3G 51
Mellison Rd. SW17 —2C 106
Mellitus St. W12 —8D 56
Mellor Clo. W on T —2H 117
Mellow Clo. Bans —6A 136
Mellow La. E. Hay —7A 52
Mellow La. W. Uxb —6A 52
Mellows Rd. Ilf —1K 47
Mellows Rd. Wall —7H 123
Mells Cres. SE9 —1K 111
Mell St. SE10 —6C 78
Melody La. N5 —1A 60
Melody Rd. SW18 —4A 90
Melody Rd. Big H —9G 141
Melon Pl. W8 —3L 73
Melon Rd. E11 —8C 46
Melon Rd. SE15 —9E 76
Melrose Av. N22 —8M 27
Melrose Av. NW2 —1F 56
Melrose Av. SW16 —7K 107
Melrose Av. SW19 —8K 89
Melrose Av. Borwd —7M 11
Melrose Av. Gnfd —5M 53
Melrose Av. Mitc —4F 106
Melrose Av. Twic —6M 85
Melrose Clo. SE12 —7E 94
Melrose Clo. Gnfd —5M 53
Melrose Clo. Hay —8E 52
Melrose Ct. Chesh —2D 6
Melrose Cres. Orp —6B 128
Melrose Dri. S'hall —2L 69
Melrose Gdns. W6 —4G 73
Melrose Gdns. Edgw —1M 39
Melrose Gdns. N Mald —7B 104
Melrose Gdns. W on T —7G 117
Melrose Ho. E14 —4M 77
(off Lanark Sq.)
Melrose Ho. NW6 —6L 57
(off Carlton Va.)
Melrose Pl. Wat —2D 8
Melrose Rd. SW13 —1D 88
Melrose Rd. SW18 —5K 89
Melrose Rd. SW19 —6L 105
Melrose Rd. W3 —4A 72
Melrose Rd. Big H —8G 141
Melrose Rd. Coul —7F 136
Melrose Rd. Pinn —2K 37
Melrose Ter. W6 —4G 73
Melrose Tudor. Wall —7J 123
(off Plough La.)
Melsa Rd. Mord —1A 122
Melstock Av. Upm —9M 51
Melthorne Dri. Ruis —8G 37
Melthorpe Gdns. SE3 —9J 79
Melton Clo. Ruis —6G 37
Melton Ct. SW7 —5B 74
Melton Ct. Sutt —9A 122
Melton Fields. Eps —1B 134
Melton Gdns. Romf —5D 50
Melton Pl. Eps —1B 134
Melton St. NW1 —6G 59
Melville Av. SW20 —4E 104
Melville Av. Gnfd —1D 54
Melville Av. S Croy —7D 124
Melville Clo. Uxb —7B 36
Melville Ct. SE8 —5J 77
Melville Ct. W12 —4F 72
(off Goldhawk Rd.)
Melville Ct. H Hill —7J 35
Melville Ct. N'wd —6B 20
Melville Gdns. N13 —5M 27
Melville Ho. SE10 —9A 78
Melville Ho. New Bar —7B 14
Melville Pl. N1 —3A 60
Melville Rd. E17 —1K 45
Melville Rd. NW10 —3B 56
Melville Rd. SW13 —9E 72
Melville Rd. Rain —7E 66
Melville Rd. Romf —7M 33
Melville Rd. Sidc —8G 97
Melville Vs. Rd. W3 —2A 72
Melvin Rd. SE20 —5G 109
Melwood Ho. E1 —9F 60
(off Watney Mkt.)
Melyn Clo. N7 —9G 43
Memel Ct. EC1 —7A 60
(off Memel St.)
Memel St. EC1 —7A 60
Memess Path. SE18 —7L 79
Memorial Av. E15 —6C 62
Memorial Clo. Houn —7K 69
Mendham Ho. SE1 —4C 76
(off Cluny Pl.)
Mendip Clo. SE26 —1G 109
Mendip Clo. SW19 —8J 89
Mendip Clo. Hay —8B 68
Mendip Clo. Wor Pk —3G 121
Mendip Ct. SE14 —7G 77
(off Avonley Rd.)
Mendip Ct. SW18 —2A 90
Mendip Dri. NW2 —7J 41
Mendip Houses. E2 —6G 61
(off Welwyn St.)
Mendip Rd. SW11 —2A 90
Mendip Rd. Bexh —9C 82
Mendip Rd. Bush —8A 10
Mendip Rd. Horn —5E 50
Mendip Rd. Ilf —3C 48
Mendora Rd. SW6 —8J 73
Mendoza Clo. Horn —3J 51
Menelik Rd. NW2 —9J 41
Menlo Gdns. SE19 —4B 108
Menlo Lodge. N13 —3K 27
(off Crothall Clo.)
Menotti St. E2 —7E 60
Menteath Ho. E14 —9L 61
(off Dod St.)
Menthone Pl. Horn —5H 51
Mentmore Clo. Harr —4G 39
Mentmore Ter. E8 —3F 60
Meon Ct. Iswth —1C 86
Meon Rd. W3 —3A 72
Meopham Rd. Mitc —5G 107
Mepham Cres. Harr —7A 22
Mepham Gdns. Harr —7A 22
Mepham St. SE1 —2L 75
Mera Dri. Bexh —3L 97
Merantun Way. SW19 —5M 105
Merbury Clo. SE13 —4B 94
Merbury Rd. SE28 —3C 80
Mercator Pl. E14 —6L 77
Mercator Rd. SE13 —3B 94
Mercer Clo. Th Dit —2E 118
Mercer Ho. SW1 —6F 74
(off Ebury Bri. Rd.)
Merceron Houses. E2 —6G 61
(off Globe Rd.)
Merceron St. E1 —7F 60
Mercer Pl. Pinn —9G 21
Mercers Clo. SE10 —5D 78
Mercer's Cotts. E1 —9J 61
(off White Horse Rd.)
Mercers Pl. W6 —5H 73
Mercers Rd. N19 —8H 43
(in two parts)
Mercer St. WC2 —9J 59
Mercer Wlk. Uxb —3A 142
Merchant Ind. Ter. NW10 —7A 56
Merchants Lodge. E17 —2L 45
(off Westbury Rd.)
Merchant St. E3 —6K 61
Merchiston Rd. SE6 —8B 94
Merchland Rd. SE9 —7A 96
Mercia Gro. SE13 —3A 94
Mercia Ho. SE5 —1A 92
(off Denmark Rd.)
Mercier Rd. SW15 —4J 89
Mercury. NW9 —8D 24
(off Concourse, The)
Mercury Cen. Felt —4E 84
Mercury Ct. E14 —5L 77
(off Homer Dri.)
Mercury Gdns. Romf —2C 50
Mercury Ho. Bren —7G 71
(off Glenhurst Rd.)
Mercury Rd. Bren —7G 71
Mercury Way. SE14 —7H 77
Mercy Ter. SE13 —4M 93
Merebank La. Croy —7K 123
Mere Clo. SW15 —6H 89
Mere Clo. Orp —4L 127
Meredith Av. NW2 —1G 57
Meredith Clo. Pinn —7H 21
Meredith Ho. N16 —1C 60
Meredith M. SE4 —3K 93
Meredith St. E13 —6E 62
Meredith St. EC1 —6M 59
Meredyth Rd. SW13 —1E 88
Mere End. Croy —2H 125
Mere Rd. Shep —1A 116
Mere Rd. Wey —5B 116
Mere Side. Orp —4L 127
Meretone Clo. SE4 —3J 93
Merevale Cres. Mord —1A 122
Mereway Rd. Twic —7B 86
Merewood Clo. Brom —6L 111
Merewood Rd. Bexh —1A 98
Mereworth Clo. Brom —9D 110
Mereworth Dri. SE18 —8M 79
Mereworth Ho. SE15 —7G 77
Merganser Ct. SE8 —7K 77
(off Edward St.)
Merganser Gdns. SE28 —4B 80
Meriden. —9J 5
Meriden Clo. Brom —4H 111
Meriden Clo. Ilf —8A 32
Meriden Ct. SW3 —6C 74
(off Chelsea Mnr. St.)
Meriden Way. Wat —9J 5
Meridian Ga. E14 —3A 78
Meridian Ho. SE10 —5C 78
(off Azof St.)
Meridian Ho. SE10 —8A 78
(off Royal Hill)
Meridian Pl. E14 —3A 78
Meridian Rd. SE7 —8H 79
Meridian Sq. E15 —3B 62
Meridian Trad. Est. SE7 —5F 78
Meridian Wlk. N17 —6C 28
Meridian Way. N18 & N9 —5G 29
Merifield Rd. SE9 —3G 95
Merino Clo. E11 —2G 47
Merino Pl. Sidc —5E 96
Merioneth Ct. W7 —8D 54
(off Copley Clo.)
Merivale Rd. SW15 —3J 89
Merivale Rd. Harr —5A 38
Merlewood Dri. Chst —5K 111
Merlewood Pl. SE9 —4K 95
Merley Ct. NW9 —6A 40
Merlin. NW9 —8D 24
(off Concourse, The)
Merlin Clo. Croy —6C 124
Merlin Clo. Ilf —5G 33
Merlin Clo. Mitc —7C 106
Merlin Clo. N'holt —6G 53
Merlin Clo. Romf —6B 34
Merlin Clo. Wall —8K 123
Merlin Clo. Wal A —7M 7
Merlin Ct. Ruis —7B 36
Merlin Ct. Short —7D 110
Merlin Cres. Edgw —8K 23
Merlin Gdns. Brom —9E 94
Merlin Gdns. Romf —6B 34
Merling Clo. Chess —7G 119
Merlin Gro. Beck —8K 109

Merlin Gro.—Milliners Ct.

Merlin Gro. Ilf —7M 31
Merlin Rd. E12 —7H 47
Merlin Rd. Romf —6B 34
Merlin Rd. Well —3E 96
Merlin Rd. N. Well —3E 96
Merlins Av. Harr —8K 37
Merlins Ct. WC1 —6L 59
(off Margery St.)
Merlin St. WC1 —6L 59
Merlin Way. Leav —7D 4
Mermagen Dri. Rain —3F 66
Mermaid Ct. SE1 —3B 76
Mermaid Ct. SE16 —2K 77
Mermaid Ho. E14 —1A 78
(off Bazely St.)
Mermaid Tower. SE8 —7K 77
(off Abinger Gro.)
Meroe Ct. N16 —7C 44
Merredene St. SW2 —5K 91
Merriam Clo. E4 —5A 30
Merrick Rd. S'hall —4K 69
Merrick Sq. SE1 —4B 76
Merridene. N21 —8M 15
Merrielands Cres. Dag —5K 65
Merrielands Retail Pk. Dag —4K 65
Merrilands Rd. Wor Pk —3G 121
Merrilees Rd. Sidc —7C 96
Merrilyn Clo. Clay —8E 118
Merriman Rd. SE3 —9G 79
Merrington Rd. SW6 —7L 73
Merrion Av. Stan —5H 23
Merritt Gdns. Chess —8G 119
Merritt Ho. Romf —5D 50
(off Frazer Clo.)
Merritt Rd. SE4 —4K 93
Merritt's Bldgs. EC2 —7C 60
(off Worship St.)
Merrivale. N14 —8H 15
Merrivale. NW1 —4G 59
(off Camden St.)
Merrivale Av. Ilf —2H 47
Merrivale M. W Dray —2H 143
Merrow Ct. Mitc —6B 106
Merrow Rd. Sutt —1H 135
Merrows Clo. N'wd —6A 20
Merrow St. SE17 —6B 76
Merrow Wlk. SE17 —6B 76
Merrow Way. New Ad —8A 126
Merrydown Way. Chst —5J 111
Merryfield. SE3 —1D 94
Merryfield Gdns. Stan —5G 23
Merryfield Ho. SE9 —9G 95
(off Grove Pk. Rd.)
Merryfields. Uxb —5B 142
(in two parts)
Merryfields Way. SE6 —6M 93
Merry Hill. —1L 21
Merryhill Clo. E4 —9M 17
Merry Hill Mt. Bush —1M 21
Merry Hill Rd. Bush —8K 9
Merryhills Clo. Big H —8H 141
Merryhills Ct. N14 —7G 15
Merryhills Dri. Enf —6H 15
Merrymeet. Bans —6D 136
Merryweather Clo. Dart —5K 99
Merryweather Ct. N19 —8G 43
Merryweather Ct. N Mald —9C 104
Mersea Ho. Bark —2M 63
Mersey Ct. King T —5H 103
Mersey Rd. E17 —1K 45
Mersey Wlk. N'holt —5L 53
Mersham Dri. NW9 —3L 39
Mersham Pl. SE20 —5F 108
Mersham Rd. T Hth —7B 108
Merten Rd. Romf —5J 49
Merthyr Ter. SW13 —7F 72
Merton. —4M 105
Merton Av. W4 —5D 72
Merton Av. N'holt —1A 54
Merton Av. Uxb —3F 142
Merton Ct. Ilf —4J 47
Merton Ct. Well —1F 96
Merton Gdns. Orp —9M 111
Merton Hall Gdns. SW20 —5J 105
Merton Hall Rd. SW19 —4J 105
Merton High St. SW19 —4M 105
Merton Ind. Pk. SW19 —5M 105
Merton La. N6 —7D 42
Merton Lodge. New Bar —7A 14
Merton Mans. SE8 —9L 77
(off Brookmill Rd.)
Merton Mans. SW20 —6H 105
Merton Park. —6L 105
Merton Pk. Pde. SW19 —5K 105
Merton Pl. SW19 —5A 106
(off Nelson Gro. Rd.)
Merton Ri. NW3 —3C 58
(in two parts)
Merton Rd. E17 —3A 46
Merton Rd. SE25 —9E 108
Merton Rd. SW18 —5L 89
Merton Rd. SW19 —4M 105
Merton Rd. Bark —3D 64
Merton Rd. Enf —2B 16
Merton Rd. Harr —6A 38
Merton Rd. Ilf —5D 48
Merton Rd. Wat —6F 8
Merton Way. Uxb —3F 142
Merton Way. W Mol —8M 101
Mertoun Ter. W1 —8D 58
(off Seymour Pl.)
Merttins Rd. SE15 & SE4 —4H 93
Meru Clo. NW5 —9E 42
Mervan Rd. SW2 —3L 91
Mervyn Av. SE9 —9A 96
Mervyn Rd. W13 —4E 70
Mervyn Rd. Shep —2A 116
Meryfield Clo. Borwd —4K 11
Messaline Av. W3 —9A 56
Messant Clo. H Wood —9J 35
Messent Rd. SE9 —4G 95
Messeter Pl. SE9 —5L 95
Messina Av. NW6 —3L 57
Messiter Ho. N1 —4K 59
(off Barnsbury Est.)
Metcalf Rd. Ashf —2A 100
Metcalf Wlk. Felt —1J 101
Meteor St. SW11 —3E 90
Meteor Way. Wall —9J 123
Metford Cres. Enf —2L 17
Metheringham Way. NW9 —8C 24
Methley St. SE11 —6L 75
Methuen Clo. Edgw —7L 23
Methuen Pk. N10 —1F 42
Methuen Rd. Belv —5M 81
Methuen Rd. Bexh —3K 97
Methuen Rd. Edgw —7L 23
Methwold Rd. W10 —8H 57
Metro Bus. Cen., The. SE26 —3K 109
Metro Central Heights. SE1 —4A 76
(off Newington Causeway)
Metro Cen. Orp —1F 128
Metro Cen., The. Wat —9A 8
Metro Cinema. —1H 75
(off Rupert St.)
Metro Ind. Cen. Iswth —1C 86
Metropolis. SE11 —4M 75
(off Oswin St.)
Metropolitan Bus. Cen. N1 —3C 60
(off Enfield Rd.)
Metropolitan Clo. E14 —8L 61
Metropolitan Sta. App. Wat —5D 8
Metropolitan Wharf. E1 —2G 77
Metro Trad. Est. Wemb —9M 39
Meux Clo. Chesh —4A 6
Mews End. Big H —9H 141
Mews Pl. Wfd G —4E 30
Mews St. E1 —2E 76
Mews, The. N1 —4A 60
Mews, The. N8 —1L 43
Mews, The. Ilf —3H 47
Mews, The. Romf —2C 50
Mews, The. Sidc —1E 112
Mews, The. Twic —5F 86
Mews, The. Wat —6G 9
(off Smith St.)
Mexborough. NW1 —4G 59
Mexfield Rd. SW15 —4K 89
Meyer Grn. Enf —2E 16
Meyer Rd. Eri —7B 82
Meymott St. SE1 —2M 75
Meynell Cres. E9 —3H 61
Meynell Gdns. E9 —3H 61
Meynell Rd. E9 —3H 61
Meynell Rd. Romf —7F 34
Meyrick Ho. E14 —8L 61
(off Burgess St.)
Meyrick Rd. NW10 —2E 56
Meyrick Rd. SW11 —2B 90
Mezen Clo. N'wd —5B 20
Miah Ter. E1 —2E 76
Miall Wlk. SE26 —1J 109
Micawber Av. Uxb —7E 142
Micawber Ct. N1 —6A 60
(off Windsor Ter.)
Micawber Ho. SE16 —3E 76
(off Llewellyn St.)
Micawber St. N1 —6A 60
Michael Cliffe Ho. EC1 —6M 59
(off Finsbury Est.)
Michael Faraday Ho. SE17 —6C 76
(off Beaconsfield Rd.)
Michael Gdns. Horn —2H 51
Michael Gaynor Clo. W7 —2D 70
Michael Manley Ind. Est. SW8 —1G 91
(off Clyston St.)
Michaelmas Clo. SW20 —7G 105
Michael Rd. E11 —6D 46
Michael Rd. SE25 —7C 108
Michael Rd. SW6 —9M 73
Michael's Clo. SE13 —3C 94
Michael Stewart Ho. SW6 —7K 73
(off Clem Attlee Ct.)
Michelangelo Ct. SE16 —6F 76
(off Stubbs Dri.)
Micheldever Rd. SE12 —5C 94
Michelham Gdns. Twic —9D 86
Michelle Ct. N12 —5A 26
Michelle Ct. W3 —1B 72
Michelle Ct. Brom —5D 110
(off Blyth Rd.)
Michelsdale Dri. Rich —3J 87
Michelson Ho. SE11 —5K 75
(off Black Prince Rd.)
Michel's Row. Rich —3J 87
Michigan Av. E12 —9K 47
Michigan Ho. E14 —4L 77
Michleham Down. N12 —4K 25
Mickledore. NW1 —5G 59
(off Ampthill Est.)
Micklefield Way. Borwd —2J 11
Mickleham Clo. Orp —6D 112
Mickleham Gdns. Sutt —8J 121
Mickleham Rd. Orp —5D 112
Mickleham Way. New Ad —9B 126
Micklethwaite Rd. SW6 —7L 73
Midas Metropolitan Ind. Est. Mord —2G 121
Mid Beckton. —9K 63
Midcroft. Ruis —6C 36
Middleborough Ho. Romf —7J 35
(off Kingsbridge Cir.)
Middle Clo. Eps —4C 134
Middle Dene. NW7 —3B 24
Middlefield. NW8 —4B 58
Middlefielde. W13 —8F 54
Middlefield Gdns. Ilf —4M 47
Middlefields. Croy —1J 139
Middle Furlong. Bush —6M 9
Middle Grn. Clo. Surb —1K 119
Middleham Ct. Dart —5M 99
(off Osbourne Rd.)
Middleham Gdns. N18 —6E 28
Middleham Rd. N18 —6E 28
Middle La. N8 —3J 43
Middle La. Eps —4C 134
Middle La. Tedd —3D 102
Middle La. M. N8 —3J 43
Middle Mill Hall. King T —7K 103
Middle Ope. Wat —1F 8
Middle Pk. Av. SE9 —5H 95
Middle Path. Harr —6B 38
Middle Rd. E13 —5E 62
Middle Rd. SW16 —6H 107
Middle Rd. E Barn —8C 14
Middle Rd. Harr —7B 38
Middle Row. W10 —7J 57
Middlesborough Rd. N18 —6E 28
Middlesex Bus. Cen. S'hall —3K 69
Middlesex County Cricket Club. —6B 58
Middlesex Ct. W4 —6D 72
Middlesex Ct. Harr —3D 38
Middlesex Pas. EC1 —8M 59
(off Bartholomew Clo.)
Middlesex Pl. E9 —2G 61
(off Elsdale St.)
Middlesex Rd. Mitc —9J 107
Middlesex St. E1 —8C 60
Middlesex Wharf. E5 —7G 45
Middle St. EC1 —8A 60
Middle St. Croy —4A 124
(in two parts)
Middle Temple Hall. —1L 75
(off Middle Temple La.)
Middle Temple La. EC4 —9L 59
Middleton Av. E4 —4K 29
Middleton Av. Gnfd —5B 54
Middleton Av. Sidc —3F 112
Middleton Bldgs. W1 —8G 59
(off Langham St.)
Middleton Clo. E4 —3K 29
Middleton Dri. SE16 —3H 77
Middleton Dri. Pinn —1E 36
Middleton Gdns. Ilf —4M 47
Middleton Gro. N7 —1J 59
Middleton Ho. E8 —3D 60
Middleton Ho. SE1 —4B 76
(off Burbage Clo.)
Middleton Ho. SW1 —5H 75
(off Causton St.)
Middleton M. N7 —1J 59
Middleton Rd. E8 —3D 60
Middleton Rd. NW11 —5L 41
Middleton Rd. Eps —2B 134
Middleton Rd. Hay —8B 52
Middleton Rd. Mord & Cars —1M 121
Middleton Rd. N Mald —7A 104
Middleton St. E2 —6F 60
Middleton Way. SE13 —3B 94
Middleway. NW11 —3M 41
Middle Way. SW16 —6H 107
Middle Way. Eri —4J 81
Middle Way. Hay —7G 53
Middle Way. Wat —1E 8
Middle Way, The. Harr —9D 22
Middle Yd. SE1 —2C 76
Midfield Av. Bexh —2A 98
Midfield Av. Swan —3E 114
Midfield Pde. Bexh —2A 98
Midfield Way. Orp —5F 112
Midford Ho. NW4 —2H 41
(off Belle Vue Est.)
Midford Pl. W1 —7G 59
Midgarth Clo. Oxs —6A 132
Midholm. Wemb —6L 39
Midholm Clo. NW11 —2M 41
Midholm Rd. Croy —5J 125
Midhope Ho. WC1 —6J 59
(off Midhope St.)
Midhope St. WC1 —6J 59
Midhurst. SE26 —3G 109
Midhurst Av. N10 —1E 42
Midhurst Av. Croy —2L 123
Midhurst Clo. Horn —9E 50
Midhurst Gdns. Uxb —4A 52
Midhurst Hill. Bexh —5L 97
Midhurst Ho. E14 —9K 61
(off Salmon La.)
Midhurst Pde. N10 —1E 42
(off Fortis Grn.)
Midhurst Rd. W13 —3E 70
Midhurst Way. E5 —9E 44
Midland Cres. NW3 —2A 58
Midland Pde. NW6 —2M 57
Midland Pl. E14 —6A 78
Midland Rd. E10 —5A 46
Midland Rd. NW1 —5H 59
Midland Ter. NW2 —8H 41
Midland Ter. NW10 —7C 56
(in two parts)
Midmoor Rd. SW12 —7G 91
Midmoor Rd. SW19 —5H 105
Midship Clo. SE16 —2H 77
Midship Point. E14 —3L 77
(off Quarterdeck, The)
Midstrath Rd. NW10 —9C 40
Midsummer Av. Houn —3K 85
Midway. Sutt —2K 121
Midway. W on T —4F 116
Midway Ho. EC1 —6M 59
(off Manningford Clo.)
Midwinter Clo. Well —2E 96
Midwood Clo. NW2 —8F 40
Miena Way. Asht —9H 133
Miers Clo. E6 —4L 63
Mighell Av. Ilf —3H 47
Milan Rd. S'hall —3K 69
Milborne Gro. SW10 —6A 74
Milborne St. E9 —2G 61
Milborough Cres. SE12 —5C 94
Milbourne Ct. Wat —4E 8
Milbourne La. Esh —8A 118
Milbrook. Esh —8A 118
Milburn Dri. W Dray —1J 143
Milburn Wlk. Eps —7C 134
Milby Ct. Borwd —3K 11
Milcote St. SE1 —3M 75
Mildenhall Ho. Romf —5L 35
(off Redcar Rd.)
Mildenhall Rd. E5 —9G 45
Mildmay Av. N1 —2B 60
Mildmay Gro. N. N1 —1B 60
Mildmay Gro. S. N1 —1B 60
Mildmay Pk. N1 —1B 60
Mildmay Pl. N16 —1C 60
Mildmay Rd. N1 —1B 60
Mildmay Rd. Ilf —8M 47
Mildmay Rd. Romf —3A 50
Mildmay St. N1 —2B 60
Mildred Av. Borwd —6L 11
Mildred Av. Hay —5B 68
Mildred Av. N'holt —1M 53
Mildred Av. Wat —6D 8
Mildred Clo. Dart —5L 99
Mildred Rd. Eri —6C 82
Mildura Ct. N8 —2K 43
Mile Clo. Wal A —6J 7
Mile End. —7K 61
Mile End Pk. —6J 61
Mile End Pl. E1 —7H 61
Mile End Rd. E1 & E3 —8G 61
Mile End, The. E17 —8H 29
Mile Rd. Wall —3F 122
Miles Bldgs. NW1 —8C 58
(off Penfold Pl.)
Miles Ct. E1 —9F 60
(off Tillman St.)
Miles Ct. Croy —4M 123
(off Cuthbert Rd.)
Miles Dri. SE28 —2C 80
Miles Ho. SE10 —6C 78
(off Tuskar St.)
Miles Lodge. Harr —3B 38
Milespit Hill. NW7 —5F 24
Miles Pl. NW8 —8B 58
(off Broadley St.)
Miles Pl. Surb —8K 103
Miles Rd. N8 —1J 43
Miles Rd. Eps —4B 134
Miles Rd. Mitc —7C 106
Miles St. SW8 —7J 75
Miles St. Bus. Est. SW8 —7J 75
Milestone Clo. N9 —2E 28
Milestone Clo. Sutt —9B 122
Milestone Green. (Junct.) —3A 88
Milestone Ho. King T —7H 103
(off Surbiton Rd.)
Milestone Rd. SE19 —3D 108
Milestone Rd. Dart —5M 99
Miles Way. N20 —2C 26
Milfoil St. W12 —1E 72
Milford Clo. SE2 —7J 81
Milford Ct. S'hall —2L 69
Milford Gdns. Croy —9G 109
Milford Gdns. Edgw —7L 23
Milford Gdns. Wemb —9H 39
Milford Gro. Sutt —6A 122
Milford La. WC2 —1L 75
Milford M. SW16 —9K 91
Milford Rd. W13 —2F 70
Milford Rd. S'hall —1L 69
Milford Towers. SE6 —6M 93
Milking La. Kes —3H 141
(in two parts)
Milk St. E16 —2M 79
Milk St. EC2 —9A 60
Milk St. Brom —3F 110
Milkwell Gdns. Wfd G —7F 30
Milkwell Yd. SE5 —9A 76
Milkwood Rd. SE24 —4M 91
Milk Yd. E1 —1G 77
Millais Av. E12 —1L 63
Millais Ct. N'holt —5H 53
(off Academy Gdns.)
Millais Gdns. Edgw —9L 23
Millais Ho. SW1 —5J 75
(off Marsham St.)
Millais Rd. E11 —9A 46
Millais Rd. Enf —7D 16
Millais Rd. N Mald —2C 120
Millais Way. Eps —6A 120
Milland Ct. Borwd —3B 12
Millard Clo. N16 —1C 60
Millard Ho. SE8 —6K 77
(off Leeway)
Millard Ter. Dag —2L 65
Mill Av. Uxb —5A 142
Millbank. SW1 —4J 75
Millbank Ct. SW1 —5J 75
(off John Islip St.)
Millbank Tower. SW1 —5J 75
(off Millbank)
Millbank Way. SE12 —4E 94
Millbourne Rd. Felt —1J 101
Mill Bri. Barn —8K 13
Mill Bri. Pl. Uxb —5A 142
Millbro. Swan —5E 114
Millbrook. Wey —6C 116
Millbrook Av. Well —3B 96
Millbrook Gdns. Chad H —4K 49
Millbrook Gdns. Gid P —9C 34
Millbrook Ho. SE15 —7E 76
(off Peckham Pk. Rd.)
Millbrook Pas. SW9 —2M 91
Millbrook Pl. NW1 —5G 59
(off Hampstead Rd.)
Millbrook Rd. N9 —1F 28
Millbrook Rd. SW9 —2M 91
Millbrook Rd. Bush —3K 9
Mill Brook Rd. St M —8G 113
Mill Clo. Cars —4E 122
Mill Clo. W Dray —4H 143
Mill Corner. Barn —3K 13
Mill Ct. E10 —8A 46
Mill Ct. Hort K —6M 115
Millcroft Ho. SE6 —1A 110
(off Melfield Gdns.)
Millender Wlk. SE16 —5G 77
Millennium Bridge. —1M 75
Millennium Bus. Cen. NW2 —7F 40
Millennium Clo. E16 —9F 62
Millennium Clo. Uxb —5A 142
Millennium Dri. E14 —5B 78
Millennium Ho. E17 —3H 45
Millennium Pl. E2 —5F 60
Millennium Sq. SE1 —3D 76
Millennium Way. SE10 —3C 78
Miller Av. Enf —2L 17
Miller Clo. Mitc —2D 122
Miller Clo. Pinn —9G 21
Miller Ct. Bexh —2A 98
Miller Rd. SW19 —3B 106
Miller Rd. Croy —3K 123
Miller's Av. E8 —1D 60
Millers Clo. NW7 —4E 24
Millers Clo. Chig —2F 32
Miller's Ct. W4 —6D 72
Millers Ct. Wemb —5J 55
(off Vicars Bri. Clo.)
Millers Grn. Clo. Enf —5M 15
Miller's La. Chig —1F 32
Millers Mdw. Clo. SE3 —4D 94
Miller's Ter. E8 —1D 60
Miller St. NW1 —5G 59
(in two parts)
Millers Way. W6 —3G 73
Millers Wharf Ho. E1 —2E 76
(off St Katherine's Way)
Miller Wlk. SE1 —2L 75
Millet Rd. Gnfd —6M 53
Mill Farm Av. Sun —4C 100
Mill Farm Bus. Pk. Houn —6J 85
Mill Farm Clo. Pinn —9G 21
Mill Farm Cres. Houn —7J 85
Millfield. N4 —7L 43
Millfield. King T —7K 103
Millfield. Sun —5B 100
Millfield Av. E17 —8J 29
Millfield Cotts. Orp —7F 112
Millfield Ho. Wat —8B 8
Millfield La. N6 —6C 42
(in two parts)
Millfield Pl. N6 —7E 42
Millfield Rd. Edgw —9A 24
Millfield Rd. Houn —7J 85
Millfields Clo. St M —8F 112
Millfields Rd. E5 —9G 45
Mill Gdns. SE26 —9F 92
Mill Grn. Mitc —2E 122
Mill Grn. Bus. Pk. Mitc —2E 122
Mill Grn. Rd. Mitc —2E 122
Millgrove St. SW11 —9E 74
Millharbour. E14 —3M 77
Millhaven Clo. Romf —4F 48
Mill Hill. —5D 24
Mill Hill. SW13 —1E 88
Mill Hill Circus. (Junct.) —5D 24
Mill Hill Gro. W3 —2A 72
Mill Hill Ind. Est. NW7 —6D 24
Mill Hill Rd. SW13 —1E 88
Mill Hill Rd. W3 —3M 71
Mill Hill Ter. W3 —2M 71
Mill Hill Yd. W3 —3M 71
Millhoo Ct. Wal A —7M 7
Mill Ho. Wfd G —5D 30
Mill Ho. Clo. Eyns —3J 131
Millhouse La. Bedm —1E 4
Millhouse Pl. SE27 —1M 107
Millicent Fawcett Ct. N17 —8D 28
Millicent Rd. E10 —6K 45
Milligan St. E14 —1K 77
Milliners Ct. Lou —4L 19

Monmouth Rd.—Mortimer Rd.

Monmouth Rd. E6 —6K 63
Monmouth Rd. N9 —2F 28
Monmouth Rd. W2 —9L 57
Monmouth Rd. Dag —1K 65
Monmouth Rd. Hay —5C 68
Monmouth Rd. Wat —5F 8
Monmouth St. WC2 —9J 59
Monnery Rd. N19 —8G 43
Monnow Rd. SE1 —6E 76
Mono La. Felt —8F 84
Monoux Almshouses. E17 —2M 45
Monoux Gro. E17 —8L 29
Monroe Cres. Enf —3F 16
Monroe Dri. SW14 —4M 87
Monro Gdns. Harr —7C 22
Monro Ind. Est. Wal X —7E 6
Monro Pl. Eps —1L 133
Monsell Rd. N4 —8L 43
Monson Rd. NW10 —5E 56
Monson Rd. SE14 —8H 77
Mons Way. Brom —1J 127
Montacute Rd. SE6 —6K 93
Montacute Rd. Bus H —9C 10
Montacute Rd. Mord —1B 122
Montacute Rd. New Ad —1A 140
Montagu Cres. N18 —4F 28
Montague Av. SE4 —3K 93
Montague Av. W7 —2D 70
Montague Av. S Croy —4C 138
Montague Clo. SE1 —2B 76
Montague Clo. W on T —2F 116
Montague Ct. Sidc —9E 96
Montague Gdns. W3 —1L 71
Montague Hall Pl. Bush —8L 9
Montague Pas. Uxb —3B 142
Montague Pl. E14 —1A 78
Montague Pl. WC1 —8H 59
Montague Pl. Swan —8D 114
Montague Rd. E8 —1E 60
Montague Rd. E11 —7D 46
Montague Rd. N8 —3K 43
Montague Rd. N15 —2E 44
Montague Rd. SW19 —4M 105
Montague Rd. W7 —2D 70
Montague Rd. W13 —9F 54
Montague Rd. Croy —3M 123
Montague Rd. Houn —2M 85
Montague Rd. Rich —5J 87
Montague Rd. S'hall —5J 69
Montague Rd. Uxb —3B 142
Montague Sq. SE15 —8G 77
Montague St. EC1 —8A 60
Montague St. WC1 —8J 59
Montague Ter. Brom —8D 110
Montague Waye. S'hall —4J 69
Montagu Gdns. N18 —4F 28
Montagu Gdns. Wall —6G 123
Montagu Mans. W1 —8D 58
Montagu M. N. W1 —8D 58
Montagu M. S. W1 —9D 58
Montagu M. W. W1 —9D 58
Montagu Pl. W1 —8D 58
Montagu Rd. N18 & N9 —5F 28
Montagu Rd. NW4 —4E 40
Montagu Rd. Ind. Est. N18 —4G 29
Montagu Row. W1 —8D 58
Montagu Sq. W1 —8D 58
Montagu St. W1 —9D 58
Montalt Rd. Wfd G —4D 30
Montana Clo. S Croy —2B 138
Montana Gdns. SE26 —2K 109
Montana Gdns. Sutt —7A 122
Montana Rd. SW17 —9E 90
Montana Rd. SW20 —5G 105
Montayne Rd. Chesh —5D 6
Montbelle Rd. SE9 —9M 95
Montbretia Clo. Orp —8G 113
Montcalm Clo. Brom —1E 126
Montcalm Clo. Hay —6F 52
Montcalm Ho. E14 —5L 77
Montcalm Rd. SE7 —8H 79
Montclare St. E2 —7D 60
Monteagle Av. Bark —2A 64
Monteagle Ct. N1 —5C 60
Monteagle Way. E5 —8E 44
Monteagle Way. SE15 —2F 92
Montefiore St. SW8 —1F 90
Montego Clo. SE24 —3L 91
Montem Rd. SE23 —6K 93
Montem Rd. N Mald —8C 104
Montem St. N4 —6K 43
Montenotte Rd. N8 —3G 43
Monterey Clo. Bex —8A 98
Monterey Pl. Shop. Cen. NW7 —5C 24
Montesole Ct. Pinn —9G 21
Montesquieu Ter. E16 —9D 62
(off Clarkson Rd.)
Montevetro. SW11 —9B 74
Montford Pl. SE11 —6L 75
Montford Rd. Sun —8E 100
Montfort Gdns. Ilf —6A 32
Montfort Ho. E2 —6G 61
(off Victoria Pk. Sq.)
Montfort Ho. E14 —4A 78
(off Galbraith St.)
Montfort Pl. SW19 —7H 89
Montgolfier Wlk. N'holt —6J 53
Montgomery Av. Esh —4C 118
Montgomery Clo. Mitc —8J 107
Montgomery Clo. Sidc —5D 96
Montgomery Ct. S Croy —7C 124
(off Birdhurst Rd.)
Montgomery Cres. Romf —5G 35
Montgomery Dri. Chesh —1E 6
Montgomery Lodge. E1 —7G 61
(off Cleveland Gro.)
Montgomery Rd. W4 —5A 72
Montgomery Rd. Edgw —6K 23
Montholme Rd. SW11 —5D 90
Monthope Rd. E1 —8E 60
(off Hopetown St., in two parts)
Montolieu Gdns. SW15 —4F 88
Montpelier Av. W5 —8G 55
Montpelier Av. Bex —6H 97
Montpelier Clo. Uxb —4E 142
Montpelier Ct. W5 —8H 55
Montpelier Ct. Brom —8D 110
(off Westmoreland Rd.)
Montpelier Gdns. E6 —6H 63
Montpelier Gdns. Romf —5G 49
Montpelier Gro. NW5 —1G 59
Montpelier M. SW7 —4C 74
Montpelier Pl. E1 —9G 61
Montpelier Pl. SW7 —4C 74
Montpelier Ri. NW11 —5J 41
Montpelier Ri. Wemb —6H 39
Montpelier Rd. N3 —8A 26
Montpelier Rd. SE15 —9F 76
Montpelier Rd. W5 —8H 55
Montpelier Rd. Purl —2M 137
Montpelier Rd. Sutt —6A 122
Montpelier Row. SE3 —1D 94
Montpelier Row. Twic —6G 87
Montpelier Sq. SW7 —3C 74
Montpelier St. SW7 —4C 74
Montpelier Ter. SW7 —3C 74
Montpelier Va. SE3 —1D 94
Montpelier Wlk. SW7 —4C 74
Montpelier Way. NW11 —5J 41
Montpellier Ho. Chig —5A 32
Montrave Rd. SE20 —3G 109
Montreal Pl. WC2 —1K 75
Montreal Rd. Ilf —5A 48
Montrell Rd. SW2 —7J 91
Montrose Av. NW6 —5J 57
Montrose Av. Edgw —9A 24
Montrose Av. Romf —9G 35
Montrose Av. Sidc —6E 96
Montrose Av. Twic —6M 85
Montrose Av. Well —2B 96
Montrose Clo. Ashf —3A 100
Montrose Clo. Well —2D 96
Montrose Clo. Wfd G —4E 30
Montrose Ct. NW9 —9A 24
Montrose Ct. NW11 —2K 41
Montrose Ct. SE6 —7D 94
Montrose Ct. SW7 —3B 74
Montrose Ct. Harr —3M 37
Montrose Cres. N12 —6A 26
Montrose Cres. Wemb —2J 55
Montrose Gdns. Mitc —6D 106
Montrose Gdns. Oxs —4B 132
Montrose Gdns. Sutt —4M 121
Montrose Ho. E14 —4L 77
Montrose Pl. SW1 —3E 74
Montrose Rd. Felt —5B 84
Montrose Rd. Harr —9C 22
Montrose Ter. W Dray —1H 143
(off Trout Rd.)
Montrose Wlk. Stan —6F 22
Montrose Way. SE23 —7H 93
Montrouge Cres. Eps —8G 135
Montserrat Av. Wfd G —7B 30
Montserrat Clo. SE19 —2B 108
Montserrat Rd. SW15 —3J 89
Monument Gdns. SE13 —4A 94
Monument Hill. Wey —6A 116
Monument Rd. Wey —6A 116
Monument St. EC3 —1B 76
Monument, The. —1B 76
(off Monument St.)
Monument Way. N17 —1D 44
Monza St. E1 —1G 77
Moodkee St. SE16 —4G 77
Moody Rd. SE15 —9D 76
Moody St. E1 —6H 61
Moon Ct. SE12 —3E 94
Moon La. Barn —5K 13
Moon St. N1 —4M 59
Moorcroft. Edgw —8M 23
Moorcroft Gdns. Brom —9J 111
Moorcroft La. Uxb —8E 142
Moorcroft Rd. SW16 —9J 91
Moorcroft Way. Pinn —3J 37
Moordown. SE18 —8M 79
Moore Clo. SW14 —2A 88
Moore Clo. Mitc —6F 106
Moore Clo. Wall —9J 123
Moore Ct. N1 —4M 59
(off Gaskin St.)
Moore Cres. Dag —4F 64
Moorehead Way. SE3 —2E 94
Moore Ho. E1 —1G 77
(off Cable St.)
Moore Ho. E2 —6G 61
(off Roman Rd.)
Moore Ho. N8 —2J 43
(off Pembroke Rd.)
Moore Ho. SE10 —6D 78
(off Armitage Rd.)
Moore Ho. Horn —4E 50
(off Globe Rd.)
Mooreland Rd. Brom —4D 110
Moore Pk. Ct. SW6 —8M 73
(off Fulham Rd.)
Moore Pk. Rd. SW6 —8L 73
Moore Rd. SE19 —3A 108
Moore St. SW3 —5D 74
Moore Wlk. E7 —9E 46
Moore Way. Sutt —1L 135
Moorey Clo. E15 —4D 62
Moorfield Av. W5 —7H 55
Moorfield Rd. N17 —9D 28
Moorfield Rd. Chess —7J 119
Moorfield Rd. Enf —3G 17
Moorfield Rd. Orp —2E 128
Moorfield Rd. Uxb —8B 142
Moorfields. EC2 —8B 60
Moorfields Highwalk. EC2 —8B 60
(off Moor La., in two parts)
Moorgate. EC2 —9B 60
Moorgate Pl. EC2 —9B 60
(off Swan All.)
Moorgreen Ho. EC1 —6M 59
(off Spencer St.)
Moorhen Clo. Eri —8F 82
Moorhouse. NW9 —8D 24
Moorhouse Rd. W2 —9L 57
Moorhouse Rd. Harr —1H 39
Moorings, The. E16 —8G 63
(off Prince Regent La.)
Moorland Clo. Romf —7M 33
Moorland Clo. Twic —6L 85
Moorland M. N1 —3L 59
Moorland Rd. SW9 —3M 91
Moorland Rd. W Dray —7G 143
Moorlands. N'holt —4J 53
Moorlands Av. NW7 —6F 24
Moor La. EC2 —8B 60
(in two parts)
Moor La. Chess —6J 119
Moor La. Rick —1A 20
Moor La. W Dray —7G 143
Moor La. Crossing. Wat —9A 8
Moormead Dri. Eps —7C 120
Moor Mead Rd. Twic —5E 86
Moor Park. —3A 20
Moor Pk. Gdns. King T —4C 104
Moor Pk. Ind. Cen. Wat —9A 8
Moor Pk. Rd. N'wd —6B 20
Moor Pl. EC2 —8B 60
Moorside Rd. Brom —9C 94
Moorsom Way. Coul —9H 137
Moor St. W1 —9H 59
Moortown Rd. Wat —4G 21
Moor Vw. Wat —9E 8
Moot Ct. NW9 —3L 39
Moran Clo. Brick W —4K 5
Moran Ho. E1 —2F 76
(off Wapping La.)
Morant Gdns. Romf —5M 33
Morant Pl. N22 —8K 27
Morant St. E14 —1L 77
Mora Rd. NW2 —9G 41
Mora St. EC1 —6A 60
Morat St. SW9 —9K 75
Moravian Clo. SW10 —7B 74
Moravian Pl. SW10 —7B 74
Moravian St. E2 —5G 61
Moray Av. Hay —2D 68
Moray Clo. Edgw —2M 23
Moray Clo. Romf —7C 34
Moray Ct. S Croy —7A 124
(off Warham Rd.)
Moray Ho. E1 —7J 61
(off Harford St.)
Moray M. N7 —7K 43
Moray Rd. N4 —7K 43
Moray Way. Romf —7B 34
Mordaunt Gdns. Dag —3J 65
Mordaunt Ho. NW10 —4B 56
Mordaunt Rd. NW10 —4B 56
Mordaunt St. SW9 —2K 91
Morden. —7M 105
Morden Ct. Mord —8M 105
Morden Ct. Pde. Mord —8M 105
Morden Gdns. Gnfd —1D 54
Morden Gdns. Mitc —8B 106
Morden Hall Rd. Mord —7M 105
Morden Hill. SE13 —1A 94
Morden La. SE13 —9A 78
Morden Park. —1J 121
Morden Rd. SE3 —1E 94
Morden Rd. SW19 —5M 105
Morden Rd. Mord & Mitc —8A 106
Morden Rd. Romf —5J 49
Morden Rd. M. SE3 —1E 94
Morden St. SE13 —9M 77
Morden Way. Sutt —2L 121
Morden Wharf. SE10 —4C 78
(off Morden Wharf Rd.)
Morden Wharf Rd. SE10 —4C 78
Mordern Ho. NW1 —7C 58
(off Harewood Av.)
Mordon Rd. Ilf —5D 48
Mordred Rd. SE6 —8C 94
Morecambe Clo. E1 —8H 61
Morecambe Clo. Horn —1F 66
Morecambe Gdns. Stan —4H 23
Morecambe St. SE17 —5A 76
Morecambe Ter. N18 —4B 28
(off Gt. Cambridge Rd.)
More Clo. E16 —9D 62
More Clo. W14 —5H 73
More Clo. Purl —3L 137
Morecombe Ho. Romf —5J 35
(off Dagnam Pk. Dri.)
Morecoombe Clo. King T —4M 103
Moree Way. N18 —4E 28
Moreland Ct. NW2 —8L 41
Moreland St. EC1 —6M 59
Moreland Way. E4 —3M 29
More La. Esh —5M 117
Morella Rd. SW12 —6D 90
Morello Av. Uxb —8F 142
Morello Clo. Swan —8B 114
Moremead. Wal A —6K 7
Moremead Rd. SE6 —1K 109
Morena St. SE6 —6M 93
Moresby Av. Surb —2M 119
Moresby Rd. E5 —6F 44
Moresby Wlk. SW8 —1G 91
More's Garden. SW3 —7B 74
(off Cheyne Wlk.)
Moretaine Rd. Ashf —9B 144
Moreton Av. Iswth —9C 70
Moreton Clo. E5 —7F 44
Moreton Clo. N15 —4B 44
Moreton Clo. NW7 —6G 25
Moreton Clo. SW1 —6G 75
(off Moreton Ter.)
Moreton Clo. Chesh —1B 6
Moreton Clo. Swan —6C 114
Moreton Ct. Dart —2D 98
Moreton Gdns. Wfd G —5J 31
Moreton Ho. SE16 —4F 76
Moreton Ind. Est. Swan —8F 114
Moreton Pl. SW1 —6G 75
Moreton Rd. N15 —4B 44
Moreton Rd. S Croy —7B 124
Moreton Rd. Wor Pk —4E 120
Moreton St. SW1 —6G 75
Moreton Ter. SW1 —6G 75
Moreton Ter. M. N. SW1 —6G 75
Moreton Ter. M. S. SW1 —6G 75
Moreton Tower. W3 —2M 71
Morford Clo. Ruis —5F 36
Morford Way. Ruis —5F 36
Morgan Av. E17 —2B 46
Morgan Clo. Dag —3L 65
Morgan Clo. N'wd —6D 20
Morgan Gdns. A'ham —2M 9
Morgan Ho. SW1 —5G 75
(off Vauxhall Bri. Rd.)
Morgan Ho. SW8 —9G 75
(off Wadhurst Rd.)
Morgan Mans. N7 —1L 59
(off Morgan Rd.)
Morgan Rd. N7 —1L 59
Morgan Rd. W10 —8K 57
Morgan Rd. Brom —4E 110
Morgan Rd. Tedd —3C 102
Morgan's La. SE1 —2C 76
Morgan's La. Hay —8B 52
Morgan St. E3 —6J 61
Morgan St. E16 —8D 62
Morgan Wlk. Beck —8M 109
Morgan Way. Rain —6G 67
Morgan Way. Wfd G —6J 31
Moriatry Clo. N7 —9J 43
Morie St. SW18 —4M 89
Morieux Rd. E10 —6K 45
Moring Rd. SW17 —1E 106
Morkyns Wlk. SE21 —9C 92
Morland Av. Croy —3C 124
Morland Av. Dart —4F 98
Morland Clo. NW11 —6M 41
Morland Clo. Hamp —2K 101
Morland Clo. Mitc —7C 106
Morland Est. E8 —3E 60
Morland Gdns. NW10 —3B 56
Morland Gdns. S'hall —2M 69
Morland Ho. NW1 —5G 59
(off Cranleigh St.)
Morland Ho. NW6 —4L 57
(off Brondesbury Rd.)
Morland Ho. SW1 —5J 75
(off Marsham St.)
Morland Ho. W11 —9J 57
(off Lancaster Rd.)
Morland Rd. E17 —3H 45
Morland Rd. SE20 —3H 109
Morland Rd. Croy —3C 124
Morland Rd. Dag —3L 65
Morland Rd. Harr —3J 39
Morland Rd. Ilf —7M 47
Morland Rd. Sutt —7A 122
Morland Way. Chesh —1E 6
Morley Av. E4 —7B 30
Morley Av. N18 —4E 28
Morley Av. N22 —9L 27
Morley Clo. Orp —4M 127
Morley Ct. E4 —5K 29
Morley Ct. Short —8D 110
Morley Cres. Edgw —2A 24
Morley Cres. Ruis —7G 37
Morley Cres. E. Stan —9G 23
Morley Cres. W. Stan —1G 39
Morley Hill. Enf —2B 16
Morley Ho. N16 —7E 44
Morley Rd. E10 —6A 46
Morley Rd. E15 —5D 62
Morley Rd. SE13 —3A 94
Morley Rd. Bark —4B 64
Morley Rd. Chst —5A 112
Morley Rd. Romf —3J 49
Morley Rd. S Croy —2D 138
Morley Rd. Sutt —3K 121
Morley Rd. Twic —5H 87
Morley St. SE1 —4L 75
Morna Rd. SE5 —1A 92
Morning La. E9 —2G 61
Morningside Rd. Wor Pk —4F 120
Mornington Av. W14 —5K 73
Mornington Av. Brom —7G 111
Mornington Av. Ilf —5L 47
Mornington Clo. Big H —9H 141
Mornington Clo. Wfd G —4E 30
Mornington Ct. NW1 —5G 59
(off Mornington Cres.)
Mornington Ct. Bex —7B 98
Mornington Cres. NW1 —5G 59
Mornington Cres. Houn —9F 68
Mornington Gro. E3 —6L 61
Mornington M. SE5 —9A 76
Mornington Pl. NW1 —5G 59
Mornington Pl. SE8 —8K 77
(off Mornington Rd.)
Mornington Rd. E4 —9B 18
Mornington Rd. E11 —5D 46
Mornington Rd. SE14 —8K 77
Mornington Rd. Ashf —2A 100
Mornington Rd. Gnfd —8M 53
Mornington Rd. Wfd G —4D 30
Mornington St. NW1 —5F 58
Mornington Ter. NW1 —4F 58
Mornington Wlk. Rich —1G 103
Morocco St. SE1 —3C 76
Morpeth Av. Borwd —2K 11
Morpeth Gro. E9 —4H 61
Morpeth Mans. SW1 —5G 75
(off Morpeth Ter.)
Morpeth Rd. E9 —4H 61
Morpeth St. E2 —6H 61
Morpeth Ter. SW1 —4G 75
Morpeth Wlk. N17 —7F 28
Morrab Gdns. Ilf —8D 48
Morrel Ct. E2 —5E 60
(off Goldsmiths Row)
Morrell Clo. New Bar —5A 14
Morris Av. E12 —1K 63
Morris Blitz Ct. N16 —9D 44
Morris Clo. Croy —9J 109
Morris Clo. Orp —5C 128
Morris Ct. E4 —3M 29
Morris Ct. Wal A —7M 7
Morris Gdns. SW18 —6L 89
Morris Gdns. Dart —4L 99
Morris Ho. E2 —6G 61
(off Roman Rd.)
Morris Ho. NW8 —7C 58
(off Salisbury St.)
Morrish Rd. SW2 —6J 91
Morrison Av. N17 —1C 44
Morrison Bldgs. N. E1 —9E 60
(off Commercial Rd.)
Morrison Bldgs. S. E1 —9E 60
(off Commercial Rd.)
Morrison Ct. Barn —6J 13
(off Manor Way)
Morrison Rd. Bark —5J 65
Morrison Rd. Hay —6F 52
Morrison St. SW11 —2E 90
Morris Pl. N4 —7L 43
Morris Rd. E14 —8M 61
Morris Rd. E15 —9C 46
Morris Rd. Dag —7K 49
Morris Rd. Iswth —2D 86
Morris Rd. Romf —7F 34
Morriss Ho. SE16 —3F 76
(off Cherry Garden St.)
Morris St. E1 —9F 60
Morriston Clo. Wat —5G 21
Morritt Ho. Wemb —1H 55
(off Talbot Rd.)
Morse Clo. E13 —6E 62
Morshead Mans. W9 —6L 57
(off Morshead Rd.)
Morshead Rd. W9 —6L 57
Morson Rd. Enf —8J 17
Morston Gdns. SE9 —1K 111
Mortain Ho. SE16 —5F 76
(off Roseberry St.)
Morten Clo. SW4 —5H 91
Morteyne Rd. N17 —8B 28
Mortgramit Sq. SE18 —4L 79
Mortham St. E15 —4C 62
Mortimer Clo. NW2 —7K 41
Mortimer Clo. SW16 —8H 91
Mortimer Clo. Bush —8M 9
Mortimer Ct. NW8 —5A 58
(off Abercorn Pl.)
Mortimer Cres. NW6 —4M 57
Mortimer Cres. Wor Pk —5B 120
Mortimer Dri. Enf —8B 16
Mortimer Est. NW6 —4M 57
(off Mortimer Pl.)
Mortimer Ho. W11 —2H 73
(off Queensdale Cres.)
Mortimer Ho. W14 —5J 73
(off N. End Rd.)
Mortimer Mkt. WC1 —7G 59
Mortimer Mkt. Cen. WC1 —7G 59
(off Mortimer Mkt.)
Mortimer Pl. NW6 —4M 57
Mortimer Rd. E6 —6K 63
Mortimer Rd. N1 —3C 60
(in two parts)
Mortimer Rd. NW10 —6G 57
Mortimer Rd. W13 —9G 55
Mortimer Rd. Big H —4G 141
Mortimer Rd. Eri —7B 82
Mortimer Rd. Mitc —5D 106
Mortimer Rd. Orp —3E 128

Myrtle Av.—New Butt La.

Myrtle Av. Ruis —5E 36
Myrtleberry Clo. E8 —2D 60
(off Beechwood Rd.)
Myrtle Clo. E Barn —1D 26
Myrtle Clo. Eri —9C 82
Myrtle Clo. Uxb —8D 142
Myrtle Clo. W Dray —4K 143
Myrtledene Rd. SE2 —6E 80
Myrtle Gdns. W7 —2C 70
Myrtle Gro. Ave —3M 83
Myrtle Gro. Enf —2B 16
Myrtle Gro. N Mald —6A 104
Myrtle Rd. E6 —4K 63
Myrtle Rd. E17 —4J 45
Myrtle Rd. N13 —3A 28
Myrtle Rd. W3 —2A 72
Myrtle Rd. Croy —5L 125
Myrtle Rd. Dart —7H 99
Myrtle Rd. Hamp H —3A 102
Myrtle Rd. Houn —1A 86
Myrtle Rd. Ilf —7M 47
Myrtle Rd. Romf —6G 35
Myrtle Rd. Sutt —7A 122
Myrtleside Clo. N'wd —7B 20
Myrtle Wlk. N1 —5C 60
Mysore Rd. SW11 —2D 90
Myton Rd. SE21 —9B 92
Mytton Ho. SW8 —8K 75
(off St Stephens Ter.)

Nadine Ct. Wall —1G 137
Nadine St. SE7 —6G 79
Nafferton Ri. Lou —7H 19
Nagasaki Wlk. SE7 —4F 78
Nagle Clo. E17 —9B 30
Nag's Head. (Junct.) —8J 43
Nags Head Ct. EC1 —7A 60
(off Golden La.)
Nags Head La. Upm & Brtwd —9M 35
Nags Head La. Well —2F 96
Nags Head Rd. Enf —6G 17
Nags Head Shop. Cen. N7 —9K 43
Nailsworth Ct. SE15 —7C 76
(off Birdlip Clo.)
Nainby Ho. SE11 —5L 75
(off Hotspur St.)
Nairne Gro. SE24 —4B 92
Nairn Grn. Wat —3E 20
Nairn Rd. Ruis —2G 53
Nairn St. E14 —8A 62
Naish Ct. N1 —4J 59
(in three parts)
Naldera Gdns. SE3 —7E 78
Nallhead Rd. Felt —2G 101
Namba Roy Clo. SW16 —1K 107
Namton Dri. T Hth —8K 107
Nan Clark's La. NW7 —2D 24
Nancy Downs. Wat —9G 9
Nankin St. E14 —9L 61
Nansen Ho. NW10 —3B 56
(off Stonebridge Pk.)
Nansen Rd. SW11 —2E 90
Nansen Village. N12 —4M 25
Nant Ct. NW2 —7K 41
Nantes Clo. SW18 —3A 90
Nantes Pas. E1 —8D 60
(off Lamb St.)
Nant Rd. NW2 —7K 41
Nant St. E2 —6F 60
Nantwich Ho. Romf —5J 35
(off Lindfield Rd.)
Naoroji St. WC1 —6L 59
Napier. NW9 —8D 24
Napier Av. E14 —6L 77
Napier Av. SW6 —2K 89
Napier Clo. SE8 —8K 77
Napier Clo. W14 —4J 73
Napier Clo. Horn —6F 50
Napier Clo. W Dray —4K 143
Napier Ct. N1 —5B 60
(off Cropley St.)
Napier Ct. SW6 —2K 89
(off Ranelagh Gdns.)
Napier Ct. Chesh —1B 6
Napier Ct. Hay —7G 53
(off Dunedin Way)
Napier Gro. N1 —5A 60
Napier Ho. Rain —6D 66
(off Dunedin Rd.)
Napier Pl. W14 —4K 73
Napier Rd. E6 —4L 63
Napier Rd. E11 —9C 46
Napier Rd. E15 —5C 62
(in two parts)
Napier Rd. N17 —1C 44
Napier Rd. NW10 —6F 56
Napier Rd. SE25 —8F 108
Napier Rd. W14 —4J 73
Napier Rd. Ashf —4B 100
Napier Rd. Belv —5K 81
Napier Rd. Brom —8F 110
Napier Rd. Enf —7H 17
Napier Rd. Iswth —3E 86
Napier Rd. H'row A —9H 143
Napier Rd. S Croy —9B 124
Napier Rd. Wat —6J 9
Napier Rd. Wemb —2H 55
Napier St. SE8 —8K 77
(off Napier Clo.)
Napier Ter. N1 —3M 59
Napier Wlk. Ashf —4B 100
Napoleon Rd. E5 —8F 44
Napoleon Rd. Twic —6F 86
Napton Clo. Hay —7J 53
Narbonne Av. SW4 —4G 91
Narboro Ct. Romf —3E 50
Narborough Clo. Uxb —7A 36
Narborough St. SW6 —1M 89
Narcissus Rd. NW6 —1L 57
Nardini. NW9 —8D 24
(off Concourse, The)
Nare Rd. Ave —1M 83
Naresby Fold. Stan —6G 23
Narford Rd. E5 —8E 44
Narrow Boat Clo. SE28 —3B 80
Narrow St. E14 —1H 77
Narrow St. W3 —2M 71
Narrow Way. Brom —1J 127
Narvic Ho. SE5 —1A 92
Nascot Pl. Wat —4F 8
Nascot Rd. Wat —4F 8
Nascot St. W12 —9G 57
Nascot St. Wat —4F 8
Nascot Wood Rd. Wat —1D 8
Naseby Clo. NW6 —3A 58
Naseby Clo. Iswth —9C 70
Naseby Ct. Sidc —1D 112
Naseby Ct. W on T —4G 117
Naseby Rd. SE19 —3B 108
Naseby Rd. Dag —8L 49
Naseby Rd. Ilf —8K 31
Nash. —8E 126
Nash Clo. Els —6K 11
Nash Clo. Sutt —5B 122
Nash Ct. E14 —2M 77
(off S. Colonnade, The)
Nash Ct. Kent —4F 38
Nashe Ho. SE1 —4B 76
(off Burbage Clo.)
Nash Grn. Brom —3E 110
Nash Ho. E17 —1M 45
Nash Ho. SW1 —6F 74
(off Lupus St.)
Nash La. Kes —9E 126
Nash Pl. E14 —2M 77
Nash Rd. N9 —2G 29
Nash Rd. SE4 —3J 93
Nash Rd. Chad H & Romf —2H 49
Nash St. NW1 —6F 58
Nash's Yd. Uxb —3B 142
Nash Way. Kent —4F 38
Nasmyth St. W6 —4F 72
Nassau Path. SE28 —2G 81
Nassau Rd. SW13 —9D 72
Nassau St. W1 —8G 59
Nassington Rd. NW3 —9D 42
Natalie Clo. Felt —6B 84
Natalie M. Twic —9B 86
Natal Rd. N11 —6J 27
Natal Rd. SW16 —3H 107
Natal Rd. Ilf —9M 47
Natal Rd. T Hth —7B 108
Natasha Ct. Romf —7G 35
Nathan Ct. N9 —9G 17
(off Causeyware Rd.)
Nathan Ho. SE11 —5L 75
(off Reedworth St.)
Nathaniel Clo. E1 —8D 60
Nathaniel Ct. E17 —5J 45
Nathans Rd. Wemb —6G 39
Nathan Way. SE28 —5B 80
National Army Mus. —7D 74
National Film Theatre. —2K 75
(off Waterloo Rd.)
National Gallery. —1H 75
National Maritime Mus. —7B 78
National Portrait Gallery. —1H 75
(off St Martin's Pl.)
National Westminster Ho. Borwd —5M 11
Nation Way. E4 —1A 30
Natural History Mus. —4B 74
Naunton Way. Horn —8H 51
Nautilus Building, The. EC1 —6L 59
(off Myddelton Pas.)
Naval Ho. E14 —1B 78
(off Quixley St.)
Naval Row. E14 —1A 78
Naval Wlk. Brom —6E 110
Navarino Gro. E8 —2E 60
Navarino Mans. E8 —2E 60
Navarino Rd. E8 —2E 60
Navarre Gdns. Romf —5M 33
Navarre Rd. E6 —5J 63
Navarre St. E2 —7D 60
Navenby Wlk. E3 —7L 61
Navestock Clo. E4 —3A 30
Navestock Cres. Wfd G —7G 31
Navestock Ho. Bark —5F 64
Navigation Dri. Enf —2L 17
Navigator Dri. S'hall —3A 70
Navy St. SW4 —2H 91
Nayland Ho. SE6 —1A 110
Naylor Gro. Enf —7H 17
Naylor Rd. N20 —2A 26
Naylor Rd. SE15 —8F 76
Nazareth Gdns. SE15 —1F 92
Nazeing Wlk. Rain —3D 66
Nazrul St. E2 —6D 60
Neagle Clo. Borwd —3A 12
Neagle Ho. NW2 —8G 41
(off Stoll Clo.)
Neal Av. S'hall —7K 53
Neal Clo. N'wd —8E 20
Neal Ct. Wal A —6M 7
Nealden St. SW9 —2K 91
Neale Clo. N2 —1A 42
Neal St. WC2 —9J 59
Neal St. Wat —7G 9
Neal's Yd. WC2 —9J 59
Near Acre. NW9 —8D 24
Neasden. —8C 40
Neasden Clo. NW10 —1C 56
Neasden Junction. (Junct.) —9C 40
Neasden La. NW10 —8C 40
Neasden La. N. NW10 —8B 40
Neasham Rd. Dag —1F 64
Neatby Ct. Chesh —1D 6
Neate St. SE5 —7C 76
(in two parts)
Neath Gdns. Mord —1A 122
Neath Ho. SE24 —5M 91
(off Dulwich Rd.)
Neathouse Pl. SW1 —5G 75
Neats Acre. Ruis —5B 36
Neatscourt Rd. E6 —8H 63
Neave Cres. Romf —8G 35
Nebraska St. SE1 —3B 76
Neckinger. SE1 —4D 76
Neckinger Est. SE16 —4D 76
Neckinger St. SE1 —3D 76
Nectarine Way. SE13 —1M 93
Needham Ho. SE11 —6L 75
(off Hotspur St.)
Needham Rd. W11 —9L 57
Needham Ter. NW2 —8H 41
Needleman St. SE16 —3H 77
Needwood Ho. N4 —6A 44
Neela Clo. Uxb —9A 36
Neeld Cres. NW4 —3F 40
Neeld Cres. Wemb —1L 55
Neeld Pde. Wemb —1K 55
Neil Clo. Ashf —2A 100
Neil Wates Cres. SW2 —7L 91
Nelgarde Rd. SE6 —6L 93
Nella Rd. W6 —7H 73
Nelldale Rd. SE16 —5G 77
Nellgrove Rd. Uxb —7F 142
Nell Gwynne Av. Shep —1B 116
Nell Gwynne Clo. Eps —3L 133
Nello James Gdns. SE27 —1B 108
Nelmes Clo. Horn —3K 51
Nelmes Cres. Horn —3J 51
Nelmes Rd. Horn —5J 51
Nelmes Way. Horn —2H 51
Nelson Clo. NW6 —6L 57
(off Cambridge Rd.)
Nelson Clo. Big H —9J 141
Nelson Clo. Croy —3M 123
Nelson Clo. Felt —7D 84
Nelson Clo. Romf —8M 33
Nelson Clo. Uxb —6F 142
Nelson Clo. W on T —3F 116
Nelson Ct. SE1 —3M 75
Nelson Ct. Eri —8D 82
(off Frobisher Rd.)
Nelson Gdns. E2 —6E 60
Nelson Gdns. Houn —5L 85
Nelson Gro. Rd. SW19 —5A 106
Nelson Ho. SW1 —7G 75
(off Dolphin Sq.)
Nelson Ho. Romf —5J 35
(off Lindfield Rd.)
Nelson Ind. Est. SW19 —5M 105
Nelson La. Uxb —6F 142
Nelson Mandela Clo. N10 —9E 26
Nelson Mandela Rd. SE3 —2G 95
Nelson Pas. EC1 —6A 60
Nelson Pl. N1 —5M 59
Nelson Pl. Sidc —1E 112
Nelson Rd. E4 —6M 29
Nelson Rd. E11 —2E 46
Nelson Rd. N8 —3K 43
Nelson Rd. N9 —2F 28
Nelson Rd. N15 —2C 44
Nelson Rd. SE10 —7A 78
Nelson Rd. SW19 —4M 105
Nelson Rd. Belv —6K 81
Nelson Rd. Brom —8G 111
Nelson Rd. Dart —5G 99
Nelson Rd. Enf —8H 17
Nelson Rd. Harr —6B 38
Nelson Rd. Houn —5L 85
Nelson Rd. H'row A —9K 143
Nelson Rd. N Mald —9B 104
Nelson Rd. Rain —5D 66
Nelson Rd. Sidc —1E 112
Nelson Rd. Stan —6G 23
Nelson Rd. Uxb —6F 142
Nelson Rd. M. SW19 —4M 105
Nelson's Column. —2J 75
Nelson Sq. SE1 —3M 75
Nelson's Row. SW4 —3H 91
Nelson St. E1 —9F 60
Nelson St. E6 —5K 63
(in two parts)
Nelson St. E16 —1D 78
(in two parts)
Nelsons Yd. NW1 —5G 59
(off Mornington Cres.)
Nelson Ter. EC1 —5M 59
Nelson Wlk. SE16 —2J 77
Nelson Wlk. Eps —1L 133
Nelwyn Av. Horn —3K 51
Nemoure Rd. W3 —1A 72
Nene Gdns. Felt —8K 85
Nene Rd. H'row A —9M 143
Nene Rd. Roundabout. H'row A —9M 143
Nepaul Rd. SW11 —1C 90
Nepean St. SW15 —5E 88
Neptune Clo. Rain —5D 66
Neptune Ct. E14 —5L 77
(off Homer Dri.)
Neptune Ct. Borwd —5L 11
Neptune Ct. Eri —8D 82
(off Frobisher Rd.)
Neptune Ho. SE16 —4G 77
(off Moodkee St.)
Neptune Rd. Harr —4B 38
Neptune Rd. H'row A —9A 68
Neptune St. SE16 —4G 77
Neptune Wlk. Eri —5B 82
Nero Ct. Bren —8H 71
Nesbit Rd. SE9 —3H 95
Nesbitt Clo. SE3 —2C 94
Nesbitts All. Barn —5K 13
Nesbitt Sq. SE19 —4C 108
Nesham St. E1 —2E 76
Ness Rd. Eri —7H 83
Ness St. SE16 —4E 76
Nesta Rd. Wfd G —6C 30
Nestles Av. Hay —4D 68
Neston Rd. Wat —1G 9
Nestor Av. N21 —8M 15
Nestor Ho. E2 —5F 60
(off Old Bethnal Grn. Rd.)
Nethan Dri. Ave —1M 83
Netheravon Rd. W4 —5D 72
Netheravon Rd. W7 —2D 70
Netheravon Rd. S. W4 —6D 72
Netherbury Rd. W5 —4H 71
Netherby Gdns. Enf —6J 15
Netherby Pk. Wey —7C 116
Netherby Rd. SE23 —6G 93
Nether Clo. N3 —7L 25
Nethercourt Av. N3 —6L 25
Netherfield Gdns. Bark —2B 64
Netherfield Rd. N12 —5M 25
Netherfield Rd. SW17 —9E 90
Netherford Rd. SW4 —1G 91
Netherhall Gdns. NW3 —2A 58
Netherhall Way. NW3 —1A 58
Netherlands Rd. Barn & New Bar —8B 14
Netherleigh Clo. N6 —6F 42
Netherpark Dri. Romf —9D 34
Nether St. N3 & N12 —8L 25
Netherton Gro. SW10 —7A 74
Netherton Rd. N15 —4B 44
Netherton Rd. Twic —4E 86
Netherwood. N2 —9B 26
Netherwood Rd. W6 —4H 73
Netherwood St. NW6 —3K 57
Nethewode Ct. Belv —4M 81
(off Lwr. Park Rd.)
Netley. SE5 —9C 76
(off Redbridge Gdns.)
Netley Clo. Cheam & Sutt —7H 121
Netley Clo. New Ad —9A 126
Netley Dri. W on T —2K 117
Netley Gdns. Mord —2A 122
Netley Rd. E17 —3K 45
Netley Rd. Bren —7J 71
Netley Rd. Ilf —3B 48
Netley Rd. Mord —2A 122
Netley St. NW1 —6G 59
Nettlecombe. NW1 —3H 59
(off Agar Gro.)
Nettlecombe Clo. Sutt —1M 135
Nettleden Av. Wemb —2L 55
Nettleden Ho. SW3 —5C 74
(off Marlborough St.)
Nettlefold Pl. SE27 —9M 91
Nettlestead Clo. Beck —4K 109
Nettleton Ct. EC2 —8A 60
(off London Wall)
Nettleton Rd. SE14 —9H 77
Nettleton Rd. H'row A —9M 143
Nettlewood Rd. SW16 —4H 107
Neuchatel Rd. SE6 —8K 93
Nevada Clo. N Mald —8A 104
Nevada St. SE10 —7A 78
Nevern Mans. SW5 —6L 73
(off Warwick Rd.)
Nevern Pl. SW5 —5L 73
Nevern Rd. SW5 —5L 73
Nevern Sq. SW5 —5L 73
Nevil Clo. N'wd —5B 20
Nevil Ho. SW9 —1M 91
(off Loughborough Est.)
Nevill Ct. EC4 —9L 59
(off E. Harding St.)
Neville Av. N Mald —5B 104
Neville Clo. E11 —8D 46
Neville Clo. NW1 —5H 59
Neville Clo. NW6 —5K 57
Neville Clo. SE15 —9E 76
Neville Clo. W3 —3A 72
Neville Clo. Bans —6M 135
Neville Clo. Esh —8K 117
Neville Clo. Houn —1M 85
Neville Clo. Sidc —1D 112
Neville Ct. NW8 —5B 58
(off Abbey Rd.)
Neville Dri. N2 —4A 42
Neville Gdns. Dag —8H 49
Neville Gill Clo. SW18 —5L 89
Neville Ho. N11 —4E 26
Neville Ho. N22 —8K 27
(off Neville Pl.)
Neville Ho. Yd. King T —6J 103
Neville Pl. N22 —8K 27
Neville Rd. E7 —3E 62
Neville Rd. NW6 —5K 57
Neville Rd. W5 —7H 55
Neville Rd. Croy —2B 124
Neville Rd. Dag —7H 49
Neville Rd. Ilf —8A 32
Neville Rd. King T —6L 103
Neville Rd. Rich —9G 87
Nevilles Ct. NW2 —8E 40
Neville St. SW7 —6B 74
Neville Ter. SW7 —6B 74
Neville Wlk. Cars —2C 122
Nevill Gro. Wat —3F 8
Nevill Rd. N16 —9C 44
Nevill Way. Lou —8J 19
Nevin Dri. E4 —1M 29
Nevin Ho. Hay —4A 68
Nevinson Clo. SW18 —5B 90
Nevis Clo. Romf —6C 34
Nevis Rd. SW17 —8E 90
Nevitt Ho. N1 —5B 60
(off Cranston Est.)
New Acres Rd. SE28 —3C 80
(in three parts)
New Addington. —2A 140
Newall Ho. SE1 —4A 76
(off Bath Ter.)
Newall Rd. H'row A —9A 68
New Arcade. Uxb —4B 142
Newark Ct. W on T —3G 117
Newark Cres. NW10 —6B 56
Newarke Ho. SW9 —1M 91
Newark Grn. Borwd —5B 12
Newark Knok. E6 —9L 63
Newark Pde. NW4 —1E 40
Newark Rd. S Croy —8B 124
Newark St. E1 —8F 60
(in two parts)
Newark Way. NW4 —2E 40
New Ash Clo. N2 —1B 42
New Atlas Wharf. E14 —4L 77
(off Glengall Causeway)
New Baltic Wharf. SE8 —6J 77
(off Evelyn St.)
New Barn Clo. Wall —8K 123
New Barnet. —6A 14
Newbarn La. W'ham & Cud —9M 141
New Barn La. Whyt —8C 138
New Barn Rd. Swan —5C 114
New Barns Av. Mitc —8H 107
(in two parts)
New Barn St. E13 —7E 62
New Barns Way. Chig —3M 31
New Beckenham. —3K 109
New Bentham Ct. N1 —3A 60
(off Ecclesbourne Rd.)
New Berry La. W on T —7H 117
Newbery Ho. N1 —3A 60
(off Northampton St.)
Newbery Rd. Eri —9D 82
Newbiggin Path. Wat —4G 21
Newbold Cotts. E1 —9G 61
Newbolt Av. Sutt —7G 121
Newbolt Ho. SE17 —6B 76
(off Brandon St.)
Newbolt Rd. Stan —5D 22
New Bond St. W1 —9F 58
Newborough Grn. N Mald —8B 104
New Brent St. NW4 —3G 41
Newbridge Point. SE23 —9H 93
(off Windrush La.)
New Bri. St. EC4 —9M 59
New Broad St. EC2 —8C 60
New B'way. W5 —1H 71
New B'way. Hamp —2B 102
New B'way. Uxb —6F 142
Newburgh Rd. W3 —2A 72
Newburgh St. W1 —9G 59
New Burlington M. W1 —1G 75
New Burlington Pl. W1 —1G 75
New Burlington St. W1 —1G 75
Newburn Ho. SE11 —6K 75
(off Newburn St.)
Newburn St. SE11 —6K 75
Newbury Av. Enf —2K 17
Newbury Clo. N'holt —2K 53
Newbury Clo. Romf —6G 35
Newbury Ct. Sidc —1D 112
Newbury Gdns. Eps —6D 120
Newbury Gdns. Romf —6H 35
Newbury Gdns. Upm —8K 51
Newbury Ho. N22 —8J 27
Newbury Ho. SW9 —1M 91
Newbury Ho. W2 —9M 57
(off Hallfield Est.)
Newbury M. NW5 —2E 58
Newbury Park. —3A 48
Newbury Rd. E4 —6A 30
Newbury Rd. Brom —7E 110
Newbury Rd. Ilf —4C 48
Newbury Rd. H'row A —9K 143
Newbury Rd. Romf —5H 35
Newbury St. EC1 —8A 60
Newbury Wlk. Romf —5H 35
Newbury Way. N'holt —2J 53
New Bus. Cen., The. NW10 —6D 56
New Butt La. SE8 —8L 77
(in two parts)

New B'way Bldgs.—Nine Elms Av.

New B'way Bldgs. W5 —1H 71
Newby. NW1 —6G 59
(off Robert St.)
Newby Clo. Enf —4C 16
Newby Pl. E14 —1A 78
Newby St. SW8 —2F 90
New Caledonian Wharf. SE16 —4K 77
Newcastle Av. Ilf —6E 32
Newcastle Clo. EC4 —9M 59
Newcastle Ct. EC4 —1A 76
(off College Hill)
Newcastle Ho. W1 —8E 58
(off Luxborough St.)
Newcastle Pl. W2 —8B 58
Newcastle Row. EC1 —7L 59
New Cavendish St. W1 —8E 58
New Change. EC4 —9A 60
New Chapel Sq. Felt —7F 84
New Charles St. EC1 —6M 59
New Charlton. —5G 79
New Chu. Rd. SE5 —8A 76
(in two parts)
New City Rd. E13 —6G 63
New Clo. SW19 —7A 106
New Clo. Felt —2J 101
New Colebrooke Ct. Cars —9E 122
(off Stanley Rd.)
New College Ct. NW3 —2A 58
(off College Cres.)
New College M. N1 —3L 59
New College Pde. NW3 —2B 58
(off College Cres.)
Newcombe Gdns. SW16 —1J 107
Newcombe Pk. NW7 —5C 24
Newcombe Pk. Wemb —4K 55
Newcombe Ri. W Dray —9C 142
Newcombe St. W8 —2L 73
Newcomen Rd. E11 —8D 46
Newcomen Rd. SW11 —2B 90
Newcomen St. SE1 —3B 76
New Compton St. WC2 —9H 59
New Concordia Wharf. SE1 —3E 76
New Cotts. Wal X —7C 6
New Ct. EC4 —1L 75
(off Fountain Ct.)
New Ct. N'holt —1M 53
Newcourt. Uxb —8A 142
Newcourt Ho. E2 —6F 60
(off Pott St.)
Newcourt St. NW8 —5C 58
New Covent Garden Market. —8H 75
New Coventry St. W1 —1H 75
New Crane Pl. E1 —2G 77
Newcroft Clo. Uxb —8D 142
New Cross. —8K 77
New Cross. (Junct.) —9K 77
New Cross Gate. —9H 77
New Cross Gate. (Junct.) —9H 77
New Cross Rd. SE15 & SE14 —8G 77
Newdales Clo. N9 —2E 28
Newdene Av. N'holt —5H 53
Newdigate Ho. E14 —9K 61
(off Norbiton Rd.)
Newell St. E14 —9K 61
New Eltham. —8A 96
New End. NW3 —9A 42
New End Sq. NW3 —9B 42
New England Ind. Est. Bark —5A 64
Newent Clo. SE15 —8C 76
New Era Est. N1 —4C 60
(off Phillipp St.)
New Farm Av. Brom —8E 110
New Farm La. N'wd —8C 20
New Fetter La. EC4 —9L 59
Newfield Clo. Hamp —5L 101
Newfield Ri. NW2 —8F 40
New Ford Rd. Wal X —7F 6
New Forest La. Chig —6L 31
Newgale Gdns. Edgw —8K 23
New Garden Dri. W Dray —3J 143
Newgate. Croy —3A 124
Newgate Clo. Felt —8J 85
Newgate St. E4 —3C 30
(in two parts)
Newgate St. EC1 —9M 59
New Globe Wlk. SE1 —2A 76
New Goulston St. E1 —9D 60
New Grn. Pl. SE19 —3C 108
Newhall Ct. Wal A —6M 7
New Hall Dri. Romf —8J 35
Newhall Gdns. W on T —4G 117
Newham Grn. N22 —8L 27
Newham's Row. SE1 —3C 76
Newham Way. E16 & E6 —8D 62
Newhaven Clo. Hay —5D 68
Newhaven Cres. Ashf —2B 100
Newhaven Gdns. SE9 —3H 95
Newhaven La. E16 —7D 62
Newhaven Rd. SE25 —9B 108
New Heston Rd. Houn —8K 69
New Horizons Ct. Bren —7G 71
Newhouse Av. Romf —1H 49
Newhouse Clo. N Mald —2C 120
Newhouse Cres. Wat —5F 4
Newhouse Wlk. Mord —2A 122
Newick Clo. Bex —5M 97
Newick Rd. E5 —9F 44
Newing Grn. Brom —4H 111
Newington. —4A 76
Newington Barrow Way. N7 —8K 43
Newington Butts. SE11 & SE1 —5M 75
Newington Causeway. SE1 —4M 75
Newington Ct. Bus. Cen. SE1
(off Newington Causeway) —4A 76
Newington Grn. N1 & N16 —1B 60
Newington Grn. Mans. N16 —1B 60
Newington Grn. Rd. N1 —2B 60
Newington Ind. Est. SE17 —5A 76
(off Crampton St.)
New Inn B'way. EC2 —7C 60
New Inn Pas. WC2 —9K 59
(off Houghton St.)
New Inn Sq. EC2 —7C 60
(off Bateman's Row)
New Inn St. EC2 —7C 60
New Inn Yd. EC2 —7C 60
New Jubilee Ct. Wfd G —7E 30
New Kelvin Av. Tedd —3C 102
New Kent Rd. SE1 —4A 76
New Kings Rd. SW6 —1K 89
New King St. SE8 —7L 77
Newland Clo. Pinn —6J 21
Newland Ct. EC1 —7B 60
(off St Luke's Est.)
Newland Dri. Enf —3F 16
Newland Gdns. W13 —3E 70
Newland Ho. N8 —1J 43
(off Newland Rd.)
Newland Ho. N8 —1J 43
(off Newland Rd.)
Newland Ho. SE14 —7H 77
(off John Williams Clo.)
Newland Rd. N8 —1J 43
Newlands. —4H 93
(Brockley)
Newlands. —3J 23
(Edgware)
Newlands. NW1 —6G 59
(off Harrington St.)
Newlands Av. Th Dit —3C 118
Newlands Clo. Edgw —3J 23
Newlands Clo. S'hall —6J 69
Newlands Clo. W on T —6J 117
Newlands Clo. Wemb —2G 55
Newlands Ct. SE9 —5L 95
Newlands Pk. SE26 —3G 109
Newlands Pl. Barn —7H 13
Newlands Quay. E1 —1G 77
Newlands Rd. SW16 —6J 107
Newlands Rd. Wfd G —2D 30
Newlands, The. Wall —9G 123
Newland St. E16 —2J 79
Newlands Wlk. Wat —6H 5
Newlands Way. Chess —7G 119
Newlands Wood. New Ad —1K 139
Newling Clo. E6 —9K 63
New London St. EC3 —1C 76
(off Hart St.)
New London Theatre. —9J 59
(off Drury La.)
New Lydenburg Commercial Est. SE7 —4G 79
New Lydenburg St. SE7 —4G 79
Newlyn. NW1 —4G 59
(off Plender St.)
Newlyn Clo. Brick W —3J 5
Newlyn Clo. Orp —6E 128
Newlyn Clo. Uxb —8E 142
Newlyn Gdns. Harr —5K 37
Newlyn Ho. Pinn —7K 21
Newlyn Rd. N17 —8D 28
Newlyn Rd. Barn —6K 13
Newlyn Rd. Well —1D 96
New Malden. —8C 104
Newman Clo. Horn —3J 51
Newman Pas. W1 —8G 59
Newman Rd. E13 —6F 62
Newman Rd. E17 —3H 45
Newman Rd. Brom —5E 110
Newman Rd. Croy —3K 123
Newman Rd. Hay —1F 68
Newman Rd. Ind. Est. Croy —2K 123
Newmans Clo. Lou —5L 19
Newman's Ct. EC3 —9B 60
(off Cornhill)
Newmans La. Lou —5L 19
Newmans La. Surb —1H 119
Newman's Row. WC2 —8K 59
Newman St. W1 —8G 59
Newman's Way. Barn —3A 14
Newman Yd. W1 —9G 59
Newmarket Av. N'holt —1L 53
Newmarket Grn. SE9 —6H 95
Newmarket Ho. Romf —5J 35
(off Lindfield Rd.)
Newmarket Way. Horn —9J 51
Newmarsh Rd. SE28 —2D 80
Newmill Ho. E3 —7A 62
New Mill Rd. Orp —5G 113
Newminster Rd. Mord —1A 122
New Mt. St. E15 —3B 62
Newnes Path. SW15 —3F 88
Newnet Clo. Cars —3D 122
Newnham Av. Ruis —6G 37
Newnham Clo. Lou —8H 19
Newnham Clo. N'holt —2A 54
Newnham Clo. T Hth —6A 108
Newnham Gdns. N'holt —2A 54
Newnham Ho. Lou —8H 19
Newnham Lodge. Belv —6L 81
(off Erith Rd.)
Newnham M. N22 —7K 27
Newnham Pde. Chesh —3D 6
Newnham Rd. N22 —8K 27
Newnhams Clo. Brom —7K 111
Newnham Ter. SE1 —4L 75
Newnham Way. Harr —3J 39
New N. Pl. EC2 —7C 60
New N. Rd. N1 —3A 60
New N. Rd. Ilf —7B 32
New N. St. WC1 —8K 59
Newnton Clo. N4 —5B 44
(in two parts)
New Oak Rd. N2 —9A 26
New Orleans Wlk. N19 —5H 43
New Oxford St. WC1 —9H 59
New Pde. Yiew —2J 143
New Pk. Av. N13 —3A 28
New Pk. Clo. N'holt —2J 53
New Pk. Est. N18 —5G 29
New Pk. Ho. N13 —4K 27
New Pk. Pde. SW2 —6J 91
(off New Pk. Rd.)
New Pk. Rd. SW2 —7H 91
New Pk. Rd. Ashf —2A 100
New Peachey La. Uxb —9B 142
Newpiece. Lou —5M 19
New Pl. New Ad —8L 125
New Pl. Sq. SE16 —4F 76
New Plaistow Rd. E15 —4C 62
New Plymouth Ho. Rain —6D 66
(off Dunedin Rd.)
New Pond Pde. Ruis —8E 36
Newport Av. E13 —7F 62
Newport Av. E14 —1B 78
Newport Clo. Enf —1J 17
Newport Ct. WC2 —1H 75
Newport Ho. E3 —6J 61
(off Strahan Rd.)
Newport Lodge. Enf —7C 16
(off Village Rd.)
Newport Mead. Wat —4H 21
Newport Pl. WC2 —1H 75
Newport Rd. E10 —7A 46
Newport Rd. E17 —2J 45
Newport Rd. SW13 —9E 72
Newport Rd. Hay —8B 52
Newport Rd. H'row A —9L 143
Newports. Swan —2B 130
Newport St. SE11 —5K 75
New Priory Ct. NW6 —3L 57
(off Mazenod Av.)
Newquay Cres. Harr —7J 37
Newquay Gdns. Wat —2F 20
Newquay Ho. SE11 —6L 75
Newquay Rd. SE6 —8M 93
New Quebec St. W1 —9D 58
New Ride. SW7 & SW1 —3B 74
New River Ct. N5 —9A 44
New River Ct. Chesh —4B 6
New River Cres. N13 —4M 27
New River Head. EC1 —6L 59
New River Wlk. N1 —3A 60
(off Canonbury Rd.)
New River Way. N4 —5B 44
New Rd. E1 —8F 60
New Rd. E4 —4M 29
New Rd. N8 —3J 43
New Rd. N9 —3E 28
New Rd. N17 —8D 28
New Rd. N22 —8A 28
New Rd. NW7 —9D 12
(Highwood Hill)
New Rd. NW7 —7J 25
(Mill Hill)
New Rd. SE2 —5H 81
New Rd. Bedf —7F 84
New Rd. Bren —7H 71
New Rd. Crox G —8A 8
New Rd. Dag & Rain —5L 65
New Rd. Els —8H 11
New Rd. Esh —5A 118
New Rd. Felt —5B 84
New Rd. Hanw —2J 101
New Rd. Harr —9D 38
New Rd. Hay —8A 68
New Rd. Hex —4D 114
New Rd. Houn —3M 85
New Rd. Ilf —7C 48
New Rd. King T —4L 103
New Rd. Let H —3C 10
New Rd. Mitc —3D 122
New Rd. Orp —2E 128
New Rd. Oxs —3D 132
New Rd. Rad —1C 10
New Rd. Rich —1G 103
New Rd. Shep —7A 100
New Rd. Swan —7D 114
New Rd. Uxb —7A 52
New Rd. Wat —6G 9
New Rd. Well —1F 96
New Rd. W Mol —8L 101
New Rd. Wey —7A 116
New Rd. Hill. Kes & Orp —1J 141
New Rochford St. NW5 —1D 58
New Row. WC2 —1J 75
Newry Rd. Twic —4E 86
Newsam Av. N15 —3B 44
Newsholme Av. N21 —7K 15
New Southgate. —5F 26
New Southgate Crematorium. N11 —3F 26
New Southgate Ind. Est. N11 —5G 27
New Spitalfields Market. —8L 45
New Spitalfields Mkt. E10 —8M 45
New Spring Gdns. Wlk. SE1 —6J 75
New Sq. WC2 —9L 59
New Sq. Felt —7A 84
New Sq. Pas. WC2 —9L 59
(off Star Yd.)
Newstead Av. Orp —5B 128
Newstead Clo. N12 —6C 26
Newstead Ct. N'holt —6J 53
Newstead Ho. Romf —4H 35
(off Troopers Dri.)
Newstead Rd. SE12 —6D 94
Newstead Wlk. Cars —2A 122
Newstead Way. SW19 —1H 105
New St. EC2 —8C 60
New St. Wat —6G 9
New St. Hill. Brom —2F 110
New St. Sq. EC4 —9L 59
Newteswell Dri. Wal A —5K 7
Newton Av. N10 —8E 26
Newton Av. W3 —3A 72
Newton Clo. E17 —4J 45
Newton Clo. Harr —7L 37
Newton Cres. Borwd —6A 12
Newton Gro. W4 —5C 72
Newton Ho. E1 —1F 76
(off Cornwall St.)
Newton Ho. E17 —1M 45
(off Prospect Hill)
Newton Ho. NW8 —4M 57
(off Abbey Rd.)
Newton Ho. SE20 —4H 109
Newton Ho. Borwd —5B 12
(off Chester Rd.)
Newton Ind. Est. Romf —2H 49
Newton Mans. W14 —7J 73
(off Queen's Club Gdns.)
Newton Point. E16 —9D 62
(off Clarkson Rd.)
Newton Rd. E15 —1B 62
Newton Rd. N15 —3E 44
Newton Rd. NW2 —9G 41
Newton Rd. SW19 —4J 105
Newton Rd. W2 —9M 57
Newton Rd. Chig —5F 32
Newton Rd. Harr —9C 22
Newton Rd. Iswth —1D 86
Newton Rd. H'row A —9J 143
Newton Rd. Purl —4G 137
Newton Rd. Well —2E 96
Newton Rd. Wemb —3K 55
Newtons Clo. Rain —3D 66
Newton St. WC1 —9J 59
Newton's Yd. SW18 —4L 89
Newton Ter. Brom —1H 127
Newton Wlk. Edgw —8M 23
Newton Way. N18 —5A 28
Newton Wood Rd. Asht —8K 133
New Tower Bldgs. E1 —2F 76
New Town. —5K 99
Newtown Rd. Den —2A 142
Newtown St. SW11 —9F 74
New Trinity Rd. N2 —1B 42
New Turnstile. WC1 —8K 59
New Union Clo. E14 —4A 78
New Union St. EC2 —8B 60
New Wanstead. E11 —4D 46
New Way Rd. NW9 —2C 40
New Wharf Rd. N1 —5J 59
New Windsor St. Uxb —4A 142
New Zealand Av. W on T —3D 116
New Zealand Way. W12 —1F 72
New Zealand Way. Rain —6D 66
Niagara Av. W5 —5G 71
Niagara Clo. Chesh —2D 6
Niagra Clo. N1 —5A 60
Niagra Ct. SE16 —4G 77
(off Canada Est.)
Nibthwaite Rd. Harr —3C 38
Nicholas Clo. Gnfd —5M 53
Nicholas Clo. Wat —1F 8
Nicholas Ct. W4 —7C 72
(off Corney Reach Way)
Nicholas Gdns. W5 —3H 71
Nicholas La. EC4 —1B 76
(in two parts)
Nicholas Pas. EC4 —1B 76
(off Nicholas La.)
Nicholas Rd. E1 —7G 61
Nicholas Rd. Croy —6J 123
Nicholas Rd. Dag —7K 49
Nicholas Rd. Els —8K 11
Nicholas Way. N'wd —8A 20
Nichola Ter. Bexh —9J 81
Nicholay Rd. N19 —6H 43
Nichol Clo. N14 —1H 27
Nicholes Rd. Houn —3L 85
Nichol La. Brom —4E 110
Nicholl Ho. N4 —6A 44
Nicholls Av. Uxb —7E 142
Nichollsfield Wlk. N7 —1K 59
Nicholls Point. E13 —4E 62
(off Park Gro.)
Nicholl St. E2 —4E 60
Nichols Clo. N4 —6L 43
(off Osborne Rd.)
Nichols Clo. Chess —8G 119
Nichols Grn. W5 —8H 55
Nicholson Ct. E17 —2J 45
Nicholson Dri. Bush —1A 22
Nicholson Ho. SE17 —6B 76
Nicholson M. King T —8J 103
Nicholson Rd. Croy —3D 124
Nicholson St. SE1 —2M 75
Nickelby Clo. SE28 —9G 65
Nickleby Clo. Uxb —9F 142
Nickleby Ho. SE16 —3E 76
(off George Row)
Nicola Clo. Harr —9B 22
Nicola Clo. S Croy —8A 124
Nicola M. Ilf —7M 31
Nicol Clo. Twic —5F 86
Nicoll Ct. N10 —7F 26
Nicoll Ct. NW10 —4C 56
Nicoll Pl. NW4 —4F 40
Nicoll Rd. NW10 —4C 56
Nicoll Way. Borwd —7B 12
Nicolson. NW9 —8C 24
Nicolson Rd. Orp —2H 129
Nicosia Rd. SW18 —6C 90
Niederwald Rd. SE26 —1J 109
Nield Rd. Hay —3D 68
Nigel Clo. N'holt —4J 53
Nigel Ct. N3 —7M 25
Nigel Fisher Way. Chess —9G 119
Nigel Ho. EC1 —8L 59
(off Portpool La.)
Nigel M. Ilf —9M 47
Nigel Playfair Av. W6 —5F 72
Nigel Rd. E7 —1G 63
Nigel Rd. SE15 —2E 92
Nigeria Rd. SE7 —8G 79
Nighthawk. NW9 —8D 24
Nightingale Av. E4 —5C 30
Nightingale Av. Harr —6F 38
Nightingale Clo. E4 —4B 30
Nightingale Clo. W4 —7A 72
Nightingale Clo. Ab L —4E 4
Nightingale Clo. Big H —7G 141
Nightingale Clo. Cars —4E 122
Nightingale Clo. Eps —4L 133
Nightingale Clo. Pinn —3G 37
Nightingale Clo. Rad —1D 10
Nightingale Corner. Orp —8H 113
Nightingale Ct. E14 —3A 78
(off Ovex Clo.)
Nightingale Ct. N4 —7K 43
(off Tollington Pk.)
Nightingale Ct. SW6 —9M 73
(off Maltings Pl.)
Nightingale Ct. Short —6C 110
Nightingale Dri. Eps —8M 119
Nightingale Gro. SE13 —4B 94
Nightingale Gro. Dart —3L 99
Nightingale Heights. SE18 —7M 79
Nightingale Ho. E1 —2E 76
(off Thomas More St.)
Nightingale Ho. N1 —4C 60
(off Wilmer Gdns.)
Nightingale Ho. SE18 —6L 79
(off Connaught M.)
Nightingale Ho. Eps —4C 134
Nightingale La. E11 —2F 46
Nightingale La. N8 —2J 43
Nightingale La. SW12 & SW4 —6D 90
Nightingale La. Brom —6G 111
Nightingale La. Rich —6J 87
Nightingale Lodge. W9 —8L 57
(off Admiral Wlk.)
Nightingale M. E3 —5H 61
Nightingale M. King T —7H 103
(off South La.)
Nightingale Pl. SE18 —7L 79
Nightingale Pl. SW10 —7A 74
Nightingale Rd. E5 —8F 44
Nightingale Rd. N9 —8G 17
Nightingale Rd. N22 —7J 27
Nightingale Rd. NW10 —5D 56
Nightingale Rd. W7 —2D 70
Nightingale Rd. Bush —7L 9
Nightingale Rd. Cars —5D 122
Nightingale Rd. Esh —7K 117
Nightingale Rd. Hamp —2L 101
Nightingale Rd. Orp —1A 128
Nightingale Rd. S Croy —3H 139
Nightingale Rd. W on T —2G 117
Nightingale Rd. W Mol —9M 101
Nightingales. Wal A —7L 7
Nightingale Sq. SW12 —6E 90
Nightingales, The. Stai —6D 144
Nightingale Va. SE18 —7L 79
Nightingale Wlk. SW4 —5F 90
Nightingale Way. E6 —8J 63
Nightingale Way. Swan —7C 114
Nikols Wlk. SW18 —3M 89
Nile Clo. N16 —8D 44
Nile Path. SE18 —7L 79
Nile Rd. E13 —5G 63
Nile St. N1 —6A 60
Nile Ter. SE15 —6D 76
Nimbus Rd. Eps —2B 134
Nimegen Way. SE22 —4C 92
Nimmo Dri. Bus H —9B 10
Nimrod. NW9 —8C 24
Nimrod Clo. N'holt —6H 53
Nimrod Ho. E16 —8F 62
(off Vanguard Clo.)
Nimrod Pas. N1 —2C 60
Nimrod Rd. SW16 —3F 106
Nina Mackay Clo. E15 —4C 62
Nine Acres Clo. E12 —1J 63
Nineacres Way. Coul —8J 137
Nine Elms. —8G 75
Nine Elms Av. Uxb —8B 142

Nine Elms Clo.—Northstead Rd.

Nine Elms Clo. Felt —7D **84**
Nine Elms Clo. Uxb —8B **142**
Nine Elms La. SW8 —8G **75**
Ninefields. Wal A —6M **7**
Nineteenth Rd. Mitc —8J **107**
Ninhams Wood. Orp —6L **127**
Ninth Av. Hay —1E **68**
Nita Ct. SE12 —7E **94**
Nithdale Rd. SE18 —8M **79**
Nithsdale Gro. Uxb —8A **36**
Niton Clo. Barn —8H **13**
Niton Rd. Rich —2L **87**
Niton St. SW6 —8H **73**
Niven Clo. Borwd —3A **12**
Noak Hill. —2J 35
Noak Hill Rd. Noak H & Romf —5F **34**
Nobel Dri. Hay —9B **68**
Nobel Ho. SE5 —1A **92**
Nobel Rd. N18 —4G **29**
Noble Corner. Houn —9L **69**
Noble Ct. E1 —1F 76
(off Cable St., in two parts)
Noble Ct. Mitc —6B **106**
Noblefield Heights. N2 —3C **42**
Noble St. EC2 —9A **60**
Noel. NW9 —8C **24**
Noel Ct. Houn —2K **85**
Noel Coward Ho. SW1 —5G 75
(off Vauxhall Bri. Rd.)
Noel Ho. NW3 —3B **58**
Noel Park. —9M 27
Noel Pk. Rd. N22 —9L **27**
Noel Rd. E6 —7J **63**
Noel Rd. N1 —5M **59**
Noel Rd. W3 —1L **71**
Noel Sq. Dag —9G **49**
Noel St. W1 —9G **59**
Noel Ter. SE23 —8G **93**
Noel Ter. Sidc —1F **112**
Noke La. St Alb —1K **5**
Nolan Way. E5 —9E **44**
Nolton Pl. Edgw —8K **23**
Nonsuch Clo. Ilf —6M **31**
Nonsuch Ct. Av. Eps —2F **134**
Nonsuch Pl. Sutt —9H **121**
Nonsuch Trad. Est. Eps —3C **134**
Nonsuch Wlk. Sutt —2G **135**
(in two parts)
Nora Gdns. NW4 —2H **41**
Norbiton. —6L 103
Norbiton Av. King T —5L **103**
Norbiton Comn. Rd. King T —7M **103**
Norbiton Hall. King T —6K **103**
Norbiton Rd. E14 —9K **61**
Norbreck Gdns. NW10 —6K **55**
Norbreck Pde. NW10 —6J **55**
Norbroke St. W12 —1D **72**
Norburn St. W10 —8J **57**
Norbury. —6K 107
Norbury Av. SW16 & T Hth —5K **107**
Norbury Av. Houn —3B **86**
Norbury Av. Wat —3G **9**
Norbury Clo. SW16 —5L **107**
Norbury Ct. Rd. SW16 —7J **107**
Norbury Cres. SW16 —5K **107**
Norbury Cross. SW16 —7J **107**
Norbury Gdns. Romf —3H **49**
Norbury Gro. NW7 —3C **24**
Norbury Hill. SW16 —4L **107**
Norbury Ri. SW16 —7J **107**
Norbury Rd. E4 —5L **29**
Norbury Rd. T Hth —6A **108**
Norbury Trad. Est. SW16 —6K **107**
Norcombe Gdns. Harr —4G **39**
Norcombe Ho. N19 —8H 43
(off Wedmore St.)
Norcott Clo. Hay —7G **53**
Norcott Rd. N16 —7E **44**
Norcroft Gdns. SE22 —6E **92**
Norcutt Rd. Twic —7C **86**
Nordenfeldt Rd. Eri —6B **82**
Norden Ho. E2 —6F 60
(off Pott St.)
Norfield Rd. Dart —1A **114**
Norfolk Av. N13 —6M **27**
Norfolk Av. N15 —4D **44**
Norfolk Av. S Croy —2D **138**
Norfolk Av. Wat —2G **9**
Norfolk Clo. N2 —1C **42**
Norfolk Clo. N13 —6M **27**
Norfolk Clo. Barn —6E **14**
Norfolk Clo. Dart —5L **99**
Norfolk Clo. Twic —5F **86**
Norfolk Ct. Barn —6J **13**
Norfolk Cres. W2 —9C **58**
Norfolk Cres. Sidc —6C **96**
Norfolk Gdns. Bexh —9K **81**
Norfolk Gdns. Borwd —6B **12**
Norfolk Gdns. Houn —4K **85**
Norfolk Ho. SE8 —9L **77**
Norfolk Ho. SE20 —5G **109**
Norfolk Ho. SW1 —5H 75
(off Page St.)
Norfolk Ho. Rd. SW16 —9H **91**
Norfolk Mans. SW11 —9D 74
(off Prince of Wales Dri.)
Norfolk M. W10 —8K 57
(off Blagrove Rd.)
Norfolk Pl. W2 —9B **58**
(in two parts)
Norfolk Pl. Well —1E **96**
Norfolk Rd. E6 —4K **63**
Norfolk Rd. E17 —9H **29**
Norfolk Rd. NW8 —4B **58**
Norfolk Rd. NW10 —3C **56**
Norfolk Rd. SW19 —4C **106**
Norfolk Rd. Bark —3C **64**
Norfolk Rd. Barn —5L **13**
Norfolk Rd. Clay —7C **118**
Norfolk Rd. Dag —1M **65**
Norfolk Rd. Enf —8F **16**
Norfolk Rd. Felt —7G **85**
Norfolk Rd. Harr —3M **37**
Norfolk Rd. Ilf —6C **48**
Norfolk Rd. Romf —4A **50**
Norfolk Rd. T Hth —7A **108**
Norfolk Rd. Upm —8L **51**
Norfolk Rd. Uxb —2B **142**
Norfolk Row. SE1 —5K **75**
(in two parts)
Norfolk Sq. W2 —9B **58**
Norfolk Sq. M. W2 —9B 58
(off London St.)
Norfolk St. E7 —1E **62**
Norfolk Ter. W6 —6J **73**
Norgrove St. SW12 —6E **90**
Norham Ct. Dart —5M 99
(off Osbourne Rd.)
Norheads La. Big H —9E **140**
Norhyrst Av. SE25 —7D **108**
Nork. —7H 135
Nork Gdns. Bans —6J **135**
Nork Ri. Bans —8H **135**
Nork Way. Bans —8G **135**
Norland Ho. W11 —2H 73
(off Queensdale Cres.)
Norland Pl. W11 —2J **73**
Norland Rd. W11 —2H 73
(off Queensdale Cres.)
Norlands Cres. Chst —5M **111**
Norland Sq. W11 —2J **73**
Norland Sq. Mans. W11 —2J 73
(off Norland Sq.)
Norley Va. SW15 —7E **88**
Norlington Rd. E10 & E11 —6A **46**
Norman Av. N22 —8M **27**
Norman Av. Eps —4D **134**
Norman Av. Felt —8J **85**
Norman Av. S'hall —1J **69**
Norman Av. S Croy —2A **138**
Norman Av. Twic —6G **87**
Normanby Clo. SW15 —4K **89**
Normanby Rd. NW10 —9D **40**
Norman Clo. N22 —8A **28**
Norman Clo. Orp —5A **128**
Norman Clo. Romf —8M **33**
Norman Clo. Wal A —6K **7**
Norman Colyer Ct. Eps —2B **134**
Norman Ct. N4 —5L **43**
Norman Ct. NW10 —3E **56**
Norman Ct. W13 —2F 70
(off Kirkfield Clo.)
Norman Ct. Ilf —5B **48**
Norman Cres. Houn —8H **69**
Norman Cres. Pinn —8G **21**
Normand Gdns. W14 —7J 73
(off Greyhound Rd.)
Normand M. W14 —7J **73**
Normand Rd. W14 —7K **73**
Normandy Av. Barn —7K **13**
Normandy Clo. SE26 —9J **93**
Normandy Dri. Hay —9A **52**
Normandy Rd. SW9 —9L **75**
Normandy Ter. E16 —9F **62**
Normandy Way. Eri —9C **82**
Norman Gro. E3 —5J **61**
Norman Hay Trad. Est. W Dray —8K **143**
Norman Ho. SW8 —8J 75
(off Wyvil Rd.)
Norman Ho. Felt —8K 85
(off Watermill Way)
Normanhurst Av. Bexh —9H **81**
Normanhurst Dri. Twic —4E **86**
Normanhurst Rd. SW2 —8K **91**
Normanhurst Rd. Orp —6F **112**
Normanhurst Rd. W on T —4H **117**
Norman Pde. Sidc —8H **97**
Norman Rd. E6 —7K **63**
Norman Rd. E11 —7B **46**
Norman Rd. N15 —3D **44**
Norman Rd. SE10 —8M **77**
Norman Rd. SW19 —4A **106**
Norman Rd. Ashf —3B **100**
Norman Rd. Belv —4M **81**
Norman Rd. Dart —7J **99**
Norman Rd. Horn —5E **50**
Norman Rd. Ilf —1M **63**
Norman Rd. Sutt —7L **121**
Norman Rd. T Hth —9M **107**
Norman's Clo. NW10 —2B **56**
Normans Clo. Uxb —7D **142**
Normansfield Av. Tedd —4G **103**
Normans Fld. Clo. Bush —9M **9**
Normanshire Av. E4 —4A **30**
Normanshire Dri. E4 —4L **29**
Norman's Mead. NW10 —2B **56**
Norman St. EC1 —6A **60**
Normanton Av. SW19 —8L **89**
Normanton Pk. E4 —2C **30**
Normanton Rd. S Croy —7C **124**
Normanton St. SE23 —8H **93**
Norman Way. N14 —2J **27**
Norman Way. W3 —8M **55**
Normington Clo. SW16 —2L **107**
Norrice Lea. N2 —3B **42**
Norris. NW9 —8D 24
(off Concourse, The)
Norris Ho. N1 —4C 60
(off Colville Est.)
Norris Ho. SE8 —6K 77
(off Grove St.)
Norris St. SW1 —1H **75**
Norris Way. Dart —2D **98**
Norroy Rd. SW15 —3H **89**
Norry's Clo. Cockf —6D **14**
Norry's Rd. Cockf —6D **14**
Norseman Clo. Ilf —6F **48**
Norseman Way. Gnfd —4M **53**
Norstead Pl. SW15 —8E **88**
N. Access Rd. E17 —4H **45**
North Acre. NW9 —8C **24**
North Acre. Bans —8K **135**
North Acton. —7B 56
N. Acton Rd. NW10 —5B **56**
Northallerton Way. Romf —5H **35**
Northall Rd. Bexh —1A **98**
Northampton Gro. N1 —1A **60**
Northampton Ho. Romf —4J 35
(off Broseley Rd.)
Northampton Pk. N1 —2A **60**
Northampton Rd. EC1 —7L **59**
Northampton Rd. Croy —4E **124**
Northampton Rd. Enf —6J **17**
Northampton Row. EC1 —7L 59
(off Rosoman Pl.)
Northampton Sq. EC1 —6M **59**
Northampton St. N1 —3A **60**
Northanger Rd. SW16 —3J **107**
North App. N'wd —2A **20**
North App. Wat —8D **4**
N. Audley St. W1 —9E **58**
North Av. N18 —4E **28**
North Av. NW10 —6G **57**
North Av. W13 —8F **54**
North Av. Cars —9E **122**
North Av. Harr —4M **37**
North Av. Hay —1E **68**
North Av. Rich —9L **71**
North Av. S'hall —1K **69**
North Av. W Vill —9C **116**
North Bank. NW8 —6C **58**
Northbank Rd. E17 —9A **30**
North Beckton. —8J 63
N. Birkbeck Rd. E11 —8B **46**
North Block. SE1 —3K 75
(off York Rd.)
Northborough Rd. SW16 —7H **107**
Northbourne. Brom —2E **126**
Northbourne Rd. SW4 —4H **91**
N. Branch Av. NW10 —6G **57**
Northbrook Dri. N'wd —8C **20**
Northbrook Rd. N22 —7J **27**
Northbrook Rd. SE13 —4C **94**
Northbrook Rd. Barn —8J **13**
Northbrook Rd. Croy —9B **108**
Northbrook Rd. Ilf —7L **47**
Northburgh St. EC1 —7M **59**
N. Carriage Dri. W2 —1C **74**
North Cheam. —6H 121
Northchurch. SE17 —6B **76**
(in three parts)
Northchurch Rd. N1 —3B **60**
(in two parts)
Northchurch Rd. Wemb —2L **55**
Northchurch Ter. N1 —3C **60**
(in two parts)
N. Circular Rd. E4 —6K **29**
N. Circular Rd. N3 —2K **41**
N. Circular Rd. N13 —5L **27**
N. Circular Rd. NW2 —8C **40**
N. Circular Rd. NW4 —5G **41**
N. Circular Rd. NW10 —5K **55**
Northcliffe Clo. Wor Pk —5C **120**
Northcliffe Dri. N20 —1K **25**
North Clo. Barn —7G **13**
North Clo. Bexh —3H **97**
North Clo. Chig —5E **32**
North Clo. Dag —4L **65**
North Clo. Felt —5B **84**
North Clo. Mord —8J **105**
N. Colonnade, The. E14 —2L **77**
North Comn. Wey —6A **116**
North Comn. Rd. W5 —1J **71**
North Comn. Rd. Uxb —1B **142**
Northcote. Oxs —6A **132**
Northcote. Pinn —9G **21**
Northcote Av. W5 —1J **71**
Northcote Av. Iswth —4E **86**
Northcote Av. S'hall —1J **69**
Northcote Av. Surb —2M **119**
Northcote M. SW11 —3C **90**
Northcote Rd. E17 —2J **45**
Northcote Rd. NW10 —3C **56**
Northcote Rd. SW11 —4C **90**
Northcote Rd. Croy —1B **124**
Northcote Rd. N Mald —7A **104**
Northcote Rd. Sidc —1C **112**
Northcote Rd. Twic —4E **86**
Northcott Av. N22 —8J **27**
Northcotts. Ab L —6B 4
(off Long Elms Clo.)
N. Countess Rd. E17 —9K **29**
North Ct. SE24 —2M **91**
North Ct. SW1 —4J 75
(off Gt. Peter St.)
North Ct. W1 —8G **59**
North Ct. Brom —5E 110
(off Palace Gro.)
North Cray. —2J 113
N. Cray Rd. Sidc & Bex —3J **113**
North Cres. E16 —7B **62**
North Cres. N3 —9K **25**
North Cres. WC1 —8H **59**
Northcroft Ct. W12 —3E **72**
Northcroft Rd. W13 —3F **70**
Northcroft Rd. Eps —9C **120**
North Crofts. SE23 —7F **92**
Northcroft Ter. W13 —3F **70**
N. Cross Rd. SE22 —4D **92**
N. Cross Rd. Ilf —2A **48**
Northdale Ct. SE25 —7D **108**
North Dene. NW7 —3B **24**
Northdene. Chig —5B **32**
North Dene. Houn —9M **69**
Northdene Gdns. N15 —4D **44**
North Down. S Croy —3C **138**
Northdown Clo. Ruis —8D **36**
Northdown Gdns. Ilf —3C **48**
Northdown Rd. Horn —5F **50**
Northdown Rd. Sutt —2L **135**
Northdown Rd. Well —1F **96**
N. Downs Cres. New Ad —1M **139**
(in two parts)
N. Downs Rd. New Ad —2M **139**
Northdown St. N1 —5J **59**
North Dri. SW16 —1G **107**
North Dri. Beck —8M **109**
North Dri. Houn —1A **86**
North Dri. Orp —6C **128**
North Dri. Romf —1G **51**
North Dri. Ruis —5C **36**
N. East Pier. E1 —2F **76**
North East Surrey Crematorium. Mord —1G **121**
North End. —8D 82
(Erith)
North End. —7A 42
(Hampstead)
North End. NW3 —7A **42**
North End. Buck H —9G **19**
North End. Croy —4A **124**
North End. Noak H —2G **35**
N. End Av. NW3 —7A **42**
N. End Cres. W14 —5K **73**
N. End Ho. W14 —5J **73**
N. End La. Orp —3L **141**
N. End Pde. W14 —5J 73
(off N. End Rd.)
N. End Rd. NW11 —6L **41**
N. End Rd. W14 & SW6 —5J **73**
Northend Rd. Eri —8D **82**
N. End Rd. Wemb —8L **39**
Northend Trad. Est. Eri —9C **82**
N. End Way. NW3 —7A **42**
Northern Av. N9 —2C **28**
Northernhay Wlk. Mord —8J **105**
Northern Perimeter Rd. H'row A —9M **143**
Northern Perimeter Rd. W. H'row A —9J **143**
Northern Rd. E13 —5F **62**
Northesk Ho. E1 —7F 60
(off Tent St.)
Northey Av. Sutt —2H **135**
N. Eyot Gdns. W6 —6D **72**
Northey St. E14 —1J **77**
North Feltham. —5F 84
N. Feltham Trad. Est. Felt —4F **84**
Northfield. Lou —6H **19**
Northfield Av. W13 & W5 —2F **70**
Northfield Av. Orp —1G **129**
Northfield Av. Pinn —2H **37**
Northfield Clo. Brom —5J **111**
Northfield Clo. Hay —4D **68**
Northfield Cres. Sutt —6J **121**
Northfield Gdns. Dag —9K **49**
Northfield Gdns. Wat —1G **9**
Northfield Ho. SE15 —7E **76**
Northfield Ind. Est. NW10 —6L **55**
Northfield Ind. Est. Wemb —4L **55**
Northfield Pde. Hay —4C **68**
Northfield Pk. Hay —4D **68**
Northfield Path. Dag —9K **49**
Northfield Pl. Wey —9A **116**
Northfield Rd. E6 —3K **63**
Northfield Rd. N16 —5C **44**
Northfield Rd. W13 —3F **70**
Northfield Rd. Barn —5C **14**
Northfield Rd. Borwd —3M **11**
Northfield Rd. Dag —9K **49**
Northfield Rd. Enf —7F **16**
Northfield Rd. Houn —7H **69**
Northfield Rd. Wal X —5E **6**
Northfields. —4F 70
Northfields. SW18 —3L **89**
Northfields. Eps —3C **134**
Northfields Prospect Bus. Cen. SW18 —3L **89**
Northfields Rd. W3 —8M **55**
North Finchley. —5A 26
Northfleet Ho. SE1 —3B 76
(off Tennis St.)
N. Flock St. SE16 —3E **76**
N. Flower Wlk. W2 —1A 74
(off Lancaster Wlk.)
North Garden. E14 —2K **77**
North Gdns. SW19 —4B **106**
North Ga. NW8 —5C 58
(off Prince Albert Rd.)
Northgate. N'wd —7A **20**
Northgate Bus. Pk. Enf —5F **16**
Northgate Dri. NW9 —4C **40**
Northgate Ho. E14 —1L 77
(off E. India Dock Rd.)
Northgate Ind. Est. Romf —8K **33**
Northgate Path. Borwd —2K **11**
N. Glade, The. Bex —6K **97**
N. Gower St. NW1 —6G **59**
North Grn. NW9 —7C **24**
North Gro. N6 —5E **42**
North Gro. N15 —3B **44**
North Harrow. —3M 37
N. Hatton Rd. H'row A —9B **68**
North Hill. N6 —4D **42**
N. Hill Av. N6 —4E **42**
N. Hill Dri. Romf —3H **35**
N. Hill Grn. Romf —4H **35**
North Hillingdon. —3A 52
North Ho. SE8 —6K **77**
N. Hyde Gdns. Hay —5E **68**
N. Hyde La. S'hall & Houn —6H **69**
N. Hyde Rd. Hay —4C **68**
Northiam. N12 —4L **25**
(in two parts)
Northiam. WC1 —6J 59
(off Cromer St.)
Northiam St. E8 & E9 —4F **60**
Northington St. WC1 —7K **59**
North Kensington. —8H 57
Northlands Av. Orp —6C **128**
Northlands St. SE5 —1A **92**
North La. Tedd —3D **102**
Northleach Ct. SE15 —7C 76
(off Birdlip Clo.)
North Lodge. New Bar —7A **14**
N. Lodge Clo. SW15 —4H **89**
North Looe. —5G 135
North Mall. N9 —2F 28
(off Plevna Rd.)
North M. WC1 —7K **59**
North Mt. N20 —2A 26
(off High Rd.)
Northolm. Edgw —4B **24**
Northolme Gdns. Edgw —8L **23**
Northolme Ri. Orp —4C **128**
Northolme Rd. N5 —9A **44**
Northolt. —3L 53
Northolt. N17 —9C 28
(off Griffin Rd.)
Northolt Av. Ruis —1F **52**
Northolt Gdns. Gnfd —1D **54**
Northolt Rd. Harr —9M **37**
Northolt Rd. H'row A —9H **143**
Northolt Way. Horn —2G **67**
N. Orbital Rd. Wat & Brick W —6H **5**
Northover. Brom —9D **94**
North Pde. Chess —7K **119**
North Pde. Edgw —9L **23**
North Pde. S'hall —9L 53
(off North Rd.)
North Pk. SE9 —5K **95**
North Pl. SW18 —4L **89**
North Pl. Mitc —4D **106**
North Pl. Tedd —3D **102**
North Pl. Wal A —6H **7**
N. Pole La. Kes —8D **126**
N. Pole Rd. W10 —8G **57**
Northport St. N1 —4B **60**
North Ride. W2 —1C **74**
North Riding. Brick W —3L **5**
North Ri. W2 —9C **58**
North Rd. N2 —9C **26**
North Rd. N6 —5E **42**
North Rd. N7 —2J **59**
North Rd. N9 —1F **28**
North Rd. SE18 —5C **80**
North Rd. SW19 —3A **106**
North Rd. W5 —4H **71**
North Rd. Belv —4M **81**
North Rd. Bren —7J **71**
North Rd. Brom —5F **110**
North Rd. Chad H —3J **49**
North Rd. Dart —5D **98**
North Rd. Edgw —8M **23**
North Rd. Felt —5B **84**
North Rd. Harr —5E **38**
North Rd. Hav —3C **34**
North Rd. Hay —8B **52**
North Rd. Ilf —7C **48**
North Rd. Purf —5M **83**
(in two parts)
North Rd. Rich —2L **87**
North Rd. S'hall —1L **69**
North Rd. Surb —1H **119**
North Rd. Wal X —6E **6**
North Rd. W on T —7G **117**
North Rd. W Dray —4K **143**
North Rd. W W'ck —3M **125**
Northrop Rd. H'row A —9C **68**
North Row. W1 —1D **74**
N. Row Bldgs. W1 —1E 74
(off North Row)
North Several. SE3 —1B **94**
North Sheen. —2L 87
Northside Rd. Brom —5E **110**
N. Side Wandsworth Comn. SW18 —4B **90**
Northspur Rd. Sutt —5L **121**
North Sq. N9 —2F 28
(off Hertford Rd.)
North Sq. NW11 —3L **41**
Northstead Rd. SW2 —8L **91**

North St. E13 —5F 62
North St. NW4 —3G 41
North St. SW4 —2G 91
North St. Bark —2M 63
(Barking Northern Relief Rd.)
North St. Bark —3A 64
(London Rd.)
North St. Bexh —3L 97
North St. Brom —5E 110
North St. Cars —5D 122
North St. Dart —6H 99
North St. Horn —5H 51
North St. Iswth —2E 86
North St. Romf —1B 50
N. Street Pas. E13 —5F 62
N. Tenter St. E1 —9D 60
North Ter. SW3 —4C 74
Northumberland All. EC3 —9C 60
(in two parts)
Northumberland Av. E12 —6G 47
Northumberland Av. WC2 —2J 75
Northumberland Av. Enf —3F 16
Northumberland Av. Horn —3G 51
Northumberland Av. Iswth —9D 70
Northumberland Av. Well —3B 96
Northumberland Clo. Eri —8A 82
Northumberland Clo. Stanw —5C 144
Northumberland Cres. Felt —5C 84
Northumberland Gdns. N9 —3D 28
Northumberland Gdns. Brom —8L 111
Northumberland Gdns. Iswth —8E 70
Northumberland Gdns. Mitc —9H 107
Northumberland Gro. N17 —7F 28
Northumberland Heath. —8A 82
Northumberland Ho. SW1 —2J 75
(off Northumberland Av.)
Northumberland Pk. N17 —7D 28
Northumberland Pk. Eri —8A 82
Northumberland Pk. Ind. Est. N17 —7F 28
Northumberland Pl. W2 —9L 57
Northumberland Pl. Rich —4H 87
Northumberland Rd. E6 —9J 63
Northumberland Rd. E17 —5L 45
Northumberland Rd. Harr —3K 37
Northumberland Rd. New Bar —8A 14
Northumberland Row. Twic —7C 86
Northumberland St. WC2 —2J 75
Northumberland Way. Eri —9A 82
Northumbria St. E14 —9L 61
N. Verbena Gdns. W6 —6E 72
Northview. N7 —8J 43
North Vw. SW19 —2G 105
North Vw. W5 —7G 55
North Vw. Pinn —5G 37
Northview. Swan —6C 114
N. View Cres. NW10 —9D 40
N. View Cres. Eps —9F 134
Northview Dri. Wfd G —9H 31
N. View Rd. N8 —2H 43
North Vs. NW1 —2H 59
North Wlk. W8 —1M 73
(off Bayswater Rd.)
North Wlk. New Ad —8M 125
(in two parts)
North Watford. —1F 8
North Way. N9 —2H 29
North Way. N11 —6G 27
North Way. NW9 —1M 39
Northway. NW11 —3M 41
Northway. Mord —7J 105
North Way. Pinn —2H 37
North Way. Uxb —3C 142
Northway. Wall —6G 123
Northway Cir. NW7 —4B 24
Northway Cres. NW7 —4B 24
Northway Gdns. NW11 —3M 41
Northway Rd. SE5 —2A 92
Northway Rd. Croy —1D 124
Northways Pde. NW3 —3B 58
(off College Cres., in two parts)
Northweald La. King T —2H 103
North Wembley. —8H 39
N. Western Av. A'ham —4M 9
N. Western Av. Wat —8B 4
(in two parts)
N. Western Commercial Cen. NW1 —3J 59
N. West Pier. E1 —2F 76
Northwest Pl. N1 —5L 59
N. Weylands Ind. Est. W on T —4J 117
North Wharf. E14 —2A 78
(off Coldharbour)
N. Wharf Rd. W2 —8B 58
Northwick Av. Harr —4E 38
Northwick Circ. Harr —4G 39
Northwick Clo. NW8 —7B 58
Northwick Clo. Harr —6F 38
Northwick Ho. W9 —7A 58
(off St John's Wood Rd.)
Northwick Pk. Rd. Harr —4D 38
Northwick Rd. Wat —4G 21
Northwick Rd. Wemb —4H 55
Northwick Ter. NW8 —7B 58
Northwick Wlk. Harr —5D 38
Northwold Dri. Pinn —9G 21
Northwold Est. E5 —7E 44
Northwold Rd. N16 & E5 —7D 44
Northwood. —6C 20
Northwood Av. Horn —9E 50
Northwood Av. Purl —4L 137
N. Wood Ct. SE25 —7E 108
Northwood Gdns. N12 —5B 26
Northwood Gdns. Gnfd —1D 54
Northwood Gdns. Ilf —2L 47
Northwood Hills. —9E 20
Northwood Hills Cir. N'wd —8E 20
Northwood Ho. SE27 —1B 108
Northwood Pl. Eri —4K 81
Northwood Rd. N6 —5F 42
Northwood Rd. SE23 —7K 93
Northwood Rd. Cars —8E 122
Northwood Rd. H'row A —9H 143
Northwood Rd. T Hth —6M 107
Northwood Way. SE19 —3B 108
Northwood Way. N'wd —7D 20
North Woolwich. —2L 79
North Woolwich Old Station Mus. —3L 79
N. Woolwich Rd. E16 —2D 78
N. Worple Way. SW14 —2B 88
Norton Almshouses. Chesh —3D 6
(off Turner's Hill)
Norton Av. Surb —2M 119
Norton Clo. E4 —5L 29
Norton Clo. Borwd —3L 11
Norton Clo. Enf —4F 16
Norton Folgate. EC2 —8C 60
Norton Folgate Almshouses. E1 —8D 60
(off Puma Ct.)
Norton Gdns. SW16 —6J 107
Norton Ho. E1 —9F 60
(off Bigland St.)
Norton Ho. E2 —5H 61
(off Mace St.)
Norton Ho. SW1 —4H 75
(off Arneway St.)
Norton Ho. SW9 —1K 91
(off Aytoun Rd.)
Norton Rd. E10 —6K 45
Norton Rd. Dag —2B 66
Norton Rd. Uxb —6B 142
Norton Rd. Wemb —2H 55
Norval Rd. Wemb —7F 38
Norvic Ho. Eri —8D 82
Norway Ga. SE16 —4J 77
Norway Pl. E14 —9K 61
Norway St. SE10 —7M 77
Norway Wlk. Rain —7G 67
Norway Wharf. E14 —9K 61
(off Norway Pl.)
Norwich Ho. E14 —9M 61
(off Cordelia St.)
Norwich Ho. Borwd —4L 11
(off Stratfield Rd.)
Norwich M. Ilf —6E 48
Norwich Pl. Bexh —3L 97
Norwich Rd. E7 —1E 62
Norwich Rd. Dag —5L 65
Norwich Rd. Gnfd —4M 53
Norwich Rd. N'wd —1D 36
Norwich Rd. T Hth —7A 108
Norwich St. EC4 —9L 59
Norwich Wlk. Edgw —7A 24
Norwich Way. Crox G —5A 8
Norwood. —3C 108
Norwood Av. Romf —5C 50
Norwood Av. Wemb —4K 55
Norwood Clo. S'hall —5L 69
Norwood Clo. Twic —8B 86
Norwood Ct. Dart —4L 99
(off Farnol Rd.)
Norwood Dri. Harr —4K 37
Norwood Gdns. Hay —7G 53
Norwood Gdns. S'hall —5K 69
Norwood Green. —5L 69
Norwood Grn. Rd. S'hall —5L 69
Norwood High St. SE27 —9M 91
Norwood Ho. E14 —1M 77
(off Poplar High St.)
Norwood New Town. —3A 108
Norwood Pk. Rd. SE27 —2A 108
Norwood Rd. SE24 —7M 91
Norwood Rd. SE27 —8M 91
Norwood Rd. Chesh —3E 6
Norwood Rd. S'hall —4J 69
Norwood Ter. S'hall —5M 69
Notley St. SE5 —8B 76
Notson Rd. SE25 —8F 108
Notting Barn Rd. W10 —7H 57
Nottingdale Sq. W11 —2J 73
Nottingham Av. E16 —8G 63
Nottingham Clo. Wat —6E 4
Nottingham Ct. WC2 —9J 59
Nottingham Ho. WC2 —9J 59
Nottingham Pl. W1 —8E 58
Nottingham Rd. E10 —4A 46
Nottingham Rd. SW17 —7D 90
Nottingham Rd. Iswth —1D 86
Nottingham Rd. S Croy —6A 124
Nottingham St. W1 —8E 58
Nottingham Ter. NW1 —7E 58
(off York Ter. W.)
Notting Hill. —1K 73
Notting Hill Ga. W11 —2L 73
Nottingwood Ho. W11 —1J 73
(off Clarendon Rd.)
Nova M. Sutt —3J 121
Novar Clo. Orp —2D 128
Nova Rd. Croy —3M 123
Novar Rd. SE9 —7A 96
Novello St. SW6 —9L 73
Novello Way. Borwd —3B 12
Nowell Rd. SW13 —7E 72
Nower Ct. Pinn —2K 37
Nower Hill. Pinn —2K 37
Noyna Rd. SW17 —9D 90
Nubia Way. Brom —9C 94
Nuding Clo. SE13 —2L 93
Nuffield Ct. Houn —8K 69
Nuffield Lodge. N6 —4G 43
Nuffield Lodge. W2 —8L 57
(off Admiral Wlk.)
Nuffield Rd. Swan —3E 114
Nugent Ind. Pk. Orp —8G 113
Nugent Rd. N19 —6J 43
Nugent Rd. SE25 —7D 108
Nugents Ct. Pinn —8J 21
Nugent's Pk. Pinn —8J 21
Nugent Ter. NW8 —5A 58
Numa Ct. Bren —8H 71
Nun Ct. EC2 —9B 60
(off Coleman St.)
Nuneaton Rd. Dag —3J 65
Nunhead. —2F 92
Nunhead Cres. SE15 —2F 92
Nunhead Est. SE15 —3F 92
Nunhead Grn. SE15 —2F 92
Nunhead Gro. SE15 —2F 92
Nunhead La. SE15 —2F 92
Nunhead Pas. SE15 —2E 92
Nunnington Clo. SE9 —9J 95
Nunns Rd. Enf —4A 16
Nuper's Hatch. —1C 34
Nupton Dri. Barn —8G 13
Nurse Clo. Edgw —8A 24
Nursery App. N12 —6C 26
Nursery Av. N3 —9A 26
Nursery Av. Bexh —2K 97
Nursery Av. Croy —4H 125
Nursery Clo. SE4 —1K 93
Nursery Clo. SW15 —3H 89
Nursery Clo. Croy —4H 125
Nursery Clo. Enf —3H 17
Nursery Clo. Eps —2C 134
Nursery Clo. Felt —6F 84
(in two parts)
Nursery Clo. Orp —2D 128
Nursery Clo. Romf —4H 49
Nursery Clo. Swan —6A 114
Nursery Clo. Wfd G —5F 30
Nursery Ct. N17 —7D 28
Nursery Ct. W13 —8E 54
Nursery Gdns. Chst —3M 111
Nursery Gdns. Enf —3H 17
Nursery Gdns. Hamp —1K 101
Nursery Gdns. Houn —4K 85
Nursery Gdns. Sun —6D 100
Nursery La. E2 —4D 60
Nursery La. E7 —2E 62
Nursery La. W10 —8G 57
Nursery La. Uxb —7B 142
Nurserymans Rd. N11 —2E 26
Nursery Rd. E9 —2G 61
Nursery Rd. N2 —8B 26
Nursery Rd. N14 —9G 15
Nursery Rd. SW9 —3K 91
Nursery Rd. SW19 —6M 105
(Merton)
Nursery Rd. SW19 —4J 105
(Wimbledon)
Nursery Rd. H Bee —3G 19
Nursery Rd. Lou —7G 19
Nursery Rd. Pinn —1G 37
Nursery Rd. Sun —6C 100
Nursery Rd. Sutt —6A 122
Nursery Rd. T Hth —8B 108
Nursery Row. Barn —5J 13
Nursery St. N17 —7D 28
Nursery, The. Eri —8D 82
Nursery Wlk. NW4 —1G 41
Nursery Wlk. Romf —5B 50
Nursery Waye. Uxb —4B 142
Nurstead Rd. Eri —8L 81
Nutbourne St. W10 —6J 57
Nutbrook St. SE15 —2E 92
Nutbrowne Rd. Dag —4K 65
Nutcroft Rd. SE15 —8F 76
Nutfield Clo. N18 —6D 28
Nutfield Clo. Cars —5C 122
Nutfield Gdns. Ilf —7D 48
Nutfield Gdns. N'holt —5G 53
Nutfield Rd. E15 —9A 46
Nutfield Rd. NW2 —8E 40
Nutfield Rd. SE22 —3D 92
Nutfield Rd. Coul —8E 136
Nutfield Rd. T Hth —8M 107
Nutfield Way. Orp —4M 127
Nutford Pl. W1 —9D 58
Nuthatch Clo. Stai —7D 144
Nuthatch Gdns. SE28 —3B 80
(in two parts)
Nuthurst Av. SW2 —8K 91
Nutkin Wlk. Uxb —3C 142
Nutley Clo. Swan —5D 114
Nutley Ter. NW3 —2A 58
Nutmead Clo. Bex —7A 98
Nutmeg Clo. E16 —7C 62
Nutmeg La. E14 —9B 62
Nuttall St. N1 —5C 60
Nutter La. E11 —4G 47
Nuttfield Clo. Crox G —8A 8
Nutt Gro. Edgw —2H 23
Nut Tree Clo. Orp —5H 129
Nutt St. SE15 —8D 76
Nutty La. Shep —7A 100
Nutwell St. SW17 —2C 106
Nuxley Rd. Belv —7K 81
Nyanza St. SE18 —7B 80
Nye Bevan Est. E5 —8H 45
Nye Bevan Ho. SW6 —8K 73
(off St Thomas's Way)
Nylands Av. Rich —9L 71
Nymans Gdns. SW20 —7F 104
Nynehead St. SE14 —8J 77
Nyon Gro. SE6 —8K 93
Nyssa Clo. Wfd G —6K 31
Nyssa Ct. E15 —6C 62
(off Teasel Way)
Nyton Clo. N19 —6J 43

Oakapple Clo. S Croy —6F 138
Oak Apple Ct. SE12 —7E 94
Oak Av. N8 —2J 43
Oak Av. N10 —7F 26
Oak Av. N17 —7B 28
Oak Av. Brick W —3L 5
Oak Av. Croy —3L 125
Oak Av. Enf —2K 15
Oak Av. Hamp —2J 101
Oak Av. Houn —8H 69
Oak Av. Upm —8M 51
Oak Av. Uxb —7A 36
Oak Av. W Dray —4L 143
Oak Bank. New Ad —8A 126
Oakbank Av. W on T —2K 117
Oakbank Gro. SE24 —3A 92
Oakbrook Clo. Brom —1F 110
Oakbury Rd. SW6 —1M 89
Oak Clo. N14 —9F 14
Oak Clo. Dart —3C 98
Oak Clo. Sutt —4A 122
Oak Clo. Wal A —7K 7
Oakcombe Clo. N Mald —5C 104
Oak Cottage Clo. SE6 —7D 94
Oak Cotts. W7 —3C 70
Oak Ct. SE15 —8D 76
(off Sumner Rd.)
Oak Ct. N'wd —6B 20
Oak Cres. E16 —8C 62
Oakcroft Bus. Cen. Chess —6K 119
Oakcroft Clo. Pinn —9F 20
Oakcroft Rd. SE13 —1B 94
Oakcroft Rd. Chess —6K 119
Oakcroft Vs. Chess —6K 119
Oakdale. N14 —1F 26
Oakdale Av. Harr —3J 39
Oakdale Av. N'wd —9E 20
Oakdale Clo. Wat —4G 21
Oakdale Ct. E4 —5A 30
Oakdale Gdns. E4 —5A 30
Oakdale Rd. E7 —3F 62
Oakdale Rd. E11 —7B 46
Oakdale Rd. E18 —9F 30
Oakdale Rd. N4 —4A 44
Oakdale Rd. SE15 & SE4 —2G 93
Oakdale Rd. SW16 —2J 107
Oakdale Rd. Eps —1B 134
Oakdale Rd. Wat —3G 21
Oakdale Way. Mitc —2E 122
Oakdene. SE15 —9F 76
Oakdene. W13 —8F 54
Oakdene. Chesh —3E 6
Oakdene. Romf —9K 35
Oakdene Av. Chst —2L 111
Oakdene Av. Eri —7A 82
Oakdene Av. Th Dit —3E 118
Oakdene Clo. Horn —4F 50
Oakdene Clo. Pinn —7K 21
Oakdene Ct. W on T —5F 116
Oakdene Dri. Surb —2A 120
Oakdene M. Sutt —3K 121
Oakdene Pk. N3 —7K 25
Oakdene Rd. Orp —9D 112
Oakdene Rd. Uxb —5F 142
Oakdene Rd. Wat —9F 4
Oakden St. SE11 —5L 75
Oake Ct. SW15 —4J 89
Oakeford Ho. W14 —4J 73
(off Russell Rd.)
Oakend Ho. N4 —5B 44
Oaken Dri. Clay —8D 118
Oakenholt Ho. SE2 —2H 81
Oaken La. Clay —6C 118
Oakenshaw Clo. Surb —2J 119
Oakes Clo. E6 —9K 63
Oakeshott Av. N6 —7E 42
Oakey La. SE1 —4L 75
Oak Farm. Borwd —7A 12
Oakfield. E4 —5M 29
Oakfield Av. Harr —1F 38
Oakfield Cen. SE20 —4F 108
Oakfield Clo. N Mald —9D 104
Oakfield Clo. Ruis —4D 36
Oakfield Clo. Wey —6A 116
Oakfield Ct. N8 —5J 43
Oakfield Ct. NW11 —5H 41
Oakfield Ct. Borwd —5M 11
Oakfield Gdns. N18 —4C 28
Oakfield Gdns. SE19 —2C 108
(in two parts)
Oakfield Gdns. Beck —9M 109
Oakfield Gdns. Cars —3C 122
Oakfield Gdns. Gnfd —7B 54
Oakfield Glade. Wey —6A 116
Oakfield Ho. E3 —8L 61
(off Gale St.)
Oakfield La. Dart —8C 98
Oakfield La. Kes —6G 127
Oakfield Lodge. Ilf —8M 47
(off Albert Rd.)
Oakfield Pk. Rd. Dart —8H 99
Oakfield Pl. Dart —8H 99
Oakfield Rd. E6 —4J 63
Oakfield Rd. E17 —9J 29
Oakfield Rd. N3 —8M 25
Oakfield Rd. N8 —4L 43
Oakfield Rd. N14 —3J 27
Oakfield Rd. SE20 —4F 108
Oakfield Rd. SW19 —9H 89
Oakfield Rd. Asht —9H 133
Oakfield Rd. Croy —3A 124
Oakfield Rd. Ilf —8M 47
Oakfield Rd. Orp —2E 128
Oakfield Rd. Ind. Est. SE20 —4F 108
Oakfields. Lou —7L 19
Oakfields. W on T —3E 116
Oakfields Rd. NW11 —4J 41
Oakfield St. SW10 —7A 74
Oakford Rd. NW5 —9G 43
Oak Gdns. Croy —4L 125
Oak Gdns. Edgw —9M 23
Oak Glade. Eps —4L 133
Oak Glade. N'wd —8A 20
Oak Glen. Horn —1J 51
Oak Grn. Ab L —5C 4
Oak Grn. Way. Ab L —5C 4
Oak Gro. NW2 —9J 41
Oak Gro. Ruis —5F 36
Oak Gro. Sun —4F 100
Oak Gro. W W'ck —3A 126
Oak Gro. Rd. SE20 —5G 109
Oakhall Ct. E11 —4F 46
Oakhall Dri. Sun —2D 100
Oak Hall Rd. E11 —4F 46
Oakham Clo. SE6 —8K 93
Oakham Clo. Barn —5D 14
Oakham Dri. Brom —8D 110
Oakhampton Rd. NW7 —7H 25
Oakhill. Clay —8E 118
Oak Hill. Eps —8B 134
Oakhill. Surb —2J 119
Oak Hill. Wfd G —7B 30
Oakhill Av. NW3 —9M 41
Oakhill Av. Pinn —9J 21
Oakhill Clo. Asht —9G 133
Oak Hill Clo. Wfd G —7B 30
Oakhill Ct. SE23 —5G 93
Oakhill Ct. SW20 —4H 105
Oak Hill Ct. Wfd G —7B 30
Oakhill Cres. Surb —2J 119
Oak Hill Cres. Wfd G —7B 30
Oakhill Dri. Surb —2J 119
Oakhill Gdns. Wey —4C 116
Oak Hill Gdns. Wfd G —8C 30
Oakhill Gro. Surb —1J 119
Oak Hill Pk. NW3 —9M 41
Oak Hill Pk. M. NW3 —9A 42
Oakhill Path. Surb —1J 119
Oakhill Pl. SW15 —4L 89
Oakhill Rd. SW15 —4K 89
Oakhill Rd. SW16 —5J 107
Oakhill Rd. Asht —9G 133
Oakhill Rd. Beck —6A 110
Oakhill Rd. Orp —3D 128
Oakhill Rd. Purf —6M 83
Oak Hill Rd. Stap A —1B 34
Oakhill Rd. Surb —1J 119
Oakhill Rd. Sutt —5M 121
Oak Hill Way. NW3 —9A 42
Oak Ho. N2 —9B 26
Oak Ho. W10 —7J 57
(off Sycamore Wlk.)
Oakhouse Rd. Bexh —4L 97
Oakhurst Av. Barn & E Barn —9C 14
Oakhurst Av. Bexh —8J 81
Oakhurst Clo. E17 —2C 46
Oakhurst Clo. Chst —5K 111
Oakhurst Clo. Ilf —8M 31
Oakhurst Clo. Tedd —2C 102
Oakhurst Gdns. E4 —1D 30
Oakhurst Gdns. E17 —2C 46
Oakhurst Gdns. Bexh —8J 81
Oakhurst Gro. SE22 —3E 92
Oakhurst Pl. Wat —6D 8
Oakhurst Ri. Cars —2C 136
Oakhurst Rd. Enf —9D 6
Oakhurst Rd. Eps —8A 120
Oakington Av. Harr —5L 37
Oakington Av. Hay —5B 68
Oakington Av. Wemb —8K 39
Oakington Ct. Enf —4M 15
(off Ridgeway, The)
Oakington Dri. Sun —6G 101
Oakington Mnr. Dri. Wemb —1L 55
Oakington Rd. W9 —7L 57
Oakington Way. N8 —5J 43
Oakland Pl. Buck H —2E 30
Oakland Rd. E15 —9B 46
Oaklands. N21 —2K 27
Oaklands. W13 —8E 54
Oaklands. Beck —5M 109
Oaklands. Kenl —6A 138
Oaklands Av. N9 —8F 16
Oaklands Av. Esh —3B 118
Oaklands Av. Iswth —7D 70
Oaklands Av. Romf —1C 50

Oaklands Av.—Old Mnr. Yd.

Oaklands Av. Sidc —6D 96
Oaklands Av. T Hth —8L 107
Oaklands Av. Wat —1F 20
Oaklands Av. W W'ck —5M 125
Oaklands Clo. Bexh —4K 97
Oaklands Clo. Chess —6G 119
Oaklands Clo. Orp —1C 128
Oaklands Clo. Wemb —1H 55
Oaklands Ct. NW10 —4C 56
(off Nicoll Rd.)
Oaklands Ct. Wat —3E 8
Oaklands Ct. Wemb —1H 55
Oaklands Dri. Twic —6A 86
Oaklands Est. SW4 —5G 91
Oaklands Gdns. Kenl —6A 138
Oaklands Ga. N'wd —6C 20
Oaklands Gro. W12 —2E 72
Oaklands La. Barn —6F 12
Oaklands La. Big H —5F 140
Oaklands M. NW2 —9H 41
(off Oaklands Rd.)
Oaklands Pk. Av. Ilf —7A 48
Oaklands Pas. NW2 —9H 41
(off Oaklands Rd.)
Oaklands Pl. SW4 —3G 91
Oaklands Rd. N20 —9K 13
Oaklands Rd. NW2 —9H 41
Oaklands Rd. SW14 —2B 88
Oaklands Rd. W7 —3D 70
(in two parts)
Oaklands Rd. Bexh —3K 97
Oaklands Rd. Brom —4C 110
Oaklands Rd. Dart —7M 99
Oaklands Way. Wall —9H 123
Oakland Way. Eps —8C 120
Oak La. E14 —1K 77
Oak La. N2 —9B 26
Oak La. N11 —6H 27
Oak La. Iswth —3C 86
Oak La. Twic —6E 86
Oak La. Wfd G —4D 30
Oaklawn Rd. Lea —9C 132
Oak Leaf Clo. Eps —4A 134
Oakleafe Gdns. Ilf —1M 47
Oaklea Pas. King T —7H 103
Oakleigh Av. N20 —2B 26
Oakleigh Av. Edgw —9M 23
Oakleigh Av. Surb —3L 119
Oakleigh Clo. N20 —3D 26
Oakleigh Clo. Swan —7C 114
Oakleigh Ct. Barn —8C 14
Oakleigh Ct. Edgw —9A 24
Oakleigh Ct. S'hall —2K 69
Oakleigh Cres. N20 —2C 26
Oakleigh Dri. Crox G —8A 8
Oakleigh Flats. Eps —6C 134
Oakleigh Gdns. N20 —1A 26
Oakleigh Gdns. Edgw —5K 23
Oakleigh Gdns. Orp —6C 128
Oakleigh M. N20 —1A 26
Oakleigh Park. —1B 26
Oakleigh Pk. Av. Chst —5L 111
Oakleigh Pk. N. N20 —1B 26
Oakleigh Pk. S. N20 —9C 14
Oakleigh Rd. Pinn —6K 21
Oakleigh Rd. Uxb —3A 52
Oakleigh Rd. N. N20 —2B 26
Oakleigh Rd. S. N11 —3E 26
Oakleigh Way. Mitc —5F 106
Oakleigh Way. Surb —3L 119
Oakley Av. W5 —1L 71
Oakley Av. Bark —3D 64
Oakley Av. Croy —6K 123
Oakley Clo. E4 —3A 30
Oakley Clo. E6 —9J 63
Oakley Clo. W7 —1C 70
Oakley Clo. Iswth —9B 70
Oakley Ct. Lou —4L 19
Oakley Cres. EC1 —5M 59
Oakley Dri. SE9 —7B 96
Oakley Dri. SE13 —5B 94
Oakley Dri. Brom —5J 127
Oakley Dri. Romf —5L 35
Oakley Gdns. N8 —3K 43
Oakley Gdns. SW3 —7C 74
Oakley Gdns. Bans —7M 135
Oakley Grange. Harr —8A 38
Oakley Ho. SW1 —5D 74
Oakley Ho. W3 —1L 71
Oakley Pk. Bex —6G 97
Oakley Pl. SE1 —6D 76
Oakley Rd. N1 —3B 60
Oakley Rd. SE25 —9F 108
Oakley Rd. Brom —5J 127
Oakley Rd. Harr —4C 38
Oakley Rd. Warl —9E 138
Oakley Sq. NW1 —5G 59
Oakley St. SW3 —7C 74
Oakley Wlk. W6 —7H 73
Oakley Yd. E2 —7D 60
(off Bacon St.)
Oak Lodge. E11 —4E 46
Oak Lodge. W8 —4M 73
(off Chantry Sq.)
Oak Lodge Av. Chig —5B 32
Oak Lodge Clo. Stan —5G 23
Oak Lodge Clo. W on T —7G 117
Oak Lodge Dri. W W'ck —2M 125
Oaklodge Way. NW7 —5D 24
Oakmead Av. Brom —1E 126
Oakmead Ct. Stan —4G 23
Oak Meade. Pinn —6L 21
Oakmead Gdns. Edgw —4B 24
Oakmead Grn. Eps —7A 134
Oakmead Pl. Mitc —5C 106
Oakmead Rd. SW12 —7E 90
Oakmead Rd. Croy —1H 123
Oakmede. Barn —6H 13
Oakmere Rd. SE2 —7E 80
Oakmont Pl. Orp —3B 128
Oakmoor Way. Chig —5C 32
Oak Pk. Gdns. SW19 —7H 89
Oak Pk. M. N16 —8D 44
Oak Path. Bush —8M 9
(off Mortimer Clo.)
Oak Pl. SW18 —4M 89
Oakridge. Brick W —2K 5
Oakridge Dri. N2 —1B 42
Oakridge La. Brom —2B 110
Oakridge Rd. Brom —1B 110
Oak Ri. Buck H —3H 31
Oak Rd. W5 —1H 71
Oak Rd. Eri —8A 82
(Mill Rd.)
Oak Rd. Eri —1E 98
(Moat La.)
Oak Rd. N Mald —6B 104
Oak Rd. Orp —9E 128
Oak Rd. Romf —8K 35
Oak Row. SW16 —6G 107
Oaks Av. SE19 —2C 108
Oaks Av. Felt —8J 85
Oaks Av. Romf —9A 34
Oaks Av. Wor Pk —5F 120
Oaks Cvn. Pk., The. Chess —5G 119
Oaksford Av. SE26 —9F 92
Oaks Gro. E4 —2C 30
Oakshade Rd. Brom —1B 110
Oakshade Rd. Oxs —6A 132
Oakshaw Rd. SW18 —6M 89
Oakshott Ct. NW1 —5H 59
(in two parts)
Oakside. Den —2A 142
Oaks La. Croy —5G 125
(in two parts)
Oaks La. Ilf —3C 48
Oaks Rd. Croy —7F 124
Oaks Rd. Kenl —6M 137
Oaks Rd. Stai & Stanw —5B 144
Oaks Shop. Cen., The. W3 —2A 72
Oaks, The. E4 —7C 30
Oaks, The. N12 —4M 25
Oaks, The. NW10 —3F 56
Oaks, The. SE18 —6A 80
Oaks, The. Borwd —3L 11
Oaks, The. Brom —1L 127
Oaks, The. Enf —5M 15
(off Bycullah Rd.)
Oaks, The. Eps —6C 134
Oaks, The. Hay —5A 52
Oaks, The. Mord —8J 105
Oaks, The. Ruis —5C 36
Oaks, The. Swan —6C 114
Oaks, The. Wat —1G 21
Oaks Track. Cars & Wall —3D 136
Oak St. Romf —3A 50
Oaks Way. Cars —9D 122
Oaks Way. Kenl —6A 138
Oaksway. Surb —3H 119
Oakthorpe Ct. N13 —5A 28
Oakthorpe Pk. Est. N13 —5A 28
Oakthorpe Rd. N13 —5L 27
Oaktree Av. N13 —3M 27
Oak Tree Clo. W5 —9G 55
Oak Tree Clo. Ab L —5B 4
Oak Tree Clo. Stan —7G 23
Oak Tree Ct. W3 —1M 71
Oaktree Ct. Els —8J 11
Oak Tree Ct. N'holt —5G 53
Oak Tree Dell. NW9 —3B 40
Oak Tree Dri. N20 —1M 25
Oak Tree Gdns. Brom —2F 110
Oaktree Gro. Ilf —1B 64
Oak Tree Ho. W9 —7L 57
(off Shirland Rd.)
Oak Tree Rd. NW8 —6C 58
Oakview Clo. Chesh —1B 6
Oakview Gdns. N2 —2B 42
Oakview Gro. Croy —3J 125
Oakview Lodge. NW11 —5K 41
(off Beechcroft Av.)
Oakview Rd. SE6 —2M 109
Oak Village. NW5 —9E 42
Oak Vs. NW11 —4K 41
(off Hendon Pk. Row)
Oak Way. N14 —9F 14
Oak Way. SW20 —8G 105
Oak Way. W3 —2C 72
Oak Way. Asht —8L 133
Oakway. Brom —6B 110
Oak Way. Croy —1H 125
Oak Way. Felt —7C 84
Oakway Clo. Bex —5J 97
Oakways. SE9 —5M 95
Oakwood. —8H 15
Oakwood. Wall —1F 136
Oakwood. Wal A —8L 7
Oakwood Av. N14 —9H 15
Oakwood Av. Beck —6A 110
Oakwood Av. Borwd —6M 11
Oakwood Av. Brom —7F 110
Oakwood Av. Eps —1L 133
Oakwood Av. Mitc —6B 106
Oakwood Av. Purl —4M 137
Oakwood Av. S'hall —1L 69
Oakwood Bus. Pk. NW10 —7B 56
Oakwood Chase. Horn —4K 51
Oakwood Clo. N14 —8J 15
Oakwood Clo. Chst —3K 111
Oakwood Clo. Dart —7M 99
Oakwood Clo. Wfd G —6J 31
Oakwood Ct. E6 —3J 63
Oakwood Ct. W14 —4K 73
Oakwood Ct. Harr —4B 38
Oakwood Ct. Swan —6A 114
(off Lawn Clo.)
Oakwood Cres. N21 —8J 15
Oakwood Cres. Gnfd —2E 54
Oakwood Dri. SE19 —3B 108
Oakwood Dri. Bexh —3A 98
Oakwood Dri. Edgw —6A 24
Oakwood Gdns. Ilf —7D 48
Oakwood Gdns. Orp —4A 128
Oakwood Gdns. Sutt —4L 121
Oakwood Hill. Lou —8K 19
Oakwood La. W14 —4K 73
Oakwood Lodge. N14 —8G 15
(off Avenue Rd.)
Oakwood Pk. Rd. N14 —9H 15
Oakwood Pl. Croy —1L 123
Oakwood Rd. NW11 —2L 41
Oakwood Rd. SW20 —5E 104
Oakwood Rd. Brick W —2K 5
Oakwood Rd. Croy —1L 123
Oakwood Rd. Orp —4A 128
Oakwood Rd. Pinn —9F 20
Oakwood Vw. N14 —8H 15
Oakworth Rd. W10 —8G 57
Oarsman Pl. E Mol —8C 102
Oasis, The. Brom —6G 111
Oast Ct. E14 —1K 77
Oasthouse Way. Orp —8F 112
Oast Lodge. W4 —8C 72
(off Corney Reach Way)
Oates Clo. Brom —7B 110
Oates Rd. Romf —5M 33
Oatfield Ho. N15 —4C 44
(off Perry Ct.)
Oatfield Rd. Orp —3D 128
Oatland Ri. E17 —9J 29
Oatlands Av. Wey —7B 116
Oatlands Chase. Wey —5C 116
Oatlands Clo. Wey —6A 116
Oatlands Dri. Wey —6A 116
Oatlands Grn. Wey —5B 116
Oatlands Mere. Wey —5B 116
Oatlands Park. —5C 116
Oatlands Rd. Enf —3G 17
Oat La. EC2 —9A 60
Oatwell Ho. SW3 —6C 74
Oban Clo. E13 —7G 63
Oban Ho. E14 —9B 62
(off Oban St.)
Oban Ho. Bark —5B 64
Oban Rd. E13 —6G 63
Oban Rd. SE25 —8B 108
Oban St. E14 —9B 62
Oberon Clo. Borwd —3A 12
Oberon Ho. N1 —5C 60
(off Arden Est.)
Oberstein Rd. SW11 —3B 90
Oborne Clo. SE24 —4M 91
O'Brien Ho. E2 —6H 61
(off Roman Rd.)
Observatory Gdns. W8 —3L 73
Observatory M. E14 —5B 78
Observatory Rd. SW14 —3A 88
Occupation La. SE18 —9M 79
Occupation La. W5 —5H 71
Occupation Rd. SE17 —6A 76
Occupation Rd. W13 —3F 70
Occupation Rd. Eps —9B 120
Occupation Rd. Wat —7F 8
Ocean Est. E1 —8J 61
(Ben Jonson Rd.)
Ocean Est. E1 —7H 61
(Mile End Rd.)
Ocean St. E1 —8H 61
Ocean Wharf. E14 —3L 77
Ockbrook. E1 —8G 61
(off Hannibal Rd.)
Ockenden M. N1 —2B 60
Ockendon Rd. N1 —2B 60
Ockham Dri. Orp —4E 112
Ockley Clo. Sidc —9C 96
Ockley Ct. Sutt —6A 122
Ockley Rd. SW16 —1J 107
Ockley Rd. Croy —2K 123
Octagon Arc. EC2 —8C 60
Octagon Ct. SE16 —2H 77
(off Rotherhithe St.)
Octavia Clo. Mitc —9C 106
Octavia Ct. Wat —4G 9
Octavia Ho. SW1 —4H 75
Octavia Ho. W10 —7J 57
Octavia Rd. Iswth —2C 86
Octavia St. SW11 —9C 74
Octavia Way. SE28 —1F 80
Octavius St. SE8 —8L 77
October Pl. NW4 —1H 41
Odard Rd. W Mol —8L 101
Oddesey Rd. Borwd —3M 11
Oddmark Rd. Bark —5B 64
Odeon Ct. E16 —8E 62
Odeon Ct. NW10 —4C 56
Odeon Leicester Square Cinema.
(off Leicester Sq.) —1H 75
Odeon Pde. Gnfd —2F 54
(off Allendale Rd.)
Odeon Swiss Cen. Cinema.
(off Leicester St.) —1H 75
Odeon West End Cinema. —1H 75
(off Panton St.)
Odessa Rd. E7 —8D 46
Odessa Rd. NW10 —5E 56
Odessa St. SE16 —3K 77
Odette Duval Ho. E1 —8G 61
(off Stepney Way)
Odger St. SW11 —1D 90
Odhams Trad. Est. Wat —1G 9
Odhams Wlk. WC2 —9J 59
Odin Ho. SE5 —1A 92
O'Donnell Ct. WC1 —7J 59
Odontological Mus., The. —9K 59
(off Lincoln Inn Fields,
Royal College of Surgeons)
O'Driscoll Ho. W12 —9F 56
Odyssey Bus. Pk. Ruis —1F 52
Offa's Mead. E9 —9K 45
Offenbach Ho. E2 —5H 61
(off Mace St.)
Offenham Rd. SE9 —1K 111
Offers Ct. King T —7K 103
Offerton Rd. SW4 —2G 91
Offham Ho. SE17 —5C 76
(off Beckway St.)
Offham Slope. N12 —5K 25
Offley Pl. Iswth —1B 86
Offley Rd. SW9 —8L 75
Offord Clo. N17 —6E 28
Offord Rd. N1 —3K 59
Offord St. N1 —3K 59
Ogden Ho. Felt —9J 85
Ogilby St. SE18 —5K 79
Ogilvie Ho. E1 —9H 61
(off Stepney Causeway)
Oglander Rd. SE15 —3D 92
Ogle St. W1 —8G 59
Oglethorpe Rd. Dag —8K 49
O'Gorman Ho. SW10 —8A 74
(off King's Rd.)
O'Grandy Ho. E17 —1M 45
Ohio Cotts. Pinn —9G 21
Ohio Rd. E13 —7D 62
Oil Mill La. W6 —6E 72
Okeburn Rd. SW17 —2E 106
Okehampton Clo. N12 —5B 26
Okehampton Cres. Well —9F 80
Okehampton Rd. NW10 —4G 57
Okehampton Rd. H Hill —6G 35
Okehampton Sq. Romf —6G 35
Okemore Gdns. Orp —8G 113
Olaf St. W11 —1H 73
Oldacre M. SW12 —6E 90
Old Av. Wey —9A 116
Old Bailey. EC4 —9M 59
Old Barge Ho. All. SE1 —1L 75
(off Barge Ho. St.)
Old Barn Clo. Sutt —9J 121
Old Barn La. Kenl —8D 138
Old Barn Rd. Eps —9A 134
Old Barn Way. Bexh —2B 98
Old Barrack Yd. SW1 —3E 74
(in two parts)
Old Barrowfield. E15 —4C 62
Old Belgate Wharf. E14 —4L 77
Old Bellgate Wharf. E14 —4L 77
Oldberry Rd. Edgw —6B 24
Old Bethnal Grn. Rd. E2 —6E 60
Old Bexley. —6M 97
Old Bexley Bus. Pk. Bex —6M 97
Old Bexley La. Bex & Dart —8B 98
(in two parts)
Old Billingsgate Mkt. EC3 —1C 76
(off Lwr. Thames St.)
Old Billingsgate Wlk. EC3 —1C 76
Old Bond St. W1 —1G 75
Oldborough Rd. Wemb —8G 39
Old Brentford. —8H 71
Old Brewer's Yd. WC2 —9J 59
Old Brewery M. NW3 —9B 42
Old Bri. Clo. N'holt —5L 53
Old Bri. St. Hamp W —6H 103
Old Broad St. EC2 —9B 60
Old Bromley Rd. Brom —2B 110
Old Brompton Rd. SW5 & SW7 —6L 73
Old Bldgs. WC2 —9L 59
(off Chancery La.)
Old Burlington St. W1 —1G 75
Oldbury Clo. Orp —8G 113
Oldbury Pl. W1 —8E 58
Oldbury Rd. Enf —4E 16
Old Castle St. E1 —9D 60
Old Cavendish St. W1 —9F 58
Old Change Ct. EC4 —9A 60
(off Carter La.)
Old Chapel Pl. SW9 —1L 91
Old Chapel Rd. Swan —2A 130
Old Charlton Rd. Shep —9A 100
Old Chelsea M. SW3 —7C 74
Old Chestnut Av. Clar P —8L 117
Old Chiswick Yd. W4 —7C 72
(off Pumping Sta. Rd.)
Old Church Ct. N11 —5F 26
Oldchurch Gdns. Romf —5B 50
Old Church La. NW9 —7B 40
Old Church La. Gnfd —6E 54
Old Church La. Stan —5F 22
Old Church Path. Esh —6A 118
Oldchurch Ri. Romf —5C 50
Old Church Rd. E1 —9H 61
Old Church Rd. E4 —4L 29
Oldchurch Rd. Romf —5B 50
Old Church St. SW3 —6B 74
Old Claygate La. Clay —8E 118
Old Compton St. W1 —1H 75
Old Cote Dri. Houn —7L 69
Old Ct. Ho. W8 —3M 73
(off Old Ct. Pl.)
Old Ct. Pl. W8 —3M 73
Old Courtyard, The. Brom —5F 110
Old Dairy M. NW5 —2F 58
Old Dairy M. SW12 —7E 90
Old Dartford Rd. F'ham —1K 131
Old Deer Pk. Gdns. Rich —2J 87
Old Devonshire Rd. SW12 —6F 90
Old Dock Clo. Rich —7L 71
Old Dover Rd. SE3 —8E 78
Oldegate Ho. E6 —3H 63
Olden La. Purl —4L 137
Old Esher Clo. W on T —7H 117
Old Esher Rd. W on T —7H 117
Old Farleigh Rd. S Croy & Warl —2G 139
Old Farm Av. N14 —9G 15
Old Farm Av. Sidc —7B 96
Old Farm Clo. SW17 —8C 90
Old Farm Clo. Houn —3K 85
Old Farm Gdns. Swan —7D 114
Old Farm Ho. Dri. Oxs —7B 132
Old Farm Pas. Hamp —5A 102
Old Farm Rd. N2 —8B 26
Old Farm Rd. Hamp —3K 101
(in two parts)
Old Farm Rd. W Dray —3H 143
Old Farm Rd. E. Sidc —8E 96
Old Farm Rd. W. Sidc —8D 96
Oldfield Clo. Brom —8K 111
Oldfield Clo. Chesh —1E 6
Oldfield Clo. Gnfd —1C 54
Oldfield Clo. Stan —5E 22
Oldfield Ct. Surb —8K 103
(off Cranes Pk. Cres.)
Oldfield Dri. Chesh —1E 6
Oldfield Farm Gdns. Gnfd —4B 54
Oldfield Gro. SE16 —5H 77
Oldfield Ho. W4 —6C 72
(off Devonshire Rd.)
Oldfield La. N. Gnfd —5B 54
Oldfield La. S. Gnfd —7A 54
Oldfield M. N6 —5G 43
Oldfield Rd. N16 —8C 44
Oldfield Rd. NW10 —3C 56
Oldfield Rd. SW19 —3J 105
Oldfield Rd. W3 —3D 72
Oldfield Rd. Bexh —1J 97
Oldfield Rd. Brom —8J 111
Oldfield Rd. Hamp —5K 101
Oldfields Cir. N'holt —2A 54
Oldfields Rd. Sutt —5K 121
Oldfields Trad. Est. Sutt —5L 121
Old Fish St. Hill. EC4 —1A 76
(off Victoria St.)
Old Fleet La. EC4 —9M 59
Old Fold Clo. Barn —3K 13
Old Fold La. Barn —3K 13
Old Fold Vw. Barn —5G 13
Old Ford. —4K 61
Old Ford. (Junct.) —5L 61
Old Ford Rd. E2 & E3 —6G 61
Old Forge Clo. Stan —4E 22
Old Forge Clo. Wat —6E 4
Old Forge Cres. Shep —1A 116
Old Forge M. W12 —3F 72
Old Forge Rd. Enf —2D 16
Old Forge Way. Sidc —1F 112
Old Gannon Clo. N'wd —4A 20
Old Gloucester St. WC1 —8J 59
Old Hall Clo. Pinn —8J 21
Old Hall Dri. Pinn —8J 21
Oldham Ter. W3 —2A 72
Old Hatch Mnr. Ruis —5D 36
Old Hill. Chst —5L 111
Old Hill. Orp —8B 128
Oldhill St. N16 —6E 44
Old Homesdale Rd. Brom —8G 111
Old Hospital Clo. SW17 —7D 90
Old Ho. Clo. SW19 —2J 105
Old Ho. Clo. Eps —2D 134
Old Ho. Gdns. Twic —5G 87
Old Howlett's La. Ruis —4B 36
Old Isleworth. —2F 86
Old Jamaica Rd. SE16 —4E 76
Old James St. SE15 —2F 92
Old Jewry. EC2 —9B 60
Old Kenton La. NW9 —3M 39
Old Kent Rd. SE1 & SE15 —5C 76
Old Kingston Rd. Wor Pk —4A 120
Old Laundry, The. Chst —5A 112
Old Lodge La. Kenl & Purl —5K 137
Old Lodge Pl. Twic —5F 86
Old Lodge Way. Stan —5E 22
Old London Rd. Sidc —4L 113
Old Macdonalds Educational Farm Pk. —1K 35
Old Maidstone Rd. Sidc —4K 113
Old Malden. —3C 120
Old Malden La. Wor Pk —5B 120
Old Mnr. Ct. NW8 —5A 58
Old Mnr. Dri. Iswth —5A 86
Old Mnr. Rd. S'hall —4H 69
Old Mnr. Way. Bexh —1B 98
Old Mnr. Way. Chst —2K 111
Old Mnr. Yd. SW5 —5M 73

Paignton Rd.—Park La.

Paignton Rd. N15 —4C 44
Paignton Rd. Ruis —8E 36
Paines Brook Rd. Romf —6K 35
Paines Brook Way. Romf —6K 35
Paines Clo. Pinn —1J 37
Paines La. Pinn —8J 21
Pain's Clo. Mitc —6F 106
Painsthorpe Rd. N16 —8C 44
Painswick Ct. SE15 —8D 76
(off Daniel Gdns.)
Painters La. Enf —8E 6
Painters Rd. Ilf —1D 48
Paisley Rd. N22 —8M 27
Paisley Rd. Cars —3B 122
Pakeman Ho. SE1 —3M 75
(off Surrey Row)
Pakeman St. N7 —8K 43
Pakenham Clo. SW12 —7E 90
Pakenham St. WC1 —6K 59
Pakington Ho. SW9 —1J 91
(off Stockwell Gdns. Est.)
Palace Av. W8 —3M 73
Palace Ct. NW3 —1M 57
Palace Ct. W2 —1M 73
(off Moscow Rd.)
Palace Ct. W2 —1M 73
(Bayswater Rd.)
Palace Ct. Brom —5F 110
(off Palace Gro.)
Palace Ct. Harr —4J 39
Palace Ct. Gdns. N10 —1G 43
Palace Dri. Wey —5A 116
Palace Gdns. Buck H —1H 31
Palace Gdns. Enf —6B 16
Palace Gdns. M. W8 —2M 73
Palace Gdns. Shop. Cen. Enf —6B 16
Palace Gdns. Ter. W8 —2L 73
Palace Ga. W8 —3A 74
Palace Gates Rd. N22 —8H 27
Palace Grn. W8 —2M 73
Palace Grn. Croy —9K 125
Palace Gro. SE19 —4D 108
Palace Gro. Brom —5F 110
Palace Mans. W14 —5J 73
(off Hammersmith Rd.)
Palace Mans. King T —8H 103
(off Palace Rd.)
Palace M. E17 —2K 45
Palace M. SW1 —5E 74
(off Eaton Ter.)
Palace M. SW6 —8L 73
Palace M. Enf —5B 16
Palace Pde. E17 —2K 45
Palace Pl. SW1 —4G 75
Palace Pl. Mans. W8 —3M 73
(off Kensington Ct.)
Palace Rd. N8 —3H 43
(in two parts)
Palace Rd. N11 —7J 27
Palace Rd. SE19 —4D 108
Palace Rd. SW2 —7K 91
Palace Rd. Brom —5F 110
Palace Rd. E Mol —7B 102
Palace Rd. King T —8H 103
Palace Rd. Ruis —9J 37
Palace Sq. SE19 —4D 108
Palace St. SW1 —4G 75
Palace Theatre. —5F 8
(off Clarendon Rd.)
Palace Theatre. —9H 59
(off Shaftesbury Av., Westminster)
Palace Vw. SE12 —8E 94
Palace Vw. Brom —7F 110
(in two parts)
Palace Vw. Croy —6K 125
Palace Vw. Rd. E4 —5M 29
Palace Way. Wey —5A 116
Palamon Ct. SE1 —6D 76
(off Cooper's Rd.)
Palamos Rd. E10 —6L 45
Palatine Av. N16 —9C 44
Palatine Rd. N16 —9C 44
Palermo Rd. NW10 —5E 56
Palestine Gro. SW19 —5B 106
Palewell Clo. Orp —6F 112
Palewell Comn. Dri. SW14 —4B 88
Palewell Pk. SW14 —4B 88
Paley Gdns. Lou —5M 19
Palfrey Pl. SW8 —8K 75
Palgrave Av. S'hall —1L 69
Palgrave Gdns. NW1 —7C 58
Palgrave Ho. SE5 —8A 76
(off Wyndham Est.)
Palgrave Ho. Twic —6A 86
Palgrave Rd. W12 —4D 72
Palissy St. E2 —6D 60
(in two parts)
Pallant Ho. SE1 —4B 76
(off Tabard St.)
Pallant Way. Orp —5L 127
Pallett Way. SE18 —9J 79
Palliser Ct. W14 —6J 73
Palliser Dri. Rain —8E 66
Palliser Ho. E1 —7H 61
(off Ernest St.)
Palliser Ho. SE10 —7B 78
(off Trafalgar Rd.)
Palliser Rd. W14 —6J 73
Pall Mall. SW1 —2G 75
Pall Mall E. SW1 —2H 75
Pall Mall Pl. SW1 —2G 75
(off Pall Mall)
Palmar Cres. Bexh —2L 97
Palmar Rd. Bexh —1L 97
Palmarsh Rd. Orp —8H 113
Palm Av. Sidc —3H 113
Palm Clo. E10 —8M 45
Palm Ct. SE15 —8D 76
(off Garnies Clo.)
Palmeira Rd. Bexh —2H 97
Palmer Av. Bush —7M 9
Palmer Av. Sutt —6G 121
Palmer Clo. Houn —9L 69
Palmer Clo. W W'ck —5B 126
Palmer Ct. NW10 —4B 56
(in two parts)
Palmer Cres. King T —7J 103
Palmer Gdns. Barn —7H 13
Palmer Pl. N7 —1L 59
Palmer Rd. E13 —7F 62
Palmer Rd. Dag —6H 49
Palmer's Ct. N11 —5G 27
(off Palmer's Rd.)
Palmersfield Rd. Bans —6L 135
Palmers Green. —4L 27
Palmers Gro. W Mol —8L 101
Palmers La. Enf —3F 16
(in two parts)
Palmers Pas. SW14 —2A 88
(off Palmers Rd.)
Palmer's Rd. E2 —5H 61
Palmer's Rd. N11 —5G 27
Palmers Rd. SW14 —2A 88
Palmers Rd. SW16 —6K 107
Palmers Rd. Borwd —3M 11
Palmerston Cen. W'stone —1D 38
Palmerston Ct. E3 —5H 61
(off Old Ford Rd.)
Palmerston Ct. Buck H —1G 31
Palmerston Ct. Surb —2H 119
Palmerston Cres. N13 —5K 27
Palmerston Cres. SE18 —7A 80
Palmerston Gro. SW19 —4L 105
Palmerston Ho. SE1 —3L 75
(off Westminster Bri. Rd.)
Palmerston Ho. W8 —2L 73
(off Kensington Pl.)
Palmerston Mans. W14 —7J 73
(off Queen's Club Gdns.)
Palmerston Rd. E7 —2F 62
Palmerston Rd. E17 —1K 45
Palmerston Rd. N22 —7K 27
Palmerston Rd. NW6 —3K 57
(in two parts)
Palmerston Rd. SW14 —3A 88
Palmerston Rd. SW19 —4L 105
Palmerston Rd. W3 —4A 72
Palmerston Rd. Buck H —2F 30
Palmerston Rd. Cars —6D 122
Palmerston Rd. Croy —9B 108
Palmerston Rd. Harr —1C 38
Palmerston Rd. Houn —9A 70
Palmerston Rd. Orp —6A 128
Palmerston Rd. Rain —5G 67
Palmerston Rd. Sutt —7A 122
Palmerston Rd. Twic —5C 86
Palmerston Way. SW8 —8F 74
Palmer St. SW1 —4H 75
Palmers Way. Chesh —2E 6
Palm Gro. W5 —4J 71
Palm Rd. Romf —3A 50
Palm Tree Ho. SE14 —8H 77
(off Barlborough St.)
Pamela Ct. N3 —6M 25
Pamela Gdns. Pinn —3F 36
Pamela Ho. E8 —4D 60
(off Haggerston Rd.)
Pamela Wlk. E8 —4E 60
(off Marlborough Av.)
Pampisford Rd. Purl & S Croy —3L 137
Pams Way. Eps —7B 120
Panama Ho. E1 —8H 61
(off Beaumont Sq.)
Pancras La. EC4 —9A 60
Pancras Rd. NW1 —5H 59
Pandora Rd. NW6 —2L 57
Panfield M. Ilf —4L 47
Panfield Rd. SE2 —4E 80
Pangbourne. NW1 —6G 59
(off Stanhope St.)
Pangbourne Av. W10 —8G 57
Pangbourne Dri. Stan —5H 23
Panhard Pl. S'hall —1M 69
Pank Av. Barn —7A 14
Pankhurst Av. E16 —2F 78
Pankhurst Clo. SE14 —8H 77
Pankhurst Clo. Iswth —2D 86
Pankhurst Pl. Wat —5G 9
Pankhurst Rd. W on T —2G 117
Panmuir Rd. SW20 —5F 104
Panmure Clo. N5 —9M 43
Panmure Ct. S'hall —9A 54
(off Osborne Rd.)
Panmure Rd. SE26 —9F 92
Panorama Ct. N6 —4G 43
Pansy Gdns. W12 —1E 72
Panter's. Swan —4D 114
Panther Dri. NW10 —1B 56
Pantile Rd. Wey —6B 116
Pantiles Clo. N13 —5M 27
Pantiles, The. NW11 —3K 41
Pantiles, The. Bexh —8K 81
Pantiles, The. Brom —7J 111
Pantiles, The. Bush —1B 22
Pantile Wlk. Uxb —3A 142
Panton St. SW1 —1H 75
Panyer All. EC4 —9A 60
(off Newgate St.)
Paper Bldgs. EC4 —1L 75
(off Crown Office Row)
Papermill Clo. Cars —6E 122
Paper Mill Wharf. E14 —1J 77
Papillons Wlk. SE3 —1E 94
Papworth Gdns. N7 —1K 59
Papworth Way. SW2 —6L 91
Parade Mans. NW4 —3F 40
Parade M. SE27 —8M 91
Parade, The. N4 —6L 43
Parade, The. SE4 —1K 93
(off Up. Brockley Rd.)
Parade, The. SE26 —9F 92
(off Wells Pk. Rd.)
Parade, The. SW11 —8D 74
Parade, The. Cars —7D 122
(off Beynon Rd.)
Parade, The. Clay —8C 118
Parade, The. Croy —1J 123
Parade, The. Dart —4D 98
Parade, The. Eps —5B 134
(in two parts)
Parade, The. Gnfd —1F 54
Parade, The. Hamp —2B 102
Parade, The. King T —6J 103
(off London Rd.)
Parade, The. Romf —6M 35
Parade, The. Sun —4D 100
Parade, The. Sutt —5K 121
Parade, The. Wat —3H 21
(Fairfield Av.)
Parade, The. Wat —5F 8
(High St.)
Parade, The. Wat —3J 21
(Parade, The)
Parade, The. Wor Pk —6D 120
Paradise Clo. Chesh —1B 6
Paradise Pas. N7 —1L 59
Paradise Pl. SE18 —5J 79
Paradise Rd. SW4 —1J 91
Paradise Rd. Rich —4H 87
Paradise Rd. Wal A —7J 7
Paradise Row. E2 —6F 60
Paradise St. SE16 —3F 76
Paradise Wlk. SW3 —7D 74
Paragon Clo. E16 —9E 62
Paragon Gro. Surb —1K 119
Paragon M. SE1 —5B 76
Paragon Pl. SE3 —1D 94
Paragon Pl. Surb —1K 119
Paragon Rd. E9 —2G 61
Paragon, The. SE3 —1D 94
Paramount Building. EC1 —7M 59
(off St John St.)
Paramount Ct. WC1 —7G 59
Paramount Ind. Est. Wat —1G 9
(off Sandown Rd.)
Parbury Ri. Chess —8J 119
Parbury Rd. SE23 —5J 93
Parchmore Rd. T Hth —6M 107
Parchmore Way. T Hth —6M 107
Pardoner Ho. SE1 —4B 76
(off Pardoner St.)
Pardoner St. SE1 —4B 76
(in two parts)
Pardon St. EC1 —7M 59
Parfett St. E1 —8E 60
(in two parts)
Parfitt Clo. NW3 —6A 42
Parfour Dri. Kenl —8A 138
Parfrey St. W6 —7G 73
Pargreaves Ct. Wemb —7L 39
Parham Dri. Ilf —4M 47
Parham Way. N10 —9G 27
Paris Garden. SE1 —2M 75
Parish Clo. Horn —7F 50
Parish Clo. Wat —7G 5
Parish Cotts. Dag —7L 49
Parish Ct. Surb —9J 103
Parish Ga. Dri. Sidc —5C 96
Parish La. SE20 —3H 109
Parish M. SE20 —4H 109
Paris Ho. E2 —5F 60
(off Old Bethnal Grn. Rd.)
Parish Wharf Pl. SE18 —5J 79
Park App. SE16 —4F 76
Park App. Well —3F 96
Park Av. E6 —4L 63
Park Av. E15 —2C 62
Park Av. N3 —8M 25
Park Av. N13 —3L 27
Park Av. N18 —4E 28
Park Av. N22 —9J 27
Park Av. NW2 —2G 57
Park Av. NW10 —5K 55
(in two parts)
Park Av. NW11 —6M 41
Park Av. SW14 —3B 88
Park Av. Bark —2A 64
Park Av. Brom —3D 110
Park Av. Bush —4H 9
Park Av. Cars —8E 122
Park Av. Enf —7B 16
Park Av. Houn —5M 85
Park Av. Ilf —6L 47
Park Av. Mitc —4F 106
Park Av. Orp —5K 127
(Farnborough Rd.)
Park Av. Orp —4E 128
(Sevenoaks Rd.)
Park Av. Ruis —4B 36
Park Av. Shep —7C 100
Park Av. S'hall —3K 69
Park Av. Wat —6E 8
Park Av. W W'ck —4A 126
Park Av. Wfd G —5F 30
Park Av. E. Eps —8E 120
Park Av. Maisonettes. Bush —4K 9
Park Av. M. Mitc —4F 106
Park Av. N. N8 —2H 43
Park Av. N. NW10 —1F 56
Park Av. Rd. N17 —7F 28
Park Av. S. N8 —2H 43
Park Av. W. Eps —8E 120
Park Boulevd. Romf —8D 34
Park Bus. Cen. NW6 —6L 57
Park Chase. Wemb —9K 39
Park Clo. E9 —4G 61
Park Clo. N20 —3B 26
Park Clo. NW2 —8F 40
Park Clo. NW10 —6K 55
Park Clo. SW1 —3D 74
Park Clo. W4 —7B 72
Park Clo. W14 —4K 73
Park Clo. Bush —5H 9
Park Clo. Cars —8D 122
Park Clo. Esh —8L 117
Park Clo. Hamp —5A 102
Park Clo. Harr —8C 22
Park Clo. Houn —4A 86
Park Clo. King T —5L 103
Park Clo. Rick —4A 20
Park Clo. W on T —4D 116
Park Ct. E4 —2A 30
Park Ct. E17 —3M 45
Park Ct. N11 —7H 27
Park Ct. N17 —7E 28
Park Ct. SE26 —3F 108
Park Ct. SW11 —9F 74
Park Ct. Harr —5J 39
Park Ct. King T —5G 103
Park Ct. N Mald —8B 104
Park Ct. S Croy —7A 124
(off Warham Rd.)
Park Ct. Uxb —4B 142
Park Ct. Wemb —1J 55
Park Cres. N3 —7M 25
Park Cres. NW1 —7F 58
Park Cres. Els —5K 11
Park Cres. Enf —6B 16
Park Cres. Eri —7A 82
Park Cres. Harr —8C 22
Park Cres. Horn —5E 50
Park Cres. Twic —7B 86
Park Cres. M. E. W1 —7F 58
Park Cres. M. W. W1 —7F 58
Park Cres. Rd. Eri —7B 82
Park Cft. Edgw —8A 24
Parkcroft Rd. SE12 —6D 94
Parkdale. N11 —6H 27
Parkdale Cres. Wor Pk —5B 120
Parkdale Rd. SE18 —6C 80
Park Dri. N21 —8A 16
Park Dri. NW11 —6M 41
Park Dri. SE7 —7J 79
Park Dri. SW14 —4B 88
Park Dri. W3 —4L 71
Park Dri. Asht —9L 133
Park Dri. Dag —8A 50
Park Dri. Har W —6B 22
Park Dri. N Har —5L 37
Park Dri. Romf —2B 50
Park Dri. Upm —9M 51
Park Dwellings. NW3 —1D 58
Park End. NW3 —9C 42
Park End. Brom —5D 110
Pk. End Rd. Romf —2C 50
Parker Clo. E16 —2J 79
Parker Ho. E14 —3L 77
(off Admirals Way)
Parker M. WC2 —9J 59
Parke Rd. SW13 —9E 72
Parke Rd. Sun —8E 100
Parker Rd. Croy —6A 124
Parkers Row. SE1 —3E 76
Parker St. E16 —2J 79
Parker St. WC2 —9J 59
Parker St. Wat —3F 8
Parkes Rd. Chig —5C 32
Pk. Farm Clo. N2 —1A 42
Pk. Farm Clo. Pinn —3F 36
Pk. Farm Ct. Hay —1C 68
Pk. Farm Rd. Brom —5H 111
Pk. Farm Rd. King T —4J 103
Pk. Farm Rd. Upm —1K 67
Parkfield. Iswth —9C 70
Parkfield Av. SW14 —3C 88
Parkfield Av. Felt —9E 84
Parkfield Av. Harr —9A 22
Parkfield Av. Hil —6F 142
Parkfield Av. N'holt —5H 53
Parkfield Clo. Edgw —6M 23
Parkfield Clo. N'holt —5J 53
Parkfield Ct. SE14 —9K 77
(off Parkfield Rd.)
Parkfield Cres. Felt —9E 84
Parkfield Cres. Harr —9A 22
Parkfield Cres. Ruis —7J 37
Parkfield Dri. N'holt —5H 53
Parkfield Gdns. Harr —1M 37
Parkfield Ho. N Har —8M 21
Parkfield Ind. Est. SW11 —1E 90
Parkfield Pde. Felt —9E 84
Parkfield Rd. NW10 —3F 56
Parkfield Rd. SE14 —9K 77
Parkfield Rd. Felt —9E 84
Parkfield Rd. Harr —8A 38
Parkfield Rd. Ick & Uxb —7A 36
Parkfield Rd. N'holt —5J 53
Parkfields. SW15 —3G 89
Parkfields. Croy —3K 125
Parkfields. Oxs —3B 132
Parkfields Av. NW9 —6B 40
Parkfields Av. SW20 —5F 104
Parkfields Clo. Cars —6E 122
Parkfields Rd. King T —2K 103
Parkfield St. N1 —5L 59
Parkfield Way. Brom —1K 127
Park Gdns. E10 —6L 45
Park Gdns. NW9 —1M 39
Park Gdns. Eri —5B 82
Park Gdns. King T —2K 103
Park Ga. N2 —1B 42
Park Ga. N21 —9K 15
Park Ga. SE3 —2D 94
Park Ga. W5 —8H 55
Parkgate Av. Barn —3A 14
Pk. Gate Clo. King T —3M 103
Pk. Gate Ct. Hamp H —3A 102
Parkgate Cres. Barn —3A 14
Parkgate Gdns. SW14 —4B 88
Parkgate M. N6 —5G 43
Parkgate Rd. SW11 —8C 74
Parkgate Rd. Orp —6M 129
Parkgate Rd. Wall —7E 122
Parkgate Rd. Wat —1G 9
Park Gates. Harr —9L 37
Park Gro. E15 —4E 62
Park Gro. N11 —7H 27
Park Gro. Bexh —3A 98
Park Gro. Brom —5F 110
Park Gro. Edgw —5K 23
Park Gro. Rd. E11 —7C 46
Parkhall Rd. N2 —2C 42
Pk. Hall Rd. SE21 —9A 92
Pk. Hall Trad. Est. SE21 —9A 92
Parkham Ct. Short —6C 110
Parkham St. SW11 —9C 74
Park Hill. SE23 —8F 92
Park Hill. SW4 —4H 91
Park Hill. W5 —8H 55
Park Hill. Brom —8J 111
Park Hill. Cars —8C 122
Park Hill. Lou —7H 19
Park Hill. Rich —5K 87
Pk. Hill Clo. Cars —7C 122
Parkhill Clo. Horn —7G 51
Pk. Hill Ct. SW17 —9D 90
Pk. Hill Ri. Croy —4C 124
Parkhill Rd. E4 —1A 30
Parkhill Rd. NW3 —1D 58
Parkhill Rd. Bex —6K 97
Pk. Hill Rd. Brom —6C 110
Pk. Hill Rd. Croy —4C 124
Parkhill Rd. Eps —3D 134
Pk. Hill Rd. Sidc —9B 96
Pk. Hill Rd. Wall —9F 122
Parkhill Wlk. NW3 —1D 58
Parkholme Rd. E8 —2E 60
Park Ho. N21 —9K 15
Park Ho. Gdns. Twic —4G 87
Park Ho. Pas. N6 —5E 42
Parkhouse St. SE5 —8B 76
Parkhurst. Eps —2A 134
Parkhurst Ct. N7 —9J 43
Parkhurst Gdns. Bex —6L 97
Parkhurst Rd. E12 —9L 47
Parkhurst Rd. E17 —2J 45
Parkhurst Rd. N7 —9J 43
Parkhurst Rd. N11 —5E 26
Parkhurst Rd. N17 —9E 28
Parkhurst Rd. N22 —6K 27
Parkhurst Rd. Bex —6L 97
Parkhurst Rd. Sutt —6B 122
Parkinson Ho. SW1 —5G 75
(off Tachbrook St.)
Parkland Av. Romf —1C 50
Parkland Av. Upm —1M 67
Parkland Ct. E15 —1C 62
(off Maryland Pk.)
Parkland Gdns. SW19 —7H 89
Parkland Gro. Ashf —9E 144
Parkland Rd. N22 —9K 27
Parkland Rd. Ashf —9E 144
Parkland Rd. Wfd G —7F 30
Parklands. N6 —6F 42
Parklands. Chig —2A 32
Parklands. Surb —9K 103
Parklands. Wal A —6J 7
Parklands Clo. SW14 —4A 88
Parklands Clo. Barn —2B 14
Parklands Clo. Chig —3A 32
Parklands Ct. Houn —1H 85
Parklands Dri. N3 —1J 41
Parklands Gro. Iswth —9D 70
Parklands Pde. Houn —1H 85
Parklands Rd. SW16 —2F 106
Parklands Way. Wor Pk —4C 120
Park La. E15 —4B 62
Park La. N9 —3C 28
Park La. N17 —7D 28
(in two parts)
Park La. W1 —1D 74
Park La. Cars & Wall —6E 122

Park La.—Pavilion Ct.

Park La. Chad H —4H 49
Park La. Chesh —1B 6
Park La. Cran & Houn —8E 68
Park La. Croy —5B 124
Park La. Elm P —2F 66
Park La. Harr —8M 37
Park La. Hay —8C 52
Park La. Horn —4D 50
Park La. Rich —3H 87
Park La. Stan —3E 22
Park La. Sutt —8J 121
Park La. Swan —6G 115
Park La. Tedd —3D 102
Park La. Wal X —6C 6
Park La. Wemb —1J 55
Park La. Clo. N17 —7E 28
Park La. Mans. Croy —5B 124
(off Edridge Rd.)
Park Langley. —8A 110
Parklawn Av. Eps —5M 133
Pk. Lawn Rd. Wey —6A 116
Park Lawns. Wemb —9K 39
Parklea Clo. NW9 —8C 24
Pk. Lee Ct. N16 —5C 44
Parkleigh Rd. SW19 —6M 105
Parkleys. Rich —1H 103
Parkleys Pde. Rich —1H 103
Park Lodge. NW8 —3B 58
Park Lorne. NW8 —6C 58
(off Park Rd.)
Park Mnr. Sutt —9A 122
(off Christchurch Pk.)
Park Mans. NW4 —3F 40
Park Mans. NW8 —5C 58
(off Allitsen Rd.)
Park Mans. SW1 —3D 74
(off Brompton Rd.)
Park Mans. SW8 —7J 75
Park Mans. SW11 —9D 74
(off Prince of Wales Dri.)
Parkmead. SW15 —5F 88
Park Mead. Harr —8M 37
Parkmead. Lou —7L 19
Park Mead. Sidc —4F 96
Parkmead Gdns. NW7 —6D 24
Park M. SE24 —6A 92
Park M. W10 —5J 57
Park M. Chst —3M 111
Park M. Rain —2E 66
Park M. Stanw —6D 144
Parkmore Clo. Wfd G —4E 30
Pk. Nook Gdns. Enf —1B 16
Park Pde. NW10 —5D 56
Park Pde. W5 —4L 71
Park Pde. Hay —9C 52
Park Pl. E14 —2L 77
Park Pl. SW1 —2G 75
Park Pl. W3 —5L 71
Park Pl. W5 —2H 71
Park Pl. Brom —5F 110
(off Park Rd.)
Park Pl. Hamp H —3A 102
Park Pl. Wemb —9K 39
Park Pl. Vs. W2 —8A 58
Park Ridings. N8 —1L 43
Park Ri. SE23 —7J 93
Park Ri. Harr —8C 22
Park Ri. Rd. SE23 —7J 93
Park Rd. E6 —4G 63
Park Rd. E10 —6L 45
Park Rd. E12 —6F 46
Park Rd. E15 —4E 62
Park Rd. E17 —3K 45
Park Rd. N2 —1B 42
Park Rd. N8 —2G 43
Park Rd. N11 —7H 27
Park Rd. N14 —1H 27
Park Rd. N15 —2M 43
Park Rd. N18 —4E 28
Park Rd. NW4 —5E 40
Park Rd. NW8 & NW1 —6C 58
Park Rd. NW9 —5B 40
Park Rd. NW10 —4C 56
Park Rd. SE25 —8C 108
Park Rd. SW19 —3B 106
Park Rd. W4 —8A 72
Park Rd. W7 —1D 70
Park Rd. Ashf —2A 100
Park Rd. Bans —7M 135
Park Rd. Barn & New Bar —6B 14
Park Rd. Beck —4K 109
Park Rd. Brom —5F 110
Park Rd. Bush —8L 9
Park Rd. Cheam & Sutt —8J 121
Park Rd. Chst —3M 111
Park Rd. Dart —6L 99
Park Rd. E Mol —8A 102
Park Rd. Enf —9E 6
Park Rd. Esh —6M 117
Park Rd. Felt —1H 101
Park Rd. Hack —4F 122
Park Rd. Hamp H —1M 101
Park Rd. Hamp W —5G 103
Park Rd. Hay —8C 52
Park Rd. High Bar —6K 13
Park Rd. Houn —4M 85
Park Rd. Ilf —8B 48
Park Rd. Iswth —9F 70
Park Rd. Kenl —7A 138
Park Rd. King T —2K 103
Park Rd. N Mald —8B 104
Park Rd. Orp —9G 113
Park Rd. Rich —5K 87
Park Rd. Stanw —5A 144
Park Rd. Sun —4F 100
Park Rd. Surb —1K 119
Park Rd. Swan —8D 114
Park Rd. Tedd —3D 102
Park Rd. Twic —5G 87
Park Rd. Uxb —3C 142
Park Rd. Wall —7F 122
Park Rd. Wal X —6D 6
Park Rd. Warl —6C 140
Park Rd. Wat —3E 8
Park Rd. Wemb —2J 55
Park Rd. E. W3 —3M 71
Park Rd. E. Uxb —5B 142
Park Rd. Ho. King T —4L 103
Park Rd. Ind. Est. Swan —7D 114
Park Rd. N. W3 —3M 71
Park Rd. N. W4 —6B 72
Park Row. SE10 —6B 78
Park Royal. —6M 55
Park Royal Junction. (Junct.) —4L 55
Pk. Royal Metro Cen. NW10 —7M 55
Pk. Royal Rd. NW10 & W3 —6A 56
Pk. Royal S. Leisure Complex. W3 —7L 55
Parkshot. Rich —3H 87
Parkside. N3 —8M 25
Parkside. NW2 —8E 40
Parkside. NW7 —6E 24
Parkside. SE3 —8D 78
Parkside. SW1 —3D 74
(off Knightsbridge)
Parkside. SW19 —9H 89
Parkside. W3 —2C 72
Parkside. W5 —1J 71
Parkside. Buck H —2F 30
Parkside. Hamp H —2B 102
Parkside. Hay —1C 68
Parkside. Sidc —8F 96
Parkside. Sutt —8J 121
Parkside. Wal X —7E 6
Parkside. Wat —8G 9
Parkside Av. SW19 —2H 105
Parkside Av. Bexh —1B 98
Parkside Av. Brom —8J 111
Parkside Av. Romf —1B 50
Parkside Bus. Est. SE8 —7J 77
Parkside Clo. SE20 —4G 109
Parkside Ct. E11 —4E 46
(off Wanstead Pl.)
Parkside Ct. N22 —6K 27
Parkside Cres. N7 —8L 43
Parkside Cres. Surb —1A 120
Parkside Cross. Bexh —1C 98
Parkside Dri. Edgw —3L 23
Parkside Dri. Wat —4C 8
Parkside Est. E9 —4G 61
Parkside Gdns. SW19 —1H 105
Parkside Gdns. Coul —9F 136
Parkside Gdns. E Barn —1D 26
Parkside Ho. Dag —8A 50
Parkside Lodge. Belv —6A 82
Parkside Pde. Dart —1D 98
(off Northend Rd.)
Parkside Rd. SW11 —9E 74
Parkside Rd. Belv —5M 81
Parkside Rd. Houn —4M 85
Parkside Rd. N'wd —5D 20
Parkside Ter. N18 —4B 28
Parkside Way. Harr —2M 37
Park Sq. Esh —6M 117
Park Sq. E. NW1 —7F 58
Park Sq. M. NW1 —7E 58
(off Up. Harley St.)
Park Sq. W. NW1 —7F 58
Parkstead Rd. SW15 —4E 88
Park Steps. W2 —1C 74
(off St George's Fields)
Parkstone Av. N18 —6D 28
Parkstone Av. Horn —4H 51
Parkstone Rd. E17 —1A 46
Parkstone Rd. SE15 —1E 92
Park St. SE1 —2A 76
Park St. W1 —1E 74
Park St. Croy —5A 124
Park St. Tedd —3C 102
Park St. La. Park & St Alb —3M 5
Park Ter. Cars —5C 122
Park Ter. Enf —2J 17
Park Ter. Wor Pk —3E 120
Park, The. N6 —4E 42
Park, The. NW11 —6M 41
Park, The. SE19 —4C 108
Park, The. SE23 —7G 93
Park, The. W5 —2H 71
Park, The. Cars —7D 122
Park, The. Sidc —2E 112
Parkthorne Clo. Harr —4M 37
Parkthorne Dri. Harr —4L 37
Parkthorne Rd. SW12 —6H 91
Park Towers. W1 —2F 74
(off Brick St.)
Park Vw. N5 —9A 44
Park Vw. N21 —9K 15
Park Vw. W3 —8A 56
Park Vw. Chad H —4H 49
Parkview. Eri —4H 81
Parkview. Gnfd —6E 54
(off Perivale La.)
Park Vw. N Mald —7D 104
Park Vw. Pinn —8K 21
Park Vw. Wemb —1M 55
Park Vw. W Dray —1J 143
Pk. View Ct. N12 —4C 26
Pk. View Ct. SE20 —5F 108
Parkview Ct. SW6 —1J 89
Parkview Ct. SW18 —4L 89
Parkview Ct. Har W —7C 22
Pk. View Cres. N11 —4F 26
Pk. View Est. E2 —5H 61
Pk. View Gdns. N22 —8L 27
Pk. View Gdns. NW4 —3G 41
Pk. View Gdns. Bark —5C 64
Pk. View Gdns. Ilf —2K 47
Pk. View Ho. E4 —5L 29
Parkview Ho. N9 —9F 16
Pk. View Ho. SE24 —5M 91
(off Hurst St.)
Parkview Ho. Wat —8H 9
Pk. View Mans. N4 —5M 43
Pk. View Rd. N3 —8M 25
Pk. View Rd. N17 —1E 44
Pk. View Rd. NW10 —9D 40
Parkview Rd. SE9 —7M 95
Pk. View Rd. W5 —8J 55
Pk. View Rd. Croy —3E 124
Pk. View Rd. Pinn —7F 20
Pk. View Rd. S'hall —2L 69
Pk. View Rd. Uxb —9D 142
Pk. View Rd. Well —2G 97
Pk. Village E. NW1 —5F 58
Pk. Village W. NW1 —5F 58
Park Vs. Romf —4H 49
Parkville Rd. SW6 —8K 73
Park Vista. SE10 —7B 78
Park Wlk. N6 —5E 42
Park Wlk. SE10 —8B 78
Park Wlk. SW10 —7A 74
Park Wlk. Barn —5B 14
Parkway. N14 —2J 27
Park Way. N20 —4D 26
Parkway. NW1 —4F 58
Park Way. NW11 —3J 41
Parkway. SW20 —8H 105
Park Way. Bex —9C 98
Park Way. Edgw —8M 23
Park Way. Enf —4L 15
Parkway. Eri —4J 81
Park Way. Felt —6F 84
Park Way. Ilf —8D 48
Parkway. New Ad —1M 139
Parkway. Rain —7E 66
Parkway. Romf —9D 34
Park Way. Ruis —6E 36
Parkway. Uxb —3E 142
Park Way. W Mol —7M 101
Park Way. Wey —5B 116
Parkway. Wfd G —5G 31
Pk. Way Ct. Ruis —6D 36
Parkway, The. Hay —4F 68
(UB3,UB4)
Parkway, The. Hay —9G 53
(UB4,UB5)
Parkway, The. Houn —1F 84
Parkway, The. Houn & S'hall —6E 68
Parkway Trad. Est. Houn —7G 69
Park West. W2 —9C 58
(off Edgware Rd.)
Park W. Pl. W2 —9C 58
Park Wharf. SE8 —6J 77
(off Evelyn St.)
Parkwood. N20 —3D 26
Parkwood. NW8 —4D 58
(off St Edmund's Ter.)
Parkwood. Beck —4L 109
Parkwood Av. Esh —3A 118
Pk. Wood Clo. Bans —7H 135
Parkwood Flats. N20 —3D 26
Parkwood Gro. Sun —7E 100
Parkwood M. N6 —4F 42
Parkwood Rd. SW19 —2K 105
Pk. Wood Rd. Bans —7H 135
Pk. Wood Rd. Bex —6K 97
Parkwood Rd. Iswth —9D 70
Pk. Wood Vw. Bans —8G 135
Parliament Ct. E1 —8C 60
(off Artillery La.)
Parliament Hill. —8D 42
Parliament Hill. NW3 —9C 42
Parliament Hill Mans. NW5 —9E 42
Parliament M. SW14 —1A 88
Parliament Sq. SW1 —3J 75
Parliament St. SW1 —3J 75
Parliament Vw. SE1 —5K 75
Parma Cres. SW11 —3D 90
Parmiter Ind. Cen. E2 —5F 60
(off Parmiter St.)
Parmiter St. E2 —5F 60
Parmoor Ct. EC1 —7A 60
(off Gee St.)
Parndon Ho. Lou —9J 19
Parnell Clo. W12 —4F 72
Parnell Clo. Ab L —3D 4
Parnell Clo. Edgw —4M 23
Parnell Ho. WC1 —8H 59
Parnell Rd. E3 —4K 61
(in two parts)
Parnham St. E14 —9J 61
(in two parts)
Parolles Rd. N19 —6G 43
Paroma Rd. Belv —4L 81
Parr Av. Eps —1F 134
Parr Clo. N9 & N18 —4F 28
Parr Ct. N1 —5B 60
(off New North Rd.)
Parr Ct. Felt —1G 101
Parrington Ho. SW4 —5H 91
Parr Rd. E6 —4H 63
Parr Rd. Stan —8H 23
Parrs Clo. S Croy —1B 138
Parrs Pl. Hamp —4L 101
Parr St. N1 —5B 60
Parry Av. E6 —9K 63
Parry Clo. Eps —9F 120
Parry Ho. E1 —2F 76
(off Green Bank)
Parry Pl. SE18 —5M 79
Parry Rd. SE25 —7C 108
Parry Rd. W10 —6J 57
(in two parts)
Parry St. SW8 —7J 75
Parsifal Rd. NW6 —1L 57
Parsley Gdns. Croy —3H 125
Parsloes Av. Dag —9H 49
Parsonage Clo. Ab L —3C 4
Parsonage Clo. Hay —9D 52
Parsonage Clo. Warl —8J 139
Parsonage Gdns. Enf —4A 16
Parsonage La. Enf —4A 16
Parsonage La. Sidc —1K 113
Parsonage La. S at H —3M 115
Parsonage Manorway. Belv —7L 81
Parsonage Rd. Rain —5G 67
Parsonage St. E14 —5A 78
Parson's Cres. Edgw —3L 23
Parsonsfield Clo. Bans —7H 135
Parsonsfield Rd. Bans —8H 135
Parsons Green. —9L 73
Parson's Grn. SW6 —9L 73
Parson's Grn. La. SW6 —9L 73
Parson's Gro. Edgw —3L 23
Parsons Hill. SE18 —4L 79
(off Powis St.)
Parsons Ho. W2 —7B 58
(off Hall Pl.)
Parsons La. Dart —9F 98
Parsons Lodge. NW6 —3M 57
(off Priory Rd.)
Parson's Mead. Croy —3M 123
Parsons Mead. E Mol —7A 102
Parson's Rd. E13 —5G 63
Parson St. NW4 —2G 41
Parthenia Rd. SW6 —9L 73
Partingdale La. NW7 —5H 25
Partington Clo. N19 —6H 43
Partridge Clo. E16 —8H 63
Partridge Clo. Barn —8G 13
Partridge Clo. Bush —1A 22
Partridge Clo. Stan —4J 23
Partridge Ct. EC1 —7M 59
(off Cyprus St.)
Partridge Dri. Orp —5A 128
Partridge Grn. SE9 —9L 95
Partridge Knoll. Purl —4M 137
Partridge Mead. Bans —7G 135
Partridge Rd. Hamp —3K 101
Partridge Rd. Sidc —9C 96
Partridge Sq. E6 —8J 63
Partridge Way. N22 —8J 27
Parvills. Wal A —5K 7
Pasadena Clo. Hay —3E 68
Pasadena Clo. Trad. Est. Hay —3F 68
Pascall Ho. SE17 —7A 76
(off Draco St.)
Pascal St. SW8 —8H 75
Pascoe Rd. SE13 —4B 94
Pasfield. Wal A —6K 7
Pasley Clo. SE17 —6M 75
Pasquier Rd. E17 —1J 45
Passage, The. Rich —4J 87
Passey Pl. SE9 —5K 95
Passfield Dri. E14 —8M 61
Passfield Path. SE28 —1F 80
Passfields. SE6 —9M 93
Passfields. W14 —6K 73
(off Star St.)
Passing All. EC1 —8M 59
(off St John St.)
Passingham Ho. Houn —7L 69
Passmore Gdns. N11 —6H 27
Passmore St. SW1 —6E 74
Pasteur Clo. NW9 —9C 24
Pasteur Ct. Harr —6F 38
Pasteur Dri. H Wood —9H 35
Pasteur Gdns. N18 —5M 27
Paston Clo. E5 —8H 45
Paston Clo. Wall —5G 123
Paston Cres. SE12 —6F 94
Pastor Ct. N6 —4G 43
Pastor St. SE11 —5M 75
(in two parts)
Pasture Clo. Bush —9A 10
Pasture Clo. Wemb —8F 38
Pasture Rd. SE6 —7D 94
Pasture Rd. Dag —9K 49
Pasture Rd. Wemb —7F 38
Pastures Mead. Uxb —2E 142
Pastures, The. N20 —1K 25
Pastures, The. Wat —9G 9
Patcham Ter. SW8 —9F 74
Patch Clo. Uxb —4D 142
Patchetts Green. —3A 10
Patching Way. Hay —8J 53
Patchway Ct. SE15 —7C 76
(off Newent Clo.)
Patent Ho. E14 —8M 61
(off Morris Rd.)
Paternoster Clo. Wal A —6M 7
Paternoster Hill. Wal A —5M 7
Paternoster Row. EC4 —9M 59
Paternoster Row. Noak H —1G 35
Paternoster Sq. EC4 —9M 59
Paterson Ct. EC1 —6B 60
(off St Lukes Est.)
Pater St. W8 —4L 73
Pates Mnr. Dri. Felt —6B 84
Pathfield Rd. SW16 —3H 107
Path, The. SW19 —5M 105
Pathway, The. Rad —1D 10
(in two parts)
Pathway, The. Wat —1H 21
Patience Rd. SW11 —1C 90
Patio Clo. SW4 —5H 91
Patmore Est. SW8 —9G 75
Patmore Ho. N16 —1C 60
Patmore La. W on T —8D 116
Patmore Lodge. N6 —2D 42
Patmore Rd. Wal A —7L 7
Patmore St. SW8 —9G 75
Patmore Way. Romf —5M 33
Patmos Lodge. SW9 —9M 75
(off Elliott Rd.)
Patmos Rd. SW9 —8M 75
Paton Clo. E3 —6L 61
Paton Ho. SW9 —1K 91
(off Stockwell Rd.)
Paton St. EC1 —6A 60
Patricia Ct. Chst —5B 112
Patricia Ct. Well —8F 80
Patricia Dri. Horn —6J 51
Patricia Gdns. Sutt —3L 135
Patrick Coman Ho. EC1 —6M 59
(off Finsbury Est.)
Patrick Connolly Gdns. E3 —6M 61
Patrick Gro. Wal A —6H 7
Patrick Pas. SW11 —1C 90
Patrick Rd. E13 —6G 63
Patrington Clo. Uxb —6A 142
Patriot Sq. E2 —5F 60
Patrol Pl. SE6 —5M 93
Pat Shaw Ho. E1 —7H 61
(off Globe Rd.)
Patshull Pl. NW5 —2G 59
Patshull Rd. NW5 —2G 59
Patten All. Rich —4H 87
Pattenden Rd. SE6 —7K 93
Patten Ho. N16 —6A 44
Patten Rd. SW18 —6C 90
Patterdale. NW1 —6F 58
(off Osnaburgh St.)
Patterdale Clo. Brom —3D 110
Patterdale Rd. SE15 —8G 77
Pattern Ho. EC1 —7M 59
Patterson Ct. SE19 —4D 108
Patterson Ct. Dart —4L 99
Patterson Rd. SE19 —3D 108
Pattina Wlk. SE16 —2J 77
(off Capstan Way)
Pattinson Point. E16 —8E 62
(off Fife Rd.)
Pattison Ho. E1 —9H 61
(off Wellesley St.)
Pattison Ho. SE1 —3A 76
(off Redcross Way)
Pattison Rd. NW2 —8L 41
Pattison Wlk. SE18 —6A 80
Paul Byrne Ho. N2 —1A 42
Paul Clo. E15 —3C 62
Paul Ct. N18 —4E 28
(off Fairfield Rd.)
Paul Ct. Romf —3A 50
Paulet Rd. SE5 —1M 91
Paul Gdns. Croy —4D 124
Paulhan Rd. Harr —2H 39
Paulin Dri. N21 —9L 15
Pauline Cres. Twic —7A 86
Pauline Ho. E1 —8E 60
(off Old Montague St.)
Paulinus Clo. Orp —6G 113
Paul Julius Clo. E14 —1B 78
Paul Robeson Clo. E6 —6L 63
Pauls Grn. Wal X —6E 6
Pauls Ho. E3 —8K 61
(off Timothy Rd.)
Paul St. E15 —4C 62
Paul St. EC2 —7B 60
Paul's Wlk. EC4 —1A 76
Paultons Sq. SW3 —7B 74
Paultons St. SW3 —7B 74
Pauntley St. N19 —6G 43
Pavan Ct. E2 —6G 61
(off Sceptre Rd.)
Paved Ct. Rich —4H 87
Paveley Dri. SW11 —8C 74
Paveley Ho. N1 —5K 59
(off Priory Grn. Est.)
Paveley St. NW8 —6C 58
Pavement M. Romf —5H 49
Pavement Sq. Croy —3E 124
Pavement, The. E11 —6A 46
(off Hainault Rd.)
Pavement, The. SW4 —3G 91
Pavement, The. W5 —4J 71
Pavement, The. Iswth —2E 86
(off South St.)
Pavet Clo. Dag —2M 65
Pavilion Ct. NW6 —6L 57
(off Cambridge Rd.)

Pavilion Lodge—Penpoll Rd.

Pavilion Lodge. Harr —6B 38
Pavilion M. N3 —1L 41
Pavilion Rd. SW1 —4D 74
Pavilion Rd. Ilf —5K 47
Pavilion Shop. Cen., The. Wal X —6E 6
Pavilions, The. Uxb —3A 142
Pavilion St. SW1 —4D 74
Pavilion Ter. Ilf —3C 48
Pavilion, The. SW8 —8H 75
Pavilion Way. Edgw —7M 23
Pavilion Way. Ruis —7G 37
Pavillion Ter. W12 —9G 57
(off Wood La.)
Pawleyne Clo. SE20 —4G 109
Pawsey Clo. E13 —4F 62
Pawsons Rd. Croy —1A 124
Paxfold. Stan —5H 23
Paxford Rd. Wemb —7F 38
Paxton Clo. Rich —1K 87
Paxton Clo. W on T —2G 117
Paxton Ct. SE12 —9G 95
Paxton Ct. SE26 —1J 109
(off Adamsrill Rd.)
Paxton Ct. Borwd —6A 12
Paxton Pl. SE27 —1C 108
Paxton Rd. N17 —7D 28
Paxton Rd. SE23 —9J 93
Paxton Rd. W4 —7C 72
Paxton Rd. Brom —4E 110
Paxton Ter. SW1 —7F 74
Paymal Ho. E1 —8G 61
(off Stepney Way)
Payne Clo. Bark —3D 64
Payne Ho. N1 —4K 59
(off Barnsbury Est.)
Paynell Ct. SE3 —2C 94
Payne Rd. E3 —5M 61
Paynesfield Av. SW14 —2B 88
Paynesfield Rd. Bus H —9D 10
Payne St. SE8 —8K 77
Paynes Wlk. W6 —7J 73
Payzes Gdns. Wfd G —6D 30
Peabody Av. SW1 —6F 74
Peabody Bldgs. E1 —1E 76
(off John Fisher St.)
Peabody Bldgs. EC1 —7A 60
(off Roscoe St.)
Peabody Bldgs. SW3 —7C 74
(off Lawrence St.)
Peabody Clo. SE10 —9M 77
Peabody Clo. SW1 —6F 74
(off Lupus St.)
Peabody Clo. Croy —3G 125
Peabody Cotts. N17 —8C 28
Peabody Ct. EC1 —7A 60
(off Roscoe St.)
Peabody Ct. SE5 —9B 76
(off Kimpton Rd.)
Peabody Est. E1 —1H 77
(off Glasmis Pl.)
Peabody Est. E2 —5F 60
(off Cambridge Cres.)
Peabody Est. EC1 —7L 59
(off Farringdon La.)
Peabody Est. EC1 —7A 60
(off Whitecross St., in two parts)
Peabody Est. N1 —4A 60
Peabody Est. SE1 —3A 76
(off Mint St.)
Peabody Est. SE1 —2L 75
(Hatfield St.)
Peabody Est. SE1 —2A 76
(Southwark St.)
Peabody Est. SE24 —6M 91
Peabody Est. SW1 —5G 75
(off Vauxhall Bri. Rd.)
Peabody Est. SW3 —7C 74
Peabody Est. SW6 —7K 73
(off Lillie Rd.)
Peabody Est. SW11 —3C 90
Peabody Est. W6 —6G 73
Peabody Est. W10 —8G 57
Peabody Hill. SE21 —7M 91
Peabody Sq. SE1 —3M 75
(in two parts)
Peabody Tower. EC1 —7A 60
(off Golden La.)
Peabody Trust. SE17 —5B 76
(off Rodney Rd.)
Peabody Yd. N1 —4A 60
Peace Clo. N14 —7F 14
Peace Clo. SE25 —8C 108
Peace Clo. Chesh —2B 6
Peace Clo. Gnfd —4B 54
Peace Dri. Wat —5E 8
Peace Gro. Wemb —8M 39
Peace Prospect. Wat —5E 8
Peace St. SE18 —7L 79
Peaches Clo. Sutt —9J 121
Peachey Clo. Uxb —9B 142
Peachey Edwards Ho. E2 —6F 60
(off Teesdale St.)
Peachey La. Uxb —8B 142
Peach Rd. W10 —6H 57
Peach Tree Av. W Dray —9D 142
Peachum Rd. SE3 —7D 78
(in two parts)
Peachwalk M. E3 —5H 61
Peacock Av. Felt —7B 84
Peacock Clo. Horn —2J 51
Peacock Gdns. S Croy —2J 139
Peacock Ind. Est. N17 —7D 28
Peacock St. SE17 —5M 75
Peacock Theatre. —9K 59
(off Portugal St.)
Peacock Wlk. E16 —9F 62
(off Mortlake Rd.)
Peacock Wlk. N6 —5F 42
Peacock Wlk. Ab L —4E 4
Peacock Yd. SE17 —6M 75
(off Iliffe St.)
Peakes Way. Chesh —1A 6
Peaketon Av. Ilf —2H 47
Peak Hill. SE26 —1G 109
Peak Hill Av. SE26 —1G 109
Peak Hill Gdns. SE26 —1G 109
Peak Ho. N4 —6A 44
(off Woodberry Down Est.)
Peaks Hill. Purl —2H 137
Peaks Hill Ri. Purl —2J 137
Peak, The. SE26 —9G 93
Peal Gdns. W13 —6E 54
Peall Rd. Croy —1K 123
Peall Rd. Ind. Est. Croy —1K 123
Pearce Clo. Mitc —6E 106
Pearcefield Av. SE23 —7G 93
Pearce Rd. W Mol —7M 101
Pear Clo. NW9 —2B 40
Pear Clo. SE14 —8J 77
Pear Ct. SE15 —8D 76
(off Thruxton Way)
Pearcroft Rd. E11 —7B 46
Peardon St. SW8 —1F 90
Peareswood Gdns. Stan —8H 23
Peareswood Rd. Eri —9D 82
Pearfield Rd. SE23 —9J 93
Pearl Clo. E6 —9L 63
Pearl Clo. NW2 —5H 41
Pearl Rd. E17 —1L 45
Pearl St. E1 —2F 76
Pearmain Clo. Shep —9A 100
Pearman St. SE1 —4L 75
Pear Pl. SE1 —3L 75
Pear Rd. E11 —8B 46
Pearsall Ho. Uxb —2E 142
Pears Av. Shep —7C 100
Pearscroft Ct. SW6 —9M 73
Pearscroft Rd. SW6 —9M 73
Pearse St. SE15 —7C 76
Pearson's Av. SE14 —9L 77
Pearson St. E2 —5D 60
Pearson Way. Dart —8K 99
Pears Rd. Houn —2A 86
Peartree. SE26 —2J 109
Peartree Av. SW17 —9A 90
Pear Tree Av. W Dray —9D 142
Pear Tree Clo. E2 —4D 60
Pear Tree Clo. Chess —7L 119
Peartree Clo. Eri —9B 82
Peartree Clo. Mitc —6C 106
Peartree Clo. S Croy —6F 138
Pear Tree Clo. Swan —6B 114
Pear Tree Ct. E18 —8F 30
Pear Tree Ct. EC1 —7L 59
Peartree Ct. Wat —9H 5
Peartree Gdns. Dag —9F 48
Peartree Gdns. Romf —9M 33
Pear Tree Ho. SE4 —2K 93
Peartree La. E1 —1G 77
Pear Tree Rd. Ashf —2A 100
Peartree Rd. Enf —5C 16
Peartrees. W Dray —1H 143
Pear Tree St. EC1 —7A 60
Pear Tree Way. SE10 —5E 78
Peary Ho. NW10 —3B 56
Peary Pl. E2 —6G 61
Pease Clo. Horn —3F 66
Peas Mead Ter. E4 —4A 30
Peatfield Clo. Sidc —9C 96
Pebble Way. W3 —2M 71
(off Steyne Rd.)
Pebworth Rd. Harr —7E 38
Peckarmans Wood. SE26 —9E 92
Peckett Sq. N5 —9A 44
Peckford Clo. SW9 —1L 91
Peckford Pl. SW9 —1L 91
Peckham. —9E 76
Peckham Gro. SE15 —8C 76
Peckham High St. SE15 —9E 76
Peckham Hill St. SE15 —8E 76
Peckham Pk. Rd. SE15 —8E 76
Peckham Rd. SE5 & SE15 —9C 76
Peckham Rye. SE15 & SE22 —2E 92
Peckham Sq. SE15 —9E 76
Pecks Yd. E1 —8D 60
(off Hanbury St.)
Peckwater St. NW5 —1G 59
Pedham Pl. Ind. Est. Swan —9E 114
Pedhoulas. N14 —3J 27
Pedlar's Wlk. N7 —1K 59
Pedley Rd. Dag —6G 49
Pedley St. E1 —7D 60
Pedro St. E5 —8H 45
Pedworth Gdns. SE16 —5G 77
Peebles Ct. S'hall —9A 54
(off Haldane Rd.)
Peek Cres. SW19 —2H 105
Peel Cen. Ind. Est. Eps —3C 134
Peel Clo. E4 —2M 29
Peel Clo. N9 —3E 28
Peel Dri. Ilf —1J 47
Peel Gro. E2 —5G 61
(in two parts)
Peel La. NW9 —1E 40
Peel Pas. W8 —2L 73
(off Peel St.)
Peel Pl. Ilf —9J 31
Peel Precinct. NW6 —5L 57
Peel Rd. E18 —8D 30
Peel Rd. Harr & W'stone —1D 38
(in two parts)
Peel Rd. Orp —7A 128
Peel Rd. Wemb —8H 39
Peel St. W8 —2L 73
Peel Way. Romf —9K 35
Peel Way. Uxb —8C 142
Peerage Way. Horn —5J 51
Peerglow Est. Enf —7G 17
Peerglow Ind. Est. Wat —1A 20
Peerless St. EC1 —6B 60
Pegamoid Rd. N18 —3G 29
Pegasus Clo. N5 —9B 44
Pegasus Ct. Ab L —5D 4
Pegasus Ct. Bren —6K 71
Pegasus Ct. King T —7H 103
Pegasus Ho. E1 —7H 61
(off Beaumont Sq.)
Pegasus Pl. SE11 —7L 75
Pegasus Pl. SW6 —9L 73
Pegasus Way. N11 —6F 26
Pegelm Gdns. Horn —5K 51
Peggotty Way. Uxb —9F 142
Pegg Rd. Houn —8H 69
Pegley Gdns. SE12 —8E 94
Pegmire La. A'ham —3A 10
Pegwell St. SE18 —8C 80
Pekin Clo. E14 —9L 61
(off Pekin St.)
Pekin Ho. E14 —9L 61
(off Pekin St.)
Pekin St. E14 —9L 61
Pelabon Ho. Twic —5H 87
(off Clevedon Rd.)
Peldon Ct. Rich —3K 87
Peldon Pas. Rich —3K 87
Peldon Wlk. N1 —4M 59
(off Popham St.)
Pelham Av. Bark —4D 64
Pelham Clo. SE5 —2C 92
Pelham Cotts. Bex —7M 97
Pelham Ct. SW3 —5C 74
(off Fulham Rd.)
Pelham Ct. Sidc —9E 96
Pelham Cres. SW7 —5C 74
Pelham Ho. W14 —5K 73
(off Mornington Av.)
Pelham Pl. SW7 —5C 74
Pelham Rd. E18 —1F 46
Pelham Rd. N15 —2D 44
Pelham Rd. N22 —9L 27
Pelham Rd. SW19 —4L 105
Pelham Rd. Beck —6G 109
Pelham Rd. Bexh —2L 97
Pelham Rd. Ilf —7B 48
Pelham's Clo. Esh —6L 117
Pelhams, The. Wat —8H 5
Pelham St. SW7 —5B 74
Pelham's Wlk. Esh —6L 117
Pelican Est. SE15 —9D 76
Pelican Ho. SE8 —5K 77
Pelican Pas. E1 —7G 61
Pelican Stairs. E1 —2G 77
Pelican Wlk. SW9 —3M 91
Pelier St. SE17 —7A 76
Pelinore Rd. SE6 —8C 94
Pella Ho. SE11 —6K 75
Pellant Rd. SW6 —8J 73
Pellatt Gro. N22 —8L 27
Pellatt Rd. SE22 —4D 92
Pellatt Rd. Wemb —7H 39
(in two parts)
Pellerin Rd. N16 —1C 60
Pellew Ho. E1 —7F 60
(off Somerford St.)
Pelling St. E14 —9L 61
Pellipar Clo. N13 —3L 27
Pellipar Gdns. SE18 —6K 79
Pellipar Rd. SE18 —6K 79
Pelly Rd. E13 —4E 62
(in two parts)
Pelter St. E2 —6D 60
(in two parts)
Pelton Av. Sutt —2M 135
Pelton Rd. SE10 —6C 78
Pembar Av. E17 —1J 45
Pemberley Chase. W Ewe —7M 119
Pemberley Clo. W Ewe —7M 119
Pember Rd. NW10 —6H 57
Pemberton Av. Romf —1F 50
Pemberton Ct. E1 —6H 61
(off Portelet Rd.)
Pemberton Gdns. N19 —8G 43
Pemberton Gdns. Romf —3J 49
Pemberton Gdns. Swan —7C 114
Pemberton Ho. SE26 —1E 108
(off High Level Dri.)
Pemberton Pl. E8 —3F 60
Pemberton Pl. Esh —5A 118
Pemberton Rd. N4 —3L 43
Pemberton Rd. E Mol —8A 102
Pemberton Row. EC4 —9L 59
Pemberton Ter. N19 —8G 43
Pembrey Way. Horn —2G 67
Pembridge Av. Twic —7K 85
Pembridge Cres. W11 —1L 73
Pembridge Gdns. W2 —1L 73
Pembridge M. W11 —1L 73
Pembridge Pl. SW15 —4L 89
Pembridge Pl. W2 —1L 73
Pembridge Rd. W11 —1L 73
Pembridge Sq. W2 —1L 73
Pembridge Vs. W11 & W2 —1L 73
Pembroke Av. Enf —2F 16
Pembroke Av. Harr —1E 38
Pembroke Av. Pinn —6H 37
Pembroke Av. Surb —9M 103
Pembroke Av. W on T —6H 117
Pembroke Bldgs. NW10 —6E 56
Pembroke Cen., The. Ruis —6D 36
Pembroke Clo. SW1 —3E 74
Pembroke Clo. Bans —9M 135
Pembroke Clo. Horn —2K 51
Pembroke Cotts. W8 —4L 73
(off Pembroke Sq.)
Pembroke Ct. W7 —9D 54
(off Copley Clo.)
Pembroke Gdns. W14 —5K 73
Pembroke Gdns. Dag —8M 49
Pembroke Gdns. Clo. W8 —4L 73
Pembroke Hall. NW4 —1G 41
(off Mulberry Clo.)
Pembroke Ho. W2 —9M 57
(off Hallfield Est.)
Pembroke Ho. W3 —3A 72
(off Park Rd. E.)
Pembroke Ho. Borwd —6L 11
(off Station Rd.)
Pembroke Lodge. Stan —6G 23
Pembroke M. E1 —7G 61
(off Wessex St.)
Pembroke M. E3 —6J 61
Pembroke M. N10 —8F 26
Pembroke M. W8 —4L 73
Pembroke Pde. Eri —6A 82
Pembroke Pl. W8 —4L 73
Pembroke Pl. Edgw —7L 23
Pembroke Pl. Iswth —1C 86
Pembroke Pl. S at H —5M 115
Pembroke Rd. E6 —8K 63
Pembroke Rd. E17 —3M 45
Pembroke Rd. N8 —2J 43
Pembroke Rd. N10 —8E 26
Pembroke Rd. N13 —3A 28
Pembroke Rd. N15 —3D 44
Pembroke Rd. SE25 —8C 108
Pembroke Rd. W8 —5K 73
Pembroke Rd. Brom —6G 111
Pembroke Rd. Eri —6A 82
Pembroke Rd. Gnfd —7M 53
Pembroke Rd. Ilf —6D 48
Pembroke Rd. Mitc —6E 106
Pembroke Rd. N'wd —3A 20
Pembroke Rd. Ruis —6C 36
Pembroke Rd. Wemb —8H 39
Pembroke Sq. W8 —4L 73
Pembroke St. N1 —3J 59
(in two parts)
Pembroke Vs. W8 —5L 73
Pembroke Vs. Rich —3H 87
Pembroke Wlk. W8 —5L 73
Pembroke Way. Hay —4A 68
Pembrook M. SW11 —3B 90
Pembry Clo. SW9 —9L 75
Pembury Av. Wor Pk —3E 120
Pembury Clo. E5 —1F 60
Pembury Clo. Brom —2D 126
Pembury Clo. Coul —6E 136
Pembury Ct. Hay —7B 68
Pembury Cres. Sidc —8J 97
Pembury Pl. E5 —1F 60
Pembury Rd. E5 —1F 60
Pembury Rd. N17 —8D 28
Pembury Rd. SE25 —8E 108
Pembury Rd. Bexh —8J 81
Pemdevon Rd. Croy —2L 123
Pemell Clo. E1 —7G 61
Pemell Ho. E1 —7G 61
(off Pemell Clo.)
Pemerich Clo. Hay —6D 68
Pempath Pl. Wemb —7H 39
Penally Pl. N1 —4B 60
Penang Ho. E1 —2F 76
(off Prusom St.)
Penang St. E1 —2F 76
Penard Rd. S'hall —4M 69
Penarth Cen. SE15 —7G 77
Penarth St. SE15 —7G 77
Penates. Esh —6B 118
Penberth Rd. SE6 —8A 94
Penbury Rd. S'hall —5K 69
Pencombe M. W11 —1K 73
Pencraig Way. SE15 —7F 76
Pencroft Dri. Dart —6G 99
Pendall Clo. Barn —6C 14
Penda Rd. Eri —8M 81
Pendarves Rd. SW20 —5G 105
Penda's Mead. E9 —9J 45
Pendell Av. Hay —8D 68
Pendennis Ho. SE8 —5J 77
Pendennis Rd. N17 —1B 44
Pendennis Rd. SW16 —1J 107
Pendennis Rd. Orp —4G 129
Penderel Rd. Houn —4L 85
Penderry Ri. SE6 —8B 94
Penderyn Way. N7 —9H 43
Pendlebury Ct. Surb —8J 103
(off Cranes Pk.)
Pendle Ct. Uxb —4F 142
Pendle Ho. SE26 —9E 92
Pendle Rd. SW16 —3F 106
Pendlestone Rd. E17 —3M 45
Pendragon Rd. Brom —9D 94
Pendragon Wlk. NW9 —4C 40
Pendrell Ho. WC2 —9H 59
(off New Compton St.)
Pendrell Rd. SE4 —1J 93
Pendrell St. SE18 —7B 80
Pendula Dri. Hay —7H 53
Pendulum M. E8 —1D 60
Penerley Rd. SE6 —7M 93
Penerley Rd. Rain —8F 66
Penfield Lodge. W9 —8L 57
(off Admiral Wlk.)
Penfields Ho. N7 —2J 59
Penfold Clo. Croy —5L 123
Penfold La. Bex —8H 97
(in two parts)
Penfold Pl. NW1 —8C 58
Penfold Rd. N9 —1H 29
Penfold St. NW8 & NW1 —7B 58
Penfold Trad. Est. Wat —3G 9
Penford Gdns. SE9 —2H 95
Penford St. SE5 —1M 91
Pengarth Rd. Bex —4H 97
Penge. —4G 109
Penge Ho. SW11 —2B 90
Penge La. SE20 —4G 109
Pengelly Clo. Chesh —3B 6
Penge Rd. E13 —4G 63
Penge Rd. SE25 & SE20 —7E 108
Penhale Clo. Orp —6E 128
Penhall Rd. SE7 —5H 79
Penhill Rd. Bex —5G 97
Penhurst Pl. SE1 —4K 75
(off Carlisle La.)
Penhurst Rd. Ilf —7M 31
Penifather La. Gnfd —6B 54
Peninsula Ct. E14 —4M 77
(off E. Ferry Rd.)
Peninsula Heights. SE1 —6J 75
Peninsula Pk. SE7 —5E 78
(off Peninsula Pk. Rd., in two parts)
Peninsular Clo. Felt —5B 84
Peninsular Pk. Rd. SE7 —5E 78
Penistone Rd. SW16 —4J 107
Penistone Wlk. Romf —6G 35
Penketh Dri. Harr —8B 38
Penley Ct. WC2 —1K 75
Penmayne Ho. SE11 —6L 75
(off Kennings Way)
Penmon Rd. SE2 —4E 80
Pennack Rd. SE15 —7D 76
Penn Almshouses. SE10 —9A 78
(off Greenwich S. St.)
Pennant M. W8 —5M 73
Pennant Ter. E17 —9K 29
Pennard Mans. W12 —3G 73
(off Goldhawk Rd.)
Pennard Rd. W12 —3G 73
Pennards, The. Sun —7G 101
Penn Clo. Gnfd —5M 53
Penn Clo. Harr —2G 39
Penn Clo. Uxb —7B 142
Penn Ct. NW9 —1B 40
Penner Clo. SW19 —8J 89
Penners Gdns. Surb —2J 119
Pennethorne Clo. E9 —4G 61
Pennethorne Ho. SW11 —2B 90
Pennethorne Rd. SE15 —8F 76
Penney Clo. Dart —6H 99
Penn Gdns. Chst —6M 111
Penn Gdns. Romf —7L 33
Penn Ho. NW8 —7C 58
(off Mallory St.)
Pennine Dri. NW2 —7H 41
Pennine La. NW2 —7J 41
Pennine Pde. NW2 —7J 41
Pennine Way. Bexh —9C 82
Pennine Way. Hay —8B 68
Pennington Clo. SE27 —1B 108
Pennington Clo. Romf —5L 33
Pennington Ct. SE16 —2J 77
Pennington Dri. N21 —7J 15
Pennington Dri. Wey —5C 116
Pennington Lodge. Surb —8J 103
(off Cranes Dri.)
Pennington St. E1 —1F 76
Pennington Way. SE12 —8F 94
Penniston Clo. N17 —9A 28
Penn La. Bex —4H 97
(in two parts)
Penn Rd. N7 —1J 59
Penn Rd. Park —1M 5
Penn Rd. Wat —3F 8
Penn St. N1 —4B 60
Penny Clo. Rain —6F 66
Penny Ct. Wat —4F 8
(off Westland Rd.)
Pennycroft. Croy —1J 139
Pennyfather La. Enf —5A 16
Pennyfields. E14 —1L 77
(in two parts)
Pennyford Ct. NW8 —7B 58
(off St John's Wood Rd.)
Penny La. Shep —2C 116
Penny M. SW12 —6F 90
Pennymoor Wlk. W9 —7K 57
(off Ashmore Rd.)
Penny Rd. NW10 —6M 55
Penny Royal. Wall —8H 123
Pennyroyal Av. E6 —9L 63
Penpoll Rd. E8 —2F 60

Penpool La.—Pickfords Wharf

Penpool La. Well —2F 96
Penrhyn Av. E17 —8K 29
Penrhyn Cres. E17 —8L 29
Penrhyn Cres. SW14 —3A 88
Penrhyn Gdns. King T —8H 103
Penrhyn Gro. E17 —8L 29
Penrhyn Rd. King T —8J 103
Penrith Clo. SW15 —4J 89
Penrith Clo. Beck —5M 109
Penrith Clo. Uxb —3B 142
Penrith Cres. Rain —1E 66
Penrith Pl. SE27 —8M 91
Penrith Rd. N15 —3B 44
Penrith Rd. Ilf —6D 32
Penrith Rd. N Mald —8B 104
Penrith Rd. Romf —6L 35
Penrith Rd. T Hth —6A 108
Penrith St. SW16 —3G 107
Penrose Av. Wat —2J 21
Penrose Dri. Eps —3L 133
Penrose Gro. SE17 —6A 76
Penrose Ho. SE17 —6A 76
(in two parts)
Penrose St. SE17 —6A 76
Penryn Ho. SE11 —6L 75
(off Seaton Clo.)
Penryn St. NW1 —5H 59
Penry St. SE1 —5C 76
Pensbury Pl. SW8 —1G 91
Pensbury St. SW8 —1G 91
Penscroft Gdns. Borwd —6B 12
Pensford Av. Rich —1L 87
Penshurst. NW5 —2E 58
Penshurst Av. Sidc —5E 96
Penshurst Gdns. Edgw —5M 23
Penshurst Grn. Brom —9D 110
Penshurst Ho. SE15 —7G 77
(off Lovelinch Clo.)
Penshurst Rd. E9 —3H 61
Penshurst Rd. N17 —7D 28
Penshurst Rd. Bexh —9K 81
Penshurst Rd. T Hth —9M 107
Penshurst Wlk. Brom —9D 110
Penshurst Way. Orp —8G 113
Penshurst Way. Sutt —9L 121
Pensilver Clo. Barn —6C 14
Penstemon Clo. N3 —6L 25
Penta Ct. Borwd —6L 11
(off Station Rd.)
Pentagon, The. W13 —1E 70
Pentavia Retail Pk. NW7 —7D 24
Pentelow Gdns. Felt —5E 84
Pentire Rd. E17 —8B 30
Pentland Av. Edgw —2M 23
Pentland Clo. NW11 —7J 41
Pentland Gdns. SW18 —5A 90
Pentland Pl. N'holt —4J 53
Pentland Rd. Bush —8A 10
Pentlands Clo. Mitc —7F 106
Pentland St. SW18 —5A 90
Pentland Way. Uxb —8A 36
Pentlow St. SW15 —2G 89
Pentlow Way. Buck H —9J 19
Pentney Rd. E4 —1B 30
Pentney Rd. SW12 —7G 91
Pentney Rd. SW20 —5J 105
Penton Dri. Chesh —2D 6
Penton Gro. N1 —5L 59
Penton Ho. N1 —5L 59
(off Donegal St.)
Penton Ho. SE2 —2H 81
Penton Pl. SE17 —6M 75
Penton Ri. WC1 —6K 59
Penton St. N1 —5L 59
Pentonville. —5K 59
Pentonville Rd. N1 —5K 59
Pentrich Av. Enf —2E 16
Pentridge St. SE15 —8D 76
Pentyre Av. N18 —5B 28
Penwerris Av. Iswth —8A 70
Penwerris Ct. Houn —8A 70
Penwith Rd. SW18 —8L 89
Penwood Ct. Pinn —2K 37
Penwood Ho. SW15 —5D 88
Penwortham Ct. N22 —9K 27
Penwortham Rd. SW16 —3F 106
Penwortham Rd. S Croy —2A 138
Penylan Pl. Edgw —7L 23
Penywern Rd. SW5 —6L 73
Penzance Gdns. Romf —6L 35
(in two parts)
Penzance Ho. SE11 —6L 75
(off Seaton Clo.)
Penzance Pl. W11 —2J 73
Penzance Rd. Romf —6L 35
Penzance St. W11 —2J 73
Peony Ct. E4 —6C 30
Peony Gdns. W12 —1E 72
Peperfield. WC1 —6K 59
(off Cromer St.)
Pepler Ho. W10 —7J 57
(off Wornington Rd.)
Pepler M. SE5 —6D 76
Peploe Rd. NW6 —5H 57
(in two parts)
Peplow Clo. W Dray —2H 143
Pepper All. Lou —4D 18
Pepper Clo. E6 —8K 63
Peppercorn Clo. T Hth —6B 108
Peppermead Sq. SE4 —4L 93
Peppermint Clo. Croy —2J 123
Peppermint Pl. E11 —8C 46
Pepper St. E14 —4M 77
Pepper St. SE1 —3A 76
Peppie Clo. N16 —7C 44
(in two parts)
Pepys Clo. Asht —9L 133
Pepys Clo. Dart —3L 99
Pepys Ct. SW4 —2F 90
Pepys Cres. E16 —2E 78
Pepys Cres. Barn —7G 13
Pepys Ho. E2 —6G 61
(off Kirkwall Pl.)
Pepys Ri. Orp —3D 128
Pepys Rd. SE14 —9H 77
Pepys Rd. SW20 —5G 105
Pepys St. EC3 —1C 76
Perceval Av. NW3 —1C 58
Perceval Ct. N'holt —1L 53
Perceval Ho. W5 —1G 71
Percheron Clo. Iswth —2D 86
Percheron Rd. Borwd —8B 12
Perch St. E8 —9D 44
Percival Clo. Oxs —3A 132
Percival Ct. N17 —7D 28
Percival Ct. Chesh —3E 6
Percival David Foundation of Chinese Art. —7H 59
(off Gordon Sq.)
Percival Gdns. Romf —4G 49
Percival Rd. SW14 —3A 88
Percival Rd. Enf —6D 16
Percival Rd. Felt —8D 84
Percival Rd. Horn —4G 51
Percival Rd. Orp —4M 127
Percival St. EC1 —7M 59
Percival Way. Eps —6B 120
Percy Bryant Rd. Sun —4C 100
Percy Bush Rd. W Dray —4K 143
Percy Cir. WC1 —6K 59
Percy Gdns. Enf —7H 17
Percy Gdns. Hay —6C 52
Percy Gdns. Iswth —2E 86
Percy Gdns. Wor Pk —3C 120
Percy M. W1 —8H 59
(off Rathbone Pl.)
Percy Pas. W1 —8G 59
(off Rathbone St.)
Percy Rd. E11 —5C 46
Percy Rd. E16 —8C 62
Percy Rd. N12 —5A 26
Percy Rd. N21 —9A 16
Percy Rd. SE20 —5H 109
Percy Rd. SE25 —9E 108
Percy Rd. W12 —3E 72
Percy Rd. Bexh —1J 97
Percy Rd. Hamp —4L 101
Percy Rd. Ilf —5E 48
Percy Rd. Iswth —3E 86
Percy Rd. Mitc —2E 122
Percy Rd. Romf —1M 49
Percy Rd. Twic —7M 85
Percy Rd. Wat —6F 8
Percy St. W1 —8H 59
Percy Way. Twic —7A 86
Percy Yd. WC1 —6K 59
Peregrine Clo. NW10 —1B 56
Peregrine Clo. Wat —7J 5
Peregrine Ct. SE8 —7L 77
(off Edward St.)
Peregrine Ct. SW16 —1K 107
Peregrine Ct. Well —9D 80
Peregrine Gdns. Croy —4J 125
Peregrine Ho. EC1 —6M 59
(off Hall St.)
Peregrine Rd. Ilf —5F 32
Peregrine Rd. Sun —6D 100
Peregrine Wlk. Horn —2F 66
Peregrine Way. SW19 —4G 105
Peregrin Rd. Wal A —7M 7
Perham Rd. W14 —6J 73
Peridot St. E6 —8J 63
Perifield. SE21 —7A 92
Perimeade Rd. Gnfd —5G 55
Periton Rd. SE9 —3H 95
Perivale. —4G 55
Perivale Gdns. W13 —7F 54
Perivale Gdns. Wat —7F 4
Perivale Grange. Gnfd —6E 54
Perivale Ind. Pk. Gnfd —5F 54
Perivale La. Gnfd —6E 54
Perivale Lodge. Gnfd —6E 54
(off Perivale La.)
Perivale New Bus. Cen. Gnfd —5G 55
Perkin Clo. Wemb —1F 54
Perkins Ho. E14 —8K 61
(off Wallwood St.)
Perkin's Rents. SW1 —4H 75
Perkins Rd. Ilf —3B 48
Perkins Sq. SE1 —2A 76
(off Porter St.)
Perks Clo. SE3 —2C 94
Perley Ho. E3 —8K 61
(off Weatherley Clo.)
Perpins Rd. SE9 —5B 96
Perran Rd. SW2 —7M 91
Perran Wlk. Bren —6J 71
Perren St. NW5 —2F 58
Perrers Rd. W6 —5F 72
Perring Est. E3 —8L 61
(off Gale St.)
Perrin Ho. NW6 —6L 57
Perrin Rd. Wemb —9F 38
Perrin's Ct. NW3 —9A 42
Perrin's La. NW3 —9A 42
Perrin's Wlk. NW3 —9A 42
Perronet Ho. SE1 —4M 75
(off Princess St.)
Perrott St. SE18 —5A 80
Perry Av. W3 —9B 56
Perry Clo. Rain —5B 66
Perry Clo. Uxb —9F 142
Perry Ct. E14 —6L 77
(off Maritime Quay)
Perry Ct. N15 —4C 44
Perryfield Way. NW9 —4D 40
Perryfield Way. Rich —9F 86
Perry Gdns. N9 —3B 28
Perry Gth. N'holt —4G 53
Perry Gro. Dart —3L 99
Perry Hall Clo. Orp —2E 128
Perry Hall Rd. Orp —1D 128
Perry Hill. SE6 —9K 93
Perry How. Wor Pk —3D 120
Perrymans Farm Rd. Ilf —4B 48
Perry Mead. Bush —8A 10
Perry Mead. Enf —4M 15
Perrymead St. SW6 —9L 73
Perryn Ct. Twic —5E 86
Perryn Ho. W3 —1C 72
Perryn Rd. SE16 —4F 76
Perryn Rd. W3 —2B 72
Perry Oaks Dri. W Dray & Houn —1A 144
Perry Ri. SE23 —9J 93
Perry Rd. Dag —8K 65
Perry's Pl. W1 —9H 59
Perry St. Chst —4B 112
Perry St. Dart —3C 98
Perry St. Gdns. Chst —3C 112
Perry St. Shaw. Chst —4C 112
Perry Va. SE23 —8G 93
Perry Way. Ave —1M 83
Persant Rd. SE6 —8C 94
Perseverance Pl. SW9 —8L 75
Perseverance Pl. Rich —3J 87
Perseverance Works. E2 —6C 60
(off Kingsland Rd.)
Persfield Clo. Eps —2D 134
Persfield M. Eps —2D 134
Pershore Clo. Ilf —3M 47
Pershore Gro. Cars —1B 122
Pert Clo. N10 —7F 26
Perth Av. NW9 —5B 40
Perth Av. Hay —7G 53
Perth Clo. SE5 —3B 92
Perth Clo. SW20 —6D 104
Perth Ho. N1 —3K 59
Perth Rd. E10 —6J 45
Perth Rd. E13 —5F 62
Perth Rd. N4 —6L 43
Perth Rd. N22 —8M 27
Perth Rd. Bark —5B 64
Perth Rd. Beck —6A 110
Perth Rd. Ilf —4L 47
Perth Ter. Ilf —5A 48
Perwell Av. Harr —6K 37
Perystreete. SE23 —8G 93
Petands Ct. Horn —8H 51
(off Randall Dri.)
Petavel Rd. Tedd —3C 102
Peter Av. NW10 —3F 56
Peter Best Ho. E1 —9F 60
(off Nelson St.)
Peterboat Clo. SE10 —5C 78
Peterborough Ct. EC4 —9L 59
Peterborough Gdns. Ilf —5J 47
Peterborough Ho. Borwd —4L 11
(off Stratfield Rd.)
Peterborough M. SW6 —1L 89
Peterborough Rd. E10 —3A 46
Peterborough Rd. SW6 —1L 89
Peterborough Rd. Cars —1C 122
Peterborough Rd. Harr —6C 38
Peterborough Vs. SW6 —9M 73
Peter Butler Ho. SE1 —3E 76
(off Wolseley St.)
Peterchurch Ho. SE15 —7F 76
(off Commercial Way)
Petergate. SW11 —3A 90
Peterhead Ct. S'hall —9A 54
(off Osborne Rd.)
Peter Ho. SW8 —8J 75
(off Luscombe Way)
Peter James Bus. Cen. Hay —3E 68
Peter James Enterprise Cen. NW10 —6A 56
Peterley Bus. Cen. E2 —5F 60
Peters Clo. Dag —6H 49
Peters Clo. Stan —6H 23
Peters Clo. Well —1C 96
Peter Scott Vis. Cen., The. —9F 72
Peters Ct. W2 —9M 57
(off Porchester Rd.)
Petersfield Av. Romf —6J 35
Petersfield Clo. N18 —5A 28
Petersfield Clo. Romf —6L 35
Petersfield Cres. Coul —7J 137
Petersfield Ri. SW15 —7F 88
Petersfield Rd. W3 —3A 72
Petersham. —7J 87
Petersham Clo. Rich —8H 87
Petersham Clo. Sutt —7K 121
Petersham Dri. Orp —6D 112
Petersham Gdns. Orp —6D 112
Petersham Ho. SW7 —5B 74
(off Kendrick M.)
Petersham La. SW7 —4A 74
Petersham M. SW7 —4A 74
Petersham Pl. SW7 —4A 74
Petersham Rd. Rich —5H 87
Petersham Ter. Mitc —5J 123
(off Richmond Grn.)
Peter's Hill. EC4 —1A 76
Peter's La. EC1 —8M 59
Peterson Ct. Lou —4L 19
Peter's Path. SE26 —1F 108
Peterstone Rd. SE2 —4F 80
Peterstow Clo. SW19 —8J 89
Peter St. W1 —1H 75
Peterwood Pk. Croy —4K 123
Peterwood Way. Croy —4K 123
Petherton Ct. Harr —4D 38
(off Gayton Rd.)
Petherton Ho. N4 —6A 44
(off Woodberry Down Est.)
Petherton Rd. N5 —1A 60
Petiver Clo. E9 —3G 61
Petley Rd. W6 —7H 73
Peto Pl. NW1 —7F 58
Peto St. N. E16 —9D 62
Peto St. S. E16 —1D 78
Petrie Clo. NW2 —2J 57
Petrie Ho. SE18 —7L 79
(off Woolwich Comn.)
Petrie Mus. of Egyptian Archaeology. —7H 59
(off Gordon Sq.)
Petros Gdns. NW3 —2A 58
Pett Clo. Horn —7F 50
Petten Clo. Orp —3H 129
Petten Gro. Orp —3G 129
Petters Rd. Asht —8K 133
Petticoat La. E1 —8C 60
Petticoat Lane Market. —9D 60
(off Middlesex St.)
Petticoat Sq. E1 —9D 60
Petticoat Tower. E1 —9D 60
(off Petticoat Sq.)
Pettits Boulevd. Romf —8C 34
Pettits Clo. Romf —9C 34
Pettits La. Romf —9C 34
Pettits La. N. Romf —8B 34
Pettits Pl. Dag —1L 65
Pettits Rd. Dag —1L 65
Pettiward Clo. SW15 —3G 89
Pettley Gdns. Romf —3B 50
Pettman Cres. SE28 —4B 80
Pettsgrove Av. Wemb —1G 55
Pett's Hill. N'holt —1M 53
Pett St. SE18 —5J 79
Petts Wood. —9A 112
Petts Wood Rd. Orp —9A 112
Petty France. SW1 —4G 75
Pettys Clo. Chesh —1D 6
Petworth Clo. N'holt —3K 53
Petworth Gdns. SW20 —7F 104
Petworth Gdns. Uxb —4A 52
Petworth Rd. N12 —5C 26
Petworth Rd. Bexh —4L 97
Petworth St. SW11 —9C 74
Petworth Way. Horn —9D 50
Petyt Pl. SW3 —7C 74
Petyward. SW3 —5C 74
Pevensey Av. N11 —5H 27
Pevensey Av. Enf —4C 16
Pevensey Clo. Iswth —8A 70
Pevensey Ct. W3 —3M 71
Pevensey Ho. E1 —8H 61
(off Ben Jonson Rd.)
Pevensey Rd. E7 —9D 46
Pevensey Rd. SW17 —1B 106
Pevensey Rd. Felt —7J 85
Peverel. E6 —9L 63
Peverel Ho. Dag —7L 49
Peveret Clo. N11 —5F 26
Peveril Ct. Dart —5M 99
(off Clifton Wlk.)
Peveril Dri. Tedd —2B 102
Peveril Ho. SE1 —4B 76
(off Rephidim St.)
Pewsey Clo. E4 —5L 29
Peyton Pl. SE10 —8A 78
Pharamond. NW2 —2H 57
Pharaoh Clo. Mitc —2D 122
Pheasant Clo. E16 —9F 62
Pheasant Clo. Purl —5M 137
Phelp St. SE17 —7B 76
Phelps Way. Hay —5D 68
Phene St. SW3 —7C 74
Philadelphia Ct. SW10 —8A 74
(off Uverdale Rd.)
Philan Way. Romf —6B 34
Philbeach Gdns. SW5 —6K 73
Phil Brown Pl. SW8 —2F 90
(off Wandsworth Rd.)
Philchurch Pl. E1 —9E 60
Philimore Clo. SE18 —6C 80
Philip Av. Romf —6B 50
Philip Av. Swan —8B 114
Philip Clo. Romf —6B 50
Philip Ct. W2 —8B 58
(off Hall Pl.)
Philip Gdns. Croy —4K 125
Philip Ho. NW6 —4M 57
(off Mortimer Pl.)
Philip La. N15 —2B 44
Philipot Path. SE9 —5K 95
Philippa Gdns. SE9 —4H 95
Philip Rd. Rain —6C 66
Philips Clo. Cars —3E 122
Philip St. E13 —7E 62
Philip Wlk. SE15 —2E 92
(in three parts)
Phillida Rd. Romf —9L 35
Phillimore Ct. Rad —1C 10
Phillimore Gdns. NW10 —4G 57
Phillimore Gdns. W8 —3L 73
Phillimore Gdns. Clo. W8 —4L 73
Phillimore Pl. W8 —3L 73
Phillimore Pl. Rad —1C 10
Phillimore Ter. W8 —4L 73
(off Allen St.)
Phillimore Wlk. W8 —4L 73
Phillipers. Wat —9H 5
Phillipp St. N1 —4C 60
(in two parts)
Phillips Clo. Dart —5F 98
Phillips Ct. Edgw —6L 23
Philpot La. EC3 —1C 76
Philpot Path. Ilf —8A 48
Philpots Clo. W Dray —1H 143
Philpot Sq. SW6 —2M 89
Philpot St. E1 —9F 60
Phineas Pett Rd. SE9 —2J 95
Phipps Bri. Rd. SW19 & Mitc —6A 106
Phipps Hatch La. Enf —2A 16
Phipps Ho. SE7 —6F 78
(off Woolwich Rd.)
Phipps Ho. W12 —1F 72
(off White City Est.)
Phipp St. EC2 —7C 60
Phoebeth Rd. SE13 —4L 93
Phoenix Bus. Cen. E3 —8L 61
Phoenix Cen. Brom —8F 110
Phoenix Clo. E8 —4D 60
Phoenix Clo. Eps —4L 133
Phoenix Clo. N'wd —4D 20
Phoenix Clo. W W'ck —4B 126
Phoenix Ct. E4 —3M 29
Phoenix Ct. E14 —5L 77
Phoenix Ct. NW1 —5H 59
(off Purchese St.)
Phoenix Ct. SE14 —7J 77
(off Chipley St.)
Phoenix Ct. Houn —4H 85
Phoenix Ct. S Croy —7D 124
Phoenix Ct. Wemb —8M 39
Phoenix Dri. Kes —6H 127
Phoenix Ho. Sutt —6M 121
Phoenix Ind. Est. Harr —2D 38
Phoenix Lodge Mans. W6 —5G 73
(off Brook Grn.)
Phoenix Pl. WC1 —7K 59
Phoenix Pl. Dart —6H 99
Phoenix Rd. NW1 —6H 59
Phoenix Rd. SE20 —3G 109
Phoenix St. WC2 —9H 59
Phoenix Theatre. —9H 59
(off Charing Cross Rd.)
Phoenix Trad. Est. Gnfd —4G 55
Phoenix Trad. Pk. Bren —6H 71
Phoenix Way. Houn —7H 69
Phoenix Wharf Rd. SE1 —3D 76
(off Tanner St.)
Phoenix Yd. WC1 —6K 59
(off Kings Cross Rd.)
Photographers' Gallery. —1J 75
Phyllis Av. N Mald —9F 104
Phyllis Ho. Croy —6M 123
(off Ashley La.)
Physic Pl. SW3 —7D 74
Piazza, The. WC2 —1J 75
(off Covent Garden)
Piazza, The. Uxb —3B 142
Picardy Manorway. Belv —4M 81
Picardy Rd. Belv —6L 81
Picardy St. Belv —4L 81
Piccadilly. W1 —2F 74
Piccadilly Arc. SW1 —2G 75
(off Piccadilly)
Piccadilly Circus. —1H 75
Piccadilly Cir. W1 —1H 75
Piccadilly Pl. W1 —1G 75
(off Piccadilly)
Piccadilly Theatre. —1G 75
(off Denman St.)
Pickard St. EC1 —6M 59
Pickering Av. E6 —5L 63
Pickering Clo. E9 —3H 61
Pickering Ct. Dart —5M 99
(off Osbourne Rd.)
Pickering Gdns. N11 —6E 26
Pickering Gdns. Croy —1D 124
Pickering Ho. W2 —9A 58
(off Hallfield Est.)
Pickering Ho. W5 —5G 71
(off Windmill Rd.)
Pickering M. W2 —9M 57
Pickering Pl. SW1 —2G 75
(off St James's St.)
Pickering St. N1 —4M 59
Pickets Clo. Bus H —1B 22
Pickets St. SW12 —6F 90
Pickett Cft. Stan —8H 23
Picketts Lock La. N9 —2G 29
Picketts Lock La. Ind. Est. N9 —2J 29
Pickford Clo. Bexh —1J 97
Pickford La. Bexh —1J 97
Pickford Rd. Bexh —2J 97
Pickfords Wharf. N1 —5A 60
Pickfords Wharf. SE1 —2B 76

Pond Clo.—Prestwood Av.

Pond Clo. SE3 —1D 94
Pond Clo. W on T —8D 116
(in two parts)
Pond Cottage La. W W'ck —3L 125
Pond Cotts. SE21 —7C 92
Ponders End. —7G 17
Ponders End Ind. Est. Enf —7J 17
Ponder St. N7 —3K 59
(in two parts)
Pond Farm Est. E5 —8G 45
Pond Fld. End. Lou —9H 19
Pondfield Ho. SE27 —2A 108
Pondfield Rd. Brom —3C 126
Pondfield Rd. Dag —1M 65
Pondfield Rd. Kenl —8M 137
(in two parts)
Pondfield Rd. Orp —5M 127
Pond Grn. Ruis —7C 36
Pond Hill Gdns. Sutt —8J 121
Pond Ho. SW3 —5C 74
Pond Lees Clo. Dag —3B 66
Pond Mead. SE21 —5B 92
Pond Path. Chst —3M 111
Pond Piece. Oxs —5A 132
Pond Pl. SW3 —5C 74
Pond Pl. Asht —9J 133
Pond Rd. E15 —5C 62
Pond Rd. SE3 —1D 94
Pondside Clo. Hay —7B 68
Pond Sq. N6 —6E 42
Ponds, The. Wey —8B 116
Pond St. NW3 —1C 58
Pond Way. Tedd —3G 103
Pondwood Ri. Orp —2C 128
Ponler St. E1 —9F 60
Ponsard Rd. NW10 —6F 56
Ponsford St. E9 —2G 61
Ponsonby Pl. SW1 —6H 75
Ponsonby Rd. SW15 —6F 88
Ponsonby Ter. SW1 —6H 75
Pontefract Ct. N'holt —1M 53
(off Newmarket Av.)
Pontefract Rd. Brom —2D 110
Ponton Rd. SW8 —8H 75
Pont St. SW1 —4D 74
Pont St. M. SW1 —4D 74
Pontypool Pl. SE1 —3M 75
Pontypool Wlk. Romf —6G 35
Pool Clo. Beck —2L 109
Pool Clo. W Mol —9K 101
Pool Ct. SE6 —8L 93
Poole Clo. Ruis —7C 36
Poole Ct. Houn —1J 85
Poole Ct. Rd. Houn —1J 85
Poole Ho. SE11 —4L 75
(off Lambeth Wlk.)
Poole Rd. E9 —2H 61
Poole Rd. Eps —8B 120
Poole Rd. Horn —5K 51
Pooles Bldgs. WC1 —7L 59
(off Mt. Pleasant)
Pooles Cotts. Rich —8H 87
Pooles La. SW10 —8A 74
Pooles La. Dag —5J 65
Pooles Pk. N4 —7L 43
Poole St. N1 —4B 60
Poole Way. Hay —6C 52
Pool Ho. NW8 —8B 58
(off Penfold St.)
Poolmans St. SE16 —3H 77
Pool Rd. Harr —5B 38
Pool Rd. W Mol —9K 101
Poolsford Rd. NW9 —2C 40
Poonah St. E1 —9G 61
Pope Clo. SW19 —3B 106
Pope Clo. Felt —7D 84
Pope Ho. SE5 —8B 76
(off Elmington Est.)
Pope Ho. SE16 —5F 76
(off Manor Est.)
Pope Rd. Brom —9H 111
Popes Av. Twic —8C 86
Popes Ct. Twic —8C 86
Popes Dri. N3 —8L 25
Popes Gro. Croy —5K 125
Popes Gro. Twic —8C 86
Pope's Head All. EC3 —9B 60
Popes La. W5 —4H 71
Popes La. Wat —1F 8
Pope's Rd. SW9 —2L 91
Pope's Rd. Ab L —4C 4
Pope St. SE1 —3C 76
Popham Clo. Hanw —9K 85
Popham Gdns. Rich —2L 87
Popham Rd. N1 —4A 60
Popham St. N1 —4M 59
(in two parts)
Pop-In Commercial Cen. Wemb —1M 55
Popinjays Row. Cheam —7H 121
(off Netley Clo.)
Poplar. —1M 77
Poplar Av. Mitc —5D 106
Poplar Av. Orp —4M 127
Poplar Av. S'hall —4M 69
Poplar Av. W Dray —1K 143
Poplar Bath St. E14 —1M 77
Poplar Bus. Pk. E14 —1A 78
Poplar Clo. E9 —1K 61
Poplar Clo. Pinn —8H 21
Poplar Ct. SW19 —2L 105
Poplar Ct. N'holt —5G 53
Poplar Ct. Twic —5G 87
Poplar Cres. Eps —8A 120
Poplar Dri. Bans —6H 135
Poplar Farm Clo. Eps —8A 120
Poplar Gdns. SE28 —1G 81
Poplar Gdns. N Mald —6B 104
Poplar Gro. N11 —6E 26
Poplar Gro. W6 —3G 73
Poplar Gro. N Mald —6B 104
Poplar Gro. Wemb —8A 40
Poplar High St. E14 —1M 77
Poplar Ho. SE4 —3K 93
(off Wickham Rd.)
Poplar Ho. SE16 —3H 77
(off Woodland Cres.)
Poplar M. W12 —2G 73
(off Uxbridge Rd.)
Poplar Mt. Belv —5M 81
Poplar Pl. SE28 —1G 81
Poplar Pl. W2 —1M 73
Poplar Pl. Hay —1E 68
Poplar Rd. SE24 —3A 92
Poplar Rd. SW19 —6L 105
Poplar Rd. Ashf —2A 100
Poplar Rd. Den —1A 142
Poplar Rd. Sutt —3K 121
Poplar Rd. S. SW19 —7L 105
Poplars Av. NW2 —2G 57
Poplars Clo. Ruis —6C 36
Poplars Clo. Wat —5F 4
Poplar Shaw. Wal A —6M 7
Poplars Rd. E17 —4M 45
Poplars, The. N14 —7F 14
Poplars, The. Borwd —3L 11
Poplar St. Romf —2A 50
Poplar Vw. Wemb —7H 39
Poplar Wlk. SE24 —2A 92
(in two parts)
Poplar Wlk. Croy —4A 124
Poplar Way. Felt —9E 84
Poplar Way. Ilf —2A 48
Poppins Ct. EC4 —9M 59
Poppleton Rd. E11 —4C 46
Poppy Clo. Wall —3E 122
Poppy La. Croy —2G 125
Porchester Clo. SE5 —3A 92
Porchester Clo. Horn —4J 51
Porchester Ct. W2 —1M 73
Porchester Gdns. W2 —1M 73
Porchester Gdns. M. W2 —9M 57
Porchester Ga. W2 —1M 73
(off Bayswater Rd., in two parts)
Porchester Ho. E1 —9F 60
(off Philpot St.)
Porchester Mead. Beck —3L 109
Porchester M. W2 —9M 57
Porchester Pl. W2 —9C 58
Porchester Rd. W2 —9M 57
Porchester Rd. King T —6M 103
Porchester Sq. W2 —9M 57
Porchester Ter. W2 —1A 74
Porchester Ter. N. W2 —9M 57
Porchfield Clo. Sutt —2M 135
Porch Way. N20 —3D 26
Porcupine Clo. SE9 —8J 95
Porden Rd. SW2 —3K 91
Porlock Av. Harr —6A 38
Porlock Ho. SE26 —9E 92
Porlock Rd. W10 —7H 57
Porlock Rd. Enf —9D 16
Porlock St. SE1 —3B 76
Porrington Clo. Chst —5K 111
Porson Ct. SE13 —2M 93
Portal Clo. SE27 —9L 91
Portal Clo. Ruis —9E 36
(in two parts)
Portal Clo. Uxb —3C 142
(in two parts)
Porta Way. E3 —7K 61
Portbury Clo. SE15 —9E 76
Port Cres. E13 —7F 62
Portcullis Ho. SW1 —3J 75
(off Bridge St.)
Portcullis Lodge Rd. Enf —5B 16
Portelet Ct. N1 —4C 60
(off De Beauvoir Est.)
Portelet Rd. E1 —6H 61
Porten Houses. W14 —4J 73
(off Porten Rd.)
Porten Rd. W14 —4J 73
Porter Rd. E6 —9K 63
Porters & Walters Almshouses. N22 —7K 27
(off Nightingale Rd.)
Porters Av. Dag —2F 64
Porter Sq. N19 —6J 43
Porter St. SE1 —2A 76
Porter St. W1 —8D 58
Porters Wlk. E1 —1F 76
(off Pennington St.)
Porters Way. W Dray —4K 143
Porteus Rd. W2 —8A 58
Portgate Clo. W9 —7K 57
Porthallow Clo. Orp —6D 128
Porthcawe Rd. SE26 —1J 109
Porthkerry Av. Well —3E 96
Portia Ct. SE11 —6M 75
(off Opal St.)
Portia Ct. Bark —3E 64
Portia Way. E3 —7K 61
Porticos, The. SW3 —7B 74
(off Kings Rd.)
Portinscale Rd. SW15 —4J 89
Portland Av. N16 —5D 44
Portland Av. N Mald —2D 120
Portland Av. Sidc —5E 96
Portland Clo. Romf —3J 49
Portland Commercial Est. Bark —5G 65
Portland Ct. SE1 —4B 76
(off Gt. Dover St.)
Portland Ct. SE14 —7J 77
(off Whitcher Clo.)
Portland Cres. SE9 —8J 95
Portland Cres. Felt —1B 100
Portland Cres. Gnfd —7M 53
Portland Cres. Stan —9H 23
Portland Dri. Chesh —4A 6
Portland Dri. Enf —2C 16
Portland Gdns. N4 —4M 43
Portland Gdns. Romf —3H 49
Portland Gro. SW8 —9K 75
Portland Heights. N'wd —4D 20
Portland Ho. SW1 —4G 75
(off Stag Pl.)
Portland M. W1 —9G 59
Portland Pl. SE25 —8E 108
(off Portland Rd.)
Portland Pl. W1 —7F 58
Portland Pl. Eps —4C 134
Portland Ri. N4 —6M 43
Portland Ri. Est. N4 —6A 44
Portland Rd. N15 —2D 44
Portland Rd. SE9 —8J 95
Portland Rd. SE25 —8E 108
Portland Rd. W11 —1J 73
Portland Rd. Ashf —9C 144
Portland Rd. Brom —1G 111
Portland Rd. Hay —6C 52
Portland Rd. King T —7J 103
Portland Rd. Mitc —6C 106
Portland Rd. S'hall —4K 69
Portland Sq. E1 —2F 76
Portland St. SE17 —6B 76
Portland Ter. Rich —3H 87
Portland Wlk. SE17 —7B 76
Portmadoc Ho. Romf —4J 35
(off Broseley Rd.)
Portman Av. SW14 —2B 88
Portman Clo. W1 —9D 58
Portman Clo. Bex —7C 98
Portman Clo. Bexh —2J 97
Portman Dri. Wfd G —9H 31
Portman Gdns. NW9 —9B 24
Portman Gdns. Uxb —3E 142
Portman Ga. NW1 —7C 58
(off Broadley Ter.)
Portman Mans. W1 —8D 58
(off Chiltern St.)
Portman M. S. W1 —9E 58
Portman Pl. E2 —6G 61
Portman Rd. King T —6K 103
Portman Sq. W1 —9E 58
Portman St. W1 —9E 58
Portman Towers. W1 —9D 58
Portmeadow Wlk. SE2 —3H 81
Portmeers Clo. E17 —4K 45
Portmore Gdns. Romf —5L 33
Portnall Rd. W9 —5K 57
Portnalls Clo. Coul —8F 136
Portnalls Ri. Coul —8F 136
Portnalls Rd. Coul —9F 136
Portnoi Clo. Romf —9B 34
Portobello Ct. Est. W11 —9K 57
Portobello M. W11 —1L 73
Portobello Rd. W10 —8J 57
Portobello Rd. W11 —9K 57
Portobello Road Market. —8J 57
Portpool La. WC1 —8L 59
Portree Clo. N22 —7K 27
Portree St. E14 —9B 62
Portrush Ct. S'hall —9A 54
(off Whitecote Rd.)
Portsdown. Edgw —5L 23
Portsdown Av. NW11 —4K 41
Portsdown M. NW11 —4K 41
Portsea Hall. W2 —9D 58
(off Portsea Pl.)
Portsea M. W2 —9C 58
(off Portsea Pl.)
Portsea Pl. W2 —9C 58
Portslade Rd. SW8 —1G 91
Portsmouth Av. Th Dit —2E 118
Portsmouth M. E16 —2F 78
Portsmouth Rd. SW15 —6F 88
Portsmouth Rd. Esh & Surb —8L 117
Portsmouth Rd. Th Dit & Surb —2E 118
Portsmouth St. WC2 —9K 59
Portsoken St. EC3 —1D 76
Portswood Pl. SW15 —5D 88
Portugal Gdns. Twic —8A 86
Portugal St. WC2 —9K 59
Portway. E15 —4D 62
Portway. Eps —1E 134
Portway Cres. Eps —1E 134
Portway Gdns. SE18 —8H 79
Pory Ho. SE11 —5K 75
Poseidon Ct. E14 —5L 77
(off Homer Dri.)
Postern Grn. Enf —4L 15
Postern, The. EC2 —8A 60
(off Wood St.)
Post La. Twic —7B 86
Postmill Clo. Croy —5G 125
Post Office All. Hamp —6M 101
Post Office App. E7 —1F 62
Post Office Ct. EC4 —9B 60
(off Barbican)
Post Office Way. SW8 —8H 75
Post Rd. S'hall —4M 69
Postway M. Ilf —8M 47
(in two parts)
Potier St. SE1 —4B 76
Potter Clo. Mitc —6F 106
Potteries, The. Barn —7L 13
Potterne Clo. SW19 —6H 89
Potters Clo. Croy —3J 125
Potters Clo. Lou —4J 19
Potters End. Pinn —6F 20
Potters Fld. Enf —6C 16
(off Lincoln Rd.)
Potters Fields. SE1 —2C 76
Potters Gro. N Mald —8A 104
Potters Heights Clo. Pinn —7F 20
Potter's La. SW16 —3H 107
Potters La. Barn —6L 13
(in two parts)
Potters La. Borwd —3A 12
Potters Lodge. E14 —6A 78
(off Manchester Rd.)
Potters M. Els —8H 11
Potters Rd. SW6 —1A 90
Potter's Rd. Barn —6M 13
Potter St. N'wd —8E 20
Potter St. Pinn —8F 20
Potter St. Hill. Pinn —6F 20
Pottery La. W11 —2J 73
Pottery Rd. Bex —8A 98
Pottery Rd. Bren —7J 71
Pottery St. SE16 —3F 76
Pott St. E2 —6F 60
Poulett Gdns. Twic —7E 86
Poulett Rd. E6 —5K 63
Poulters Wood. Kes —7H 127
Poulton Av. Sutt —5B 122
Poulton Clo. E8 —2F 60
Poultry. EC2 —9B 60
Pound Clo. Orp —4B 128
Pound Clo. Surb —3G 119
Pound Ct. Dri. Orp —4B 128
Poundfield. Wat —8D 4
Poundfield Rd. Lou —7L 19
Pound Grn. Bex —6L 97
Pound La. NW10 —2E 56
Pound La. Eps —4A 134
Pound Pk. Rd. SE7 —5H 79
Pound Pl. SE9 —5L 95
Pound Rd. Bans —9K 135
Pound St. Cars —7D 122
Pound Way. Chst —4A 112
Pountney Rd. SW11 —2E 90
Poverest. —9E 112
Poverest Rd. Orp —9D 112
Povey Ho. SE17 —5C 76
(off Tatum St.)
Powder Mill La. Dart —8J 99
Powder Mill La. Twic —6K 85
Powdermill La. Wal A —6H 7
Powdermill M. Wal A —6H 7
(off Powdermill La.)
Powell Clo. Chess —7H 119
Powell Clo. Edgw —6K 23
Powell Clo. Wall —9J 123
Powell Ct. E17 —1M 45
Powell Ct. S Croy —6M 123
(off Bramley Hill)
Powell Gdns. Dag —9L 49
Powell Rd. E5 —8F 44
Powell Rd. Buck H —9G 19
Powell's Wlk. W4 —7C 72
Power Dri. Enf —9F 6
Powergate Bus. Pk. NW10 —6B 56
Power Rd. W4 —5L 71
Powers Ct. Twic —6H 87
Powerscroft Rd. E5 —9G 45
Powerscroft Rd. Sidc —3G 113
Power Works. Eri —9E 82
Powis Ct. W11 —9K 57
(off Powis Gdns.)
Powis Ct. Bus H —1B 22
(off Rutherford Way)
Powis Gdns. NW11 —5K 41
Powis Gdns. W11 —9K 57
Powis M. W11 —9K 57
Powis Pl. WC1 —7J 59
Powis Rd. E3 —6M 61
Powis Sq. W11 —9K 57
(in two parts)
Powis St. SE18 —4L 79
Powis Ter. W11 —9K 57
Powlett Ho. NW1 —2F 58
(off Powlett Pl.)
Powlett Pl. NW1 —3E 58
Pownall Gdns. Houn —3M 85
Pownall Rd. E8 —4E 60
Pownall Rd. Houn —3M 85
Pownsett Ter. Ilf —1A 64
Powster Rd. Brom —2E 110
Powys Clo. Bexh —7H 81
Powys Ct. N11 —5J 27
Powys Ct. Borwd —5B 12
Powys La. N14 & N13 —4J 27
Poynders Ct. SW4 —5G 91
Poynders Gdns. SW4 —6G 91
Poynders Rd. SW4 —5G 91
Poynings Clo. Orp —4G 129
Poynings Rd. N19 —8G 43
Poynings Way. N12 —5L 25
Poynings Way. H Wood —8J 35
Poyntell Cres. Chst —5B 112
Poynter Ct. N'holt —5H 53
(off Gallery Gdns.)
Poynter Ho. NW8 —7B 58
(off Fisherton St.)
Poynter Ho. W11 —2H 73
(off Queensdale Cres.)
Poynter Rd. Enf —7D 16
Poynton Rd. N17 —9E 28
Poyntz Rd. SW11 —1D 90
Poyser St. E2 —5F 60
Praed M. W2 —9B 58
Praed St. W2 —9B 58
Pragel St. E13 —5G 63
Pragnell Rd. SE12 —8F 94
Prague Pl. SW2 —4J 91
Prah Rd. N4 —7L 43
Prairie St. SW8 —1E 90
Pratt M. NW1 —4G 59
Pratts La. W on T —6H 117
Pratts Pas. King T —6J 103
Pratt St. NW1 —4G 59
Pratt Wlk. SE11 —5K 75
Prayle Gro. NW2 —6H 41
Preachers Ct. EC1 —7M 59
(off Charterhouse Sq.)
Prebend Gdns. W6 & W4 —5D 72
(in two parts)
Prebend Mans. W4 —5D 72
(off Chiswick High Rd.)
Prebend St. N1 —4A 60
Precinct Rd. Hay —1E 68
Precincts, The. Mord —1L 121
Precinct, The. N1 —4A 60
(in two parts)
Precinct, The. W Mol —7M 101
Premier Corner. W9 —5K 57
Premier Ct. Enf —2H 17
Premiere Pl. E14 —1L 77
Premier Ho. N1 —3M 59
Premier Pk. Rd. NW10 —5M 55
Premier Pl. SW15 —3J 89
Prendergast Rd. SE3 —2C 94
Prentice Ct. SW19 —2K 105
Prentis Rd. SW16 —1H 107
Prentiss Ct. SE7 —5H 79
Presburg Rd. N Mald —9C 104
Presburg St. E5 —8H 45
Prescelly Pl. Edgw —8K 23
Prescot St. E1 —1D 76
Prescott Av. Orp —1M 127
Prescott Clo. SW16 —4J 107
Prescott Clo. Horn —6F 50
Prescott Ho. SE5 —7M 75
(off Hillingdon St.)
Prescott Pl. SW4 —2H 91
Prescott Rd. Chesh —1E 6
Presentation M. SW2 —8K 91
Preshaw Cres. Mitc —7C 106
President Dri. E1 —2F 76
President Ho. EC1 —6M 59
President Quay. E1 —2D 76
(off St Katherine's Way)
President St. EC1 —6A 60
(off Central St.)
Press Ho. NW10 —8B 40
Press Rd. NW10 —8B 40
Press Rd. Uxb —2B 142
Prestage Way. E14 —1A 78
Prestbury Cres. Bans —8D 136
Prestbury Rd. E7 —3G 63
Prestbury Sq. SE9 —1K 111
Prested Rd. SW11 —3C 90
Prestige Way. NW4 —3G 41
Preston. —6J 39
Preston Av. E4 —6B 30
Preston Clo. SE1 —5C 76
Preston Clo. Twic —9C 86
Preston Ct. New Bar —6A 14
Preston Ct. Sidc —1D 112
(off Crescent, The)
Preston Ct. W on T —3G 117
Preston Dri. E11 —3G 47
Preston Dri. Bexh —9H 81
Preston Dri. Eps —8C 120
Preston Gdns. NW10 —2D 56
Preston Gdns. Enf —1J 17
Preston Gdns. Ilf —4J 47
Preston Gro. Asht —9G 133
Preston Hill. Harr —5J 39
Preston Ho. SE1 —4D 76
(off Stanworth St.)
Preston Ho. SE17 —5C 76
(off Preston Clo.)
Preston Ho. Dag —8L 49
(off Uvedale Rd.)
Preston Pl. NW2 —2E 56
Preston Pl. Rich —4J 87
Preston Rd. E11 —4C 46
Preston Rd. SE19 —3M 107
Preston Rd. SW20 —4D 104
Preston Rd. Romf —4H 35
Preston Rd. Wemb & Harr —6J 39
Preston's Rd. E14 —1A 78
Prestons Rd. Brom —5E 126
Preston Waye. Harr —6J 39
Prestwich Ter. SW4 —4G 91
Prestwick Clo. S'hall —6J 69
Prestwick Ct. S'hall —1A 70
(off Baird Av.)
Prestwick Rd. Wat —5F 20
Prestwood. Wat —2J 21
Prestwood Av. Harr —2F 38

Queenswood Cres.—Ravensbury Gro.

Queenswood Cres. Wat —6E 4
Queenswood Gdns. E11 —6F 46
Queenswood Pk. N3 —9J 25
Queens Wood Rd. N10 —4F 42
Queenswood Rd. SE23 —9H 93
Queenswood Rd. Sidc —4D 96
Queen's Yd. W1 —8G 59
Queen Victoria. (Junct.) —5G 121
Queen Victoria Av. Wemb —3H 55
Queen Victoria Memorial. —3G 75
Queen Victoria Seaman's Rest. E14
(off E. India Dock Rd.) —9M 61
Queen Victoria St. EC4 —1M 75
Queen Victoria Ter. E1 —1F 76
(off Sovereign Clo.)
Quemerford Rd. N7 —1K 59
Quendon Dri. Wal A —6K 7
Quendon Ho. W10 —7G 57
(off Sutton Way)
Quenington Ct. SE15 —7D 76
Quentin Ho. SE1 —3L 75
(off Gray St., in two parts)
Quentin Pl. SE13 —2C 94
Quentin Rd. SE3 —2C 94
Quentins Dri. Berr G —8M 141
Quernmore Clo. Brom —3E 110
Quernmore Rd. N4 —4L 43
Quernmore Rd. Brom —3E 110
Querrin St. SW6 —1A 90
Quested Ct. E8 —1F 60
(off Brett Rd.)
Questor. Dart —8J 99
Quex M. NW6 —4L 57
Quex Rd. NW6 —4L 57
Quick Rd. W4 —6C 72
Quicksilver Pl. N22 —9K 27
Quicks Rd. SW19 —4M 105
Quick St. N1 —5M 59
Quick St. M. N1 —5M 59
Quickswood. NW3 —3C 58
Quiet Nook. Brom —5H 127
Quill La. SW15 —3H 89
Quillot, The. W on T —7D 116
Quill St. N4 —8L 43
Quill St. W5 —5J 55
Quilp St. SE1 —3A 76
(in two parts)
Quilter Gdns. Orp —3G 129
Quilter Ho. W10 —6K 57
Quilter Rd. Orp —3G 129
Quilter St. E2 —6E 60
Quilter St. SE18 —6D 80
Quinta Dri. Barn —7F 12
Quintin Av. SW20 —5K 105
Quintin Clo. Pinn —2F 36
Quinton Clo. Beck —7A 110
Quinton Clo. Houn —8F 68
Quinton Clo. Wall —6F 122
Quinton Ho. SW8 —8J 75
(off Wyvil Rd.)
Quinton Rd. Th Dit —3E 118
Quinton St. SW18 —8A 90
Quinton Way. Wal A —8J 7
Quixley St. E14 —1B 78
Quorn Rd. SE22 —3C 92

Rabbit La. W on T —9E 116
Rabbit Row. W8 —2L 73
Rabbits Rd. E12 —9J 47
Rabbs Mill Ho. Uxb —5A 142
Rabournmead Dri. N'holt —1J 53
Raby Rd. N Mald —8B 104
Raby St. E14 —9J 61
Raccoon Way. Houn —1G 85
Rachel Clo. Ilf —1B 48
Rachel Point. E5 —9E 44
Racine. SE5 —9C 76
(off Peckham Rd.)
Rackham M. SW16 —3G 107
Rackman Clo. Well —1F 96
Rackstraw Ho. NW3 —3D 58
Racton Rd. SW6 —7L 73
Radbourne Av. W5 —5G 71
Radbourne Clo. E5 —9H 45
Radbourne Ct. Harr —4F 38
Radbourne Cres. E17 —9B 30
Radbourne Rd. SW12 —6G 91
Radcliffe Av. NW10 —5E 56
Radcliffe Av. Enf —3A 16
Radcliffe Gdns. Cars —1C 136
Radcliffe Ho. SE16 —5F 76
(off Anchor St.)
Radcliffe M. Hamp H —2A 102
Radcliffe Path. SW8 —1F 90
Radcliffe Rd. N21 —1M 27
Radcliffe Rd. SE1 —4C 76
Radcliffe Rd. Croy —4D 124
Radcliffe Rd. Harr —9E 22
Radcliffe Sq. SW15 —5H 89
Radcliffe Way. N'holt —6H 53
Radcot Point. SE23 —9H 93
Radcot St. SE11 —6L 75
Raddington Rd. W10 —8J 57
Radfield Way. Sidc —6B 96
Radford Ho. E14 —8M 61
(off St Leonard's Rd.)
Radford Ho. N7 —1K 59
Radford Rd. SE13 —5A 94
Radford Way. Bark —6D 64
Radipole Rd. SW6 —9K 73
Radius Pk. Felt —3D 84
Radland Rd. E16 —9D 62
Radlet Av. SE26 —9F 92
Radlett Clo. E7 —2D 62
Radlett Pl. NW8 —4C 58
Radlett Rd. A'ham —2M 9
Radlett Rd. Wat —5G 9
Radley Av. Ilf —9E 48
Radley Clo. Felt —7D 84
Radley Ct. SE16 —3H 77
Radley Gdns. Harr —2J 39
Radley Ho. NW1 —7D 58
(off Gloucester Pl.)
Radley Ho. SE2 —3H 81
(off Wolvercote Rd.)
Radley M. W8 —4L 73
Radley Rd. N17 —9C 28
Radley's La. E18 —9E 30
Radleys Mead. Dag —2M 65
Radley Sq. E5 —7G 45
Radley Ter. E16 —8D 62
(off Hermit Rd.)
Radlix Rd. E10 —6L 45
Radnor Av. Harr —3C 38
Radnor Av. Well —4F 96
Radnor Clo. Chst —3C 112
Radnor Clo. Mitc —8J 107
Radnor Ct. W7 —9D 54
(off Copley Clo.)
Radnor Ct. Har W —8D 22
Radnor Cres. SE18 —8E 80
Radnor Cres. Ilf —3K 47
Radnor Gdns. Enf —3C 16
Radnor Gdns. Twic —8D 86
Radnor Gro. Uxb —5E 142
Radnor Hall Mobile Homes. Borwd —7J 11
Radnor M. W2 —9B 58
Radnor Pl. W2 —9C 58
Radnor Rd. NW6 —4J 57
Radnor Rd. SE15 —8E 76
Radnor Rd. Harr —3B 38
Radnor Rd. Twic —7D 86
Radnor St. EC1 —6A 60
Radnor Ter. W14 —5K 73
Radnor Ter. Sutt —9L 121
Radnor Wlk. E14 —5L 77
(off Barnsdale Av.)
Radnor Wlk. SW3 —6C 74
Radnor Wlk. Croy —1J 125
Radnor Way. NW10 —7M 55
Radstock Av. Harr —1E 38
Radstock Clo. N11 —6E 26
Radstock Ho. H Hill —5H 35
(off Darlington Gdns.)
Radstock St. SW11 —8C 74
(in two parts)
Raebarn Gdns. Barn —7F 12
Raeburn Av. Dart —4F 98
Raeburn Av. Surb —3M 119
Raeburn Clo. NW11 —4A 42
Raeburn Clo. King T —4H 103
Raeburn Ho. N'holt —5H 53
(off Academy Gdns.)
Raeburn Rd. Edgw —8L 23
Raeburn Rd. Hay —5B 52
Raeburn Rd. Sidc —5C 96
Raeburn St. SW2 —3J 91
Raffles Ct. NW4 —2F 40
Raffles Sq. E15 —3B 62
Rafford Way. Brom —6F 110
R.A.F. Northolt. —2E 52
Raggleswood. Chst —5L 111
Raglan Av. Wal X —7D 6
Raglan Clo. Houn —4K 85
Raglan Ct. SE12 —4E 94
Raglan Ct. S Croy —7M 123
Raglan Ct. Wemb —9K 39
Raglan Gdns. Wat —1F 20
Raglan Rd. E17 —3A 46
Raglan Rd. SE18 —6M 79
Raglan Rd. Belv —5K 81
Raglan Rd. Brom —8G 111
Raglan Rd. Enf —9D 16
Raglan St. NW5 —2F 58
Raglan Ter. Harr —9M 37
Raglan Way. N'holt —2A 54
Ragley Clo. W3 —3A 72
Raider Clo. Romf —8L 33
Railey M. NW5 —1G 59
Railpit La. Warl —7C 140
Railshead Rd. Iswth —3F 86
Railton Rd. SE24 —3L 91
Railway App. N4 —4L 43
Railway App. SE1 —2B 76
Railway App. Harr —2D 38
Railway App. Twic —6E 86
Railway App. Wall —7F 122
Railway Arches. E10 —5M 45
(off Capworth St.)
Railway Arches. E11 —7C 46
(off Leytonstone High Rd.)
Railway Arches. E11 —6B 46
(off Sidings, The)
Railway Arches. E17 —3L 45
(off Yunus Khan Clo.)
Railway Av. SE16 —3G 77
(in two parts)
Railway Children Wlk. Brom —8E 94
Railway Cotts. SW19 —1M 105
Railway Cotts. W6 —3G 73
(off Sulgrave Rd.)
Railway Cotts. Borwd —6L 11
(off Station Rd.)
Railway Cotts. Twic —5L 85
Railway Cotts. Wat —3F 8
Railway Gro. SE14 —8K 77
Railway M. E3 —6L 61
(off Wellington Way)
Railway M. W11 —9J 57
Railway Pas. Tedd —3E 102
Railway Pl. SW19 —3K 105
Railway Pl. Belv —4L 81
Railway Ri. SE22 —3C 92
Railway Rd. Tedd —1C 102
Railway Rd. Wal X —6F 6
Railway Side. SW13 —2C 88
(in two parts)
Railway St. N1 —5J 59
Railway St. Romf —5G 49
Railway Ter. E17 —8A 30
Railway Ter. SE13 —4M 93
Railway Ter. Coul —7H 137
(off Station App.)
Railway Ter. Felt —7E 84
Rainborough Clo. NW10 —2A 56
Rainbow Av. E14 —6M 77
Rainbow Ct. SE14 —7J 77
(off Chipley St.)
Rainbow Ct. Wat —8G 9
Rainbow Ind. Est. W Dray —1H 143
Rainbow Quay. SE16 —4J 77
Rainbow St. SE5 —8C 76
Rainer Clo. Chesh —2D 6
Raine St. E1 —2F 76
Rainham. —7E 66
Rainham Clo. SE9 —5B 96
Rainham Clo. SW11 —5C 90
Rainham Hall. —7E 66
Rainham Ho. NW1 —4G 59
(off Bayham Pl.)
Rainham Rd. NW10 —6G 57
Rainham Rd. Horn & Rain —1D 66
Rainham Rd. N. Dag —7L 49
Rainham Rd. S. Dag —9M 49
Rainham Trad. Est. Rain —7D 66
Rainhill Way. E3 —6L 61
(in two parts)
Rainsborough Av. SE8 —5J 77
Rainsford Clo. Stan —4G 23
Rainsford Rd. NW10 —5M 55
(in two parts)
Rainsford St. W2 —9C 58
Rainsford Way. Horn —6E 50
Rainton Rd. SE7 —6E 78
Rainville Rd. W6 —7G 73
Raisins Hill. Pinn —1G 37
Raith Av. N14 —3H 27
Raleana Rd. E14 —2A 78
Raleigh Av. Hay —8F 52
Raleigh Av. Wall —6H 123
Raleigh Clo. NW4 —3G 41
Raleigh Clo. Eri —7D 82
Raleigh Clo. Pinn —5H 37
Raleigh Clo. Ruis —7D 36
Raleigh Ct. SE16 —2H 77
(off Clarence M.)
Raleigh Ct. W12 —3G 73
(off Scott's Rd.)
Raleigh Ct. W13 —8F 54
Raleigh Ct. Beck —5M 109
Raleigh Ct. Eri —8D 82
Raleigh Ct. Wall —8F 122
Raleigh Dri. N20 —3C 26
Raleigh Dri. Clay —7B 118
Raleigh Dri. Surb —3A 120
Raleigh Gdns. SW2 —5K 91
Raleigh Gdns. Mitc —7D 106
(in two parts)
Raleigh Ho. E14 —3M 77
(off Admirals Way)
Raleigh Ho. SW1 —7H 75
(off Dolphin Sq.)
Raleigh M. N1 —4M 59
(off Packington St.)
Raleigh M. Orp —7D 128
Raleigh Rd. N2 —9C 26
Raleigh Rd. N8 —2L 43
Raleigh Rd. SE20 —4H 109
Raleigh Rd. Enf —6B 16
Raleigh Rd. Felt —9D 84
Raleigh Rd. Rich —2K 87
Raleigh Rd. S'hall —6J 69
Raleigh St. N1 —4M 59
Raleigh Way. N14 —1H 27
Raleigh Way. Felt —2G 101
Ralph Brook Ct. N1 —6B 60
(off Chart St.)
Ralph Ct. W2 —9M 57
(off Queensway)
Ralph Perring Ct. Beck —8L 109
Ralston St. SW3 —6D 74
Ralston Way. Wat —2H 21
Ramac Ind. Est. SE7 —5F 78
Rama Clo. SW16 —4J 107
Rama Ct. Harr —7C 38
Ramac Way. SE7 —5F 78
Rama La. SE19 —4D 108
Ramar Ho. E1 —8E 60
(off Hanbury St.)
Rambler Clo. SW16 —1G 107
Rame Clo. SW17 —2E 106
Ramilles Clo. SW2 —5J 91
Ramillies Pl. W1 —9G 59
Ramillies Rd. NW7 —2C 24
Ramillies Rd. W4 —5B 72
Ramillies Rd. Sidc —5F 96
Ramillies St. W1 —9G 59
Ramney Dri. Enf —9E 6
Ramones Ter. Mitc —8J 107
Ramornie Clo. W on T —7K 117
Rampart St. E1 —9F 60
Ram Pas. King T —6H 103
Rampayne St. SW1 —6H 75
Ram Pl. E9 —2G 61
Rampton Clo. E4 —3L 29
Ramsay Gdns. Romf —8G 35
Ramsay Ho. NW8 —5C 58
(off Townshend Est.)
Ramsay M. SW3 —7C 74
Ramsay Pl. Harr —6C 38
Ramsay Rd. E7 —9C 46
Ramsay Rd. W3 —4A 72
Ramscroft Clo. N9 —9C 16
Ramsdale Rd. SW17 —2E 106
Ramsden. —3G 129
Ramsden Clo. Orp —3G 129
Ramsden Dri. Romf —7L 33
Ramsden Rd. N11 —5D 26
Ramsden Rd. SW12 —5E 90
Ramsden Rd. Eri —8B 82
Ramsden Rd. Orp —2F 128
Ramsey Clo. NW9 —4D 40
Ramsey Clo. Gnfd —1B 54
Ramsey Ct. Croy —4M 123
(off Church St.)
Ramsey Ho. SW9 —8L 75
(off Vassall Rd.)
Ramsey Rd. T Hth —1K 123
Ramsey St. E2 —7E 60
Ramsey Wlk. N1 —2B 60
(off Handa Wlk.)
Ramsey Way. N14 —9G 15
Ramsfort Ho. SE16 —5F 76
(off Camilla Rd.)
Ramsgate Clo. E16 —2F 78
Ramsgate St. E8 —2D 60
Ramsgill App. Ilf —2D 48
Ramsgill Dri. Ilf —3D 48
Rams Gro. Romf —2J 49
Ram St. SW18 —4M 89
Ramulis Dri. Hay —7H 53
Ramuswood Av. Orp —7C 128
Rancliffe Gdns. SE9 —3J 95
Rancliffe Rd. E6 —5J 63
Randall Av. NW2 —7C 40
Randall Clo. SW11 —9C 74
Randall Clo. Eri —7A 82
Randall Ct. NW7 —7E 24
Randall Dri. Horn —9G 51
Randall Pl. SE10 —8A 78
Randall Rd. SE11 —6K 75
Randall Row. SE11 —5K 75
Randalls Rents. SE16 —4K 77
(off Gulliver St.)
Randell's Rd. N1 —4J 59
(in two parts)
Randisbourne Gdns. SE6 —9M 93
Randle Rd. Rich —1G 103
Randlesdown Rd. SE6 —1L 109
(in two parts)
Randolph App. E16 —9G 63
Randolph Av. W9 —5M 57
Randolph Clo. Bexh —2A 98
Randolph Clo. King T —2A 104
Randolph Ct. H End —7L 21
(off Avenue, The)
Randolph Cres. W9 —7A 58
Randolph Gdns. NW6 —5M 57
Randolph Gro. Romf —3G 49
Randolph M. W9 —7A 58
Randolph Rd. E17 —3M 45
Randolph Rd. W9 —7A 58
Randolph Rd. Brom —3K 127
Randolph Rd. Eps —6D 134
Randolph Rd. S'hall —3K 69
Randolph St. NW1 —3G 59
Randon Clo. Harr —9M 21
Ranelagh Av. SW6 —2K 89
Ranelagh Av. SW13 —1E 88
Ranelagh Bri. W2 —8M 57
Ranelagh Clo. Edgw —4L 23
Ranelagh Dri. Edgw —4L 23
Ranelagh Dri. Twic —3F 86
Ranelagh Gdns. E11 —3G 47
Ranelagh Gdns. SW6 —2J 89
Ranelagh Gdns. W4 —8A 72
Ranelagh Gdns. W6 —5D 72
Ranelagh Gdns. Ilf —6K 47
Ranelagh Gdns. Mans. SW6 —2J 89
(off Ranelagh Gdns.)
Ranelagh Gro. SW1 —6E 74
Ranelagh Ho. SW3 —6D 74
(off Elystan Pl.)
Ranelagh M. W5 —3H 71
Ranelagh Pl. N Mald —9C 104
Ranelagh Rd. E6 —4L 63
Ranelagh Rd. E11 —9C 46
Ranelagh Rd. E15 —5C 62
Ranelagh Rd. N17 —1C 44
Ranelagh Rd. N22 —8K 27
Ranelagh Rd. NW10 —5D 56
Ranelagh Rd. SW1 —6G 75
Ranelagh Rd. W5 —3H 71
Ranelagh Rd. S'hall —2H 69
Ranelagh Rd. Wemb —2H 55
Ranfurly Rd. Sutt —4L 121
Rangbourne Ho. N7 —1J 59
Rangefield Rd. Brom —2C 110
Rangemoor Rd. N15 —3D 44
Ranger's House. —9B 78
Ranger's Rd. E4 —9C 18
Rangers Sq. SE10 —9B 78
Rangeworth Pl. Sidc —9D 96
Rangoon St. EC3 —9D 60
(off Crutched Friars)
Rankin Clo. NW9 —1C 40
Rankine Ho. SE1 —4A 76
(off Bath Ter.)
Ranleigh Gdns. Bexh —8K 81
Ranmere St. SW12 —7F 90
Ranmoor Clo. Harr —2B 38
Ranmoor Gdns. Harr —2B 38
Ranmore Av. Croy —5D 124
Ranmore Path. Orp —8E 112
Ranmore Pl. Wey —7A 116
(off Princes Rd.)
Ranmore Rd. Sutt —1H 135
Rannoch Clo. Edgw —2M 23
Rannoch Rd. W6 —7G 73
Rannock Av. NW9 —5B 40
Ranskill Ct. Borwd —3L 11
Ranskill Rd. Borwd —3L 11
Ransom Clo. Wat —9G 9
Ransome's Dock Bus. Cen. SW11 —8C 74
Ransom Rd. SE7 —5G 79
Ranston St. NW1 —8C 58
Ranulf Rd. NW2 —9K 41
Ranwell Clo. E3 —4K 61
Ranworth Clo. Eri —1C 98
Ranworth Rd. N9 —2G 29
Ranyard Clo. Chess —5K 119
Raphael Av. Romf —1D 50
Raphael Ct. SE16 —6F 76
(off Stubbs Dri.)
Raphael Dri. Th Dit —2D 118
Raphael Dri. Wat —4H 9
Raphael St. SW7 —3D 74
Rapier Clo. Purf —5K 83
Rapley Ho. E2 —6E 60
(off Turin St.)
Rashleigh Ct. SW8 —1F 90
Rashleigh Ho. WC1 —6J 59
(off Thanet St.)
Rasper Rd. N20 —2A 26
Rastell Av. SW2 —8H 91
Ratcliff. —9J 61
Ratcliffe Clo. SE12 —6E 94
Ratcliffe Clo. Uxb —6B 142
Ratcliffe Cross St. E1 —9H 61
Ratcliffe Ho. E14 —9J 61
Ratcliffe La. E14 —9J 61
Ratcliffe Orchard. E1 —1H 77
Ratcliff Rd. E7 —1G 63
Rathbone Ho. NW6 —4L 57
Rathbone Mkt. E16 —8D 62
Rathbone Pl. W1 —8H 59
Rathbone Point. E5 —9E 44
Rathbone Sq. Croy —6A 124
Rathbone St. E16 —8D 62
Rathbone St. W1 —8G 59
Rathcoole Av. N8 —3K 43
Rathcoole Gdns. N8 —3K 43
Rathfern Rd. SE6 —7K 93
Rathgar Av. W13 —2F 70
Rathgar Clo. N3 —9K 25
Rathgar Rd. SW9 —2M 91
Rathlin Wlk. N1 —2B 60
Rathmell Dri. SW4 —5H 91
Rathmore Rd. SE7 —6F 78
Rats La. Lou —2F 18
Rattray Ct. SE6 —8D 94
Rattray Rd. SW2 —3L 91
Raul Rd. SE15 —1E 92
Raveley St. NW5 —9G 43
(in two parts)
Raven Clo. NW9 —9C 24
Ravendale Rd. Sun —6D 100
Ravenet St. SW11 —9F 74
Ravenfield Rd. SW17 —9D 90
Ravenhill Rd. E13 —5G 63
Raven Ho. SE16 —5H 77
(off Tawny Way)
Ravenings Pde. Ilf —6E 48
Ravenna Rd. SW15 —4H 89
Ravenoak Way. Chig —5C 32
Ravenor Ct. Gnfd —7M 53
Ravenor Pk. Rd. Gnfd —6M 53
Raven Rd. E18 —9G 31
Raven Row. E1 —8F 60
Ravensbourne Av. Brom —4B 110
Ravensbourne Av. Stai —7C 144
Ravensbourne Ct. SE6 —6L 93
Ravensbourne Cres. Romf —1K 51
Ravensbourne Gdns. W13 —8F 54
Ravensbourne Gdns. Ilf —8L 31
Ravensbourne Ho. NW8 —8C 58
(off Broadley St.)
Ravensbourne Ho. Brom —2B 110
Ravensbourne Mans. SE8 —7L 77
(off Berthon St.)
Ravensbourne Pk. SE6 —6L 93
Ravensbourne Pk. Cres. SE6 —6K 93
Ravensbourne Pl. SE13 —1M 93
Ravensbourne Rd. SE6 —6K 93
Ravensbourne Rd. Brom —7E 110
Ravensbourne Rd. Dart —2E 98
Ravensbourne Rd. Twic —5G 87
Ravensbury Av. Mord —9A 106
Ravensbury Ct. Mitc —8B 106
(off Ravensbury Gro.)
Ravensbury Gro. Mitc —8B 106

Regal Ct.—Ridgeway Clo.

Regal Ct. N18 —5D 28
Regal Cres. Wall —5F 122
Regal Dri. N11 —5F 26
Regal La. NW1 —4E 58
Regal Pl. E3 —6K 61
Regal Pl. SW6 —8M 73
(off Maxwell Rd.)
Regal Row. SE15 —9G 77
Regal Way. Harr —4J 39
Regal Way. Wat —2G 9
Regan Ho. N18 —6D 28
Regan Way. N1 —5C 60
Regarder Rd. Chig —5E 32
Regarth Av. Romf —4C 50
Regatta Ho. Tedd —1E 102
Regatta Point. Bren —7K 71
Regency Clo. W5 —9J 55
Regency Clo. Chig —5A 32
Regency Clo. Hamp —2K 101
Regency Ct. Enf —7B 16
Regency Ct. Sutt —6M 121
Regency Ct. Tedd —3F 102
Regency Cres. NW4 —9H 25
Regency Dri. Ruis —6C 36
Regency Gdns. Horn —5G 51
Regency Gdns. W on T —3G 117
Regency Ho. NW1 —7F 58
(off Osnaburgh St.)
Regency Lawn. NW5 —8F 42
Regency Lodge. NW3 —3B 58
(off Adelaide Rd.)
Regency Lodge. Buck H —2H 31
Regency M. NW10 —2E 56
Regency M. SW9 —8M 75
Regency M. Beck —4A 110
Regency M. Iswth —4C 86
Regency Pl. SW1 —5H 75
Regency St. SW1 —5H 75
Regency Ter. SW7 —6B 74
(off Fulham Rd.)
Regency Wlk. Croy —1J 125
Regency Wlk. Rich —4J 87
(off Grosvenor Av.)
Regency Way. Bexh —2H 97
Regent Av. Uxb —3F 142
Regent Bus. Cen. Hay —3F 68
Regent Clo. N12 —5A 26
Regent Clo. Harr —4J 39
Regent Clo. Houn —9F 68
Regent Ct. N3 —7M 25
Regent Ct. N20 —2A 26
Regent Ct. NW8 —6C 58
(off North Bank)
Regent Gdns. Ilf —5E 48
Regent Ga. Wal X —7D 6
Regent Ho. W14 —5J 73
(off Windsor Way)
Regent Ho. Eps —3C 134
Regent Pl. SW19 —2A 106
Regent Pl. W1 —1G 75
Regent Pl. Croy —3D 124
Regent Rd. SE24 —5M 91
Regent Rd. Surb —9K 103
Regents Av. N13 —5L 27
Regent's Bri. Gdns. SW8 —8J 75
Regents Canal Ho. E14 —9J 61
(off Commercial Rd.)
Regents Clo. Hay —8D 52
Regents Clo. S Croy —8C 124
Regents Clo. Stan —4J 23
Regents Ct. E8 —4D 60
(off Pownall Rd.)
Regents Ct. Brom —4D 110
Regents Ct. King T —5J 103
(off Sopwith Way)
Regents Dri. Kes —7H 127
Regents Ga. Ho. E14 —1J 77
Regents M. NW8 —5A 58
Regent's Park. —5F 58
Regent's Pk. —6E 58
Regents Pk. Est. NW1 —6G 59
(off Robert St.)
Regent's Pk. Gdns. M. NW1 —4D 58
Regent's Pk. Ho. NW1 —6C 58
(off Park Rd.)
Regent's Pk. Open Air Theatre. —6E 58
Regents Pk. Rd. N3 —1K 41
Regent's Pk. Rd. NW1 —3D 58
(in two parts)
Regent's Pk. Ter. NW1 —4F 58
Regent's Pl. SE3 —1E 94
Regents Pl. Lou —9H 19
Regents Plaza. NW6 —5M 57
(off Kilburn High Rd.)
Regent Sq. E3 —6M 61
Regent Sq. WC1 —6J 59
Regent Sq. Belv —5M 81
Regent's Row. E8 —4E 60
Regent St. NW10 —6H 57
Regent St. SW1 —1H 75
Regent St. W1 —9F 58
Regent St. W4 —6L 71
Regent St. Wat —2F 8
Regents Wharf. E8 —4F 60
(off Wharf Pl.)
Regents Wharf. N1 —5K 59
Regina Clo. Barn —5H 13
Regina Ho. SE20 —5H 109
Reginald Pl. SE8 —8L 77
(off Deptford High St.)
Reginald Rd. E7 —3E 62
Reginald Rd. SE8 —8L 77
Reginald Rd. N'wd —8D 20
Reginald Rd. Romf —8L 35
Reginald Sq. SE8 —8L 77
Regina Point. SE16 —3G 77
Regina Rd. N4 —6K 43
Regina Rd. SE25 —7E 108
Regina Rd. W13 —2E 70
Regina Rd. S'hall —5J 69
Regina Ter. W13 —2E 70
Regis Ct. N8 —2K 43
Regis Ct. NW1 —8D 58
(off Melcombe Pl.)
Regis Ho. W1 —8E 58
(off Beaumont St.)
Regis Pl. SW2 —3K 91
Regis Rd. NW5 —1F 58
Regnart Bldgs. NW1 —6G 59
(off Euston St.)
Reid Clo. Coul —8F 136
Reid Clo. Pinn —2E 36
Reidhaven Rd. SE18 —5C 80
Reigate Av. Sutt —3L 121
Reigate Rd. Brom —9D 94
Reigate Rd. Eps & Tad —2D 134
Reigate Rd. Ilf —7D 48
Reigate Way. Wall —7J 123
Reighton Rd. E5 —8E 44
Reinickendorf Av. SE9 —5A 96
Relay Rd. W12 —2G 73
Relf Rd. SE15 —2E 92
Reliance Arc. SW9 —3L 91
Reliance Sq. EC2 —7C 60
(off Anning St.)
Relko Ct. Eps —3B 134
Relko Gdns. Sutt —7B 122
Relton M. SW7 —4C 74
Rembold Ho. SE10 —9A 78
(off Blissett St.)
Rembrandt Clo. E14 —4B 78
Rembrandt Clo. SW1 —6E 74
(off Graham Ter.)
Rembrandt Ct. SE16 —6F 76
(off Stubbs Dri.)
Rembrandt Ct. Eps —8D 120
Rembrandt Rd. SE13 —3C 94
Rembrandt Rd. Edgw —9L 23
Rembrandt Way. W on T —4F 116
Remembrance Rd. E7 —9H 47
Remington Rd. E6 —9J 63
Remington Rd. N15 —4B 44
Remington St. EC1 —5M 59
Remnant St. WC2 —9K 59
Remsted Ho. NW6 —4M 57
(off Mortimer Cres.)
Remus Building, The. EC1 —6L 59
(off Hardwick St.)
Remus Rd. E3 —3L 61
Renaissance Ho. Eps —5C 134
(off Up. High St.)
Rendle Clo. Croy —9D 108
Rendlesham Av. Rad —1D 10
Rendlesham Rd. E5 —9E 44
Rendlesham Rd. Enf —3M 15
Renforth St. SE16 —4G 77
Renfree Way. Shep —1A 116
Renfrew Clo. E6 —1L 79
Renfrew Ct. Houn —1J 85
Renfrew Ho. E17 —9K 29
Renfrew Rd. SE11 —5M 75
Renfrew Rd. Houn —1H 85
Renfrew Rd. King T —4M 103
Renmans, The. Asht —8K 133
Renmuir St. SW17 —3D 106
Rennell St. SE13 —2A 94
Rennels Way. Iswth —1C 86
Renness Rd. E17 —1J 45
Rennets Clo. SE9 —4C 96
Rennets Wood Rd. SE9 —4B 96
Rennie Clo. Ashf —9B 144
Rennie Cotts. E1 —7G 61
(off Pemell Clo.)
Rennie Ct. SE1 —2M 75
(off Stamford St.)
Rennie Est. SE16 —5F 76
Rennie Ho. SE1 —4A 76
(off Bath Ter.)
Rennie St. SE1 —2M 75
(in two parts)
Renoir Ct. SE16 —6F 76
(off Stubbs Dri.)
Renown Clo. Croy —3M 123
Renown Clo. Romf —8L 33
Rensburg Rd. E17 —3H 45
Renshaw Clo. Belv —7K 81
Renters Av. NW4 —4G 41
Renton Clo. SW2 —5K 91
Renton Dri. Orp —2H 129
Renwick Ind. Est. Bark —5F 64
Renwick Rd. Bark —7F 64
Repens Way. Hay —7H 53
Rephidim St. SE1 —4C 76
Replingham Rd. SW18 —7K 89
Reporton Rd. SW6 —8J 73
Repository Rd. SE18 —7K 79
Repton Av. Hay —5B 68
Repton Av. Romf —1E 50
Repton Av. Wemb —9G 39
Repton Clo. Cars —7C 122
Repton Ct. Beck —5M 109
Repton Ct. Ilf —8K 31
Repton Dri. Romf —2E 50
Repton Gdns. Romf —1E 50
Repton Gro. Ilf —8K 31
Repton Ho. E14 —9J 61
Repton Ho. SW1 —5G 75
(off Charlwood St.)
Repton Rd. Harr —2K 39
Repton Rd. Orp —5E 128
Repton St. E14 —9J 61
Repulse Clo. Romf —8L 33
Reservoir Clo. T Hth —8B 108
Reservoir Rd. N14 —7G 15
Reservoir Rd. SE4 —1J 93
Reservoir Rd. Lou —3F 18
Reservoir Rd. Ruis —2B 36
Resolution Wlk. SE18 —4K 79
Restavon Cvn. Site. Berr G —8M 141
Restell Clo. SE3 —7C 78
Restmor Way. Wall —4E 122
Reston Clo. Borwd —2L 11
Reston Path. Borwd —2L 11
Reston Pl. SW7 —3A 74
Restons Cres. SE9 —5B 96
Restoration Sq. SW11 —9B 74
Restormel Clo. Houn —4L 85
Restormel Ho. SE11 —5L 75
(off Chester Way)
Retcar Clo. N19 —7F 42
Retcar Pl. N19 —7F 42
(off Retcar Clo.)
Retford Clo. Borwd —2L 11
Retford Clo. Romf —6L 35
Retford Path. Romf —6L 35
Retford Rd. Romf —6K 35
Retford St. N1 —5C 60
Retingham Way. E4 —2M 29
Retles Ct. Harr —5C 38
Retreat Clo. Harr —3G 39
Retreat Ho. E9 —2G 61
Retreat Pl. E9 —2G 61
Retreat Rd. Rich —4H 87
Retreat, The. NW9 —3B 40
Retreat, The. SW14 —2C 88
Retreat, The. Harr —5L 37
Retreat, The. K Lan —4A 4
Retreat, The. Orp —8F 128
Retreat, The. Surb —1K 119
Retreat, The. T Hth —8B 108
Retreat, The. Wor Pk —4F 120
Retreat Way. Chig —3F 32
Reubens Ct. W4 —6M 71
(off Chaseley Dri.)
Reunion Row. E1 —1F 76
Reveley Sq. SE16 —3J 77
Revell Ri. SE18 —7D 80
Revell Rd. King T —6M 103
Revell Rd. Sutt —8K 121
Revelon Rd. SE4 —3J 93
Revelstoke Rd. SW18 —8K 89
Reventlow Rd. SE9 —7A 96
Reverdy Rd. SE1 —5E 76
Reverend Clo. Harr —8M 37
Revesby Rd. Cars —1B 122
Review Rd. NW2 —7D 40
Review Rd. Dag —4M 65
Rewell St. SW6 —8A 74
Rewley Rd. Cars —1B 122
Rex Clo. Romf —7M 33
Rex Pl. W1 —1E 74
Reydon Av. E11 —3G 47
Reynard Clo. SE4 —2J 93
Reynard Clo. Brom —7L 111
Reynard Dri. SE19 —4D 108
Reynard Mills Trad. Est. Bren —6G 71
Reynard Pl. SE14 —7J 77
Reynardson Rd. N17 —7A 28
Reynards Way. Brick W —2K 5
Reynolds Av. E12 —1L 63
Reynolds Av. Chad H & Romf —5G 49
Reynolds Av. Chess —9J 119
Reynolds Clo. NW11 —5M 41
Reynolds Clo. SW19 —5B 106
Reynolds Clo. Cars —3D 122
Reynolds Ct. Romf —1H 49
Reynolds Dri. Edgw —1K 39
Reynolds Ho. NW8 —5B 58
(off Wellington Rd.)
Reynolds Ho. SW1 —5H 75
(off Erasmus St.)
Reynolds Pl. SE3 —8F 78
Reynolds Pl. Rich —5K 87
Reynolds Rd. SE15 —3G 93
Reynolds Rd. W4 —4A 72
Reynolds Rd. Hay —7G 53
Reynolds Rd. N Mald —2B 120
Reynolds Way. Croy —6C 124
Rheidol M. N1 —5A 60
Rheidol Ter. N1 —4A 60
Rheingold Way. Wall —1J 137
Rhein Ho. N8 —1J 43
(off Campsfield Rd.)
Rheola Clo. N17 —8D 28
Rhoda St. E2 —7D 60
Rhodes Av. N22 —8G 27
Rhodes Ho. N1 —6B 60
(off Provost Est.)
Rhodes Ho. W12 —2F 72
(off White City Est.)
Rhodesia Rd. E11 —7B 46
Rhodesia Rd. SW9 —1J 91
Rhodesmoor Ho. Ct. Mord —1L 121
Rhodes St. N7 —1K 59
Rhodes Way. Wat —4H 9
Rhodeswell Rd. E14 —8J 61
Rhodrons Av. Chess —7J 119
Rhondda Gro. E3 —6J 61
Rhyl Rd. Gnfd —5D 54
Rhyl St. NW5 —2E 58
Rhys Av. N11 —7H 27
Rialto Rd. Mitc —6E 106
Ribble Clo. Wfd G —6G 31
Ribblesdale Av. N11 —6E 26
Ribblesdale Av. N'holt —2M 53
Ribblesdale Ho. NW6 —4L 57
(off Kilburn Va.)
Ribblesdale Rd. N8 —2K 43
Ribblesdale Rd. SW16 —3F 106
Ribblesdale Rd. Dart —7M 99
Ribbon Dance M. SE5 —9B 76
Ribchester Av. Gnfd —6D 54
Ribston Clo. Brom —3K 127
Ricardo Path. SE28 —2G 81
Ricardo St. E14 —9M 61
Ricards Rd. SW19 —2K 105
Riccall Ct. NW9 —8C 24
(off Pageant Av.)
Rice Pde. Orp —9B 112
Riceyman Ho. WC1 —6L 59
(off Lloyd Baker St.)
Richard Anderson Ct. SE14 —8H 77
(off Monson Rd.)
Richard Burbidge Mans. SW13 —7G 73
(off Brasenose Dri.)
Richard Clo. SE18 —5J 79
Richard Fell Ho. E12 —9L 47
(off Walton Rd.)
Richard Ho. SE16 —5G 77
(off Silwood St.)
Richard Ho. Dri. E16 —9H 63
Richard Neale Ho. E1 —1F 76
(off Cornwall St.)
Richards Av. Romf —4A 50
Richards Clo. Bush —9B 10
Richards Clo. Harr —3E 38
Richards Clo. Hay —7B 68
Richards Clo. Uxb —4E 142
Richards Fld. Eps —1B 134
Richard Sharples Ct. Sutt —9A 122
Richardson Clo. E8 —4D 60
Richardson Ct. SW4 —1J 91
(off Studley Rd.)
Richardson Rd. E15 —5C 62
Richardson's M. W1 —7G 59
(off Warren St.)
Richards Pl. E17 —1L 45
Richard's Pl. SW3 —5C 74
Richard St. E1 —9F 60
Richbell Clo. Asht —9H 133
Richbell Pl. WC1 —8K 59
Richborne Ter. SW8 —8K 75
Richborough Clo. Orp —8H 113
Richborough Ho. SE15 —7G 77
(off Sharratt St.)
Richborough Rd. NW2 —9J 41
Richens Clo. Houn —1B 86
Riches Rd. Ilf —7A 48
Richfield Rd. Bush —9A 10
Richford Ga. W6 —4G 73
Richford Rd. E15 —4D 62
Richford St. W6 —3G 73
Rich Ind. Est. SE15 —7F 76
Richland Av. Coul —6E 136
Richlands Av. Eps —6E 120
Rich La. SW5 —6M 73
Richman Ho. SE8 —6K 77
(off Grove St.)
Richmer Rd. Eri —8E 82
Richmond. —4H 87
Richmond Av. E4 —5B 30
Richmond Av. N1 —4K 59
Richmond Av. NW10 —2G 57
Richmond Av. SW20 —5J 105
Richmond Av. Felt —5C 84
Richmond Av. Uxb —2F 142
Richmond Bri. Twic & Rich —5H 87
Richmond Bldgs. W1 —9H 59
Richmond Circus. (Junct.) —3J 87
Richmond Clo. E17 —4K 45
Richmond Clo. Borwd —7B 12
Richmond Clo. Chesh —2C 6
Richmond Clo. Eps —6C 134
Richmond Cotts. W14 —5J 73
(off Hammersmith Rd.)
Richmond Ct. SW1 —3D 74
(off Sloane St.)
Richmond Ct. Lou —7H 19
Richmond Ct. Mitc —7B 106
Richmond Ct. Wemb —8K 39
Richmond Cres. E4 —5B 30
Richmond Cres. N1 —4K 59
Richmond Cres. N9 —1E 28
Richmond Dri. Shep —1B 116
Richmond Dri. Wat —4C 8
Richmond Gdns. NW4 —3E 40
Richmond Gdns. Harr —7D 22
Richmond Grn. Croy —5J 123
Richmond Gro. N1 —3M 59
(in two parts)
Richmond Gro. Surb —1K 119
Richmond Hill. Rich —5J 87
Richmond Hill Ct. Rich —5J 87
Richmond Ho. NW1 —5F 58
(off Park Village E.)
Richmond Ho. SE17 —6B 76
(off Portland St.)
Richmond Mans. Twic —5H 87
Richmond M. W1 —9H 59
Richmond M. Tedd —2D 102
Richmond Pde. Twic —5G 87
(off Richmond Rd.)
Richmond Pk. —7M 87
Richmond Pk. Lou —9H 19
Richmond Pk. Rd. SW14 —4A 88
Richmond Pk. Rd. King T —5J 103
Richmond Pl. SE18 —5A 80
Richmond Rd. E4 —1B 30
Richmond Rd. E7 —1F 62
Richmond Rd. E8 —3D 60
Richmond Rd. E11 —7B 46
Richmond Rd. N2 —9A 26
Richmond Rd. N11 —6J 27
Richmond Rd. N15 —4C 44
Richmond Rd. SW20 —5F 104
Richmond Rd. W5 —3J 71
Richmond Rd. Coul —7F 136
Richmond Rd. Croy —5J 123
Richmond Rd. Ilf —8A 48
Richmond Rd. Iswth —2E 86
Richmond Rd. King T —1H 103
Richmond Rd. New Bar —7M 13
Richmond Rd. Romf —4D 50
Richmond Rd. T Hth —7M 107
Richmond Rd. Twic —6F 86
Richmond St. E13 —5E 62
Richmond Ter. SW1 —3J 75
Richmond Way. E11 —7E 46
Richmond Way. W12 & W14 —3H 73
Richmond Way. Crox G —6A 8
Richmount Gdns. SE3 —2E 94
Rich St. E14 —1K 77
Rickard Clo. NW4 —2F 40
Rickard Clo. SW2 —7L 91
Rickard Clo. W Dray —4H 143
Rickards Clo. Surb —4J 119
Ricketts Hill Rd. Tats —9H 141
Rickett St. SW6 —7L 73
Rickman Hill. Coul —9F 136
Rickman Hill Rd. Coul —9F 136
Rickman Ho. E1 —6G 61
(off Rickman St.)
Rickman St. E1 —7G 61
Rickmansworth Rd. N'wd —5A 20
Rickmansworth Rd. Pinn —9F 20
Rickmansworth Rd. Wat —6C 8
Rick Roberts Way. E15 —4A 62
Rickthorne Rd. N19 —7J 43
Rickyard Path. SE9 —3J 95
Riddell Ct. SE5 —6D 76
Ridding La. Gnfd —1D 54
(in two parts)
Riddlesdown. —5A 138
Riddlesdown Av. Purl —3A 138
Riddlesdown Rd. Purl —2A 138
(in two parts)
Riddons Rd. SE12 —9G 95
Rideout St. SE18 —5K 79
Rider Clo. Sidc —5C 96
Ride, The. Bren —6F 70
Ride, The. Enf —5G 17
Ridgdale St. E3 —5M 61
Ridge Av. N21 —9A 16
Ridge Av. Dart —5D 98
Ridgebrook Rd. SE3 —2H 95
Ridge Clo. NW4 —9H 25
Ridge Clo. NW9 —2B 40
Ridge Clo. SE28 —3B 80
Ridge Ct. SE22 —6E 92
Ridge Crest. Enf —3K 15
Ridgecroft Clo. Bex —7A 98
Ridgefield. Wat —1C 8
Ridge Hill. NW11 —6J 41
Ridgehurst Av. Wat —7D 4
Ridge La. Wat —1D 8
Ridge Langley. S Croy —2E 138
Ridgemont Gdns. Edgw —4A 24
Ridgemont Pl. Horn —4H 51
Ridgemount. Wey —4C 116
Ridgemount Av. Coul —9F 136
Ridgemount Av. Croy —3H 125
Ridgemount Clo. SE20 —4F 108
Ridgemount Gdns. Enf —5M 15
Ridge Pk. Purl —2H 137
Ridge Rd. N8 —4K 43
Ridge Rd. N21 —1A 28
Ridge Rd. NW2 —8K 41
Ridge Rd. Mitc —4F 106
Ridge Rd. Sutt —3J 121
Ridge St. Wat —2F 8
Ridges Yd. Croy —5M 123
Ridge, The. Barn —7K 13
Ridge, The. Bex —6K 97
Ridge, The. Coul —6J 137
Ridge, The. Eps —9A 134
Ridge, The. Orp —4B 128
Ridge, The. Purl —2G 137
Ridge, The. Surb —9L 103
Ridge, The. Twic —6B 86
Ridgeview Clo. Barn —8H 13
Ridgeview Rd. N20 —3M 25
Ridge Way. SE19 —3C 108
Ridgeway. Brom —4E 126
Ridge Way. Cray —5D 98
Ridgeway. Eps —4A 134
Ridge Way. Felt —9J 85
Ridgeway. Rich —5J 87
Ridge Way. Wfd G —4G 31
Ridgeway Av. Barn —8D 14
Ridgeway Clo. Oxs —6A 132

…elle Clo.—Rosedale Ho.

…elle Clo. SW11 —3B 90
Rochelle St. E2 —6D 60
(in two parts)
Rochemont Wlk. E8 —4E 60
(off Pownell Rd.)
Roche Rd. SW16 —5K 107
Rochester Av. E13 —4G 63
Rochester Av. Brom —6F 110
Rochester Av. Felt —8D 84
Rochester Clo. SW16 —4J 107
Rochester Clo. Enf —3C 16
Rochester Clo. Sidc —5F 96
Rochester Ct. E2 —7F 60
(off Wilmot St.)
Rochester Ct. NW1 —3G 59
(off Rochester Sq.)
Rochester Dri. Bex —5K 97
Rochester Dri. Pinn —3H 37
Rochester Dri. Wat —8G 5
Rochester Gdns. Croy —5C 124
Rochester Gdns. Ilf —5K 47
Rochester Ho. SE1 —3B 76
Rochester Ho. SE15 —7G 77
(off Sharratt St.)
Rochester M. NW1 —3G 59
Rochester M. W5 —5G 71
Rochester Pde. Felt —8E 84
Rochester Pl. NW1 —2G 59
Rochester Rd. NW1 —2G 59
Rochester Rd. Cars —6D 122
Rochester Rd. Dart —6L 99
Rochester Rd. N'wd —1D 36
Rochester Row. SW1 —5G 75
Rochester Sq. NW1 —3G 59
Rochester St. SW1 —4H 75
Rochester Ter. NW1 —2G 59
Rochester Wlk. SE1 —2B 76
(off Stoney St.)
Rochester Way. SE3 & SE9 —9F 78
Rochester Way. Dart —6B 98
Rochester Way Relief Rd. SE3 & SE9 —9F 78
Roche Wlk. Cars —1B 122
Rochford. N17 —9C 28
(off Griffin Rd.)
Rochford Av. Romf —3G 49
Rochford Av. Wal A —7K 7
Rochford Clo. E6 —5H 63
Rochford Clo. Horn —2F 66
Rochford Wlk. E8 —3E 60
Rochford Way. Croy —1J 123
Rochfort Ho. SE8 —6K 77
Rock Av. SW14 —2B 88
Rockbourne M. SE23 —7H 93
Rockbourne Rd. SE23 —7H 93
Rockchase Gdns. Horn —4J 51
Rock Circus. —1H 75
(off Piccadilly Circus)
Rock Clo. Mitc —6B 106
Rockell's Pl. SE22 —5F 92
Rockfield Ho. NW4 —2H 41
(off Belle Vue Est.)
Rockfield Ho. SE10 —7A 78
(off Welland St.)
Rockford Av. Gnfd —5E 54
Rock Gdns. Dag —1M 65
Rock Gro. Way. SE16 —5E 76
(in two parts)
Rockhall Rd. NW2 —9H 41
Rockhampton Clo. SE27 —1L 107
Rockhampton Rd. SE27 —1L 107
Rockhampton Rd. S Croy —8C 124
Rock Hill. SE26 —1D 108
Rock Hill. Orp —8M 129
Rockingham Av. Horn —4F 50
Rockingham Clo. SW15 —3D 88
Rockingham Clo. Uxb —4A 142
Rockingham Ga. Bush —8A 10
Rockingham Pde. Uxb —3A 142
Rockingham Rd. Uxb —4A 142
Rockingham St. SE1 —4A 76
Rockland Rd. SW15 —3J 89
Rocklands Dri. Stan —9F 22
Rockley Ct. W14 —3H 73
(off Rockley Rd.)
Rockley Rd. W14 —3H 73
Rockmount Rd. SE18 —6D 80
Rockmount Rd. SE19 —3B 108
Rocks La. SW13 —9E 72
Rock St. N4 —7L 43
Rockware Av. Gnfd —4B 54
Rockware Av. Bus. Cen. Gnfd —4B 54
Rockways. Barn —8D 12
Rockwell Gdns. SE19 —2C 108
Rockwell Rd. Dag —1M 65
Rockwood Pl. W12 —3G 73
Rocliffe St. N1 —5M 59
Rocombe Cres. SE23 —6G 93
Rocque Ho. SW6 —8K 73
(off Estcourt Rd.)
Rocque La. SE3 —2D 94
Rodale Mans. SW18 —5M 89
Rodborough Ct. W9 —7L 57
(off Hermes Clo.)
Rodborough Rd. NW11 —6L 41
Roden Gdns. Croy —1C 124
Rodenhurst Rd. SW4 —5G 91
Roden St. N7 —8K 43
Roden St. Ilf —8L 47
Roden Way. Ilf —8L 47
(off Roden St.)
Rodeo Clo. Eri —9F 82
Roderick Ho. SE16 —5G 77
(off Raymouth Rd.)
Roderick Rd. NW3 —9D 42
Rodgers Clo. Els —8H 11
Rodgers Ho. SW4 —6H 91
(off Clapham Pk. Est.)
Rodin Ct. N1 —4M 59
(off Essex Rd.)
Roding Av. Wfd G —6J 31
Roding Gdns. Lou —8J 19
Roding Ho. N1 —4L 59
(off Barnsbury Est.)
Roding La. Buck H & Chig —1H 31
Roding La. N. Wfd G —6J 31
Roding La. S. Ilf & Wfd G —2H 47
Roding M. E1 —2E 76
Roding Rd. E5 —9H 45
Roding Rd. E6 —8M 63
Roding Rd. Lou —7J 19
Rodings Row. Barn —6J 13
(off Leecroft Rd.)
Rodings, The. Wfd G —6G 31
Roding Trad. Est. Bark —3M 63
Roding Vw. Buck H —1H 31
Roding Way. Rain —5H 67
Rodmarton St. W1 —8D 58
Rodmell. WC1 —6J 59
(off Regent Sq.)
Rodmell Clo. Hay —7J 53
Rodmell Slope. N12 —5K 25
Rodmere St. SE10 —6C 78
Rodmill La. SW2 —6J 91
Rodney Clo. Croy —3M 123
Rodney Clo. N Mald —9C 104
Rodney Clo. Pinn —5J 37
Rodney Clo. W on T —3G 117
Rodney Ct. NW8 —7A 58
Rodney Ct. Barn —5K 13
Rodney Gdns. Pinn —3F 36
Rodney Gdns. W W'ck —6E 126
Rodney Grn. W on T —4G 117
Rodney Ho. E14 —5M 77
(off Cahir St.)
Rodney Ho. N1 —5K 59
(off Donegal St.)
Rodney Ho. SW1 —6G 75
(off Dolphin Sq.)
Rodney Ho. W11 —1L 73
(off Pembridge Cres.)
Rodney Pl. E17 —9J 29
Rodney Pl. SE17 —5A 76
Rodney Pl. SW19 —5A 106
Rodney Rd. E11 —2F 46
Rodney Rd. SE17 —5A 76
Rodney Rd. Mitc —7C 106
Rodney Rd. N Mald —9C 104
Rodney Rd. Twic —5L 85
Rodney Rd. W on T —4G 117
Rodney St. N1 —5K 59
Rodney Way. Romf —8M 33
Rodway Rd. SW15 —6E 88
Rodway Rd. Brom —5F 110
Rodwell Clo. Ruis —6G 37
Rodwell Pl. Edgw —6L 23
Rodwell Rd. SE22 —5D 92
Roe. NW9 —7D 24
Roebourne Way. E16 —2L 79
Roebuck Clo. Felt —1F 100
Roebuck Ho. SW1 —4G 75
(off Palace Ho.)
Roebuck La. N17 —6D 28
Roebuck La. Buck H —9G 19
Roebuck Rd. Chess —7L 119
Roebuck Rd. Ilf —5F 32
Roebuck Trad. Est. Ilf —6F 32
Roedean Av. Enf —3G 17
Roedean Clo. Enf —3G 17
Roedean Clo. Orp —6F 128
Roedean Cres. SW15 —5C 88
Roedean Dri. Romf —2C 50
Roe End. NW9 —2A 40
Roe Green. —2A 40
Roe Grn. NW9 —3A 40
Roehampton. —6E 88
Roehampton Clo. SW15 —3E 88
Roehampton Dri. Chst —3A 112
Roehampton Ga. SW15 —5C 88
Roehampton High St. SW15 —6E 88
Roehampton Lane. (Junct.) —7F 88
Roehampton La. SW15 —3E 88
Roehampton Va. SW15 —9D 88
Roe La. NW9 —2M 39
Rofant Rd. N'wd —6C 20
Roffey Clo. Purl —8M 137
Roffey St. E14 —3A 78
Rogate Ho. E5 —8E 44
Roger Dowley Ct. E2 —5G 61
Roger Harriss Almshouses. E15 —4D 62
(off Gift La.)
Roger Reede's Almshouses. Romf —2C 50
Rogers Ct. Swan —8E 114
Rogers Est. E2 —6G 61
Rogers Gdns. Dag —1L 65
Rogers Ho. SW1 —5H 75
(off Page St.)
Roger's Ho. Dag —8L 49
Rogers La. Warl —9K 139
Rogers Rd. E16 —9D 62
Rogers Rd. SW17 —1B 106
Rogers Rd. Dag —1L 65
Rogers Ruff. N'wd —8A 20
Roger St. WC1 —7K 59
Rogers Wlk. N12 —3M 25
Rohere Ho. EC1 —6A 60
Rojack Rd. SE23 —7H 93
Rokeby Gdns. Wfd G —8E 30
Rokeby Pl. SW20 —4F 104
Rokeby Rd. SE4 —1K 93
Rokeby Rd. Harr —1B 38
Rokeby St. E15 —4B 62
Roke Clo. Kenl —6A 138
Rokell Ho. Beck —2M 109
(off Beckenham Hill Rd.)
Roke Lodge Rd. Kenl —5M 137
Roke Rd. Kenl —7A 138
Rokesby Clo. Well —1B 96
Rokesby Pl. Wemb —1H 55
Rokesly Av. N8 —3J 43
Roland Gdns. SW7 —6A 74
Roland Ho. SW7 —6A 74
(off Cranley M.)
Roland M. E1 —8H 61
Roland Rd. E17 —2B 46
Roland Way. SE17 —6B 76
Roland Way. SW7 —6A 74
Roland Way. Wor Pk —4D 120
Roles Gro. Romf —2H 49
Rolfe Clo. Barn —6C 14
Rolinsden Way. Kes —7H 127
Rolland Ho. W7 —8C 54
Rollesby Rd. Chess —8L 119
Rollesby Way. SE28 —9G 65
Rolleston Av. Orp —1M 127
Rolleston Clo. Orp —2M 127
Rolleston Rd. S Croy —9B 124
Roll Gdns. Ilf —3L 47
Rollins St. SE15 —7G 77
Rollit Cres. Houn —4L 85
Rollit St. N7 —1L 59
Rollo Rd. Swan —4D 114
Rolls Bldgs. EC4 —9L 59
Rollscourt Av. SE24 —4A 92
Rolls Pk. Av. E4 —5L 29
Rolls Pk. Rd. E4 —5M 29
Rolls Pas. WC2 —9L 59
(off Chancery La.)
Rolls Rd. SE1 —6D 76
Rolt St. SE8 —7J 77
(in two parts)
Rolvenden Gdns. Brom —4H 111
Rolvenden Pl. N17 —8E 28
Roman Clo. W3 —3M 71
Roman Clo. Felt —4G 85
Roman Clo. Rain —5B 66
Romanfield Rd. SW2 —6K 91
Roman Gdns. K Lan —3A 4
Roman Ho. EC2 —8A 60
(off Wood St.)
Romanhurst Av. Brom —8C 110
Romanhurst Gdns. Brom —8C 110
Roman Ind. Est. Croy —2C 124
Roman Ri. SE19 —3B 108
Roman Rd. E2 & E3 —6G 61
Roman Rd. E3 —4K 61
Roman Rd. E6 —7H 63
Roman Rd. N10 —7F 26
Roman Rd. NW2 —8G 41
Roman Rd. W4 —5C 72
Roman Rd. Ilf —2M 63
Roman Sq. SE28 —2E 80
Roman Wlk. Rad —1D 10
Roman Way. N7 —2K 59
Roman Way. SE15 —8G 77
Roman Way. Cars —1D 136
Roman Way. Croy —4M 123
Roman Way. Dart —4C 98
Roman Way. Enf —7D 16
Romany Gdns. E17 —8J 29
Romany Gdns. Sutt —2L 121
Romany Ri. Orp —3A 128
Roma Read Clo. SW15 —6F 88
Roma Rd. E17 —1J 45
Romayne Ho. SW4 —2H 91
Romberg Rd. SW17 —9E 90
Romborough Gdns. SE13 —4A 94
Romborough Way. SE13 —4A 94
Rom Cres. Romf —5D 50
Romeland. Els —8H 11
Romeland. Wal A —6J 7
Romero Clo. SW9 —2K 91
Romero Sq. SE3 —3G 95
Romeyn Rd. SW16 —9K 91
Romford. —3C 50
Romford Greyhound Stadium. —4A 50
Romford Ice Rink. —5C 50
Romford Rd. E15 & E7 —2C 62
Romford Rd. Ave —1M 83
Romford Rd. Chig —3F 32
Romford Rd. Romf —7J 33
Romford St. E1 —8E 60
Romilly Dri. Wat —4J 21
Romilly Rd. N4 —7M 43
Romilly St. W1 —1H 75
Romily Ct. SW6 —1J 89
Rommany Rd. SE27 —1B 108
(in two parts)
Romney Chase. Horn —4L 51
Romney Clo. N17 —8F 28
Romney Clo. NW11 —6A 42
Romney Clo. SE14 —8G 77
Romney Clo. Ashf —2A 100
Romney Clo. Chess —6J 119
Romney Clo. Harr —5L 37
Romney Ct. NW3 —2C 58
Romney Ct. W12 —3H 73
(off Shepherd's Bush Grn.)
Romney Dri. Brom —4H 111
Romney Dri. Harr —5L 37
Romney Gdns. Bexh —9K 81
Romney M. W1 —8E 58
Romney Pde. Hay —5B 52
Romney Rd. SE10 —7B 78
Romney Rd. Hay —5B 52
Romney Rd. N Mald —1B 120
Romney Row. NW2 —7H 41
(off Brent Ter.)
Romney St. SW1 —4J 75
Romola Rd. SE24 —7M 91
Romsey Clo. Orp —6M 127
Romsey Gdns. Dag —4H 65
Romsey Rd. W13 —1E 70
Romsey Rd. Dag —4H 65
Romulus Ct. Bren —8H 71
Rom Valley Way. Romf —5C 50
Ronald Av. E15 —6C 62
Ronald Buckingham Ct. SE16 —3G 77
(off Kenning St.)
Ronald Clo. Beck —8K 109
Ronald Ct. Brick W —2K 5
Ronald Ct. New Bar —5M 13
Ronald Ho. SE3 —3G 95
Ronald Rd. Romf —8L 35
Ronaldshay. N4 —6L 43
Ronalds Rd. N7 —1L 59
(in three parts)
Ronalds Rd. Brom —5E 110
Ronaldstone Rd. Sidc —5C 96
Ronald St. E1 —9G 61
Rona Rd. NW3 —9E 42
Ronart St. W'stone —1D 38
Rona Wlk. N1 —2B 60
(off Ramsey Wlk.)
Rondel Ct. Bex —5J 97
Rondu Rd. NW2 —1J 57
Ronelean Rd. Surb —4K 119
Roneo Corner. Horn —6D 50
Roneo Link. Horn —6D 50
Ronfearn Av. Orp —9H 113
Ron Leighton Way. E6 —4J 63
Ronneby Clo. Wey —5C 116
Ronver Rd. SE12 —7D 94
Rood La. EC3 —1C 76
Rookby Ct. N21 —2M 27
Rook Clo. Horn —3E 66
Rook Clo. Wemb —8M 39
Rookeries Clo. Felt —9F 84
Rookery Clo. NW9 —3D 40
Rookery Cres. Dag —3M 65
Rookery Dri. Chst —1A 128
Rookery Gdns. Orp & St M —9G 113
Rookery La. Brom —1H 127
Rookery Rd. SW4 —3G 91
Rookery Rd. Orp —2K 141
Rookery, The. —9F 8
Rookery Way. NW9 —3D 40
Rookesley Rd. Orp —2H 129
Rooke Way. SE10 —6D 78
Rookfield Av. N10 —2G 43
Rookfield Clo. N10 —2G 43
Rookley Clo. Sutt —1M 135
Rooksmead Rd. Sun —6E 100
Rooks Ter. W Dray —3J 143
Rookstone Rd. SW17 —2D 106
Rook Wlk. E6 —9H 63
Rookwood Av. N Mald —8E 104
Rookwood Av. Wall —6H 123
Rookwood Gdns. E4 —2D 30
Rookwood Ho. Bark —5B 64
Rookwood Rd. N16 —5D 44
Roosevelt Way. Dag —2B 66
Rootes Dri. W10 —8H 57
Ropemaker Rd. SE16 —3J 77
Ropemaker's Field. E14 —1K 77
Ropemakers Fields. E14 —1K 77
Ropemaker St. EC2 —8B 60
Roper La. SE1 —3C 76
Ropers Av. E4 —5M 29
Ropers Orchard. SW3 —7C 74
(off Danvers St.)
Roper St. SE9 —4K 95
Ropers Wlk. SW2 —6L 91
Roper Way. Mitc —6E 106
Ropery Bus. Pk. SE7 —5G 79
Ropery St. E3 —7K 61
Rope St. SE16 —5J 77
Rope Wlk. Sun —7G 101
Rope Wlk. Gdns. E1 —9E 60
Rope Yd. Rails. SE18 —4M 79
Ropley St. E2 —5E 60
Rosa Alba M. N5 —9A 44
Rosalind Ct. Bark —3E 64
(off Meadow Rd.)
Rosalind Ho. N1 —5C 60
(off Arden Ho.)
Rosaline Rd. SW6 —8J 73
Rosaline Ter. SW6 —8J 73
(off Rosaline Rd.)
Rosamond St. SE26 —9F 92
Rosamund Clo. S Croy —6B 124
Rosamun St. S'hall —5J 69
Rosary Clo. Houn —1J 85
Rosary Gdns. SW7 —5A 74
Rosary Gdns. Ashf —1A 100
Rosary Gdns. Bush —9C 10
Rosaville Rd. SW6 —8K 73
Roscoe St. EC1 —7A 60
(in two parts)
Roscoe St. Est. EC1 —7A 60
Roscoff Clo. Edgw —8A 24
Roseacre Clo. W13 —8F 54
Roseacre Clo. Horn —5K 51
Roseacre Rd. Well —2F 96
Rose All. EC2 —8C 60
(off Bishopsgate)
Rose All. SE1 —2A 76
Rose & Crown Ct. EC2 —9A 60
(off Foster La.)
Rose & Crown Pas. Isw'th —9E 70
Rose & Crown Yd. SW1 —2G 75
Roseary Clo. W Dray —5H 143
Rose Av. E18 —9F 30
Rose Av. Mitc —5D 106
Rose Av. Mord —9A 106
Rosebank. SE20 —4F 108
Rosebank. SW6 —8G 73
Rosebank. W3 —9B 56
Rosebank. Eps —6A 134
Rosebank. Wal A —6L 7
Rosebank Av. Horn —1G 67
Rosebank Av. Wemb —9D 38
Rose Bank Clo. N12 —5C 26
Rosebank Clo. Tedd —3E 102
Rosebank Gdns. E3 —5K 61
Rosebank Gdns. W3 —9B 56
Rosebank Gro. E17 —1K 45
Rosebank Rd. E17 —4M 45
Rosebank Rd. W7 —3C 70
Rosebank Vs. E17 —2L 45
Rosebank Wlk. NW1 —3H 59
Rosebank Wlk. SE18 —5J 79
Rosebank Way. W3 —9B 56
Rose Bates Dri. NW9 —2L 39
Roseberry Av. T Hth —6A 108
Roseberry Ct. Wat —3E 8
Roseberry Gdns. N4 —4M 43
Roseberry Gdns. Dart —6G 99
Roseberry Gdns. Orp —5C 128
Roseberry Pl. E8 —2D 60
Roseberry St. SE1 —5F 76
Rosebery Av. E12 —2J 63
Rosebery Av. EC1 —7L 59
Rosebery Av. N17 —9E 28
Rosebery Av. Eps —6C 134
Rosebery Av. Harr —9J 37
Rosebery Av. N Mald —6D 104
Rosebery Av. Sidc —6C 96
Rosebery Clo. Mord —1H 121
Rosebery Ct. EC1 —7L 59
(off Rosebery Av.)
Rosebery Gdns. N8 —3J 43
Rosebery Gdns. W13 —9E 54
Rosebery Gdns. Sutt —6M 121
Rosebery Ho. E2 —5H 61
(off Sewardstone Rd.)
Rosebery Ind. Est. N17 —9F 28
Rosebery Ind. Pk. N17 —9F 28
Rosebery M. N10 —9G 27
Rosebery Rd. N9 —3E 28
Rosebery Rd. N10 —9G 27
Rosebery Rd. SW2 —5J 91
Rosebery Rd. Bush —9M 9
Rosebery Rd. Houn —4A 86
Rosebery Rd. King T —6M 103
Rosebery Rd. Sutt —8K 121
Rosebery Sq. EC1 —7L 59
(off Rosebery Av.)
Rosebery Sq. King T —6M 103
Rosebine Av. Twic —6B 86
Rosebriars. Esh —7A 118
(in two parts)
Rosebriar Wlk. Wat —9D 4
Rosebury Rd. SW6 —1M 89
Rosebury Sq. Wfd G —7L 31
Rosebury Va. Ruis —7E 36
Rose Bush Ct. NW3 —1D 58
Rosebushes. Eps —8F 134
Rose Cotts. Brick —3M 5
Rose Cotts. Kes —3G 141
Rose Ct. E1 —8D 60
(off Wentworth St.)
Rose Ct. Chesh —1A 6
Rose Ct. S Harr —7A 38
Rose Ct. Wemb —5J 55
(off Vicars Bri. Clo.)
Rosecourt Rd. Croy —1K 123
Rosecroft. N14 —2H 27
Rosecroft Av. NW3 —8L 41
Rosecroft Clo. Big H —9K 141
Rosecroft Clo. Orp —1G 129
Rosecroft Ct. N'wd —6A 20
Rosecroft Dri. Wat —9C 4
Rosecroft Gdns. NW2 —8E 40
Rosecroft Gdns. Twic —7B 86
Rosecroft Rd. S'hall —7L 53
Rosecroft Wlk. Pinn —3H 37
Rosecroft Wlk. Wemb —1H 55
Rosedale. —1A 6
Rosedale. Asht —9G 133
Rose Dale. Orp —4M 127
Rosedale Av. Chesh —2A 6
Rosedale Av. Hay —8B 52
Rosedale Clo. SE2 —4F 80
Rosedale Clo. W7 —3D 70
Rosedale Clo. Brick W —3J 5
Rosedale Clo. Dart —6M 99
Rosedale Clo. Stan —6F 22
Rosedale Ct. N5 —9M 43
Rosedale Ct. Harr —9D 38
Rosedale Gdns. Dag —3F 64
Rosedale Ho. N16 —6B 44

St Mary's App.—Saltram Cres.

St Mary's App. E12 —1K 63
St Mary's Av. E11 —5F 46
St Mary's Av. N3 —9J 25
St Mary's Av. Brom —7C 110
St Mary's Av. N'wd —5C 20
St Mary's Av. Stanw —6B 144
St Mary's Av. Tedd —3D 102
St Mary's Av. Central. S'hall —5M 69
St Mary's Av. N. S'hall —5M 69
St Mary's Av. S. S'hall —5M 69
St Mary's Clo. N17 —8D 28
St Mary's Clo. Chess —9K 119
St Mary's Clo. Eps —9D 120
St Mary's Clo. Orp —6F 112
St Mary's Clo. Stanw —6B 144
St Mary's Clo. Sun —8E 100
St Mary's Clo. Wat —6F 8
(off Church St.)
St Mary's Ct. E6 —7K 63
St Mary's Ct. SE7 —8H 79
St Mary's Ct. W5 —3H 71
St Mary's Ct. W12 —4D 72
St Mary's Ct. Wall —6G 123
St Mary's Cres. NW4 —1F 40
St Mary's Cres. Hay —1D 68
St Mary's Cres. Iswth —8B 70
St Mary's Cres. Stanw —6B 144
St Mary's Dri. Felt —6A 84
St Mary's Est. SE16 —3G 77
(off St Marychurch St.)
St Mary's Flats. NW1 —6H 59
St Mary's Gdns. SE11 —5L 75
St Mary's Ga. W8 —4M 73
St Mary's Grn. N2 —9A 26
St Mary's Grn. Big H —9G 141
St Mary's Gro. N1 —2M 59
St Mary's Gro. SW13 —2F 88
St Mary's Gro. W4 —7M 71
St Mary's Gro. Big H —9G 141
St Mary's Gro. Rich —3K 87
St Mary's Ho. N1 —4M 59
(off St Mary's Path)
St Mary's La. N Ock & Upm —7L 51
St Mary's Mans. W2 —8B 58
St Mary's M. NW6 —3M 57
(in two parts)
St Marys M. Rich —8G 87
St Mary's Path. N1 —4M 59
St Mary's Pl. SE9 —5K 95
St Mary's Pl. W5 —3H 71
St Mary's Pl. W8 —4M 73
St Mary's Rd. E10 —8A 46
St Mary's Rd. E13 —5F 62
St Mary's Rd. N8 —2J 43
St Mary's Rd. N9 —1F 28
St Mary's Rd. NW10 —4C 56
St Mary's Rd. NW11 —5J 41
St Mary's Rd. SE15 —9G 77
St Mary's Rd. SE25 —7C 108
St Mary's Rd. SW19 —2J 105
St Marys Rd. W5 —3H 71
St Mary's Rd. Barn —9D 14
St Mary's Rd. Bex —7A 98
St Mary's Rd. Chesh —2C 6
St Mary's Rd. Dit H —2G 119
St Mary's Rd. E Mol —9B 102
St Mary's Rd. Hay —1D 68
St Mary's Rd. Ilf —7B 48
St Mary's Rd. S Croy —2B 138
St Mary's Rd. Surb —1H 119
St Mary's Rd. Swan —8B 114
St Mary's Rd. Wat —6F 8
St Mary's Rd. Wey —6B 116
St Mary's Rd. Wor Pk —4C 120
St Mary's Sq. W2 —8B 58
St Mary's Sq. W5 —3H 71
St Mary's Ter. W2 —8B 58
St Mary's Tower. EC1 —7A 60
(off Fortune St.)
St Mary St. SE18 —5K 79
St Mary's Vw. Harr —3G 39
St Mary's Vw. Wat —6G 9
(off King St.)
St Mary's Wlk. SE11 —5L 75
St Mary's Wlk. Hay —1D 68
St Mary's Way. Chig —5L 31
St Matthew Clo. Uxb —9B 142
St Matthew's Av. Surb —3J 119
St Matthew's Clo. Rain —3E 66
St Matthews Clo. Wat —8H 9
St Matthews Ct. E10 —5M 45
(off Capworth St.)
St Matthews Ct. N10 —9E 26
St Matthews Ct. SE1 —4A 76
(off Meadow Row)
St Matthew's Dri. Brom —7K 111
St Matthews Ho. SE17 —7B 76
(off Phelp St.)
St Matthew's Lodge. NW1 —5G 59
(off Oakley Sq.)
St Matthew's Rd. SW2 —3K 91
St Matthew's Rd. W5 —2J 71
St Matthew's Row. E2 —6E 60
St Matthew St. SW1 —4H 75
St Matthias Clo. NW9 —3D 40
St Maur Rd. SW6 —9K 73
St Mellion Clo. SE28 —9H 65
St Merryn Clo. SE18 —8B 80
St Merryn Ct. Beck —4L 109
St Michael's All. EC3 —9B 60
St Michael's Av. N9 —9G 17
St Michael's Av. Wemb —2L 55
St Michaels Clo. E16 —8H 63
St Michael's Clo. N3 —9K 25
St Michael's Clo. N12 —5C 26
St Michael's Clo. Brom —7J 111
St Michael's Clo. Eri —3H 81
St Michael's Clo. W on T —4G 117
St Michael's Clo. Wor Pk —4D 120
St Michaels Ct. E14 —8A 62
(off St Leonards Rd.)
St Michael's Ct. SE1 —3A 76
(off Trinity St.)
St Michael's Ct. Wey —7A 116
(off Princes Rd.)
St Michael's Cres. Pinn —4J 37
St Michaels Dri. Wat —6F 4
St Michael's Flats. NW1 —5H 59
(off Aldenham St.)
St Michael's Gdns. W10 —8J 57
St Michael's Pde. Wat —2F 8
St Michael's Ri. Well —9F 80
St Michael's Rd. NW2 —9G 41
St Michael's Rd. SW9 —1K 91
St Michael's Rd. Croy —3A 124
St Michael's Rd. Wall —8G 123
St Michael's Rd. Well —2F 96
St Michael's St. W2 —9B 58
St Michaels Ter. N6 —6E 42
(off South Gro.)
St Michael's Ter. N22 —8J 27
St Mildred's Ct. EC2 —9B 60
St Mildreds Rd. SE6 —6C 94
St Mirren Ct. New Bar —7A 14
St Neots Clo. Borwd —2L 11
St Neot's Rd. Romf —7K 35
St Nicholas Av. Horn —8E 50
St Nicholas Cen. Sutt —7M 121
St Nicholas Clo. Els —8H 11
St Nicholas Clo. Uxb —9B 142
St Nicholas Ct. King T —8J 103
(off Surbiton Rd.)
St Nicholas' Flats. NW1 —5H 59
(off Werrington St.)
St Nicholas Glebe. SW17 —2E 106
St Nicholas Ho. SE8 —7L 77
(off Deptford Grn.)
St Nicholas Rd. SE18 —6D 80
St Nicholas Rd. Sutt —7M 121
St Nicholas Rd. Th Dit —1D 118
St Nicholas St. SE8 —9K 77
St Nicholas Way. Sutt —6M 121
St Nicolas La. Chst —5J 111
St Ninian's Ct. N20 —3D 26
St Norbert Grn. SE4 —3J 93
St Norbert Rd. SE4 —4H 93
St Normans Way. Eps —2E 134
St Olaf Ho. SE1 —2B 76
(off Tooley St.)
St Olaf's Rd. SW6 —8J 73
St Olaf Stairs. SE1 —2B 76
(off Tooley St.)
St Olave's Ct. EC2 —9B 60
St Olave's Est. SE1 —3C 76
St Olave's Gdns. SE11 —5L 75
St Olave's Mans. SE11 —5L 75
(off Walnut Tree Wlk.)
St Olave's Rd. E6 —4L 63
St Olave's Ter. SE1 —3C 76
(off Fair St.)
St Olaves Wlk. SW16 —6G 107
St Onge Pde. Enf —5B 16
(off Southbury Rd.)
St Oswald's Pl. SE11 —6K 75
St Oswald's Rd. SW16 —5M 107
St Oswulf St. SW1 —5H 75
(off Erasmus St.)
St Owen Ho. SE1 —4C 76
(off Fendall St.)
St Pancras. —6J 59
St Pancras Commercial Cen. NW1 —4G 59
(off Pratt St.)
St Pancras Ct. N2 —9B 26
St Pancras Way. NW1 —3G 59
St Patrick's Ct. E4 —7C 30
St Paul Clo. Uxb —8B 142
St Paul's All. EC4 —9M 59
(off St Paul's Chyd.)
St Paul's Av. NW2 —2F 56
St Paul's Av. SE16 —2H 77
St Paul's Av. Harr —2K 39
St Paul's Cathedral. —9A 60
St Paul's Chyd. EC4 —9M 59
(in two parts)
St Pauls Clo. SE7 —6H 79
St Paul's Clo. W5 —3K 71
St Paul's Clo. Ashf —2A 100
St Paul's Clo. Ave —1M 83
St Paul's Clo. Cars —3C 122
St Paul's Clo. Chess —6H 119
St Paul's Clo. Hay —6B 68
St Paul's Clo. Houn —1J 85
St Pauls Ct. SW4 —4H 91
St Paul's Ct. Houn —2J 85
St Pauls Courtyard. SE8 —8L 77
St Paul's Cray. —6F 112
St Paul's Cray Rd. Chst —5B 112
St Paul's Cres. NW1 —3H 59
(in two parts)
St Paul's Dri. E15 —1B 62
St Paul's M. NW1 —3H 59
St Paul's Pl. N1 —2B 60
St Pauls Pl. Ave —1M 83
St Paul's Ri. N13 —6M 27
St Paul's Rd. N1 —2M 59
St Paul's Rd. N17 —7E 28
St Paul's Rd. Bark —4A 64
St Paul's Rd. Bren —7H 71
St Paul's Rd. Eri —8A 82
St Paul's Rd. Rich —2K 87
St Paul's Rd. T Hth —7A 108
St Paul's Shrubbery. N1 —2B 60
St Paul's Sq. Brom —6D 110
St Paul's Studios. W6 —6J 73
(off Talgarth Rd.)
St Pauls Ter. SE17 —7M 75
St Pauls Tower. E10 —5M 45
(off Beaumont Rd.)
St Paul St. N1 —4A 60
(in two parts)
St Pauls Vw. Apartments. WC1 —6L 59
(off Amwell St.)
St Paul's Wlk. King T —4L 103
St Pauls Way. E3 —8K 61
St Paul's Way. N3 —7M 25
St Pauls Way. Wal A —6K 7
St Pauls Way. Wat —4G 9
St Paul's Wood Hill. Orp —6C 112
St Peter's All. EC3 —9B 60
(off Cornhill)
St Peter's Av. E2 —5E 60
St Peter's Av. E17 —2C 46
St Peters Av. N2 —7C 26
St Peter's Av. N18 —4E 28
St Peters Av. Berr G —8M 141
St Petersburgh M. W2 —1M 73
St Petersburgh Pl. W2 —1M 73
St Peter's Cen. E1 —2F 76
(off Watts St.)
St Peters Chu. Clo. N1 —4M 59
(off Devonia Rd.)
St Peter's Clo. E2 —5E 60
St Peter's Clo. SW17 —8C 90
St Peter's Clo. Barn —7F 12
St Peters Clo. Bus H —1B 22
St Peter's Clo. Chst —4B 112
St Peter's Clo. Ilf —2C 48
St Peter's Clo. Ruis —7H 37
St Peter's Ct. NW4 —3G 41
St Peters Ct. W Mol —8L 101
St Peter's Gdns. SE27 —9L 91
St Peter's Gro. W6 —5E 72
St Peters Ho. SE17 —7B 76
St Peter's Ho. WC1 —6J 59
(off Regent Sq.)
St Peter's La. St P —6E 112
St Peters Pl. W9 —7M 57
St Peter's Rd. N9 —1F 28
St Peter's Rd. W6 —6E 72
St Peter's Rd. Croy —6B 124
St Peter's Rd. King T —6L 103
St Peter's Rd. S'hall —8L 53
St Peter's Rd. Twic —4F 86
St Peters Rd. Uxb —8B 142
St Peter's Rd. W Mol —8L 101
St Peter's Sq. E2 —5E 60
St Peter's Sq. W6 —5D 72
St Peter's St. N1 —4M 59
St Peter's St. S Croy —7B 124
St Peter's St. M. N1 —5M 59
(off St Peters St.)
St Peter's Ter. SW6 —8K 73
St Peter's Vs. W6 —5E 72
St Peter's Way. N1 —3C 60
St Peter's Way. W5 —8H 55
St Peter's Way. Hay —6B 68
St Peter's Wharf. W4 —6E 72
St Philip Ho. WC1 —6L 59
(off Lloyd Baker St.)
St Philips Av. N2 —7C 26
St Philip's Av. Wor Pk —4F 120
St Philip's Ga. Wor Pk —4F 120
St Philip Sq. SW8 —1F 90
St Philip's Rd. E8 —2E 60
St Philips Rd. Surb —1H 119
St Philip St. SW8 —1F 90
St Philip's Way. N1 —4A 60
St Quentin Rd. Well —2D 96
St Quintin Av. W10 —8G 57
St Quintin Gdns. W10 —8G 57
St Quintin Rd. E13 —6F 62
St Raphael's Way. NW10 —1A 56
St Regis Clo. N10 —9F 26
St Regis Heights. NW3 —8M 41
St Richard's Ho. NW1 —6H 59
(off Eversholt St.)
St Ronan's Clo. Barn —2B 14
St Ronan's Cres. Wfd G —7E 30
St Rule St. SW8 —1G 91
St Saviour's College. SE27 —1B 108
St Saviour's Ct. N10 —9F 26
(off Alexandra Pk. Rd.)
St Saviours Ct. Harr —3C 38
St Saviour's Est. SE1 —3D 76
St Saviour's Rd. SW2 —4K 91
St Saviour's Rd. Croy —1M 123
St Saviour's Wharf. SE1 —3D 76
(off Shad Thames)
St Saviour's Wharf. SE1 —3D 76
(off Mill St.)
Saints Clo. SE27 —1M 107
Saints Dri. E7 —1H 63
St Silas Pl. NW5 —2E 58
St Simon's Av. SW15 —4G 89
St Stephen's Av. E17 —3A 46
St Stephen's Av. W12 —3F 72
(in two parts)
St Stephen's Av. W13 —9F 54
St Stephen's Av. Asht —8J 133
St Stephen's Clo. E17 —3M 45
St Stephen's Clo. NW8 —4C 58
St Stephen's Clo. S'hall —8L 53
St Stephens Ct. N8 —4K 43
St Stephens Ct. W13 —9F 54
St Stephen's Ct. Enf —8C 16
(off Park Av.)
St Stephen's Cres. W2 —9L 57
St Stephen's Cres. T Hth —7L 107
St Stephen's Gdns. SW15 —4K 89
St Stephen's Gdns. W2 —9L 57
(in two parts)
St Stephen's Gdns. Twic —5G 87
St Stephens Gro. SE13 —2A 94
St Stephens Ho. SE17 —7B 76
(off Lytham St.)
St Stephens M. W2 —8L 57
St Stephens Pde. E7 —3G 63
St Stephen's Pas. Twic —5G 87
St Stephen's Rd. E3 —4J 61
St Stephen's Rd. E6 —3G 63
St Stephen's Rd. E17 —3M 45
St Stephen's Rd. W13 —9F 54
St Stephen's Rd. Barn —7H 13
St Stephens Rd. Enf —1H 17
St Stephen's Rd. Houn —5L 85
St Stephen's Rd. W Dray —2H 143
St Stephen's Row. EC4 —9B 60
(off Walbrook)
St Stephen's Ter. SW8 —8K 75
St Stephen's Wlk. SW7 —5A 74
(off Southwell Gdns.)
St Swithins La. EC4 —1B 76
St Swithun's Rd. SE13 —5B 94
St Theresa Clo. Eps —6A 134
St Theresa Ct. E4 —9B 18
St Theresa's Rd. Felt —3D 84
St Thomas Clo. Surb —3K 119
St Thomas Ct. E10 —5M 45
(off Beaumont Rd.)
St Thomas Ct. Bex —6L 97
St Thomas Ct. Pinn —8J 21
St Thomas Dri. Orp —3A 128
St Thomas Dri. Pinn —8J 21
St Thomas Gdns. Ilf —2A 64
St Thomas Ho. E1 —9H 61
(off W. Arbour St.)
St Thomas Rd. E16 —9E 62
St Thomas Rd. N14 —9H 15
St Thomas Rd. W4 —7A 72
St Thomas Rd. Belv —3A 82
St Thomas's Gdns. NW5 —2E 58
St Thomas's Pl. E9 —3G 61
St Thomas's Rd. N4 —7L 43
St Thomas's Rd. NW10 —4C 56
St Thomas's Sq. E9 —3G 61
St Thomas St. SE1 —2B 76
St Thomas's Way. SW6 —8K 73
St Timothys M. Brom —5F 110
St Ursula Gro. Pinn —3H 37
St Ursula Rd. S'hall —9L 53
St Vincent Clo. SE27 —2M 107
St Vincent De Paul Ho. E1 —8G 61
(off Jubilee St.)
St Vincent Ho. SE1 —4D 76
(off Fendall St.)
St Vincent Rd. Twic —5A 86
St Vincent Rd. W on T —5F 116
St Vincents Av. Dart —4L 99
St Vincent's Cotts. Wat —6F 8
(off Marlborough Rd.)
St Vincent's Hamlet. —1M 35
St Vincents Rd. Dart —5L 99
St Vincent St. W1 —8E 58
St Vincents Vs. Dart —5J 99
St Wilfrid's Clo. Barn —7C 14
St Wilfrid's Rd. New Bar —7C 14
St Winefride's Av. E12 —1K 63
St Winifreds. Kenl —7A 138
St Winifred's Clo. Chig —5A 32
St Winifred's Rd. Big H —9K 141
St Winifred's Rd. Tedd —3F 102
Saladin Dri. Purf —5L 83
Sala Ho. SE3 —3F 94
Salamanca Pl. SE1 —5K 75
Salamanca St. SE1 & SE11 —5K 75
Salamander Clo. King T —2G 103
Salamander Quay. King T —5H 103
Salamons Way. Rain —9C 66
Salcombe Dri. Mord —3H 121
Salcombe Dri. Romf —4K 49
Salcombe Gdns. NW7 —6G 25
Salcombe Pk. Lou —7H 19
Salcombe Rd. E17 —5K 45
Salcombe Rd. N16 —1C 60
Salcombe Rd. Ashf —9C 144
Salcombe Way. Hay —6B 52
Salcombe Way. Ruis —7E 36
Salcot Cres. New Ad —2A 140
Salcott Rd. SW11 —4C 90
Salcott Rd. Croy —5J 123
Salehurst Clo. Harr —3J 39
Salehurst Rd. SE4 —5K 93
Salem Pl. Croy —5A 124
Salem Rd. W2 —1M 73
Sale Pl. W2 —8C 58
Sale St. E2 —7E 60
Salford Ho. E14 —5A 78
(off Seyssel St.)
Salford Rd. SW2 —7H 91
Salhouse Clo. SE28 —9G 65
Salisbury Av. N3 —1K 41
Salisbury Av. Bark —3B 64
Salisbury Av. Sutt —8K 121
Salisbury Av. Swan —8E 114
Salisbury Clo. SE17 —5B 76
Salisbury Clo. Wor Pk —5D 120
Salisbury Ct. EC4 —9M 59
Salisbury Ct. Cars —7D 122
Salisbury Ct. Enf —6B 16
(off London Rd.)
Salisbury Ct. N'holt —1M 53
(off Newmarket Av.)
Salisbury Cres. Chesh —5D 6
Salisbury Gdns. SW19 —4J 105
Salisbury Gdns. Buck H —2H 31
Salisbury Hall Gdns. E4 —6L 29
Salisbury Ho. E14 —9M 61
(off Hobday St.)
Salisbury Ho. EC2 —8B 60
(off London Wall)
Salisbury Ho. N1 —4M 59
(off St Mary's Path)
Salisbury Ho. SW1 —6H 75
(off Drummond Ga.)
Salisbury Ho. SW9 —8L 75
(off Cranmer Rd.)
Salisbury Ho. Stan —6E 22
Salisbury Mans. N4 —3M 43
Salisbury M. SW6 —8K 73
Salisbury Pas. SW6 —8K 73
(off Dawes Rd.)
Salisbury Pavement. SW6 —8K 73
(off Dawes Rd.)
Salisbury Pl. SW9 —8M 75
Salisbury Pl. W1 —8D 58
Salisbury Rd. E4 —3L 29
Salisbury Rd. E7 —2E 62
Salisbury Rd. E10 —7A 46
Salisbury Rd. E12 —1H 63
Salisbury Rd. E17 —3A 46
Salisbury Rd. N4 —3M 43
Salisbury Rd. N9 —3E 28
Salisbury Rd. N22 —8M 27
Salisbury Rd. SE25 —1E 124
Salisbury Rd. SW19 —4J 105
Salisbury Rd. W13 —3F 70
Salisbury Rd. Bans —6M 135
Salisbury Rd. Barn —5J 13
Salisbury Rd. Bex —7L 97
Salisbury Rd. Brom —9J 111
Salisbury Rd. Cars —8D 122
Salisbury Rd. Dag —2M 65
Salisbury Rd. Enf —1K 17
Salisbury Rd. Felt —7G 85
Salisbury Rd. Harr —3B 38
Salisbury Rd. Houn —2G 85
Salisbury Rd. Ilf —7C 48
Salisbury Rd. H'row A —4A 84
Salisbury Rd. N Mald —7B 104
Salisbury Rd. Pinn —2E 36
Salisbury Rd. Rich —3J 87
Salisbury Rd. Romf —3F 50
Salisbury Rd. S'hall —5J 69
Salisbury Rd. Uxb —5A 142
Salisbury Rd. Wat —2F 8
Salisbury Rd. Wor Pk —6B 120
Salisbury Sq. EC4 —9L 59
Salisbury St. NW8 —7C 58
Salisbury St. W3 —3A 72
Salisbury Ter. SE15 —2G 93
Salisbury Wlk. N19 —7G 43
Salix Clo. Sun —4F 100
Salix Ct. N3 —6L 25
Salliesfield. Twic —5B 86
Sally Murray Clo. E12 —9L 47
(off Grantham Rd.)
Salmen Rd. E13 —5D 62
Salmond Clo. Stan —6E 22
Salmon La. E14 —9J 61
Salmon M. NW6 —1L 57
Salmon Rd. Belv —6L 81
Salmon Rd. Dart —2K 99
Salmons Rd. N9 —1E 28
Salmons Rd. Chess —8J 119
Salmon St. E14 —9K 61
Salmon St. NW9 —6M 39
Salomons Rd. E13 —8G 63
Salop Rd. E17 —4H 45
Saltash Clo. Sutt —6K 121
Saltash Rd. Ilf —7B 32
Saltash Rd. Well —9G 81
Saltbox Hill. Big H —5F 140
Saltcoats Rd. W4 —3C 72
Saltcroft Clo. Wemb —6M 39
Saltdene. N4 —6K 43
Salter Clo. Harr —9K 37
Salterford Rd. SW17 —3E 106
Salter Rd. SE16 —2H 77
Salters Ct. EC4 —9A 60
(off Bow La.)
Salters Gdns. Wat —3E 8
Salters Hall Ct. EC4 —1B 76
(off Cannon St.)
Salter's Hill. SE19 —2B 108
Salters Rd. E17 —2B 46
Salters Rd. W10 —7H 57
Salter St. E14 —1K 77
Salter St. NW10 —6E 56
Salterton Rd. N7 —8K 43
Saltford Clo. Eri —6C 82
Salt Hill Clo. Uxb —1C 142
Saltley Clo. E6 —9J 63
Saltoun Rd. SW2 —3L 91
Saltram Clo. N15 —2D 44
Saltram Cres. W9 —6K 57

Seymour Clo.—Sheridan Ct.

Seymour Clo. Lou —8J 19
Seymour Clo. Pinn —8K 21
Seymour Ct. E4 —2D 30
Seymour Ct. N10 —9E 26
Seymour Ct. N21 —8K 15
Seymour Ct. NW2 —7F 40
Seymour Dri. Brom —3K 127
Seymour Gdns. SE4 —2J 93
Seymour Gdns. Felt —1G 101
Seymour Gdns. Ilf —6K 47
Seymour Gdns. Ruis —6H 37
Seymour Gdns. Surb —9K 103
Seymour Gdns. Twic —6F 86
Seymour Ho. NW1 —6H 59
(off Churchway)
Seymour Ho. WC1 —7J 59
(off Tavistock Pl.)
Seymour Ho. Sutt —8M 121
(off Mulgrave Rd.)
Seymour M. W1 —9E 58
Seymour M. Ewe —2E 134
Seymour Pl. SE25 —8F 108
Seymour Pl. W1 —8D 58
Seymour Rd. E4 —1M 29
Seymour Rd. E6 —5H 63
Seymour Rd. E10 —6K 45
Seymour Rd. N3 —7M 25
Seymour Rd. N8 —3L 43
Seymour Rd. N9 —2F 28
Seymour Rd. SW18 —6K 89
Seymour Rd. SW19 —9H 89
Seymour Rd. W4 —5A 72
Seymour Rd. Cars —7E 122
Seymour Rd. E Mol —9A 102
Seymour Rd. Hamp H —2A 102
Seymour Rd. King T —5H 103
Seymour Rd. Mitc —2E 122
Seymour Rd. Ind. Est. E10 —6K 45
Seymours, The. Lou —3L 19
Seymour St. W2 & W1 —9D 58
Seymour Ter. SE20 —5F 108
Seymour Vs. SE20 —5F 108
Seymour Wlk. SW10 —7A 74
Seymour Way. Sun —4D 100
Seyssel St. E14 —5A 78
Shaa Rd. W3 —1B 72
Shacklegate La. Tedd —1C 102
Shackleton Clo. SE23 —8F 92
Shackleton Ct. E14 —6L 77
(off Maritime Quay)
Shackleton Ct. W12 —3F 72
Shackleton Ho. E1 —2G 77
(off Prusom St.)
Shackleton Ho. NW10 —3B 56
Shackleton Rd. S'hall —1K 69
Shackleton Way. Ab L —5E 4
(off Lysander Way)
Shacklewell. —9D 44
Shacklewell Grn. E8 —9D 44
Shacklewell Ho. E8 —9D 44
Shacklewell La. N16 —1D 60
Shacklewell Rd. N16 —9D 44
Shacklewell Row. E8 —9D 44
Shacklewell St. E2 —6D 60
Shadbolt Clo. Wor Pk —4D 120
Shad Thames. SE1 —2D 76
Shadwell. —1F 76
Shadwell Ct. N'holt —5K 53
Shadwell Dri. N'holt —6K 53
Shadwell Gdns. E1 —1G 77
(off Sutton St.)
Shadwell Pier Head. E1 —1G 77
Shadwell Pl. E1 —1G 77
(off Shadwell Gdns.)
Shadybush Clo. Bush —9A 10
Shady La. Wat —4F 8
Shaef Way. Tedd —4E 102
Shafter Rd. Dag —2A 66
Shaftesbury. Lou —5H 19
Shaftesbury Av. WC1 & WC2 —9J 59
Shaftesbury Av. Enf —4H 17
Shaftesbury Av. Felt —5E 84
Shaftesbury Av. Harr & S Harr —6M 37
Shaftesbury Av. Kent —3H 39
Shaftesbury Av. New Bar —6A 14
Shaftesbury Av. S'hall —5L 69
Shaftesbury Cen. W10 —7H 57
(off Barlby Rd.)
Shaftesbury Circ. S Harr —6A 38
Shaftesbury Ct. E6 —9L 63
(off Sapphire Clo.)
Shaftesbury Ct. N1 —5B 60
(off Shaftesbury St)
Shaftesbury Ct. SW6 —9M 73
(off Maltings Pl.)
Shaftesbury Ct. SW16 —9H 91
Shaftesbury Ct. Crox G —7A 8
Shaftesbury Gdns. NW10 —7C 56
Shaftesbury La. Dart —3M 99
Shaftesbury Lodge. E14 —9M 61
(off Upper N. St.)
Shaftesbury M. SE1 —4B 76
(off Falmouth Rd.)
Shaftesbury M. SW4 —4G 91
Shaftesbury M. W8 —4L 73
(off Stratford Rd.)
Shaftesbury Pde. S Harr —6A 38
Shaftesbury Pl. EC2 —8A 60
(off London Wall)
Shaftesbury Pl. W14 —5K 73
(off Warwick Rd.)
Shaftesbury Point. E13 —5E 62
(off High St.)
Shaftesbury Rd. E4 —1B 30
Shaftesbury Rd. E7 —3G 63
Shaftesbury Rd. E10 —6L 45
Shaftesbury Rd. E17 —4M 45
Shaftesbury Rd. N18 —6C 28
Shaftesbury Rd. N19 —6J 43
Shaftesbury Rd. Beck —6K 109
Shaftesbury Rd. Cars —2B 122
Shaftesbury Rd. Rich —2J 87
Shaftesbury Rd. Romf —4D 50
Shaftesbury Rd. Wat —5G 9
Shaftesburys, The. Bark —5A 64
Shaftesbury St. N1 —5A 60
(in two parts)
Shaftesbury Theatre. —9J 59
(off Shaftesbury Av.)
Shaftesbury Way. K Lan —1A 4
Shaftesbury Way. Twic —9B 86
Shaftesbury Waye. Hay —8G 53
Shafto M. SW1 —4D 74
Shafton M. E9 —4H 61
Shafton Rd. E9 —4H 61
Shaftsbury Ct. SE5 —3B 92
Shaftsbury Ct. Eri —9D 82
(off Selkirk Dri.)
Shafts Ct. EC3 —9C 60
Shahjalal Ho. E2 —5E 60
(off Pritchards Rd.)
Shakespeare Av. N11 —5G 27
Shakespeare Av. NW10 —4B 56
Shakespeare Av. Felt —5E 84
Shakespeare Av. Hay —9E 52
(in two parts)
Shakespeare Ct. New Bar —5M 13
Shakespeare Cres. E12 —2K 63
Shakespeare Cres. NW10 —4B 56
Shakespeare Dri. Harr —4K 39
Shakespeare Gdns. N2 —2D 42
Shakespeare Ho. N14 —2H 27
Shakespeare Ind. Est. Wat —2E 8
Shakespeare Rd. E17 —9H 29
Shakespeare Rd. N3 —8L 25
Shakespeare Rd. NW7 —4D 24
Shakespeare Rd. SE24 —4M 91
Shakespeare Rd. W3 —2A 72
Shakespeare Rd. W7 —1D 70
Shakespeare Rd. Bexh —9J 81
Shakespeare Rd. Dart —3L 99
Shakespeare Rd. Romf —4D 50
Shakespeare's Globe Exhibition. —2A 76
(off Shakespeare's Globe Theatre)
Shakespeare's Globe Theatre. —2A 76
Shakespeare Sq. Ilf —6A 32
Shakespeare St. Wat —2F 8
Shakespeare Tower. EC2 —8A 60
(off Beech St.)
Shakespeare Way. Felt —1G 101
Shakspeare M. N16 —9C 44
Shakspeare Wlk. N16 —9C 44
Shalcomb St. SW10 —7A 74
Shalcross Dri. Chesh —3F 6
Shalden Ho. SW15 —5D 88
Shaldon Dri. Mord —9J 105
Shaldon Dri. Ruis —8G 37
Shaldon Rd. Edgw —9K 23
Shaldon Way. W on T —5G 117
Shalfleet Dri. W10 —1H 73
Shalford Clo. Orp —6A 128
Shalford Ct. N1 —5M 59
(off Charlton Pl.)
Shalford Ho. SE1 —4B 76
Shalimar Gdns. W3 —1A 72
Shalimar Rd. W3 —1A 72
Shallons Rd. SE9 —1M 111
Shalstone Rd. SW14 —2M 87
Shalston Vs. Surb —1K 119
Shamrock Rd. Croy —1K 123
Shamrock St. SW4 —2H 91
Shamrock Way. N14 —1F 26
Shandon Rd. SW4 —5G 91
Shand St. SE1 —3C 76
Shandy St. E1 —8H 61
Shanklin Clo. Chesh —2A 6
Shanklin Gdns. Wat —4G 21
Shanklin Ho. E17 —9K 29
Shanklin Rd. N8 —3H 43
Shannon Clo. NW2 —8H 41
Shannon Clo. S'hall —6H 69
Shannon Corner. (Junct.) —8E 104
Shannon Corner Retail Pk. N Mald —8E 104
Shannon Ct. N16 —8C 44
Shannon Ct. Croy —3A 124
(off Tavistock Rd.)
Shannon Gro. SW9 —3K 91
Shannon Pl. NW8 —5C 58
Shannon Way. Ave —1M 83
Shannon Way. Beck —3M 109
Shanti Ct. SW18 —7L 89
Shap Cres. Cars —3D 122
Shapland Way. N13 —5K 27
Shap St. E2 —5D 60
Shapwick Clo. N11 —5D 26
Shardcroft Av. SE24 —4M 91
Shardeloes Rd. SE14 —1K 93
Shard's Sq. SE15 —7E 76
Sharland Clo. T Hth —1L 123
Sharman Ct. Sidc —1E 112
(off Carlton Rd.)
Sharnbrooke Clo. Well —2G 97
Sharnbrook Ho. W14 —7L 73
Sharon Clo. Eps —5A 134
Sharon Clo. Surb —3G 119
Sharon Ct. S Croy —7A 124
(off Warham Rd.)
Sharon Gdns. E9 —4G 61
Sharon Rd. W4 —6B 72
Sharon Rd. Enf —4J 17
Sharpe Clo. W7 —8D 54
Sharp Ho. SW8 —2F 90
Sharp Ho. Twic —5H 87
Sharpleshall St. NW1 —3D 58
Sharpness Clo. Hay —8J 53
Sharpness Ct. SE15 —8D 76
(off Daniel Gdns.)
Sharp's La. Ruis —5B 36
Sharp Way. Dart —2K 99
Sharratt St. SE15 —7G 77
Sharsted St. SE17 —6M 75
Sharvel La. N'holt —4F 52
Sharwood. WC1 —5K 59
(off Penton Ri.)
Shaver's Pl. SW1 —1H 75
(off Coventry St.)
Shaw Av. Bark —5J 65
Shawbrooke Rd. SE9 —4G 95
Shawbury Rd. SE22 —4D 92
Shaw Clo. SE28 —2F 80
Shaw Clo. Bus H —2C 22
Shaw Clo. Chesh —1C 6
Shaw Clo. Eps —3D 134
Shaw Clo. Horn —6F 50
Shaw Clo. S Croy —4D 138
Shaw Ct. W3 —4A 72
(off All Saints Rd.)
Shaw Cres. S Croy —4D 138
Shaw Dri. W on T —2G 117
Shawfield Ct. W Dray —4J 143
Shawfield Pk. Brom —6H 111
Shawfield St. SW3 —6C 74
Shawford Ct. SW15 —6E 88
Shawford Rd. Eps —8B 120
Shaw Gdns. Bark —5J 65
Shaw Ho. E14 —9J 61
(off Blount St.)
Shaw Ho. E16 —2L 79
(off Claremont St.)
Shaw Ho. Belv —6K 81
Shawley Cres. Eps —9G 135
Shawley Way. Eps —9F 134
Shaw Path. Brom —9D 94
Shaw Rd. SE22 —3C 92
Shaw Rd. Brom —9D 94
Shaw Rd. Enf —3H 17
Shaws Cotts. SE23 —9J 93
Shaws Path. King T —5G 103
(off High St.)
Shaw Sq. E17 —8J 29
Shaw Way. Wall —9J 123
Shaxton Cres. New Ad —1A 140
Shearing Dri. Cars —2A 122
Shearling Way. N7 —2J 59
Shearman Rd. SE3 —3D 94
Shears Clo. Dart —8G 99
Shears Ct. Sun —4C 100
Shears, The. (Junct.) —4C 100
Shearwater Ct. SE8 —7K 77
(off Abinger Gro.)
Shearwater Rd. Sutt —7K 121
Shearwater Way. Hay —9H 53
Shearwood Cres. Dart —2D 98
Sheath's La. Oxs —5A 132
Sheaveshill Av. NW9 —2C 40
Sheaveshill Ct. NW9 —2B 40
Sheaveshill Pde. NW9 —2C 40
(off Sheaveshill Av.)
Sheen Comn. Dri. Rich —3L 87
Sheen Ct. Rich —3L 87
Sheen Ct. Rd. Rich —3L 87
Sheendale Rd. Rich —3K 87
Sheenewood. SE26 —1F 108
Sheen Ga. Gdns. SW14 —3A 88
Sheengate Mans. SW14 —3B 88
Sheen Gro. N1 —4L 59
Sheen La. SW14 —4A 88
Sheen Pk. Rich —3J 87
Sheen Rd. Orp —8D 112
Sheen Rd. Rich —4J 87
Sheen Way. Wall —7K 123
Sheen Wood. SW14 —4A 88
Sheepbarn La. Warl —4D 140
Sheepcot Dri. Wat —7G 5
Sheepcote Clo. Houn —8E 68
Sheepcote La. SW11 —1D 90
Sheepcote La. Orp & Swan —1K 129
Sheepcote Rd. Harr —4D 38
Sheepcotes Rd. Romf —2J 49
Sheepcot La. Wat —6E 4
(in two parts)
Sheephouse Way. N Mald —3B 120
Sheep La. E8 —4F 60
Sheep Wlk. M. SW19 —3H 105
Sheerness M. E16 —3M 79
Sheerwater Rd. E16 —8H 63
Sheffield Dri. Romf —5L 35
Sheffield Gdns. Romf —5L 35
Sheffield Rd. H'row A —5A 84
Sheffield Sq. E3 —6K 61
Sheffield St. WC2 —9K 59
Sheffield Ter. W8 —2L 73
Sheffield Way. H'row A —4B 84
Shefton Ri. N'wd —7E 20
Sheila Clo. Romf —7M 33
Sheila Rd. Romf —7M 33
Sheilings, The. Horn —3K 51
Shelbourne Clo. Pinn —1K 37
Shelbourne Pl. Beck —4K 109
Shelbourne Rd. N17 —9F 28
Shelburne Dri. Houn —5L 85
Shelburne Rd. N7 —9K 43
Shelbury Clo. Sidc —9E 96
Shelbury Rd. SE22 —4F 92
Sheldon Av. N6 —5C 42
Sheldon Av. Ilf —9M 31
Sheldon Clo. SE12 —4F 94
Sheldon Clo. SE20 —5F 108
Sheldon Ct. SW8 —9J 75
(off Lansdowne Grn.)
Sheldon Ct. Barn —6M 13
Sheldon Rd. N18 —4C 28
Sheldon Rd. NW2 —9H 41
Sheldon Rd. Bexh —9K 81
Sheldon Rd. Dag —3J 65
Sheldon St. Croy —5A 124
Sheldrake Clo. E16 —2K 79
Sheldrake Ct. E6 —5J 63
(off St Bartholomew's Rd.)
Sheldrake Ho. SE16 —5H 77
(off Tawny Way)
Sheldrake Pl. W8 —3L 73
Sheldrick Clo. SW19 —6B 106
Shelduck Clo. E15 —1D 62
Shelduck Ct. SE8 —7K 77
(off Pilot Clo.)
Sheldwich Ter. Brom —1J 127
Shelford Pl. N16 —8B 44
Shelford Ri. SE19 —4D 108
Shelford Rd. Barn —8G 13
Shelgate Rd. SW11 —4C 90
Shell Clo. Brom —1J 127
Shellduck Clo. NW9 —9C 24
Shelley. N8 —1J 43
(off Boyton Rd.)
Shelley Av. E12 —2J 63
Shelley Av. Gnfd —6B 54
Shelley Av. Horn —7D 50
Shelley Clo. SE15 —1F 92
Shelley Clo. Bans —7H 135
Shelley Clo. Coul —9K 137
Shelley Clo. Edgw —4L 23
Shelley Clo. Gnfd —6B 54
Shelley Clo. Hay —8E 52
Shelley Clo. N'wd —5D 20
Shelley Clo. Orp —5C 128
Shelley Ct. E10 —5M 45
(off Skelton's La.)
Shelley Ct. E11 —2F 46
(off Makepeace Rd.)
Shelley Ct. N19 —6K 43
Shelley Ct. SW3 —7D 74
(off Tite St.)
Shelley Ct. Wal A —6M 7
(off Ninefields)
Shelley Cres. Houn —9H 69
Shelley Cres. S'hall —9K 53
Shelley Dri. Well —9C 80
Shelley Gdns. Wemb —7G 39
Shelley Gro. Lou —6K 19
Shelley Ho. E2 —6G 61
(off Cornwall Av.)
Shelley Ho. SE17 —6A 76
(off Browning St.)
Shelley Ho. SW1 —7G 75
(off Churchill Gdns.)
Shelley Rd. NW10 —4B 56
Shelley Way. SW19 —3B 106
Shellness Rd. E5 —1F 60
Shell Rd. SE13 —2M 93
Shellwood Rd. SW11 —1D 90
Shelmerdine Clo. E3 —8L 61
Shelson Av. Felt —9D 84
Shelton Av. Warl —9G 139
Shelton Clo. Warl —9G 139
Shelton Rd. SW19 —5L 105
Shelton St. WC2 —9J 59
(in two parts)
Shene Ho. EC1 —8L 59
(off Bourne Est.)
Shenfield Ho. SE18 —9H 79
(off Portway Gdns.)
Shenfield Rd. Wfd G —7F 30
Shenfield St. N1 —5C 60
(in two parts)
Shenley Av. Ruis —7D 36
Shenley Rd. SE5 —9C 76
Shenley Rd. Borwd —6L 11
Shenley Rd. Dart —5L 99
Shenley Rd. Houn —9J 69
Shenstone. W5 —2G 71
Shenstone Clo. Dart —3B 98
Shenstone Gdns. Romf —8G 35
Shenwood Ct. Borwd —1L 11
Shepherd Clo. W1 —1E 74
(off Lees Pl.)
Shepherdess Pl. N1 —6A 60
Shepherdess Wlk. N1 —5A 60
Shepherd Ho. E14 —9M 61
(off Annabel Clo.)
Shepherd Mkt. W1 —2F 74
Shepherd's Bush. —3G 73
Shepherd's Bush Grn. W12 —3G 73
Shepherd's Bush Mkt. W12 —3G 73
Shepherd's Bush Pl. W12 —3H 73
Shepherd's Bush Rd. W6 —5G 73
Shepherd's Clo. N6 —4F 42
Shepherd's Clo. Orp —5D 128
Shepherds Clo. Romf —3H 49
Shepherds Clo. Uxb —7A 142
Shepherds Ct. W12 —3H 73
(off Shepherd's Bush Grn.)
Shepherds Grn. Chst —4B 112
Shepherd's Hill. N6 —4F 42
Shepherds Hill. Romf —9L 35
Shepherds La. E9 —2H 61
Shepherd's La. Dart —7E 98
Shepherds Leas. SE9 —3A 96
Shepherd's Path. NW3 —1B 58
(off Lyndhurst Rd.)
Shepherds Path. N'holt —2J 53
(off Arnold Rd.)
Shepherds Pl. W1 —1E 74
Shepherd's Rd. Wat —5D 8
Shepherd St. W1 —2F 74
Shepherds Wlk. NW2 —7E 40
Shepherd's Wlk. NW3 —1B 58
Shepherds Wlk. Bus H —2B 22
Shepherds Way. S Croy —9H 125
Shepiston La. Hay —5M 143
Shepley Clo. Cars —5E 122
Shepley Clo. Horn —1H 67
Shepley M. Enf —1L 17
Sheppard Clo. Enf —3F 16
Sheppard Clo. King T —8J 103
Sheppard Dri. SE16 —6F 76
Sheppard Ho. E2 —5E 60
(off Warner Pl.)
Sheppard Ho. SW2 —7L 91
Sheppards College. Brom —5E 110
(off London Rd.)
Sheppard St. E16 —7D 62
Shepperton. —1A 116
Shepperton Bus. Pk. Shep —9A 100
Shepperton Clo. Borwd —3B 12
Shepperton Ct. Shep —1A 116
Shepperton Ct. Dri. Shep —9A 100
Shepperton Rd. N1 —4A 60
Shepperton Rd. Orp —1A 128
Sheppey Clo. Eri —8F 82
Sheppey Gdns. Dag —3G 65
Sheppey Rd. Dag —3F 64
Sheppey's La. K Lan & Ab L —2A 4
Sheppey Wlk. N1 —2A 60
Shepton Houses. E2 —6G 61
(off Welwyn St.)
Sherard Ct. N7 —8J 43
Sherard Rd. SE9 —4J 95
Sheraton Bus. Cen. Gnfd —5G 55
Sheraton Clo. Els —7K 11
Sheraton Dri. Eps —5A 134
Sheraton Ho. SW1 —7F 74
(off Churchill Gdns.)
Sheraton M. Wat —6C 8
Sheraton St. W1 —9H 59
Sherborne Av. Enf —4G 17
Sherborne Av. S'hall —5L 69
Sherborne Clo. Eps —9G 135
Sherborne Clo. Hay —9G 53
Sherborne Cotts. Wat —7G 9
(off Muriel Av.)
Sherborne Cres. Cars —2C 122
Sherborne Gdns. NW9 —1L 39
Sherborne Gdns. W13 —8F 54
Sherborne Gdns. Romf —5L 33
Sherborne Gdns. Shep —2C 116
Sherborne Ho. SW1 —6F 74
Sherborne Ho. SW8 —8K 75
(off Bolney St.)
Sherborne La. EC4 —1B 76
Sherborne Pl. N'wd —6B 20
Sherborne Rd. Bedf & Felt —7B 84
(in two parts)
Sherborne Rd. Chess —7J 119
Sherborne Rd. Orp —8D 112
Sherborne Rd. Sutt —4L 121
Sherborne St. N1 —4B 60
Sherborne Way. Crox G —7A 8
Sherboro Rd. N15 —4D 44
Sherbourne Ct. Sutt —8A 122
Sherbourne Ho. Wat —8B 8
Sherbourne Pl. Stan —6E 22
Sherbrooke Clo. Bexh —3L 97
Sherbrooke Ho. E2 —5G 61
(off Bonner Rd.)
Sherbrooke Rd. SW6 —8J 73
Sherbrook Gdns. N21 —9M 15
Shere Av. Sutt —2G 135
Shere Clo. Chess —7H 119
Sheredan Rd. E4 —5B 30
Shere Ho. SE1 —4B 76
(off Gt. Dover St.)
Shere Rd. Ilf —3L 47
Sherfield Clo. N Mald —8M 103
Sherfield Gdns. SW15 —5D 88
Sheridan Bldgs. WC2 —9J 59
(off Martlett Ct.)
Sheridan Clo. Romf —7G 35
Sheridan Clo. Swan —8D 114
Sheridan Clo. Uxb —7A 52
Sheridan Ct. NW6 —3A 58
(off Belsize Rd.)
Sheridan Ct. W7 —1D 70
(off Milton Rd.)
Sheridan Ct. Croy —6C 124
(off Coombe Rd.)
Sheridan Ct. Dart —3L 99
Sheridan Ct. Harr —4B 38

Sheridan Ct.—Silvester Rd.

Sheridan Ct. Houn —4J 85
Sheridan Ct. N'holt —1M 53
Sheridan Cres. Chst —6M 111
Sheridan Gdns. Harr —4H 39
Sheridan Ho. E1 —9G 61
(off Tarling St.)
Sheridan Ho. SE11 —5L 75
(off Wincott St.)
Sheridan Lodge. Brom —8G 111
(off Homesdale Rd.)
Sheridan M. E11 —4F 46
(off High St.)
Sheridan Pl. SW13 —2D 88
Sheridan Pl. Hamp —5M 101
Sheridan Rd. E7 —8D 46
Sheridan Rd. E12 —1J 63
Sheridan Rd. SW19 —5K 105
Sheridan Rd. Belv —5L 81
Sheridan Rd. Bexh —2J 97
Sheridan Rd. Rich —9G 87
Sheridan Rd. Wat —9H 9
Sheridan St. E1 —9F 60
Sheridan Ter. N'holt —1M 53
Sheridan Wlk. NW11 —4L 41
Sheridan Wlk. Cars —7D 122
Sheridan Way. Beck —5K 109
Sheriden Pl. Harr —5C 38
Sheriff Way. Wat —6E 4
Sheringham. NW8 —4B 58
Sheringham Av. E12 —9K 47
Sheringham Av. N14 —7H 15
Sheringham Av. Felt —9E 84
Sheringham Av. Romf —4A 50
Sheringham Av. Twic —7K 85
Sheringham Ct. Enf —5M 15
Sheringham Ct. Felt —9E 84
(off Sheringham Av.)
Sheringham Dri. Bark —1D 64
Sheringham Ho. NW1 —8C 58
(off Lisson St.)
Sheringham Rd. N7 —2K 59
Sheringham Rd. SE20 —7G 109
Sheringham Tower. S'hall —1M 69
Sherington Av. Pinn —7L 21
Sherington Rd. SE7 —7F 78
Sherland Rd. Twic —7D 86
Sherlies Av. Orp —4C 128
Sherlock Ct. NW8 —4B 58
(off Dorman Way)
Sherlock Holmes Mus. —7D 58
(off Baker St.)
Sherlock M. W1 —8E 58
Shermanbury Pl. Eri —8D 82
Sherman Rd. Brom —5E 110
Shernbroke Rd. Wal A —7M 7
Shernhall St. E17 —1A 46
Sherrard Rd. E7 & E12 —2G 63
Sherrards Way. Barn —7L 13
Sherrick Grn. Rd. NW10 —1F 56
Sherriff Rd. NW6 —2L 57
Sherringham Av. N17 —9E 28
Sherrin Rd. E10 —9M 45
Sherrock Gdns. NW4 —2E 40
Sherry M. Bark —3B 64
Sherston Ct. SE17 —5M 75
(off Newington Butts)
Sherston Ct. WC1 —6L 59
(off Attneave St.)
Sherwin Ho. SE11 —7L 75
(off Kennington Rd.)
Sherwin Rd. SE14 —9H 77
Sherwood. NW6 —3J 57
Sherwood Av. E18 —1F 46
Sherwood Av. SW16 —4H 107
Sherwood Av. Gnfd —2C 54
Sherwood Av. Hay —7F 52
Sherwood Av. Ruis —4C 36
Sherwood Clo. E17 —9K 29
Sherwood Clo. SW13 —2F 88
Sherwood Clo. W13 —2F 70
Sherwood Clo. Bex —5G 97
Sherwood Ct. SW11 —2A 90
Sherwood Ct. W1 —8D 58
Sherwood Ct. S Croy —7A 124
(off Nottingham Rd.)
Sherwood Ct. S Harr —7M 37
Sherwood Ct. Wat —7D 4
Sherwood Gdns. E14 —5L 77
Sherwood Gdns. SE16 —6E 76
Sherwood Gdns. Bark —3B 64
Sherwood Pk. Av. Sidc —6E 96
Sherwood Pk. Rd. Mitc —8G 107
Sherwood Pk. Rd. Sutt —7L 121
Sherwood Rd. NW4 —1G 41
Sherwood Rd. SW19 —4K 105
Sherwood Rd. Coul —8G 137
Sherwood Rd. Croy —2F 124
Sherwood Rd. Hamp H —2A 102
Sherwood Rd. Harr —7A 38
Sherwood Rd. Ilf —2B 48
Sherwood Rd. Well —1C 96
Sherwoods Rd. Wat —9J 9
Sherwood St. N20 —3B 26
Sherwood St. W1 —1G 75
Sherwood Ter. N20 —3B 26
Sherwood Way. W W'ck —4A 126
Shetland Clo. Borwd —8B 12
Shetland Rd. E3 —5K 61
Shewens Rd. Wey —6B 116
Shield Dri. Bren —7E 70
Shieldhall St. SE2 —5G 81
Shield Rd. Ashf —1A 100
Shifford Path. SE23 —9H 93
Shillaker Ct. W3 —2D 72
Shillibeer Pl. W1 —8C 58
(off York St.)
Shillibeer Wlk. Chig —3D 32
Shillingford St. N1 —3M 59
Shilling Pl. W7 —3E 70
Shillingstone Ho. W14 —4J 73
(off Russell Rd.)
Shinfield St. W12 —9G 57
Shingle Ct. Wal A —6M 7
Shingle End. Bren —8G 71
Shinglewell Rd. Eri —8L 81
Shinners Clo. SE25 —9E 108
Ship All. W4 —7L 71
Ship & Mermaid Row. SE1 —3B 76
Shipka Rd. SW12 —7F 90
Shiplake Ho. E2 —6D 60
(off Arnold Cir.)
Ship La. SW14 —2A 88
Ship La. S at H —5H 115
Shipman Rd. E16 —9F 62
Shipman Rd. SE23 —8H 93
Ship St. SE8 —9L 77
Ship Tavern Pas. EC3 —1C 76
Shipton Clo. Dag —8H 49
Shipton Ho. E2 —5D 60
(off Shipton St.)
Shipton St. E2 —5D 60
Shipway Ter. N16 —8D 44
Shipwright Rd. SE16 —3J 77
Shipwright Yd. SE1 —2C 76
Ship Yd. E14 —6M 77
Shirburn Clo. SE23 —6G 93
Shirbutt St. E14 —1M 77
Shirebrook Rd. SE3 —2H 95
Shire Ct. Eps —9D 120
Shire Ct. Eri —4H 81
Shirehall Clo. NW4 —4H 41
Shirehall Gdns. NW4 —4H 41
Shirehall La. NW4 —4H 41
Shirehall Pk. NW4 —3H 41
Shirehall Rd. Dart —2G 115
Shire Horse Way. Iswth —2D 86
Shire La. Kes & Orp —1J 141
(in two parts)
Shire La. Orp —7C 128
Shiremeade. Borwd —7K 11
Shire M. Whit —5A 86
Shire Pl. SW18 —6A 90
Shire Pl. Bren —8G 71
Shires, The. Ham —1J 103
Shires, The. Wat —4F 4
Shirland M. W9 —6K 57
Shirland Rd. W9 —6K 57
Shirlbutt St. E14 —1M 77
Shirley. —4H 125
Shirley Av. Bex —6H 97
Shirley Av. Cheam —1K 135
Shirley Av. Croy —3G 125
Shirley Av. Sutt —6B 122
Shirley Chu. Rd. Croy —5G 125
Shirley Clo. Chesh —2C 6
Shirley Clo. Dart —3G 99
Shirley Clo. Houn —4A 86
Shirley Ct. SW16 —4J 107
Shirley Ct. Lou —4K 19
Shirley Cres. Beck —8J 109
Shirley Dri. Houn —4A 86
Shirley Gdns. W7 —2D 70
Shirley Gdns. Bark —2C 64
Shirley Gdns. Horn —7G 51
Shirley Gro. N9 —9G 17
Shirley Gro. SW11 —2E 90
Shirley Heights. Wall —1G 137
Shirley Hills Rd. Croy —7G 125
Shirley Ho. SE5 —8B 76
(off Picton St.)
Shirley Ho. Dri. SE7 —8G 79
Shirley Oaks. —3H 125
Shirley Oaks Rd. Croy —3H 125
Shirley Pk. Croy —4G 125
Shirley Pk. Rd. Croy —3F 124
Shirley Rd. E15 —3C 62
Shirley Rd. W4 —3B 72
Shirley Rd. Ab L —5D 4
Shirley Rd. Croy —2F 124
Shirley Rd. Enf —5A 16
Shirley Rd. Sidc —9C 96
Shirley Rd. Wall —1G 137
Shirleys Clo. E17 —3M 45
Shirley St. E16 —9D 62
Shirley Way. Croy —5J 125
Shirlock Rd. NW3 —9D 42
Shobden Rd. N17 —8B 28
Shobroke Clo. NW2 —8G 41
Shoebury Rd. E6 —3K 63
Shoelands Ct. NW9 —1B 40
Shoe La. EC4 —9L 59
Sholden Gdns. Orp —9G 113
Shooters Av. Harr —2G 39
Shooters Hill. —9L 79
Shooters Hill. SE18 & Well —9K 79
Shooters Hill Rd. SE3 & SE18 —8G 79
Shooters Hill Rd. SE10 & SE3 —9A 78
Shooters Rd. Enf —3M 15
Shoot Up Hill. NW2 —1J 57
Shord Hill. Kenl —8B 138
Shore Bus. Cen. E9 —3G 61
Shore Clo. Felt —6E 84
Shore Clo. Hamp —3J 101
Shoreditch. —6C 60
Shoreditch Ct. E8 —3D 60
(off Queensbridge Rd.)
Shoreditch High St. E1 —7C 60
Shore Gro. Felt —8K 85
Shoreham Clo. SW18 —4M 89
Shoreham Clo. Bex —7H 97
Shoreham Clo. Croy —1G 125
Shoreham La. Orp —8L 129
Shoreham Rd. Eyns —8G 131
Shoreham Rd. Orp —5F 112
Shoreham Rd. E. H'row A —4C 144
Shoreham Rd. W. H'row A —4C 144
Shoreham Way. Brom —1E 126
Shore Ho. SW8 —2F 90
Shore M. E9 —3G 61
(off Shore Rd.)
Shore Pl. E9 —3G 61
Shore Rd. E9 —3G 61
Shorncliffe Rd. SE1 —6D 76
Shorndean St. SE6 —7A 94
Shorne Clo. Orp —8H 113
Shorne Clo. Sidc —5F 96
Shornefield Clo. Brom —7L 111
Shornells Way. SE2 —5G 81
Shorrold's Rd. SW6 —8K 73
Shortcroft Mead Ct. NW10 —1E 56
(off Cooper Rd.)
Shortcroft Rd. Eps —9D 120
Shortcrofts Rd. Dag —2K 65
Shorter St. EC3 —1D 76
Short Ga. N12 —4K 25
Short Hedges. Houn —9L 69
Short Hill. Harr —6C 38
Shortlands. —6C 110
Shortlands. W6 —5H 73
Shortlands. Hay —7B 68
Shortlands Clo. N18 —3B 28
Shortlands Clo. Belv —4K 81
Shortlands Gdns. Brom —6C 110
Shortlands Gro. Brom —7B 110
Shortlands Ho. E17 —3K 45
Shortlands Rd. E10 —5M 45
Shortlands Rd. Brom —7B 110
Shortlands Rd. King T —4K 103
Short La. Brick W —2J 5
Short La. Stai —6D 144
Shortmead Dri. Chesh —4E 6
Short Path. SE18 —7M 79
Short Rd. E11 —7C 46
Short Rd. W4 —7C 72
Short Rd. H'row A —5C 144
Shorts Cft. NW9 —2M 39
Shorts Gdns. WC2 —9J 59
Shorts Rd. Cars —6C 122
Short St. NW4 —2G 41
Short St. SE1 —3L 75
Short Wall. E15 —6A 62
Short Way. N12 —6C 26
Short Way. SE9 —2J 95
Short Way. Twic —6A 86
Shortwood Av. Stai —9A 144
Shorwell Ct. Purf —6M 83
Shotfield. Wall —8F 122
Shott Clo. Sutt —7A 122
Shottendane Rd. SW6 —9L 73
Shottery Clo. SE9 —9J 95
Shottfield Av. SW14 —3C 88
Shottsford. W11 —9L 57
(off Ledbury Rd.)
Shoulder of Mutton All. E14 —1J 77
Shouldham St. W1 —8C 58
Showers Way. Hay —2E 68
Shrapnel Clo. SE18 —8J 79
Shrapnel Rd. SE9 —2K 95
Shrewsbury Av. SW14 —3A 88
Shrewsbury Av. Harr —2J 39
Shrewsbury Clo. Surb —4J 119
Shrewsbury Ct. EC1 —7A 60
(off Whitecross St.)
Shrewsbury Cres. NW10 —4B 56
Shrewsbury Ho. SW8 —7K 75
(off Meadow Rd.)
Shrewsbury La. SE18 —9M 79
Shrewsbury M. W2 —8L 57
(off Chepstow Rd.)
Shrewsbury Rd. E7 —1H 63
Shrewsbury Rd. N11 —6G 27
Shrewsbury Rd. W2 —9L 57
Shrewsbury Rd. Beck —7J 109
Shrewsbury Rd. Cars —2C 122
Shrewsbury Rd. H'row A —5A 84
Shrewsbury St. W10 —7G 57
Shrewsbury Wlk. Iswth —2E 86
Shrewton Rd. SW17 —4D 106
Shroffold Rd. Brom —1C 110
Shropshire Clo. Mitc —8J 107
Shropshire Ct. W7 —9D 54
(off Copley Clo.)
Shropshire Pl. WC1 —7G 59
Shropshire Rd. N22 —7K 27
Shroton St. NW1 —8C 58
Shrubberies, The. E18 —9E 30
Shrubberies, The. Chig —5A 32
Shrubbery Clo. N1 —4A 60
Shrubbery Gdns. N21 —9M 15
Shrubbery Rd. N9 —3E 28
Shrubbery Rd. SW16 —1J 107
Shrubbery Rd. S'hall —2L 69
Shrubbery, The. E11 —3F 46
Shrubbery, The. Surb —3J 119
Shrubbery, The. Upm —8M 51
Shrubland Clo. N20 —1B 26
Shrubland Gro. Wor Pk —5G 121
Shrubland Rd. E8 —4E 60
Shrubland Rd. E10 —5L 45
Shrubland Rd. E17 —3L 45
Shrubland Rd. Bans —8K 135
Shrublands Av. Croy —5L 125
Shrublands Clo. SE26 —9G 93
Shrublands Clo. Chig —6A 32
Shrubsall Clo. SE9 —7J 95
Shuna Wlk. N1 —2B 60
Shurland Av. Barn —8B 14
Shurland Gdns. SE15 —8D 76
Shurlock Av. Swan —6B 114
Shurlock Dri. Orp —6A 128
Shuters Sq. W14 —6K 73
Shuttle Clo. Sidc —6D 96
Shuttlemead. Bex —6K 97
Shuttle Rd. Dart —2E 98
Shuttle St. E1 —7E 60
Shuttleworth Rd. SW11 —1C 90
Sibella Rd. SW4 —1H 91
Sibley Clo. Bexh —4J 97
Sibley Ct. Uxb —8A 52
Sibley Gro. E12 —3J 63
Sibthorpe Rd. SE12 —5F 94
Sibthorp Rd. Mitc —6D 106
Sibton Rd. Cars —2C 122
Sicilian Av. WC1 —8J 59
(off Vernon Pl.)
Sickle Corner. Dag —7M 65
Sidbury St. SW6 —9J 73
Sidcup. —1E 112
Sidcup By-Pass. Chst & Sidc —9B 96
Sidcup High St. Sidc —1E 112
Sidcup Hill. Sidc —1F 112
Sidcup Hill Gdns. Sidc —2G 113
Sidcup Pl. Sidc —2E 112
Sidcup Rd. SE12 & SE9 —4G 95
Sidcup Technical Cen. Sidc —3H 113
Siddeley Dri. Houn —2J 85
Siddons Ho. W2 —8B 58
(off Harbet Rd.)
Siddons La. NW1 —7D 58
Siddons Rd. N17 —8E 28
Siddons Rd. SE23 —8J 93
Siddons Rd. Croy —5L 123
Side Rd. E17 —3K 45
Sidewood Rd. SE9 —7B 96
Sidford Ho. SE1 —4L 75
(off Cosser St.)
Sidford Pl. SE1 —4L 75
Sidgwick Ho. SW9 —1K 91
(off Lingham St.)
Sidings M. N7 —8L 43
Sidings, The. E11 —6A 46
Sidings, The. Lou —8J 19
Sidlaw Ho. N16 —6D 44
Sidmouth Av. Iswth —1C 86
Sidmouth Clo. Wat —2F 20
Sidmouth Ct. Dart —7M 99
(off Churchill Clo.)
Sidmouth Dri. Ruis —8E 36
Sidmouth Ho. SE15 —8E 76
(off Lympstone Gdns.)
Sidmouth Ho. W1 —9C 58
(off Cato St.)
Sidmouth Pde. NW10 —3G 57
Sidmouth Rd. E10 —8A 46
Sidmouth Rd. NW2 —3G 57
Sidmouth Rd. Orp —9F 112
(in two parts)
Sidmouth Rd. Well —8G 81
Sidmouth St. WC1 —6K 59
Sidney Av. N22 —5K 27
Sidney Boyd Ct. NW6 —3L 57
Sidney Clo. Uxb —3A 142
Sidney Elson Way. E6 —5L 63
Sidney Est. E1 —9G 61
(Bromhead St.)
Sidney Est. E1 —8G 61
(Wolsey St.)
Sidney Gdns. Bren —7H 71
Sidney Godley (VC) Ho. E2 —6G 61
(off Digby St.)
Sidney Gro. EC1 —5M 59
Sidney Ho. E2 —5H 61
(off Old Ford Rd.)
Sidney Miller Ct. W3 —2M 71
(off Crown St.)
Sidney Rd. E7 —8E 46
Sidney Rd. N22 —7K 27
Sidney Rd. SE25 —9E 108
Sidney Rd. SW9 —1K 91
Sidney Rd. Beck —6J 109
Sidney Rd. Harr —1A 38
Sidney Rd. Twic —5E 86
Sidney Rd. W on T —2E 116
Sidney Sq. E1 —8G 61
Sidney St. E1 —8F 60
Sidworth St. E8 —3F 60
Siebert Rd. SE3 —7E 78
Siege Ho. E1 —9F 60
(off Sidney St.)
Siemens Rd. SE18 —4H 79
Sienna Ter. NW2 —7E 40
Sigdon Pas. E8 —1E 60
Sigdon Rd. E8 —1E 60
Sigers, The. Pinn —4F 36
Sigmund Freud Statue. —2B 58
(off Adelaide Rd.)
Signmakers Yd. NW1 —4F 58
(off Delancey St.)
Sigrist Sq. King T —5J 103
Silbury Av. Mitc —5C 106
Silbury Ho. SE26 —9E 92
Silbury St. N1 —6B 60
Silchester Rd. W10 —9H 57
Silecroft Rd. Bexh —9L 81
Silesia Bldgs. E8 —3F 60
Silex St. SE1 —3M 75
Silicone Bus. Cen. Gnfd —5G 55
Silk Clo. SE12 —4E 94
Silk Ct. E2 —6E 60
(off Squirries St.)
Silkfield Rd. NW9 —3C 40
Silk Ho. NW9 —1B 40
Silk Mill Ct. Wat —8F 8
Silk Mill Rd. Wat —9F 8
Silk Mills Pas. SE13 —1M 93
Silk Mills Path. SE13 —1M 93
Silk Mills Sq. E9 —2K 61
Silks Ct. E11 —6D 46
Silkstream Pde. Edgw —8A 24
Silkstream Rd. Edgw —8A 24
Silk St. EC2 —8A 60
Sillitoe Ho. N1 —4B 60
(off Colville Est.)
Silsoe Ho. NW1 —5F 58
Silsoe Rd. N22 —9K 27
Silver Birch Av. E4 —5K 29
Silverbirch Clo. N11 —6E 26
Silver Birch Clo. SE28 —2E 80
Silver Birch Clo. Dart —1C 114
Silver Birch Gdns. E6 —7K 63
Silver Birch M. Ilf —6A 32
Silverbirch Wlk. NW5 —2E 58
Silverburn Ho. SW9 —9M 75
(off Lothian Rd.)
Silver Chase Ct. Enf —2M 15
Silvercliffe Gdns. Barn —6C 14
Silver Clo. SE14 —8J 77
Silver Clo. Harr —7B 22
Silver Cres. W4 —5M 71
Silverdale. NW1 —6G 59
(off Hampstead Rd.)
Silverdale. SE26 —1G 109
Silverdale. Enf —6J 15
Silverdale Av. Ilf —3C 48
Silverdale Av. Oxs —6A 132
Silverdale Av. W on T —4D 116
Silverdale Cen., The. Wemb —4K 55
Silverdale Clo. W7 —2C 70
Silverdale Clo. N'holt —1K 53
Silverdale Clo. Sutt —6K 121
Silverdale Dri. SE9 —8J 95
Silverdale Dri. Horn —1F 66
Silverdale Dri. Sun —6F 100
Silverdale Factory Cen. Hay —4E 68
Silverdale Gdns. Hay —3E 68
Silverdale Ho. EC1 —7M 59
(off Goswell Rd.)
Silverdale Ind. Est. Hay —4E 68
Silverdale Rd. E4 —6B 30
Silverdale Rd. Bexh —1M 97
Silverdale Rd. Bush —7J 9
Silverdale Rd. Hay —3D 68
Silverdale Rd. Pet W —8A 112
Silverdale Rd. St P —7E 112
Silver Dell. Wat —9D 4
Silverglade Bus. Pk. Chess —4G 133
Silverhall St. Iswth —2E 86
Silver Hill. Well E —1A 12
Silverholme Clo. Harr —5J 39
Silver Jubilee Way. Houn —1F 84
Silverland St. E16 —2K 79
Silver La. Purl —4H 137
Silver La. W W'ck —4B 126
Silverleigh Rd. T Hth —8K 107
Silvermead. E18 —8E 30
Silvermere Av. Romf —6M 33
Silvermere Ct. Purl —4L 137
Silvermere Rd. SE6 —6M 93
Silver Pl. W1 —9G 59
Silver Rd. SE13 —2M 93
(in two parts)
Silver Rd. W12 —1H 73
Silver Spring Clo. Eri —7M 81
Silverston Way. Stan —6G 23
Silver St. N18 —4B 28
Silver St. Enf —5B 16
Silver St. Wal A —7J 7
Silverthorn. NW8 —4M 57
(off Abbey Rd.)
Silverthorne Rd. SW8 —1F 90
Silverthorn Gdns. E4 —2L 29
Silverton Rd. W6 —7H 73
Silvertown. —2H 79
Silvertown Way. E16 —9C 62
Silver Tree Clo. W on T —5E 116
Silvertree La. Gnfd —6B 54
Silver Trees. Brick W —3K 5
Silver Wlk. SE16 —2J 77
Silver Way. Hil —5F 142
Silver Way. Romf —1M 49
Silver Wing Ind. Est. Croy —8K 123
Silverwood Clo. Beck —4L 109
Silverwood Clo. Croy —1K 139
Silverwood Clo. N'wd —8A 20
Silvester Ho. E1 —9F 60
(off Varden St.)
Silvester Ho. E2 —6G 61
(off Sceptre Rd.)
Silvester Ho. W11 —9K 57
(off Basing St.)
Silvester Rd. SE22 —4D 92

Silvester St.—Southborough Rd.

Silvester St. SE1 —3B 76
Silvocea Way. E14 —9B 62
Silwood Est. SE16 —5G 77
Silwood St. SE16 —5G 77
Simla Ho. SE1 —3B 76
(off Kipling Est.)
Simmil Rd. Clay —7C 118
Simmons Clo. N20 —2C 26
Simmons Clo. Chess —8G 119
Simmons La. E4 —2B 30
Simmons Rd. SE18 —6M 79
Simmons Way. N20 —2C 26
Simms Clo. Cars —4C 122
Simms Rd. SE1 —5E 76
Simnel Rd. SE12 —6F 94
Simon Clo. W11 —1K 73
Simon Ct. W9 —6L 57
(off Saltram Cres.)
Simon Ct. Bush —8L 9
Simonds Rd. E10 —7L 45
Simone Clo. Brom —5H 111
Simone Ct. SE26 —9G 93
Simone Dri. Kenl —8A 138
Simon Peter Ct. Enf —4M 15
Simons Ct. N16 —7D 44
Simons Wlk. E15 —1B 62
Simpson Clo. N21 —7J 15
Simpson Dri. W3 —9B 56
Simpson Ho. NW8 —6C 58
Simpson Ho. SE11 —6K 75
Simpson Rd. Houn —5K 85
Simpson Rd. Rain —2D 66
Simpson Rd. Rich —1G 103
Simpson's Rd. E14 —1M 77
Simpsons Rd. Brom —7E 110
Simpson St. SW11 —1C 90
Simpson Way. Surb —1G 119
Simrose Ct. SW18 —4L 89
Sims Clo. Romf —2D 50
Sims Wlk. SE3 —3D 94
Sinclair Ct. Croy —4C 124
Sinclair Dri. Sutt —1M 135
Sinclair Gdns. W14 —3H 73
Sinclair Gro. NW11 —4H 41
Sinclair Ho. WC1 —6J 59
(off Sandwich St.)
Sinclair Mans. W14 —3H 73
(off Richmond Way)
Sinclair Pl. SE4 —5L 93
Sinclair Rd. E4 —5K 29
Sinclair Rd. W14 —3H 73
Sinclare Clo. Enf —3D 16
Sinderby Clo. Borwd —3K 11
Singapore Rd. W13 —2E 70
Singer St. EC1 —6B 60
Single Street. —7M 141
Single St. Berr G —7M 141
Singleton Clo. SW17 —4D 106
Singleton Clo. Croy —2A 124
Singleton Clo. Horn —9D 50
Singleton Rd. Dag —1K 65
Singleton Scarp. N12 —5L 25
Singret Pl. Cow —7A 142
Sinnott Rd. E17 —8H 29
Sion Ct. Twic —7F 86
Sion Rd. Twic —7F 86
Sippets Ct. Ilf —6B 48
Sipson. —7L 143
Sipson Clo. W Dray —7L 143
Sipson La. W Dray & Hay —7L 143
Sipson Rd. W Dray —4K 143
(in two parts)
Sipson Way. W Dray —8L 143
Sir Abraham Dawes Cotts. SW15 —3J 89
Sir Alexander Clo. W3 —2D 72
Sir Alexander Rd. W3 —2D 72
Sir Cyril Black Way. SW19 —4L 105
Sirdar Rd. N22 —1M 43
Sirdar Rd. W11 —1H 73
Sirdar Rd. Mitc —3E 106
Sir Henry Floyd Ct. Stan —2F 22
Sirinham Point. SW8 —7K 75
(off Meadow Rd.)
Sirius Building. E1 —1H 77
(off Jardine Rd.)
Sirius Rd. N'wd —5E 20
Sir John Soane's Mus. —9K 59
Sir Nicholas Garrow Ho. W10
(off Kensal Rd.) —7J 57
Sir Oswald Stoll Foundation, The.
(off Fulham Rd.) SW6 —8M 73
Sir Oswald Stoll Mans. SW6
(off Fulham Rd.) —8M 73
Sir William Atkins Ho. Eps —6B 134
Sir William Powell's Almshouses. SW6 —1J 89
Sise La. EC4 —9B 60
(off Queen Victoria St.)
Siskin Clo. Borwd —6L 11
Siskin Clo. Bush —6J 9
Siskin Ho. SE16 —5H 77
(off Tawny Way)
Siskin Ho. Wat —8B 8
Sisley Rd. Bark —4C 64
Sispara Gdns. SW18 —5K 89
Sissinghurst Clo. Brom —2C 110
Sissinghurst Ho. SE15 —7G 77
(off Sharratt St.)
Sissinghurst Rd. Croy —2E 124
Sister Mabel's Way. SE15 —8E 76
Sisters Av. SW11 —2D 90
Sistova Rd. SW12 —7F 90
Sisulu Pl. SW9 —2L 91
Sittingbourne Av. Enf —8B 16
Sitwell Gro. Stan —5D 22
Siverst Clo. N'holt —2M 53
Sivill Ho. E2 —6D 60
(off Columbia Rd.)
Siviter Way. Dag —3M 65
Siward Rd. N17 —8B 28
Siward Rd. SW17 —9A 90
Siward Rd. Brom —7F 110
Six Acres Est. N4 —7L 43
Six Bridges Ind. Est. SE1 —6E 76
Sixth Av. E12 —9K 47
Sixth Av. W10 —6J 57
Sixth Av. Hay —2D 68
Sixth Av. Wat —8H 5
Sixth Cross Rd. Twic —9A 86
Skardu Rd. NW2 —1J 57
Skarnings Ct. Wal A —6M 7
Skeena Hill. SW18 —6J 89
Skeet Hill La. Orp —3J 129
Skeffington Rd. E6 —4K 63
Skeggs Ho. E14 —4A 78
(off Glengall St.)
Skegness Ho. N7 —3K 59
(off Sutterton St.)
Skelbrook St. SW18 —8A 90
Skelgill Rd. SW15 —3K 89
Skelley Rd. E15 —3D 62
Skelton Clo. E8 —2D 60
Skelton Rd. E7 —2E 62
Skelton's La. E10 —5M 45
Skelwith Rd. W6 —7G 73
Skenfrith Ho. SE15 —7F 76
(off Commercial Way)
Skerne Rd. King T —5H 103
Sketchley Gdns. SE16 —6H 77
Sketty Rd. Enf —5D 16
Skibbs La. Orp —7J 129
Skid Hill La. Warl —4D 140
Skiers St. E15 —4C 62
Skiffington Clo. SW2 —7L 91
Skillen Lodge. Pinn —8H 21
Skinner Ct. E2 —5F 60
Skinner Pl. SW1 —5E 74
(off Bourne St.)
Skinners La. EC4 —1A 76
Skinners La. Asht —9H 133
Skinners La. Houn —9M 69
Skinner's Row. SE10 —9M 77
Skinner St. EC1 —6L 59
Skipsey Av. E6 —6K 63
Skipton Clo. N11 —6E 26
Skipton Dri. Hay —4A 68
Skipton Ho. SE4 —3J 93
Skipwith Ho. EC1 —8L 59
(off Bourne Est.)
Skipworth Rd. E9 —4G 61
Skomer Wlk. N1 —2A 60
Skua Ct. SE8 —7K 77
(off Dorking Clo.)
Skyline Plaza Building. E1 —9E 60
(off Commercial Rd.)
Skylines. E14 —3A 78
Sky Peals Rd. Wfd G —7B 30
Skyport Dri. Harm & W Dray —8H 143
Sladebrook Rd. SE3 —2H 95
Slade Ct. New Bar —5M 13
Sladedale Rd. SE18 —6C 80
Slade Gdns. Eri —9D 82
Slade Green. —9E 82
Slade Grn. Rd. Eri —8F 82
Slade Ho. Houn —5K 85
Sladen Pl. E5 —9F 44
Slades Clo. Enf —5L 15
Slades Dri. Chst —1M 111
Slades Gdns. Enf —4L 15
Slades Hill. Enf —5L 15
Slades Ri. Enf —5L 15
Slade, The. SE18 —7C 80
Slade Tower. E10 —7L 45
(off Leyton Grange Est.)
Slade Wlk. SE17 —7M 75
Slagrove Pl. SE4 —4L 93
Slaidburn St. SW10 —7A 74
Slaithwaite Rd. SE13 —3A 94
Slaney Ct. NW10 —3G 57
Slaney Pl. N7 —1L 59
Slaney Rd. Romf —3C 50
Slater Clo. SE18 —6L 79
Slatter. NW9 —7D 24
Slattery Rd. Felt —7H 85
Sleaford Grn. Wat —3H 21
Sleaford Ind. Est. SW8 —8G 75
Sleaford St. SW8 —8G 75
Sledmere Ct. Felt —7C 84
Sleigh Ho. E2 —6G 61
(off Bacton St.)
Slewins Clo. Horn —3G 51
Slewins La. Horn —3G 51
Slewyn Ct. Wemb —8A 40
Slievemore Clo. SW4 —2H 91
Sligo Ho. E1 —7H 61
(off Beaumont Gro.)
Slindon Ct. N16 —8D 44
Slingsby Pl. WC2 —1J 75
Slippers Pl. SE16 —4F 76
Slipway Ho. E14 —6M 77
(off Burrells Wharf Sq.)
Sloane Av. SW3 —5C 74
Sloane Ct. E. SW3 —6E 74
Sloane Ct. W. SW3 —6E 74
Sloane Gdns. SW1 —5E 74
Sloane Gdns. Orp —5A 128
Sloane Sq. SW1 —5D 74
Sloane St. SW1 —3D 74
Sloane Ter. SW1 —5E 74
Sloane Ter. Mans. SW1 —5E 74
Sloane Wlk. Croy —1K 125
Slocum Clo. SE28 —1G 81
Sloman Ho. W10 —6J 57
(off Beethoven St.)
Slough La. NW9 —3A 40
Sly St. E1 —9F 60
Smaldon Clo. W Dray —4L 143
Smallberry Av. Iswth —1D 86
Smallbrook M. W2 —9B 58
Smalley Clo. N16 —8D 44
Smalley Rd. Est. N16 —8D 44
(off Smalley Clo.)
Smallholdings Rd. Eps —6G 135
(in two parts)
Smallwood Rd. SW17 —1B 106
Smarden Clo. Belv —6L 81
Smarden Gro. SE9 —1K 111
Smart Clo. Romf —8F 34
Smart's La. Lou —6H 19
Smart's Pl. N18 —5E 28
Smart's Pl. WC1 —9J 59
Smart St. E2 —6H 61
Smeaton Clo. Chess —8H 119
Smeaton Clo. Wal A —5L 7
Smeaton Ct. SE1 —4A 76
Smeaton Rd. SW18 —6L 89
Smeaton Rd. Enf —1L 17
Smeaton Rd. Wfd G —5K 31
Smeaton St. E1 —2F 76
Smedley St. SW8 & SW4 —1H 91
Smeed Rd. E3 —3L 61
Smiles Pl. SE13 —1A 94
Smitham Bottom La. Purl —3G 137
Smitham Downs Rd. Purl —5H 137
Smith Clo. SE16 —2H 77
Smithfield St. EC1 —8M 59
Smith Hill. Bren —7J 71
Smithies Ct. E15 —1A 62
Smithies Rd. SE2 —5F 80
Smith's Ct. W1 —1H 75
(off Gt. Windmill St.)
Smithson Rd. N17 —8B 28
Smiths Point. E13 —4E 62
(off Brooks Rd.)
Smith Sq. SW1 —4J 75
Smith St. SW3 —6D 74
Smith St. Surb —1K 119
Smith St. Wat —6G 9
Smith's Yd. SW18 —8A 90
Smiths Yd. Croy —5A 124
(off St George's Wlk.)
Smith Ter. SW3 —6D 74
Smithwood Clo. SW19 —7J 89
Smithy St. E1 —8G 61
Smock Wlk. Croy —1A 124
Smokehouse Yd. EC1 —8M 59
(off St John St.)
Smoothfield. Houn —3L 85
Smugglers Way. SW18 —3M 89
Smug Oak. —3M 5
Smug Oak Grn. Bus. Cen. Brick W —3M 5
Smug Oak La. Brick W & Col S —3M 5
Smyrk's Rd. SE17 —6C 76
Smyrna Rd. NW6 —3L 57
Smythe Rd. S at H —5L 115
Smythe St. E14 —1M 77
Snakes La. Barn —5F 14
Snakes La. E. Wfd G —6G 31
Snakes La. W. Wfd G —5E 30
Snaresbrook. —3E 46
Snaresbrook Dri. Stan —4H 23
Snaresbrook Hall. E18 —2E 46
Snaresbrook Rd. E11 —2C 46
Snarsgate St. W10 —8G 57
Sneath Av. NW11 —5K 41
Snellings Rd. W on T —7G 117
Snells Pk. N18 —6D 28
Sneyd Rd. NW2 —1G 57
Snipe Clo. Eri —8F 82
Snodland Clo. Orp —2L 141
Snowberry Clo. E11 —9B 46
Snowbury Rd. SW6 —1M 89
Snowden Av. Hil & Uxb —5F 142
Snowden Dri. NW9 —4C 40
Snowden St. EC2 —7C 60
Snowdon Cres. Hay —4A 68
Snowdon Rd. H'row A —5A 84
Snowdown Clo. SE20 —5G 109
Snowdrop Clo. Hamp —3L 101
Snowdrop Path. Romf —7H 35
Snow Hill. EC1 —8M 59
Snow Hill Ct. EC1 —9M 59
(in two parts)
Snowman Ho. NW6 —4M 57
Snowsfields. SE1 —3B 76
Snowshill Rd. E12 —1J 63
Snowy Fielder Waye. Iswth —1F 86
Soames St. SE15 —2D 92
Soames Wlk. N Mald —5C 104
Soane Ct. NW1 —3G 59
(off St Pancras Way)
Sobraon Ho. King T —4K 103
(off Elm Rd.)
Socket La. Hayes —1F 126
Soham Rd. Enf —1K 17
Soho. —9G 59
Soho Sq. W1 —9H 59
Soho St. W1 —9H 59
Soho Theatre & Writers Cen.
(off Dean St.) —9H 59
Sojourner Truth Clo. E8 —2F 60
Solander Gdns. E1 —1G 77
Solar Ct. N3 —7M 25
Solar Ct. Wat —7D 8
Solar Ho. E6 —8L 63
(off Alpine Way)
Solarium Ct. SE1 —5D 76
(off Alscot Rd.)
Solar Way. Enf —9F 6
Soldene Ct. N7 —1K 59
(off George's Rd.)
Solebay St. E1 —7J 61
Solent Ho. E1 —8J 61
(off Ben Jonson Rd.)
Solent Ri. E13 —6E 62
Solent Rd. NW6 —1L 57
Solent Rd. H'row A —5D 144
Soley M. WC1 —6L 59
Solna Av. SW15 —4G 89
Solna Rd. N21 —1B 28
Soloman Av. N18 —4E 28
Solomon's Pas. SE15 —3F 92
Soloms Ct. Rd. Bans —9B 136
(in two parts)
Solon New Rd. SW4 —3J 91
Solon New Rd. Est. SW4 —3J 91
Solon Rd. SW2 —3J 91
Solway Clo. E8 —2D 60
(off Queensbridge Rd.)
Solway Clo. Houn —2J 85
Solway Ho. E1 —7H 61
(off Ernest St.)
Solway Rd. N22 —8M 27
Solway Rd. SE22 —3E 92
Somaford Gro. Barn —8B 14
Somali Rd. NW2 —1K 57
Somerby Rd. Bark —3B 64
Somercoates Clo. Barn —5C 14
Somer Ct. SW6 —7L 73
(off Anselm Rd.)
Somerden Rd. Orp —2H 129
Somerfield Ho. SE16 —6H 77
Somerfield Rd. N4 —7M 43
Somerford Clo. Eastc & Pinn —2E 36
Somerford Gro. N16 —9D 44
Somerford Gro. N17 —7E 28
(in two parts)
Somerford Gro. Est. N16 —9D 44
Somerford St. E1 —7F 60
Somerford Way. SE16 —3J 77
Somerhill Av. Sidc —6F 96
Somerhill Rd. Well —1F 96
Somerleyton Pas. SW9 —3M 91
Somerleyton Rd. SW9 —3L 91
Somersby Gdns. Ilf —3K 47
Somers Clo. NW1 —5H 59
Somers Cres. W2 —9C 58
Somerset Av. SW20 —6F 104
Somerset Av. Chess —6H 119
Somerset Av. Well —4D 96
Somerset Clo. N17 —9B 28
Somerset Clo. Eps —1B 134
Somerset Clo. N Mald —1C 120
Somerset Clo. W on T —7F 116
Somerset Clo. Wfd G —8E 30
Somerset Ct. W7 —9D 54
(off Copley Clo.)
Somerset Ct. Buck H —2G 31
Somerset Est. SW11 —9B 74
Somerset Gdns. N6 —5E 42
Somerset Gdns. N17 —7C 28
Somerset Gdns. SE13 —1M 93
Somerset Gdns. SW16 —7K 107
Somerset Gdns. Horn —6L 51
Somerset Gdns. Tedd —2C 102
Somerset Hall. N17 —7C 28
Somerset House. —1K 75
Somerset Lodge. Bren —7H 71
Somerset Rd. E17 —4L 45
Somerset Rd. N17 —1D 44
Somerset Rd. N18 —5D 28
Somerset Rd. NW4 —2G 41
Somerset Rd. SW19 —9H 89
Somerset Rd. W4 —4B 72
Somerset Rd. W13 —2F 70
Somerset Rd. Bren —7G 71
Somerset Rd. Dart —5F 98
Somerset Rd. Enf —2L 17
Somerset Rd. Harr —3A 38
Somerset Rd. King T —6K 103
Somerset Rd. New Bar —7M 13
Somerset Rd. Orp —2E 128
Somerset Rd. S'hall —8K 53
Somerset Rd. Tedd —2C 102
Somerset Sq. W14 —3J 73
Somerset Waye. Houn —7J 69
Somersham Rd. Bexh —1J 97
Somers Pl. SW2 —6K 91
Somers Rd. E17 —2K 45
Somers Rd. SW2 —5K 91
Somers Town. —6H 59
Somers Way. Bush —9A 10
Somerton Av. Rich —2M 87
Somerton Clo. Purl —7L 137
Somerton Rd. NW2 —8J 41
Somerton Rd. SE15 —3F 92
Somertrees Av. SE12 —8F 94
Somervell Rd. Harr —1K 53
Somerville Av. SW13 —7F 72
Somerville Point. SE16 —3K 77
Somerville Rd. SE20 —4H 109
Somerville Rd. Dart —5K 99
Somerville Rd. Romf —4G 49
Sonderburg Rd. N7 —7K 43
Sondes St. SE17 —7B 76
Sonia Clo. Wat —9G 9
Sonia Ct. Edgw —7K 23
Sonia Ct. Harr —4D 38
Sonia Gdns. N12 —4A 26
Sonia Gdns. NW10 —9D 40
Sonia Gdns. Houn —8L 69
Sonning Gdns. Hamp —3J 101
Sonning Ho. E2 —6D 60
(off Swanfield St.)
Sonning Rd. SE25 —1E 124
Sontan Ct. Twic —7B 86
Soper Clo. E4 —5K 29
Soper Clo. SE23 —7H 93
Soper M. Enf —2L 17
Sophia Clo. N7 —2K 59
Sophia Ho. W6 —6G 73
(off Queen Caroline St.)
Sophia Rd. E10 —6M 45
Sophia Rd. E16 —9F 62
Sophia Sq. SE16 —1J 77
(off Sovereign Cres.)
Sopwith. NW9 —7D 24
Sopwith Av. Chess —7J 119
Sopwith Clo. Big H —8H 141
Sopwith Clo. King T —2K 103
Sopwith Rd. Houn —8G 69
Sopwith Way. SW8 —8F 74
Sopwith Way. King T —5J 103
Sorbie Clo. Wey —8B 116
Sorensen Ct. E10 —7M 45
(off Leyton Grange Est.)
Sorrel Bank. Croy —2J 139
Sorrel Clo. SE28 —2E 80
Sorrel Gdns. E6 —8J 63
Sorrel La. E14 —9B 62
Sorrell Clo. SE14 —8J 77
Sorrell Clo. SW9 —1L 91
Sorrel Wlk. Romf —1D 50
Sorrento Rd. Sutt —5L 121
Sotheby Rd. N5 —8M 43
Sotheran Clo. E8 —4E 60
Sotheron Rd. SW6 —8M 73
Sotheron Rd. Wat —5G 9
Soudan Rd. SW11 —9D 74
Souldern Rd. W14 —4H 73
Souldern St. Wat —7F 8
Sounds Lodge. Swan —1A 130
S. Access Rd. E17 —5J 45
South Acre. NW9 —9D 24
Southacre. W2 —9C 58
(off Hyde Pk. Cres.)
Southacre Way. Pinn —8G 21
South Acton. —3M 71
S. Africa Rd. W12 —2F 72
Southall. —2K 69
Southall Ct. S'hall —1K 69
Southall Enterprise Cen. S'hall —3L 69
Southall Green. —4J 69
Southall Ho. Romf —6J 35
(off Kingsbridge Cir)
Southall La. Cran & Houn —7F 68
Southall Pl. SE1 —3B 76
Southampton Bldgs. WC2 —8L 59
Southampton Gdns. Mitc —9J 107
Southampton Pl. WC1 —8J 59
Southampton Rd. NW5 —1D 58
Southampton Rd. H'row A —5C 144
Southampton Row. WC1 —8J 59
Southampton St. WC2 —1J 75
Southampton Way. SE5 —8B 76
Southampton Way. Stanw —5C 144
Southam St. W10 —7J 57
South App. N'wd —3B 20
S. Audley St. W1 —1E 74
South Av. E4 —9M 17
South Av. N2 —2M 41
South Av. NW10 —7G 57
South Av. Cars —9E 122
South Av. Rich —1L 87
South Av. S'hall —1K 69
South Av. Gdns. S'hall —1K 69
South Bank. Surb —1J 119
Southbank. Th Dit —2F 118
South Bank Bus. Cen. SW8 —7H 75
Southbank Bus. Cen. SW11 —9D 74
South Bank Cen. —2K 75
S. Bank Ter. Surb —1J 119
South Barnet. —1E 26
South Beddington. —8H 123
S. Birkbeck Rd. E11 —8B 46
S. Black Lion La. W6 —6E 72
South Block. SE1 —3K 75
(off Westminster Bri. Rd.)
S. Bolton Gdns. SW5 —6A 74
S. Border, The. Purl —3H 137
Southborough. —9K 111
(Bromley)
Southborough. —3J 119
(Surbiton)
Southborough Clo. Surb —3H 119
Southborough Ho. SE17 —6C 76
(off Surrey Gro.)
Southborough La. Brom —9J 111
Southborough Rd. E9 —4H 61

Spencer M.—Stane Way

Spencer M. W6 —7J 73
(off Queen's Club Gdns.)
Spencer Park. —4B 90
Spencer Pk. SW18 —4B 90
Spencer Pk. E Mol —9A 102
Spencer Pl. N1 —3M 59
Spencer Pl. Croy —2B 124
Spencer Ri. NW5 —9F 42
Spencer Rd. E6 —4H 63
Spencer Rd. E17 —9A 30
Spencer Rd. N8 —3K 43
(in two parts)
Spencer Rd. N11 —4F 26
Spencer Rd. N17 —8E 28
Spencer Rd. SW11 —3B 90
Spencer Rd. SW19 —3J 105
Spencer Rd. SW20 —5F 104
Spencer Rd. W3 —2A 72
Spencer Rd. W4 —8A 72
Spencer Rd. Brom —4D 110
Spencer Rd. E Mol —8A 102
Spencer Rd. Harr —9C 22
Spencer Rd. Ilf —6D 48
Spencer Rd. Iswth —9A 70
Spencer Rd. Mitc —7E 106
Spencer Rd. Mit J —2E 122
Spencer Rd. Rain —6B 66
Spencer Rd. S Croy —7C 124
Spencer Rd. Twic —9C 86
Spencer Rd. Wemb —7G 39
Spencer St. EC1 —6M 59
Spencer St. S'hall —3H 69
Spencer Wlk. NW3 —9B 42
Spencer Wlk. SW15 —3H 89
Spenlow Ho. SE16 —4E 76
(off Jamaica Rd.)
Spenser Cres. Upm —5M 51
Spenser Gro. N16 —1C 60
(in two parts)
Spenser M. SE21 —8B 92
Spenser Rd. SE24 —4M 91
Spenser St. SW1 —4G 75
Spensley Wlk. N16 —8B 44
Speranza Rd. SE18 —6D 80
Sperling Rd. N17 —9C 28
Spert St. E14 —1J 77
Speyside. N14 —8G 15
Spey St. E14 —8A 62
Spey Way. Romf —7C 34
Spezia Rd. NW10 —5E 56
Spice Ct. E1 —1E 76
(off Asher Way)
Spice Quay Heights. SE1 —2D 76
Spicer Clo. SW9 —1M 91
Spicer Clo. W on T —1G 117
Spicer Ct. Enf —5C 16
Spicers Fld. Oxs —5B 132
Spice's Yd. Croy —6A 124
Spielman Rd. Dart —3K 99
Spigurnell Rd. N17 —8B 28
Spikes Bri. Rd. S'hall —9J 53
Spilsby Clo. NW9 —8C 24
Spilsby Rd. H Hill & Romf —7H 35
Spindle Clo. SE18 —4J 79
Spindlewood Gdns. Croy —6C 124
Spindrift Av. E14 —5L 77
Spinel Clo. SE18 —6D 80
Spingate Clo. Horn —1H 67
Spinnaker Ct. Hamp W —5H 103
(off Becketts Pl.)
Spinnaker Ho. E14 —3L 77
(off Byng St.)
Spinnells Rd. Harr —6K 37
Spinney Clo. Beck —8M 109
Spinney Clo. N Mald —9C 104
Spinney Clo. Rain —5C 66
Spinney Clo. W Dray —1J 143
Spinney Clo. Wor Pk —4D 120
Spinney Cft. Oxs —7B 132
Spinney Dri. Felt —6A 84
Spinney Gdns. SE19 —2D 108
Spinney Gdns. Dag —1J 65
Spinney Oak. Brom —6J 111
Spinneys, The. Brom —6K 111
Spinney, The. N21 —9L 15
Spinney, The. SW13 —8F 72
Spinney, The. SW16 —9G 91
Spinney, The. Barn —4M 13
Spinney, The. Chesh —3B 6
Spinney, The. Eps —5C 134
Spinney, The. Lou —6M 19
Spinney, The. Oxs —4A 132
Spinney, The. Purl —3M 137
Spinney, The. Sidc —2J 113
Spinney, The. Stan —4J 23
Spinney, The. Sun —5E 100
Spinney, The. Sutt —6G 121
Spinney, The. Swan —6C 114
Spinney, The. Wat —3E 8
Spinney, The. Wemb —8E 38
Spire Ho. W2 —1A 74
(off Lancaster Ga.)
Spires Shop. Cen., The. Barn —5J 13
Spires, The. Dart —8H 99
Spirit Quay. E1 —2E 76
Spitalfields. —8D 60
Spital Sq. E1 —8C 60
Spital St. E1 —8E 60
Spital St. Dart —5H 99
Spital Yd. EC2 —8C 60
Spitfire Est., The. Houn —6G 69
Spitfire Rd. H'row A —5A 84
Spitfire Rd. Wall —9K 123
Spitfire Way. Houn —6G 69
Splendour Wlk. SE16 —6G 77
(off Verney Rd.)
Spode Ho. SE11 —4L 75
(off Lambeth Wlk.)
Spode Wlk. NW6 —1M 57
Spondon Rd. N15 —2E 44
Spoonbill Way. Hay —8H 53
Spooner Ho. Houn —7L 69
Spooners Dri. Park —1M 5
Spooners M. W3 —2B 72
Spooner Wlk. Wall —7J 123
Sportsbank St. SE6 —6A 94
Spottons Gro. N17 —8A 28
Spout Hill. Croy —7L 125
Spout La. N. Stai —3A 144
Spratt Hall Rd. E11 —4E 46
Spray La. Twic —5C 86
Spray St. SE18 —5M 79
Spread Eagle Wlk. Eps —5B 134
Spreighton Rd. W Mol —8M 101
Spriggs Ho. N1 —3M 59
(off Canonbury Rd.)
Sprimont Pl. SW3 —6D 74
Springall St. SE15 —8F 76
Springalls Wharf. SE16 —3E 76
(off Bermondsey Wall W.)
Spring Bank. N21 —8K 15
Springbank Av. Horn —1G 67
Springbank Rd. SE13 —5B 94
Springbank Wlk. NW1 —3H 59
Springbourne Ct. Beck —5A 110
(in two parts)
Spring Bri. M. W5 —1H 71
Springbridge Rd. W5 —1H 71
Spring Clo. Barn —7H 13
Spring Clo. Borwd —3L 11
Spring Clo. Dag —6H 49
Spring Clo. La. Sutt —8J 121
Spring Corner. Felt —9E 84
Spring Cotts. Surb —9H 103
Spring Ct. NW6 —2K 57
Spring Ct. Eps —1D 134
Spring Ct. Rd. Enf —2L 15
Springcroft Av. N2 —2D 42
Spring Crofts. Bush —7L 9
Springdale M. N16 —9B 44
Springdale Rd. N16 —9B 44
Spring Dri. Pinn —4E 36
Springfarm Clo. Rain —6H 67
Springfield. E5 —6F 44
Springfield. Bus H —1B 22
Springfield Av. N10 —1G 43
Springfield Av. SW20 —7K 105
Springfield Av. Hamp —3M 101
Springfield Av. Swan —8D 114
Springfield Clo. N12 —5M 25
Springfield Clo. Crox G —7A 8
Springfield Clo. Stan —3E 22
Springfield Ct. NW3 —3C 58
(off Eton Av.)
Springfield Ct. Ilf —1M 63
Springfield Ct. King T —8J 103
(off Springfield Rd.)
Springfield Ct. Wall —7F 122
Springfield Dri. Ilf —3A 48
Springfield Gdns. E5 —6F 44
Springfield Gdns. NW9 —3B 40
Springfield Gdns. Brom —8K 111
Springfield Gdns. Ruis —6F 36
Springfield Gdns. Upm —8M 51
Springfield Gdns. W W'ck —4M 125
Springfield Gdns. Wfd G —7G 31
Springfield Gro. SE7 —7G 79
Springfield Gro. Sun —5D 100
Springfield La. NW6 —4M 57
Springfield Mt. NW9 —3C 40
Springfield Pde. M. N13 —4L 27
Springfield Pl. N Mald —8A 104
Springfield Ri. SE26 —9F 92
(in two parts)
Springfield Rd. E4 —1C 30
Springfield Rd. E6 —3L 63
Springfield Rd. E15 —6C 62
Springfield Rd. E17 —4K 45
Springfield Rd. N11 —5F 26
Springfield Rd. N15 —2E 44
Springfield Rd. NW8 —4A 58
Springfield Rd. SE26 —2F 108
Springfield Rd. SW19 —2K 105
Springfield Rd. W7 —2C 70
Springfield Rd. Bexh —2M 97
Springfield Rd. Brom —8K 111
Springfield Rd. Chesh —5E 6
Springfield Rd. Eps —2G 135
Springfield Rd. Harr —4C 38
Springfield Rd. Hay —2G 69
Springfield Rd. King T —7J 103
Springfield Rd. Tedd —2E 102
Springfield Rd. T Hth —5A 108
Springfield Rd. Twic —7L 85
Springfield Rd. Wall —7F 122
Springfield Rd. Wat —6F 4
Springfield Rd. Well —2F 96
Springfields. New Bar —7M 13
(off Somerset Rd.)
Springfields. Wal A —7L 7
Springfield Wlk. NW6 —4M 57
Springfield Wlk. Orp —3C 128
(off Andover Rd.)
Spring Gdns. N5 —1A 60
Spring Gdns. SW1 —2H 75
(in two parts)
Spring Gdns. Big H —9G 141
Spring Gdns. Horn —9F 50
Spring Gdns. Orp —8F 128
Spring Gdns. Romf —3A 50
Spring Gdns. Wall —7G 123
Spring Gdns. Wat —8G 5
Spring Gdns. W Mol —9M 101
Spring Gdns. Wfd G —7G 31
Spring Grove. —9C 70
Spring Gro. SE19 —4D 108
Spring Gro. W4 —6L 71
Spring Gro. Hamp —5M 101
Spring Gro. Lou —8H 19
Spring Gro. Mitc —5E 106
Spring Gro. Cres. Houn —9A 70
Spring Gro. Rd. Houn & Iswth —9M 69
Spring Gro. Rd. Rich —4K 87
Springhead Rd. Eri —7D 82
Spring Hill. E5 —5E 44
Spring Hill. SE26 —1G 109
Springhill Clo. SE5 —2B 92
Springholm Clo. Big H —9G 141
Spring Ho. WC1 —6L 59
(off Margery St.)
Springhurst Clo. Croy —6K 125
Spring Lake. Stan —4F 22
Spring La. E5 —5F 44
Spring La. N10 —1E 42
Spring La. SE25 —1F 124
Spring M. W1 —8D 58
Spring M. Eps —1D 134
Spring Park. —5L 125
Spring Pk. Av. Croy —4H 125
Spring Pk. Dri. N4 —6A 44
Springpark Dri. Beck —7A 110
Spring Pk. Rd. Croy —4H 125
Spring Pas. SW15 —2H 89
Spring Path. NW3 —1B 58
Spring Pl. N3 —1L 41
Spring Pl. NW5 —1F 58
Springpond Rd. Dag —1J 65
Springrice Rd. SE13 —5B 94
Spring Rd. Felt —9D 84
Spring Shaw Rd. Orp —5E 112
Spring St. W2 —9B 58
Spring St. Eps —1D 134
Spring Ter. Rich —4J 87
Spring Tide Clo. SE15 —9E 76
Spring Va. Bexh —3M 97
Springvale Av. Bren —6H 71
Spring Va. Clo. Swan —5D 114
Spring Va. N. Dart —6H 99
Springvale Retail Pk. Orp —7G 113
Spring Va. S. Dart —6H 99
Spring Va. Ter. W14 —4H 73
Springvale Way. Orp —7G 113
Spring Villa Rd. Edgw —7L 23
Spring Wlk. E1 —8E 60
Springwater. WC1 —8K 59
(off New North St.)
Springwater Clo. SE18 —9L 79
Springway. Harr —5B 38
Springwell Av. NW10 —4D 56
Springwell Clo. SW16 —1K 107
Springwell Ct. Houn —1H 85
Springwell Rd. SW16 —1L 107
Springwell Rd. Houn —1H 85
Springwood Ct. S Croy —6C 124
(off Birdhurst Rd.)
Springwood Cres. Edgw —2M 23
Springwood Way. Romf —3E 50
Sprowston M. E7 —2E 62
Sprowston Rd. E7 —1E 62
Spruce Ct. W5 —4J 71
Sprucedale Clo. Swan —6C 114
Sprucedale Gdns. Croy —6H 125
Sprucedale Gdns. Wall —1J 137
Spruce Hills Rd. E17 —9A 30
Spruce Ho. SE16 —3H 77
(off Woodland Cres.)
Spruce Pk. Short —8D 110
Spruce Rd. Big H —8H 141
Sprules Rd. SE4 —1J 93
Spur Clo. Ab L —6B 4
Spurfield. W Mol —7M 101
Spurgeon Av. SE19 —5B 108
Spurgeon Rd. SE19 —5B 108
Spurgeon St. SE1 —4B 76
Spurling Rd. SE22 —3D 92
Spurling Rd. Dag —2K 65
Spurrell Av. Bex —1B 114
Spur Rd. N15 —2B 44
Spur Rd. SE1 —3L 75
(off Station App. Rd.)
Spur Rd. SW1 —3G 75
Spur Rd. Edgw —4J 23
Spur Rd. Felt —3F 84
Spur Rd. Iswth —8E 70
Spur Rd. Orp —4E 128
Spurstowe Rd. E8 —2F 60
Spurstowe Ter. E8 —2F 60
Spur, The. Chesh —1D 6
Spurway Pde. Ilf —3K 47
(off Woodford Av.)
Squadrons App. Horn —2G 67
Square Rigger Row. SW11 —2A 90
Square, The. W6 —6G 73
Square, The. Cars —7E 122
Square, The. Ilf —5L 47
Square, The. Rich —4H 87
Square, The. Swan —7B 114
Square, The. Uxb —2B 68
Square, The. Wat —1F 8
Square, The. W Dray —9G 143
Square, The. Wey —6A 116
Square, The. Wfd G —5E 30
Squarey St. SW17 —9A 90
Squire Gdns. NW8 —6B 58
(off Grove End Rd.)
Squires Ct. SW4 —9J 75
Squires Ct. SW19 —1L 105
Squires Fld. Hex —5E 114
Squires La. N3 —9M 25
Squires Mt. NW3 —8B 42
Squires, The. Romf —4A 50
Squires Wlk. Ashf —4B 100
Squires Way. Dart —1B 114
Squires Wood Dri. Chst —4J 111
Squirrel Clo. Houn —2G 85
Squirrel Clo. Orp —3C 128
Squirrel M. W13 —1D 70
Squirrels Clo. N12 —4A 26
Squirrels Clo. Uxb —3E 142
Squirrels Ct. Wor Pk —4E 120
(off Avenue, The)
Squirrels Drey. Short —6C 110
(off Park Hill Rd.)
Squirrels Grn. Wor Pk —4D 120
Squirrel's Heath. —1H 51
Squirrels Heath Av. Romf —1F 50
Squirrels Heath La. Romf & Horn —2G 51
Squirrels Heath Rd. Romf —1J 51
Squirrel's La. Buck H —3H 31
Squirrels, The. SE13 —2B 94
Squirrels, The. Bush —8B 10
Squirrels, The. Pinn —1K 37
Squirrels Trad. Est., The. Hay —4D 68
Squirrels Way. Eps —6B 134
Squirries St. E2 —6E 60
Stable Clo. N'holt —5L 53
Stables End. Orp —5A 128
Stables Mkt., The. NW1 —3F 58
Stables M. SE27 —2A 108
Stables, The. Buck H —9G 19
Stables Way. SE11 —6L 75
Stable Wlk. N2 —8B 26
Stable Way. W10 —9G 57
Stable Yd. SW1 —3G 75
(off St James' Pal.)
Stable Yd. SW15 —2G 89
Stable Yd. Rd. SW1 —3G 75
Stableyard, The. SW9 —1K 91
Stacey Av. N18 —4G 29
Stacey Clo. E10 —3B 46
Stacey St. N7 —8L 43
Stacey St. WC2 —9H 59
Stack Ho. SW1 —5E 74
(off Cundy St.)
Stackhouse St. SW3 —4D 74
(off Pavilion Rd.)
Stacy Path. SE5 —8C 76
Stadium Bus. Cen. Wemb —8M 39
Stadium Retail Pk. Wemb —8L 39
Stadium Rd. SE18 —8K 79
Stadium Rd. E. NW4 —5F 40
Stadium St. SW10 —8A 74
Stadium Way. Dart —4C 98
Stadium Way. Wemb —9K 39
Staffa Rd. E10 —6J 45
Stafford Av. Horn —1H 51
Stafford Clo. E17 —4K 45
(in two parts)
Stafford Clo. N14 —7G 15
Stafford Clo. NW6 —6L 57
(in two parts)
Stafford Clo. Chesh —2B 6
Stafford Clo. Sutt —8J 121
Stafford Ct. SW8 —8J 75
Stafford Ct. W7 —9D 54
(off Copley Clo.)
Stafford Cripps Ho. E2 —6G 61
(off Globe Rd.)
Stafford Cripps Ho. SW6 —7K 73
(off Clem Attlee Ct.)
Stafford Cross Bus. Pk. Croy —7K 123
Stafford Gdns. Croy —7K 123
Stafford Ind. Est. Horn —1H 51
Stafford Mans. SW1 —4G 75
(off Stafford Pl.)
Stafford Mans. SW4 —3J 91
Stafford Mans. SW11 —8D 74
(off Albert Bri. Rd.)
Stafford Pl. SW1 —4G 75
Stafford Pl. Rich —6K 87
Stafford Rd. E3 —5K 61
Stafford Rd. E7 —3G 63
Stafford Rd. NW6 —6L 57
Stafford Rd. Harr —7A 22
Stafford Rd. N Mald —7A 104
Stafford Rd. Ruis —9D 36
Stafford Rd. Sidc —1C 112
Stafford Rd. Wall & Croy —8G 123
Staffordshire St. SE15 —9E 76
Stafford Sq. Wey —6B 116
Stafford St. W1 —2G 75
Stafford Ter. W8 —4L 73
Staff St. EC1 —6B 60
Stag Clo. Edgw —9M 23
Stag Ct. King T —5L 103
(off Coombe Rd.)
Staggart Grn. Chig —5D 32
Stagg Hill. Barn —1C 14
Stag Lane. (Junct.) —8D 88
Stag La. SW15 —9D 88
Stag La. Buck H —2F 30
Stag La. Edgw & NW9 —9M 23
Stag Leys Clo. Bans —7B 136
Stag Pl. SW1 —4G 75
Stags Way. Iswth —8D 70
Stainbank Rd. Mitc —7F 106
Stainby Clo. W Dray —4J 143
Stainby Rd. N15 —2D 44
Stainer Ho. SE3 —3G 95
Stainer Rd. Borwd —3H 11
Stainer St. SE1 —2B 76
Staines Av. Sutt —4H 121
Staines Rd. Felt & Houn —7E 144
Staines Rd. Ilf —1A 64
Staines Rd. Twic —9L 85
Staines Rd. E. Sun —4E 100
Staines Rd. W. Ashf & Sun —4A 100
Staines Wlk. Sidc —3G 113
Stainford Clo. Ashf —2B 100
Stainforth Rd. E17 —2L 45
Stainforth Rd. Ilf —5B 48
Staining La. EC2 —9A 60
Stainmore Clo. Chst —5B 112
Stainsbury St. E2 —5G 61
Stainsby Pl. E14 —9L 61
Stainsby Rd. E14 —9L 61
Stains Clo. Chesh —1E 6
Stainton Rd. SE6 —5B 94
Stainton Rd. Enf —3G 17
Stalbridge Flats. W1 —9E 58
(off Lumley St.)
Stalbridge St. NW1 —8C 58
Stalham St. SE16 —4F 76
Stalham Way. Ilf —8M 31
Stalisfield Pl. Dow —2L 141
Stambourne Way. SE19 —4C 108
Stambourne Way. W W'ck —4A 126
Stamford Brook Arches. W6 —5E 72
Stamford Brook Av. W6 —4D 72
Stamford Brook Gdns. W6 —4D 72
Stamford Brook Mans. W6 —5D 72
(off Goldhawk Rd.)
Stamford Brook Rd. W6 —4D 72
Stamford Clo. N15 —3E 44
Stamford Clo. NW3 —8A 42
(off Heath St.)
Stamford Clo. Harr —7C 22
Stamford Clo. S'hall —1L 69
Stamford Ct. W6 —5E 72
Stamford Dri. Brom —8D 110
Stamford Gdns. Dag —3G 65
Stamford Ga. SW6 —8M 73
Stamford Green. —5M 133
Stamford Grn. Rd. Eps —5M 133
Stamford Gro. E. N16 —6E 44
Stamford Gro. W. N16 —6E 44
Stamford Hill. —6D 44
Stamford Hill. N16 —7D 44
Stamford Lodge. N16 —5D 44
Stamford Rd. E6 —4J 63
Stamford Rd. N1 —3C 60
Stamford Rd. N15 —3E 44
Stamford Rd. Dag —4F 64
Stamford Rd. W on T —5H 117
Stamford Rd. Wat —4F 8
Stamford St. SE1 —2L 75
Stamp Pl. E2 —5D 60
Stanard Clo. N16 —5C 44
Stanborough Av. Borwd —1L 11
Stanborough Clo. Borwd —2L 11
Stanborough Clo. Hamp —3K 101
Stanborough Pk. Wat —8F 4
Stanborough Pas. E8 —2D 60
Stanborough Rd. Houn —2B 86
Stanbridge Pl. N21 —2M 27
Stanbridge Rd. SW15 —2G 89
Stanbrook Rd. SE2 —3F 80
Stanbury Av. Wat —1C 8
Stanbury Ct. NW3 —2D 58
Stanbury Rd. SE15 —1F 92
(in two parts)
Stancroft. NW9 —3C 40
Standale Gro. Ruis —3A 36
Standard Ind. Est. E16 —3K 79
Standard Pl. EC2 —6C 60
(off Rivington St.)
Standard Rd. NW10 —7A 56
Standard Rd. Belv —6L 81
Standard Rd. Bexh —3J 97
Standard Rd. Dow & Orp —2L 141
Standard Rd. Enf —2J 17
Standard Rd. Houn —2J 85
Standen Av. Horn —8J 51
Standen Rd. SW18 —6K 89
Standfield. Ab L —4C 4
Standfield Gdns. Dag —2L 65
Standfield Rd. Dag —1L 65
Standish Ho. SE3 —3F 94
(off Elford Clo.)
Standish Ho. W6 —5E 72
(off St Peter's Gro.)
Standish Rd. W6 —5E 72
Standlake Point. SE23 —9H 93
Stane Clo. SW19 —4M 105
Stane Pas. SW16 —2J 107
Stanesgate Ho. SE15 —8E 76
(off Friary Est.)
Stane Way. SE18 —8H 79

Steadman Ct.—Stratford Studios

Steadman Ct. EC1 —7A 60
(off Old St.)
Steadman Ho. Dag —8L 49
(off Uvedale Rd.)
Stead St. SE17 —5B 76
Steam Farm La. Felt —3D 84
Stean St. E8 —4D 60
Stebbing Ho. W11 —2H 73
(off Queensdale Cres.)
Stebbing Way. Bark —5E 64
Stebondale St. E14 —5A 78
Stedham Pl. WC1 —9J 59
(off New Oxford St.)
Stedman Clo. Bex —9C 98
Steed Clo. Horn —7F 50
Steedman St. SE17 —5A 76
Steeds Rd. N10 —8D 26
Steeds Way. Lou —5J 19
Steele Ho. E15 —5C 62
(off Eve Rd.)
Steele Rd. E11 —9C 46
Steele Rd. N17 —1C 44
Steele Rd. NW10 —5A 56
Steele Rd. W4 —4A 72
Steele Rd. Iswth —3E 86
Steele's M. N. NW3 —2D 58
Steele's M. S. NW3 —2D 58
Steele's Rd. NW3 —2D 58
Steele's Studios. NW3 —2D 58
Steele Wlk. Eri —8M 81
Steel's La. E1 —9G 61
Steel's La. Oxs —6A 132
Steelyard Pas. EC4 —1B 76
(off Allhallows La.)
Steen Way. SE22 —4C 92
Steep Clo. Orp —8D 128
Steep Hill. SW16 —9H 91
Steep Hill. Croy —6C 124
Steeplands. Bush —9M 9
Steeple Clo. SW6 —1J 89
Steeple Clo. SW19 —2J 105
Steeple Ct. E1 —7F 60
Steeple Heights Dri. Big H —9H 141
Steeplestone Clo. N18 —5A 28
Steeple Wlk. N1 —4A 60
(off Basire St.)
Steerforth St. SW18 —8A 90
Steers Mead. Mitc —5D 106
Steers Way. SE16 —3J 77
Stelfox Ho. WC1 —6K 59
(off Penton Ri.)
Stella Rd. SW17 —3D 106
Stelling Rd. Eri —8B 82
Stellman Clo. E5 —8E 44
Stembridge Rd. SE20 —6F 108
Sten Clo. Enf —1L 17
Stephan Clo. E8 —4E 60
Stephen Av. Rain —2E 66
Stephen Clo. Orp —5D 128
Stephendale Rd. SW6 —2M 89
Stephen Fox Ho. W4 —6C 72
(off Chiswick La.)
Stephen M. W1 —8H 59
Stephen Pl. SW4 —2G 91
Stephen Rd. Bexh —2A 98
Stephens Clo. Romf —5G 35
Stephens Ct. E16 —7D 62
Stephens Ct. SE4 —2J 93
Stephens Lodge. N12 —3A 26
(off Woodside La.)
Stephenson Ct. Cheam —9J 121
(off Station App.)
Stephenson Ho. SE1 —4A 76
Stephenson Rd. E17 —3J 45
Stephenson Rd. W7 —9D 54
Stephenson Rd. Twic —6L 85
Stephenson St. E16 —7C 62
Stephenson St. NW10 —6C 56
Stephenson Way. NW1 —7G 59
Stephenson Way. Wat & Bush —6H 9
Stephen's Rd. E15 —4C 62
Stephen St. W1 —8H 59
Stepney. —8H 61
Stepney Causeway. E1 —9H 61
Stepney Grn. E1 —8G 61
Stepney Grn. Ct. E1 —8H 61
(off Stepney Grn.)
Stepney High St. E1 —8H 61
Stepney Way. E1 —8F 60
Sterling Av. Edgw —4K 23
Sterling Av. Wal X —7D 6
Sterling Clo. NW10 —3E 56
Sterling Gdns. SE14 —7J 77
Sterling Ho. SE3 —3F 94
Sterling Pl. W5 —5J 71
Sterling Rd. Enf —3B 16
Sterling St. SW7 —4C 74
Sterling Way. N18 —5B 28
Stern Clo. Bark —5G 65
Sterndale Rd. W6 —4H 73
Sterndale Rd. Dart —6K 99
Sterne St. W12 —3H 73
Sternhall La. SE15 —2E 92
Sternhold Av. SW2 —8H 91
Sterry Cres. Dag —1L 65
Sterry Dri. Eps —6C 120
Sterry Dri. Th Dit —1C 118
Sterry Gdns. Dag —2L 65
Sterry Rd. Bark —4D 64
Sterry Rd. Dag —9L 49
Sterry St. SE1 —3B 76
Steucers La. SE23 —7J 93
Stevannie Ct. Belv —6L 81
Steve Biko La. SE6 —1L 109
Steve Biko Rd. N7 —8L 43
Steve Biko Way. Houn —2L 85
Stevedale Rd. Well —1G 97
Stevedore St. E1 —2F 76
Stevenage Cres. Borwd —3J 11
Stevenage Rd. E6 —2L 63
Stevenage Rd. SW6 —8H 73
Stevens Av. E9 —2G 61
Stevens Clo. Beck —3L 109
Stevens Clo. Bex —1B 114
Stevens Clo. Eps —4C 134
Stevens Clo. Hamp —2J 101
Stevens Clo. Pinn —3G 37
Stevens Grn. Bus H —1A 22
Stevens La. Clay —9E 118
Stevenson Clo. SE16 —6E 76
Stevenson Clo. Barn —9B 14
Stevenson Clo. Eri —8F 82
Stevenson Ho. NW8 —4A 58
(off Boundary Rd.)
Stevens Pl. Purl —5M 137
Stevens Rd. Dag —8F 48
Stevens St. SE1 —4C 76
Stevens Way. Chig —4C 32
Steventon Rd. W12 —1D 72
Steward Clo. Chesh —3E 6
Stewards Holte Wlk. N11 —4F 26
Steward St. E1 —8C 60
(in two parts)
Stewards Wlk. Romf —3C 50
Stewart Av. Upm —8M 51
Stewart Clo. NW9 —4A 40
Stewart Clo. Ab L —5D 4
Stewart Clo. Chst —2M 111
Stewart Clo. Hamp —3J 101
Stewart Quay. Hay —3C 68
Stewart Rainbird Ho. E12 —1L 63
(off Parkhurst Rd.)
Stewart Rd. E15 —9B 46
Stewartsby Clo. N18 —5A 28
Stewart's Gro. SW3 —6B 74
Stewart's Rd. SW8 —8G 75
Stewart St. E14 —3A 78
Stew La. EC4 —1A 76
Steyne Ho. W3 —2A 72
(off Horn La.)
Steyne Rd. W3 —2M 71
Steyning Clo. Kenl —8M 137
Steyning Gro. SE9 —1K 111
Steynings Way. N12 —5L 25
Steyning Way. Houn —3G 85
Steynton Av. Bex —8H 97
Stickland Rd. Belv —5L 81
Stickleton Clo. Gnfd —6M 53
Stifford Ho. E1 —8G 61
(off Stepney Way)
Stilecroft Gdns. Wemb —8F 38
Stile Hall Gdns. W4 —6L 71
Stile Hall Pde. W4 —6L 71
Stileman Ho. E3 —8K 61
(off Ackroyd Dri.)
Stile Path. Sun —7E 100
Stiles Clo. Brom —1K 127
Stiles Clo. Eri —6M 81
Stillingfleet Rd. SW13 —7E 72
Stillington St. SW1 —5G 75
Stillness Rd. SE23 —5J 93
Stillwell Dri. Uxb —7D 142
Stilton Cres. NW10 —3B 56
Stilton Path. Borwd —2L 11
Stilwell Roundabout. Uxb —1L 143
Stipularis Dri. Hay —7H 53
Stirling Av. Pinn —6H 37
Stirling Av. Shep —7C 100
Stirling Clo. SW16 —5H 107
Stirling Clo. Bans —9K 135
Stirling Clo. Rain —6F 66
Stirling Clo. Uxb —6A 142
Stirling Corner. (Junct.) —8B 12
Stirling Corner. Borwd & Barn —8B 12
Stirling Ct. W13 —1F 70
Stirling Dri. Orp —7F 128
Stirling Gro. Houn —1A 86
Stirling Ho. SE18 —6M 79
Stirling Ho. Borwd —6A 12
Stirling Rd. E13 —5F 62
Stirling Rd. E17 —1J 45
Stirling Rd. N17 —8E 28
Stirling Rd. N22 —8M 27
Stirling Rd. SW9 —1J 91
Stirling Rd. W3 —4M 71
Stirling Rd. Harr —1D 38
Stirling Rd. Hay —1F 68
Stirling Rd. H'row A —5D 144
Stirling Rd. Twic —6L 85
Stirling Rd. Path. E17 —1J 45
Stirling Wlk. Surb —1M 119
Stirling Way. Ab L —5E 4
Stirling Way. Borwd —8B 12
Stirling Way. Croy —2J 123
Stiven Cres. Harr —8K 37
Stoats Nest Rd. Coul —6J 137
Stoats Nest Village. Coul —7J 137
Stockbeck. NW1 —5G 59
(off Ampthill Est.)
Stockbury Rd. Croy —1G 125
Stockdale Rd. Dag —7K 49
Stockdove Way. Gnfd —6D 54
Stocker Gdns. Dag —3G 65
Stock Exchange. —9B 60
Stockfield Rd. SW16 —9K 91
Stockfield Rd. Clay —7C 118
Stockham's Clo. S Croy —2B 138
Stock Hill. Big H —8H 141
Stockholm Ho. E1 —1E 76
(off Swedenborg Gdns.)
Stockholm Rd. SE16 —6G 77
Stockholm Way. E1 —2E 76
Stockhurst Clo. SW15 —1G 89
Stockingswater La. Enf —4K 17
Stockland Rd. Romf —4B 50
Stock La. Dart —9G 99
Stockleigh Hall. NW8 —5C 58
(off Prince Albert Rd.)
Stockley Clo. W Dray —3M 143
Stockley Country Pk. —1L 143
Stockley Farm Rd. W Dray —4M 143
Stockley Park. —2M 143
Stockley Rd. Uxb & W Dray —9E 142
Stockley Rd. W Dray —5M 143
Stock Orchard Cres. N7 —1K 59
Stock Orchard St. N7 —1K 59
Stockport Rd. SW16 —5H 107
Stocksfield Rd. E17 —1A 46
Stocks Pl. E14 —1K 77
Stock St. E13 —5E 62
Stockton Clo. New Bar —6A 14
Stockton Gdns. N17 —7A 28
Stockton Gdns. NW7 —3C 24
Stockton Ho. E2 —6F 60
(off Ellsworth St.)
Stockton Ho. S Harr —6L 37
Stockton Rd. N17 —7A 28
Stockton Rd. N18 —6E 28
Stockwell. —1K 91
Stockwell Av. SW9 —2K 91
Stockwell Clo. Brom —6F 110
Stockwell Clo. Chesh —1A 6
Stockwell Gdns. SW9 —9K 75
Stockwell Gdns. Est. SW9 —1J 91
Stockwell Grn. SW9 —1K 91
Stockwell Grn. Ct. SW9 —1K 91
Stockwell La. SW9 —1K 91
Stockwell La. Chesh —1A 6
(in two parts)
Stockwell M. SW9 —1K 91
Stockwell Pk. Cres. SW9 —1K 91
Stockwell Pk. Est. SW9 —1K 91
Stockwell Pk. Rd. SW9 —9K 75
Stockwell Pk. Wlk. SW9 —2L 91
Stockwell Rd. SW9 —1K 91
Stockwell St. SE10 —7A 78
Stockwell Ter. SW9 —9K 75
Stodart Rd. SE20 —5G 109
Stoddart Ho. SW8 —7K 75
Stofield Gdns. SE9 —9H 95
Stoford Clo. SW19 —6J 89
Stoke Av. Ilf —6E 32
Stokenchurch St. SW6 —9M 73
Stoke Newington. —8D 44
Stoke Newington Chu. St. N16 —8B 44
Stoke Newington Comn. N16 —7D 44
Stoke Newington High St. N16 —8D 44
Stoke Newington Rd. N16 —1D 60
Stoke Pl. NW10 —6D 56
Stoke Rd. King T —4A 104
Stoke Rd. Rain —5H 67
Stoke Rd. W on T —5G 117
Stokesay Ct. Dart —5M 99
(off Osbourne Rd.)
Stokesby Rd. Chess —8K 119
Stokes Cotts. Ilf —8A 32
Stokes Ct. N2 —2C 42
Stokesheath Rd. Oxs —3A 132
Stokesley St. W12 —9D 56
Stokes Rd. E6 —7J 63
Stokes Rd. Croy —1H 125
Stokley Ct. N8 —2J 43
Stoll Clo. NW2 —8G 41
Stompond La. W on T —4E 116
Stoms Path. SE6 —2L 109
Stonard Rd. N13 —3L 27
Stonard Rd. Dag —1F 64
Stonards Hill. Lou —8K 19
Stondon Ho. E15 —4D 62
(off John St.)
Stondon Pk. SE23 —5J 93
Stondon Wlk. E6 —5H 63
Stonebanks. W on T —2E 116
Stonebridge. —4B 56
Stonebridge Pk. NW10 —3B 56
Stonebridge Rd. N15 —3D 44
Stonebridge Shop. Cen. NW10 —4B 56
Stonebridge Way. Wemb —2M 55
Stone Bldgs. WC2 —8K 59
(off Chancery La.)
Stonechat Sq. E6 —8J 63
Stone Clo. SW4 —1G 91
Stone Clo. Dag —7K 49
Stone Clo. W Dray —2K 143
Stonecot Clo. Sutt —3J 121
Stonecot Hill. Sutt —3J 121
Stone Ct. Eri —6D 82
Stone Cres. Felt —6D 84
Stonecroft Clo. Barn —6F 12
Stonecroft Rd. Eri —8A 82
Stonecroft Way. Croy —2J 123
Stonecrop Clo. NW9 —1B 40
Stonecutter St. EC4 —9M 59
Stonefield. N7 —7K 43
Stonefield Clo. Bexh —2L 97
Stonefield Clo. Ruis —1J 53
Stonefield St. N1 —4L 59
Stonefield Way. SE7 —8H 79
Stonefield Way. Ruis —9J 37
Stonegate Clo. Orp —7G 113
Stonegrove. —5K 23
Stonegrove. Edgw —4J 23
Stone Gro. Ct. Edgw —5K 23
Stonegrove Gdns. Edgw —5K 23
Stone Hall. W8 —4M 73
(off St Margarets's La.)
Stonehall Av. Ilf —4J 47
Stone Hall Gdns. W8 —4M 73
Stone Hall Pl. W8 —4M 73
Stone Hall Rd. N21 —9K 15
Stoneham Rd. N11 —5G 27
Stonehill Clo. SW14 —4B 88
Stonehill Ct. E4 —9M 17
Stonehill Green. —4A 114
Stonehill Rd. SW14 —4A 88
Stone Hill Rd. W4 —6L 71
Stonehills Ct. SE21 —9C 92
Stonehill Woods Pk. Sidc —3M 113
Stonehorse Rd. Enf —7G 17
Stonehouse. NW1 —4G 59
(off Plender St.)
Stone Ho. Ct. EC3 —9C 60
(off Houndsditch)
Stone Lake Ind. Pk. SE7 —5G 79
Stone Lake Retail Pk. SE7 —5G 79
Stoneleigh. —7E 120
Stoneleigh Av. Enf —2F 16
Stoneleigh Av. Wor Pk —6E 120
Stoneleigh B'way. Eps —7E 120
Stoneleigh Clo. Wal X —6D 6
Stoneleigh Ct. Ilf —1J 47
Stoneleigh Cres. Eps —7D 120
Stoneleigh M. E3 —5J 61
Stoneleigh Pk. Wey —8A 116
Stoneleigh Pk. Av. Croy —1H 125
Stoneleigh Pk. Rd. Eps —8D 120
Stoneleigh Pl. W11 —1H 73
Stoneleigh Rd. N17 —1D 44
Stoneleigh Rd. Cars —2C 122
Stoneleigh Rd. Ilf —1J 47
Stoneleigh St. W11 —1H 73
Stoneleigh Ter. N19 —7F 42
Stonell's Rd. SW11 —5D 90
Stonemasons Clo. N15 —2B 44
Stonenest St. N4 —6K 43
Stone Pk. Av. Beck —8L 109
Stone Pl. Wor Pk —4E 120
Stone Rd. Brom —9D 110
Stones All. Wat —6F 8
Stones Cross Rd. Swan —9A 114
Stones End St. SE1 —3A 76
Stone's Rd. Eps —4C 134
Stone St. Croy —7L 123
Stonewall. E6 —8L 63
Stonewold Ct. W5 —9H 55
Stonewood Rd. Eri —6C 82
Stoney All. SE18 —1L 95
Stoneyard La. E14 —1M 77
Stoneycroft Clo. SE12 —6D 94
Stoneycroft Rd. Wfd G —6J 31
Stoneydeep. Tedd —1E 102
Stoneydown. E17 —2J 45
Stoneydown Av. E17 —2J 45
Stoneydown Ho. E17 —2J 45
(off Blackhorse Rd.)
Stoneyfield Rd. Coul —9K 137
Stoneyfields Gdns. Edgw —4A 24
Stoneyfields La. Edgw —5A 24
Stoney La. E1 —9D 60
Stoney La. SE19 —3D 108
Stoney St. SE1 —2B 76
Stonhouse St. SW4 —3H 91
Stonny Cft. Asht —9K 133
Stonor Rd. W14 —5K 73
Stonycroft Clo. Enf —4J 17
Stony Hill. W End —9K 117
Stony Path. Lou —3K 19
Stonyshotts. Wal A —7L 7
Stopes St. SE15 —8D 76
Stopford Rd. E13 —4E 62
Stopford Rd. SE17 —6M 75
Stopher Ho. SE1 —3M 75
(off Webber St.)
Store Rd. E16 —3L 79
Storers Quay. E14 —5B 78
Store St. E15 —1B 62
Store St. WC1 —8H 59
Storey Ct. NW8 —6B 58
(off St John's Wood Rd.)
Storey Ho. E14 —1M 77
(off Cottage St.)
Storey Rd. E17 —2K 45
Storey Rd. N6 —4D 42
Storey's Ga. SW1 —3H 75
Storey St. E16 —2L 79
Stories M. SE5 —1C 92
Stories Rd. SE5 —2C 92
Stork Rd. E7 —2D 62
Storksmead Rd. Edgw —7C 24
Stork's Rd. SE16 —4E 76
Stormont Rd. N6 —5D 42
Stormont Rd. SW11 —2E 90
Stormont Way. Chess —7G 119
Stormount Dri. Hay —3A 68
Storrington. WC1 —6J 59
(off Regent Sq.)
Storrington Rd. Croy —3D 124
Story St. N1 —3K 59
Stothard Ho. E1 —7G 61
(off Amiel St.)
Stothard St. E1 —7G 61
Stott Clo. SW18 —5B 90
Stoughton Av. Sutt —7H 121
Stoughton Clo. SE11 —5K 75
Stoughton Clo. SW15 —7E 88
Stour Av. S'hall —4L 69
Stourcliffe Clo. W1 —9D 58
Stourcliffe St. W2 —9D 58
Stour Clo. Kes —6G 127
Stourhead Clo. SW19 —6H 89
Stourhead Gdns. SW20 —7E 104
Stourhead Ho. SW1 —6H 75
(off Tachbrook St.)
Stour Rd. E3 —3L 61
Stour Rd. Dag —7L 49
Stour Rd. Dart —2E 98
Stourton Av. Felt —1K 101
Stowage. SE8 —7L 77
Stow Cres. E17 —7J 29
Stowe Cres. Ruis —4A 36
Stowe Gdns. N9 —1D 28
Stowe Ho. NW11 —4A 42
Stowell Av. New Ad —2B 140
Stowell Ho. N8 —2J 43
(off Pembroke Rd.)
Stowe Pl. N15 —1C 44
Stowe Rd. W12 —3F 72
Stowe Rd. Orp —6F 128
Stowting Rd. Orp —6C 128
Stoxmead. Harr —8B 22
Stracey Rd. E7 —9E 46
Stracey Rd. NW10 —4B 56
Strachan Pl. SW19 —3G 105
Stradbroke Dri. Chig —6L 31
Stradbroke Gro. Buck H —1H 31
Stradbroke Gro. Ilf —1J 47
Stradbroke Pk. Chig —6M 31
Stradbroke Rd. N5 —9A 44
Stradbrook Clo. Harr —8K 37
Stradella Rd. SE24 —5A 92
Strafford Av. Ilf —9L 31
Strafford Ho. SE8 —6K 77
(off Grove St.)
Strafford Rd. W3 —3A 72
Strafford Rd. Barn —5J 13
Strafford Rd. Houn —2K 85
Strafford Rd. Twic —6E 86
Strafford St. E14 —3L 77
Strahan Rd. E3 —6J 61
Straight Rd. Romf —5F 34
Straightsmouth. SE10 —8A 78
Straight, The. S'hall —3H 69
Strait Rd. E6 —1J 79
Strakers Rd. SE15 —3F 92
Strale Ho. N1 —4C 60
(off Whitmore Est.)
Strand. WC2 —1J 75
Strand Ct. SE18 —6C 80
Strandfield Clo. SE18 —6C 80
Strand La. WC2 —1K 75
Strand On The Green. —7L 71
Strand on the Grn. W4 —7L 71
Strand Pl. N18 —4C 28
Strand School App. W4 —7L 71
Strand Theatre. —1K 75
(off Aldwych)
Strangeways. Wat —9C 4
Strang Ho. N1 —4A 60
Strang Print Room. —7H 59
(off Gower St.)
Strangways Ter. W14 —4K 73
Stranraer Rd. H'row A —5C 144
Stranraer Way. N1 —3J 59
Stranraer Way. Stanw —5C 144
Strasburg Rd. SW11 —9E 74
Stratfield Pk. Clo. N21 —9M 15
Stratfield Rd. Borwd —5L 11
Stratford. —3B 62
Stratford Av. Uxb —5D 142
Stratford Cen., The. E15 —3B 62
Stratford Circus Arts Cen. —2B 62
Stratford Clo. Bark —3E 64
Stratford Clo. Dag —3A 66
Stratford Ct. N Mald —8B 104
Stratford Ct. Wat —3F 8
Stratford Gro. SW15 —3H 89
Stratford Ho. Romf —6H 35
(off Dartfields)
Stratford Ho. Av. Brom —7J 111
Stratford Marsh. —3M 61
Stratford New Town. —1A 62
Stratford Office Village, The. E15 —3C 62
(off Romford Rd.)
Stratford Pl. W1 —9F 58
Stratford Rd. E13 —4D 62
(in two parts)
Stratford Rd. NW4 —2H 41
Stratford Rd. W8 —4L 73
Stratford Rd. Hay —7F 52
Stratford Rd. H'row A —5F 144
Stratford Rd. S'hall —5J 69
Stratford Rd. T Hth —8L 107
Stratford Rd. Wat —4E 8
Stratford Shop. Cen. E15 —3B 62
(off Stratford Cen., The)
Stratford Studios. W8 —4L 73

Sycamore Rd.—Teddington Pk.

Sycamore Rd. Dart —7H 99
Sycamore St. EC1 —7A 60
Sycamore Wlk. W10 —7J 57
Sycamore Wlk. Ilf —2A 48
Sycamore Way. Tedd —3G 103
Sycamore Way. T Hth —9L 107
Sydcote. SE21 —7A 92
Sydenham. —1G 109
Sydenham Av. N21 —7K 15
Sydenham Av. SE26 —2F 108
Sydenham Clo. Romf —1D 50
Sydenham Cotts. SE12 —8G 95
Sydenham Ct. Croy —3B 124
(off Sydenham Rd.)
Sydenham Hill. SE23 & SE26 —7F 92
Sydenham Pk. SE26 —9G 93
Sydenham Pk. Mans. SE26 —9G 93
(off Sydenham Pk.)
Sydenham Pk. Rd. SE26 —9G 93
Sydenham Pl. SE27 —9M 91
Sydenham Ri. SE23 —8F 92
Sydenham Rd. SE26 —1G 109
Sydenham Rd. Croy —3A 124
Sydmons Ct. SE23 —6G 93
Sydner M. N16 —9D 44
Sydner Rd. N16 —9D 44
Sydney Av. Purl —4K 137
Sydney Clo. SW3 —5B 74
Sydney Ct. Hay —7G 53
Sydney Gro. NW4 —3G 41
Sydney M. SW3 —5B 74
Sydney Pl. SW7 —5B 74
Sydney Rd. E11 —4F 46
Sydney Rd. N8 —2L 43
Sydney Rd. N10 —8E 26
Sydney Rd. SE2 —6H 81
Sydney Rd. SW20 —6H 105
Sydney Rd. W13 —2E 70
Sydney Rd. Bexh —3H 97
Sydney Rd. Enf —5B 16
(in two parts)
Sydney Rd. Felt —7E 84
Sydney Rd. Ilf —9A 32
Sydney Rd. Rich —3J 87
Sydney Rd. Sidc —1C 112
Sydney Rd. Sutt —6L 121
Sydney Rd. Tedd —2D 102
Sydney Rd. Wat —7C 8
Sydney Rd. Wfd G —4E 30
Sydney St. SW3 —6C 74
Sylvana Clo. Uxb —4D 142
Sylvan Av. N3 —9L 25
Sylvan Av. N22 —7K 27
Sylvan Av. NW7 —6C 24
Sylvan Av. Horn —4J 51
Sylvan Av. Romf —4K 49
Sylvan Clo. S Croy —2F 138
Sylvan Ct. N12 —3M 25
Sylvan Est. SE19 —5D 108
Sylvan Gdns. Surb —2H 119
Sylvan Gro. NW2 —9H 41
Sylvan Gro. SE15 —7F 76
Sylvan Hill. SE19 —5C 108
Sylvan Rd. E7 —2E 62
Sylvan Rd. E11 —3E 46
Sylvan Rd. E17 —3L 45
Sylvan Rd. SE19 —5D 108
Sylvan Wlk. Brom —7K 111
Sylvan Way. Chig —3F 32
Sylvan Way. Dag —9F 48
Sylvan Way. W W'ck —6C 126
Sylverdale Rd. Croy —5M 123
Sylverdale Rd. Purl —5M 137
Sylvester Av. Chst —3K 111
Sylvester Gdns. Ilf —5F 32
Sylvester Path. E8 —2F 60
Sylvester Rd. E8 —2F 60
Sylvester Rd. E17 —5K 45
Sylvester Rd. N2 —9A 26
Sylvester Rd. Wemb —1G 55
Sylvestrus Clo. King T —5L 103
Sylvia Av. Pinn —6J 21
Sylvia Ct. N1 —5B 60
Sylvia Ct. Wemb —3M 55
Sylvia Gdns. Wemb —3M 55
Sylvia Pankhurst Ho. Dag —8L 49
(off Wythenshawe Rd.)
Symes M. NW1 —5G 59
Symington Ho. SE1 —4B 76
(off Deverell St.)
Symington M. E9 —1H 61
Symister M. N1 —6C 60
(off Coronet St.)
Symonds Ct. Chesh —1D 6
Symons St. SW3 —5D 74
Syon Ga. Way. Bren —8E 70
Syon House & Pk. —9G 71
Syon La. Iswth —7D 70
Syon Lodge. SE12 —6E 94
Syon Pk. Gdns. Iswth —8D 70
Syracuse Av. Rain —6J 67
Syringa Ho. SE4 —2K 93

Tabard Ct. E14 —9A 62
(off Lodore St.)
Tabard Garden Est. SE1 —4B 76
Tabard Ho. SE1 —4B 76
(off Manciple St.)
Tabard St. SE1 —3B 76
Tabarin Way. Eps —8G 135
Tabernacle Av. E13 —7E 62
Tabernacle St. EC2 —7B 60
Tableer Av. SW4 —4G 91
Tabley Rd. N7 —9J 43
Tabor Ct. Sutt —8J 121
Tabor Gdns. Sutt —8K 121
Tabor Gro. SW19 —4J 105
Tabor Rd. W6 —4F 72
Tachbrook Est. SW1 —6H 75
Tachbrook M. SW1 —5G 75
Tachbrook Rd. Felt —6D 84
Tachbrook Rd. S'hall —5H 69
Tachbrook Rd. Uxb —5A 142
Tachbrook Rd. W Dray —2J 143
Tachbrook St. SW1 —5G 75
(in two parts)
Tack M. SE4 —2L 93
Tadema Ho. NW8 —7B 58
(off Penfold St.)
Tadema Rd. SW10 —8A 74
Tadlow. King T —7L 103
(off Washington Rd.)
Tadlows Clo. Upm —1M 67
Tadmor Clo. Sun —8D 100
Tadmor St. W12 —2H 73
Tadworth Av. N Mald —8D 104
Tadworth Ho. SE1 —3M 75
(off Webber St.)
Tadworth Pde. Horn —9F 50
Tadworth Rd. NW2 —7E 40
Taeping St. E14 —5M 77
Taffrail Ho. E14 —6M 77
(off Burrells Wharf Sq.)
Taffy's Row. Mitc —7C 106
Taft Way. E3 —6M 61
Tailworth St. E1 —8E 60
(off Chicksand St.)
Tailworth St. Houn —1A 86
Tait Ct. SW8 —9J 75
(off Lansdowne Grn.)
Tait Ho. SE1 —2L 75
(off Greet St.)
Tait Rd. Croy —2C 124
Takeley Clo. Romf —9B 34
Takeley Clo. Wal A —6K 7
Takhar M. SW11 —1C 90
Talacre Rd. NW5 —2E 58
Talbot Av. N2 —1B 42
Talbot Av. Wat —9J 9
Talbot Clo. N15 —2D 44
Talbot Ct. EC3 —1B 76
(off Gracechurch St.)
Talbot Ct. NW9 —8B 40
Talbot Cres. NW4 —3E 40
Talbot Gdns. Ilf —7E 48
Talbot Gro. Ho. W11 —9J 57
(off Lancaster Rd.)
Talbot Ho. E14 —9M 61
(off Giraud St.)
Talbot Pl. SE3 —1C 94
Talbot Rd. E6 —5L 63
Talbot Rd. E7 —9E 46
Talbot Rd. N6 —4E 42
Talbot Rd. N15 —2D 44
Talbot Rd. N22 —9G 27
Talbot Rd. SE22 —3C 92
Talbot Rd. W11 & W2 —9K 57
(in two parts)
Talbot Rd. W13 —2E 70
Talbot Rd. Cars —7E 122
Talbot Rd. Dag —2K 65
Talbot Rd. Harr —9D 22
Talbot Rd. Iswth —3E 86
Talbot Rd. S'hall —5J 69
Talbot Rd. T Hth —8B 108
Talbot Rd. Twic —7C 86
Talbot Rd. Wemb —2H 55
Talbot Sq. W2 —9B 58
Talbot Wlk. NW10 —2C 56
Talbot Wlk. W11 —9J 57
Talbot Yd. SE1 —2B 76
Talcott Path. SW2 —7L 91
Talfourd Pl. SE15 —9D 76
Talfourd Rd. SE5 —9D 76
Talgarth Ho. Romf —6J 35
(off Kingsbridge Cir.)
Talgarth Mans. W14 —6J 73
(off Talgarth Rd.)
Talgarth Rd. W6 & W14 —6H 73
Talgarth Wlk. NW9 —3C 40
Talia Ho. E14 —4A 78
(off Manchester Rd.)
Talina Cen. SW6 —9A 74
Talisman Clo. Ilf —6F 48
Talisman Sq. SE26 —1E 108
Talisman Way. Eps —8G 135
Talisman Way. Wemb —8K 39
Tallack Clo. Harr —7C 22
Tallack Rd. E10 —6K 45
Tall Elms Clo. Brom —9D 110
Tallents Clo. S at H —4M 115
Talleyrand Ho. SE5 —1A 92
(off Lilford Rd.)
Tallis Clo. E16 —9F 62
Tallis Gro. SE7 —7F 78
Tallis St. EC4 —1L 75
Tallis Vw. NW10 —2B 56
Tallis Way. Borwd —3H 11
Tall Pines. Eps —3D 134
Tall Trees. SW16 —7K 107
Tall Trees Clo. Horn —3J 51
Talma Gdns. Twic —5C 86
Talmage Clo. SE23 —6G 93
Talman Gro. Stan —6H 23
Talma Rd. SW2 —3L 91
Talwin St. E3 —6M 61
Tamar Clo. E3 —4K 61
Tamar Dri. Ave —9M 67
Tamar Ho. SE11 —6L 75
(off Kennington La.)
Tamarind Ct. W8 —4M 73
(off St Margaret's La.)
Tamarind Yd. E1 —2E 76
(off Kennet St.)
Tamarisk Sq. W12 —1D 72
Tamar Sq. Wfd G —6F 30
Tamar St. SE7 —4J 79
Tamar Way. N17 —1E 44
Tamesis Gdns. Wor Pk —4C 120
Tamian Ind. Est. Houn —3G 85
Tamian Way. Houn —3G 85
Tamworth. N7 —2J 59
Tamworth Av. Wfd G —6C 30
Tamworth La. Mitc —6F 106
Tamworth Pk. Mitc —7F 106
Tamworth Pl. Croy —4A 124
Tamworth Rd. Croy —4M 123
Tamworth St. SW6 —7L 73
Tamworth Vs. Mitc —8F 106
Tancred Rd. N4 —5M 43
Tandem Cen. Retail Pk. SW19 —5B 106
Tandem Way. SW19 —5B 106
Tandridge Dri. Orp —3B 128
Tandridge Gdns. S Croy —5D 138
Tandridge Pl. Orp —3B 128
Tanfield Av. NW2 —9D 40
Tanfield Rd. Croy —6A 124
Tangent Link. H Hill —8H 35
Tangier Rd. Rich —3L 87
Tangier Way. Tad —9J 135
Tangier Wood. Tad —9J 135
Tangleberry Clo. Brom —8K 111
Tangle Tree Clo. N3 —9M 25
Tanglewood Clo. Croy —5G 125
Tanglewood Clo. Stan —2C 22
Tanglewood Clo. Uxb —7E 142
Tanglewood Ct. St M —7G 113
Tanglewood Way. Felt —9F 84
Tangley Gro. SW15 —5D 88
Tangley Pk. Rd. Hamp —2K 101
Tangmere. N17 —9B 28
(off Willan Rd.)
Tangmere. WC1 —6K 59
(off Sidmouth St.)
Tangmere Cres. Horn —2F 66
Tangmere Gdns. N'holt —5G 53
(in two parts)
Tangmere Gro. King T —2H 103
Tangmere Way. NW9 —9C 24
Tanhurst Ho. SW2 —6K 91
(off Redlands Way)
Tanhurst Wlk. SE2 —4H 81
Tankerton Houses. WC1 —6J 59
(off Tankerton St.)
Tankerton Rd. Surb —4K 119
Tankerton St. WC1 —6J 59
Tankerton Ter. Croy —1K 123
Tankerville Rd. SW16 —4H 107
Tank Hill Rd. Purf —5L 83
Tank La. Purf —5L 83
Tankridge Rd. NW2 —7F 40
Tanner Ho. SE1 —3C 76
(off Tanner St.)
Tanneries, The. E1 —7G 61
(off Cephas Av.)
Tanner Point. E13 —4E 62
(off Pelly Rd.)
Tanners Clo. W on T —1F 116
Tanners End La. N18 —4C 28
Tanner's Hill. SE8 —9K 77
Tanners Hill. Ab L —4D 4
Tanners La. B'side & Ilf —1A 48
Tanner St. SE1 —3C 76
(in two parts)
Tanner St. Bark —2A 64
Tanners Wood Clo. Ab L —5C 4
Tanners Wood Ct. Ab L —5C 4
Tanners Wood La. Ab L —5C 4
Tannery Clo. Beck —9H 109
Tannery Clo. Dag —8M 49
Tannington Ter. N5 —8M 43
Tannsfeld Rd. SE26 —2H 109
Tansley Clo. N7 —1H 59
Tanswell St. SE1 —3L 75
Tansy Clo. E6 —9L 63
Tansy Clo. Romf —6J 35
Tantallon Rd. SW12 —7E 90
Tant Av. E16 —9D 62
Tantony Gro. Romf —1H 49
Tanworth Clo. N'wd —6A 20
Tanworth Gdns. Pinn —9F 20
Tanyard La. Bex —6L 97
Tanza Rd. NW3 —9D 42
Tapestry Clo. Sutt —9M 121
Tapley Ho. SE1 —3E 76
(off Wolseley St.)
Tapling Trad. Est. W Dray —1H 143
Taplow. SE17 —6B 76
(off Thurlow St.)
Taplow Ct. Mitc —8C 106
Taplow Ho. E2 —6D 60
(off Palissy St.)
Taplow Rd. N13 —4A 28
Taplow St. N1 —5A 60
Tappesfield Rd. SE15 —2G 93
Tapp St. E1 —7F 60
Tapster St. Barn —5K 13
Tara Ct. Beck —6M 109
Taranto Ho. E1 —8H 61
(off Master's St.)
Tarbert Rd. SE22 —4C 92
Tarbert Wlk. E1 —1G 77
Target Clo. Felt —5C 84
Target Ho. W13 —2F 70
(off Sherwood Clo.)
Target Roundabout. (Junct.) —4K 53
Tariff Cres. SE8 —5K 77
Tariff Rd. N17 —6E 28
Tarleton Ct. N22 —9L 27
Tarleton Gdns. SE23 —8F 92
Tarling Clo. Sidc —9F 96
Tarling Ho. E1 —9F 60
(off Tarling St.)
Tarling Rd. E16 —9D 62
Tarling Rd. N2 —9A 26
Tarling St. E1 —9G 61
Tarling St. Est. E1 —9G 61
Tarmac Way. W Dray —8G 143
Tarn Bank. Enf —7J 15
Tarns, The. NW1 —6G 59
(off Varndell St.)
Tarn St. SE1 —4A 76
Tarnwood Pk. SE9 —6K 95
Tarnworth Rd. Romf —5L 35
Tarplett Ho. SE14 —7G 77
(off John Williams Clo.)
Tarquin Ho. SE26 —1E 108
(off High Level Dri.)
Tarragon Clo. SE14 —8J 77
Tarragon Gro. SE26 —3H 109
Tarranbrae. NW6 —3J 57
Tarrant Ho. E2 —6G 61
(off Roman Rd.)
Tarrant Pl. W1 —8D 58
Tarrington Clo. SW16 —9H 91
Tartan Ho. E14 —9A 62
(off Dee St.)
Tarver Rd. SE17 —6M 75
Tarves Way. SE10 —8M 77
Tash Pl. N11 —5F 26
Tasker Clo. Hay —8A 68
Tasker Ho. E14 —8K 61
(off Wallwood St.)
Tasker Ho. Bark —5B 64
Tasker Rd. NW3 —1D 58
Tasman Ct. E14 —5M 77
(off Westferry Rd.)
Tasman Ct. Sun —4C 100
Tasman Ho. E1 —2F 76
(off Clegg St.)
Tasmania Ter. N18 —6A 28
Tasman Rd. SW9 —2J 91
Tasman Wlk. E16 —9H 63
Tasso Rd. W6 —7J 73
Tasso Yd. W6 —7J 73
(off Tasso Rd.)
Tatam Rd. NW10 —3B 56
Tatchbury Ho. SW15 —5D 88
(off Tunworth Cres.)
Tate Britain. —5J 75
Tate Gdns. Bush —9C 10
Tate Ho. E2 —5H 61
(off Mace St.)
Tate Modern. —2M 75
Tate Rd. E16 —2K 79
(in two parts)
Tate Rd. Sutt —7L 121
Tatnell Rd. SE23 —5J 93
Tatsfield Ho. SE1 —4B 76
(off Pardoner St.)
Tattenham Corner Rd. Eps —9D 134
Tattenham Cres. Eps —9E 134
Tattenham Way. Tad —9H 135
Tattersall Clo. SE9 —4J 95
Tatton Cres. N16 —5D 44
Tatum St. SE17 —5B 76
Tauber Clo. Els —6K 11
Tauheed Clo. N4 —7A 44
Taunton Av. SW20 —6F 104
Taunton Clo. Bexh —1B 98
Taunton Clo. Ilf —6D 32
Taunton Clo. Sutt —3L 121
Taunton Dri. N2 —9A 26
Taunton Dri. Enf —5L 15
Taunton Ho. W2 —9A 58
(off Hallfield Est.)
Taunton Ho. Romf —5K 35
(off Redcar Rd.)
Taunton M. NW1 —7D 58
Taunton Pl. NW1 —7D 58
Taunton Rd. SE12 —4C 94
Taunton Rd. Gnfd —4M 53
Taunton Rd. Romf —4G 35
Taunton Way. Stan —9J 23
Tavern Clo. Cars —2C 122
Taverners Clo. W11 —2J 73
Taverner Sq. N5 —9A 44
Taverners Way. E4 —1C 30
Tavern La. SW9 —1L 91
Tavern Quay. SE16 —5J 77
Tavistock Av. E17 —1H 45
Tavistock Av. Gnfd —5E 54
Tavistock Clo. N16 —1C 60
Tavistock Clo. Romf —8H 35
Tavistock Ct. WC1 —7H 59
(off Tavistock Sq.)
Tavistock Ct. Croy —3B 124
(off Tavistock Rd.)
Tavistock Cres. W11 —8K 57
(in three parts)
Tavistock Cres. Mitc —8J 107
Tavistock Gdns. Ilf —9C 48
Tavistock Ga. Croy —3B 124
Tavistock Gro. Croy —2B 124
Tavistock Ho. WC1 —7H 59
Tavistock M. E18 —2E 46
Tavistock M. W11 —9K 57
Tavistock Pl. E18 —2E 46
Tavistock Pl. N14 —9F 14
Tavistock Pl. WC1 —7J 59
Tavistock Rd. E7 —9D 46
Tavistock Rd. E15 —2D 62
Tavistock Rd. E18 —1E 46
Tavistock Rd. N4 —4B 44
Tavistock Rd. NW10 —5D 56
Tavistock Rd. W11 —9K 57
(in two parts)
Tavistock Rd. Brom —8D 110
Tavistock Rd. Cars —3B 122
Tavistock Rd. Croy —3B 124
Tavistock Rd. Edgw —8L 23
Tavistock Rd. Uxb —1B 52
Tavistock Rd. Wat —3H 9
Tavistock Rd. Well —9G 81
Tavistock Rd. W Dray —2H 143
Tavistock Sq. WC1 —7H 59
Tavistock St. WC2 —1J 75
(in two parts)
Tavistock Ter. N19 —8H 43
Tavistock Tower. SE16 —4J 77
Tavistock Wlk. Cars —3B 122
Taviton St. WC1 —7H 59
Tavy Bri. SE2 —3G 81
Tavy Bri. Cen. SE2 —3G 81
Tavy Clo. SE11 —6L 75
(off White Hart St., in two parts)
Tawney Rd. SE28 —1F 80
Tawny Av. Upm —1M 67
Tawny Clo. W13 —2F 70
Tawny Clo. Felt —9E 84
Tawny Way. SE16 —5H 77
Tayben Av. Twic —5C 86
Taybridge Rd. SW11 —2E 90
Tay Bldgs. SE1 —4C 76
(off Decima St.)
Tayburn Clo. E14 —9A 62
Tayfield Clo. Uxb —8A 36
Tayler Ct. NW8 —4B 58
(off Dorman Way)
Tayles Hill Dri. Eps —2D 134
Taylor Av. Rich —1M 87
Taylor Clo. N17 —7E 28
Taylor Clo. SE8 —7K 77
Taylor Clo. Eps —3L 133
Taylor Clo. Hamp H —2A 102
Taylor Clo. Houn —9A 70
Taylor Clo. Orp —6D 128
Taylor Clo. Romf —7L 33
Taylor Ct. E15 —1A 62
Taylor Ct. SE20 —6G 109
(off Elmers End Rd.)
Taylor Rd. Asht —9H 133
Taylor Rd. Mitc —4C 106
Taylor Rd. Wall —7F 122
Taylor Row. Dart —9G 99
Taylor Row. Noak H —2G 35
Taylors Bldgs. SE18 —5M 79
Taylors Clo. Sidc —9D 96
Taylors Ct. Felt —8E 84
Taylors Grn. W3 —9C 56
Taylors La. NW10 —3C 56
Taylor's La. SE26 —1F 108
Taylors La. Barn —3K 13
Taylorsmead. NW7 —5E 24
Taylor Ter. Chesh —1E 6
Taymount Grange. SE23 —8G 93
Taymount Ri. SE23 —8G 93
Tayport Clo. N1 —3J 59
Tayside Ct. SE5 —3B 92
Tayside Dri. Edgw —3M 23
Tay Way. Romf —8D 34
Taywood Rd. N'holt —6K 53
Teak Clo. SE16 —2J 77
Teal Av. Orp —8H 113
Tealby Ct. N7 —1K 59
(off George's Rd.)
Teal Clo. E16 —8H 63
Teal Clo. S Croy —3H 139
Teal Ct. NW10 —2B 56
Teal Ct. SE8 —7K 77
(off Abinger Gro.)
Teal Dri. N'wd —7A 20
Teale St. E2 —5E 60
Teal Ho. Wat —9J 5
Tealing Dri. Eps —6B 120
Teal Pl. Sutt —7K 121
Teardrop Ind. Est. Swan —9F 114
Teasel Clo. Croy —3H 125
Teasel Way. E15 —6C 62
Teazlewood Pk. Lea —9E 132
Tebworth Rd. N17 —7D 28
Teck Clo. Iswth —1E 86
Tedder Clo. Chess —7G 119
Tedder Clo. Ruis —1E 52
Tedder Clo. Uxb —3D 142
Tedder Rd. S Croy —9G 125
Teddington. —2E 102
Teddington Bus. Pk. Tedd —3D 102
(off Station Rd.)
Teddington Clo. Eps —2B 134
Teddington Pk. Tedd —2D 102

Thistlebrook—Tinworth St.

Thistlebrook. SE2 —4G 81
Thistle Ct. Dart —7M 99
(off Churchill Clo.)
Thistlecroft Gdns. Stan —8H 23
Thistlecroft Rd. W on T —6G 117
Thistledene. Th Dit —1C 118
Thistledene Av. Harr —8J 37
Thistledene Av. Romf —5M 33
Thistle Gro. SW10 —6A 74
Thistle Ho. E14 —9A 62
(off Dee St.)
Thistlemead. Chst —6M 111
Thistle Mead. Lou —5L 19
Thistlewaite Rd. E5 —8F 44
Thistlewood Clo. N7 —7K 43
Thistlewood Cres. New Ad —4B 140
Thistleworth Clo. Iswth —8B 70
Thistleworth Marina. Iswth —3F 86
(off Railshead Rd.)
Thistley Clo. N12 —6C 26
Thistley Ct. SE8 —7M 77
Thomas A'Beckett Clo. Wemb —9D 38
Thomas Baines Rd. SW11 —2B 90
Thomas Burt Ho. E2 —6F 60
(off Canrobert St.)
Thomas Ct. E17 —3M 45
Thomas Cribb M. E6 —9L 63
Thomas Darby Ct. W11 —9J 57
(off Lancaster Rd.)
Thomas Dean Rd. SE26 —1K 109
Thomas Dinwiddy Rd. SE12 —8F 94
Thomas Doyle St. SE1 —4M 75
Thomas England Ho. Romf —4B 50
(off Waterloo Gdns.)
Thomas Hewlett Ho. Harr —9C 38
Thomas Hollywood Ho. E2 —5G 61
(off Approach Rd.)
Thomas Ho. Sutt —9M 121
Thomas La. SE6 —6L 93
Thomas More Highwalk. EC2
(off Beech St.) —8A 60
Thomas More Ho. EC2 —8A 60
(off Beech St.)
Thomas More Sq. E1 —1E 76
(off Thomas More St.)
Thomas More St. E1 —1E 76
Thomas More Way. N2 —1A 42
Thomas Neals Shop. Mall. WC2
(off Earlham St.) —9J 59
Thomas N. Ter. E16 —8D 62
(off Barking Rd.)
Thomas Pl. W8 —4M 73
Thomas Rd. E14 —9K 61
Thomas Rd. Ind. Est. E14 —8L 61
(in two parts)
Thomas Sims Ct. Horn —2F 66
Thomas St. SE18 —5M 79
Thomas Turner Path. Croy —4A 124
(off George St.)
Thomas Wall Clo. Sutt —7M 121
Thomas Watson Cottage Homes.
(off Leecroft Rd.) Barn —6J 13
Thompson Av. Rich —2L 87
Thompson Clo. Ilf —7A 48
Thompson Ho. SE14 —7G 77
(off John Williams Clo.)
Thompson Rd. SE22 —5D 92
Thompson Rd. Dag —8K 49
Thompson Rd. Uxb —4C 142
Thompson's Av. SE5 —8A 76
Thompson's La. Lou —2E 18
Thomson Cres. Croy —3L 123
Thomson Ho. E14 —9L 61
(off Saracen St.)
Thomson Ho. SE17 —5C 76
(off Tatum St.)
Thomson Ho. SW1 —6H 75
(off Bessborough Pl.)
Thomson Ho. S'hall —1J 69
(off Broadway, The)
Thomson Rd. Harr —1C 38
Thorburn Sq. SE1 —5E 76
Thorburn Way. SW19 —5B 106
Thoresby St. N1 —6A 60
Thorkhill Gdns. Th Dit —3E 118
Thorkhill Rd. Th Dit —3E 118
Thornaby Gdns. N18 —6E 28
Thornaby Ho. E2 —6F 60
(off Canrobert St.)
Thorn Av. Bus H —1A 22
Thorn Bank. Edgw —6L 23
Thornbury. NW4 —2F 40
(off Prince of Wales Clo.)
Thornbury Av. Iswth —8B 70
Thornbury Clo. N16 —1C 60
Thornbury Ct. W11 —1L 73
(off Chepstow Vs.)
Thornbury Ct. Iswth —8C 70
Thornbury Ct. S Croy —7B 124
(off Blunt Rd.)
Thornbury Gdns. Borwd —6A 12
Thornbury Ho. Romf —5H 35
(off Bridgewater Wlk.)
Thornbury Rd. SW2 —5J 91
Thornbury Rd. Iswth —8B 70
Thornbury Sq. N6 —6G 43
Thornby Rd. E5 —8G 45
Thorncliffe Rd. SW4 —5J 91
Thorncliffe Rd. S'hall —6K 69
Thorn Clo. Brom —1L 127
Thorn Clo. N'holt —6K 53
Thorncombe Rd. SE22 —4C 92
Thorncroft. Horn —4F 50
Thorncroft Rd. Sutt —7M 121
Thorncroft St. SW8 —8J 75
Thorndean St. SW18 —8A 90
Thorndene. SE28 —1F 80
Thorndene Av. N11 —1E 26
Thorndike Av. N'holt —4H 53
Thorndike Clo. SW10 —8A 74
Thorndike Ho. SW1 —6H 75
(off Vauxhall Bri. Rd.)
Thorndike St. SW1 —5H 75
Thorndon Clo. Orp —6D 112
Thorndon Gdns. Eps —7C 120
Thorndon Rd. Orp —6D 112
Thorndyke Ct. Pinn —6K 21
Thorne Clo. E11 —9C 46
Thorne Clo. E16 —9E 62
Thorne Clo. Ashf —4A 100
Thorne Clo. Eri —7M 81
Thorne Ho. E2 —6G 61
(off Roman Rd.)
Thorne Ho. E14 —4A 78
(off Launch St.)
Thorne Ho. Clay —9F 118
Thorneloe Gdns. Croy —7L 123
Thorne Pas. SW13 —1C 88
Thorne Rd. SW8 —8J 75
Thornes Clo. Beck —7A 110
Thorne St. SW13 —2C 88
Thornet Wood Rd. Brom —7L 111
Thornewill Ho. E1 —1G 77
(off Cable St.)
Thorney. —4G 143
Thorney Ct. SW7 —3A 74
(off Palace Ga.)
Thorney Cres. SW11 —8B 74
Thorneycroft Clo. W on T —1G 117
Thorneycroft Dri. Enf —1L 17
Thorney Hedge Rd. W4 —5M 71
Thorney Mill Rd. Iver & W Dray —4G 143
Thorney St. SW1 —5J 75
Thornfield Av. NW7 —8J 25
Thornfield Ct. NW7 —8J 25
Thornfield Ho. E14 —1L 77
(off Rosefield Gdns.)
Thornfield Pde. NW7 —7J 25
(off Holders Hill Rd.)
Thornfield Rd. W12 —3F 72
(in four parts)
Thornfield Rd. Bans —9L 135
Thornford Rd. SE13 —4A 94
Thorngate Rd. W9 —7L 57
Thorngrove Rd. E13 —4F 62
Thornham Gro. E15 —1B 62
Thornham St. SE10 —7M 77
Thornhaugh M. WC1 —7H 59
Thornhaugh St. WC1 —7H 59
Thornhill Av. SE18 —8C 80
Thornhill Av. Surb —4J 119
Thornhill Bri. Wharf. N1 —4K 59
Thornhill Cres. N1 —3K 59
Thornhill Gdns. E10 —7M 45
Thornhill Gdns. Bark —3C 64
Thornhill Gro. N1 —3K 59
Thornhill Ho. W4 —6C 72
(off Wood St.)
Thornhill Houses. N1 —3L 59
Thornhill Rd. E10 —7M 45
Thornhill Rd. N1 —3L 59
Thornhill Rd. Croy —2A 124
Thornhill Rd. N'wd —4A 20
Thornhill Rd. Surb —4J 119
Thornhill Sq. N1 —3K 59
Thorn Ho. Borwd —4A 12
(off Elstree Way)
Thornicroft Ho. SW9 —1K 91
(off Stockwell Rd.)
Thorn La. Rain —5H 67
Thornlaw Rd. SE27 —1L 107
Thornley Clo. N17 —7E 28
Thornley Dri. Harr —7M 37
Thornsbeach Rd. SE6 —7A 94
Thornsett Pl. SE20 —6F 108
Thornsett Rd. SE20 —6F 108
Thornsett Rd. SW18 —7M 89
Thornsett Ter. SE20 —6F 108
(off Croydon Rd.)
Thorn Ter. SE15 —2G 93
Thornton Av. SW2 —7H 91
Thornton Av. W4 —5C 72
Thornton Av. Croy —1K 123
Thornton Av. W Dray —4K 143
Thornton Clo. W Dray —4K 143
Thornton Dene. Beck —6L 109
Thornton Gdns. SW12 —7H 91
Thornton Gro. Pinn —6L 21
Thornton Heath. —8A 108
Thornton Heath Pond. (Junct.) —9L 107
Thornton Hill. SW19 —4J 105
Thornton Ho. SE17 —5C 76
(off Townsend St.)
Thornton Pl. W1 —8D 58
Thornton Rd. E11 —7B 46
Thornton Rd. N18 —3G 29
Thornton Rd. SW12 —6H 91
Thornton Rd. SW14 —3B 88
Thornton Rd. SW19 —3H 105
Thornton Rd. Barn —5J 13
Thornton Rd. Belv —5M 81
Thornton Rd. Brom —2E 110
Thornton Rd. Cars —3B 122
Thornton Rd. Croy & T Hth —2K 123
Thornton Rd. Ilf —9M 47
Thornton Rd. E. SW19 —3H 105
Thornton Row. T Hth —9L 107
Thornton's Farm Av. Romf —6A 50
Thornton St. SW9 —1L 91
Thornton Way. NW11 —3M 41
Thorntree Ct. W5 —8J 55
Thorntree Rd. SE7 —6H 79
Thornville Gro. Mitc —6B 106
Thornville St. SE8 —9L 77
Thornwell Ct. W7 —3C 70
(off Du Burstow Ter.)
Thornwood Clo. E18 —9F 30
Thornwood Ho. Buck H —9J 19
Thornwood Rd. SE13 —4C 94
Thornycroft Ho. W4 —6C 72
(off Fraser St.)
Thorogood Gdns. E15 —1C 62
Thorogood Way. Rain —4C 66
Thorold Clo. S Croy —2H 139
Thorold Ho. SE1 —3A 76
(off Pepper St.)
Thorold Rd. N22 —7J 27
Thorold Rd. Ilf —7M 47
Thorparch Rd. SW8 —9H 75
Thorpebank Rd. W12 —2E 72
Thorpe Clo. SE26 —1H 109
Thorpe Clo. W10 —9J 57
Thorpe Clo. New Ad —3A 140
Thorpe Clo. Orp —4C 128
Thorpe Ct. Enf —5M 15
Thorpe Cres. E17 —9K 29
Thorpe Cres. Wat —9G 9
Thorpedale Gdns. Ilf —2L 47
Thorpedale Rd. N4 —7J 43
Thorpe Hall Rd. E17 —8A 30
Thorpe Ho. N1 —4K 59
(off Barnsbury Est.)
Thorpe Lodge. Horn —4J 51
Thorpe Pk. —8J 107
Thorpe Rd. E6 —4K 63
Thorpe Rd. E7 —9D 46
Thorpe Rd. E17 —9A 30
Thorpe Rd. N15 —4C 44
Thorpe Rd. Bark —3B 64
Thorpe Rd. King T —4J 103
Thorpewood Av. SE26 —8F 92
Thorpland Av. Uxb —8A 36
Thorsden Way. SE19 —2C 108
Thorverton Rd. NW2 —8J 41
Thoydon Rd. E3 —5J 61
Thrale Rd. SW16 —1G 107
Thrale St. SE1 —2A 76
Thrapston Ho. Romf —5J 35
(off Lindfield Rd.)
Thrasher Clo. E8 —4D 60
Thrawl St. E1 —8D 60
Thrayle Ho. SW9 —2K 91
(off Benedict Rd.)
Threadgold Ho. N1 —2B 60
(off Dovercourt Est.)
Threadneedle St. EC2 —9B 60
Three Barrels Wlk. EC4 —1A 76
(off Queen St. Pl.)
Three Bridges Bus. Cen. S'hall —3A 70
Three Colt Corner. E2 & E1 —7E 60
(off Cheshire St.)
Three Colts La. E2 —7F 60
Three Colt St. E14 —9K 61
Three Corners. Bexh —1M 97
Three Cranes Wlk. EC4 —1A 76
(off Bell Wharf La.)
Three Cups Yd. WC1 —8K 59
(off Sandland St.)
Three Kings Yd. W1 —1F 74
Three Mill La. E3 —6A 62
Three Oak La. SE1 —3D 76
Three Quays. EC3 —1C 76
(off Tower Hill)
Three Quays Wlk. EC3 —1C 76
Three Valleys Way. Bush —7H 9
Threshers Pl. W11 —1J 73
Thriffwood. SE26 —9G 93
Thrift Farm La. Borwd —4A 12
Thrigby Rd. Chess —8K 119
Thring Ho. SW9 —1K 91
(off Stockwell Rd.)
Throckmorten Rd. E16 —9F 62
Throgmorton Av. EC2 —9B 60
(in two parts)
Throgmorton St. EC2 —9B 60
Throstle Pl. Wat —5G 5
Throwley Clo. SE2 —4G 81
(in two parts)
Throwley Rd. Sutt —7M 121
Throwley Way. Sutt —6M 121
Thrums. Wat —1F 8
Thrupp Clo. Mitc —6F 106
Thrupp's Av. W on T —7H 117
Thrupp's La. W on T —7H 117
Thrush Grn. Harr —2L 37
Thrush St. SE17 —6A 76
Thurbarn Rd. SE6 —2M 109
Thurland Ho. SE16 —5F 76
(off Camilla Rd.)
Thurland Rd. SE16 —4E 76
Thurlby Clo. Harr —4E 38
Thurlby Clo. Wfd G —5K 31
Thurlby Cft. NW4 —1G 41
(off Mulberry Clo.)
Thurlby Rd. SE27 —1L 107
Thurlby Rd. Wemb —2H 55
Thurleigh Av. SW12 —5E 90
Thurleigh Rd. SW12 —6D 90
Thurleston Av. Mord —9J 105
Thurlestone Av. N12 —6D 26
Thurlestone Av. Ilf —9D 48
Thurlestone Clo. Shep —1A 116
Thurlestone Ct. S'hall —9M 53
(off Howard Rd.)
Thurlestone Pde. Shep —1A 116
(off High St.)
Thurlestone Rd. SE27 —9L 91
Thurloe Clo. SW7 —5C 74
Thurloe Ct. SW3 —5C 74
(off Fulham Ct.)
Thurloe Gdns. Romf —4D 50
Thurloe Pl. SW7 —5B 74
Thurloe Pl. M. SW7 —5B 74
(off Thurloe Pl.)
Thurloe Sq. SW7 —5C 74
Thurloe St. SW7 —5B 74
Thurlow Clo. E4 —6M 29
Thurlow Gdns. Ilf —6B 32
Thurlow Gdns. Wemb —1H 55
Thurlow Hill. SE21 —7A 92
Thurlow Ho. SW16 —9J 91
Thurlow Pk. Rd. SE21 —8M 91
Thurlow Rd. NW3 —1B 58
Thurlow Rd. W7 —3E 70
Thurlow St. SE17 —6B 76
(in two parts)
Thurlow Ter. NW5 —1E 58
Thurlow Wlk. SE17 —6C 76
(in two parts)
Thurlstone Rd. Ruis —8E 36
Thurnby Ct. Twic —9C 86
Thurnscoe. NW1 —4G 59
(off Pratt St.)
Thurrock Commercial Cen. Ave —3K 83
Thursland Rd. Sidc —2J 113
Thursley Cres. New Ad —9A 126
Thursley Gdns. SW19 —8H 89
Thursley Ho. SW2 —6K 91
(off Holmewood Gdns.)
Thursley Rd. SE9 —9K 95
Thurso Clo. Romf —6M 35
Thurso Ho. NW6 —5M 57
Thurso St. SW17 —1B 106
Thurstan Dwellings. WC2 —9J 59
(off Newton St.)
Thurstan Rd. SW20 —4F 104
Thurston Ind. Est. SE13 —2M 93
Thurston Rd. SE13 —1M 93
Thurston Rd. S'hall —9K 53
Thurtle Rd. E2 —5D 60
Thwaite Clo. Eri —7A 82
Thyer Clo. Orp —6A 128
Thyra Gro. N12 —6M 25
Tibbatts Rd. E3 —7M 61
Tibbenham Pl. SE6 —8L 93
Tibbenham Wlk. E13 —5D 62
Tibberton Sq. N1 —4A 60
Tibbet's Clo. SW19 —7H 89
Tibbet's Corner. (Junct.) —6H 89
Tibbet's Ride. SW15 —6H 89
Tibbles Clo. Wat —8J 5
Tibbs Hill Rd. Ab L —3D 4
Tiber Gdns. N1 —4J 59
Ticehurst Clo. Orp —4E 112
Ticehurst Rd. SE23 —8J 93
Tichmarsh. Eps —2A 134
Tickford Clo. SE2 —3G 81
Tickford Ho. NW8 —6C 58
Tidal Basin Rd. E16 —1D 78
Tidbury Ct. SW8 —8G 75
(off Stewart's Rd.)
Tidenham Gdns. Croy —5C 124
Tideside Ct. SE18 —4J 79
Tideswell Rd. SW15 —3G 89
Tideswell Rd. Croy —5L 125
Tideway Clo. Rich —1F 102
Tideway Ct. SE16 —2H 77
Tideway Ho. E14 —3L 77
(off Strafford St.)
Tideway Ind. Est. SW8 —7G 75
(off Kirtling St.)
Tideway Wlk. SW8 —7G 75
Tidey St. E3 —8L 61
Tidford Rd. Well —1D 96
Tidworth Rd. E3 —7L 61
Tiepigs La. W W'ck & Brom —4C 126
Tierney Ct. Croy —4C 124
Tierney Rd. SW2 —7J 91
Tiffany Heights. SW18 —6L 89
Tiger La. Brom —8F 110
Tiger Way. E5 —9F 44
Tilbrook Rd. SE3 —2G 95
Tilbury Clo. SE15 —8D 76
Tilbury Clo. Orp —6F 112
Tilbury Ho. SE14 —7H 77
(off Myers La.)
Tilbury Rd. E6 —5K 63
Tilbury Rd. E10 —5A 46
Tildesley Rd. SW15 —5G 89
Tile Farm Rd. Orp —5B 128
Tilehouse Clo. Borwd —5K 11
Tilehurst Point. SE2 —3H 81
Tilehurst Rd. SW18 —7B 90
Tilehurst Rd. Sutt —7J 121
Tile Kiln La. N6 —6F 42
Tile Kiln La. N13 —5A 28
(in two parts)
Tile Kiln La. Bex —8A 98
(in two parts)
Tile Kiln La. Hare —5A 36
Tile Kiln Studios. N6 —6G 43
Tile Yd. E14 —9K 61
Tileyard Rd. N7 —3J 59
Tilford Av. New Ad —1A 140
Tilford Gdns. SW19 —7H 89
Tilford Ho. SW2 —6K 91
(off Holmewood Gdns.)
Tilia Clo. Sutt —7K 121
Tilia Rd. E5 —9F 44
Tilia Wlk. SW9 —3M 91
Till Av. F'ham —2K 131
Tilleard Ho. W10 —6J 57
(off Herries St.)
Tiller Rd. E14 —4L 77
Tillett Clo. NW10 —2A 56
Tillett Sq. SE16 —3J 77
Tillet Way. E2 —6E 60
Tillingbourne Gdns. N3 —1K 41
Tillingbourne Grn. Orp —8D 112
Tillingbourne Way. N3 —2K 41
Tillingham Ct. Wal A —6M 7
Tillingham Way. N12 —4L 25
Tilling Rd. NW2 —6G 41
Tilling Way. Wemb —8H 39
Tillman St. E1 —9F 60
Tilloch St. N1 —3K 59
Tillotson Ct. SW8 —8H 75
(off Wandsworth Rd.)
Tillotson Rd. N9 —2D 28
Tillotson Rd. Harr —7M 21
Tillotson Rd. Ilf —5L 47
Tilmans Mead. F'ham —3K 131
Tilney Ct. EC1 —7A 60
Tilney Ct. Buck H —2E 30
Tilney Dri. Buck H —2E 30
Tilney Gdns. N1 —2B 60
Tilney Rd. Dag —2K 65
(in two parts)
Tilney Rd. S'hall —5G 69
Tilney St. W1 —2E 74
Tilson Gdns. SW12 —6J 91
Tilson Ho. SW2 —6J 91
Tilson Rd. N17 —8E 28
Tilston Clo. E11 —8D 46
Tilton St. SW6 —7J 73
Tiltwood, The. W3 —1A 72
Tilt Yd. App. SE9 —5K 95
Timber Clo. Chst —6L 111
Timbercroft. Eps —6C 120
Timbercroft La. SE18 —7C 80
Timberdene. NW4 —9H 25
Timberdene Av. Ilf —8M 31
Timberland Clo. SE15 —8E 76
Timberland Rd. E1 —9F 60
Timberling Gdns. S Croy —1B 138
Timber Mill Way. SW4 —2H 91
Timber Pond Rd. SE16 —2H 77
Timberslip Dri. Wall —1H 137
Timbers, The. Sutt —8J 121
Timber St. EC1 —7A 60
Timbertop Rd. Big H —9G 141
Timberwharf Rd. N16 —4E 44
Timber Wharves Est. E14 —5L 77
(off Copeland Dri.)
Timbrell Pl. SE16 —2K 77
Time Sq. E8 —1D 60
Times Sq. Sutt —7M 121
Timor Ho. E1 —7J 61
(off Duckett St.)
Timothy Clo. SW4 —4G 91
Timothy Clo. Bexh —4J 97
Timothy Ho. Eri —3J 81
(off Kale Rd.)
Timothy Rd. E3 —8K 61
Timsbury Wlk. SW15 —7E 88
Tindale Clo. S Croy —3B 138
Tindall Clo. Romf —9K 35
Tindal St. SW9 —9M 75
Tinderbox All. SW14 —2B 88
Tine Rd. Chig —5C 32
(in two parts)
Tinniswood Clo. N5 —1L 59
Tinsley Rd. E1 —8G 61
Tintagel Clo. Eps —6D 134
Tintagel Ct. Horn —6L 51
Tintagel Cres. SE22 —3D 92
Tintagel Dri. Stan —4H 23
Tintagel Gdns. SE22 —3D 92
Tintagel Rd. Orp —4G 129
Tintern Av. NW9 —1M 39
Tintern Clo. SW15 —4J 89
Tintern Clo. SW19 —3A 106
Tintern Ct. W13 —1E 70
Tintern Gdns. N14 —9J 15
Tintern Ho. NW1 —5F 58
(off Augustus St.)
Tintern Ho. SW1 —5F 74
(off Abbots Mnr.)
Tintern Path. NW9 —4C 40
(off Fryent Gro.)
Tintern Rd. N22 —8A 28
Tintern Rd. Cars —3B 122
Tintern St. SW4 —3J 91
Tintern Way. Harr —6M 37
Tinto Rd. E16 —7E 62
Tinwell M. Borwd —7B 12
Tinworth St. SE1 —6J 75

Trafford Ho.—Tufton St.

Trafford Ho. N1 —5B 60
(off Cranston Est.)
Trafford Rd. T Hth —9K 107
Traitors' Gate. —2D 76
(off Tower of London, The)
Tralee Ct. SE16 —6F 76
(off Masters Dri.)
Tramsheds Ind. Est. Croy —2H 123
Tramway Av. E15 —3C 62
Tramway Av. N9 —9F 16
Tramway Path. Mitc —8C 106
(in three parts)
Tranley M. NW3 —9C 42
Tranmere Ct. Sutt —9A 122
Tranmere Rd. N9 —9D 16
Tranmere Rd. SW18 —8A 90
Tranmere Rd. Twic —6M 85
Tranquil Pas. SE3 —1D 94
Tranquil Ri. Eri —6C 82
Tranquil Va. SE3 —1C 94
Transay Wlk. N1 —2B 60
Transept St. NW1 —8C 58
Transmere Clo. Orp —1A 128
Transmere Rd. Orp —1A 128
Transom Clo. SE16 —5J 77
Transom Sq. E14 —6M 77
Transport Av. Bren —6E 70
Tranton Rd. SE16 —4E 76
Trappes Ho. SE16 —5F 76
(off Camilla Rd.)
Trap's Hill. Lou —5K 19
Traps La. N Mald —5C 104
Travellers Site. E17 —6K 29
Travellers Way. Houn —1G 85
Travers Clo. E17 —8H 29
Travers Ho. SE10 —7B 78
(off Trafalgar Gro.)
Travers Rd. N7 —8L 43
Travis Ho. SE10 —9A 78
Treacy Clo. Bus H —2A 22
Treadgold St. W11 —1H 73
Treadway St. E2 —5F 60
Treadwell Rd. Eps —8C 134
Treasury Pas. SW1 —3J 75
(off Downing St.)
Treaty Cen. Houn —2M 85
Treaty St. N1 —4K 59
Trebeck St. W1 —2F 74
Trebovir Rd. SW5 —6L 73
Treby St. E3 —7K 61
Trecastle Way. N7 —9H 43
Tredegar M. E3 —6K 61
Tredegar Rd. E3 —5K 61
Tredegar Rd. N11 —7H 27
Tredegar Rd. Dart —8E 98
Tredegar Sq. E3 —6K 61
Tredegar Ter. E3 —6K 61
Trederwen Rd. E8 —4E 60
Tredown Rd. SE26 —2G 109
Tredwell Clo. SW2 —8K 91
Tredwell Clo. Brom —8J 111
Tredwell Rd. SE27 —1M 107
Treebourne Rd. Big H —9G 141
Tree Clo. Rich —7H 87
Treemount Ct. Eps —5C 134
Treen Av. SW13 —2D 88
Tree Rd. E16 —9G 63
Treeside Clo. W Dray —5H 143
Tree Top M. Dag —2B 66
Treetops Clo. SE2 —6J 81
Treetops Clo. N'wd —5B 20
Treeview Clo. SE19 —5C 108
Treewall Gdns. Brom —1F 110
Trefgarne Rd. Dag —7L 49
Trefil Wlk. N7 —9J 43
Trefoil Ho. Eri —3J 81
(off Kale Rd.)
Trefoil Rd. SW18 —4A 90
Trefusis Ct. Houn —9F 68
Trefusis Wlk. Wat —3C 8
Tregaron Av. N8 —4J 43
Tregaron Gdns. N Mald —8C 104
Tregarvon Rd. SW11 —3E 90
Tregenna Av. Harr —9L 37
Tregenna Clo. N14 —7G 15
Tregenna Ct. S Harr —9L 37
Tregony Rd. Orp —6D 128
Trego Rd. E9 —3L 61
Tregothnan Rd. SW9 —2J 91
Tregunter Rd. SW10 —7M 73
Trehearn Rd. Ilf —7B 32
Treherne Ct. SW9 —9M 75
Treherne Ct. SW17 —1E 106
Trehern Rd. SW14 —2B 88
Trehurst St. E5 —1J 61
Trelawney Est. E9 —2G 61
Trelawney Ho. SE1 —3A 76
(off Pepper St.)
Trelawney Rd. Ilf —7B 32
Trelawn Rd. E10 —8A 46
Trelawn Rd. SW2 —4L 91
Trellick Clo. E17 —2M 45
Trellick Tower. W10 —7K 57
(off Golborne Rd.)
Trellis Sq. E3 —6K 61
Treloar Gdns. SE19 —3B 108
Tremadoc Rd. SW4 —3H 91
Tremaine Clo. SE4 —1L 93
Tremaine Rd. SE20 —6F 108
Trematon Ho. SE11 —6L 75
(off Kennings Way)
Trematon Pl. Tedd —4G 103
Tremlett Gro. N19 —8G 43
Tremlett M. N19 —8G 43
Trenance Gdns. Ilf —8E 48
Trenchard Av. Ruis —9F 36
Trenchard Clo. NW9 —8C 24
Trenchard Clo. Stan —6E 22
Trenchard Clo. W on T —7G 117
Trenchard Ct. NW4 —3E 40
Trenchard Ct. Mord —1L 121
Trenchard St. SE10 —6B 78
Trenchold St. SW8 —7J 75
Trendell Ho. E14 —9L 61
(off Dod St.)
Trenear Clo. Orp —6E 128
Trenham Dri. Warl —8G 139
Trenholme Clo. SE20 —4F 108
Trenholme Rd. SE20 —4F 108
Trenholme Ter. SE20 —4F 108
Trenmar Gdns. NW10 —6F 56
Trent Av. W5 —4G 71
Trentbridge Clo. Ilf —6D 32
Trent Ct. S Croy —7A 124
(off Nottingham Rd.)
Trent Gdns. N14 —8F 14
Trentham Dri. Orp —8E 112
Trentham St. SW18 —7L 89
Trent Ho. SE15 —3G 93
Trent Ho. King T —5H 103
Trent Pk. Country Pk. —3F 14
Trent Rd. SW2 —4K 91
Trent Rd. Buck H —1F 30
Trent Way. Hay —5C 52
Trent Way. Wor Pk —5G 121
Trentwood Side. Enf —5K 15
Treport St. SW18 —6M 89
Tresco Clo. Brom —3C 110
Trescoe Gdns. Harr —5J 37
Trescoe Gdns. Romf —5A 34
Tresco Gdns. Ilf —7E 48
Tresco Ho. SE11 —6L 75
(off Sancroft St.)
Tresco Rd. SE15 —3F 92
Tresham Cres. NW8 —7C 58
Tresham Rd. Bark —3D 64
Tresham Wlk. E9 —1G 61
Tresidder Ho. SW4 —6H 91
Tresilian Av. N21 —7K 15
Tressell Clo. N1 —3M 59
Tressillian Cres. SE4 —2L 93
Tressillian Rd. SE4 —3K 93
Tress Pl. SE1 —2M 75
(off Blackfriars Rd.)
Trestis Clo. Hay —7H 53
Treswell Rd. Dag —4J 65
Tretawn Gdns. NW7 —4C 24
Tretawn Pk. NW7 —4C 24
Trevanion Rd. W14 —5J 73
Treve Av. Harr —5B 38
Trevellance Way. Wat —6H 5
Trevelyan Av. E12 —9K 47
Trevelyan Clo. Dart —3K 99
Trevelyan Cres. Harr —5H 39
Trevelyan Gdns. NW10 —4G 57
Trevelyan Ho. E2 —6H 61
(off Morpeth St.)
Trevelyan Ho. SE5 —8M 75
(off John Ruskin St.)
Trevelyan Rd. E15 —9D 46
Trevelyan Rd. SW17 —2C 106
Trevenna Ho. SE23 —9H 93
(off Dacres Rd.)
Trevera Ct. Enf —7J 17
Trevera Ct. Wal X —6E 6
(off Eleanor Rd.)
Treveris St. SE1 —2M 75
Treverton St. W10 —7J 57
Treverton Towers. W10 —8H 57
(off Treverton St.)
Treves Clo. N21 —7K 15
Treves Ho. E1 —7E 60
(off Vallance Rd.)
Treville St. SW15 —6F 88
Treviso Rd. SE23 —8H 93
Trevithick Clo. Felt —7D 84
Trevithick Dri. Dart —3K 99
Trevithick Ho. SE16 —5F 76
(off Rennie Est.)
Trevithick St. SE8 —7L 77
Trevone Ct. SW2 —6J 91
(off Doverfield Rd.)
Trevone Gdns. Pinn —4J 37
Trevor Clo. Brom —2D 126
Trevor Clo. E Barn —8B 14
Trevor Clo. Harr —7D 22
Trevor Clo. Iswth —4D 86
Trevor Clo. N'holt —5G 53
Trevor Cres. Ruis —9D 36
Trevor Gdns. Edgw —8B 24
Trevor Gdns. N'holt —5G 53
Trevor Gdns. Ruis —9E 36
Trevor Pl. SW7 —3C 74
Trevor Rd. SW19 —4J 105
Trevor Rd. Edgw —8B 24
Trevor Rd. Hay —3C 68
Trevor Rd. Wfd G —7E 30
Trevor Sq. SW7 —3D 74
Trevor St. SW7 —3C 74
Trevor Wlk. SW7 —3C 74
(off Trevor Pl.)
Trevose Ho. SE11 —6K 75
(off Orsett St.)
Trevose Rd. E17 —8B 30
Trevose Way. Wat —3G 21
Trewenna Dri. Chess —7H 119
Trewince Rd. SW20 —5G 105
Trewint St. SW18 —8A 90
Trewsbury Ho. SE2 —2H 81
Trewsbury Rd. SE26 —2H 109
Triandra Way. Hay —8H 53
Triangle Bus. Cen., The. NW10 —6D 56
Triangle Cen. S'hall —2B 70
Triangle Ct. E16 —8H 63
Triangle Pas. Barn —6A 14
Triangle Pl. SW4 —3H 91
Triangle Rd. E8 —4F 60
Triangle, The. E8 —4F 60
Triangle, The. EC1 —7M 59
(off Cyrus St.)
Triangle, The. N13 —4K 27
Triangle, The. Bark —2A 64
Triangle, The. King T —6M 103
Triangle, The. Sidc —6E 96
(off Burnt Oak La.)
Triangle, The. Wemb —1K 55
Trickett Ho. Sutt —1M 135
Tricycle Theatre. —3K 57
(off Kilburn High Rd.)
Trident Bus. Cen. SW17 —2D 106
Trident Gdns. N'holt —6H 53
Trident Ho. E14 —9A 62
(off Blair St.)
Trident Rd. Wat —7D 4
Trident St. SE16 —5H 77
Trident Way. S'hall —4F 68
Trig La. EC4 —1A 76
Trigo Ct. Eps —3B 134
Trigon Rd. SW8 —8K 75
Trilby Rd. SE23 —8H 93
Trillo Ct. Ilf —5C 48
Trimdon. NW1 —4G 59
Trimmer Wlk. Bren —7J 71
Trim St. SE14 —7K 77
Trinder Gdns. N19 —6J 43
Trinder Rd. N19 —6J 43
Trinder Rd. Barn —7G 13
Tring Av. W5 —2K 71
Tring Av. S'hall —9K 53
Tring Av. Wemb —2L 55
Tring Clo. Ilf —3B 48
Tring Clo. Romf —4K 35
Tring Ct. Twic —1E 102
Tring Gdns. Romf —4J 35
Tring Grn. Romf —4J 35
Tring Ho. Wat —9C 8
Tring Wlk. Romf —4J 35
Trinidad Gdns. Dag —3B 66
Trinidad Ho. E14 —1K 77
(off Gill St.)
Trinidad St. E14 —1K 77
Trinity Av. N2 —1B 42
Trinity Av. Enf —8D 16
Trinity Buoy Wharf. E14 —1C 78
(off Orchard Pl.)
Trinity Bus. Pk. E4 —6K 29
Trinity Chu. Pas. SW13 —7F 72
Trinity Chu. Rd. SW13 —7F 72
Trinity Chu. Sq. SE1 —4A 76
Trinity Clo. E8 —2D 60
Trinity Clo. E11 —7C 46
Trinity Clo. NW3 —9B 42
Trinity Clo. SE13 —3B 94
Trinity Clo. SW4 —3G 91
Trinity Clo. Brom —3J 127
Trinity Clo. Houn —3J 85
Trinity Clo. N'wd —6C 20
Trinity Clo. S Croy —1C 138
Trinity Clo. Stanw —5A 144
Trinity Cotts. Rich —2K 87
Trinity Ct. SE1 —4A 76
(off Brockham St.)
Trinity Ct. SE7 —5H 79
Trinity Ct. SE25 —1C 124
Trinity Ct. SE26 —9G 93
Trinity Ct. W2 —9A 58
(off Gloucester Ter.)
Trinity Ct. WC1 —7K 59
(off Gray's Inn Rd.)
Trinity Ct. Croy —4A 124
Trinity Ct. Dart —7M 99
(off Churchill Clo.)
Trinity Ct. Enf —4A 16
Trinity Cres. SW17 —8D 90
Trinity Gdns. E16 —8D 62
Trinity Gdns. SW9 —3K 91
Trinity Gdns. Dart —5H 99
Trinity Grn. E1 —7G 61
Trinity Gro. SE10 —9A 78
Trinity Hall Clo. Wat —5G 9
Trinity Hospital Almshouses. SE10 —6B 78
(off High Bri.)
Trinity Ho. SE1 —4A 76
(off Bath Ter.)
Trinity Ho. Wal X —5E 6
Trinity La. Wal X —5E 6
Trinity M. SE20 —5F 108
Trinity M. W10 —9H 57
Trinity Path. SE23 —9G 93
Trinity Pier. E14 —1C 78
Trinity Pl. EC3 —1D 76
Trinity Pl. Bexh —3K 97
Trinity Ri. SW2 —7L 91
Trinity Rd. N2 —1B 42
Trinity Rd. N22 —7J 27
(in two parts)
Trinity Rd. SW18 & SW17 —3A 90
Trinity Rd. SW19 —3L 105
Trinity Rd. Ilf —1A 48
Trinity Rd. Rich —2K 87
Trinity Rd. S'hall —2J 69
Trinity Sq. EC3 —1C 76
Trinity St. E16 —8D 62
Trinity St. SE1 —3A 76
(in two parts)
Trinity St. Enf —4A 16
Trinity Tower. E1 —1E 76
(off Vaughan Way)
Trinity Wlk. NW3 —2A 58
Trinity Way. E4 —6K 29
Trinity Way. W3 —1C 72
Trio Pl. SE1 —3A 76
Tristan Ct. SE8 —7K 77
(off Dorking Clo)
Tristan Sq. SE3 —2C 94
Tristram Clo. E17 —1B 46
Tristram Rd. Brom —1D 110
Triton Ho. E14 —5M 77
(off Cahir St.)
Triton Sq. NW1 —7G 59
Tritton Av. Croy —6J 123
Tritton Rd. SE21 —9B 92
Triumph Clo. Hay —9A 68
Triumph Ho. Bark —6E 64
Triumph Rd. E6 —9K 63
Triumph Trad. Est. N17 —6E 28
Trocadero Entertainment Cen. —1H 75
Trocette Mans. SE1 —4C 76
(off Bermondsey St.)
Trojan Ct. NW6 —3J 57
Trojan Ind. Est. NW10 —2D 56
Trojan Way. Croy —5K 123
Troon Clo. SE16 —6F 76
Troon Clo. SE28 —9H 65
Troon Ho. E1 —9J 61
(off White Horse Rd.)
Troon St. E1 —9J 61
Troopers Dri. Romf —4H 35
Trosley Rd. Belv —7L 81
Trossachs Rd. SE22 —4C 92
Trothy Rd. SE1 —5E 76
Trotman Ho. SE14 —9G 77
(off Pomeroy St.)
Trotters Bottom. Barn —1E 12
Trotter Way. Eps —4M 133
Trott Rd. N10 —7D 26
Trott St. SW11 —9C 74
Trot Wood. Chig —5B 32
Troughton Rd. SE7 —6F 78
Troutbeck. NW1 —6F 58
(off Albany St.)
Troutbeck Rd. SE14 —9J 77
Trout La. W Dray —1G 143
Trout Rd. W Dray —2H 143
Trouville Rd. SW4 —5G 91
Trowbridge Rd. E9 —2K 61
Trowbridge Rd. Romf —6H 35
Trowley Ri. Ab L —4C 4
Trowlock Av. Tedd —3G 103
Trowlock Way. Tedd —3H 103
Troy Ct. SE18 —5M 79
Troy Ct. W8 —4L 73
(off Kensington High St.)
Troy Ind. Est. Harr —3D 38
Troy Rd. SE19 —3B 108
Troy Town. SE15 —2E 92
Trubshaw Rd. S'hall —4M 69
Truesdale Rd. E6 —9K 63
Trulock Ct. N17 —7E 28
Trulock Rd. N17 —7E 28
Truman Clo. Edgw —7M 23
Trumans Rd. N16 —1D 60
Trumble Gdns. T Hth —8M 107
Trumpers Way. W7 —4C 70
Trumper Way. Uxb —3A 142
Trumpington Rd. E7 —9D 46
Trump St. EC2 —9A 60
Trundlers Way. Bush —1C 22
Trundle St. SE1 —3A 76
(off Weller St.)
Trundley's Rd. SE8 —6H 77
Trundley's Ter. SE8 —5H 77
Trunks All. Swan —6M 113
Truro Gdns. Ilf —5J 47
Truro Ho. Pinn —7K 21
Truro Rd. E17 —2K 45
Truro Rd. N22 —7J 27
Truro St. NW5 —2E 58
Truro Wlk. Romf —6G 35
Truro Way. N'holt —6C 52
Truslove Rd. SE27 —2L 107
Trussley Rd. W6 —4G 73
Truston's Gdns. Horn —5E 50
Trust Rd. Wal X —7E 6
Trust Wlk. SE21 —7M 91
Tryfan Clo. Ilf —3H 47
Tryon Cres. E9 —4G 61
Tryon St. SW3 —6D 74
Trystings Clo. Clay —8E 118
Tuam Rd. SE18 —7B 80
Tubbenden Clo. Orp —5C 128
Tubbenden Dri. Orp —6B 128
Tubbenden La. Orp —6B 128
Tubbenden La. S. Orp —7B 128
Tubbs Rd. NW10 —5D 56
Tucker St. Wat —7G 9
Tucklow Wlk. SW15 —6D 88
Tuck Rd. Rain —2E 66
Tudor Av. E17 —5K 45
Tudor Av. Chesh —4A 6
Tudor Av. Hamp —4L 101
Tudor Av. Romf —1E 50
Tudor Av. Wat —2H 9
Tudor Av. Wor Pk —5F 120
Tudor Clo. N6 —5G 43
Tudor Clo. NW3 —1C 58
Tudor Clo. NW7 —6E 24
Tudor Clo. NW9 —7A 40
Tudor Clo. SW2 —5K 91
Tudor Clo. Ashf —9C 144
Tudor Clo. Bans —7J 135
Tudor Clo. Chesh —4B 6
Tudor Clo. Chess —7J 119
Tudor Clo. Chig —4L 31
Tudor Clo. Chst —5K 111
Tudor Clo. Dart —5F 98
Tudor Clo. Eps —2D 134
Tudor Clo. Hamp —2A 102
Tudor Clo. Pinn —3E 36
Tudor Clo. S Croy —7F 138
Tudor Clo. Sutt —7H 121
Tudor Clo. Wall —9G 123
Tudor Clo. Wfd G —5F 30
Tudor Ct. N1 —2C 60
Tudor Ct. N22 —7J 27
Tudor Ct. SE9 —3J 95
Tudor Ct. SE16 —2H 77
(off Princes Riverside Rd.)
Tudor Ct. W3 —3L 71
Tudor Ct. Big H —9J 141
Tudor Ct. Borwd —4J 11
Tudor Ct. Crock —2A 130
Tudor Ct. Felt —1G 101
Tudor Ct. Romf —6M 35
Tudor Ct. Sidc —9E 96
Tudor Ct. Stanw —5C 144
Tudor Ct. Tedd —3D 102
Tudor Ct. N. Wemb —1L 55
Tudor Ct. S. Wemb —1L 55
Tudor Cres. Enf —3A 16
Tudor Cres. Ilf —6M 31
Tudor Dri. King T —2H 103
Tudor Dri. Mord —1H 121
Tudor Dri. Romf —2E 50
Tudor Dri. W on T —3H 117
Tudor Dri. Wat —2H 9
Tudor Enterprise Pk. Harr —8D 38
(HA1)
Tudor Enterprise Pk. Harr —1B 38
(HA3)
Tudor Est. NW10 —5M 55
Tudor Gdns. NW9 —7A 40
Tudor Gdns. SW13 —2C 88
Tudor Gdns. W3 —8L 55
Tudor Gdns. Harr —9B 22
Tudor Gdns. Romf —2E 50
Tudor Gdns. Twic —7D 86
Tudor Gdns. Upm —7M 51
Tudor Gdns. W W'ck —5A 126
Tudor Gro. E9 —3G 61
Tudor Ho. E9 —3G 61
Tudor Ho. W14 —5H 73
(off Windsor Way)
Tudor Ho. Pinn —9G 21
(off Pinner Hill Rd.)
Tudor Mnr. Gdns. Wat —5H 5
Tudor M. Romf —3D 50
Tudor Pde. SE9 —3J 95
Tudor Pde. Romf —5H 49
Tudor Pl. SE19 —4D 108
Tudor Pl. Mitc —4C 106
Tudor Rd. E4 —6M 29
Tudor Rd. E6 —4G 63
Tudor Rd. E9 —4F 60
Tudor Rd. N9 —9F 16
Tudor Rd. SE19 —4D 108
Tudor Rd. SE25 —9F 108
Tudor Rd. Ashf —3B 100
Tudor Rd. Bark —4D 64
Tudor Rd. Barn —5L 13
Tudor Rd. Bush —7A 110
Tudor Rd. Hamp —4L 101
Tudor Rd. Harr —9B 22
Tudor Rd. Hay —9B 52
Tudor Rd. Houn —3B 86
Tudor Rd. King T —4L 103
Tudor Rd. Pinn —9G 21
Tudor Rd. S'hall —1J 69
Tudor Sq. Hay —8B 52
Tudor Stacks. SE24 —3A 92
Tudor St. EC4 —1L 75
Tudor Wlk. Bex —5J 97
Tudor Wlk. Wat —1H 9
Tudor Wlk. Wey —5A 116
Tudor Way. N14 —1H 27
Tudor Way. W3 —3L 71
Tudor Way. Orp —1B 128
Tudor Way. Uxb —2E 142
Tudor Way. Wal A —6K 7
Tudor Well Clo. Stan —5F 22
Tudor Works. Hay —2H 69
Tudway Rd. SE3 —2F 94
Tuffnell Ct. Chesh —1D 6
(off Coopers Wlk.)
Tufnail Rd. Dart —5K 99
Tufnell Park. —9G 43
Tufnell Pk. Rd. N19 & N7 —9G 43
Tufter Rd. Chig —5D 32
Tufton Ct. SW1 —4J 75
(off Tufton St.)
Tufton Gdns. W Mol —6M 101
Tufton Rd. E4 —4L 29
Tufton St. SW1 —4J 75

Viscount St.—Wanborough Dri.

Viscount St. EC1 —7A 60
Viscount Way. H'row A —3C 84
Vista Av. Enf —4H 17
Vista Dri. Ilf —3H 47
Vista, The. SE9 —5H 95
Vista, The. Sidc —2D 112
Vista Way. Harr & Kent —4J 39
Vittoria Ho. N1 —4K 59
(off High Rd.)
Viveash Clo. Hay —4D 68
Vivian Av. NW4 —3F 40
Vivian Av. Wemb —1L 55
Vivian Clo. Wat —1E 20
Vivian Comma Clo. N4 —8M 43
Vivian Ct. N12 —5M 25
Vivian Gdns. Wat —1E 20
Vivian Gdns. Wemb —1L 55
Vivian Mans. NW4 —3F 40
(off Vivian Av.)
Vivian Rd. E3 —5J 61
Vivian Sq. SE15 —2F 92
Vivian Way. N2 —3B 42
Vivien Clo. Chess —9J 119
Vivienne Clo. Twic —5H 87
Voce Rd. SE18 —8B 80
Voewood Clo. N Mald —1D 120
Vogans Mill. SE1 —3D 76
Vogler Ho. E1 —1G 77
(off Cable St.)
Vogue Ct. Brom —5F 110
Vollasky Ho. E1 —8E 60
(off Daplyn St.)
Voltaire Rd. SW4 —2H 91
Voltaire Way. Hay —1C 68
Volt Av. NW10 —6B 56
Volta Way. Croy —3K 123
Voluntary Pl. E11 —4E 46
Vorley Rd. N19 —7G 43
Voss Ct. SW16 —3J 107
Voss St. E2 —6E 60
Voyager Bus. Est. SE16 —4E 76
(off Spa Rd.)
Voyagers Clo. SE28 —9G 65
Vulcan Clo. E6 —9L 63
Vulcan Clo. Wall —9K 123
(off Handley Page Rd.)
Vulcan Ga. Enf —4L 15
Vulcan Rd. SE4 —1K 93
Vulcan Sq. E14 —5M 77
Vulcan Ter. SE4 —1K 93
Vulcan Way. N7 —2K 59
Vulcan Way. New Ad —2C 140
Vyner Rd. W3 —1B 72
Vyner St. E2 —4F 60
Vyner's Way. Uxb —1E 142
Vyne, The. Bexh —2M 97
Vyse Clo. Barn —6G 13

Wadard Ter. Swan —9G 115
Wadbrook St. King T —6H 103
Wadding St. SE17 —5B 76
Waddington Clo. Enf —6C 16
Waddington Rd. E15 —1B 62
Waddington St. E15 —2B 62
Waddington Way. SE19 —4A 108
Waddon. —5L 123
Waddon Clo. Croy —5L 123
Waddon Ct. Rd. Croy —5L 123
Waddon Marsh Way. Croy —3K 123
Waddon New Rd. Croy —5M 123
Waddon Pk. Av. Croy —6L 123
Waddon Rd. Croy —5L 123
Waddon Way. Croy —8L 123
Wade Av. Orp —2H 129
Wade Ct. N10 —7F 26
Wade Ho. SE1 —3E 76
(off Parkers Row)
Wade Ho. Enf —7B 16
Wades Gro. N21 —9L 15
Wades Hill. N21 —8L 15
Wades La. Tedd —2E 102
Wadeson St. E2 —5F 60
Wade's Pl. E14 —1M 77
Wadeville Av. Romf —4J 49
Wadeville Clo. Belv —7L 81
Wadham Av. E17 —7M 29
Wadham Clo. Shep —2A 116
Wadham Gdns. NW3 —4C 58
Wadham Gdns. Gnfd —2B 54
Wadham Rd. E17 —7M 29
Wadham Rd. SW15 —3J 89
Wadham Rd. Ab L —4D 4
Wadhurst Clo. SE20 —6F 108
Wadhurst Rd. SW8 —9G 75
Wadhurst Rd. W4 —4B 72
Wadley Rd. E11 —5C 46
Wadsworth Bus. Cen. Gnfd —5G 55
Wadsworth Clo. Enf —7H 17
Wadsworth Clo. Gnfd —5G 55
Wadsworth Rd. Gnfd —5F 54
Wager St. E3 —7K 61
Waggoners Roundabout. (Junct.) —9F 68
Waggon La. N17 —6E 28
Waggon M. N14 —1G 27
Waggon Rd. Barn —1A 14
Waghorn Rd. E13 —4G 63
Waghorn Rd. Harr —1H 39
Waghorn St. SE15 —2E 92
Wagner St. SE15 —8G 77
Wagstaff Gdns. Dag —3G 65
Wagtail Clo. NW9 —9C 24
Wagtail Gdns. S Croy —2J 139
Wagtail Wlk. Beck —9A 110
Wagtail Way. Orp —8H 113
Waid Clo. Dart —5K 99
Waight's Ct. King T —5J 103
Wainfleet Av. Romf —9A 34
Wainford Clo. SW19 —6H 89
Wainwright Gro. Iswth —3B 86
Waite Davies Rd. SE12 —6D 94
Waite St. SE15 —7D 76
Waithman St. EC4 —9M 59
(off Apothecary St.)
Wakefield Ct. SE26 —3G 109
Wakefield Gdns. SE19 —4C 108
Wakefield Gdns. Ilf —4J 47
Wakefield Ho. SE15 —9E 76
Wakefield M. WC1 —6J 59
Wakefield Rd. N11 —5H 27
Wakefield Rd. N15 —3D 44
Wakefield Rd. Rich —4H 87
Wakefield St. E6 —4H 63
Wakefield St. N18 —5E 28
Wakefield St. WC1 —7J 59
Wakefields Wlk. Chesh —4E 6
Wakeford Clo. SW4 —4G 91
Wakehams Hill. Pinn —1K 37
Wakeham St. N1 —2B 60
Wakehurst Rd. SW11 —4C 90
Wakeling Rd. W7 —8D 54
Wakeling St. E14 —9J 61
Wakelin Ho. N1 —3M 59
(off Sebbon St.)
Wakelin Ho. SE23 —6J 93
Wakelin Rd. E15 —5C 62
Wakeman Rd. NW10 —6G 57
Wakemans Hill Av. NW9 —3B 40
Wakerfield Clo. Horn —3K 51
Wakering Rd. Bark —2A 64
(in two parts)
Wakerings, The. Bark —2A 64
Wakerley Clo. E6 —9K 63
Wake Rd. Lou —2G 19
Wakley St. EC1 —6M 59
Walberswick St. SW8 —8J 75
Walbrook. EC4 —1B 76
(in three parts)
Walbrook Ho. N9 —2G 29
(off Huntingdon Rd.)
Walbrook Wharf. EC4 —1A 76
(off Bell Wharf La.)
Walburgh St. E1 —9F 60
Walburton Rd. Purl —5G 137
Walcorde Av. SE17 —5A 76
Walcot Gdns. SE11 —5L 75
(off Kennington Rd.)
Walcot Rd. Enf —4K 17
Walcot Sq. SE11 —5L 75
Walcott St. SW1 —5G 75
Waldair Ct. E16 —3M 79
Waldeck Gro. SE27 —9M 91
Waldeck Rd. N15 —2M 43
Waldeck Rd. SW14 —2A 88
Waldeck Rd. W4 —7L 71
Waldeck Rd. W13 —9F 54
Waldeck Rd. Dart —6K 99
Waldeck Ter. SW14 —2A 88
(off Waldeck Rd.)
Waldegrave Av. Tedd —2D 102
Waldegrave Ct. Bark —4B 64
Waldegrave Ct. Upm —6M 51
Waldegrave Gdns. Twic —8D 86
Waldegrave Gdns. Upm —6M 51
Waldegrave Pk. Twic —1D 102
Waldegrave Rd. N8 —1L 43
Waldegrave Rd. SE19 —4D 108
Waldegrave Rd. W5 —1K 71
Waldegrave Rd. Brom —8J 111
Waldegrave Rd. Dag —7G 49
Waldegrave Rd. Tedd —1D 102
Waldegrove. Croy —5D 124
Waldemar Av. SW6 —9J 73
Waldemar Av. W13 —2G 71
Waldemar Rd. SW19 —2L 105
Walden Av. N13 —4A 28
Walden Av. Chst —1K 111
Walden Av. Rain —5B 66
Walden Clo. Belv —6K 81
Walden Ct. SW8 —9H 75
Walden Gdns. T Hth —7K 107
Walden Ho. SW1 —5E 74
(off Pimlico Rd.)
Waldenhurst Rd. Orp —2H 129
Walden Pde. Chst —3K 111
(in two parts)
Walden Rd. N17 —8B 28
Walden Rd. Chst —3K 111
Walden Rd. Horn —4H 51
Waldens Clo. Orp —2H 129
Waldenshaw Rd. SE23 —7G 93
Waldens Rd. Orp —2J 129
Walden St. E1 —9F 60
Walden Way. NW7 —6H 25
Walden Way. Horn —4H 51
Walden Way. Ilf —7C 32
Waldo Clo. SW4 —4G 91
Waldo Ind. Est. Brom —7H 111
Waldo Pl. Mitc —4C 106
Waldorf Clo. S Croy —1M 137
Waldo Rd. NW10 —6E 56
(in two parts)
Waldo Rd. Brom —7H 111
Waldram Cres. SE23 —7G 93
Waldram Pk. Rd. SE23 —7H 93
Waldram Pl. SE23 —7G 93
Waldrist Way. Eri —3K 81
Waldron Gdns. Brom —7B 110
Waldronhyrst. S Croy —6M 123
Waldron M. SW3 —7B 74
Waldron Rd. SW18 —9A 90
Waldron Rd. Harr —6C 38
Waldron's Path. S Croy —6A 124
Waldrons, The. Croy —6M 123
Waldrons Yd. S Harr —7B 38
Waldstock Rd. SE28 —1E 80
Waleran Clo. Stan —5D 22
Walerand Rd. SE13 —1A 94
Waleran Flats. SE1 —5C 76
Wales Av. Cars —7C 122
Wales Clo. SE15 —8F 76
Wales Farm Rd. W3 —8B 56
Waleton Acres. Wall —8G 123
Waley St. E1 —8J 61
Walfield Av. N20 —9M 13
Walford Ho. E1 —9F 60
Walford Rd. N16 —9C 44
Walford Rd. Uxb —5A 142
Walfrey Gdns. Dag —3J 65
Walham Green. —9M 73
Walham Grn. Ct. SW6 —8M 73
(off Waterford Rd.)
Walham Gro. SW6 —8L 73
Walham Ri. SW19 —3J 105
Walham Yd. SW6 —8L 73
Walkato Lodge. Buck H —1G 31
Walkden Rd. Chst —2L 111
Walker Clo. N11 —4G 27
Walker Clo. SE18 —5A 80
Walker Clo. W7 —2C 70
Walker Clo. Dart —2D 98
Walker Clo. Felt —6D 84
Walker Clo. Hamp —3K 101
Walker Ho. NW1 —5H 59
Walker's Ct. W1 —1H 75
(off Brewer St.)
Walkerscroft Mead. SE21 —7A 92
Walkers Pl. SW15 —3J 89
Walkfield Dri. Eps —9F 134
Walkinshaw Ct. N1 —3A 60
(off Rotherfield St.)
Walkley Rd. Dart —4F 98
Walks, The. N2 —1B 42
Walk, The. N13 —3L 27
(off Fox La.)
Walk, The. Horn —7K 51
Walk, The. Sun —4D 100
Wallace Clo. SE28 —1H 81
Wallace Clo. Shep —8B 100
Wallace Clo. Uxb —5C 142
Wallace Collection. —9E 58
Wallace Ct. NW1 —8C 58
(off Old Marylebone Rd.)
Wallace Cres. Cars —7D 122
Wallace Fields. Eps —5E 134
Wallace Ho. N7 —2K 59
(off Caledonian Rd.)
Wallace Rd. N1 —2A 60
Wallace Way. N19 —7H 43
(off St John's Way)
Wallbrook Bus. Cen. Houn —2F 84
Wallbutton Rd. SE4 —1J 93
Wallcote Av. NW2 —6H 41
Wall Ct. N4 —6K 43
(off Stroud Grn. Rd.)
Wallend. —4L 63
Wall End Ct. E6 —4L 63
(off Wall End Rd.)
Wall End Rd. E6 —3K 63
Wallenger Av. Romf —1F 50
Waller Dri. N'wd —9E 20
Waller Rd. SE14 —9H 77
Wallers Clo. Dag —4J 65
Wallers Clo. Wfd G —6K 31
Waller's Hoppet. Lou —4K 19
Waller Way. SE10 —8M 77
Wallflower St. W12 —1D 72
Wallgrave Rd. SW5 —5M 73
Wallhouse Rd. Eri —8F 82
Wallingford Av. W10 —8H 57
Wallingford Ho. Romf —6J 35
(off Kingsbridge Rd.)
Wallingford Rd. Uxb —5A 142
Wallington. —8G 123
Wallington Clo. Ruis —4A 36
Wallington Corner. Wall —6F 122
(off Manor Rd. N.)
Wallington Ct. Wall —8F 122
(off Stanley Pk. Rd.)
Wallington Green. (Junct.) —6F 122
Wallington Rd. Ilf —5D 48
Wallington Sq. Wall —8F 122
Wallis All. SE1 —3A 76
(off Marshalsea Rd.)
Wallis Clo. SW11 —2B 90
Wallis Clo. Dart —9D 98
Wallis Clo. Horn —6F 50
Wallis Ho. SE14 —9J 77
Wallis M. N8 —1L 43
(off Courcy Rd.)
Wallis Rd. E9 —2K 61
Wallis Rd. S'hall —9M 53
Wallis's Cotts. SW2 —6J 91
Wallman Pl. N22 —8K 27
Wallorton Gdns. SW14 —3B 88
Wallside. EC2 —8A 60
(off Beech St.)
Wall St. N1 —2B 60
Wallwood Rd. E11 —5B 46
Wallwood St. E3 —8K 61
Wallwood St. E14 —8K 61
Walmar Clo. Barn —3B 14
Walmer Clo. E4 —2M 29
Walmer Clo. Farnb —6B 128
Walmer Clo. Romf —9M 33
Walmer Ct. Surb —9J 103
(off Cranes Pk.)
Walmer Gdns. W13 —3E 70
Walmer Ho. W10 —9H 57
(off Bramley Rd.)
Walmer Pl. W1 —8D 58
(off Walmer St.)
Walmer Rd. W10 —9G 57
Walmer Rd. W11 —1J 73
Walmer St. W1 —8D 58
Walmer Ter. SE18 —5A 80
Walmgate Rd. Gnfd —4F 54
Walmington Fold. N12 —6L 25
Walm La. NW2 —2G 57
Walney Wlk. N1 —2A 60
Walnut Av. W Dray —4L 143
Walnut Clo. SE8 —7K 77
Walnut Clo. Cars —7D 122
Walnut Clo. Eps —7D 134
Walnut Clo. Eyns —5H 131
Walnut Clo. Hay —1C 68
Walnut Clo. Ilf —2A 48
Walnut Ct. E17 —2A 46
Walnut Ct. W5 —3J 71
Walnut Ct. W8 —4M 73
(off St Mary's Pl.)
Walnut Fields. Eps —1D 134
Walnut Gdns. E15 —1C 62
Walnut Grn. Bush —4K 9
Walnut Gro. Bans —6H 135
Walnut Gro. Enf —7B 16
Walnut M. Sutt —9A 122
Walnut Rd. E10 —7L 45
Walnuts Rd. Orp —3F 128
Walnuts, The. Orp —3E 128
Walnut Tree Av. Dart —8J 99
Walnut Tree Av. Mitc —7C 106
Walnut Tree Clo. SW13 —9D 72
Walnut Tree Clo. Bans —4J 135
Walnut Tree Clo. Chesh —4D 6
Walnut Tree Clo. Chst —5B 112
Walnut Tree Clo. Shep —7A 100
Walnut Tree Cotts. SW19 —2J 105
Walnut Tree Ho. SW10 —7M 73
(off Tregunter Rd.)
Walnut Tree Rd. SE10 —6C 78
(in two parts)
Walnut Tree Rd. Bren —7J 71
Walnut Tree Rd. Dag —7J 49
Walnut Tree Rd. Eri —6C 82
Walnut Tree Rd. Houn —7K 69
Walnut Tree Rd. Shep —6A 100
Walnut Tree Wlk. SE11 —5L 75
Walnut Way. Buck H —3H 31
Walnut Way. Ruis —2G 53
Walnut Way. Swan —6B 114
Walpole Av. Rich —1K 87
Walpole Clo. W13 —3G 71
Walpole Clo. Pinn —6L 21
Walpole Ct. W14 —4H 73
(off Blythe Rd.)
Walpole Ct. Twic —8C 86
Walpole Cres. Tedd —2D 102
Walpole Gdns. W4 —6A 72
Walpole Gdns. Twic —8C 86
Walpole Ho. SE1 —3L 75
(off Westminster Bri. Rd.)
Walpole Lodge. W5 —2G 71
Walpole M. NW8 —4B 58
Walpole M. SW19 —3B 106
Walpole Pl. SE18 —5M 79
Walpole Pl. Tedd —2D 102
Walpole Rd. E6 —3G 63
Walpole Rd. E17 —2J 45
Walpole Rd. E18 —8D 30
Walpole Rd. N17 —9A 28
(in two parts)
Walpole Rd. SW19 —3B 106
Walpole Rd. Brom —9H 111
Walpole Rd. Croy —4B 124
Walpole Rd. Surb —2J 119
Walpole Rd. Tedd —2D 102
Walpole Rd. Twic —8C 86
Walpole St. SW3 —6D 74
Walpole Way. Barn —7G 13
Walrond Av. Wemb —1J 55
Walsham Clo. N16 —6E 44
Walsham Clo. SE28 —1H 81
Walsham Ho. SE14 —1H 93
Walsham Ho. SE17 —6B 76
(off Blackwood St.)
Walsham Rd. SE14 —1H 93
Walsham Rd. Felt —6F 84
Walsh Cres. New Ad —4C 140
Walshford Way. Borwd —2L 11
Walsingham. NW8 —4B 58
Walsingham Gdns. Eps —6C 120
Walsingham Ho. E4 —9B 18
Walsingham Lodge. SW13 —9E 72
Walsingham Mans. SW6 —8M 73
(off Fulham Rd.)
Walsingham Pk. Chst —6B 112
Walsingham Pl. SW11 —5E 90
Walsingham Rd. E5 —8E 44
Walsingham Rd. W13 —2E 70
Walsingham Rd. Enf —6B 16
Walsingham Rd. Mitc —9D 106
Walsingham Rd. New Ad —2A 140
Walsingham Rd. Orp —5F 112
Walsingham Wlk. Belv —7L 81
Walston Ho. SW1 —6H 75
(off Aylesford St.)
Walter Besant Ho. E1 —6H 61
(off Bancroft Rd.)
Walter Ct. W3 —9A 56
(off Lynton Ter.)
Walter Grn. Ho. SE15 —9G 77
(off Lausanne Rd.)
Walter Hurford Pde. E12 —9L 47
Walter Rodney Clo. E6 —2K 63
Walters Clo. SE17 —5B 76
(off Brandon St.)
Walters Ho. SE11 —7M 75
(off Brandon Est.)
Walters Mead. Asht —9J 133
Walters Rd. SE25 —8C 108
Walters Rd. Enf —6G 17
Walter St. E2 —6H 61
Walter St. King T —5J 103
Walters Way. SE23 —5H 93
Walters Yd. Brom —6E 110
Walter Ter. E1 —9H 61
Walterton Rd. W9 —7K 57
Walter Wlk. Edgw —6A 24
Waltham Abbey. —6J 7
Waltham Abbey Church. —6J 7
Waltham Abbey Gatehouse. —6J 7
Waltham Abbey Tourist Info. Cen. —6J 7
Waltham Av. NW9 —4L 39
Waltham Av. Hay —4A 68
Waltham Clo. Dart —5E 98
Waltham Clo. Orp —3H 129
Waltham Cross. —6E 6
Waltham Cross Eleanor Cross. —7E 6
Waltham Dri. Edgw —9L 23
Waltham Gdns. Enf —9C 6
Waltham Ho. NW8 —4A 58
Waltham Pk. Way. E17 —8L 29
Waltham Rd. Cars —2B 122
Waltham Rd. S'hall —4J 69
Waltham Rd. Wfd G —6J 31
Walthamstow. —2L 45
Walthamstow Av. E4 —6K 29
Walthamstow Bus. Cen. E17 —9A 30
Walthamstow Greyhound Stadium. —7M 29
Waltham Way. E4 —3K 29
Waltheof Av. N17 —8B 28
Waltheof Gdns. N17 —8B 28
Walton & Hersham F.C. —4E 116
Walton Av. Harr —1K 53
Walton Av. N Mald —8D 104
Walton Av. Sutt —5K 121
Walton Bri. Shep & W on T —2C 116
Walton Bri. Rd. Shep —2C 116
Walton Clo. E5 —8H 45
Walton Clo. NW2 —7F 40
Walton Clo. SW8 —8J 75
Walton Clo. Harr —2B 38
Walton Ct. New Bar —7A 14
Walton Ct. S Croy —7A 124
(off Warham Rd.)
Walton Cft. Harr —9C 38
Walton Dri. NW10 —2B 56
Walton Dri. Harr —2B 38
Walton Gdns. W3 —8M 55
Walton Gdns. Felt —1D 100
Walton Gdns. Wal A —6H 7
Walton Gdns. Wemb —7J 39
Walton Grn. New Ad —1M 139
Walton Ho. E2 —7D 60
Walton Ho. E4 —5L 29
(off Chingford Mt. Rd.)
Walton Ho. E17 —1M 45
(off Drive, The)
Walton La. Shep —2B 116
Walton La. Wey & W on T —4A 116
Walton-On-Thames. —3E 116
Walton Pk. W on T —4H 117
Walton Pk. La. W on T —4H 117
Walton Pl. SW3 —4D 74
Walton Rd. E12 —9L 47
(in three parts)
Walton Rd. E13 —5G 63
Walton Rd. N15 —2D 44
Walton Rd. Bush —6H 9
Walton Rd. E Mol & W Mol —8K 101
Walton Rd. Eps —9D 134
(in two parts)
Walton Rd. Harr —2B 38
Walton Rd. Romf —7K 33
Walton Rd. Sidc —8G 97
Walton Rd. W on T & W Mol —9G 101
Walton St. SW3 —5C 74
Walton St. Enf —3B 16
Walton Way. W3 —8M 55
Walton Way. Mitc —8G 107
Walt Whitman Clo. SE24 —3M 91
Walverns Clo. Wat —8G 9
Walworth. —6A 76
Walworth Pl. SE17 —6A 76
Walworth Rd. SE1 & SE17 —5A 76
Walwyn Av. Brom —7H 111
Wanborough Dri. SW15 —7F 88

Waterside—Wellmeadow Rd.

Waterside. Beck —5K 109
Waterside. Dart —4C 98
Water Side. Uxb —8A 142
Waterside. W Dray —8G 143
Waterside Bus. Cen. Iswth —3F 86
Waterside Clo. E3 —4K 61
Waterside Clo. SE16 —3E 76
Waterside Clo. Bark —9E 48
Waterside Clo. H Wood —7L 35
Waterside Clo. N'holt —6K 53
Waterside Clo. Surb —4J 119
Waterside Dri. W on T —9E 100
Waterside Ho. E14 —3M 77
(off Admirals Way)
Waterside Pl. NW1 —4E 58
Waterside Point. SW11 —8C 74
Waterside Rd. S'hall —4L 69
Waterside Trad. Cen. W7 —4C 70
Waterside Way. SW17 —1A 106
Watersmeet Way. SE28 —9G 65
Waterson St. E2 —6C 60
Waters Pl. SW15 —1G 89
Watersplash Clo. King T —7J 103
Watersplash La. Hay —5E 68
(in two parts)
Waters Rd. SE6 —9C 94
Waters Rd. King T —6M 103
Waters Sq. King T —7M 103
Water St. WC2 —1L 75
(off Maltravers St.)
Waterton. Swan —8B 114
Water Tower Clo. Uxb —1C 142
Water Tower Hill. Croy —6B 124
Water Tower Pl. N1 —4L 59
Waterview Ho. E14 —8J 61
(off Carr St.)
Waterworks Corner. (Junct.) —8C 30
Waterworks La. E5 —7H 45
Waterworks Rd. SW2 —5K 91
Waterworks Yd. Croy —5A 124
Watery La. SW20 —6K 105
Watery La. Hay —6C 68
Watery La. N'holt —5G 53
Watery La. Sidc —3F 112
Wates Way. Mitc —1D 122
Wateville Rd. N17 —8A 28
Watford. —6F 8
Watford Arches Retail Pk. Wat —7H 9
Watford By-Pass. Edgw —4M 23
Watford By-Pass. Stan & Edgw —9F 10
Watford Clo. SW11 —9C 74
Watford Enterprise Cen. Wat —8C 8
Watford F.C. —7F 8
Watford Fld. Rd. Wat —7G 9
Watford Heath. —1H 21
Watford Heath. Wat —9H 9
Watford Heath Farm. Wat —9J 9
Watford Ho. Romf —5K 35
(off Redruth Rd.)
Watford Mus. —6G 9
Watford Rd. E16 —8E 62
Watford Rd. Crox G & Rick —8A 8
Watford Rd. Els —8F 10
Watford Rd. Harr & Wemb —5E 38
Watford Rd. N'wd —7D 20
Watford Rd. Rad —1C 10
Watford Way. NW4 —2E 40
Watford Way. NW7 & NW4 —4C 24
Watkin Rd. Wemb —8M 39
Watkins Ct. N'wd —8D 20
Watkinson Rd. N7 —2K 59
Watling. —7B 24
Watling Av. Edgw —8A 24
Watling Ct. EC4 —9A 60
(off Watling St.)
Watling Ct. Els —8H 11
Watling Farm Clo. Stan —1G 23
Watling Gdns. NW2 —2J 57
Watling Ga. NW9 —2C 40
Watlings Clo. Croy —1J 125
Watling St. EC4 —9A 60
Watling St. SE15 —7C 76
Watling St. Bexh —3M 97
Watling St. Dart & Bean —6L 99
Watling St. Rad & Els —2F 10
Watlington Gro. SE26 —2J 109
Watney Cotts. SW14 —2A 88
Watney Mkt. E1 —9F 60
Watney Rd. SW14 —2A 88
Watney's Rd. Mitc —9H 107
Watney St. E1 —9F 60
Watson Av. E6 —3L 63
Watson Av. Sutt —4J 121
Watson Clo. N16 —1B 60
Watson Clo. SW19 —3C 106
Watson Gdns. H Wood —9J 35
Watson's M. W1 —8C 58
Watsons Rd. N22 —8K 27
Watson's St. SE8 —8L 77
Watson St. E13 —5F 62
Watsons Yd. NW2 —7E 40
Wattendon Rd. Kenl —8M 137
Wattisfield Rd. E5 —8G 45
Watts Bri. Rd. Eri —7D 82
Watts Clo. N15 —3C 44
Watts Gro. E3 —8L 61
Watts La. Chst —5M 111
Watts La. Tedd —2E 102
Watts Point. E13 —4E 62
(off Brooks Rd.)
Watts Rd. Th Dit —2E 118
Watts St. E1 —2F 76
Watts St. SE15 —9D 76
Wat Tyler Ho. N8 —1J 43
(off Boyton Rd.)
Wat Tyler Rd. SE10 & SE3 —1A 94
Wauthier Clo. N13 —5M 27
Wavel Ct. E1 —2G 77
(off Garnet St.)
Wavel Ct. Croy —7B 124
(off Hurst Rd.)
Wavell Clo. Chesh —1E 6
Wavell Dri. Sidc —5C 96
Wavel M. N8 —2H 43
Wavel M. NW6 —3M 57
Wavel Pl. SE26 —1D 108
Wavendon Av. W4 —6B 72
Waveney Av. SE15 —3F 92
Waveney Clo. E1 —2E 76
Waveney Ho. SE15 —3F 92
Waverley Av. E4 —4K 29
Waverley Av. E17 —1B 46
Waverley Av. Kenl —8C 138
Waverley Av. Surb —1M 119
Waverley Av. Sutt —4M 121
Waverley Av. Twic —7K 85
Waverley Av. Wemb —1K 55
Waverley Clo. E18 —8G 31
Waverley Clo. Brom —9H 111
Waverley Clo. Hay —5B 68
Waverley Clo. W Mol —9L 101
Waverley Ct. NW6 —3J 57
Waverley Ct. SE26 —2G 109
Waverley Ct. Enf —5A 16
Waverley Cres. SE18 —6B 80
Waverley Cres. Romf —7G 35
Waverley Gdns. E6 —8J 63
Waverley Gdns. NW10 —5K 55
Waverley Gdns. Bark —5C 64
Waverley Gdns. Ilf —9A 32
Waverley Gdns. N'wd —8E 20
Waverley Gro. N3 —1J 41
Waverley Ind. Est. Harr —1B 38
Waverley Pl. N4 —7M 43
Waverley Pl. NW8 —5B 58
Waverley Rd. E17 —1A 46
Waverley Rd. E18 —8G 31
Waverley Rd. N8 —4J 43
Waverley Rd. N17 —7F 28
Waverley Rd. SE18 —6A 80
Waverley Rd. SE25 —8F 108
Waverley Rd. Enf —5M 15
Waverley Rd. Eps —7F 120
Waverley Rd. Harr —7J 37
Waverley Rd. Rain —7F 66
Waverley Rd. S'hall —1L 69
Waverley Rd. Stoke D & Oxs —6A 132
Waverley Vs. N17 —9D 28
Waverley Way. Cars —8C 122
Waverton Ho. E3 —4K 61
Waverton Rd. SW18 —6A 90
Waverton St. W1 —2E 74
Wavertree Ct. SW2 —7J 91
Wavertree Rd. E18 —9E 30
Wavertree Rd. SW2 —7K 91
Waxlow Cres. S'hall —9L 53
Waxlow Ho. Hay —8H 53
Waxlow Rd. NW10 —5A 56
Waxwell Clo. Pinn —9H 21
Waxwell Farm Ho. Pinn —9H 21
Waxwell La. Pinn —9H 21
Wayborne Gro. Ruis —4A 36
Waye Av. Houn —9E 68
Wayfarer Rd. N'holt —6H 53
Wayfield Link. SE9 —5B 96
Wayford St. SW11 —1C 90
Wayland Av. E8 —1E 60
Wayland Clo. E8 —1E 60
Wayland Ho. SW9 —1L 91
(off Robsart St.)
Waylands. Hay —8B 52
Waylands. Swan —8D 114
Waylands Mead. Beck —5M 109
Waylett Ho. SE11 —6K 75
(off Loughborough St.)
Waylett Pl. SE27 —9M 91
Waylett Pl. Wemb —9H 39
Wayman Ct. E8 —2F 60
Wayne Clo. Orp —5D 128
Wayneflete Tower Av. Esh —5L 117
Wayne Kirkum Way. NW6 —1K 57
Waynflete Av. Croy —5M 123
Waynflete Sq. W10 —1H 73
Waynflete St. SW18 —8A 90
Wayside. NW11 —6J 41
Wayside. SW14 —4A 88
Wayside. New Ad —8M 125
Wayside Av. Bush —8B 10
Wayside Av. Horn —7H 51
Wayside Clo. N14 —8G 15
Wayside Clo. Romf —1D 50
Wayside Ct. Brick W —3K 5
Wayside Ct. Twic —5G 87
Wayside Ct. Wemb —8L 39
Wayside Gdns. Dag —1L 65
Wayside Gro. SE9 —1K 111
Wayside M. Ilf —3L 47
Wayville Rd. Dart —6M 99
Weald Clo. SE16 —6F 76
Weald Clo. Brom —4J 127
Weald La. Harr —9B 22
Weald Ri. Harr —7D 22
Weald Rd. Brtwd & S Wea —1K 35
Weald Rd. Uxb —5E 142
Weald Sq. E5 —7E 44
Wealdstone. —1C 38
Wealdstone Rd. Sutt —4K 121
Weald, The. Chst —3K 111
Weald Way. Hay —6C 52
Weald Way. Romf —4M 49
Wealdwood Gdns. Pinn —6M 21
Weale Rd. E4 —3B 30
Weall Clo. Purl —4K 137
Weall Ct. Pinn —2J 37
Weall Grn. Wat —5F 4
Weardale Gdns. Enf —3B 16
Weardale Rd. SE13 —3B 94
Wearmouth Ho. E3 —8K 61
(off Joseph St.)
Wear Pl. E2 —6F 60
(in two parts)
Wearside Rd. SE13 —3M 93
Weatherbury. W2 —9L 57
(off Talbot Rd.)
Weatherbury Ho. N19 —8H 43
(off Wedmore St.)
Weatherley Clo. E3 —8K 61
Weaver Clo. E6 —1M 79
Weaver Clo. Croy —6D 124
Weavers Clo. Iswth —3C 86
Weavers Ho. E11 —4E 46
(off New Wanstead)
Weavers La. SE1 —2C 76
Weavers Ter. SW6 —7L 73
(off Micklethwaite Rd.)
Weaver St. E1 —7E 60
Weavers Way. NW1 —4H 59
Weaver Wlk. SE27 —1A 108
Webb Clo. W10 —7G 57
Webber Clo. Els —8H 11
Webber Clo. Eri —8F 82
Webber Row. SE1 —3M 75
(in two parts)
Webber St. SE1 —3L 75
Webb Est. E5 —5E 44
Webb Gdns. E13 —7E 62
Webb Ho. SW8 —8H 75
Webb Ho. Dag —8L 49
(off Kershaw Rd.)
Webb Ho. Felt —9J 85
Webb Pl. NW10 —6D 56
Webb Rd. SE3 —7D 78
Webbscroft Rd. Dag —9M 49
Webb's Rd. SW11 —3D 90
Webbs Rd. Hay —6F 52
Webb St. SE1 —4C 76
Webheath. NW6 —3K 57
Webster Clo. Horn —8H 51
Webster Clo. Oxs —6A 132
Webster Clo. Wal A —6M 7
Webster Gdns. W5 —2H 71
Webster Rd. E11 —8A 46
Webster Rd. SE16 —4E 76
Weddell Ho. E1 —7H 61
(off Duckett St.)
Wedderburn Rd. NW3 —1B 58
Wedderburn Rd. Bark —4C 64
Wedgewood Clo. N'wd —7A 20
Wedgewood Ct. Bex —6K 97
Wedgewood Ct. Brom —7D 110
(off Cumberland Rd.)
Wedgewood Ho. SW1 —6F 74
(off Churchill Gdns.)
Wedgwood Ho. E2 —6H 61
(off Warley St.)
Wedgwood Ho. SE11 —4L 75
(off Lambeth Wlk.)
Wedgwood M. W1 —9H 59
Wedgwood Wlk. NW6 —1M 57
(off Dresden Clo.)
Wedgwood Way. SE19 —4A 108
Wedlake Clo. Horn —6J 51
Wedlake St. W10 —7J 57
Wedmore Av. Ilf —8L 31
Wedmore Ct. N19 —7H 43
Wedmore Gdns. N19 —7H 43
Wedmore M. N19 —8H 43
Wedmore Rd. Gnfd —6B 54
Wedmore St. N19 —8H 43
Wednesbury Gdns. Romf —7K 35
Wednesbury Grn. Romf —7K 35
Wednesbury Rd. Romf —7K 35
Weech Rd. NW6 —9L 41
Weedington Rd. NW5 —1E 58
Weedon Ho. W12 —9E 56
Weekley Sq. SW11 —2B 90
Weigall Rd. SE12 —4E 94
Weighhouse St. W1 —9E 58
Weighton M. SE20 —6F 108
Weighton Rd. SE20 —6F 108
Weighton Rd. Harr —8B 22
Weihurst Ct. Sutt —7C 122
Weihurst Gdns. Sutt —7B 122
Weirdale Av. N20 —2D 26
Weir Hall Av. N18 —6B 28
Weir Hall Gdns. N18 —5B 28
Weir Hall Rd. N18 & N17 —5B 28
Weir Rd. SW12 —6G 91
Weir Rd. SW19 —9M 89
Weir Rd. Bex —6M 97
Weir Rd. W on T —1E 116
Weirside Gdns. W Dray —2H 143
Weir's Pas. NW1 —6H 59
Weiss Rd. SW15 —2H 89
Welbeck Av. Brom —1E 110
Welbeck Av. Hay —7F 52
Welbeck Av. Sidc —7E 96
Welbeck Clo. N12 —5B 26
Welbeck Clo. Borwd —5L 11
Welbeck Clo. Eps —9E 120
Welbeck Clo. N Mald —9D 104
Welbeck Ct. W14 —5K 73
(off Addison Bri. Pl.)
Welbeck Ho. W1 —9F 58
(off Welbeck St.)
Welbeck Rd. E6 —6H 63
Welbeck Rd. Barn —8C 14
Welbeck Rd. Harr —6M 37
Welbeck Rd. Sutt & Cars —4B 122
Welbeck St. W1 —8E 58
Welbeck Vs. N21 —2A 28
Welbeck Wlk. Cars —3B 122
Welbeck Way. W1 —9F 58
Welbourne Rd. N17 —1D 44
Welby Ho. N19 —5H 43
Welby St. SE5 —9M 75
Welch Pl. Pinn —8F 20
Welcome Ct. E17 —5L 45
(off Boundary Rd.)
Welcomes Rd. Kenl —9A 138
Welcome Ter. Whyt —8D 138
Welcote Dri. N'wd —6B 20
Weldon Clo. Ruis —2F 52
Weldon Ct. N21 —7K 15
Weldon Dri. W Mol —8K 101
Weld Pl. N11 —5F 26
(in two parts)
Welfare Rd. E15 —3C 62
Welford Clo. E5 —8H 45
Welford Ct. NW1 —3F 58
(off Castlehaven Rd.)
Welford Ct. SW8 —1G 91
Welford Pl. SW19 —1J 105
Welham Rd. SW17 & SW16 —2E 106
Welhouse Rd. Cars —3C 122
Wellacre Rd. Harr —4F 38
Wellan Clo. Sidc —4F 96
Welland Ct. SE6 —8K 93
(off Oakham Clo.)
Welland Gdns. Gnfd —5D 54
Welland Ho. SE15 —3G 93
Welland M. E1 —2E 76
Wellands Clo. Brom —6K 111
Welland St. SE10 —7A 78
Well App. Barn —7G 13
Wellbrook Rd. Orp —6L 127
Wellby Ct. E13 —4G 63
Well Clo. SW16 —1K 107
Well Clo. Ruis —8J 37
Wellclose Sq. E1 —1E 76
(in two parts)
Wellclose St. E1 —1E 76
Wellcome Av. Dart —3J 99
Wellcome Cen. for Medical Science. —7H 59
(off Euston Rd.)
Well Cottage Clo. E11 —4G 47
Well Ct. EC4 —9A 60
(in two parts)
Welldon Ct. Harr —3C 38
Welldon Cres. Harr —3C 38
Well End. —2B 12
Well End Rd. Borwd —1A 12
Weller Ho. SE16 —3E 76
(off George Row)
Weller Pl. Orp —3L 141
Wellers Ct. NW1 —5J 59
Wellers Gro. Chesh —1A 6
Weller St. SE1 —3A 76
Wellesford Clo. Bans —9K 135
Wellesley Av. W6 —4F 72
Wellesley Av. N'wd —5D 20
Wellesley Clo. SE7 —6G 79
Wellesley Ct. NW2 —7E 40
Wellesley Ct. NW8 —6A 58
(off Maida Va.)
Wellesley Ct. Sutt —3J 121
Wellesley Ct. Rd. Croy —4B 124
Wellesley Cres. Twic —8C 86
Wellesley Gro. Croy —4B 124
Wellesley Ho. SW1 —6F 74
(off Ebury Bri. Rd.)
Wellesley Lodge. Sutt —9L 121
(off Worcester Rd.)
Wellesley Mans. W14 —6K 73
(off Edith Vs.)
Wellesley Pde. Twic —9C 86
Wellesley Pk. M. Enf —4M 15
Wellesley Pas. Croy —4A 124
Wellesley Pl. NW1 —6H 59
Wellesley Pl. NW5 —1E 58
Wellesley Rd. E11 —3E 46
Wellesley Rd. E17 —4L 45
Wellesley Rd. N22 —9L 27
Wellesley Rd. NW5 —1E 58
Wellesley Rd. W4 —6L 71
Wellesley Rd. Croy —3A 124
Wellesley Rd. Harr —3C 38
Wellesley Rd. Ilf —7M 47
Wellesley Rd. Sutt —8A 122
Wellesley Rd. Twic —9B 86
Wellesley St. E1 —8H 61
Wellesley Ter. N1 —6A 60
Wellfield Av. N10 —1F 42
Wellfield Gdns. Cars —1C 136
Wellfield Rd. SW16 —1J 107
Wellfields. Lou —5L 19
Wellfield Wlk. SW16 —2K 107
(in two parts)
Wellfit St. SE24 —2M 91
Wellgarth. Gnfd —2F 54
Wellgarth Rd. NW11 —6M 41
Well Gro. N20 —1A 26
Well Hall Pde. SE9 —3K 95
Well Hall Rd. SE9 —2J 95
Well Hall Roundabout. (Junct.) —3K 95
Well Hill. —8M 129
Well Hill. Orp —8M 129
Well Hill La. Orp —8M 129
Wellhouse La. Barn —6G 13
Wellhouse Rd. Beck —8L 109
Welling. —2F 96
Wellingborough Ho. Romf —5K 35
(off Redruth Rd.)
Welling High St. Well —2F 96
Wellington. N8 —2J 43
(in two parts)
Wellington Av. E4 —2L 29
Wellington Av. N9 —3F 28
Wellington Av. N15 —4D 44
Wellington Av. SE18 —4M 79
Wellington Av. Houn —4L 85
Wellington Av. Pinn —8K 21
Wellington Av. Sidc —5E 96
Wellington Av. Wor Pk —5G 121
Wellington Bldgs. SW1 —6E 74
Wellington Clo. SE14 —9H 77
Wellington Clo. W11 —9L 57
Wellington Clo. Dag —3A 66
Wellington Clo. W on T —3D 116
Wellington Clo. Wat —3K 21
Wellington Ct. NW8 —5B 58
(off Wellington Rd.)
Wellington Ct. SW1 —3D 74
(off Knightsbridge)
Wellington Ct. SW6 —9M 73
(off Maltings Pl.)
Wellington Ct. Hamp —2B 102
Wellington Ct. Pinn —8K 21
(off Wellington Rd.)
Wellington Ct. Stanw —6C 144
Wellington Cres. N Mald —7A 104
Wellington Dri. Dag —3A 66
Wellington Dri. Purl —2K 137
Wellington Est. E2 —5G 61
Wellington Gdns. SE7 —7G 79
Wellington Gdns. Twic —1B 102
Wellington Gro. SE10 —8B 78
Wellington Hill. Lou —1E 18
Wellington Ho. W5 —6J 55
Wellington Ho. N'holt —3L 53
(off Farmlands, The)
Wellington Ho. Wat —4G 9
(off Exeter Clo.)
Wellingtonia Av. Hav —4A 34
Wellington Mans. E10 —6L 45
Wellington M. N7 —2K 59
(off Roman Way)
Wellington M. SE7 —7G 79
Wellington M. SE22 —3E 92
Wellington M. SW16 —9H 91
Wellington Mus. —3E 74
Wellington Pde. Sidc —4E 96
Wellington Pk. Est. NW2 —6E 40
Wellington Pas. E11 —3E 46
(off Wellington Rd.)
Wellington Pl. E11 —3E 46
Wellington Pl. N2 —3C 42
Wellington Pl. NW8 —6B 58
Wellington Rd. E6 —4K 63
Wellington Rd. E7 —9D 46
Wellington Rd. E10 —6J 45
Wellington Rd. E11 —3E 46
Wellington Rd. E17 —2J 45
Wellington Rd. NW8 —5B 58
Wellington Rd. NW10 —6H 57
Wellington Rd. SW19 —8L 89
Wellington Rd. W5 —4G 71
Wellington Rd. Belv —6K 81
Wellington Rd. Bex —4H 97
Wellington Rd. Brom —8G 111
Wellington Rd. Croy —2M 123
Wellington Rd. Dart —5G 99
Wellington Rd. Enf —7C 16
Wellington Rd. Felt —4C 84
Wellington Rd. Hamp & Twic —2B 102
Wellington Rd. Harr —1C 38
Wellington Rd. Orp —1F 128
Wellington Rd. Pinn —8K 21
Wellington Rd. Uxb —4A 142
Wellington Rd. Wat —4F 8
Wellington Rd. N. Houn —2K 85
Wellington Rd. S. Houn —3K 85
Wellington Row. E2 —6D 60
Wellington Sq. SW3 —6D 74
Wellington St. SE18 —5L 79
Wellington St. WC2 —1K 75
Wellington St. Bark —4A 64
Wellington Ter. E1 —2F 76
Wellington Ter. N8 —1L 43
(off Turnpike La.)
Wellington Ter. W11 —1L 73
Wellington Ter. Harr —6B 38
Wellington Way. E3 —6L 61
Welling United F.C. —2G 97
Welling Way. SE9 & Well —2A 96
Well La. SW14 —4A 88
Wellmeadow Rd. SE13 & SE6 —5C 94
(in two parts)
Wellmeadow Rd. W7 —5E 70

Wellow Wlk.—Westgate Rd.

Wellow Wlk. Cars —3B 122
Well Pl. NW3 —8B 42
Well Rd. NW3 —8B 42
Well Rd. Barn —7G 13
Wells Clo. N'holt —6G 53
Wells Ct. NW6 —5L 57
(off Cambridge Av.)
Wells Dri. NW9 —6B 40
Wells Gdns. Dag —1M 65
Wells Gdns. Ilf —5J 47
Wells Gdns. Rain —2D 66
Wells Ho. EC1 —6L 59
(off Spa Grn. Est.)
Wells Ho. SE16 —4G 77
(off Howland Est.)
Wells Ho. W5 —2H 71
(off Grove Rd.)
Wells Ho. Bark —3E 64
(off Margaret Bondfield Av.)
Wells Ho. Brom —2F 110
(off Pike Clo.)
Wells Ho. Eps —6L 133
Wells Ho. Rd. NW10 —8C 56
Wellside Clo. Barn —6G 13
Wellside Gdns. SW14 —3A 88
Wells M. W1 —8G 59
Wellsmoor Gdns. Brom —7L 111
Wells Pk. Rd. SE26 —9E 92
Wells Path. N'holt —6C 52
Wellsprings Cres. Wemb —8M 39
Wells Ri. NW8 —4D 58
Wells Rd. W12 —3G 73
Wells Rd. Brom —6K 111
Wells Rd. Eps —6L 133
Wells Sq. WC1 —6K 59
Wells St. W1 —8G 59
Wellstead Av. N9 —9H 17
Wellstead Rd. E6 —5L 63
Wells Ter. N4 —7L 43
Wells, The. —6L 133
Wells, The. N14 —9H 15
Wellstones. Wat —6F 8
Well St. E9 —3G 61
Well St. E15 —2C 62
Wells Way. SE5 —7B 76
Wells Way. SW7 —4B 74
Wells Yd. N7 —1L 59
Wells Yd. Wat —5F 8
Well Wlk. NW3 —9B 42
Well Way. Eps —7L 133
Wellwood Clo. Coul —6J 137
Wellwood Rd. Ilf —6E 48
Welsby Ct. W5 —8G 55
Welsford St. SE1 —5E 76
(in two parts)
Welsh Clo. E13 —6E 62
Welsh Ho. E1 —2F 76
(off Wapping La.)
Welshpool Ho. E8 —4E 60
Welshpool St. E8 —4E 60
(in two parts)
Welshside Wlk. NW9 —4C 40
Welstead Ho. E1 —9F 60
(off Cannon St. Rd.)
Welstead Way. W4 —5D 72
Welsummer Way. Chesh —1D 6
Weltje Rd. W6 —5E 72
Welton Ct. SE5 —9C 76
Welton Ho. E1 —8H 61
(off Stepney Way)
Welton Rd. SE18 —8C 80
Welwyn Av. Felt —5D 84
Welwyn St. E2 —6G 61
Welwyn Way. Hay —7C 52
Wembley. —1J 55
Wembley Arena. —9L 39
Wembley Arena. —9L 39
Wembley Commercial Cen. Wemb —7H 39
Wembley Conference Centre. —9L 39
Wembley Hill Rd. Wemb —8K 39
Wembley Park. —8L 39
Wembley Pk. Bus. Cen. Wemb —9M 39
Wembley Pk. Dri. Wemb —9K 39
Wembley Retail Pk. Wemb —9M 39
Wembley Rd. Hamp —5L 101
Wembley Stadium. —1L 55
Wembley Stadium Ind. Est. Wemb —9M 39
Wembley Way. Wemb —2M 55
Wemborough Rd. Stan —8F 22
Wembury M. N6 —5G 43
Wembury Rd. N6 —5F 42
Wemyss Rd. SE3 —1D 94
Wendela Ct. Harr —7C 38
Wendell Rd. W12 —4D 72
Wenderholme. S Croy —7B 124
(off South Pk. Hill Rd.)
Wendle Ct. SW8 —7J 75
Wendling Rd. Sutt —3B 122
Wendon St. E3 —4K 61
Wendover. SE17 —6C 76
(in two parts)
Wendover Clo. Hay —7J 53
Wendover Ct. NW2 —8L 41
Wendover Ct. NW10 —7M 55
Wendover Ct. W1 —8E 58
(off Chiltern St.)
Wendover Ct. Brom —7F 110
(off Wendover Rd.)
Wendover Dri. N Mald —1D 120
Wendover Ho. W1 —8E 58
(off Chiltern St.)
Wendover Ho. Wat —9C 8
(off Chenies Way)
Wendover Rd. NW10 —5D 56
Wendover Rd. SE9 —2H 95
Wendover Rd. Brom —8F 110
Wendover Way. Bush —8A 10
Wendover Way. Horn —1G 67
Wendover Way. Orp —1E 128
Wendover Way. Well —4E 96
Wend, The. Coul —6H 137
Wendy Clo. Enf —8D 16
Wendy Way. Wemb —4J 55
Wenham Ho. SW8 —8G 75
(off Ascalon St.)
Wenlake Ho. EC1 —7A 60
(off Old St.)
Wenlock Barn Est. N1 —5B 60
(off Wenlock St.)
Wenlock Ct. N1 —5B 60
Wenlock Gdns. NW4 —2F 40
Wenlock Rd. N1 —5A 60
Wenlock Rd. Edgw —7M 23
Wenlock St. N1 —5A 60
Wennington. —1J 83
Wennington Rd. E3 —5H 61
Wennington Rd. Rain & Wen —7E 66
Wensdale Ho. E5 —7E 44
Wensley Av. Wfd G —7D 30
Wensley Clo. SE9 —5K 95
Wensley Clo. Romf —5L 33
Wensleydale Av. Ilf —9J 31
Wensleydale Gdns. Hamp —4M 101
Wensleydale Pas. Hamp —5L 101
Wensleydale Rd. Hamp —3L 101
Wensley Rd. N18 —6F 28
Wenta Bus. Cen. Wat —1H 9
Wentbridge Path. Borwd —2L 11
Wentland Clo. SE6 —8B 94
Wentland Rd. SE6 —8B 94
Wentway Ct. W13 —7D 54
(off Ruislip Rd. E.)
Wentworth Av. N3 —7L 25
Wentworth Av. Els —7K 11
Wentworth Clo. N3 —7M 25
Wentworth Clo. SE28 —9H 65
Wentworth Clo. Ashf —9F 144
Wentworth Clo. Hayes —4E 126
Wentworth Clo. Mord —2L 121
Wentworth Clo. Orp —7C 128
Wentworth Clo. Surb —4H 119
Wentworth Clo. Wat —2D 8
Wentworth Ct. W6 —7J 73
(off Laundry Rd.)
Wentworth Ct. Twic —9C 86
Wentworth Cres. SE15 —8E 76
Wentworth Cres. Hay —4B 68
Wentworth Dri. Dart —5E 98
Wentworth Dri. Pinn —3E 36
Wentworth Dwellings. E1 —9D 60
(off Wentworth St.)
Wentworth Fields. Hay —5B 52
Wentworth Gdns. N13 —3M 27
Wentworth Hill. Wemb —6K 39
Wentworth M. E3 —7J 61
Wentworth Pk. N3 —7L 25
Wentworth Pl. Stan —6F 22
Wentworth Rd. E12 —9H 47
Wentworth Rd. NW11 —4K 41
Wentworth Rd. Barn —5H 13
Wentworth Rd. Croy —2L 123
Wentworth Rd. S'hall —5G 69
Wentworth St. E1 —9D 60
Wentworth Way. Pinn —2J 37
Wentworth Way. Rain —6F 66
Wentworth Way. S Croy —6E 138
Wenvoe Av. Bexh —1M 97
Wepham Clo. Hay —8H 53
Wernbrook St. SE18 —7A 80
Werndee Rd. SE25 —8E 108
Werneth Hall Rd. Ilf —1L 47
Werrington St. NW1 —5G 59
Werter Rd. SW15 —3J 89
Wescott Way. Uxb —5A 142
Wesleyan Pl. NW5 —9F 42
Wesley Av. E16 —2F 78
Wesley Av. NW10 —6B 56
Wesley Av. Houn —1J 85
Wesley Clo. N7 —7K 43
Wesley Clo. SE17 —5M 75
Wesley Clo. Harr —7A 38
Wesley Clo. Orp —7G 113
Wesley Rd. E10 —5A 46
Wesley Rd. N2 —8C 26
Wesley Rd. NW10 —4A 56
Wesley Rd. Hay —1E 68
Wesley's House Mus. —7B 60
Wesley Sq. W11 —9J 57
Wesley St. W1 —8E 58
Wessex Av. SW19 —7L 105
Wessex Clo. Ilf —4C 48
Wessex Clo. King T —5M 103
Wessex Clo. Th Dit —4D 118
Wessex Ct. Barn —6H 13
Wessex Ct. Beck —5J 109
Wessex Ct. Stanw —5C 144
Wessex Dri. Eri —1C 98
Wessex Dri. Pinn —7J 21
Wessex Gdns. NW11 —6J 41
Wessex Ho. SE1 —6D 76
Wessex La. Gnfd —6B 54
Wessex Rd. H'row A —3A 144
Wessex St. E2 —6G 61
Wessex Way. NW11 —6J 41
Westacott. Hay —8C 52
Westacott Clo. N19 —6H 43
West Acres. Esh —9K 117
West Acton. —9L 55
Westall Rd. Lou —5M 19
West App. Orp —9A 112
W. Arbour St. E1 —9H 61
West Av. E17 —2M 45
West Av. N2 —1M 41
West Av. N3 —6L 25
West Av. NW4 —3H 41
West Av. Hay —1D 68
West Av. Pinn —4K 37
West Av. S'hall —1K 69
West Av. Wall —7J 123
W. Avenue Rd. E17 —2L 45
West Bank. N16 —5C 44
West Bank. Bark —4M 63
West Bank. Enf —4A 16
Westbank Rd. Hamp H —3A 102
West Barnes. —8F 104
W. Barnes La. N Mald & SW20 —9E 104
West Beckton. —9H 63
West Bedfont. —5D 144
Westbeech Rd. N22 —1L 43
Westbere Dri. Stan —5H 23
Westbere Rd. NW2 —9J 41
West Block. SE1 —3K 75
(off Addington St.)
Westbourne Av. W3 —9B 56
Westbourne Av. Sutt —4J 121
Westbourne Bri. W2 —8A 58
Westbourne Clo. Hay —7G 53
Westbourne Cres. W2 —1B 74
Westbourne Cres. M. W2 —1B 74
(off Westbourne Cres.)
Westbourne Dri. SE23 —8H 93
Westbourne Gdns. W2 —9M 57
Westbourne Green. —9K 57
Westbourne Gro. W11 & W2 —1K 73
Westbourne Gro. M. W11 —9L 57
Westbourne Gro. Ter. W2 —9M 57
Westbourne Ho. SW1 —6F 74
Westbourne Ho. Houn —7L 69
Westbourne Pde. Hil —7F 142
Westbourne Pk. Pas. W2 —8L 57
(off Alfred Rd., in two parts)
Westbourne Pk. Rd. W11 & W2 —9J 57
Westbourne Pk. Vs. W2 —8L 57
Westbourne Pl. N9 —3F 28
Westbourne Rd. N7 —2K 59
Westbourne Rd. SE26 —3H 109
Westbourne Rd. Bexh —8H 81
Westbourne Rd. Croy —1D 124
Westbourne Rd. Felt —9D 84
Westbourne Rd. Uxb —7F 142
Westbourne St. W2 —1B 74
Westbourne Ter. SE23 —8H 93
(off Waldram Pk. Rd.)
Westbourne Ter. W2 —9A 58
Westbourne Ter. M. W2 —9A 58
Westbourne Ter. Rd. W2 —8M 57
Westbourne Ter. Rd. Bri. W2
(off Westbourne Ter. Rd.) —8A 58
Westbridge Clo. W12 —3E 72
Westbridge Rd. SW11 —9B 74
West Brompton. —7M 73
Westbrook Av. Hamp —4K 101
Westbrook Clo. Barn —5B 14
Westbrook Cres. Cockf —5B 14
Westbrook Dri. Orp —3H 129
Westbrooke Cres. Well —2G 97
Westbrooke Rd. Sidc —8B 96
Westbrooke Rd. Well —2F 96
(in two parts)
Westbrook Ho. E2 —6G 61
(off Victoria Pk. Sq.)
Westbrook Rd. SE3 —9F 78
Westbrook Rd. Houn —8K 69
Westbrook Rd. T Hth —5B 108
Westbrook Sq. Barn —5B 14
Westbury Av. N22 —1M 43
Westbury Av. Clay —8D 118
Westbury Av. S'hall —7L 53
Westbury Av. Wemb —3J 55
Westbury Clo. Ruis —5E 36
Westbury Clo. Shep —1A 116
Westbury Clo. Whyt —9D 138
Westbury Ct. Bark —4B 64
(off Westbury Rd.)
Westbury Gro. N12 —6L 25
Westbury Ho. E17 —2K 45
Westbury La. Buck H —2G 31
Westbury Lodge Clo. Pinn —1H 37
Westbury Pl. Bren —7H 71
Westbury Rd. E7 —2F 62
Westbury Rd. E17 —2K 45
Westbury Rd. N11 —6J 27
Westbury Rd. N12 —6L 25
Westbury Rd. SE20 —5H 109
Westbury Rd. W5 —9J 55
Westbury Rd. Bark —4B 64
Westbury Rd. Beck —7J 109
Westbury Rd. Brom —5H 111
Westbury Rd. Buck H —2G 31
Westbury Rd. Chesh —3D 6
Westbury Rd. Croy —1B 124
Westbury Rd. Felt —7H 85
Westbury Rd. Ilf —7L 47
Westbury Rd. N Mald —8B 104
Westbury Rd. N'wd —4C 20
Westbury Rd. Wat —7F 8
Westbury Rd. Wemb —3J 55
Westbury St. SW8 —1G 91
(off Portslade Rd.)
Westbury Ter. E7 —2F 62
Westcar La. W on T —8F 116
W. Carriage Dri. W2 —1C 74
W. Central St. WC1 —9J 59
W. Centre Av. NW10 —7F 56
West Chantry. Harr —8M 21
Westchester Dri. NW4 —1H 41
West Clo. N9 —3D 28
West Clo. Ashf —9C 144
West Clo. Barn —7F 12
West Clo. Cockf —6E 14
West Clo. Gnfd —5A 54
West Clo. Hamp —3J 101
West Clo. Rain —7F 66
West Clo. Wemb —6K 39
Westcombe Av. Croy —2J 123
Westcombe Ct. SE3 —8D 78
Westcombe Dri. Barn —7L 13
Westcombe Hill. SE3 —8E 78
Westcombe Lodge Dri. Hay —8B 52
Westcombe Pk. Rd. SE3 —7C 78
West Comn. Rd. Brom & Kes —3E 126
West Comn. Rd. Uxb —1B 142
Westcoombe Av. SW20 —5D 104
Westcote Ri. Ruis —5A 36
Westcote Rd. SW16 —2G 107
West Cotts. NW6 —1L 57
Westcott Clo. N15 —4D 44
Westcott Clo. Brom —9K 111
Westcott Clo. New Ad —1M 139
Westcott Cres. W7 —9C 54
Westcott Ho. E14 —1L 77
(off E. India Dock Rd.)
Westcott Rd. SE17 —7M 75
Westcott Way. Sutt —2G 135
West Ct. E17 —2L 45
West Ct. Houn —8A 70
West Ct. Wemb —7G 39
Westcroft Clo. NW2 —9J 41
Westcroft Clo. Enf —2G 17
Westcroft Gdns. Mord —7K 105
Westcroft Rd. Cars & Wall —6E 122
Westcroft Sq. W6 —5E 72
Westcroft Way. NW2 —9J 41
W. Cromwell Rd. W14 & SW5 —6K 73
W. Cross Cen. Bren —7E 70
W. Cross Route. W10 —1H 73
W. Cross Way. Bren —7F 70
Westdale Pas. SE18 —7M 79
Westdale Rd. SE18 —7M 79
Westdean Av. SE12 —7F 94
W. Dean Clo. SW18 —5M 89
West Dene. Sutt —8J 121
W. Dene Dri. H Hill —5H 35
W. Dene Way. Wey —5C 116
Westdown Rd. E15 —9A 46
Westdown Rd. SE6 —6L 93
West Drayton. —3J 143
W. Drayton Pk. Av. W Dray —4J 143
W. Drayton Rd. Uxb —9F 142
West Dri. SW16 —1G 107
West Dri. Cars —2B 136
West Dri. Harr —6B 22
West Dri. Sutt —1H 135
West Dri. Tad —9H 135
West Dri. Wat —9F 4
West Dri. Gdns. Harr —6B 22
West Dulwich. —8B 92
West Ealing. —1F 70
W. Ealing Bus. Cen. W13 —1E 70
W. Eaton Pl. SW1 —5E 74
W. Eaton Pl. M. SW1 —5E 74
(off W. Eaton Pl.)
Wested La. Swan —2E 130
(in two parts)
W. Ella Rd. NW10 —3C 56
West End. —8K 117
(Esher)
West End. —5H 53
(Northolt)
W. End Av. E10 —3B 46
W. End Av. Pinn —2H 37
Westend Clo. NW10 —3A 56
W. End Ct. NW6 —3M 57
W. End Ct. Pinn —2H 37
W. End Gdns. Esh —7K 117
W. End Gdns. N'holt —5G 53
W. End La. NW6 —1L 57
W. End La. Barn —6H 13
W. End La. Esh —9K 117
W. End La. Hay —8A 68
W. End La. Pinn —1H 37
W. End Rd. Ruis & N'holt —7C 36
W. End Rd. S'hall —2J 69
Westerdale Rd. SE10 —6E 78
Westerfield Rd. N15 —3D 44
Westergate. W5 —8J 55
Westergate Ho. King T —8H 103
(off Portsmouth Rd.)
Westergate Rd. SE2 —7J 81
Westerham. NW1 —4G 59
(off Bayham St.)
Westerham Av. N9 —3B 28
Westerham Clo. Sutt —2L 135
Westerham Dri. Sidc —5F 96
Westerham Ho. SE1 —4B 76
(off Law St.)
Westerham Lodge. Beck —4L 109
(off Park Rd.)
Westerham Rd. E10 —5M 45
Westerham Rd. Kes —9H 127
Westerley Cres. SE26 —2K 109
Western Av. NW11 —4H 41
Western Av. W5 & W3 —7K 55
Western Av. Dag —2A 66
Western Av. Den & Uxb —1A 142
Western Av. Gnfd & W5 —5B 54
Western Av. Romf —9G 35
Western Av. Uxb & N'holt —2A 52
Western Av. Bus. Pk. W3 —7M 55
Western Beach Apartments. E16 —1E 78
Western Circus. (Junct.) —1D 72
Western Ct. N3 —6L 25
Western Ct. W3 —9B 56
Western Ct. W9 —5K 57
(off Carlton Va.)
Western Ct. Romf —3C 50
(off Chandlers Way)
Western Dri. Shep —1B 116
Western Gdns. W5 —1L 71
Western International Mkt. S'hall —5F 68
Western La. SW12 —6E 90
Western Mans. New Bar —7M 13
(off Gt. North Rd.)
Western M. W9 —7K 57
Western Pde. New Bar —7L 13
Western Pathway. Rain & Horn —3F 66
Western Perimeter Rd. W Dray & H'row A —2A 144 & 9G 143
Western Pl. SE16 —3G 77
Western Rd. E13 —5G 63
Western Rd. E17 —3A 46
Western Rd. N2 —2D 42
Western Rd. N22 —9K 27
Western Rd. NW10 —7A 56
Western Rd. SW9 —2L 91
Western Rd. SW19 & Mitc —5B 106
Western Rd. W5 —1H 71
Western Rd. Romf —3C 50
Western Rd. S'hall —5G 69
Western Rd. Sutt —7L 121
Western Ter. W6 —6E 72
(off Chiswick Mall)
Western Vw. Hay —3D 68
Westernville Gdns. Ilf —5A 48
Western Way. SE28 —4B 80
Western Way. Barn —8L 13
West Ewell. —9C 120
Westferry Cir. E14 —2L 77
Westferry Rd. E14 —1K 77
West Fld. Asht —9K 133
Westfield. Lou —7H 19
Westfield Av. S Croy —5B 138
Westfield Av. Wat —2H 9
Westfield Clo. NW9 —1A 40
Westfield Clo. SW10 —8A 74
Westfield Clo. Enf —5J 17
Westfield Clo. Sutt —6K 121
Westfield Clo. Wal X —4F 6
Westfield Ct. Surb —9H 103
(off Portsmouth Rd)
Westfield Dri. Harr —2H 39
Westfield Gdns. Harr —2H 39
Westfield Ho. SE16 —5H 77
(off Rotherhithe New Rd.)
Westfield Ho. SW18 —7M 89
Westfield La. Harr —3H 39
(in two parts)
Westfield Pk. Pinn —7K 21
Westfield Pk. Dri. Wfd G —6J 31
Westfield Rd. NW7 —3B 24
Westfield Rd. W13 —2E 70
Westfield Rd. Beck —6K 109
Westfield Rd. Bexh —2A 98
Westfield Rd. Croy —4M 123
Westfield Rd. Dag —9J 49
Westfield Rd. Mitc —6C 106
Westfield Rd. Surb —9H 103
Westfield Rd. Sutt —6K 121
Westfield Rd. W on T —2J 117
Westfields. SW13 —2D 88
Westfields Av. SW13 —2C 88
Westfields Rd. W3 —8M 55
Westfield St. SE18 —4H 79
Westfield Wlk. Wal X —4F 6
Westfield Way. E1 —6J 61
Westfield Way. Ruis —8C 36
W. Garden Pl. W2 —9C 58
West Gdns. E1 —1F 76
West Gdns. SW17 —3C 106
West Gdns. Eps —2C 134
Westgate. W5 —6J 55
Westgate Clo. Eps —7B 134
Westgate Ct. SE12 —7E 94
(off Burnt Ash Hill)
Westgate Ct. SW9 —2L 91
(off Canterbury Cres.)
Westgate Ct. Wal X —8D 6
Westgate M. W10 —7J 57
(off West Row)
Westgate Rd. SE25 —8F 108
Westgate Rd. Beck —6M 109

Winchester St.—Wolsey Clo.

Winchester St. W3 —2A 72
Winchester Wlk. SE1 —2B 76
Winchester Way. Crox G —7A 8
Winchet Wlk. Croy —1G 125
Winchfield Clo. Harr —4G 39
Winchfield Ho. SW15 —5D 88
Winchfield Rd. SE26 —2J 109
Winch Ho. E14 —4M 77
(off Tiller Rd.)
Winch Ho. SW10 —8A 74
(off King's Rd.)
Winchilsea Cres. W Mol —6A 102
Winchilsea Ho. NW8 —6B 58
(off St John's Wood Rd.)
Winchmore Hill. —9L 15
Winchmore Hill Rd. N14 & N21 —1H 27
Winchmore Vs. N21 —9K 15
(off Winchmore Hill Rd.)
Winckley Clo. Harr —3K 39
Wincott St. SE11 —5L 75
Wincrofts Dri. SE9 —3B 96
Windall Clo. SE19 —5E 108
Windborough Rd. Cars —9E 122
Windermere. NW1 —6F 58
(off Albany St.)
Windermere Av. N3 —1L 41
Windermere Av. NW6 —4J 57
Windermere Av. SW19 —7M 105
Windermere Av. Horn —1E 66
Windermere Av. Ruis —5G 37
Windermere Av. Wemb —5G 39
Windermere Clo. Dart —7F 98
Windermere Clo. Felt —7D 84
Windermere Clo. Orp —5M 127
Windermere Clo. Stai —7C 144
Windermere Ct. SW13 —7D 72
Windermere Ct. Kenl —7M 137
Windermere Ct. Wat —4E 8
Windermere Ct. Wemb —5G 39
Windermere Gdns. Ilf —3J 47
Windermere Gro. Wemb —6G 39
Windermere Hall. Edgw —5K 23
Windermere Ho. E3 —7K 61
Windermere Ho. New Bar —6M 13
Windermere Point. SE15 —8G 77
(off Old Kent Rd.)
Windermere Rd. N10 —8F 26
Windermere Rd. N19 —7G 43
Windermere Rd. SW15 —1C 104
Windermere Rd. SW16 —5G 107
Windermere Rd. W5 —4G 71
Windermere Rd. Bexh —1A 98
Windermere Rd. Coul —7J 137
Windermere Rd. Croy —3D 124
Windermere Rd. S'hall —8K 53
Windermere Rd. W W'ck —4C 126
Windermere Way. W Dray —2J 143
Winders Rd. SW11 —1C 90
(in two parts)
Windfield Clo. SE26 —1H 109
Windham Av. New Ad —2B 140
Windham Rd. Rich —2K 87
Windings, The. S Croy —3D 138
Winding Way. Dag —8G 49
Winding Way. Harr —9C 38
Windlass Pl. SE8 —5J 77
Windlesham Gro. SW19 —7H 89
Windley Clo. SE23 —8G 93
Windmill. WC1 —8K 59
(off New North St.)
Windmill Av. Eps —3D 134
Windmill Av. S'hall —2A 70
Windmill Bridge Ho. Croy —3C 124
(off Freemasons Rd.)
Windmill Bus. Cen. S'hall —2A 70
Windmill Bus. Village. Sun —5C 100
Windmill Clo. SE1 —5E 76
(off Beatrice Rd.)
Windmill Clo. SE13 —1A 94
Windmill Clo. Eps —4D 134
Windmill Clo. Sun —4C 100
Windmill Clo. Surb —3G 119
Windmill Clo. Upm —7L 51
Windmill Clo. Wal A —7L 7
Windmill Ct. NW2 —2J 57
Windmill Ct. W5 —5G 71
(off Windmill Rd.)
Windmill Dri. SW4 —4F 90
Windmill Dri. Kes —6G 127
Windmill End. Eps —4D 134
Windmill Gdns. Enf —5L 15
Windmill Grn. Shep —2C 116
(off Walton La.)
Windmill Gro. Croy —1A 124
Windmill Hill. NW3 —8A 42
Windmill Hill. Enf —5M 15
Windmill Hill. Ruis —5D 36
Windmill La. E15 —2B 62
Windmill La. Barn —8D 12
Windmill La. Bus H —1C 22
Windmill La. Chesh & Wal X —3E 6
Windmill La. Eps —4D 134
Windmill La. Gnfd —8A 54
Windmill La. S'hall & Iswth —2A 70
Windmill La. Surb —1F 118
Windmill M. W4 —5C 72
Windmill Pas. W4 —5C 72
Windmill Ri. King T —4M 103
Windmill Rd. N18 —4B 28
Windmill Rd. SW18 —5B 90
Windmill Rd. SW19 —1F 104
Windmill Rd. W4 —5C 72
Windmill Rd. W5 & Bren —5G 71
Windmill Rd. Croy —2A 124
Windmill Rd. Hamp H —2M 101
Windmill Rd. Mitc —9G 107
Windmill Rd. Sun —5C 100
Windmill Rd. W. Sun —6C 100
Windmill Row. SE11 —6L 75
Windmill St. W1 —8H 59
(in two parts)
Windmill St. Bus H —1C 22
Windmill Ter. Shep —2C 116
Windmill Wlk. SE1 —2L 75
Windmill Way. Ruis —6D 36
Windover Av. NW9 —2B 40
Windrose Clo. SE16 —3H 77
Windrush. SE28 —2F 80
Windrush. N Mald —8M 103
Windrush Clo. N17 —8C 28
Windrush Clo. SW11 —3B 90
Windrush Clo. W4 —9A 72
Windrush La. SE23 —9H 93
Windrush Rd. NW10 —4B 56
Windsock Clo. SE16 —5K 77
Windsor Av. E17 —9J 29
Windsor Av. SW19 —5A 106
Windsor Av. Edgw —4M 23
Windsor Av. N Mald —9A 104
Windsor Av. Sutt —5J 121
Windsor Av. Uxb —4F 142
Windsor Av. W Mol —7L 101
Windsor Cen., The. N1 —4M 59
(off Windsor St.)
Windsor Clo. N3 —9J 25
Windsor Clo. SE27 —1A 108
Windsor Clo. Borwd —3L 11
Windsor Clo. Bren —7F 70
Windsor Clo. Chesh —3A 6
Windsor Clo. Chst —2M 111
Windsor Clo. Harr —8L 37
Windsor Clo. N'wd —9E 20
Windsor Cotts. SE14 —8K 77
(off Amersham Gro.)
Windsor Ct. N12 —5D 26
Windsor Ct. N14 —9G 15
Windsor Ct. NW3 —9L 41
Windsor Ct. NW11 —4J 41
(off Golders Grn. Rd.)
Windsor Ct. SE16 —1H 77
(off King & Queen Wharf)
Windsor Ct. SW3 —6C 74
(off Jubilee Pl.)
Windsor Ct. SW11 —1B 90
Windsor Ct. W2 —1M 73
(off Moscow Rd.)
Windsor Ct. King T —8H 103
(off Palace Rd.)
Windsor Ct. Pinn —1H 37
Windsor Ct. Sun —4E 100
Windsor Ct. Whyt —9D 138
Windsor Cres. Harr —8L 37
Windsor Cres. Wemb —8M 39
Windsor Dri. Ashf —9B 144
Windsor Dri. Barn —8D 14
Windsor Dri. Dart —5E 98
Windsor Dri. Orp —8E 128
Windsor Gdns. W9 —8L 57
Windsor Gdns. Croy —5J 123
Windsor Gdns. Hay —4B 68
Windsor Gro. SE27 —1A 108
Windsor Hall. E16 —2F 78
(off Wesley Av., in two parts)
Windsor Ho. E2 —6H 61
(off Knottisford St.)
Windsor Ho. N1 —5A 60
Windsor Ho. NW1 —6F 58
(off Cumberland Mkt.)
Windsor Ho. N'holt —2L 53
(off Farmlands, The)
Windsor M. SE6 —7A 94
Windsor M. SE23 —7J 93
Windsor M. SW18 —6A 90
(off Wilna Rd.)
Windsor Pk. Rd. Hay —8D 68
Windsor Pl. SW1 —4G 75
Windsor Rd. E4 —4M 29
Windsor Rd. E7 —1F 62
Windsor Rd. E10 —7M 45
Windsor Rd. E11 —6E 46
Windsor Rd. N3 —9J 25
Windsor Rd. N7 —8J 43
Windsor Rd. N13 —3L 27
Windsor Rd. N17 —9E 28
Windsor Rd. NW2 —2F 56
Windsor Rd. W5 —1J 71
(in two parts)
Windsor Rd. Barn —8H 13
Windsor Rd. Bexh —3L 97
Windsor Rd. Dag —8J 49
Windsor Rd. Enf —9D 6
Windsor Rd. Harr —8A 22
Windsor Rd. Horn —5G 51
Windsor Rd. Houn —1F 84
Windsor Rd. Ilf —9M 47
Windsor Rd. King T —4J 103
Windsor Rd. Rich —1K 87
Windsor Rd. S'hall —4K 69
Windsor Rd. Sun —3E 100
Windsor Rd. Tedd —2B 102
Windsor Rd. T Hth —6M 107
Windsor Rd. Wat —2G 9
Windsor Rd. Wor Pk —4E 120
Windsors, The. Buck H —2J 31
Windsor St. N1 —4M 59
Windsor St. Uxb —3A 142
Windsor Ter. N1 —6A 60
Windsor Wlk. SE5 —1B 92
Windsor Wlk. W on T —3H 117
Windsor Wlk. Wey —7A 116
Windsor Way. W6 —5H 73
Windsor Wharf. E9 —2L 61
Windsor Wood. Wal A —6L 7
Windspoint Dri. SE15 —7F 76
Windus Rd. N16 —6D 44
Windus Wlk. N16 —6D 44
Windward Clo. Enf —8D 6
Windycroft Clo. Purl —5H 137
Windy Ridge. Brom —5J 111
Windy Ridge Clo. SW19 —2H 105
Wine Clo. E1 —1G 77
Wine Office Ct. EC4 —9L 59
Winery La. King T —7K 103
Winfields Mobile Home Pk. Wat —3M 9
Winford Ct. SE15 —9F 76
Winford Ho. E3 —3K 61
Winford Pde. S'hall —9M 53
(off Brunel Pl.)
Winforton St. SE10 —9A 78
Winfrith Rd. SW18 —6A 90
Wingate Cres. Croy —1J 123
Wingate Rd. W6 —4F 72
Wingate Rd. Ilf —1M 63
Wingate Rd. Sidc —3G 113
Wingate Trad. Est. N17 —7E 28
Wingfield Ct. Sidc —8D 96
Wingfield Ct. Wat —8A 8
Wingfield Ho. E2 —6D 60
(off Virginia Rd.)
Wingfield Ho. NW6 —5M 57
(off Tollgate Gdns.)
Wingfield M. SE15 —2E 92
Wingfield Rd. E15 —9C 46
Wingfield Rd. E17 —3M 45
Wingfield Rd. King T —3K 103
Wingfield St. SE15 —2E 92
Wingfield Way. Ruis —2F 52
Wingford Rd. SW2 —5J 91
Wingletye La. Horn —2K 51
Wingmore Rd. SE24 —2A 92
Wingrad Ho. E1 —8G 61
(off Jubilee St.)
Wingrave. SE17 —5B 76
(in three parts)
Wingrave Rd. W6 —7G 73
Wingreen. NW8 —4M 57
(off Abbey Rd.)
Wingrove. E4 —9L 17
Wingrove Ct. Romf —3A 50
Wingrove Dri. Purf —6M 83
Wingrove Rd. SE6 —8C 94
Wings Clo. Sutt —6L 121
Winicotte Ho. W2 —8B 58
(off Paddington Grn.)
Winifred Av. Horn —9H 51
Winifred Pl. N12 —5A 26
Winifred Rd. SW19 —5L 105
Winifred Rd. Coul —8E 136
Winifred Rd. Dag —7J 49
Winifred Rd. Dart —4F 98
Winifred Rd. Eri —6C 82
Winifred Rd. Hamp H —1L 101
Winifred St. E16 —2K 79
Winifred Ter. E13 —5E 62
(off Victoria Rd.)
Winifred Ter. Enf —9D 16
Winifred Whittington Ho. Rain —8F 66
Winkfield Rd. E13 —5F 62
Winkfield Rd. N22 —8L 27
Winkley Ct. N10 —2F 42
(off St James's La.)
Winkley Ct. S Harr —8L 37
Winkley St. E2 —5F 60
Winkworth Cotts. E1 —7G 61
(off Cephas St.)
Winkworth Pl. Bans —6K 135
Winkworth Rd. Bans —6L 135
Winlaton Rd. Brom —1B 110
Winmill Rd. Dag —8K 49
Winnett St. W1 —1H 75
Winningales Ct. Ilf —9J 31
Winnings Wlk. N'holt —2J 53
Winnington Clo. N2 —4B 42
Winnington Ho. SE5 —8A 76
(off Wyndham Est.)
Winnington Rd. N2 —4B 42
Winnington Rd. Enf —2G 17
Winnipeg Dri. Grn St —8D 128
Winnock Rd. W Dray —2H 143
Winn Rd. SE12 —7E 94
Winns Av. E17 —1K 45
Winns Comn. Rd. SE18 —7C 80
Winns M. N15 —2C 44
Winns Ter. E17 —1L 45
Winsbeach. E17 —9B 30
Winscombe Cres. W5 —7H 55
Winscombe St. NW5 —8F 42
Winscombe Way. Stan —5E 22
Winsford Rd. SE6 —9K 93
Winsford Ter. N18 —5B 28
Winsham Gro. SW11 —4E 90
Winsham Ho. NW1 —6H 59
(off Churchway)
Winslade Rd. SW2 —4J 91
Winslade Way. SE6 —6M 93
Winsland M. W2 —9B 58
Winsland St. W2 —9B 58
Winsley St. W1 —9G 59
Winslow. SE17 —6C 76
Winslow Clo. NW10 —8C 40
Winslow Clo. Pinn —4F 36
Winslow Gro. E4 —2C 30
Winslow Rd. W6 —7G 73
Winslow Way. Felt —9H 85
Winslow Way. W on T —5G 117
Winsmoor Ct. Enf —5M 15
Winsor Park. —8M 63
Winsor Ter. E6 —8L 63
Winstanley Est. SW11 —2B 90
Winstanley Rd. SW11 —2B 90
Winstead Gdns. Dag —1A 66
Winston Av. NW9 —5C 40
Winston Churchill's Britain at War Experience. —2C 76
(off Tooley St.)
Winston Clo. Harr —6D 22
Winston Clo. Romf —2M 49
Winston Ct. Brom —5F 110
(off Widmore Rd.)
Winston Ct. Harr —7M 21
Winston Ho. N1 —5B 60
(off Cherbury St.)
Winston Ho. W13 —3E 70
(off Salisbury Rd.)
Winston Ho. WC1 —7H 59
(off Endsleigh St.)
Winston Rd. N16 —9B 44
Winston Wlk. W4 —4B 72
Winston Way. Ilf —8M 47
Winstre Rd. Borwd —3L 11
Winter Av. E6 —4J 63
Winterborne Av. Orp —5B 128
Winterbourne Gro. Wey —8A 116
Winterbourne Ho. W11 —1J 73
(off Portland Rd.)
Winterbourne Rd. SE6 —7K 93
Winterbourne Rd. Dag —7G 49
Winterbourne Rd. T Hth —8L 107
Winter Box Wlk. Rich —4K 87
Winterbrook Rd. SE24 —5A 92
Winterburn Clo. N11 —6E 26
Winterdown Gdns. Esh —8K 117
Winterdown Rd. Esh —8K 117
Winterfold Clo. SW19 —8J 89
Wintergreen Clo. E6 —8J 63
Winterleys. NW6 —5K 57
(off Albert Rd.)
Winter Lodge. SE16 —6E 76
(off Fern Wlk.)
Winter's Ct. E4 —3M 29
Winterslow Ho. SE5 —1A 92
(off Flaxman Rd.)
Winters Rd. Th Dit —2F 118
Winterstoke Gdns. NW7 —5E 24
Winterstoke Rd. SE6 —7K 93
Winters Way. Wal A —6M 7
Winterton Ct. SE20 —6E 108
Winterton Ct. King T —5H 103
(off Lwr. Teddington Rd.)
Winterton Ho. E1 —9G 61
(off Deancross St.)
Winterton Pl. SW10 —7A 74
Winterwell Rd. SW2 —4J 91
Winthorpe Rd. SW15 —3J 89
Winthrop Ho. W12 —1F 72
(off White City Est.)
Winthrop St. E1 —8F 60
Winthrop Wlk. Wemb —8J 39
Winton App. Crox G —7A 8
Winton Av. N11 —7G 27
Winton Clo. N9 —9H 17
Winton Ct. Swan —8C 114
Winton Cres. Crox G —7A 8
Winton Dri. Chesh —2E 6
Winton Dri. Crox G —8A 8
Winton Gdns. Edgw —7K 23
Winton Rd. Orp —6M 127
Winton Way. SW16 —2L 107
Wireless Rd. Big H —7H 141
Wirrall Ho. SE26 —9E 92
Wirral Wood Clo. Chst —3L 111
Wisbeach Rd. Croy —9B 108
Wisbech. N4 —6K 43
(off Lorne Rd.)
Wisborough Rd. S Croy —1D 138
Wisden Ho. SW8 —7K 75
Wisdom Ct. Iswth —2E 86
(off South St.)
Wisdons Clo. Dag —6M 49
Wise La. NW7 —5E 24
Wise La. W Dray —4H 143
Wiseman Rd. E10 —7L 45
Wise Rd. E15 —4B 62
Wiseton Rd. SW17 —7C 90
Wisham Wlk. N13 —6J 27
Wishart Rd. SE3 —1H 95
Wishford Ct. Asht —9K 133
Wisley Ct. S Croy —2B 138
Wisley Ho. SW1 —6H 75
(off Rampayne St.)
Wisley Rd. SW11 —4E 90
Wisley Rd. Orp —4E 112
Wistaria Clo. Orp —4M 127
Wisteria Clo. NW7 —5D 24
Wisteria Clo. Ilf —1M 63
Wisteria Dri. NW7 —6D 24
Wisteria Gdns. Swan —6B 114
Wisteria Gdns. Wfd G —5E 30
Wisteria Rd. SE13 —3B 94
Witanhurst La. N6 —6E 42
Witan St. E2 —6F 60
Witham Clo. Lou —8J 19
Witham Ct. E10 —8M 45
Witham Rd. SE20 —7G 109
Witham Rd. W13 —2E 70
Witham Rd. Dag —1L 65
Witham Rd. Iswth —9B 70
Witham Rd. Romf —3F 50
Withens Clo. Orp —8G 113
Witherby Clo. Croy —7C 124
Witherings, The. Horn —3J 51
Witherington Rd. N5 —1L 59
Withers Clo. Chess —8G 119
Withers Mead. NW9 —8D 24
Withers Pl. EC1 —7A 60
Witherston Way. SE9 —8L 95
Withycombe Rd. SW19 —6H 89
Withy Ho. E1 —7H 61
(off Globe Rd.)
Withy La. Ruis —3A 36
Withy Mead. E4 —3B 30
Withy Pl. Park —1M 5
Witley Ct. WC1 —7J 59
(off Coram St.)
Witley Cres. New Ad —8A 126
Witley Gdns. S'hall —5K 69
Witley Ho. SW2 —6J 91
Witley Ind. Est. S'hall —5K 69
Witley Rd. N19 —7G 43
Witney Clo. Pinn —6K 21
Witney Path. SE23 —9H 93
Wittenham Way. E4 —3B 30
Wittering Clo. King T —2H 103
Wittering Wlk. Horn —2G 67
Wittersham Rd. Brom —2D 110
Witts Ho. King T —7K 103
(off Winery La.)
Wivenhoe Clo. SE15 —2F 92
Wivenhoe Ct. Houn —3K 85
Wivenhoe Rd. Bark —5E 64
Wiverton Rd. SE26 —3G 109
Wixom Ho. SE3 —3G 95
Wix Rd. Dag —4H 65
Wix's La. SW4 —2F 90
Woburn. W13 —8F 54
(off Clivedon Ct.)
Woburn Av. Horn —9E 50
Woburn Av. Purl —3L 137
Woburn Clo. SE28 —9H 65
Woburn Clo. SW19 —3A 106
Woburn Clo. Bush —8A 10
Woburn Ct. E18 —9E 30
Woburn Ct. SE16 —6F 76
(off Masters Dri.)
Woburn Ct. Croy —3A 124
Woburn M. WC1 —7H 59
Woburn Pl. WC1 —7J 59
Woburn Rd. Cars —3C 122
Woburn Rd. Croy —3A 124
Woburn Sq. WC1 —7H 59
Woburn Tower. N'holt —6H 53
(off Broomcroft Av.)
Woburn Wlk. WC1 —6H 59
Wodehouse Av. SE5 —9D 76
Wodehouse Ct. W3 —4A 72
(off Vincent Rd.)
Wodehouse Rd. Dart —3L 99
Woffington Clo. King T —5G 103
Woking Clo. SW15 —3D 88
Wolcot Ho. NW1 —5G 59
(off Aldenham St.)
Woldham Pl. Brom —8G 111
Woldham Rd. Brom —8G 111
Wolds Dri. Orp —6L 127
Wolfe Clo. Brom —1E 126
Wolfe Clo. Hay —6F 52
Wolfe Cres. SE7 —6H 79
Wolfe Cres. SE16 —3H 77
Wolfe Ho. W12 —1F 72
(off White City Est.)
Wolferton Rd. E12 —9K 47
Wolffe Gdns. E15 —2D 62
Wolfington Rd. SE27 —1M 107
Wolfram Clo. SE13 —4C 94
Wolftencroft Clo. SW11 —2C 90
Wollaston Clo. SE1 —5A 76
Wollett Ct. NW1 —3G 59
(off St Pancras Way)
Wolmer Clo. Edgw —4L 23
Wolmer Gdns. Edgw —3L 23
Wolseley Av. SW19 —8L 89
Wolseley Gdns. W4 —7M 71
Wolseley Rd. E7 —3F 62
Wolseley Rd. N8 —4H 43
Wolseley Rd. N22 —8K 27
Wolseley Rd. W4 —5A 72
Wolseley Rd. Harr & W'stone —1C 38
Wolseley Rd. Mitc —2E 122
Wolseley Rd. Romf —5B 50
Wolseley St. SE1 —3E 76
Wolsey Av. E6 —6L 63
Wolsey Av. E17 —1K 45
Wolsey Av. Chesh —2A 6
Wolsey Av. Th Dit —9D 102
Wolsey Bus. Pk. Wat —9B 8
Wolsey Clo. SW20 —4F 104
Wolsey Clo. Houn —3A 86
Wolsey Clo. King T —5M 103
Wolsey Clo. S'hall —4A 70
Wolsey Clo. Wor Pk —6E 120

Woodside Pk. Av.—Wynnstay Gdns.

Woodside Pk. Av. E17 —2B 46
Woodside Pk. Rd. N12 —4M 25
Woodside Pl. Wemb —4J 55
Woodside Rd. E13 —7G 63
Woodside Rd. N22 —7K 27
Woodside Rd. SE25 —1F 124
Woodside Rd. Ab L & Wat —4E 4
Woodside Rd. Bexh —3B 98
Woodside Rd. Brick W —3K 5
Woodside Rd. Brom —9J 111
Woodside Rd. King T —4J 103
Woodside Rd. N Mald —6B 104
Woodside Rd. N'wd —7D 20
Woodside Rd. Purl —5H 137
Woodside Rd. Sidc —9C 96
Woodside Rd. Sutt —5A 122
Woodside Rd. Wfd G —4E 30
Woodside Way. Croy —1G 125
Woodside Way. Mitc —5F 106
Woods M. W1 —1D 74
Woodsome Lodge. Wey —8A 116
Woodsome Rd. NW5 —8E 42
Woods Pl. SE1 —4C 76
Woodspring Rd. SW19 —8J 89
Woods Rd. SE15 —9F 76
Woodstead Gro. Edgw —6J 23
Woods, The. N'wd —5E 20
Woodstock Av. NW11 —5J 41
Woodstock Av. W13 —4E 70
Woodstock Av. Iswth —4E 86
Woodstock Av. Romf —5M 35
Woodstock Av. S'hall —6K 53
Woodstock Av. Sutt —2K 121
Woodstock Clo. Bex —7K 97
Woodstock Clo. Stan —9J 23
Woodstock Ct. SE11 —6K 75
Woodstock Ct. SE12 —5E 94
Woodstock Ct. Eps —5B 134
Woodstock Cres. N9 —8F 16
Woodstock Gdns. Beck —5M 109
Woodstock Gdns. Hay —8D 52
Woodstock Gdns. Ilf —7E 48
Woodstock Grange. W5 —2J 71
Woodstock Gro. W12 —3H 73
Woodstock La. N. Surb —4G 119
Woodstock La. S. Clay & Chess —7F 118
Woodstock M. W1 —8E 58
(off Westmoreland St.)
Woodstock Ri. Sutt —2K 121
Woodstock Rd. E7 —3G 63
Woodstock Rd. E17 —9B 30
Woodstock Rd. N4 —6L 43
Woodstock Rd. NW11 —5K 41
Woodstock Rd. W4 —5C 72
Woodstock Rd. Bus H —9C 10
Woodstock Rd. Cars —7E 122
Woodstock Rd. Coul —8F 136
Woodstock Rd. Croy —5B 124
Woodstock Rd. Wemb —4K 55
Woodstock St. W1 —9F 58
Woodstock Ter. E14 —1M 77
Woodstock, The. (Junct.) —2K 121
Woodstock Way. Mitc —6F 106
Woodstone Av. Eps —7E 120
Wood Street. (Junct.) —1A 46
Wood St. E16 —1F 78
Wood St. E17 —1A 46
Wood St. EC2 —9A 60
Wood St. W4 —6C 72
Wood St. Barn —6H 13
Wood St. King T —6H 103
Wood St. Mitc —2E 122
Wood St. Swan —6G 115
Woodsway. Oxs —6C 132
Woodsyre. SE26 —1D 108
Woodthorpe Rd. SW15 —3F 88
Woodthorpe Rd. Ashf —9C 144
Woodtree Clo. NW4 —9H 25
Wood Va. N10 —3G 43
Wood Va. SE23 —7F 92
Woodvale Av. SE25 —7D 108
Woodvale Ct. Brom —5F 110
(off Widmore Rd.)
Wood Va. Est. SE23 —6G 93
Woodvale Wlk. SE27 —2A 108
Woodvale Way. NW11 —8H 41
Woodview. Chess —3G 133
Woodview Av. E4 —4A 30
Woodview Clo. N4 —5M 43
Woodview Clo. SW15 —1B 104
Woodview Clo. Orp —4A 128
Woodview Clo. S Croy —6F 138
Woodview Rd. Swan —6A 114
Woodville. SE3 —9F 78
Woodville Clo. SE12 —4E 94
Woodville Clo. Tedd —1E 102
Woodville Ct. SE19 —5D 108
Woodville Ct. Wat —4E 8
Woodville Gdns. NW2 —5H 41
Woodville Gdns. W5 —9J 55
Woodville Gdns. Ilf —1M 47
Woodville Gdns. Ruis —5A 36
Woodville Gdns. Surb —2H 119
Woodville Gro. Well —2E 96
Woodville Ho. SE1 —4D 76
(off Grange Wlk.)
Woodville Rd. E11 —6D 46
Woodville Rd. E17 —2K 45
Woodville Rd. E18 —9F 30
Woodville Rd. N1 —1C 60
Woodville Rd. NW6 —5K 57
Woodville Rd. NW11 —5H 41
Woodville Rd. W5 —9H 55
Woodville Rd. Barn & New Bar —5M 13
Woodville Rd. Mord —8L 105
Woodville Rd. Rich —9F 86
Woodville Rd. T Hth —8A 108
Woodville St. SE18 —5J 79
Woodville, The. W5 —9H 55
(off Woodville Rd.)
Woodward Av. NW4 —3E 40
Woodward Clo. Clay —8D 118
Woodwarde Rd. SE22 —5C 92
Woodward Gdns. Dag —3G 65
Woodward Gdns. Stan —7D 22
Woodward Rd. Dag —3F 64
Woodward's Footpath. Twic —5A 86
Wood Way. Orp —4L 127
Woodway Cres. Harr —4E 38
Woodwaye. Wat —9G 9
Woodwell St. SW18 —4A 90
Wood Wharf. SE10 —7A 78
Wood Wharf Bus. Pk. E14 —2M 77
(in two parts)
Woodyard Clo. NW5 —1E 58
Woodyard La. SE21 —6C 92
Woodyates Rd. SE12 —5E 94
Woolacombe Rd. SE3 —9G 79
Woolacombe Way. Hay —5C 68
Woolcombes Ct. SE16 —2H 77
(off Princes Riverside Rd.)
Wooler St. SE17 —6B 76
Woolf Clo. SE28 —2F 80
Woolf Ct. W3 —4A 72
(off Vincent Rd.)
Woolf M. WC1 —7H 59
(off Burton Pl.)
Woolgar M. N16 —1C 60
(off Gillett St.)
Woolhampton Way. Chig —3F 32
Woollard St. Wal A —7J 7
Woollaston Rd. N4 —4M 43
Woollett Clo. Cray —3E 98
Woolley Ho. SW9 —2M 91
(off Loughborough Rd.)
Woollon Ho. E1 —9G 61
(off Clark St.)
Woolmead Av. NW9 —5E 40
Woolmer Clo. Borwd —2L 11
Woolmerdine Ct. Bush —5H 9
Woolmer Gdns. N18 —5E 28
Woolmer Rd. N18 —5E 28
Woolmore St. E14 —1A 78
Woolneigh St. SW6 —2M 89
Woolridge Way. E9 —3G 61
Wool Rd. SW20 —3F 104
Woolstaplers Way. SE16 —4E 76
Woolston Clo. E17 —9H 29
Woolstone Rd. SE23 —8J 93
Woolwich. —4L 79
Woolwich Chu. St. SE18 —4J 79
Woolwich Comn. SE18 —7L 79
Woolwich Dockyard Ind. Est. SE18 —4J 79
Woolwich High St. SE18 —4L 79
Woolwich Ind. Est. SE28 —4C 80
(Hadden Rd.)
Woolwich Ind. Est. SE28 —4D 80
(Kellner Rd.)
Woolwich Mnr. Way. E6 & E16 —7K 63
Woolwich New Rd. SE18 —6L 79
Woolwich Rd. SE2 & Belv —7H 81
Woolwich Rd. SE10 & SE7 —6D 78
Woolwich Rd. Bexh —2L 97
Wooster Gdns. E14 —9B 62
Wooster M. Harr —1A 38
Wooster Pl. SE1 —5B 76
(off Searles Rd.)
Wootton Clo. Eps —8D 134
Wootton Clo. Horn —3H 51
Wootton Gro. N3 —8L 25
Wootton St. SE1 —2L 75
Worbeck Rd. SE20 —6F 108
Worcester Av. N17 —7E 28
Worcester Clo. NW2 —8F 40
Worcester Clo. Croy —4L 125
Worcester Clo. Mitc —6E 106
Worcester Ct. N12 —5M 25
Worcester Ct. W7 —9D 54
(off Copley Clo.)
Worcester Ct. Harr —1C 38
Worcester Ct. W on T —4G 117
Worcester Ct. Wor Pk —5C 120
Worcester Cres. NW7 —3C 24
Worcester Cres. Wfd G —4F 30
Worcester Dri. W4 —3C 72
Worcester Dri. Ashf —2A 100
Worcester Gdns. Gnfd —2B 54
Worcester Gdns. Ilf —5J 47
Worcester Gdns. Wor Pk —5C 120
Worcester Ho. SE11 —4L 75
(off Kennington Rd.)
Worcester Ho. SW9 —8L 75
(off Cranmer Rd.)
Worcester Ho. W2 —9A 58
(off Hallfield Est.)
Worcester Ho. Borwd —4L 11
(off Stratfield Rd.)
Worcester M. NW6 —2M 57
Worcester Park. —3E 120
Worcester Pk. Rd. Wor Pk —5B 120
Worcester Rd. E12 —9K 47
Worcester Rd. E17 —9H 29
Worcester Rd. SW19 —2K 105
Worcester Rd. Cow & Uxb —8A 142
Worcester Rd. Sutt —9L 121
Worcesters Av. Enf —2E 16
Wordsworth Av. E12 —3J 63
Wordsworth Av. E18 —1D 46
Wordsworth Av. Gnfd —6B 54
Wordsworth Av. Kenl —7B 138
Wordsworth Clo. Romf —8G 35
Wordsworth Ct. Harr —5C 38
Wordsworth Dri. Cheam & Sutt —6G 121
Wordsworth Ho. NW6 —6L 57
(off Stafford Rd.)
Wordsworth Pde. N15 —2M 43
Wordsworth Pl. NW3 —1D 58
Wordsworth Rd. N16 —9C 44
Wordsworth Rd. SE1 —5D 76
Wordsworth Rd. SE20 —4H 109
Wordsworth Rd. Hamp —1K 101
Wordsworth Rd. Wall —8G 123
Wordsworth Rd. Well —9C 80
Wordsworth Wlk. NW11 —2L 41
Wordsworth Way. Dart —3L 99
Wordsworth Way. W Dray —5J 143
Worfield St. SW11 —8C 74
Worgan St. SE11 —6K 75
Worgan St. SE16 —5H 77
Worland Rd. E15 —3C 62
World Bus. Cen. H'row A —9A 68
World of Silk. —4C 98
(off Bourne Rd.)
World's End. —5K 15
Worlds End Est. SW10 —8B 74
World's End La. N21 & Enf —7K 15
Worlds End La. Orp —8D 128
World's End Pas. SW10 —8B 74
(off Worlds End. Est)
World's End Pl. SW10 —8B 74
(off Worlds End Est.)
Worlidge St. W6 —6G 73
Worlingham Rd. SE22 —3D 92
Wormholt Rd. W12 —1E 72
Wormwood St. EC2 —9C 60
(in two parts)
Wormyngford Ct. Wal A —6M 7
Wornington Rd. W10 —7J 57
(in two parts)
Wornum Ho. W10 —5J 57
(off Kilburn La.)
Woronzow Rd. NW8 —4B 58
Worple Av. SW19 —4H 105
Worple Av. Iswth —4E 86
Worple Clo. Harr —6K 37
Worple Rd. SW20 & SW19 —6G 105
Worple Rd. Eps —7B 134
Worple Rd. Iswth —3E 86
Worple Rd. M. SW19 —3K 105
Worple St. SW14 —2B 88
Worple Way. Harr —6K 37
Worple Way. Rich —4J 87
Worship St. EC2 —7B 60
Worslade Rd. SW17 —1B 106
Worsley Bri. Rd. SE26 & Beck —1K 109
Worsley Ho. SE23 —8F 92
Worsley Rd. E11 —9C 46
Worsopp Dri. SW4 —4G 91
Worth Clo. Orp —6C 128
Worthfield Clo. Eps —9B 120
Worth Gro. SE17 —6B 76
Worthing Clo. E15 —4C 62
Worthing Rd. Houn —7K 69
Worthington Clo. Mitc —8F 106
Worthington Ho. EC1 —6L 59
(off Myddelton Pas.)
Worthington Rd. Surb —3K 119
Wortley Rd. E6 —3H 63
Wortley Rd. Croy —2L 123
Worton Ct. Iswth —3C 86
Worton Gdns. Iswth —1B 86
Worton Hall Ind. Est. Iswth —3C 86
Worton Rd. Iswth —3B 86
Worton Way. Iswth —1B 86
Wotton Ct. E14 —1B 78
(off Jamestown Way)
Wotton Grn. Orp —8H 113
Wotton Rd. NW2 —8G 41
Wotton Rd. SE8 —7K 77
Wotton Way. Sutt —2G 135
Wouldham Rd. E16 —9D 62
Wragby Rd. E11 —8C 46
Wrampling Pl. N9 —1E 28
Wrangthorn Wlk. Croy —6L 123
Wray Av. Ilf —1L 47
Wrayburn Ho. SE16 —3E 76
(off Llewellyn St.)
Wray Clo. Horn —5G 51
Wray Cres. N4 —7J 43
Wrayfield Rd. Sutt —5H 121
Wray Rd. Sutt —1K 135
Wraysbury Clo. Houn —4J 85
Wrays Way. Hay —7C 52
Wrekin Rd. SE18 —8A 80
Wren Av. NW2 —1G 57
Wren Av. S'hall —5K 69
Wren Clo. E16 —9D 62
Wren Clo. N9 —1H 29
Wren Clo. Orp —7H 113
Wren Clo. S Croy —1H 139
Wren Ct. Croy —6B 124
(off Coombe Rd.)
Wren Cres. Bush —1A 22
Wren Dri. Wal A —7M 7
Wren Dri. W Dray —4H 143
Wren Gdns. Dag —1H 65
Wren Gdns. Horn —6D 50
Wren Ho. E3 —5J 61
(off Gernon Rd.)
Wren Ho. SW1 —6H 75
(off Aylesford St.)
Wren Ho. Hamp W —6H 103
(off High St.)
Wren Landing. E14 —2L 77
Wrenn Ho. SW13 —7G 73
Wren Path. SE28 —4B 80
Wren Rd. SE5 —9B 76
Wren Rd. Dag —1H 65
Wren Rd. Sidc —1G 113
Wren's Av. Ashf —1A 100
Wrens Hill. Oxs —7A 132
Wren's Pk. Ho. E5 —7F 44
Wren St. WC1 —7K 59
Wrentham Av. NW10 —5H 57
Wrenthorpe Rd. Brom —1C 110
Wrenwood Way. Pinn —2F 36
Wrestlers Ct. EC3 —9C 60
(off Clark's Pl.)
Wrexham Rd. E3 —5L 61
Wrexham Rd. Romf —3H 35
Wricklemarsh Rd. SE3 —1F 94
(in two parts)
Wrigglesworth St. SE14 —8H 77
Wright Clo. SE13 —3B 94
Wright Rd. N1 —2C 60
Wright Rd. Houn —8G 69
Wrights All. SW19 —3G 105
Wrightsbridge Rd. S Wea —1K 35
Wright's Bldgs. Wat —4F 8
(off Langley Rd.)
Wrights Clo. Dag —9M 49
Wrights Grn. SW4 —3H 91
Wright's La. W8 —4M 73
Wrights Pl. NW10 —2A 56
Wright's Rd. E3 —5K 61
(in two parts)
Wrights Rd. SE25 —7C 108
Wrights Row. Wall —6F 122
Wrights Wlk. SW14 —2B 88
Wrigley Clo. E4 —5B 30
Wrington Ho. Romf —5K 35
(off Redruth Rd.)
Writtle Ho. NW9 —9D 24
Writtle Wlk. Rain —4C 66
Wrotham Ho. SE1 —4B 76
(off Law St.)
Wrotham Ho. Beck —4K 109
(off Sellindge Clo.)
Wrotham Rd. NW1 —3G 59
Wrotham Rd. W13 —2G 71
Wrotham Rd. Barn —4J 13
Wrotham Rd. Well —9G 81
Wroth's Path. Lou —3K 19
Wrottesley Rd. NW10 —5E 56
Wrottesley Rd. SE18 —7A 80
Wroughton Rd. SW11 —4D 90
Wroughton Ter. NW4 —2F 40
Wroxall Rd. Dag —2G 65
Wroxham Gdns. N11 —7H 27
Wroxham Rd. SE28 —1H 81
Wroxham Way. Ilf —8M 31
Wroxton Rd. SE15 —1G 93
Wrythe Grn. Cars —5D 122
Wrythe Grn. Rd. Cars —5D 122
Wrythe La. Cars —3A 122
Wrythe, The. —5D 122
Wulfstan St. W12 —8D 56
Wyatt Clo. SE16 —3K 77
Wyatt Clo. Bush —9B 10
Wyatt Clo. Felt —7H 85
Wyatt Clo. Hay —8E 52
Wyatt Ct. Wemb —3J 55
Wyatt Dri. SW13 —7F 72
Wyatt Ho. NW8 —7B 58
(off Frampton St.)
Wyatt Ho. SE3 —1D 94
Wyatt Ho. Twic —5H 87
Wyatt Pk. Rd. SW2 —8J 91
Wyatt Rd. E7 —2E 62
Wyatt Rd. N5 —8A 44
Wyatt Rd. Dart —2D 98
Wyatts La. E17 —1A 46
Wybert St. NW1 —7G 59
Wyborne Ho. NW10 —3A 56
Wyborne Way. NW10 —3A 56
Wyburn Av. Barn —5K 13
Wyche Gro. S Croy —9B 124
Wych Elm Clo. Horn —5L 51
Wych Elm Lodge. Brom —4D 110
Wych Elm Pas. King T —4K 103
Wych Elm Rd. Horn —4L 51
Wych Elms. Park —1M 5
Wycherley Clo. SE3 —8D 78
Wycherley Cres. New Bar —8M 13
Wychcombe Studios. NW3 —2D 58
Wychwood Av. Edgw —6H 23
Wychwood Av. T Hth —7A 108
Wychwood Clo. Edgw —6H 23
Wychwood Clo. Sun —3E 100
Wychwood End. N6 —5G 43
Wychwood Gdns. Ilf —2K 47
Wychwood Way. SE19 —3B 108
Wychwood Way. N'wd —7D 20
Wyclif Ct. EC1 —6M 59
(off Wyclif St.)
Wycliffe Clo. Well —9D 80
Wycliffe Ct. Ab L —5C 4
Wycliffe Rd. SW11 —1E 90
Wycliffe Rd. SW19 —3M 105
Wyclif St. EC1 —6M 59
Wycombe Gdns. NW11 —7L 41
Wycombe Ho. NW8 —7C 58
(off Grendon St.)
Wycombe Pl. SW18 —5A 90
Wycombe Rd. N17 —8E 28
Wycombe Rd. Ilf —3K 47
Wycombe Rd. Wemb —4L 55
Wydehurst Rd. Croy —2E 124
Wydell Clo. Mord —1H 121
Wydeville Mnr. Rd. SE12 —1F 110
Wye Clo. Ashf —1A 100
Wye Clo. Orp —2D 128
Wye Clo. Ruis —4A 36
Wye Ct. W13 —8F 54
(off Malvern Way)
Wyemead Cres. E4 —2C 30
Wye St. SW11 —1B 90
Wyeths M. Eps —5D 134
Wyeths Rd. Eps —5D 134
Wyevale Clo. Pinn —1E 36
Wyfields. Ilf —8M 31
Wyfold Ho. SE2 —3H 81
(off Wolvercote Rd.)
Wyfold Rd. SW6 —8J 73
Wyhill Wlk. Dag —3A 66
Wyke Clo. Iswth —7D 70
Wyke Gdns. W7 —4E 70
Wykeham Av. Dag —2G 65
Wykeham Av. Horn —4H 51
Wykeham Clo. W Dray —6L 143
Wykeham Ct. N11 —2E 26
(off Wykeham Rd.)
Wykeham Ct. NW4 —3G 41
(off Wykeham Rd.)
Wykeham Grn. Dag —2G 65
Wykeham Hill. Wemb —6K 39
Wykeham Ri. N20 —1J 25
Wykeham Rd. NW4 —2G 41
Wykeham Rd. Harr —2F 38
Wyke Rd. E3 —3L 61
Wyke Rd. SW20 —6G 105
Wylchin Clo. Pinn —1D 36
Wyldes Clo. NW11 —6A 42
Wyldfield Gdns. N9 —2D 28
Wyld Way. Wemb —2M 55
Wyleu St. SE23 —6J 93
Wylie Rd. S'hall —4L 69
Wyllen Clo. E1 —7G 61
Wylo Dri. Barn —8E 12
Wymans Way. E7 —9G 47
Wymering Mans. W9 —6L 57
(off Wymering Rd., in two parts)
Wymering Rd. W9 —6L 57
Wymond St. SW15 —2G 89
Wynan Rd. E14 —6M 77
Wynash Gdns. Cars —7C 122
Wynaud Ct. N22 —6K 27
Wyncham Av. Sidc —7C 96
Wyncham Ho. Sidc —8E 96
(off Longlands Rd.)
Wynchgate. N14 & N21 —1H 27
Wynchgate. Harr —7C 22
Wynchgate. N'holt —1K 53
Wyncote Way. S Croy —1H 139
Wyncroft Clo. Brom —7K 111
Wyndale Av. NW9 —4L 39
Wyndcliff Rd. SE7 —7F 78
Wyndcroft Clo. Enf —5M 15
Wyndham Clo. Orp —3A 128
Wyndham Clo. Sutt —9L 121
Wyndham Ct. W7 —5E 70
Wyndham Cres. N19 —8G 43
Wyndham Cres. Houn —5L 85
Wyndham Deedes Ho. E2 —5E 60
(off Hackney Rd.)
Wyndham Est. SE5 —8A 76
Wyndham Ho. E14 —3M 77
(off Marsh Wall)
Wyndham M. W1 —8D 58
Wyndham Pl. W1 —8D 58
Wyndham Rd. E6 —3H 63
Wyndham Rd. SE5 —8A 76
Wyndham Rd. W13 —4F 70
Wyndham Rd. Barn —1D 26
Wyndham Rd. King T —4K 103
(in two parts)
Wyndhams Theatre. —1J 75
(off St Martin's La.)
Wyndham St. W1 —8D 58
Wyndham Yd. W1 —8D 58
Wyneham Rd. SE24 —4B 92
Wynell Rd. SE23 —9H 93
Wynford Gro. Orp —7F 112
Wynford Ho. N1 —5K 59
(off Priory Grn. Est.)
Wynford Pl. Belv —7L 81
Wynford Rd. N1 —5K 59
Wynford Way. SE9 —9K 95
Wynlie Gdns. Pinn —9F 20
Wynndale Rd. E18 —8F 30
Wynne Ho. SE14 —9H 77
Wynne Rd. SW9 —1L 91
Wynnstay Gdns. W8 —4L 73

HOSPITALS and HOSPICES
covered by this atlas
with their map square reference

N.B. Where Hospitals and Hospices are not named on the map, the reference
given is for the road in which they are situated.

ACTON HOSPITAL —3L **71**
Gunnersbury La.
LONDON
W3 8EG
Tel: 020 83831133

ARCHERY HOUSE —5M **99**
Bow Arrow La.
DARTFORD
DA2 6PB
Tel: 01322 622222

ASHFORD HOSPITAL —8C **144**
London Rd.
ASHFORD
TW15 3AA
Tel: 01784 884488

ATHLONE HOUSE —6D **42**
Hampstead La.
LONDON
N6 4RX
Tel: 020 83485231

ATKINSON MORLEY'S HOSPITAL —4F **104**
31 Copse Hill
LONDON
SW20 0NE
Tel: 020 89467711

BARKING HOSPITAL —3D **64**
Upney La.
BARKING
IG11 9LX
Tel: 0208 9838000

BARNES HOSPITAL —2C **88**
S. Worple Way
LONDON
SW14 8SU
Tel: 020 88784981

BARNET HOSPITAL —6H **13**
Wellhouse La.
BARNET
EN5 3DJ
Tel: 020 82164000

BECKENHAM HOSPITAL —6K **109**
379 Croydon Rd.
BECKENHAM
BR3 3QL
Tel: 020 82896600

BECONTREE DAY HOSPITAL —7J **49**
508 Becontree Av.
DAGENHAM
RM8 3HR
Tel: 0208 9841234

BELVEDERE DAY HOSPITAL —4E **56**
341 Harlesden Rd.
LONDON
NW10 3RX
Tel: 020 84593562

BELVEDERE PRIVATE CLINIC —6G **81**
Knee Hill
LONDON
SE2 0AT
Tel: 020 83114464

BETHLEM ROYAL HOSPITAL, THE
—2L **125**
Monks Orchard Rd.
BECKENHAM
BR3 3BX
Tel: 020 87776611

BEXLEY HOSPITAL —8C **98**
Old Bexley La.
BEXLEY
DA5 2BW
Tel: 01322 526282

BLACKHEATH BMI HOSPITAL, THE —2D **94**
40-42 Lee Ter.
LONDON
SE3 9UD
Tel: 020 83187722

BOLINGBROKE HOSPITAL —4C **90**
Bolingbroke Gro.
LONDON
SW11 6HN
Tel: 020 72237411

BRITISH HOME & HOSPITAL FOR INCURABLES —2M **107**
Crown La.
LONDON
SW16 3JB
Tel: 020 86708261

BROMLEY HOSPITAL —8F **110**
Cromwell Av.
BROMLEY
BR2 9AJ
Tel: 020 82897000

BUSHEY BUPA HOSPITAL —9D **10**
Heathbourne Rd.
Bushey Heath
BUSHEY
WD23 1RD
Tel: 020 89509090

CAMDEN MEWS DAY HOSPITAL —2G **59**
1-5 Camden M.
LONDON
NW1 9DB
Tel: 020 75304780

CANE HILL FORENSIC MENTAL HEALTH UNIT —9G **137**
Brighton Rd.
COULSDON
CR5 3YL
Tel: 01737 556300

CARSHALTON WAR MEMORIAL HOSPITAL —8D **122**
The Park,
CARSHALTON
SM5 3DB
Tel: 020 86475534

CASSEL HOSPITAL, THE —1H **103**
1 Ham Comn.
RICHMOND
TW10 7JF
Tel: 020 89408181

CENTRAL MIDDLESEX HOSPITAL —6A **56**
Acton La.
LONDON
NW10 7NS
Tel: 020 89655733

CHADWELL HEATH HOSPITAL —3F **48**
Grove Rd.
ROMFORD
RM6 4XH
Tel: 020 89838000

CHARING CROSS HOSPITAL —7H **73**
Fulham Pal. Rd.
LONDON
W6 8RF
Tel: 020 88461234

CHASE FARM HOSPITAL —2L **15**
127 The Ridgeway
ENFIELD
EN2 8JL
Tel: 020 83666600

CHELSEA & WESTMINSTER HOSPITAL —7A **74**
369 Fulham Rd.
LONDON
SW10 9NH
Tel: 020 87468000

CHELSFIELD PARK HOSPITAL —7J **129**
Bucks Cross Rd.
ORPINGTON
BR6 7RG
Tel: 01689 877855

CHESHUNT COMMUNITY HOSPITAL —4E **6**
King Arthur Ct., Cheshunt
WALTHAM CROSS
EN8 8XN
Tel: 01992 622157

CLAYPONDS HOSPITAL —5J **71**
Sterling Pl.
LONDON
W5 4RN
Tel: 020 85604011

CLEMENTINE CHURCHILL HOSPITAL, THE —8D **38**
Sudbury Hill
HARROW
HA1 3RX
Tel: 020 88723872

COLINDALE HOSPITAL —9C **24**
Colindale Av.
LONDON
NW9 5HG
Tel: 020 89522381

COTTAGE DAY HOSPITAL —9C **90**
Springfield University Hospital
61 Glenburnie Rd.
LONDON
SW17 7DJ
Tel: 020 86826514

CROMWELL HOSPITAL, THE —5M **73**
162-174 Cromwell Rd.
LONDON
SW5 0TU
Tel: 020 74602000

DEVONSHIRE HOSPITAL, THE —8E **58**
29-31 Devonshire St.
LONDON
W1N 1RF
Tel: 020 74867131

EALING HOSPITAL —3B **70**
Uxbridge Rd.
SOUTHALL
UB1 3HW
Tel: 020 89675000

EAST HAM MEMORIAL HOSPITAL —3H **63**
Shrewsbury Rd.
LONDON
E7 8QR
Tel: 0208 5865000

EASTMAN DENTAL HOSPITAL & DENTAL INSTITUTE, THE
—7K **59**
256 Gray's Inn Rd.
LONDON
WC1X 8LD
Tel: 020 79151000

EDENHALL MARIE CURIE CENTRE —1B **58**
11 Lyndhurst Gdns.
LONDON
NW3 5NS
Tel: 020 77940066

EDGWARE COMMUNITY HOSPITAL —7M **23**
Burnt Oak Broadway
EDGWARE
HA8 0AD
Tel: 020 89522381

EPSOM DAY SURGERY UNIT —5D **134**
The Old Cottage Hospital
Alexandra Rd.
EPSOM
KT17 4BL
Tel: 01372 739002

EPSOM GENERAL HOSPITAL —7A **134**
Dorking Rd.
EPSOM
KT18 7EG
Tel: 01372 735735

ERITH & DISTRICT HOSPITAL —7B **82**
Park Cres., ERITH
DA8 3EE
Tel: 020 83022678

FARNBOROUGH HOSPITAL —6L **127**
Farnborough Comn., ORPINGTON
BR6 8ND
Tel: 01689 814000

FARNBOROUGH HOSPITAL (ANNEXE) —6E **128**
Sevenoaks Rd.
ORPINGTON
BR6 9JU
Tel: 01689 815000

FINCHLEY MEMORIAL HOSPITAL —7A **26**
Granville Rd.
LONDON
N12 0JE
Tel: 020 83493121

FLORENCE NIGHTINGALE DAY HOSPITAL —8C **58**
1B Harewood Row
LONDON
NW1 6SE
Tel: 020 7259940

FLORENCE NIGHTINGALE HOSPITAL —8C **58**
11-19 Lisson Gro.
LONDON
NW1 6SH
Tel: 020 72583828

GAINSBOROUGH CLINIC, THE —4L **75**
22 Barkham Ter.
LONDON
SE1 7PW
Tel: 020 79285633

GARDEN HOSPITAL, THE —1G **41**
46-50 Sunny Gdns. Rd.
LONDON
NW4 1RP
Tel: 020 84574500

GOODMAYES HOSPITAL —3E **48**
Barley La.
ILFORD
IG3 8XJ
Tel: 020 89838000

GORDON HOSPITAL —5H **75**
Bloomburg St.
LONDON
SW1V 2RH
Tel: 020 87468733

GREAT ORMOND STREET HOSPITAL FOR CHILDREN
—7J **59**
Gt. Ormond St.
LONDON
WC1N 3JH
Tel: 020 74059200

GREENWICH & BEXLEY COTTAGE HOSPICE —6G **81**
185 Bostall Hill
LONDON
SE2 0QX
Tel: 020 83122244

GREENWICH DISTRICT HOSPITAL —6D **78**
Vanbrugh Hill
LONDON
SE10 9HE
Tel: 020 88588141

GROVELANDS PRIORY HOSPITAL —1J **27**
The Bourne
LONDON
N14 6RA
Tel: 020 88828191

GUY'S HOSPITAL —2B **76**
St Thomas St.
LONDON
SE1 9RT
Tel: 020 79555000

GUY'S NUFFIELD HOUSE —3B **76**
Newcomen St.
LONDON
SE1 1YR
Tel: 020 79554257

HAMMERSMITH & NEW QUEEN CHARLOTTE'S
HOSPITAL —9F **56**
Du Cane Rd., LONDON
W12 0HS
Tel: 020 83831000

HARLEY STREET CLINIC, THE —8F **58**
35 Weymouth St., LONDON
W1N 4BJ
Tel: 020 79357700

HAROLD WOOD HOSPITAL —8J **35**
Gubbins La., ROMFORD
RM3 0BE
Tel: 01708 345533

HAYES GROVE PRIORY HOSPITAL —4E **126**
Prestons Rd., BROMLEY
BR2 7AS
Tel: 020 84627722

HEART HOSPITAL, THE —8E **58**
16-18 Westmoreland St.
LONDON
W1G 8PH
Tel: 020 75738888

HENDERSON HOSPITAL —1M **135**
Homeland Dri.
SUTTON
SM2 5LY
Tel: 020 86611611

HIGHGATE PRIVATE HOSPITAL —4D **42**
17 View Rd.
LONDON
N6 4DJ
Tel: 020 83414182

HILLINGDON HOSPITAL —8D **142**
Pield Heath Rd.
UXBRIDGE
UB8 3NN
Tel: 01895 238282

HOLLY HOUSE HOSPITAL —2F **30**
High Rd.
BUCKHURST HILL
IG9 5HX
Tel: 0208 5053311

HOMERTON HOSPITAL —1H **61**
Homerton Row
LONDON
E9 6SR
Tel: 020 85105555

HORNSEY CENTRAL HOSPITAL —3H **43**
Park Rd.
LONDON
N8 8JL
Tel: 020 82191700

HOSPITAL FOR TROPICAL DISEASES —7G **59**
Mortimer Mkt., Capper St.
LONDON
WC1E 6AU
Tel: 020 73879300

HOSPITAL OF ST JOHN & ST ELIZABETH —5B **58**
60 Grove End Rd.
LONDON
NW8 9NH
Tel: 020 72865126

KING EDWARD VII'S HOSPITAL FOR OFFICERS —8E **58**
5-10 Beaumont St.
LONDON
W1N 2AA
Tel: 020 74864411

KING GEORGE HOSPITAL —3E **48**
Barley La.
ILFORD
IG3 8YB
Tel: 020 89838000

KING'S COLLEGE HOSPITAL —1B **92**
Denmark Hill
LONDON
SE5 9RS
Tel: 020 77374000

KING'S COLLEGE HOSPITAL, DULWICH —3C **92**
East Dulwich Gro.
LONDON
SE22 8PT
Tel: 020 77374000

KING'S OAK BMI HOSPITAL, THE —2L **15**
The Ridgeway
ENFIELD
EN2 8SD
Tel: 020 83709500

KINGSBURY COMMUNITY HOSPITAL —2L **39**
Honeypot La.
LONDON
NW9 9QY
Tel: 020 89031323

KINGSTON HOSPITAL —5M **103**
Galsworthy Rd.
KINGSTON UPON THAMES
KT2 7QB
Tel: 020 85467711

LATIMER DAY HOSPITAL —8G **59**
40 Hanson St., LONDON
W1W 6UL
Tel: 020 73809187

LEWISHAM UNIVERSITY HOSPITAL —4M **93**
Lewisham High St., LONDON
SE13 6LH
Tel: 020 83333000

LISTER HOSPITAL, THE —6F **74**
Chelsea Bri. Rd.
LONDON
SW1W 8RH
Tel: 020 77303417

LITTLE BROOK HOSPITAL —5M **99**
Bow Arrow La.
DARTFORD
DA2 6PH
Tel: 01322 622222

LIVINGSTONE HOSPITAL —6K **99**
East Hill
DARTFORD
DA1 1SA
Tel: 01322 622222

LONDON BRIDGE HOSPITAL —2B **76**
27 Tooley St.
LONDON
SE1 2PR
Tel: 020 74073100

LONDON CHEST HOSPITAL —5G **61**
Bonner Rd.
LONDON
E2 9JX
Tel: 020 73777000

LONDON CLINIC, THE —7E **58**
20 Devonshire Pl.
LONDON
W1N 2DH
Tel: 020 79354444

LONDON FOOT HOSPITAL —7G **59**
33 & 40 Fitzroy Sq.
LONDON
W1P 6AY
Tel: 020 75304500

LONDON INDEPENDENT HOSPITAL —8H **61**
1 Beaumont Sq.
LONDON
E1 4NL
Tel: 020 77900990

LONDON LIGHTHOUSE —9J **57**
111-117 Lancaster Rd.
LONDON
W11 1QT
Tel: 020 77921200

LONDON WELBECK HOSPITAL —8E **58**
27 Welbeck St.
LONDON
W1G 8EN
Tel: 020 72242242

MAITLAND DAY HOSPITAL —9G **45**
143-153 Lwr. Clapton Rd.
LONDON
E5 8EQ
Tel: 020 89195600

MAUDSLEY HOSPITAL, THE —1B **92**
Denmark Hill
LONDON
SE5 8AZ
Tel: 020 77036333

MAYDAY UNIVERSITY HOSPITAL —1M **123**
Mayday Rd.
THORNTON HEATH
CR7 7YE
Tel: 020 84013000

MEADOW HOUSE HOSPICE —3B **70**
Ealing Hospital, Uxbridge Rd.
SOUTHALL
UB1 3HW
Tel: 020 8967 5179

MEADOWS, THE, E.M.I UNIT —2K **11**
Castleford Clo.
BOREHAMWOOD
WD6 4AL
Tel: 020 89534954

MEMORIAL HOSPITAL —1L **95**
Shooters Hill
LONDON
SE18 3RZ
Tel: 020 88565511

MIDDLESEX HOSPITAL, THE —8G **59**
Mortimer St., LONDON
W1N 8AA
Tel: 020 76368333

MILDMAY MISSION HOSPITAL —6D **60**
Hackney Rd., LONDON
E2 7NA
Tel: 020 76136300

Hospitals & Hospices

MOLESEY HOSPITAL —9L **101**
High St.
WEST MOLESEY
KT8 2LU
Tel: 020 89414481

MOORFIELDS EYE HOSPITAL —6B **60**
162 City Rd.
LONDON
EC1V 2PD
Tel: 020 72533411

MORLAND ROAD DAY HOSPITAL —3L **65**
Morland Rd.
DAGENHAM
RM10 9HU
Tel: 0208 5932343

NATIONAL HOSPITAL FOR NEUROLOGY &
        NEUROSURGERY (FINCHLEY), THE —2C **42**
Gt. North Rd.
LONDON
N2 0NW
Tel: 020 78373611

NATIONAL HOSPITAL FOR NEUROLOGY &
        NEUROSURGERY, THE —7J **59**
Queen Sq.
LONDON
WC1N 3BG
Tel: 020 78373611

NELSON HOSPITAL —6K **105**
Kingston Rd.
LONDON
SW20 8DB
Tel: 020 82962000

NEW EPSOM & EWELL COTTAGE HOSPITAL, THE
        —3J **133**
W. Park Rd.
EPSOM
KT19 8PH
Tel: 01372 734834

NEW VICTORIA HOSPITAL —5C **104**
184 Coombe La. W.
KINGSTON UPON THAMES
KT2 7EG
Tel: 020 89499000

NEWHAM GENERAL HOSPITAL —7G **63**
Glen Rd.
LONDON
E13 8SL
Tel: 020 74764000

NORTH LONDON HOSPICE —3A **26**
47 Woodside Av.
LONDON
N12 8TT
Tel: 020 83438841

NORTH LONDON NUFFIELD HOSPITAL, THE —4L **15**
Cavell Dri.
ENFIELD
EN2 7PR
Tel: 020 83662122

NORTH MIDDLESEX HOSPITAL, THE —5C **28**
Sterling Way
LONDON
N18 1QX
Tel: 020 88872000

NORTHWICK PARK HOSPITAL —5E **38**
Watford Rd.
HARROW
HA1 3UJ
Tel: 020 88643232

NORTHWOOD & PINNER COMMUNITY HOSPITAL —8E **20**
Pinner Rd.
NORTHWOOD
HA6 1DE
Tel: 01923 824182

OBSTETRIC HOSPITAL, THE —7G **59**
Huntley St.
LONDON
WC1E 6DH
Tel: 020 73879300

OLDCHURCH HOSPITAL —4C **50**
Oldchurch Rd.
ROMFORD
RM7 0BE
Tel: 01708 746090

PARKLANDS DAY HOSPITAL —4J **133**
West Park Hospital
Horton La.
EPSOM
KT19 8PB
Tel: 01883 388300

PARKSIDE HOSPITAL —9H **89**
53 Parkside
LONDON
SW19 5NX
Tel: 020 89718000

PEACE HOSPICE, THE —5E **8**
Peace Dri.
WATFORD
WD1 3AD
Tel: 01923 330330

PENNY SANGHAM DAY HOSPITAL —4K **69**
Osterley Pk. Rd.
SOUTHALL
UB2 4EU
Tel: 020 85719676

PLAISTOW HOSPITAL —5G **63**
Samson St.
LONDON
E13 9EH
Tel: 020 85866200

PORTLAND HOSPITAL FOR WOMEN & CHILDREN, THE
        —7F **58**
209 Gt. Portland St.
LONDON
W1N 6AH
Tel: 020 75804400

PRINCESS ALICE HOSPICE —7L **117**
W. End La.
ESHER
KT10 8NA
Tel: 01372 468811

PRINCESS GRACE HOSPITAL —7E **58**
42-52 Nottingham Pl.
LONDON
W1M 3FD
Tel: 020 74861234

PRINCESS LOUISE HOSPITAL —8H **57**
St Quintin Av.
LONDON
W10 6DL
Tel: 020 89690133

PROSPECT HOUSE, E.M.I. UNIT —5E **8**
Peace Dri.
WATFORD
WD1 3XE
Tel: 01923 693900

PURLEY AND DISTRICT WAR MEMORIAL HOSPITAL
        —3L **137**
Brighton Rd.
PURLEY
CR8 2YL
Tel: 020 84013000

QUEEN ELIZABETH HOSPITAL —8J **79**
Stadium Rd.
LONDON
SE18 4QH
Tel: 020 88565533

QUEEN MARY'S HOSPITAL —3E **112**
Frognal Av.
SIDCUP
DA14 6LT
Tel: 020 83022678

QUEEN MARY'S HOSPITAL —8A **42**
23 E. Heath Rd.
LONDON
NW3 1DU
Tel: 020 74314111

QUEEN MARY'S HOSPITAL FOR CHILDREN —3A **122**
Wrythe La.
CARSHALTON
SM5 1AA
Tel: 020 82962000

QUEEN MARY'S UNIVERSITY HOSPITAL —5E **88**
Roehampton La., LONDON
SW15 5PN
Tel: 020 87896611

REDFORD LODGE PSYCHIATRIC HOSPITAL —2E **28**
15 Church St., LONDON
N9 9DY
Tel: 020 89561234

RICHARD HOUSE CHILDREN'S HOSPICE —1H **79**
Richard Ho. Dri., LONDON
E16 3RG
Tel: 020 75110222

RICHMOND HEALTHCARE HAMLET —2J **87**
Kew Foot Rd., RICHMOND
TW9 2TE
Tel: 020 89403331

RODING HOSPITAL (BUPA) —1H **47**
Roding La. S.
ILFORD
IG4 5PZ
Tel: 020 85511100

ROEHAMPTON PRIORY HOSPITAL —3D **88**
Priory La.
LONDON
SW15 5JJ
Tel: 020 88768261

ROYAL BROMPTON HOSPITAL —6C **74**
Sydney St.
LONDON
SW3 6NP
Tel: 020 73528121

ROYAL BROMPTON HOSPITAL (ANNEXE) —6B **74**
Fulham Rd.
LONDON
SW3 6HP
Tel: 020 73528121

ROYAL FREE HOSPITAL, THE —1C **58**
Pond St.
LONDON
NW3 2QG
Tel: 020 77940500

ROYAL HOSPITAL FOR NEURO-DISABILITY —5J **89**
West Hill
LONDON
SW15 3SW
Tel: 020 87804500

ROYAL LONDON HOMOEOPATHIC HOSPITAL, THE —8J **59**
Gt. Ormond St.
LONDON
WC1N 3HR
Tel: 020 78378833

ROYAL LONDON HOSPITAL (MILE END) —7H **61**
Bancroft Rd.
LONDON
E1 4DG
Tel: 020 73777920

ROYAL LONDON HOSPITAL (WHITECHAPEL) —8F **60**
Whitechapel Rd.
LONDON
E1 1BB
Tel: 020 73777000

ROYAL MARSDEN HOSPITAL (FULHAM), THE —6B **74**
Fulham Rd.
LONDON
SW3 6JJ
Tel: 020 73528171

ROYAL MARSDEN HOSPITAL (SUTTON), THE —2A **136**
Downs Rd.
SUTTON
SM2 5PT
Tel: 020 86426011

ROYAL NATIONAL ORTHOPAEDIC HOSPITAL —2F **22**
Brockley Hill
STANMORE
HA7 4LP
Tel: 020 89542300

ROYAL NATIONAL ORTHOPAEDIC HOSPITAL
        (OUTPATIENTS) —7F **58**
45-51 Bolsover St.
LONDON
W1P 8AQ
Tel: 020 89542300

ROYAL NATIONAL THROAT, NOSE & EAR HOSPITAL
        —6K **59**
330 Gray's Inn Rd.
LONDON
WC1X 8DA
Tel: 020 79151300

ROYAL NATIONAL THROAT, NOSE & EAR HOSPITAL -
        SPEECH & LANGUAGE UNIT —8G **55**
10 Castlebar Hill
LONDON
W5 1TD
Tel: 020 89978480

ST ANDREW'S AT HARROW —7C **38**
Bowden House Clinic
London Rd.
HARROW
HA1 3JL
Tel: 020 89667000

ST ANDREW'S HOSPITAL —7M **61**
Devas St.
LONDON
E3 3NT
Tel: 020 74764000

ST ANN'S HOSPITAL —3A **44**
St Ann's Rd.
LONDON
N15 3TH
Tel: 020 84426000

ST ANTHONY'S HOSPITAL —4H **121**
London Rd.
LONDON
SM3 9DW
Tel: 020 83376691

ST BARTHOLOMEW'S HOSPITAL —8M **59**
West Smithfield
LONDON
EC1A 7BE
Tel: 020 73777000

ST BERNARD'S HOSPITAL —3B **70**
Uxbridge Rd.
SOUTHALL
UB1 3EU
Tel: 020 89675000

ST CHARLES HOSPITAL —8H **57**
Exmoor St.
LONDON
W10 6DZ
Tel: 020 89692488

ST CHRISTOPHER'S HOSPICE —2G **109**
51-59 Lawrie Pk. Rd.
LONDON
SE26 6DZ
Tel: 020 87789252

ST CLEMENT'S HOSPITAL —6K **61**
2A Bow Rd.
LONDON
E3 4LL
Tel: 020 73777000

ST EBBA'S —1A **134**
Hook Rd.
EPSOM
KT19 8QJ
Tel: 01883 388300

ST FRANCIS HOSPICE —3C **34**
The Hall, Broxhill Rd.
Havering-atte-Bower
ROMFORD
RM4 1QH
Tel: 01708 753319

ST GEORGE'S HOSPITAL (TOOTING) —2B **106**
Blackshaw Rd.
LONDON
SW17 0QT
Tel: 020 86721255

ST GEORGES HOSPITAL (HORNCHURCH) —1J **67**
117 Suttons La.
HORNCHURCH
RM12 6RS
Tel: 01708 465000

ST HELIER HOSPITAL —3A **122**
Wrythe La.
CARSHALTON
SM5 1AA
Tel: 020 82962000

ST JOHN'S AND AMYAND HOUSE —6E **86**
Strafford Rd.
TWICKENHAM
TW1 3AD
Tel: 020 87449943

ST JOHN'S HOSPICE —5B **58**
Hospital of St John & St Elizabeth
60 Grove End Rd.
LONDON
NW8 9NH
Tel: 020 72865126

ST JOSEPH'S HOSPICE —4F **60**
Mare St.
LONDON
E8 4SA
Tel: 020 85256000

ST LUKE'S HOSPITAL FOR THE CLERGY —7G **59**
14 Fitzroy Sq.
LONDON
W1T 6AH
Tel: 020 73884954

ST LUKE'S KENTON GRANGE HOSPICE —3B **38**
Kenton Grange
Kenton Rd.
HARROW
HA3 0YG
Tel: 020 83828000

ST LUKE'S WOODSIDE HOSPITAL —2E **42**
Woodside Av.
LONDON
N10 3HU
Tel: 020 82191800

ST MARY'S HOSPITAL —9B **58**
Praed St.
LONDON
W2 1NY
Tel: 020 77256666

ST PANCRAS HOSPITAL —4H **59**
4 St Pancras Way
LONDON
NW1 0PE
Tel: 020 75303500

ST RAPHAEL'S HOSPICE —3H **121**
St. Anthony's Hospital
London Rd.
SUTTON
SM3 9DW
Tel: 020 83354575

ST THOMAS' HOSPITAL —4K **75**
Lambeth Pal. Rd.
LONDON
SE1 7EH
Tel: 020 79289292

SHIRLEY OAKS HOSPITAL —2G **125**
Poppy La.
CROYDON
CR9 8AB
Tel: 020 86555500

SLOANE HOSPITAL, THE —5B **110**
125-133 Albemarle Rd.
BECKENHAM
BR3 5HS
Tel: 020 84666911

SOUTH BROMLEY HOSPICE CARE —6D **128**
109 Sevenoaks Rd.
ORPINGTON
BR6 9JX
Tel: 01689 605300

SOUTH LONDON AND MAUDSLEY TRUST —2J **91**
108 Landor Rd.
LONDON
SW9 9NT
Tel: 020 74116100

SOUTHWOOD HOSPITAL —5E **42**
70 Southwood La.
LONDON
N6 5SP
Tel: 020 83408778

SPRINGFIELD UNIVERSITY HOSPITAL —9C **90**
61 Glenburnie Rd.
LONDON
SW17 7DJ
Tel: 020 86826000

STONE HOUSE HOSPITAL —5M **99**
Cotton La.
DARTFORD
DA2 6AU
Tel: 01322 622222

SURBITON HOSPITAL —1J **119**
Ewell Rd.
SURBITON
KT6 6EZ
Tel: 020 83997111

SUTTON GENERAL HOSPITAL —2M **135**
Cotswold Rd.
SUTTON
SM2 5NF
Tel: 020 82962000

TEDDINGTON MEMORIAL HOSPITAL —3C **102**
Hampton Rd.
TEDDINGTON
TW11 0JL
Tel: 020 84088210

THORPE COOMBE HOSPITAL —1A **46**
714 Forest Rd.
LONDON
E17 3HP
Tel: 020 85208971

TOLWORTH HOSPITAL —4L **119**
Red Lion Rd.
SURBITON
KT6 7QU
Tel: 020 83900102

TRINITY HOSPICE —3F **90**
30 Clapham Comn. N. Side
LONDON
SW4 0RN
Tel: 020 77871000

UNITED ELIZABETH GARRETT ANDERSON & SOHO HOSPITALS FOR WOMEN —6H **59**
144 Euston Rd.
LONDON
NW1 2AP
Tel: 020 73872501

UNIVERSITY COLLEGE HOSPITAL —7G **59**
Gower St.
LONDON
WC1E 6AU
Tel: 020 73879300

UPTON DAY HOSPITAL —3J **97**
14 Upton Rd.
BEXLEYHEATH
DA6 8LQ
Tel: 020 83017900

WALTON COMMUNITY HOSPITAL —4F **116**
Rodney Rd.
WALTON-ON-THAMES
KT12 3LD
Tel: 01932 220060

WATFORD GENERAL HOSPITAL —7F **8**
60 Vicarage Rd.
WATFORD
WD18 0HB
Tel: 01923 244366

WELLINGTON HOSPITAL, THE —6B **58**
8a Wellington Pl.
LONDON
NW8 9LE
Tel: 020 75865959

WEST MIDDLESEX UNIVERSITY HOSPITAL —1E **86**
Twickenham Rd.
ISLEWORTH
TW7 6AF
Tel: 020 85602121

WEST PARK HOSPITAL —4J **133**
Horton La.
EPSOM
KT19 8PB
Tel: 01883 388300

WESTERN OPHTHALMIC HOSPITAL —8D **58**
153 Marylebone Rd.
LONDON
NW1 5QH
Tel: 020 78866666

WHIPPS CROSS HOSPITAL —4B **46**
Whipps Cross Rd.
LONDON
E11 1NR
Tel: 020 85395522

WHITTINGTON NHS TRUST —7G **43**
Highgate Hill
LONDON
N19 5NF
Tel: 020 72723070

WILLESDEN COMMUNITY HOSPITAL —3E **56**
Harlesden Rd.
LONDON
NW10 3RY
Tel: 020 84591292

RAIL, CROYDON TRAMLINK, DOCKLANDS LIGHT RAILWAY AND LONDON UNDERGROUND STATIONS

with their map square reference

Abbey Wood Station. Rail —4G **81**
Acton Central Station. Rail —2B **72**
Acton Main Line Station. Rail —9A **56**
Acton Town Station. Tube —3L **71**
Addington Village Stop. CT —8L **125**
Addiscombe Stop. CT —3E **124**
Albany Park Station. Rail —8H **97**
Aldgate East Station. Tube —9D **60**
Aldgate Station. Tube —9D **60**
Alexandra Palace Station. Rail —9J **27**
All Saints Station. DLR —1M **77**
Alperton Station. Tube —4H **55**
Ampere Way Stop. CT —3K **123**
Anerley Station. Rail —5F **108**
Angel Road Station. Rail —5G **29**
Angel Station. Tube —5L **59**
Archway Station. Tube —7G **43**
Arena Stop. CT —9G **109**
Arnos Grove Station. Tube —5G **27**
Arsenal Station. Tube —8L **43**
Ashford Station. Rail —9D **144**
Ashtead Station. Rail —9J **133**
Avenue Road Stop. CT —6H **109**

Baker Street Station. Tube —7D **58**
Balham Station. Rail & Tube —7F **90**
Bank Station. Tube & DLR —9B **60**
Banstead Station. Rail —6K **135**
Barbican Station. Rail & Tube —8A **60**
Barking Station. Rail & Tube —3A **64**
Barkingside Station. Tube —1B **48**
Barnehurst Station. Rail —1A **98**
Barnes Bridge Station. Rail —1D **88**
Barnes Station. Rail —2E **88**
Barons Court Station. Tube —6J **73**
Battersea Park Station. Rail —8F **74**
Bayswater Station. Tube —1M **73**
Beckenham Hill Station. Rail —2A **110**
Beckenham Junction Station. Rail & CT —5L **109**
Beckenham Road Stop. CT —5J **109**
Beckton Park Station. DLR —1K **79**
Beckton Station. DLR —8L **63**
Becontree Station. Tube —2H **65**
Beddington Lane Stop. CT —1G **123**
Belgrave Walk Stop. CT —8B **106**
Bellingham Station. Rail —9M **93**
Belmont Station. Rail —2M **135**
Belsize Park Station. Tube —1C **58**
Belvedere Station. Rail —4M **81**
Bermondsey Station. Tube —4E **76**
Berrylands Station. Rail —8M **103**
Bethnal Green Station. Rail —7F **60**
Bethnal Green Station. Tube —6G **61**
Bexley Station. Rail —7L **97**
Bexleyheath Station. Rail —1J **97**
Bickley Station. Rail —7J **111**
Bingham Road Stop. CT —3E **124**
Birkbeck Stop. CT —7G **109**
Blackfriars Station. Rail & Tube —1M **75**
Blackheath Station. Rail —2D **94**
Blackhorse Lane Stop. CT —2E **124**
Blackhorse Road Station. Rail & Tube —2H **45**
Blackwall Station. DLR —1A **78**
Bond Street Station. Tube —9F **58**
Borough Station. Tube —3A **76**
Boston Manor Station. Tube —5E **70**
Bounds Green Station. Tube —6H **27**
Bow Church Station. DLR —6L **61**
Bow Road Station. Tube —6L **61**
Bowes Park Station. Rail —7J **27**
Brent Cross Station. Tube —5H **41**
Brentford Station. Rail —7G **71**
Bricket Wood Station. Rail —3L **5**
Brimsdown Station. Rail —4J **17**
Brixton Station. Rail & Tube —3L **91**
Brockley Station. Rail —2J **93**
Bromley North Station. Rail —5E **110**
Bromley South Station. Rail —7E **110**
Bromley-by-Bow Station. Tube —6A **62**
Brondesbury Park Station. Rail —4J **57**

Brondesbury Station. Rail —3K **57**
Bruce Grove Station. Rail —9D **28**
Buckhurst Hill Station. Tube —2H **31**
Burnt Oak Station. Tube —8A **24**
Bush Hill Park Station. Rail —8D **16**
Bushey Station. Rail —8H **9**

Caledonian Road & Barnsbury Station. Rail
—3K **59**
Caledonian Road Station. Tube —2K **59**
Cambridge Heath Station. Rail —5F **60**
Camden Road Station. Rail —3G **59**
Camden Town Station. Tube —4F **58**
Canada Water Station. Tube —3G **77**
Canary Wharf Station. DLR —2L **77**
Canning Town Station. Rail, DLR & Tube —9C **62**
Cannon Street Station. Rail & Tube —1B **76**
Canonbury Station. Rail —1A **60**
Canons Park Station. Tube —7J **23**
Carpenders Park Station. Rail —3H **21**
Carshalton Beeches Station. Rail —8D **122**
Carshalton Station. Rail —6D **122**
Castle Bar Park Station. Rail —8D **54**
Catford Bridge Station. Rail —6L **93**
Catford Station. Rail —6L **93**
Chadwell Heath Station. Rail —5H **49**
Chalk Farm Station. Tube —3E **58**
Chancery Lane Station. Tube —8L **59**
Charing Cross Station. Rail & Tube —2J **75**
Charlton Station. Rail —6G **79**
Cheam Station. Rail —9J **121**
Chelsfield Station. Rail —7F **128**
Cheshunt Station. Rail —3F **6**
Chessington North Station. Rail —7J **119**
Chessington South Station. Rail —9H **119**
Chigwell Station. Tube —3M **31**
Chingford Station. Rail —9C **18**
Chislehurst Station. Rail —6L **111**
Chiswick Park Station. Tube —5A **72**
Chiswick Station. Rail —8A **72**
Church Street Stop. CT —4A **124**
City Thameslink Station. Rail —9M **59**
Clapham Common Station. Tube —3G **91**
Clapham High Street Station. Rail —2H **91**
Clapham Junction Station. Rail —2C **90**
Clapham North Station. Tube —2J **91**
Clapham South Station. Tube —5F **90**
Clapton Station. Rail —7F **44**
Claygate Station. Rail —8C **118**
Clock House Station. Rail —5J **109**
Cockfosters Station. Tube —6E **14**
Colindale Station. Tube —1C **40**
Colliers Wood Station. Tube —4B **106**
Coombe Lane Stop. CT —7G **125**
Coulsdon South Station. Rail —8H **137**
Covent Garden Station. Tube —1J **75**
Crayford Station. Rail —5D **98**
Cricklewood Station. Rail —9H **41**
Crofton Park Station. Rail —4K **93**
Crossharbour Station. DLR —4M **77**
Crouch Hill Station. Rail —5K **43**
Croxley Green Station. Rail —7B **8**
Croxley Station. Tube —8A **8**
Crystal Palace Station. Rail —3E **108**
Custom House Station. Rail & DLR —1F **78**
Cutty Sark Station. DLR —7A **78**
Cyprus Station. DLR —1L **79**

Dagenham Dock Station. Rail —6K **65**
Dagenham East Station. Tube —1A **66**
Dagenham Heathway Station. Tube —2K **65**
Dalston Kingsland Station. Rail —1C **60**
Dartford Station. Rail —5J **99**
Denmark Hill Station. Rail —1B **92**
Deptford Bridge Station. DLR —9L **77**
Deptford Station. Rail —8L **77**
Devons Road Station. DLR —7M **61**
Dollis Hill Station. Tube —1E **56**
Drayton Green Station. Rail —9D **54**

Drayton Park Station. Rail —9L **43**
Dundonald Road Stop. CT —4K **105**

Ealing Broadway Station. Rail & Tube —1H **71**
Ealing Common Station. Tube —2K **71**
Earl's Court Station. Tube —5M **73**
Earlsfield Station. Rail —7A **90**
East Acton Station. Tube —9D **56**
East Croydon Station. Rail & CT —4B **124**
East Dulwich Station. Rail —3C **92**
East Finchley Station. Tube —2C **42**
East Ham Station. Tube —3J **63**
East India Station. DLR —1B **78**
East Putney Station. Tube —4J **89**
Eastcote Station. Tube —5G **37**
Eden Park Station. Rail —9L **109**
Edgware Road Station. Tube —8C **58**
Edgware Road Station. Tube —8C **58**
Edgware Station. Tube —6M **23**
Edmonton Green Station. Rail —2E **28**
Elephant & Castle Station. Rail & Tube —5A **76**
Elm Park Station. Rail —9F **50**
Elmers End Station. Rail & CT —8H **109**
Elmstead Woods Station. Rail —3J **111**
Elstree & Borehamwood Station. Rail —6L **11**
Eltham Station. Rail —4K **95**
Elverson Road Station. DLR —1M **93**
Embankment Station. Tube —2J **75**
Emerson Park Station. Rail —5J **51**
Enfield Chase Station. Rail —5A **16**
Enfield Lock Station. Rail —1J **17**
Enfield Town Station. Rail —5C **16**
Epsom Downs Station. Rail —7F **134**
Epsom Station. Rail —5B **134**
Erith Station. Rail —6C **82**
Esher Station. Rail —4B **118**
Essex Road Station. Rail —3A **60**
Euston Square Station. Tube —7G **59**
Euston Station. Rail & Tube —6H **59**
Ewell East Station. Rail —2F **134**
Ewell West Station. Rail —1C **134**
Eynsford Station. Rail —6H **131**

Fairlop Station. Tube —8B **32**
Falconwood Station. Rail —3B **96**
Farningham Road Station. Rail —6M **115**
Farringdon Station. Rail & Tube —8M **59**
Feltham Station. Rail —7F **84**
Fenchurch Street Station. Rail —1C **76**
Fieldway Stop. CT —9M **125**
Finchley Central Station. Tube —8L **25**
Finchley Road & Frognal Station. Rail —1A **58**
Finchley Road Station. Tube —2A **58**
Finsbury Park Station. Rail & Tube —7L **43**
Forest Gate Station. Rail —1E **62**
Forest Hill Station. Rail —8G **93**
Fulham Broadway Station. Tube —8L **73**
Fulwell Station. Rail —1B **102**

Gallions Reach Station. DLR —1M **79**
Gants Hill Station. Tube —4L **47**
Garston Station. Rail —8J **5**
George Street Stop. CT —4A **124**
Gidea Park Station. Rail —2F **50**
Gipsy Hill Station. Rail —2C **108**
Gloucester Road Station. Tube —5A **74**
Golders Green Station. Tube —6L **41**
Goldhawk Road Station. Tube —3G **73**
Goodge Street Station. Tube —8H **59**
Goodmayes Station. Rail —6E **48**
Gordon Hill Station. Rail —3M **15**
Gospel Oak Station. Rail —9E **42**
Grange Hill Station. Tube —4B **32**
Grange Park Station. Rail —7M **15**
Gravel Hill Stop. CT —8J **125**
Great Portland Street Station. Tube —7F **58**
Green Park Station. Tube —2G **75**
Greenford Station. Rail & Tube —4B **54**

Rail, Croydon Tramlink, Docklands Light Railway & London Underground Stations

South Ealing Station. Tube —4H **71**
South Greenford Station. Rail —6C **54**
South Hampstead Station. Rail —3A **58**
South Harrow Station. Tube —8A **38**
South Kensington Station. Tube —5B **74**
South Kenton Station. Rail & Tube —6G **39**
South Merton Station. Rail —7K **105**
South Quay Station. DLR —3M **77**
South Ruislip Station. Rail & Tube —1G **53**
South Tottenham Station. Rail —3D **44**
South Wimbledon Station. Tube —4M **105**
South Woodford Station. Tube —9F **30**
Southall Station. Rail —3K **69**
Southbury Station. Rail —6F **16**
Southfields Station. Tube —7K **89**
Southgate Station. Tube —1H **27**
Southwark Station. Tube —2M **75**
Stamford Brook Station. Tube —5D **72**
Stamford Hill Station. Rail —5C **44**
Stanmore Station. Tube —4H **23**
Stepney Green Station. Tube —7H **61**
Stockwell Station. Tube —1J **91**
Stoke Newington Station. Rail —7D **44**
Stonebridge Park Station. Rail & Tube —3M **55**
Stoneleigh Station. Rail —7E **120**
Stratford (Low Level) Station. Rail —3B **62**
Stratford Station. Rail, Tube & DLR —3B **62**
Strawberry Hill Station. Rail —9D **86**
Streatham Common Station. Rail —4H **107**
Streatham Hill Station. Rail —8J **91**
Streatham Station. Rail —2H **107**
Sudbury & Harrow Road Station. Rail —1F **54**
Sudbury Hill Station. Tube —9C **38**
Sudbury Hill, Harrow Station. Rail —9C **38**
Sudbury Town Station. Tube —2F **54**
Sunbury Station. Rail —5E **100**
Sundridge Park Station. Rail —4F **110**
Surbiton Station. Rail —1J **119**
Surrey Quays Station. Tube —5H **77**
Sutton Common Station. Rail —4M **121**
Sutton Station. Rail —8A **122**
Swanley Station. Rail —8B **114**
Swiss Cottage Station. Tube —3B **58**
Sydenham Hill Station. Rail —9D **92**
Sydenham Station. Rail —1G **109** .
Syon Lane Station. Rail —8E **70**

Teddington Station. Rail —3E **102**
Temple Station. Tube —1K **75**
Thames Ditton Station. Rail —2D **118**
Theobalds Grove Station. Rail —5D **6**
Therapia Lane Stop. CT —2J **123**
Thornton Heath Station. Rail —8A **108**

Tolworth Station. Rail —4M **119**
Tooting Bec Station. Tube —9E **90**
Tooting Broadway Station. Tube —2C **106**
Tooting Station. Rail —3D **106**
Tottenham Court Road Station. Tube —9H **59**
Tottenham Hale Station. Rail & Tube —1F **44**
Totteridge & Whetstone Station. Tube —2A **26**
Tower Gateway Station. DLR —1D **76**
Tower Hill Station. Tube —1D **76**
Tufnell Park Station. Tube —9G **43**
Tulse Hill Station. Rail —8M **91**
Turkey Street Station. Rail —1G **17**
Turnham Green Station. Tube —5C **72**
Turnpike Lane Station. Tube —1M **43**
Twickenham Station. Rail —6E **86**

Upminster Bridge Station. Tube —7L **51**
Upminster Station. Rail & Tube —7M **51**
Upney Station. Tube —3D **64**
Upper Halliford Station. Rail —6C **100**
Upper Holloway Station. Rail —7H **43**
Upper Warlingham Station. Rail —9E **138**
Upton Park Station. Tube —4G **63**
Uxbridge Station. Tube —3B **142**

Vauxhall Station. Rail & Tube —6J **75**
Victoria Coach Station. Bus —5F **74**
Victoria Station. Rail & Tube —4F **74**

Waddon Marsh Stop. CT —3K **123**
Waddon Station. Rail —6L **123**
Wallington Station. Rail —8F **122**
Waltham Cross Station. Rail —7F **6**
Walthamstow Central Station. Rail & Tube —3L **45**
Walthamstow Queens Road Station. Rail —3L **45**
Walton-On-Thames Station. Rail —6E **116**
Wandle Park Stop. CT —4L **123**
Wandsworth Common Station. Rail —7D **90**
Wandsworth Road Station. Rail —1G **91**
Wandsworth Town Station. Rail —3M **89**
Wanstead Park Station. Rail —9F **46**
Wanstead Station. Tube —4F **46**
Wapping Station. Tube —2G **77**
Warren Street Station. Tube —7G **59**
Warwick Avenue Station. Tube —7A **58**
Waterloo East Station. Rail —2L **75**
Waterloo International Station. Rail —3K **75**
Waterloo Station. Rail & Tube —3L **75**
Watford High Street Station. Rail —6G **9**
Watford Junction Station. Rail —4G **9**
Watford North Station. Rail —1G **9**

Watford Stadium Station. Rail —8E **8**
Watford Station. Tube —5D **8**
Watford West Station. Rail —7D **8**
Wellesley Road Stop. CT —4B **124**
Welling Station. Rail —1E **96**
Wembley Central Station. Rail & Tube —1J **55**
Wembley Park Station. Tube —8L **39**
Wembley Stadium Station. Rail —1K **55**
West Acton Station. Tube —9L **55**
West Brompton Station. Rail & Tube —7L **73**
West Croydon Station. Rail & CT —3A **124**
West Drayton Station. Rail —2J **143**
West Dulwich Station. Rail —8B **92**
West Ealing Station. Rail —1F **70**
West Finchley Station. Tube —6M **25**
West Ham Station. Tube —6C **62**
West Ham Station. Rail —6C **62**
West Hampstead Station. Rail —2L **57**
West Hampstead Station. Tube —2M **57**
West Hampstead Thameslink Station. Rail —2L **57**
West Harrow Station. Tube —4A **38**
West India Quay Station. DLR —1L **77**
West Kensington Station. Tube —6K **73**
West Norwood Station. Rail —1M **107**
West Ruislip Station. Rail & Tube —7A **36**
West Sutton Station. Rail —6L **121**
West Wickham Station. Rail —2A **126**
Westbourne Park Station. Tube —8K **57**
Westcombe Park Station. Rail —6E **78**
Westferry Station. DLR —1L **77**
Westminster Station. Tube —3J **75**
White City Station. Tube —1G **73**
White Hart Lane Station. Rail —7D **28**
Whitechapel Station. Tube —8F **60**
Whitton Station. Rail —6A **86**
Whyteleafe Station. Rail —9D **138**
Willesden Green Station. Tube —2G **57**
Willesden Junction Station. Rail & Tube —6D **56**
Wimbledon Chase Station. Rail —6J **105**
Wimbledon Park Station. Tube —9L **89**
Wimbledon Station. Rail, CT & Tube —3K **105**
Winchmore Hill Station. Rail —9M **15**
Wood Green Station. Tube —9L **27**
Wood Street, Walthamstow Station. Rail —2B **46**
Woodford Station. Tube —6F **30**
Woodgrange Park Station. Rail —1H **63**
Woodmansterne Station. Rail —8F **136**
Woodside Park Station. Tube —4M **25**
Woodside Stop. CT —1F **124**
Woolwich Arsenal Station. Rail —5M **79**
Woolwich Dockyard Station. Rail —5K **79**
Worcester Park Station. Rail —3E **120**